Oxford

Basic

AMERICAN

DICTIONARY

for learners
of English

OXFORD

UNIVERSITY PRESS

OXFORD
UNIVERSITY PRESS

Great Clarendon Street, Oxford OX2 6DP

Oxford University Press is a department of the University of Oxford.
It furthers the University's objective of excellence in research, scholarship,
and education by publishing worldwide in

Oxford New York

Auckland Cape Town Dar es Salaam Hong Kong Karachi
Kuala Lumpur Madrid Melbourne Mexico City Nairobi
New Delhi Shanghai Taipei Toronto

With offices in

Argentina Austria Brazil Chile Czech Republic France Greece
Guatemala Hungary Italy Japan Poland Portugal Singapore
South Korea Switzerland Thailand
Turkey Ukraine Vietnam

OXFORD and OXFORD ENGLISH are registered trademarks
of Oxford University Press in the UK and in certain
other countries

© Oxford University Press 2011

Database right Oxford University Press (maker)

First published 2011

2015 2014 2013 2012 2011
10 9 8 7 6 5 4 3 2

ISBN: 978 0 19 439969 2   Pack for paperback and CD-ROM
ISBN: 978 0 19 439964 7   Paperback in pack
ISBN: 978 0 19 439968 5   CD-ROM in pack

Printed in China

Contents

Reference Pages

Acknowledgments

Publishing Manager
Alison Waters

Senior Editor
Jennifer Bradbery

Editors
Daniel Barron
Carol Braham
Kerri Hamberg
Lisa Isenman
Marina Padakis
Suzanne Webb
Ben Weller

Academic Word List
Averil Coxhead, Victoria University of Wellington, New Zealand

Designers
A–Z design by Peter Burgess
Cover design by Maj-Britt Hagsted

Typesetting
Text capture and processing by Oxford University Press
Typesetting by Data Standards Limited

Oxford American Dictionaries Advisory Board
The publisher would like to thank the Board members for their invaluable advice and contribution to the development of the series.
Advisory Board members:
Jayme Adelson-Goldstein, ESL Curriculum Consultant, Lighthearted Learning, Northridge, CA
Cheryl Boyd Zimmerman, Ph.D. Associate Professor, TESOL Coordinator, California State University, Fullerton, CA
Keith S. Folse, Ph.D. Professor of TESOL, University of Central Florida, Orlando, FL
Alison Rice, Director, International English Language Institute Hunter College, City University of New York, NY

Foreword

Jayme Adelson-Goldstein

In the twenty years that I've worked as an author on the *Oxford Picture Dictionary (OPD)* program, I can't tell you how often I've wished for an **American English** dictionary that would serve as the "next step" between the OPD and higher-level learners' dictionaries, of which there are several. At the highest level, there is the new *Oxford Advanced American Dictionary*, with its wealth of language development opportunities for advanced-level learners. And for learners who are beginning their studies, there's the *Oxford Picture Dictionary*, with thematic illustrations providing immediate access to meaning and fundamental vocabulary-building activities. But what about the low intermediate learner? Advanced-level dictionaries are an exercise in frustration for this learner, and picture dictionaries may be too rudimentary. What will help these learners start building the rich, active vocabulary that is key to their academic and workplace success? I would suggest that the book you hold in your hands, the *Oxford Basic American Dictionary*, is the answer to that question.

For years, I've observed how monolingual text dictionaries overwhelm low intermediate learners; especially when the pages are dense and the definitions complex. By contrast, the *Oxford Basic American Dictionary* is easy to navigate. The uncluttered, clean look of its pages and the clear, basic language used in each entry, simplify the look-up process for students, encouraging learner autonomy that in turn boosts confidence and develops all-round language skills. The photos and illustrations that support definitions throughout, help learners make the transition from a picture dictionary to a text dictionary. And, just like a picture dictionary, the pictures here do more than clarify a word's meaning, they also help create a broader understanding of a word in context.

Beyond being a look-up tool, dictionaries can play an important role in our learners' vocabulary development. By highlighting the 2000 most important and useful words to learn in English, the *Oxford Basic American Dictionary* helps learners identify key words they need in their everyday active vocabulary. Thanks to clear labeling within dictionary entries, words on the Academic Word List or words related to various content areas (for example science words, math words) are clearly marked so that learners can build their academic vocabulary too.

Of course, the real test of a learner's dictionary is whether it prepares users to move the word from the page into real-life communication. This dictionary incorporates authentic and level-appropriate examples, collocations, synonyms, antonyms, pronunciation, and/or register information in its entries. The numerous collocation and thesaurus notes expand learners' understanding and correct usage of new vocabulary.

After spending weeks reading through this wonderful new dictionary, I've come to see it as much more than "a book of words from A–Z." It is a bridge into the world of text dictionaries, a low-intermediate vocabulary book, a self-study tool, and a supplement to language skill development for intermediate-low ESOL programs. But ultimately, I think of this dictionary as a treasure map – encouraging learners to travel its pages, looking for one word while unexpectedly discovering another and another – and learning to love the language along the way.

I encourage you to turn the page and discover the *Oxford Basic American Dictionary*.

> **Jayme Adelson-Goldstein** is the co-author of the best-selling *Oxford Picture Dictionary*, the series director for *Step Forward: English for Everyday Life*, and several other ESL texts. Over the past 25 years, she has been a classroom teacher, teacher educator, and curriculum developer in the ESOL field.

Guide to the Dictionary
Finding Words and Phrases

The **2000 keywords**
(= the most important words
to learn) are in orange with
a 🔑 symbol. You can find a
full list of keywords on
pages R2–R10.

park¹ 🔑 /pɑrk/ *noun* [*count*]
a place with grass and trees, where anyone can
go to walk, play games, or relax: *We had a picnic
in the park.* • *Central Park* ⊃ Look at **national
park**.

Words with the **same
spelling**, but different
parts of speech, have
different numbers.

park² 🔑 /pɑrk/ *verb* (parks, park·ing, parked)
to stop and leave a vehicle somewhere for a
time: *You can't park on this street.* • *My car is
parked across from the bank.*
▶ **park·ing** /'pɑrkɪŋ/ *noun* [*noncount*]: *The sign
says "No Parking." • I can't find a parking space.*

Related words are given
below the main word.

con·sid·er·a·tion /kən,sɪdə'reɪʃn/ *noun*
[*noncount*]
1 (*formal*) thinking carefully about something:
*After a lot of consideration, I decided not to accept
the job.* ⊃ **SYNONYM thought**
2 being kind, and caring about other people's
feelings: *He shows no **consideration for** anyone
else.*
take something into consideration to think
carefully about something when you are
deciding: *We must take the cost into
consideration when planning our vacation.*

Dots in a word show how
it is divided into syllables.

Different meanings are
marked with numbers.

Idioms and **phrasal verbs**
(which have a special
meaning) are shown below
the main words.

a·nal·o·gy [AWL] /ə'nælədʒi/ *noun* [*count*] (*plural*
a·nal·o·gies)
a comparison between two things that shows
how they are similar: *to **make an analogy**
between the human brain and a computer*

An **AWL** symbol means that
a word is in the **Academic
Word List.**

prime num·ber /,praɪm 'nʌmbər/ *noun* [*count*]
(**MATH**) a number that can only be divided by
itself and 1. The numbers 7, 17, and 41 are
prime numbers.

Content area vocabulary is
labeled to show words that
are often used in a particular
academic subject.

Understanding and Using Words

wake 🔑 /weɪk/ (also **wake up**) *verb* (wakes,
wak·ing, woke /woʊk/, has wok·en /'woʊkən/)
1 to stop sleeping: *What time did you **wake up**
this morning?*
2 to make someone stop sleeping: *The noise
woke me **up**. • Don't wake the baby.*

All **verb forms** are
given.

The **meaning** (or
definition) is written in
simple English.

Example sentences
help you to understand
a word and show you
how it is used.

tooth 🔑 /tuθ/ *noun* [*count*] (*plural* teeth /tiθ/)
1 one of the hard, white things in your mouth
that you use for eating: *I brush my teeth after
every meal.* ⊃ Look at the picture at **mouth**.

The **part of speech** (for
example **noun**, **verb**, or
adjective) is always given.

Irregular **plural forms**
are given.

fun·ny 🔑 /'fʌni/ *adjective* (fun·ni·er, fun·ni·est)
1 making you laugh or smile: *a funny story* •
He's so funny! ⊃ **SYNONYM amusing**

Comparative and
superlative forms are
given, unless they are
formed with *more* or
most.

The **pronunciation** of all
words is given.

thumb 🔑 /θʌm/ *noun* [*count*]

ⓘ **PRONUNCIATION**
The word **thumb** sounds like **come**, because
we don't say the letter **b** in this word.

the short thick finger at the side of your hand ⊃
Look at the picture at **hand**.

Some difficult words have
notes giving extra help on
pronunciation.

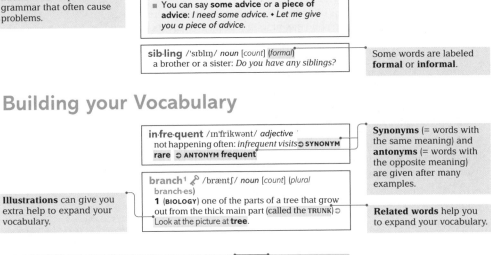

The **grammar of nouns** is given.

wait·er /'weɪt̬ər/ *noun* [count]
a man who brings food and drinks to your table in a restaurant

ad·vice /əd'vaɪs/ *noun* [noncount]
words that you say to help someone decide what to do: *The book **gives** some good **advice on** traveling overseas.* ◆ *I **took** the doctor's **advice** (= I did what the doctor told me to do) and stayed in bed.*

Words that often go together (**collocations**) are highlighted.

Many words have **grammar notes**, which give you extra information on points of grammar that often cause problems.

Grammar

- Be careful! You cannot say "an advice."
- You can say **some advice** or **a piece of advice**: *I need some advice.* ◆ *Let me give you a piece of advice.*

sib·ling /'sɪblɪŋ/ *noun* [count] (*formal*)
a brother or a sister: *Do you have any siblings?*

Some words are labeled **formal** or **informal**.

Building your Vocabulary

in·fre·quent /ɪn'frikwənt/ *adjective*
not happening often: *infrequent visits* ⊃ SYNONYM **rare** ⊃ ANTONYM **frequent**

Synonyms (= words with the same meaning) and **antonyms** (= words with the opposite meaning) are given after many examples.

Illustrations can give you extra help to expand your vocabulary.

branch¹ /bræntʃ/ *noun* [count] (*plural* branch·es)
1 (BIOLOGY) one of the parts of a tree that grow out from the thick main part (called the TRUNK) ⊃ Look at the picture at **tree**.

Related words help you to expand your vocabulary.

You will find many note boxes to help you learn more words. Look at pages x–xii for a full list of notes in this dictionary.

Word building

- A young cat is called a **kitten**.
- A cat **purrs** when it is happy.
- When a cat makes a loud noise, it **meows**: *My cat meows when he's hungry.*

Collocations

Higher education

applying
- **apply for** college
- **apply to** a college/a university/Harvard
- **get into/go to** college/Princeton

studying
- **major in/minor in** biology/philosophy
- **work toward** a B.A./a law degree/a master's degree

finishing
- **finish/graduate from** college
- **earn/receive/get** a degree/a bachelor's degree/a master's degree

Which word?

Hear or listen?

- When you **hear** something, sounds come to your ears: *I **heard** the door close.*
- When you **listen to** something, you are trying to hear it: *I **listen to** the radio every morning.*

Thesaurus

intelligent good at learning, understanding, and thinking quickly and clearly: *He's a very intelligent man.* ◆ *She asked a lot of intelligent questions.*

smart quick at learning and understanding things; able to make good decisions: *She's smarter than her brother.* ◆ *Accepting that job was a smart career move.* ◆ *OK, I admit it wasn't the smartest thing I ever did (= it was a stupid thing to do).*

brilliant extremely intelligent: *a brilliant young scientist/musician* ◆ *He has one of the most brilliant minds in the country.*

bright (used especially about young people) intelligent; quick to learn: *She's probably the brightest student in the class.* ◆ *a bright boy/girl/kid*

Content Area Vocabulary

Words in this dictionary are given a subject label if they are often used in a particular academic subject, for example the word **radius** is used in **mathematics**:

> **ra·di·us** /ˈreɪdiəs/ *noun* [count] (*plural* **ra·di·i** /ˈreɪdiaɪ/)
> (**MATH**) the length of a straight line from the center of a circle to the outside ⇒ Look at the picture at **circle**.

Sometimes, different meanings of a word are used in different content areas, for example the noun **pitch** has one meaning that is used in **sports** and another meaning that is used in **music**:

> **pitch²** /pɪtʃ/ *noun* (*plural* **pitch·es**)
> **1** [count] (**SPORTS**) an act of throwing a baseball to a player who tries to hit it: *He hit the first pitch of the game into center field.*
> **2** [noncount] (**MUSIC**) how high or low a sound is

If you are using English to study other subjects, these labels will show you which words are useful to learn. This is the list of the subject labels used in this dictionary:

Art	**Health**
Biology	**History**
Business	**Math**
Chemistry	**Music**
Computers	**Physics**
English Language Arts	**Politics**
General Science	**Religion**
Geography	**Sports**

List of Illustrations

At or near these words in the dictionary, you will find pictures to help you to understand words or to show you a group of related items.

snowboarding	stereo	tiger	volcano
soap	stethoscope	toad	waffle
soccer	string	toaster	also pancake
solid	stroller	tongs	wallet
different solid shapes	submarine	toothpaste	wastebasket
spade	sunset	toy	watch
spider	surfing	tractor	waterfall
sponge	SUV	trapezoid	wavelength
spoon	swan	tree	whale
sports car	swing	parts of a tree	wheelbarrow
spring	switch	trophy	wheelchair
squeeze	swollen	truck	windsurfing
also squash, press,	syringe	tub	wolf
crush	tambourine	turkey	wrench
squirrel	tape measure	tweezers	wring
starfish	teddy bear	USB flash drive	xylophone
stationery	telescope	vacuum cleaner	zebra
stationery items	tennis	van	zipper
station wagon	thermometer	vegetable	
steering wheel	thread	different vegetables	
the inside of a car	thumbtack	vest	

List of Notes

In this dictionary, we have put special note boxes at lots of entries. These note boxes contain extra information to help you expand your vocabulary.

Thesaurus

Look up the words in **blue** to find **Thesaurus** boxes. Here you can find out about words with similar meanings, as well as information to help you choose the right word.

afraid / scared / frightened / terrified
angry / mad / furious / annoyed
attractive / beautiful / good-looking / pretty /
  handsome
break / crack / smash / snap / burst
cold / cool / freezing / chilly
cook / boil / fry / bake / roast / grill / broil
cut / chop / slice / carve
discussion / conversation / talk / debate / chat
fat / overweight / heavy / obese
field / court / stadium / ballpark / track
hate / can't stand / dislike / despise / loathe
hot / warm / lukewarm / boiling
hurt / ache / burn / sting

intelligent / smart / brilliant / bright
job / work / employment / career / profession
like / love / be fond of / adore
look / watch / see
piece / slice / chunk / lump / slab
price / cost / charge / fee / expense
purpose / aim / plan / intention / goal
road / street / highway / lane / avenue
stuff / things / belongings / property
talk / speak / discuss / communicate
thin / slim / skinny / lean / underweight
trip / travel / journey / expedition / voyage
wind / hurricane / tornado / breeze / gale
wrong / false / incorrect / mistaken / inaccurate

Collocations

Look up the words in **blue** below to find **Collocations** boxes. These contain useful words and phrases that are often used together.

appearance – Physical Appearance
clothes – Clothes and Appearance
cooking – Cooking
diet – Diet and Exercise
e-mail – E-mail
environment – The Environment
exam – Work and Exams

higher education – Higher Education
illness – Illnesses
injury – Injuries
Internet – The Internet
movie – The Movies
music – Music
nature – The Natural World

phone – Phones
school – School
shopping – Shopping

television – Television
weather – The Weather

Word Building

Look up the words in **blue** to find **Word building** boxes, which contain related vocabulary.

account – types of bank accounts
bad – words that mean "bad"
bank – money and banks
bus – traveling by bus
card – playing cards
cat – words connected with cats
cell phone – using cell phones
chicken – chickens
clean – ways of cleaning
clock – clocks and watches
coffee – types of coffee
cow – cows and their meat
elementary school – the U.S. school system
glad – ways to say you are happy
government – the U.S. government
horse – words connected with horses

hospital – going to hospital
job – talking about jobs
light – words connected with lights
lion – words connected with lions
money – different forms of money
month – months of the year
name – types of names
operate – doctors who operate
orchestra – the sections of an orchestra
pig – pigs and their meat
stepmother – members of the family
storm – types of storms
supermarket – shopping in a supermarket
thief – people who steal
tide – high tide, low tide
wedding – talking about weddings

Which Word?

Look up the words in **blue** to find **Which word?** boxes. These tell you the difference between similar words.

a or an
act, action, or activity
actually or currently
allow or let
alone or lonely
already or yet
also or too
among or between
asleep or sleeping
bat, racket, club, or stick

been or gone
bored or boring
borrow or lend
bring or take
clothes or clothing
do or make
everyone or someone
farther or further
fast or quick
hear or listen

invaluable or worthless
its or it's
lay or lie
mistake or fault
say or tell
for or since
some or any
steal or rob
university or college
want or would like

Prefixes and Suffixes

Look up the words in **blue** to find out the meanings of the most common prefixes and suffixes, and to see useful examples.

Prefixes

anti-   mini-
de-   mis-
dis-   non-
il-   over-
im-   re-
in-   self-
inter-   semi-
ir-   un-
mid-   under-

Suffixes

-able   -ment
-en   -ness
-free   -ous
-ful   -ology
-ing   -proof
-ish   -ward
-ist
-less
-ly

Spelling

Note boxes at these entries will help you remember how to spell these difficult words:

accommodations	dairy	environment	loose	recommend
address	desert	exaggerate	millennium	successful
affect	dessert	forty	necessary	unnecessary
angle	diary	grammar	opposite	until
ceiling	disappointed	immediately	possession	
committee	embarrassed	independent	receive	

Pronunciation

Note boxes at these entries will help you to pronounce these difficult words:

although	design	increase	record	though
answer	double	island	refuse	thread
birth	doubt	juice	rough	through
blow	dumb	knead	row	throw
bow	enough	lamb	sew	thumb
bread	excuse	lead	shirt	tongue
breast	flour	learn	should	touch
bury	friend	live	shoulder	use
buy	fruit	low	skirt	warm
climb	great	money	some	wear
close	guard	object	son	weigh
contrast	half	owe	suit	whole
cough	heart	own	sword	wind
could	height	pear	tear	yacht
daughter	high	present	their	

Grammar

Look up the words in **blue** to find information about these grammar points:

advice – *advice* as a noncount noun
afternoon – which preposition: *in* or *on*?
always – the position of *always* in a sentence
apostrophe – using apostrophes
arrive – which preposition: *in* or *at*?
billion – *billion* or *billions*?
can – the different forms of *can*
church – which preposition: *in*, *to*, or *at*?
enough – using *enough* and *too*
far – using *far* and *a long way*
glasses – *glasses* as a plural noun
home – using *home* as an adverb
infinitive – with or without *to*?
information – *information* as a noncount noun
luggage – *luggage* as a noncount noun

million – *million* or *millions*?
modal verb – the grammar of modal verbs
Ms. – using Miss, Mrs., Ms., and Mr.
much – using *much* and *a lot (of)*
must – using *must* and *don't have to*
o'clock – using *o'clock*
own – using *own* correctly
pants – *pants* as a plural noun
play – using *play* with instruments, games, and
    sports
school – using *a* and *the* with school
so – using *so* and *such*
used to – using *used to* in questions and negatives
will – the different forms of *will*
would – the different forms of *would*

Research Contributors

The publisher would like to acknowledge the following individuals for their invaluable feedback during the development of this series of dictionaries:

Gianna Acevedo Alamo, Volusia County Schools, FL; Francesca Armendaries, Golden West College, Orange County, CA; Brian Arnold, Virginia Commonwealth University, Richmond, VA; Kenneth Aubens, Westside Education and Career Center, Los Angeles, CA; Beth Backes, Tidewater Community College, VA; Kitty Barrera, University of Houston, Language and Culture Center, TX; Susan Boland, Tidewater Community College, VA; Linda Bolet, Houston Community College & South West College, TX; Nancy Boyer, Golden West College, Orange County, CA; Sandra J Briggs, San Mateo Union High School District, San Francisco, CA; Adriana Casas, School of Continuing Education, Orange County, CA; Glyn Cassorla, Hunter College, CUNY, NY; Lucy Castillo, Houston Community College & South West College, TX; Cynthia Cen, Newcomer High School, San Francisco, CA; Gwen Charvis, Lone Star College, North Harris, TX; Roland Cirilo, Lone Star College, Fairbanks, TX; Tricia Collins, Tidewater Community College, VA; Mary Colonna, Columbia University, NY; Eugenia D Coutavas, Hunter College, CUNY, NY; Nancy Cuda, Tidewater Community College, VA; David Dahnke, Lone Star College, North Harris, TX; Karen Del Colle, Bergen County Community College, NJ; Stan Dicarlo, Westside Education and Career Center, Los Angeles, CA; Dorothy Doggett, Houston Community College & South West College, TX; Joyce Doyle, Houston Community College and South West College, TX; Tom Edminster, Abraham Lincoln High School, San Francisco, CA; Tatiana Erokina, Golden West College & Santa Ana College, CA; Gail Fernandez, Bergen County Community College, NJ; Katherine Fouche, University of Texas, Austin, TX; Ma. Alma Garza Cano, Houston Community College & South West College, TX; Jenny Georgerian, Virginia Commonwealth University, Richmond, VA; Caroline Gibbs, City College of San Francisco, CA; Linda Gilette, City College of San Francisco, CA; Betty Gilfillan, Houston Community College & South West College, TX; Terry Guthrie, City College of San Francisco, CA; Janet Harclerode, Santa Monica College, Los Angeles, CA; Deborah Hardin, University of Houston, Language and Culture Center, TX; Lisse Hildebrandt, Virginia Commonwealth University, Richmond, VA; Eva Hodjera, Golden West College, Orange County, CA; Kate Hoffman, School District of Manatee County, FL; Matt Holsten, City College of San Francisco, CA; Katie Hurter, Lone Star College, North Harris, TX; Bill Jiang, Bergen County Community College, NJ; Johnnie Johnson-Hafernik, University of San Francisco, CA; Harold Kahn, Bergen County Community College, NJ; Gursharan Kandola, University of Houston, Language and Culture Center, TX; John Keene, California State University, Long Beach, CA; Gail Kellersberger, University of Houston, Downtown, TX; Jane Kenefick, Columbia University, NY; Jeannie Keng-Suh, Bergen County Community College, NJ; Milena Kristov, Bergen County Community College, NJ; Kathy Lenz, California State University, Long Beach, CA; Deborah Levy, City College of San Francisco, CA; Lynn Levy, City College of San Francisco, CA; Victoria Loeb, Houston Community College, TX; Thi Thi Ma, City College of San Francisco, CA; Veronica Martir, Hunter College, CUNY, NY; Susan McAlister, University of Houston, Language and Culture Center, TX; Nadya Mcann, San Francisco State University, American Language Institute, CA; Jim McKinney, City College of San Francisco, CA; Shant Melkonian, Hunter College, CUNY, NY; Carmen Menendez, Volusia County Schools, FL; Florin Mihai, University of Central Florida, FL; Jay Mojica, City College of San Francisco, CA; Svetlana Montgomery, St Lucie County Public Schools District Office, FL; Susan Morgan, Houston Community College & South West College, TX; Susan Morse, University of California, Irvine, CA; Gretchen Mowens, San Francisco State University, American Language Institute, CA; Janet Muzal, Lone Star College, North Harris, TX; Dina Paglia, Hunter College, CUNY, NY; Irina Patten, Lone Star College, Fairbanks, TX; Arturo V. Ponce, Whittier Union HS District, Los Angeles, CA; Maria Ponce, San Francisco Unified School District, CA; Valentina Purtel, School of Continuing Education, Orange County, CA; Candace Revilla, Golden West College, Orange County, CA; Maureen Roller, Bergen County Community College, NJ; Barbara Russell, Virginia Commonwealth University, VA; Azize Ruttler, Bergen County Community College, NJ; Fayruz Sabha, Golden West College, Santa Ana College & Long Beach CC, CA; Peg Sarosy, San Francisco State University, American Language Institute, CA; Alice Savage, Lone Star College, TX; Shira Seaman, Hunter College, CUNY, NY; Kathy Sherak, San Francisco State University, American Language Institute, CA; Larry A. Sims, University of California, Irvine, CA; Lyna Soler Marin, St Lucie County Public Schools District Office, FL; Jennifer Swoyer, Northside ISD Adult Education, Dallas, TX; Mo-Shuet Tam, City College of San Francisco, CA; Dawn Venable, Virginia Commonwealth University, VA; Steve Vogel, Hunter College, CUNY, NY; Martha Young, Virginia Commonwealth University, VA; Jana Zanetto, City College of San Francisco, CA.

A a

A /eɪ/ *noun* [count, noncount] (*plural* **A's, a's** /eɪz/)
1 the first letter of the English alphabet: *"Apple" begins with an "A."*
2 A the highest grade given for a test or piece of work: *I got an A on my chemistry exam.*

a 🔑 /ə; eɪ/ (*also* **an** /ən; æn/) *article*
1 one or any: *Would you like a drink?* ◆ *A dog has four legs.* ◆ *He's a teacher.*
2 each, or for each: *She calls her mother three times a week.* ◆ *The salary is $45,000 a year.*

Which word?

A or an?

■ You use **an** in front of words that start with a vowel sound. Be careful! It is the sound that is important, not the spelling.

■ Words like *university* and *euro* take **a** instead of **an**, and words that begin with a silent "h," like *hour*, take **an** instead of **a.**

■ Look at these examples: *a box* ◆ *a singer* ◆ *a university* ◆ *an apple* ◆ *an hour* ◆ *an SUV* ◆ *an umbrella.*

a·ban·don ᴀᴡʟ /əˈbændən/ *verb* (**a·ban·dons, a·ban·don·ing, a·ban·doned**)
1 to leave someone or something completely: *He abandoned his car in the snow.*
2 to stop doing something before it is finished: *When the rain started, we abandoned our game.*

ab·bey /ˈæbi/ *noun* [count] (*plural* **ab·beys**)
(**RELIGION**) a building where religious men or women (called **MONKS** and **NUNS**) live or lived

ab·bre·vi·ate /əˈbriviˌeɪt/ *verb* (**ab·bre·vi·ates, ab·bre·vi·at·ing, ab·bre·vi·at·ed**)
to make a word shorter by not saying or writing some of the letters: *The word "telephone" is often abbreviated to "phone."*

ab·bre·vi·a·tion /əˌbriviˈeɪʃn/ *noun* [count]
(**ENGLISH LANGUAGE ARTS**) a short form of a word: *TV is an abbreviation for "television."*

ABCs (*also* **ABC's**) /ˌeɪ bi ˈsiz/ *noun* [plural]
the letters of the English alphabet: *We learned our ABC's in preschool.*

ab·do·men /ˈæbdəmən/ *noun* [count] (*formal*)
(**BIOLOGY**) the front middle part of your body, which contains your stomach

a·bil·i·ty 🔑 /əˈbɪləti/ *noun* [count, noncount] (*plural* **a·bil·i·ties**)
the power and knowledge to do something: *She has the ability to pass the test, but she needs to work harder.*

a·ble 🔑 /ˈeɪbl/ *adjective*
having the power, knowledge, time, etc. to do something: *Will you be able to come to the party?* ◆ *Is Sue able to swim?* ⊃ ANTONYM **unable** ⊃ Look at **can¹**.

Suffix

–able
(in adjectives)
1 possible to: *acceptable* ◆ *adorable* ◆ *curable* ◆ *unpredictable* (= *that you cannot predict*)
2 having a particular quality: *comfortable* ◆ *fashionable*

ab·nor·mal ᴀᴡʟ /æbˈnɔrml/ *adjective*
different from what is normal or usual, in a way that worries you or that is unpleasant: *They thought the boy's behavior was abnormal.* ◆ *abnormal behavior* ⊃ ANTONYM **normal**
▶ **ab·nor·mal·ly** ᴀᴡʟ /æbˈnɔrməli/ *adverb*: *abnormally high temperatures*

a·board /əˈbɔrd/ *adverb, preposition*
on or onto a ship, train, bus, or airplane: *Are all the passengers aboard the ship?* ◆ *Welcome aboard Flight 603 to Miami.*

a·bol·ish /əˈbɑlɪʃ/ *verb* (**a·bol·ish·es, a·bol·ish·ing, a·bol·ished**)
to stop or end something by law: *The senator has promised to abolish the tax if he is elected president.*
▶ **ab·o·li·tion** /ˌæbəˈlɪʃn/ *noun* [noncount]: *the abolition of slavery*

a·bout¹ 🔑 /əˈbaʊt/ *adverb*
1 (*also* **a·round**) a little more or less than; a little before or after: *She's about 30 years old.* ◆ *There were about 2,000 people at the concert.* ◆ *I got there at about two o'clock.*
2 almost; nearly: *Dinner is just about ready.*
be about to do something to be going to do something very soon: *The movie is about to start.*

a·bout² 🔑 /əˈbaʊt/ *preposition*
of; on the subject of: *a book about cats* ◆ *We talked about the problem.* ◆ *What are you thinking about?*

a·bove 🔑 /əˈbʌv/ *adverb, preposition*
1 in a higher place; higher than someone or something: *I looked up at the sky above.* ◆ *My bedroom is above the kitchen.* ◆ *There is a picture on the wall above the fireplace.* ⊃ ANTONYM **below**
2 more than a number or price: *children aged ten and above* ⊃ ANTONYM **below, under**
above all more than any other thing; what is most important: *He's handsome and intelligent and, above all, he's kind!*

a·bridged /əˈbrɪdʒd/ *adjective*
(used about a book) shorter than the original: *an abridged version of a novel*

---

a·broad /ə'brɔd/ *adverb*
in or to another country: *She lives abroad.* ♦ *He plans to spend his junior year studying abroad.*

a·brupt /ə'brʌpt/ *adjective*
1 sudden and unexpected: *an abrupt change of plans*
2 seeming rude and unfriendly: *I'm sorry for being so abrupt with you.*
▶ **a·brupt·ly** /ə'brʌptli/ *adverb*: *The conversation ended abruptly.*

ab·sence /'æbsəns/ *noun* [count, noncount]
a time when a person or thing is not there: *frequent absences from school due to illness* ♦ *I am doing Julie's job **in** her **absence**.*

ab·sent /'æbsənt/ *adjective*
not there: *Taylor was absent from school today.*

ab·sent·mind·ed /ˌæbsənt'maɪndəd/ *adjective*
often forgetting or not noticing things, perhaps because you are thinking about something else: *Grandma is getting more absentminded as she gets older.* ⊃ SYNONYM **forgetful**

ab·so·lute /'æbsəlut/ *adjective*
complete: *I've never played chess before. I'm an absolute beginner.* ♦ *The whole trip was an absolute disaster.*

ab·so·lute·ly /'æbsəˌlutli; ˌæbsə'lutli/ *adverb*
1 completely: *I was absolutely certain that it was her.*
2 (used when you are strongly agreeing with someone) yes; certainly: *"It's a good idea, isn't it?" "Oh, absolutely!"*

ab·sorb /əb'sɔrb/ *verb* (ab·sorbs, ab·sorb·ing, ab·sorbed)
(GENERAL SCIENCE) to take in something like liquid or heat, and hold it: *The dry ground absorbed all the rain.*

ab·sorb·ent /əb'sɔrbənt/ *adjective*
(GENERAL SCIENCE) able to take in and hold something, especially liquid: *an absorbent cloth*

ab·sorb·ing /əb'sɔrbɪŋ/ *adjective*
very interesting: *an absorbing book*

ab·stract AWL /'æbstrækt/ *adjective*
1 about an idea, not a real thing: *abstract thought*
2 not like a real thing: *an abstract painting*

ab·surd /əb'sərd/ *adjective*
so silly that it makes you laugh: *The guards look absurd in that new uniform.* ⊃ SYNONYM **ridiculous**

a·bun·dant /ə'bʌndənt/ *adjective* (formal)
existing in large quantities; more than enough: *an abundant supply of food*
▶ **a·bun·dance** /ə'bʌndəns/ *noun* [noncount, singular]: *There was **an abundance of** fish near the reef.* ♦ *These flowers grow here **in abundance**.*

a·buse¹ /ə'byuz/ *verb* (a·bus·es, a·bus·ing, a·bused)
1 to use something in a wrong or bad way: *The manager often abuses her power.*
2 to treat someone in a cruel or violent way: *The child had been physically abused.*
3 to say rude things to someone: *He said he was verbally abused by the bus driver.*

a·buse² /ə'byus/ *noun*
1 [noncount, singular] using something in a wrong or bad way: *the dangers of drug abuse* ♦ *an abuse of power*
2 [noncount] being cruel or unkind to someone: *The child had suffered verbal and physical abuse.*
3 [noncount] rude words: *The cab driver shouted abuse at the cyclist.* ♦ *racial abuse*
▶ **a·bu·sive** /ə'byusiv/ *adjective*: *an abusive remark*

AC /ˌeɪ 'si/ short for **air conditioning**

ac·a·dem·ic AWL /ˌækə'dɛmɪk/ *adjective*
connected with education, especially in schools and colleges: *Our academic year begins in September.*

a·cad·e·my AWL /ə'kædəmi/ *noun* [count] (plural a·cad·e·mies)
1 a school that teaches people certain skills: *a military academy*
2 an official group of people who are important in art, science, or literature: *the Academy of Motion Picture Arts and Sciences*

ac·cel·er·ate /ək'sɛləreɪt/ *verb* (ac·cel·er·ates, ac·cel·er·at·ing, ac·cel·er·at·ed)
to go, or to make a vehicle go faster: *She accelerated up the steep hill.*

ac·cel·er·a·tor /ək'sɛləreɪtər/ *noun* [count]
the part of a vehicle that you press with your foot when you want it to go faster: *She hit the accelerator and passed the bus.* ⊃ SYNONYM **gas pedal** ⊃ Look at the picture at **steering wheel**.

ac·cent /'æksɛnt/ *noun* [count] (ENGLISH LANGUAGE ARTS)
1 the way a person from a certain place or country speaks a language: *She speaks English with a strong southern accent.*
2 saying one word or part of a word more strongly than another: *In the word "because," the accent is on the second part of the word.*
3 (in writing) a mark, usually above a letter, that changes the sound of the letter: *Fiancé has an accent on the "e."*

ac·cept /ək'sɛpt/ *verb* (ac·cepts, ac·cept·ing, ac·cept·ed)
1 to say "yes" when someone asks you to have or do something: *Please accept this gift.* ♦ *I accepted the invitation to his party.*
2 to believe that something is true: *She can't accept that her son is dead.*

3 to allow someone to join a group, a school, an organization, etc.: *She was accepted at Yale and plans to start in the fall.* ⊃ Look at **reject**.

ac·cept·a·ble 🔑 /ək'sɛptəbl/ *adjective*
allowed by most people; good enough: *It's not acceptable to make so many mistakes.* ⊃ **ANTONYM unacceptable**

ac·cep·tance /ək'sɛptəns/ *noun* [noncount]
taking something that someone offers you or asks you to have: *Her quick acceptance of the offer surprised me.*

ac·cess¹ **AWL** /'æksɛs/ *noun* [noncount]
a way to go into a place or to use something: *We don't **have access to** the yard from our apartment.* ◆ *Do you **have access to** a computer at home?*

ac·cess² **AWL** /'æksɛs/ *verb* (ac·cess·es, ac·cess·ing, ac·cessed)
(**COMPUTERS**) to find information on a computer: *Click on the icon to access a file.*

ac·ces·si·ble **AWL** /ək'sɛsəbl/ *adjective*
1 possible to be reached or entered: *The island is only accessible by boat.*
2 easy to get, use, or understand: *This DVD makes history more accessible to kids.* ⊃ **ANTONYM inaccessible**

ac·ci·dent 🔑 /'æksədənt/ *noun* [count]
something bad that happens by chance: *I **had an accident** when I was driving to work – my car hit a tree.* ◆ *I'm sorry I broke your watch – it was an accident.*
by accident by chance; not because you planned it: *I took Jane's book by accident. I thought it was mine.*

ac·ci·den·tal /,æksə'dɛntl/ *adjective*
If something is **accidental**, it happens by chance and is not planned: *Police do not know if the plane crash was accidental or caused by a bomb.*
▸ **ac·ci·den·tal·ly** /,æksə'dɛntli/ *adverb*: *He accidentally broke the window.*

ac·com·mo·date **AWL** /ə'kɑmədeɪt/ *verb* (ac·com·mo·dates, ac·com·mo·dat·ing, ac·com·mo·dat·ed)
to have enough space for a particular number of people: *Each apartment can accommodate up to six people.*

ac·com·mo·da·tions /ə,kɑmə'deɪʃnz/ *noun* [plural]

a place to stay or live: *It's difficult to find cheap accommodations in New York.*

ac·com·pa·ny **AWL** /ə'kʌmpəni/ *verb* (ac·com·pa·nies, ac·com·pa·ny·ing, ac·com·pa·nied)
1 (formal) to go with someone to a place: *Four teachers accompanied the class on their school trip.*
2 to happen at the same time as something else: *Thunder is usually accompanied by lightning.*
3 (**MUSIC**) to play music while someone sings or plays another instrument: *You sing, and I'll accompany you on the guitar.*

ac·com·plish /ə'kɑmplɪʃ/ *verb* (ac·com·plish·es, ac·com·plish·ing, ac·com·plished)
to succeed in doing something difficult that you planned to do: *The first part of the plan has been safely accomplished.* ⊃ **SYNONYM achieve**

ac·com·plish·ment /ə'kɑmplɪʃmənt/ *noun* [count]
something difficult that someone has succeeded in doing or learning: *He was proud of his academic accomplishments.* ⊃ **SYNONYM achievement**

ac·cord /ə'kɔrd/ *noun*
of your own accord because you want to, not because someone has asked you: *She left the job of her own accord.*

ac·cord·ing·ly /ə'kɔrdɪŋli/ *adverb*
in a way that is suitable: *I realized that I was in danger and **acted accordingly**.*

ac·cord·ing to 🔑 /ə'kɔrdɪŋ tə; ə'kɔrdɪŋ tʊ/ *preposition*
as someone or something says: *According to Daniel, this movie is really good.* ◆ *The church was built in 1868, according to this book.*

ac·count¹ 🔑 /ə'kaʊnt/ *noun* [count]
1 an arrangement with a bank that lets you keep your money there: *I deposited the money into my account.* ◆ *to open an account*

Word building

- There are two main types of **bank account**. If you have a **checking account**, you can take your money out at any time by using a **check** or an **ATM card** (= a card that you put into a machine, which gives you money).
- A **savings account** lets you keep your money in the bank to use later. You receive extra money, called **interest**, for keeping your money there.

2 accounts [plural] lists of all the money that a person or business receives and pays: *Who keeps* (= writes) *the accounts for your business?*
3 words that someone says or writes about something that happened: *She **gave** the police a **full account** of the robbery.*
on account of something because of something: *Our school was closed on account of bad weather.*

take something into account; take account of something to remember something when you are thinking about other things: *John is always last, but you must take his age into account – he is much younger than the other children.*

ac·count² /əˈkaʊnt/ *verb* (ac·counts, ac·count·ing, ac·count·ed)
account for something
1 to explain or give a reason for something: *How can you account for the missing pieces?*
2 to make the amount that is mentioned: *Sales to Texas accounted for 60% of our total sales last year.*

ac·count·ant /əˈkaʊntnt/ *noun* [count]
a person whose job is to make lists of all the money that people or businesses receive and pay: *Nicky is an accountant.*

ac·cu·mu·late **AWL** /əˈkyumyəleɪt/ *verb* (ac·cu·mu·lates, ac·cu·mu·lat·ing, ac·cu·mu·lat·ed)
to increase over a period of time; to collect things over a period of time: *Germs accumulate quickly in bathrooms.* ◆ *We've accumulated a lot of junk over the years.*
▶ **ac·cu·mu·la·tion** **AWL** /əˌkyumyəˈleɪʃn/ *noun* [count, noncount]: *an accumulation of wealth*

ac·cu·ra·cy **AWL** /ˈækyərəsi/ *noun* [noncount]
the quality of being exactly right, with no mistakes

ac·cu·rate ✎ **AWL** /ˈækyərət/ *adjective*
exactly right; with no mistakes: *He gave an accurate description of the thief.* ⊃ ANTONYM **inaccurate**
▶ **ac·cu·rate·ly** **AWL** /ˈækyərətli/ *adverb*: *The map was accurately drawn.* ⊃ ANTONYM **inaccurately**

ac·cuse ✎ /əˈkyuz/ *verb* (ac·cus·es, ac·cus·ing, ac·cused)
to say that someone has done something wrong or broken the law: *His classmates accused him of cheating on the test.* ◆ *She was accused of murder.*
▶ **ac·cu·sa·tion** /ˌækyəˈzeɪʃn/ *noun* [count, noncount]: *The accusations were not true.*

ac·cus·tomed /əˈkʌstəmd/ *adjective*
familiar with something and accepting it as normal or usual: *My eyes slowly grew accustomed to the dark.* ◆ *I was not accustomed to such hot weather.* ⊃ SYNONYM **used to**

ace /eɪs/ *noun* [count]
a PLAYING CARD (= one of 52 cards used for playing games) which has only one shape on it. An **ace** has either the lowest or the highest value in a game of cards: *the ace of hearts*

ache¹ /eɪk/ *noun* [count]
(HEALTH) a pain that lasts for a long time: *I have an ache in my side.* ◆ *She has an earache.*

ache² /eɪk/ *verb* (aches, ach·ing, ached)
(HEALTH) to hurt; to give you pain: *She was aching all over.* ◆ *My legs ached after the long walk.* ⊃ Look at the note at **hurt¹**.

a·chieve ✎ **AWL** /əˈtʃiv/ *verb* (a·chieves, a·chiev·ing, a·chieved)
to do or finish something well after trying hard: *He worked hard and achieved his aim of becoming a doctor.*

a·chieve·ment ✎ **AWL** /əˈtʃivmənt/ *noun* [count, noncount]
something that someone has done after trying hard: *Climbing Mount Everest was his greatest achievement.* ◆ *She felt a great sense of achievement.*

ac·id ✎ /ˈæsɪd/ *noun* [count]
(CHEMISTRY) a liquid substance that burns things or makes holes in metal: *the acid in your stomach*

a·cid rain /ˌæsɪd ˈreɪn/ *noun* [noncount]
(GEOGRAPHY) rain that has chemicals in it from factories, for example. It causes damage to trees, rivers, and buildings.

ac·knowl·edge **AWL** /əkˈnɑlɪdʒ/ *verb* (ac·knowl·edg·es, ac·knowl·edg·ing, ac·knowl·edged)
1 to agree or accept that something is true: *He acknowledged that he had made a mistake.*
2 to write to someone who has sent you a letter, etc. to say that you have received it: *She never acknowledged my letter.*
3 to show that you have noticed someone: *He acknowledged me with a wave.*
▶ **ac·knowl·edg·ment** **AWL** (also **ac·knowl·edge·ment**) /əkˈnɑlɪdʒmənt/ *noun* [count, noncount]: *I didn't receive an acknowledgment of my application.*

ac·ne /ˈækni/ *noun* [noncount]
(HEALTH) a skin problem, common among young people, that causes red spots, especially on the face

a·corn /ˈeɪkɔrn/ *noun* [count]
a small nut with a base like a cup. Acorns grow on large trees (called OAK TREES).

acorn

a·cous·tic /əˈkustɪk/ *adjective*
1 (PHYSICS) connected with sound or the way people hear sounds
2 (MUSIC) (of a musical instrument) not electric: *an acoustic guitar* ⊃ Look at the picture at **guitar**.

ac·quain·tance /əˈkweɪntns/ *noun* [count]
a person that you know a little but who is not a close friend

ac·quire `AWL` /əˈkwaɪər/ *verb* (ac·quires, ac·quir·ing, ac·quired) (*formal*)
to get or buy something: *He acquired some English from watching American television shows.*

a·cre /ˈeɪkər/ *noun* [*count*]
a unit for measuring an area of land; 4,840 square yards: *a farm of 40 acres*

ac·ro·bat /ˈækrəbæt/ *noun* [*count*]
a person who performs difficult acts such as walking on high ropes, especially in a CIRCUS (= a show that travels to different towns)

a·cross 🔎 /əˈkrɔs/ *adverb, preposition*
1 from one side to the other side of something: *We walked across the field.* ♦ *A smile spread across her face.* ♦ *The river was about fifty feet across.*
2 on the other side of something: *There is a bank just across the road.*
across from on the opposite side of someone or something: *He sat across from me at lunch.* ♦ *The house across the street from us is for sale.*

act¹ 🔎 /ækt/ *verb* (acts, act·ing, act·ed)
1 to do something, or to behave in a certain way: *Doctors acted quickly to save the boy's life after the accident.* ♦ *Stop acting like a child!*
2 to pretend to be someone else in a play, movie, or television program ⊃ **SYNONYM perform**
act as something to do the job of another person, usually for a short time: *He acted as manager while his boss was away.*

act² 🔎 /ækt/ *noun* [*count*]
1 a thing that you do: *an act of kindness*

Which word?

Act, action, or activity?

■ **Act** and **action** can have the same meaning: *It was a brave act.* ♦ *It was a brave action.*
■ **Act**, but not **action**, can be followed by **of**: *It was an act of bravery.*
■ We say **activity** for something that is done regularly: *I like outdoor activities such as walking and skiing.*

2 one of the main parts of a play or an OPERA (= a musical play): *This play has five acts.*
3 a law that a government makes: *an act of Congress* ♦ *the Civil Rights Act*
4 behavior that hides your true feelings: *She seems very happy, but she's just **putting on an act**.*
in the act (of doing something) while doing something wrong: *I caught him in the act of stealing the money.*

act·ing /ˈæktɪŋ/ *noun* [*noncount*]
being in plays or movies: *Have you ever done any acting?*

ac·tion 🔎 /ˈækʃn/ *noun*
1 [*noncount*] doing things, especially for a particular purpose: *Now is the time for action!* ♦ *If we don't **take action** quickly, it'll be too late!*
2 [*count*] something that you do: *The little girl copied her mother's actions.*
3 [*noncount*] exciting things that happen: *I like movies with a lot of action in them.* ♦ *an **action-packed** movie*
in action doing something; working: *We watched the machine in action.*

ac·ti·vate /ˈæktəveɪt/ *verb* (ac·ti·vates, ac·ti·vat·ing, ac·ti·vat·ed)
to make something start working: *Any small movement can activate the alarm.*

ac·tive 🔎 /ˈæktɪv/ *adjective*
1 If you are **active**, you are always busy and able to do a lot of things: *My grandmother is 75 but she's still very active.*
2 (**ENGLISH LANGUAGE ARTS**) (used about a verb or sentence) when the person or thing doing the action is the subject of the verb: *In the sentence "The dog bit him," the verb is active.* ⊃ **ANTONYM passive**

ac·tiv·i·ty 🔎 /ækˈtɪvəti/ *noun* (*plural* ac·tiv·i·ties)
1 [*noncount*] a lot of things happening and people doing things: *On the day of the festival there was a lot of activity in the streets.*
2 [*count*] something that you do, usually regularly and because you enjoy it: *The hotel offers a range of sports activities.*

ac·tor 🔎 /ˈæktər/ *noun* [*count*]
a man or woman who acts in plays, movies, or television programs

ac·tress 🔎 /ˈæktrəs/ *noun* [*count*] (*plural* ac·tress·es)
a woman who acts in plays, movies, or television programs

ac·tu·al 🔎 /ˈæktʃuəl/ *adjective*
that really happened; real: *The actual damage to the car was not as bad as we thought.* ♦ *They seemed to be good friends but **in actual fact** they hated each other.*

ac·tu·al·ly 🔎 /ˈæktʃuəli; ˈæktʃəli/ *adverb*
1 really; in fact: *You don't actually believe her, do you?* ♦ *I can't believe I'm actually going to Australia!*
2 a word that you use to disagree politely or when you say something new: *I don't agree. I thought the movie was very good, actually.* ♦ *"Let's go out tonight." "Actually, I'd like to stay in and watch a movie."*

Which word?

- Be careful! **Actually** does **not** mean "now."
- We can say **currently** or **right now** instead: *He's currently working in China.* ◆ *I'm studying for my exams right now.*

ac·u·punc·ture /'ækyə,pʌŋktʃər/ *noun* [noncount]
(**HEALTH**) a way of treating an illness or stopping pain by putting thin needles into parts of the body

a·cute /ə'kyut/ *adjective*
very serious; very great: *an acute shortage of food*

a·cute an·gle /ə'kyut ,æŋgl/ *noun* [count]
(**MATH**) an angle of less than 90° ⊃ Look at the picture at **angle**.

A.D. /,eɪ 'di/ *abbreviation*
(**HISTORY, RELIGION**) A.D. in a date shows that it was after Christ was born: *1066 A.D.* ⊃ Look at **B.C.**

ad /æd/ *noun* [count] (*informal*) short for **advertisement**: *a TV ad*

a·dapt **AWL** /ə'dæpt/ *verb* (a·dapts, a·dapt·ing, a·dapt·ed)
1 to change the way that you do things because you are in a new situation: *He has adapted very well to being in a new school.*
2 to change something so that you can use it in a different way: *The car was adapted for use as a taxi.*

a·dapt·a·ble **AWL** /ə'dæptəbl/ *adjective*
able to change in a new situation: *He'll get used to his new school soon. Children are very adaptable.*

ad·ap·ta·tion **AWL** /,ædəp'teɪʃn; ,ædæp'teɪʃn/ *noun* [count]
(**ENGLISH LANGUAGE ARTS**) a movie, play, or TV show that is based on a book: *The movie is a new adaptation of a novel by Jane Austen.*

add /æd/ *verb* (adds, add·ing, add·ed)
1 to put something with something else: *Mix the flour with the milk and then add the eggs.* ◆ *Add your name to the list.*
2 (**MATH**) to put numbers together so that you get a total: *If you add 2 and 5 together, you get 7.* ◆ *Add $4 to the total, to cover postage.* ⊃ **ANTONYM subtract**
3 to say something more: *"Go away – and don't come back again," she added.*
add up to find the total of several numbers: *The waiter hadn't added up the check correctly.*
add up to something to have as a total: *The numbers add up to exactly 100.*

ad·dict /'ædɪkt/ *noun* [count]
(**HEALTH**) a person who cannot stop wanting something that is bad for them: *a drug addict*
▸ **ad·dict·ed** *adjective*: *to be addicted to drugs*

ad·dic·tion /ə'dɪkʃn/ *noun* [count, noncount]
(**HEALTH**) the condition of being unable to stop taking drugs or doing something that is bad for you: *She has a drug addiction.*

ad·di·tion /ə'dɪʃn/ *noun*
1 [noncount] (**MATH**) putting numbers together: *We learned addition and subtraction in elementary school.*
2 [count] a thing or person that is added to something: *They have a new addition to their family* (= a new baby).
in addition; in addition to something as well as: *He speaks five languages in addition to English.*

ad·di·tion·al /ə'dɪʃənl/ *adjective*
added; extra: *There is a small additional charge for the use of the swimming pool.*

ad·dress¹ /ə'drɛs; 'ædrɛs/ *noun* [count] (*plural* ad·dress·es)

🛈 **SPELLING**
Remember! You spell **address** with DD and SS.

1 the number of the building and the name of the street and town where someone lives or works: *Her address is 408 Broadway, Fargo, North Dakota.* ◆ *Are you still living at that address?*
2 (**COMPUTERS**) a group of words and symbols that tells you where you can find someone or something using a computer: *What is your e-mail address?*

ad·dress² /ə'drɛs/ *verb* (ad·dress·es, ad·dress·ing, ad·dressed)
1 to write on a letter or package the name and address of the person you are sending it to: *The letter was addressed to Jim Watson.*
2 to make a formal speech to a group of people: *The president will address the assembly.*

ad·e·quate **AWL** /'ædɪkwət/ *adjective*
enough for what you need: *They are very poor and do not have adequate food or clothing.* ⊃ **ANTONYM inadequate**
▸ **ad·e·quate·ly** **AWL** /'ædɪkwətli/ *adverb*

ad·ja·cent **AWL** /ə'dʒeɪsnt/ *adjective*
next to something: *She works in the office adjacent to mine.* ◆ *There was a fire in the adjacent building.*

ad·jec·tive /'ædʒɪktɪv/ *noun* [count]
(**ENGLISH LANGUAGE ARTS**) a word you use with a noun that tells you more about it: *In the phrase "this soup is hot," "hot" is an adjective.*

ad·just **AWL** /əˈdʒʌst/ *verb* (ad·justs, ad·just·ing, ad·just·ed)
to make a small change to something, to make it better: *You can adjust the height of this chair.*
▶ **ad·just·ment** **AWL** /əˈdʒʌstmənt/ *noun* [count, noncount]: *After a few **minor adjustments**, the room looked perfect.*

ad·just·a·ble /əˈdʒʌstəbl/ *adjective*
that can be changed or put in the right position: *an adjustable mirror*

ad·min·is·tra·tion **AWL** /ədˌmɪnəˈstreɪʃn/ *noun*
1 [count] (POLITICS) the government of a country, especially the U.S.: *the Obama Administration*
2 [noncount] (BUSINESS) controlling or managing something, for example a business, an office, or a school

ad·min·i·stra·tive **AWL** /ədˈmɪnəˌstreɪtɪv/ *adjective*
(BUSINESS) connected with organizing and managing a business, country, etc.: *an administrative assistant*

ad·min·is·tra·tor **AWL** /ədˈmɪnəˌstreɪtər/ *noun* [count]
(BUSINESS) a person whose job is to organize or manage a system, a department, or an organization: *school administrators*

ad·mi·ra·ble /ˈædmərəbl/ *adjective*
that you admire; excellent: *Her positive attitude to life is admirable.*

ad·mi·ral /ˈædmərəl/ *noun* [count]
a very important officer in the navy

ad·mire /ədˈmaɪər/ *verb* (ad·mires, ad·mir·ing, ad·mired)
to think or say that someone or something is very good: *I really **admire** you **for** doing such a difficult job.* ◆ *They were admiring the view from the top of the tower.*
▶ **ad·mi·ra·tion** /ˌædməˈreɪʃn/ *noun* [noncount]: *I have great admiration for her work.*

ad·mis·sion /ədˈmɪʃn/ *noun*
1 [count, noncount] allowing someone to go into a school, club, public place, etc.: *All those who were not wearing a tie were **refused admission to** the club.* ◆ *Maria is hoping to gain admission to Princeton University* (= she would like to study there). ◆ *College admissions have increased again this year.*
2 [noncount] the amount of money that you have to pay to go into a place: *Admission to the zoo is $10.*
3 [count] when you agree that you did something wrong or bad: *an **admission of** guilt*

ad·mit /ədˈmɪt/ *verb* (ad·mits, ad·mit·ting, ad·mit·ted)
1 to say that you have done something wrong or that something bad is true: *He admitted*

stealing the money. ◆ *I admit that I made a mistake.* ⊃ ANTONYM **deny**
2 to allow someone or something to go into a place: *This ticket admits one person to the museum.*

ad·o·les·cence /ˌædəˈlɛsns/ *noun* [noncount]
the period of a person's life between being a child and becoming an adult

ad·o·les·cent /ˌædəˈlɛsnt/ *noun* [count]
a young person who is developing from a child into an adult ⊃ SYNONYM **teenager**

a·dopt /əˈdɑpt/ *verb* (a·dopts, a·dopt·ing, a·dopt·ed)
to take the child of another person into your family and treat them as your own child by law: *They adopted Mikey after his parents died.*

a·dor·a·ble /əˈdɔrəbl/ *adjective*
very attractive and easy to love: *Your puppy is so adorable!* ⊃ SYNONYM **cute**

a·dore /əˈdɔr/ *verb* (a·dores, a·dor·ing, a·dored)
to love someone or something very much: *She adores her grandchildren.* ⊃ Look at the note at **like**[1].

a·dult 🔑 **AWL** /əˈdʌlt; ˈædʌlt/ *noun* [count]
a person or an animal that has grown to the full size; not a child: *Adults as well as children will enjoy this movie.*
▶ **a·dult** **AWL** *adjective*: *an adult ticket* ◆ *adult education*

a·dult·hood **AWL** /əˈdʌlthʊd/ *noun* [noncount]
the time when you are an adult: *His asthma attacks stopped when he **reached adulthood**.*

ad·vance /ədˈvæns/ *noun* [count, noncount]
progress or a new development in something: *major **advances in** computer technology*
in advance before something happens: *You should buy tickets for the concert well in advance.*

ad·vanced 🔑 /ədˈvænst/ *adjective*
of or for someone who is already good at something; difficult: *an advanced English class*

ad·van·tage 🔑 /ədˈvæntɪdʒ/ *noun* [count, noncount]
something that helps you or that is useful: *One **advantage of** camping is that it's cheap.* ◆ *He **has the advantage of** being able to speak two languages fluently.* ⊃ ANTONYM **disadvantage**
take advantage of something to make good use of something to help yourself: *Buy now and take advantage of these special prices!*

ad·ven·ture 🔑 /ədˈvɛntʃər/ *noun* [count, noncount]
something exciting that you do or that happens to you: *She wrote a book about her adventures in South America.* ◆ *He left home to travel, hoping for excitement and adventure.*

ad·ven·tur·ous /əd'vɛntʃərəs/ *adjective*
An **adventurous** person likes to do exciting, dangerous things.

ad·verb /'ædvərb/ *noun* [*count*]
(**ENGLISH LANGUAGE ARTS**) a word that tells you how, when, or where something happens: *In the phrase "please speak slowly," "slowly" is an adverb.*

ad·ver·tise /'ædvər,taɪz/ *verb* (**ad·ver·tis·es, ad·ver·tis·ing, ad·ver·tised**)
to put information in a newspaper, on television, on the Internet, on a wall, etc. in order to make people want to buy something or do something: *I saw those sneakers advertised in a magazine.* ◆ *It's very expensive to advertise on television.*
▶ **ad·ver·tis·ing** /'ædvər,taɪzɪŋ/ *noun* [*noncount*]
the activity or business of telling people about things to buy: *He works in advertising.* ◆ *The magazine gets a lot of money from advertising.*

ad·ver·tise·ment /,ædvər'taɪzmənt/ (also *informal* **ad**) *noun* [*count*]
information in a newspaper, on television, on the Internet, on a wall, etc. that tries to make people buy something or do something: *an advertisement for a new kind of candy bar*

ad·vice /əd'vaɪs/ *noun* [*noncount*]
words that you say to help someone decide what to do: *The book gives some good advice on traveling overseas.* ◆ *I took the doctor's advice* (= I did what the doctor told me to do) *and stayed in bed.*

Grammar

■ Be careful! You cannot say "an advice."
■ You can say **some advice** or **a piece of advice**: *I need some advice.* ◆ *Let me give you a piece of advice.*

ad·vise /əd'vaɪz/ *verb* (**ad·vis·es, ad·vis·ing, ad·vised**)
to tell someone what you think they should do: *The doctor advised him to lose weight.*
▶ **ad·vis·er** (also **ad·vis·or**) /əd'vaɪzər/ *noun* [*count*]
a person who gives advice, for example to a company or the government

aer·o·bics /ɛ'roʊbɪks/ *noun* [*noncount*]
(**SPORTS**) physical exercises that people often do in classes, with music

aer·o·sol /'ɛrəsɔl/ *noun* [*count*]
a container with liquid in it. You press a button to make the liquid come out in a lot of very small drops.

af·fair /ə'fɛr/ *noun*
1 [*count*] something that happens; an event: *The wedding was a very quiet affair.*

2 affairs [*plural*] important events and situations: *the Department of Military Affairs* (= connected with the army, navy, etc.) ◆ *We talked about current affairs* (= the political and social events that are happening at the present time).
3 [*singular*] something private that you do not want other people to know about: *What happened between us is my affair. I don't want to talk about it.*
4 [*count*] a sexual relationship between two people, usually one that is secret: *Her husband was having an affair.*

af·fect /ə'fɛkt/ **AWL** *verb* (**af·fects, af·fect·ing, af·fect·ed**)

🛈 **SPELLING**
Be careful! Don't confuse **affect**, which is a verb, with **effect**, which is a noun. If you **affect** something, then you have an **effect** on it.

to make something or someone change in a particular way, especially a bad way: *Smoking can affect your health.* ◆ *His parents' divorce affected the child deeply.*

af·fec·tion /ə'fɛkʃn/ *noun* [*count, noncount*]
a feeling of loving or liking someone: *She has great affection for her aunt.*

af·fec·tion·ate /ə'fɛkʃənət/ *adjective*
showing that you love or like someone very much: *a very affectionate child*
▶ **af·fec·tion·ate·ly** /ə'fɛkʃənətli/ *adverb*: *He smiled affectionately at his son.*

af·ford /ə'fɔrd/ *verb* (**af·fords, af·ford·ing, af·ford·ed**)
to have enough money to buy or do something: *I can't afford a vacation this year.* ◆ *We couldn't afford a car in those days.*
▶ **af·ford·a·ble** /ə'fɔrdəbl/ *adjective*: *good food at affordable prices*

a·fraid /ə'freɪd/ *adjective*
If you are **afraid** of something, it makes you feel fear: *Some people are afraid of snakes.* ◆ *I was afraid to open the door.*
I'm afraid … a polite way of saying that you are sorry: *I'm afraid I broke your calculator.* ◆ *I'm afraid that I can't come to your party.*

Thesaurus

afraid feeling fear; worried that something bad might happen. This word cannot come before a noun, so you can say "the man is afraid" but NOT "an afraid man": *Are you afraid of spiders?* ◆ *Alex is afraid of going out after dark.* ◆ *We were afraid to go into the cave.* ◆ *He's afraid that he'll fall.*
scared a more informal word than *afraid*, which is used more in spoken than written English: *I'm really scared of heights.* ◆

Everyone was too **scared to** move. ◆ The thieves **got scared** and ran away. ◆ Are you **scared about** the exam tomorrow?

frightened a more formal word than *afraid*, which is used more in written than spoken English: *a frightened child* ◆ *She is not frightened of anything.* ◆ *He was frightened that the glass would break.*

terrified very afraid: *to be terrified of spiders* ◆ *He was terrified that he would fall.* ◆ *You look terrified!*

Af·ri·can A·mer·i·can /ˌæfrɪkən əˈmɛrɪkən/ *noun* [count]
an American whose family came from Africa
▶ **Af·ri·can-A·mer·i·can** *adjective*: *an African-American actor*

af·ter¹ 🔑 /ˈæftər/ *preposition*
1 later than someone or something: *Jenny arrived after dinner.* ◆ *After doing my homework, I went out.*
2 behind or following someone or something: *Ten comes after nine.* ◆ *Russell finished after Evans in the race.*
3 (used when telling the time) later than: *We left at a quarter after seven* (= 7:15).
4 trying to get or catch someone or something: *The police officer ran after her.*
after all
1 used when you thought something different would happen: *I was worried about the test, but it wasn't difficult after all.*
2 used to mean "do not forget": *She doesn't understand. After all, she's only two.*
be after something to be trying to get or find something: *What kind of work are you after?*

af·ter² 🔑 /ˈæftər/ *conjunction, adverb*
at a time later than someone or something: *We arrived after the movie had started.* ◆ *Ava left at ten o'clock and I left soon after.* ◆ *Call me tomorrow or the day after* (= the day after tomorrow).

af·ter·noon 🔑 /ˌæftərˈnun/ *noun* [count]
the part of a day between 12 o'clock in the middle of the day and the evening: *We had lunch and in the afternoon we went for a walk.* ◆ *I saw Sue this afternoon.* ◆ *Yesterday afternoon I went shopping.*

Grammar

- We usually say **in the afternoon**: *We went to the beach in the afternoon.*
- If we include a day or date then we usually use **on**: *I'll see you on Monday afternoon.*

good afternoon (*formal*) words that you say when you see someone for the first time in the afternoon

af·ter·shave /ˈæftərʃeɪv/ *noun* [count, noncount]
a liquid with a nice smell that men sometimes put on their faces after they SHAVE (= cut the hair off their face)

af·ter·ward 🔑 /ˈæftərwərd/ (also **af·ter·wards** /ˈæftərwərdz/) *adverb*
later; after another thing has happened: *We had dinner and went to see a movie afterward.*

a·gain 🔑 /əˈgɛn/ *adverb*
1 one more time; once more: *Could you say that again, please?* ◆ *I will never see him again.*
2 in the way that someone or something was before: *You'll feel better again soon.*
again and again many times: *I've told you again and again not to do that!*

a·gainst 🔑 /əˈgɛnst/ *preposition*
1 on the other side, for example in a game, fight, etc.: *They played baseball against a team from another town.*
2 not agreeing with or supporting someone or something: *Many people are against the plan.* ⊃ ANTONYM for
3 touching someone or something for support: *I put the ladder against the wall.*
4 in order to stop something: *Have you had a shot against the disease?*

age 🔑 /eɪdʒ/ *noun*
1 [count, noncount] the amount of time that someone or something has been in the world: *She is seven years of age.* ◆ *I started work at the age of 16.* ◆ *Children of all ages will enjoy this movie.* ◆ *He needs some friends his own age.*

> ⓘ **STYLE**
> When we want to ask someone's age, we say **How old are you?**
> To say your age, you say **I am 14** or **I'm 14 years old** (but NOT "I am 14 years").

2 [noncount] being old: *Her hair was gray with age.*
3 [count] a certain time in history: *the computer age* ◆ *the history of art through the ages* ◆ *the Stone Age* (= when people used stone tools)
4 ages [plural] (*informal*) a very long time: *We waited ages for a bus.* ◆ *She's lived here for ages.*

ag·ed 🔑 /eɪdʒd/ *adjective*
of the age mentioned: *They have two children, aged three and five.*

a·gen·cy /ˈeɪdʒənsi/ *noun* [count] (*plural* **a·gen·cies**)
(BUSINESS) the work or office of someone who does business for others: *A travel agency plans trips for people.*

a·gen·da /əˈdʒɛndə/ *noun* [count]
a list of all the things to be talked about in a meeting: *The next item on the agenda is the class field trip.*

---

a·gent /ˈeɪdʒənt/ *noun* [count]
(**BUSINESS**) a person who does business for another person or for a company: *a real-estate agent* ◆ *a travel agent*

ag·gra·vate /ˈæɡrəveɪt/ *verb* (ag·gra·vates, ag·gra·vat·ing, ag·gra·vat·ed)
1 to make something worse: *The people were poor, and the war only aggravated the situation.*
2 to make someone angry: *His constant humming really aggravates me.* ➔ **SYNONYM irritate**

ag·gres·sion /əˈɡrɛʃn/ *noun* [noncount]
angry behavior or feelings that make you want to attack other people: *Do violent video games lead to aggression?*

ag·gres·sive /əˈɡrɛsɪv/ *adjective*
If you are **aggressive**, you are ready to argue or fight: *He often gets aggressive after drinking alcohol.*

ag·ile /ˈædʒl; ˈædʒaɪl/ *adjective*
able to move quickly and easily: *an agile athlete*
▸ **a·gil·i·ty** /əˈdʒɪləti/ *noun* [noncount]: *a test of speed and agility*

ag·i·tat·ed /ˈædʒəˌteɪtəd/ *adjective*
worried or upset about something: *When it started to get dark, she became more and more agitated.*

a·go /əˈɡoʊ/ *adverb*
before now; in the past: *His wife died five years ago.* ◆ *I learned to drive a long time ago.*
long ago a very long time in the past: *Long ago there were no cars or airplanes.*

a·gon·iz·ing /ˈæɡəˌnaɪzɪŋ/ *adjective*
very painful: *an agonizing pain*

ag·o·ny /ˈæɡəni/ *noun* [count, noncount] (*plural* ag·o·nies)
very great pain: *He screamed in agony.*

a·gree /əˈɡri/ *verb* (a·grees, a·gree·ing, a·greed)
1 to have the same opinion as another person about something: *Martin thinks we should go by train, but I don't agree.* ◆ *I agree with you.* ➔ **ANTONYM disagree**
2 to say "yes" when someone asks you to do something: *Amy agreed to give me the money.* ➔ **ANTONYM refuse**
3 to decide something with another person: *We agreed to meet on March 3rd.* ◆ *Liz and I agreed on a price.*

a·gree·a·ble /əˈɡriəbl/ *adjective* (*formal*)
pleasant or nice

a·gree·ment /əˈɡrimənt/ *noun*
1 [noncount] having the same opinion as someone or something: *She nodded her head in agreement.* ➔ **ANTONYM disagreement**

2 [count] a plan or decision that two or more people have made together: *The leaders reached an agreement after five days of talks.*

ag·ri·cul·ture /ˈæɡrəˌkʌltʃər/ *noun* [noncount]
keeping animals and growing plants for food ➔ **SYNONYM farming**
▸ **ag·ri·cul·tur·al** /ˌæɡrəˈkʌltʃərəl/ *adjective*: *agricultural workers*

a·head /əˈhɛd/ *adverb*
1 in front of someone or something: *We could see a light ahead of us.*
2 before or more advanced than someone or something: *Inga and Nils arrived a few minutes ahead of us.* ◆ *New York is three hours ahead of Los Angeles.*
3 into the future: *We have a lot of work ahead of us.* ◆ *We must think ahead so we're not surprised.*
4 winning in a game, competition, etc.: *The Lions were ahead 14-0 at halftime.*
go ahead used to give someone permission to do something: *"Can I borrow your bike?" "Sure, go ahead."*

aid **AWL** /eɪd/ *noun* [noncount]
1 help, or something that gives help: *He walks with the aid of a cane.* ◆ *She wears a hearing aid* (= a small thing that you put in your ear so you can hear better).
2 money, food, etc. that is sent to a country or to people in order to help them: *We sent aid to the earthquake victims.*
▸ **aid** **AWL** *verb* (aids, aid·ing, aid·ed) (*formal*)
to help someone or something: *Sleep aids recovery from any illness.* ➔ Look at **first aid**.

AIDS /eɪdz/ *noun* [noncount]
(**HEALTH**) a very serious illness which destroys the body's ability to fight other illnesses: *the AIDS virus*

aim¹ /eɪm/ *noun*
1 [count] something that you want and plan to do: *Kate's aim is to find a good job.* ➔ Look at the note at **purpose**.
2 [noncount] the act of pointing something at a person or thing before trying to hit them with it: *She picked up the gun, took aim, and fired.*

aim² /eɪm/ *verb* (aims, aim·ing, aimed)
1 to try or plan to do something: *He's aiming to leave at nine o'clock.*
2 to plan something for a certain person or group: *This book is aimed at teenagers.*
3 to point something, for example a gun, at someone or something that you want to hit: *He aimed his gun at the target and fired.*

air¹ /ɛr/ *noun* [noncount]
1 the mixture of gases that surrounds the earth and that you take in through your nose and mouth when you breathe: *Can we open a window? I need some fresh air.*

2 the space around and above things: *He threw the ball up **into the air**.*
3 travel in a vehicle that can fly, such as an airplane: *It's more expensive to travel **by air** than by train.*
on air; on the air on the radio or on television: *This radio station is on the air 24 hours a day.*

air² /ɛr/ *verb* (airs, air·ing, aired)
1 to tell people what you think about something: *The discussion gave people a chance to **air** their **views**.*
2 to send out sound or pictures by radio or television: *All the major networks aired the president's speech.* ⊃ SYNONYM **broadcast**

air con·di·tion·er /ˈɛr kənˌdɪʃnər/ *noun* [count]
a machine that keeps the air cool and dry

air con·di·tion·ing /ˌɛr kənˈdɪʃnɪŋ/ *noun* [noncount] (abbreviation **AC**)
a system that keeps the air in a room, building, car, etc. cool and dry
▶ **air-con·di·tioned** /ˌɛr kənˈdɪʃnd/ *adjective*: *air-conditioned offices*

air·craft /ˈɛrkræft/ *noun* [count] (*plural* **air·craft**)
any vehicle that can fly, for example an airplane

air·fare /ˈɛrfɛr/ *noun* [count]
the money that you pay to travel by plane: *How much is the airfare from New York to Chicago?*

air force /ˈɛr fɔrs/ *noun* [count]
the airplanes and other vehicles that can fly, which a country uses for fighting, and the people who fly them

air·line /ˈɛrlaɪn/ *noun* [count]
a company that takes people or things to different places by airplane: *Which airline are you flying with?*

air·mail /ˈɛrmeɪl/ *noun* [noncount]
the system of sending things like letters and packages by airplane: *I sent the package by airmail.* ◆ *I sent it airmail.*

air·plane /ˈɛrpleɪn/ *noun* [count]
a vehicle with wings that can fly through the air
⊃ SYNONYM **plane**

air·port /ˈɛrpɔrt/ *noun* [count]
a place where people get on and off airplanes, with buildings where passengers can wait: *I'll meet you at the airport.*

air·y /ˈɛri/ *adjective* (air·i·er, air·i·est)
having a lot of fresh air inside: *a light and airy room*

aisle /aɪl/ *noun* [count]
a way between lines of seats in something such as a church or an airplane

a·jar /əˈdʒɑr/ *adjective*
(used about a door) open a little, but not much: *I left the door ajar.*

a·larm¹ /əˈlɑrm/ *noun*
1 [count] something that tells you about danger, for example by making a loud noise: *Does your car have an alarm?* ◆ *a burglar alarm* ◆ *a fire alarm*
2 [count] = **alarm clock**
3 [noncount] a sudden feeling of fear: *He heard a noise, and jumped out of bed **in alarm**.*

a·larm² /əˈlɑrm/ *verb* (a·larms, a·larm·ing, a·larmed)
to make someone or something feel suddenly afraid or worried: *The noise alarmed the bird and it flew away.*
▶ **a·larmed** /əˈlɑrmd/ *adjective*: *She was alarmed to hear that Peter was sick.*

a·larm clock /əˈlɑrm klɑk/ (also **a·larm**) *noun* [count]
a clock that makes a noise to wake you up: *She set the alarm clock for 6 a.m.*

alarm clock

al·bum /ˈælbəm/ *noun* [count]
1 (MUSIC) a collection of songs on one CD, tape, etc.: *The band is about to release their third album.* ⊃ Look at **single²**.
2 a book in which you can keep stamps, photographs, etc. that you have collected: *a photo album*

al·co·hol /ˈælkəhɔl; ˈælkəhɑl/ *noun* [noncount]
1 the clear liquid in drinks such as beer and wine that can make people act in an unusual way
2 drinks like wine, beer, etc. that contain alcohol

al·co·hol·ic¹ /ˌælkəˈhɔlɪk; ˌælkəˈhɑlɪk/ *adjective*
containing alcohol: *an alcoholic drink*

al·co·hol·ic² /ˌælkəˈhɔlɪk; ˌælkəˈhɑlɪk/ *noun* [count]
a person who cannot stop drinking large amounts of alcohol

a·lert /əˈlɚt/ *adjective*
watching, listening, etc. for something with all your attention: *A good driver is always alert.*

al·gae /ˈældʒi/ *noun* [plural]
(BIOLOGY) very simple plants that grow in water

al·ge·bra /ˈældʒəbrə/ *noun* [noncount]
(MATH) a type of mathematics in which letters and symbols are used to represent numbers

al·i·bi /ˈæləbaɪ/ *noun* [count] (*plural* al·i·bis)
something that proves you were in a different place when a crime happened and so could not have done it: *Do you have an alibi for the night of the robbery?*

a·li·en /ˈeɪliən/ *noun* [count]
1 (*formal*) a person who is not a citizen of the country where they are living or working: *an illegal alien*
2 a person or an animal that comes from another planet: *aliens from outer space*

a·li·en·ate /ˈeɪliəneɪt/ *verb* (a·li·en·ates, a·li·en·at·ing, a·li·en·at·ed)
to make someone feel that he or she does not belong in a group: *She felt* **alienated from** *the other students in her class.*

a·lign /əˈlaɪn/ *verb* (a·ligns, a·lign·ing, a·ligned)
to arrange things in a straight line: *to align the tires of a car*

a·like /əˈlaɪk/ *adjective, adverb*
1 very similar: *The two sisters are very alike.*
2 in the same way: *The book is popular with adults and children alike.*

al·i·mo·ny /ˈæləmoʊni/ *noun* [noncount]
money that you have to pay by law to the person you were married to after you have divorced

a·live 🔑 /əˈlaɪv/ *adjective*
living; not dead: *Are your grandparents alive?*

all¹ 🔑 /ɔl/ *adjective, pronoun*
1 every part of something; the whole of something: *She ate all the bread.* ◆ *It rained all day.*
2 every one of a group: *All cats are animals but not all animals are cats.* ◆ *I invited thirty people to the party, but not* **all of** *them came.* ◆ *Are you all listening?*
3 everything that; the only thing that: *All I ate yesterday was one banana.*
(**not**) **at all** in any way: *I didn't enjoy it at all.*

all² 🔑 /ɔl/ *adverb*
completely: *She lives all alone.* ◆ *He was dressed all in black.*
all along from the beginning: *I knew all along that she was lying.*
all over everywhere: *We looked all over for that ring.*

al·lege /əˈlɛdʒ/ *verb* (al·leg·es, al·leg·ing, al·leged)
to say that someone has done something wrong when you do not have proof that this is true: *She alleged that he had stolen money from her hotel room.*

al·ler·gic /əˈlərdʒɪk/ *adjective*
(**HEALTH**) having an ALLERGY: *He's* **allergic to** *peanuts.*

al·ler·gy /ˈælərdʒi/ *noun* [count] (*plural* **al·ler·gies**)
(**HEALTH**) a medical condition that makes you sick when you eat, touch, or breathe something that does not normally make other people sick: *She has an* **allergy to** *cats.*

al·ley /ˈæli/ (also **al·ley·way** /ˈæliweɪ/) *noun* [count]
a narrow path between buildings

al·li·ance /əˈlaɪəns/ *noun* [count]
(**POLITICS**) an agreement between countries or groups of people to work together and help each other

al·li·ga·tor /ˈæləgeɪtər/ *noun* [count]
a big animal with a long body, a big mouth, and sharp teeth that lives in the lakes and rivers of the southern U.S. ⊃ Look at the picture at **crocodile**.

al·lo·cate **AWL** /ˈæləkeɪt/ *verb* (al·lo·cates, al·lo·cat·ing, al·lo·cat·ed)
to decide to use something for a particular purpose: *The government allocated more of its resources to education.*
▸ **al·lo·ca·tion** **AWL** /ˌæləˈkeɪʃn/ *noun* [count, noncount]: *the allocation of funds for research*

al·low 🔑 /əˈlaʊ/ *verb* (al·lows, al·low·ing, al·lowed)
to say that someone can have or do something: *My parents allow me to stay out late on weekends.* ◆ *Smoking is not allowed in theaters.* ◆ *You're not allowed to park your car here.*

Which word?

Allow or let?

- **Allow** is used in both formal and informal English. **Let** is very common in spoken English.
- You **allow** someone **to do** something, but you **let** someone **do** something (without "to"): *Jenny was allowed to stay up late last night.* ◆ *Her parents let her stay up late.*
- You cannot use **let** in the passive. You must use **allow** and **to**: *They let him take the test again.* ◆ *He was allowed to take the test again.*

al·low·ance /əˈlaʊəns/ *noun* [count]
an amount of money that you receive regularly to help you pay for something that you need: *Her parents give her an allowance of ten dollars a week.*

all right 🔑 /ɔl ˈraɪt/ *adjective, adverb, exclamation*
1 good, or good enough: *Is everything all right?*
2 well; not hurt: *I was sick, but I'm all right now.*
3 used to say "yes, I agree" when someone asks you to do something: *"Can you get me a glass of water?" "All right."*

al·ly /ˈælaɪ/ *noun* [count] (*plural* **al·lies**)
(**POLITICS**) a person or country that agrees to help another person or country, for example in a war

al·mond /ˈɑmənd/ *noun* [*count*]
a flat, pale nut that you can eat ⟳ Look at the picture at **nut**.

al·most 🔑 /ˈɔlmoʊst/ *adverb*
nearly; not exactly or completely: *It's almost three o'clock.* • *I almost fell into the river!*

a·lone 🔑 /əˈloʊn/ *adjective, adverb*
1 without any other person: *I don't like being alone in the house.* • *My grandmother lives alone.*
⟳ SYNONYM **on your own**, **by yourself**
2 only: *You alone can help me.*

Which word?

Alone or lonely?
■ **Alone** means that you are not with other people: *She lived alone in an apartment downtown.*
■ **Lonely** means that you are unhappy because you are not with other people: *He felt lonely at the new school without his old friends.*

a·long¹ 🔑 /əˈlɔŋ/ *preposition*
1 from one end of something toward the other end: *We walked along the road.*
2 in a line next to something long: *There are trees along the river bank.*

a·long² 🔑 /əˈlɔŋ/ *adverb*
1 forward: *He drove along very slowly.*
2 with someone: *We're going for a walk. Why don't you come along too?*

a·long·side /əˌlɔŋˈsaɪd/ *preposition, adverb*
next to something: *Put your bike alongside mine.*
• *Nick caught up with me and rode alongside.*

a·loud /əˈlaʊd/ *adverb*
in a normal speaking voice that other people can hear: *I read the story aloud to my sister.*

al·pha·bet 🔑 /ˈælfəbɛt/ *noun* [*count*]
(**ENGLISH LANGUAGE ARTS**) all the letters of a language: *The English alphabet starts with A and ends with Z.*

al·pha·bet·i·cal /ˌælfəˈbɛtɪkl/ *adjective*
in the order of the alphabet: *Put these words in alphabetical order* (= with words beginning with A first, then B, then C, etc.)
▶ **al·pha·bet·i·cal·ly** /ˌælfəˈbɛtɪkli/ *adverb*: *The books are listed alphabetically.*

al·read·y 🔑 /ɔlˈrɛdi/ *adverb*
before now or before then: *"Would you like some lunch?" "No, thank you – I've already eaten."* • *We ran to the station but the train had already left.*

Which word?

Already or yet?
■ **Yet** means the same as **already**, but you only use **yet** in negative sentences and questions.
■ Look at these examples: *I have read this book already.* • *I haven't read this book yet.* • *Have you read the book yet?*

al·so 🔑 /ˈɔlsoʊ/ *adverb*
a word you use to say that one more thing is true: *He plays several instruments and also writes music.* • *The food is wonderful, and also very cheap.* ⟳ SYNONYM **too**

Which word?

Also or too?
■ You use **also** in writing, but you usually use **too** in spoken English.
■ **Also** usually goes before a main verb or after "is," "are," "were," etc.: *He also enjoys reading.* • *He has also been to Australia.*
■ **Too** usually goes at the end of a phrase or sentence: *We're going to the movies tomorrow. Would you like to come too?*

al·tar /ˈɔltər/ *noun* [*count*]
(**RELIGION**) a high table used in a religious ceremony

al·ter AWL /ˈɔltər/ *verb* (al·ters, al·ter·ing, al·tered)
to make something different in some way; to change: *We altered our plans and will now stay for a week instead of ten days.* • *He had altered so much I hardly recognized him.*

al·ter·a·tion AWL /ˌɔltəˈreɪʃn/ *noun* [*count, noncount*]
a small change: *We want to make a few alterations to the house before we move in.*

al·ter·nate¹ AWL /ˈɔltərnət/ *adjective*
1 one out of every two: *He works alternate weeks* (= he works the first week, he doesn't work the second week, he works again the third week, etc.).
2 with first one thing, then the other, then the first thing again, etc.: *The cake had alternate layers of chocolate and vanilla.*
3 that you can use, do, etc. instead of something else: *We took an alternate route to avoid the traffic.*

al·ter·nate² AWL /ˈɔltərneɪt/ *verb* (al·ter·nates, al·ter·nat·ing, al·ter·nat·ed)
If two things **alternate**, first one thing happens and then the other, and then the first thing happens again, etc.: *She seemed to alternate between loving him and hating him.*

al·ter·na·tive¹ AWL /ɔlˈtərnətɪv/ *adjective*
1 that you can use, do, etc. instead of something else: *We need to develop alternative sources of energy.*

2 different from the usual style, customs, beliefs, etc.: *alternative medicine*

al·ter·na·tive² AWL /ɔl'tərnəṭɪv/ *noun* [count]
a thing that you can choose instead of another thing: *We could go by train – the alternative is to take the car.*

al·ter·na·tive·ly AWL /ɔl'tərnəṭɪvli/ *adverb*
used to talk about a second possible thing you can do: *We can go by bus. Alternatively, I could take the car.*

al·though 🔑 /ɔl'ðoʊ/ *conjunction*

> **ⓘ PRONUNCIATION**
> The word **although** ends with the same sound as **go**.

1 despite something: *Although she was sick, she went to work.*
2 but: *I love dogs, although I wouldn't have one as a pet.* ⟳ SYNONYM **though**

al·ti·tude /'æltətud/ *noun* [count, noncount]
(GEOGRAPHY) the height of something above the level of the ocean: *The plane climbed to an altitude of 30,000 feet.*

al·to·geth·er /ˌɔltə'gɛðər/ *adverb*
1 completely: *At the age of 65, he stopped working altogether.*
2 counting everything or everyone: *There were ten of us altogether.*

a·lu·mi·num /ə'lumənəm/ *noun* [noncount]
(symbol **Al**)
(CHEMISTRY) a light metal that has a silver color: *aluminum foil* (= for example, for wrapping food)

al·ways 🔑 /'ɔlweɪz/ *adverb*
1 at all times; every time: *I've always lived in Texas.* • *The train is always late.*
2 all through the past until now: *I've always wanted a dog.*
3 forever: *I will always remember that day.*
4 again and again: *My sister is always borrowing my clothes!*

> **Grammar**
>
> ▪ **Always** usually goes before the main verb or after "is," "are," "were," etc.: *He always wears those shoes.* • *Jill is always late.*
> ▪ **Always** can go at the beginning of a sentence when you are telling someone to do something: *Always stop and look before you cross the road.*

am /əm; æm/ form of **be**

a.m. /ˌeɪ 'ɛm/ *abbreviation*
You use **a.m.** after a time to show that it is between midnight and 12 o'clock in the day: *I*

always start work at 9 a.m. (= 9 o'clock in the morning) ⟳ Look at **p.m.**

am·a·teur /'æmətʃər/ *noun* [count]
(SPORTS) a person who does a sport or an activity because they enjoy it, but not for money as a job: *Only amateurs can take part in the tournament.* ⟳ ANTONYM **professional**
▸ **am·a·teur** *adjective*: *an amateur photographer*

a·maze /ə'meɪz/ *verb* (a·maz·es, a·maz·ing, a·mazed)
to surprise someone very much, or to be difficult for someone to believe: *It amazes me that anyone could be so stupid!*

a·mazed /ə'meɪzd/ *adjective*
very surprised: *She was amazed to discover the truth about her father.* • *I was amazed at her knowledge of baseball.*

a·maze·ment /ə'meɪzmənt/ *noun* [noncount]
great surprise: *She looked at me in amazement.*

a·maz·ing /ə'meɪzɪŋ/ *adjective*
If something is **amazing**, it surprises you very much and is difficult to believe: *I have an amazing story to tell you.* • *The concert was amazing – I didn't want it to end.* ⟳ SYNONYM **incredible**
▸ **a·maz·ing·ly** /ə'meɪzɪŋli/ *adverb*: *Maria plays the violin amazingly well.*

am·bas·sa·dor /æm'bæsədər/ *noun* [count]
(POLITICS) an important person who represents his or her country in a foreign country: *the U.S. ambassador to Italy*

am·big·u·ous AWL /ˌæm'bɪgyuəs/ *adjective*
having more than one possible meaning: *His answer was ambiguous, so I'm not sure if he wants the job or not.*

am·bi·tion /æm'bɪʃn/ *noun*
1 [noncount] a very strong wish to be successful, to have power, etc.: *Louise is intelligent, but she has no ambition.*
2 [count] something that you really want to do: *My ambition is to become a doctor.*

am·bi·tious /æm'bɪʃəs/ *adjective*
A person who is **ambitious** wants to be successful, to have power, etc.

am·bu·lance /'æmbyələns/ *noun* [count]
a vehicle that takes people who are sick or hurt to the hospital

am·bush /'æmbʊʃ/ *noun* [count]
a sudden surprise attack: *The soldier was killed in an ambush.*

a·me·ba /ə'mibə/ *noun* [count] (plural a·me·bas or a·me·bae /ə'mibi/) = **amoeba**

a·mend AWL /ə'mɛnd/ *verb* (a·mends, a·mend·ing, a·mend·ed)
to change a law, document, statement, etc. in order to correct a mistake or improve it: *The law needs to be amended.*

a·mend·ment `AWL` /əˈmɛndmənt/ *noun* [*count*]
(**POLITICS**) a change that is made to a law or
document: *The 19th Amendment to the U.S.
Constitution gave women the right to vote.*

A·mer·i·can /əˈmɛrɪkən/ *adjective*
from or connected with the U.S.: *I'm Mexican,
but my wife is American.* • *American history*
▶ **A·mer·i·can** *noun* [*count*]: *We are all Americans.*

am·mo·nia /əˈmoʊniə/ *noun* [*noncount*]
(**CHEMISTRY**) a clear gas with a strong smell, or a
liquid made with this gas and used for cleaning

am·mu·ni·tion /ˌæmyəˈnɪʃn/ *noun* [*noncount*]
things that you throw or shoot from a gun to
hurt people or damage things: *They only
stopped shooting when they had no more
ammunition.*

am·nes·ty /ˈæmnəsti/ *noun* [*count, noncount*]
(*plural* **am·nes·ties**)
(**POLITICS**) a time when a government forgives
political crimes and allows some prisoners to go
free

a·moe·ba /əˈmibə/
noun [*count*] (*plural*
a·moe·bas or
a·moe·bae /əˈmibi/)
(**BIOLOGY**) a very small
animal that consists
of only one cell

amoeba

nucleus

a·mong 🔑 /əˈmʌŋ/ (*also* **a·mongst** /əˈmʌŋst/)
preposition
1 in the middle of a group of people or things: *I
often feel nervous when I'm among strangers.*
2 for or by more than two things or people: *He
divided the money among his six children.*
3 in a particular group of people or things:
*There is a lot of anger among students about the
new law.*

Which word?

Among or between?

■ We use **among** when we are talking about
more than two people or things: *You're
among friends here.*
■ If there are only two people or things, we
use **between**: *Sarah and I divided the cake
between us.* • *I was standing between Alice
and Cathy.*

a·mount¹ 🔑 /əˈmaʊnt/ *noun* [*count*]
how much there is of something: *He spent a
large amount of money.*

a·mount² /əˈmaʊnt/ *verb* (**a·mounts,**
a·mount·ing, a·mount·ed)
amount to something to make a certain
amount when you add everything together: *The
cost of the repairs amounted to $500.*

amp /æmp/ *noun* [*count*]
(**PHYSICS**) a measure of electricity

am·phib·i·an /æmˈfɪbiən/ *noun* [*count*]
(**BIOLOGY**) an animal that can live both on land
and in water: *frogs, toads, and other amphibians*

am·ple /ˈæmpl/ *adjective*
enough or more than enough: *We have ample
time to make a decision.*

am·pli·fi·er /ˈæmpləˌfaɪər/ *noun* [*count*]
(**MUSIC**) an electrical machine that makes sounds
louder ⊃ Look at the picture at **guitar.**

am·pu·tate /ˈæmpyəteɪt/ *verb* (**am·pu·tates,**
am·pu·tat·ing, am·pu·tat·ed)
(**HEALTH**) to cut off a person's arm, leg, finger, or
toe for medical reasons: *His leg was so badly
injured that it had to be amputated.*

a·muse 🔑 /əˈmyuz/ *verb* (**a·mus·es, a·mus·ing,**
a·mused)
1 to make someone smile or laugh: *Rick's joke
did not amuse his mother.*
2 to keep someone happy and busy: *We played
games to amuse ourselves on the long bus ride.*

a·mused /əˈmyuzd/ *adjective*
thinking that something is funny and wanting
to laugh or smile: *He was amused to see how
seriously she took the game.*

a·muse·ment /əˈmyuzmənt/ *noun* [*noncount*]
the feeling that you have when something
makes you laugh or smile: *We watched **in
amusement** as the dog chased its tail.*

a·muse·ment park /əˈmyuzmənt pɑrk/ *noun*
[*count*]
a large park which has a lot of things that you
can ride and play on and many different
activities to enjoy

a·mus·ing /əˈmyuzɪŋ/ *adjective*
Something or someone that is **amusing** makes
you smile or laugh: *an amusing story* ⊃ **SYNONYM**
funny

an 🔑 /ən; æn/ *article*
1 one or any: *I ate an apple.*
2 each, or for each: *It costs $4 an hour to park
your car here.* ⊃ Look at the note at **a.**

a·nal·o·gy `AWL` /əˈnælədʒi/ *noun* [*count*] (*plural*
a·nal·o·gies)
a comparison between two things that shows
how they are similar: *to **make an analogy**
between the human brain and a computer*

---

a·nal·y·sis 🔑 **AWL** /ə'næləsıs/ *noun* [count, noncount] (plural **a·nal·y·ses** /ə'næləsiz/)
the process of carefully examining the different parts of something: *Some samples of the water were sent to a laboratory **for analysis**.*

an·a·lyst **AWL** /'ænəlɪst/ *noun* [count]
a person whose job is to analyze things carefully: *a political analyst*

an·a·lyt·ic·al **AWL** /ˌænə'lɪtɪkl/ (also **an·a·lyt·ic** /ˌænə'lɪtɪk/) *adjective*
looking carefully at different parts of something in order to understand or explain it: *analytical methods for research*

an·a·lyze 🔑 **AWL** /'ænəlaɪz/ *verb* (an·a·lyz·es, an·a·lyz·ing, an·a·lyzed)
to look at or think about the different parts of something carefully so that you can understand it: *They will analyze the statistics.*

a·nat·o·my /ə'nætəmi/ *noun* (plural a·nat·o·mies) (BIOLOGY)
1 [noncount] the scientific study of the structure of human or animal bodies
2 [count] the structure of a living thing: *the anatomy of a frog*
▶ **a·nat·om·i·cal** /ˌænə'tɑmɪkl/ *adjective*

an·ces·tor /'ænsɛstər/ *noun* [count]
(HISTORY) Your **ancestors** are the people in your family who lived a long time before you: *My ancestors came from Ireland.*

an·chor /'æŋkər/
noun [count]
anchor
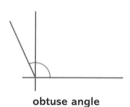
1 a heavy metal thing that you drop into the water from a boat to stop the boat from moving away
2 a person whose job is to read news reports on TV and introduce news reports from other people: *a local news anchor*

an·cient 🔑 /'eɪnʃənt/ *adjective*
(HISTORY) very old; from a time long ago: *ancient buildings*

and 🔑 /ənd; ən/ *conjunction*
1 a word that joins words or parts of sentences together: *ham and eggs • The cat was black and white. • They sang and danced all evening.*
2 (MATH) a word you use when you are adding two numbers together: *Twelve and six is eighteen.* ⊃ **SYNONYM plus**

an·ec·dote /'ænɪkdoʊt/ *noun* [count]
a short, interesting, or funny story about a real person or event

a·ne·mi·a /ə'nimiə/ *noun* [noncount]
(HEALTH) a medical condition in which there are not enough red cells in the blood
▶ **a·ne·mic** /ə'nimɪk/ *adjective*

an·es·thet·ic /ˌænəs'θɛtɪk/ *noun* [count, noncount]
(HEALTH) a drug that a doctor gives you so that you will not feel any pain during an operation: *The patient will be **under anesthetic** for around an hour.*

an·gel /'eɪndʒl/ *noun* [count]
(RELIGION) a spirit who carries messages from God. In pictures, **angels** are usually dressed in white and they have wings.

an·ger¹ 🔑 /'æŋgər/ *noun* [noncount]
the strong feeling that you have when something has happened or someone has done something that you do not like: *She was shaking with anger.*

an·ger² /'æŋgər/ *verb* (an·gers, an·ger·ing, an·gered)
to make someone feel angry

angles

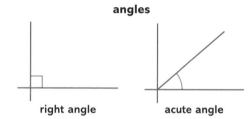

right angle   acute angle

obtuse angle

an·gle 🔑 /'æŋgl/ *noun* [count] (MATH)

> ℹ SPELLING
> Remember! You spell **angle** with L before E. You spell **angel** with E before L.

the space between two lines that meet. **Angles** are measured in **degrees**: *an angle of 40°*

an·gry 🔑 /'æŋgri/ *adjective* (an·gri·er, an·gri·est)
If you are **angry**, you feel or show anger: *My dad was **angry at** me when I got home late. • There's no need to **get angry**.*
▶ **an·gri·ly** /'æŋgrəli/ *adverb*: *"Someone took my book!" she shouted angrily.*

an·guish /ˈæŋɡwɪʃ/ *noun* [noncount] (*formal*)
a feeling of great unhappiness or mental pain: *her anguish at the death of her son*

an·i·mal 🔑 /ˈænəml/ *noun* [count]
1 any living thing that can move and feel but is not a person, a bird, a fish, or an insect: *Cats, horses, and rats are animals.* ⊃ Look at the note at **nature**.
2 any living thing that can move and feel, including people, birds, etc.: *Humans are social animals.*

an·i·mat·ed /ˈænəmeɪtəd/ *adjective*
1 full of interest and energy: *an animated discussion* ⊃ SYNONYM **lively**
2 If a movie is **animated**, drawings or models of people and animals are made to look as if they can really move and talk: *animated cartoons*

an·i·ma·tion /ˌænəˈmeɪʃn/ *noun*
1 [noncount] the process of making movies, videos, and computer games in which drawings or models of people and animals seem to move: *computer animation*
2 [count] a movie which is made in this way: *The website includes several animations.*

an·kle /ˈæŋkl/ *noun* [count]
the part of your leg where it joins your foot ⊃ Look at the picture at **leg**.

an·ni·ver·sa·ry /ˌænəˈvərsəri/ *noun* [count]
(*plural* **an·ni·ver·sa·ries**)
a day that is exactly a year or a number of years after a special or important event: *Today is their 25th wedding anniversary.* ◆ *It happened on the anniversary of her husband's death.*

an·nounce 🔑 /əˈnaʊns/ *verb* (**an·nounc·es, an·nounc·ing, an·nounced**)
to tell a lot of people something important: *The teacher announced the winner of the competition.* ◆ *She announced that she was going to have a baby.*

an·nounce·ment /əˈnaʊnsmənt/ *noun* [count]
important information that someone tells a lot of people: *Ladies and gentlemen, I'd like to **make an announcement**.*

an·nounc·er /əˈnaʊnsər/ *noun* [count]
a person whose job is to tell us about programs on radio or television

an·noy /əˈnɔɪ/ *verb* (**an·noys, an·noy·ing, an·noyed**)
to make someone a little angry: *It really annoys me when my brother leaves his clothes all over the floor.*

an·noy·ance /əˈnɔɪəns/ *noun* [noncount]
the feeling of being a little angry: *She could not hide her annoyance when I arrived late.*

an·noyed /əˈnɔɪd/ *adjective*
a little angry: *I was annoyed when he didn't call me.* ◆ *My dad is **annoyed with** me.* ⊃ Look at the note at **angry**.

an·noy·ing /əˈnɔɪɪŋ/ *adjective*
If a person or thing is **annoying**, they make you a little angry: *It's annoying when people don't listen to you.*

an·nu·al AWL /ˈænyuəl/ *adjective*
1 happening or done once a year or every year: *There is an annual meeting in June.*
2 for a period of one year: *Their annual income* (= the money they earn in a year) *is less than $20,000.*
▶ **an·nu·al·ly** AWL /ˈænyuəli/ *adverb*: *Payments will be made annually.*

a·non·y·mous /əˈnɑnəməs/ *adjective*
1 If a person is **anonymous**, other people do not know their name: *An anonymous caller told the police about the bomb.*
2 If something is **anonymous**, you do not know who did, gave, or made it: *She received an anonymous letter.*

a·no·rex·i·a /ˌænəˈrɛksiə/ *noun* [noncount]
(HEALTH) an illness that makes someone afraid of being fat. People with **anorexia** eat very little and so become very thin and sick.
▶ **a·no·rex·ic** /ˌænəˈrɛksɪk/ *adjective*: *She was anorexic as a teenager.*

an·oth·er 🔑 /əˈnʌðər/ *adjective, pronoun*
1 one more thing or person of the same kind: *Would you like another drink?* ◆ *I like these cookies – can I have another one?*
2 a different thing or person: *I can't see you tomorrow – can we meet another day?* ◆ *If that pen doesn't work, I can give you another.*

æ **cat**   ɛ **ten**   i **see**   ɪ **sit**   ɑ **hot**   ɔ **saw**   ʌ **cup**   ʊ **put**   u **too**   **17**

an·swer[1] 🔊 /'ænsər/ *verb* (an·swers, an·swer·ing, an·swered)

1 to say or write something back when someone has asked you something or written to you: *I asked him if he was hungry but he didn't answer.* ◆ *I couldn't answer all the test questions.*
2 to write a letter or message to someone who has written to you: *She didn't answer my e-mail.*
🔊 SYNONYM **reply**
answer the door to open the door when someone knocks or rings the bell: *Can you answer the door, please?*
answer the phone to pick up the telephone when it rings, and speak

an·swer[2] 🔊 /'ænsər/ *noun* [count]
1 something that you say or write when you reply to someone or something: *Thanks for the offer, but the answer is still no.* ◆ *I never received an **answer to** my e-mail.*
2 a way of stopping a problem: *I didn't have any money, so the only answer was to borrow some.*
3 the correct reply to a question in a test or an exam: *What was the **answer to** question 4?* ◆ *All the answers are at the back of the book.*
4 when someone opens the door or picks up the telephone because someone has knocked or called: *I knocked on the door and waited but there was **no answer**.*

an·swer·ing ma·chine /'ænsərɪŋ məˌʃin/ *noun* [count]
a machine that answers the telephone for you and keeps messages so that you can listen to them later: *He wasn't at home, so I left a message on his answering machine.* 🔊 Look at **voice mail**.

ant /ænt/ *noun* [count]
a very small insect that lives in big groups in the ground and works very hard 🔊 Look at the picture at **insect**.

the Ant·arc·tic /ði ænt'ɑrktɪk/ *noun* [singular]
(**GEOGRAPHY**) the very cold lands in the most southern part of the world: *an expedition to the Antarctic* 🔊 Look at **the Arctic**. 🔊 Look at the picture at **earth**.

an·te·lope
/'æntəloʊp/ *noun*
[count] (*plural*
an·te·lope or
an·te·lopes*)
a wild animal with
long horns and long
thin legs, which can
run fast

antelope

horn

an·ten·na /æn'tɛnə/ *noun* [count]
1 (*plural* an·ten·nas) a long metal stick on a building, car, etc. that receives radio or television signals
2 (*plural* an·ten·nae /æn'tɛni/) one of the two long thin parts on the heads of some insects, and of some animals that live in shells, which they use to feel and touch things 🔊 Look at the picture at **insect**.

Prefix

anti-

(in nouns and adjectives) against: *an antismoking campaign* ◆ *an antiwar demonstration* ◆ *antiterrorist legislation* ◆ *antisocial behavior*

an·ti·bi·ot·ic /ˌæntɪbaɪ'ɑtɪk/ *noun* [count]
(**HEALTH**) a medicine which fights illness in a person's body: *The doctor gave me some antibiotics for a chest infection.*

an·tic·i·pate AWL /æn'tɪsəpeɪt/ *verb*
(an·tic·i·pates, an·tic·i·pat·ing, an·tic·i·pat·ed)
to think that something will happen and be ready for it: *We didn't anticipate so many problems.*

an·tic·i·pa·tion AWL /ænˌtɪsə'peɪʃn/ *noun*
[noncount]
excited feelings about something that is going to happen: *They lined up outside the stadium in excited anticipation.*

an·ti·per·spi·rant /ˌænti'pərspərənt/ *noun*
[count, noncount]
a substance that you put on your body to reduce sweat, especially under your arms

an·tique /æn'tik/ *noun* [count]
an old thing that is worth a lot of money: *These chairs are antiques.*
▶ **an·tique** *adjective*: *an antique vase*

an·ti·sep·tic /ˌæntə'sɛptɪk/ *noun* [count, noncount]
(**HEALTH**) a liquid or cream that you put on a cut, etc. to stop infection: *Put some antiseptic on that scratch.*
▶ **an·ti·sep·tic** *adjective*: *antiseptic cream*

ant·ler /'æntlər/ *noun* [count]
(**BIOLOGY**) a horn that looks like a tree branch on the head of a male DEER (= a wild animal that eats grass): *a pair of antlers* 🔊 Look at the picture at **deer**.

an·to·nym /'æntənɪm/ *noun* [count]
(**ENGLISH LANGUAGE ARTS**) a word that means the opposite of another word: *"Old" is the antonym of "young."* 🔊 Look at **synonym**.

anx·i·e·ty /æŋ'zaɪəti/ *noun* [count, noncount]
(*plural* anx·i·e·ties)
the feeling of being worried or afraid

anx·ious /ˈæŋkʃəs/ *adjective*
1 worried and afraid: *She seemed anxious about the meeting.*
2 If you are **anxious** to do something, you want to do it very much: *My family is anxious to meet you.*
▶ **anx·ious·ly** /ˈæŋkʃəsli/ *adverb*: *We waited anxiously.*

an·y¹ /ˈɛni/ *adjective, pronoun*
1 a word that you use instead of "some" in questions and after "not" and "if": *Do you have any money?* • *I don't speak any Spanish.* • *She asked if I had any milk.* • *I want some chocolate but there isn't any.* ⊃ Look at the note at **some**.
2 used for saying that it does not matter which thing or person you choose: *Come any day next week.* • *Take any book you want.*

an·y² /ˈɛni/ *adverb*
used in negative sentences or questions to make an adjective or an adverb stronger: *I can't walk any faster.* • *Is your dad feeling any better?*

an·y·bod·y /ˈɛniˌbʌdi; ˈɛniˌbɑdi/ another word for **anyone**

an·y·how /ˈɛnihaʊ/ (*informal*) another word for **anyway**

an·y·more /ˌɛniˈmɔr/ (also **an·y more**) *adverb*
used at the end of negative sentences and questions to mean "now": *She doesn't live here anymore.* • *Why doesn't he talk to me anymore?*

an·y·one /ˈɛniwʌn/ (also **an·y·bod·y**) *pronoun*
1 used in questions and negative sentences to mean "any person": *There wasn't anyone there.* • *Did you see anyone you know?* • *Would anyone like more to eat?*
2 any person; it does not matter who: *Anyone can learn to swim.*

an·y·place /ˈɛnipleɪs/ (*informal*) another word for **anywhere**

an·y·thing /ˈɛniθɪŋ/ *pronoun*
1 used in questions and negative sentences to mean "a thing of any kind": *Is there anything in that box?* • *I can't see anything.* • *"Would you like anything else?" asked the waitress.*
2 any thing or things; it does not matter what: *I'm so hungry, I could eat anything!* • *I'll do anything you say.*
not anything like someone or **something** not the same as someone or something in any way: *She isn't anything like her sister.*

an·y·time /ˈɛnitaɪm/ *adverb*
at any time; it does not matter when: *Feel free to call me anytime.*

an·y·way /ˈɛniweɪ/ (also *informal* **an·y·how**) *adverb*
1 a word that you use when you give a second, more important reason for something: *I don't want to go out tonight, and anyway I don't have any money.*
2 despite something: *It was very expensive, but she bought it anyway.* • *I'm afraid I'm busy tonight, but thanks for the invitation anyway.*
3 a word that you use when you start to talk about something different or when you go back to something you talked about earlier: *That's what John told me. Anyway, how are you?*

an·y·where /ˈɛniwɛr/ (also *informal* **an·y·place**) *adverb*
1 used in negative sentences and in questions instead of "somewhere": *I can't find my pen anywhere.* • *Are you going anywhere this summer?*
2 in, at, or to any place, when it does not matter where: *Just put the box down anywhere.*

a·part /əˈpɑrt/ *adverb*
1 away from the others, or from each other: *The two houses are 500 feet apart.* • *My mother and father live apart now.*
2 into parts: *He took my radio apart to repair it.*
apart from someone or **something** except for: *There's no one here, apart from me.* • *I like all vegetables apart from carrots.*

a·part·ment /əˈpɑrtmənt/ *noun* [*count*]
a group of rooms for living in, usually on one floor of a house or big building: *My apartment is on the third floor.* • *an apartment building* (= a building with a lot of apartments in it)

ap·a·thy /ˈæpəθi/ *noun* [*noncount*]
a feeling of not being interested in or enthusiastic about anything

ape /eɪp/ *noun* [*count*]
an animal like a big MONKEY (= an animal that lives in hot countries and can climb trees), with no tail and with long arms. There are different types of **ape**: *Gorillas and chimpanzees are apes.*

a·piece /əˈpis/ *adverb*
each: *She gave the kids $5 apiece.*

a·pol·o·get·ic /əˌpɑləˈdʒɛt̮ɪk/ *adjective*
feeling or showing that you are sorry about something: *The waiter was very apologetic when he spilled my food.*

a·pol·o·gize /əˈpɑlədʒaɪz/ *verb* (**a·pol·o·giz·es, a·pol·o·giz·ing, a·pol·o·gized**)
to say that you are sorry about something that you have done: *I apologized to John for losing his book.*

a·pol·o·gy /əˈpɑlədʒi/ *noun* [*count, noncount*]
(*plural* **a·pol·o·gies**)
words that you say or write to show that you are sorry about something you have done: *Please accept my apology.*

a·pos·tro·phe /əˈpɑstrəfi/ *noun* [*count*]
(**ENGLISH LANGUAGE ARTS**) the sign (') that you use in writing

Grammar

- You use an **apostrophe** to show that you have left a letter out of a word or that a number is missing, for example in *I'm* (= I am) and *'09* (=2009).
- You also use it to show that something belongs to someone or something: *the boy's room*.
- If the apostrophe comes after the letter "s," it shows that there is more than one person: *the boys' room* (= a room which is shared by two or more boys).

ap·palled /ə'pɔld/ *adjective*
feeling shocked at something bad: *She was appalled by his violent behavior.*

ap·pa·rat·us /ˌæpə'ræṭəs/ *noun* [count, noncount] (plural **ap·pa·rat·us·es**)
(**GENERAL SCIENCE**) the set of tools or equipment used for doing a job or an activity: *a piece of laboratory apparatus* ◆ *a diver's breathing apparatus*

ap·par·ent **AWL** /ə'pærənt/ *adjective*
1 that seems to be real or true but may not be: *His apparent interest in the proposal surprised everyone.*
2 easy to see or understand; clear: *It was apparent that she didn't like him.* ⊃ **SYNONYM obvious**

ap·par·ent·ly ♪ **AWL** /ə'pærəntli/ *adverb*
You use **apparently** to talk about what people say, or how something appears, when you do not know if it is true or not: *Apparently, he's already been married twice.* ◆ *He was apparently undisturbed by the news.*

ap·peal¹ /ə'pil/ *verb* (**ap·peals**, **ap·peal·ing**, **ap·pealed**)
1 to ask in a serious way for something that you want very much: *Aid workers in the disaster area appealed for food and clothing.*
2 to be attractive or interesting to someone: *Living in a big city doesn't appeal to me.*
3 to officially ask someone in authority to change a decision: *He decided to appeal his conviction.*

ap·peal² /ə'pil/ *noun*
1 [count] asking a lot of people for money, help, or information: *The police made an appeal for witnesses to come forward.*
2 [noncount] a quality that makes someone or something attractive or interesting: *I can't understand the appeal of stamp collecting.*
3 [count] a formal request to someone in authority to change a decision: *an appeal to the Supreme Court*

ap·peal·ing /ə'pilɪŋ/ *adjective*
attractive or interesting: *A vacation in Hawaii sounds very appealing!*

ap·pear ♪ /ə'pɪr/ *verb* (**ap·pears**, **ap·pear·ing**, **ap·peared**)
1 to suddenly be seen; to come into sight: *The sun suddenly appeared from behind a cloud.* ◆ *We waited for an hour but he didn't appear.* ⊃ **ANTONYM disappear**
2 to seem: *She appears to be very happy at her new school.* ◆ *It appears that I was wrong.*
3 to perform in a movie, play, etc.: *She is currently appearing in a Broadway musical.*

ap·pear·ance ♪ /ə'pɪrəns/ *noun*
1 [count, noncount] the way that someone or something looks or seems: *A new hairstyle can completely change your appearance.* ⊃ Look at the note at **clothes**.
2 [count] when someone or something arrives in a place; when someone or something is seen: *Jane's appearance at the party surprised everyone.* ◆ *Is this your first appearance on television?*

Collocations

Physical Appearance

face
- blue/green/brown **eyes**
- pale/flushed/rosy **cheeks**
- white/perfect/crooked **teeth**
- a long/short/neat **beard**

hair and skin
- pale/fair/dark **skin**
- smooth/wrinkled **skin**
- straight/curly/wavy **hair**
- a bald/shaved **head**

ap·pen·di·ci·tis /əˌpɛndə'saɪṭəs/ *noun* [noncount]
(**HEALTH**) an illness in which your APPENDIX becomes very painful and usually has to be removed

ap·pen·dix **AWL** /ə'pɛndɪks/ *noun* [count]
1 (plural **ap·pen·dix·es**) (**BIOLOGY**) a small tube inside your body near your stomach, which can become painful: *She had to have her appendix removed.*
2 (plural **ap·pen·dix·es** or **ap·pen·di·ces** /ə'pɛndəsiz/) (**ENGLISH LANGUAGE ARTS**) a section at the end of a book that gives extra information: *Further statistics can be found in the appendix.*

ap·pe·tite /'æpətaɪt/ *noun* [count, noncount]
the feeling that you want to eat: *When he was sick he completely lost his appetite.*

ap·pe·tiz·er /'æpətaɪzər/ *noun* [count]
a small amount of food that you eat as the first part of a meal

ap·plaud /ə'plɔd/ *verb* (ap·plauds, ap·plaud·ing, ap·plaud·ed)
to make a noise by hitting your hands together to show that you like something: *We all applauded loudly at the end of the song.* ⊃ **SYNONYM clap**

ap·plause /ə'plɔz/ *noun* [noncount]
when a lot of people hit their hands together to show that they like something: *There was loud applause from the audience.*

ap·ple 🔑 /'æpl/ *noun* [count]
a hard round fruit with green or red skin: *an apple tree* ⊃ Look at the picture at **fruit**.

ap·ple ci·der /ˌæpl 'saɪdər/ *noun* [count, noncount]
a drink made from apples

ap·pli·ance /ə'plaɪəns/ *noun* [count]
a useful machine for doing something in the house: *Washing machines and irons are electrical appliances.*

ap·pli·cant /'æplɪkənt/ *noun* [count]
a person who APPLIES (= officially asks) for a job or a place at a college, for example: *There were six applicants for the job.*

ap·pli·ca·tion /ˌæplə'keɪʃn/ *noun*
1 [count, noncount] writing to ask for something, for example a job: *Please turn in your application by December 2.* ◆ *You will need to fill out an application form* (= a special piece of paper that you use to apply for something).
2 [count] (COMPUTERS) a computer program that is designed to do a particular job

ap·ply 🔑 /ə'plaɪ/ *verb* (ap·plies, ap·ply·ing, ap·plied)
1 to write to ask for something: *Why don't you apply for the job?* ◆ *Steve has applied to medical school.*
2 to be about someone or something; to be important to someone or something: *This law applies to all young people over the age of sixteen.*
3 to put or spread something onto a surface: *Apply the cream to the infected area twice a day.*

ap·point /ə'pɔɪnt/ *verb* (ap·points, ap·point·ing, ap·point·ed)
to choose someone for a job or position: *The bank has appointed a new manager.*

ap·point·ment 🔑 /ə'pɔɪntmənt/ *noun* [count]
an arrangement to see someone at a particular time: *I have an appointment with the doctor at ten o'clock.* ◆ *You need to call them to make an appointment.*

ap·pre·ci·ate 🔑 AWL /ə'priʃieɪt/ *verb*
(ap·pre·ci·ates, ap·pre·ci·at·ing, ap·pre·ci·at·ed)
1 to be grateful for something that someone has done for you: *Thank you for your help. I appreciate it.*

2 to enjoy something or understand how good someone or something is: *Van Gogh's paintings were only appreciated after his death.* ◆ *My boss doesn't appreciate me.*
3 to understand that something is true: *I don't think you appreciate how expensive it will be.*

ap·pre·ci·a·tion AWL /əˌpriʃi'eɪʃn/ *noun* [noncount]
1 understanding and enjoyment of how good someone or something is: *She shows little appreciation of good music.*
2 the feeling of being grateful for something that someone has done for you: *We gave her some flowers to show our appreciation for her hard work.*

ap·pren·tice /ə'prɛntəs/ *noun* [count]
a person, especially a young person, who is learning to do a job: *an apprentice electrician*

ap·proach¹ AWL /ə'proʊtʃ/ *verb* (ap·proach·es, ap·proach·ing, ap·proached)
to come near to someone or something in distance or time: *As you approach the town, you'll see a church on your right.* ◆ *Their final exams were approaching.*

ap·proach² AWL /ə'proʊtʃ/ *noun* (plural ap·proach·es)
1 [count] a way of doing something: *This is a new approach to learning languages.*
2 [noncount] coming near or nearer to someone or something: *the approach of winter*

ap·pro·pri·ate 🔑 AWL /ə'proʊpriət/ *adjective*
suitable or right for a particular situation, person, etc.: *Jeans and T-shirts are not appropriate for a job interview.* ⊃ ANTONYM **inappropriate**

▶ **ap·pro·pri·ate·ly** AWL /ə'proʊpriətli/ *adverb*: *Please come appropriately dressed.*

ap·prov·al /ə'pruvl/ *noun* [noncount]
1 feeling, showing, or saying that something or someone is good or right: *Tania's parents gave the marriage their approval.* ⊃ ANTONYM **disapproval**
2 official permission to do something: *We finally got approval for our building plans.*

ap·prove 🔑 /ə'pruv/ *verb* (ap·proves, ap·prov·ing, ap·proved)
1 to think or say that something or someone is good or right: *My parents don't approve of my friends.* ◆ *She doesn't approve of smoking.* ⊃ ANTONYM **disapprove**
2 to officially agree to something or say that something is correct: *Has your boss approved your vacation days?*

ap·prox·i·mate AWL /ə'prɑksəmət/ *adjective*
almost correct but not exact: *The approximate time of arrival is three o'clock.*

---

ap·prox·i·mate·ly AWL /əˈprɑksəmətli/ *adverb*
about; more or less: *I live approximately two miles from the station.* ➷ SYNONYM **roughly**

a·pri·cot /ˈæprɪkɑt; ˈeɪprɪkɑt/ *noun* [count]
a small soft yellow or orange fruit with a large seed inside

A·pril 🔑 /ˈeɪprəl/ *noun* [count, noncount]
(abbreviation **Apr.**)
the fourth month of the year

a·pron /ˈeɪprən/ *noun* [count]
a thing that you wear over the front of your clothes to keep them clean, especially when you are cooking

ap·ti·tude /ˈæptətud/ *noun* [count, noncount]
a natural ability or skill at doing something: *He has an aptitude for learning languages.*

a·quar·i·um /əˈkwɛriəm/ *noun* [count]
1 a large glass container filled with water, in which fish are kept
2 a building where people can go to see fish and other water animals

a·quat·ic /əˈkwætɪk/ *adjective*
(BIOLOGY) living or happening in or on water: *aquatic plants* • *sailing and other aquatic sports*

arc /ɑrk/ *noun* [count]
(MATH) a curved line; part of a circle ➷ Look at the picture at **circle**.

ar·cade /ɑrˈkeɪd/ *noun* [count]
a large room with machines and games that you put coins in to play: *a video game arcade*

arch /ɑrtʃ/ *noun*
[count] (*plural* **arch·es**)
a part of a bridge, building, or wall that is in the shape of a half circle

arch

ar·chae·ol·o·gist
(also **ar·che·ol·o·gist**)
/ˌɑrkiˈɑlədʒɪst/ *noun*
[count]
a person who studies or knows a lot about
ARCHAEOLOGY

ar·chae·ol·o·gy (also **ar·che·ol·o·gy**)
/ˌɑrkiˈɑlədʒi/ *noun* [noncount]
the study of the past by looking at objects or parts of old buildings that are found in the ground
▶ **ar·chae·o·log·i·cal** (also **ar·che·o·log·i·cal**) /ˌɑrkiəˈlɑdʒəkl/ *adjective*: *archaeological remains*

ar·chi·tect /ˈɑrkətɛkt/ *noun* [count]
a person whose job is to design and plan buildings

ar·chi·tec·ture /ˈɑrkəˌtɛktʃər/ *noun* [noncount]
1 the study of designing and making buildings: *He has a degree in architecture.*

2 (ART) the design or style of a building or buildings: *Do you like modern architecture?*

the Arc·tic /ði ˈɑrktɪk/ *noun* [singular]
(GEOGRAPHY) the very cold land and countries in the most northern part of the world ➷ Look at **the Antarctic.** ➷ Look at the picture at **earth**.

are /ər; ɑr/ form of **be**

ar·e·a 🔑 AWL /ˈɛriə/ *noun*
1 [count] a part of a city, country, or the world: *Do you live in this area?* • *the desert areas of South America*
2 [count, noncount] (MATH) the size of a flat place. If a room is twelve feet wide and ten feet long, it has an **area** of 120 square feet.
3 [count] a space that you use for a particular activity: *The restaurant has a nonsmoking area* (= a part where you must not smoke).

ar·e·a code /ˈɛriə ˌkoʊd/ *noun* [count]
the numbers for a particular area, which you use when you are making a telephone call from outside the area: *One of the area codes for Chicago is 312.*

a·re·na /əˈrinə/ *noun* [count] (*plural* **a·re·nas**)
a place with seats around it where you can watch sports or concerts

aren't /ɑrnt/ short for **are not**

ar·gue 🔑 /ˈɑrgyu/ *verb* (**ar·gues**, **ar·gu·ing**, **ar·gued**)
1 to talk with someone in an angry way because you do not agree: *My parents argue a lot about money.* • *I often argue with my brother.*
2 to say why you think something is right or wrong: *Billy argued that war is not the answer.*

ar·gu·ment 🔑 /ˈɑrgyəmənt/ *noun* [count]
1 an angry discussion between people who do not agree with each other: *They had an argument about where to go on vacation.* • *I had an argument with my father.*
2 the reason or reasons that you give to support your opinion about something: *What are the arguments for and against higher taxes?*

ar·gu·men·ta·tive /ˌɑrgyəˈmɛntətɪv/ *adjective*
often involved in or enjoying arguments: *Stop being so argumentative!*

ar·id /ˈærɪd/ *adjective*
(GEOGRAPHY) with little or no rain and so very dry: *This region has an arid climate.*

a·rise /əˈraɪz/ *verb* (**a·ris·es**, **a·ris·ing**, **a·rose** /əˈroʊz/, has **a·ris·en** /əˈrɪzn/) (*formal*)
If a problem or difficult situation **arises**, it happens or starts to exist.

a·rith·me·tic /əˈrɪθmətɪk/ *noun* [noncount]
(MATH) working with numbers, for example by adding or multiplying, to find the answer to a math problem: *I'm not very good at mental arithmetic.*

arm¹ 🔊 /ɑrm/ *noun* [count]
the part of your body from your shoulder to your hand: *Put your arms in the air.* ✦ *He was carrying a book under his arm.* ⟹ Look at the picture at **body**.
arm in arm with your arm holding another person's arm: *The two friends walked arm in arm.*

arm² /ɑrm/ *verb* (arms, arm·ing, armed)
to provide weapons for someone or yourself: *The rebel group armed themselves with guns.*
▶ **armed** /ɑrmd/ *adjective*
carrying a gun or other weapon: *The robbers are armed and dangerous.* ⟹ Look at **the armed forces**.

ar·ma·dil·lo
/ˌɑrməˈdɪloʊ/ *noun* [count] (plural ar·ma·dil·los)
a small American animal that eats insects. Its body is covered in a shell of hard plates.

armadillo

arm·chair /ˈɑrmtʃɛr/ *noun* [count]
a soft, comfortable chair with side parts where you can put your arms: *She was asleep in an armchair.* ⟹ Look at the picture at **chair**.

the armed forc·es /ði ˌɑrmd ˈfɔrsɪz/ *noun* [plural]
a country's soldiers who fight on land, on water, or in the air ⟹ SYNONYM **the military**

ar·mor /ˈɑrmər/ *noun* [noncount]
metal clothes that men wore long ago to cover their bodies when they were fighting: *a suit of armor*
▶ **ar·mored** /ˈɑrmərd/ *adjective*: *an armored car*

arm·pit /ˈɑrmpɪt/ *noun* [count]
the part of your body under your arm, where your arm joins your body

arms /ɑrmz/ *noun* [plural]
guns, bombs, and other weapons for fighting: *to develop nuclear arms*

ar·my 🔊 /ˈɑrmi/ *noun* [count] (plural ar·mies)
(POLITICS) a large group of soldiers who fight on land in a war: *He joined the army when he was 18.* ✦ *the U.S. Army* ⟹ Look at **navy**.

a·ro·ma /əˈroʊmə/ *noun* [count]
a pleasant smell: *the aroma of freshly baked bread*

a·rose form of **arise**

a·round 🔊 /əˈraʊnd/ *preposition, adverb*
1 in or to different places or in different directions: *Her clothes were lying around the room.* ✦ *We walked around for an hour looking for a restaurant.* ✦ *The children were running around the house.*

2 in the opposite direction or in another direction: *Turn around and go back the way you came.*
3 on or to all sides of something, often in a circle: *We sat around the table.* ✦ *He ran around the track.* ✦ *There is a wall around the yard.*
4 in a place; near here: *Is there a bank around here?* ✦ *Is Helen around? I want to speak to her.*
5 (also a·bout) a little more or less than; a little before or after: *I'll see you around seven* (= at about 7 o'clock).

ar·range 🔊 /əˈreɪndʒ/ *verb* (ar·rang·es, ar·rang·ing, ar·ranged)
1 to put things in a certain order or place: *Arrange the chairs in a circle.*
2 to make a plan for the future: *I arranged to meet Tim at six o'clock.*

ar·range·ment 🔊 /əˈreɪndʒmənt/ *noun* [count]
1 a plan or preparation that you make so that something can happen in the future: *They are making the arrangements for their wedding.*
2 a group of things put together so that they look nice: *a flower arrangement*

ar·rest¹ 🔊 /əˈrɛst/ *verb* (ar·rests, ar·rest·ing, ar·rest·ed)
When the police **arrest** someone, they take that person away to ask them questions about a crime: *The man was arrested for selling drugs.*

ar·rest² /əˈrɛst/ *noun* [count, noncount]
the act of arresting someone: *The police made five arrests.* ✦ *The wanted man is now under arrest* (= has been arrested).

ar·ri·val /əˈraɪvl/ *noun*
1 [count, noncount] coming to a place: *My brother met me at the airport on my arrival.* ⟹ ANTONYM **departure**
2 [count] a person or thing that has arrived: *We brought in extra chairs for the late arrivals.*

ar·rive 🔊 /əˈraɪv/ *verb* (ar·rives, ar·riv·ing, ar·rived)
1 to come to a place: *What time did you arrive last night?* ✦ *What time does the train arrive in Chicago?* ✦ *They arrived at the station ten minutes late.* ⟹ ANTONYM **leave**, **depart**
2 to come or happen: *Summer has arrived!*

Grammar

■ Be careful! We use **arrive in** with the name of a city or country and **arrive at** with a building such as a station, an airport, or a school.

ar·ro·gant /ˈærəgənt/ *adjective*
A person who is **arrogant** thinks that they are better and more important than other people.
▶ **ar·ro·gance** /ˈærəgəns/ *noun* [noncount]: *He had the arrogance to think that he should decide for us.*

ar·row 🔑 /'æroʊ/ *noun* [*count*]
1 a long thin piece of wood or metal with a point at one end ⊃ Look at the picture at **bow³**.
2 the sign (→) that shows where something is or where you should go: *The arrow is pointing left.*

ar·son /'ɑrsn/ *noun* [*noncount*]
the crime of setting fire to a building on purpose

art 🔑 /ɑrt/ *noun*
1 [*noncount*] (**ART**) making things such as paintings and drawings for people to look at: *He's studying art at college.*
2 [*noncount*] (**ART**) things like paintings and drawings that someone has made: *modern art* ◆ *an art gallery*
3 the arts [*plural*] things like films, plays, and literature: *How much money does the government spend on the arts?*
4 [*count, usually singular*] a skill, or something that needs skill: *the art of letter writing*
5 arts [*plural*] the subjects you can study in school or college which are not science subjects, for example history or languages: *She has a Bachelor of Arts degree in history.*

ar·ter·y /'ɑrtəri/ *noun* [*count*] (*plural* **ar·ter·ies**)
(**BIOLOGY**) one of the tubes in your body that carry blood away from your heart to other parts of your body ⊃ Look at **vein**. ⊃ Look at the picture at **body**.

ar·thri·tis /ɑr'θraɪtəs/ *noun* [*noncount*]
(**HEALTH**) a disease that causes pain when you bend your arms, fingers, knees, etc.

ar·ti·choke /'ɑrtə,tʃoʊk/ *noun* [*count*]
a green vegetable with a lot of thick pointed leaves that looks like a flower. You eat the bottom part of the leaves and its center when it is cooked.

ar·ti·cle 🔑 /'ɑrtɪkl/ *noun* [*count*]
1 a piece of writing in a newspaper or magazine: *Did you read the article about young fashion designers?*
2 a thing: *Many of the articles in the store are half price.* ◆ *articles of clothing* (= things like skirts, coats, and pants)
3 (**ENGLISH LANGUAGE ARTS**) the words "a" and "an" (called the **INDEFINITE ARTICLE**), or "the" (called the **DEFINITE ARTICLE**)

ar·ti·fi·cial 🔑 /ˌɑrtə'fɪʃl/ *adjective*
not natural or real, but made by people: *artificial flowers* ◆ *These drinks contain no artificial colors or flavors.*
▶ **ar·ti·fi·cial·ly** /ˌɑrtə'fɪʃəli/ *adverb*

ar·ti·fi·cial in·tel·li·gence /ˌɑrtə'fɪʃl ɪn'tɛlədʒəns/ *noun* [*noncount*] (abbreviation **AI**)
(**COMPUTERS**) the study of the way in which computers can copy the way humans think

art·ist 🔑 /'ɑrtɪst/ *noun* [*count*]
(**ART**) a person who makes art, especially paintings or drawings: *Andy Warhol was a famous American artist.*

ar·tis·tic 🔑 /ɑr'tɪstɪk/ *adjective* (**ART**)
1 good at painting, drawing, or making other things connected with art: *He's very artistic – his drawings are excellent.*
2 connected with art: *the artistic director of the theater*

as 🔑 /əz; æz/ *conjunction, preposition*
1 while something else is happening: *Just as I was leaving the house, the phone rang.*
2 as ... as words that you use to compare people or things; the same amount: *Paul is as tall as his father.* ◆ *I don't have as many clothes as you do.* ◆ *I'd like it done as soon as possible.*
3 used to say that someone or something has a particular job or purpose: *She works as a secretary for a big company.* ◆ *I used my shoe as a hammer.*
4 in the same way: *Please do as I tell you!*
5 (*formal*) because: *As she was sick, she didn't go to school.*

ASAP (also **asap**) /ˌeɪ ɛs eɪ 'pi; 'eɪsæp/ *abbreviation* (*informal*)
as soon as possible: *I'd like the report on my desk ASAP.*

as·cend /ə'sɛnd/ *verb* (**as·cend**, **as·cend·ing**, **as·cend·ed**) (*formal*)
to go up: *The results are arranged in ascending order* (= from the lowest to the highest). ⊃ **ANTONYM descend**
▶ **as·cent** /ə'sɛnt/ *noun* [*count*]: *the first ascent of Mount Everest* ⊃ **ANTONYM descent**

ash /æʃ/ *noun* [*noncount*]
the gray powder that is left after something has completely burned: *cigarette ash*

a·shamed 🔑 /ə'ʃeɪmd/ *adjective*
feeling sorry and unhappy because you have done something wrong, or because you are not as good as other people: *I felt ashamed about lying to my parents.* ◆ *She was ashamed of her old clothes.*

a·shore /ə'ʃɔr/ *adverb*
onto the land from the ocean or a river: *We left the boat and went ashore.*

ash·tray /'æʃtreɪ/ *noun* [*count*]
a small dish for cigarette **ASH** and the ends of cigarettes

a·side /ə'saɪd/ *adverb*
on or to one side; away: *He set the letter aside while he did his homework.*

ask 🔑 /æsk/ *verb* (**asks**, **ask·ing**, **asked**)
1 to try to get an answer by using a question: *I asked him what time it was.* ◆ *"What's your*

name?" she asked. ◆ Liz asked the teacher a question.

2 to say that you would like someone to do something for you: *I asked Sara to drive me to the station.*

3 to try to get permission to do something: *I asked my teacher if I could go home.* ◆ *I asked if I could go home early.*

4 to invite someone to go somewhere with you: *Mark asked me to dinner on Saturday.*

ask for someone to say that you want to speak to someone: *Call this number and ask for Mrs. Green.*

ask for something to say that you want someone to give you something: *He asked for a new bike for his birthday.*

a·sleep 🔊 /ə'slip/ *adjective*
sleeping: *The baby is asleep in the bedroom.* ◆ *He fell asleep* (= started sleeping) *in front of the fire.*
⊃ ANTONYM **awake**

Which word?

Asleep or sleeping?

▪ You use **sleeping**, not **asleep**, before a noun: *She put the sleeping child in his crib.*
▪ We use **fall asleep** or **go to sleep** to talk about starting to sleep: *Laura fell asleep as soon as she got into bed.* ◆ *Tom read for half an hour before he went to sleep.*

---

as·par·a·gus /ə'spærəgəs/ *noun* [noncount]
thin green plants with pointed ends that are eaten as a vegetable

as·pect AWL /'æspɛkt/ *noun* [count]
one of the qualities or parts of a situation, idea, problem, etc.: *Spelling is one of the most difficult aspects of learning English.*

as·phalt /'æsfɔlt/ *noun* [noncount]
a thick black substance that is used for making the surface of roads

as·pi·rin /'æsprən/ *noun* [count, noncount] (*plural* as·pi·rin or as·pi·rins)
(HEALTH) a medicine that stops pain: *I took an aspirin for my headache.*

as·sas·sin /ə'sæsn/ *noun* [count]
a person who kills a famous or important person: *Lincoln's assassin, John Wilkes Booth, was a professional actor.*

as·sas·si·nate /ə'sæsəneɪt/ *verb* (as·sas·si·nates, as·sas·si·nat·ing, as·sas·si·nat·ed)
to kill an important or famous person: *John F. Kennedy was assassinated in 1963.*
▶ **as·sas·si·na·tion** /ə,sæsə'neɪʃn/ *noun* [count, noncount]: *an assassination attempt*

as·sault /ə'sɔlt/ *verb* (as·saults, as·sault·ing, as·sault·ed)
to attack or hurt someone: *He assaulted a policeman.*
▶ **as·sault** *noun* [count, noncount]: *an assault on an old lady*

as·sem·ble AWL /ə'sɛmbl/ *verb* (as·sem·bles, as·sem·bling, as·sem·bled)
1 to come together, or bring people or things together in a group: *The leaders assembled in Washington for the meeting.*
2 to fit the parts of something together: *instructions for assembling a bookcase*

as·sem·bly AWL /ə'sɛmbli/ *noun* [count, noncount] (*plural* as·sem·blies)
a meeting of a big group of people for a special reason: *Our school assembly is at 9:30 in the morning.*

as·ser·tive /ə'sərtɪv/ *adjective*
acting and talking in a confident way so that people listen to you or do what you want: *If you want them to listen to you, you need to be more assertive.*

as·sess AWL /ə'sɛs/ *verb* (as·sess·es, as·sess·ing, as·sessed)
to judge how good, bad, or important something is: *It's difficult to assess the effects of the price increases.*
▶ **as·sess·ment** AWL /ə'sɛsmənt/ *noun* [count, noncount]: *I made a careful assessment of the risks involved.*

as·set /'æsɛt/ *noun* [count]
a person or thing that is useful to someone or something: *She's a great asset to the organization.*

as·sign AWL /ə'saɪn/ *verb* (as·signs, as·sign·ing, as·signed)
to give someone a particular job to do: *The teacher assigned us four pages of math homework.*

as·sign·ment AWL /ə'saɪnmənt/ *noun* [count, noncount]
a job or piece of work that someone is given to do: *You have to complete three writing assignments each semester.* ◆ *a reporter on assignment in Mexico* (= working there)

as·sist AWL /ə'sɪst/ *verb* (as·sists, as·sist·ing, as·sist·ed) (*formal*)
to help someone: *The driver assisted her with her suitcases.*

as·sis·tance AWL /ə'sɪstəns/ *noun* [noncount] (*formal*)
help: *I cannot move this piano without your assistance.*

---

as·sis·tant AWL /ə'sɪstənt/ *noun* [*count*]
a person who helps someone in a more important position: *Ms. Dixon is not here today. Would you like to speak to her assistant?*

as·so·ci·ate¹ /ə'soʊʃi,eɪt/ *verb* (as·so·ci·ates, as·so·ci·at·ing, as·so·ci·at·ed)
1 to make a connection between things or people in your mind: *Most people associate Colorado with snow and skiing.* ◆ *These illnesses are associated with smoking.*
2 to spend time with someone

as·so·ci·ate² /ə'soʊʃiət/ *noun* [*count*]
(**BUSINESS**) a person that you know through your work: *a business associate*

as·so·ci·ate's de·gree /ə'soʊʃiəts dɪ,gri/ (also **as·so·ci·ate de·gree**) *noun* [*count*]
a degree that you get after studying for two years at a college or university in the U.S. ↪ Look at **bachelor's degree**.

as·so·ci·a·tion /ə,soʊsi'eɪʃn/ *noun* [*count*]
a group of people who join or work together for a special reason: *the American Medical Association*

as·sort·ed /ə'sɔrtəd/ *adjective*
of different types; mixed: *a box of assorted chocolates*

as·sume AWL /ə'sum/ *verb* (as·sumes, as·sum·ing, as·sumed)
to think that something is true although you are not really sure: *Kate isn't here today, so I assume that she's sick.*

as·sump·tion AWL /ə'sʌmpʃn/ *noun* [*count*]
something that you think is true, although you are not really sure: *It's unfair to make assumptions about a person before you get to know them.*

as·sure AWL /ə'ʃʊr/ *verb* (as·sures, as·sur·ing, as·sured)
to tell someone what is true or certain so that they feel less worried: *I assure you that the dog isn't dangerous.*

as·ter·isk /'æstərɪsk/ *noun* [*count*]
(**ENGLISH LANGUAGE ARTS**) the symbol (*) that you use to make people notice something in a piece of writing

as·ter·oid /'æstərɔɪd/ *noun* [*count*]
any of the many small planets that go around the sun

asth·ma /'æzmə/ *noun* [*noncount*]
(**HEALTH**) an illness that makes breathing difficult: *He had an asthma attack.*
▶ **asth·mat·ic** /æz'mætɪk/ *adjective*: *My daughter is asthmatic.*

a·ston·ish /ə'stɑnɪʃ/ *verb* (a·ston·ish·es, a·ston·ish·ing, a·ston·ished)
to surprise someone very much: *The news astonished everyone.*

a·ston·ished /ə'stɑnɪʃt/ *adjective*
very surprised: *I was astonished to hear that he was getting married.*

a·ston·ish·ing /ə'stɑnɪʃɪŋ/ *adjective*
If something is **astonishing**, it surprises you very much: *an astonishing story*

a·ston·ish·ment /ə'stɑnɪʃmənt/ *noun* [*noncount*]
a feeling of great surprise: *He looked at me in astonishment when I told him the news.*

as·trol·o·gy /ə'strɑlədʒi/ *noun* [*noncount*]
the study of the positions and movements of the stars and planets and the way that some people believe they affect people and events
▶ **as·trol·o·ger** /ə'strɑlədʒər/ *noun* [*count*]
a person who studies or knows a lot about **astrology** ↪ Look at **horoscope, the zodiac**.

as·tro·naut /'æstrənɔt; 'æstrənət/ *noun* [*count*]
a person who works and travels in space

as·tron·o·my /ə'strɑnəmi/ *noun* [*noncount*]
the study of the sun, moon, planets, and stars
▶ **as·tron·o·mer** /ə'strɑnəmər/ *noun* [*count*]
a person who studies or knows a lot about **astronomy**

as·tute /ə'stut/ *adjective*
good at judging people or situations: *an astute observer*

at 🔑 /ət; æt/ *preposition*
1 a word that shows where: *They are at school.* ◆ *Jen is at home.* ◆ *The answer is at the bottom of the page.*
2 a word that shows when: *I go to bed at eleven o'clock.* ◆ *At night you can see the stars.*
3 toward someone or something: *Look at the picture.* ◆ *I smiled at her.* ◆ *Someone threw paint at the mayor.*
4 a word that shows what someone is doing or what is happening: *The two countries are at war.* ◆ *We were hard at work.*
5 a word that shows how much, how fast, how old, etc.: *We were traveling at about 50 miles per hour.* ◆ *She got married at nineteen* (= when she was nineteen years old).
6 a word that shows how well someone or something does something: *I'm not very good at math.*
7 because of something: *We laughed at his jokes.*
8 the symbol @, used in e-mail addresses after a person's name ↪ Look at the note at **dot**.

ate form of **eat**

a·the·ist /'eɪθiɪst/ *noun* [*count*]
(**RELIGION**) a person who does not believe that there is a God

ath·lete /'æθlit/ *noun* [*count*]
(**SPORTS**) a person who is good at sports like running or jumping, especially one who takes

part in sports competitions: *Athletes from all over the world go to the Olympic Games.*

ath·let·ic /æθ'lɛṭɪk/ *adjective*
1 (SPORTS) connected with sports: *athletic ability*
2 (HEALTH) having a fit, strong, and healthy body

ath·let·ics /æθ'lɛṭɪks/ *noun* [*noncount*]
(SPORTS) sports of any kind: *college athletics*

at·las /'ætləs/ *noun* [*count*] (*plural* at·las·es)
(GEOGRAPHY) a book of maps: *an atlas of the world*

ATM /ˌeɪ ti 'ɛm/ *noun* [*count*]
a machine that you can get money from by using a special plastic card ⊃ Look at the note at **account**[1].

at·mos·phere /'ætməsfɪr/ *noun*
1 the atmosphere [*singular*] (GENERAL SCIENCE) the mixture of gases around the earth: *pollution of the atmosphere*
2 [*count*] the air in a place: *a smoky atmosphere*
3 [*count, noncount*] the feeling that places or people give you: *The atmosphere in the office was very friendly.*

atom

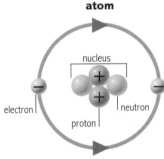

nucleus

electron

neutron

proton

at·om /'æṭəm/ *noun* [*count*]
(PHYSICS, CHEMISTRY) one of the very small things that everything is made of: *Water is made of atoms of hydrogen and oxygen.* ⊃ Look at **molecule**.

a·tom·ic /ə'tɑmɪk/ *adjective* (CHEMISTRY, PHYSICS)
1 of or about atoms: *atomic physics*
2 using the great power that is made by breaking atoms: *an atomic bomb* • *atomic energy*

at·tach /ə'tætʃ/ *verb* (at·tach·es, at·tach·ing, at·tached)
to join or fix one thing to another thing: *I attached the photo to the letter.* • *Please attach a copy of the document* (= send it with the e-mail).

at·tached AWL /ə'tætʃt/ *adjective*
liking someone or something very much: *We've grown very attached to this house.*

at·tach·ment AWL /ə'tætʃmənt/ *noun*
1 [*count, noncount*] a strong feeling of love or liking for someone or something: *a child's strong attachment to its parents*

2 [*count*] (COMPUTERS) a document that you send to someone using e-mail

at·tack[1] /ə'tæk/ *noun*
1 [*count, noncount*] a violent act which is done in order to hurt someone or damage something: *There was a terrorist attack on the city.*
2 [*count*] (HEALTH) a time when you are sick: *an attack of the flu*

at·tack[2] /ə'tæk/ *verb* (at·tacks, at·tack·ing, at·tacked)
to start fighting or hurting someone or something: *The army attacked the city.* • *The old man was attacked and his money was stolen.*

at·tain AWL /ə'teɪn/ *verb* (at·tains, at·tain·ing, at·tained)
to succeed in getting or achieving something, especially after a lot of effort: *He attained his goal of becoming a pilot.*

at·tempt /ə'tɛmpt/ *verb* (at·tempts, at·tempt·ing, at·tempt·ed)
to try to do something that is difficult: *He attempted to sail around the world.* ⊃ SYNONYM **try**
▶ **at·tempt** *noun* [*count*]: *She made no attempt to help me.* • *a brave attempt at breaking the world record*

at·tend /ə'tɛnd/ *verb* (at·tends, at·tend·ing, at·tend·ed)
to go to or be present at a place: *Did you attend the meeting?* • *The children attend a public school.*

at·ten·dance /ə'tɛndəns/ *noun*
1 [*noncount*] being present at a place, for example at school: *Attendance at these lectures is mandatory.*
2 [*count, noncount*] the number of people who go to an organized event: *Movie attendance rose again last year.*

at·ten·dant /ə'tɛndənt/ *noun* [*count*]
a person whose job is to serve or help people in a public place: *a parking lot attendant* ⊃ Look at **flight attendant**.

at·ten·tion /ə'tɛnʃn/ *noun* [*noncount*]
1 looking or listening carefully and with interest: *I shouted in order to attract her attention* (= make her notice me). • *Can I have your attention, please?* (= please listen to me)
2 special care or action: *to require medical attention*
pay attention to look or listen carefully: *Please pay attention to what I'm saying.*

at·ten·tive /ə'tɛntɪv/ *adjective*
watching, listening to, or thinking about someone or something carefully: *an attentive audience*

at·tic /ˈætɪk/ *noun* [count]
the room or space under the roof of a house: *My old clothes are in a box in the attic.*

at·ti·tude 🔊 **AWL** /ˈætəˌtud/ *noun* [count]
the way you think or feel about something: *What's your **attitude toward** marriage?*

at·tor·ney /əˈtərni/ *noun* [count] (*plural* at·tor·neys)
a lawyer, especially one who helps people or talks for them in a court of law ⮂ **SYNONYM lawyer**

at·tract 🔊 /əˈtrækt/ *verb* (at·tracts, at·tract·ing, at·tract·ed)
1 to make someone like someone or something: *He was **attracted to** her.* ◆ *I had always been **attracted by** the idea of working overseas.*
2 to make someone or something come somewhere: *Moths are attracted to light.* ◆ *The new book has attracted a lot of publicity.*

at·trac·tion /əˈtrækʃn/ *noun*
1 [count, noncount] a feeling of liking someone or something very much: *I can't understand his attraction to her.*
2 [count] something that is interesting or enjoyable: *The Washington Monument is a major tourist attraction.*

at·trac·tive 🔊 /əˈtræktɪv/ *adjective*
1 A person who is **attractive** is nice to look at: *He's very attractive.*
2 Something that is **attractive** pleases you or interests you: *That's an attractive offer.* ⮂
ANTONYM unattractive

Thesaurus

attractive can be used about any person who is nice to look at: *He's polite and attractive.* ◆ *a group of attractive young women*
beautiful (usually used to describe a woman or girl) very attractive: *a beautiful, intelligent woman* ◆ *She looked beautiful that night.*
good-looking (used more about men than women) attractive: *The band's lead singer is very good-looking.* ◆ *a good-looking young actor*
pretty (usually about a girl or young woman) attractive: *She has a very pretty face.* ◆ *a pretty little girl in a pink dress*
handsome (usually used about a man or boy) attractive: *You look so handsome in that suit!* ◆ *a polite, handsome man*

a·typ·i·cal /eɪˈtɪpɪkl/ *adjective* (formal)
not typical or usual: *atypical behavior* ⮂ **ANTONYM typical**

auc·tion /ˈɔkʃn/ *noun* [count]
a sale where each thing is sold to the person who will give the most money for it
▸ **auc·tion** *verb* (auc·tions, auc·tion·ing, auc·tioned)
to sell something at an auction

au·di·ence /ˈɔdiəns/ *noun* [count]
the people who are watching or listening to a movie, play, concert, television program, etc.: *Several audience members left before the end of the show.*

au·di·o /ˈɔdioʊ/ *adjective*
(**MUSIC**) connected with the recording of sound: *audio equipment*

au·di·o·vis·u·al /ˌɔdioʊˈvɪʒuəl/ *adjective*
using both sound and pictures: *audiovisual aids for the classroom*

au·di·tion¹ /ɔˈdɪʃn/ *noun* [count]
a short performance by an actor, a singer, etc. to find out if he or she is good enough to be in a play, show, etc.

au·di·tion² /ɔˈdɪʃn/ *verb* (au·di·tion, au·di·tion·ing, au·di·tioned)
to take part in an AUDITION: *He auditioned for the part of Othello.*

au·di·to·ri·um /ˌɔdəˈtɔriəm/ *noun* [count] (*plural* au·di·to·ri·ums or au·di·to·ri·a /ˌɔdəˈtɔriə/)
a large room like a theater where people sit and watch a performance, listen to a speaker, etc.: *School assemblies are held in the auditorium.*

Au·gust 🔊 /ˈɔɡʌst/ *noun* [count, noncount] (abbreviation **Aug.**)
the eighth month of the year

aunt 🔊 /ænt; ɑnt/ *noun* [count]
the sister of your mother or father, or the wife of your uncle: *Aunt Mary*

au·then·tic /ɔˈθɛntɪk/ *adjective*
real and true: *That's not an authentic Picasso painting – it's just a copy.*

au·thor **AWL** /ˈɔθər/ *noun* [count]
(**ENGLISH LANGUAGE ARTS**) a person who writes books or stories: *Who is your favorite author?*

au·thor·i·tar·i·an /əˌθɔrəˈtɛriən/ *adjective*
not allowing people the freedom to decide things for themselves: *an authoritarian government* ◆ *authoritarian parents*

au·thor·i·ta·tive **AWL** /əˈθɔrəˌteɪtɪv/ *adjective*
1 having authority; demanding or expecting that people obey you: *an authoritative tone of voice*
2 that you can trust as true and correct: *the most authoritative book on the subject*

au·thor·i·ty 🖋 **AWL** /ə'θɔrəṭi/ *noun* (*plural* au·thor·i·ties)
1 [*noncount*] the power to tell people what they must do: *The police have the **authority** to stop cars.*
2 [*count*] (**POLITICS**) a group of people that tell other people what they must do: *the city authorities*
3 [*count*] a person with special knowledge: *She's an **authority** on criminal law.* ⊃ **SYNONYM expert**

au·thor·ize /'ɔθəraɪz/ *verb* (au·thor·i·zes, au·thor·i·zing, au·thor·ized)
to give official permission for something, or for someone to do something: *He authorized his assistant to sign letters for him.*
▶ **au·thor·i·za·tion** /ˌɔθərə'zeɪʃn/ *noun* [*noncount*]: *No one is allowed in this area without authorization.*

au·to /'ɔt̬oʊ/ *noun* [*count*] (*plural* au·tos) (*formal*)
a car: *auto insurance*

au·to·bi·og·ra·phy /ˌɔt̬əbaɪ'ɑgrəfi/ *noun* [*count*] (*plural* au·to·bi·og·ra·phies)
(**ENGLISH LANGUAGE ARTS**) a book that a person has written about their life

au·to·graph /'ɔt̬əgræf/ *noun* [*count*]
a famous person's name, which they themselves have written: *He asked Madonna for her autograph.*

au·to·mat·ed **AWL** /'ɔt̬əmeɪt̬əd/ *adjective*
operated by machine, without needing people: *The factory has a fully automated system.*

au·to·mat·ic **AWL** /ˌɔt̬ə'mæt̬ɪk/ *adjective*
1 If a machine is **automatic**, it can work by itself, without people controlling it: *automatic doors*
2 that you do without thinking: *Breathing is automatic.*
▶ **au·to·mat·i·cal·ly** **AWL** /ˌɔt̬ə'mæt̬ɪkli/ *adverb*: *This light comes on automatically at five o'clock.* ◆ *I automatically turned right, because that's the way I usually go.*

au·to·mo·bile /ˌɔt̬əmə'bil/ *noun* [*count*]
a car: *the automobile industry*

au·top·sy /'ɔˌtɑpsi/ *noun* [*count*] (*plural* au·top·sies)
(**HEALTH**) an examination of a dead body to find out the cause of death: *to perform an autopsy*

au·tumn /'ɔt̬əm/ *noun* [*count, noncount*] (*formal*)
the part of the year between summer and winter: *In autumn, the leaves begin to fall from the trees.* ⊃ **SYNONYM fall**

a·vail·a·ble 🖋 **AWL** /ə'veɪləbl/ *adjective*
ready for you to use, have, or see: *I called the hotel to ask if there were any rooms available.* ◆ *I'm sorry – the manager is not available this afternoon.*

av·a·lanche /'ævəlæntʃ/ *noun* [*count*]
(**GEOGRAPHY**) a very large amount of snow that falls quickly down the side of a mountain

av·e·nue /'ævənu/ *noun* [*count*]
a street in a town or city: *I live on McClean Avenue.* ⊃ The short way of writing "Avenue" in addresses is Ave.: *109 Fifth Ave.* ⊃ Look at the note at **road**.

av·er·age¹ 🖋 /'ævrɪdʒ/ *noun*
1 [*count*] (**MATH**) the result you get when you add two or more amounts together and then divide the total by the number of amounts you added: *The average of 2, 3, and 7 is 4 (2 + 3 + 7 = 12, and 12 ÷ 3 = 4).*
2 [*noncount*] the normal amount, quality, etc.: *On average, I buy a newspaper about twice a week.*

av·er·age² 🖋 /'ævrɪdʒ/ *adjective*
1 (**MATH**) (used about a number) found by calculating the AVERAGE¹(1): *The average age of the students is 19.*
2 normal or usual: *The average student gets around 5 hours of homework a week.*

av·er·age³ /'ævrɪdʒ/ *verb* (av·er·ag·es, av·er·ag·ing, av·er·aged)
to do or get something as an average: *If we average 55 miles an hour, we should get there by 4 o'clock.*

a·vi·a·tion /ˌeɪvi'eɪʃn/ *noun* [*noncount*]
the process or activity of designing, building, or flying airplanes, etc.: *the aviation industry*

av·id /'ævɪd/ *adjective*
very enthusiastic about something, usually something you do in your free time: *an avid golfer*

av·o·ca·do /ˌɑvə'kɑdoʊ; ˌævə'kɑdoʊ/ *noun* [*count*] (*plural* av·o·ca·dos)
a fruit that is wider at one end than the other, with tough dark green skin and a large hard part (called a PIT) inside: *According to this recipe, I need four ripe avocados.*

avocado

a·void 🖋 /ə'vɔɪd/ *verb* (a·voids, a·void·ing, a·void·ed)
1 to stop something from happening; to try not to do something: *He always tried to avoid arguments if possible.* ◆ *She has to avoid eating too much chocolate.*
2 to stay away from someone or something: *We crossed the road to avoid our teacher.*

a·void·a·ble /ə'vɔɪdəbl/ *adjective*
If something is **avoidable**, it is not necessary and can be prevented. ⊃ **ANTONYM unavoidable**

a·wait /ə'weɪt/ *verb* (a·waits, a·wait·ing, a·wait·ed) (*formal*)
to wait for something: *Please await further instructions.*

a·wake /ə'weɪk/ *adjective*
not sleeping: *The children are still awake.* ◆ *It was 2 a.m. and I was still* **wide** (= completely) *awake.* ◑ ANTONYM **asleep**

a·ward¹ /ə'wɔrd/ *noun* [count]
a prize or money that you give to someone who has done something very well: *She won the award for best actress.*

a·ward² /ə'wɔrd/ *verb* (a·wards, a·ward·ing, a·ward·ed)
to officially give a prize to someone: *He was awarded first prize in the writing competition.*

a·ware AWL /ə'wɛr/ *adjective*
If you are **aware** of something, you know about it: *He's not aware of the problem.* ◆ *I was aware that someone was watching me.* ◑ ANTONYM **unaware**

a·ware·ness AWL /ə'wɛrnə/ *noun* [noncount, singular]
knowing something; knowing that something exists and is important: *an awareness of the importance of healthy eating* ◆ *to raise awareness of the risks of smoking*

a·way /ə'weɪ/ *adverb*
1 to or in another place: *She ran away from him.* ◆ *He put his books away.*
2 from a place: *The ocean is two miles away.*
3 not here: *Sorry, but Mr. Russell is away from his desk at the moment.* ◑ SYNONYM **absent**
4 in the future: *Our vacation is only three weeks away.*

awe /ɔ/ *noun* [noncount]
a feeling of great respect because you admire something very much: *As a young boy he was in awe of his uncle.*

awe·some /'ɔsəm/ *adjective*
1 (*informal*) very good; excellent: *I just bought this awesome new computer!* ◆ *Wow! That's totally awesome!* ◑ SYNONYM **great**

2 making you feel impressed and perhaps a little afraid: *an awesome sight*

aw·ful /'ɔfl/ *adjective*
very bad: *The pain was awful.* ◆ *What awful weather!* ◑ Look at the note at **bad**.

aw·ful·ly /'ɔfli/ *adverb*
very: *It was awfully hot.* ◆ *I'm awfully sorry!* ◑ SYNONYM **terribly**

a·while /ə'waɪl/ *adverb*
for a short amount of time: *Why don't you stay awhile?*

awk·ward /'ɔkwərd/ *adjective*
1 difficult or causing problems: *This big box will be awkward to carry.* ◆ *an awkward question*
2 not comfortable; making you feel embarrassed: *I felt awkward at the party because I didn't know anyone.*
3 not able to move your body in an easy way: *He's very awkward when he dances.*

awn·ing /'ɔnɪŋ/ *noun* [count]
a piece of material above a door or window to keep off the sun or rain

ax (also **axe**) /æks/ *noun* [count] (*plural* **ax·es**)
a tool for cutting wood: *He chopped down the tree with an ax.*

ax·is /'æksəs/ *noun* [count] (*plural* **ax·es** /'æksiz/)
1 (PHYSICS) a line we imagine through the middle of an object, around which the object turns: *The earth rotates on its axis.* ◑ Look at the picture at **earth**.
2 (MATH) a fixed line used for marking measurements on a picture showing numbers and amounts (a GRAPH): *the horizontal axis* ◆ *the vertical axis*

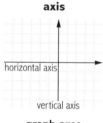

axis

horizontal axis

vertical axis

graph axes

ax·le /'æksl/ *noun* [count]
a bar that connects a pair of wheels on a vehicle

B b

B, b /bi/ *noun* [count, noncount] (*plural* B's, b's /biz/)
1 the second letter of the English alphabet: *"Ball" begins with a "B."*
2 B the second highest grade given for a test or piece of work, lower than an A: *I got a B on my math exam.*

B.A. /ˌbi ˈeɪ/ *noun* [count]
the degree that you receive when you complete a program of study at a college or university in an ARTS subject (= a subject that is not a science subject). **B.A.** is short for "Bachelor of Arts." ⮑ Look at **B.S., M.A., bachelor's degree.**

ba·by /ˈbeɪbi/ *noun* [count] (*plural* ba·bies)
a very young child: *She's going to have a baby.* ◆ *a baby boy* ◆ *a baby girl*

ba·by car·riage /ˈbeɪbi ˌkærɪdʒ/ (also **ba·by bug·gy** /ˈbeɪbi ˌbʌgi/) *noun* [count]
a thing that a baby lies in to go out. It has wheels so that you can push it.

ba·by·sit /ˈbeɪbɪsɪt/ *verb* (ba·by·sits, ba·by·sit·ting, ba·by·sat /ˈbeɪbisæt/)
to take care of a child for a short time while the parents are not at home

ba·by·sit·ter /ˈbeɪbɪsɪt̬ər/ *noun* [count]
a person who takes care of a child for a short time while the parents are not at home

bach·e·lor /ˈbætʃələr/ *noun* [count]
a man who has never married

bach·e·lor's de·gree /ˈbætʃələrz dɪˌgri/ *noun* [count]
a degree that you get after studying for four years at a college or university: *She has a bachelor's degree in English literature from Stanford University.* ⮑ Look at **associate's degree, master's degree.**

back¹ /bæk/ *noun* [count]
1 the part of a person or an animal that is between the neck and the part of your body that you sit on (the BUTTOCKS): *He lay on his back and looked up at the sky.* ◆ *She was standing with her back to me so I couldn't see her face.*
2 the part of something that is behind or farthest from the front: *The answers are at the back of the book.* ◆ *Write your address on the back of the check.* ◆ *We sat in the back of the car.*
behind someone's back when someone is not there, so that they do not know about it: *Don't talk about Kate behind her back.*

back² /bæk/ *adjective*
farthest from the front: *the back door* ◆ *back teeth*

back³ /bæk/ *adverb*
1 in or to the place where someone or something was before: *I'll be back* (= I will return) *at six o'clock.* ◆ *Go back to sleep.* ◆ *We walked to the store and back.*
2 away from the front: *I looked back to see if she was coming.* ◆ *Could everyone move back a little, please?* ⮑ **ANTONYM forward**
3 as a way of returning or answering something: *He paid me back the money.* ◆ *I wrote her a letter, but she didn't write back.* ◆ *I was out when she called, so I called her back.*
back and forth from one place to another and back again, many times: *She travels back and forth between Boston and New York.*

back⁴ /bæk/ *verb* (backs, back·ing, backed)
1 to move backward or to make something move backward: *She backed the car out of the garage.*
2 to give help or support to someone or something: *The governor is backing the proposal.*
back away to move away backward: *Sally backed away from the big dog.*
back down to stop demanding something or saying that you are right: *You deserve that raise. Don't back down now.*
back out to not do something that you promised or agreed to do: *You promised you would come with me. You can't back out of it now!*
back up to move backward, especially in a vehicle: *Back up a little, then the other cars can go by.*
back someone up to support someone: *I'm going to say what I really think at the meeting. Will you back me up?*
back something up
1 to say or show that something is true: *All the evidence backed up what the woman had said.*
2 (COMPUTERS) to make a copy of information in your computer that you do not want to lose

back·ache /ˈbækeɪk/ *noun* [count, noncount]
(HEALTH) a continuous pain in your back: *I have a terrible backache.*

back·bone /ˈbækboʊn/ *noun* [count]
(BIOLOGY) the line of bones down the back of your body ⮑ **SYNONYM spine**

back·ground /ˈbækgraʊnd/ *noun*
1 [count] the type of family that a person comes from and the education and experience that they have: *She comes from a poor background.*
2 [singular] (ART) the things at the back in a picture: *This is a photo of my house with the mountains in the background.* ⮑ **ANTONYM foreground**
3 [noncount] the facts or events that are connected with a situation: *I need to get some background information.*

back·log /'bæklɔg; 'bæklɑg/ *noun* [count]
work, etc. that has not yet been done and needs to be done: *I have a huge backlog of e-mails to answer.*

back·pack¹ /'bækpæk/ *noun* [count]
a large bag that you carry on your back when you are traveling ⊃ Look at the picture at **bag**.

back·pack² /'bækpæk/ *verb* (back·packs, back·pack·ing, back·packed)
to go walking or traveling with your clothes, etc. in a BACKPACK
▶ **back·pack·ing** /'bækpækɪŋ/ *noun* [noncount]: *We **went backpacking** around Europe last summer.*

back·side /'bæksaɪd/ *noun* [count] (*informal*)
the part of your body that you sit on

back·stage /ˌbæk'steɪdʒ/ *adverb*
in the part of a theater where the performers get dressed, wait, etc.: *We got to go backstage and meet the band after the concert.*

back·stroke /'bækstroʊk/ *noun* [noncount]
(**SPORTS**) a way of swimming on your back

back·up /'bækʌp/ *noun*
1 [noncount] extra help or support that you can get if necessary: *The police had backup from the army.*
2 [count] (**COMPUTERS**) a copy of information that you have put in your computer and which you do not want to lose: *Always make a backup of your computer files.*

back·ward¹ /'bækwərd/ (also **back·wards** /'bækwərdz/) *adverb*
1 toward a place or a position that is behind: *Could everyone take a step backward?* ⊃ **ANTONYM forward**
2 with the back or the end first: *If you say the alphabet backward, you start with "Z."*
backward and forward first in one direction and then in the other, many times: *The dog ran backward and forward, fetching sticks.*

back·ward² /'bækwərd/ *adjective*
1 in the direction behind you: *a backward step*
2 slow to learn or change: *Our teaching methods are backward compared to some countries.*

back·yard /ˌbæk'yɑrd/ *noun* [count]
the area behind and around a house: *Everyone was in our backyard, sitting or lying on the grass.*

ba·con /'beɪkən/ *noun* [noncount]
long thin pieces of meat from a pig: *We had bacon and eggs for breakfast.*

bac·te·ri·a /bæk'tɪriə/ *noun* [plural]
(**BIOLOGY**) very small things that live in air, water, earth, plants, and animals. Some **bacteria** can make us sick.

bad /bæd/ *adjective* (worse, worst)
1 not good or nice: *The weather was very bad.* ◆ *He had some bad news – his uncle died.* ◆ *a bad smell*
2 serious: *She had a bad accident.*
3 not done or made well: *bad driving*
4 not able to work or do something well: *My eyesight is bad.* ◆ *Do you think he's a bad teacher?*
5 too old to eat; not fresh: *bad eggs*
6 not good; morally wrong: *In cowboy movies, the bad guys always wear black hats.*

Word building

- If something is very bad, you can say **awful**, **dreadful**, or **terrible**: *I've had a terrible day.*
- Something that is not nice or someone who is unkind is **horrible**: *He's always saying horrible things to me.*

bad at something If you are **bad at something**, you cannot do it well: *I'm very bad at sports.*
bad for you If something is **bad for you**, it can make you sick: *Smoking is bad for you.*
go bad to become too old to eat: *This fish has gone bad.*
not bad (*informal*) pretty good: *"What was the movie like?" "Not bad."*
too bad (*informal*) words that you use when you are sorry or feel bad about something: *It's too bad he lost his job.*

badge /bædʒ/ *noun* [count]
a small piece of metal, cloth, or plastic with a design or words on it that you wear on your clothes: *a police officer's badge*

badg·er /'bædʒər/ *noun* [count]
an animal with black and white lines on its head that lives in holes in the ground and comes out at night

bad·ly /'bædli/ *adverb* (worse, worst)
1 in a way that is not good enough; not well: *She played badly.* ◆ *These clothes are badly made.*
2 very much: *I badly need a vacation.* ◆ *He was badly hurt in the accident.*

bad·min·ton /'bædmɪntn/ *noun* [noncount]
(**SPORTS**) a game for two or four players who try to hit a kind of light ball with feathers on it over a high net, using a RACKET (= a piece of equipment that you hold in your hand): *Do you want to play badminton?*

bag /bæg/ *noun* [count]
a thing made of cloth, paper, leather, etc., for holding and carrying things: *Would you like me to put this in a bag for you?* ◆ *He put the apples in a paper bag.* ◆ *Can you help me carry the grocery bags into the house?* ⊃ Look at **handbag**.

bags

briefcase   fanny pack   purse
strap

suitcase   grocery bag   backpack

ba·gel /ˈbeɪgl/ *noun* [count]
a type of bread in the shape of a ring

bagel

bag·gage /ˈbæɡɪdʒ/ *noun* [noncount]
the bags that you take with you when you travel: *We put all our baggage in the car.* ⊃ SYNONYM **luggage**

bag·gy /ˈbæɡi/ *adjective* (bag·gi·er, bag·gi·est)
If clothes are **baggy**, they are big and loose: *He was wearing baggy jeans.*

bag·pipes /ˈbæɡpaɪps/ *noun* [plural]
(MUSIC) a musical instrument that is often played in Scotland

bail /beɪl/ *noun* [noncount]
money that is paid so that someone does not have to stay in prison until the day he or she has to appear in a court of law: *The judge set bail at $50,000.* ◆ *He was released on bail until his trial.*

bait /beɪt/ *noun* [noncount]
food that is used to catch animals or fish with

bake /beɪk/ *verb* (bakes, bak·ing, baked)
to cook food, for example bread, in an oven: *My brother baked a cake for my birthday.* ◆ *a baked potato* (= a whole potato cooked in its skin in an oven) ⊃ Look at the note at **cook¹**.

bak·er /ˈbeɪkər/ *noun* [count]
a person who makes and sells bread and cakes

bak·er·y /ˈbeɪkəri/ *noun* [count] (plural bak·er·ies)
a place where bread and cakes are made or sold

bal·ance¹ /ˈbæləns/ *noun*
1 [noncount] the ability to keep steady with an equal amount of weight on each side of the body: *I struggled to keep my balance on my new skates.* ◆ *She lost her balance and fell off her bike.*
2 [singular] when two things are the same, so that one is not bigger or more important, for example: *You need to find a balance between work and play.*

3 [count] the amount of money in someone's bank account: *You can check your bank balance online.*

bal·ance² /ˈbæləns/ *verb* (bal·anc·es, bal·anc·ing, bal·anced)
1 to put your body or something else into a position where it is steady and does not fall: *He balanced the bag on his head.* ◆ *She balanced on one leg.*
2 to have or to give different things equal value, importance, etc.: *to balance work and home life*

bal·anced /ˈbælənst/ *adjective*
consisting of good or equal amounts of different parts or things: *Eating a balanced diet will help you stay healthy.*

bal·co·ny /ˈbælkəni/ *noun* [count] (plural bal·co·nies)
1 a small area on the outside wall of a building, above the ground, where you can stand or sit
2 an area of seats upstairs in a theater: *We have balcony seats.*

bald /bɔld/ *adjective*
with no hair or not much hair on your head: *My dad is going bald* (= losing his hair). ⊃ Look at the picture at **hair**.

bald ea·gle /ˌbɔld ˈiɡl/ *noun* [count]
a large bird with brown feathers on its body and white feathers on its head and neck. It is the official symbol of the U.S.

bald eagle

ball /bɔl/ *noun* [count]
1 (SPORTS) a round thing that you use in games and sports: *Throw the ball to me.* ◆ *a basketball* ◆ *a tennis ball*
2 any round thing: *a ball of string* ◆ *a snowball*
3 a big formal party where people dance
be on the ball (*informal*) to know what is happening and to think or act quickly: *This job involves a lot of deadlines, so you really have to be on the ball.*

bal·le·ri·na /ˌbæləˈrinə/ *noun* [count]
a woman who dances in BALLETS

bal·let /bæˈleɪ/ *noun*
1 [noncount] a style of dance that tells a story with music but no words: *Do you like ballet?* ◆ *a ballet dancer*
2 [count] a performance of a story, told with dancing and music but no words: *I went to see a ballet.*

bal·loon /bəˈlun/ *noun* [count]
1 a small rubber bag that you blow air into and use as a toy or to decorate a room: *We are going*

to hang red, white, and blue balloons around the room for the party.
2 = hot-air balloon

bal·lot /ˈbælət/ *noun* (**POLITICS**)
1 [*count*] a piece of paper that you use when you vote: *Put an "X" next to the candidate's name on the ballot.* ◆ *Voters will **cast their ballots** (= vote) on election day.*
2 [*count, noncount*] when people vote for someone or something by writing secretly on a piece of paper: *We **held a ballot** to choose a new president.*

ballpark /ˈbɔlpɑrk/ *noun* [*count*]
(**SPORTS**) a field or sports center where baseball is played ⊃ Look at the note at **field**.
a ballpark figure a number that is not exact, but is more or less correct: *Can you give me a ballpark figure as to what this will cost?*

ball·point pen /ˌbɔlpɔɪnt ˈpɛn/ *noun* [*count*]
a pen that has a very small ball at the end that rolls a special liquid (called **INK**) onto the paper ⊃ Look at the picture at **stationery**.

ba·lo·ney /bəˈloʊni/ *noun* [*noncount*]
1 (*informal*) words or ideas that have no meaning or that are not true: *What a bunch of baloney!* ⊃ **SYNONYM nonsense**
2 = bologna

bam·boo /ˌbæmˈbu/ *noun* [*count, noncount*] (*plural* bam·boos)
a tall plant that grows in hot countries and is often used for making furniture: *Bamboos are fast-growing, woody plants.* ◆ *a bamboo chair* ◆ ***bamboo shoots** (= young bamboo plants that can be eaten)*

ban /bæn/ *verb* (bans, ban·ning, banned)
to say that something must not happen; to not allow something: *The movie was banned.*
▶ **ban** *noun* [*count*]: *There is **a ban on** smoking in public places.*

ba·nan·a /bəˈnænə/ *noun* [*count*]
a long curved yellow fruit ⊃ Look at the picture at **fruit**.

band 🔑 /bænd/ *noun* [*count*]
1 a thin flat piece of material that you put around something, for example to hold it together: *I put a **rubber band** around the letters.* ◆ *The hat had a red band around it.*
2 (**MUSIC**) a group of people who play music together: *a rock band* ◆ *a jazz band*
3 a line of color or material on something that is different from the rest of it: *She wore a red sweater with a green band across the middle.*

band·age¹ /ˈbændɪdʒ/ *noun* [*count*]
(**HEALTH**) a long piece of cloth that you tie around a part of the body that is hurt

band·age² /ˈbændɪdʒ/ *verb* (band·ag·es, band·ag·ing, band·aged)
(**HEALTH**) to put a BANDAGE around a part of the body: *The nurse bandaged my foot.*

Band-Aid™   **bandage**

Band-Aid™ /ˈbænd eɪd/ *noun* [*count*]
(**HEALTH**) a small piece of sticky material that you put over a cut on your body to keep it clean

ban·dan·na /bænˈdænə/ *noun* [*count*]
a square piece of cloth that you wear around your neck or head

ban·dit /ˈbændət/ *noun* [*count*]
a person who attacks and robs people who are traveling: *They were killed by bandits in the mountains.*

bang¹ /bæŋ/ *verb* (bangs, bang·ing, banged)
to make a loud noise by hitting something hard or by closing something: *He **banged** his head **on** the ceiling.* ◆ *Don't bang the door!*

bang² /bæŋ/ *noun* [*count*]
1 a sudden, very loud noise: *He shut the door with a bang.*
2 a short, strong knock or hit, especially one that causes pain and injury: *He fell and got a **bang on** the head.*

bangs /bæŋz/ *noun* [*plural*]
the short hair that hangs down above your eyes: *She decided to cut her bangs.* ⊃ Look at the picture at **hair**.

ban·is·ter /ˈbænəstər/ *noun* [*count*]
a long piece of wood or metal that you hold on to when you go up or down stairs

ban·jo /ˈbændʒoʊ/ *noun* [*count*] (*plural* ban·jos)
(**MUSIC**) a musical instrument with a long thin neck, a round body, and four or more strings

banjo

bank¹ 🔑 /bæŋk/ *noun* [*count*]
1 a place that keeps money safe for people: *I have $500 in the bank.*
2 (**GEOGRAPHY**) the land along the side of a river: *People were fishing along the banks of the river.*

bank² /bæŋk/ *verb* (banks, bank·ing, banked)
to keep your money in a particular bank: *Who do you **bank with**?*

bank on someone or **something** to expect and trust someone to do something, or something to happen: *The boss might give you the day off but I wouldn't bank on it.*

bank ac·count /'bæŋk ə,kaʊnt/ *noun* [*count*]
an arrangement that you have with a bank that lets you keep your money there: *I'd like to open a bank account.*

Word building

- If you have a **bank account**, you can **deposit** money (= **pay** it **in**) or **withdraw** it (= **take** it **out**): *I'd like to withdraw $50, please.*
- If you don't want to **spend** your money, you can **save** it (= keep it in the bank).

---

bank·er /'bæŋkər/ *noun* [*count*]
(**BUSINESS**) a person who owns a bank or who has an important job in a bank

bank·ing /'bæŋkɪŋ/ *noun* [*noncount*]
the type of business done by banks: *She chose a career in banking.*

bank·rupt /'bæŋkrʌpt/ *adjective*
not able to continue in business because you cannot pay the money that you owe: *His business went bankrupt after a year.*

ban·ner /'bænər/ *noun* [*count*]
a long piece of cloth with words on it. People carry **banners** to show what they think: *The banner said "Stop the war."*

ban·quet /'bæŋkwət/ *noun* [*count*]
a formal dinner for a large number of people, usually as a special event

bap·tism /'bæptɪzəm/ *noun* [*count, noncount*]
(**RELIGION**) a religious ceremony when someone is BAPTIZED

bap·tize /'bæptaɪz/ *verb* (**bap·tiz·es, bap·tiz·ing, bap·tized**)
(**RELIGION**) to put water on someone and give them a name, to show that they belong to the Christian Church

bar¹ 🖉 /bɑr/ *noun* [*count*]
1 a place where people can go and buy drinks, especially alcoholic drinks: *There's a bar in the hotel.*
2 a place where you can get a particular kind of food or drink: *a snack bar*
3 a long, high table where you buy drinks in a bar: *We stood at the bar.*
4 a long thin piece of metal or wood: *There were iron bars on the windows.*
5 a small block of something hard: *a candy bar* • *a bar of soap* ⊃ Look at the picture at **soap**.
behind bars (*informal*) in prison: *His killer is now safely behind bars.*

bar² /bɑr/ *verb* (**bars, bar·ring, barred**)
1 to put something across a place so that people cannot pass: *A line of police barred the road.*
2 to say officially that someone must not do something or go somewhere: *Journalists were barred from taking photographs of the event.*

bar·be·cue /'bɑrbɪkyu/ *noun* [*count*] (abbreviation **BBQ**)
a meal or a party where you cook food on a fire outside: *We had a barbecue on the beach.*
▶ **bar·be·cue** *verb* (**bar·be·cues, bar·be·cu·ing, bar·be·cued**): *barbecued steak*

barbed wire /,bɑrbd 'waɪər/ *noun* [*noncount*]
wire with a lot of sharp points on it. Some fences are made of **barbed wire**.

barbed wire

bar·ber /'bɑrbər/ *noun* [*count*]
a person whose job is to cut men's hair
▶ **bar·ber·shop** /'bɑrbərʃɑp/ *noun* [*count*]
a place where a barber works

bar code /'bɑr koʊd/ *noun* [*count*]
a pattern of black lines that is printed on things you buy. It contains information that a computer reads to find the price.

bar code

bare /bɛr/ *adjective*
1 (used about a part of the body) with no clothes covering it: *He had bare feet* (= he wasn't wearing shoes or socks).
2 without anything covering it or in it: *They had taken the paintings down, so the walls were all bare.*

bare·foot /'bɛrfʊt/ *adjective, adverb*
with no shoes or socks on your feet: *The children ran barefoot along the beach.*

bare·ly /'bɛrli/ *adverb*
almost not; only just: *She barely ate anything.* ⊃ **SYNONYM hardly**

bar·gain¹ /'bɑrgən/ *noun* [*count*]
something that is cheaper than usual: *At just $10, the dress was a real bargain!*

bar·gain² /'bɑrgən/ *verb* (**bar·gains, bar·gain·ing, bar·gained**)
to try to agree on a good price for something: *She may sell the car for less if you bargain with her.*

barge /bɑrdʒ/ *noun* [*count*]
a long boat with a flat bottom for carrying things or people on rivers or CANALS (= artificial rivers)

---

bark¹ /bɑrk/ *noun*
1 [*noncount*] the hard surface of a tree ⊃ Look at the picture at **tree**.
2 [*count*] the short loud sound that a dog makes

bark² /bɑrk/ *verb* (barks, bark·ing, barked)
If a dog **barks**, it makes short loud sounds: *The dog always **barks** at people it doesn't know.*

bar·ley /ˈbɑrli/ *noun* [*noncount*]
a plant that we use for food and for making beer and some other drinks

barn /bɑrn/ *noun* [*count*]
a large building on a farm for storing grain or keeping animals in

bar·racks /ˈbærəks/ *noun* [*plural*]
a building or group of buildings where soldiers live: *an army barracks*

bar·rel /ˈbærəl/ *noun* [*count*]
1 a big container for liquids, with round sides and flat ends: *a beer barrel ◆ a barrel of oil*
2 the long metal part of a gun that a bullet goes through

bar·ren /ˈbærən/ *adjective*
(**GEOGRAPHY**) (used about land) not good enough for plants to grow on

bar·ri·cade /ˈbærəkeɪd/ *noun* [*count*]
a line of things arranged across a road, etc. to stop people from getting past
▶ **bar·ri·cade** *verb* (bar·ri·cades, bar·ri·cad·ing, bar·ri·cad·ed): *He barricaded the door to keep the police out.*

bar·ri·er /ˈbæriər/ *noun* [*count*]
1 a wall or fence that stops you from going somewhere: *The police put up barriers to hold back the crowd.*
2 something that causes problems or makes it impossible for something to happen: *I would love to live in Japan, but I'm worried about the language barrier.*

bar·tend·er /ˈbɑrtɛndər/ *noun* [*count*]
a person whose job is to make and serve drinks in a bar

base¹ 🔑 /beɪs/ *noun* [*count*]
1 the bottom part of something; the part that something stands on: *The lamp has a heavy base. ◆ the base of a column*
2 a person's or a company's main home or office: *She travels all over the world, but Philadelphia is her base.*
3 a place where soldiers in the army, navy, etc. live and work: *an army base*
4 (**SPORTS**) one of the four points that a player must touch before scoring in baseball: *The batter hit the ball and ran to first base.*

base² 🔑 /beɪs/ *verb* (ba·ses, bas·ing, based)
be based somewhere If a person or a company **is based in** a place, that is where they

have their main home or office: *The company is based in Seattle.*
base something on something to make or develop something, using another thing as a starting point: *The movie is based on a true story.*

baseball

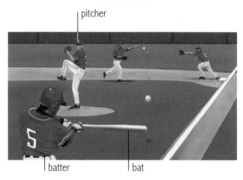
pitcher
batter | bat

base·ball 🔑 /ˈbeɪsbɔl/ *noun* (**SPORTS**)
1 [*noncount*] a game in which two teams hit a ball with a wooden stick (called a **BAT**) and then score points by running around four fixed points (called **BASES**) on a large field: *We played baseball in the park.*
2 [*count*] a ball for playing this game

base·ment /ˈbeɪsmənt/ *noun* [*count*]
part of a building that is under the level of the ground: *a basement apartment*

ba·ses
1 /ˈbeɪsəz/ plural of **base**¹
2 /ˈbeɪsiz/ plural of **basis**

bash /bæʃ/ *verb* (bash·es, bash·ing, bashed)
(*informal*)
to hit someone or something very hard: *I fell and bashed my knee.*

ba·sic 🔑 /ˈbeɪsɪk/ *adjective*
1 most important and necessary: *A person's basic needs are food, clothes, and a place to live.*
2 simple; including only what is necessary: *This class teaches basic computer skills.*

ba·si·cal·ly /ˈbeɪsɪkli/ *adverb*
1 in the most important ways: *She's a little strange but basically a very nice person.*
2 used when you are saying what is important about a situation: *Basically, all I want is to be left alone.*

ba·sics /ˈbeɪsɪks/ *noun* [*plural*]
the things that you need most or are the most important: *You can get all the basics at the local store. ◆ This course will teach you the basics of digital photography.*

ba·sin /ˈbeɪsn/ *noun* [*count*]
(**GEOGRAPHY**) a place where the earth's surface is

lower than the area around it: *the Great Basin in the western U.S.*

ba·sis 🔊 /ˈbeɪsəs/ *noun* (*plural* **ba·ses** /ˈbeɪsiz/)
1 [*singular*] the way something is done or organized: *We meet on a regular basis* (= often).
2 [*singular*] the reason why something is done: *We made our decision on the basis of your report.*
3 [*count*] a starting point, from which something develops: *Her notes formed the basis of a book.*

bas·ket /ˈbæskət/
noun [*count*]
1 a container made of thin sticks or thin pieces of plastic or metal, which you use for holding or carrying things: *a bread basket* • *a shopping basket* ⊃ Look at **wastebasket**.
2 (**SPORTS**) a net that hangs from a metal ring high up at each end of a **BASKETBALL** court

basket

— hoop

— basket

bas·ket·ball /ˈbæskətbɔl/ *noun* (**SPORTS**)
1 [*noncount*] a game for two teams of five players who try to throw a ball into a high net
2 [*count*] a ball for playing this game

bass /beɪs; bæs/ *adjective*
(**MUSIC**) with a deep sound: *She plays the bass guitar.* • *a bass drum* ⊃ Look at the picture at **guitar**.

bat¹ /bæt/ *noun* [*count*]
1 (**SPORTS**) a piece of wood for hitting the ball in baseball ⊃ Look at the picture at **baseball**.

Which word?

- The thing that you use to hit the ball has different names in different sports.
- You use a **bat** in baseball.
- You use a **racket** to play tennis, badminton, and squash.
- To play golf, you use a **club**.
- In hockey, you use a **stick**.

2 an animal like a mouse with wings. Bats come out and fly at night.

bat

bat² /bæt/ (**bats, bat·ting, bat·ted**) *verb* (**SPORTS**) to try to hit a ball in baseball: *Who's batting first for the Orioles?*

batch /bætʃ/ *noun* [*count*] (*plural* **batch·es**)
a group of things: *She made a batch of cookies.*

bath 🔊 /bæθ/ *noun* [*count*] (*plural* **baths** /bæθs; bæðz/)
washing your body in a large container (called a **BATHTUB**) that you fill with water: *I took a bath this morning.*

bathe /beɪð/ *verb* (**bathes, bath·ing, bathed**)
to wash yourself or someone else in a large container (called a **BATHTUB**) filled with water: *I bathe every morning.* • *Have you bathed the baby yet?*

bath·ing suit /ˈbeɪðɪŋ ˌsut/ *noun* [*count*]
a piece of clothing that you wear to go swimming: *The hotel has a pool, so pack your bathing suit.* ⊃ **SYNONYM swimsuit**

bath·robe
/ˈbæθroʊb/ *noun*
[*count*]
a piece of clothing, like a loose soft coat, that you put on after taking a bath or shower

bathrobe

bath·room 🔊
/ˈbæθrum/ *noun*
[*count*]
a room where there is a toilet, and usually also a **BATHTUB** or shower: *Can I go to the bathroom* (= use the toilet)?

Culture

- People usually say **the bathroom** in their homes.
- In public places, people say **the restroom, ladies' room** or **men's room**.

bath·tub /ˈbæθtʌb/ (*also informal* **tub** /tʌb/) *noun* [*count*]
a large container that you fill with water and sit in to wash your body

bat·ter /ˈbæt̬ər/ *noun*
1 [*noncount*] a mixture of flour, eggs, milk, etc. used for making food such as cakes: *pancake batter*
2 [*count*] (**SPORTS**) a person who hits the ball in baseball ⊃ Look at the picture at **baseball**.

bat·ter·y /ˈbæt̬əri/ *noun* [*count*] (*plural* **bat·ter·ies**)
(**PHYSICS**) a thing that gives electricity. You put **batteries** inside things like toys, radios, and cars to make them work.

bat·tle¹ /ˈbæt̬l/ *noun*
1 [*count, noncount*] (**HISTORY**) a fight between armies in a war: *the Battle of Bunker Hill* • *He was killed in battle.*
2 [*count*] trying very hard to do something difficult: *After three years, she lost her battle against cancer.*

bat·tle² /ˈbætl/ *verb* (bat·tles, bat·tling, bat·tled)
to try very hard to do something difficult: *The doctors battled to save her life.*

bay /beɪ/ *noun* [count] (*plural* bays)
(**GEOGRAPHY**) a part of the coast where the land goes in to form a curve: *There was a ship in the bay.* • *San Francisco Bay*

BBQ abbreviation of **barbecue**

B.C. /ˌbi ˈsi/ *abbreviation*
(**HISTORY, RELIGION**) B.C. in a date shows it was before Christ was born: *Julius Caesar died in 44 B.C.* ꙮ Look at **A.D.**

be

Full forms	Short forms	Negative short forms
present tense		
I am	I'm	I'm not
you are	you're	you aren't
he/she/it is	he's/she's/it's	he/she/it isn't
we are	we're	we aren't
they are	they're	they aren't
past tense		
I was	—	I wasn't
you were	—	you weren't
he/she/it was	—	he/she/it wasn't
we were	—	we weren't
they were	—	they weren't
present participle		
being		
past participle		
been		

be /bi/ *verb*
1 there is/there are to exist or be present in a place: *There are a lot of trees in our yard.* • *I tried calling them but there was no answer.* • *Is there a post office near here?*
2 a word that you use when you are giving the name of people or things, describing them or giving more information about them: *I'm (= I am) Ben.* • *The movie was excellent.* • *John is a doctor.* • *Roberta's Italian.* • *"What color is your car?" "It's red."* • *Today is Friday.*
3 a word that you use to give the position of someone or something or the place where they are: *Jen's (= Jen is) in her office.* • *Where are the scissors?*
4 a word that you use to talk about the age of someone or something or to talk about time: *"How old is she?" "She's twelve."* • *Her birthday was in May.* • *It's six o'clock.*

5 (**ENGLISH LANGUAGE ARTS**) a word that you use with another verb: *"What are you doing?" "I'm (= I am) reading."*
6 (**ENGLISH LANGUAGE ARTS**) a word that you use with part of another verb to show that something happens to someone or something: *This cheese is made in France.* • *The house was built in 1910.*
7 a word that shows that something must or will happen: *They are to be married in June.*

beach /bitʃ/ *noun* [count] (*plural* beach·es)
(**GEOGRAPHY**) a piece of land next to an ocean or a lake that is covered with sand or stones: *a sandy beach* • *We lay on the beach in the sun.*

bea·con /ˈbikən/ *noun* [count]
a strong light or other signal that is used as a warning or guide for boats, airplanes, etc.

bead /bid/ *noun* [count]
a small ball of wood, glass, or plastic with a hole in the middle. **Beads** are put on a string to make jewelry.

beak /bik/ *noun* [count]
the hard pointed part of a bird's mouth ꙮ Look at the picture at **bird**.

beak·er /ˈbikər/ *noun* [count]
(**GENERAL SCIENCE**) a glass container with a flat bottom, used by scientists for pouring liquids

beam¹ /bim/ *noun* [count]
1 (**PHYSICS**) a line of light: *a laser beam*
2 a long heavy piece of wood that holds up a roof or ceiling

beam² /bim/ *verb* (beams, beam·ing, beamed)
1 to send out light and warmth: *The sun beamed down on them.*
2 to have a big happy smile on your face

bean /bin/ *noun* [count]
a seed, or a seed container, that we use as food: *green beans* • *coffee beans*

bear¹ /bɛr/ *noun* [count]
a big wild animal with thick fur

bear

bear² /bɛr/ *verb* (bears, bear·ing, bore /bɔr/, has borne /bɔrn/)
1 to be able to accept something unpleasant without complaining: *The pain was difficult to bear.*
2 to hold someone or something up so that they do not fall: *The ice is too thin to bear your weight.*
bear left; bear right to turn toward the left or right: *When the road splits, bear left.*
bear in mind that…; bear something in mind to remember or consider something: *When you're packing, bear in mind that the*

weather will be much colder in Maine. ♦ *Thanks, I'll bear that in mind.*

can't bear someone or something to hate someone or something: *I can't bear this music.* ♦ *He can't bear having nothing to do.*

beard 🔊 /bɪrd/ *noun* [count]
the hair on a man's chin: *He has a beard.*

beast /bist/ *noun* [count]
1 (*formal*) a wild animal
2 an unkind or cruel person

beat¹ 🔊 /bit/ *verb* (beats, beat·ing, beat, has beat·en /'bitn/)
1 (SPORTS) to win a fight or game against a person or group of people: *Daniel always beats me at tennis.* ♦ *Our team was beaten 2-1.*
2 to hit someone or something very hard many times: *She beat the dust out of the rug.* ♦ *The rain was beating on the roof.*
3 to make the same sound or movement many times: *His heart was beating fast.*
4 to mix food quickly with a fork, for example: *Beat the eggs and sugar together.*

beat someone up to hit or kick someone hard, many times: *He was badly beaten up by a gang of teenagers.*

beat² /bit/ *noun* [count]
1 a single sound that comes again and again: *the beat of the drum* ⊃ Look at **heartbeat**.
2 (MUSIC) the strong pattern of sounds that a piece of music has: *We danced to the beat.*

beau·ti·cian /byu'tɪʃn/ *noun* [count]
a person whose job is to give special treatments to your face and body to make you look good

beau·ti·ful 🔊 /'byuṭəfl/ *adjective*
1 very pretty or attractive: *a beautiful woman* ⊃ Look at the note at **attractive**.
2 very nice to see, hear, or smell: *Those flowers are beautiful.* ♦ *What a beautiful song!*
▶ **beau·ti·ful·ly** /'byuṭəfli/ *adverb*: *Louis sang beautifully.*

beau·ty 🔊 /'byuṭi/ *noun* [noncount]
the quality of being beautiful: *She was a woman of great beauty.* ♦ *the beauty of the mountains*

bea·ver /'bivər/ *noun* [count]
an animal with brown fur, a wide flat tail, and sharp teeth. It builds walls across rivers to hold back the water (called DAMS).

beaver

be·cause 🔊 /bɪ'kɔz; bɪ'kʌz/ *conjunction*
for the reason that: *He was angry because I was late.*

because of something as a result of something or someone: *We stayed at home because of the rain.*

beck·on /'bɛkən/ *verb* (beck·ons, beck·on·ing, beck·oned)
to move your finger to show that you want someone to come nearer

be·come 🔊 /bɪ'kʌm/ *verb* (be·comes, be·com·ing, be·came /bɪ'keɪm/, has be·come)
to begin to be something: *She became a doctor in 2002.* ♦ *The weather is becoming colder.*

> ❗ **STYLE**
> In conversation, we usually say **get** instead of **become** with adjectives. It is less formal: *The weather is getting colder.* ♦ *She got nervous as the exam date came closer.*

what became of...? used to ask what has happened to someone or something: *What became of that student who used to live with you?*

bed 🔊 /bɛd/ *noun* [count]
1 a thing that you sleep on: *It was time to go to bed.* ♦ *The children are in bed.* ♦ *to make the bed* (= to make it ready for someone to sleep in)
2 (GEOGRAPHY) the bottom of a river or the ocean

bed and break·fast /ˌbɛd ən 'brɛkfəst/ (abbreviation **B and B, B&B**) *noun* [count]
a small hotel where you pay for a room to sleep in and a meal the next morning: *I stayed in a bed and breakfast.*

bed·clothes /'bɛdkloʊðz/ *noun* [plural]
the sheets and covers that you use on a bed

bed·room 🔊 /'bɛdrum/ *noun* [count]
a room where you sleep

bed·side /'bɛdsaɪd/ *noun* [singular]
the area that is next to a bed: *She sat at his bedside all night long.* ♦ *A book lay open on the bedside table.*

bed·spread /'bɛdsprɛd/ *noun* [count]
a large cover for a bed that you put on top of the sheets and other covers

bed·time /'bɛdtaɪm/ *noun* [count, noncount]
the time when someone usually goes to bed: *Come on, it's past your bedtime.*

bee /bi/ *noun* [count]
a black and yellow insect that flies and makes a sweet food that we eat (called HONEY) ⊃ Look at the picture at **insect**.

beef /bif/ *noun* [noncount]
meat from a cow: *roast beef* ⊃ Look at the note at **cow**.

bee·hive /'bihaɪv/ *noun* [count]
a thing that BEES live in

been /bɪn; bin/
1 form of **be**
2 form of **go¹**
have been to to have gone to a place and come back again: *Have you ever been to Canada?*

Which word?

Been or gone?

- If someone has **been** to a place, they have traveled there and returned: *I've been to Mexico three times.* ◆ *You were away a long time. Where have you been?*
- If someone has **gone** to a place, they have traveled there and they are still there now: *Judy isn't here. She has gone to New York.* ◆ *Mom has gone out, but she'll be back soon.*

beep /bip/ *verb* (beeps, beep·ing, beeped)
to make a short high noise: *Why is the computer beeping?*
▸ **beep** *noun* [count]: *Please leave a message after the beep.*

beer /bɪr/ *noun*
1 [noncount] an alcoholic drink made from grain: *a bottle of beer*
2 [count] a glass, bottle, or can of beer: *Three beers, please.*

beet /bit/ *noun* [count]
a round dark red vegetable that you cook before you eat

bee·tle /ˈbitl̩/ *noun* [count]
an insect with hard wings and a shiny body ⊃ Look at the picture at **insect**.

be·fore¹ /bɪˈfɔr/ *preposition, conjunction*
1 earlier than someone or something; earlier than the time that: *He arrived before me.* ◆ *I said goodbye before I left.* ◆ *Ellen worked in a hospital before getting this job.* ◆ *They should be here before long* (= soon).
2 in front of someone or something: *B comes before C in the alphabet.* ⊃ **ANTONYM after**

be·fore² /bɪˈfɔr/ *adverb*
at an earlier time; in the past: *I've never met them before.* ◆ *I've seen this movie before.*

be·fore·hand /bɪˈfɔrhænd/ *adverb*
at an earlier time than something: *Tell me beforehand if you are going to be late.*

beg /bɛg/ *verb* (begs, beg·ging, begged)
1 to ask for money or food because you are very poor: *There are a lot of people begging in the streets.*
2 to ask someone for something strongly, or with a lot of feeling: *She begged me to stay with her.* ◆ *He begged for help.*
I beg your pardon (formal) polite words that you say to mean "I am sorry" or "could you repeat that, please?": *I beg your pardon, I didn't mean to step on your foot.* ◆ *I beg your pardon, could you say that again?*

beg·gar /ˈbɛgər/ *noun* [count]
a person who asks other people for money or food

be·gin /bɪˈgɪn/ *verb* (be·gins, be·gin·ning, be·gan /bɪˈgæn/, has be·gun /bɪˈgʌn/)
1 to start to do something or start to happen: *I'm beginning to feel cold.* ◆ *The movie begins at 7:30.* ⊃ **SYNONYM start**
2 to start in a particular way: *The name John begins with a "J."* ⊃ **ANTONYM end**
to begin with at first; at the beginning: *To begin with, they were very happy.*

be·gin·ner /bɪˈgɪnər/ *noun* [count]
a person who is starting to do or learn something

be·gin·ning /bɪˈgɪnɪŋ/ *noun* [count]
the time or place where something starts; the first part of something: *I didn't see the beginning of the show.* ⊃ **ANTONYM end**

be·gun form of **begin**

be·half **AWL** /bɪˈhæf/ *noun*
on behalf of someone; on someone's behalf for someone; in the place of someone: *Mr. Smith is away, so I am writing to you on his behalf.*

be·have /bɪˈheɪv/ *verb* (be·haves, be·hav·ing, be·haved)
to do and say things in a particular way: *They behaved very kindly toward me.* ◆ *The children behaved badly all day.*
behave yourself to be good; to do and say the right things: *Did the children behave themselves?*

be·hav·ior /bɪˈheɪvyər/ *noun* [noncount]
the way you are; the way that you do and say things: *He was sent out of the class for bad behavior.*

be·hind /bɪˈhaɪnd/ *preposition, adverb*
1 at or to the back of someone or something: *I hid behind the wall.* ◆ *I drove off, and Jim followed behind.*
2 slower or less good than someone or something; slower or less good than you should be: *She is behind with her work because she's often sick.*
3 in the place where someone or something was before: *I got off the train and left my bag behind* (= on the train).
4 responsible for causing or starting something: *What was the reason behind his sudden change of opinion?*

beige /beɪʒ/ *adjective*
having a light brown color: *beige pants*
▸ **beige** *noun* [count, noncount]

be·ing¹ /ˈbiɪŋ/ form of **be**

be·ing² /ˈbiɪŋ/ *noun* [count]
a person or living thing: *a being from another planet*

be·lief /bɪˈlif/ *noun* [count]
a sure feeling that something is true or real: *his belief in God* ◆ *Divorce is against their religious beliefs.*

be·liev·a·ble /bɪ'livəbl/ *adjective*
that you can believe ⊃ ANTONYM **unbelievable**

be·lieve 🔑 /bɪ'liv/ *verb* (be·lieves, be·liev·ing, be·lieved)
1 to feel sure that something is true; to feel sure that what someone says is true: *Long ago, people **believed that** the earth was flat.* ◆ *She says she didn't take the money. Do you believe her?*
2 to think that something is true or possible, although you are not sure: *"Does Paul still work here?" "I **believe so**."*
believe in someone or **something** to feel sure that someone or something exists: *Do you believe in ghosts?*

bell 🔑 /bɛl/ *noun* [count]
a metal thing that makes a sound when something hits or touches it: *The church bells were ringing.* ◆ *I rang the bell and he answered the door.*

bel·ly /'bɛli/ *noun* [count] (*plural* **bel·lies**) (*informal*)
the part of your body between your chest and your legs ⊃ SYNONYM **stomach**

bel·ly but·ton /'bɛli ˌbʌtn/ *noun* [count] (*informal*)
the small hole in the middle of your stomach ⊃ SYNONYM **navel**

be·long 🔑 /bɪ'lɔŋ/ *verb* (be·longs, be·long·ing, be·longed)
1 to be someone's: *"Who does this pen **belong to**?" "It **belongs to** me."*
2 to be a member of a group or an organization: *Which political party do you **belong to**?*
3 to have its right or usual place: *That chair belongs in my room.*

be·long·ings /bɪ'lɔŋɪŋz/ *noun* [plural]
the things that you own: *They lost all their belongings in the fire.* ⊃ Look at the note at **thing**.

be·lov·ed /bɪ'lʌvd; bɪ'lʌvəd/ *adjective* (*formal*)
loved very much: *their beloved daughter*

be·low 🔑 /bɪ'loʊ/ *preposition, adverb*
1 in or to a lower place than someone or something: *From the plane we could see the mountains below.* ◆ *He dove below the surface of the water.* ◆ *Do not write below this line.* ⊃ ANTONYM **above**
2 less than a number or price: *The temperature was below zero.*

belt 🔑 /bɛlt/ *noun* [count]
a long piece of cloth or leather that you wear around the middle of your body ⊃ Look at **safety belt**, **seat belt**. ⊃ Look at the picture at **clothes**.

bench /bɛntʃ/ *noun*
[count] (*plural* bench·es)
a long seat for two or more people, usually made of wood: *a park bench*

bench

bend¹ 🔑 /bɛnd/ *verb* (bends, bend·ing, bent /bɛnt/, has bent)
1 to make something that was straight into a curved shape: *Bend your legs!*
2 to be or become curved: *The road bends to the left.*
bend down; **bend over** to move your body forward and down: *She bent down to put on her shoes.*

bend² /bɛnd/ *noun* [count]
a part of a road or river that is not straight: *Drive slowly – there's a bend in the road.*

be·neath /bɪ'niθ/ *preposition, adverb*
in or to a lower place than someone or something: *From the tower, they looked down on the city beneath.* ◆ *The boat sank beneath the waves.* ⊃ SYNONYM **below**, **underneath** ⊃ ANTONYM **above**

ben·e·fi·cial AWL /ˌbɛnə'fɪʃl/ *adjective*
having a good or useful effect: *Regular exercise is **beneficial to** your health.*

ben·e·fit¹ 🔑 AWL /'bɛnəfɪt/ *noun*
1 [count] something that is good or helpful: *What are the **benefits of** having a computer?* ◆ *I did it **for your benefit** (= to help you).*
2 [count, noncount] (**POLITICS**, **BUSINESS**) money or other advantages that you get from your job, the government, or a company you belong to: *unemployment benefits* ◆ *All our employees receive medical benefits in addition to their salary.*

ben·e·fit² AWL /'bɛnəfɪt/ *verb* (ben·e·fits, ben·e·fit·ing, ben·e·fit·ed or ben·e·fit·ting, ben·e·fit·ted)
to be good or helpful for someone: *The new law will benefit families with children.*
benefit from something to get something good or useful from something: *She will benefit from a vacation.*

bent¹ form of **bend¹**

bent² /bɛnt/ *adjective*
not straight; curved: *Do this exercise with your knees bent.* ◆ *This knife is bent.* ⊃ ANTONYM **straight**

be·ret /bə'reɪ/ *noun* [count]
a soft flat round hat ⊃ Look at the picture at **hat**.

berries

blueberries   **raspberries**   **strawberries**

ber·ry /'bɛri/ *noun* [count] (*plural* ber·ries)
a small soft fruit with seeds in it: *Those berries are poisonous.* ◆ *raspberries*

æ cat   ɛ ten   i see   ɪ sit   ɑ hot   ɔ saw   ʌ cup   ʊ put   u too

be·side 🔊 /bɪˈsaɪd/ preposition
at the side of someone or something: *Come and sit beside me.* ➔ SYNONYM **next to**
beside the point not important or closely connected with the main thing you are talking about: *I know it was an accident, but that's beside the point. Go and apologize.*

be·sides /bɪˈsaɪdz/ preposition, adverb
as well as someone or something; also: *We have lots of things in common besides music.* ◆ *I don't really want to go. Besides, it's too late now.*

best¹ 🔊 /bɛst/ adjective (good, bet·ter, best)
better than all others: *This is the best pizza I've ever eaten!* ◆ *Tom is my best friend.* ◆ *Joe's the best player on the team.* ➔ ANTONYM **worst**

best² 🔊 /bɛst/ adverb
1 in the most excellent way: *I work best in the morning.*
2 more than all others: *Which picture do you like best?* ➔ SYNONYM **most** ➔ ANTONYM **least**

best³ 🔊 /bɛst/ noun [singular]
the person or thing that is better than all others: *Mike and Ian are good at tennis but Paul is the best.*
at best if everything goes as well as possible: *At best, it will be ready by the end of March.*
do your best to do all that you can: *I don't know if I can finish the work today, but I'll do my best.*

best man /ˌbɛst ˈmæn/ noun [singular]
a man at a wedding who helps the man who is getting married (the GROOM)

best sell·er /ˌbɛst ˈsɛlər/ noun [count]
a book or other product that is bought by large numbers of people

bet /bɛt/ verb (bets, bet·ting, bet, has bet)
to risk money on a race or a game by saying what the result will be. If you are right, you win money: *I bet you $5 that our team will win.*
I bet (informal) I am sure: *I bet it will rain tomorrow.* ◆ *I bet you can't climb that tree.*
you bet (informal) words you use to mean "Yes, of course!": *"Are you coming too?" "You bet!"*
▶ **bet** noun [count]: *I lost the bet.*

be·tray /bɪˈtreɪ/ verb (be·trays, be·tray·ing, be·trayed)
1 to harm your country or your friends by giving information to an enemy: *She betrayed the whole group to the secret police.*
2 to hurt someone who trusts you by doing something dishonest or harmful: *When parents get divorced, children often feel betrayed.*

bet·ter¹ 🔊 /ˈbɛtər/ adjective (good, bet·ter, best)
1 of a higher standard or quality; not as bad as something else: *This book is better than that one.*
2 (HEALTH) less sick: *I was sick yesterday, but I feel better now.* ➔ ANTONYM **worse**

bet·ter² 🔊 /ˈbɛtər/ adverb
in a more excellent or pleasant way; not as badly: *You speak Spanish better than I do.*
be better off to be happier, richer, etc.: *I'm better off now that I have a new job.* ◆ *You look sick – you'd be better off in bed.*
had better should; ought to: *You'd better go now if you want to catch the train.*

be·tween 🔊 /bɪˈtwin/ preposition, adverb
1 in the space in the middle of two things or people: *The letter B comes between A and C.* ◆ *I sat between Suzy and Brian.* ◆ *I see her most weekends but not very often in between.* ➔ Look at the note at **among**.
2 to and from two places: *The boat sails between Manhattan and Staten Island.*
3 for or by two or more people or things: *We shared the cake between us* (= each of us had some cake).
4 more than one thing but less than another thing: *The meal will cost between $20 and $25.*
5 after one time and before the next time: *I'll meet you between 4 and 4:30.*
6 a word that you use when you compare two people or things: *What is the difference between "some" and "any"?*

bev·er·age /ˈbɛvərɪdʒ/ noun [count] (formal)
a drink: *We have a selection of beverages.*

be·ware /bɪˈwɛr/ verb
beware of someone or **something** to be careful because someone or something is dangerous: *Beware of the dog!* (= words written on a sign)

be·wil·dered /bɪˈwɪldərd/ adjective
If you are **bewildered**, you do not understand something or you do not know what to do: *I was completely bewildered by his sudden change of mood.* ➔ SYNONYM **confused**

be·yond 🔊 /bɪˈyɑnd/ preposition, adverb
1 on the other side of something; farther than something: *The road continues beyond the town up into the hills.* ◆ *We could see the lake and the mountains beyond.*
2 later than a particular time: *Most people don't work beyond the age of 65.* ◆ *The party went on beyond midnight.*

bi·as AWL /ˈbaɪəs/ noun [count, noncount] (plural bi·as·es)
a strong positive or negative feeling towards a person, a group, or an opinion that is not fair or not based on facts: *a bias against women drivers*
▶ **bi·ased** AWL /ˈbaɪəst/ adjective: *a biased piece of writing* ➔ ANTONYM **unbiased**

bib /bɪb/ noun [count]
a piece of cloth or plastic that a baby wears under its chin when he or she is eating

| tʃ **chin** | dʒ **June** | v **van** | θ **thin** | ð **then** | s **so** | z **zoo** | ʃ **she**

the Bi·ble /ðə ˈbaɪbl/ *noun* [*count*]
(**RELIGION**) the book of great religious importance to Christian and Jewish people
▸ **bib·li·cal** /ˈbɪblɪkl/ *adjective* connected to the Bible: *biblical stories*

bib·li·og·ra·phy /ˌbɪbliˈɑgrəfi/ *noun* [*count*]
(*plural* **bib·li·og·ra·phies**)
(**ENGLISH LANGUAGE ARTS**) a list of books, articles, etc. on a particular subject, or the ones a writer has used to write a book or paper: *Remember to include all of your sources in your bibiography.*

bicycle

handlebars · saddle
spoke
pedal · chain · tire

bi·cy·cle /ˈbaɪsɪkl/ (also *informal* **bike** /baɪk/) *noun* [*count*]
a vehicle with two wheels. You sit on a **bicycle** and move your legs to make the wheels turn: *Can you **ride a bicycle**?*

bid¹ /bɪd/ *verb* (bids, bid·ding, bid, has bid)
1 to offer some money because you want to buy something: *He bid $10,000 **for** the painting.*
2 to offer to do work or provide a service for a particular price: *A Canadian company is **bidding for** the contract.*

bid² /bɪd/ *noun* [*count*]
1 an offer of money for something that you want to buy: *She made a **bid of** $250 **for** the vase.*
2 a formal offer to do work or provide a service for a particular price: *We got bids from three moving companies and chose the cheapest one.*
3 an attempt to do or get something: *a **bid for** power*

big /bɪg/ *adjective* (big·ger, big·gest)
1 not small; large: *Chicago is a big city.* • *This shirt is **too big** for me.* • *How big is your apartment?* ⊃ **ANTONYM small**
2 great or important: *a big problem*
3 older: *Amy is my big sister.* ⊃ **ANTONYM little**

the big bang /ðə ˌbɪg ˈbæŋ/ *noun* [*singular*]
(**PHYSICS**) the large explosion that some scientists believe created the universe

bike /baɪk/ *noun* [*count*] (*informal*)
a bicycle or a motorcycle: *I go to school **by bike**.*

bi·ki·ni /bɪˈkini/ *noun* [*count*]
a piece of clothing in two pieces that women wear for swimming

bi·lin·gual /ˌbaɪˈlɪŋgwəl/ *adjective*
1 (**ENGLISH LANGUAGE ARTS**) able to speak two languages very well: *Their children are bilingual.*
2 having or using two languages: *a bilingual dictionary*

bill¹ /bɪl/ *noun* [*count*]
1 a piece of paper that shows how much money you must pay for something: *We didn't have enough money to pay the phone bill.*
2 a piece of paper money: *He gave me a $20 bill.* • *a ten-dollar bill* ⊃ Look at the picture at **money**.
3 (**POLITICS**) a plan for a possible new law: *The bill was discussed in Congress.*
4 the hard pointed or curved part of a bird's mouth: *a duck's bill* ⊃ **SYNONYM beak**

bill² /bɪl/ *verb* (bills, bill·ing, billed)
to send someone a bill for something: *The company billed me for several items I didn't order.*

bill·board /ˈbɪlbɔrd/ *noun* [*count*]
a large board on the outside of a building or near a road, where advertisements are put

bil·lion /ˈbɪlyən/ *number*
1,000,000,000: *five billion dollars* • *The company is worth **billions of** dollars.*

Grammar

- Be careful! When you use **billion** with a number, don't add an "s": *six billion dollars.*
- If there is no number mentioned, then add an "s": *billions of dollars.*

bin /bɪn/ *noun* [*count*]
a large container that is used for storing or holding things: *Put those empty cans in the recycling bin.*

bind /baɪnd/ *verb* (binds, bind·ing, bound /baʊnd/, has bound)
to tie string or rope around something to hold it firmly: *They bound the prisoner's arms and legs together.*

binge /bɪndʒ/ *verb* (bin·ges, bing·ing or binge·ing, binged) (*informal*)
to eat or drink too much, especially when you cannot control yourself: *to **binge on** junk food*

bin·go /ˈbɪŋgoʊ/ *noun* [*noncount*]
a game where each player has a card with numbers on it, and the person who controls the game calls numbers out. If that person calls out the right numbers on your card, you win the game.

bin·oc·u·lars
/bɪˈnɑkyələrz/ *noun* [*plural*]
special glasses that you use to see things that are far away ⊃ Look at **telescope**.

binoculars

a pair of binoculars

bi·o·de·grad·a·ble /ˌbaɪoʊdɪˈɡreɪdəbl/ *adjective*
(**BIOLOGY**) Biodegradable substances can go
back into the earth and so do not damage the
environment: *There is growing demand for
biodegradable products.*

bi·og·ra·phy /baɪˈɑɡrəfi/ *noun* [count] (*plural*
bi·og·ra·phies)
(**ENGLISH LANGUAGE ARTS**) the story of a person's
life that another person writes: *a biography of
George Washington* ⊃ Look at **autobiography**.

bi·o·log·i·cal /ˌbaɪəˈlɑdʒɪkl/ *adjective*
(**BIOLOGY**) connected with the scientific study of
plants, animals, and other living things:
biological research

bi·ol·o·gy /baɪˈɑlədʒi/ *noun* [noncount]
the study of the life of animals and plants:
Biology is my favorite subject.
▶ **bi·ol·o·gist** /baɪˈɑlədʒɪst/ *noun* [count]
a person who studies **biology**

bird

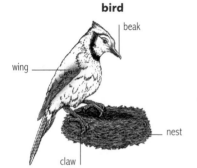

beak

wing

nest

claw

bird 🔊 /bərd/ *noun* [count]
an animal with feathers and wings: *Crows and
robins are birds.*

bird of prey /ˌbərd əv ˈpreɪ/ *noun* [count]
a bird that catches and eats other birds and
small animals: *Eagles are birds of prey.*

birth 🔊 /bərθ/ *noun* [count, noncount]

> ℹ️ **PRONUNCIATION**
> The word **birth** sounds like **earth**.

the time when a baby comes out of its mother;
being born: *the birth of a baby* • *What's your date
of birth* (= the date when you were born)?
give birth to have a baby: *Last week my sister
gave birth to her second child.*

birth cer·tif·i·cate /ˈbərθ sərˌtɪfəkət/ *noun*
[count]
an official document that shows when and
where you were born, and who your parents
are: *You need to bring a copy of your birth
certificate and a photo ID.*

birth con·trol /ˈbərθ kənˌtroʊl/ *noun* [noncount]
ways of controlling the number of children you

have: *methods of birth control* ⊃ Look at
contraceptive.

birth·day 🔊 /ˈbərθdeɪ/ *noun* [count] (*plural*
birth·days)
the day each year that is the same as the date
when you were born: *My birthday is on May 2.* •
Happy Birthday! • *a birthday present* • *a birthday
cake with sixteen candles on it*

birth·place /ˈbərθpleɪs/ *noun* [count]
(**HISTORY**) the house or area where a person was
born, or the place where something began:
Greece is the birthplace of the Olympic Games.

bis·cuit /ˈbɪskət/ *noun* [count]
a type of soft, round bread. People often eat
biscuits warm with butter.

bish·op /ˈbɪʃəp/ *noun* [count]
(**RELIGION**) an important priest in the Christian
church, who takes care of all the churches in a
large area

bi·son /ˈbaɪsn/ *noun* [count] (*plural* bi·son)
a large wild animal that looks like a cow with a
large head, curved horns, and thick fur on its
head and neck: *a herd of bison* ⊃ **SYNONYM
buffalo**

bit /bɪt/ *noun* [count]
1 a small piece or amount of something: *There
were bits of broken glass on the floor.* • *I think
these strawberries need a little bit more sugar.*
2 (**COMPUTERS**) the smallest unit of information
that is stored in a computer's memory
a bit; a little bit
1 a little; slightly: *You look a bit tired.* • *This one's
a little bit cheaper than that one.*
2 a short time or distance: *Let's wait a bit.*
bit by bit slowly, or a little at a time: *Bit by bit, I
started to feel better.*
quite a bit (*informal*) a lot: *It must have rained
quite a bit during the night.*

bite¹ 🔊 /baɪt/ *verb* (bites, bit·ing, bit /bɪt/, has
bit·ten /ˈbɪtn/)
1 to cut something with your teeth: *That dog bit
my leg!*
2 If an insect or snake **bites** you, it hurts you by
pushing a small sharp part into your skin: *I was
bitten by mosquitoes.*

bite² 🔊 /baɪt/ *noun*
1 [count] a piece of food that you can put in your
mouth: *He took a bite of his sandwich.*
2 [count] (**HEALTH**) a painful place on your skin
made by an insect or an animal: *a snake bite*
3 [singular] (*informal*) a small meal: *Would you like
a bite to eat before you go?*

bit·ter 🔊 /ˈbɪtər/ *adjective*
1 angry and sad about something that has
happened: *He felt very bitter about losing his job.*
2 Bitter food has a sharp, unpleasant taste: *The
coffee was bitter.*

3 very cold: *a bitter wind*
▶ **bit·ter·ness** /ˈbɪtərnəs/ *noun* [*noncount*]: *The strike caused great bitterness.*

bi·zarre /bɪˈzɑr/ *adjective*
very strange: *He has a bizarre sense of humor.* ⊃ **SYNONYM weird**
▶ **bi·zarre·ly** /bɪˈzɑrli/ *adverb*: *bizarrely dressed teenagers*

black¹ 🔑 /blæk/ *adjective* (black·er, black·est)
1 with the color of the sky at night: *a black dog*
2 belonging to a race of people with dark skin: *Martin Luther King Jr. was a famous black leader.* ⊃ **SYNONYM African-American**
3 (used about coffee) without milk: *Two black coffees, please.*

black² /blæk/ *noun*
1 [*noncount*] the color of the sky at night: *She was dressed in black.*
2 blacks [*plural*] people who belong to a race of people with dark skin ⊃ **SYNONYM African American**
black and white with the colors black, white, and gray only: *black-and-white photographs*

black·ber·ry /ˈblækˌbɛri/ *noun* [*count*] (*plural* black·ber·ries)
a small, soft, black fruit that grows on a bush

black·bird /ˈblækbərd/ *noun* [*count*]
a bird with black feathers

black·board /ˈblækbɔrd/ (also **chalk·board** /ˈtʃɔkbɔrd/) *noun* [*count*]
a dark board that a teacher writes on with a white substance (called **CHALK**): *The teacher wrote her name on the blackboard.* ⊃ Look at **whiteboard**.

black eye /ˌblæk ˈaɪ/ *noun* [*count*]
a dark area of skin around a person's eye where someone or something has hit them: *He got a black eye in a fight.*

black·mail /ˈblækmeɪl/ *noun* [*noncount*]
saying that you will tell something bad about someone if they do not give you money or do something for you
▶ **black·mail** *verb* (black·mails, black·mail·ing, black·mailed): *She blackmailed him into giving her thousands of dollars.*

black·out /ˈblækaʊt/ *noun* [*count*]
1 a time when there is no light because the electricity is not working: *We had a blackout for six hours after the storm.*
2 (**HEALTH**) a period when you are unconscious for a short time: *to have a blackout*

black·smith /ˈblæksmɪθ/ *noun* [*count*]
a person whose job is to make and repair things made of iron

blad·der /ˈblædər/ *noun* [*count*]
(**BIOLOGY**) the part of your body where waste liquid (called **URINE**) collects before leaving your body

blade /bleɪd/ *noun* [*count*]
1 the flat sharp part of something such as a knife or a tool ⊃ Look at the picture at **shears**.
2 a single flat leaf of grass: *a few blades of grass*

blame 🔑 /bleɪm/ *verb* (blames, blam·ing, blamed)
to say that a certain person or thing made something bad happen: *The other driver **blamed** me **for** the accident.*
▶ **blame** *noun* [*noncount*]: *Eve took the blame for the mistake.*

bland /blænd/ *adjective* (bland·er, bland·est)
1 ordinary and not very interesting: *I find her songs kind of bland.*
2 Bland food does not have a strong taste: *a bland diet of rice and fish*

blank¹ /blæŋk/ *adjective*
1 with no writing, pictures, or anything else on it: *a blank piece of paper*
2 without feelings, understanding, or interest: *She had a blank expression on her face.* ◆ *I tried to remember the answer, but my mind **went blank** (= I couldn't remember anything).*
▶ **blank·ly** /ˈblæŋkli/ *adverb*: *to stare at someone blankly*

blank² /blæŋk/ *noun* [*count*]
an empty space on a document, where you can write an answer or some information: *Fill in the blanks in the following exercise.*

blan·ket /ˈblæŋkət/ *noun* [*count*]
a thick cover that you put on a bed

blare /blɛr/ *verb* (blares, blar·ing, blared)
to make a loud, unpleasant noise: *A car drove by with the radio blaring.*

blast¹ /blæst/ *noun* [*count*]
1 when a bomb explodes: *Two people were killed in the blast.*
2 a sudden movement of air: *a blast of cold air*
3 a sudden loud noise: *The driver gave a few blasts on his horn.*

blast² /blæst/ *verb* (blasts, blast·ing, blast·ed)
to make a hole in something with an explosion: *They blasted through the mountain to make a tunnel.*

blast·off /ˈblæstɔf/ *noun* [*noncount*]
the time when a **SPACECRAFT** (= a vehicle that travels into space) leaves the ground

bla·tant /ˈbleɪtnt/ *adjective*
very clear or obvious: *It was a blatant lie.*

blaze¹ /bleɪz/ *noun*
1 [*count*] a large and often dangerous fire: *It took firefighters four hours to put out the blaze.*

---

2 [*singular*] a very bright show of light or color: *The garden was a blaze of color.*

blaze² /bleɪz/ *verb* (blaz·es, blaz·ing, blazed)
to burn in a strong and bright way: *a blazing fire*

blaz·er /'bleɪzər/ *noun* [*count*]
a jacket that looks like part of a suit but does not have matching pants

bleach¹ /blitʃ/ *noun* [*noncount*]
a strong chemical substance used for making clothes whiter or for cleaning things: *Use some bleach on it to kill the germs.*

bleach² /blitʃ/ *verb* (bleach·es, bleach·ing, bleached)
to become or to make something white or lighter in color by using a chemical or by leaving it in the sun: *She bleaches her hair blonde.*

bleach·ers /'blitʃərz/ *noun* [*plural*]
(**SPORTS**) lines of long seats where people sit to watch sports games, etc.: *We sat in the bleachers.*

bleak /blik/ *adjective* (bleak·er, bleak·est)
1 A **bleak** situation is not hopeful or encouraging: *The country's future looks bleak.*
2 cold and gray: *It was a bleak winter's day.*

bleed /blid/ *verb* (bleeds, bleed·ing, bled /blɛd/, has bled)
(**HEALTH**) to lose blood: *I cut my hand and it's bleeding.*

blem·ish /'blɛmɪʃ/ *noun* [*count*] (*plural* blem·ish·es)
a mark that spoils the way something looks: *makeup to cover pimples and other blemishes*

blend /blɛnd/ *verb* (blends, blend·ing, blend·ed)
1 to mix: *Blend the sugar and the butter together.*
2 to look or sound good together: *These colors blend very well.*
▶ **blend** *noun* [*count*]: *This is a blend of two different kinds of coffee.*

blend·er /'blɛndər/ *noun* [*count*]
an electric machine that is used for mixing soft food or liquid

bless /blɛs/ *verb* (bless·es, bless·ing, blessed)
(**RELIGION**) to ask for God's help for someone or something: *The priest blessed the young couple.*
Bless you! words that you say to someone when they SNEEZE (= make a loud noise through their nose)

bless·ing /'blɛsɪŋ/ *noun* [*count*]
1 something that is good or that helps you: *Having such a supportive family has been a real blessing.*
2 If you have someone's **blessing**, they agree with what you are doing and will support you: *They got married without their parents' blessing.*

3 (**RELIGION**) God's help and protection, or a prayer asking for this: *The rabbi said a blessing.*

blew form of **blow¹**

blimp /blɪmp/ *noun* [*count*]
a big thing that is filled with gas so it can float. It is made of soft material and looks like a long round balloon: *the Goodyear Blimp*

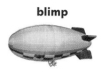
blimp

blind¹ /blaɪnd/ *adjective* (blind·er, blind·est)
not able to see: *My grandad is going blind.* ◆ *He trains guide dogs for the blind* (= people who are not able to see).
▶ **blind·ness** /'blaɪndnəs/ *noun* [*noncount*]: *The disease can cause blindness.*

blind² /blaɪnd/ *verb* (blinds, blind·ing, blind·ed)
to make someone unable to see: *I was blinded for a couple of seconds by the glare of the sun.*

blind³ /blaɪnd/ *noun* [*count*]
a piece of cloth or other material that you pull down to cover a window

blind·fold /'blaɪndfoʊld/ *noun* [*count*]
a piece of cloth that you put over someone's eyes so that they cannot see
▶ **blind·fold** *verb* (blind·folds, blind·fold·ing, blind·fold·ed): *The prisoners were blindfolded and pushed into vans.*

blind

blink /blɪŋk/ *verb* (blinks, blink·ing, blinked)
1 to shut and open your eyes very quickly ⊃ Look at **wink**.
2 (used about a light) to come on and go off again quickly: *I don't know why that light is blinking on my computer.*
▶ **blink** *noun* [*count*]

bliss /blɪs/ *noun* [*noncount*]
perfect happiness: *married bliss*
▶ **bliss·ful** /'blɪsfl/ *adjective*: *a blissful smile*

blis·ter /'blɪstər/ *noun* [*count*]
(**HEALTH**) a small painful place on your skin that is full of liquid. Rubbing or burning can cause blisters: *My new shoes gave me blisters.*

bliz·zard /'blɪzərd/ *noun* [*count*]
a very bad storm with snow and strong winds ⊃ SYNONYM **snowstorm**

bloat·ed /'bloʊt̬əd/ *adjective*
If you feel **bloated**, your stomach feels uncomfortable because it is too full: *I felt really bloated after that huge lunch.*

blob /blɑb/ *noun* [count]
a small amount of a thick liquid: *There are blobs of paint on the floor.*

block¹ 🔊 /blɑk/ *noun* [count]
1 a big heavy of something, with flat sides: *a block of wood* • *The bridge is made of concrete blocks.*
2 a group of buildings with streets all around it: *We drove around the block looking for the hotel.* • *My house is two blocks from here.*
3 a thing that stops someone or something from moving forward: *The police put road blocks around the town.*
4 a number of similar things that form a group: *We booked a block of seats for the baseball game.*

block² /blɑk/ *verb* (blocks, block·ing, blocked)
1 to stop someone or something from moving forward: *A fallen tree blocked the road.*
2 to stop someone from seeing something: *Can you sit down? You're blocking my view.*

block·age /ˈblɑkɪdʒ/ *noun* [count]
a thing that is preventing something from passing: *There must be a blockage in the pipe somewhere.*

blog /blɑg/ *noun* [count]
a personal record that someone puts on their website saying what they do every day and what they think about things
▶ **blog·ger** /ˈblɑgər/ *noun* [count]
a person who writes a **blog**

blond /blɑnd/ (also **blonde**) *adjective*
with hair that has a light color: *He has blond hair.* • *She is tall and blonde.*
▶ **blonde** *noun* [count]
a woman who has **blond** hair: *She's a natural blonde.*

blood 🔊 /blʌd/ *noun* [noncount]
the red liquid inside your body: *He lost a lot of blood in the accident.* ➔ The verb is **bleed**.

blood pres·sure /ˈblʌd prɛʃər/ *noun* [noncount]
(HEALTH, BIOLOGY) the force with which blood moves around the body: *He has **high blood pressure**.*

blood·shed /ˈblʌdʃɛd/ *noun* [noncount]
the killing of people, especially during a war: *They hoped the peace talks would prevent more bloodshed.*

blood·stream /ˈblʌdstrim/ *noun* [singular]
(BIOLOGY) the blood as it flows through the body: *It takes a few minutes for the drug to enter your bloodstream.*

blood·thirst·y /ˈblʌdˌθərsti/ *adjective*
wanting to hurt and kill people: *a bloodthirsty dictator*

blood ves·sel /ˈblʌd ˌvɛsl/ *noun* [count]
(BIOLOGY) one of the tubes in your body that blood flows through

blood·y /ˈblʌdi/ *adjective* (blood·i·er, blood·i·est)
1 with a lot of killing: *It was a bloody war.*
2 covered with blood: *a bloody nose*

bloom¹ /blum/ *verb* (blooms, bloom·ing, bloomed)
to produce flowers: *Roses bloom in the summer.*

bloom² /blum/ *noun*
in bloom with its flowers open: *The dogwood trees are in bloom.*

blos·som /ˈblɑsəm/ *noun* [count, noncount]
the flowers on a tree, especially a fruit tree: *The apple tree is covered in blossom.*
▶ **blos·som** *verb* (blos·soms, blos·som·ing, blos·somed): *The cherry trees are blossoming.*

blouse /blaʊs/ *noun* [count]
a piece of clothing like a shirt that a woman or girl wears on the top part of her body ➔ Look at the picture at **clothes**.

blow¹ 🔊 /bloʊ/ *verb* (blows, blow·ing, blew /blu/, has blown /bloʊn/)

ⓘ **PRONUNCIATION**
The word **blow** sounds like **go**.

1 When air or wind **blows**, it moves: *The wind was blowing from the ocean.*
2 to move something through the air: *The wind blew my hat off.*
3 to send air out from your mouth: *Please blow into this tube.*
4 (MUSIC) to send air out from your mouth into a musical instrument, for example, to make a noise: *The referee blew his whistle.*
blow up; blow something up
1 to explode or make something explode, for example with a bomb: *The plane blew up.* • *They blew up the station.*
2 to fill something with air: *We blew up some balloons for the party.*
blow your nose to clear your nose by blowing strongly through it onto a piece of cloth or paper (called a HANDKERCHIEF or TISSUE)

blow² 🔊 /bloʊ/ *noun* [count]
1 a hard hit from someone's hand or a weapon: *He felt a blow on the back of his head.*
2 something that happens suddenly and that makes you very unhappy: *Her father's death was a terrible blow.*

blow-dry /ˈbloʊ draɪ/ *verb* (blow-dries, blow-dry·ing, blow-dried)
to dry someone's hair using a small machine that blows out hot air (a HAIR DRYER): *I didn't have time to blow-dry my hair.*

blue¹ 🔑 /blu/ *adjective* (blu·er, blu·est)
1 having the color of a clear sky when the sun shines: *He wore a blue shirt.* • *dark blue curtains* • *Her eyes are bright blue.*
2 (*informal*) sad: *I'm feeling a little blue today.*

blue² 🔑 /blu/ *noun* [count, noncount]
the color of a clear sky when the sun shines: *She was dressed in blue.* ⊃ Look at **blues**.

blue·ber·ry /'blu,bɛri/ *noun* [count] (*plural* blue·ber·ries)
a small, round, dark blue fruit that grows on a bush: *blueberry muffins* ⊃ Look at the picture at **berry**.

blue-col·lar /,blu 'kɑlər/ *adjective*
(**BUSINESS**) connected with people who do physical work with their hands rather than office work: *blue-collar workers* ⊃ Look at **white-collar**.

blues /bluz/ *noun* [plural]
(**MUSIC**) a type of slow, sad music with a strong rhythm, developed by African-American musicians in the Southern U.S.: *to sing **the blues*** • *a blues band*

bluff /blʌf/ *verb* (bluffs, bluff·ing, bluffed)
to try to make people believe something is true when it is not: *She won't really tell Mom and Dad. She's just bluffing.*

blunt /blʌnt/ *adjective* (blunt·er, blunt·est)
1 with an edge or point that is not sharp: *He only had a blunt knife to cut the rope.* ⊃ ANTONYM **sharp**
2 If you are **blunt**, you say what you think in a way that is not polite.
▶ **blunt·ly** /'blʌntli/ *adverb*: *"Go away," she said bluntly.*

blur /blər/ *noun* [count, usually singular]
something that you cannot see clearly or remember well: *Without my glasses, everything's a blur.* • *The events of the day were just a blur.*

blur·ry /'bləri/ *adjective* (blurr·i·er, blurr·i·est)
not clear: *I can't read the words – they're all blurry.*

blurt /blərt/ *verb* (blurts, blurt·ing, blurt·ed)
blurt something out to say something suddenly or without thinking: *The teacher told us to wait, but James just blurted out the answer.*

blush /blʌʃ/ *verb* (blush·es, blush·ing, blushed)
If you **blush**, your face suddenly becomes red, for example because you are embarrassed: *She blushed when he looked at her.*

Blvd. abbreviation of **boulevard**

boar /bɔr/ (also **wild boar**) *noun* [count]
a wild pig

board¹ 🔑 /bɔrd/ *noun*
1 [count] a long, thin, flat piece of wood: *I nailed a board across the broken window.* • *floorboards*
2 [count] a flat piece of wood, for example, that you use for a special purpose: *There is a list of names on the bulletin board.* • *an ironing board* • *a chessboard* ⊃ Look at **blackboard**.
3 [count] (**BUSINESS**) a group of people who have a special job, for example controlling a company: *the board of directors*
4 [noncount] the meals that are provided when you live at a college or stay at a hotel, etc.: *The tuition fees do not include **room and board**.*
on board on a ship or an airplane: *How many passengers are on board?*

board² /bɔrd/ *verb* (boards, board·ing, board·ed)
to get on a ship, bus, train, or airplane: *We said goodbye and boarded the train.* • *Flight 193 to Denver is now boarding* (= is ready for passengers to get on).

board·ing pass /'bɔrdɪŋ pæs/ *noun* [count]
a card that you must show when you get on an airplane or a ship

board·ing school /'bɔrdɪŋ skul/ *noun* [count]
a school where the students live

boast /boʊst/ *verb* (boasts, boast·ing, boast·ed)
to talk in a way that shows you are too proud of something that you have or something that you can do: *He's always **boasting about** what a good football player he is.*
▶ **boast·ful** /'boʊstfl/ *adjective*: *I know you won, but you don't need to be so boastful about it.*

boat 🔑 /boʊt/ *noun* [count]
a vehicle for traveling on water: *a fishing boat* • *We traveled by boat.* ⊃ Look at **ship**.

bob /bɑb/ *verb* (bobs, bob·bing, bobbed)
to move quickly up and down: *The boats in the harbor were **bobbing up and down** in the water.*

bod·y 🔑 /'bɑdi/ *noun* (*plural* bod·ies)
1 [count] the whole physical form of a person or an animal: *the human body*
2 [count] all of a person or animal except the legs, arms, and head: *The baby mice have thin bodies and big heads.*
3 [count] a dead person: *The police found a body in the river.*
4 [singular] the main part of something: *the body of a plane* (= the part where the seats are)

bod·y·build·ing /'bɑdi,bɪldɪŋ/ *noun* [noncount]
(**SPORTS**) making the muscles of your body bigger and stronger by doing exercise
▶ **bod·y·build·er** /'bɑdi,bɪldər/ *noun* [count]
a person who does **bodybuilding**

body

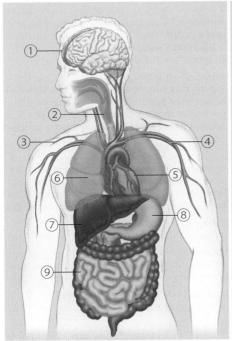

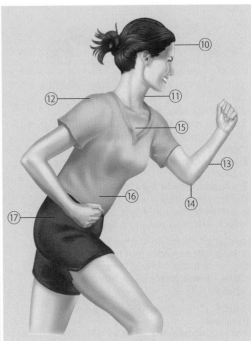

internal organs   the body

①	brain	④	vein	⑦	liver	⑩	head	⑬	arm	⑯	stomach
②	throat	⑤	heart	⑧	stomach	⑪	neck	⑭	elbow	⑰	hip
③	artery	⑥	lung	⑨	intestines	⑫	shoulder	⑮	chest		

bod·y·guard /ˈbɑdigɑrd/ *noun* [*count*]
a person or group of people whose job is to
keep an important person safe: *The president's
bodyguards all carry guns.*

bo·gus /ˈboʊɡəs/ *adjective*
pretending to be real or true: *a bogus contract*

boil 🔑 /bɔɪl/ *verb* (**boils**, **boil·ing**, **boiled**)
1 (**GENERAL SCIENCE**) When a liquid **boils**, it
becomes very hot and makes steam and
bubbles: *Water boils at 212°F.*
2 to heat a liquid until it **boils**: *I boiled some
water for the pasta.*
3 to cook something in extremely hot water:
Boil the rice in a pan. • *a boiled egg* ⊃ Look at the
note at **cook**¹.
boil over to boil and flow over the sides of a
pan: *Don't let the milk boil over.*

boil·er /ˈbɔɪlər/ *noun* [*count*]
a big metal container that heats water for a
building

boil·ing /ˈbɔɪlɪŋ/ (also **boil·ing hot**) *adjective*
(*informal*)
very hot: *I'm boiling.* • *It's boiling hot in here.* ⊃
Look at the note at **hot**.

boil·ing point /ˈbɔɪlɪŋ ˌpɔɪnt/ *noun* [*count*]
(**GENERAL SCIENCE**) the temperature at which a
liquid starts to boil

bois·ter·ous /ˈbɔɪstərəs/ *adjective*
noisy and full of energy: *The kids were a little too
boisterous on the school bus.*

bold /boʊld/ *adjective* (**bold·er**, **bold·est**)
1 brave and not afraid: *It was very bold of you to
ask for more money.*
2 that you can see clearly: *bold colors*
▶ **bold·ly** /ˈboʊldli/ *adverb*: *He boldly said that he
disagreed.*

bo·lo·gna (also **ba·lo·ney**) /bəˈloʊni/ *noun*
[*noncount*]
a meat that people often eat for lunch, made
from different types of cooked meats: *a bologna
sandwich*

bolts

bolt

bolt | nut

bolt /boʊlt/ *noun* [count]
1 a thick metal pin that you use with another piece of metal (called a NUT) to fasten things together
2 a piece of metal that you move across a door to lock it
3 a sudden bright light in the sky during a storm: *a bolt of lightning*
▸ **bolt** *verb* (bolts, bolt·ing, bolt·ed)
to lock a door by putting a **bolt** across it

bomb¹ /bɑm/ *noun* [count]
a thing that explodes and hurts or damages people or things: *Aircraft dropped bombs on the city.* ✦ *A bomb went off* (= exploded) *at the station.*

bomb² /bɑm/ *verb* (bombs, bomb·ing, bombed)
to attack people or a place with bombs: *The city was bombed in the war.*

bomb·er /'bɑmər/ *noun* [count]
1 a type of airplane that drops bombs
2 a person who makes a bomb explode somewhere

bond AWL /bɑnd/ *noun* [count]
something that joins people or groups of people together: *a strong bond of friendship*

bone /boʊn/ *noun* [count]
one of the hard white parts inside the body of a person or an animal: *She broke a bone in her foot.* ✦ *This fish has a lot of bones in it.*

bon·fire /'bɑn,faɪər/ *noun* [count]
a big fire that you make outside

bon·net /'bɑnət/ *noun* [count]
a soft hat that you tie under your chin

bo·nus /'boʊnəs/ *noun* [count] (*plural* bon·us·es)
1 (BUSINESS) an extra payment that is added to what you usually get: *to receive an annual bonus*
2 something good that you get in addition to what you expected: *My cell phone service includes free texts as an **added bonus**.*

bon·y /'boʊni/ *adjective* (bon·i·er, bon·i·est)
very thin, so that you can see the shape of the bones: *long bony fingers*

boo /bu/ *exclamation, noun* [count] (*plural* boos)
1 a word people use to show that they do not like someone or something: *The speech was met with boos from the audience.*
2 a sound that you make to frighten or surprise someone: *He jumped out from behind the door and shouted "Boo!"*
▸ **boo** *verb* (boos, boo·ing, booed)
to shout "boo": *The audience booed.*

book¹ /bʊk/ *noun* [count]
a thing that you read or write in, which has a lot of pieces of paper joined together inside a cover: *I'm reading a book by Mark Twain.* ✦ *an address book* (= a book that you write people's addresses in)

book² /bʊk/ *verb* (books, book·ing, booked)
to arrange to do or have something later, for example a seat on an airplane or a room at a hotel: *He booked a flight to Los Angeles.* ✦ *The hotel is **fully booked*** (= all the rooms are full).

book·case /'bʊk,keɪs/ *noun* [count]
a piece of furniture that you put books in

book·let /'bʊklət/ *noun* [count]
a small thin book that gives information about something

book·store /'bʊkstɔr/ *noun* [count]
a store that sells books

boom¹ /bum/ *noun* [count]
1 a loud deep sound: *There was a huge boom, and then silence.*
2 (BUSINESS) a period in which something increases or develops very quickly: *a boom in car sales*

boom² /bum/ *verb* (booms, boom·ing, boomed)
to make a loud deep sound: *We heard the guns booming in the distance.*

boost /bust/ *verb* (boosts, boost·ing, boost·ed)
to make something increase in number, value, or strength: *Lower prices have boosted sales.* ✦ *What can we do to **boost her confidence** (= make her feel more confident)?*

boot /but/ *noun* [count]
a shoe that covers your foot and usually part of your leg ⊃ Look at the picture at **shoe**.

booth /buθ/ *noun* [count] (*plural* booths /buθs; buðz/)
a small room or space that is separated from the rest of the area: *a voting booth* ✦ *a phone booth*

bor·der /'bɔrdər/ *noun* [count]
1 (GEOGRAPHY) a line between two countries or states: *You need a passport to cross the border.* ⊃ Look at **boundary**.
2 a line along the edge of something: *a white tablecloth with a blue border*

bore¹ form of **bear**¹

bore² /bɔr/ *verb* (bores, bor·ing, bored)
1 to make someone feel bored, especially by talking too much: *He bores everyone with his long stories.*
2 to make a thin round hole in something: *These insects bore holes in wood.*

bore³ /bɔr/ *noun* [count]
a person who talks a lot in a way that is not interesting

bored 🔑 /bɔrd/ *adjective*
not interested; unhappy because you have nothing interesting to do: *I'm **bored with** this book.* ◆ *The children were **bored stiff** (= extremely bored).*
▶ **bore·dom** /'bɔrdəm/ *noun* [noncount]: *I started to eat too much out of boredom.*

Which word?

Bored or boring?

- If you have nothing to do, or if what you are doing does not interest you, then you are **bored**: *Grace was so bored that she went home.*
- The person or thing that makes you feel like this is **boring**: *The movie was very boring.*

bor·ing 🔑 /'bɔrɪŋ/ *adjective*
not interesting: *That class was so boring!*

born 🔑 /bɔrn/ *adjective*
be born to start your life: *He was born in 1996.* ◆ *Where were you born?*

borne form of **bear²**

bor·ough /'bərou/ *noun* [count]
(GEOGRAPHY) a town or an part of a city that has its own local government: *Brooklyn is a borough of New York City.*

bor·row 🔑 /'barou; 'bɔrou/ *verb* (bor·rows, bor·row·ing, bor·rowed)
to take and use something that you will give back after a short time: *I **borrowed** some books **from** the library.* ◆ *Can I borrow your pen?*

Which word?

Borrow or lend?

- If you **borrow** something, you have it for a short time and you must give it back: *I borrowed a DVD from Alex for the weekend.*
- If you **lend** something, you give it to someone for a short time: *Alex lent me a DVD for the weekend.*

boss¹ 🔑 /bɔs/ *noun* [count] (plural boss·es)
a person who is in charge of other people at work and tells them what to do: *I asked my boss for a vacation.*

boss² /bɔs/ *verb* (boss·es, boss·ing, bossed)
boss someone around to tell someone what to do, in a way that bothers them: *I wish you'd stop bossing me around.*

boss·y /'bɔsi/ *adjective* (boss·i·er, boss·i·est)
A **bossy** person likes to tell other people what to do: *My sister is very bossy.*

bot·a·ny /'batn·i/ *noun* [noncount]
(BIOLOGY) the scientific study of plants
▶ **bot·a·nist** /'batn·ɪst/ *noun* [count]
a person who studies plants

both 🔑 /bouθ/ *adjective, pronoun*
the two; not only one but also the other: *Hold it in both hands.* ◆ *Both her brothers are doctors.* ◆ *Both of us like dancing.* ◆ *We both like dancing.*
both … and not only … but also: *She is both rich and intelligent.*

both·er 🔑 /'baðər/ *verb* (both·ers, both·er·ing, both·ered)
1 to disturb someone or make them angry, worried, or upset: *Don't bother me now – I'm busy!* ◆ *Is this music bothering you?* ◆ *I'm sorry to bother you, but there's someone on the phone for you.* ◆ *My ankle is still bothering (= hurting) me.*
2 to spend extra time or energy doing something: *Don't **bother with** the dishes – I'll do them later.* ◆ *He didn't even **bother to** say goodbye.*

bot·tle 🔑 /'batl/ *noun* [count]
a glass or plastic container for liquids, with a thin part at the top: *a beer bottle* ◆ *They drank two bottles of water.* ⊃ Look at the picture at **container**.

bot·tom¹ 🔑 /'batəm/ *noun*
1 [count, usually singular] the lowest part of something: *They live **at the bottom of** the hill.* ◆ *The book was at the bottom of my bag.* ◆ *Look at the picture at the bottom of the page.* ⊃ ANTONYM **top**
2 [count] the flat surface on the outside of an object, on which it stands: *There's a label on the bottom of the box.* ⊃ ANTONYM **top**
3 [singular] the lowest position compared to other people or groups: *I was always at the bottom of the class in math.* ⊃ ANTONYM **top**
4 [count] (informal) the part of your body that you sit on

bot·tom² 🔑 /'batəm/ *adjective*
lowest: *Put the book on the bottom shelf.* ⊃ ANTONYM **top**

bought form of **buy**

boul·der /'bouldər/ *noun* [count]
a very big rock

boul·e·vard /ˈbʊləvɑrd/ *noun* [*count*]
a wide street in a town or city ⊃ The short way of writing "Boulevard" in street names is Blvd.: *Sunset Blvd*

bounce /baʊns/ *verb* (bounc·es, bounc·ing, bounced)
1 (used about a ball) to move away quickly after hitting something hard; to make a ball do this: *The ball **bounced off** the wall.* • *The boy was bouncing a basketball.*
2 to jump up and down many times: *The children were bouncing on their beds.*

bounc·er /ˈbaʊnsər/ *noun* [*count*]
a person whose job is to control who goes in to a bar or club, and to make people leave if they are causing trouble: *The bouncer checked our IDs.*

bounc·y /ˈbaʊnsi/ *adjective* (bounc·i·er, bounc·i·est)
that BOUNCES well or that can make things BOUNCE: *a bouncy ball* • *a bouncy surface*

bound¹ form of **bind**

bound² /baʊnd/ *adjective*
1 sure to do something: *She works very hard, so she's **bound to** do well in her exams.*
2 having a legal or moral duty to do something: *She is not legally bound to pay for the damage.*
3 going to a place: *This ship is **bound for** Miami.*

bound³ /baʊnd/ *verb* (bounds, bound·ing, bound·ed)
to run with long steps: *The dog bounded up the steps.*

bound·a·ry /ˈbaʊndəri/ *noun* [*count*] (*plural* bound·a·ries)
a real or imagined line that marks the edges of something: *This fence is the **boundary between** the two yards.* • *scientists who push back the boundaries of knowledge* ⊃ Look at **border**.

bou·quet /boʊˈkeɪ; buˈkeɪ/ *noun* [*count*]
a group of flowers that is arranged in an attractive way: *He gave her a bouquet of roses.*

bou·tique /buˈtik/ *noun* [*count*]
(BUSINESS) a small store that sells expensive clothes, gifts, etc.: *a designer boutique*

bow¹ /baʊ/ *verb* (bows, bow·ing, bowed)

to bend your head or body forward to show respect: *The actors bowed at the end of the play.*

bow² /baʊ/ *noun* [*count*]
1 an act of BOWING: *He **made a bow** and left the stage.*
2 the front end of a ship or boat ⊃ Look at **stern²**.

bows

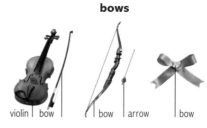

violin | bow | bow | arrow | bow

bow³ /boʊ/ *noun* [*count*]

1 a knot with two loose round parts and two loose ends that you use when you are tying shoes, etc.
2 a curved piece of wood with a tight string between the two ends. You use a **bow** to send arrows through the air.
3 (MUSIC) a long thin piece of wood with hair stretched across it that you use for playing some musical instruments: *a violin bow*

bow·el /ˈbaʊəl/ *noun* [*count*]
(BIOLOGY) one of the tubes that takes waste food away from your stomach to the place where it leaves your body

bowl¹ 🥄 /boʊl/ *noun* [*count*]
a deep round dish that is used for holding food or liquids: *a sugar bowl* • *a bowl of soup* ⊃ Look at the picture at **cereal**.

bowl² /boʊl/ *verb* (bowls, bowl·ing, bowled)
(SPORTS) to roll the ball in a game of BOWLING

bowl·ing /ˈboʊlɪŋ/ *noun* [*noncount*]
(SPORTS) a game in which you roll a heavy ball down a special track toward a group of wooden objects shaped like bottles (called PINS) and try to knock them all down: *We **go bowling** every Friday night.*

bowling

bow tie /ˈboʊ taɪ/ *noun* [*count*]
a tie in the shape of a BOW³(1) that some men wear on formal occasions

box¹ 🥄 /bɑks/ *noun* [*count*] (*plural* box·es)
1 a container with straight sides. A **box** often has a lid: *Put the books in a cardboard box.* • *a box of chocolates* • *a matchbox* ⊃ Look at the picture at **container**.

2 a square or similar shape on a piece of paper for people to write information in: *Write your name in the box below.*

box² /bɑks/ *verb* (box·es, box·ing, boxed)
(SPORTS) to fight with your hands, wearing thick gloves, as a sport

box·er /'bɑksər/ *noun* [count]
(SPORTS) a person who BOXES as a sport: *Muhammad Ali, the famous boxer*

box·er shorts /'bɑksər ˌʃɔrts/ (also **box·ers** /'bɑksərz/) *noun* [plural]
men's underwear that looks like a pair of short pants

box·ing /'bɑksɪŋ/ *noun* [noncount]
(SPORTS) the sport of fighting with your hands, while wearing thick gloves

box of·fice /'bɑks ˌɔfəs/ *noun* [count]
a place where you buy tickets in a theater, etc.

boy /bɔɪ/ *noun* [count] (plural **boys**)
a male child; a young man: *They have three children, two boys and a girl.* ◆ *The older boys at school used to tease him.*

boy·cott /'bɔɪkɑt/ *verb* (boy·cotts, boy·cott·ing, boy·cott·ed)
(BUSINESS, POLITICS) to refuse to buy, use, or take part in something as a way of making a protest: *Several athletes boycotted the Olympics* (= they did not take part) *in protest.*
▶ **boy·cott** *noun* [count]: *a boycott of American goods*

boy·friend /'bɔɪfrɛnd/ *noun* [count]
a boy or man who someone has a romantic relationship with: *She has had a lot of boyfriends.*

the Boy Scouts /ðə ˈbɔɪ skaʊts/ *noun* [singular]
a special club for boys, which does a lot of activities with them and teaches them useful skills
▶ **Boy Scout** *noun* [count]
a boy who is a member of **the Boy Scouts**

bra /brɑ/ *noun* [count] (plural **bras**)
a thing that a woman wears under her other clothes to cover and support the soft round parts at the front of her body (her BREASTS)

brace·let /'breɪslət/ *noun* [count]
a pretty piece of metal, wood, or plastic that you wear around your arm ⊃ Look at the picture at **jewelry**.

brac·es /'breɪsəz/ *noun* [plural]
(HEALTH) wires that children wear on their teeth to make them grow straight: *My dentist told me I need braces.*

brack·et /'brækət/ *noun* [count]
1 (ENGLISH LANGUAGE ARTS) one of the two marks, [ ], that you put around extra information in a text ⊃ Look at **parentheses**.

2 a particular range of ages, prices, pay, etc.: *the 18-24 age bracket* (= people aged between 18 and 24) ◆ *to be in a high income bracket*

brag /bræg/ *verb* (brags, brag·ging, bragged)
to talk in a way that shows you are too proud of something that you have or something that you can do: *She's always bragging about how smart she is.* ⊃ SYNONYM **boast**

braid /breɪd/ *noun* [count]
a long piece of hair that someone has divided into three parts and put over and under each other: *She wears her hair in braids.* ⊃ Look at the picture at **hair**.
▶ **braid** *verb* (braids, braid·ing, braid·ed): *She braided her hair.*

Braille /breɪl/ *noun* [noncount]
a system of printing using little round marks that you can read by touching them. It is used by people who are not able to see (BLIND people).

brain /breɪn/ *noun*
1 [count] the part inside the head of a person or an animal that thinks and feels: *The brain controls the rest of the body.* ⊃ Look at the picture at **body**.
2 [count, noncount] the ability to think clearly; being intelligent: *He doesn't have the brains to be a doctor.*

brain·storm /'breɪnstɔrm/ *verb* (brain·storms, brain·storm·ing, brain·stormed)
to try to think of as many ideas as possible in a short time: *Let's brainstorm some new ways to raise money.*

brain·wash /'breɪnwɑʃ; 'breɪnwɔʃ/ *verb* (brain·wash·es, brain·wash·ing, brain·washed)
to make someone believe something by using strong mental pressure: *They were brainwashed into giving away all their money.*

brain·y /'breɪni/ *adjective* (brain·i·er, brain·i·est) (informal)
intelligent: *Laura's even brainier than her sister.* ⊃ SYNONYM **smart**

brake¹ /breɪk/ *noun* [count]
the part of a vehicle that you use to make it go slower or stop: *I put my foot on the brake.* ⊃ Look at the picture at **steering wheel**.

brake² /breɪk/ *verb* (brakes, brak·ing, braked)
to use a BRAKE: *A dog ran into the road and the driver braked suddenly.*

bran /bræn/ *noun* [noncount]
the brown covering of grain that is left when the grain is made into flour: *bran muffins*

branch¹ /bræntʃ/ *noun* [count] (plural branch·es)
1 (BIOLOGY) one of the parts of a tree that grow out from the thick main part (called the TRUNK) ⊃ Look at the picture at **tree**.

2 (BUSINESS) an office or a store that is part of a big company: *This bank has branches all over the country.*
3 one part of an academic subject or area of study: *Psychiatry is a branch of medicine.*

branch² /bræntʃ/ *verb* (branch·es, branch·ing, branched)
branch out to start doing something new and different: *He started as a clothing designer, then branched out into furniture.*

brand /brænd/ *noun* [count]
(BUSINESS) the name of a product that a particular company makes: *Which brand of coffee do you buy?*

bran·dish /ˈbrændɪʃ/ *verb* (bran·dish·es, bran·dish·ing, bran·dished)
to wave something in the air in a violent or excited way: *He came out of the building brandishing a gun.*

brand new /ˌbrænd ˈnu/ *adjective*
completely new: *a brand new car*

bran·dy /ˈbrændi/ *noun* [count, noncount] (plural bran·dies)
a strong alcoholic drink made from wine: *a glass of brandy* • *Two brandies, please.*

brash /bræʃ/ *adjective* (brash·er, brash·est)
too confident and direct: *He has a brash manner, which some people don't like.*

brass /bræs/ *noun* [noncount]
1 a hard yellow metal: *brass buttons*
2 the group of musical instruments that are made of **brass**: *music for piano, strings, and brass* ⊃ Look at the note at **orchestra**.

brat /bræt/ *noun* [count]
a child who behaves badly: *Stop acting like a spoiled brat!*

brave 🔑 /breɪv/ *adjective* (brav·er, brav·est)
ready to do dangerous or difficult things without fear: *brave soldiers* • *Try to be brave.*
▶ **brave·ly** /ˈbreɪvli/ *adverb*: *He fought bravely in the war.*
▶ **brav·er·y** /ˈbreɪvəri/ *noun* [noncount]: *He won a medal for bravery.*

bread 🔑 /brɛd/ *noun* [noncount]

ⓘ **PRONUNCIATION**
The word **bread** sounds like **red**.

food made from flour and baked in an oven: *I bought a loaf of bread.* • *a slice of bread and butter*

breadth /brɛdθ/ *noun* [count, noncount]
how far it is from one side of something to the other: *We measured the length and breadth of the yard.* ⊃ SYNONYM **width** ⊃ The adjective is **broad**.

break¹ 🔑 /breɪk/ *verb* (breaks, break·ing, broke /broʊk/, has bro·ken /ˈbroʊkən/)
1 to make something go into smaller pieces, for example by dropping it or hitting it: *Did you break the window?* • *She broke her arm.*
2 to go into smaller pieces, for example by falling or hitting: *I dropped the cup and it broke.*
3 to stop working; to damage a machine so that it stops working: *You broke my phone!*
4 to do something that is against the law or against what has been agreed or promised: *People who break the law must be punished.* • *I never break my promises.*
5 to stop doing something for a short time: *Let's break for lunch now and meet back here at 2 p.m.*
break down
1 If a machine or car **breaks down**, it stops working: *We were late because our car broke down.*
2 If a person **breaks down**, they start to cry: *He broke down when he heard the news.*
break in; break into something to go into a place by breaking a door or window so that you can steal something: *Thieves broke into the house. They broke in through a window.*
break off to take away a piece of something by breaking it: *He broke off another piece of chocolate for me.*
break out
1 to start suddenly: *A fire broke out last night.*
2 to get free from a place like a prison: *Four prisoners broke out of jail last night.*
break up to end a relationship with someone: *Mia and Carl just broke up.* • *Susy broke up with her boyfriend last week.*

Thesaurus

break to go, or to make something go into smaller pieces: *She dropped the cup and it broke into pieces.* • *I'm sorry, I broke one of your dinner plates.* • *He broke the chocolate in two and gave me half.* • *She fell and broke her arm.*

crack (used about something hard) to break so that a line appears, but without dividing into smaller pieces; to break something in this way: *The ice cracked as I stepped on it.* • *This mirror is cracked.* • *He cracked a tooth playing football.*

smash to break into many pieces in a violent and noisy way; to break something in this way: *The glass bowl smashed into a thousand pieces.* • *Several windows had been smashed.* • *He smashed the box open and took the jewelry from inside.*

bread

a loaf of bread

slice

snap to break suddenly into two pieces with a sharp noise; to break something in this way: *Suddenly, the cable snapped.* • *The weight of the snow snapped the branch in two.*

burst to break open suddenly; to make something break in this way: *That balloon will burst if you blow it up any more.* • *Don't burst that balloon!* • *The dam burst under the weight of the water.*

break² /breɪk/ *noun* [count]
1 a place where something opens or has broken: *The sun shone through a break in the clouds.*
2 a short time when you stop doing something: *We worked all day without a break.*
3 an opportunity to do something; a chance to be successful: *He got his big break when he appeared on "American Idol."*
give someone a break to stop bothering someone or being unfair to them: *Give me a break! I've been working all day!*

break·down /ˈbreɪkdaʊn/ *noun* [count]
1 a time when a machine, car, etc. stops working: *We had a breakdown on the highway.*
2 the failure or end of something: *The breakdown of the talks could lead to more violence.*
3 another word for **nervous breakdown**

break·fast /ˈbrɛkfəst/ *noun* [count, noncount]
the first meal of the day: *I had breakfast at seven o'clock.* • *to eat a big breakfast*

break-in /ˈbreɪk ˌɪn/ *noun* [count]
the act of entering a building by force, especially to steal something: *The police reported several break-ins in the area.*

break·through /ˈbreɪkθru/ *noun* [count]
something important that you discover or develop: *to made a breakthrough in cancer research*

break·up /ˈbreɪkʌp/ *noun* [count]
the end of a relationship between two people: *the breakup of a marriage*

breast /brɛst/ *noun* [count]

ⓘ **PRONUNCIATION**
The word **breast** sounds like **test**.

1 one of the two soft round parts of a woman's body that can give milk
2 the front part of a bird's body

breast·stroke /ˈbrɛststroʊk; ˈbrɛstroʊk/ *noun* [noncount]
(**SPORTS**) a way of swimming on your front in which you push both arms forward and then pull them back to your sides in a circle: *Can you do the breaststroke?* ⊃ Look at **crawl²**.

breath /brɛθ/ *noun* [count, noncount]
the air that you take in and let out through your nose and mouth: *Take a deep breath.* • *He has bad breath* (= breath that smells bad).
hold your breath to stop breathing for a short time: *We all held our breath as the winner was announced.*
out of breath breathing very quickly: *She was out of breath after climbing the stairs.*
under your breath If you say something **under your breath**, you say it quietly because you do not want people to hear: *"Idiot!" he muttered under his breath.*

breathe /brið/ *verb* (breathes, breath·ing, breathed)
to take in and let out air through your nose and mouth: *The doctor told me to breathe in and then breathe out again slowly.*

breath·less /ˈbrɛθləs/ *adjective*
(**HEALTH**) breathing quickly or with difficulty: *Running made them hot and breathless.*

breath·tak·ing /ˈbrɛθˌteɪkɪŋ/ *adjective*
very beautiful, surprising, or exciting: *We had a breathtaking view of the mountains.*

breed¹ /brid/ *verb* (breeds, breed·ing, bred /brɛd/, has bred)
1 (**BIOLOGY**) When animals **breed**, they produce young animals: *Birds breed in the spring.*
2 to keep animals so that they will produce baby animals: *They breed horses on their farm.*

breed² /brid/ *noun* [count]
a kind of animal: *There are many different breeds of dog.*

breeze /briz/ *noun* [count]
a light wind ⊃ Look at the note at **wind¹**.

brew·er·y /ˈbruəri/ *noun* [count] (plural brew·er·ies)
a place where beer is made

bribe /braɪb/ *noun* [count]
money or a gift that you give to someone to make them do something for you, especially something dishonest
▶ **bribe** *verb* (bribes, brib·ing, bribed): *The prisoner bribed the guard to let him go free.*

brib·er·y /ˈbraɪbəri/ *noun* [noncount]
the act of giving or taking **BRIBES**: *the bribery of public officials*

brick /brɪk/ *noun* [count, noncount]
a small block of **CLAY** (= a type of earth) that has been baked until it is hard. **Bricks** are used for building: *a brick wall*

brick·lay·er /ˈbrɪkˌleɪər/ *noun* [count]
a person whose job is to build things with bricks

brid·al /ˈbraɪdl/ *adjective*
connected with a BRIDE or a wedding: *a bridal shower* (= a party before a wedding where people give presents to the bride)

bride /braɪd/ *noun* [count]
a woman on the day of her wedding: *the bride and groom*

bride·groom /ˈbraɪdɡrum/ *noun* [count] (*formal*)
a man on the day of his wedding ⊃ SYNONYM **groom**

brides·maid /ˈbraɪdzmeɪd/ *noun* [count]
a girl or woman who helps a BRIDE at her wedding ⊃ Look at **maid of honor**.

bridge /brɪdʒ/ *noun* [count]
a thing that is built over a road, railroad, or river so that people, trains, or cars can cross it: *We walked over the bridge.*

brief AWL /brif/ *adjective* (brief·er, brief·est)
short or quick: *a brief telephone call* ◆ *Please be brief.*
in brief in a few words: *Here is the news in brief* (= words said on a radio or television program).
▶ **brief·ly** AWL /ˈbrifli/ *adverb*: *He had spoken to Emma only briefly.*

brief·case /ˈbrifkeɪs/ *noun* [count]
a flat case that you use for carrying papers, especially when you go to work ⊃ Look at the picture at **bag**.

brief·ing AWL /ˈbrifɪŋ/ *noun* [count, noncount]
instructions or information that someone is given before something happens: *a press briefing* (= where information is given to journalists)

bright /braɪt/ *adjective* (bright·er, bright·est)
1 with a lot of light: *It was a bright sunny day.* ◆ *That lamp is very bright.*
2 with a strong color: *a bright yellow shirt*
3 intelligent; able to learn things quickly: *She is the brightest child in the class.* ⊃ Look at the note at **intelligent**.
▶ **bright·ly** /ˈbraɪtli/ *adverb*: *brightly colored clothes*
▶ **bright·ness** /ˈbraɪtnəs/ *noun* [noncount]: *the brightness of the sun*

bright·en /ˈbraɪtn/ *verb* (bright·ens, bright·en·ing, bright·ened) (also **bright·en up**)
to become brighter or happier; to make something brighter: *Her face brightened when she saw him.* ◆ *These flowers will brighten the room up.*

bril·liant /ˈbrɪlyənt/ *adjective*
1 with a lot of light; very bright: *brilliant sunshine*
2 extremely intelligent: *a brilliant student* ⊃ Look at the note at **intelligent**.
▶ **bril·liance** /ˈbrɪlyəns/ *noun* [noncount]: *the brilliance of the light*
▶ **bril·liant·ly** /ˈbrɪlyəntli/ *adverb*

brim /brɪm/ *noun* [count]
1 the edge around the top of something like a cup, bowl, or glass: *The bowl was full to the brim.*
2 the wide part around the bottom of a hat

bring /brɪŋ/ *verb* (brings, bring·ing, brought /brɔt/, has brought)
1 to take something or someone with you to a place: *Could you bring me a glass of water?* ◆ *Can I bring a friend to the party?*
2 to make something happen: *Money doesn't always bring happiness.*
bring something about to cause something to happen: *to bring about changes in people's lives*
bring something back
1 to return something: *I brought back the book you lent me.*
2 to make you remember something: *These old photographs bring back a lot of happy memories.*
bring something on to cause something: *Her headaches are brought on by stress.*
bring someone up to take care of a child until they are grown up: *He was brought up by his aunt after his parents died.* ⊃ The noun is **upbringing**.
bring something up to start to talk about something: *Can you bring up this problem at the next meeting?*

Which word?

Bring or take?
■ You **bring** something with you to the place where you are going: *Bring your vacation pictures to show me.* ◆ *He always brings me flowers.* ◆ *Can I bring a friend to the party?*
■ You **take** something to a different place: *Don't forget to take your passport.* ◆ *Take an umbrella when you go out today.*

brisk /brɪsk/ *adjective* (brisk·er, brisk·est)
quick and using a lot of energy: *We went for a brisk walk.*
▶ **brisk·ly** /ˈbrɪskli/ *adverb*: *to walk briskly*

bris·tle /ˈbrɪsl/ *noun* [count]
a short thick hair like the hair on a brush

brit·tle /ˈbrɪtl/ *adjective*
Something that is **brittle** is hard but breaks easily: *This glass is very brittle.*

broad /brɔd/ *adjective* (broad·er, broad·est)
1 large from one side to the other: *a broad river* ⊃ SYNONYM **wide**

2 including many different people or things: *We offer a* **broad range** *of products.* ⊃ ANTONYM **narrow** ⊃ The noun is **breadth**.

broad·band /'brɔdbænd/ *noun* [noncount]
(COMPUTERS) a way of connecting a computer to the Internet, which lets you send and receive a lot of information quickly: *Do you have broadband?*

broad·cast /'brɔdkæst/ *verb* (broad·casts, broad·cast·ing, broad·cast, has broad·cast)
to send out sound or pictures by radio or television: *The Olympics are broadcast live around the world.*
▶ **broad·cast** *noun* [count]: *a news broadcast*
▶ **broad·cast·er** /'brɔdkæstər/ *noun* [count]
a person whose job is to talk on radio or television

broad·ly /'brɔdli/ *adverb*
1 with a big, wide smile: *He smiled broadly as he shook my hand.*
2 generally: *Broadly speaking, the plan will work like this…*

broc·co·li /'brɑkəli/ *noun* [noncount]
a vegetable with green or purple flowers that you eat ⊃ Look at the picture at **vegetables**.

bro·chure /brou'ʃʊr/ *noun* [count]
a thin book with pictures of things you can buy or places you can go on vacation: *a travel brochure*

broil /brɔɪl/ *verb* (broils, broil·ing, broiled)
to cook something under or over direct heat: *broiled salmon* ⊃ Look at the note at **cook¹**.

broil·er /'brɔɪlər/ *noun* [count]
a part of an oven that cooks food with heat from above: *Roast the peppers under the broiler.*

broke¹ form of **break¹**

broke² /brouk/ *adjective* (informal)
having no money: *I can't go out tonight. I'm totally broke.*

bro·ken¹ form of **break¹**

bro·ken² /'broukən/ *adjective*
in pieces or not working: *a broken window* • *"What's the time?" "I don't know – my watch is broken."* • *The TV is broken.* ⊃ The verb is **break**.

bronze /brɑnz/ *noun* [noncount]
a dark red-brown metal: *a bronze medal*

brook /brʊk/ *noun*
[count]
(GEOGRAPHY) a very small river

broom /brum/ *noun*
[count]
a brush with a long handle that you use for cleaning the floor

broom

broth /brɔθ/ *noun* [noncount]
a thin soup: *chicken broth*

broth·er /'brʌðər/ *noun* [count]
a man or boy who has the same parents as you: *My younger brother is named Mark.* • *Gavin and Nick are brothers.* • *Do you have any* **brothers and sisters**?

broth·er-in-law /'brʌðər ɪn lɔ/ *noun* [count]
(plural **broth·ers-in-law**)
1 the brother of your wife or husband
2 the husband of your sister ⊃ Look at **sister-in-law**.

broth·er·ly /'brʌðərli/ *adjective*
showing feelings of kindness and love, like a brother would show: *brotherly love*

brought form of **bring**

brow /braʊ/ *noun* [count] (formal)
the part of your face above your eyes ⊃ SYNONYM **forehead**

brown /braʊn/ *adjective* (brown·er, brown·est)
having the color of soil or wood: *She has dark hair and brown eyes.*
▶ **brown** *noun* [count, noncount]: *You look good in brown.*

browse /braʊz/ *verb* (brows·es, brows·ing, browsed)
1 to spend time looking through a store or book without a clear idea of what you are looking for: *I browsed through the catalog but didn't see anything I wanted to buy.*
2 (COMPUTERS) to look for and read information on a computer: *to browse the Internet*

brows·er /'braʊzər/ *noun* [count]
(COMPUTERS) a program that lets you look at pages on the Internet: *a Web browser*

bruise /bruz/ *noun* [count]
a dark mark on your skin that comes after something hits it
▶ **bruise** *verb* (bruis·es, bruis·ing, bruised): *He fell and bruised his leg.*

brunch /brʌntʃ/ *noun* [count, noncount] (plural brunch·es)
a late morning meal that you eat instead of breakfast and lunch: *to go out for brunch*

bru·nette /ˌbru'nɛt/ *noun* [count]
a woman with dark brown hair

brunt /brʌnt/ *noun*
bear, take, etc. **the brunt of something** to suffer the main force or the worst part of something: *The West Coast bore the brunt of the storm.*

brushes

hairbrush   toothbrush   paintbrushes

brush¹ /brʌʃ/ *noun* [count] (*plural* **brush·es**)
a thing that you use for cleaning, painting, or making your hair neat: *a clothes brush*

brush² /brʌʃ/ *verb* (**brush·es, brush·ing, brushed**)
to clean or make something neat with a brush: *I **brush** my **teeth** twice a day.* • *Brush your hair!*

Brus·sels sprout /ˈbrʌsl ˌspraʊt/ (also **brus·sels sprout**) *noun* [count]
a very small round green vegetable consisting of a tight ball of leaves

bru·tal /ˈbruṭl/ *adjective*
very cruel: *a brutal murder*
▶ **bru·tal·ly** /ˈbruṭl·i/ *adverb*: *She was brutally attacked.*

bru·tal·i·ty /bruˈtæləṭi/ *noun* [count, noncount]
(*plural* **bru·tal·i·ties**)
very cruel and violent behavior: *complaints of police brutality*

B.S. /ˌbi ˈes/ *noun* [count]
the degree that you receive when you complete a program of study at a college or university in a science subject. B.S. is short for "Bachelor of Science." ⤳ Look at **B.A., M.S., bachelor's degree.**

bub·ble¹ /ˈbʌbl/ *noun* [count]
a small ball of air or gas inside a liquid: *The children **blew bubbles** under the water.*

bub·ble² /ˈbʌbl/ *verb* (**bub·bles, bub·bling, bub·bled**)
to make a lot of bubbles: *When water boils, it bubbles.*

buck /bʌk/ *noun* [count]
1 (*informal*) a dollar: *I spent ten bucks on lunch.*
2 a male DEER (= a wild animal that eats grass)

buck·et /ˈbʌkət/ *noun*
[count]
a round metal or plastic container with a handle. You use a **bucket** for carrying water, for example.

bucket

buck·le /ˈbʌkl/ *noun*
[count]
a metal or plastic thing on the end of a belt or on a shoe that you use for fastening it

bud /bʌd/ *noun* [count]
a leaf or flower before it opens: *The trees are covered in buds.*

Bud·dhism /ˈbudɪzəm; ˈbʊdɪzəm/ *noun*
[noncount]
(**RELIGION**) the religion that is based on the teaching of Buddha

Bud·dhist /ˈbudɪst; ˈbʊdɪst/ *noun* [count]
(**RELIGION**) a person who follows the religion of BUDDHISM
▶ **Bud·dhist** *adjective*: *a Buddhist temple*

bud·dy /ˈbʌdi/ *noun* [count] (*plural* **bud·dies**)
a male friend: *I spent the weekend with some college buddies.*

budge /bʌdʒ/ *verb* (**budg·es, budg·ing, budged**)
to move a little or to make something move a little: *I tried to move the rock but it wouldn't budge.*

budg·et /ˈbʌdʒət/ *noun* [count, noncount]
a plan of how much money you will have and how you will spend it: *We have a weekly budget for food.*
▶ **budg·et** *verb* (**budg·ets, budg·et·ing, budg·et·ed**): *I am budgeting very carefully because I want to buy a new car.*

buf·fa·lo /ˈbʌfəloʊ/
noun [count] (*plural*
buf·fa·lo or **buf·fa·loes**)
a large wild animal
that looks like a cow
with a large head,
curved horns, and
thick fur on its head
and neck ⤳ Look at
bison.

buffalo

buf·fet /bəˈfeɪ; bʊˈfeɪ/ *noun* [count]
a meal when all the food is on a big table and you take what you want: *a buffet lunch*

bug¹ /bʌg/ *noun* [count]
1 a small insect
2 (**HEALTH**) an illness that is not serious: *I caught a bug.*
3 (**COMPUTERS**) a fault in a machine, especially a computer system or program

bug² /bʌg/ *verb* (**bugs, bugg·ing, bugged**)
(*informal*)
to bother or worry someone: *The kids have been bugging me all day.*

build /bɪld/ *verb* (**builds, build·ing, built** /bɪlt/, **has built**)
to make something by putting parts together: *He built a wall in front of the house.* • *The bridge is built of stone.*

build·er /ˈbɪldər/ *noun* [count]
a person or company that builds things, especially houses and buildings

build·ing 🔑 /ˈbɪldɪŋ/ *noun*
1 [*count*] a structure with a roof and walls. Houses, schools, churches, and stores are all **buildings**: *There are a lot of old buildings in this town.*
2 [*noncount*] the process or business of making buildings: *the building industry* ➔ SYNONYM **construction**

built form of **build**

bulb /bʌlb/ *noun* [*count*]
1 (also **light bulb**) the glass part of an electric lamp that gives light ➔ Look at the picture at **lamp**.
2 (BIOLOGY) a round thing that some plants grow from: *a tulip bulb* ➔ Look at the picture at **plant**.

bulge /bʌldʒ/ *verb* (bulg·es, bulg·ing, bulged)
to go out in a round shape from something that is usually flat: *My stomach is bulging – I have to get some exercise.*
▶ **bulge** *noun* [*count*]: *a bulge in the wall*

bulk AWL /bʌlk/ *noun*
1 [*singular*] the main part of something; most of something: *It was supposed to be a group project, but I did the bulk of the work.*
2 [*noncount*] the large size, weight, or amount of something: *The sheer bulk of the stone table made it impossible for us to move.*
in bulk in large quantities: *It's cheaper to buy in bulk.*

bulk·y AWL /ˈbʌlki/ *adjective* (bulk·i·er, bulk·i·est)
big, heavy, and difficult to carry: *a bulky package*

bull /bʊl/ *noun* [*count*]
the male of the cow and of some other animals ➔ Look at the picture at **cow**.

bull·doz·er
/ˈbʊldoʊzər/ *noun* [*count*]
a big heavy machine that moves earth and makes land flat

bulldozer

bul·let 🔑 /ˈbʊlət/ *noun* [*count*]
a small piece of metal that comes out of a gun: *The bullet hit him in the leg.*

bul·le·tin /ˈbʊlətn/ *noun* [*count*]
a short newspaper that a club or an organization publishes: *the monthly church bulletin*

bul·le·tin board /ˈbʊlətn bɔrd/ *noun* [*count*]
a board on a wall for information: *The teacher put the exam results on the bulletin board.*

bul·let·proof /ˈbʊlətpruf/ *adjective*
made of a strong material that stops bullets from passing through it: *a bulletproof vest*

bull's-eye /ˈbʊlz aɪ/ *noun* [*count*]
(SPORTS) the center of a round object (called a TARGET) that you try to hit when you are shooting or throwing things in certain sports: *to hit the bull's-eye*

bul·ly /ˈbʊli/ *noun* [*count*] (*plural* **bul·lies**)
a person who hurts or frightens a weaker person
▶ **bul·ly** *verb* (bul·lies, bul·ly·ing, bul·lied): *She was bullied by the older girls at school.*

bum /bʌm/ *noun* [*count*] (*informal*)
a person who is very lazy or who does no work

bump¹ /bʌmp/ *verb* (bumps, bump·ing, bumped)
1 to hit someone or something when you are moving: *She bumped into a chair.*
2 to hit a part of your body against something hard: *I bumped my knee on the table.*
bump into someone to meet someone by chance: *I bumped into David today.*

bump² /bʌmp/ *noun* [*count*]
1 the action or sound of something hitting a hard surface: *He fell and hit the ground with a bump.*
2 a round raised area on your body where you have hit it: *I have a bump on my head.*
3 a small part on something flat that is higher than the rest: *The car hit a bump in the road.*

bump·er /ˈbʌmpər/ *noun* [*count*]
a bar on the front and back of a car which helps to protect the car if it hits something ➔ Look at the picture at **car**.

bump·y /ˈbʌmpi/ *adjective* (bump·i·er, bump·i·est)
not flat or smooth: *We had a bumpy flight.* ◆ *The road was very bumpy.* ➔ ANTONYM **smooth**

bun /bʌn/ *noun* [*count*]
a small round piece of bread: *a hamburger bun*

bunch /bʌntʃ/ *noun* [*count*] (*plural* **bunch·es**)
a group of things that grow together or that you tie or hold together: *a bunch of grapes* ◆ *two bunches of flowers*
a bunch of …; a whole bunch of … (*informal*) a large group of people or things; a lot of something: *I have a bunch of stuff to do today.* ◆ *A whole bunch of us went out for pizza after work.*

bun·dle /ˈbʌndl/ *noun* [*count*]
a group of things that you tie or wrap together: *a bundle of old newspapers*

bunk /bʌŋk/ *noun* [*count*]
1 a narrow bed that is attached to a wall, for example on a ship or train
2 (also **bunk bed**) one of a pair of beds built one on top of the other

bun·ny /ˈbʌni/ *noun* [count] (*plural* **bun·nies**)
a child's word for RABBIT (= a small animal with long ears)

buoy /ˈbui; bɔi/ *noun* [count] (*plural* **buoys**)
a thing that floats in water to show boats where there are dangerous places

bur·den /ˈbərdn/ *noun* [count]
something that you have to do that worries you, or that causes difficulty or hard work: *I don't want to be a* **burden to** *my children when I'm old.*

bu·reau /ˈbyʊroʊ/ *noun* [count]
1 (POLITICS) a government department: *the Federal Bureau of Investigation*
2 (BUSINESS) an organization or a company that provides information: *a visitor's bureau*

bu·reauc·ra·cy /byʊˈrɑkrəsi/ *noun* [noncount]
the system of official rules and processes that a government or an organization has, which people often think is too complicated: *You have to deal with so much bureaucracy to get your passport.*
▶ **bu·reau·crat·ic** /ˌbyʊrəˈkrætɪk/ *adjective*: *bureaucratic procedures*

burg·er /ˈbərgər/ *noun* [count]
meat that is cut into very small pieces and made into a flat round shape, which you eat between two pieces of bread: *a burger and fries* ⊃
SYNONYM **hamburger**

bur·glar /ˈbərglər/ *noun* [count]
a person who goes into a building to steal things

bur·glar·ize /ˈbərglərɑɪz/ *verb* (**bur·glar·iz·es**, **bur·glar·iz·ing**, **bur·glar·ized**)
to go into a building illegally, usually using force, and steal from it: *Our house was burglarized.*

bur·gla·ry /ˈbərgləri/ *noun* [count, noncount]
(*plural* **bur·gla·ries**)
the crime of going into a house to steal things: *He was arrested for burglary.* ⬧ *There was a burglary at the house next door.*

bur·i·al /ˈbɛriəl/ *noun* [count, noncount]
the time when a dead body is put in the ground ⊃ The verb is **bury**.

bur·ied, bur·ies forms of **bury**

burn¹ 🔎 /bərn/ *verb* (**burns**, **burn·ing**, **burned** or **burnt** /bərnt/, **has burned** or **has burnt**)
1 to make flames and heat; to be on fire: *Paper burns easily.* ⬧ *She escaped from the burning building.*
2 to harm or destroy someone or something with fire or heat: *I burned my fingers on a match.* ⬧ *We burned the wood on the fire.* ⬧ *Her hand was badly burned.*
3 to feel very hot and painful: *Your forehead's burning. You must have a fever.* ⬧ *Her cheeks*

burned with embarrassment. ⊃ Look at the note at **hurt¹**.
burn down; **burn something down** to burn, or to make a building burn, until there is nothing left: *Their house burned down.*

burn² /bərn/ *noun* [count]
(HEALTH) a place on your body where fire or heat has hurt it: *I have a burn on my arm.*

burp /bərp/ *verb* (**burps**, **burp·ing**, **burped**)
to make a noise from your mouth when air suddenly comes up from your stomach: *He burped loudly.*
▶ **burp** *noun* [count]: *I heard a loud burp.*

bur·row /ˈbəroʊ/ *noun* [count]
a hole or tunnel in the ground made by some animals for them to live in. RABBITS (= small animals with long ears) live in **burrows**.
▶ **bur·row** *verb* (**bur·rows**, **bur·row·ing**, **bur·rowed**)
to dig a hole in the ground: *These animals burrow for food.*

burst¹ 🔎 /bərst/ *verb* (**bursts**, **burst·ing**, **burst**, **has burst**)
1 to break open suddenly or to make something do this: *The bag was so full that it burst.* ⬧ *He burst the balloon.* ⊃ Look at the note at **break¹**.
2 to go or come suddenly: *Steve burst into the room.*
burst into something to start doing something suddenly: *She read the letter and burst into tears* (= started to cry). ⬧ *The car burst into flames* (= started to burn).
burst out laughing to suddenly start to laugh: *When she saw my hat, she burst out laughing.*

burst² /bərst/ *noun* [count]
something that happens suddenly and quickly: *a sudden* **burst of** *activity*

bur·y 🔎 /ˈbɛri/ *verb* (**bur·ies**, **bur·y·ing**, **bur·ied**, **has bur·ied**)

> ❶ **PRONUNCIATION**
> The word **bury** sounds like **very**.

1 to put a dead body in the ground: *She wants to be buried next to her mother.* ⊃ The noun is **burial**.
2 to put something in the ground or under something: *The dog buried the bone in the yard.*

bus 🔎 /bʌs/ *noun* [count] (*plural* **bus·es** or **bus·ses**)
a large vehicle that carries a lot of people along the road and stops often so they can get on and off: *We went to the city by bus.* ⬧ *Where do you* **get off** *the bus?*

Word building

- You can get on or off a **bus** at a **bus stop**, and the place where most bus routes start is the **bus station**.

ə **about**   y **yes**   w **woman**   t̬ **butter**   eɪ **say**   aɪ **five**   ɔɪ **boy**   aʊ **now**   oʊ **go**

■ The **bus driver** will take the money (your **fare**) and give you your **ticket**. If you need to change to a different bus on the same trip, the driver will give you a ticket called a **transfer** that you can use on the other bus without paying again.

■ You can buy a **one-way ticket**, or a **round-trip ticket** if you want to come back again: *Round-trip to St. Paul, please.*

■ Note that we travel **on the bus** or **by bus**: *"How do you get to school?" "By bus."*

bush 🔊 /bʊʃ/ *noun* [count] (*plural* **bush·es**)
a plant like a small tree with a lot of branches: *a rose bush*

bush·el /'bʊʃl/ *noun* [count]
a unit for measuring grain and fruit, equal to 64 pints or 35.2 liters: *a bushel of apples*

busi·ness 🔊 /'bɪznəs/ *noun* (*plural* **busi·ness·es**)
1 [noncount] buying and selling things: *I want to go into business when I leave school.* ◆ *Business is not very good this year.*
2 [noncount] the work that you do as your job: *The manager will be away on business next week.* ◆ *a business trip*
3 [count] a place where people sell or make things, for example a store or factory
it's none of your business; mind your own business words that you use to tell someone rudely that you do not want to tell them about something private: *"Where are you going?" "Mind your own business!"*

busi·ness·man /'bɪznəs,mæn; 'bɪznəs,mən/ *noun* [count] (*plural* **busi·ness·men** /'bɪznəs,mən/)
a man who works in business, especially in a top position

busi·ness·wom·an /'bɪznəs,wʊmən/ *noun* [count] (*plural* **busi·ness·wom·en** /'bɪznəs,wɪmən/)
a woman who works in business, especially in a top position

bus sta·tion /'bʌs ,steɪʃn/ *noun* [count]
a building where buses start and end their trips

bus stop /'bʌs stɑp/ *noun* [count]
a place where buses stop and people get on and off ⊃ SYNONYM **stop**

bust¹ /bʌst/ *adjective*
go bust (*informal*) If a company or business **goes bust**, it has to close because it has lost too much money.

bust² /bʌst/ *noun* [count]
1 (ART) a model of a person's head, shoulders, and chest: *a bust of John F. Kennedy*
2 a woman's chest or the measurement around her chest: *Her bust size is 34B.*

bus·y 🔊 /'bɪzi/ *adjective* (**bus·i·er**, **bus·i·est**)
1 with a lot of things that you must do; working or not free: *Mr. Jones can't see you now – he's busy.*
2 with a lot of things happening: *I had a busy morning.* ◆ *The stores are always busy at Christmas.*
3 (used about a telephone) being used: *The line is busy – I'll try again later.*
▶ **bus·i·ly** /'bɪzəli/ *adverb*: *He was busily writing a letter.*

but¹ 🔊 /bʌt; bət/ *conjunction*
a word that you use to show something different: *My sister speaks Spanish but I don't.* ◆ *He studied hard, but he didn't pass the exam.* ◆ *The weather was sunny but cold.*

but² /bʌt; bət/ *preposition*
except: *She eats **nothing but** chocolate.*

butch·er /'bʊtʃər/ *noun* [count]
a person or store that sells meat: *She went to the butcher for some lamb chops.*

butt /bʌt/ *noun* [count]
1 (*informal*) the part of your body that you sit on ⊃ SYNONYM **buttocks**
2 a short piece of a cigarette that is left after it has been smoked

but·ter 🔊 /'bʌtər/ *noun* [noncount]
a soft yellow food that is made from milk. You put it on bread or use it in cooking: *She spread butter on the bread.*
▶ **but·ter** *verb* (**but·ters**, **but·ter·ing**, **but·tered**)
to put butter on bread: *I buttered the toast.*

butterfly

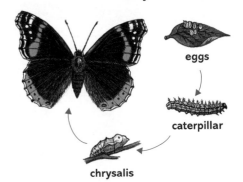

eggs

caterpillar

chrysalis

but·ter·fly /'bʌtərflaɪ/ *noun* [count] (*plural* **but·ter·flies**)
an insect with big wings that usually have bright colors

but·ter·scotch /'bʌtərskɑtʃ/ *noun* [noncount]
a type of brown candy made by boiling butter and brown sugar together

but·tock /'bʌtək/ *noun* [count]
one of the two parts of your body that you sit on

but·ton 🔑 /'bʌtn/ *noun* [*count*]
1 a small round thing on clothes that holds them together. You push it through a small hole (called a BUTTONHOLE).
2 a small thing on a machine that you push: *Press* this **button** to ring the bell.
3 a small piece of plastic or metal with a picture or words on the front and a pin on the back, which you wear on your clothes: *Everyone was wearing a campaign button.*

buy 🔑 /baɪ/ *verb* (**buys**, **buy·ing**, **bought** /bɔt/, **has bought**)

> ℹ️ **PRONUNCIATION**
> The word **buy** sounds like **my**.

to give money to get something: *I bought a new watch.* ◆ *He **bought** the car **from** a friend.* ⊃ **ANTONYM sell**
▶ **buy·er** /'baɪər/ *noun* [*count*]: *We've found a buyer for our house!* ⊃ **ANTONYM seller**

buzz /bʌz/ *verb* (**buzz·es**, **buzz·ing**, **buzzed**)
to make the sound that an insect such as a BEE (= a black and yellow insect) makes when it flies: *A fly was buzzing against the window.*
▶ **buzz** *noun* [*count*] (*plural* **buzz·es**): *the buzz of insects*

buz·zard /'bʌzərd/ *noun* [*count*]
a large bird that eats dead animals

buzz·er /'bʌzər/ *noun* [*count*]
a piece of equipment that makes a buzzing sound: *Press the buzzer in the lobby and I'll let you in.*

by¹ 🔑 /baɪ/ *preposition*
1 very near: *The telephone is by the door.* ◆ *They live by the ocean.* ⊃ **SYNONYM beside**
2 from one side of someone or something to the other: *He walked by me without speaking.* ⊃ **SYNONYM past**
3 not later than: *I must finish this work by six o'clock.* ⊃ **SYNONYM before**
4 using or doing something: *I go to work by train.* ◆ *He paid by check.* ◆ *You turn the computer on by pressing this button.*
5 a word that shows who or what did something: *a painting by Picasso* ◆ *She was caught by the police.*
6 as a result of something: *I got on the wrong bus by mistake.* ◆ *We met by chance.*
7 used for showing the measurements of an area: *The table is six feet by three feet* (= six feet long and three feet wide).

by² /baɪ/ *adverb*
past: *She drove by without stopping.*

bye 🔑 /baɪ/ (also **bye-bye** /'baɪbaɪ; ˌbaɪ'baɪ/) *exclamation*
goodbye: *Bye! See you tomorrow.*

by·stand·er /'baɪˌstændər/ *noun* [*count*]
a person who is near something when it happens but is not involved: *Several innocent bystanders were hurt when the gangs started to fight.*

byte /baɪt/ *noun* [*count*]
(**COMPUTERS**) a unit of information in a computer ⊃ Look at **gigabyte**, **kilobyte**, **megabyte**.

Cc

C, c /si/ *noun* [count, noncount] (*plural* C's, c's /siz/)
1 the third letter of the English alphabet: *"Car" begins with a "C."*
2 C (**GENERAL SCIENCE**) abbreviation of **Celsius, centigrade**: *Water freezes at 0°C.*
3 C a grade that is given to a student for average work. A C is lower than a B: *I only got a C on my math test.*

cab /kæb/ *noun* [count]
1 another word for **taxi**
2 the part of a truck, train, or bus where the driver sits

cab·bage /'kæbɪdʒ/ *noun* [count, noncount]
a large round vegetable with thick green or white leaves ➲ Look at the picture at **vegetable**.

cab·in /'kæbən/ *noun* [count]
1 a small simple house made of wood: *a log cabin at the edge of the lake*
2 the part of an airplane where people sit: *the passengers in the first-class cabin*
3 a small bedroom on a ship

cab·i·net 🔑 /'kæbənət/ *noun* [count]
1 a piece of furniture that you can keep things in: *a medicine cabinet* ◆ *a file cabinet* (= one that you use in an office to keep documents in)
2 (also **Cab·i·net**) (**POLITICS**) a group of the most important people in the government ➲ Look at the note at **government**.

ca·ble /'keɪbl/ *noun*
1 [count, noncount] a set of wires that carry electricity or messages: *a printer cable*
2 (also **ca·ble tel·e·vi·sion** /ˌkeɪbl 'tɛləvɪʒn/, **ca·ble TV** /ˌkeɪbl ˌtiˈvi/) [noncount] a way of sending television programs along wires in the ground: *Do your hotel rooms have cable?* ◆ *a cable TV channel*
3 [count] a strong, thick, metal rope

cac·tus /'kæktəs/ *noun*
[count] (*plural* **cac·ti** /'kæktaɪ/ or **cac·tus·es**)
a plant with a lot of sharp points, which grows in hot dry places

cactus

pot

ca·fé (also **ca·fe**)
/kæˈfeɪ/ *noun* [count]
a place where you can buy a drink and something to eat

caf·e·te·ri·a /ˌkæfəˈtɪriə/ *noun* [count]
a restaurant where you choose and pay for your meal and then carry it to a table. Places like factories, schools, and hospitals often have **cafeterias**.

caf·feine /kæˈfin/ *noun* [noncount]
the substance in coffee and tea that makes you feel more active and awake ➲ Look at **decaffeinated**.

cage /keɪdʒ/ *noun* [count]
a place with bars around it where animals or birds are kept so that they cannot escape

cake 🔑 /keɪk/ *noun* [count, noncount]
a sweet food that you make from flour, eggs, sugar, and butter and bake in the oven: *a chocolate cake* ◆ *Would you like a piece of cake?*
a piece of cake (*informal*) something that is very easy to do

cal·ci·um /'kælsiəm/ *noun* [noncount] (symbol **Ca**) (**CHEMISTRY**) a chemical substance that is found in foods such as milk and cheese. It helps to make bones and teeth strong.

cal·cu·late 🔑 /'kælkyəleɪt/ *verb* (cal·cu·lates, cal·cu·lat·ing, cal·cu·lat·ed)
(**MATH**) to find an amount or a number by using mathematics: *Can you calculate how much the vacation will cost?*

cal·cu·la·tion /ˌkælkyəˈleɪʃn/ *noun* [count, noncount]
(**MATH**) finding an answer by using mathematics: *I need to do a few calculations before I can give you an answer.*

cal·cu·la·tor
/'kælkyəˌleɪtər/
noun [count]
(**MATH**) a small electronic instrument that you use for calculating numbers

calculator

cal·en·dar
/'kæləndər/ *noun* [count]
a list of the days, weeks, and months of one year

calf /kæf/ *noun* [count] (*plural* **calves** /kævz/)
1 a young cow
2 the back of your leg, below your knee

call¹ 🔑 /kɔl/ *verb* (calls, call·ing, called)
1 to speak loudly and clearly so that someone who is far away can hear you: *"Breakfast is ready," she called.* ◆ *She called out the names of the winners.*
2 to contact someone by telephone: *I'll call you later.* ◆ *Who's calling, please?*
3 to give a name to someone or something: *They called the baby Sophie.*
4 to ask someone to come: *He was so sick that we had to call the doctor.*

be called to have as a name: *What was that town called?*
call someone back to contact someone by telephone again: *I can't talk now – I'll call you back later.*
call collect to make a telephone call that the person who receives the call will pay for
call something off to say that a planned activity or event will not happen: *The baseball game was called off because of bad weather.* ⟳
SYNONYM cancel

call² 🔑 /kɔl/ *noun* [count]
1 a loud sound or shout: *a call for help*
2 an act of using the telephone or a conversation on the telephone: *I **got a call** from James.* ◆ *I don't have time to talk now – I'll **give you a call** later.*
3 a short visit to someone: *The doctor has several calls to make this morning.*
4 a request or demand for something: *There have been calls for the senator's resignation.*

call·er /'kɔlər/ *noun* [count]
a person who is making a telephone call to someone: *The caller suddenly hung up* (= ended the telephone call).

calm¹ 🔑 /kɑm/ *adjective* (calm·er, calm·est)
1 quiet, and not excited or afraid: *Try to stay calm – there's no danger.*
2 without big waves: *calm waters*
3 without much wind: *calm weather*
▶ **calm·ly** /'kɑmli/ *adverb*: *He spoke calmly about the accident.*

calm² /kɑm/ *verb* (calms, calm·ing, calmed)
calm down to become less afraid or excited; to make someone less afraid or excited: *Calm down and tell me what happened.*

cal·o·rie /'kæləri/ *noun* [count]
a unit for measuring the energy value of food. Food that has a lot of **calories** in it can make you fat: *a low-calorie drink*

calves plural of **calf**

cam·cord·er /'kæmkɔrdər/ *noun* [count]
a camera that you can carry around and use for recording moving pictures and sound

came form of **come**

cam·el /'kæml/ *noun* [count]
a large animal with one or two round parts (called **HUMPS**) on its back. **Camels** carry people and things in hot dry places.

camel

cam·er·a 🔑 /'kæmrə/ *noun* [count]
a thing that you use for taking photographs or moving pictures: *I need some new film for my camera.*

cam·er·a·man /'kæmrəmæn/ *noun* [count] (*plural* cam·er·a·men /'kæmrəmɛn/)
a person who operates a video camera for a movie or television company

cam·ou·flage /'kæməflɑʒ/ *noun* [noncount]
1 materials or colors that soldiers use to make themselves and their equipment less easy to see: *army troops **in camouflage***
2 the way an animal's color or shape makes it difficult to see: *The polar bear's white coat provides camouflage in the snow.*
▶ **cam·ou·flage** *verb* (cam·ou·flag·es, cam·ou·flag·ing, cam·ou·flaged): *The soldiers camouflaged themselves with leaves.*

camp¹ 🔑 /kæmp/ *noun* [count, noncount]
1 a place where people live in a kind of small house made of cloth (called a **TENT**) for a short time: *They returned to camp tired and hungry.*
2 a place where children go during school vacations to do special activities: *a summer camp* ◆ *I'm going to tennis camp this year.*

camp² 🔑 /kæmp/ *verb* (camps, camp·ing, camped)
to live in a kind of small house made of cloth (called a **TENT**) for a short time: *The children camped in the backyard overnight.*
▶ **camp·ing** /'kæmpɪŋ/ *noun* [noncount]
sleeping or spending a vacation in a tent: *We **went camping** last summer.*

cam·paign¹ /kæm'peɪn/ *noun* [count]
a plan to do a number of things in order to get a special result: *a campaign to stop people from smoking*

cam·paign² /kæm'peɪn/ *verb* (cam·paigns, cam·paign·ing, cam·paigned)
to take part in planned activities in order to get a special result: *The school is **campaigning for** new computer equipment.*

camp·ing /'kæmpɪŋ/ *noun* [noncount]
sleeping or spending a vacation in a kind of small house made of heavy cloth (called a **TENT**): *Camping is no fun in the rain.*

camp·site /'kæmpsaɪt/ *noun* [count]
a place where you can camp

cam·pus /'kæmpəs/ *noun* [count, noncount] (*plural* cam·pus·es)
the area where the buildings of a college are: *a college campus* ◆ *Do you live **on campus**?*

can¹ /kən; kæn/ modal verb

Grammar

- The negative form of **can** is **cannot** or **can't**: *She can't swim.*
- The past tense of **can** is **could**: *We could walk to the beach from our hotel.*
- The future tense of **can** is **will be able to**: *You will be able to see it if you stand on this chair.*

1 to be able to do something; to be strong enough, intelligent enough, etc. to do something: *She can speak three languages.* ◆ *Can you cook?*
2 to be possible or likely to happen: *It can be very cold in the mountains in the winter.*
3 a word that you use with verbs like "see," "hear," "smell," and "taste": *I can smell something burning.* ◆ *"What's that noise?" "I can't hear anything."*
4 to be allowed to do something: *You can go now.* ◆ *He asked if he could have some more soup.* ◆ *The doctor says she can't go back to school yet.*
5 a word that you use when you ask someone to do something: *Can you hand me that screwdriver?* ⊃ Look at the note at **modal verb**.

can² /kæn/ noun [count]
a metal container for food or a drink that keeps it fresh: *a can of soup* ◆ *a can of beans* ◆ *an empty soda can* ⊃ Look at the picture at **container**.

Ca·na·di·an /kə'neɪdiən/ adjective
(GEOGRAPHY) from or connected with Canada: *a Canadian novelist*
▶ **Ca·na·di·an** noun [count]: *She married a Canadian.*

ca·nal /kə'næl/ noun [count]
(GEOGRAPHY) a path that is made through the land and filled with water so that boats can travel on it: *the Panama Canal*

ca·nar·y /kə'nɛri/ noun [count] (plural ca·nar·ies)
a small yellow bird that people often keep as a pet

can·cel /'kænsl/ verb (can·cels, can·cel·ing, can·celed)
to decide that a planned activity or event will not happen: *Soccer practice was canceled because the field was too wet.*

can·cel·la·tion /ˌkænsə'leɪʃn/ noun [count, noncount]
a decision that a planned activity or event will not happen: *the cancellation of the president's visit*

can·cer /'kænsər/ noun [count, noncount]
(HEALTH) a very dangerous disease that makes some very small parts in the body (called CELLS)

grow too fast: *She has lung cancer.* ◆ *He died of cancer.*

can·di·date /'kændədeɪt/ noun [count]
a person who wants to be chosen for something: *There were a lot of candidates for the job.*

can·dle /'kændl/ noun [count]
a round stick of WAX (= solid oil or fat) with a piece of string in the middle (called a WICK), which burns to give light

candle

can·dle·stick /'kændl,stɪk/ noun [count]
a thing that holds a CANDLE

can·dy /'kændi/ noun [count, noncount] (plural can·dies)
sweet food made of sugar or chocolate, or a piece of this food: *Can I have a piece of candy?* ◆ *She gave him a candy bar for a treat.* ◆ *a bowl of pink and yellow candies*

cane /keɪn/ noun
1 [count] a long stick that you lean on if you have trouble walking: *My grandfather walks with a cane.*
2 [count, noncount] the long central parts of some plants, for example BAMBOO (= a tall plant that grows in hot countries), which can be used for making furniture: *sugar cane* ◆ *a cane chair*

canned /kænd/ adjective
in a can: *canned drinks*

can·ni·bal /'kænəbl/ noun [count]
a person who eats other people

can·non /'kænən/ noun [count] (plural can·non or can·nons)
an old type of big gun that fires big stone or metal balls

can·not /'kænɑt; kə'nɑt/ form of **can¹**

ca·noe /kə'nu/ noun [count]
(SPORTS) a light, narrow boat that you move through the water using a flat piece of wood (called a PADDLE)
▶ **ca·noe·ing** /kə'nuɪŋ/ noun [noncount]: *We went canoeing on the river.*

canoe

can o·pen·er /'kæn ˌoʊpənər/ noun [count]
a tool for opening cans of food ⊃ Look at the picture at **kitchen**.

can't /kænt/ short for **cannot**

can·ta·loupe /ˈkæntl·oʊp/ noun [count, noncount]
a big round fruit (called a MELON). It has a thick hard skin and is orange inside.

can·vas /ˈkænvəs/ noun [noncount]
a strong heavy cloth, used for making bags, TENTS (= that you sleep in when you are camping) and SAILS (= the cloth on boats that catches the wind), or for painting pictures on

can·yon /ˈkænyən/ noun [count]
(GEOGRAPHY) a deep valley with sides of rock that go up very quickly (that are STEEP): the Grand Canyon

cap /kæp/ noun [count]
1 a soft hat with a hard curved part at the front to keep the sun off your face: a baseball cap ⊃ Look at the picture at **hat**.
2 a thing that covers the top of a bottle or tube: Put the cap back on the bottle.

ca·pa·bil·i·ty AWL /ˌkeɪpəˈbɪləti/ noun [count, noncount] (plural **ca·pa·bil·i·ties**)
the ability to do something: The computer virus has the capability of destroying your hard drive.

ca·pa·ble 🖉 AWL /ˈkeɪpəbl/ adjective
1 able to do something: You are **capable of** passing the exam if you work harder.
2 able to do things well: a capable student ⊃
ANTONYM **incapable**

ca·pac·i·ty AWL /kəˈpæsəti/ noun (plural **ca·pac·i·ties**)
1 [usually singular, noncount] how much a container or space can hold: The gas tank has a capacity of 16 gallons. ◆ The stadium was filled **to capacity**.
2 [singular] the ability to do or understand something: a capacity for hard work

cape /keɪp/ noun [count]
1 a piece of clothing that covers your body and your arms, but does not have separate sleeves
2 (GEOGRAPHY) a piece of land that goes out into the ocean: Cape Canaveral

cap·i·tal 🖉 /ˈkæpətl/ noun
1 [count] (POLITICS) the most important city in a country or state, where the government is: Austin is the capital of Texas.
2 [noncount] (BUSINESS) a large amount of money that you use to start a business, etc.: When she had enough capital, she opened a restaurant.
3 (also **cap·i·tal let·ter**) [count] (ENGLISH LANGUAGE ARTS) a big letter of the alphabet, used at the beginning of sentences: Please fill out the form **in capitals**. ◆ Names of people and places begin with a capital letter.

cap·i·tal·ism /ˈkæpətəlɪzəm/ noun [noncount]
(BUSINESS, POLITICS) a system in which businesses are owned by individual people or groups, and not by the government ⊃ Look at **communism**, **socialism**.
▶ **cap·i·tal·ist** adjective, noun [count]: a capitalist society

cap·i·tal pun·ish·ment /ˌkæpətl ˈpʌnɪʃmənt/ noun [noncount]
punishment by death for serious crimes ⊃ Look at **the death penalty**.

cap·puc·ci·no /ˌkæpəˈtʃinoʊ/ noun [count] (plural **cap·puc·ci·nos**)
a cup of coffee that has hot milk with bubbles in it on top: Two cappuccinos, please. ⊃ Look at **espresso**, **latte**.

cap·size /ˈkæpsaɪz/ verb (**cap·siz·es**, **cap·siz·ing**, **cap·sized**)
If a boat **capsizes**, it turns over in the water: During the storm, the boat capsized.

cap·sule /ˈkæpsl/ noun
a type of pill shaped like a tube that is filled with medicine

cap·tain /ˈkæptən/ noun [count]
1 the person who is in charge of a ship or an airplane: The captain sent a message by radio for help.
2 an important officer in the army, navy, police force, etc.: an army captain
3 (SPORTS) the leader of a group of people: He's the captain of the school basketball team.

cap·tion /ˈkæpʃn/ noun [count]
the words above or below a picture in a book or newspaper, which tell you about it

cap·tive /ˈkæptɪv/ noun [count]
a person who is not free ⊃ SYNONYM **prisoner**

cap·tiv·i·ty /kæpˈtɪvəti/ noun [noncount]
being kept in a place that you cannot leave: Wild animals are often unhappy **in captivity**.

cap·ture /ˈkæptʃər/ verb (**cap·tures**, **cap·tur·ing**, **cap·tured**)
1 to catch someone and keep them somewhere so that they cannot leave: The police captured the criminals.
2 to take control of a place: The town was captured by rebels.
▶ **cap·ture** noun [noncount]: the capture of the escaped prisoners

car

car 🖉 /kɑr/ noun [count]
1 (also **au·to·mo·bile** /ˌɔtəməˈbil/) a vehicle with

four wheels, usually with enough space for four or five people: *What kind of car do you drive?*
2 one of the parts of a train that carries people or goods: *I got a cup of coffee in the dining car.*

car·a·mel /'kærəml/ *noun* [count, noncount]
a type of brown candy that is made from sugar, butter, and milk

car·bo·hy·drate /ˌkɑrboʊˈhaɪdreɪt/ *noun* [count, noncount]
(**BIOLOGY**) one of the substances in food, for example sugar, which gives your body energy: *Bread and rice contain carbohydrates.*

car·bon /'kɑrbən/ *noun* [noncount] (symbol **C**)
(**CHEMISTRY**) a chemical that is in all living things, and that DIAMONDS (= clear, very hard, expensive stones) are made of: *Coal is made up of carbon and hydrogen.*

car·bon di·ox·ide /ˌkɑrbən daɪˈɑksaɪd/ *noun* [noncount] (symbol CO_2)
(**CHEMISTRY**) a gas that has no color or smell that people and animals breathe out

car·bon foot·print /ˌkɑrbən ˈfʊtprɪnt/ *noun* [count]
the amount of CARBON DIOXIDE that a person, business, or country produces: *Here are some ways to reduce your carbon footprint…*

car·bon mon·ox·ide /ˌkɑrbən məˈnɑksaɪd/ *noun* [noncount] (symbol **CO**)
(**CHEMISTRY**) a poisonous gas that is produced when car engines burn gasoline

card /kɑrd/ *noun* [count]
1 a piece of thick paper with writing or pictures on it: *I sent a birthday card to my friend.* ◆ *John gave Kate his business card and asked her to call him at the office.* ➋ Look at **credit card**, **phone card**, **postcard**.
2 (also **play·ing card**) one of a set of 52 cards (called a DECK OF CARDS) that you use to play games: *Let's play cards tonight.* ➋ Look at the picture at **playing card**.

Word building

- A **deck of cards** has four groups of thirteen cards, called **suits**.
- Two suits are red (**hearts** and **diamonds**) and two are black (**clubs** and **spades**).

card·board /'kɑrdbɔrd/ *noun* [noncount]
very thick paper that is used for making boxes, etc.

car·di·gan /'kɑrdɪgən/ *noun* [count]
a piece of clothing which fastens at the front like a jacket and is often made of wool

car·di·nal /'kɑrdnəl/ *noun* [count]
1 (**RELIGION**) an important priest in the Roman Catholic church

2 (**MATH**) (also **car·di·nal num·ber** /ˌkɑrdnəl ˈnʌmbər/) a whole number, for example 1, 2, 3 ➋ Look at **ordinal number**.

care¹ /kɛr/ *noun* [noncount]
thinking about what you are doing so that you do not make a mistake or break something: *Wash these glasses with care!*
take care
1 to be careful: *Take care when you cross the road.*
2 (*informal*) used when you are saying "goodbye" to someone: *Bye! Take care!*
take care of someone or **something** to keep someone or something safe, well, or in good condition: *She is taking care of her sister's baby today.* ◆ *Take care of your violin by keeping it in its case.*
take care of something to organize or deal with something: *Don't worry about cooking dinner – I'll take care of it.*

care² /kɛr/ *verb* (cares, car·ing, cared)
to think that someone or something is important: *The only thing he cares about is money.* ◆ *I don't care who wins – I'm not interested in football.*
care for someone to do the things for someone that they need: *After the accident, her parents cared for her until she was better.*
who cares? (*informal*) words that you use to show you do not think something is important or interesting: *"Who do you think is going to win the game?" "Who cares?"*

ca·reer /kəˈrɪr/ *noun* [count]
a job that you learn to do and then do for many years: *He is considering a career in teaching.* ◆ *His career was always more important to him than his family.* ➋ Look at the note at **job**.

care·ful /'kɛrfl/ *adjective*
thinking about what you are doing so that you do not make a mistake or have an accident: *Careful! The plate is very hot.* ◆ *Be careful! There's a car coming.* ◆ *He was careful not to hurt her feelings.*
▶ **care·ful·ly** /'kɛrfli/ *adverb*: *Please listen carefully.*

care·less /'kɛrləs/ *adjective*
not thinking enough about what you are doing so that you make mistakes: *Careless drivers can cause accidents.*
▶ **care·less·ly** /'kɛrləsli/ *adverb*: *She threw her coat carelessly on the floor.*
▶ **care·less·ness** /'kɛrləsnəs/ *noun* [noncount]

care·tak·er /'kɛrteɪkər/ *noun* [count]
a person whose job is to take care of a house or other building when the owner is away

car·go /ˈkɑrgoʊ/ *noun* [*count, noncount*] (*plural* **car·goes** or **car·gos**)
the things that a ship or an airplane carries: *a cargo of wheat*

car·na·tion /kɑrˈneɪʃn/ *noun* [*count*]
a pink, white, or red flower with a nice smell

car·ni·val /ˈkɑrnəvl/ *noun* [*count*]
an event with rides and games for children, or a public festival that takes place in the streets: *I got cotton candy at our school carnival.* • *the New Orleans carnival season*

car·ni·vore /ˈkɑrnəvɔr/ *noun* [*count*]
(**BIOLOGY**) an animal that eats meat ➴ Look at **herbivore, omnivore**.
▶ **car·niv·o·rous** /ˌkɑrˈnɪvərəs/ *adjective*: *Lions are carnivorous animals.*

car·ol /ˈkærəl/ *noun* [*count*]
(**MUSIC, RELIGION**) a Christian song that people sing at Christmas

car·ou·sel /ˌkærəˈsɛl/ *noun* [*count*]
a big round machine with models of animals or cars on it. Children can ride on it as it turns. ➴
SYNONYM merry-go-round

car·pen·ter /ˈkɑrpəntər/ *noun* [*count*]
a person whose job is to make things from wood
▶ **car·pen·try** /ˈkɑrpəntri/ *noun* [*noncount*]
making things from wood

car·pet /ˈkɑrpət/ *noun* [*count*]
a soft covering for a floor that is often made of wool and is usually the same size as the floor ➴ Look at **rug**.

car·riage /ˈkærɪdʒ/ *noun* [*count*]
a road vehicle, usually with four wheels, that is pulled by horses and was used in the past to carry people

car·ried form of **carry**

car·rot /ˈkærət/ *noun* [*count, noncount*]
a long, thin, orange vegetable: *a pound of carrots* • *grated carrot* ➴ Look at the picture at **vegetable**.

car·ry 🖉 /ˈkæri/ *verb* (**car·ries, car·ry·ing, car·ried, has car·ried**)
1 to hold something and take it to another place or keep it with you: *He carried the suitcase to my room.* • *I can't carry this box – it's too heavy.* • *Do the police carry guns in your country?*

ⓘ STYLE
You use **wear**, not **carry**, to talk about having clothes on your body: *She is wearing a red dress and carrying a black bag.*

2 to move people or things: *Special fast trains carry people downtown.*
be or **get carried away** to be so excited that you forget what you are doing: *I got carried away and started shouting at the television.*

carry out something to do or finish what you have planned: *The bridge was closed while they carried out the repairs.*

carts

luggage cart   shopping cart

cart /kɑrt/ *noun* [*count*]
1 a thing on wheels that you use for carrying things: *He filled his **shopping cart** with food for the party.*
2 a wooden vehicle with wheels that a horse usually pulls

car·ton /ˈkɑrtn/ *noun* [*count*]
a container made of very thick paper (called **CARDBOARD**) or plastic: *a carton of milk* ➴ Look at the picture at **container**.

car·toon /kɑrˈtun/ *noun* [*count*]
1 (**ART**) a funny drawing, for example in a newspaper
2 a television program or movie that tells a story by using moving drawings, computer images, etc. instead of real people and places: *The kids like to watch cartoons on Saturday mornings.*

car·tridge /ˈkɑrtrɪdʒ/ *noun* [*count*]
a small case containing something that is used inside a machine or a gun: *I need to replace the ink cartridge in my printer.*

carve /kɑrv/ *verb* (**carves, carv·ing, carved**)
1 (**ART**) to cut wood or stone to make a picture or shape: *Her father carved a little horse for her out of wood.*
2 to cut meat into thin pieces after you have cooked it: *My mom always carves the turkey on Thanksgiving.* ➴ Look at the note at **cut¹**.

case 🖉 /keɪs/ *noun* [*count*]
1 a situation or an example of something: *In some cases, students had to wait six weeks for their exam results.* • *There were four cases of this disease in the school last month.*
2 a crime that the police must find an answer to: *a murder case*
3 a question that people in a court of law must decide about: *a divorce case*
4 a container or cover for keeping something in: *Put the camera back in its case.* • *a pencil case* ➴ Look at **briefcase, suitcase**.
in any case words that you use when you give a second reason for something: *I don't want to see*

the movie, and in any case I'm too busy. ⊃
SYNONYM anyway
in case because something might happen: *Take
an umbrella in case it rains.* • *You probably won't
need to call, but take my number* **just in case**.
in that case if that is the situation: *"There's no
coffee." "Well, in that case we'll have tea."*

cash¹ 🔑 /kæʃ/ *noun* [noncount]
money in coins and bills: *Are you paying* **in cash**
or by credit card? ⊃ Look at the note at **money**.

cash² /kæʃ/ *verb* (**cash·es, cash·ing, cashed**)
to give someone a check and get money for it:
I'd like to cash this check, please.

cash·ier /kæˈʃɪər/ *noun* [count]
the person whose job is to take money from
customers in a store, restaurant, etc.

cash ma·chine /ˈkæʃ məˌʃin/ *noun* [count]
another word for **ATM**

cash reg·is·ter /ˈkæʃ ˌrɛdʒəstər/ (also **reg·is·ter**)
noun [count]
a machine in a store that is used to add the cost
of things and store money

ca·si·no /kəˈsinoʊ/ *noun* [count] (*plural* **ca·si·nos**)
a place where people play games in which they
can win and lose money

cas·se·role /ˈkæsəroʊl/ *noun* [count, noncount]
a type of food that you make by cooking meat
and vegetables in liquid for a long time in the
oven: *I made a casserole for dinner.* • *chicken
casserole*

cas·sette /kəˈsɛt/ *noun* [count]
(**MUSIC**) a plastic box with special tape inside for
recording and playing sound or pictures: *a
cassette tape* • *an old cassette player*

cast¹ /kæst/ *noun* [count]
all the actors in a movie, play, or television
show: *The whole cast was excellent.*

cast² /kæst/ *verb* (**casts, cast·ing, cast, has cast**)
to choose an actor for a particular part in a
movie, play, or television show: *She always
seems to be cast in the same sort of role.*
cast a spell to use magic words that have the
power to change someone or something: *The
witch cast a spell* **on** *the handsome prince.*

cas·tle /ˈkæsl/ *noun* [count]
a large old building that was built in the past to
keep people safe from attack: *a medieval castle*

ca·su·al /ˈkæʒuəl/ *adjective*
1 (used about clothes) not formal: *I wear casual
clothes like jeans and T-shirts when I'm not at
work.*
2 showing that you are not worried about
something; relaxed: *She gave us a casual wave
as she passed.*

▶ **ca·su·al·ly** /ˈkæʒəli/ *adverb*: *They dressed
casually for the beach party.*

ca·su·al·ty /ˈkæʒuəlti/ *noun* [count] (*plural*
ca·su·al·ties)
a person who is hurt or killed in an accident or a
war: *Both sides suffered heavy casualties* (= a lot
of people were hurt or killed).

cats

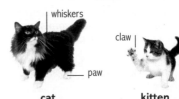

whiskers
claw
paw
cat   **kitten**

cat 🔑 /kæt/ *noun* [count]
1 a small animal with soft fur that people keep
as a pet

Word building

■ A young cat is called a **kitten**.
■ A cat **purrs** when it is happy.
■ When a cat makes a loud noise, it **meows**:
  My cat meows when he's hungry.

2 a wild animal of the cat family: *the big cats,
such as tigers and lions*

cat·a·log (also **cat·a·logue**) /ˈkætlag/ *noun* [count]
a list of all the things that you can buy from a
company or see somewhere: *a mail order
catalog*

ca·tas·tro·phe /kəˈtæstrəfi/ *noun* [count]
a sudden disaster that causes great suffering or
damage: *major catastrophes such as floods and
earthquakes*
▶ **cat·a·stroph·ic** /ˌkætəˈstrɑfɪk/ *adjective*: *The
flood had a catastrophic effect.*

catch¹ 🔑 /kætʃ/ *verb* (**catch·es, catch·ing,
caught** /kɔt/, **has caught**)
1 (**SPORTS**) to take and hold something that is
moving: *He threw the ball to me and I caught it.*
2 to find and hold someone or something: *They
caught a fish in the river.* • *The man ran so fast
that the police couldn't catch him.*
3 to see someone when they are doing
something wrong: *They caught the thief stealing
the painting.*
4 to be early enough for a bus, train, etc. that is
going to leave: *You should run if you want to
catch the bus.* ⊃ **ANTONYM miss**
5 (**HEALTH**) to get an illness: *She caught a cold.*
6 to get stuck in or on something by mistake: *I
caught my coat in the car door.*
catch fire to start to burn: *The house caught fire.*

catch on
1 to become popular or fashionable: *The idea never really caught on in this country.*
2 to understand or realize something: *It took me a while to catch on.*
catch up to do something quickly so that you are not behind others: *If you miss a class, you can do some work at home to catch up.* ◆ *Quick! Run and catch up with the others!*

catch² /kætʃ/ *noun* [count] (*plural* **catch·es**)
1 (**SPORTS**) the act of catching something, for example a ball: *That was a great catch!* ➲ Look at **miss²**.
2 a device for fastening something and keeping it closed: *I can't wear this necklace – the catch is broken.*
3 a hidden problem in something that seems to be very good: *That sounds too easy. What's the catch?*

catch·y /ˈkætʃi/ *adjective* (**catch·i·er, catch·i·est**)
(used about a tune or a song) easy to remember

cat·e·go·rize **AWL** /ˈkæṭəɡəˌraɪz/ *verb*
(**cat·e·go·riz·es, cat·e·go·riz·ing, cat·e·go·rized**)
to put people or things into groups according to what type they are: *Do we categorize a tomato as a fruit or a vegetable?*

cat·e·go·ry **AWL** /ˈkæṭəˌɡɔri/ *noun* [count] (*plural* **cat·e·go·ries**)
a group of people or things that are similar to each other: *The results can be divided into three main categories.*

ca·ter·ing /ˈkeɪṭərɪŋ/ *noun* [noncount]
the activity or business of providing food and drinks at events: *Who is doing the catering for your wedding?*

cat·er·pil·lar /ˈkæṭəpɪlər/ *noun* [count]
a small animal with a long body and a lot of legs. A **caterpillar** later becomes an insect that has large wings with bright colors (called a **BUTTERFLY**). ➲ Look at the picture at **butterfly**.

ca·the·dral /kəˈθidrəl/ *noun* [count]
(**RELIGION**) a big important church

Cath·o·lic /ˈkæθəlɪk/ (also **Ro·man Cath·o·lic**)
noun [count]
(**RELIGION**) a member of the Christian church that has the Pope as its head
▶ **Cath·o·lic** (also **Ro·man Cath·o·lic**) *adjective*: *a Catholic priest*

cat·tle /ˈkæṭl/ *noun* [plural]
cows that are kept for their milk or meat: *a herd* (= a group) *of cattle*

caught form of **catch**

cau·li·flow·er /ˈkɔlɪˌflaʊər; ˈkɑlɪˌflaʊər/ *noun*
[count, noncount]
a large vegetable with green leaves outside and

a round white part in the middle ➲ Look at the picture at **vegetable**.

cause¹ /kɔz/ *noun* [count]
1 a thing or person that makes something happen: *Bad driving is the **cause of** most road accidents.*
2 something that people care about and want to help: *They gave the money to **a good cause** – it was used to build a new hospital.*

cause² /kɔz/ *verb* (**causes, caus·ing, caused**)
to be the reason why something happens: *What caused the accident?* ◆ *The fire was caused by a cigarette.*

cau·tion /ˈkɔʃn/ *noun* [noncount]
great care, because of possible danger: *Caution! Wet floor.*

cau·tious /ˈkɔʃəs/ *adjective*
careful because there may be danger: *He is always cautious about driving at night.*
▶ **cau·tious·ly** /ˈkɔʃəsli/ *adverb*: *He cautiously pushed open the door and looked into the room.*

cave /keɪv/ *noun* [count]
(**GEOGRAPHY**) a large hole in the side of a mountain or under the ground: *Thousands of years ago, people lived in caves.*

cav·i·ty /ˈkævəṭi/ *noun* [count] (*plural* **cav·i·ties**)
1 an empty space inside something solid: *the chest cavity*
2 (**HEALTH**) a hole in a tooth: *You'll get cavities if you eat too much candy.*

cc /ˌsi ˈsi/ *abbreviation*
1 letters that are used on e-mails or business letters to show that you are sending a copy to another person. The letters **cc** stand for "carbon copy."
2 short for **cubic centimeter**: *a 1,200cc engine*

CD /ˌsi ˈdi/ *noun* [count]
(**MUSIC**) compact disc; a small, round piece of hard plastic on which you can record sound or store information

CD play·er /ˌsi ˈdi ˌpleɪər/ *noun* [count]
(**MUSIC**) a machine that you use to play music from CDs

CD-ROM /ˌsi di ˈrɑm/ *noun* [count]
(**COMPUTERS**) a CD on which you can store large amounts of information, sound, and pictures, to use on a computer

cease **AWL** /sis/ *verb* (**ceas·es, ceas·ing, ceased**)
(*formal*)
to stop: *Fighting in the area has now ceased.*

cease·fire /ˈsisˌfaɪər/ *noun* [count]
an agreement between two groups to stop fighting each other

tʃ **ch**in   dʒ **J**une   v **v**an   θ **th**in   ð **th**en   s **s**o   z **z**oo   ʃ **sh**e

ceil·ing /ˈsilɪŋ/ *noun* [count]
the top part of the inside of a room

cel·e·brate /ˈsɛləbreɪt/ *verb* (**cel·e·brates, cel·e·brat·ing, cel·e·brat·ed**)
to do something to show that you are happy, for a special reason or because it is a special day: *If you do well on your exams, we'll have a party to celebrate.* ◆ *Grandma celebrated her 90th birthday last week.*

cel·e·bra·tion /ˌsɛləˈbreɪʃn/ *noun* [count, noncount]
a time when you enjoy yourself because you have a special reason to be happy: *birthday celebrations* ◆ *I think this is a cause for celebration!*

ce·leb·ri·ty /səˈlɛbrəti/ *noun* (*plural* **ce·leb·ri·ties**)
a famous person: *a TV celebrity* ⊃ Look at **star**¹(3).

cel·er·y /ˈsɛləri/ *noun* [noncount]
a vegetable with long green and white sticks that can be eaten without being cooked: *a stalk of celery* ⊃ Look at the picture at **vegetable**.

cell /sɛl/ *noun* [count]
1 (BIOLOGY) the smallest part of any living thing. All plants and animals are made up of **cells**: *red blood cells*
2 a small room for one or more prisoners in a prison or police station
3 (*informal*) another word for **cell phone**: *Call me on my cell.*

cel·lar /ˈsɛlər/ *noun* [count]
a room in the part of a building that is under the ground: *a wine cellar* ⊃ Look at **basement**.

cel·lo /ˈtʃɛloʊ/ *noun* [count] (*plural* **cel·los**)
(MUSIC) a large wooden musical instrument with strings. You sit down to play it and hold it between your knees. ⊃ Look at the picture at **instrument**.

cell phone /ˈsɛl foʊn/ (also **cell·phone**) (also *informal* **cell** /sɛl/) *noun* [count]
a telephone that you can carry around with you: *I won't be in the office today, but you can reach me on my cell phone.* ◆ *What's your cell phone number?*

Word building

Cell phones
- **Cell phones** can be used anywhere there is a **signal**.
- If you **call** someone but cannot **get through**, you can leave a **message** on their voice mail or you can **text** them (= send them a text message).
- When the **battery** in your phone **runs out**, you have to **recharge** it.
⊃ Look at the note at **phone**¹.

Cel·si·us /ˈsɛlsiəs/ (also **cen·ti·grade**) *noun* [noncount] (abbreviation **C**)
(GENERAL SCIENCE) a way of measuring temperature. Water freezes at 0° **Celsius** and boils at 100° **Celsius**. ⊃ Look at **Fahrenheit**.

ce·ment /səˈmɛnt/ *noun* [noncount]
a gray powder that becomes hard like stone when you mix it with water and leave it to dry. **Cement** is used in building for sticking bricks or stones together, or for making very hard surfaces.

cem·e·ter·y /ˈsɛməˌtɛri/ *noun* [count] (*plural* **cem·e·ter·ies**)
(RELIGION) an area of ground where dead people are put under the earth

cen·sor /ˈsɛnsər/ *verb* (**cen·sors, cen·sor·ing, cen·sored**)
to remove the parts of a book, movie, etc. that might upset people or that contain secret information
▶ **cen·sor·ship** /ˈsɛnsərʃɪp/ *noun* [noncount]: *government censorship of radio and television programs*

cen·sus /ˈsɛnsəs/ *noun* [count] (*plural* **cen·sus·es**)
the act of officially counting all the people who live in a country, and finding information about them: *The last census took place in 2010.*

cent /sɛnt/ *noun* [count]
a small coin or unit of money. There are 100 **cents** in a dollar. ⊃ Look at **penny**.

cen·ter /ˈsɛntər/ *noun* [count]
1 the part in the middle of something: *The flower has a yellow center with white petals.* ◆ *I don't like having the center seat on an airplane.* ⊃ Look at the picture at **circle**.
2 a place where people come to do a particular activity: *a shopping center* ◆ *The hotel has a new fitness center.*
3 (SPORTS) a player whose position is in the middle in sports like basketball

cen·ti·grade /ˈsɛntəgreɪd/ *noun* [noncount]
(GENERAL SCIENCE) another word for **Celsius**

cen·ti·li·ter /ˈsɛntəlitər/ *noun* [count] (abbreviation **cl**)
(GENERAL SCIENCE) a measure of liquid. There are 100 **centiliters** in a **liter**.

cen·ti·me·ter /ˈsɛntəˌmitər/ *noun* [count] (abbreviation **cm**)
a measure of length. There are 100 **centimeters** in a **meter**.

cen·ti·pede /ˈsɛntəpid/ *noun* [count]
a small animal like an insect, with a long thin body and very many legs

cen·tral 🔑 /ˈsɛntrəl/ *adjective*
in the middle part of something: *The hotel is in a central location, close to downtown and the airport.*

cen·tu·ry 🔑 /ˈsɛntʃəri/ *noun* [count] (*plural* **cen·tu·ries**)
a period of 100 years: *People have been making wine in this area for centuries.* ◆ *We are living at the beginning of the twenty-first century.*

ce·re·al /ˈsɪriəl/ *noun* [count, noncount]
1 a food made from grain, which you can eat for breakfast with milk: *I had a bowl of cereal for breakfast.*
2 a plant that farmers grow so that we can eat the grain: *Wheat and oats are cereals.*

cer·e·mo·ny 🔑 /ˈserəmoʊni/ *noun* [count] (*plural* **cer·e·mo·nies**)
a formal public or religious event: *the opening ceremony of the Olympic Games* ◆ *a wedding ceremony*
▶ **cer·e·mo·ni·al** /ˌserəˈmoʊniəl/ *adjective*: *a ceremonial occasion*

cer·tain 🔑 /ˈsərtn/ *adjective*
1 sure about something; without any doubt: *I'm certain that I've seen her before.* ◆ *Are you certain about that?* ⊃ **ANTONYM uncertain**
2 used for talking about a particular thing or person without saying what or who they are: *Do you want the work to be finished by a certain date?* ◆ *It's cheaper to call at certain times of the day.*
for certain without any doubt: *I don't know for certain where she is.*
make certain to check something so that you are sure about it: *Please make certain that the window is closed before you leave.*

cer·tain·ly 🔑 /ˈsərtnli/ *adverb*
1 without any doubt: *She is certainly the best swimmer on the team.* ⊃ **SYNONYM definitely**
2 (*formal*) used when answering questions to mean "of course": *"Will you open the door for me, please?" "Certainly."* ◆ *"Are you going to tell him the bad news?" "Certainly not!"*

cer·tif·i·cate /sərˈtɪfəkət/ *noun* [count]
an important piece of paper that shows that something is true: *Your **birth certificate** shows when and where you were born.*

ce·sar·e·an /sɪˈzɛriən/ (also **ce·sar·e·an sec·tion** /sɪˈzɛriən ˈsɛkʃn/) *noun* [count]
(**HEALTH**) an operation in which a mother's body is cut open so her baby can be taken out: *She had a cesarean.*

chain¹ 🔑 /tʃeɪn/ *noun*
1 [count, noncount] a line of metal rings that are joined together: *She wore a gold chain around her neck.* ◆ *My bicycle chain is broken.* ◆ *a length of chain* ⊃ Look at the picture at **bicycle**, **jewelry**.
2 [count] (**BUSINESS**) a group of stores, restaurants, hotels, etc. that are owned by one person or company: *The mall has most of the major chain stores* (= stores that are part of a chain).

chain² 🔑 /tʃeɪn/ *verb* (**chains**, **chain·ing**, **chained**)
to attach someone or something to a place with a **chain**: *The dog was **chained to** a tree.*

chairs

chair   armchair

cushion

stool   sofa/couch

chair 🔑 /tʃɛr/ *noun*
1 [count] a piece of furniture for one person to sit on, with four legs, a seat, and a back: *a table and four chairs*
2 [singular] = **chairperson**: *the chair of the history department*

chair·per·son /ˈtʃɛrˌpərsn/ *noun* [count] (also **chair**) (also **chair·man** /ˈtʃɛrmən/, **chair·wom·an** /ˈtʃɛrˌwʊmən/)
(**BUSINESS**) a person who controls a meeting, group, or university department

chalk /tʃɔk/ *noun* [count, noncount]
(**ART**) small sticks made of a soft white rock that you use for writing or drawing: *The teacher wrote the answer on the board with a piece of chalk.* ◆ *a box of colored chalks*

chalk·board /ˈtʃɔkbɔrd/ *noun* [count] another word for **blackboard**

chal·lenge¹ 🔑 **AWL** /ˈtʃæləndʒ/ *noun* [count]
1 a new or difficult thing that makes you try hard: *Climbing the mountain will be a real challenge.*
2 an invitation to fight or play a game against someone

chal·lenge² **AWL** /ˈtʃæləndʒ/ *verb* (**chal·leng·es**, **chal·leng·ing**, **chal·lenged**)
1 to ask someone to play a game with you or fight with you to see who wins: *The boxer challenged the world champion to a fight.*

2 to refuse to accept a set of rules; to say that you think someone or something is wrong: *She does not like anyone challenging her authority.*

chal·leng·er AWL /'tʃæləndʒər/ *noun* [count]
a person who takes part in a competition or an election to win a position that someone else already has: *the senator's challenger in the election*

chal·leng·ing AWL /'tʃæləndʒɪŋ/ *adjective*
difficult in an interesting way that tests your ability: *a challenging piece of work*

cham·pagne /ʃæm'peɪn/ *noun* [noncount]
a French white wine with a lot of bubbles

cham·pi·on /'tʃæmpiən/ *noun* [count]
(**SPORTS**) a person who is the best at a sport or game: *a chess champion* ◆ *the world champion*

cham·pi·on·ship /'tʃæmpiən,ʃɪp/ *noun* [count]
(**SPORTS**) a competition to find the best player or team in a sport or game: *Our team won the championship this year.*

chance /tʃæns/ *noun*
1 [count] a possibility that something may happen: *There's no chance that she'll come now.* ◆ *She has a good chance of becoming the next president.* ◆ *He doesn't stand (= have) a chance of passing the exam.*
2 [count] a time when you can do something: *It was their last chance to escape.* ◆ *Be quiet and give her a chance to explain.* ⊃ SYNONYM **opportunity**
3 [noncount] when something happens that you cannot control or that you have not planned: *We must plan this carefully. I don't want to leave anything to chance.* ◆ *We met by chance at the train station.* ⊃ SYNONYM **luck**
take a chance to do something when it is possible that something bad may happen because of it: *We may lose money, but we'll just have to take that chance.*

chan·cel·lor /'tʃænsələr/ *noun* [count]
1 (**POLITICS**) the head of the government in some countries: *the German chancellor*
2 the head of some universities: *the chancellor of Washington University*

chan·de·lier /,ʃændə'lɪr/ *noun* [count]
a large frame that hangs from the ceiling and holds many small lights: *a crystal chandelier*

change¹ /tʃeɪndʒ/ *verb* (chang·es, chang·ing, changed)
1 to become different: *She has changed a lot since the last time I saw her – she looks much older.* ◆ *Water changes into ice when it gets very cold.*
2 to make something different: *At this restaurant they change the menu every week.*
3 to put or take something in place of another thing: *to change a lightbulb* ◆ *He changed the day of the meeting from Monday to Tuesday.* ◆ *I need*

to change some money (= exchange money into the money of another country) *at the airport.*
4 (also **get changed**) to put on different clothes: *I need to change before I go out.* ◆ *You need to get changed for soccer practice.* ◆ *He changed out of his suit and into his running shorts.*
5 to get off a train, bus, or airplane and get on another one: *To get to San Francisco, I have to change planes in Chicago.*

change² /tʃeɪndʒ/ *noun*
1 [count] when something becomes different: *The new administration has made a lot of changes.* ◆ *There has been a change in the weather.*
2 [noncount] the money that you get back if you pay more than the amount something costs: *If a newspaper costs $1.50 and you pay with two dollar bills, you will get 50 cents change.*
3 [noncount] small pieces of money; coins: *I don't have any change on me.*
for a change because you want something different: *Today we had lunch in a restaurant for a change.*

chan·nel AWL /'tʃænl/ *noun* [count]
1 a TV station: *Which channel is the game on?*
2 (**GEOGRAPHY**) a long narrow place where water can go: *the English Channel* (= the area of water between England and France)

chant /tʃænt/ *verb* (chants, chant·ing, chant·ed)
to say or sing a word or phrase many times: *The protesters chanted antiwar slogans.*
▶ **chant** *noun* [count]: *a religious chant*

cha·os /'keɪɑs/ *noun* [noncount]
when everything is confused and nothing is organized: *The house was in chaos after the party.* ◆ *The accident caused total chaos on the highway.*

chap·el /'tʃæpl/ *noun* [count]
(**RELIGION**) a room or a small church where Christians go to speak to God (to PRAY)

chap·er·one /'ʃæpə,roʊn/ *noun* [count]
an older person who goes to social events for younger people to make sure they behave correctly
▶ **chap·er·one** *verb* (chap·er·ones, chap·er·on·ing, chap·er·oned): *We need more volunteers to chaperone the school dance.*

chap·ter AWL /'tʃæptər/ *noun* [count]
(**ENGLISH LANGUAGE ARTS**) one of the parts of a book: *Turn to Chapter 4.*

char·ac·ter /'kærəktər/ *noun*
1 [count, usually singular] the qualities that make someone or something different from other people or things: *He has a strong character.* ◆ *The new factory will change the character of the town.*
2 [count] a person in a book, play, television show, or movie: *Homer Simpson is a cartoon character.*

char·ac·ter·is·tic 🔑 /ˌkærəktəˈrɪstɪk/ *noun*
[count]
a quality that someone or something has: *personal characteristics such as age, height, and weight*

char·coal /ˈtʃɑrkoʊl/ *noun* [noncount]
a black substance that is made from burning wood. It is used as a fuel or for drawing: *a charcoal grill • a charcoal drawing*

charge¹ 🔑 /tʃɑrdʒ/ *noun* [count, noncount]
1 the money that you must pay for something: *There is a charge of $200 for the use of the party room. • We deliver free of charge.* ⊃ Look at the note at **price**.
2 when the police say that someone has done something wrong: *a murder charge*
be in charge of someone or **something** to take care of or be responsible for someone or something: *Tom is in charge of his baby brother while his mom is out.*

charge² 🔑 /tʃɑrdʒ/ *verb* (charg·es, charg·ing, charged)
1 to ask someone to pay a particular price for something: *The mechanic charged me $500 for the repairs.*
2 to buy something with a small card made of plastic (called a CREDIT CARD) instead of cash: *I charged the tickets on my credit card.*
3 to say that someone has done something wrong: *The police have charged him with murder.*
4 to run quickly and with a lot of force: *The bull charged. • The children charged into the room.*
5 to put electricity into something: *I need to charge my phone.*

cha·ris·ma /kəˈrɪzmə/ *noun* [noncount]
a special quality that some people have, which makes other people like them
▶ **cha·ris·mat·ic** /ˌkærəzˈmætɪk/ *adjective*: *a charismatic leader*

char·i·ty 🔑 /ˈtʃærəti/ *noun* (plural char·i·ties)
1 [count, noncount] an organization that collects money to help people who need it: *The United Way is a charity. • They give a lot of money to charity.*
2 [noncount] being kind and helping other people

charm¹ /tʃɑrm/ *noun*
1 [noncount] the quality of being pleasant or attractive: *The historic houses add to the charm of the town.*
2 [count] a small thing that you wear because you think it will bring good luck: *She wears a chain with a lucky charm on it.*

charm² /tʃɑrm/ *verb* (charms, charm·ing, charmed)
to make someone like you: *The baby charmed everyone with her smile.*

charm·ing /ˈtʃɑrmɪŋ/ *adjective*
very pleasant or attractive: *Have you met the new principal? He's really charming.*

chart AWL /tʃɑrt/ *noun* [count]
1 a drawing that gives information about something: *a temperature chart*
2 (GEOGRAPHY) a map of the ocean or the sky
3 the charts (MUSIC) an official list of the songs, CDs, etc. that have sold the most in a particular week: *What's number 1 on the charts this week?*

chase 🔑 /tʃeɪs/ *verb* (chas·es, chas·ing, chased)
to run behind someone or something and try to catch them: *The dog chased the cat around the yard. • The police chased after the thief but he escaped.*
▶ **chase** *noun* [count]: *The movie includes an exciting car chase.*

chat¹ /tʃæt/ *verb* (chats, chat·ting, chat·ted)
to talk in a friendly, informal way with someone: *We chatted on the phone for a few minutes.*

chat² /tʃæt/ *noun* [count]
a friendly talk: *Let's have a chat about it later.* ⊃ Look at the note at **discussion**.

chat room /ˈtʃæt rum/ *noun* [count]
(COMPUTERS) an area on the Internet where you can join in a discussion with other people

chat·ter /ˈtʃæt̬ər/ *verb* (chat·ters, chat·ter·ing, chat·tered)
to talk quickly about things that are not very important: *Stop chattering and finish your work.*

cheap 🔑 /tʃip/ *adjective* (cheap·er, cheap·est)
1 costing little money: *That restaurant is very good, and relatively cheap. • Computers are getting cheaper all the time.* ⊃ ANTONYM **expensive**
2 low in price and quality: *I don't like that dress – it looks cheap.*
3 not wanting to spend money: *He's too cheap to take her out to a nice restaurant.*

cheat 🔑 /tʃit/ *verb* (cheats, cheat·ing, cheat·ed)
to do something that is not honest or fair: *She cheated on the exam.*
▶ **cheat** *noun* [count]
a person who **cheats**: *That man's a liar and a cheat.*

check¹ 🔑 /tʃɛk/ *verb* (checks, check·ing, checked)
1 to look at something to see that it is right, good, or safe: *Do these math problems, and then use a calculator to check your answers. • Before my long drive to Miami, I checked the oil. • Check that all the windows are closed before you leave.*
2 to make a mark like this ✓ by something: *Check the box next to the right answer.*
check in to tell the person at the desk in a hotel or an airport that you have arrived: *I have to*

tʃ **ch**in   dʒ **J**une   v **v**an   θ **th**in   ð **th**en   s **s**o   z **z**oo   ʃ **sh**e

check in an hour before my flight. ⊃ The noun is
check-in.
check out to pay your bill and leave a hotel ⊃
The noun is **checkout.**
check someone or **something out**
1 to find out if something is correct: *We need to
check out those rumors that the business is
closing.*
2 (*informal*) to look at a person or thing that
seems interesting: *Hey, check out Mike's new
sports car!*

check² /tʃɛk/ *noun* [*count*]
1 a look to see that everything is right, good, or
safe: *They **do** regular safety **checks on** all their
products.* • *a security check*
2 a piece of paper from a bank that you can
write on and use to pay for things: *I gave him a
check for $50.* • *Can I pay **by check**?*
3 a piece of paper that shows how much money
you must pay for food in a restaurant: *"Would
you like anything else?" "No, just the check
please."*
4 (also **check mark** /'tʃɛk mɑrk/) a small mark
like this ✓: *Put a check next to the names of the
people who have paid.*

check·book /'tʃɛkbʊk/ *noun* [*count*]
a book of CHECKS²(2)

checked /tʃɛkt/ *adjective* (also **check·ered**
/'tʃɛkərd/)
with a pattern of squares: *a checked shirt* ⊃ Look
at the picture at **pattern.**

check·ers /'tʃɛkərz/ *noun* [*noncount*]
a game that two people play with round flat
pieces on a board that has 64 squares in two
different colors: *Do you want to play checkers?*

check-in /'tʃɛk ɪn/ *noun*
1 [*count, noncount*] the place where you go first
when you arrive at an airport, to show your
ticket, etc.: *There was a long line at check-in.*
2 [*noncount*] the act of telling someone you have
arrived at a hotel, an airport, etc.: *Do you know
your check-in time?*

check mark /'tʃɛk mɑrk/ *noun* [*count*] another
word for **check²**(4)

check·out /'tʃɛkaʊt/ *noun*
1 (also **check-out coun·ter** /'tʃɛkaʊt ˌkaʊntər/)
[*count*] the place in a large store where you pay
for things
2 [*noncount*] the time when you leave a hotel at
the end of your stay: *What time is checkout?*

check·up /'tʃɛkʌp/ *noun* [*count*]
(**HEALTH**) a general examination by a doctor to
make sure that you are healthy: *You should visit
your dentist for a checkup twice a year.*

ched·dar /'tʃɛdər/ *noun* [*noncount*]
a type of hard yellow or orange cheese

cheek /tʃik/ *noun* [*count*]
one of the two soft parts of your face below your
eyes ⊃ Look at the picture at **face.**

cheer¹ /tʃɪr/ *verb* (**cheers, cheer·ing, cheered**)
to shout to show that you like something or to
encourage someone: *The crowd cheered loudly
when the players ran onto the field.*
cheer up; cheer someone up to become or to
make someone happier: *Cheer up! You'll feel
better soon.* • *We gave Julie some flowers to cheer
her up.*

cheer² /tʃɪr/ *noun* [*count*]
a loud shout that shows that you are pleased:
*The crowd **gave a** loud **cheer** as the singer came
onto the stage.*

cheer·ful /'tʃɪrfl/ *adjective*
happy: *a cheerful smile* • *You don't look very
cheerful today. What's the matter?*
▶ **cheer·ful·ly** /'tʃɪrfəli/ *adverb*

cheer·lead·er /'tʃɪrlidər/ *noun* [*count*]
(**SPORTS**) a person who wears special clothes,
and dances and shouts at a sports game to
encourage the crowd to make a noise: *She was a
cheerleader in high school.*

cheese /tʃiz/ *noun* [*count, noncount*]
a yellow or white food made from milk: *bread
and cheese*

cheese·burg·er /'tʃizˌbərgər/ *noun* [*count*]
a HAMBURGER (= a flat, round piece of meat in
between two round pieces of bread), with a slice
of cheese on top of the meat

cheese·cake
/'tʃizkeɪk/ *noun*
[*count, noncount*]
a type of cake that is
made from soft white
cheese, sugar, and
eggs on a base made
of crushed cookies

cheesecake

**a slice of
cheesecake**

chef /ʃɛf/ *noun* [*count*]
a professional cook, especially the chief cook in
a hotel or restaurant

chem·i·cal¹ /'kɛmɪkl/ *adjective* 〔AWL〕
(**CHEMISTRY**) connected with chemistry or
chemicals: *a chemical experiment*

chem·i·cal² /'kɛmɪkl/ *noun* [*count*] 〔AWL〕
(**CHEMISTRY**) a solid or liquid substance that is
used or produced in a chemical process

chem·ist /'kɛmɪst/ *noun* [*count*]
(**CHEMISTRY**) a scientist who does research and
experiments with chemicals

chem·is·try /'kɛməstri/ *noun* [*noncount*]
the science that studies gases, liquids, and
solids to find out what they are and how they
behave

che·mo·ther·a·py /ˌkimoʊˈθɛrəpi/ (also *informal* **che·mo** /ˈkimoʊ/) *noun* [*noncount*]
(**HEALTH**) the treatment of a disease using chemicals: *Cancer patients are usually treated using chemotherapy.*

cher·ish /ˈtʃɛrɪʃ/ *verb* (**cher·ish·es, cher·ish·ing, cher·ished**)
to love and take care of someone or something: *Her ring is her most cherished possession.*

cher·ry /ˈtʃɛri/ *noun* [*count*] (*plural* **cher·ries**)
a small round red or black fruit that has a large seed inside it (called a **PIT**) ⊃ Look at the picture at **fruit**.

chess /tʃɛs/ *noun* [*noncount*]
a game that two people play on a board with black and white squares on it (called a **CHESSBOARD**). Each player has sixteen pieces that can be moved around the board in different ways.

chess

chest /tʃɛst/ *noun* [*count*]
1 the top part of the front of your body ⊃ Look at the picture at **body**.
2 a large, strong box with a lid that you use for storing or carrying things

chest·nut /ˈtʃɛsnʌt/ *noun* [*count*]
a smooth, brown nut with a sharp point, or the tree that this nut grows on: *roasted chestnuts*

chest of draw·ers /ˌtʃɛst əv ˈdrɔrz/ *noun* [*count*] (*plural* **chests of draw·ers**)
a large piece of furniture with parts that you can pull out (called **DRAWERS**). A **chest of drawers** is usually used for keeping clothes in.

chew /tʃu/ *verb* (**chews, chew·ing, chewed**)
to use your teeth to break up food in your mouth when you are eating: *You should chew your food thoroughly.*

chew·ing gum /ˈtʃuɪŋ gʌm/ *noun* [*noncount*] = **gum** (2)

chic /ʃik/ *adjective* (**chic·er, chic·est**)
fashionable and attractive: *a chic new restaurant*

chick /tʃɪk/ *noun* [*count*]
a baby bird, especially a baby chicken: *a hen with her chicks*

chick·en /ˈtʃɪkən/ *noun*
1 [*count*] a bird that people often keep for its eggs and its meat

chicken

2 [*noncount*] the meat from this bird: *roast chicken*

chick·en pox /ˈtʃɪkən pɑks/ (also **chick·en·pox**) *noun* [*noncount*]
(**HEALTH**) a disease, especially of children. When you have the **chicken pox** you feel very hot and get red spots on your skin that make you want to scratch.

chief¹ /tʃif/ *noun* [*count*]
the leader of a group of people: *the chief of a Native American tribe* ◆ *police chiefs*

chief² /tʃif/ *adjective*
most important: *Bad driving is one of the chief causes of road accidents.*

chief·ly /ˈtʃifli/ *adverb*
not completely, but mostly: *His success was due chiefly to hard work.* ⊃ **SYNONYM** **mainly**

child /tʃaɪld/ *noun* [*count*] (*plural* **child·ren** /ˈtʃɪldrən/)
1 a young boy or girl: *There are 30 children in the class.*
2 a daughter or son: *Do you have any children?* ◆ *One of her children got married last year.*

child·care /ˈtʃaɪldkɛr/ *noun* [*noncount*]
taking care of children, especially while the parents are at work: *childcare facilities for working parents*

child·hood /ˈtʃaɪldhʊd/ *noun* [*count, noncount*]
the time when you are a child: *She had a happy childhood.*

child·ish /ˈtʃaɪldɪʃ/ *adjective*
like a child: *Don't be so childish! It's only a game.*
⊃ **SYNONYM** **immature**

chil·i /ˈtʃɪli/ *noun* (*plural* **chil·ies**)
1 [*count*] (also **chil·i pep·per**) a small green or red vegetable that has a very strong hot taste: *chili powder*

chilies

2 [*noncount*] a dish made with **chilis**, and usually meat

chill /tʃɪl/ *verb* (**chills, chill·ing, chilled**)
1 to make someone or something colder: *Chill the white wine before you serve it.*
2 (also **chill out**) (*informal*) to relax and not worry about things: *When I get home from work, I like to chill out in front of the TV.*
▶ **chill** *noun* [*singular*]

a feeling of being cold: *There's a chill in the air this morning.*

chill·y /'tʃɪli/ *adjective* (chill·i·er, chill·i·est)
cold: *a chilly morning* ⊃ Look at the note at **cold¹**.

chime /tʃaɪm/ *verb* (chimes, chim·ing, chimed)
to make the sound that a bell makes: *The clock chimed midnight.*

chim·ney /'tʃɪmni/ *noun* [count] (*plural* chim·neys)
a large pipe over a fire that lets smoke go outside into the air

chim·pan·zee
/ˌtʃɪmpæn'zi/ *noun* [count]
an African animal like a large MONKEY with no tail

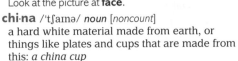

chimpanzee

chin 🔑 /'tʃɪn/ *noun* [count]
the part of your face below your mouth ⊃ Look at the picture at **face**.

chi·na /'tʃaɪnə/ *noun* [noncount]
a hard white material made from earth, or things like plates and cups that are made from this: *a china cup*

chip¹ /tʃɪp/ *noun* [count]
1 a small piece of something, such as wood, chocolate, or glass: *a chocolate chip cookie*
2 the place where a small piece of wood, stone, or other material has broken off a larger piece: *This plate has a chip in it.*
3 (also **po·ta·to chip**) a very thin piece of potato cooked in hot oil and eaten cold: *I put out chips and dip for the party.*
4 (COMPUTERS) a very small thing inside a computer that makes it work ⊃ SYNONYM **microchip**

chip² /tʃɪp/ *verb* (chips, chip·ping, chipped)
to break or lose a small piece off something hard: *My son fell off his bike and chipped his tooth.*

chip·munk
/'tʃɪpmʌŋk/ *noun* [count]
a small animal with a long, thick tail and brown fur with lines of black and white on its back

chipmunk

chirp /tʃərp/ *verb* (chirps, chirp·ing, chirped)
to make the short high sound that small birds make

chis·el /'tʃɪzl/ *noun* [count]
a tool with a sharp end that is used for cutting or shaping wood, stone, etc.

chlo·ride /'klɔraɪd/ *noun* [count, noncount]
(CHEMISTRY) a substance that is a mixture of CHLORINE and another chemical: *sodium chloride*

chlo·rine /'klɔrin/ *noun* [noncount] (symbol **Cl**)
(CHEMISTRY) a yellow-green gas with a strong smell, which is used for making water safe to drink or to swim in

choc·o·late 🔑 /'tʃɑklət/ *noun*
1 [noncount] a dark brown sweet food that is made from seeds (called COCOA BEANS) that grow on trees in hot countries: *Do you like chocolate?* ◆ *I would love a piece of chocolate right now.* ◆ *a chocolate cake*
2 [count] a piece of candy made of **chocolate**: *a box of chocolates*

choc·o·late chip /ˌtʃɑklət 'tʃɪp/ *noun* [count]
a small piece of chocolate used in baking: *chocolate chip cookies*

choice 🔑 /tʃɔɪs/ *noun*
1 [count] the act of choosing between two or more people or things: *You **made** the right choice.*
2 [noncount] the right or chance to choose: *We **have no choice**. We have to leave.*
3 [count] the things that you can choose from: *The menu has **a choice of** six different soups.*
4 [count] the person or thing that someone has chosen: *She was my choice for student council president.*

choir /'kwaɪər/ *noun* [count]
(MUSIC) a group of people who sing together: *a school choir*

choke /tʃoʊk/ *verb* (chokes, chok·ing, choked)
to be or to make someone not able to breathe because something is stopping air from getting in: *He was **choking on** a fish bone.* ◆ *Loosen the dog's collar – it's choking him.*

cho·les·ter·ol /kə'lɛstərɔl/ *noun* [noncount]
(HEALTH, BIOLOGY) a substance in your body that can cause heart disease if there is too much of it: *a new medication to help lower your cholesterol*

choose 🔑 /tʃuz/ *verb* (choos·es, choos·ing, chose /tʃoʊz/, has cho·sen /'tʃoʊzn/)
to decide which thing or person you want: *She chose the chocolate cake.* ◆ *Mike had to choose between getting a job or going to college.* ⊃ The noun is **choice**.

chop¹ /tʃɑp/ *verb* (chops, chop·ping, chopped)
to cut something into pieces with a knife, etc.: *Chop up an onion into small pieces.* ◆ *We chopped some wood for the fire.* ⊃ Look at the note at **cut¹**.
chop something down to cut a tree, etc. at the bottom so that it falls down
chop something off to remove something from something else by cutting it: *to chop a branch off a tree*

chop² /tʃɑp/ *noun* [count]
a thick slice of meat with a piece of bone in it: *a lamb chop*

chop·sticks /ˈtʃɑpstɪks/ *noun* [plural]
a pair of thin sticks that are used for eating with, especially in some Asian countries

chopsticks

chord /kɔrd/ *noun* [count]
(**MUSIC**) two or more musical notes that are played at the same time

chore /tʃɔr/ *noun* [count]
a job that is not interesting but that you must do: *doing the household chores*

cho·re·og·ra·phy /ˌkɔriˈɑgrəfi/ *noun* [noncount]
the arrangement of movements for a dance

cho·rus /ˈkɔrəs/ *noun* [count] (plural **cho·rus·es**)
(**MUSIC**)
1 a part of a song that you repeat
2 a large group of people who sing together ⟳
SYNONYM choir

chose, cho·sen forms of **choose**

chow·der /ˈtʃaʊdər/ *noun* [count]
a thick soup, usually made with fish: *clam chowder*

Christ /kraɪst/ = **Jesus**

chris·ten /ˈkrɪsn/ *verb* (chris·tens, chris·ten·ing, chris·tened)
(**RELIGION**) to give a name to a baby and make him or her a member of the Christian church in a special ceremony
▸ **chris·ten·ing** /ˈkrɪsnɪŋ/ *noun* [count]
the ceremony when a baby is **christened**

Chris·tian /ˈkrɪstʃən/ *noun* [count]
(**RELIGION**) a person who believes in Jesus Christ and what he taught
▸ **Chris·tian** *adjective*: *the Christian church*

Chris·ti·an·i·ty /ˌkrɪstʃiˈænəti/ *noun* [noncount]
(**RELIGION**) the religion that follows what Jesus Christ taught

Christ·mas /ˈkrɪsməs/ *noun* [count, noncount]
(**RELIGION**) the period of time around and including December 25, when Christians remember the birth of Christ: *Merry Christmas!* ◆ *Where are you spending Christmas this year?*

Culture

- Christmas is an important festival in the U.S.
- The day before **Christmas Day** is called **Christmas Eve**.
- Many children believe that **Santa Claus** visits them at Christmas to bring presents,

and they hang **Christmas stockings** for him to fill with presents.
- People send **Christmas cards** and give presents to their friends and family. Many people go to church at Christmas and sing **Christmas carols**.
- People put special trees (called **Christmas trees**) in their homes, and decorate them with small lights and other pretty things.
- **Christmas** is sometimes written informally as **Xmas**.

chrome /kroʊm/ *noun* [noncount]
a hard, shiny metal that is used to cover other metals: *a chrome bumper on a car*

chro·mo·some /ˈkroʊməsoʊm/ *noun* [count]
(**BIOLOGY**) the part of a cell that decides the sex, character, size, etc. that a person, plant, or animal will have

chron·ic /ˈkrɑnɪk/ *adjective*
(**HEALTH**) (used about a disease or problem) that continues for a long time and is hard to get rid of: *a chronic backache* ◆ *chronic unemployment*

chron·o·log·i·cal /ˌkrɑnəˈlɑdʒɪkl/ *adjective*
arranged in the order in which events happened: *a list of Civil War battles in chronological order*

chrys·a·lis /ˈkrɪsəlɪs/ *noun* [count] (plural **chrys·a·lis·es**)
(**BIOLOGY**) the form of an insect while it is changing into an adult inside a hard case ⟳ Look at the picture at **butterfly**.

chub·by /ˈtʃʌbi/ *adjective* (chub·bi·er, chub·bi·est)
slightly fat: *a baby with chubby cheeks*

chunk /tʃʌŋk/ *noun* [count]
a large piece or part of something: *A large chunk of my income goes to paying rent.* ⟳ Look at the note at **piece**.

church 🔑 /tʃɜrtʃ/ *noun* [count, noncount] (plural **church·es**)
(**RELIGION**) a building where Christians go to speak to God (to **PRAY**): *They go to church every Sunday.*

Grammar

- When we talk about going to a ceremony (a **service**) in a church we say **in church**, **to church** or **at church** without "a" or "the": *Was Mr. Poole at church today?*
- We use **a** or **the** to talk about the building: *the church where we got married* ◆ *a historic church.*

chute /ʃut/ *noun* [*count*]
a narrow space that you drop or slide things down: *a laundry chute*

ci·der /ˈsaɪdər/ (also **ap·ple ci·der**) *noun* [*count, noncount*]
a drink made from apples

ci·gar /sɪˈɡɑr/ *noun* [*count*]
a thick roll of dried leaves (called TOBACCO) that some people smoke. **Cigars** are larger than cigarettes.

cig·a·rette 🔑 /ˈsɪɡərɛt/ *noun* [*count*]
a thin tube of white paper filled with dried leaves (called TOBACCO), which some people smoke: *He smoked two packs of cigarettes a day.*

cin·e·ma /ˈsɪnəmə/ *noun* [*noncount*] (*formal*)
movies in general: *French cinema during the twentieth century*

cin·na·mon /ˈsɪnəmən/ *noun* [*noncount*]
a brown powder that is used to give flavor to sweet foods: *cinnamon toast* (= toast with butter, cinnamon, and sugar)

circle

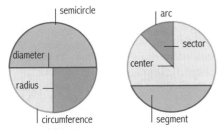

cir·cle¹ 🔑 /ˈsərkl/ *noun* [*count*]
1 a round shape; a ring: *There are 360 degrees in a circle.* ⊃ Look at the picture at **shape**.
2 a group of people who are friends, or who have the same interest or job: *He has a large circle of friends.*

cir·cle² /ˈsərkl/ *verb* (**cir·cles, cir·cling, cir·cled**)
to move in a circle, or to draw a circle around something: *Vultures circled overhead.* ◆ *Circle the correct answer in your book.*

cir·cuit /ˈsərkət/ *noun* [*count*]
(**PHYSICS**) the complete path of electricity through a wire, etc.: *an electrical circuit*

cir·cu·lar /ˈsərkyələr/ *adjective*
with the shape of a circle: *a circular table* ⊃
SYNONYM round

cir·cu·late /ˈsərkyəleɪt/ *verb* (**cir·cu·lates, cir·cu·lat·ing, cir·cu·lat·ed**)
to move around: *Blood circulates around the body.*

cir·cu·la·tion /ˌsərkyəˈleɪʃn/ *noun* [*noncount*]
(**BIOLOGY**) the movement of blood around the body

cir·cum·fer·ence /sərˈkʌmfrəns/ *noun* [*count*]
(**MATH**) the distance around a circle ⊃ Look at the picture at **circle**.

cir·cum·stanc·es **AWL** /ˈsərkəmstænsɪz/ *noun* [*plural*]
the facts that are true in a particular situation
under no circumstances never; not for any reason: *Under no circumstances should you go out alone at night.*
under the circumstances as the result of a particular situation: *It's not an ideal solution, but it's the best we can do under the circumstances.*

cir·cus /ˈsərkəs/ *noun* [*count*] (*plural* **cir·cus·es**)
a performance by a company of people and often trained animals which travels to different places: *The kids enjoyed seeing the acrobats, clowns, and elephants at the circus.*

cite **AWL** /saɪt/ *verb* (**cites, cit·ing, cit·ed**)
to mention something as an example, to support what you are saying: *She cited rising crime figures as an example of the city's problems.*

cit·i·zen 🔑 /ˈsɪt̬əzn/ *noun* [*count*]
a person who belongs to a country or a city: *She became an American citizen in 1995.*

cit·i·zen·ship /ˈsɪt̬əzənʃɪp/ *noun* [*noncount*]
the legal right to belong to a particular country: *to apply for citizenship*

cit·rus fruit /ˈsɪtrəs frut/ *noun* [*count, noncount*]
a fruit such as an orange or a lemon

cit·y 🔑 /ˈsɪt̬i/ *noun* [*count*] (*plural* **cit·ies**)
a big and important town: *the city of New York* ◆ *city streets*

cit·y hall (also **City Hall**) /ˌsɪt̬i ˈhɔl/ *noun* [*count*]
(**POLITICS**) the government of a city and the offices it uses: *We're going to fight city hall to get our roads repaired.* ◆ *We got married at City Hall.*

civ·ic /ˈsɪvɪk/ *adjective*
(**POLITICS**) connected with a city or town, or the people who live there: *a civic leader* ◆ *our civic responsibilities*

civ·il **AWL** /ˈsɪvl/ *adjective*
1 connected with the public, not with the army or a church: *a civil wedding* (= not a religious one)
2 connected with the legal rights of people, but not criminal issues: *civil law*
3 polite, but not very friendly: *You may not like him, but try at least to be civil.*

ci·vil·ian /səˈvɪlyən/ *noun* [*count*]
a person who does not belong to the army, navy, etc. or to the police

civ·i·li·za·tion /ˌsɪvələˈzeɪʃn/ *noun* [*count, noncount*]
the way people live together in a society with laws, education, and a government: *the ancient*

civilizations of Greece and Rome • *Western civilization*

civ·i·lized /ˈsɪvəlaɪzd/ *adjective*
1 (used about a society) well organized and having a highly developed culture
2 polite and reasonable: *a civilized conversation*

civ·il rights /ˌsɪvl ˈraɪts/ *noun* [*plural*]
a person's legal rights to freedom and to equal treatment in society: *Martin Luther King Jr. was a civil rights leader during the 1960s.*

civ·il serv·ant /ˌsɪvl ˈsərvənt/ *noun* [*count*]
(**POLITICS**) a person who works in THE CIVIL SERVICE

the civ·il serv·ice /ðə ˌsɪvl ˈsərvəs/ *noun* [*singular*]
(**POLITICS**) the government departments in a country, and the people who work for them

civ·il war /ˌsɪvl ˈwɔr/ *noun* [*count, noncount*]
(**HISTORY, POLITICS**) a war between groups of people who live in the same country: *The Civil War began in 1861.*

cl abbreviation of **centiliter**

claim¹ /kleɪm/ *verb* (claims, claim·ing, claimed)
1 to say that something is true: *He claims that he did the work without help.*
2 to ask for something because it is yours: *If no one claims the camera you found, you can have it.*

claim² /kleɪm/ *noun* [*count*]
1 saying that something is true: *No one believed his claim that he had found the money on the street.*
2 something that you ask for because you think you have a right to it: *After the car accident, he made a claim to his insurance company to pay for repairs.*

clam /klæm/ *noun* [*count*]
a type of fish with a round shell in two parts that can open and close: *fried clams*

clamp¹ /klæmp/ *verb* (clamps, clamp·ing, clamped)
to hold something firmly in a particular position: *Her lips were clamped shut.*
clamp down on someone or **something** (*informal*) to take strong action in order to stop or control something: *The police are clamping down on street crime.*

clamp² /klæmp/ *noun* [*count*]
a tool that holds two things together very firmly

clang /klæŋ/ *verb* (clangs, clang·ing, clanged)
to make a loud sound, like metal when you hit it with something: *The iron gates clanged shut.*

clap /klæp/ *verb* (claps, clap·ping, clapped)
to hit your hands together to make a noise, usually to show that you like something: *At the end of the concert the audience clapped loudly.*

clar·i·fy **AWL** /ˈklærəfaɪ/ *verb* (clar·i·fies, clar·i·fy·ing, clar·i·fied)
to make something clear and easy to understand: *I hope that what I say will clarify the situation.*
▶ **clar·i·fi·ca·tion** **AWL** /ˌklærəfəˈkeɪʃn/ *noun* [*noncount*]: *That report needs some clarification.*

clar·i·net /ˌklærəˈnɛt/ *noun* [*count*]
(**MUSIC**) a musical instrument made of wood with holes in it. You play it by blowing into it. ➋ Look at the picture at **instrument**.

clar·i·ty **AWL** /ˈklærəti/ *noun* [*noncount*]
the quality of being clear and easy to understand: *clarity of expression* • *Your written arguments lack clarity.* ➋ The adjective is **clear**.

clash¹ /klæʃ/ *verb* (clash·es, clash·ing, clashed)
1 to fight or argue about something: *Police clashed with demonstrators.*
2 If colors or patterns **clash**, they do not look good together: *That red tie clashes with your shirt.*

clash² /klæʃ/ *noun* [*count*] (*plural* clash·es)
1 a fight or a serious argument: *a clash between police and demonstrators*
2 a big difference: *a clash of cultures*

clasp¹ /klæsp/ *verb* (clasps, clasp·ing, clasped)
to hold someone or something firmly: *He clasped the dog's leash tightly.* ➋ SYNONYM **grip**

clasp² /klæsp/ *noun* [*count*]
a metal object that fastens or holds something together: *the clasp on a necklace* ➋ Look at the picture at **jewelry**.

class 🔑 /klæs/ *noun* (*plural* class·es)
1 [*count*] a group of children or students who learn together: *There is a new girl in my class.* • *The whole class passed the exam.* • *the class of '09* (= the group of students who finished their studies in 2009)
2 [*count, noncount*] the time when you learn something with a teacher: *Classes begin at nine o'clock.* • *No cell phones are allowed in class.*
3 [*count*] a group of people or things that are the same in some way: *There are many different classes of insects.* • *the middle class* (= people who are neither rich nor poor)
4 [*count*] how good, comfortable, etc. something is: *It costs more to travel first class.*

clas·sic¹ **AWL** /ˈklæsɪk/ *adjective*
(**ENGLISH LANGUAGE ARTS**) important and having a value that will last: *the classic novel "Pride and Prejudice"*

clas·sic² **AWL** /ˈklæsɪk/ *noun* [*count*]
(**ENGLISH LANGUAGE ARTS**) a book, movie, or piece of music that is so good that it is still popular many years after it was written or made: *"Charlotte's Web," written by E. B. White, is a children's classic.*

clas·si·cal `AWL` /'klæsɪkl/ *adjective*
1 in a style that people have used for a long time because they think it is good: *classical dance* ⊃
SYNONYM traditional ⊃ **ANTONYM modern**
2 (**MUSIC**) Classical music is written for instruments that are not electronic, and is considered to be serious and important: *I prefer rock to classical music.*
3 connected with ancient Greece or Rome: *classical Greek architecture*

clas·si·fied ad /ˌklæsəfaɪd 'æd/ *noun* [*count*]
a small advertisement that you put in a newspaper, on the Internet, etc. if you want to buy or sell something, rent an apartment, etc.

clas·si·fy /'klæsəfaɪ/ *verb* (clas·si·fies, clas·si·fy·ing, clas·si·fied)
to put someone or something into a group with others that are similar: *Would you classify the movie as a drama or a thriller?*
▸ **clas·si·fi·ca·tion** /ˌklæsəfə'keɪʃn/ *noun* [*count, noncount*]: *the classification of different species of butterflies*

class·mate /'klæsmeɪt/ *noun* [*count*]
a person who is in the same class as you at school or college

class·room /'klæsrum/ *noun* [*count*]
a room where you learn in a school or college

class·y /'klæsi/ *adjective* (class·i·er, class·i·est)
(*informal*)
having high quality or style; expensive: *He took me to a classy restaurant.*

clat·ter /'klætər/ *verb* (clat·ters, clat·ter·ing, clat·tered)
to make the loud noise of hard things hitting each other: *The dishes clattered in the cupboard when he slammed the door.*
▸ **clat·ter** *noun* [*count, usually singular*]: *the clatter of horses' hoofs*

clause `AWL` /klɔz/ *noun* [*count*]
1 (**ENGLISH LANGUAGE ARTS**) a part of a sentence that has a verb in it: *The sentence "After we had finished eating, we went out." contains two clauses.*
2 a part of a legal document that says that something must or must not be done: *There is a clause in the rental agreement forbidding pets.*

claus·tro·pho·bi·a /ˌklɔstrə'foʊbiə/ *noun*
[*noncount*]
(**HEALTH**) a very strong fear of being in a small or closed space

claw /klɔ/ *noun* [*count*]
one of the hard pointed parts on the feet of some animals and birds: *Cats have sharp claws.* ⊃ Look at the picture at **cat**.

clay /kleɪ/ *noun* [*noncount*]
a kind of heavy earth that becomes hard when it is dry: *clay pots*

clean¹ /klin/ *adjective* (clean·er, clean·est)
1 not dirty: *clean clothes* ◆ *Are your hands clean?*
⊃ **ANTONYM dirty**
2 having no record of crimes or offenses: *Do you have a clean driving record?*

clean² /klin/ *verb* (cleans, clean·ing, cleaned)
to remove the dirt or marks from something; to make something clean: *Sam cleaned the kitchen floor.*
clean something out to clean the inside of something: *I found my old jacket when I cleaned out my closet.*
clean up; clean something up to make a place clean and neat: *You need to clean up your room before you go out.* ◆ *She helped me clean up after the party.*

Word building

- When you **clean** or **clean up** your home, you **do housework**.
- You **wash** something with water and often soap. You **wipe** a surface with a wet cloth and you **dust** a surface with a dry cloth.
- You **sweep** the floor with a **broom**.

clean·er /'klinər/ *noun* [*count*]
1 a person whose job is to clean people's houses or other buildings: *an office cleaner*
2 a substance or special machine used for cleaning something: *a carpet cleaner*
3 the cleaners = dry cleaners: *Could you pick up my suit from the cleaners on your way home?*

clear¹ /klɪr/ *adjective* (clear·er, clear·est)
1 easy to see, hear, or understand: *She spoke in a loud, clear voice.* ◆ *These instructions aren't very clear.* ◆ *It's clear that he's not happy.* ◆ *I made it clear to him that he was no longer welcome here.*
⊃ **ANTONYM unclear**
2 easy to see through: *clear glass*
3 free from marks: *a clear sky* (= without clouds)
◆ *clear skin* (= without spots)
4 with nothing blocking the way: *Most roads are now clear of snow.*

clear² /klɪr/ *verb* (clears, clear·ing, cleared)
1 to remove things from a place because you do not want or need them there: *They cleared the snow from the path.* ◆ *When you're finished eating, clear the table* (= take away the dirty plates).
2 to become clear: *It rained in the morning, but in the afternoon the sky cleared.*
clear something out to make something neat and clean by getting rid of things that you do not want

---

clear·ance /ˈklɪrəns/ *noun* [*noncount*]
1 official permission to do something: *You need special **security clearance** to enter the building.*
2 getting rid of something that is old and not wanted: *a clearance sale*

clear·ly 🖉 /ˈklɪrli/ *adverb*
1 in a way that is easy to see, hear, or understand: *When you make your speech, try to speak slowly and clearly.* • *The notes explain very clearly what you have to do.*
2 without any doubt: *She is clearly very intelligent.* ⊃ SYNONYM **obviously**

cler·gy /ˈklərdʒi/ *noun* [*plural*]
(RELIGION) the people who perform religious services: *a member of the clergy*

cler·gy·man /ˈklərdʒimən/ (also **cler·gy·wom·an** /ˈklərdʒiwʊmən/) *noun* [*count*] (plural **cler·gy·men** /ˈklərdʒimɛn/, **cler·gy·wom·en** /ˈklərdʒiwɪmən/)
(RELIGION) a member of the CLERGY

clerk /klərk/ *noun* [*count*]
1 a person whose job is to do written work or keep records or accounts in an office, a bank, etc.
2 a person who works in a store ⊃ SYNONYM **salesclerk**
3 a person whose job is to help people arriving at or leaving a hotel: *Leave your keys with the clerk at the front desk.*

clev·er /ˈklɛvər/ *adjective* (**clev·er·er**, **clev·er·est**)
intelligent and showing skill; quick at learning and understanding things: *a clever strategy*
▶ **clev·er·ly** /ˈklɛvərli/ *adverb*

cli·ché /kliˈʃeɪ/ *noun* [*count*]
(ENGLISH LANGUAGE ARTS) a phrase or an idea that has been used too many times before, so it does not mean much: *The saying "life begins at 40" is such a cliché.*

click¹ /klɪk/ *verb* (**clicks**, **click·ing**, **clicked**)
1 to make a short, sharp sound: *The door clicked shut.*
2 (COMPUTERS) to press one of the buttons on a computer mouse: *To open a file, **click on** the menu.* • *Click the OK button to start.* ⊃ Look at **double-click**.

click² /klɪk/ *noun* [*count*]
1 a short, sharp sound: *the click of a switch*
2 (COMPUTERS) the act of pressing a button on a computer mouse: *You can do this with a click of the mouse.*

cli·ent /ˈklaɪənt/ *noun* [*count*]
(BUSINESS) a person who pays a professional or business person for help or advice: *The lawyer claimed that her client was innocent.*

cliff /klɪf/ *noun* [*count*]
(GEOGRAPHY) a high area of rock by the ocean, with one side that goes up very quickly (that is STEEP)

cliff
lighthouse | cliff

cli·mate 🖉 /ˈklaɪmət/ *noun* [*count, noncount*]
(GEOGRAPHY) the normal weather conditions of a place: *Coffee will not grow in a cold climate.*

cli·mate change /ˈklaɪmət ˌtʃeɪndʒ/ *noun* [*noncount*]
(GEOGRAPHY) changes in the earth's weather, espcially the fact that the earth's atmosphere is getting hotter: *Scientists are very worried about the effects of global climate change.* ⊃ Look at **global warming**.

cli·max /ˈklaɪmæks/ *noun* [*count*] (plural **cli·max·es**)
the most important part of something or of a period of time: *Winning an Oscar was the **climax** of his career.*

climb 🖉 /klaɪm/ *verb* (**climbs**, **climb·ing**, **climbed**)

> ℹ PRONUNCIATION
> The word **climb** sounds like **time**.

1 to go up toward the top of something: *They climbed the mountain.* • *The cat climbed to the top of the tree.*
2 to move to or from a place when it is not easy to do it: *The boys climbed through a hole in the fence.*
3 to move to a higher level: *The road climbs steeply.*
▶ **climb** *noun* [*count*]: *It was a long climb to the top of the mountain.*

climb·er /ˈklaɪmər/ *noun* [*count*]
(SPORTS) a person who climbs mountains or rocks as a sport: *a rock climber*

climb·ing /ˈklaɪmɪŋ/ *noun* [*noncount*]
(SPORTS) the sport of climbing mountains or rocks: *He was injured in a climbing accident.*

cling /klɪŋ/ *verb* (**clings**, **cling·ing**, **clung** /klʌŋ/, has **clung**)
to hold tight or stick to someone or something: *The girl was crying and **clinging to** her mother.* • *His wet clothes **clung to** his body.*

clin·ic /ˈklɪnɪk/ *noun* [*count*]
(HEALTH) a place where you can go to get help or advice from a doctor about a particular medical problem

clip¹ /klɪp/ *noun* [*count*]
a small piece of metal or plastic for holding things together or in place: *a hair clip* ⊃ Look at **paper clip**.

clip² /klɪp/ *verb* (clips, clip·ping, clipped)
to join something to another thing with a CLIP: *Clip the photo to the top of the letter.* ◆ *Do your earrings clip on?*

clip·board
/ˈklɪpbɔrd/ *noun* [*count*]
1 a small board with a part that holds papers at the top
2 (**COMPUTERS**) a place where information from a computer file is kept for a short time, before it is added to another file

clipboard

clock /klɑk/ *noun* [*count*]
a thing that shows you what time it is: *an alarm clock*

Word building

- A small clock that you wear on your wrist is called a **watch**.
- You say that a clock or watch is **fast** if it shows a time that is later than the real time. You say that it is **slow** if it shows a time that is earlier than the real time.

clock·wise /ˈklɑkwaɪz/ *adjective, adverb*
in the direction that the hands of a clock move: *Turn the handle clockwise.* ⊃ **ANTONYM counterclockwise**

clog /klɑg/ *noun* [*count*]
a type of shoe with no back and a thick base made of wood: *a pair of clogs*

clone /kloʊn/ *noun* [*count*]
(**BIOLOGY**) an exact copy of a plant or an animal, created from one of its cells
▶ **clone** *verb* (clones, clon·ing, cloned): *Scientists first cloned a sheep in 1996.*

close¹ /kloʊz/ *verb* (clos·es, clos·ing, closed)

ⓘ PRONUNCIATION
When the word **close** is a verb, it has a /z/ sound as in **grows** or **nose**.
When the word **close** is an adjective, it has a /s/ sound as in **dose**.

1 to shut: *Please close the window.* ◆ *Close your eyes!* ◆ *The door closed quietly.*
2 to stop being open, so that people cannot go there: *What time does the bank close?* ⊃ **ANTONYM open**
close down; close something down to stop all business at a store, factory, etc.: *The store*

closed down when the owner died. ◆ *Health inspectors closed the restaurant down.*

close² /kloʊs/ *adjective, adverb* (clos·er, clos·est)
1 near: *We live close to the train station.* ◆ *The photographer asked us to stand closer together* (= with less space between us).
2 If people are **close**, they know each other well and like each other very much: *I'm very close to my sister.* ◆ *John and I are close friends.*
3 (used about a competition or race) only won by a small amount: *a close game*
4 careful: *Take a close look at this picture.*
a close call a bad thing that almost happened: *I wasn't hurt, but it was a pretty close call.*
▶ **close·ly** /ˈkloʊsli/ *adverb*: *Paul entered, followed closely by Mike.* ◆ *We watched her closely* (= carefully).

closed /kloʊzd/ *adjective*
not open: *The store is closed on Sundays.* ◆ *Keep your eyes closed.* ⊃ **SYNONYM shut** ⊃ **ANTONYM open**

closed-cir·cuit tel·e·vi·sion /ˌkloʊzd ˌsərkət ˈtɛləvɪʒn/ *noun* [*noncount*] (abbreviation **CCTV**)
a type of television system with cameras in public places, used to prevent crime

clos·et /ˈklɑzət/ *noun* [*count*]
a space in a wall with a door that reaches the ground, used for storing clothes, shoes, etc.: *a walk-in closet*

clo·sure /ˈkloʊʒər/ *noun* [*count, noncount*]
the act of closing a business: *the closure of factories in Detroit*

clot /klɑt/ *noun* [*count*]
(**HEALTH**) a lump that forms when blood dries or gets thick: *a blood clot*
▶ **clot** *verb* (clots, clot·ting, clot·ted): *This medication stops blood from clotting.*

cloth /klɔθ/ *noun*
1 [*noncount*] material made of wool, cotton, etc. that you use for making clothes and other things ⊃ **SYNONYM fabric**
2 [*count*] a piece of **cloth** that you use for a special job: *Do you have a cloth I can use to wipe the floor with?* ⊃ Look at **tablecloth**, **washcloth**.

clothes /kloʊðz/ *noun* [*plural*]
things like pants, shirts, and dresses that you wear to cover your body: *She was wearing new clothes.* ◆ *Take off those wet clothes.*

Collocations

Clothes and appearance

clothes
- **be wearing** a new outfit/a uniform/jeans
- **wear** jewelry/a watch/glasses/contact lenses/perfume

clothes

jacket — tie — shirt — pocket — sleeve — belt — jeans — suit — pants

collar — blouse — skirt

dress

overcoat   jacket   sweater   T-shirt   shorts

- **put on/take off** your clothes/coat/shoes
- **change into** a pair of jeans/your pajamas
- be fashionably/well **dressed**
- be/get **dressed for** work/school/dinner

appearance

- **brush/comb** your hair
- **wash/shampoo/blow-dry** your hair
- **have/get** a haircut/your hair cut/a new hairstyle
- **have/get** a makeover/your nails done
- **use/wear/put on** makeup/cosmetics/lipstick

cloth·ing 🔊 /ˈkloʊðɪŋ/ *noun* [noncount]
clothes, especially a particular type of clothes: *You will need waterproof clothing.* ◆ *He checked the pockets of each piece of clothing before putting it in the washing machine.*

Which word?

Clothes or clothing?

- **Clothes** is a plural noun: *I need to buy some new clothes.* ◆ *Look at all these clothes!*
- **Clothing** is a more formal word for clothes, and can be used to talk about single items: *a piece of clothing* ◆ *an item of clothing.*

cloud 🔊 /klaʊd/ *noun*
1 [count, noncount] (GEOGRAPHY) a white or gray shape in the sky that is made of small drops of water: *Look at those dark clouds. It's going to rain.*
2 [count] a large collection of dust or smoke that looks like a **cloud**: *clouds of smoke*

cloud·y /ˈklaʊdi/ *adjective* (cloud·i·er, cloud·i·est)
If the weather is **cloudy**, the sky is full of clouds: *a cloudy day*

clove /kloʊv/ *noun* [count]
1 the small dried flower of a tree that grows in hot countries, used as a spice in cooking. **Cloves** look like small nails.
2 one of the small separate sections of GARLIC (= a vegetable of the onion family with a strong taste and smell, used in cooking): *Crush two cloves of garlic.* ⊃ Look at the picture at **garlic**.

clo·ver /ˈkloʊvər/ *noun* [count]
a small plant with leaves that usually have three parts to them: *Have you ever found a four-leaf clover?*

clown /klaʊn/ *noun* [count]
a person who wears funny clothes and a big red nose and does silly things to make people laugh

club 🔊 /klʌb/ *noun*
1 [count] a group of people who do something together, or the place where they meet: *to be a member of a club* ◆ *the school's chess club* ◆ *Do you belong to a country club?* (= where people play sports and go to social events)
2 [count] (also **nightclub** /ˈnaɪtklʌb/) a place where people go to listen to music, dance, etc.
3 [count] a heavy stick with one thick end, used as a weapon
4 [count] (SPORTS) a long thin stick that is used for hitting a ball when playing GOLF (= a game played on grass in which you hit a small ball into a number of holes) ⊃ Look at the note at **bat**[1].
5 **clubs** [plural] the group of playing cards (called a SUIT) that have the shape ♣ on them:

the three of clubs ⇒ Look at the picture at **playing card**.

club·bing /'klʌbɪŋ/ *noun* [*noncount*]
the activity of going out to places called CLUBS or NIGHTCLUBS, where you can listen to music and dance at night: *They go clubbing every Saturday night.*

club so·da /ˌklʌb 'soʊdə/ *noun* [*noncount*]
water with bubbles in it ⇒ SYNONYM **soda water**

clue /klu/ *noun* [*count*]
something that helps to find the answer to a problem, or to know the truth: *The police are looking for clues to help them find the missing man.* ⇒ Look at the picture at **crossword puzzle**.
have no clue (*informal*) to know nothing about something: *"What's his name?" "I have no clue."*

clum·sy /'klʌmzi/ *adjective* (**clum·si·er**, **clum·si·est**)
If you are **clumsy**, you often drop things or do things badly because you do not move in an easy or careful way: *I just broke another glass. I'm so clumsy!*
▸ **clum·si·ly** /'klʌmzəli/ *adverb*: *He clumsily knocked the cup off the table.*

clung form of **cling**

clus·ter /'klʌstər/ *noun* [*count*]
a group of people or things that are close together: *a cluster of grapes*

clutch¹ /klʌtʃ/ *verb* (**clutch·es**, **clutch·ing**, **clutched**)
to hold something tight: *The boy clutched his mother's hand.* ⇒ SYNONYM **grip**

clutch² /klʌtʃ/ *noun* [*count*] (*plural* **clutch·es**)
(in some vehicles) the part that your foot presses while your hand moves the stick that changes the engine speed

clut·ter /'klʌtər/ *noun* [*noncount*]
things that are where they are not wanted or needed, and which make a place messy: *I can't stand all this clutter!*
▸ **clut·tered** /'klʌtərd/ *adjective*: *a cluttered desk*

cm abbreviation of **centimeter**

Co. /koʊ/ abbreviation of **company**(1)

c/o /ˌsi 'oʊ/ *abbreviation*
You use **c/o** (short for CARE OF) when you are writing to someone who is staying at another person's house: *Ms. S. Garcia, c/o Mr. Michael Nolan*

coach¹ /koʊtʃ/ *noun* (*plural* **coach·es**)
1 [*count*] (**SPORTS**) a person who trains a person or team in a sport: *a baseball coach*
2 [*noncount*] the cheapest type of seats on an airplane: *I used to fly business class for work, but now I fly coach.*

coach² /koʊtʃ/ *verb* (**coach·es**, **coach·ing**, **coached**)
to teach someone to play a sport or do something better: *She is coaching the Olympic volleyball team.*

coal /koʊl/ *noun* [*noncount*]
a hard black substance that comes from under the ground and gives out heat when you burn it: *a coal mine*

coarse /kɔrs/ *adjective* (**coars·er**, **coars·est**)
made of thick pieces so that it is not smooth: *coarse salt • coarse material* ⇒ ANTONYM **fine**

coast 🔑 /koʊst/ *noun* [*count*]
(**GEOGRAPHY**) the part of the land that is next to the ocean: *We drove along the coast. • They reported seeing sharks just off the coast.*

Culture

- The area of the United States next to the Pacific Ocean is called the **West Coast**.
- The area next to the Atlantic Ocean is called the **East Coast**: *They live on the West Coast. • Boston and other East Coast cities.*

coast·al /'koʊstl/ *adjective*
(**GEOGRAPHY**) at or near a coast: *coastal areas*

the Coast Guard /ðə 'koʊst ɡɑrd/ *noun* [*count*]
an organization that watches people's activities on the ocean and helps people or ships who are in danger

coast·line /'koʊstlaɪn/ *noun* [*count*]
(**GEOGRAPHY**) the edge of the land next to the ocean: *a rocky coastline*

coat¹ 🔑 /koʊt/ *noun* [*count*]
1 a piece of clothing that you wear over your other clothes when you are outside: *Put your coat on – it's cold today.*
2 the hair or fur that covers an animal: *a dog with a smooth coat*
3 a layer of something that covers a surface: *a coat of paint*

coat² /koʊt/ *verb* (**coats**, **coat·ing**, **coat·ed**)
to put a thin covering of something over another thing: *Their shoes were coated with mud.*

coat hang·er /'koʊt ˌhæŋər/ *noun* [*count*]
another word for **hanger**

cob·web /'kɑbwɛb/ *noun* [*count*]
a net, especially one that is old and full of dust, that a spider made to catch insects

cock·pit /'kɑkpɪt/ *noun* [*count*]
the part of an airplane where the pilot sits

cock·roach /'kɑkroʊtʃ/ *noun* [*count*] (*plural* **cock·roach·es**) (also *informal* **roach**)
a large brown insect that you find in houses, especially dirty ones

cock·tail /ˈkɑkteɪl/ *noun* [*count*]
a drink usually made of alcohol mixed with fruit juices or other types of drinks: *a cocktail party*

co·coa /ˈkoʊkoʊ/ *noun*
1 [*noncount*] a dark brown powder made from the seeds (called COCOA BEANS) of a tree that grows in hot countries. **Cocoa** is used in making chocolate.
2 [*count, noncount*] a drink of hot milk mixed with this powder: *a cup of cocoa*

co·co·nut /ˈkoʊkənʌt/ *noun* [*count*]
a large fruit that grows on trees in hot countries. **Coconuts** are brown and hard on the outside, and they have sweet white food and liquid inside.

coconuts

cod /kɑd/ *noun* [*count*]
(*plural* **cod**)
a large fish that lives in the ocean and that you can eat

code AWL /koʊd/ *noun*
1 [*count, noncount*] a way of writing secret messages, using letters, numbers, or special signs: *The list of names was written **in code**.*
2 [*count*] a group of numbers or letters that helps you find something: *a bar code* (= a pattern of lines printed on things that you buy, that a computer can read) ⊃ Look at **area code**, **zip code**.
3 [*count*] a set of rules for a group of people: *Does your school have a dress code* (= a set of rules about what you are allowed to wear)*?*

cof·fee /ˈkɔfi/ *noun*
1 [*noncount*] a brown powder made from the seeds (called COFFEE BEANS) of a tree that grows in hot countries. You use it for making a drink.
2 [*noncount*] a drink made by adding hot water to this powder: *Would you like coffee or tea?* ◆ *a cup of coffee*
3 [*count*] a cup of this drink: *Two large coffees, please.*

Word building

■ **Black** coffee has no milk in it.
■ **Decaffeinated** coffee, also called **decaf**, has had the caffeine taken out.

cof·fee shop /ˈkɔfi ʃɑp/ *noun* [*count*]
a small, informal restaurant that serves cheap meals, coffee, and other drinks

cof·fee ta·ble /ˈkɔfi ˌteɪbl/ *noun* [*count*]
a small, low table that you put magazines, cups, or other similar things on

cof·fin /ˈkɔfən/ *noun* [*count*]
a box that a dead person's body is put in

co·her·ent AWL /koʊˈhɪrənt/ *adjective*
clear, organized, and easy to understand: *a coherent argument* ⊃ ANTONYM **incoherent**
▶ **co·her·ent·ly** AWL /koʊˈhɪrəntli/ *adverb*

coil¹ /kɔɪl/ *verb* (coils, coil·ing, coiled)
to make something into a lot of circles that are joined together: *The snake coiled itself around a branch.*

coil² /kɔɪl/ *noun* [*count*]
a long piece of rope or wire that goes around in circles: *a coil of rope*

coin 🔑 /kɔɪn/ *noun* [*count*]
a piece of money made of metal: *The soda machine takes both bills and coins.* ⊃ Look at the picture at **money**.

co·in·cide AWL /ˌkoʊɪnˈsaɪd/ *verb* (co·in·cides, co·in·cid·ing, co·in·cid·ed)
1 to happen at the same time as something else: *My trip to Cape Cod coincided with the president's visit.*
2 to be the same or very similar: *Our views coincide completely.*

co·in·ci·dence AWL /koʊˈɪnsədəns/ *noun* [*count*]
two or more similar things happening at the same time or in the same place by chance, in a surprising way: *What a coincidence! I was just thinking about you when you called!*

co·in·ci·den·tal AWL /koʊˌɪnsəˈdɛntl/ *adjective*
happening by chance; not planned

co·la /ˈkoʊlə/ *noun* [*count, noncount*]
a sweet brown drink with bubbles in it

cold¹ 🔑 /koʊld/ *adjective* (cold·er, cold·est)
1 not hot or warm; with a low temperature: *Put your coat on – it's cold outside.* ◆ *I'm cold. Will you turn up the heat?* ◆ *hot and cold water* ⊃ ANTONYM **hot**
2 not friendly or kind: *She gave him a cold, hard look.*
▶ **cold·ly** /ˈkoʊldli/ *adverb*: *She looked at me coldly.*

Thesaurus

cold with a temperature that is lower than usual or lower than the human body; (used about food or drink) not heated: *I'm not going into the lake – the water's too cold.* ◆ *Should I turn the heat on? I'm cold.* ◆ *to look/ feel cold* ◆ *Would you like a cold drink?* ◆ *We're having cold chicken for lunch.*

cool (used especially about the weather) a little cold, often in a pleasant way: *It's hot outside but it's nice and cool in here.* ◆ *a cool breeze* (= a light wind) ◆ *Let's sit in the shade and keep cool.*

tʃ **ch**in   dʒ **J**une   v **v**an   θ **th**in   ð **th**en   s **s**o   z **z**oo   ʃ **sh**e

freezing (*informal*) (used about the temperature or people) extremely cold: *It's freezing outside.* • *freezing temperatures* • *I'm freezing! Close the window!* • *freezing cold weather* ⊃ ANTONYM **boiling**

chilly (used especially about the weather) too cold to be comfortable: *a chilly morning in November* • *Bring a coat. It might get chilly later.* • *She was beginning to feel chilly.*

cold² /koʊld/ *noun*
1 [*noncount*] cold weather: *Don't go out in the cold.*
2 [*count*] (**HEALTH**) a common illness of the nose and throat. When you have a **cold**, you often cannot breathe through your nose and your throat hurts: *I think I'm getting a cold.* • *Come in out of the rain, or you'll catch a cold.*

cold-blood·ed /ˌkoʊld ˈblʌdəd/ *adjective*
(**BIOLOGY**) having a body temperature that changes with the temperature of the air: *Reptiles are cold-blooded.* ⊃ Look at **warm-blooded**.

col·lapse **AWL** /kəˈlæps/ *verb* (col·laps·es, col·laps·ing, col·lapsed)
1 to fall down suddenly: *The building collapsed in the earthquake.* • *She collapsed in the street and was rushed to hospital.*
2 to fail suddenly and completely: *The economy collapsed, leaving thousands of people out of work.*
▶ **col·lapse** **AWL** *noun* [*count, noncount*]: *the collapse of the bridge* • *the economic collapse*

col·lar /ˈkɑlər/ *noun* [*count*]
1 the part of your clothes that goes around your neck ⊃ Look at the picture at **clothes**.
2 a band that you put around the neck of a dog or cat ⊃ Look at **blue-collar, white-collar**.

col·league **AWL** /ˈkɑlig/ *noun* [*count*]
a person who works with you

col·lect¹ /kəˈlɛkt/ *verb* (col·lect, col·lect·ing, col·lect·ed)
1 to take things from different people or places and put them together: *The teacher will collect the test booklets at the end of the exam.*
2 to bring together things that are the same in some way, in order to study or enjoy them: *My son collects stamps.*

col·lect² /kəˈlɛkt/ *adjective, adverb*
(used about a telephone call) to be paid for by the person who receives the call: *a collect call* • *I called my parents collect from Toronto.*

col·lec·tion /kəˈlɛkʃn/ *noun*
1 [*count*] a group of similar things that someone has brought together: *The Art Institute of Chicago has a large collection of modern paintings.* • *a music collection*

2 [*count, noncount*] taking something from a place or from people: *garbage collection*

col·lec·tor /kəˈlɛktər/ *noun* [*count*]
a person who collects things: *a stamp collector* • *a tax collector*

col·lege /ˈkɑlɪdʒ/ *noun*
1 [*count, noncount*] a place where you can go to study after you have finished high school: *She's going to college next year.* • *My brother is in college.* • *an art college* ⊃ Look at the note at **higher education, university**.
2 [*count*] a main division of a university: *The history department is part of the College of Arts and Sciences.*

col·lide /kəˈlaɪd/ *verb* (col·lides, col·lid·ing, col·lid·ed)
to move fast toward someone or something, and hit them hard: *The two trucks collided.* • *He ran along the corridor and collided with his teacher.* ⊃ SYNONYM **crash**

col·li·sion /kəˈlɪʒn/ *noun* [*count*]
when things or people COLLIDE: *The driver of the car was killed in the collision.* ⊃ SYNONYM **crash**

col·lo·ca·tion /ˌkɑləˈkeɪʃn/ *noun* [*count*]
(**ENGLISH LANGUAGE ARTS**) a combination of words that people use very often: *"Burst into tears" and "take a walk" are English collocations.*

co·logne /kəˈloʊn/ *noun* [*count, noncount*]
a liquid that you put on your body to make yourself smell nice: *Do you ever wear cologne?* • *a selection of men's colognes*

co·lon /ˈkoʊlən/ *noun* [*count*]
1 (**ENGLISH LANGUAGE ARTS**) the mark (:) that you use in writing, for example before a list
2 (**BIOLOGY**) the large tube inside your body below your stomach, which carries waste out of your body

colo·nel /ˈkərnl/ *noun* [*count*]
an officer of a high level in the army

co·lo·ni·al /kəˈloʊniəl/ *adjective* (**HISTORY**)
1 connected with or being part of a COLONY: *Spain used to be a major colonial power.*
2 connected with the U.S. at the time when it was still a British COLONY: *people who lived in colonial times*

col·o·nize /ˈkɑlənaɪz/ *verb* (col·o·niz·es, col·o·niz·ing, col·o·nized)
(**POLITICS**) to take control of another country or place and make it a COLONY
▶ **col·o·ni·za·tion** /ˌkɑlənəˈzeɪʃn/ *noun* [*noncount*]: *the colonization of Latin America by Spain and Portugal*

col·o·ny /ˈkɑləni/ *noun* [*count*] (*plural* col·o·nies)
(**POLITICS**) a country or an area that is ruled by another country: *the 13 original colonies (= that*

used to be ruled by Britain, and are now part of the United States)

col·or¹ 🔊 /'kʌlər/ *noun* [*count, noncount*]
Red, blue, yellow, and green are all **colors**: *"What color are your new shoes?" "Black."* ♦ *The leaves change color in the fall.*
...of color A person, man, or woman **of color** does not have white skin.

🛈 **STYLE**
Some words that we use to talk about color are **light, pale, dark, deep,** and **bright**.

col·or² /'kʌlər/ *verb* (**col·ors, col·or·ing, col·ored**)
to put color on something using pens, pencils, etc.: *The kids colored their pictures with crayons.*

col·or-blind /'kʌlər ˌblaɪnd/ (also **col·or·blind**) *adjective*
(**BIOLOGY**) not able to see the difference between some colors, especially red and green

col·ored /'kʌlərd/ *adjective*
having a particular color or different colors: *She was wearing a brightly colored sweater.* ♦ *colored paper*

col·or·ful /'kʌlərfl/ *adjective*
with a lot of bright colors: *a colorful dress*

col·or·ing /'kʌlərɪŋ/ *noun*
1 [*noncount*] the colors of an animal or of a person's hair, skin, etc.: *You can tell that it's a male bird by its bright red coloring.*
2 [*count, noncount*] a substance that is used to give a color to food: *We used green food coloring for the frosting.*

col·or·less /'kʌlərləs/ *adjective*
without color: *a colorless liquid*

col·umn 🔊 /'kɑləm/ *noun* [*count*]
1 a tall solid piece of stone that supports part of a building
2 a long thin section of writing on one side or part of a page: *Each page of this dictionary has two columns.*
3 a piece of writing by a particular writer, which is published regularly in a newspaper, magazine, etc.: *She writes a weekly column for the local paper.*

co·ma /'koʊmə/ *noun* [*count*] (*plural* **co·mas**)
(**HEALTH**) a state like a very deep sleep, which often lasts for a long time and is caused by a serious illness or injury: *She was in a coma for several days after the accident.*

comb¹ /koʊm/ *noun*
[*count*]
a flat piece of metal or
plastic with thin parts
like teeth. You use it
to make your hair neat.

comb

comb² /koʊm/ *verb* (**combs, comb·ing, combed**)
to make your hair neat with a **comb**: *Have you combed your hair?*

com·bat /'kɑmbæt/ *noun* [*noncount*]
fighting, especially in a war: *Two soldiers were killed in combat yesterday.*

com·bi·na·tion 🔊 /ˌkɑmbə'neɪʃn/ *noun* [*count, noncount*]
two or more things joined together: *The building is a combination of new and old styles.* ⊃
SYNONYM mixture

com·bine 🔊 /kəm'baɪn/ *verb* (**com·bined, com·bin·ing, com·bined**)
to join; to mix two or more things together: *The two schools combined and moved to a larger building.*

come 🔊 /kʌm/ *verb* (**comes, com·ing, came** /keɪm/, **has come**)
1 to move toward the person who is speaking or the place that you are talking about: *Come here, please.* ♦ *The dog came when I called him.* ♦ *Here comes Matt* (= Matt is coming). ♦ *I'm sorry, but I can't come to your party.*
2 to arrive at or reach a place: *If you follow that path, you will come to the river.* ♦ *A letter came for you this morning.*
3 to go somewhere with the person who is speaking: *I'm going to a party tonight. Do you want to come with me?*
4 to be in a particular position: *June comes after May.*
5 to be available: *Does this shirt come in a size large?*
come about to happen: *How did this situation come about?*
come across something to find something when you are not looking for it: *I came across these old photos yesterday.*
come along to go somewhere with someone: *I'm going to the mall. Do you want to come along?*
come apart to break into pieces: *This old coat is coming apart.*
come back to return: *What time will you be coming back?*
come down to fall or become lower: *The price of oil is coming down.*
come down with something to get an illness: *I think I'm coming down with a cold.*
come from somewhere or **something**
1 The place that you **come from** is where you were born or where you live: *I come from Texas.* ♦ *Where do you come from?*
2 to be made from something or produced somewhere: *Wool comes from sheep.*
come in to enter a place: *Come in and sit down.*
come off something to become removed from something: *The handle has come off this cup.*

come on! words that you use for telling someone to hurry or to try harder: *Come on! We'll be late!*

come out to appear: *The rain stopped and the sun came out.* ◆ *His first novel came out in 2004.*

come over to visit a person in their house not very far away: *Can you come over for dinner tomorrow night?*

come up
1 to happen: *I'm going to be late tonight – something's come up at work.*
2 to be mentioned or discussed: *The subject of religion came up.*

come up with something to find an answer or a solution to something: *I'm trying to come up with new ways of saving money.*

how come …? (*informal*) why…?: *How come you're here so early?*

to come in the future: *You'll regret it in years to come.*

come·back /ˈkʌmbæk/ *noun* [*count*]
a return to a strong or important position that you had before: *The former world champion is hoping to **make a comeback**.*

co·me·di·an /kəˈmidiən/ *noun* [*count*]
a person whose job is to make people laugh

com·e·dy /ˈkɑmədi/ *noun* [*count*] (*plural* **com·e·dies**)
a funny play or movie: *a romantic comedy*

com·et /ˈkɑmət/ *noun* [*count*]
a thing in the sky that moves around the sun. A **comet** looks like a bright star with a tail.

com·fort¹ /ˈkʌmfərt/ *noun*
1 [*noncount*] having everything your body needs; being without pain or problems: *They have enough money to live **in comfort**.*
2 [*count*] a person or thing that helps you or makes life better: *Her children were a **comfort to** her when she was sick.*

com·fort² /ˈkʌmfərt/ *verb* (**com·forts**, **com·fort·ing**, **com·fort·ed**)
to make someone feel less unhappy or worried: *A mother was comforting her crying son.*

com·fort·a·ble /ˈkʌmftərbl/ *adjective*
1 nice to sit in, to be in, or to wear: *This is a very comfortable bed.* ◆ *comfortable shoes*
2 physically relaxed; without pain or fear that something bad will happen: *Sit down and **make yourself comfortable**.* ◆ *Are you **comfortable with** letting him stay in your house while you're away?*
⊃ ANTONYM **uncomfortable**
▶ **com·fort·a·bly** /ˈkʌmftərbli/ *adverb*: *If you're all sitting comfortably, then I'll begin.*

com·ic¹ /ˈkɑmɪk/ (also **com·i·cal** /ˈkɑmɪkl/) *adjective*
funny: *a comic scene in a play*

com·ic² /ˈkɑmɪk/ *noun* (also **com·ic book** /ˈkɑmɪk bʊk/) [*count*]
a magazine for children, with pictures that tell a story

com·ma /ˈkɑmə/ *noun* [*count*] (*plural* **com·mas**)
(**ENGLISH LANGUAGE ARTS**) a mark (,) that you use in writing to separate parts of a sentence or things in a list

com·mand¹ /kəˈmænd/ *noun*
1 [*count*] words that tell you that you must do something: *The soldiers must obey their general's commands.* ⊃ SYNONYM **order**
2 [*count*] (**COMPUTERS**) an instruction to a computer to do something: *Use the Find command to look for a word in the file.*
3 [*noncount*] the power to tell people what to do: *Who is **in command of** this ship?* ⊃ SYNONYM **control**

com·mand² /kəˈmænd/ *verb* (**com·mands**, **com·mand·ing**, **com·mand·ed**)
to tell someone that they must do something: *He **commanded** us **to** leave immediately.* ⊃ SYNONYM **order**

com·mem·o·rate /kəˈmɛməreɪt/ *verb* (**com·mem·o·rates**, **com·mem·o·rat·ing**, **com·mem·o·rat·ed**)
to make people remember a special event: *a concert to commemorate the anniversary of his death*

com·ment¹ **AWL** /ˈkɑmɛnt/ *noun* [*count, noncount*]
something that you say that shows what you think about something: *She **made** some interesting **comments** about the book.*
no comment words that people say when they do not want to answer a question or say anything at all: *"Senator, how do you respond to these accusations?" "No comment."*

com·ment² **AWL** /ˈkɑmɛnt/ *verb* (**com·ments**, **com·ment·ing**, **com·ment·ed**)
to say what you think about something: *A lot of people at school **commented on** my new watch.*

com·men·tar·y **AWL** /ˈkɑmənˌtɛri/ *noun* [*count, noncount*] (*plural* **com·men·tar·ies**)
when someone describes an event while it is happening, especially on the radio or television: *a sports commentary*

com·men·ta·tor **AWL** /ˈkɑmənteɪtər/ *noun* [*count*]
a person who gives a COMMENTARY on the radio or television

com·merce /ˈkɑmərs/ *noun* [*noncount*]
(**BUSINESS**) the business of buying and selling things

com·mer·cial¹ /kə'mərʃl/ *adjective*
1 connected with buying and selling things: *commercial law*
2 (**BUSINESS**) making a profit: *His last movie was not a commercial success* (= it did not make any money).

com·mer·cial² /kə'mərʃl/ *noun* [*count*]
an advertisement on the television or radio

com·mis·sion **AWL** /kə'mɪʃn/ *noun*
1 [*count*] an official group of people who are in charge of something: *the Federal Trade Commission*
2 [*count, noncount*] (**BUSINESS**) money that you get for selling something: *He earns a 10% commission for every insurance product he sells.*

com·mit **AWL** /kə'mɪt/ *verb* (com·mits, com·mit·ting, com·mit·ted)
to do something bad: *This man has* **committed** *a very serious* **crime**.

com·mit·ment **AWL** /kə'mɪtmənt/ *noun*
1 [*count*] a promise to do something: *When I make a commitment, I always stick to it.*
2 [*noncount*] being prepared to give a lot of your time and attention to something: *I admire his commitment to his work.*

com·mit·ted **AWL** /kə'mɪtəd/ *adjective*
prepared to give a lot of your time and attention to something: *We are* **committed to** *raising standards in schools.*

com·mit·tee /kə'mɪti/ *noun* [*count*]

> **ℹ SPELLING**
> Remember! You spell **committee** with **MM**, **TT**, and **EE**.

a group of people that other people choose to discuss or decide something: *She's* **on the** *planning* **committee**.

com·mon¹ /'kɑmən/ *adjective* (com·mon·er, com·mon·est)
1 happening often or found in many places: *Back pain is a common medical problem.* ⟳
ANTONYM rare
2 shared by two or more people, or by everyone in a group: *They share a common interest in photography.*

com·mon² /'kɑmən/ *noun*
have something in common to be like someone in a certain way, or to have the same interests as someone: *Paul and I are good friends. We have a lot in common.*

com·mon sense /ˌkɑmən 'sɛns/ *noun*
[*noncount*]
the ability to think about things and do the right thing based on your experience: *If you aren't sure how to handle the situation, just use your common sense.*

com·mu·ni·cate **AWL** /kə'myunəkeɪt/ *verb* (com·mu·ni·cates, com·mu·ni·cat·ing, com·mu·ni·cat·ed)
to share and exchange information, ideas, or feelings with someone: *Parents often find it difficult to* **communicate with** *their children.* ⟳ Look at the note at **talk¹**.

com·mu·ni·ca·tion **AWL** /kəˌmyunə'keɪʃn/ *noun*
1 [*noncount*] sharing or exchanging information, feelings, or ideas with someone: *Communication is difficult when two people don't speak the same language.*
2 communications [*plural*] ways of sending or receiving information, especially telephones, radio, computers, etc.: *a communications satellite*

com·mu·nism /'kɑmyənɪzəm/ *noun* [*noncount*]
(**POLITICS**) the political system in which the government owns and controls all factories, farms, etc. and everyone is equal ⟳ Look at **capitalism, socialism**.
▶ **com·mu·nist** /'kɑmyənɪst/ *adjective, noun* [*count*]: *a communist country*

com·mu·ni·ty **AWL** /kə'myunəti/ *noun* (plural com·mu·ni·ties)
1 the community [*singular*] all the people who live in a place; the place where they live: *The mayor discussed how to reduce crime in the community.*
2 [*count*] a group of people who join together, for example because they have the same interests or religion: *the Jewish community in New York*

com·mu·ni·ty col·lege /kə'myunəti ˌkɑlɪdʒ/ *noun* [*count*]
a college near where you live, where you can learn a skill or prepare for another college or university ⟳ Look at **junior college**.

com·mute /kə'myut/ *verb* (com·mutes, com·mut·ing, com·mut·ed)
to travel a long way from home to work every day: *She lives in New Jersey and commutes to New York.*
▶ **com·mut·er** /kə'myutər/ *noun* [*count*]
a person who **commutes**

com·pact /'kɑmpækt; kəm'pækt/ *adjective*
small, or smaller than usual: *a compact car*

com·pact disc /ˌkɑmpækt 'dɪsk/ *noun* [*count*]
= CD

com·pan·ion /kəm'pænyən/ *noun* [*count*]
a person or animal that travels with you or spends time with you

com·pa·ny /'kʌmpəni/ *noun* (plural com·pa·nies)
1 [*count*] (**BUSINESS**) a group of people who work together to make or sell things: *an advertising company* • *the Student Loans Company* ⟳ The

short way of writing "Company" in names is Co.: *Milton and Co.*

2 [*noncount*] being with a person or people: *I always enjoy Mark's company.*

keep someone company to be or go with someone: *Please stay and keep me company for a while.*

com·pa·ra·ble /ˈkɑmpərəbl/ *adjective*
similar in size or quality to something else: *Salaries here are **comparable to** salaries paid by other companies.*

com·par·a·tive /kəmˈpærəṭɪv/ *noun* [*count*]
(**ENGLISH LANGUAGE ARTS**) the form of an adjective or adverb that shows more of something: *The comparative of "bad" is "worse."*
▸ **com·par·a·tive** *adjective*: *"Longer" is the comparative form of "long."* ⊃ Look at **superlative**.

com·pare 🔑 /kəmˈpɛr/ *verb* (com·pares, com·par·ing, com·pared)
to think about or look at people or things together so that you can see how they are different: *Compared to the place where I grew up, this place is exciting.* ◆ *Write an essay that compares and contrasts the teachings of Martin Luther King and Malcolm X.* ◆ *Compare your answers with your neighbor's.*

com·par·i·son 🔑 /kəmˈpærəsn/ *noun* [*count, noncount*]
looking at or understanding how things are different or the same: *It's hard to **make comparisons** between athletes from different sports.*

by or **in comparison** when you compare two or more people or things: *In comparison with many other people, they're rich.*

com·part·ment /kəmˈpɑrtmənt/ *noun* [*count*]
a separate part inside a box, bag, or other container: *The suitcase had a secret compartment at the back.*

compass

north
northwest   northeast
west   east
southwest   southeast
south

com·pass /ˈkʌmpəs/ *noun* [*count*] (*plural* com·pass·es)
1 (**GEOGRAPHY**) a thing for finding direction, with a needle that always points north: *You need a map and a compass.*

2 (**MATH**) an instrument with two long thin parts joined together at the top that is used for drawing circles: *Use a compass to draw a circle with a radius of two inches.*

com·pas·sion /kəmˈpæʃn/ *noun* [*noncount*]
the strong feeling that you have when you understand and feel sorry for someone who is suffering: *to have compassion for the victims of a crime*

com·pat·i·ble **AWL** /kəmˈpæṭəbl/ *adjective*
able to exist or be used together: *Is this software **compatible with** my computer?*
▸ **com·pat·i·bil·i·ty** **AWL** /kəmˌpæṭəˈbɪləṭi/ *noun* [*noncount*]

com·pen·sate **AWL** /ˈkɑmpənseɪt/ *verb* (com·pen·sates, com·pen·sat·ing, com·pen·sat·ed)
1 to take away the bad effect of something, or make it smaller: *She **compensated for** her lack of experience by working hard.*
2 to pay someone money because you have injured them or lost or damaged their property: *The airline compensated passengers for their lost luggage.*

com·pen·sa·tion **AWL** /ˌkɑmpənˈseɪʃn/ *noun* [*noncount*]
money that you pay someone, especially because you have injured them or damaged their property: *I got $10,000 **in compensation** for my injuries.*

com·pete /kəmˈpit/ *verb* (com·petes, com·pet·ing, com·pet·ed)
to try to win a race or a competition: *The world's best athletes compete in the Olympic Games.*

com·pe·tent /ˈkɑmpəṭənt/ *adjective*
having the ability or skill for something: *She's a very competent teacher.*
▸ **com·pe·tent·ly** /ˈkɑmpəṭəntli/ *adverb*

com·pe·ti·tion 🔑 /ˌkɑmpəˈtɪʃn/ *noun*
1 [*count*] a game or test that people try to win: *I entered the painting competition and won first prize.*
2 [*noncount*] trying to win or be better than someone else: *We were **in competition with** a team from another school.*

com·pet·i·tive /kəmˈpɛṭəṭɪv/ *adjective*
1 in which people or organizations COMPETE against each other: *competitive sports*
2 wanting to win or be better than other people: *She's very competitive.*

com·pet·i·tor /kəmˈpɛṭəṭər/ *noun* [*count*]
a person, company, product, etc. that is COMPETING against others

com·plain /kəmˈpleɪn/ *verb* (com·plains, com·plain·ing, com·plained)
to say that you do not like something or that you are unhappy about something: *She is always complaining about the weather.* • *He complained to the waiter that his soup was cold.*

com·plaint /kəmˈpleɪnt/ *noun* [*count*]
when you say that you do not like something: *We made a complaint to the hotel manager about the dirty rooms.*

com·plete¹ /kəmˈplit/ *adjective*
1 with none of its parts missing: *I own a complete set of Shakespeare's plays.* ⊃ SYNONYM whole ⊃ ANTONYM incomplete
2 in every way: *Their visit was a complete surprise.* ⊃ SYNONYM total
3 finished: *The work is complete.* ⊃ ANTONYM incomplete

com·plete² /kəmˈplit/ *verb* (com·pletes, com·plet·ing, com·plet·ed)
1 to finish doing or making something: *She went to college for three years but never completed her bachelor's degree.*
2 to write all the necessary information on something, for example a form: *Complete the following exercise using the table above.*

com·plete·ly /kəmˈplitli/ *adverb*
in every way: *The money has completely disappeared.* • *I completely forgot that it was your birthday!* ⊃ SYNONYM totally

com·plex¹ AWL /kəmˈplɛks/ *adjective*
difficult to understand because it has a lot of different parts: *a complex problem* ⊃ SYNONYM complicated ⊃ ANTONYM simple

com·plex² AWL /ˈkɑmplɛks/ *noun* [*count*] (*plural* com·plex·es)
a group of buildings: *a sports complex*

com·plex·ion /kəmˈplɛkʃn/ *noun* [*count*]
the natural color and quality or the skin on your face: *a healthy complexion*

com·pli·cat·ed /ˈkɑmpləˌkeɪtəd/ *adjective*
difficult to understand because it has a lot of different parts: *I can't explain how to play the game. It's too complicated.* ⊃ ANTONYM simple

com·pli·ca·tion /ˌkɑmpləˈkeɪʃn/ *noun* [*count*]
something that makes a situation more difficult

com·pli·ment /ˈkɑmpləmənt/ *noun* [*count*]
something nice that you say about someone: *She gets lots of compliments on her piano playing.*
▸ **com·pli·ment** /ˈkɑmpləmɛnt/ *verb* (com·pli·ments, com·pli·ment·ing, com·pli·ment·ed): *They complimented me on my cooking.*

com·po·nent AWL /kəmˈpoʊnənt/ *noun* [*count*]
one of the parts that form something: *computer components*

com·pose /kəmˈpoʊz/ *verb* (com·pos·es, com·pos·ing, com·posed)
(MUSIC) to write something, especially music: *Verdi composed many operas.*
be composed of something to be made or formed from different parts or people: *Water is composed of oxygen and hydrogen.*

com·pos·er /kəmˈpoʊzər/ *noun* [*count*]
(MUSIC) a person who writes music: *My favorite composer is Mozart.*

com·po·si·tion /ˌkɑmpəˈzɪʃn/ *noun* [*count*]
a piece of writing or music

com·post /ˈkɑmpoʊst/ *noun* [*noncount*]
a mixture of dead plants, old food, etc. that is added to soil to help plants grow: *a compost heap*

com·pound AWL /ˈkɑmpaʊnd/ *noun* [*count*]
1 (CHEMISTRY) something that is made of two or more parts: *Salt is a chemical compound.*
2 (ENGLISH LANGUAGE ARTS) a word that is made from two or more other words: *"Roommate" and "good-looking" are compounds.*
3 a closed area with a group of buildings inside it: *a prison compound*

com·pre·hen·sion /ˌkɑmprɪˈhɛnʃn/ *noun* [*count, noncount*]
understanding something that you hear or read: *a test in reading comprehension*

com·pre·hen·sive AWL /ˌkɑmprɪˈhɛnsɪv/ *adjective*
including everything or almost everything: *a comprehensive list of all the schools in the area*

com·prise AWL /kəmˈpraɪz/ *verb* (com·pris·es, com·pris·ing, com·prised)
to be made from two or more things; to have things as parts: *an association comprising local politicians and employers* ⊃ SYNONYM consist of something

com·pro·mise¹ /ˈkɑmprəmaɪz/ *noun* [*count, noncount*]
an agreement between people when each person gets part, but not all, of what they wanted: *After long talks, the workers and management reached a compromise.*

com·pro·mise² /ˈkɑmprəmaɪz/ *verb* (com·pro·mis·es, com·pro·mis·ing, com·pro·mised)
to accept less than you want, in order to reach an agreement: *There will be no peace agreement unless both sides are prepared to compromise.*

com·pul·so·ry /kəmˈpʌlsəri/ *adjective*
If something is **compulsory**, you must do it: *School is compulsory for all children between the ages of five and sixteen.* ⊃ ANTONYM optional

computer

screen | monitor

mouse

key

keyboard

com·put·er 🔑 **AWL** /kəm'pyut̬ər/ *noun* [*count*]
a machine that can store and find information, calculate amounts, and control other machines: *All the work is done **by computer**.* ◆ *He spends a lot of time **on the computer**, sending e-mails.* ◆ *a **computer program** (= information that tells a computer what to do)* ◆ *They played **computer games** after school.*

con¹ /kɑn/ *noun* [*count*]
1 a problem that makes something difficult or less good: *What are the **pros and cons** (= advantages and disadvantages) of buying a used car?* ⊃ SYNONYM **disadvantage**
2 (*informal*) a trick to get money from someone: *The e-mail about the investment opportunity is a total con.*

con² /kɑn/ *verb* (**cons, con·ning, conned**) (*informal*)
to trick or cheat someone, especially in order to get money: *He **conned** her **into** investing in a company that didn't really exist.*

con·ceal /kən'sil/ *verb* (**con·ceals, con·ceal·ing, con·cealed**) (*formal*)
to hide something: *They concealed the bomb in a suitcase.*

con·ceit·ed /kən'sit̬əd/ *adjective*
too proud of yourself and what you can do

con·ceive **AWL** /kən'siv/ *verb* (**con·ceives, con·ceiv·ing, con·ceived**)
1 (*formal*) to think of or imagine something: *He conceived the idea during his trip to Antarctica.*
2 (BIOLOGY) to get pregnant

con·cen·trate 🔑 **AWL** /'kɑnsntreɪt/ *verb* (**con·cen·trates, con·cen·trat·ing, con·cen·trat·ed**)
to give all your attention to something: *Stop looking out of the window and **concentrate on** your work!* ◆ *Be quiet and let him concentrate.*

con·cen·tra·tion **AWL** /ˌkɑnsn'treɪʃn/ *noun* [*noncount*]
the ability to give all your attention to something: *You need total concentration for this type of work.*

con·cept **AWL** /'kɑnsɛpt/ *noun* [*count*]
an idea, or a basic truth about something: *This course teaches the basic concepts of mathematics.* ◆ *It's hard to understand the concept of infinity.*

con·cern¹ /kən'sərn/ *verb* (**con·cerns, con·cern·ing, con·cerned**)
1 to be important or interesting to someone: *Please pay attention because this information concerns all of you.* ⊃ SYNONYM **affect**
2 to be about something: *The story concerns a young boy and his parents.*
3 to worry someone: *It concerns me that she is always late.*

con·cern² /kən'sərn/ *noun*
1 [*noncount*] a feeling of being worried: *There is a lot of concern about this problem.*
2 [*count*] something that is important or interesting to someone: *Her problems are not my concern.*

con·cerned /kən'sərnd/ *adjective*
worried about something: *They are very **concerned about** their son's health.*
as far as I am concerned in my personal opinion: *As far as I'm concerned, he can stay here as long as he wants.*

con·cern·ing /kən'sərnɪŋ/ *preposition* (*formal*)
about something: *He asked several questions concerning the future of the company.*

con·cert 🔑 /'kɑnsərt/ *noun* [*count*]
(MUSIC) a public performance of music: *a rock concert*

con·cise /kən'saɪs/ *adjective*
(ENGLISH LANGUAGE ARTS) giving a lot of information in a few words: *His summary was clear and concise.*

con·clude **AWL** /kən'klud/ *verb* (**con·cludes, con·clud·ing, con·clud·ed**)
1 to decide something, after you have studied or thought about it: *The report **concluded that** the working conditions were unsafe.*
2 (*formal*) to end or make something end: *The ambassador concluded his tour with a visit to a local hospital.* ◆ *I would like to **conclude by** thanking our guest speaker.*

con·clu·sion 🔑 **AWL** /kən'kluʒn/ *noun* [*count*]
1 what you believe or decide after thinking carefully about something: *We **came to the conclusion** that you were right all along.*
2 the end of something, for example a movie or a piece of writing: *Your essay should include a clear conclusion.*

con·crete /'kɑŋkrit/ *noun* [*noncount*]
a hard gray material used for building things: *a concrete floor*

con·cus·sion /kən'kʌʃn/ *noun* [count]
(**HEALTH**) an injury to the brain, caused by hitting your head: *She was taken to the hospital with a concussion.*

con·demn /kən'dɛm/ *verb* (con·demns, con·demn·ing, con·demned)
1 to say strongly that someone or something is very bad or wrong: *Many people condemned the government's decision.*
2 to say that someone must be punished in a certain way: *The murderer was condemned to death.* ⊃ **SYNONYM sentence**

con·den·sa·tion /ˌkɑndən'seɪʃn/ *noun* [noncount]
(**GENERAL SCIENCE**) small drops of liquid that form when warm air touches a cold surface: *condensation on the windows*

con·dense /kən'dɛns/ *verb* (con·dens·es, con·dens·ing, con·densed)
1 (**CHEMISTRY**) to change or make something change from a gas to a liquid
2 to make something smaller or shorter so that it fills less space: *We'll have to condense these three chapters into one.*

con·di·tion 🖉 /kən'dɪʃn/ *noun*
1 [noncount, singular] the state that someone or something is in: *The car was cheap and in good condition, so I bought it.*
2 conditions [plural] the situation in which people live, work, or do things: *The prisoners lived in terrible conditions.*
3 [count] something that must happen before another thing can happen: *One of the conditions of the job is that you agree to work on Saturdays.*
4 [count] (**HEALTH**) a medical problem that you have for a long time: *He has a heart condition.*
on the condition that… only if: *You can go to the party on the condition that you come home before midnight.*

con·di·tion·er /kən'dɪʃənər/ *noun* [count, noncount]
a substance that keeps something in good condition: *Use conditioner for dry hair.*

con·do·min·i·um /ˌkɑndə'mɪniəm/ *noun* [count] (also informal **con·do** /'kɑndoʊ/ plural con·dos)
an apartment or apartment building that is owned by the people who live in it

con·duct¹ AWL /kən'dʌkt/ *verb* (con·ducts, con·duct·ing, con·duct·ed)
1 to organize or do an activity: *They are going to conduct an experiment.*
2 (**MUSIC**) to stand in front of a group of musicians and control what they do: *The orchestra was conducted by Peter Jones.*
3 (**PHYSICS, CHEMISTRY**) to allow heat or electricity to pass through something: *Rubber doesn't conduct electricity.*

con·duct² AWL /'kɑndʌkt/ *noun* [noncount] (formal)
the way someone behaves ⊃ **SYNONYM behavior**

con·duc·tor /kən'dʌktər/ *noun* [count]
1 (**MUSIC**) a person who stands in front of a group of musicians (called an **ORCHESTRA**) and controls what they do
2 a person who sells or checks people's tickets on a train

cone /koʊn/ *noun* [count]
1 (**MATH**) a shape with one flat round end and one pointed end: *an orange traffic cone* ◆ *an ice cream cone* ⊃ Look at the picture at **solid.**
2 the hard fruit of some trees (called **PINE** and **FIR**): *a pine cone*

con·fer·ence AWL /'kɑnfrəns/ *noun* [count]
a large meeting, where many people with the same job or interests come together to discuss their views: *an international conference on climate change*

con·fess /kən'fɛs/ *verb* (con·fess·es, con·fess·ing, con·fessed)
to say that you have done something wrong: *She confessed that she had stolen the money.* ◆ *He confessed to the crime.* ⊃ **SYNONYM admit** ⊃ **ANTONYM deny**

con·fes·sion /kən'fɛʃn/ *noun* [count]
when you say that you have done something wrong: *She made a full confession to the police.*

con·fide /kən'faɪd/ *verb* (con·fides, con·fid·ing, con·fid·ed)
confide in someone to talk to someone about something secret or private, because you trust them: *He confided in his brother.*

con·fi·dence 🖉 /'kɑnfədəns/ *noun* [noncount]
the feeling that you can do something well: *She answered the questions with confidence.* ◆ *I'm sure you'll pass the test. I have great confidence in you.*
in confidence If someone tells you something in confidence, it is a secret.

con·fi·dent 🖉 /'kɑnfədənt/ *adjective*
sure that you can do something well, or that something will happen: *I'm confident that our team will win.*
▶ **con·fi·dent·ly** /'kɑnfədəntli/ *adverb*: *She walked confidently to the front of the class.*

con·fi·den·tial /ˌkɑnfə'dɛnʃl/ *adjective*
If someone tells you something that is confidential, you should keep it a secret and not tell other people: *confidential information*

con·firm AWL /kən'fərm/ *verb* (con·firms, con·firm·ing, con·firmed)
to say that something is true or that something will happen: *Please write and confirm the date of your arrival.*

con·fir·ma·tion AWL /ˌkɑnfərˈmeɪʃn/ *noun*
[*noncount*]
saying that something is true or will definitely
happen

con·fis·cate /ˈkɑnfəskeɪt/ *verb* (con·fis·cates,
con·fis·cat·ing, con·fis·cat·ed)
to officially take something away from someone
as a punishment: *We will confiscate any cell
phones used inside the school building.*

con·flict¹ AWL /ˈkɑnflɪkt/ *noun* [*count, noncount*]
a fight or an argument

con·flict² AWL /kənˈflɪkt/ *verb* (con·flicts,
con·flict·ing, con·flict·ed)
to disagree or be different: *These results **conflict
with** earlier research results.*

con·form AWL /kənˈfɔrm/ *verb* (con·forms,
con·form·ing, con·formed)
to behave in a way that other people and society
expect you to behave: *New students in the school
feel a lot of pressure to conform.*

con·front /kənˈfrʌnt/ *verb* (con·fronts,
con·front·ing, con·front·ed)
1 to think about something that is difficult or
unpleasant: *to confront a problem*
2 to stand in front of someone, for example
because you want to fight him or her: *The
protesters were confronted by riot police.*

con·fron·ta·tion /ˌkɑnfrənˈteɪʃn/ *noun* [*count,
noncount*]
a fight or an argument: *I want to avoid any
confrontation.*

con·fuse 🔊 /kənˈfyuz/ *verb* (con·fus·es,
con·fus·ing, con·fused)
1 to mix someone's ideas, so that they cannot
think clearly or understand: *They confused me
by asking so many questions.*
2 to think that one thing or person is another
thing or person: *I often **confuse** Lee **with** his
brother. They look so similar.*
▶ **con·fus·ing** /kənˈfyuzɪŋ/ *adjective*
difficult to understand: *This map is very
confusing.*

con·fused 🔊 /kənˈfyuzd/ *adjective*
not able to think clearly: *The waiter **got confused**
and brought everyone the wrong drink.*

con·fu·sion /kənˈfyuʒn/ *noun* [*noncount*]
not being able to think clearly or understand
something: *He looked at me **in confusion** when I
asked him a question.*

con·ges·tion /kənˈdʒɛstʃən/ *noun* [*noncount*]
(**HEALTH**) the state of being very full of
something: *severe traffic congestion* • *medicine
to relieve nasal congestion*
▶ **con·gest·ed** /kənˈdʒɛstəd/ *adjective*: *The
highway is always congested during rush hour.* • *I
have a bad cold and am completely congested.*

con·grat·u·late /kənˈɡrætʃəleɪt/ *verb*
(con·grat·u·lates, con·grat·u·lat·ing,
con·grat·u·lat·ed)
to tell someone that you are pleased about
something that they have done: *I congratulated
Sue **on** passing her exam.*

con·grat·u·la·tions /kənˌɡrætʃəˈleɪʃnz/ *noun*
[*plural*]
something you say to someone when you are
pleased about something they have done:
***Congratulations on** your new job!*

con·gre·ga·tion /ˌkɑŋɡrəˈɡeɪʃn/ *noun* [*count*]
(**RELIGION**) a group of people who attend a
particular church: *He has been a member of the
congregation for 20 years.*

Con·gress /ˈkɑŋɡrəs/ *noun* [*singular*]
(**POLITICS**) a group of people who make the laws
in the U.S. and some other countries: *He ran for
Congress* (= tried to win the election) *in 2008.* ⊃
Look at the note at **government**.

con·gress·man /ˈkɑŋɡrəsmən/ (also
con·gress·wom·an /ˈkɑŋɡrəsˌwʊmən/) *noun*
[*count*] (*plural* **con·gress·men** /ˈkɑŋɡrəsmən/,
con·gress·wom·en /ˈkɑŋɡrəsˌwɪmən/)
(**POLITICS**) a member of the U.S. Congress,
especially the House of Representatives ⊃ Look
at **senator**.

con·ju·gate /ˈkɑndʒəɡeɪt/ *verb* (con·ju·gates,
con·ju·gat·ing, con·ju·gat·ed)
(**ENGLISH LANGUAGE ARTS**) to give the different
forms of a verb: *Can you conjugate the verb "to
be"?*

con·junc·tion /kənˈdʒʌŋkʃn/ *noun* [*count*]
(**ENGLISH LANGUAGE ARTS**) a word that joins other
words or parts of a sentence: *"And," "or", and
"but" are conjunctions.*
in conjunction with someone or **something**
together with someone or something

con·nect 🔊 /kəˈnɛkt/ *verb* (con·nects,
con·nect·ing, con·nect·ed)
1 to join one thing to another thing: *This cord
connects the computer **to** the printer.* • *The suburb
is connected to the city by a new subway line.*
2 to have a connection with another person or
thing: *There is no evidence to connect her to the
crime.*

con·nec·tion 🔊 /kəˈnɛkʃn/ *noun* [*count*]
1 the way that one thing is joined or related to
another: *We had a bad connection on the phone,
so I couldn't hear him very well.* • *Is there a
connection between violence on TV and crime?*
2 a train, an airplane, or a bus that leaves a
place soon after another arrives, so that people
can change from one to the other: *The train was
late, so I **missed** my **connection**.*

---

in connection with something (*formal*) about something: *A man has been arrested in connection with the murder of the teenager.*

con·quer /ˈkɑŋkər/ *verb* (**con·quers, con·quer·ing, con·quered**)
(**POLITICS**) to take control of a country or city and its people by force: *The Spanish conquered the Incas in South America.*
▶ **con·quer·or** /ˈkɑŋkərər/ *noun* [*count*]

con·quest /ˈkɑŋkwɛst/ *noun* [*count, noncount*]
an act of taking control of land or people: *the conquest of South America*

con·science /ˈkɑnʃəns/ *noun* [*count, noncount*]
the feeling inside you about what is right and wrong: *He has a **guilty conscience** (= he feels that he has done something wrong).*

con·sci·en·tious /ˌkɑnʃiˈɛnʃəs/ *adjective*
careful to do things correctly and well: *She's a very conscientious student.*

con·scious /ˈkɑnʃəs/ *adjective*
1 If you are **conscious** of something, you know about it: *I was **conscious that** someone was watching me.* ⊃ **SYNONYM aware**
2 awake and able to see, hear, feel, and think: *The patient was conscious during the operation.* ⊃ **ANTONYM unconscious**
▶ **con·scious·ly** /ˈkɑnʃəsli/ *adverb*

con·scious·ness /ˈkɑnʃəsnəs/ *noun* [*noncount*]
the state of being able to see, hear, feel, and think: *As she fell, she hit her head and **lost consciousness**.*

con·sec·u·tive /kənˈsɛkyətɪv/ *adjective*
coming or happening one after the other: *This is the team's fourth consecutive win.*

con·sen·sus **AWL** /kənˈsɛnsəs/ *noun* [*singular, noncount*]
an agreement among all members of a group: *to **reach a consensus** • There is no consensus among experts about the causes of global warming.*

con·sent¹ **AWL** /kənˈsɛnt/ *noun* [*noncount*]
agreeing to let someone do something: *The girl's parents **gave** their **consent to** the operation.* ⊃ **SYNONYM permission**

con·sent² **AWL** /kənˈsɛnt/ *verb* (**con·sent, con·sent·ing, con·sent·ed**) (*formal*)
to agree to something: *He finally **consented to** his daughter's marriage.*

con·se·quence **AWL** /ˈkɑnsəkwɛns/ *noun* [*count*]
a result of something that has happened: *Their actions had terrible consequences. • My rent just went up, and **as a consequence**, I hardly have any money.*

con·se·quent·ly **AWL** /ˈkɑnsəkwɛntli/ *adverb*
because of that: *He didn't study enough, and consequently failed the test.* ⊃ **SYNONYM therefore**

con·ser·va·tion /ˌkɑnsərˈveɪʃn/ *noun* [*noncount*]
1 taking good care of the natural world: *the conservation of the rain forests*
2 not allowing something to be wasted, damaged, or destroyed: *energy conservation*
▶ **con·ser·va·tion·ist** /ˌkɑnsərˈveɪʃənɪst/ *noun* [*count*]
a person who believes in protecting the natural world

con·ser·va·tive /kənˈsərvətɪv/ *adjective*
1 not liking change or new ideas: *the conservative opinions of his parents* ⊃ **SYNONYM traditional**
2 (**POLITICS**) supporting a free market, low taxes, and old ideas about family, etc.: *conservative politicians* ⊃ **ANTONYM liberal**

con·serve /kənˈsərv/ *verb* (**con·serves, con·serv·ing, con·served**)
to avoid wasting something: *to conserve water*

con·si·der /kənˈsɪdər/ *verb* (**con·si·ders, con·si·der·ing, con·si·dered**)
1 to think carefully about something: *I'm considering applying for another job. • We must consider what to do next.*
2 to think that something is true: *I consider her to be a good teacher.*
3 to think about the feelings of other people when you do something: *I can't just quit my job! I have to consider my family.*

con·sid·er·a·ble **AWL** /kənˈsɪdərəbl/ *adjective* (*formal*)
great or large: *The car cost a considerable amount of money.*
▶ **con·sid·er·a·bly** **AWL** /kənˈsɪdərəbli/ *adverb*: *My apartment is considerably smaller than yours.*

con·sid·er·ate /kənˈsɪdərət/ *adjective*
A person who is **considerate** is kind, and thinks and cares about other people: *Please be more considerate and don't play loud music late at night.* ⊃ **ANTONYM inconsiderate**

con·sid·er·a·tion /kənˌsɪdəˈreɪʃn/ *noun* [*noncount*]
1 (*formal*) thinking carefully about something: *After a lot of consideration, I decided not to accept the job.* ⊃ **SYNONYM thought**
2 being kind, and caring about other people's feelings: *He shows no **consideration for** anyone else.*
take something into consideration to think carefully about something when you are deciding: *We must take the cost into consideration when planning our vacation.*

con·sid·er·ing /kən'sɪdərɪŋ/ *preposition, conjunction*
a word you use to show that a particular fact is important when you make a statement about something: *Considering you've only been studying for a year, you speak English very well.*

con·sist 🔑 **AWL** /kən'sɪst/ *verb* (con·sists, con·sist·ing, con·sist·ed)
consist of something to be made from two or more things; to have things as parts: *Pasta consists of flour and water.*

con·sist·en·cy **AWL** /kən'sɪstənsi/ *noun* (*plural* con·sist·en·cies)
1 [*noncount*] always having the same standard, opinions, behavior, etc.: *There doesn't seem to be any consistency in his work.*
2 [*count, noncount*] how thick or smooth a liquid substance is: *The mixture should have a thick, sticky consistency.*

con·sist·ent **AWL** /kən'sɪstənt/ *adjective*
always the same: *His work isn't very consistent.* ⊃ **ANTONYM inconsistent**
▶ **con·sist·ent·ly** **AWL** /kən'sɪstəntli/ *adverb*: *We must try to keep a consistently high standard.*

con·so·la·tion /ˌkɑnsə'leɪʃn/ *noun* [*count, noncount*]
a thing or person that makes you feel better when you are sad: *If it's any consolation, you weren't the only person who failed the test.*

con·sole¹ /kən'soʊl/ *verb* (con·soles, con·sol·ing, con·soled)
to make someone happier when they are sad about something ⊃ **SYNONYM comfort**

con·sole² /'kɑnsoʊl/ *noun* [*count*]
(**COMPUTERS**) a piece of equipment with buttons and switches on it which you connect to a computer to play games

con·sol·i·date /kən'sɑlədeɪt/ *verb* (con·sol·i·dates, con·sol·i·dat·ing, con·sol·i·dat·ed)
to join things together into one: *to consolidate your debts into one payment*
▶ **con·sol·i·da·tion** /kənˌsɑlə'deɪʃn/ *noun* [*noncount*]: *debt consolidation*

con·so·nant /'kɑnsənənt/ *noun* [*count*]
(**ENGLISH LANGUAGE ARTS**) any letter of the alphabet except a, e, i, o, and u: *The letters "t," "m," "s," and "b" are all consonants.* ⊃ Look at **vowel**.

con·spic·u·ous /kən'spɪkyuəs/ *adjective*
easily seen or noticed: *She felt very conspicuous in her bright orange shirt.*
▶ **con·spic·u·ous·ly** /kən'spɪkyuəsli/ *adverb*

con·spir·a·cy /kən'spɪrəsi/ *noun* [*count, noncount*] (*plural* **con·spir·a·cies**)
a secret plan by a group of people to do something bad

con·stant 🔑 **AWL** /'kɑnstənt/ *adjective*
1 happening all the time: *the constant noise of traffic*
2 not changing at all: *You use less gas if you drive at a constant speed.*
▶ **con·stant·ly** **AWL** /'kɑnstəntli/ *adverb*: *The situation is constantly changing.*

con·stel·la·tion /ˌkɑnstə'leɪʃn/ *noun* [*count*]
a group of stars that forms a pattern and has a name

con·sti·tute **AWL** /'kɑnstətut/ *verb* (con·sti·tutes, con·sti·tut·ing, con·sti·tut·ed) (*formal*)
to be one of the parts that form something: *Women constitute a high proportion of part-time workers.*

con·sti·tu·tion **AWL** /ˌkɑnstə'tuʃn/ (also Con·sti·tu·tion) *noun* [*count*]
(**POLITICS**) the laws of a country, a state, or an organization: *rights guaranteed by the U.S. Constitution*
▶ **con·sti·tu·tion·al** **AWL** /ˌkɑnstə'tuʃənl/ *adjective*: *constitutional amendments* (= changes to the laws in a constitution) ⊃ Look at **unconstitutional**.

con·struct **AWL** /kən'strʌkt/ *verb* (con·structs, con·struct·ing, con·struct·ed)
to build something: *The bridge was constructed out of stone.*

con·struc·tion **AWL** /kən'strʌkʃn/ *noun*
1 [*noncount*] building something: *the construction of a new airport* • *This web site is under construction* (= in the process of being created).
2 [*count*] (*formal*) something that people have built

con·sul /'kɑnsl/ *noun* [*count*]
(**POLITICS**) a person who works in a foreign city and helps people from his or her country who are living or visiting there

con·sult **AWL** /kən'sʌlt/ *verb* (con·sults, con·sult·ing, con·sult·ed)
to ask someone or to look in a book when you want to know something: *If the pain doesn't go away, you should consult a doctor.*

con·sult·ant **AWL** /kən'sʌltnt/ *noun* [*count*]
(**BUSINESS**) a person who knows a lot about a subject and gives advice to other people about it: *a management consultant*

con·sul·ta·tion **AWL** /ˌkɑnsl'teɪʃn/ *noun* [*count, noncount*]
a meeting to discuss something, or to get advice or information: *The company president was in consultation with the workers' unions.* • *a consultation with a doctor*

containers

| **bags** | **bottles** | **boxes** | **cans** |
| **cartons** | **packages** | **tubes** | **jars** |

con·sume **AWL** /kən'sum/ *verb* (con·sumes, con·sum·ing, con·sumed) (*formal*)
to eat, drink, or use something: *This car consumes a lot of fuel.*

con·sum·er **AWL** /kən'sumər/ *noun* [count]
(**BUSINESS**) a person who buys or uses something: *Consumers want more information about the food they buy.*

con·sump·tion **AWL** /kən'sʌmpʃn/ *noun* [noncount]
eating, drinking, or using something: *This car has a high fuel consumption* (= it uses a lot of fuel).

con·tact¹ 🔑 **AWL** /'kɑntækt/ *noun*
1 [noncount] meeting, talking to, or writing to someone: *Until Lauren went to school, she had little contact with other children.* ◆ *Are you still in contact with the people you met on vacation?* ◆ *Doctors come into contact with* (= meet) *a lot of people.*
2 [noncount] the state of touching someone or something: *Don't let the cleaning products come into contact with your food.*
3 [count] a person you know who may be able to help you: *business contacts*

con·tact² 🔑 **AWL** /'kɑntækt/ *verb* (con·tacts, con·tact·ing, con·tact·ed)
to call or write to someone, or go to see them: *If you see this man, please contact the police.*

con·tact lens /'kɑntækt lɛnz/ *noun* [count] (*plural* con·tact lens·es)
a small, round piece of thin plastic that you wear in your eye so that you can see better ⊃ Look at **glasses**.

con·ta·gious /kən'teɪdʒəs/ *adjective*
(**HEALTH**) A **contagious** disease passes from one person to another person if they are close to each other. ⊃ Look at **infectious**.

con·tain 🔑 /kən'teɪn/ *verb* (con·tains, con·tain·ing, con·tained)
to have something inside: *This box contains 12 bottles of wine.* ◆ *Chocolate contains a lot of sugar.*

con·tain·er 🔑 /kən'teɪnər/ *noun* [count]
a thing that you can put other things in. Boxes and bottles are **containers**.

con·tam·i·nate /kən'tæməneɪt/ *verb* (con·tam·i·nates, con·tam·i·nat·ing, con·tam·i·nat·ed)
to make something dirty or harmful by adding something dangerous: *The town's drinking water was contaminated with poisonous chemicals.*
▶ **con·tam·i·na·tion** /kən,tæmə'neɪʃn/ *noun* [noncount]: *contamination from the accident at the nuclear power plant*

con·tem·plate /'kɑntəmpleɪt/ *verb* (con·tem·plates, con·tem·plat·ing, con·tem·plat·ed)
to think about something, or the possibility of doing something: *After losing her job, she contemplated going back to school.*

con·tem·po·rar·y¹ **AWL** /kən'tɛmpə,rɛri/ *adjective*
1 belonging to the present time: *contemporary art* ⊃ **SYNONYM modern**
2 belonging to the same time as someone or something else

con·tem·po·rar·y² **AWL** /kən'tɛmpə,rɛri/ *noun* [count] (*plural* con·tem·po·rar·ies)
a person who lives or does something at the same time as someone else

con·tempt /kən'tɛmpt/ *noun* [noncount]
the feeling that someone or something is without value and does not deserve any respect at all: *She looked at him with contempt.*

con·tent¹ /kən'tɛnt/ *adjective*
happy or satisfied with what you have: *She is not content with the money she has – she wants more.*

con·tent² /'kɑntɛnt/ *noun*
1 contents [*plural*] what is inside something: *I poured the contents of the bottle into a bowl.* ◆ *The contents page of a book tells you what is in it.*
2 [*singular*] the main ideas or facts in a book, an essay, a speech, etc.: *The content of the essay is good, but there are too many spelling mistakes.*

con·tent·ed /kən'tɛntəd/ *adjective*
happy or satisfied, especially because your life is good: *a contented smile*

con·test /'kɑntɛst/ *noun* [*count*]
a game or competition that people try to win: *a beauty contest*

con·tes·tant /kən'tɛstənt/ *noun* [*count*]
a person who tries to win a CONTEST: *There are six contestants in the race.*

con·text **AWL** /'kɑntɛkst/ *noun* [*count*]
1 the situation in which something happens or that caused something to happen: *Let me put the event into context.* ◆ *the historical context of the Civil War*
2 (**ENGLISH LANGUAGE ARTS**) the words that come before and after another word or sentence: *You can often understand the meaning of a word by looking at its context.*

con·ti·nent /'kɑntənənt/ *noun* [*count*]
(**GEOGRAPHY**) one of the seven main areas of land in the world, for example Africa, Asia, or Europe
▶ **con·ti·nen·tal** /ˌkɑntə'nɛntl/ *adjective*: *a continental climate*

con·tin·u·al /kən'tɪnyuəl/ *adjective*
happening often: *We have had continual problems with this machine.*
▶ **con·tin·u·al·ly** /kən'tɪnyuəli/ *adverb*: *He is continually late for work.*

con·tin·ue /kən'tɪnyu/ *verb* (con·tin·ues, con·tin·u·ing, con·tin·ued)
1 to not stop happening or doing something: *If the pain continues, see your doctor.* ◆ *The rain continued all afternoon.*
2 to start again after stopping: *Let's have lunch now and continue the meeting this afternoon.*
3 to go farther in the same direction: *We continued along the path until we came to the river.*

con·tin·u·ing ed·u·ca·tion /kən'tɪnyuɪŋ ˌɛdʒə'keɪʃn/ *noun* [*noncount*]
classes for adults that are not part of the formal education system: *continuing education courses in photography and graphic design* ⟹ Look at **higher education**.

con·ti·nu·i·ty /ˌkɑntə'nuəti/ *noun* [*noncount*]
continuing without stopping, or staying the same: *Staying with the same doctor provides continuity in your treatment.*

con·tin·u·ous /kən'tɪnyuəs/ *adjective*
not stopping: *a continuous line* ◆ *a continuous noise*
▶ **con·tin·u·ous·ly** /kən'tɪnyuəsli/ *adverb*: *It rained continuously for five hours.*

con·tour /'kɑntʊr/ *noun* [*count*]
the shape of the outside of something: *I could just make out the contours of the house in the dark.*

con·tra·cep·tive /ˌkɑntrə'sɛptɪv/ *noun* [*count*]
(**HEALTH**) a drug or an object that stops a woman from becoming pregnant
▶ **con·tra·cep·tion** /ˌkɑntrə'sɛpʃn/ *noun* [*noncount*]
(**HEALTH**) the ways of stopping a woman from becoming pregnant ⟹ Look at **birth control**.

con·tract¹ **AWL** /'kɑntrækt/ *noun* [*count*]
an official piece of paper that says that someone agrees to do something: *The museum renewed the director's contract for another five years.*

con·tract² **AWL** /kən'trækt/ *verb* (con·tracts, con·tract·ing, con·tract·ed)
to become or make something smaller: *Metals contract as they cool.* ⟹ **ANTONYM expand**

con·trac·tion /kən'trækʃn/ *noun* [*count*]
(**ENGLISH LANGUAGE ARTS**) a short form of a word or words: *"Isn't" is a contraction of "is not."*

con·tra·dict **AWL** /ˌkɑntrə'dɪkt/ *verb* (con·tra·dicts, con·tra·dict·ing, con·tra·dict·ed)
to say that something is wrong or not true: *I didn't want to contradict him, but I think he was wrong.*
▶ **con·tra·dic·tion** **AWL** /ˌkɑntrə'dɪkʃn/ *noun* [*count*]: *There is a contradiction between the two descriptions of what happened.*

con·tra·dic·to·ry **AWL** /ˌkɑntrə'dɪktəri/ *adjective*
opposite to or not matching something else: *Contradictory reports appeared in the newspapers.*

con·trar·y¹ **AWL** /'kɑnˌtrɛri/ *adjective*
contrary to something very different from something; opposite to something: *Contrary to the doctor's orders, he didn't stay in bed.*

con·trar·y² **AWL** /'kɑnˌtrɛri/ *noun*
on the contrary (*formal*) the opposite is true; certainly not: *"Is business slow?" "On the contrary, sales are higher than ever."*

con·trast¹ **AWL** /'kɑntræst/ *noun* [*count*]

> ℹ **PRONUNCIATION**
> When the word **contrast** is a noun, you say the first part of the word louder: **CON**trast. When the word **contrast** is a verb, you say the second part of the word louder: **con**TRAST.

a difference between things that you can see clearly: *There is a big* **contrast between** *the climate in the valley and the climate in the hills.*

con·trast² **AWL** /kən'træst/ *verb* (**con·trasts, con·trast·ing, con·trast·ed**)
to look at or think about two or more things together and see the differences between them: *The book* **contrasts** *life today* **with** *life 100 years ago.*

con·trib·ute 🖋 **AWL** /kən'trɪbyut/ *verb* (**con·trib·utes, con·trib·ut·ing, con·trib·ut·ed**)
to give or be a part of something with other people: *We* **contributed** *$100* **to** *the disaster fund.* ◆ *He didn't contribute anything to the conversation.*
▶ **con·trib·u·tor** **AWL** /kən'trɪbyət̮ər/ *noun* [*count*]
a person who contributes to something

con·tri·bu·tion 🖋 **AWL** /ˌkɑntrə'byuʃn/ *noun* [*count*]
something that you give when other people are giving too: *Would you like to* **make a contribution to** *the charity?*

con·trol¹ 🖋 /kən'troʊl/ *noun*
1 [*noncount*] the power to make people or things do what you want: *Who has* **control of** *the Senate?* ◆ *You don't have any* **control over** *the weather.* ◆ *The driver* **lost control** *and the bus went into the river.*
2 **controls** [*plural*] the parts of a machine that you press or move to make it work: *airplane controls*
be in control to have the power or ability to deal with something: *The police are now in control of the area after last night's violence.*
be or **get out of control** to be or become impossible to deal with: *The situation got out of control and people started fighting.*
be under control If things **are under control**, you are able to deal with them successfully: *Don't worry, everything's under control.*

con·trol² 🖋 /kən'troʊl/ *verb* (**con·trols, con·trol·ling, con·trolled**)
to make people or things do what you want: *He can't control his dog.* ◆ *This switch controls the heating.*
▶ **con·trol·ler** /kən'troʊlər/ *noun* [*count*]
a person who controls something: *an air traffic controller*

con·tro·ver·sial **AWL** /ˌkɑntrə'vərʃl/ *adjective*
Something that is **controversial** makes people argue and disagree with each other: *a controversial new law*

con·tro·ver·sy **AWL** /'kɑntrəvərsi/ *noun* [*count, noncount*] (*plural* **con·tro·ver·sies**)
public discussion and disagreement about something: *The new power plant caused a lot of controversy.*

con·ven·ience /kən'vinyəns/ *noun* [*noncount*]
being easy to use or making things easy for someone: *For convenience, I usually do all my grocery shopping in the same place.* ◆ **ANTONYM inconvenience**

con·ven·ience store /kən'vinyəns ˌstɔr/ *noun* [*count*]
a store that stays open late and sells food and other small items

con·ven·ient 🖋 /kən'vinyənt/ *adjective*
1 useful, easy, or quick to do; not causing problems: *Let's meet on Friday. What's the most convenient time for you?*
2 near to a place or easy to get to: *I like to buy food at the farmer's market, but it's not very convenient.* ◆ **ANTONYM inconvenient**
▶ **con·ven·ient·ly** /kən'vinyəntli/ *adverb*: *Our office is conveniently located near a subway stop.*

con·vent /'kɑnvɛnt/ *noun* [*count*]
(**RELIGION**) a place where religious women (called **NUNS**) live and work ◆ Look at **monastery**.

con·ven·tion **AWL** /kən'vɛnʃn/ *noun* [*count*]
(**BUSINESS**) a large meeting of people who do the same job, belong to the same organization, etc.: *the Democratic Party Convention* ◆ *a convention center* (= a large building where conventions are held) ◆ **SYNONYM conference**

con·ven·tion·al **AWL** /kən'vɛnʃənl/ *adjective*
following what is normal or the way things have been done for a long time: *a conventional laptop computer* ◆ *conventional attitudes* ◆ **ANTONYM unconventional**

con·ver·sa·tion 🖋 /ˌkɑnvər'seɪʃn/ *noun* [*count, noncount*]
a talk between two or more people: *She* **had a long conversation with** *her friend on the phone.* ◆ *a topic of conversation* ◆ Look at the note at **discussion**.

con·verse¹ **AWL** /kən'vərs/ *verb* (**con·vers·es, con·vers·ing, con·versed**) (*formal*)
to have a conversation with someone

con·verse² **AWL** /'kɑnvərs/ *noun* [*singular*] **the converse** (*formal*)
the opposite of a situation or statement: *Building new roads increases traffic, and the converse is equally true: reducing the number and size of roads means less traffic.*

con·ver·sion **AWL** /kən'vərʒn/ *noun* [*count, noncount*]
1 changing from one form, system, or use to another: *a conversion table for miles and kilometers*
2 (**RELIGION**) becoming a member of a different religion

ə **about**   y **yes**   w **woman**   t̮ **butter**   eɪ **say**   aɪ **five**   ɔɪ **boy**   aʊ **now**   oʊ **go**

con·vert `AWL` /kən'vərt/ *verb* (con·verts, con·vert·ing, con·vert·ed)
1 to change something into another thing: *They converted the house into offices.* ◆ *How do you convert pounds into kilos?*
2 (**RELIGION**) to change to a different religion: *She converted to Islam.*

con·vert·i·ble `AWL` /kən'vərṭəbl/ *noun* [count]
a car with a roof that can be folded down or taken off

con·vey /kən'veɪ/ *verb* (con·veys, con·vey·ing, con·veyed)
to make ideas, feelings, etc. known to someone: *The color red conveys a sense of energy and strength.*

con·vict¹ /kən'vɪkt/ *verb* (con·victs, con·vict·ing, con·vict·ed)
to decide in a court of law that someone has done something wrong: *She was **convicted of** murder and sent to prison.*

con·vict² /'kɑnvɪkt/ *noun* [count]
a person who is guilty of a crime and is in prison

con·vic·tion /kən'vɪkʃn/ *noun*
1 [count, noncount] the action of finding someone guilty in a court of law: *He has several previous convictions for burglary.*
2 [count] a very strong opinion or belief: *religious convictions*

con·vince 🔊 `AWL` /kən'vɪns/ *verb* (con·vinc·es, con·vinc·ing, con·vinced)
1 to make someone believe something: *I couldn't **convince** him **that** I was right.*
2 to persuade someone to do something: *She tried to convince me to go with her.*
▶ **con·vinced** `AWL` /kən'vɪnst/ *adjective*
completely sure about something: *I'm **convinced that** I've seen her somewhere before.* ⊃
ANTONYM unconvinced

cook¹ 🔊 /kʊk/ *verb* (cooks, cook·ing, cooked)
to make food ready to eat by heating it: *My father cooked us dinner.* ◆ *I am learning how to cook.*
▶ **cooked** /kʊkt/ *adjective*: *cooked chicken*

Thesaurus

cook to make food ready to eat by heating it: *My mother taught me how to cook.* ◆ *Who is going to cook dinner tonight?* ◆ *What's the best way to cook salmon?* ◆ *He cooked us a wonderful meal.*
boil to cook vegetables, rice, eggs, etc. in boiling water (= water heated to 212°F): *Boil the rice for 15 minutes.* ◆ *Put the potatoes on to boil.* ◆ *Do you like boiled cabbage?*

fry to cook food in a shallow pan of hot oil: *Fry the onion and garlic for five minutes.* ◆ *There was a smell of bacon frying in the kitchen.* ◆ *fried chicken/fish/rice*
bake to cook food in an oven without any extra fat or liquid: *to bake bread/cookies* ◆ *We baked him a cake for his birthday.* ◆ *baked potatoes*
roast to cook large pieces of meat in an oven or over a fire; to cook vegetables in oil or fat in an oven: *The turkey is roasting in the oven.* ◆ *You should boil the potatoes for a little while before you roast them.*
grill to cook meat or fish on metal bars over a fire: *to grill steak/chicken/burgers/fish on the barbecue* ◆ *grilled salmon*
broil to cook food under or over direct heat: *to broil salmon/a steak* ◆ *We ate broiled chicken with vegetables.*

cook² /kʊk/ *noun* [count]
a person who cooks: *She works as a cook in a big hotel.* ◆ *He is a good cook.*

cook·book /'kʊkbʊk/ *noun* [count]
a book that has instructions for preparing different types of food

cook·ie 🔊 /'kʊki/ *noun* [count]
a kind of cake that is small, thin, and sweet: *Let's bake cookies.* ◆ *a chocolate chip cookie*

cook·ing 🔊 /'kʊkɪŋ/ *noun* [noncount]
1 making food ready to eat: *Who **does the cooking** in your family?* ◆ *cooking lessons*
2 the food that you cook: *He missed his mom's cooking when he went to college.*

Collocations

Cooking

preparing
- **chop/slice** the onions
- **peel** the potatoes/an orange
- **grate** the cheese/a carrot
- **mix (together)** all the ingredients

cooking
- **heat** the oven/the broiler/some oil in a frying pan
- **melt** the butter/chocolate/cheese
- **cook** food/fish/meat/rice
- **bake** bread/a cake/cookies/muffins
- **boil** potatoes/an egg/water
- **fry/stir-fry** the chicken/vegetables
- **grill/broil/barbecue** fish/meat/steak
- **roast** chicken/turkey/potatoes
- **steam** rice/vegetables
- **microwave** food/popcorn/your dinner

cool¹ 🔊 /kul/ *adjective* (**cool·er**, **cool·est**)
1 a little cold; not hot or warm: *cool weather* • *It was a cool evening, so I put on a sweater.* ⊃ Look at the note at **cold¹**.
2 (*informal*) very good or fashionable: *Those shoes are so cool!* ⊃ **ANTONYM uncool**
3 not excited or angry ⊃ **SYNONYM calm**
4 (*informal*) People say **Cool!** to show that they think something is a good idea: *"We're going to Dave's party tomorrow night." "Cool!"*

cool² /kul/ *verb* (**cools**, **cool·ing**, **cooled**)
to make something less hot; to become less hot: *Take the cake out of the oven and let it cool.*
cool down; **cool off**
1 to become less hot: *We swam in the river to cool off after our long walk.*
2 to become less excited or angry

cool·er /'kulər/ *noun* [*count*]
a small box that you fill with ice to keep food and drinks cold: *Do we have a cooler to bring to the beach?* ⊃ Look at **water cooler**.

co·op·er·ate AWL /koʊˈɑpəreɪt/ *verb*
(**co·op·er·ates**, **co·op·er·at·ing**, **co·op·er·at·ed**)
to work together with someone else in a helpful way: *She agreed to cooperate with the police in their investigation.* • *If everyone cooperates, we'll be finished soon.*

co·op·er·a·tion AWL /koʊˌɑpəˈreɪʃn/ *noun*
[*noncount*]
help that you give by doing what someone asks you to do: *Thank you for your cooperation.*

co·op·er·a·tive AWL /koʊˈɑprətɪv/ *adjective*
helpful by doing what you are asked to do

co·or·di·nate¹ AWL /koʊˈɔrdəneɪt/ *verb*
(**co·or·di·nates**, **co·or·di·nat·ing**, **co·or·di·nat·ed**)
to organize different things or people so that they work well together: *She coordinated all of the hospital volunteers.*
▶ **co·or·di·na·tor** AWL /koʊˈɔrdəneɪtər/ *noun*
[*count*]: *a project coordinator*

co·or·di·nate² AWL /koʊˈɔrdənət/ *noun* [*count*]
(**GEOGRAPHY**) one of the two numbers or letters that are used to find a position on a map

co·or·di·na·tion AWL /koʊˌɔrdəˈneɪʃn/ *noun*
[*noncount*]
1 the organization of different people or things so that they work well together: *There wasn't enough coordination between the committees.*
2 the ability to control the movements of your body well: *You need good hand-eye coordination to play golf.*

cop /kɑp/ *noun* [*count*] (*informal*)
a police officer: *a traffic cop*

cope /koʊp/ *verb* (**copes**, **cop·ing**, **coped**)
to deal with something, although it is difficult: *He finds it difficult to cope with all the pressure at work.*

cop·ies, cop·ied forms of **copy²**

cop·per /'kɑpər/ *noun* [*noncount*] (symbol **Cu**)
(**CHEMISTRY**) a common metal with a color between brown and red: *copper wire*

cop·y¹ 🔊 /'kɑpi/ *noun* [*count*] (*plural* **cop·ies**)
1 a thing that is made to look exactly like another thing: *This isn't a real Van Gogh painting. It's only a copy.* • *The secretary made two copies of the letter.*
2 one example of a book or newspaper: *Two million copies of this newspaper are sold every day.*

cop·y² 🔊 /'kɑpi/ *verb* (**cop·ies**, **cop·y·ing**, **cop·ied**, **has cop·ied**)
1 to write, draw, or make something exactly the same as something else: *The teacher asked us to copy the list of words into our books.* • *Copy the table and paste it into a new document.*
2 to do or try to do the same as someone else: *He copies everything his brother does.* ⊃ **SYNONYM imitate**
3 to cheat by looking at someone else's work and writing down what they have written: *If I catch you copying off anyone you will get a zero on your test.*

cop·y·right /'kɑpiˌraɪt/ *noun* [*count, noncount*]
the legal right to be the only person who can print, copy, etc. a piece of writing, music, or other work: *Who owns the copyright on this song?*

cor·al /'kɔrəl/ *noun* [*noncount*]
(**BIOLOGY**) a hard red, pink, or white substance that forms in the ocean from the bones of very small animals: *a coral reef* (= a line of rock in the ocean formed by coral)

cord /kɔrd/ *noun*
[*count*]
1 a piece of wire covered with plastic, which carries electricity to electrical equipment: *a power cord*
2 strong, thick string

cord

cord
wire

cor·du·roy
/'kɔrdərɔɪ/ *noun* [*noncount*]
a thick, soft, cotton cloth with lines on it, used for making clothes: *corduroy pants*

core AWL /kɔr/ *noun* [*count*]
1 the middle part of some kinds of fruit, where the seeds are: *an apple core*

2 the central or most important part of something: *Environmental protection is at the core of our policies.*
3 the central part of an object: *the earth's core*
▶ **core** AWL *adjective*
the most important: *core subjects* (= subjects that all students have to study) *such as English and mathematics*

cork /kɔrk/ *noun*
1 [*noncount*] a light, soft material that comes from the outside of a particular tree
2 [*count*] a round piece of **cork** that you put in a bottle to close it

cork·screw /'kɔrkˌskru/ *noun* [*count*]
a thing that you use for pulling CORKS out of bottles ⊃ Look at the picture at **kitchen**.

corn /kɔrn/ *noun*
[*noncount*]
a tall plant with big yellow seeds that you can eat: *a can of corn •
We had fried chicken and corn for dinner.*

corn

cor·ner /'kɔrnər/
noun [*count*]
a place where two lines, walls, or roads meet: *Put the lamp in the corner of the room. • The restaurant is on the corner of East Avenue and Union Street. • He drove around the corner to look for a parking space.*

corn·flakes /'kɔrnfleɪks/ *noun* [*plural*]
small pieces of dried food that you eat with milk for breakfast

corn·y /'kɔrni/ *adjective* (corn·i·er, corn·i·est)
(*informal*)
used, seen, heard, etc. too often to be interesting: *a corny joke*

cor·po·rate AWL /'kɔrpərət/ *adjective*
(BUSINESS) connected with a big company or group of companies: *corporate planning*

cor·po·ra·tion AWL /ˌkɔrpə'reɪʃn/ *noun* [*count*]
(BUSINESS) a big company ⊃ Look at **incorporated**.

corpse /kɔrps/ *noun* [*count*]
the body of a dead person

cor·rect¹ /kə'rɛkt/ *adjective*
right or true; with no mistakes: *Let me make sure I have your correct address. • All your answers were correct.* ⊃ ANTONYM **incorrect**
▶ **cor·rect·ly** /kə'rɛktli/ *adverb*: *Have I spelled your name correctly?* ⊃ ANTONYM **incorrectly**

cor·rect² /kə'rɛkt/ *verb* (cor·rects, cor·rect·ing, cor·rect·ed)
to show where the mistakes are in something and make it right: *The class did the exercises and*

the teacher corrected them. • Please correct me if I make a mistake.

cor·rec·tion /kə'rɛkʃn/ *noun* [*count*]
a change that makes something right or better: *The teacher made a few corrections to my essay.*

cor·re·spond AWL /ˌkɔrə'spɑnd/ *verb*
(cor·re·sponds, cor·re·spond·ing, cor·re·spond·ed)
1 to be the same, or almost the same, as something: *Does the name on the envelope correspond with the name inside the letter?*
2 to write letters to and receive them from someone: *She corresponded with him for two years while he was overseas.*

cor·re·spon·dence AWL /ˌkɔrə'spɑndəns/ *noun* [*noncount*]
the letters a person sends and receives: *Her secretary reads all her correspondence.*

cor·re·spond·ent /ˌkɔrə'spɑndənt/ *noun* [*count*]
a person who reports news or writes articles for a newspaper, etc.: *our Middle East correspondent, Andrew Rosen*

cor·ri·dor /'kɔrədər/ *noun* [*count*]
a long, narrow part inside a building with rooms on each side of it

cor·rupt /kə'rʌpt/ *adjective*
doing or involving illegal or dishonest things in order to get money or some other advantage: *corrupt officials • The whole system is corrupt.*
▶ **cor·rupt** *verb* (cor·rupts, cor·rupt·ing, cor·rupt·ed): *These politicians have been corrupted by power.*

cor·rup·tion /kə'rʌpʃn/ *noun* [*noncount*]
behavior that is illegal or dishonest, especially by people in official positions: *accusations of corruption in the police department*

cos·met·ic /kɑz'mɛtɪk/ *adjective*
used or done in order to make your face or body more attractive: *cosmetic surgery*

cos·met·ics /kɑz'mɛtɪks/ *noun* [*plural*]
special powders or creams that you use on your face to make yourself more attractive

cost¹ /kɔst/ *noun*
1 [*count*] the money that you have to pay for something: *The cost of the repairs was very high. • the cost of living* (= the amount of money you need to pay for food, clothes, and somewhere to live) ⊃ Look at the note at **price**.
2 [*singular, noncount*] what you lose or give to have another thing: *He saved the child at the cost of his own life.*
at all costs; **at any cost** no matter what you must do to make it happen: *We must win at all costs.*

cost² /kɔst/ *verb* (costs, cost·ing, cost, has cost)
1 to have the price of: *This plant cost $4.* ◆ *How much did the book cost?*
2 to make you lose something: *One mistake cost him his job.*

cost·ly /'kɔstli/ *adjective* (cost·li·er, cost·li·est)
costing a lot of money: *The repairs will be very costly.* ⊃ SYNONYM **expensive**

cos·tume /'kɑstum/ *noun* [count, noncount]
the special clothes that people wear to look like a different person, animal, or thing: *The dancers wore beautiful costumes.* ◆ *a Halloween costume* ◆ *a costume party*

cot·tage /'kɑtɪdʒ/ *noun* [count]
a small house in the country

cot·ton /'kɑtn/ *noun* [noncount]
1 a natural cloth that is made from the soft white hairs around the seeds of a plant that grows in hot countries: *a cotton shirt* ◆ *100% cotton* (= made of cotton only)
2 soft, light material made from cotton that you often use for cleaning your skin: *Use a cotton ball to apply the lotion.*

cot·ton can·dy /ˌkɑtn 'kændi/ *noun* [noncount]
a type of soft, sticky candy made from melted sugar and served on a stick: *We bought cotton candy at the town fair.*

couch /kaʊtʃ/ *noun* [count] (*plural* couch·es)
a long, comfortable seat for two or more people to sit on ⊃ SYNONYM **sofa** ⊃ Look at the picture at **chair.**

cou·gar /'kugər/ *noun* [count]
a large wild cat that lives in western North America ⊃ SYNONYM **mountain lion**

cough¹ /kɔf/ *verb* (coughs, cough·ing, coughed)

ⓘ PRONUNCIATION
The word **cough** sounds like **off.**

to send air out of your throat with a sudden loud noise: *The smoke made me cough.*

cough² /kɔf/ *noun* [count]
1 when you send air out of your throat with a sudden loud noise: *He gave a little cough before he started to speak.*
2 (HEALTH) an illness that makes you cough a lot: *I have a bad cough.*

could /kəd; kʊd/ *modal verb*

ⓘ PRONUNCIATION
The word **could** sounds like **good,** because we don't say the letter l in this word.

1 the word for "can" in the past: *He could run very fast when he was young.* ◆ *I could hear the birds singing.*

2 a word that shows what is or may be possible: *I don't know where Mom is. She could be in the kitchen.* ◆ *It could rain tomorrow.*
3 a word that you use to ask something in a polite way: *Could you open the door?* ◆ *Could I have another drink, please?*
4 a word that you use to make a suggestion: *We could go out to dinner tonight if you're free.* ⊃ Look at the note at **modal verb.**

could·n't /'kʊdnt/ short for **could not**: *It was dark and I couldn't see anything.*

could've /'kʊdəv/ (*informal*) short for **could have**: *He could've gone to college but he didn't want to.*

coun·cil /'kaʊnsl/ *noun* [count]
a group of people who are chosen to work together and to make rules and decide things: *The city council is planning to widen the road.*

coun·sel /'kaʊnsl/ *verb* (coun·sels, coun·sel·ing, coun·seled)
to give professional advice and help to someone with a problem: *She counsels teenagers suffering from depression.*
▶ **coun·se·lor** /'kaʊnsələr/ *noun* [count]
a person whose job is to give professional advice: *a college counselor*

coun·sel·ing /'kaʊnsəlɪŋ/ *noun* [noncount]
professional advice about a problem: *Many students come to us for counseling.* ◆ *marriage counseling*

count¹ /kaʊnt/ *verb* (counts, count·ing, count·ed)
1 to say numbers one after the other in the correct order: *Can you count to ten in Spanish?*
2 to look at people or things to see how many there are: *I counted the chairs – there are 32.*
3 to include someone or something when you are finding a total: *There were twenty people on the bus, not counting the driver.*
4 to be important or accepted: *Every point in this game counts.* ◆ *Your throw won't count if you go over the line.*
count on someone or **something** to feel sure that someone or something will do what you want: *Can I count on you to help me?*

count² /kaʊnt/ *noun* [count]
a time when you count things: *After an election there is a count of all the votes.*
keep count of something to know how many there are of something: *Try to keep count of the number of tickets you sell.*
lose count to not know how many there are of something: *I've lost count of how many times he's told that joke!*

count·a·ble noun /'kaʊntəbl ˌnaʊn/ *noun* [count] another word for **count noun**

count·down /ˈkaʊntdaʊn/ *noun* [count]
the act of saying numbers backward to zero just before something important happens: *the countdown to takeoff*

coun·ter /ˈkaʊntər/ *noun* [count]
1 a long, high table in a kitchen where you prepare food or eat: *She wiped off the counter with a sponge.* ◆ *The kids sat at the kitchen counter doing their homework.*
2 a long, high table in a store, bar, hotel, etc. that is between the people who work there and the customers: *The man **behind the counter** showed me some earrings.*

coun·ter·clock·wise /ˌkaʊntərˈklɑkwaɪz/ *adjective, adverb*
in the opposite direction to the hands of a clock: *Turn the handle counterclockwise.* ⊃ **ANTONYM clockwise**

coun·ter·feit /ˈkaʊntərfɪt/ *adjective*
not real, but copied so that it looks like the real thing: *counterfeit money*

count·less /ˈkaʊntləs/ *adjective*
very many: *I have tried to call him countless times.*

count noun /ˈkaʊnt naʊn/ (also **count·a·ble noun**) *noun* [count]
(**ENGLISH LANGUAGE ARTS**) Count nouns are ones that you can use in the plural or with "a" or "an": *The words "chair" and "idea" are count nouns.* ⊃ Look at **noncount noun**.

coun·try /ˈkʌntri/ *noun* (plural **coun·tries**)
1 [count] (**GEOGRAPHY, POLITICS**) an area of land with its own people and government: *Argentina, Brazil, and other South American countries*
2 the country [noncount] land that is away from towns and cities: *They bought a house **in the country**.*

coun·try mu·sic /ˈkʌntri ˌmyuzɪk/ (also **coun·try and west·ern** /ˌkʌntri ənd ˈwɛstərn/) *noun* [noncount]
(**MUSIC**) a type of popular music based on music from the southern and western U.S.

coun·try·side /ˈkʌntrisaɪd/ *noun* [noncount]
land with fields, woods, farms, etc. that is away from towns and cities: *The hotel has magnificent views of the surrounding countryside.*

coun·ty /ˈkaʊnti/ *noun* [count] (plural **coun·ties**)
(**POLITICS**) one part of a state that has its own local government: *a county courthouse* ◆ *Orange County, California*

coup /ku/ *noun* [count] (plural **coups** /kuz/)
(**POLITICS**) a situation where a group of people suddenly take control of a government by force: *He seized power in a military coup in the late 1990s.*

cou·ple 🔑 **AWL** /ˈkʌpl/ *noun*
1 a couple [singular] two or a small number of people or things: *I invited **a couple of** friends over for lunch.* ◆ *I'll be back in **a couple of** minutes.*
2 [count] two people who are married or in a romantic relationship: *A young couple lives next door.*

cou·pon /ˈkupɑn; ˈkyupɑn/ *noun* [count]
a small piece of paper that you can use to buy things at a lower price, or that you can collect and use instead of money to buy things

cour·age /ˈkʌrɪdʒ/ *noun* [noncount]
not being afraid, or not showing that you are afraid when you do something dangerous or difficult: *She **showed** great **courage** in the face of danger.* ⊃ **SYNONYM bravery**
▶ **cou·ra·geous** /kəˈreɪdʒəs/ *adjective*: *a courageous young man* ⊃ **SYNONYM brave**

cour·i·er /ˈkʌriər; ˈkʊriər/ *noun* [count]
a person whose job is to deliver important papers, packages, etc. somewhere: *He had a summer job as a bike courier.*

course 🔑 /kɔrs/ *noun*
1 [count] a set of classes on a certain subject: *He's **taking a course** in computer programming.*
2 [count] one separate part of a meal: *a three-course meal* ◆ *I had chicken for my **main course**.*
3 [count] (**SPORTS**) a piece of ground for some sports: *a golf course* ◆ *a racecourse*
4 [noncount] the direction that something moves in: *We followed the course of the river.* ◆ *The plane had to **change course** because of the storm.*
5 [noncount] the time when something is happening: *His cell phone rang six times during the **course of** dinner.*
of course certainly: *Of course I'll help you.* ◆ *"Can I use your phone?" "Of course." ◆ "Are you angry with me?" "Of course not!"*

court 🔑 /kɔrt/ *noun*
1 [count, noncount] the place where a judge or a group of people (called a **JURY**) decide if a person has done something wrong, and what the punishment will be: *a court of law* ◆ *The man will appear **in court** tomorrow.*
2 [count] (**SPORTS**) a piece of ground where you can play certain sports: *a tennis court* ◆ *a basketball court* ⊃ Look at the note at **field**.

cour·te·ous /ˈkərṭiəs/ *adjective*
polite and showing respect for other people

cour·te·sy /ˈkərṭəsi/ *noun* [noncount]
polite behavior that shows respect for other people

court·house /ˈkɔrthaʊs/ *noun* [count]
a building where courts of law and other government offices are

court·room /ˈkɔrtrum/ noun [count]
a room where trials or other court cases are held: *Everyone stood when the judge entered the courtroom.*

court·yard /ˈkɔrtyɑrd/ noun [count]
an open space without a roof, inside a building or between buildings

cous·in 🔑 /ˈkʌzn/ noun [count]
the child of your aunt or uncle: *Do your cousins live here in the States?*

cov·er¹ 🔑 /ˈkʌvər/ verb (cov·ers, cov·er·ing, cov·ered)
1 to put one thing over another thing to hide it or to keep it safe or warm: *Cover the floor **with** old newspapers before you start painting.* • *She covered her eyes during the scary part of the movie.*
2 to be all over something or someone: *Snow covered the ground.* • *The children **were covered in** mud.*
3 to include or to deal with something: *The exam will cover all of the major Civil War battles.*

cov·er² 🔑 /ˈkʌvər/ noun [count]
1 a thing that you put over another thing, for example to keep it safe: *a plastic cover for a computer*
2 the outside part of a book or magazine: *The book had a picture of the author **on the cover**.*

cov·er·alls /ˈkʌvərɔlz/ noun [plural]
a piece of clothing that covers your legs, body, and arms. You wear it over your other clothes to keep them clean when you are working.

cov·er·ing 🔑 /ˈkʌvərɪŋ/ noun [count]
something that covers another thing: *window coverings*

cov·er let·ter /ˈkʌvər ˌlɛtər/ noun [count]
a letter that you send with a package or document that gives more information about it: *Please submit a cover letter with your résumé.*

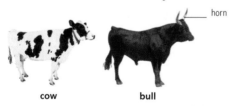

horn

cow   bull

cow 🔑 /kaʊ/ noun [count]
a big, female farm animal that is kept for its milk or meat

Word building

- The male cow is called a **bull**, and a young cow is a **calf**.
- Meat from a cow is called **beef** and meat from a calf is called **veal**.

cow·ard /ˈkaʊərd/ noun [count]
a person who is afraid when there is danger or a problem
▸ **cow·ard·ly** /ˈkaʊərdli/ adjective

cow·boy /ˈkaʊbɔɪ/ noun [count]
a man who rides a horse and whose job is to take care of cows: *cowboy boots*

cow·girl /ˈkaʊgərl/ noun [count]
a woman who rides a horse and whose job is to take care of cows

co·work·er /ˈkoʊwərkər/ noun [count]
someone who works with you, doing the same kind of job as you: *I got a ride home from one of my coworkers.* ⊃ **SYNONYM colleague**

coy·o·te /kaɪˈoʊţi/ noun [count]
a wild dog that lives mainly in western North America

coyote

co·zy /ˈkoʊzi/ adjective (co·zi·er, co·zi·est)
warm and comfortable: *a cozy room*

crab /kræb/ noun [count]
an animal that lives in and near the ocean. It has a hard shell and ten legs. ⊃ Look at the picture at **crustacean**.

crack¹ 🔑 /kræk/ verb (cracks, crack·ing, cracked)
1 to break, but not into separate pieces: *The glass will crack if you pour boiling water into it.* • *This cup is cracked.* ⊃ Look at the note at **break¹**.
2 to make a sudden loud noise
crack down on someone or **something** to become stricter when dealing with bad or illegal behavior: *The police are cracking down on drug dealers.*

crack² /kræk/ noun [count]
1 a thin line on something where it has broken, but not into separate pieces: *There's a crack in this glass.*
2 a narrow space between two things or two parts of something: *a crack in the curtains*
3 a sudden loud noise: *a crack of thunder*

crack·down /ˈkrækdaʊn/ noun [count]
action to stop bad or illegal behavior: *a police crackdown on street crime*

crack·er /ˈkrækər/ noun [count]
a thin, dry type of bread that you can eat with cheese

crack·le /ˈkrækl/ verb (crack·les, crack·ling, crack·led)
to make a lot of short sharp sounds: *Dry wood crackles when you burn it.*

cra·dle /ˈkreɪdl/ *noun* [*count*]
a small bed for a baby, which can be moved from side to side ⊃ Look at **crib**.

craft /kræft/ *noun* [*count*]
a job or activity for which you need skill with your hands: *Pottery is a traditional craft.*

crafts·man /ˈkræftsmən/ *noun* [*count*] (*plural* crafts·men /ˈkræftsmən/)
a person who is good at making things with their hands: *furniture made by local craftsmen*

craft·y /ˈkræfti/ *adjective* (craft·i·er, craft·i·est)
good at getting what you want in a way that is not completely honest

cram /kræm/ *verb* (crams, cram·ming, crammed)
1 to push too many people or things into a small space: *She crammed her clothes into a bag.*
2 to study and try to learn a lot a short time before a test or exam: *He stayed up all night cramming for his biology exam.*

cramp /kræmp/ *noun* [*count*]
(**HEALTH**) a sudden pain that you get in a muscle, for example in your leg, or in your stomach

cramped /kræmpt/ *adjective*
not having enough space: *There were five of us living in a cramped apartment.*

cran·ber·ry /ˈkrænˌbɛri/ *noun* [*count*] (*plural* cran·ber·ries)
a small red fruit with a sharp taste that grows on a bush: *turkey with cranberry sauce*

crane /kreɪn/ *noun* [*count*]
a big machine with a long metal arm for lifting heavy things

crash¹ /kræʃ/ *verb* (crash·es, crash·ing, crashed)
1 to have an accident in a car or other vehicle and hit something: *The bus **crashed into** a tree.* ◆ *I crashed my father's car.*
2 to fall or hit something with a loud noise: *The tree crashed to the ground.*
3 (**COMPUTERS**) If a computer **crashes**, it suddenly stops working.
4 (**BUSINESS**) (used about money or business) to suddenly lose value or fail: *A lot of banks have closed since the market crashed.*

crash² /kræʃ/ *noun* [*count*] (*plural* crash·es)
1 an accident when something that is moving hits another thing: *He was killed **in a car crash**.* ◆ *a plane crash*
2 a loud noise when something falls or hits another thing: *I heard a crash as the tree fell.*
3 (**BUSINESS**) (used about money or business) a sudden fall in the value or price of something: *a stock market crash*

crate /kreɪt/ *noun* [*count*]
a big box for carrying bottles or other things

cra·ter /ˈkreɪtər/ *noun* [*count*]
1 the hole in the top of a VOLCANO ⊃ Look at the picture at **volcano**.
2 a large hole in the ground, caused by something large hitting it: *craters on the moon*

crawl¹ /krɔl/ *verb* (crawls, crawl·ing, crawled)
to move slowly on your hands and knees, or with your body close to the ground: *Babies crawl before they can walk.* ◆ *A spider crawled across the floor.*

crawl² /krɔl/ **the crawl** *noun* [*noncount*]
(**SPORTS**) a way of swimming on your front ⊃ Look at **breaststroke**.

cray·on /ˈkreɪɑn/ *noun* [*count*]
(**ART**) a soft, thick pencil that comes in many colors: *The kids were drawing pictures with crayons.*

craze /kreɪz/ *noun* [*count*]
something that a lot of people are very interested in: *the **latest craze** in video games*

cra·zy 🔑 /ˈkreɪzi/ *adjective* (cra·zi·er, cra·zi·est) (*informal*)
1 stupid; not sensible: *You must be crazy to ride a bike at night with no lights.*
2 very angry: *My mom will **go crazy** if I get home late.*
3 If you are **crazy about** something or someone, you like it or them very much: *She's crazy about basketball.* ◆ *He's crazy about her.*
4 (**HEALTH**) sick in your mind: *He's acting like he's totally crazy.*
like crazy (*informal*) very much, fast, hard, etc.: *I had to pedal like crazy to make it up the hill.*

creak /krik/ *verb* (creaks, creak·ing, creaked)
to make a noise like a door that needs oil, or like an old wooden floor when you walk on it
▶ **creak** *noun* [*count*]: *The door opened with a creak.*

cream¹ 🔑 /krim/ *noun*
1 [*noncount*] the thick liquid on the top of milk
2 [*count, noncount*] a thick liquid that you put on your skin, for example to keep it soft: *hand cream*
3 [*noncount*] a color between white and yellow

cream² 🔑 /krim/ *adjective*
with a color between white and yellow: *She was wearing a cream dress.*

cream cheese /ˌkrim ˈtʃiz/ *noun* [*noncount*]
a type of soft, white cheese: *a bagel with cream cheese*

cream·y /ˈkrimi/ *adjective* (cream·i·er, cream·i·est)
1 with cream in it, or thick and smooth like cream: *a creamy sauce*
2 having a color like cream: *creamy skin*

crease /kris/ *noun* [*count*]
a line or fold in a piece of clothing, paper, etc., especially one that should not be there: *You need to iron this shirt – it's full of creases.*
▸ **crease** *verb* (creas·es, creas·ing, creased)
to get or make something get **creases**: *Don't sit on my jacket – you'll crease it.*

cre·ate 🖉 **AWL** /kri'eɪt/ *verb* (cre·ates, cre·at·ing, cre·at·ed)
to make something happen or exist: *Do you believe that God created the world?* ◆ *We plan to create more jobs in the area.*

cre·a·tion **AWL** /kri'eɪʃn/ *noun*
1 [*noncount*] making something new: *the creation of the world*
2 [*count*] a new thing that someone has made: *This is our chef's latest creation – a white chocolate mousse.*

cre·a·tive **AWL** /kri'eɪṭɪv/ *adjective*
A person who is **creative** has a lot of new ideas or is good at making new things: *She's a fantastic designer – she's so creative.*

cre·a·tiv·i·ty **AWL** /ˌkrieɪ'tɪvəṭi/ *noun* [*noncount*]
the ability to produce new things or ideas using skill or imagination: *teaching that encourages creativity*

cre·a·tor **AWL** /kri'eɪṭər/ *noun* [*count*]
a person who makes something new: *the creator of the new drama*

crea·ture /'kriṭʃər/ *noun* [*count*]
any living thing that is not a plant: *birds, fish, and other creatures* ◆ *This story is about creatures from another planet.*

cred·it¹ **AWL** /'krɛdət/ *noun*
1 [*noncount*] a way of buying something where you pay for it later: *I bought my car on credit.*
2 [*count*] money that is added to a bank or other account: *A credit of $65 will be added to your account.* ⊃ ANTONYM **debit**
3 [*noncount*] saying that someone has done something well: *I did the work but John took all the credit for it!*
4 [*count*] a unit of study at a school or college: *This history course is worth three credits.*
5 the credits [*plural*] the list of the names of people who made a movie or television program, usually shown at the end

cred·it² **AWL** /'krɛdət/ (cred·its, cred·it·ing, cred·it·ed) *verb*
to add money to someone's bank account: *$500 has been credited to your account.* ⊃ ANTONYM **debit**

cred·it card 🖉 /'krɛdət kɑrd/ *noun* [*count*]
a plastic card from a bank that you can use to buy something and pay for it later: *Can I pay by credit card?* ⊃ Look at **debit card**.

creek /krik/ *noun* [*count*]
(**GEOGRAPHY**) a small river ⊃ SYNONYM **stream**

creep /krip/ *verb* (creeps, creep·ing, crept /krɛpt/, has crept)
to move quietly and carefully so that no one hears or sees you: *I crept into the room where the kids were sleeping.* ◆ *The cat crept toward the bird.*

creep·y /'kripi/ *adjective* (creep·i·er, creep·i·est) (*informal*)
making you feel nervous or afraid: *a creepy ghost story* ⊃ SYNONYM **spooky**

cre·mate /'krimeɪt; krɪ'meɪt/ *verb* (cre·mates, cre·mat·ing, cre·mat·ed)
to burn the body of a dead person
▸ **cre·ma·tion** /krɪ'meɪʃn/ *noun* [*count, noncount*]
the act of burning the body of a dead person, or the ceremony at which this happens

crept form of **creep**

cres·cent /'krɛsnt/ *noun* [*count*]
the shape of the moon when it is less than half a circle

crest /krɛst/ *noun* [*count*]
the top part of a hill or a wave: *surfers riding the crest of the wave*

crev·ice /'krɛvəs/ *noun* [*count*]
a narrow crack in a rock or wall

crew /kru/ *noun* [*count*]
1 all the people who work on a ship or an airplane
2 a group of people who work together: *a camera crew* (= people who film things for television, etc.)

crib /krɪb/ *noun* [*count*]
a bed with high sides for a baby ⊃ Look at **cradle**.

crib

crick·et /'krɪkət/ *noun*
1 [*count*] a small, brown insect that jumps and makes a loud high noise by rubbing its wings together
2 [*noncount*] (**SPORTS**) a game in which two teams hit a ball and then score points by running between two sets of sticks: *We watched a cricket match.*

cried form of **cry¹**

cries
1 form of **cry¹**
2 plural of **cry²**

crime 🖉 /kraɪm/ *noun*
1 [*count*] something that someone does that is against the law: *Murder and robbery are serious crimes.* ◆ *They had committed a crime.*

2 [*noncount*] illegal behavior or activities: *The new police chief promised to* **fight crime.** ◆ *an increase in the* **crime rate**

crim·i·nal[1] 🔑 /ˈkrɪmənl/ *adjective*
connected with crime: *Deliberate damage to public property is a* **criminal offense.** ◆ *She is studying criminal law.*

crim·i·nal[2] 🔑 /ˈkrɪmənl/ *noun* [*count*]
a person who does something that is against the law: *a high-security prison for dangerous criminals*

crim·son /ˈkrɪmzn/ *adjective*
having a dark red color, like blood
▶ **crim·son** *noun* [*noncount*]

cringe /krɪndʒ/ *verb* (**cringe, cring·ing, cringed**)
1 to feel embarrassed: *Those embarrassing home movies* **make me cringe.**
2 to move away from someone or something because you are scared: *The dog cringed in terror when the man raised his arm.*

cri·sis 🔑 /ˈkraɪsəs/ *noun* [*count*] (*plural* **cri·ses** /ˈkraɪsiz/)
a time when something very dangerous or serious happens: *a political crisis*

crisp /krɪsp/ *adjective* (**crisp·er, crisp·est**)
1 hard and dry: *Store the crackers in a tin to keep them crisp.*
2 fresh and not soft: *crisp apples*
3 (used about the air or weather) cold and dry: *a crisp fall day*

crisp·y /ˈkrɪspi/ *adjective* (**crisp·i·er, crisp·i·est**)
(of food) hard and dry in a good way: *crispy potato chips*

cri·te·ri·a **AWL** /kraɪˈtɪriə/ *noun* [*plural*]
the standards that you use when you decide something or form an opinion: *What are your criteria for deciding who gets the prize?*

crit·ic /ˈkrɪtɪk/ *noun* [*count*]
1 a person who says that someone or something is wrong or bad: *critics of the current administration*
2 a person who writes about a book, movie, or play and says if they like it or not: *The critics loved his new movie.*

crit·i·cal /ˈkrɪtɪkl/ *adjective*
1 If you are **critical** of someone or something, you say that they are wrong or bad: *They were very* **critical of** *my work.*
2 very important: *We have reached a critical stage in our negotiations.* ⟳ **SYNONYM crucial**
3 very serious or dangerous: *The patient is in* **critical condition.**
▶ **crit·i·cal·ly** /ˈkrɪtɪkli/ *adverb*: *She's critically injured.*

crit·i·cism 🔑 /ˈkrɪtəsɪzəm/ *noun*
1 [*count, noncount*] what you think is bad about someone or something: *I listened to all their criticisms of my plan.*
2 [*noncount*] (**ENGLISH LANGUAGE ARTS**) a description of the good and bad points of a play, movie, book, etc.: *literary criticism*

crit·i·cize 🔑 /ˈkrɪtəsaɪz/ *verb* (**crit·i·ciz·es, crit·i·ciz·ing, crit·i·cized**)
to say that someone or something is wrong or bad: *She was* **criticized for** *not following orders.*

croak /kroʊk/ *verb* (**croaks, croak·ing, croaked**)
1 If a **FROG** (= a small green animal that lives in or near water) **croaks**, it makes a low rough sound.
2 to speak in a low, rough voice: *"My throat's really sore,"* he croaked.
▶ **croak** *noun* [*count*]

alligator

crocodile

croc·o·dile /ˈkrɑkədaɪl/ *noun* [*count*]
a big animal with a long tail and a big mouth with sharp teeth. **Crocodiles** live in rivers in hot countries: *A crocodile is a reptile.*

crook·ed /ˈkrʊkəd/ *adjective*
not straight: *That picture is crooked.*

crop /krɑp/ *noun* [*count*]
all the plants of one kind that a farmer grows at one time: *There was a good* **crop of** *potatoes last year.* ◆ *Rain is good for the crops.*

cross[1] 🔑 /krɔs/ *verb* (**cross·es, cross·ing, crossed**)
1 to go from one side of something to the other: *Be careful when you cross the street.*
2 to put one thing over another thing: *She sat down and* **crossed** *her* **legs.**
cross your mind (used about a thought or an idea) to come into your mind: *It never even crossed my mind that she was lying.*
cross something off to remove something written down, by drawing a line through it: *Sarah will be out of town, so you can cross her name off the guest list.*
cross something out to draw a line through a word or words, for example because you have made a mistake: *I crossed out the misspelled word and wrote it again correctly.*

cross² /krɔs/ *noun* [count] (*plural* **cross·es**)
1 something with the shape X or †: *She wears a cross* (= a symbol of the Christian religion) *around her neck.*
2 something that is a mixture of two different things: *a fruit that is **a cross between** a peach **and** a plum*

cross·ing /'krɔsɪŋ/ *noun* [count]
a place where you can cross something, for example a road or a river

cross-leg·ged /'krɔs ˌlɛɡəd/ *adjective, adverb*
sitting on the floor with your legs pulled up in front of you and with one leg or foot over the other: *The kids sat cross-legged on the carpet.*

cross ref·er·ence /'krɔs ˌrɛfrəns/ *noun* [count]
(**ENGLISH LANGUAGE ARTS**) a note in a book that tells you to look in another place in the book for more information

cross·roads /'krɔsroʊdz/ *noun* [count] (*plural* **cross·roads**)
a place where two roads meet and cross each other

cross sec·tion /'krɔs ˌsɛkʃn/ *noun*
1 [count, noncount] (**GENERAL SCIENCE**) a picture of what the inside of something would look like if you cut through it: *a cross section of the human brain*
2 [count] a group of people that are typical of a larger group: *The families in the study represent a cross section of society.*

cross·walk /'krɔswɔk/ *noun* [count]
a place where cars must stop so that people can cross the road

cross·word puz·zle **crossword puzzle**
/'krɔswərd ˌpʌzl/ (also
cross·word) *noun*
[count]
a game where you
have to write words
in square spaces
across and down the
page

clues

crouch /kraʊtʃ/ *verb*
(**crouch·es, crouch·ing,**
crouched)
to bend your legs and back so that your body is close to the ground: *I crouched under the table to hide.*

crow /kroʊ/ *noun* [count]
a large black bird that makes a loud noise

crowd¹ /kraʊd/ *noun* [count]
a lot of people together: *There was a huge crowd at the football game.*

crowd² /kraʊd/ *verb* (**crowds, crowd·ing,**
crowd·ed)
to come together in a big group: *The journalists **crowded around** the movie star.*

crowd·ed /'kraʊdəd/ *adjective*
full of people: *The streets were very crowded.* • *a crowded bus*

crown¹ /kraʊn/ *noun* [count]
a circle made of valuable metal and stones (called **JEWELS**) that a king or queen wears on his or her head

crown² /kraʊn/ *verb* (**crowns, crown·ing,**
crowned)
to put a **CROWN** on the head of a new king or queen in an official ceremony: *The current queen **was crowned** in 1953.*

cru·cial **AWL** /'kruʃl/ *adjective*
very important: *a crucial moment* ⊃ **SYNONYM** **critical**

crude /krud/ *adjective* (**crud·er, crud·est**)
1 simple and not showing much skill or care: *The method was crude but effective.*
2 rude in a way that many people do not like: *crude jokes*

crude oil /ˌkrud 'ɔɪl/ *noun* [noncount]
oil that is in its natural state, before it is treated with chemicals

cru·el /'kruəl/ *adjective* (**cru·el·er, cru·el·est**)
A person who is **cruel** is unkind and likes to hurt other people or animals: *I think it's cruel to keep animals in cages.*
▶ **cru·el·ly** /'kruəli/ *adverb*: *He was treated cruelly when he was young.*

cru·el·ty /'kruəlti/ *noun* [noncount]
behavior that is unkind and hurts other people or animals

cruise¹ /kruz/ *noun* [count]
a vacation when you travel on a ship and visit different places: *They **went on a cruise** to Alaska.*

cruise² /kruz/ *verb* (**cruis·es, cruis·ing, cruised**)
1 to travel on a ship as a vacation, visiting different places: *They cruised around the Caribbean.*
2 to stay at the same speed in a car, plane, etc.: *cruising along at 60 miles an hour*

crumb /krʌm/ *noun* [count]
a very small piece of bread, cake, or cookie

crum·ble /'krʌmbl/ *verb* (**crum·bles, crum·bling,**
crum·bled)
to break into very small pieces: *The old church walls are crumbling.*

crum·ple /'krʌmpl/ *verb* (**crum·ples, crum·pling,**
crum·pled)
to be crushed or to crush something into a smaller shape: *She crumpled the paper into a ball and threw it away.*

crunch /krʌntʃ/ *verb* (crunch·es, crunch·ing, crunched)
1 to make a loud noise when you eat something that is hard: *She crunched on her apple noisily.*
2 to make a noise like the sound of something being crushed: *The leaves crunched under our feet as we walked.*
▸ **crunch** *noun* [singular]: *the crunch of their boots on the snow*

crunch·y /ˈkrʌntʃi/ *adjective* (crunch·i·er, crunch·i·est)
hard and dry, so that it makes a noise when you eat it or walk on it: *a crunchy salad*

crush 🔑 /krʌʃ/ *verb* (crush·es, crush·ing, crushed)
to press something very hard so that you break or damage it: *Put the melons in another bag so they won't crush the eggs.* ⊃ Look at the picture at **squeeze**.

crust /krʌst/ *noun* [count]
1 the hard part on the outside of bread
2 a hard layer or surface around something soft or liquid: *the earth's crust*

crustaceans

shell | claw
crab

lobster

crus·ta·cean /krʌˈsteɪʃn/ *noun* [count]
(BIOLOGY) any animal with a soft body in several sections and covered with a hard shell: *crabs, lobsters, and other crustaceans*

crutch /krʌtʃ/ *noun* [count] (*plural* crutch·es)
a long stick that you put under your arm to help you walk when you have hurt your leg: *He broke his leg and now he's on crutches.*

cry¹ 🔑 /kraɪ/ *verb* (cries, cry·ing, cried, has cried)
1 to have drops of water falling from your eyes because you are unhappy or hurt: *The baby cries a lot.*
2 to shout or make a loud noise: *"Help!" he cried.* ♦ *She cried out in pain.*

cry² /kraɪ/ *noun* [count] (*plural* cries)
a loud noise that you make to show strong feelings such as pain, fear, or excitement: *He gave a cry of pain.* ♦ *We heard her cries and ran to help.*

crys·tal /ˈkrɪstl/ *noun*
1 [count] (CHEMISTRY) a shape that some substances make when they become solid: *salt crystals*

2 [count, noncount] a kind of rock that looks like glass
3 [noncount] very good quality glass: *crystal wine glasses*

cub /kʌb/ *noun* [count]
a young animal, such as a young LION or BEAR

cube¹ /kyub/ *noun* [count] (MATH)
1 a shape like a box with six square sides all the same size ⊃ Look at the picture at **solid**.
2 the number that you get if you multiply a number by itself twice: *The cube of 5 (= 5³) is 125 (= 5x5x5).*
▸ **cu·bic** /ˈkyubɪk/ *adjective*: *a cubic foot (= a space like a cube that is one foot long on each side)* • *64 cubic centimeters*

cube² /kyub/ *verb* (cubes, cub·ing, cubed)
(MATH) to multiply a number by itself twice: *Four cubed is 64 (= 4x4x4).*

cu·bi·cle /ˈkyubɪkl/ *noun* [count]
a small room that is made by separating off part of a larger room: *a shower cubicle*

cu·cum·ber /ˈkyuˌkʌmbər/ *noun* [count]
a long vegetable with a green skin, which we often eat in salads ⊃ Look at the picture at **vegetable**.

cud·dle /ˈkʌdl/ *verb* (cud·dles, cud·dling, cud·dled)
to hold someone or something in your arms to show love: *He cuddled his favorite teddy bear.* ⊃ SYNONYM **hug**

cud·dly /ˈkʌdli/ *adjective* (cud·dli·er, cud·dli·est)
soft and pleasant to hold close to you: *a cuddly teddy bear*

cue /kyu/ *noun* [count]
a word or movement that is a signal for someone else to say or do something: *When Julia starts to cry, that's your cue to come onto the stage.*

cuff /kʌf/ *noun* [count]
the end part of a sleeve, near your hand

cul·prit /ˈkʌlprət/ *noun* [count]
a person who has done something wrong: *Police still can't find the culprit.*

cult /kʌlt/ *noun* [count]
(RELIGION) a type of religious group, especially one that is considered unusual: *Their daughter joined a cult.*

cul·ti·vate /ˈkʌltəveɪt/ *verb* (cul·ti·vates, cul·ti·vat·ing, cul·ti·vat·ed)
1 to use land for growing plants: *Only a small area of the island was cultivated.*
2 to try to get someone's friendship or support: *He cultivated links with colleagues in other colleges.*
▸ **cul·ti·va·tion** /ˌkʌltəˈveɪʃn/ *noun* [noncount]: *cultivation of the land*

cul·tur·al **AWL** /ˈkʌltʃərəl/ *adjective*
1 connected with the ideas, customs, and way of life of a group of people or a country: *There are many cultural differences between our two countries.* ⊃ Look at **multicultural**.
2 connected with art, music, or literature: *a cultural event*

cul·ture 🔑 **AWL** /ˈkʌltʃər/ *noun*
1 [count] the customs, ideas, and way of life of a group of people or a country: *the language and culture of the Aztecs*
2 [noncount] art, music, literature, and the theater: *The city is a center of culture.*

cul·ture shock /ˈkʌltʃər ˌʃɑk/ *noun* [noncount]
a feeling of being surprised, confused, or uncomfortable when you go to a country that is very different from your own

cun·ning /ˈkʌnɪŋ/ *adjective*
intelligent, especially in a bad or dishonest way: *a cunning trick*

cups

cup — saucer
cup and saucer

handle
mug

cup 🔑 /kʌp/ *noun* [count]
1 a small round container with a handle, which you can drink from: *a cup and saucer*
2 a unit of measurement used in cooking, equal to eight ounces: *Add half a cup of sugar and two cups of flour.*
3 (**SPORTS**) a large metal thing like a cup, which you get as a prize for winning a competition

cup·board /ˈkʌbərd/ *noun* [count]
a piece of furniture with shelves and doors, where you keep things like food: *kitchen cupboards*

cur·a·ble /ˈkyʊrəbl/ *adjective*
(**HEALTH**) (used about a disease) that can be made better ⊃ **ANTONYM incurable**

curb¹ /kərb/ *noun* [count]
the edge of a path next to a road: *They stood on the curb waiting to cross the street.*

curb² /kərb/ *verb* (curbs, curb·ing, curbed)
to control or limit something, especially something bad: *Apparently, this pill curbs your appetite.*

cure¹ /kyʊr/ *verb* (cures, cur·ing, cured) (**HEALTH**)
1 to make a sick person well again: *The doctors can't cure her.*
2 to make an illness go away: *Can this disease be cured?* ⊃ The adjective is **curable**.

cure² /kyʊr/ *noun* [count]
(**HEALTH**) something that makes an illness go away: *a cure for cancer*

cur·few /ˈkərfyu/ *noun* [count]
1 a time when children must arrive home in the evening: *My parents set my curfew at 10:00* (= I have to be home by 10pm).
2 a time after which people are not allowed to go outside their homes: *After the rebel attack, the government imposed a curfew on the city.*

cu·ri·os·i·ty /ˌkyʊriˈɑsəti/ *noun* [noncount]
wanting to know about things: *I was full of curiosity about the letter.*

cu·ri·ous /ˈkyʊriəs/ *adjective*
If you are **curious**, you want to know about something: *They were very curious about the people who lived upstairs.*
▶ **cu·ri·ous·ly** /ˈkyʊriəsli/ *adverb*: *"Where are you going?" she asked curiously.*

curl¹ /kərl/ *verb* (curls, curl·ing, curled)
to form or make something form into a round or curved shape: *to curl your hair*
curl up to put your arms, legs, and head close to your body: *The cat curled up by the fire.*

curl² /kərl/ *noun* [count]
a piece of hair in a round shape

curl·y 🔑 /ˈkərli/ *adjective* (curl·i·er, curl·i·est)
with a lot of CURLS: *He has curly hair.* ⊃ **ANTONYM straight** ⊃ Look at the picture at **hair**.

cur·ren·cy **AWL** /ˈkərənsi/ *noun* [count] (plural cur·ren·cies)
the money that a country uses: *The currency of the United States is the dollar.*

cur·rent¹ /ˈkərənt/ *adjective*
happening or used now: *current fashions*
▶ **cur·rent·ly** /ˈkərəntli/ *adverb*
now; at the moment: *He is currently working in Seattle.*

cur·rent² /ˈkərənt/ *noun* [count]
1 air or water that is moving: *It is dangerous to swim here because of the strong current.*
2 (**PHYSICS**) electricity that is going through a wire

cur·ric·u·lum /kəˈrɪkyələm/ *noun* [count] (plural cur·ric·u·la /kəˈrɪkyələ/ or cur·ric·u·lums)
all the subjects that you study in a school or college: *Latin is not part of the curriculum at our school.* ⊃ Look at **syllabus**.

cur·ry /ˈkəri/ *noun* [count, noncount] (plural cur·ries)
an Indian dish of meat or vegetables cooked with spices and often eaten with rice: *chicken curry*

curse /kərs/ *noun* [count]
1 a rude word that some people use when they are very angry ⊃ **SYNONYM swear word**

2 a word or phrase that has a magic power to make something bad happen: *The family seemed to be under a curse* (= lots of bad things happened to them).

▶ **curse** *verb* (**curse, curs·ing, cursed**)
to use rude language because you are angry: *When he stood up, he hit his head and cursed loudly.* ⊃ **SYNONYM swear**

cur·sor /'kərsər/ *noun* [count]
(**COMPUTERS**) a small sign on a computer screen that shows where on the screen you are working

cur·tain /'kərtn/ *noun* [count]
a piece of cloth that you can move to cover a window: *Could you open the curtains, please?*

curve[1] /kərv/ *noun* [count]
a line that is not straight; a bend: *a curve on a graph*

curve[2] /kərv/ *verb* (**curves, curv·ing, curved**)
to make a round shape; to bend: *The road curves to the right.*

▶ **curved** /kərvd/ *adjective*: *a table with curved legs* • *a curved line* ⊃ Look at the picture at **line**.

cush·ion /'kʊʃn/ *noun* [count]
a cloth bag filled with something soft, which you put on a chair ⊃ Look at the picture at **chair**.

cus·to·dy /'kʌstədi/ *noun* [noncount]
1 the legal right to take care of someone or something: *She got full custody of the children after the divorce.*
2 the state of being kept in prison for a short time: *He was taken into police custody.*

cus·tom /'kʌstəm/ *noun* [count]
something that a group of people usually do: *the custom of giving gifts at Christmas* • *It's a local custom.*

cus·tom·er /'kʌstəmər/ *noun* [count]
a person who buys things from a store or other business

cus·tom·ize /'kʌstəmaɪz/ *verb* (**cus·tom·iz·es, cus·tom·iz·ing, cus·tom·ized**)
to change something to make it more suitable for you: *We can customize your car with leather seats.*

cus·toms /'kʌstəmz/ *noun* [plural]
the place at an airport or a port where you must show what you have brought with you from another country: *a customs officer*

cut[1] /kʌt/ *verb* (**cuts, cut·ting, cut, has cut**)
1 to break or damage something with something sharp, for example a knife or scissors: *I cut the apple in half* (= into two parts). • *She cut her finger on some broken glass.*
2 to take one piece from something bigger using a knife or scissors: *Can you cut me a piece of cake, please?*

3 to make something shorter with a knife or scissors: *Did you get your hair cut ?*
be cut off to be kept alone, away from other people: *When I went away to college, I really felt cut off from my friends.*
cut down on something to use, do, or buy less of something: *You should cut down on sweets.*
cut something down to cut something so that it falls down: *We cut down the old tree.*
cut something off
1 to remove something from something larger by cutting: *Peel the cucumber and cut off the ends.*
2 to stop the supply of something: *The workmen cut off the electricity.*
cut something out
1 to take something from the place where it was by using scissors, etc.: *I cut the picture out of the newspaper.*
2 (*informal*) to stop saying or doing something that you do not like: *Cut it out! That hurts!*
cut something up to cut something into pieces with a knife, etc.

Thesaurus

cut to divide something into two or more pieces with a knife, etc.: *Cut the sandwich in half* (= into two equal pieces). • *She cut the bread into thick slices.* • *He cut up the meat on his plate.*

chop to cut something into pieces with something sharp, such as a knife: *Chop the carrots up into small pieces.* • *Add the finely chopped onions.* • *Roughly chop the herbs.*

slice to cut something into thin pieces (called **slices**): *Slice the cucumber thinly.* • *a loaf of sliced bread* • *Should I slice the cake now?*

carve to cut a large piece of cooked meat into smaller pieces for eating: *Dinner is ready. Who's going to carve the turkey?*

cut[2] /kʌt/ *noun* [count]
1 (**HEALTH**) an injury on the skin, made by something sharp like a knife: *He had a deep cut on his leg.*
2 a hole or opening in something, made with something sharp: *Make a small cut in the material.*
3 making something smaller or less: *a cut in government spending* • *job cuts*

cute /kyut/ *adjective* (**cut·er, cut·est**)
1 pretty and attractive: *a cute little baby*
2 (*informal*) sexually attractive: *There were so many cute guys at the party.*

cy·ber·space /'saɪbər,speɪs/ *noun* [noncount]
(**COMPUTERS**) a place that is not real, where e-mails go when you send them from one computer to another

---

cy·cle AWL /'saɪkl/ *noun* [count]
a series of events that happen again and again, always in the same order: *the life cycle of a frog*

cy·cli·cal AWL /'saɪklɪkl; 'sɪklɪkl/ (also **cy·clic** /'saɪklɪk; 'sɪklɪk/) *adjective*
repeated many times in the same order: *the cyclical pattern of the economy*

cy·cling AWL /'saɪklɪŋ/ *noun* [noncount]
(**SPORTS**) the sport or activity of riding a bicycle

cy·clist /'saɪklɪst/ *noun* [count]
(**SPORTS**) a person who rides a bicycle as a sport: *Cyclists from all over the world competed in the race.*

cy·clone /'saɪkloʊn/ *noun* [count]
(**GEOGRAPHY**) a very strong wind that moves in a circle and causes a storm

cyl·in·der /'sɪləndər/ *noun* [count]
(**MATH**) a long round shape, like a tube or a can of food ⊃ Look at the picture at **solid**.

▶ **cy·lin·dri·cal** /sə'lɪndrɪkl/ *adjective*: *a cylindrical shape*

cym·bal /'sɪmbl/ *noun* [count]
(**MUSIC**) one of a pair of round metal plates used as a musical instrument

cymbal

a pair of cymbals

cyn·ic /'sɪnɪk/ *noun* [count]
a person who believes that people only do things for themselves, not to help others: *You're such a cynic. Maybe he doesn't even care about the money.*

▶ **cyn·i·cal** /'sɪnɪkl/ *adjective*: *a cynical comment about modern politics*

Dd

D, d /di/ *noun* [count] (*plural* **D's, d's** /diz/)
1 the fourth letter of the English alphabet: *"Dog" begins with a "D."*
2 **D** a low grade for a test or piece of work. A **D** is the lowest grade with which you can pass: *I got a D on my chemistry test.*

D.A. short for **district attorney**

dab¹ /dæb/ *noun* [count]
a small quantity of something that is put on a surface: *a dab of paint*

dab² /dæb/ *verb* (**dabs, dab·bing, dabbed**)
to touch something lightly and quickly: *She dabbed the cut with a cotton ball.*
dab something on something to put something on something else lightly: *to dab some antiseptic on a wound*

dad /dæd/ *noun* [count] (*informal*)
father: *Let's go, Dad!* ◆ *This is my dad.*

dad·dy /'dædi/ *noun* [count] (*plural* **dad·dies**)
a word for "father" that children use

daf·fo·dil /'dæfədɪl/ *noun* [count]
a yellow flower that grows in the spring

dag·ger /'dægər/
noun [count]
a short pointed knife that people use as a weapon ➔ Look at **sword**.

dagger

dai·ly /'deɪli/
adjective, *adverb*
happening or coming every day or once a day: *There are daily flights between Miami and Dallas.* ◆ *a daily newspaper* ◆ *The museum is open daily from 9 a.m. to 5 p.m.*

dai·ry /'dɛri/ *noun* (*plural* **dai·ries**)

> **ⓘ SPELLING**
> Be careful! Don't confuse **dairy** and **diary**. You spell **dairy** with **AI**.

1 [count] a place where milk is kept, or where milk products like butter and cheese are made
2 [noncount] food made from milk, for example cheese or butter: *Don't give her a yogurt – she doesn't eat dairy.* ◆ *dairy products*

dai·sy /'deɪzi/ *noun* [count] (*plural* **dai·sies**)
a small flower with a yellow center, which usually grows wild in grass

dam /dæm/ *noun* [count]
a wall that is built across a river to hold the water back

dam·age¹ /'dæmɪdʒ/ *noun* [noncount]
harm or injury that is caused when something is broken or spoiled: *He had an accident, but he didn't do any damage to his car.*

dam·age² /'dæmɪdʒ/ *verb* (**dam·ag·es, dam·ag·ing, dam·aged**)
to break or harm something: *The house was badly damaged by the fire.*
▶ **dam·ag·ing** /'dæmədʒɪŋ/ *adjective*: *Cars have a damaging effect on the environment.*

damn /dæm/ *exclamation*
a rude word that people sometimes use when they are angry: *Damn! I'm late and I can't find my keys!*

damp /dæmp/ *adjective* (**damp·er, damp·est**)
a little wet: *a cold, damp house*

dance¹ /dæns/ *verb* (**danc·es, danc·ing, danced**)
to move your body to music: *Bob really knows how to dance!* ◆ *I danced with her all night.*
▶ **danc·ing** /'dænsɪŋ/ *noun* [noncount]: *Will there be dancing at the party?*

dance² /dæns/ *noun*
1 [count, noncount] movements that you do to music
2 [count] a party where people dance: *My parents met at a dance.*

danc·er /'dænsər/ *noun* [count]
a person who dances: *Baryshnikov is a famous ballet dancer.* ◆ *I'm not a very good dancer.*

dan·de·li·on /'dændəlaɪən/ *noun* [count]
a small yellow flower that grows wild in grass

dan·druff /'dændrəf/ *noun* [noncount]
small pieces of dead skin in a person's hair

dan·ger /'deɪndʒər/ *noun*
1 [noncount] the possibility that something bad may happen: *If you don't stop smoking, your health may be in serious danger.*
2 [count] a person or thing that may bring harm or trouble: *These chemicals are a danger to the environment.*

dan·ger·ous /'deɪndʒərəs/ *adjective*
A person or thing that is **dangerous** may hurt you: *It's dangerous to ride a motorcycle without a helmet.* ◆ *a dangerous disease*
▶ **dan·ger·ous·ly** /'deɪndʒərəsli/ *adverb*: *She drives dangerously.*

dan·gle /'dæŋgl/ *verb* (**dan·gles, dan·gling, dan·gled**)
to hang down and swing from side to side; to hold something so it hangs in this way: *She sat on the dock with her legs dangling over the water.*

dare /dɛr/ *verb* (**dares, dar·ing, dared**)
dare do something to be brave enough to do something: *I didn't dare ask for more money.*

---

dare someone to do something to ask someone to do something dangerous or silly to see if they are brave enough: *I dare you to jump off that wall!*

don't you dare words that you use for telling someone very strongly not to do something: *Don't you dare read my letters!*

how dare you words that show you are very angry about something that someone has done: *How dare you speak to me like that!*

dar·ing /'dɛrɪŋ/ *adjective*
not afraid to do dangerous things: *a daring attack* ⊃ SYNONYM **brave**

dark¹ /dɑrk/ *adjective* (dark·er, dark·est)
1 with no light, or not much light: *It was so dark that I couldn't see anything.* • *It gets dark very early in the winter.* ⊃ ANTONYM **light**
2 A **dark** color is nearer to black than to white: *a dark green skirt* • *He has dark brown eyes.* ⊃ ANTONYM **light, pale**
3 A person who is **dark** has brown or black hair or skin: *a thin, dark woman* ⊃ ANTONYM **fair**

dark² /dɑrk/ *noun* [singular]
where there is no light: *Cats can see in the dark.* • *Are you afraid of the dark?*

after dark after the sun goes down in the evening

before dark before the sun goes down in the evening: *Make sure you get home before dark.*

dark·ness /'dɑrknəs/ *noun* [noncount]
when there is no light: *The whole house was in darkness.*

dar·ling /'dɑrlɪŋ/ *noun* [count]
a name that you call someone that you love: *Are you all right, darling?*
▶ **dar·ling** *adjective*: *our darling daughter*

dart /dɑrt/ *verb* (darts, dart·ing, dart·ed)
to move quickly and suddenly: *He darted across the road.*

darts /dɑrts/ *noun* [plural]
a game in which you throw a small metal arrow (called a DART) at a round board with numbers on it (called a DARTBOARD)

dash¹ /dæʃ/ *noun* [count] (plural dash·es)
1 a sudden short run somewhere: *He made a dash for the bus but just missed it.* • *Owen ran the 100-yard dash (= a race of 100 yards) in less than ten seconds.*
2 a small amount of something that you add to something else: *Add a dash of lemon juice.*
3 (ENGLISH LANGUAGE ARTS) a mark (–) that you use in writing

dash² /dæʃ/ *verb* (dash·es, dash·ing, dashed)
to run quickly somewhere: *I dashed into a coffee shop when it started to rain.*

dash·board /'dæʃbɔrd/ *noun* [count]
the part of a car in front of the driver where most of the switches and controls are ⊃ Look at the picture at **steering wheel**.

da·ta AWL /'deɪtə; 'dætə/ *noun* [plural]
facts or information: *We are studying the data that we have collected.*

da·ta·base /'deɪtəbeɪs; 'dætəbeɪs/ *noun* [count]
(COMPUTERS) information that is stored in a computer in an organized system that lets you look at it and use it in different ways: *Information about every car is stored in the police database.*

date¹ /deɪt/ *noun* [count]
1 the number of the day, the month, and sometimes the year: *"What's the date today?" "It's February first."* • *Today's date is December 12, 2010.* • *What is your date of birth?*
2 a romantic meeting when two people go out somewhere: *He asked her out on a date.*
3 a small sweet brown fruit that comes from a tree which grows in hot countries

out of date not modern: *The machinery they use is completely out of date.*

up to date with all the newest information: *Is this list of names up to date?*

date² /deɪt/ *verb* (dates, dat·ing, dat·ed)
1 to write the day's date on something: *The letter is dated January 4, 2011.*
2 to have a romantic relationship with someone: *Are you dating anyone right now?*

dat·ed /'deɪtəd/ *adjective*
old-fashioned: *It's a good movie, but it looks really dated now.* • *a dated hairstyle*

daugh·ter /'dɔtər/ *noun* [count]

> 🛈 PRONUNCIATION
> The word **daughter** sounds like **water**, because we don't say the letters **gh** in this word.

a girl or woman who is someone's child: *They have two daughters and a son.* • *My oldest daughter is a doctor.*

daugh·ter-in-law /'dɔtər ɪn lɔ/ *noun* [count] (plural daugh·ters-in-law)
the wife of your son ⊃ Look at **son-in-law**.

daunt /dɔnt/ *verb* (daunts, daunt·ing, daunt·ed)
to make someone feel nervous or worried by being too big or difficult: *She said the job was really hard, but I wasn't daunted.*
▶ **daunt·ing** /'dɔntɪŋ/ *adjective*: *The thought of having to change schools was really daunting.* • *a daunting task*

dawn /dɔn/ *noun* [count, noncount]
the time in the early morning when the sun comes up ⊃ Look at **dusk**.

day / /deɪ/ *noun* [count] (*plural* **days**)
1 a time of 24 hours from midnight to the next midnight: *There are seven days in a week.* ◆ *I was in Las Vegas for a few days.* ◆ *"What day is it today?" "Tuesday."*
2 the time when it is light outside: *Most people work during the day and sleep at night.*
3 a time in the past: *In my grandparents' day, people didn't have cell phones.*
one day
1 on a certain day in the past: *One day, a letter arrived.*
2 (also **some day**) at some time in the future: *I hope to become a doctor one day.* ◆ *Some day I'll be rich and famous.*
the day after tomorrow not tomorrow, but the next day
the day before yesterday not yesterday, but the day before
the other day a few days ago: *I went to see my cousin the other day.*
these days (*informal*) used to talk about the present, especially when you are comparing it with the past: *These days kids grow up so quickly.*
  ❺ SYNONYM **nowadays**

day·break /ˈdeɪbreɪk/ *noun* [noncount]
the time of day when light first appears: *He left at daybreak.*

day·care /ˈdeɪkɛr/ (also **day care**) *noun* [noncount]
care for small children while their parents are working; a place that offers this service: *a daycare center* ◆ *My wife takes the kids to daycare every morning.*

day·dream /ˈdeɪdrim/ *noun* [count]
happy thoughts that make you forget about what you should be doing now: *She stared out of the window, lost in a daydream.*
▶ **day·dream** *verb* (**day·dreams, day·dream·ing, day·dreamed**): *He daydreamed about being so rich that he could buy anything he wanted.*

day·light /ˈdeɪlaɪt/ *noun* [noncount]
the light from the sun during the day: *These colors look different in daylight.*

day off /ˌdeɪ ˈɔf/ *noun* [count] (*plural* **days off**)
a day when you do not go to work or school: *She hasn't taken a day off in six months.*

day·time /ˈdeɪtaɪm/ *noun* [noncount]
the time when it is day and not night: *I prefer to study in the daytime and go out at night.* ❺
ANTONYM **nighttime**

daze /deɪz/ *noun*
in a daze not able to think normally; confused: *I was in a daze, and walked into the street without looking.*

dazed /deɪzd/ *adjective*
not able to think normally; confused: *He had a dazed look on his face.*

daz·zle /ˈdæzl/ *verb* (**daz·zles, daz·zling, daz·zled**)
to impress someone very much: *He was dazzled by her beauty.*

Prefix

de-
(in verbs, and related nouns, adjectives, and adverbs) removing something: *decaffeinated coffee* ◆ *defrost the refrigerator*

dead¹ / /dɛd/ *adjective*
1 not alive now: *All my grandparents are dead.* ◆ *Throw away those dead flowers.*
2 no longer working because it doesn't have any power: *The batteries in this flashlight are dead.* ◆ *I picked up the phone, but the line was dead.*
3 very quiet: *This town is completely dead at night.*
4 complete: *There was dead silence when she finished speaking.*
a dead end a street that is only open at one end

dead² /dɛd/ *adverb* (*informal*)
completely or very: *I'm dead tired.*

dead·line /ˈdɛdlaɪn/ *noun* [count]
a day or time before which you must do something: *The deadline for finishing this essay is next Tuesday.*

dead·ly¹ /ˈdɛdli/ *adjective* (**dead·li·er, dead·li·est**)
Something that is **deadly** may kill people or other living things: *a deadly weapon*

dead·ly² /ˈdɛdli/ *adverb* (*informal*)
extremely: *I'm deadly serious.*

deaf /dɛf/ *adjective* (**deaf·er, deaf·est**)
(HEALTH) not able to hear anything or not able to hear very well: *My grandma's starting to go deaf.* ◆ *television subtitles for the deaf* (= people who cannot hear)
▶ **deaf·ness** /ˈdɛfnəs/ *noun* [noncount]: *In old age she was troubled by deafness.*

deaf·en /ˈdɛfən/ *verb* (**deaf·ens, deaf·en·ing, deaf·ened**)
to make a very loud noise so that someone cannot hear well: *We were deafened by the loud music.*
▶ **deaf·en·ing** /ˈdɛfəniŋ/ *adjective*: *a deafening noise*

deal¹ / /dil/ *verb* (**deals, deal·ing, dealt** /dɛlt/, **has dealt**)
1 to give cards to players in a game of cards: *Start by dealing seven cards to each player.*

2 (BUSINESS) to buy and sell something in business: *Our firm **deals with** customers all over the world.* ◆ *We **deal in** insurance.*
deal something out to give something to a number of people: *The profits will be dealt out among us.*
deal with something
1 to take action in a particular situation in order to solve a problem or do a particular job: *I am too busy to deal with this problem now.*
2 to be about a particular subject: *The first chapter of the book deals with letter writing.*

deal² /dil/ *noun* [count]
(BUSINESS) an agreement, usually about buying, selling, or working: *Let's **make a deal** – I'll help you today if you help me tomorrow.*
a good deal; a great deal a lot: *I've spent a great deal of time on this report.*

deal·er /'dilər/ *noun* [count]
1 a person who buys and sells things: *a car dealer*
2 the person who gives the cards to the players in a game of cards

dear¹ 🔑 /dɪr/ *adjective* (dear·er, dear·est)
1 Dear a word that you use before a person's name at the beginning of a letter: *Dear Mr. Carter,...* ◆ *Dear Sir or Madam,...*
2 that you love very much: *She was a dear friend.*

dear² /dɪr/ *exclamation*
something you say if you are surprised or upset: *Oh dear! It's starting to rain again.* ◆ *Dear me! What a mess!*

dear³ /dɪr/ *noun* [count] (*informal*)
a word that you use when you are speaking to someone that you love: *Hello, dear.*

death 🔑 /dɛθ/ *noun* [count, noncount]
when a life finishes: *He became manager of the company after his father's death.* ◆ *There are thousands of deaths in car accidents every year.* ◆ *The police do not know the **cause of death**.* ⊃ Look at **birth**.

the death pen·al·ty /ðə 'dɛθ ˌpɛn·lti/ *noun* [*singular*]
the legal punishment of being killed for a crime ⊃ Look at **capital punishment**.

de·bat·a·ble AWL /dɪ'beɪtəbl/ *adjective*
not certain; that you could argue about: *It's debatable whether computers really make things easier.*

de·bate AWL /dɪ'beɪt/ *noun*
1 [count] a public meeting where people with different opinions discuss something important ⊃ Look at the note at **discussion**.
2 [noncount] general discusssion about something, when people express different opinions: *There's been a lot of debate about global warming.*

▶ **de·bate** AWL *verb* (de·bates, de·bat·ing, de·bat·ed): *Politicians will be debating the new plans later this week.*

deb·it¹ /'dɛbɪt/ *noun* [count]
an amount of money that is taken out of a bank account ⊃ ANTONYM **credit**

deb·it² /'dɛbɪt/ *verb* (deb·its, deb·it·ing, deb·it·ed)
to take an amount of money out of a bank account: *The payment will be debited from your account.* ⊃ ANTONYM **credit**

deb·it card /'dɛbɪt kɑrd/ *noun* [count]
a plastic card that you can use to pay for things directly from your bank account: *Can I pay by debit card?* ⊃ Look at **credit card**.

de·bris /də'bri/ *noun* [noncount]
pieces of something that has been destroyed: *debris from the plane crash*

debt 🔑 /dɛt/ *noun* [count]
money that you must pay back to someone: *The company has borrowed a lot of money and it still has debts.*
in debt If you are **in debt**, you must pay money to someone.

debt·or /'dɛtər/ *noun* [count]
a person who owes money

de·but /deɪ'byu/ *noun* [count]
the first appearance in public of an actor, etc.: *She made her movie debut in 2006.*

Dec. abbreviation of **December**

de·cade AWL /'dɛkeɪd/ *noun* [count]
a period of ten years: *The country has become richer in the past decade.*

de·caf·fein·at·ed /ˌdi'kæfəneɪtəd/ (also informal **de·caf** /'dikæf/) *adjective*
(used about coffee or tea) with all or most of the substance that makes you feel awake (called CAFFEINE) taken out: *I only drink decaffeinated coffee in the evening.*

de·cay /dɪ'keɪ/ *verb* (de·cays, de·cay·ing, de·cayed)
to become bad or be slowly destroyed: *If you don't clean your teeth, they will decay.*
▶ **de·cay** *noun* [noncount]: *tooth decay*

de·ceit /dɪ'sit/ *noun* [noncount]
dishonest behavior; trying to make someone believe something that is not true: *She was tired of his lies and deceit.*
▶ **de·ceit·ful** /dɪ'sitfl/ *adjective*: *deceitful behavior* ⊃ SYNONYM **dishonest**

de·ceive /dɪ'siv/ *verb* (de·ceives, de·ceiv·ing, de·ceived)
to deliberately make someone believe something that is not true: *She **deceived** me **into** thinking she was a police officer.* ◆ *You're*

t∫ **ch**in　　　dʒ **J**une　　　v **v**an　　　θ **th**in　　　ð **th**en　　　s **s**o　　　z **z**oo　　　∫ **sh**e

deceiving yourself if you think he'll change his mind.

De·cem·ber 🔊 /dɪˈsɛmbər/ *noun* [count, noncount] (abbreviation **Dec.**)
the twelfth month of the year

de·cen·cy /ˈdisənsi/ *noun* [noncount]
moral or correct behavior: *At least she **had the decency to** admit that it was her fault.*

de·cent /ˈdisənt/ *adjective*
1 good enough; right: *You can't wear jeans for a job interview – you should buy some decent clothes.*
2 honest and good: *decent people*

de·cep·tion /dɪˈsɛpʃn/ *noun* [count, noncount]
making someone believe something that is not true: *They had all been fooled by his deception.*

de·cep·tive /dɪˈsɛptɪv/ *adjective*
giving someone a false impression: *The water is deceptive. It's much deeper than it looks.*

de·ci·bel /ˈdɛsəbɛl/ *noun* [count]
a measurement of how loud a sound is

de·cide 🔊 /dɪˈsaɪd/ *verb* (de·cides, de·cid·ing, de·cid·ed)
to choose something after thinking about the possibilities: *I can't decide what color to paint my room.* • *We've decided to go to Florida for our vacation.* • *She decided that she didn't want to come.*

dec·i·mal /ˈdɛsəml/ *noun* [count]
(**MATH**) part of a number, written after the mark (.): *Three quarters written as a decimal is 0.75.*

> ⓘ **STYLE**
> We say "0.75" as "zero point seven five."

dec·i·mal point /ˌdɛsəml ˈpɔɪnt/ *noun* [count]
(**MATH**) a small round mark, used to separate a whole number from a DECIMAL: *To multiply 1.55 by 10, move the decimal point one place to the right.*

de·ci·sion 🔊 /dɪˈsɪʒn/ *noun* [count]
choosing something after thinking; deciding: *I have to **make** a **decision about** what I'm going to do when I finish school.*

de·ci·sive /dɪˈsaɪsɪv/ *adjective*
1 able to make decisions quickly: *It's no good hesitating. Be decisive.* ⊃ ANTONYM **indecisive**
2 making something certain or final: *the decisive battle of the war*

deck /dɛk/ *noun* [count]
1 one of the floors of a ship, airplane, or bus: *He stood on the lower deck of the ship and looked out to sea.*
2 a set of 52 cards for playing games ⊃ Look at the picture at **playing card**.

3 a wooden floor that is built outside the back of a house, where you can sit and relax: *Let's go sit out on the deck.*

de·clare /dɪˈklɛr/ *verb* (de·clares, de·clar·ing, de·clared)
1 to say very clearly what you think or what you will do, often to a lot of people: *He declared that he was not a thief.* • *The country declared war on its enemy.*
2 to give information about goods or money so that you can pay tax on them or it: *You must declare all your income on this form.*
▶ **dec·la·ra·tion** /ˌdɛkləˈreɪʃn/ *noun* [count, noncount]: *a declaration of support* • *the Declaration of Independence*

de·cline **AWL** /dɪˈklaɪn/ *verb* (de·clines, de·clin·ing, de·clined)
to become weaker, smaller, or worse: *The standard of education has declined.*
▶ **de·cline** **AWL** *noun* [count, noncount]: *a decline in sales*

de·com·pose /ˌdikəmˈpoʊz/ *verb* (de·com·pos·es, de·com·pos·ing, de·com·posed)
to be slowly destroyed by natural chemical processes: *a decomposing corpse*
▶ **de·com·po·si·tion** /ˌdikɑmpəˈzɪʃn/ *noun* [noncount]

dec·o·rate 🔊 /ˈdɛkəreɪt/ *verb* (dec·o·rates, dec·o·rat·ing, dec·o·rat·ed)
to make something look more attractive by adding things to it: *We decorated the room with flowers.* • *to decorate a Christmas tree*

dec·o·ra·tion /ˌdɛkəˈreɪʃn/ *noun* [count, noncount]
something that you add to a thing to make it look more attractive: *Christmas decorations*

dec·o·ra·tive /ˈdɛkərətɪv/ *adjective*
added to make something look attractive: *a tablecloth with a decorative lace edge*

de·crease /dɪˈkris/ *verb* (de·creas·es, de·creas·ing, de·creased)
to become or to make something smaller or less: *The number of employees has decreased from 200 to 100.* ⊃ ANTONYM **increase**
▶ **de·crease** /ˈdikris/ *noun* [count, noncount]: *There was a **decrease in** the number of people living in the area.* ⊃ ANTONYM **increase**

ded·i·cate /ˈdɛdəˌkeɪt/ *verb* (ded·i·cates, ded·i·cat·ing, ded·i·cat·ed)
to give all of your energy, time, effort, etc. to something: *He dedicated his life to helping the poor.*
▶ **ded·i·cat·ed** /ˈdɛdəkeɪtəd/ *adjective*: *a team of dedicated volunteers*

ded·i·ca·tion /ˌdɛdəˈkeɪʃn/ *noun* [*noncount*]
wanting to give your time and energy to something, because you feel it is important: *I admire her dedication to her career.*

de·duct /dɪˈdʌkt/ *verb* (**de·ducts, de·duct·ing, de·duct·ed**)
to take something such as money or points away from a total amount: *Your pension will be automatically **deducted from** your salary.* ◆ *I will deduct points for spelling mistakes.*

deed /did/ *noun* [*count*]
1 (*formal*) something that you do; an action: *Cleaning the house for her grandmother was a good deed.*
2 a legal document which shows that you own a house or building

deep¹ 🔊 /dip/ *adjective* (**deep·er, deep·est**)
1 Something that is **deep** goes down a long way: *Be careful – the water is very deep.* ◆ *There were deep cuts in his face.* ⊃ **ANTONYM shallow**
2 You use **deep** to say or ask how far something is from the top to the bottom: *The hole was about six feet deep and three feet wide.* ⊃ The noun is **depth**.
3 A **deep** sound is low and strong: *He has a deep voice.* ⊃ **ANTONYM high**
4 A **deep** color is strong and dark: *She has deep blue eyes.* ⊃ **ANTONYM pale, light**
5 If you are in a **deep** sleep, it is difficult for someone to wake you up: *She was in such a deep sleep that she didn't hear me calling her.*
6 **Deep** feelings are very strong: *deep sadness*

deep² /dip/ *adverb*
a long way down or inside something: *creatures that live deep in the ocean*

deep-fried /ˌdip ˈfraɪd/ *adjective*
cooked in oil that covers the food completely: *deep-fried onion rings*

deep·ly 🔊 /ˈdipli/ *adverb*
strongly or completely: *They were deeply disturbed by the accident.*

deer /dɪr/ *noun* [*count*]
(*plural* **deer**)
a wild animal that eats grass and can run fast. Male **deer** have horns that look like branches (called ANTLERS).

deer

antlers

de·feat 🔊 /dɪˈfit/ *verb*
(**de·feats, de·feat·ing, de·feat·ed**)
to win a fight or game against a person or group of people: *The army defeated the rebels.*
▶ **de·feat** *noun* [*count, noncount*]: *It was another defeat for the team.* ◆ *She refused to **admit defeat** and kept on trying.* ⊃ **ANTONYM victory**

de·fect /ˈdifɛkt/ *noun* [*count*]
something that is wrong with something: *a speech defect* ◆ *defects in the education system*
▶ **de·fec·tive** /dɪˈfɛktɪv/ *adjective*: *The accident was caused by defective brakes.*

de·fend /dɪˈfɛnd/ *verb* (**de·fends, de·fend·ing, de·fend·ed**)
1 to fight to keep away people or things that attack: *They **defended** the city **against** the enemy.*
2 to say that someone has not done something wrong: *My sister defended me when Dad said I was lazy.* ◆ *He had a lawyer to defend him in court.*
3 (SPORTS) to try to stop another person or team from scoring in a game
▶ **de·fend·er** /dɪˈfɛndər/ *noun* [*count*]
a person who defends someone or something, especially in sports

de·fend·ant /dɪˈfɛndənt/ *noun* [*count*]
a person who is accused of a crime in a court of law

de·fense /dɪˈfɛns/ *noun*
1 [*count, noncount*] fighting against people who attack, or keeping away dangerous people or things: *They fought the war **in defense of** their country.* ◆ *the body's defenses against disease*
2 [*noncount*] (POLITICS) the military equipment, forces, etc. for protecting a country: *the Defense Department* ◆ *to reduce defense spending*
3 **the defense** [*singular*] the lawyers who are representing the person who is accused of something in a court of law: *The defense presented their case.* ⊃ Look at **prosecution**(2).
4 /ˈdifɛns/ [*noncount*] (SPORTS) the players on a sports team who try to stop the other team from scoring; the action of these players: *He broke through the defense to score a touchdown.*

de·fen·sive /dɪˈfɛnsɪv/ *adjective*
1 that protects someone or something from attack: *The troops took up a defensive position.* ⊃ **ANTONYM offensive**
2 showing that you feel someone is criticizing you: *When she asked why he was late, he got very defensive.*
▶ **de·fen·sive·ly** /dɪˈfɛnsɪvli/ *adverb*: *"It wasn't my idea," she said defensively.*

de·fi·ant /dɪˈfaɪənt/ *adjective*
refusing to do what someone tells you: *From the age of fifteen she became more defiant.*
▶ **de·fi·ance** /dɪˈfaɪəns/ *noun* [*noncount*]: *As an act of defiance, they played their music too loud.* ⊃ The verb is **defy**.

def·i·cit /ˈdɛfəsɪt/ *noun* [*count*]
(POLITICS) the amount by which the money you receive is less than the money you have spent: *a country's budget deficit*

　ə **about**　y **yes**　w **woman**　t̬ **butter**　eɪ **say**　aɪ **five**　ɔɪ **boy**　aʊ **now**　oʊ **go**

de·fied, de·fies forms of **defy**

de·fine `AWL` /dɪ'faɪn/ *verb* (de·fines, de·fin·ing, de·fined)
(**ENGLISH LANGUAGE ARTS**) to say what a word means: *How do you define "rich"?* ⇥ The noun is **definition**.

def·i·nite ♪ `AWL` /'dɛfənət/ *adjective*
Something that is **definite** is clear, fixed, and unlikely to change: *I want a definite answer, "yes" or "no."* ◆ *There has been a definite change in her attitude.*

def·i·nite ar·ti·cle /,dɛfənət 'ɑrtɪkl/ *noun* [count]
(**ENGLISH LANGUAGE ARTS**) in English grammar, the word "the" ⇥ Look at **indefinite article**.

def·i·nite·ly ♪ `AWL` /'dɛfənətli/ *adverb*
certainly: *I'll definitely consider your advice.* ◆ *It's definitely the best restaurant in town.*

def·i·ni·tion ♪ `AWL` /,dɛfə'nɪʃn/ *noun* [count]
(**ENGLISH LANGUAGE ARTS**) a group of words that tell you what another word means

de·fin·i·tive `AWL` /dɪ'fɪnətɪv/ *adjective*
in a form that is so good that it cannot be improved: *the definitive guide to New York restaurants*

de·for·es·ta·tion /di,fɔrə'steɪʃn/ *noun* [noncount]
(**GEOGRAPHY**) cutting down trees over a large area

de·formed /dɪ'fɔrmd/ *adjective*
having a shape that is not normal or natural

de·frost /,dɪ'frɔst/ *verb* (de·frosts, de·frost·ing, de·frost·ed)
1 to make food warmer so that it is no longer frozen: *Defrost the chicken completely before cooking.*
2 to remove the ice from something: *to defrost the refrigerator*

de·fy /dɪ'faɪ/ *verb* (de·fies, de·fy·ing, de·fied, has de·fied)
If you **defy** someone or something, you do something that they say you should not do: *She defied her parents and stayed out all night.*

de·grade /dɪ'greɪd/ *verb* (de·grades, de·grad·ing, de·grad·ed)
to make people respect someone less: *That type of movie really degrades women.*
▶ **de·grad·ing** /dɪ'greɪdɪŋ/ *adjective*: *Asking people for money is so degrading.*

de·gree ♪ /dɪ'gri/ *noun*
1 [count] (**GENERAL SCIENCE**) a measurement of temperature: *Water boils at 212 degrees Fahrenheit (212°F).*
2 [count] (**MATH**) a measurement of angles (= the space between two lines that meet): *There are 90 degrees (90°) in a right angle.*

3 [count] Universities and colleges give **degrees** to students who have completed a program there: *She has a degree in Mathematics.*
4 [count, noncount] a certain amount or level: *There's always a degree of risk involved in rock climbing.* ◆ *I feel sorry for her to some degree.*

de·hy·drat·ed /,di'haɪdreɪtəd/ *adjective*
(**HEALTH**) having lost too much water from your body: *Make sure to drink plenty of fluids so you don't get dehydrated.*
▶ **de·hy·dra·tion** /,dihaɪ'dreɪʃn/ *noun* [noncount]: *The survivors were suffering from dehydration.*

de·lay¹ /dɪ'leɪ/ *verb* (de·lays, de·lay·ing, de·layed)
1 to make someone or something late: *My train was delayed for two hours because of the bad weather.*
2 to not do something until a later time: *Can we delay our meeting until next week?*

de·lay² /dɪ'leɪ/ *noun* [count, noncount] (*plural* de·lays)
a time when someone or something is late: *There was a long delay at the airport.* ◆ *You must pay the money without delay* (= immediately).

del·e·gate¹ /'dɛləgət/ *noun* [count]
a person who has been chosen to speak or make decisions for a group of people, especially at a meeting

del·e·gate² /'dɛləgeɪt/ *verb* (del·e·gates, del·e·gat·ing, del·e·gat·ed)
to give someone with a lower job a particular task to do: *You should delegate more work to your assistant.*

de·lete /dɪ'lit/ *verb* (de·letes, de·let·ing, de·let·ed)
to remove something that is written or that is stored on a computer: *I deleted some important files on my computer by accident.*

del·i /'dɛli/ *noun* [count] (*plural* del·is) (*informal*) = **delicatessen**: *the deli counter at the grocery store*

de·lib·er·ate /dɪ'lɪbərət/ *adjective*
If something is **deliberate**, then it is planned and not done by mistake: *Was it an accident or was it deliberate?*

de·lib·er·ate·ly ♪ /dɪ'lɪbərətli/ *adverb*
If you do something **deliberately**, you wanted or planned to do it: *The police think that someone started the fire deliberately.*

del·i·ca·cy /'dɛlɪkəsi/ *noun* [count] (*plural* del·i·ca·cies)
a type of food that is considered particularly good: *Try this dish – it's a local delicacy.*

del·i·cate /'dɛlɪkət/ *adjective*
1 If something is **delicate**, you can break or damage it very easily: *I have delicate skin, so I use special soap.*

---

2 light and pleasant; not strong: *delicate colors like pale pink and pale blue* • *The food had a delicate flavor.*

del·i·ca·tes·sen /ˌdɛlɪkəˈtɛsn/ (also *informal* **del·i** /ˈdɛli/) *noun* [count]
a store that sells foods such as meat, cheese, and salads that are ready to eat and do not need to be cooked

de·li·cious /dɪˈlɪʃəs/ *adjective*
very good to eat: *This soup is delicious.*

de·light¹ /dɪˈlaɪt/ *noun* [noncount]
great happiness: *The children shrieked with delight when they saw the puppy.* ⊃ SYNONYM **joy**

de·light² /dɪˈlaɪt/ *verb* (de·lights, de·light·ing, de·light·ed)
to make someone very pleased or happy

de·light·ed /dɪˈlaɪtəd/ *adjective*
very pleased or happy: *I'm delighted to meet you.*

de·light·ful /dɪˈlaɪtfl/ *adjective*
very pleasant or attractive: *We stayed in a delightful little hotel.*

de·liv·er 🔑 /dɪˈlɪvər/ *verb* (de·liv·ers, de·liv·er·ing, de·liv·ered)
1 to take something to the place where it must go: *The mailman delivered two letters this morning.* • *We deliver free within the local area.*
2 to help a mother to give birth to her baby: *to* **deliver a baby**

de·liv·er·y /dɪˈlɪvəri/ *noun* [count, noncount] (*plural* de·liv·er·ies)
1 the act of taking something to the place where it must go: *Please allow 28 days for delivery.* • *We are waiting for a delivery of bread.*
2 the process of giving birth to a baby: *an easy delivery*

del·ta /ˈdɛltə/ *noun* [count] (*plural* del·tas)
(GEOGRAPHY) an area of land where a river divides into smaller rivers flowing toward the ocean: *the Mississippi River delta*

de·luxe /dɪˈlʌks/ *adjective*
of extremely high quality and more expensive than usual: *a deluxe hotel*

de·mand¹ 🔑 /dɪˈmænd/ *noun* [count]
saying strongly that you must have something: *a* **demand for** *higher pay*
in demand wanted by a lot of people: *Good teachers are always in demand.*

de·mand² 🔑 /dɪˈmænd/ *verb* (de·mands, de·mand·ing, de·mand·ed)
to say strongly that you must have something: *The workers are demanding more money.* • *She demanded to see the manager.*

de·mand·ing /dɪˈmændɪŋ/ *adjective*
1 requiring a lot of effort, care, skill, etc.: *a demanding job*

2 (used about a person) always wanting attention or expecting things from other people: *Young children can be very demanding.* • *a demanding boss*

dem·o /ˈdɛmoʊ/ *noun* [count] (*plural* dem·os) (*informal*) short for **demonstration**(1): *They gave us a demo of the new software.*

de·moc·ra·cy /dɪˈmɑkrəsi/ *noun* (*plural* de·moc·ra·cies) (POLITICS)
1 [noncount] a system of government where the people choose their leader by voting
2 [count] a country with a government that the people choose: *We live in a democracy.*

Dem·o·crat /ˈdɛməkræt/ *noun* [count]
(POLITICS) a person in THE DEMOCRATIC PARTY in the U.S. ⊃ Look at **Republican**.

dem·o·crat·ic /ˌdɛməˈkrætɪk/ *adjective* (POLITICS)
1 If a country, etc. is **democratic**, the people in it can choose its leaders or decide about the way it is organized.
2 **Democratic** connected with THE DEMOCRATIC PARTY in the U.S.: *the Democratic senator*
▶ **dem·o·crat·i·cal·ly** /ˌdɛməˈkrætɪkli/ *adverb*: *a democratically elected government*

the Dem·o·crat·ic Par·ty /ðə ˌdɛməˈkrætɪk ˌpɑrti/ *noun* [singular]
(POLITICS) one of the two main political parties in the U.S. ⊃ Look at **the Republican Party**.

de·mol·ish /dɪˈmɑlɪʃ/ *verb* (de·mol·ish·es, de·mol·ish·ing, de·mol·ished)
to break a building so that it falls down: *The warehouse is due to be demolished next year.*
▶ **dem·o·li·tion** /ˌdɛməˈlɪʃn/ *noun* [count, noncount]: *The demolition of the factory will make room for more houses.*

de·mon /ˈdimən/ *noun* [count]
an evil spirit

dem·on·strate AWL /ˈdɛmənstreɪt/ *verb* (dem·on·strates, dem·on·strat·ing, dem·on·strat·ed)
1 to show something clearly: *He demonstrated how to operate the machine.*
2 (POLITICS) to walk or stand in public with a group of people to show that you have strong feelings about something: *Thousands of people demonstrated against the war.* ⊃ SYNONYM **protest**
▶ **dem·on·stra·tor** AWL /ˈdɛmənstreɪtər/ *noun* [count]
(POLITICS) a person who takes part in a public protest: *antiwar demonstrators*

dem·on·stra·tion AWL /ˌdɛmənˈstreɪʃn/ *noun*
1 [count, noncount] (also *informal* **dem·o**) showing how to do something, or how something works: *He gave us a cooking demonstration.*
2 [count] (POLITICS) a group of people walking or standing together in public to show that they

have strong feelings about something: *antigovernment demonstrations*

de·mote /dɪˈmoʊt/ *verb* (de·motes, de·mot·ing, de·mot·ed)
to move someone to a lower position or level, often as a punishment: *Isabel was demoted from manager to assistant.* ➔ **ANTONYM promote**

den /dɛn/ *noun* [count]
1 the place where a wild animal lives
2 a room in a house where people go to relax, watch television, etc.: *They were all watching TV in the den.*

de·ni·al **AWL** /dɪˈnaɪəl/ *noun*
1 [count] a statement that something is not true: *The mayor issued a public denial about his involvement in the scandal.*
2 [noncount] refusing to accept that something is true: *He's been in denial ever since she left.* ➔ The verb is **deny**.

de·nied, de·nies **AWL** forms of **deny**

den·im /ˈdɛnəm/ *noun* [noncount]
strong cotton material that is used for making jeans and other clothes. **Denim** is often blue: *a denim jacket*

de·nom·i·na·tor /dɪˈnɑməneɪtər/ *noun* [count]
(**MATH**) the number below the line in a FRACTION, for example 4 in ¾ ➔ Look at **numerator**.

de·note **AWL** /dɪˈnoʊt/ *verb* (formal) (de·notes, de·not·ing, de·not·ed)
to mean something: *The red triangle denotes danger.* ➔ **SYNONYM represent**

dense /dɛns/ *adjective*
1 with a lot of things or people close together: *dense forests*
2 thick and difficult to see through: *The accident happened in dense fog.*

den·si·ty /ˈdɛnsəṭi/ *noun* (plural den·si·ties)
1 [noncount] how many people or things are in a place, compared to how big it is: *the population density*
2 [count, noncount] (**PHYSICS**) how heavy something is, compared to how big it is: *Lead has a high density.*

dent /dɛnt/ *noun* [count]
a place where a flat surface, especially metal, has been hit and pushed in but not broken: *There's a big dent in the side of my car.*
▶ **dent** *verb* (dents, dent·ing, dent·ed): *I dropped the can and dented it.*

den·tal /ˈdɛntl/ *adjective*
connected with teeth: *dental care* • *dental floss* (= a kind of string for cleaning between teeth)

den·tist 🔑 /ˈdɛntɪst/ *noun* [count]
(**HEALTH**) a person whose job is to take care of your teeth: *You should go to the dentist for a checkup.* • *I have to leave early – I have a dentist appointment.*

de·ny 🔑 **AWL** /dɪˈnaɪ/ *verb* (de·nies, de·ny·ing, de·nied, has de·nied)
to say that something is not true: *He denied that he had stolen the car.* • *They denied breaking the window.* ➔ **ANTONYM admit** ➔ The noun is **denial**.

de·o·dor·ant /diˈoʊdərənt/ *noun* [count, noncount]
a substance that you put on your body to stop bad smells

de·part /dɪˈpɑrt/ *verb* (de·parts, de·part·ing, de·part·ed) (formal)
to leave a place: *The next flight to Baltimore departs from gate 3.* ➔ **ANTONYM arrive** ➔ The noun is **departure**.

de·part·ment 🔑 /dɪˈpɑrtmənt/ *noun* [count]
one of the parts of a college, school, government, store, big company, etc.: *The book department is on the second floor.* • *the sales department*

de·part·ment store /dɪˈpɑrtmənt ˌstɔr/ *noun* [count]
a big store that sells a lot of different things: *Macy's is a famous department store in New York.*

de·par·ture /dɪˈpɑrtʃər/ *noun* [count, noncount]
leaving a place: *Arrivals and departures are shown on the screen.* • *Passengers should check in at least one hour before departure.* ➔ **ANTONYM arrival**

de·pend 🔑 /dɪˈpɛnd/ *verb* (de·pends, de·pend·ing, de·pend·ed)
depend on someone or **something**
1 to trust someone; to feel sure that someone or something will do what you want: *I know I can depend on my friends to help me.*
2 to need someone or something: *She still depends on her parents for money because she doesn't have a job.*
it depends; that depends words that you use to show that something is not certain: *I don't know whether I'll see him. It depends what time he gets here.* • *"Can you lend me some money?" "That depends. How much do you want?"*

de·pend·a·ble /dɪˈpɛndəbl/ *adjective*
that can be trusted: *The bus service is usually very dependable.* ➔ **SYNONYM reliable**

de·pend·ence /dɪˈpɛndəns/ *noun* [noncount]
the state of needing someone or something: *The country is trying to reduce its dependence on imported oil.* ➔ **ANTONYM independence**

de·pend·ent[1] /dɪˈpɛndənt/ *noun* [count]
a person, especially a child, who depends on another person for a home, food, money, etc.

de·pend·ent² /dɪˈpɛndənt/ *adjective*
If you are **dependent** on someone or something, you need them: *A baby is completely dependent on its parents.* ⊃ **ANTONYM independent**

de·port /dɪˈpɔrt/ *verb* (de·ports, de·port·ing, de·port·ed)
(**POLITICS**) to force someone to leave a country: *Many illegal immigrants were deported.*
▶ **de·por·ta·tion** /ˌdipɔrˈteɪʃn/ *noun* [count, noncount]: *After being arrested, she faced deportation.*

de·pos·it¹ /dɪˈpɑzət/ *noun* [count]
1 money that you pay to show that you want something and that you will pay the rest later: *We paid a deposit on the car.*
2 extra money that you pay when you rent something. You get it back if you do not damage or lose what you have rented: *If you damage the apartment, they'll keep your deposit.*
3 money that you pay into a bank: *I'd like to make a deposit, please.*

de·pos·it² /dɪˈpɑzət/ *verb* (de·pos·its, de·pos·it·ing, de·pos·it·ed)
to put something somewhere to keep it safe: *The money was deposited in the bank.*

de·pot /ˈdipoʊ/ *noun* [count]
a place where a lot of goods or vehicles are stored: *a bus depot*

de·press **AWL** /dɪˈprɛs/ *verb* (de·press·es, de·press·ing, de·pressed)
to make someone feel sad: *This wet weather really depresses me.*
▶ **de·press·ing** **AWL** /dɪˈprɛsɪŋ/ *adjective*: *That movie about the war was very depressing.*

de·pressed **AWL** /dɪˈprɛst/ *adjective*
very unhappy for a long period of time: *He's been very depressed since he lost his job.*

de·pres·sion 🔊 **AWL** /dɪˈprɛʃn/ *noun*
1 [noncount] (**HEALTH**) a feeling of being unhappy, which lasts for a long time: *She often suffers from depression.*
2 [count, noncount] (**BUSINESS**) a time when a country's economy is bad and many people do not have a job: *the Great Depression of the 1930s* ⊃ Look at **recession**.

de·prive /dɪˈpraɪv/ *verb* (de·prives, de·priv·ing, de·prived)
to stop someone or something from having something: *The prisoners were deprived of food.*
▶ **dep·ri·va·tion** /ˌdɛprəˈveɪʃn/ *noun* [noncount]: *people suffering from sleep deprivation*

de·prived /dɪˈpraɪvd/ *adjective*
not having enough of the basic things in life such as food, money, etc.: *She came from a deprived background.*

depth /dɛpθ/ *noun*
1 [count, noncount] how deep something is; how far it is from the top of something to the bottom: *What is the depth of the swimming pool?* • *The hole was 6 feet in depth.* ⊃ Look at the picture at **dimension**.
2 [noncount] the amount of emotion, knowledge, etc. a person has: *the depth of his feelings for her* ⊃ The adjective is **deep**.

dep·u·ty /ˈdɛpyəṭi/ *noun* [count] (plural dep·u·ties)
the person in a company, school, etc., who does the work of the leader when they are not there: *the deputy chief of police*

de·riv·a·tive **AWL** /dəˈrɪvəṭɪv/ *noun* [count]
(**ENGLISH LANGUAGE ARTS**) a word that is made from another word: *"Happiness" is a derivative of "happy."*

de·rive **AWL** /dɪˈraɪv/ *verb* (de·rives, de·riv·ing, de·rived)
be derived from something to come or develop from something: *The name "Los Angeles" is derived from the Spanish word for angels.*

de·scend /dɪˈsɛnd/ *verb* (de·scends, de·scend·ing, de·scend·ed) (formal)
to go down: *The plane started to descend.* ⊃ **ANTONYM ascend**
be descended from someone to have someone as a relative in the past: *He claims he is descended from royalty.*

de·scen·dant /dɪˈsɛndənt/ *noun* [count]
Your **descendants** are your children, your children's children (called **GRANDCHILDREN**) and everyone in your family who lives after you: *She claims to be a descendant of George Washington.*

de·scent /dɪˈsɛnt/ *noun* [count]
going down: *The plane began its descent into Newark Airport.*

de·scribe 🔊 /dɪˈskraɪb/ *verb* (de·scribes, de·scrib·ing, de·scribed)
to say what someone or something is like or what happened: *Can you describe the man you saw?* • *She described the accident to the police.*

de·scrip·tion 🔊 /dɪˈskrɪpʃn/ *noun* [count, noncount]
words that tell what someone or something is like or what happened: *I gave the police a description of the thief.*

des·ert¹ 🔊 /ˈdɛzərt/ *noun* [count, noncount]

> ℹ **SPELLING**
> Remember! You spell **desert** with one S.

(**GEOGRAPHY**) a large, dry area of land with very few plants: *the Sahara Desert*

de·sert² /dɪˈzərt/ *verb* (de·serts, de·sert·ing, de·sert·ed)
to leave a person or place when it is wrong to go: *He deserted his wife and children.*

de·sert·ed /dɪˈzərtəd/ *adjective*
empty, because all the people have left: *At night the streets are deserted.*

de·serve /dɪˈzərv/ *verb* (de·serves, de·serv·ing, de·served)
to be good or bad enough to have something: *You have worked very hard and you deserve a rest.* • *They stole money from the elderly, so they deserve to go to prison.*

de·sign¹ AWL /dɪˈzaɪn/ *noun*

> ℹ️ PRONUNCIATION
> The word **design** sounds like **fine**, because we don't say the letter g in this word.

1 [noncount] the way that something is planned, made, or arranged: *The basic design of the car is similar to our earlier model.*
2 [count] a drawing that shows how to make something: *Have you seen the designs for the new shopping center?*
3 [count] a pattern of lines, shapes, and colors on something: *The wallpaper has a design of blue and green squares on it.* ⊃ SYNONYM **pattern**

de·sign² AWL /dɪˈzaɪn/ *verb* (de·signs, de·sign·ing, de·signed)
to draw a plan that shows how to make something: *The building was designed by a German architect.*

de·sign·er AWL /dɪˈzaɪnər/ *noun* [count]
a person whose job is to make drawings that show how something will be made: *a fashion designer*

de·sir·a·ble /dɪˈzaɪrəbl/ *adjective*
wanted by many people: *The apartment is in a very desirable location.*

de·sire /dɪˈzaɪər/ *noun* [count, noncount]
a feeling of wanting something very much: *a desire for peace*

desk /dɛsk/ *noun* [count]
1 a type of table, often with drawers, that you sit at to write or work: *The students took their books out of their desks.*
2 a table or place in a building where someone gives information, etc.: *Ask at the information desk.*

desk·top /ˈdɛsktɑp/ (also **desk·top com·put·er** /ˌdɛsktɑp kəmˈpyutər/) *noun* [count]
(COMPUTERS) a computer that is designed to sit on top of a desk ⊃ Look at **laptop**.

des·o·late /ˈdɛsələt/ *adjective*
(used about a place) empty in a way that seems sad: *a desolate border town*

des·o·la·tion /ˌdɛsəˈleɪʃn/ *noun* [noncount]: *All the factories closed, leaving the town in a state of desolation.*

de·spair /dɪˈspɛr/ *noun* [noncount]
a feeling of not having hope: *He was in despair because he had no money and nowhere to live.*
▶ **de·spair** *verb* (de·spairs, de·spair·ing, de·spaired): *We began to despair of ever finding somewhere to live.*

des·per·ate /ˈdɛspərət/ *adjective*
1 If you are **desperate**, you have no hope and you are ready to do anything to get what you want: *She is so desperate for a job that she will work anywhere.*
2 very serious: *There is a desperate need for food in some parts of the world.*
▶ **des·per·ate·ly** /ˈdɛspərətli/ *adverb*: *He is desperately unhappy.*

des·per·a·tion /ˌdɛspəˈreɪʃn/ *noun* [noncount]
the feeling of having no hope, which makes you do anything to get what you want: *In desperation, she sold her ring to get money for food.*

de·spise /dɪˈspaɪz/ *verb* (de·spis·es, de·spis·ing, de·spised)
to hate someone or something: *I despise people who tell lies.* ⊃ Look at the note at **hate¹**.

de·spite /dɪˈspaɪt/ *preposition*
although something happened or is true; not noticing or not caring about something: *We decided to go out despite the bad weather.* ⊃ SYNONYM **in spite of**

des·sert /dɪˈzərt/ *noun* [count, noncount]

> ℹ️ SPELLING
> Remember! You spell **dessert** with SS.

something sweet that you eat at the end of a meal: *a chocolate dessert* • *We had ice cream for dessert.*

des·ti·na·tion /ˌdɛstəˈneɪʃn/ *noun* [count]
the place where someone or something is going: *They were very tired when they finally reached their destination.*

des·tined /ˈdɛstənd/ *adjective*
sure to be or do something in the future: *He was destined for success.*

des·ti·ny /ˈdɛstəni/ *noun* (plural des·ti·nies)
1 [count] the things that happen to you in your life, especially the things that you cannot control: *She felt that it was her destiny to become famous.*
2 [noncount] a power that some people believe controls their lives: *Destiny brought them together.* ⊃ SYNONYM **fate**

---

de·stroy 🔑 /dɪˈstrɔɪ/ *verb* (de·stroys, de·stroy·ing, de·stroyed)
to break something completely so that you cannot use it again or so that it is gone: *The house was destroyed by fire.*

de·struc·tion /dɪˈstrʌkʃn/ *noun* [noncount]
breaking something completely so that you cannot use it again or so that it is gone: *the **destruction of** the city by bombs*

de·struc·tive /dɪˈstrʌktɪv/ *adjective*
causing a lot of harm or damage: *earthquakes and other destructive forces of nature*

de·tach /dɪˈtætʃ/ *verb* (de·tach·es, de·tach·ing, de·tached)
to separate something from another thing that it is joined to: *Please complete and detach the form below.* ⊃ ANTONYM **attach**

de·tail 🔑 /ˈditeɪl; dɪˈteɪl/ *noun* [count, noncount]
one fact or piece of information about something: *Tell me quickly what happened – I don't need to know all the details.* ♦ *For more details, please call this number.* ♦ *This work involves close attention to detail.*
in detail with all the small parts: *Tell me about your plan in detail.*

de·tailed /ˈditeɪld; dɪˈteɪld/ *adjective*
giving a lot of information: *a detailed description*

de·tain /dɪˈteɪn/ *verb* (de·tains, de·tain·ing, de·tained)
to stop someone from leaving a place: *He was detained by immigration officials at the airport.*

de·tect **AWL** /dɪˈtɛkt/ *verb* (de·tects, de·tect·ing, de·tect·ed)
to discover or notice something that is difficult to see: *The tests detected a small amount of blood on his clothes.*

de·tec·tive **AWL** /dɪˈtɛktɪv/ *noun* [count]
a person whose job is to find out who did a crime. **Detectives** are usually police officers: *Sherlock Holmes is a famous detective in stories.*

de·tec·tor **AWL** /dɪˈtɛktər/ *noun* [count]
a machine that is used for finding or noticing something: *a metal detector* ♦ *a smoke detector*

de·ten·tion /dɪˈtɛnʃn/ *noun* [count, noncount]
the punishment of being kept at school after the other children have gone home: *They can't give me a detention for this!*

de·ter /dɪˈtər/ *verb* (de·ters, de·ter·ring, de·terred)
to make someone decide not to do something: *Even the high prices didn't deter people from buying tickets.*

de·ter·gent /dɪˈtərdʒənt/ *noun* [count, noncount]
a liquid or powder that you use for washing clothes and dishes: *What brand of laundry detergent do you use?*

de·te·ri·o·rate /dɪˈtɪriəˌreɪt/ *verb* (de·te·ri·o·rates, de·te·ri·o·rat·ing, de·te·ri·o·rat·ed)
to get worse: *Her health deteriorated as she got older.*
▸ **de·te·ri·o·ra·tion** /dɪˌtɪriəˈreɪʃn/ *noun* [count, noncount]

de·ter·mi·na·tion 🔑 /dɪˌtərməˈneɪʃn/ *noun* [noncount]
being sure that you want to do something: *She has shown great **determination to** succeed.*

de·ter·mine /dɪˈtərmən/ *verb* (de·ter·mines, de·ter·min·ing, de·ter·mined)
1 (formal) to discover the facts about something: *We need to determine the cause of the accident.*
2 to decide or have an influence on something: *The results of the test will determine what treatment you need.*

de·ter·mined 🔑 /dɪˈtərmənd/ *adjective*
very sure that you want do something: *She is **determined to** win the match.*

de·test /dɪˈtɛst/ *verb* (de·tests, de·test·ing, de·test·ed)
to hate someone or something very much: *They have always detested each other.*

det·o·nate /ˈdɛtnˌeɪt/ *verb* (det·o·nates, det·o·nat·ing, det·o·nat·ed)
to explode or to make something explode: *The mine detonated, killing five soldiers.* ♦ *Terrorists detonated a bomb in the capital.*

de·tour /ˈditʊr/ *noun* [count]
a longer way to a place when you cannot go by the usual way: *The bridge was closed so we had to **take a detour**.*

dev·as·tate /ˈdɛvəˌsteɪt/ *verb* (dev·as·tates, dev·as·tat·ing, dev·as·tat·ed)
1 to destroy something or damage it very badly: *War devastated the country.*
2 to make someone extremely upset: *This tragedy has devastated the community.*
▸ **dev·as·tat·ing** /ˈdɛvəˌsteɪtɪŋ/ *adjective*: *The storm had a devastating effect on the island.*

dev·as·tat·ed /ˈdɛvəˌsteɪtəd/ *adjective*
extremely upset: *He was devasted when his wife left him.*

de·vel·op 🔑 /dɪˈvɛləp/ *verb* (de·vel·ops, de·vel·op·ing, de·vel·oped)
1 to grow slowly, increase, or change into something else; to make someone or something do this: *Children **develop into** adults.*
2 to begin to have something: *She developed the disease at the age of 27.*
3 When a photograph is **developed**, special chemicals are used on the film so that you can see the picture.

de·vel·op·ing /dɪˈvɛləpɪŋ/ *adjective*
(used about a poor country) that is trying to develop or improve its economy: *a developing country* • *the developing nations*

de·vel·op·ment 🖋 /dɪˈvɛləpmənt/ *noun*
1 [noncount] becoming bigger or more complete; growing: *We studied the development of babies in their first year of life.*
2 [count] something new that happens: *There are new developments in science almost every day.*
3 [count, noncount] a piece of land with new buildings on it; the process of building on a piece of land: *a new housing development*

de·vi·ate **AWL** /ˈdivieɪt/ *verb* (de·vi·ates, de·vi·at·ing, de·vi·at·ed)
to change or become different from what is normal or expected: *He never deviated from his original plan.*

de·vice 🖋 **AWL** /dɪˈvaɪs/ *noun* [count]
a tool or piece of equipment that you use for doing a special job: *a device for opening cans*

dev·il /ˈdɛvl/ *noun* **the Devil** [singular]
(RELIGION) the most powerful evil spirit, according to some religions

de·vi·ous /ˈdiviəs/ *adjective*
intelligent in a way that is not honest: *a devious plan*

de·vote **AWL** /dɪˈvoʊt/ *verb* (de·votes, de·vot·ing, de·vot·ed)
to give a lot of time or energy to something: *She devoted her life to helping the poor.* • *Schools should devote more time to science subjects.*

de·vot·ed **AWL** /dɪˈvoʊtəd/ *adjective*
If you are **devoted** to someone or something, you love them very much: *John is devoted to his wife and children.*

de·vo·tion **AWL** /dɪˈvoʊʃn/ *noun* [noncount]
1 great love for someone or something: *a mother's devotion to her children*
2 the act of giving a lot of time and energy to someone or something: *devotion to duty*

de·vour /dɪˈvaʊər/ *verb* (de·vours, de·vour·ing, de·voured)
to eat something quickly because you are very hungry: *He devoured everything on his plate and asked for more.*

de·vout /dɪˈvaʊt/ *adjective*
(RELIGION) very religious: *a devout Catholic family*

dew /du/ *noun* [noncount]
small drops of water that form on plants and grass in the night: *In the morning, the grass was wet with dew.*

di·a·be·tes /ˌdaɪəˈbitiz/ *noun* [noncount]
(HEALTH) a disease that makes it difficult for your body to control the level of sugar in your blood
▶ **di·a·bet·ic** /ˌdaɪəˈbɛtɪk/ *noun* [count]
a person who has **diabetes**

di·ag·nose /ˌdaɪəgˈnoʊs/ *verb* (di·ag·nos·es, di·ag·nos·ing, di·ag·nosed)
(HEALTH) to find out and say what illness a person has: *She was diagnosed with diabetes.*

di·ag·no·sis /ˌdaɪəgˈnoʊsəs/ *noun* [count, noncount] (*plural* di·ag·no·ses /ˌdaɪəgˈnoʊsiz/)
(HEALTH) the act of finding out or saying what illness a person has: *to make a diagnosis*

di·ag·o·nal /daɪˈægənl/ *adjective*
(MATH) going from one corner of a square to another: *Draw a diagonal line.* ⊃ Look at the picture at **line**.
▶ **di·ag·o·nal·ly** /daɪˈægənəli/ *adverb*: *Walk diagonally across the field to the far corner, and then turn left.*

di·a·gram 🖋 /ˈdaɪəgræm/ *noun* [count]
a picture that explains something: *This diagram shows all the parts of an engine.*

di·al¹ /ˈdaɪəl/ *noun* [count]
a round part of a clock or other piece of equipment with numbers or letters on it, which shows the time, speed, temperature, etc.: *Check the tire pressure on the dial.*

di·al² /ˈdaɪəl/ *verb* (di·als, di·al·ing, di·aled)
to use a telephone by pushing buttons or turning the DIAL to call a number: *You must have dialed the wrong number.*

di·a·lect /ˈdaɪəlɛkt/ *noun* [count, noncount]
(ENGLISH LANGUAGE ARTS) the form of a language that people speak in one part of a country: *a local dialect*

di·a·logue (also **di·a·log**) /ˈdaɪəlɔg; ˈdaɪəlɑg/ *noun* [count, noncount]
words that people say to each other in a book, play, or movie

di·am·e·ter /daɪˈæmətər/ *noun* [count, noncount]
(MATH) a straight line across a circle, through the center ⊃ Look at the picture at **circle**.

di·a·mond /ˈdaɪmənd/ *noun*
1 [count, noncount] a hard stone that looks like clear glass and is very expensive: *The ring has a large diamond in it.* • *a diamond necklace*
2 [count] the shape ◇
3 [count] (SPORTS) a field where baseball is played
4 diamonds [plural] the group of playing cards (called a SUIT) that have red ◇ shapes on them: *the eight of diamonds* ⊃ Look at the picture at **playing card**.

di·a·per /ˈdaɪpər/ *noun* [count]
a piece of cloth or strong paper that a baby wears around its bottom and between its legs: *It's time to* **change** *the baby's* **diaper**.

di·ar·rhe·a /ˌdaɪəˈriə/ *noun* [noncount]
(**HEALTH**) an illness that makes you pass waste material from your body very often and in liquid form: *an attack of diarrhea*

di·a·ry /ˈdaɪəri/ *noun* [count] (*plural* **di·a·ries**)

> ⓘ **SPELLING**
>
> Be careful! Don't confuse **diary** and **dairy**. You spell **diary** with **IA**.

a book where you write what you have done each day: *Do you* **keep a diary** (= write in a diary every day)? ⊃ **SYNONYM journal**

dice¹ /daɪs/ (also **die** /daɪ/) *noun* [count] (*plural* **dice**)
a small piece of wood or plastic with spots on the sides for playing games: *Throw the dice.*

dice

dice² /daɪs/ *verb* (**dices, dic·ing, diced**)
to cut something into small square pieces: *Dice the carrots and add them to the soup.*

dic·tate /ˈdɪkteɪt/ *verb* (**dic·tates, dic·tat·ing, dic·tat·ed**)
1 to say words so that another person can write them: *She* **dictated** *a letter* **to** *her secretary.*
2 to tell someone what to do in a way that seems unfair: *Parents can't dictate to their children how they should run their lives.*

dic·ta·tion /dɪkˈteɪʃn/ *noun* [count, noncount]
words that you say or read so that another person can write them down

dic·ta·tor /ˈdɪkteɪt̬ər/ *noun* [count]
(**POLITICS**) a person who has complete control of a country
▶ **dic·ta·tor·ship** /dɪkˈteɪt̬ərʃɪp/ *noun* [count]
a country that is ruled by a **dictator**: *a military dictatorship*

dic·tion·ar·y /ˈdɪkʃəˌnɛri/ *noun* [count] (*plural* **dic·tion·ar·ies**)
(**ENGLISH LANGUAGE ARTS**) a book that gives words from A to Z and explains what each word means: *Look up the words in your dictionary.*

did form of **do**

did·n't /ˈdɪdnt/ short for **did not**

die¹ /daɪ/ *verb* (**dies, dy·ing, died, has died**)
to stop living: *People, animals, and plants die if they don't have water.* ◆ *She* **died of** *cancer.*
be dying for something (*informal*) to want to have something very much: *It's so hot! I'm dying for a drink.*

be dying to do something to want to do something very much: *My brother is dying to meet you.*
die down to slowly become less strong: *The storm died down.*
die out to disappear or stop happening: *This species died out in the 19th century.*

die² /daɪ/ *noun* [count] (*plural* **dice** /daɪs/) another word for **dice**

die·sel /ˈdizl/ *noun*
1 [noncount] a type of heavy oil that is used in some engines as fuel: *a diesel engine* ◆ *a taxi that runs on diesel*
2 [count] a vehicle that uses **diesel**: *My new car's a diesel.*

di·et¹ /ˈdaɪət/ *noun*
1 [count, noncount] the food that you usually eat: *It is important to have a healthy diet.*
2 [count] (**HEALTH**) special foods that you eat when you are sick or when you want to get thinner: *You'll need to* **go on a diet** *if you want to lose some weight.* ◆ *No cake for me, thanks. I'm* **on a diet**.

Collocations

Diet and Exercise

healthy eating
- **eat** a healthy/balanced diet
- **be on/go on** a diet
- **avoid/cut down on** alcohol/caffeine/fatty foods

staying healthy
- **be/get/stay** healthy/in shape
- **put on/gain/lose** weight/a few pounds
- **watch/control** your weight

exercise
- **get** regular/plenty of exercise
- **do** yoga/aerobics
- **play** football/hockey/tennis
- **go** cycling/jogging/swimming

di·et² /ˈdaɪət/ *verb* (**di·ets, di·et·ing, di·et·ed**)
(**HEALTH**) to try to lose weight by eating less food or only eating certain kinds of food: *She's always dieting but never seems to lose any weight.*

dif·fer /ˈdɪfər/ *verb* (**dif·fers, dif·fer·ing, dif·fered**)
to be different: *How does this printer* **differ from** *the more expensive one?*

dif·fer·ence /ˈdɪfrəns/ *noun* [count, noncount]
the way that one thing is not the same as another thing: *What's the* **difference between** *this computer and that cheaper one?* ◆ *What's the* **difference in** *price between these two bikes?* ◆ *Sarah looks exactly like her sister – I can't* **tell the difference** *between them.*

make a difference to change or have an effect on someone or something: *Marriage made a big difference in her life.*

make no difference; not make any difference to not change anything; to not be important: *It makes no difference to us if the baby is a girl or a boy.*

dif·fer·ent 🔑 /'dɪfrənt/ *adjective*
1 not the same: *These two shoes are different sizes!* • *Football is very different from soccer.*
2 many and not the same: *They sell 30 different flavors of ice cream.*
▶ **dif·fer·ent·ly** /'dɪfrəntli/ *adverb*: *He's very quiet at home but he behaves differently at school.*

dif·fer·en·ti·ate **AWL** /ˌdɪfə'rɛnʃieɪt/ *verb* (dif·fer·en·ti·ates, dif·fer·en·ti·at·ing, dif·fer·en·ti·at·ed)
to see or show how things are different: *It's hard to **differentiate between** the male and the female of the species.*

dif·fi·cult 🔑 /'dɪfɪkəlt/ *adjective*
1 not easy to do or understand: *a difficult problem* • *The exam was very difficult.* • *It's difficult to learn a new language.* ⊃ **SYNONYM hard** ⊃ **ANTONYM easy**
2 A person who is **difficult** is not easy to please or will not do what you want: *She's a very difficult child.*

dif·fi·cul·ty 🔑 /'dɪfɪkəlti/ *noun* (plural dif·fi·cul·ties)
1 [count, noncount] a problem; something that is not easy to do or understand: *I have difficulty understanding German.* • *My grandfather walks with difficulty now.* • *to get into financial difficulties*
2 [noncount] how hard something is: *The questions start easy and increase in difficulty.*

dig 🔑 /dɪg/ *verb* (digs, dig·ging, dug /dʌg/, has dug)
to move earth and make a hole in the ground: *You need to dig the garden before you plant the seeds.* • *They dug a tunnel through the mountain for the new railroad.*
dig something up to take something from the ground by **digging**: *They dug up some old coins in their field.*

di·gest /dɪ'dʒɛst/ *verb* (di·gests, di·gest·ing, di·gest·ed)
(**BIOLOGY**) When your stomach **digests** food, it changes it so that your body can use it.
▶ **di·ges·tion** /daɪ'dʒɛstʃən/ *noun* [noncount]: *Vegetables are usually cooked to help digestion.*

di·ges·tive sys·tem /daɪ'dʒɛstɪv ˌsɪstəm/ *noun* [count]
(**BIOLOGY**) the many parts inside the body that **DIGEST** food

dig·it /'dɪdʒət/ *noun* [count]
(**MATH**) any of the numbers from 0 to 9: *What is your ten digit telephone number?*

dig·i·tal /'dɪdʒətl/ *adjective*
1 (**COMPUTERS**) using an electronic system that changes sounds or pictures into numbers before it stores or sends them: *a digital camera*
2 A **digital** clock or watch shows the time in numbers.

dig·ni·fied /'dɪgnəfaɪd/ *adjective*
behaving in a calm, serious way that makes other people respect you

dig·ni·ty /'dɪgnəti/ *noun* [noncount]
calm and serious behavior that makes other people respect you: *to behave with dignity*

di·lem·ma /də'lɛmə/ *noun* [count]
a situation when you have to make a difficult choice between two things: *to be in a dilemma*

dil·i·gent /'dɪlɪdʒənt/ *adjective* (formal)
showing care and effort in your work: *a diligent student*

di·lute /daɪ'lut/ *verb* (di·lutes, di·lut·ing, di·lut·ed)
to add water to another liquid: *You need to dilute this paint before you use it.*

dim /dɪm/ *adjective* (dim·mer, dim·mest)
not bright or clear: *The light was so dim that we couldn't see anything.*
▶ **dim·ly** /'dɪmli/ *adverb*: *The room was dimly lit and full of smoke.*

dime /daɪm/ *noun* [count]
a coin that is worth ten cents ⊃ Look at the picture at **money**.

dimensions

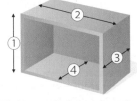

① height
② length
③ width
④ depth

di·men·sion **AWL** /də'mɛnʃn/ *noun* [count]
a measurement of how long, wide, or high something is: *What are the dimensions of the room?*
▶ **–di·men·sion·al** **AWL** /-də'mɛnʃənl/ *adjective*
(used to make adjectives) having the number of **DIMENSIONS** mentioned: *a three-dimensional object* (= one that has length, height, and width)

di·min·ish **AWL** /də'mɪnɪʃ/ *verb* (di·min·ish·es, di·min·ish·ing, di·min·ished) (formal)
to become or make something smaller or less important: *Her determination to succeed never diminished.* ⊃ **SYNONYM decrease**

din /dɪn/ *noun* [singular]
a very loud, unpleasant noise: *We had to shout over the din of the helicopters.*

din·er /ˈdaɪnər/ *noun* [count]
1 a restaurant that serves cheap, simple food in an informal atmosphere: *Let's go to the diner for breakfast.*
2 a person who is eating in a restaurant

din·ing room /ˈdaɪnɪŋ rum/ *noun* [count]
a room where people eat

din·ner /ˈdɪnər/ *noun* [count, noncount]
the largest meal of the day. You have **dinner** in the evening, or sometimes in the middle of the day: *What time do you usually have dinner?* ◆ *What's for dinner?* ⊃ Look at the note at **meal**.

di·no·saur /ˈdaɪnəsɔr/ *noun* [count]
a big wild animal that lived a very long time ago: *dinosaur fossils*

dip¹ /dɪp/ *verb* (dips, dip·ping, dipped)
to put something into a liquid for a short time and then take it out again: *Dip your hand in the water to see how hot it is.*

dip² /dɪp/ *noun* [count, noncount]
a thick sauce that you DIP pieces of food into before eating them: *chips and dip* ◆ *an onion dip*

di·plo·ma /dəˈploʊmə/ *noun* [count]
a piece of paper that shows you have passed an exam or finished special studies: *a high school diploma*

di·plo·ma·cy /dəˈploʊməsi/ *noun* [noncount]
1 (POLITICS) the activity of managing relations between countries: *There is a danger of war if diplomacy fails.*
2 being able to deal well with people in difficult situations: *He handled the meeting with great diplomacy.*

dip·lo·mat /ˈdɪpləmæt/ *noun* [count]
(POLITICS) a person whose job is to speak and do things for their country in another country

dip·lo·mat·ic /ˌdɪpləˈmætɪk/ *adjective*
1 (POLITICS) connected with managing relations between countries: *diplomatic talks*
2 careful not to say or do things that may make people unhappy or angry: *a diplomatic answer* ⊃ SYNONYM **tactful**
▸ **dip·lo·mat·i·cal·ly** /ˌdɪpləˈmætɪkli/ *adverb*

di·rect¹ /dəˈrɛkt/ *adjective, adverb*
1 as straight as possible, without turning or stopping: *Which is the most direct route to the stadium from here?* ◆ *We got a direct flight* (= a flight that does not stop) *to San Francisco.* ◆ *The 6:45 train goes direct to Boston.*
2 from one person or thing to another person or thing, with no one or nothing between them: *You should keep this plant out of direct sunlight.* ◆ *They are in direct contact with the hijackers.*

3 saying what you mean in a clear way: *She has a very direct manner, which some people do not like.* ⊃ Look at **indirect**.

di·rect² /dəˈrɛkt/ *verb* (di·rects, di·rect·ing, di·rect·ed)
1 to tell someone how to get to a place: *Can you direct me to the train station, please?*
2 to manage or control someone or something: *A police officer was in the middle of the road, directing traffic.*
3 to be in charge of actors in a play or a movie: *The movie was directed by Martin Scorsese.*

di·rec·tion /dəˈrɛkʃn/ *noun*
1 [count, noncount] where a person or thing is going or looking: *They got lost because they went in the wrong direction.*
2 directions [plural] words that tell you how to get to a place or how to do something: *Let's stop and ask for directions.* ◆ *Simple directions for building the model are printed on the box.*

di·rect·ly /dəˈrɛktli/ *adverb*
in a direct line or way: *He refused to answer my question directly.* ◆ *The supermarket is directly opposite the bank.* ◆ *Lung cancer is directly related to smoking.*

di·rect ob·ject /dəˌrɛkt ˈɑbdʒɛkt/ *noun* [count]
(ENGLISH LANGUAGE ARTS) the person or thing that is directly affected by the action of a verb: *In "I met him in town," the word "him" is the direct object.*

di·rec·tor /dəˈrɛktər/ *noun* [count]
1 (BUSINESS) a person who controls a business or a group of people
2 a person in charge of a movie or play who tells the actors what to do

di·rec·to·ry /dəˈrɛktəri/ *noun* [count] (*plural* di·rec·to·ries)
1 a book or list of people's addresses and telephone numbers: *a telephone directory*
2 (COMPUTERS) a file containing a group of other files or programs in a computer

dirt /dərt/ *noun* [noncount]
a substance that is not clean, for example mud or dust: *The children came in from the yard covered in dirt.*

dirt·y /ˈdərti/ *adjective* (dirt·i·er, dirt·i·est)
not clean: *Your hands are dirty – go and wash them!* ⊃ ANTONYM **clean**

Prefix

dis-
(in nouns, verbs, adjectives, and adverbs) not; the opposite of: *a disability* ◆ *a disagreement* ◆ *to disappear* ◆ *to dislike* ◆ *to be dishonest* ◆ *to be disloyal*

dis·a·bil·i·ty /ˌdɪsə'bɪləti/ *noun* [*count, noncount*]
(*plural* **dis·a·bil·i·ties**)
(**HEALTH**) a physical or mental condition that means you cannot use a part of your body completely or easily, or that you cannot learn easily: *people with severe learning disabilities*

dis·a·bled /dɪs'eɪbəld/ *adjective*
(**HEALTH**) not able to use a part of your body well: *Peter is disabled – he lost a leg in an accident.* ◆ *The hotel has improved facilities for **the disabled** (= people who are disabled).*

dis·ad·van·tage 🔑 /ˌdɪsəd'væntɪdʒ/ *noun*
[*count*]
a problem that makes something difficult or less good: *One **disadvantage** of living in the country is the lack of public transportation.* ➔ **ANTONYM advantage**

dis·a·gree 🔑 /ˌdɪsə'gri/ *verb* (**dis·a·grees, dis·a·gree·ing, dis·a·greed**)
to have a different opinion from someone else: *I said it was a good movie, but Jason **disagreed** with me.* ◆ *My sister and I **disagree** about everything!* ➔ **ANTONYM agree**

dis·a·gree·ment 🔑 /ˌdɪsə'grimənt/ *noun* [*count, noncount*]
a situation where people have different opinions about something and often argue: *We sometimes **have disagreements** about money.* ◆ *There was some disagreement about what to do next.*

dis·ap·pear 🔑 /ˌdɪsə'pɪr/ *verb* (**dis·ap·pears, dis·ap·pear·ing, dis·ap·peared**)
If a person or thing **disappears**, they go away so people cannot see them: *The sun disappeared behind the clouds.* ◆ *The police are looking for a woman who disappeared on Sunday.* ➔ **ANTONYM appear**
▶ **dis·ap·pear·ance** /ˌdɪsə'pɪrəns/ *noun* [*count, noncount*]: *Everyone was worried about the child's disappearance.*

dis·ap·point /ˌdɪsə'pɔɪnt/ *verb* (**dis·ap·points, dis·ap·point·ing, dis·ap·point·ed**)
to make you sad because what you wanted did not happen: *I'm sorry to disappoint you, but I can't come to your party.*
▶ **dis·ap·point·ing** /ˌdɪsə'pɔɪntɪŋ/ *adjective*: *Peter received some disappointing news.*

dis·ap·point·ed /ˌdɪsə'pɔɪntəd/ *adjective*

ℹ️ **SPELLING**
Remember! You spell **disappointed** with one **S** and **PP**.

If you are **disappointed**, you feel sad because what you wanted did not happen: *Sue was disappointed when she didn't win the prize.*

dis·ap·point·ment /ˌdɪsə'pɔɪntmənt/ *noun*
1 [*noncount*] a feeling of sadness because what you wanted did not happen: *She couldn't hide her disappointment when she lost the match.*
2 [*count*] something that makes you sad because it is not what you had hoped: *Sarah's party was a disappointment – only four people came.*

dis·ap·prov·al /ˌdɪsə'pruvl/ *noun* [*noncount*]
a feeling that something is bad or that someone is behaving badly: *She shook her head in disapproval.* ➔ **ANTONYM approval**

dis·ap·prove /ˌdɪsə'pruv/ *verb* (**dis·ap·proves, dis·ap·prov·ing, dis·ap·proved**)
to think that someone or something is bad: *Joe's parents **disapproved** of his new girlfriend.* ➔ **ANTONYM approve**

dis·as·ter 🔑 /dɪ'zæstər/ *noun*
1 [*count*] something very bad that happens and that may hurt a lot of people: *Floods and earthquakes are natural disasters.*
2 [*count, noncount*] a very bad situation or event: *Our vacation was a disaster! It rained all week!*

dis·as·trous /dɪ'zæstrəs/ *adjective*
very bad; that causes great trouble: *The heavy rain brought disastrous floods.*

dis·be·lief /ˌdɪsbɪ'lif/ *noun* [*noncount*]
the feeling of not believing someone or something: *"It can't be true!" he shouted in disbelief.*

disc /dɪsk/ *noun* [*count*] = **disk**

dis·ci·ple /dɪ'saɪpl/ *noun* [*count*]
(**RELIGION**) a person who follows a teacher, especially a religious one

dis·ci·pline /'dɪsəplɪn/ *noun* [*noncount*]
teaching you to control yourself and follow rules: *Children learn discipline at school.*
▶ **dis·ci·pline** *verb* (**dis·ci·plines, dis·ci·plin·ing, dis·ci·plined**): *You must discipline yourself to work harder.*

disc jock·ey /'dɪsk ˌdʒɑki/ *noun* [*count*]
(abbreviation **DJ**)
(**MUSIC**) a person whose job is to play records and talk about music on the radio or in a club

dis·co /'dɪskoʊ/ *noun* [*count*] (*plural* **dis·cos**)
(**MUSIC**) a place where people dance and listen to popular music

dis·com·fort /dɪs'kʌmfərt/ *noun* [*noncount*]
a slight feeling of pain: *You may feel some discomfort after the surgery.* ➔ **ANTONYM comfort**

dis·con·nect /ˌdɪskə'nɛkt/ *verb* (**dis·con·nects, dis·con·nect·ing, dis·con·nect·ed**)
to stop a supply of water, gas, or electricity from going to a piece of equipment or a building: *Your phone will be disconnected if you don't pay the bill.* ➔ **ANTONYM connect**

---

dis·count /'dɪskaʊnt/ *noun* [*count, noncount*]
money that someone takes away from the price of something to make it cheaper: *Seniors often get a **discount on** rail travel.*

dis·cour·age /dɪs'kərɪdʒ/ *verb* (dis·cour·ag·es, dis·cour·ag·ing, dis·cour·aged)
to make someone not want to do something: *Kate's parents tried to **discourage** her from leaving school.* ⊃ ANTONYM **encourage**
▸ **dis·cour·ag·ing** /dɪs'kərɪdʒɪŋ/ *adjective*
making you feel less confident about something: *The results were discouraging.* ⊃ ANTONYM **encouraging**

dis·cov·er 🔊 /dɪs'kʌvər/ *verb* (dis·cov·ers, dis·cov·er·ing, dis·cov·ered)
to find or learn something for the first time: *Who discovered Australia? ◆ I was in the store when I discovered that I didn't have any money.*

dis·cov·er·y /dɪs'kʌvəri/ *noun* [*count, noncount*]
(*plural* dis·cov·er·ies)
finding or learning something for the first time: *Scientists have **made** an important new discovery.*

dis·creet /dɪ'skrit/ *adjective*
careful in what you say, so that you do not cause problems for someone: *When you work in counseling, you have to be discreet.*
▸ **dis·creet·ly** /dɪ'skritli/ *adverb*: *She handled the matter discreetly.*

dis·cre·tion /dɪ'skrɛʃn/ *noun* [*noncount*]
1 the freedom and power to make decisions by yourself: *You decide what is best. Use your discretion.*
2 care in what you say, so that you do not cause problems for someone: *You can rely on my discretion.*

dis·crim·i·nate AWL /dɪ'skrɪməneɪt/ *verb*
(dis·crim·i·nates, dis·crim·i·nat·ing, dis·crim·i·nat·ed)
to treat one person or group in a worse way than others: *This company **discriminates against** women – it pays them less than men for doing the same work.*
▸ **dis·crim·i·na·tion** AWL /dɪˌskrɪmə'neɪʃn/ *noun*
[*noncount*]: *religious discrimination* (= treating someone in an unfair way because their religion is not the same as yours)

dis·cuss 🔊 /dɪ'skʌs/ *verb* (dis·cuss·es, dis·cuss·ing, dis·cussed)
to talk or write about something in a serious way: *I discussed the problem with my parents.* ⊃ Look at the note at **talk¹**.

dis·cus·sion 🔊 /dɪ'skʌʃn/ *noun* [*count, noncount*]
talking about something in a serious way: *We **had** an interesting **discussion about** politics.*

dis·ease 🔊 /dɪ'ziz/ *noun* [*count, noncount*]
(HEALTH) an illness, especially one that you can catch from another person: *Malaria and measles are diseases.*

dis·grace /dɪs'greɪs/ *noun*
1 [*noncount*] when other people stop thinking well of you, because you have done something bad: *He's **in disgrace** because he stole money from his brother.*
2 [*singular*] a person or thing that gives a very bad impression, making people feel ashamed: *The sidewalks are covered with trash. **It's a disgrace!***

dis·grace·ful /dɪs'greɪsfl/ *adjective*
very bad, making other people feel sorry and embarrassed: *The way the hockey players behaved was disgraceful.*

dis·guise¹ /dɪs'gaɪz/ *verb* (dis·guis·es, dis·guis·ing, dis·guised)
to change the appearance of someone or something, so that people will not know who or what they are: *They **disguised** themselves **as** guards and escaped from the prison.*

dis·guise² /dɪsˈgaɪz/ *noun* [count, noncount]
things that you wear so that people do not know who you are: *She is so famous that she has to go shopping **in disguise**.*

dis·gust¹ /dɪsˈgʌst/ *noun* [noncount]
a strong feeling of not liking something: *They left the restaurant **in disgust** because the food was so bad.*

dis·gust² /dɪsˈgʌst/ *verb* (dis·gusts, dis·gust·ing, dis·gust·ed)
to make someone have a strong feeling of not liking something: *The violence in the movie really disgusted me.*
▶ **dis·gust·ed** /dɪsˈgʌstəd/ *adjective*: *I was disgusted to find a fly in my soup.*

dis·gust·ing /dɪsˈgʌstɪŋ/ *adjective*
very unpleasant or bad: *What a disgusting smell!*

dish /dɪʃ/ *noun* (plural dish·es)
1 [count] a container for food. You can use a **dish** to cook food in an oven, or to put food on the table.
2 [count] a type of food prepared in a particular way: *We had a fish dish and a vegetarian dish.*
3 the dishes [plural] all the plates, cups, etc. that you use during a meal: *I'll wash the dishes.*

dish·cloth /ˈdɪʃklɔθ/ *noun* [count]
a cloth used for washing dirty dishes

dis·hon·est /dɪsˈɑnəst/ *adjective*
A person who is **dishonest** says things that are not true, or steals or cheats. ➔ ANTONYM **honest**
▶ **dis·hon·es·ty** /dɪsˈɑnəsti/ *noun* [noncount]

dish tow·el /ˈdɪʃ ˌtaʊəl/ *noun* [count]
a small towel that is used for drying plates, cups, etc.

dish·wash·er /ˈdɪʃwɑʃər/ *noun* [count]
a machine that washes things like plates, glasses, knives, and forks

dis·il·lu·sioned /ˌdɪsəˈluʒənd/ *adjective*
disappointed because someone or something is not as good as you first thought: *I soon became disillusioned with the job.*

dis·in·fect /ˌdɪsənˈfɛkt/ *verb* (dis·in·fects, dis·in·fect·ing, dis·in·fect·ed)
(HEALTH) to clean something with a liquid that kills BACTERIA (= the small living things that sometimes carry disease): *to disinfect a wound*

dis·in·fec·tant /ˌdɪsənˈfɛktənt/ *noun* [count, noncount]
a substance that you use for cleaning something very well

dis·in·te·grate /dɪsˈɪntəgreɪt/ *verb* (dis·in·te·grates, dis·in·te·grat·ing, dis·in·te·grat·ed)
to break into many small pieces: *The spacecraft exploded and disintegrated.*

disk /dɪsk/ *noun* [count]
1 (COMPUTERS) a flat piece of plastic that stores information for use by a computer: *Please insert a disk into Drive D.* ➔ Look at **floppy disk**, **hard disk**.
2 a round flat object: *He wears a plastic disk around his neck.*
3 = CD: *Put the disk in the CD player.*

disk drive /ˈdɪsk draɪv/ *noun* [count]
(COMPUTERS) a piece of electrical equipment that passes information to or from a computer disk

dis·like /dɪsˈlaɪk/ *verb* (dis·likes, dis·lik·ing, dis·liked)
to not like someone or something: *I dislike getting up early.* ➔ Look at the note at **hate¹**.
▶ **dis·like** *noun* [count, noncount]: *I have a strong dislike of hospitals.*

dis·lo·cate /dɪsˈloʊkeɪt; ˈdɪsloʊkeɪt/ *verb* (dis·lo·cates, dis·lo·cat·ing, dis·lo·cat·ed)
(HEALTH) to put a bone out of its correct position: *He dislocated his shoulder.*

dis·loy·al /dɪsˈlɔɪəl/ *adjective*
not supporting your friends, family, country, etc.: *He was accused of being **disloyal** to the government.* ➔ ANTONYM **loyal**

dis·mal /ˈdɪzməl/ *adjective*
very bad and making you feel sad: *It was a wet, dismal day.*

dis·may /dɪsˈmeɪ/ *noun* [noncount]
a strong feeling of being surprised and worried: *John looked at me **in dismay** when I told him about the accident.*
▶ **dis·mayed** /dɪsˈmeɪd/ *adjective*: *I was dismayed to find that someone had stolen my bike.*

dis·miss /dɪsˈmɪs/ *verb* (dis·miss·es, dis·miss·ing, dis·missed)
1 (formal) to make someone leave their job: *He was dismissed for stealing money from the company.* ➔ SYNONYM **fire**
2 to decide not to think about something or someone: *She dismissed the idea as ridiculous.*
3 to allow someone to leave a place: *The lesson finished and the teacher dismissed the class.*

dis·miss·al /dɪsˈmɪsl/ *noun* [count, noncount]
the act of making someone leave their job: *a case of unfair dismissal*

dis·o·be·di·ent /ˌdɪsəˈbidiənt/ *adjective*
not doing what someone tells you to do: *a disobedient child* ➔ ANTONYM **obedient**
▶ **dis·o·be·di·ence** /ˌdɪsəˈbidiəns/ *noun* [noncount] ➔ ANTONYM **obedience**

dis·o·bey /ˌdɪsəˈbeɪ/ *verb* (dis·o·beys, dis·o·bey·ing, dis·o·beyed)
to not do what someone tells you to do: *She disobeyed her parents and went to the party.* ➔ ANTONYM **obey**

dis·or·der /dɪsˈɔrdər/ *noun*
1 [*noncount*] a messy or confused state: *His finances are in complete disorder.* ➔ **ANTONYM order**
2 [*count, noncount*] (**HEALTH**) an illness: *eating disorders such as anorexia*

dis·or·gan·ized /dɪsˈɔrgənaɪzd/ *adjective*
badly planned; not able to plan well: *The meeting was very disorganized.* ✦ *He's a very disorganized person.* ➔ **ANTONYM organized**

dis·o·ri·ent·ed /dɪsˈɔriəntəd/ *adjective*
confused about where you are: *When I came out of the subway I felt disoriented.*

dis·patch /dɪˈspætʃ/ *verb* (**dis·patch·es, dis·patch·ing, dis·patched**) (*formal*)
to send something somewhere: *Troops have been dispatched to the area.*

dis·pen·ser /dɪˈspɛnsər/ *noun* [*count*]
a machine or container that you can get things like money, drinks, etc. from: *a soap dispenser*

dis·place **AWL** /dɪsˈpleɪs/ *verb* (**dis·plac·es, dis·plac·ing, dis·placed**)
to remove and take the place of someone or something: *Federer was finally displaced as the world's top tennis player.*
▶ **dis·place·ment** **AWL** /dɪsˈpleɪsmənt/ *noun* [*noncount*]: *the displacement of civilians during the war*

dis·play¹ **AWL** /dɪˈspleɪ/ *verb* (**dis·plays, dis·play·ing, dis·played**)
to show something so that people can see it: *All kinds of toys were displayed in the store window.*

dis·play² **AWL** /dɪˈspleɪ/ *noun* [*count*] (*plural* **dis·plays**)
something that people look at: *a fireworks display*
on display in a place where people can see it and where it will attract attention: *The paintings are on display in the museum.*

dis·pos·a·ble **AWL** /dɪˈspoʊzəbl/ *adjective*
intended to be thrown away after being used once or for a short time: *a disposable camera* ✦ *disposable razor blades*

dis·pose **AWL** /dɪˈspoʊz/ *verb* (**dis·pos·es, dis·pos·ing, dis·posed**)
dispose of something to throw or give something away because you do not want it: *Where can I dispose of this garbage?*
▶ **dis·pos·al** **AWL** /dɪˈspoʊzl/ *noun* [*noncount*]: *the disposal of nuclear waste*

dis·prove /ˌdɪsˈpruv/ *verb* (**dis·proves, dis·prov·ing, dis·proved**)
to show that something is not true: *We're trying to disprove the theory that chocolate is bad for you.*

dis·pute /dɪˈspyut/ *noun* [*count, noncount*]
an argument or disagreement between people with different ideas: *There was a dispute about which driver caused the accident.*

dis·qual·i·fy /dɪsˈkwɑləfaɪ/ *verb* (**dis·qual·i·fies, dis·qual·i·fy·ing, dis·qual·i·fied**)
to officially stop someone from doing something or taking part in something: *He was found cheating, and was disqualified from the competition.*
▶ **dis·qual·i·fi·ca·tion** /dɪsˌkwɑləfəˈkeɪʃn/ *noun* [*count, noncount*]

dis·re·spect·ful /ˌdɪsrɪˈspɛktfl/ *adjective*
showing a lack of respect: *Stop being so disrespectful!*
▶ **dis·re·spect·ful·ly** /ˌdɪsrɪˈspɛktfli/ *adverb*

dis·rupt /dɪsˈrʌpt/ *verb* (**dis·rupts, dis·rupt·ing, dis·rupt·ed**)
to stop something from happening as or when it should: *The storm disrupted all flights from Chicago.*
▶ **dis·rup·tion** /dɪsˈrʌpʃn/ *noun* [*count, noncount*]: *disruptions to the bus service*
▶ **dis·rup·tive** /dɪsˈrʌptɪv/ *adjective*: *disruptive behavior*

dis·sat·is·fied /dɪˈsæt̬əsˌfaɪd/ *adjective*
not pleased with something: *I am very dissatisfied with your work.* ➔ **ANTONYM satisfied**

dis·solve /dɪˈzɑlv/ *verb* (**dis·solves, dis·solv·ing, dis·solved**)
If a solid **dissolves**, it becomes part of a liquid: *Sugar dissolves in water.*

dis·tance 🔑 /ˈdɪstəns/ *noun*
1 [*count, noncount*] how far it is from one place to another place: *It's a short distance from my house to the station.* ✦ *In America we usually measure distance in miles.*
2 [*singular*] a place that is far from someone or something: *From a distance, he looks pretty young.* ✦ *I could see a light in the distance.*

dis·tant 🔑 /ˈdɪstənt/ *adjective*
1 far away in space or time: *distant countries*
2 not very friendly: *He can sometimes seem cold and distant.*

dis·till /dɪˈstɪl/ *verb* (**dis·tills, dis·till·ing, dis·tilled**)
(**CHEMISTRY**) to make a liquid pure by heating it until it becomes a gas and then collecting the liquid that forms when the gas is cool: *distilled water*
▶ **dis·til·la·tion** /ˌdɪstəˈleɪʃn/ *noun* [*count, noncount*]

dis·tinct **AWL** /dɪˈstɪŋkt/ *adjective*
1 easy to hear, see, or smell; clear: *There is a distinct smell of burning in this room.*
2 clearly different: *Spanish and Portuguese are two distinct languages.*
▶ **dis·tinct·ly** **AWL** /dɪˈstɪŋktli/ *adverb*
very clearly: *I distinctly heard him say his name was Robert.*

dis·tinc·tion `AWL` /dɪ'stɪŋkʃn/ *noun* [count, noncount]
1 a clear or important difference between things or people: *We need to **make a distinction** between legal and illegal drugs.*
2 the quality of being excellent or famous for what you have achieved: *a pianist **of distinction***

dis·tinc·tive `AWL` /dɪ'stɪŋktɪv/ *adjective*
clearly different and therefore easy to recognize: *a distinctive flavor*

dis·tin·guish /dɪ'stɪŋgwɪʃ/ *verb* (dis·tin·guish·es, dis·tin·guish·ing, dis·tin·guished)
to see, hear, etc. the difference between two things or people: *Some people can't **distinguish between** me and my twin sister.*

dis·tin·guished /dɪ'stɪŋgwɪʃt/ *adjective*
famous or important: *a distinguished actor*

dis·tort `AWL` /dɪ'stɔrt/ *verb* (dis·torts, dis·tort·ing, dis·tort·ed)
to change the shape or sound of something so that it seems strange: *Her face was distorted with grief.*
▸ **dis·tor·tion** `AWL` /dɪ'stɔrʃn/ *noun* [count, noncount]: *sound distortion*

dis·tract /dɪ'strækt/ *verb* (dis·tracts, dis·tract·ing, dis·tract·ed)
If a person or thing **distracts** you, they stop you from thinking about what you are doing: *The noise distracted me from my homework.*

dis·trac·tion /dɪ'strækʃn/ *noun* [count, noncount]
something that takes your attention away from what you were doing or thinking about: *It's hard to work at home because there are so many distractions.*

dis·tress /dɪ'strɛs/ *noun* [noncount]
1 a strong feeling of pain or sadness
2 being in danger and needing help: *a ship **in distress***
▸ **dis·tress** *verb* (dis·tress·es, dis·tress·ing, dis·tressed): *It distressed her to see her mother crying.*

dis·tress·ing /dɪ'strɛsɪŋ/ *adjective*
making you feel sad or upset: *The news of her death was extremely distressing.*

dis·trib·ute `AWL` /dɪ'strɪbyut/ *verb* (dis·trib·utes, dis·trib·ut·ing, dis·trib·ut·ed)
to give or send things to a number of people: *New books are distributed on the first day of school.*
▸ **dis·tri·bu·tion** `AWL` /,dɪstrə'byuʃn/ *noun* [noncount]: *the distribution of newspapers*

dis·trict /'dɪstrɪkt/ *noun* [count]
a part of a country or city: *the city's financial district*

dis·trict at·tor·ney /,dɪstrɪkt ə'tərni/
(abbreviation **D.A.**) *noun* [count] (*plural* **dis·trict at·tor·neys**)
(**POLITICS**) a lawyer working for the government, whose job is to prove in a court of law that someone is guilty of a crime

dis·turb 🔑 /dɪ'stərb/ *verb* (dis·turbs, dis·turb·ing, dis·turbed)
1 to stop someone from doing something, for example thinking, working, or sleeping: *I'm sorry to disturb you, but there's a phone call for you.* ◆ *Do not disturb* (= a sign that you put on a door to tell people not to come in).
2 to worry someone: *We were disturbed by the news that John was in the hospital.*
▸ **dis·turb·ing** /dɪ'stərbɪŋ/ *adjective*
making you worried or upset: *The new crime statistics are very disturbing.*

dis·tur·bance /dɪ'stərbəns/ *noun*
1 [count, noncount] a thing that stops you from doing something, for example thinking, working, or sleeping
2 [count] when a group of people fight or make a lot of noise and trouble: *The police threatened to arrest anyone who **caused** a **disturbance**.*

ditch /dɪtʃ/ *noun* [count] (*plural* **ditch·es**)
a long narrow hole at the side of a road or field, which holds or carries away water

dit·to /'dɪt̬oʊ/ *adverb* (*informal*)
a word that you use to mean "me too": *"I'm starving." "Ditto (= I'm starving too)!"*

dive /daɪv/ *verb*
(dives, div·ing, dived or **dove** /doʊv/, has dived)
1 to jump into water with your arms and head first: *Sam **dived into** the pool.*
2 to swim underwater wearing breathing equipment, collecting or looking at things: *The main purpose of his vacation to Bermuda was to **go diving**.* ◆ *The birds were diving for fish.*
3 to move down quickly and suddenly: *She had to dive to catch the ball.*
▸ **div·ing** *noun* [noncount]: *The resort has facilities for sailing, waterskiing, and diving.*

dive

diving board

swim trunks

div·er /'daɪvər/ *noun* [count]
a person who goes underwater using special equipment: *Police divers found a body in the lake.*

di·verse `AWL` /də'vərs/ *adjective*
very different from each other: *people with diverse backgrounds*

---

di·ver·sion /dəˈvərʒn/ *noun* [*count*]
a way that you must go when the usual way is closed: *There was a diversion around the town because of a car accident.*

di·ver·si·ty AWL /dəˈvərsəti/ *noun* [*noncount*]
a range of many people or things that are different from each other: *the cultural diversity of a big city* ➔ SYNONYM **variety**

di·vert /dəˈvərt/ *verb* (di·verts, di·vert·ing, di·vert·ed)
to make something go a different way: *Our flight was **diverted to** another airport because of the bad weather.*

di·vide 🖊 /dəˈvaɪd/ *verb* (di·vides, di·vid·ing, di·vid·ed)
1 to share or cut something into smaller parts: *The teacher **divided** the class **into** groups of three.* ♦ *The book is divided into ten chapters.*
2 to separate into parts: *When the road divides, go left.*
3 (MATH) to find out how many times one number goes into a bigger number: *36 **divided** by 4 is 9 (= 36 ÷ 4 = 9).*

di·vine /dəˈvaɪn/ *adjective*
(RELIGION) of, like, or from God or a god: *a divine message*

div·ing board /ˈdaɪvɪŋ bɔrd/ *noun* [*count*]
a board at the side of a swimming pool that you use to jump into the water ➔ Look at the picture at **dive.**

di·vi·sion 🖊 /dəˈvɪʒn/ *noun*
1 [*noncount*] sharing or cutting something into parts: *the **division of** the class into two teams*
2 [*noncount*] (MATH) finding out how many times one number goes into a bigger number ➔ Look at **multiplication.**
3 [*count*] (BUSINESS) one of the parts of a big company: *He works in the sales division.*

di·vorce 🖊 /dəˈvɔrs/ *noun* [*count, noncount*]
the end of a marriage by law: *They are **getting** a divorce.*
▶ **di·vorce** *verb* (di·vorc·es, di·vorc·ing, di·vorced): *He divorced his wife.*

di·vorced /dəˈvɔrst/ *adjective*
no longer married: *I'm not married – I'm divorced.* ♦ *They **got divorced** last year.*

diz·zy /ˈdɪzi/ *adjective* (diz·zi·er, diz·zi·est)
If you feel **dizzy**, you feel that everything is turning around and around and that you are going to fall: *The room was very hot and I started to feel dizzy.*

DJ /ˈdi dʒeɪ/ short for **disc jockey**

DNA /ˌdi ɛn ˈeɪ/ *noun* [*noncount*]
(BIOLOGY) the chemical in cells that controls what characteristics animals and plants will have: *a DNA test*

do

Full forms	Negative short forms
present tense	
I **do**	I **don't**
you **do**	you **don't**
he/she/it **does**	he/she/it **doesn't**
we **do**	we **don't**
they **do**	they **don't**
past tense	
did	**didn't**
present participle	
doing	
past participle	
done	

do¹ 🖊 /du/ *verb* (does /dəz; dʌz/, do·ing, did /dɪd/, has done /dʌn/)
1 a word that you use with another verb to make a question: *Do you want an apple?*
2 a word that you use with another verb when you are saying "not": *I like baseball but I don't (= do not) like tennis.*
3 a word that you use in place of saying something again: *She doesn't speak English, but I do (= I speak English).* ♦ *"I like football." "So do I."* ♦ *"I don't speak Chinese." "Neither do I."*
4 a word that you use before another verb to make it stronger: *"Why didn't you buy any milk?" "I did buy some – it's in the fridge."*

do² 🖊 /du/ *verb* (does /dʌz/, do·ing, did /dɪd/, has done /dʌn/)
1 to carry out an action: *What are you doing?* ♦ *He did the cooking.* ♦ *What did you **do with** my key? (= where did you put it?)*
2 to make progress or develop: *"How's your son doing at school?" "He's doing well."* ♦ *How are you doing (= how are you)?*
3 to have a job: *"What do you do?" "I'm a doctor."*
4 to finish something; to find the answer: *I did my homework.* ♦ *I can't do this math problem – it's too difficult.*
5 to be good enough; to be enough: *Will this soup do for dinner?*

Which word?

Do or make?

■ We use the verb **do** for many of the jobs we do at home. We **do the dishes, the laundry** and **the ironing.**
■ We always use **make** for beds: *Make your bed after breakfast.*

could do with something to want or need something: *I could do with a cup of coffee.*

do something over to do something again, usually because you did not do it well enough the first time: *If you don't do a good job on your homework, you'll have to do it over.*

do without; do without something to manage without having something: *If the store is closed, we'll just have to do without coffee.*

have to do with someone or **something** to be connected with someone or something: *I'm not sure what his job is – I think it has something to do with computers.* • *Don't read that letter. It has nothing to do with you!*

dock /dɑk/ *noun* [*count*]
a place by an ocean, lake, or river where ships go, so that people can move things on and off them or repair them
▶ **dock** *verb* (docks, dock·ing, docked)
(used about a ship) to sail into a port and stop at the **dock**: *The ship had docked at Long Beach.*

doc·tor /'dɑktər/ *noun* [*count*] (abbreviation **Dr.**)
1 (HEALTH) a person whose job is to make sick people well again: *Doctor Toby sees patients every morning.* • *If you're feeling sick you should go to the doctor.*
2 a person who has the highest degree from a university

doc·tor·ate /'dɑktərət/ *noun* [*count*]
the highest university degree

doc·u·ment AWL /'dɑkyəmənt/ *noun* [*count*]
1 an official paper with important information on it: *a legal document*
2 (COMPUTERS) a computer file that contains writing

doc·u·men·ta·ry /ˌdɑkyə'mɛntri/ *noun* [*count*] (*plural* doc·u·men·ta·ries)
a movie, or a television or radio program about true things: *I watched an interesting documentary about Japan on TV last night.*

doc·u·men·ta·tion AWL /ˌdɑkyəmən'teɪʃn/ *noun* [*noncount*]
the documents that are needed for something, or that show something is true: *What documentation do I need to get a new passport?*

dodge /dɑdʒ/ *verb* (dodg·es, dodg·ing, dodged)
1 to move quickly to avoid something or someone: *He ran across the busy road, dodging the cars.*
2 to avoid doing something that you should do: *He was accused of dodging (= not paying) his taxes.*

does form of **do**

does·n't /'dʌznt/ short for **does not**

dogs

dog   puppy

dog /dɔg/ *noun* [*count*]
an animal that many people keep as a pet or to guard buildings

doll /dɑl/ *noun* [*count*]
a toy like a very small person ⊃ Look at the picture at **toy**.

dol·lar /'dɑlər/ *noun* [*count*] (symbol **$**)
a unit of money that people use in the U.S., Canada, and some other countries. There are 100 **cents** in a dollar: *This table cost four hundred dollars.* • *a five-dollar bill*

dolphin

dol·phin /'dɑlfən/ *noun* [*count*]
an intelligent animal that lives in the ocean

do·main AWL /doʊ'meɪn/ *noun* [*count*]
1 area of knowledge or activity: *The information is now in the public domain* (= the public knows about it).
2 (COMPUTERS) a set of Internet addresses that end with the same group of letters, for example ".com" or ".org"

dome /doʊm/ *noun* [*count*]
the round roof of a building: *the dome of the cathedral*

do·mes·tic AWL /də'mɛstɪk/ *adjective*
1 connected with the home or family: *Cooking and cleaning are domestic jobs.* • *Many cats and dogs are **domestic animals*** (= animals that live in your home with you).
2 not international; only inside one country: *a domestic flight* (= to a place in the same country)

dom·i·nant AWL /'dɑmənənt/ *adjective*
1 more powerful or important than others: *His mother was the dominant influence in his life.*
2 (BIOLOGY) A **dominant** physical characteristic, for example brown eyes, appears in a child even if he or she has only one GENE (= a thing that controls what a living thing will be like) for this characteristic.

dom·i·nate `AWL` /'dɑmənert/ *verb* (dom·i·nates, dom·i·nat·ing, dom·i·nat·ed)
to control someone or something because you are stronger or more important: *She always dominates the conversation at dinner parties.*
▸ **dom·i·na·tion** `AWL` /,dɑmə'neɪʃn/ *noun* [*noncount*]

dom·i·no /'dɑmənoʊ/ *noun* [*count*] (*plural* dom·i·noes or dom·i·nos)
one of a set of small flat pieces of wood or plastic, used to play a game (called DOMINOES)

dominoes

do·nate /'doʊneɪt/ *verb* (do·nates, do·nat·ing, do·nat·ed)
to give something, especially money, to people who need it: *They donated $10,000 to the hospital.*
▸ **do·na·tion** /doʊ'neɪʃn/ *noun* [*count*]: *He made a donation to the charity.*

done¹ form of **do**

done² /dʌn/ *adjective*
1 finished: *Are you almost done? We need to leave soon.*
2 cooked enough: *The meat is ready, but the vegetables are still not done.*

don·key /'dɑŋki; 'dɔŋki/ *noun* [*count*]
an animal like a small horse with long ears

donkey

do·nor /'doʊnər/ *noun* [*count*]
1 (**HEALTH**) someone who gives blood or a part of his or her body to help a sick person: *a blood donor*
2 someone who gives something, for example money, to help an organization

don't /doʊnt/ short for **do not**

donut /'doʊnʌt/ *noun* [*count*] = **doughnut**

doo·dle /'dudl/ *verb* (doo·dles, doo·dling, doo·dled)
to make small drawings, especially when you are bored or thinking about something else: *I often doodle when I'm on the phone.*

doom /dum/ *noun* [*noncount*]
death or a terrible event in the future that you cannot avoid: *a terrible sense of doom* (= a feeling that something bad is going to happen)

door 🔑 /dɔr/ *noun* [*count*]
the way into a building or room; a piece of wood, glass, or metal that you use to open and close the way into a building, room, car, etc.: *Can you close the door, please?* ◆ *I knocked on the*
door. ◆ *There is someone at the door.* ◆ *Will you* **answer the door** (= go to open the door when someone knocks or rings the bell)*?*
next door in the next house, room, or building: *Mary lives next door to us.*

door·bell /'dɔrbɛl/ *noun* [*count*]
a bell outside a house, which you ring to tell people inside that you want to go in

door·knob /'dɔrnɑb/ *noun* [*count*]
a round object on a door, which you use to open and close it

door·mat /'dɔrmæt/ *noun* [*count*]
a piece of material on the floor in front of a door for cleaning your shoes on

door·step /'dɔrstɛp/ *noun* [*count*]
a step in front of a door outside a building

door·way /'dɔrweɪ/ *noun* [*count*]
an opening for going into a building or room: *Mike was waiting in the doorway when they arrived.*

dor·mi·to·ry /'dɔrmə,tɔri/ *noun* [*count*] (*plural* dor·mi·to·ries) (also *informal* **dorm** /dɔrm/)
a building at a college or university where students live

dos·age /'doʊsɪdʒ/ *noun* [*count, usually singular*]
(**HEALTH**) the amount of medicine you should take and how often you should take it: *the recommended daily dosage*

dose /doʊs/ *noun* [*count, usually singular*]
(**HEALTH**) an amount of medicine that you take at one time: *Take a dose of cough medicine before you go to bed.*

dot 🔑 /dɑt/ *noun* [*count*]
a small round mark: *A lowercase letter "i" has a dot over it.*

ℹ STYLE
We use **dot** when we say a person's e-mail address. For the address **ann@smith.com** we say "Ann **at** smith **dot** com."

---

on the dot (*informal*) at exactly the right time: *Please be here at nine o'clock on the dot.*

dot·ted line /,dɑţəd 'laɪn/ *noun* [*count*]
a line of dots that sometimes shows where you have to write something: *Please sign* (= write your name) *on the dotted line.* ↪ Look at the picture at **line**.

dou·ble¹ 🔑 /'dʌbl/ *adjective*

ℹ PRONUNCIATION
The word **double** sounds like **bubble**.

---

1 two times as much or as many: *a double portion of fries*
2 with two parts that are the same: *double doors* ◆ *You spell "necessary" with a double "s."*

---

3 made for two people or things: *a double bed* ◆ *a double room* ⟹ Look at **single**¹(4).

dou·ble² /'dʌbl/ *verb* (dou·bles, dou·bling, dou·bled)
to become, or make something become, twice as much or as many: *The price of gas has almost doubled in two years.*

dou·ble bass /ˌdʌbl 'beɪs/ *noun* [count]
(MUSIC) the largest musical instrument with strings, which you usually play standing up ⟹ Look at the picture at **instrument**.

dou·ble-check /ˌdʌbl 'tʃɛk/ *verb* (dou·ble-checks, dou·ble-check·ing, dou·ble-checked)
to check something again, or very carefully: *Have you double-checked to make sure you have your passport?*

dou·ble-click /ˌdʌbl 'klɪk/ *verb* (dou·ble-clicks, dou·ble-click·ing, dou·ble-clicked)
(COMPUTERS) to quickly press a button twice on a computer control (called a MOUSE): *To start the program, just **double-click on** the icon.*

doubt¹ 🔑 /daʊt/ *noun* [count, noncount]

> ⓘ **PRONUNCIATION**
> The word **doubt** sounds like **out**, because we do not say the letter **b** in this word.

a feeling that you are not sure about something: *She says the story is true but I have my doubts about it.*
in doubt not sure: *If you are in doubt, ask your teacher.*
no doubt I am sure: *Paul isn't here yet, but no doubt he will come later.*
without a doubt; without doubt definitely: *It was without doubt the coldest winter for many years.*

doubt² 🔑 /daʊt/ *verb* (doubts, doubt·ing, doubt·ed)
to not feel sure about something; to think that something is probably not true or probably will not happen: *I doubt if he will come.* ◆ *It might rain tomorrow, but I doubt it.*

doubt·ful /'daʊtfl/ *adjective*
not certain or not likely: *It is **doubtful whether** he will walk again.*

doubt·less /'daʊtləs/ *adverb* (formal)
almost certainly: *Doubtless she'll be late!*

dough /doʊ/ *noun* [noncount]
flour, water, and other things mixed together. It is used to make bread, cookies, etc.

dough·nut (also **do·nut**) /'doʊnʌt/ *noun* [count]
a small round cake, often in the shape of a ring, which is cooked in oil

dove¹ /dʌv/ *noun* [count]
a bird that is often used as a sign of peace

dove² /doʊv/ form of **dive**

down¹ 🔑 /daʊn/ *adverb*, *preposition*
1 in or to a lower place; not up: *The sun goes down in the evening.* ◆ *We ran down the hill.* ◆ *Put that box down on the floor.*
2 from standing to sitting or lying: *Sit down.* ◆ *Lie down on the bed.*
3 at or to a lower level: *Prices are going down.* ◆ *Turn that music down!* (= so that it is not so loud)
4 along: *He lives just down the street.* ◆ *Go down the road until you reach the traffic lights.*
5 on paper; on a list: *Write these words down.* ◆ *Have you got me down for the trip?*

down² /daʊn/ *adjective*
1 sad: *You seem a little down today.*
2 lower than before: *Unemployment is down again this month.*
3 (COMPUTERS) (used about computers) not working: *I can't get that information right now because the system is down.*

down·fall /'daʊnfɔl/ *noun* [singular]
when someone loses their power or stops being successful: *The scandal led to the senator's downfall.*

down·hill /ˌdaʊn'hɪl/ *adverb*
down, toward the bottom of a hill: *My bicycle can go fast downhill.*

down·load /'daʊnloʊd/ *verb* (down·loads, down·load·ing, down·load·ed)
(COMPUTERS) If you **download** a computer program or information from the Internet, you make a copy of it on your own computer: *I downloaded some music files from their website.* ⟹ Look at **upload**.

down·size /'daʊnsaɪz/ *verb* (down·siz·es, down·siz·ing, down·sized)
(BUSINESS) to reduce the number of people who work at a company in order to save money

down·stairs 🔑 /ˌdaʊn'stɛrz/ *adverb*
to or on a lower floor of a building: *I went downstairs to make breakfast.* ⟹ ANTONYM **upstairs**
▶ **down·stairs** /'daʊnstɛrz/ *adjective*: *She lives in the downstairs apartment.*

down·town /ˌdaʊn'taʊn/ *adverb*, *adjective*
in or toward the center of a city, especially its main business area: *She works downtown.* ◆ *downtown Denver* ⟹ Look at **uptown**.

down·ward 🔑 /'daʊnwərd/ (also **down·wards** /'daʊnwərdz/) *adverb*
toward the ground or toward a lower level: *She was lying **face downward** on the grass.* ⟹ ANTONYM **upward**

doze /doʊz/ *verb* (doz·es, doz·ing, dozed)
to sleep lightly for a short time: *My grandfather was dozing in his armchair.*

doze off to go to sleep, especially during the day: *I dozed off in front of the television.*

doz·en /ˈdʌzn/ *noun* [count] (*plural* **doz·en**)
twelve: *a dozen red roses* ✦ *two dozen boxes* ✦ *half a dozen eggs*
dozens of (*informal*) a lot of: *They invited dozens of people to the party.*

Dr. abbreviation of **Doctor**

draft¹ **AWL** /dræft/ *noun*
1 [count] (**ENGLISH LANGUAGE ARTS**) a piece of writing or a drawing that you will probably change and improve; not the final copy: *the first draft of an essay*
2 [count] cold air that comes into a room: *Can you shut the window? I can feel a draft.*
3 the draft [singular] the system of making someone join the armed forces: *He moved to Canada to avoid the draft during the Vietnam War.*

draft² **AWL** /dræft/ *verb* (**drafts**, **draft·ing**, **draft·ed**)
1 to make a first or early copy of a piece of writing: *I'll draft a letter and show it to you before I send it.*
2 to force someone to join the armed forces: *He was drafted into the army.*

draft·y /ˈdræfti/ *adjective* (**draft·i·er**, **draft·i·est**)
a **drafty** room or building has cold air blowing through it: *a drafty old house*

drag /dræg/ *verb* (**drags**, **drag·ging**, **dragged**)
1 to pull something along the ground slowly, often because it is heavy: *He couldn't lift the bag, so he dragged it out of the store.*
2 If something **drags**, it seems to go slowly because it is not interesting: *Time drags when you're waiting for a bus.*

drag·on /ˈdrægən/ *noun* [count]
a big, dangerous animal with fire in its mouth, which you only find in stories

drag·on·fly /ˈdrægən
ˌflaɪ/ *noun* [count]
(*plural* **drag·on·flies**)
an insect that often
flies near water and
that has four wings
and a long, thin body

dragonfly

drain¹ /dreɪn/ *noun*
[count]
a pipe that carries away dirty water from a building: *The drain is blocked.*
go down the drain (*informal*) to be wasted: *All our hard work has gone down the drain.*

drain² /dreɪn/ *verb* (**drains**, **drain·ing**, **drained**)
1 to flow away: *The water drained away slowly.*
2 to let liquid flow away from something, so that it becomes dry: *Drain and rinse the pasta.*

3 to become dry because liquid is flowing away: *Leave the dishes to drain.*

drain·pipe /ˈdreɪnpaɪp/ *noun* [count]
a pipe that takes water from the roof of a building to a **DRAIN¹** when it rains

dra·ma **AWL** /ˈdrɑmə/ *noun*
1 [count] a story that you watch in the theater or on television, or listen to on the radio: *a TV drama*
2 [noncount] the study of plays and acting: *She went to drama school.*
3 [count, noncount] an exciting thing that happens: *There was a big drama at school when one of the teachers fell in the swimming pool!*

dra·mat·ic **AWL** /drəˈmætɪk/ *adjective*
1 sudden, great, or exciting: *The finish of the race was very dramatic.*
2 connected with plays or the theater: *a dramatic society*
▸ **dra·mat·i·cal·ly** **AWL** /drəˈmætɪkli/ *adverb*:
Prices went up dramatically.

dram·a·tist **AWL** /ˈdræmətɪst/ *noun* [count]
a person who writes plays

drank form of **drink¹**

drapes /dreɪps/ *noun* [plural]
long pieces of heavy material that you can move to cover a window: *velvet drapes*

dras·tic /ˈdræstɪk/ *adjective*
having a sudden, very strong effect: *We have made some drastic changes.*
▸ **dras·ti·cal·ly** /ˈdræstɪkli/ *adverb*

draw¹ 🖋 /drɔ/ *verb* (**draws**, **draw·ing**, **drew** /dru/, has **drawn** /drɔn/)
1 (**ART**) to make a picture with a pen or a pencil: *She drew a picture of a horse.* ✦ *He has drawn a car.* ✦ *My sister draws well.*
2 to pull or take something from a place: *I drew my chair up closer to the fire.* ✦ *He drew a knife from his pocket.*
3 to pull something to make it move: *The carriage was drawn by two horses.* ✦ *It's too bright in here, we'll have to draw the curtains* (= close them).
4 (*formal*) to move or come: *The train drew into the station.*
5 to attract or interest someone: *The concert drew a large crowd.*
draw back to move away from someone or something: *He came close but she drew back.*
draw up to come to a place and stop: *A taxi drew up outside the house.*
draw something up to write something: *They drew up a list of people who they wanted to invite.*

draw² /drɔ/ *noun* [count]
a person, thing, or event that attracts a lot of people: *The festival is always a big draw for young people.*

　　ə **about**　　y **yes**　　w **woman**　　ţ **butter**　　eɪ **say**　　aɪ **five**　　ɔɪ **boy**　　aʊ **now**　　oʊ **go**

draw·back /'drɔbæk/ noun [count]
a disadvantage or problem: *His lack of experience is a major drawback.*

draw·er 🔑 /drɔr/ noun [count]
a thing like a box that you can pull out from a desk, for example: *There's some paper in the top drawer of my desk.*

draw·ing 🔑 /'drɔɪŋ/ noun (ART)
1 [count] a picture made with a pen or a pencil, but not paint: *He did a **drawing** of the old farmhouse.*
2 [noncount] the art of drawing pictures with a pen or a pencil: *Katherine is very good at drawing.*
3 [count] the act of choosing something, for example the winner of a prize, often by taking a piece of paper out of a container: *The raffle drawing will take place today at 5p.m.*

drawn form of **draw¹**

dread¹ /drɛd/ verb (dreads, dread·ing, dread·ed)
to be very afraid of something that is going to happen: *I'm dreading the exam.*

dread² /drɛd/ noun [noncount, singular]
great fear that something bad might happen: *She lived **in dread** of the cancer returning.*

dread·ful /'drɛdfl/ adjective (formal)
very bad: *There's been a dreadful accident.*
▶ **dread·ful·ly** /'drɛdfli/ adverb

dream¹ 🔑 /drim/ noun [count]
1 pictures or events that happen in your mind when you are asleep: *I had a **dream about** school last night.* ⊃ Look at **nightmare**.
2 something nice that you hope for: *His dream was to give up his job and live in the country.*

dream² 🔑 /drim/ verb (dreams, dream·ing, dreamed or dreamt /drɛmt/, has dreamed or has dreamt)
1 to have a picture or idea in your mind when you are asleep: *I **dreamed about** you last night.* ◆ *I **dreamt that** I was flying.*
2 to hope for something nice in the future: *She **dreams of** becoming a famous actress.*

dream·er /'drimər/ noun [count]
a person who thinks a lot about ideas or plans that will probably never happen

drea·ry /'drɪri/ adjective (drear·i·er, drear·i·est)
not at all interesting or attractive, in a way that makes you feel sad: *a dreary winter day*

drench /drɛntʃ/ verb (drench·es, drench·ing, drenched)
to make someone or something completely wet: *I forgot my umbrella and **got** totally **drenched**.*

dress¹ 🔑 /drɛs/ noun (plural dress·es)
1 [count] a piece of clothing with a top part and a skirt, which a woman or girl wears ⊃ Look at the picture at **clothes**.

2 [noncount] clothes: *Many companies are allowing employees to come to work in **casual dress**.*

dress² 🔑 /drɛs/ verb (dress·es, dress·ing, dressed)
1 to put clothes on yourself or another person: *I **got dressed** and went downstairs for breakfast.* ◆ *She dressed quickly and went out.* ◆ *He washed and dressed the baby.* ⊃ ANTONYM **undress**
2 to wear a particular style, type, or color of clothes: *She dresses like a movie star.* ◆ *He was **dressed in** black.*
dress up
1 to put on special clothes for fun, so that you look like another person or a thing: *The children **dressed up as** ghosts.*
2 to put on your best clothes: *They dressed up to go to the theater.*

dress·er /'drɛsər/ noun [count]
a piece of furniture with drawers, used for storing clothes

dress·ing /'drɛsɪŋ/ noun
1 [count, noncount] a sauce for food, especially for salads
2 [noncount] another word for **stuffing**: *turkey with dressing*
3 [count] (HEALTH) a thing for covering a part of your body that is hurt: *You should put a dressing on that cut.*

drew form of **draw¹**

drib·ble /'drɪbl/ verb (drib·bles, drib·bling, drib·bled)
1 (used about a liquid) to fall in small drops; to pour a liquid in this way: *Paint dribbled down the can.*
2 (SPORTS) to make a ball move forward by using many short hits or kicks: *to dribble a basketball*

dried form of **dry²**

dri·er
1 form of **dry¹**
2 = **dryer**

dries form of **dry²**

dri·est form of **dry¹**

drift /drɪft/ verb (drifts, drift·ing, drift·ed)
to move slowly in the air or on water: *The empty boat drifted out to sea.* ◆ *The balloon drifted away.*

drill¹ /drɪl/ noun [count]
drill
1 a tool that you use for making holes: *an electric drill* ◆ *a dentist's drill*
2 a way of learning something by repeating it many times: *We did a drill to memorize verb endings.*

3 practice for what you should do in an emergency: *a **fire drill***

drill² /drɪl/ *verb* (drills, drill·ing, drilled)
1 to make a hole in something using a DRILL: *Drill two holes in the wall.*
2 to teach someone by making them repeat something many times: *Mrs. Chang drilled her third graders in the times tables.*

drink¹ 🎵 /drɪŋk/ *verb* (drinks, drink·ing, drank /dræŋk/, has drunk /drʌŋk/)
1 to take in liquid, for example water, milk, or coffee, through your mouth: *What do you want to drink?* ◆ *She was drinking a cup of coffee.*
2 to drink alcohol: *"Would you like some wine?" "No, thank you. I don't drink."*

drink² 🎵 /drɪŋk/ *noun* [count, noncount]
1 liquid, for example water, milk, or coffee, that you take in through your mouth: *Would you like a drink?* ◆ *Can I **have a drink** of water?*
2 drink with alcohol in it, for example beer or wine: *There was lots of food and drink at the party.*

drip /drɪp/ *verb* (drips, drip·ping, dripped)
1 to fall slowly in small drops: *Water was dripping through the roof.*
2 If something **drips**, liquid falls from it in small drops: *The faucet is dripping.*
▶ **drip** *noun* [count]
a small drop of liquid that falls from something: *Use a bucket to catch the drips.*

drive¹ 🎵 /draɪv/ *verb* (drives, driv·ing, drove /droʊv/, has driv·en /'drɪvn/)
1 to control a car, bus, etc. and make it go where you want to go: *Can you drive?* ◆ *She usually drives to work.*
2 to take someone to a place in a car: *My parents drove me to the airport.*

drive² 🎵 /draɪv/ *noun*
1 [count] a trip in a car: *It's a long drive from Los Angeles to San Francisco.* ◆ *We went for a drive in my sister's car.*
2 [singular] used in the name of some streets: *We live at 1120 Lakeside Drive.*
3 [noncount] the energy and determination you need to succeed: *He has the drive to win the election.*
4 [count] (COMPUTERS) the part of a computer that reads and stores information: *I saved my work on the C: drive*

drive-in /'draɪv ɪn/ *noun* [count]
a place where you can go to eat or to watch a movie while you are sitting in your car

driv·en form of **drive¹**

driv·er 🎵 /'draɪvər/ *noun* [count]
a person who controls a car, bus, train, etc.: *John is a good driver.* ◆ *a taxi driver*

driv·er's li·cense /'draɪvərz ˌlaɪsns/ *noun* [count]
an official document that shows that you are allowed to drive a car, etc.: *Can I see your driver's license, please?*

drive-through (also *informal* **drive-thru**) /'draɪv θru/ *noun* [count]
a part of a restaurant, bank, etc. where you can be served without getting out of your car

drive·way /'draɪvweɪ/ *noun* [count] (*plural* drive·ways)
a wide hard path or private road that goes from the street to one house: *She parked her car in the driveway.*

driv·ing /'draɪvɪŋ/ *noun* [noncount]
controlling a car, bus, etc.: *He failed his **driving test**.* ◆ *dangerous driving*

drool /drul/ *verb* (drools, drool·ing, drooled)
to let liquid (called SALIVA) come out from your mouth: *The baby just drooled on my shirt.*

droop /drup/ *verb* (droops, droop·ing, drooped)
to bend or hang down: *Flowers droop if you don't put them in water.*

drop¹ 🎵 /drɑp/ *verb* (drops, drop·ping, dropped)
1 to let something fall: *I dropped my watch and it broke.*
2 to fall: *The glass dropped from her hands.*
3 to become lower or less: *The temperature has dropped.*
4 (also **drop someone off**) to stop your car and let someone get out: *Could you drop me at the station?* ◆ *He dropped me off at the bus stop.*
5 to stop doing something: *I'm going to drop geography* (= stop studying it) *at school next year.*

drop by; **drop in** to visit someone who does not know that you are coming: *We were in the area, so we thought we'd drop in and see you.*
drop off to fall asleep: *She dropped off in front of the TV.*
drop out to leave or stop doing something before you have finished: *His parents are worried that he'll drop out of school.*

drop² 🎵 /drɑp/ *noun* [count]
1 a very small amount of liquid: *drops of rain* ◆ *a drop of blood*
2 a fall in the amount or level of something: *a **drop in** temperature* ◆ *a drop in prices*

drop·out /'drɑpaʊt/ *noun* [count]
a person who leaves school, college, etc. before finishing their studies: *high school dropouts*

drought /draʊt/ *noun* [count, noncount]
(GEOGRAPHY) a long time when there is not enough rain: *Hundreds of people died in the drought.*

drove form of **drive**¹

drown /draʊn/ *verb* (drowns, drown·ing, drowned)
to die under water because you cannot breathe; to make someone die in this way: *The boy fell in the river and drowned.* • *Twenty people were drowned in the floods.*

drow·sy /ˈdraʊzi/ *adjective* (drow·si·er, drow·si·est)
feeling tired and wanting to sleep: *The heat made him very drowsy.*
▸ **drow·si·ness** /ˈdraʊzinəs/ *noun* [*noncount*]: *This medicine can cause drowsiness.*

drug /drʌg/ *noun* [*count*] (**HEALTH**)
1 an illegal chemical substance that people take because it makes them feel happy or excited: *He doesn't smoke or **take drugs**.* • *She's worried that her daughter is **on drugs** (= regularly using illegal drugs).* • *Heroin is a dangerous drug.*
2 a chemical substance used as a medicine, which you take when you are sick to make you better: *drug companies* • *Some drugs can only be obtained with a prescription from a doctor.*

drug ad·dict /ˈdrʌg ˌædɪkt/ *noun* [*count*]
(**HEALTH**) a person who cannot stop using drugs

drug·store /ˈdrʌgstɔr/ *noun* [*count*]
(**HEALTH**) a store where you can buy medicines and other things such as soap, newspapers, and candy

drum /drʌm/ *noun* [*count*]
1 (**MUSIC**) a musical instrument that you hit with special sticks (called **DRUMSTICKS**) or with your hands: *He plays the drums in a band.*
2 a big round container for oil: *an oil drum*

drum | drumstick | drum

drum·mer /ˈdrʌmer/ *noun* [*count*]
(**MUSIC**) a person who plays a DRUM

drunk¹ form of **drink**¹

drunk² /drʌŋk/ *adjective*
If a person is **drunk**, they have drunk too much alcohol: *He gets drunk every Friday night.*

dry¹ /draɪ/ *adjective* (dri·er, dri·est)
1 with no water or liquid in it or on it: *The laundry isn't dry yet.* ⊃ **ANTONYM wet**
2 with no rain: *dry weather* ⊃ **ANTONYM wet**
3 not sweet: *dry white wine*

dry² /draɪ/ *verb* (dries, dry·ing, dried, has dried)
to become or make something dry: *Our clothes were drying in the sun.* • *Dry your hands on this towel.* • *If you wash the dishes, I'll dry them.*
dry out to become completely dry: *Leave your shoes by the fire to dry out.*
dry up (used about rivers, lakes, etc.) to become completely dry: *There was no rain for several months and all the rivers dried up.*

dry-clean /ˈdraɪ klin/ *verb* (dry-cleans, dry-clean·ing, dry-cleaned)
to make clothes clean by using chemicals, not water: *I had my suit dry-cleaned.*

dry clean·ers /ˈdraɪ ˌklinərs/ *noun* [*count*]
a store where you take clothes and other things to be DRY-CLEANED

dry·er (also **dri·er**) /ˈdraɪər/ *noun* [*count*]
a machine for drying something: *Take the clothes out of the washing machine and put them in the dryer.* • *a hair dryer*

du·al /ˈduəl/ *adjective*
having two parts; double: *the dual role of mother and working woman* • *dual citizenship*

du·bi·ous /ˈdubiəs/ *adjective*
1 not sure or certain: *I'm very dubious about whether we're doing the right thing.* ⊃ **SYNONYM doubtful**
2 that may not be honest or safe: *dubious financial dealings*

duck¹ /dʌk/ *noun*
1 [*count*] a bird that lives on and near water. You often see **ducks** on farms or in parks. ⊃ Look at **duckling**.
2 [*noncount*] meat from a **duck**: *roast duck with orange sauce*

duck

duck² /dʌk/ *verb* (ducks, duck·ing, ducked)
to move your head down quickly, so that something does not hit you or so that someone does not see you: *He saw the ball coming toward him and ducked.*

duck·ling /ˈdʌklɪŋ/ *noun* [*count*]
a young DUCK

duct /dʌkt/ *noun* [*count*]
a tube that carries liquid, gas, etc.: *We got into the building through the air duct.* • *tear ducts (= in the eye)*

dude /dud/ *noun* [*count*] (*informal*)
a boy or man: *Hey dude, what's up?*

due /du/ *adjective*
1 If something is **due** at a certain time, you expect it to happen or come then: *When's the baby due?* • *The new road is **due to** open in April.*

---

2 If an amount of money is **due**, you must pay it: *My rent is due at the beginning of the month.*
3 ready for something: *My car is **due for** an inspection.*
due to something because of something; caused by something: *The accident was due to bad driving.*

du·el /'duəl/ *noun* [count]
(HISTORY) a formal type of fight with guns or other weapons that was used in the past to decide an argument between two men

du·et /du'ɛt/ *noun* [count]
(MUSIC) music for two people to sing or play on musical instruments: *Jim and Christy sang a duet.* ⊃ Look at **solo**².

dug form of **dig**

dull /dʌl/ *adjective* (dull·er, dull·est)
1 not interesting or exciting: *Life is never dull in a big city.* ⊃ SYNONYM **boring**
2 not strong or loud: *a dull pain*
3 not bright: *It was a dull, cloudy day.*
4 not sharp: *a dull knife* ⊃ SYNONYM **blunt**

dumb /dʌm/ *adjective* (informal)

> ℹ **PRONUNCIATION**
> The word **dumb** sounds like **gum**, because we don't say the letter **b** in this word.

not intelligent; stupid: *That was a dumb thing to do!* ⊃ ANTONYM **smart**

dum·my /'dʌmi/ *noun* [count] (plural **dum·mies**)
1 a model of the human body, used for showing clothes in a store window or while you are making clothes: *a tailor's dummy*
2 (informal) a stupid person: *I felt like such a dummy.*

dump¹ /dʌmp/ *verb* (dumps, dump·ing, dumped)
1 to take something to a place and leave it there because you do not want it: *They dumped their garbage by the side of the road.*
2 to put something down without being careful: *Don't dump your clothes on the floor!*
3 (informal) to end a romantic relationship with someone: *I can't believe he dumped me for another girl!*

dump² /dʌmp/ *noun* [count]
1 a place where people take things they do not want: *a garbage dump*
2 (informal) a dirty, messy, or unpleasant place: *This place is a real dump!*

dune /dun/ *noun* [count]
(GEOGRAPHY) a small hill of sand near the ocean or in a desert: *a sand dune*

dun·geon /'dʌndʒən/ *noun* [count]
a dark, underground room used as a prison: *the castle dungeons*

dunk /dʌŋk/ *verb* (dunks, dunk·ing, dunked)
1 to put something into a liquid for a short time: *to dunk a cookie into milk*
2 (SPORTS) (in BASKETBALL) to jump very high and throw the ball hard down into the BASKET (= the round net)

du·plex /'duplɛks/ *noun* [count] (plural **du·plex·es**)
a house that is divided into two separate homes, with a separate door for each one

du·pli·cate /'duplәkeɪt/ *verb* (du·pli·cates, du·pli·cat·ing, du·pli·cat·ed)
1 to make an exact copy of something
2 to do something that has already been done: *We don't want to duplicate the work of the other departments.*

du·ra·ble /'dʊrәbl/ *adjective*
likely to last for a long time without getting weaker: *a durable fabric*
▶ **du·ra·bil·i·ty** /ˌdʊrә'bɪlәti/ *noun* [noncount]

dur·ing 🔑 /'dʊrɪŋ/ *preposition*
1 all the time that something is happening: *The sun gives us light during the day.*
2 at some time while something else is happening: *She died during the night.* ◆ *I fell asleep during the movie.*

dusk /dʌsk/ *noun* [noncount]
the time in the evening when it is almost dark ⊃ Look at **dawn**.

dust¹ 🔑 /dʌst/ *noun* [noncount]
dry dirt that is like powder: *The old table was covered in dust.*

dust² /dʌst/ *verb* (dusts, dust·ing, dust·ed)
to take dust off something with a cloth: *I dusted the furniture.*

dustpan

brush

dust·pan /'dʌstpæn/ *noun* [count]
a flat container with a handle that you use for getting dust or garbage off the floor

dust·y /'dʌsti/ *adjective* (dust·i·er, dust·i·est)
covered with dust: *The furniture was very dusty.*

du·ti·ful /'dutɪfl/ *adjective*
doing everything that you are expected to do: *a dutiful son*
▶ **du·ti·ful·ly** /'dutɪfli/ *adverb*: *He told me to follow him, and I dutifully obeyed.*

du·ty 🔑 /'duṭi/ *noun* [*count, noncount*] (*plural* du·ties)

1 something that you must do because it is part of your job or because you think it is right: *It is your duty to take care of your parents when they get older.* ◆ *One of the duties of a secretary is to type letters.*
2 money (called TAX) that you pay to the government when you bring things into a country from another country

off duty not working: *The police officer was off duty.*

on duty working: *Some nurses at the hospital are on duty all night.*

du·ty-free /ˌduṭi 'fri/ *adjective, adverb*
Duty-free goods are things that you can bring into a country without paying money to the government. You can buy goods **duty-free** on airplanes or ships and at airports.

DVD 🔑 /ˌdi vi 'di/ *noun* [*count*]
(**COMPUTERS**) a small plastic disk that you record movies and music on. You can play a **DVD** on a computer or a special machine (called a DVD PLAYER): *Is the movie available on DVD?*

dwarf /dwɔrf/ *noun* [*count*]
1 (in children's stories) a very small person: *Snow White and the Seven Dwarfs*
2 (**BIOLOGY**) a person, animal, or plant that is much smaller than the usual size

dye /daɪ/ *verb* (dyes, dye·ing, dyed)
to change the color of something by using a special liquid or substance: *She dyed her hair blond.*
▶ **dye** *noun* [*count, noncount*]
a substance that you use to change the color of something, for example cloth or hair: *purple hair dye*

dy·ing form of **die**[1]

dy·nam·ic **AWL** /daɪ'næmɪk/ *adjective*
full of energy and ideas: *a dynamic teacher*

dy·na·mite /'daɪnəmaɪt/ *noun* [*noncount*]
a powerful substance that can explode: *a stick of dynamite*

Ee

E, e /i/ *noun* [count, noncount] (plural E's, e's /iz/)
the fifth letter of the English alphabet: *"Egg"
begins with an "E."*

each 🔑 /itʃ/ *adjective, pronoun*
every person or thing in a group: *Each student
buys a book and a tape.* • *He gave a present to
each of the children.* • *These T-shirts are $5 each.*

each oth·er 🔑 /ˌitʃ ˈʌðər/ *pronoun*
used for saying that someone does the same
thing as another person: *Gary and Susy looked at
each other* (= Gary looked at Susy and Susy
looked at Gary).

ea·ger /ˈigər/ *adjective*
If you are **eager** to do something, you want to
do it very much: *She's eager to help with the
party.*
▶ **ea·ger·ly** /ˈigərli/ *adverb*: *The children were
waiting eagerly for the movie to begin.*
▶ **ea·ger·ness** /ˈigərnəs/ *noun* [noncount]: *I
couldn't hide my eagerness to get home.*

ea·gle /ˈigl/ *noun* [count]
a very large bird that can see very well. It
catches and eats small birds and animals. ➷ Look
at **bald eagle**.

ear 🔑 /ɪr/ *noun* [count]
one of the two parts of your body that you use to
hear with: *Elephants have big ears.* ➷ Look at the
picture at **face**.

ear·ache /ˈɪreɪk/ *noun* [count]
(**HEALTH**) pain inside your ear: *I have an earache.*

ear·ly 🔑 /ˈərli/ *adjective, adverb* (ear·li·er,
ear·li·est)
1 near the beginning of a period of time: *Come
in the early afternoon.* • *She was in her early
twenties* (= aged between 20 and about 23 or
24). • *I have to get up early tomorrow.*
2 before the usual or right time: *The train
arrived ten minutes early.* • *You're early! It's only
six-thirty.* • *I was early for class.* ➷ **ANTONYM late**
an early night an evening when you go to bed
earlier than usual: *I'm really tired, I think I'll
make it an early night.*

earn 🔑 /ərn/ *verb* (earns, earn·ing, earned)
1 to get money by working: *How much do
teachers earn in your country?* • *She earns about
$50,000 a year.*
2 to get something because you have worked
well or done something good: *You've earned a
vacation!*

earn·ings /ˈərnɪŋz/ *noun* [plural]
money that you earn by working

ear·phones /ˈɪrfoʊnz/ *noun* [plural]
(**MUSIC**) things that you put in or over your ears
so that you can listen to music without other
people hearing it ➷ Look at **headphones**.

ear·ring /ˈɪrɪŋ/ *noun* [count]
a piece of jewelry that you wear on your ear: *a
pair of silver earrings* ➷ Look at the picture at
jewelry.

the earth

the Arctic | the North Pole
axis
line of longitude
northern hemisphere
southern hemisphere
equator
the South Pole | the Antarctic | line of latitude

earth 🔑 /ərθ/ *noun*
1 usually **the earth, the Earth** [singular] this
world; the planet that we live on: *The moon
travels around the earth.* • *They live in one of the
hottest places on earth.*
2 [singular] the surface of the world; land: *The
satellite fell toward earth.* • *The earth shook.*
3 [noncount] the substance that plants grow in:
Cover the seeds with earth. ➷ **SYNONYM soil**
how, who, what, where, etc. on earth...?
(informal) used in questions when you are very
surprised or want to say something very
strongly: *What on earth are you doing?* • *Where
on earth is Paul? He's two hours late!*

earth·quake /ˈərθkweɪk/ *noun* [count]
(**GEOGRAPHY**) a sudden strong shaking of the
ground

earth·worm /ˈərθwərm/ *noun* [count]
a small, long, thin animal with no legs or eyes
that lives in the soil

ease¹ /iz/ *noun*
with ease with no difficulty: *She answered the
questions with ease.* ➷ **SYNONYM easily**
be or **feel at ease** to be or feel comfortable and
relaxed: *Everyone was so friendly that I felt
completely at ease.*

ease² /iz/ *verb* (eas·es, eas·ing, eased)
to become or to make something less painful or
serious: *They waited for the rain to ease.* • *This
should ease the pain.*

ea·sel /ˈizl/ *noun*
[count]
(**ART**) a frame that an
artist uses to hold a
picture while it is
being painted

easel

eas·i·ly /ˈizəli/
adverb
with no difficulty: *I
can easily call and
check the time of the
movie.* ◆ *He passed the
test easily.* ⊃ The
adjective is **easy.**

east /ist/ *noun* [*singular*] (abbreviation **E.**)
(**GEOGRAPHY**)
1 the direction you look in to see the sun come
up in the morning: *Which way is east?* ◆ *There
was a cold wind from the east.* ⊃ Look at the picture
at **compass**.
2 the east or **the East** the part of any country,
city, etc. that is further to the east than the other
parts: *He grew up in the East, but moved to
California after college.*
3 the East the countries of Asia, for example
China and Japan
▶ **east** *adjective, adverb*: *an east wind* (= that
comes from the east) ◆ *They live on the East
Coast.* ◆ *We traveled east.*

Eas·ter /ˈistər/ *noun* [*noncount*]
(**RELIGION**) a Sunday in March or April, and the
days around it, when Christians think about
Christ coming back to life

Culture

- **Easter** is a popular festival, with many
  traditions in the U.S.
- People think about new life and the coming
  of spring. They celebrate this by decorating
  and coloring eggs and eating chocolate.

Eas·ter egg /ˈistər ɛg/ *noun* [count]
an egg that you decorate for Easter

east·ern /ˈistərn/ *adjective*
(**GEOGRAPHY**) in or of the east of a place: *eastern
Pennsylvania*

eas·y /ˈizi/ *adjective* (eas·i·er, eas·i·est)
1 not difficult to do or understand: *The
homework was very easy.* ◆ *English isn't an easy
language to learn.*
2 without problems or pain: *He has had an easy
life.* ⊃ **ANTONYM difficult, hard** ⊃ Look at **easily.**
take it easy; take things easy to relax and not
worry or work too much: *After my exams I'm
going to take it easy for a few days.*

eas·y·go·ing /ˌiziˈgoʊɪŋ/ *adjective*
calm, relaxed, and not easily worried or upset:
*Her parents are pretty easygoing, so she has a lot
of freedom to do what she wants.*

eat /it/ *verb* (eats, eat·ing, ate /eɪt/, has
eat·en /ˈitn/)
1 to put food in your mouth and swallow it: *Who
ate all the chocolates?* ◆ *Would you like something
to eat?*
2 to have a meal: *What time should we eat?*
eat out to have a meal in a restaurant: *We don't
eat out very often.*

eaves·drop /ˈivzdrɑp/ *verb* (eaves·drops,
eaves·drop·ping, eaves·dropped)
to listen secretly to other people talking: *They
caught him **eavesdropping on** their conversation.*

ec·cen·tric /ɪkˈsɛntrɪk/ *adjective*
(used about people or their behavior) strange or
unusual: *He's a little eccentric, but he's a great
teacher.*

ech·o /ˈɛkoʊ/ *noun* [count] (*plural* ech·oes)
a sound that a surface such as a wall sends back
so that you hear it again
▶ **ech·o** *verb* (ech·oes, ech·o·ing, ech·oed): *His
footsteps echoed in the
empty hall.*

e·clipse /ɪˈklɪps/ *noun*
[count]
a time when the
moon passes
between the earth
and the sun so that we
cannot see the sun's
light, or when the
earth's shadow falls
on the moon so that
we cannot see the
moon's light: *a total eclipse of the sun*

eclipse

solar eclipse

e·col·o·gist /ɪˈkɑlədʒɪst/ *noun* [count]
(**BIOLOGY**) a person who studies or knows a lot
about **ECOLOGY**

e·col·o·gy /ɪˈkɑlədʒi/ *noun* [*noncount*]
(**BIOLOGY**) the relationship between living things
and everything around them; the study of this
subject
▶ **ec·o·log·i·cal** /ˌikəˈlɑdʒɪkl/ *adjective*: *an
ecological disaster*

ec·o·nom·ic /ˌɛkəˈnɑmɪk/ *adjective* **AWL**
(**BUSINESS, POLITICS**) connected with the way that
people and countries spend money and make,
buy, and sell things: *The country has serious
economic problems.*

ec·o·nom·i·cal **AWL** /ˌɛkəˈnɑmɪkl/ *adjective*
costing or using less time, money, etc. than
usual: *This car is very economical to run* (= it
does not use a lot of gas).

▶ **ec·o·nom·i·cal·ly** **AWL** /ˌɛkəˈnɑmɪkli/ *adverb*:
The service could be run more economically.

ec·o·nom·ics **AWL** /ˌɛkəˈnɑmɪks/ *noun* [noncount]
(**BUSINESS**, **POLITICS**) the study of the way that
people and countries spend money and make,
buy, and sell things

e·con·o·mist **AWL** /ɪˈkɑnəmɪst/ *noun* [count]
(**BUSINESS**, **POLITICS**) a person who studies or
knows a lot about ECONOMICS

e·con·o·mize /ɪˈkɑnəmaɪz/ *verb* (e·con·o·miz·es,
e·con·o·miz·ing, e·con·o·mized)
to save money, time, etc.; to use less of
something: *We're trying to economize by eating
in restaurants less often.*

e·con·o·my 🖋 **AWL** /ɪˈkɑnəmi/ *noun* (*plural*
e·con·o·mies)
1 (**BUSINESS**, **POLITICS**) [count] the way that a
country spends its money and makes, buys, and
sells things: *the economies of Japan and
Germany*
2 [count, noncount] using money or things well
and carefully: *We need to make some economies.*

e·co·sys·tem /ˈikoʊˌsɪstəm/ *noun* [count]
(**GEOGRAPHY**, **BIOLOGY**) all the plants and animals
in a particular area, and the environment that
they live in

edge 🖋 /ɛdʒ/ *noun* [count]
1 the part along the end or side of something:
She stood at the water's edge. ◆ *the edge of the
table*
2 the sharp part of a knife or tool
be on edge to be nervous or worried

ed·i·ble /ˈɛdəbl/ *adjective*
good or safe to eat: *The food was barely edible* (=
almost too bad to eat). ⊃ **ANTONYM inedible**

ed·it **AWL** /ˈɛdət/ *verb* (ed·its, ed·it·ing, ed·it·ed)
(**ENGLISH LANGUAGE ARTS**) to prepare a piece of
writing, film, etc. to be published or released:
Paul edited the report. ◆ *The violent scene was
edited out of the movie.*

e·di·tion **AWL** /ɪˈdɪʃn/ *noun* [count]
(**ENGLISH LANGUAGE ARTS**) one of a number of
books, magazines, or newspapers that appear
at the same time: *the evening edition of the
newspaper*

ed·i·tor **AWL** /ˈɛdəṭər/ *noun* [count]
(**ENGLISH LANGUAGE ARTS**) a person whose job is
to prepare or control a book or a newspaper
before it is printed

ed·i·to·ri·al¹ **AWL** /ˌɛdəˈtɔriəl/ *noun* [count]
(**ENGLISH LANGUAGE ARTS**) an article in a
newspaper that gives the writer's opinion on an
important issue

ed·i·to·ri·al² **AWL** /ˌɛdəˈtɔriəl/ *adjective*
(**ENGLISH LANGUAGE ARTS**) connected with the
work of preparing newspapers, books, etc. to be
published or released: *the magazine's editorial
department*

ed·u·cate 🖋 /ˈɛdʒəkeɪt/ *verb* (ed·u·cates,
ed·u·cat·ing, ed·u·cat·ed)
to teach or train someone, especially in school:
Where was she educated? ◆ *We must educate
young people about the dangers of smoking.*

ed·u·cat·ed /ˈɛdʒəkeɪṭəd/ *adjective*
having studied and learned a lot to a high level:
He's smart and well educated. ⊃ **ANTONYM
uneducated**

ed·u·ca·tion 🖋 /ˌɛdʒəˈkeɪʃn/ *noun* [noncount,
singular]
teaching people at a school or college:
Education is extremely important. ◆ *He had a
good education.*
▶ **ed·u·ca·tion·al** /ˌɛdʒəˈkeɪʃənl/ *adjective*:
educational programs

eel /il/ *noun* [count]
a long fish that looks
like a snake

eel

ef·fect 🖋 /ɪˈfɛkt/ *noun*
[count, noncount]
a change that
happens because of
something: *We are studying the effects of heat on
different metals.* ◆ *Her shouting had little effect on
him.*
take effect to begin to work: *It takes about 20
minutes for the medicine to take effect.*

ef·fec·tive /ɪˈfɛktɪv/ *adjective*
Something that is **effective** works well: *Jogging
is an effective way to stay in shape.* ⊃ **ANTONYM
ineffective**
▶ **ef·fec·tive·ly** /ɪˈfɛktɪvli/ *adverb*: *She dealt with
the situation effectively.*

ef·fi·cient /ɪˈfɪʃnt/ *adjective*
working well, without making mistakes or
wasting energy: *Our secretary is very efficient.* ◆
an efficient way of working ⊃ **ANTONYM inefficient**
▶ **ef·fi·cien·cy** /ɪˈfɪʃnsi/ *noun* [noncount]: *ways of
increasing efficiency at the factory*
▶ **ef·fi·cient·ly** /ɪˈfɪʃntli/ *adverb*: *Try to use your
time more efficiently.*

ef·fort 🖋 /ˈɛfərt/ *noun* [count, noncount]
the physical or mental energy that you need to
do something: *Thank you for all your efforts.* ◆ *He
made an effort to arrive on time.*

ef·fort·less /ˈɛfərtləs/ *adjective*
needing little or no effort, so that it seems easy:
She makes ice skating look effortless.
▶ **ef·fort·less·ly** /ˈɛfərtləsli/ *adverb*

EFL /ˌi ɛf ˈɛl/ *abbreviation*
(**ENGLISH LANGUAGE ARTS**) EFL is short for "English as a foreign language" (= the teaching of English to people who speak other languages) ⟳ Look at **ESL**.

e.g. /ˌi ˈdʒi/ short for **for example**: *popular sports, e.g. football, baseball, and swimming*

egg /ɛg/ *noun*
1 (**BIOLOGY**) [*count*] a round or OVAL (= almost round) object that has a baby bird, fish, insect, or snake inside it: *The hen has laid an egg.*
2 [*count, noncount*] an egg that we eat, especially from a chicken: *a boiled egg*

egg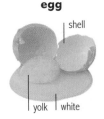

shell

yolk | white

egg·plant /ˈɛgplænt/ *noun* [*count, noncount*]
a large purple vegetable that is white inside

e·go /ˈigoʊ/ *noun* [*count*] (*plural* **e·gos**)
the opinion that you have of yourself: *He has a big ego* (= he has a high opinion of himself).

eight /eɪt/ *number*
8

eight·een /eɪˈtin/ *number*
18
▶ **eight·eenth** /ˌeɪˈtinθ/ *pronoun, adjective, adverb, noun* [*count*]
18th: *He met Emma just before his eighteenth birthday.*

eighth /eɪtθ/ *pronoun, adjective, adverb, noun* [*count*]
1 8th: *I was eighth in line for tickets.*
2 one of eight equal parts of something; ⅛

eight·y /ˈeɪti/ *number*
1 80
2 the eighties [*plural*] the numbers, years, or temperatures between 80 and 89
in your eighties between the ages of 80 and 89
▶ **eight·i·eth** /ˈeɪtiəθ/ *pronoun, adjective, adverb, noun* [*count*]
80th: *My grandpa just celebrated his eightieth birthday.*

ei·ther[1] /ˈiðər/ *adjective, pronoun*
1 one of two things or people: *There is cake and ice cream. You can have either.* ◆ *Either one of us could help you.*
2 each: *There are trees along either side of the street.*

ei·ther[2] /ˈiðər/ *adverb*
(used in sentences with "not") also: *Lydia can't swim, and I can't either.*
either...or words that show two different things or people that you can choose: *You can*

have either tea or coffee. ◆ *I will either write or call.*

e·lab·o·rate /ɪˈlæbərət/ *adjective*
not simple; with a lot of different parts: *The carpet has a very elaborate pattern.* ⟳ **SYNONYM complicated**
▶ **e·lab·o·rate·ly** /ɪˈlæbərətli/ *adverb*: *The rooms were elaborately decorated.*

e·las·tic /ɪˈlæstɪk/ *noun* [*noncount*]
material that becomes longer when you pull it and then goes back to its usual size: *This skirt needs some new elastic in the waist.*
▶ **e·las·tic** *adjective*: *elastic material*

el·bow /ˈɛlboʊ/ *noun* [*count*]
the part in the middle of your arm where it bends: *She fell and broke her elbow.* ⟳ Look at the picture at **body**.

eld·er /ˈɛldər/ *adjective* (*formal*)
older, especially of two members of the same family: *My elder brother lives abroad.*

eld·er·ly /ˈɛldərli/ *adjective*
(used about people) a polite way of saying "old": *an elderly lady* ◆ *health care for* **the elderly** (= people who are elderly)

eld·ers /ˈɛldərz/ *noun* [*plural*]
people who are older than you: *My parents taught me to respect my elders.*

eld·est /ˈɛldəst/ *adjective* (*formal*)
oldest of three or more people, especially members of the same family: *Their eldest son is at college.*

e·lect /ɪˈlɛkt/ *verb* (**e·lects, e·lect·ing, e·lect·ed**)
(**POLITICS**) to choose someone to be a leader by voting for him or her: *The new president was elected last year.*

e·lec·tion /ɪˈlɛkʃn/ *noun* [*count, noncount*]
(**POLITICS**) a time when people choose someone to be a leader by voting for him or her: *The election will be held on Tuesday.*

e·lec·tric /ɪˈlɛktrɪk/ *adjective*
using or providing electricity: *an electric stove* ◆ *an electric outlet*

e·lec·tri·cal /ɪˈlɛktrɪkl/ *adjective*
of or using electricity: *an electrical appliance* (= a machine that uses electricity)

e·lec·tri·cian /ɪˌlɛkˈtrɪʃn/ *noun* [*count*]
a person whose job is to make and repair electrical systems and equipment: *John's an electrician. He'll be able to fix the light for you.*

e·lec·tri·ci·ty /ɪˌlɛkˈtrɪsəti/ *noun* [*noncount*]
(**PHYSICS**) power that comes through wires. Electricity can make heat and light, and makes machines work.

e·lec·tric shock /ɪˌlɛktrɪk ˈʃɑk/ *noun* [count]
a sudden painful feeling that you get if
electricity goes through your body

e·lec·trode /ɪˈlɛktroʊd/ *noun* [count]
(**PHYSICS**) a point at which electricity enters or
leaves an electrical device

e·lec·tron /ɪˈlɛktrɑn/ *noun* [count]
(**CHEMISTRY**, **PHYSICS**) a very small piece of matter
with a negative electric charge, found in all
atoms ⊃ Look at **neutron**, **proton**. ⊃ Look at the
picture at **atom**.

e·lec·tron·ic 🔑 /ɪˌlɛkˈtrɑnɪk/ *adjective*
1 (**GENERAL SCIENCE**) Electronic equipment
includes things like computers and televisions.
They use electricity and very small electrical
parts (called **MICROCHIPS** and **TRANSISTORS**) to
make them work: *an electronic calculator*
2 (**COMPUTERS**) done using a computer:
electronic bill paying
▶ **e·lec·tron·i·cal·ly** /ɪˌlɛkˈtrɑnɪkli/ *adverb*

e·lec·tron·ics /ɪˌlɛkˈtrɑnɪks/ *noun* [noncount]
(**GENERAL SCIENCE**) the technology that is used to
make things like computers and televisions: *the
electronics industry*

el·e·gant /ˈɛləɡənt/ *adjective*
with a beautiful style or shape: *She looked very
elegant in her new black dress.* ◆ *elegant furniture*
▶ **el·e·gance** /ˈɛləɡəns/ *noun* [noncount]

el·e·ment AWL /ˈɛləmənt/ *noun* [count]
1 an important part of something: *Cost was an
important element in our decision.*
2 (**CHEMISTRY**) a simple chemical, for example
iron or gold: *Water is made of the elements
hydrogen and oxygen.*

el·e·men·ta·ry /ˌɛləˈmɛntəri/ *adjective*
connected with the early stages of learning; not
difficult: *an elementary dictionary* ◆ *elementary
physics*

el·e·men·ta·ry school /ˌɛləˈmɛntəri skul/ *noun*
[count, noncount] (also **grade school**)
a school for children who are around five to
eleven years old

Word building

- In the U.S., children start **elementary
  school** when they are 5. The first year of
  this is called **kindergarten**.
- When children are around 11 years old,
  they move to **middle school** (or **junior
  high school**), and when they reach the age
  of around 14, they start **high school**.
- Each year of school is called a **grade**. When
  a child is around 6 years old they are in **first
  grade**, and the last year of high school is
  the **twelfth grade**.

el·e·phant /ˈɛləfənt/
noun [count]
a very big, wild
animal from Africa or
Asia, with a long nose
(called a **TRUNK**) that
hangs down

elephant

tusk

trunk

el·e·va·tion
/ˌɛləˈveɪʃn/ *noun*
[count]
(**GEOGRAPHY**) the height of a place, especially its
height above the level of the ocean: *Denver is at
an elevation of 5,280 feet.*

el·e·va·tor /ˈɛləveɪtər/ *noun* [count]
a machine that takes people and things up and
down in a high building: *Should we use the stairs
or take the elevator?*

e·lev·en 🔑 /ɪˈlɛvən/ *number*
11
▶ **e·lev·enth** /ɪˈlɛvənθ/ *pronoun, adjective,
adverb, noun* [count]
11th

elf /ɛlf/ *noun* [count] (*plural* **elves** /ɛlvz/)
a very small person in stories who has pointed
ears and magic powers

el·i·gi·ble /ˈɛlɪdʒəbl/ *adjective*
allowed to do something, because you have the
right skills, you are the right age, etc.: *You need
a degree in biology to be eligible for the program.*
◆ *When are you eligible to vote in your country?*
▶ **el·i·gi·bil·i·ty** /ˌɛlɪdʒəˈbɪləti/ *noun* [noncount]

e·lim·i·nate AWL /ɪˈlɪməneɪt/ *verb* (**e·lim·i·nates,
e·lim·i·nat·ing, e·lim·i·nat·ed**)
1 to remove something that is not needed or
wanted: *We must try to eliminate waste.*
2 to stop someone from going further in a
competition, etc.: *We lost both games, so our
team was eliminated from the competition.*

e·lite /ɪˈlit/ eɪˈlit/ *noun* [count]
a group of people who are thought to be the best
or most important because they are rich,
intelligent, etc.: *the ruling elite* (= the people that
control the area, the country, etc.) ◆ *an elite
group of business leaders*

e·lope /ɪˈloʊp/ *verb* (**e·lopes, e·lop·ing, e·loped**)
to run away secretly to get married

el·o·quent /ˈɛləkwənt/ *adjective* (*formal*)
able to use language and express your opinions
well: *an eloquent speech*
▶ **el·o·quent·ly** /ˈɛləkwəntli/ *adverb*: *He spoke
eloquently about his work.*

else 🔑 /ɛls/ *adverb*
1 more; extra: *What else would you like?* ◆ *Is
anyone else coming to the party?*
2 different: *This café's full; let's go somewhere
else.* ◆ *It's not mine – it must be someone else's.* ◆

*There was **nothing else** to eat, so we had eggs again.*

or else if not, then: *Go now, or else you'll be late.* ➔ SYNONYM **otherwise**

else·where /ˈɛlswɛr/ *adverb* (*formal*)
in or to another place: *He can't find a job near home, so he's looking elsewhere.*

elves plural of **elf**

e-mail 🖉 (also **e.mail**) /ˈimeɪl/ *noun* (**COMPUTERS**)
1 [*noncount*] a system for sending messages from one computer to another: *to send a message by e-mail* ◆ *What's your e-mail address?*
2 [*count*] a message that is written on one computer and sent to another: *I'll send you an e-mail.*
▶ **e-mail** (also **e.mail**) *verb* (e-mails, e-mail·ing, e-mailed): *E-mail me when you arrive.* ◆ *I'll e-mail the documents to her.*

Collocations

E-mail
- **have/set up** an e-mail account
- **check/read** your e-mail
- **receive/get/open** an e-mail
- **send/forward/delete** an e-mail
- **write/answer/reply to** an e-mail
- **attach** a file/a picture/a document
- **contain/open/send** an attachment

e·man·ci·pate /ɪˈmænsəpeɪt/ *adjective*
(e·man·ci·pates, e·man·ci·pat·ing, e·man·ci·pat·ed) (*formal*)
(**HISTORY**) to give someone the same legal, social, and political rights as other people: *Lincoln emancipated the slaves after the Civil War.*
▶ **e·man·ci·pa·tion** /ɪˌmænsəˈpeɪʃn/ *noun* [*noncount*]: *the emancipation of women*

em·bar·rass 🖉 /ɪmˈbærəs/ *verb* (em·bar·rass·es, em·bar·rass·ing, em·bar·rassed)
to make someone feel shy or worried about what other people think of them: *Please don't embarrass me in front of my friends.*
▶ **em·bar·rass·ing** /ɪmˈbærəsɪŋ/ *adjective*: *I couldn't remember her name – it was so embarrassing!*

em·bar·rassed 🖉 /ɪmˈbærəst/ *adjective*

> ⓘ SPELLING
>
> Remember! You spell **embarrassed** with **RR** and **SS**.

If you are **embarrassed**, you feel shy or worried about what other people think of you: *He felt embarrassed at being the center of attention.*

em·bar·rass·ment /ɪmˈbærəsmənt/ *noun*
[*noncount*]
the feeling that you have when you are embarrassed: *His face was red with embarrassment.*

em·bas·sy /ˈɛmbəsi/ *noun* [*count*] (*plural* em·bas·sies)
(**POLITICS**) a group of people whose job is to speak and act for their government in another country, or the building where they work: *To get a visa, you should apply to the American embassy.*

em·blem /ˈɛmbləm/ *noun* [*count*]
an object or a symbol that represents something: *America's national emblem, the bald eagle*

em·brace /ɪmˈbreɪs/ *verb* (em·brac·es, em·brac·ing, em·braced) (*formal*)
to put your arms around someone to show that you love them: *She embraced each member of her family.* ➔ SYNONYM **hug**

em·broi·der /ɪmˈbrɔɪdər/ *verb* (em·broi·ders, em·broi·der·ing, em·broi·dered)
to decorate cloth by sewing patterns on it
▶ **em·broi·dered** /ɪmˈbrɔɪdərd/ *adjective*: *an embroidered blouse*

em·broi·der·y /ɪmˈbrɔɪdəri/ *noun* [*noncount*]
patterns that are sewn onto cloth to decorate it

em·bry·o /ˈɛmbrioʊ/ *noun* [*count*] (*plural* em·bry·os)
(**BIOLOGY**) a human or animal when it is starting to grow before it is born

em·er·ald /ˈɛmərəld/ *noun* [*count*]
a green JEWEL (= valuable stone): *an emerald ring*
▶ **em·er·ald** (also **em·er·ald green** /ˌɛmərəld ˈgrin/) *adjective*
bright green: *an emerald green dress*

e·merge AWL /ɪˈmərdʒ/ *verb* (e·merg·es, e·merg·ing, e·merged)
to come out from a place: *The moon emerged from behind the clouds.*

e·mer·gen·cy 🖉 /ɪˈmərdʒənsi/ *noun* [*count, noncount*] (*plural* e·mer·gen·cies)
a sudden dangerous situation, when people need help quickly: *Come quickly, doctor! It's an emergency!* ◆ *In an emergency, call 911 for help.* ◆ *an emergency exit* (= a way out of a building that can be used in an emergency)

e·mer·gen·cy room /ɪˈmərdʒənsi ˌrum/ *noun* [*count*] (abbreviation **ER**)
(**HEALTH**) the place in a hospital where you go if you have been hurt in an accident, or if you have suddenly become very sick

---

em·i·grate /ˈɛməgreɪt/ *verb* (em·i·grates, em·i·grat·ing, em·i·grat·ed)
to leave your country and go to live in another country: *They **emigrated to** Australia in the 1990s.* ⊃ Look at **immigrate**.
▶ **em·i·gra·tion** /ˌɛməˈgreɪʃn/ *noun* [*noncount*]: *emigration by poor people in search of work* ⊃ Look at **immigration**.

e·mis·sions /ɪˈmɪʃnz/ *noun* [*plural*]
(**GENERAL SCIENCE**) gas, heat, etc. that is sent out into the air: *carbon emissions* ◆ *I need to get an emissions test for my car* (= to check that emissions are not too high).

e·mit /ɪˈmɪt/ *verb* (e·mit, e·mit·ting, e·mit·ted)
(*formal*)
to send out something such as gas, heat, light, a sound, etc.: *The factory is emitting toxic chemicals.*

e·mo·tion 🔑 /ɪˈmoʊʃn/ *noun* [*count, noncount*]
a strong feeling, for example love or anger: *They expressed mixed emotions at the news.* ◆ *His voice was filled with emotion.*

e·mo·tion·al /ɪˈmoʊʃənl/ *adjective*
1 connected with feelings: *emotional problems*
2 showing strong feelings, sometimes by crying: *He got very **emotional** when we said goodbye.*

em·pa·thize /ˈɛmpəθaɪz/ *verb* (em·pa·thiz·es, em·pa·thiz·ing, em·pa·thized)
to understand how another person feels, especially because you have been in a similar situation: *She empathized with his feelings of betrayal.*

em·pa·thy /ˈɛmpəθi/ *noun* [*noncount*]
the ability to understand how other people feel

em·per·or /ˈɛmpərər/ *noun* [*count*]
(**HISTORY, POLITICS**) a man who rules a group of countries (called an **EMPIRE**): *the Emperor Napoleon* ⊃ Look at **empress**.

em·pha·sis **AWL** /ˈɛmfəsəs/ *noun* [*count, noncount*] (*plural* em·pha·ses /ˈɛmfəsiz/)
1 special importance that is given to something: *Our school places a lot of **emphasis on** science.*
2 (**ENGLISH LANGUAGE ARTS**) the force that you give to a word or phrase when you are speaking; a way of writing a word to show that it is important: *In the word "photographer" the emphasis is on the second syllable.* ◆ *I underlined the word "urgent" **for emphasis**.* ⊃ **SYNONYM stress**

em·pha·size **AWL** /ˈɛmfəsaɪz/ *verb*
(em·pha·siz·es, em·pha·siz·ing, em·pha·sized)
to say something strongly to show that it is important: *She emphasized the importance of hard work.* ⊃ **SYNONYM stress**

em·pire /ˈɛmpaɪər/ *noun* [*count*]
(**POLITICS, HISTORY**) a group of countries that is controlled by one country: *the Roman Empire*

em·ploy 🔑 /ɛmˈplɔɪ/ *verb* (em·ploys, em·ploy·ing, em·ployed)
to pay someone to do work for you: *The factory employs 800 workers.* ⊃ Look at **unemployed**.

em·ploy·ee /ɛmˈplɔɪ; ˌɛmplɔrˈi/ *noun* [*count*]
a person who works for someone: *This company treats its employees very well.*

em·ploy·er /ɛmˈplɔɪər/ *noun* [*count*]
a person or company that pays other people to do work

em·ploy·ment 🔑 /ɛmˈplɔɪmənt/ *noun* [*noncount*]
having a job that you are paid to do: *It can be hard for young people to **find employment**.* ⊃ Look at **unemployment**. ⊃ Look at the note at **job**.

em·pow·er /ɪmˈpaʊər/ *verb* (em·pow·ers, em·pow·er·ing, em·pow·ered)
to give someone more control over their own life or the situation they are in: *The feminist movement empowered women and gave them more confidence.*

em·press /ˈɛmprəs/ *noun* [*count*] (*plural* em·press·es)
(**POLITICS, HISTORY**) a woman who rules a group of countries (called an **EMPIRE**), or the wife of an **EMPEROR** (= a man who rules a group of countries)

emp·ty¹ 🔑 /ˈɛmpti/ *adjective* (emp·ti·er, emp·ti·est)
with nothing or no one inside or on it: *The auditorium was almost empty.* ◆ *an empty box* ⊃ Look at the picture at **full**.

emp·ty² /ˈɛmpti/ *verb* (emp·ties, emp·ty·ing, emp·tied, has emp·tied)
1 to take everything out of something: *The waiter emptied the ashtrays.* ◆ *We **emptied** our bags **out** onto the floor.*
2 to become **empty**: *The movie finished and the theater started to empty.*

Suffix

-en

(in verbs) to make or become: *harden* ◆ *lessen* ◆ *shorten* ◆ *weaken*

en·a·ble **AWL** /ɛˈneɪbl/ *verb* (en·a·bles, en·a·bling, en·a·bled) (*formal*)
to make it possible for someone to do something: *Your help **enabled** me **to** finish the work on time.*

en·close /ɪnˈkloʊz/ *verb* (en·clos·es, en·clos·ing, en·closed)
1 to put something inside a letter or package: *I enclose a check for $100.*
2 to put something, for example a wall or fence, around a place on all sides: *The prison is enclosed by a high wall.*

en·clo·sure /ɪnˈkloʊʒər/ *noun* [count]
a piece of land inside a wall, fence, etc. that is used for a particular purpose: *a wildlife enclosure*

en·coun·ter¹ AWL /ɪnˈkaʊntər/ *verb* (en·coun·ters, en·coun·ter·ing, en·coun·tered)
to experience something (a danger, difficulty, etc.): *I've never encountered any discrimination at work.*

en·coun·ter² AWL /ɪnˈkaʊntər/ *noun* [count]
a meeting or event, especially an unpleasant one that you were not expecting: *an encounter with the police*

en·cour·age /ɪnˈkərɪdʒ/ *verb* (en·cour·ag·es, en·cour·ag·ing, en·cour·aged)
to give someone hope or help so that they do something or continue doing something: *We encouraged him to write a book about his adventures.* ⊃ ANTONYM discourage
▸ **en·cour·ag·ing** /ɪnˈkərɪdʒɪŋ/ *adjective*: *Ann's grades in school are very encouraging.*

en·cour·age·ment /ɪnˈkərɪdʒmənt/ *noun* [noncount]
the act of encouraging someone; something you say that gives someone hope and confidence: *My parents have always given me a lot of encouragement.* ◆ *a few words of encouragement*

en·cy·clo·pe·di·a /ɛnˌsaɪkləˈpidiə/ *noun* [count]
(plural en·cy·clo·pe·di·as)
a book or CD that gives information about a lot of different things: *an encyclopedia of world history*

end¹ /ɛnd/ *noun* [count]
the farthest or last part of something: *Turn right at the end of the street.* ◆ *They were sitting at the other end of the room.* ◆ *I'm going on vacation at the end of June.* ◆ *We were sad because the vacation was coming to an end.*
end to end in a line with the ends touching: *They put the tables end to end.*
for...on end for a very long time: *He watches TV for hours on end.*
in the end finally; at last: *In the end it was midnight when we got home.*
make ends meet to have enough money for your needs: *After her husband died it was difficult to make ends meet.*
put an end to something to stop something from happening: *We must put an end to this terrible war.*

end² /ɛnd/ *verb* (ends, end·ing, end·ed)
to stop or to finish something: *What time does the movie end?* ◆ *The road ends here.* ◆ *Most adverbs in English end in "-ly."* ◆ *We ended our vacation with a few days on the beach.*
end up to finally be in a place or doing something when you did not plan it: *If she continues to steal, she'll end up in prison.* ◆ *I ended up doing all the work myself.*

en·dan·ger /ɪnˈdeɪndʒər/ *verb* (en·dan·gers, en·dan·ger·ing, en·dan·gered)
to cause danger to someone or something: *Smoking endangers your health.*

en·dan·gered /ɪnˈdeɪndʒərd/ *adjective*
(used about animals, plants, etc.) in danger of disappearing from the world (becoming EXTINCT): *The panda is an endangered species.*

end·ing /ˈɛndɪŋ/ *noun* [count]
the last part of something, for example a word, story, or movie: *Nouns with the ending "–ch" form the plural with "–es."* ◆ *The movie has a happy ending.*

end·less /ˈɛndləs/ *adjective*
never stopping or finishing; very long: *The journey seemed endless.*
▸ **end·less·ly** /ˈɛndləsli/ *adverb*: *He talks endlessly about nothing.*

en·dorse /ɪnˈdɔrs/ *verb* (en·dors·es, en·dors·ing, en·dorsed)
to give official support to a person, plan, product, etc.: *The union endorsed the Democratic candidate for president.*

en·dur·ance /ɪnˈdʊrəns/ *noun* [noncount]
the ability to continue doing something painful or uncomfortable without complaining: *Running a marathon is a test of endurance.*

en·dure /ɪnˈdʊr/ *verb* (en·dures, en·dur·ing, en·dured) (formal)
to suffer something that is painful or uncomfortable, usually without complaining: *The pain was almost too great to endure.* ⊃ SYNONYM bear

en·e·my /ˈɛnəmi/ *noun* (plural en·e·mies)
1 a person who hates you: *He has made a lot of enemies.*
2 the enemy [singular] the army or country that your country is fighting against in a war: *The enemy is attacking from the north.*

en·er·get·ic AWL /ˌɛnərˈdʒɛtɪk/ *adjective*
full of energy so that you can do a lot of things
▸ **en·er·get·i·cal·ly** AWL /ˌɛnərˈdʒɛtɪkli/ *adverb*

en·er·gize /ˈɛnərdʒaɪz/ *verb* (en·er·giz·es, en·er·giz·ing, en·er·gized)
to give someone more energy: *The audience was energized by his speech.*

---

en·er·gy [AWL] /ˈɛnərdʒi/ *noun* [noncount]
1 the ability to be active without getting tired: *Children are usually* **full of energy**.
2 (PHYSICS) the power from electricity, gas, oil, etc. that is used to make machines work and to make heat and light: *It is important to try to save energy.* ◆ *atomic energy*

en·force [AWL] /ɪnˈfɔrs/ *verb* (en·forc·es, en·forc·ing, en·forced)
to make sure that people follow laws or rules: *How will they enforce the new law?*

en·gaged /ɪnˈgeɪdʒd/ *adjective*
If two people are **engaged**, they have agreed to get married: *Louise is* **engaged** *to Michael.* ◆ *They* **got engaged** *last year.*

en·gage·ment /ɪnˈgeɪdʒmənt/ *noun* [count]
an agreement to marry someone

en·gine /ˈɛndʒən/ *noun* [count]
1 a machine that makes things move: *a car engine*
2 the front part of a train, which pulls the rest

en·gi·neer /ˌɛndʒəˈnɪr/ *noun* [count]
a person whose job is to plan, make, or repair things like machines, roads, or bridges: *My brother is an electrical engineer.*

en·gi·neer·ing /ˌɛndʒəˈnɪrɪŋ/ *noun* [noncount]
planning and making things like machines, roads, or bridges: *She's studying chemical engineering at college.*

En·glish /ˈɪŋglɪʃ/ *noun* [noncount]
(ENGLISH LANGUAGE ARTS) the language that is spoken in the U.S., Canada, Britain, Australia, etc.: *Do you speak English?*

en·hance [AWL] /ɪnˈhæns/ *verb* (en·hanc·es, en·hanc·ing, en·hanced)
to improve someone or something, or to make someone or something more attractive: *an opportunity to enhance the reputation of the company* ◆ *makeup that enhances your best features*

en·joy /ɪnˈdʒɔɪ/ *verb* (en·joys, en·joy·ing, en·joyed)
to like something very much: *I enjoy playing soccer.* ◆ *Did you enjoy your dinner?*
enjoy yourself to be happy; to have a good time: *I really enjoyed myself at the party.*

en·joy·a·ble /ɪnˈdʒɔɪəbl/ *adjective*
Something that is **enjoyable** makes you happy: *Thank you for a very enjoyable evening.*

en·joy·ment /ɪnˈdʒɔɪmənt/ *noun* [count, noncount]
a feeling of enjoying something: *I get a lot of enjoyment from traveling.* ➔ SYNONYM **pleasure**

en·large /ɪnˈlɑrdʒ/ *verb* (en·larg·es, en·larg·ing, en·larged)
to make something bigger: *Reading will enlarge your vocabulary.*
▸ **en·large·ment** /ɪnˈlɑrdʒmənt/ *noun* [count, noncount]: *an enlargement of a photograph*

e·nor·mous [AWL] /ɪˈnɔrməs/ *adjective*
very big: *an enormous dog* ➔ SYNONYM **huge**
▸ **e·nor·mous·ly** [AWL] /ɪˈnɔrməsli/ *adverb*
very, or very much: *The movie was enormously successful.*

e·nough /ɪˈnʌf/ *adjective, pronoun, adverb*

> ⓘ PRONUNCIATION
>
> The word **enough** sounds like **stuff**, because sometimes the letters **–gh** sound like **f**, in words like **enough**, **rough** and **tough**.

as much or as many as you need: *There isn't* **enough** *food* **for** *ten people.* ◆ *You're too thin – you don't eat enough.* ◆ *Is she old* **enough to** *drive?*

Grammar

- If you have **enough** of something, you have the right amount: *There's enough cake for everyone.*
- In negative sentences **enough** means "less than": *The coffee isn't hot enough.*
- For "more than" we use **too**: *The coffee is too hot.*

en·roll /ɪnˈroʊl/ *verb* (en·rolls, en·roll·ing, en·rolled)
to join a group, for example a school, college, or class. You usually pay money (called a FEE) when you **enroll**: *I've* **enrolled in** *an English course.*

en·sure [AWL] /ɪnˈʃʊr/ *verb* (en·sures, en·sur·ing, en·sured) (also **in·sure**) (formal)
to make sure that something happens: *Please* **ensure that** *all the lights are switched off before you leave.* ➔ SYNONYM **make sure**

en·ter /ˈɛntər/ *verb* (en·ters, en·ter·ing, en·tered)
1 (formal) to come or go into a place: *They stopped talking when she entered the room.* ◆ *Do not enter without knocking.*
2 to give your name to someone because you want to do something like run in a race or take an exam: *I entered a competition last month and won a prize.*
3 to put information on paper or in a computer: *Please enter your name and address at the top of the form.* ◆ *I've entered the data into the computer.*

en·ter·prise /ˈɛntərpraɪz/ *noun* [count]
a new plan, project, or business: *a business enterprise*

en·ter·tain 🔊 /ˌɛntərˈteɪn/ *verb* (en·ter·tains, en·ter·tain·ing, en·ter·tained)
1 to say or do things that other people find interesting or funny: *She entertained us all with her funny stories.*
2 to give food and drink to visitors in your house: *We're entertaining friends this evening.*

en·ter·tain·er /ˌɛntərˈteɪnər/ *noun* [count]
a person whose job is to help people have a good time, for example by singing, dancing, or telling jokes

en·ter·tain·ing /ˌɛntərˈteɪnɪŋ/ *adjective*
funny and interesting: *The talk was informative and entertaining.*

en·ter·tain·ment 🔊 /ˌɛntərˈteɪnmənt/ *noun* [count, noncount]
anything that ENTERTAINS people, for example movies, concerts, or television: *There isn't much entertainment for young people in this town.*

en·thu·si·asm 🔊 /ɛnˈθuziæzəm/ *noun* [noncount]
a strong feeling of wanting to do something or liking something: *The students showed great enthusiasm for the new project.*

en·thu·si·ast /ɛnˈθuziæst/ *noun* [count]
a person who is very interested in an activity or a subject: *car enthusiasts*

en·thu·si·as·tic 🔊 /ɪnˌθuziˈæstɪk/ *adjective*
full of enthusiasm: *The kids are very enthusiastic about sports.*
▶ **en·thu·si·as·ti·cal·ly** /ɪnˌθuziˈæstɪkli/ *adverb*

en·tire /ɪnˈtaɪər/ *adjective*
whole or complete: *We spent the entire day at the beach.*

en·tire·ly /ɪnˈtaɪərli/ *adverb*
completely: *That is an entirely different question.* ◆ *I entirely agree with you.*

en·ti·tle /ɪnˈtaɪt̮l/ *verb* (en·ti·tles, en·ti·tling, en·ti·tled)
1 to give someone the right to have or do something: *I've worked hard, so I think I'm entitled to a vacation.*
2 to give a title to a book, a play, etc.: *His latest book is entitled "Aquarium."*

en·trance 🔊 /ˈɛntrəns/ *noun*
1 [count] the door, gate, or opening where you go into a place: *I'll meet you at the entrance to the museum.* ➔ ANTONYM **exit**
2 [count] coming or going into a place: *He made his entrance onto the stage.* ➔ ANTONYM **exit**
3 [noncount] the right to go into a place: *They were refused entrance to the club because they were wearing jeans.*

en·trée (also **en·tree**) /ˈɑntreɪ/ *noun* [count]
the main course of a meal, especially in a restaurant: *The fixed price menu includes an appetizer, an entrée, and a dessert.*

en·tre·pre·neur /ˌɑntrəprəˈnər/ *noun* [count]
(BUSINESS) a person who makes money by starting or running businesses

en·try /ˈɛntri/ *noun* (plural en·tries)
1 [noncount] the act of going into a place: *The thieves gained entry (= got in) through a window.* ➔ SYNONYM **entrance**
2 [noncount] the right to go into a place: *There's a sign that says "No Entry."* ◆ *They were refused entry into the country.*
3 [count] (also **en·try·way** /ˈɛntriweɪ/) a door, gate, or passage where you enter a building: *We stood in the entry of the building until the rain stopped.* ➔ SYNONYM **entrance**
4 [count] a person or thing that is entered in a competition: *The standard of the entries was very high.*
5 [count] one item that is written down in a list, dictionary, diary, etc.: *an entry in a dictionary*

en·ve·lope /ˈɛnvəloʊp; ˈɑnvəloʊp/ *noun* [count]
a paper cover for a letter: *Did you write his address on the envelope?*

en·vied, en·vies forms of **envy**²

en·vi·ous /ˈɛnviəs/ *adjective*
wanting what someone else has: *She's envious of her sister's success.* ➔ SYNONYM **jealous** ➔ The noun and verb are both **envy**.

en·vi·ron·ment 🔊 AWL /ɛnˈvaɪərnmənt/ *noun*

> ⓘ **SPELLING**
> Be careful! Remember to put **N** before **M** in **environment**.

1 the environment [singular] the air, water, land, animals, and plants around us: *We must do more to protect the environment.*
2 [count, noncount] the conditions in which you live, work, etc.: *Children need a happy home environment.*

Collocations

The environment

environmental damage
- **cause** climate change/global warming
- **produce** pollution/carbon dioxide/CO_2
- **destroy/harm** the environment/wildlife
- **pollute** the environment/the air/rivers and lakes/the oceans

protecting the environment
- **reduce/limit** pollution/emissions
- **protect/save** the planet/the rain forests/ an endangered species

energy and resources
- **save/consume/waste** energy
- **dump/throw away** garbage/trash/waste
- **recycle** bottles/packaging/paper/waste

■ **get/generate/produce** electricity from wind/solar power

en·vi·ron·men·tal [AWL] /ɛn,vaɪərn'mɛntl/ *adjective*
1 connected with the natural conditions in which people, animals, and plants live; connected with the environment: *We talked about pollution and other environmental problems.*
2 connected with the conditions in which you live, work, etc.: *Ice on the street created an environmental hazard.*
▶ **en·vi·ron·men·tal·ly** [AWL] /ɛn,vaɪərn'mɛntəli/ *adverb*: *environmentally friendly* packaging (= that does not harm the environment)

en·vi·ron·men·tal·ist [AWL] /ɛn,vaɪərn'mɛntəlɪst/ *noun* [count]
a person who tries to protect the environment
▶ **en·vi·ron·men·tal·ism** /ɛn,vaɪərn'mɛntəlɪzəm/ *noun* [noncount]

en·vy¹ /'ɛnvi/ *noun* [noncount]
a sad or angry feeling of wanting what another person has: *I couldn't hide my envy of her success.* • *They looked with envy at her new clothes.* ⊃ SYNONYM **jealousy**

en·vy² /'ɛnvi/ *verb* (en·vies, en·vy·ing, en·vied, has en·vied)
to want something that someone else has; to feel ENVY: *I envy you! You always seem so happy!*

en·zyme /'ɛnzaɪm/ *noun* [count]
(BIOLOGY) a substance, produced by all living things, which helps a chemical change to happen more quickly, without being changed itself

ep·ic /'ɛpɪk/ *noun* [count]
a long movie or book that contains a lot of action: *His latest movie is a historical epic.*

ep·i·dem·ic /,ɛpə'dɛmɪk/ *noun* [count]
(HEALTH) a disease that many people in a place have at the same time: *a flu epidemic*

ep·i·lep·sy /'ɛpəlɛpsi/ *noun* [noncount]
(HEALTH) a disease of the brain that can cause a person to become unconscious suddenly, sometimes with violent movements that they cannot control

ep·i·sode /'ɛpəsoʊd/ *noun* [count]
a program on television or radio that is part of a longer story: *You can see the final episode of the series on Monday.*

e·qual¹ 🔧 /'ikwəl/ *adjective*
the same in size, amount, value, or level as something or someone else: *Women want equal pay for equal work.* • *Divide the pie into six equal pieces.* ⊃ ANTONYM **unequal**

e·qual² /'ikwəl/ *verb* (e·quals, e·qual·ing, e·qualed)
1 to be exactly the same amount as something: *Two plus two equals four (2+2=4).*
2 to be as good as someone or something: *This achievement is unlikely ever to be equaled.*

e·qual³ /'ikwəl/ *noun* [count]
a person who has the same ability or rights as someone else: *She treats everyone as her equal.*

e·qual·i·ty /ɪ'kwɑləti/ *noun* [noncount]
being the same or having the same rights: *People are still fighting for racial equality.* ⊃ ANTONYM **inequality**

e·qual·ly /'ikwəli/ *adverb*
1 in the same way: *Diet and exercise are equally important.*
2 in equal parts or amounts: *The money was divided equally among her four children.*

e·qual sign /'ikwəl saɪn/ (also **e·quals sign**) *noun* [count]
(MATH) the symbol (=), used in mathematics

e·qua·tion [AWL] /ɪ'kweɪʒn/ *noun* [count]
(MATH) a statement that two quantities are equal: *In the equation $2x+5=11$, what is the value of x?*

e·qua·tor /ɪ'kweɪt̬ər/ *noun* the equator [singular]
(GEOGRAPHY) the line on maps around the middle of the world. Countries near the **equator** are very hot. ⊃ Look at the picture at **earth**.
▶ **e·qua·to·ri·al** /,ikwə'tɔriəl/ *adjective*: *equatorial rain forests*

e·qui·lat·er·al tri·an·gle /,ikwɪlæt̬ərəl 'traɪæŋgl/ *noun* [count]
(MATH) a shape with three straight sides that are all the same length

equilateral triangle

e·qui·nox /'ikwə,nɑks/ *noun* [count]
one of the two times in the year when the sun is above the EQUATOR, and day and night are of equal length: *the spring equinox* • *the fall equinox*

e·quip [AWL] /ɪ'kwɪp/ *verb* (e·quips, e·quip·ping, e·quipped)
to get or have all the things that are needed for doing something: *Before setting out, they equipped themselves with a map.* • *The kitchen is well equipped.*

e·quip·ment 🔧 [AWL] /ɪ'kwɪpmənt/ *noun* [noncount]
special things that you need for doing something: *sports equipment* • *a piece of equipment*

e·quiv·a·lent AWL /ɪˈkwɪvələnt/ *adjective*
equal in value, amount, meaning, importance, etc.: *One mile is roughly equivalent to 1.6 kilometers.*
▶ **e·quiv·a·lent** AWL *noun* [count]: *Send $20, or the equivalent in your own currency.*

ER /ˌi ˈɑr/ short for **emergency room**

e·ra /ˈɪrə; ˈɛrə/ *noun* [count]
(HISTORY) a period of time in history: *the Prohibition era*

e·rase /ɪˈreɪs/ *verb* (e·ras·es, e·ras·ing, e·rased)
to remove something completely (for example a pencil mark, a computer file, etc.): *I like to use a pencil so that I can erase my mistakes.*

e·ras·er /ɪˈreɪsər/ *noun* [count]
(ART) a small piece of rubber that you use for removing marks that you have made with a pencil, pen, etc. ⊃ Look at the picture at **stationery**.

e·rect¹ /ɪˈrɛkt/ *adjective* (formal)
standing or pointing straight up: *He stood with his head erect.*

e·rect² /ɪˈrɛkt/ *verb* (e·rects, e·rect·ing, e·rect·ed) (formal)
to build something or to make something stand up straight: *Police erected barriers to keep the crowds back.*

e·rode AWL /ɪˈroʊd/ *verb* (e·rodes, e·rod·ing, e·rod·ed)
(GEOGRAPHY) to destroy something slowly, especially caused by the weather, the ocean, etc.: *The cliffs have been eroded by ocean waves.*
▶ **e·ro·sion** AWL /ɪˈroʊʒn/ *noun* [noncount]: *the erosion of the coastline*

e·rot·ic /ɪˈrɑtɪk/ *adjective*
causing sexual excitement: *an erotic picture*

er·rand /ˈɛrənd/ *noun* [count]
a short trip to do something, for example to buy something at a store: *I have to run a few errands for my mom.*

er·rat·ic /ɪˈrætɪk/ *adjective*
changing without reason; that you can never be sure of: *erratic behavior*
▶ **er·rat·i·cal·ly** /ɪˈrætɪkli/ *adverb*: *She was driving erratically.*

er·ror 🔑 AWL /ˈɛrər/ *noun* [count]
something that is done wrong: *The letter was sent to the wrong address because of a computer error.* ◆ *I think you have made an error in calculating the total.* ⊃ SYNONYM **mistake**

e·rupt /ɪˈrʌpt/ *verb* (e·rupts, e·rupt·ing, e·rupt·ed)
(GEOGRAPHY) When a VOLCANO (= a mountain with a hole in the top) **erupts**, smoke, hot rocks, or liquid rock (called LAVA) suddenly come out: *The volcano could erupt at any time.*
▶ **e·rup·tion** /ɪˈrʌpʃn/ *noun* [count, noncount]: *a volcanic eruption*

es·ca·la·tor /ˈɛskəleɪtər/ *noun* [count]
moving stairs that carry people up and down

es·cape¹ 🔑 /ɪˈskeɪp/ *verb* (es·capes, es·cap·ing, es·caped)
1 to get free from someone or something: *The bird escaped from its cage.* ◆ *Two prisoners escaped, but were later caught.*
2 to manage to avoid something dangerous or unpleasant: *The pilot escaped death by seconds.*

es·cape² /ɪˈskeɪp/ *noun* [count, noncount]
escaping from a place, or from a dangerous or unpleasant situation: *As soon as he turned away, she would make her escape.* ◆ *She had a lucky escape* (= something bad almost happened to her) *when a truck crashed into her car.*

es·cort¹ /ɛsˈkɔrt/ *verb* (es·corts, es·cort·ing, es·cort·ed)
to go with someone, for example to protect them or to make sure that they arrive somewhere: *The police escorted her out of the building.*

es·cort² /ˈɛskɔrt/ *noun* [count]
one or more people or vehicles that go with someone to protect them: *He always travels with an armed escort.*

ESL /ˌi ɛs ˈɛl/ *abbreviation*
ESL is short for "English as a second language" (= the teaching of English to speakers of other languages who are living in a country where people speak English). ⊃ Look at **EFL**.

es·pe·cial·ly 🔑 /ɪˈspɛʃəli/ *adverb*
1 more than usual, or more than others: *I hate getting up early, especially in winter.* ◆ *She loves animals, especially horses.*
2 for a particular person or thing: *I bought these flowers especially for you.*

es·pres·so /ɛˈsprɛsoʊ/ *noun* [count] (plural es·pres·sos)
a cup of strong black coffee ⊃ Look at **cappuccino**, **latte**.

es·say /ˈɛseɪ/ *noun* [count]
a short piece of writing about a particular subject: *Our teacher asked us to write an essay on our favorite author.*

es·sence /ˈɛsns/ *noun* [noncount]
the basic or most important quality of something: *The essence of the problem is that there is not enough money available.*

es·sen·tial /ɪˈsɛnʃl/ *adjective*
If something is **essential**, it is completely necessary and you must have or do it: *It is essential that you study hard for this exam.* ⊃ SYNONYM **vital**

es·tab·lish AWL /ɪˈstæblɪʃ/ *verb* (es·tab·lish·es, es·tab·lish·ing, es·tab·lished)
to start something new: *The school was established in 1932.*

---

es·tab·lish·ment AWL /ɪˈstæblɪʃmənt/ *noun*
1 [*count*] (*formal*) an organization, business, or store: *a commercial establishment*
2 [*noncount*] the act of creating or starting something: *the establishment of a new tax system*

es·tate AWL /ɪˈsteɪt/ *noun* [*count*]
1 a large piece of land in the country, which one person or family owns
2 all the money and property that someone leaves when they die: *His estate was left to his daughter when he died.* ⊃ Look at **real estate**.

es·ti·mate¹ AWL /ˈɛstəmət/ *noun* [*count*]
1 a judgment about the size or cost of something before you have all the facts and figures: *Can you give me a **rough estimate of** how many people will be there?*
2 a statement that says how much a piece of work will cost: *The builders gave me an estimate for the roof repairs.*

es·ti·mate² AWL /ˈɛstəmeɪt/ *verb* (**es·ti·mates, es·ti·mat·ing, es·ti·mat·ed**)
to say how much you think something will cost, how big something is, or how long it will take to do something: *The builders **estimated that** it would take a week to repair the roof.*

etc. 🔊 /ɛt ˈsɛtərə/ *abbreviation*
You use **etc.** at the end of a list to show that there are other things, but you are not going to name them all: *Remember to take some paper, a pen, etc.* ⊃ Etc. is short for "et cetera."

e·ter·nal /ɪˈtɚnl/ *adjective*
existing or continuing forever: *They believe in eternal life* (= life after death).

e·ter·ni·ty /ɪˈtɚnəti/ *noun* [*noncount*]
time that has no end; the state or time after death

eth·ic AWL /ˈɛθɪk/ *noun*
1 ethics [*plural*] moral beliefs that control or influence a person's behavior: *a **code of ethics** for the medical profession*
2 [*singular*] a system of moral beliefs or rules of behavior: *a strong work ethic*

eth·i·cal AWL /ˈɛθɪkl/ *adjective*
1 connected with beliefs about what is right or wrong: *an ethical question*
2 morally correct: *She didn't break the law, but her behavior certainly wasn't ethical.*

eth·nic AWL /ˈɛθnɪk/ *adjective*
connected with or belonging to a group of people that share a particular culture: *New York City is home to many different **ethnic minorities**.*

et·y·mol·o·gy /ˌɛtəˈmɑlədʒi/ *noun* [*count, noncount*] (*plural* **et·y·mol·o·gies**)
(**ENGLISH LANGUAGE ARTS**) the study of the history of words and their meanings, or the history of one particular word: *What is the etymology of this word?* ♦ *She's an expert in etymology.*

eu·ro /ˈyʊroʊ/ *noun* [*count*] (*plural* **eu·ros**) (symbol €)
a unit of money that people use in many European countries: *All prices are in euros.*

e·vac·u·ate /ɪˈvækyueɪt/ *verb* (**e·vac·u·ates, e·vac·u·at·ing, e·vac·u·at·ed**)
to take people away from a dangerous place to a safer place: *The area near the factory was evacuated after the explosion.*
▸ **e·vac·u·a·tion** /ɪˌvækyuˈeɪʃn/ *noun* [*count, noncount*]: *the evacuation of cities during the war*

e·val·u·ate AWL /ɪˈvælyueɪt/ *verb* (**e·val·u·ates, e·val·u·at·ing, e·val·u·at·ed**)
to form an opinion about how good something is, after thinking about it carefully: *We need to evaluate the program to see if it is still effective.*
▸ **e·val·u·a·tion** AWL /ɪˌvælyuˈeɪʃn/ *noun* [*count, noncount*]: *an evaluation of our training procedures*

e·vap·o·rate /ɪˈvæpəreɪt/ *verb* (**e·vap·o·rates, e·vap·o·rat·ing, e·vap·o·rat·ed**)
(**PHYSICS**) If a liquid **evaporates**, it changes into a gas: *Water evaporates if you heat it.*

eve /iv/ *noun* [*count*]
the day before a special day: *December 24 is **Christmas Eve**.* ♦ *I went to a party on **New Year's Eve*** (= December 31).

e·ven¹ 🔊 /ˈivən/ *adverb*
1 a word that you use to say that something is surprising: *The game is so easy that even a child can play it.* ♦ *He didn't laugh – he didn't even smile.*
2 a word that you use to make another word stronger: *Their house is even smaller than ours.*
even if it does not change anything if: *Even if you run, you won't catch the bus.*
even so although that is true: *I didn't have any lunch, but even so I'm not hungry.*
even though although: *I went to the party, even though I was tired.*

e·ven² /ˈivən/ *adjective*
1 flat and smooth: *The game must be played on an even surface.* ⊃ **ANTONYM uneven**
2 not changing: *The wine should be stored at an even temperature.*
3 the same; equal: *Sara won the first game and I won the second, so we're even.*
4 (**MATH**) Even numbers can be divided exactly by two: *4, 6, 8, and 10 are even numbers.* ⊃ **ANTONYM odd**
get even with someone (*informal*) to hurt someone who has hurt you

tʃ **ch**in   dʒ **J**une   v **v**an   θ **th**in   ð **th**en   s **s**o   z **z**oo   ʃ **sh**e

eve·ning 🔑 /ˈivnɪŋ/ *noun* [count, noncount]
the part of the day between the end of the
afternoon and the night: *What are you doing this
evening?* • *Most people watch television in the
evening.* • *John came on Monday evening.*
good evening (*formal*) words that you say when
you see someone for the first time in the
evening

e·ven·ly /ˈivənli/ *adverb*
in a smooth, regular, or equal way: *The teams
were evenly balanced.* • *Spread the mixture
evenly in the pan.*

e·vent 🔑 /ɪˈvɛnt/ *noun* [count]
1 something important that happens: *My
sister's wedding was a big event for our family.*
2 a race or competition: *The next event will be
the high jump.*

e·vent·ful /ɪˈvɛntfl/ *adjective*
full of important or exciting things happening:
It's been a pretty eventful week!

e·ven·tu·al **AWL** /ɪˈvɛntʃuəl/ *adjective*
happening as a result at the end of a period of
time or of a process: *We still don't know what the
eventual cost will be.*

e·ven·tu·al·ly **AWL** /ɪˈvɛntʃəli/ *adverb*
after a long time: *The bus eventually arrived two
hours late.*

ev·er 🔑 /ˈɛvər/ *adverb*
at any time: *"Have you ever been to Africa?" "No,
I haven't."* • *I **hardly ever** (= almost never) see
Peter.*
ever since in all the time since: *I've known Lucy
ever since we were children.* ➔ Look at **forever**.

ev·er·green /ˈɛvərgrin/ *noun* [count]
a tree or bush that has green leaves all through
the year

eve·ry 🔑 /ˈɛvri/ *adjective*
1 all of the people or things in a group: *She
knows every student in the school.*
2 used for saying how often something
happens: *He calls **every evening**.* • *I see Robert
every now and then (= sometimes, but not
often).* • *She comes **every other day** (= for
example on Monday, Wednesday, and Friday
but not on Tuesday or Thursday).*

eve·ry·bod·y 🔑 /ˈɛvriˌbɑdi; ˈɛvriˌbʌdi/ *pronoun*
another word for **everyone**

eve·ry·day /ˈɛvrideɪ/ *adjective*
normal; not special: *Computers are now part of
everyday life.*

eve·ry·one 🔑 /ˈɛvriwʌn/ (also **eve·ry·bod·y**)
pronoun
each person; all people: *Everyone knows Tom.* •
Everyone has a chance to win.

eve·ry·thing 🔑 /ˈɛvriθɪŋ/ *pronoun*
1 each thing; all things: *Sam lost everything in
the fire.* • *Everything in that store is very
expensive.*
2 the most important thing: *Money isn't
everything, you know.*

eve·ry·where 🔑 /ˈɛvriwɛr/ *adverb*
in all places or to all places: *I've looked
everywhere for my pen, but I can't find it.*

e·vict /ɪˈvɪkt/ *verb* (e·victs, e·vict·ing, e·vict·ed)
to officially force someone to leave the house
they are living in: *They were evicted for not
paying the rent.*

ev·i·dence 🔑 **AWL** /ˈɛvədəns/ *noun* [noncount]
the facts, signs, or objects that make you believe
that something is true: *The police searched the
room, looking for evidence.* • *There is evidence of
a link between smoking and cancer.*
give evidence to say what you know about
someone or something in a court of law: *The
man who saw the accident will give evidence in
court.*

ev·i·dent **AWL** /ˈɛvədənt/ *adjective*
easy to see or understand: *It was evident that the
damage was very serious.* ➔ **SYNONYM obvious**

ev·i·dent·ly **AWL** /ˈɛvədəntli/ *adverb*
clearly; that can be easily seen or understood:
She was evidently very upset. ➔ **SYNONYM
obviously**

e·vil¹ 🔑 /ˈivl/ *adjective*
morally bad and cruel: *an evil person*

e·vil² /ˈivl/ *noun* [count, noncount]
something that causes bad or harmful things to
happen: *the struggle between good and evil* •
illegal drugs and other evils of modern society

ev·o·lu·tion **AWL** /ˌɛvəˈluʃn/ *noun* [noncount]
(**BIOLOGY**) the development of plants and
animals from simple early forms, which
happens over a long period of time: *Darwin's
theory of evolution*
▶ **ev·o·lu·tion·ary** **AWL** /ˌɛvəˈluʃneri/ *adjective*:
evolutionary theories

e·volve **AWL** /ɪˈvɑlv/ *verb* (e·volves, e·volv·ing,
e·volved)
1 to develop slowly over time: *His style of
painting has evolved over the past 20 years.*
2 (**BIOLOGY**) If plants or animals **evolve**, they
change slowly over a long period of time from

simple forms to more advanced ones: *The three species evolved from a single ancestor.*

ex·act 🔑 /ɪgˈzækt/ *adjective*
completely correct: *We need to know the exact time the incident occurred.*

ex·act·ly 🔑 /ɪgˈzæktli/ *adverb*
1 You use **exactly** when you are asking for or giving information that is completely correct: *Can you tell me exactly what happened?* • *It cost exactly $10.* ➔ SYNONYM **precisely**
2 in every way or detail: *This shirt is exactly what I wanted.* ➔ SYNONYM **just**
3 You use **exactly** to agree with someone: *"So you mean someone in this room must be the thief?" "Exactly."*

ex·ag·ger·ate 🔑 /ɪgˈzædʒəreɪt/ *verb*
(ex·ag·ger·ates, ex·ag·ger·at·ing, ex·ag·ger·at·ed)

> ℹ️ **SPELLING**
> Remember! You spell **exaggerate** with **GG**.

to say that something is bigger, better, worse, etc. than it really is: *Don't exaggerate! I was only two minutes late, not twenty.*
▸ **ex·ag·ger·a·tion** /ɪgˌzædʒəˈreɪʃn/ *noun* [count, noncount]: *It's a bit of an exaggeration to say she can't speak English!*

ex·am 🔑 /ɪgˈzæm/ *noun* [count]
a test of what you know or can do: *We have an English exam next week.* • *"Did you pass all your exams?" "No, I failed history."*

Collocations

Work and exams

doing
- **do** your homework/an assignment/a paper/an essay
- **write** a paper/an essay/a report
- **turn in/hand in** your homework/an assignment/a paper
- **take** a test/an exam/a quiz

passing/failing
- **grade** homework/a test
- **pass/do well on** a test/an exam/a quiz
- **fail** a test/an exam/a class
- **get** a good grade/an A/a B/a diploma

ex·am·i·na·tion 🔑 /ɪgˌzæməˈneɪʃn/ *noun*
1 [count, noncount] the act of looking carefully at someone or something: *a medical examination*
2 [count] (*formal*) another word for **exam**

ex·am·ine 🔑 /ɪgˈzæmən/ *verb* (ex·am·ines, ex·am·in·ing, ex·am·ined)
1 to look carefully at something or someone: *The doctor examined her, but could find nothing wrong.* • *Have the car examined by an expert before you buy it.*

2 (*formal*) to ask questions to find out what someone knows or what they can do: *You will be examined on everything you have learned this year.*

ex·am·ple 🔑 /ɪgˈzæmpl/ *noun* [count]
something that shows what other things of the same kind are like: *This dictionary gives many examples of how words are used in sentences.*
for example used for giving an example: *Do you speak any other languages, for example Spanish or French?* ➔ The short way of writing "for example" is **e.g.**

ex·as·per·at·ed /ɪgˈzæspəˌreɪtɪd/ *adjective*
feeling angry with something or someone: *"Oh, come on!" she said, clearly exasperated with me.*

ex·ceed AWL /ɪkˈsid/ *verb* (ex·ceeds, ex·ceed·ing, ex·ceed·ed)
to be more than a particular number or amount: *The weight must not exceed 20 pounds.* ➔ The noun is **excess**.

ex·cel /ɪkˈsɛl/ *verb* (ex·cels, ex·cel·ling, ex·celled) (*formal*)
to be very good at doing something: *Anne excels in sports.*

ex·cel·lence /ˈɛksələns/ *noun* [noncount]
being very good: *This school is known for academic excellence.*

ex·cel·lent 🔑 /ˈɛksələnt/ *adjective*
very good: *She speaks excellent Spanish.*

ex·cept 🔑 /ɪkˈsɛpt/ *preposition*
not including someone or something: *The restaurant is open every day except Sunday.* • *Everyone went to the party except for me.*
except that used before you say something that makes a statement not completely true: *I don't know what he looks like, except that he's very tall.*

ex·cep·tion /ɪkˈsɛpʃn/ *noun* [count]
a person or thing that is not the same as the others: *Most of his books are good, but this one is an exception.*
with the exception of someone or **something** except: *I like all vegetables with the exception of cabbage.* ➔ SYNONYM **apart from**

ex·cep·tion·al /ɪkˈsɛpʃənl/ *adjective*
very good, especially if this is unusual: *She is an exceptional pianist.*
▸ **ex·cep·tion·al·ly** /ɪkˈsɛpʃənli/ *adverb*: *He was an exceptionally good student.*

ex·cess /ɪkˈsɛs/ *noun* [singular]
more than is necessary or usual: *An excess of stress can make you sick.*
▸ **ex·cess** /ˈɛksɛs/ *adjective*: *Cut any excess fat off the meat.* ➔ The verb is **exceed**.

ə **about**   y **yes**   w **woman**   t̬ **butter**   eɪ **say**   aɪ **five**   ɔɪ **boy**   aʊ **now**   oʊ **go**

ex·ces·sive /ɪkˈsɛsɪv/ *adjective*
too much or too great: *I think $40 for a steak is excessive.* • *The police officer was accused of using excessive force.*
▸ **ex·ces·sive·ly** /ɪkˈsɛsɪvli/ *adverb*

ex·change[1] 🔑 /ɪksˈtʃeɪndʒ/ *noun* [count, noncount]
giving or receiving something in return for something else: *a useful exchange of information* • *We can offer free accommodations in exchange for some help in the house.* ⊃ Look at **stock exchange**.

ex·change[2] 🔑 /ɪksˈtʃeɪndʒ/ *verb* (ex·chang·es, ex·chang·ing, ex·changed)
to give one thing and get another thing for it: *I would like to exchange this skirt for a bigger size.* • *We exchanged phone numbers.*

ex·change rate /ɪksˈtʃeɪndʒ ˌreɪt/ *noun* [count]
(**BUSINESS**) how much money from one country you can buy with money from another country: *The exchange rate is 0.7 euros to the dollar.*

ex·cite /ɪkˈsaɪt/ *verb* (ex·cites, ex·cit·ing, ex·cit·ed)
to make a person feel very happy or enthusiastic so that they are not calm: *Please don't excite the children too much or they won't sleep tonight.*

ex·cit·ed 🔑 /ɪkˈsaɪtəd/ *adjective*
not calm, for example because you are happy about something that is going to happen: *He's getting very excited about his vacation.*

ex·cite·ment 🔑 /ɪkˈsaɪtmənt/ *noun* [noncount]
a feeling of being excited: *There was great excitement in the stadium before the game began.*

ex·cit·ing 🔑 /ɪkˈsaɪtɪŋ/ *adjective*
Something that is **exciting** makes you have strong feelings of happiness and enthusiasm: *an exciting story* • *Her new job sounds very exciting.*

ex·claim /ɪkˈskleɪm/ *verb* (ex·claims, ex·claim·ing, ex·claimed)
to say something suddenly and loudly because you are surprised or angry: *"I don't believe it!" she exclaimed.*

ex·cla·ma·tion /ˌɛkskləˈmeɪʃn/ *noun* [count]
(**ENGLISH LANGUAGE ARTS**) a short word or phrase that you use to show surprise, pain, happiness, etc.: *"Oh," "Hey," and "Wow" are exclamations.* • *He gave an exclamation of surprise.* ⊃ SYNONYM **interjection**

ex·cla·ma·tion point /ˌɛkskləˈmeɪʃn ˌpɔɪnt/ *noun* [count]
(**ENGLISH LANGUAGE ARTS**) a mark (!) that you use in writing to show loud or strong words, or surprise

ex·clude 🔺AWL /ɪkˈsklud/ *verb* (ex·cludes, ex·clud·ing, ex·clud·ed)
1 to deliberately not include something: *The price excludes tax.* ⊃ ANTONYM **include**
2 to not allow a person to enter a place or do an activity: *Students were excluded from the meeting.*

ex·clud·ing 🔺AWL /ɪkˈskludɪŋ/ *preposition*
without: *The meal cost $45, excluding drinks.* ⊃ ANTONYM **including**

ex·cur·sion /ɪkˈskərʒn/ *noun* [count]
a short trip to see something interesting or to enjoy yourself: *We're going on an excursion to the island on Sunday.*

ex·cuse[1] 🔑 /ɪkˈskyus/ *noun* [count]

> ℹ️ **PRONUNCIATION**
> When the word **excuse** is a noun, it ends with a sound like **juice** or **loose**.
> When the word **excuse** is a verb, it ends with a sound like **shoes** or **choose**.

words you say or write to explain why you have done something wrong: *You're late! What's your excuse this time?* • *There's no excuse for rudeness.*

ex·cuse[2] 🔑 /ɪkˈskyuz/ *verb* (ex·cus·es, ex·cus·ing, ex·cused)
used when you want to say that you are sorry for something that is not very bad: *Please excuse us for being late – we missed the bus.*
excuse me
1 words you use when you want to start talking to someone you do not know: *Excuse me, could you tell me the time?*
2 words you use to say that you are sorry: *Did I step on your foot? Excuse me.*
3 Excuse me? words you use to ask someone to repeat what they just said: *"Is this your bag?" "Excuse me?" "I asked if this was your bag."*

ex·e·cute /ˈɛksəkyut/ *verb* (ex·e·cutes, ex·e·cut·ing, ex·e·cut·ed)
to kill a person as a legal punishment: *He was executed for murder.*
▸ **ex·e·cu·tion** /ˌɛksəˈkyuʃn/ *noun* [count, noncount]: *the execution of prisoners*

ex·ec·u·tive[1] /ɪɡˈzɛkyətɪv/ *noun* [count]
(**BUSINESS**) a person who has an important position in a business or organization

ex·ec·u·tive[2] /ɪɡˈzɛkyətɪv/ *adjective*
1 (**BUSINESS**) connected with managing and making decisions in a business or organization: *an executive director of a company* • *executive decisions*
2 (**POLITICS**) connected with the part of the government that makes decisions about running the country: *the executive branch of the federal government* ⊃ Look at the note at **government**.

---

ex·empt /ɪɡ'zɛmpt/ *adjective*
If you are **exempt** from something, you do not have to do it: *Are full-time students exempt from jury duty?*

ex·er·cise¹ /'ɛksərsaɪz/ *noun*
1 [*noncount*] (**HEALTH**) moving your body to keep it strong and well: *Swimming is very good exercise.* ⊃ Look at the note at **diet¹**.
2 [*count*] (**HEALTH**) a special movement that you do to keep your body strong and well: *This exercise is good for your back.*
3 [*count*] a piece of work that you do to learn something: *Please do exercises 1 and 2 for homework.*

ex·er·cise² /'ɛksərsaɪz/ *verb* (ex·er·cis·es, ex·er·cis·ing, ex·er·cised)
(**HEALTH**) to move your body to keep it strong and well: *They exercise in the park every morning.*

ex·er·tion /ɪɡ'zərʃn/ *noun* [*noncount*]
using your body in a way that takes a lot of effort: *You should avoid any physical exertion for the next four weeks.*

ex·hale /ɛks'heɪl/ *verb* (ex·hales, ex·hal·ing, ex·haled)
(**BIOLOGY**) to let air, smoke, etc. out of your body by breathing: *He sat back and exhaled deeply.* ⊃ **ANTONYM inhale**

ex·haust¹ /ɪɡ'zɔst/ *noun*
1 [*noncount*] the waste gas that comes out of a vehicle, an engine, or a machine: *car exhaust*
2 (also **ex·haust pipe** /ɪɡ'zɔst paɪp/) a pipe through which waste gases come out, for example on a car ⊃ **SYNONYM tailpipe**

ex·haust² /ɪɡ'zɔst/ *verb* (ex·hausts, ex·haust·ing, ex·haust·ed)
to make you feel very tired: *The long trip exhausted us.*
▶ **ex·haust·ing** /ɪɡ'zɔstɪŋ/ *adjective*: *Teaching young children can be exhausting.*

ex·haust·ed /ɪɡ'zɔstəd/ *adjective*
very tired: *I'm exhausted – I think I'll go to bed.*

ex·haus·tion /ɪɡ'zɔstʃən/ *noun* [*noncount*]
being extremely tired: *suffering from exhaustion*

ex·hib·it¹ **AWL** /ɪɡ'zɪbət/ (also **ex·hi·bi·tion** /ˌɛksə'bɪʃn/) *noun* [*count, noncount*]
(**ART**) an object or a group of objects that are arranged in a museum, etc. so that people can look at them: *a special exhibit of works by local artists* • *Her paintings will be on exhibit through the end of August.*

ex·hib·it² **AWL** /ɪɡ'zɪbət/ *verb* (ex·hib·its, ex·hib·it·ing, ex·hib·it·ed)
(**ART**) to show something in a public place for people to look at: *Her photographs have been exhibited all over the world.*

ex·hi·bi·tion **AWL** /ˌɛksə'bɪʃn/ *noun* [*count, noncount*] another word for **exhibit¹**

ex·ile /'ɛgzaɪl; 'ɛksaɪl/ *noun* (**POLITICS**)
1 [*noncount*] having to live away from your own country, especially for political reasons or as a punishment: *Napoleon spent the last years of his life in exile.*
2 [*count*] a person who has to live away from their own country

ex·ist /ɪɡ'zɪst/ *verb* (ex·ists, ex·ist·ing, ex·ist·ed)
to be real; to live: *Does life exist on other planets?* • *That word does not exist.*

ex·is·tence /ɪɡ'zɪstəns/ *noun* [*noncount*]
being real; living: *It is the oldest language in existence.*

ex·ist·ing /ɪɡ'zɪstɪŋ/ *adjective*
that is already there or being used now: *Under the existing law, you are not allowed to work in this country.*

ex·it /'ɛgzət; 'ɛksət/ *noun* [*count*]
1 a way out of a building: *Where is the exit?* • *an emergency exit* ⊃ **ANTONYM entrance**
2 a place where cars can leave a highway: *We need to get off at the next exit.*

ex·ot·ic /ɪɡ'zɑṭɪk/ *adjective*
strange or interesting because it comes from another country: *exotic fruits*

ex·pand **AWL** /ɪk'spænd/ *verb* (ex·pands, ex·pand·ing, ex·pand·ed)
to become bigger or to make something bigger: *Metals expand when they are heated.* • *We hope to expand the business this year.* ⊃ Look at **contract²**.
▶ **ex·pan·sion** **AWL** /ɪk'spænʃn/ *noun* [*noncount*]: *The city's rapid expansion has caused a lot of problems.*

ex·pect /ɪk'spɛkt/ *verb* (ex·pects, ex·pect·ing, ex·pect·ed)
1 to think that someone or something will come, or that something will happen: *I'm expecting a letter.* • *We expected it to be hot in Hawaii, and it was .* • *She's expecting a baby* (= she is going to have a baby) *in June.*
2 If you are **expected** to do something, you must do it: *I am expected to work every Saturday.*

ex·pec·ta·tion /ˌɛkspɛk'teɪʃn/ *noun* [*count, noncount*]
a belief that something will happen: *Against all expectations, we enjoyed ourselves.*

ex·pe·di·tion /ˌɛkspə'dɪʃn/ *noun* [*count*]
a long trip to find or do something special: *an expedition to the South Pole* ⊃ Look at the note at **trip¹**.

ex·pel /ɪk'spɛl/ *verb* (ex·pels, ex·pel·ling, ex·pelled)
to send someone away from a school, an organization, or a country: *The boys were expelled from school for smoking.*

ex·pense /ɪkˈspɛns/ *noun*
1 [*count, noncount*] the cost of something: *Having a car is a big expense.* ➲ Look at the note at **price**.
2 expenses [*plural*] money that you spend on a certain thing: *The company pays our **travel** **expenses**.*

ex·pen·sive 🔑 /ɪkˈspɛnsɪv/ *adjective*
Something that is **expensive** costs a lot of money: *expensive clothes* ✦ *The meal was very expensive.* ➲ **ANTONYM cheap**

ex·pe·ri·ence¹ 🔑 /ɪkˈspɪriəns/ *noun*
1 [*noncount*] knowing about something because you have seen it or done it: *She has four years' teaching experience.* ✦ *Do you have much **experience of** working with children?*
2 [*count*] something that has happened to you: *He wrote a book about his experiences in South America.*

ex·pe·ri·ence² 🔑 /ɪkˈspɪriəns/ *verb*
(ex·pe·ri·enc·es, ex·pe·ri·enc·ing, ex·pe·ri·enced)
If you **experience** something, it happens to you: *Everyone experiences failure at some time in their lives.*

ex·pe·ri·enced /ɪkˈspɪriənst/ *adjective*
If you are **experienced**, you know about something because you have done it many times before: *She's an experienced driver.* ➲ **ANTONYM inexperienced**

ex·per·i·ment /ɪkˈspɛrəmənt/ *verb*
(ex·per·i·ments, ex·per·i·ment·ing, ex·per·i·ment·ed)
to do an experiment or to test something: *I don't think it's right to **experiment on** animals.* ✦ *young people who **experiment with** (= try) illegal drugs*

ex·per·i·ment 🔑 /ɪkˈspɛrəmənt/ *noun* [*count*]
(**GENERAL SCIENCE**) a scientific test that you do to find out what will happen or to see if something is true: *They have to **do experiments** to find out if the drug is safe for humans.*

ex·pert 🔑 **AWL** /ˈɛkspərt/ *noun* [*count*]
a person who knows a lot about something: *He's an **expert on** American literature.* ✦ *a computer expert*

ex·per·tise **AWL** /ˌɛkspərˈtiz/ *noun* [*noncount*]
knowing a lot about a particular subject, activity, or job: *scientific expertise*

ex·pire /ɪkˈspaɪər/ *verb* (ex·pires, ex·pir·ing, ex·pired)
to come to the end of the time when you can use an official document: *I need to renew my driver's license before it expires next month.*

ex·plain 🔑 /ɪkˈspleɪn/ *verb* (ex·plains, ex·plain·ing, ex·plained)
1 to tell someone about something so that they understand it: *The teacher usually **explains** the new words **to** us.* ✦ *He **explained how** to use the machine.*

2 to give a reason for something: *I **explained** why we needed the money.*

ex·pla·na·tion 🔑 /ˌɛkspləˈneɪʃn/ *noun* [*count, noncount*]
something that helps someone understand something, or a reason for something: *Did they **give** any **explanation for** their behavior?*

ex·plic·it **AWL** /ɪkˈsplɪsət/ *adjective*
clear; making something easy to understand: *She gave me explicit instructions not to touch anything.*
▶ **ex·plic·it·ly** **AWL** /ɪkˈsplɪsətli/ *adverb*: *He was explicitly forbidden to stay out past midnight.*

ex·plode 🔑 /ɪkˈsploʊd/ *verb* (ex·plodes, ex·plod·ing, ex·plod·ed)
to burst suddenly with a very loud noise: *A bomb exploded in the city center, killing two people.* ➲ The noun is **explosion**.

ex·ploit **AWL** /ɪkˈsplɔɪt/ *verb* (ex·ploits, ex·ploit·ing, ex·ploit·ed)
to treat someone badly to get what you want: *Some employers exploit workers, making them work long hours for low pay.*

ex·plore 🔑 /ɪkˈsplɔr/ *verb* (ex·plores, ex·plor·ing, ex·plored)
to travel around a new place to learn about it: *They explored the area on foot.*
▶ **ex·plo·ra·tion** /ˌɛkspləˈreɪʃn/ *noun* [*count, noncount*]: *the exploration of space*

ex·plor·er /ɪkˈsplɔrər/ *noun* [*count*]
a person who travels around a new place to learn about it: *The first European explorers arrived in America in the 15th century.*

ex·plo·sion 🔑 /ɪkˈsploʊʒn/ *noun* [*count*]
the sudden bursting and loud noise of something such as a bomb exploding: *There was an explosion, and pieces of glass flew everywhere.* ➲ The verb is **explode**.

ex·plo·sive /ɪkˈsploʊsɪv/ *adjective*
(**CHEMISTRY**) Something that is **explosive** can cause an explosion: *an explosive gas*
▶ **ex·plo·sive** *noun* [*count*]
(**CHEMISTRY**) a substance that can make things explode

ex·port¹ **AWL** /ɛkˈspɔrt/ *verb* (ex·ports, ex·port·ing, ex·port·ed)
(**BUSINESS**) to sell things to another country: *Japan **exports** cars **to** the United States.* ➲ **ANTONYM import**
▶ **ex·port·er** **AWL** /ɛkˈspɔrtər/ *noun* [*count*]: *the world's biggest exporter of oil* ➲ **ANTONYM importer**

ex·port² **AWL** /ˈɛkspɔrt/ *noun* (**BUSINESS**)
1 [*noncount*] selling things to another country:
These cars are made for export.
2 [*count*] something that you sell to another
country: *The country's main exports are tea and
cotton.* ⊃ **ANTONYM import**

ex·pose **AWL** /ɪkˈspoʊz/ *verb* (**ex·pos·es,**
ex·pos·ing, ex·posed)
1 to show something that is usually covered or
hidden: *He undid his top button, exposing his
neck.* ◆ *The newspaper exposed her terrible secret.*
2 to put someone in a difficult or dangerous
situation: *A baby's skin should not be exposed to
the sun for too long.*

ex·po·sure **AWL** /ɪkˈspoʊʒər/ *noun* [*noncount*]
being put in a difficult or dangerous situation:
Exposure to radiation is harmful.

ex·press¹ /ɪkˈsprɛs/ *verb* (**ex·press·es,**
ex·press·ing, ex·pressed)
to say or show how you think or feel: *She
expressed her ideas well.*

ex·press² /ɪkˈsprɛs/ *adjective*
that goes or is sent very quickly: *an express bus* ◆
express mail
▶ **ex·press** *adverb*: *I sent the package express.*

ex·pres·sion 🔎 /ɪkˈsprɛʃn/ *noun* [*count*]
1 the look on your face that shows how you feel:
an expression of surprise
2 (**ENGLISH LANGUAGE ARTS**) a word or group of
words; a way of saying something: *The
expression "to drop off" means "to fall asleep."*

ex·pres·sive /ɪkˈsprɛsɪv/ *adjective*
showing feelings or thoughts: *an expressive
piece of music* ◆ *Hannah has a very expressive
face.*

ex·press·way /ɪkˈsprɛsweɪ/ (also **free·way**
/ˈfriweɪ/) *noun* [*count*]
a wide road where vehicles can travel fast: *Turn
right and get on the expressway.*

ex·pul·sion /ɪkˈspʌlʃn/ *noun* [*count, noncount*]
the official act of making someone leave a
school, an organization, or a country: *There
have been three expulsions from school this year.*
⊃ The verb is **expel.**

ex·qui·site /ɪkˈskwɪzət/ *adjective*
extremely beautiful: *She has an exquisite face.*

ex·tend /ɪkˈstɛnd/ *verb* (**ex·tends, ex·tend·ing,**
ex·tend·ed)
1 to make something longer or bigger: *I'm
extending my vacation for another week.*
2 to reach or stretch over an area: *The park
extends as far as the river.*

ex·tend·ed fam·i·ly /ɪkˌstɛndəd ˈfæməli/ *noun*
[*count*] (*plural* **ex·tend·ed fam·i·lies**)
a large family group that includes uncles, aunts,
cousins, grandparents, etc.: *Are you planning to*
*invite your whole extended family to the
wedding?*

ex·ten·sion /ɪkˈstɛnʃn/ *noun*
1 [*count, noncount*] the act of making something
bigger or longer: *the extension of the president's
powers*
2 [*count*] a new part that you add to a building to
make it bigger: *They built an extension on the
back of the house.*
3 [*count*] extra time that you are allowed to do
something: *I need to ask my tutor for an
extension on my English paper.*
4 [*count*] one of the telephones in a building that
is connected to the main telephone: *Can I have
extension 4110, please?*

ex·ten·sive /ɪkˈstɛnsɪv/ *adjective*
large in area or amount: *The house has extensive
grounds.* ◆ *Many buildings suffered extensive
damage.*

ex·tent /ɪkˈstɛnt/ *noun* [*noncount*]
how big something is: *I had no idea of the full
extent of the problem* (= how big it was).
to a certain extent; to some extent used to
show that you do not think something is
completely true: *I agree with you to a certain
extent.*

ex·te·ri·or /ɪkˈstɪriər/ *noun* [*count, usually singular*]
the outside part of something, especially a
building: *We painted the exterior of the house
white.* ⊃ **ANTONYM interior**
▶ **ex·te·ri·or** *adjective*: *an exterior door* ⊃ **ANTONYM
interior**

ex·ter·nal **AWL** /ɪkˈstərnl/ *adjective*
on, of, or from the outside: *external walls* ⊃
ANTONYM internal

ex·tinct /ɪkˈstɪŋkt/ *adjective*
(**BIOLOGY**) If a type of animal or plant is **extinct**, it
does not exist now: *Dinosaurs became extinct
millions of years ago.*
▶ **ex·tinc·tion** /ɪkˈstɪŋkʃn/ *noun* [*noncount*]: *The
panda is in danger of extinction.*

ex·tin·guish /ɪkˈstɪŋgwɪʃ/ *verb* (**ex·tin·guish·es,**
ex·tin·guish·ing, ex·tin·guished) (*formal*)
to make something stop burning: *It took several
hours to extinguish the fire.* ⊃ **SYNONYM put out**

ex·tra¹ 🔎 /ˈɛkstrə/ *adjective, adverb*
more than what is usual: *I've put an extra blanket
on your bed because it's cold tonight.* ◆ *The room
costs $100, and you have to pay extra for
breakfast.*

ex·tra² /ˈɛkstrə/ *noun* [*count*]
1 a person in a movie, etc. who has a small, not
important part, for example in a crowd
2 something that costs more, or that is not
usually included: *All the little extras added $300
to the cost of the computer.*

ex·tract[1] AWL /ɪkˈstrækt/ *verb* (**ex·tracts**, **ex·tract·ing**, **ex·tract·ed**) (*formal*)
to take something out, especially with difficulty: *We'll have to extract two teeth to make room for the new ones.*

ex·tract[2] AWL /ˈɛkstrækt/ *noun* [count]
(**ENGLISH LANGUAGE ARTS**, **MUSIC**) a part of a book, piece of music, etc. that shows what the rest is like: *We're reading extracts of Thoreau and Emerson this semester.*

ex·tra·cur·ric·u·lar /ˌɛkstrəkəˈrɪkyələr/ *adjective*
not part of the usual studies at a school or college: *His extracurricular activities include sports and music lessons.*

ex·traor·di·nar·y /ɪkˈstrɔrdəˌnɛri/ *adjective*
very unusual or strange: *What an extraordinary thing to say!*

ex·trav·a·gant /ɪkˈstrævəgənt/ *adjective*
If you are **extravagant**, you spend too much money: *He's pretty extravagant – he goes everywhere by taxi.*
▶ **ex·trav·a·gance** /ɪkˈstrævəgəns/ *noun* [count, noncount]
the act or habit of spending too much money: *There are no limits to his extravagance.*

ex·treme 🔑 /ɪkˈstrim/ *adjective*
1 very great or strong: *the extreme cold of the Arctic*
2 If you say that a person is **extreme**, you mean that their ideas are too strong.
3 as far away as possible: *They came from the extreme north of Alaska.*

ex·treme·ly 🔑 /ɪkˈstrimli/ *adverb*
very: *He's extremely good-looking.*

ex·treme sports /ɪkˌstrim ˈspɔrts/ *noun* [plural]
(**SPORTS**) sports that are very exciting and often dangerous to do

ex·tro·vert /ˈɛkstrəvərt/ *noun* [count]
a person who is confident and prefers being with other people to being alone ⊃ **ANTONYM introvert**

eye 🔑 /aɪ/ *noun* [count]
one of the two parts in your head that you see with: *She has blue eyes.* ♦ *Open your eyes!*

catch someone's eye
1 to make someone look at you: *Try to catch the waiter's eye the next time he comes this way.*
2 If something **catches your eye**, you see it suddenly: *Her bright yellow hat caught my eye.*
in someone's eyes in the opinion of someone: *Richard is 42, but in his mother's eyes, he's still a little boy!*
keep an eye on someone or **something** to watch someone or something to make sure it is safe: *Will you keep an eye on my bag while I go to the restroom?*
see eye to eye with someone to agree with someone: *Mr. Harper doesn't always see eye to eye with his neighbors.*

eye

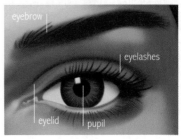
eyebrow · eyelashes · eyelid · pupil

eye·ball /ˈaɪbɔl/ *noun* [count]
(**BIOLOGY**) the whole eye, including the part that is inside the head

eye·brow /ˈaɪbraʊ/ *noun* [count]
one of the two lines of hair above your eyes

eye·glass·es /ˈaɪglæsəz/ *noun* [plural] = **glasses**

eye·lash /ˈaɪlæʃ/ *noun* [count] (*plural* **eye·lash·es**)
(also **lash** /læʃ/)
one of the hairs that grow in a line on your **EYELID**: *She has beautiful long eyelashes.*

eye·lid /ˈaɪlɪd/ *noun* [count]
the piece of skin that can move to close your eye

eye·shad·ow /ˈaɪˌʃædoʊ/ *noun* [noncount]
color that is put on the skin over the eyes to make them look more attractive

eye·sight /ˈaɪsaɪt/ *noun* [noncount]
the ability to see: *Your eyesight is very good.*

Ff

F, f /ɛf/ *noun* [count, noncount]
1 (*plural* **F's, f's** /ɛfs/) the sixth letter of the English alphabet: *"Father" begins with an "F."*
2 F (**GENERAL SCIENCE**) abbreviation of **Fahrenheit**: *Water freezes at 32°F.*
3 F the lowest grade that is given for a test or piece of work. An F means that the person has failed: *I got an F on my essay and had to write it again.*

fa·ble /ˈfeɪbl/ *noun* [count]
(**ENGLISH LANGUAGE ARTS**) a short story, usually about animals, that teaches people a lesson (called a **MORAL**)

fab·ric /ˈfæbrɪk/ *noun* [count, noncount]
cloth that is used for making things such as clothes: *cotton fabrics*

fab·u·lous /ˈfæbyələs/ *adjective*
very good: *The food smells fabulous!* ⊃ **SYNONYM wonderful**

face

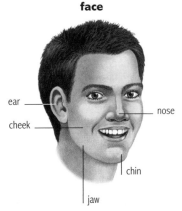

ear
cheek
nose
chin
jaw

face¹ /feɪs/ *noun* [count]
1 the front part of your head: *Have you washed your face?* ◆ *She had a smile on her face.* ⊃ Look at the note at **appearance**.
2 the front or one side of something: *a clock face* ◆ *He put the cards face down on the table.*
face to face If two people are **face to face**, they are looking straight at each other: *They stood face to face.*
keep a straight face to not smile or laugh when something is funny: *I couldn't keep a straight face when he dropped his watch in the soup!*
make a face to move your mouth and eyes to show that you do not like something: *She made a face when she saw what was for dinner.*

to someone's face If you say something **to someone's face**, you say it when that person is with you: *I wanted to say that I was sorry to her face, not on the phone.*

face² /feɪs/ *verb* (**fac·es, fac·ing, faced**)
1 to have your face or front toward something: *Can you all face the front of the class, please?* ◆ *My bedroom faces the backyard.*
2 to deal with an unfriendly person or a difficult situation: *I can't face going to work today – I'm too sick.*
let's face it (*informal*) we must agree that it is true: *Let's face it – you're not very good at math.*

face-lift (also **face·lift**) /ˈfeɪslɪft/ *noun* [count]
a medical operation to make your face look younger

fa·cial /ˈfeɪʃl/ *adjective*
connected with the face: *a facial expression* ◆ *facial hair*

fa·cil·i·tate **AWL** /fəˈsɪləteɪt/ *verb* (**fa·cil·i·tates, fa·cil·i·tat·ing, fa·cil·i·tat·ed**) (*formal*)
to make something possible or easier: *teaching techniques that facilitate learning*

fa·cil·i·ties **AWL** /fəˈsɪlətiz/ *noun* [plural]
services, rooms, equipment, etc. that make it possible to do something: *Our school has very good sports facilities.*

fact /fækt/ *noun* [count]
something that you know has happened or is true: *It's a fact that the earth travels around the sun.*
in fact; in actual fact used to show that something is true; really: *I thought she was 21 years old, but in actual fact she's only 19.* ◆ *I think I saw him – in fact, I'm sure I did.*

fac·tor **AWL** /ˈfæktər/ *noun* [count]
1 one of the things that influence a situation, a decision, etc.: *Cost was a major factor in deciding where I went to college.*
2 (**MATH**) a whole number by which a larger number can be divided: *2, 3, 4, and 6 are factors of 12.*

fac·to·ry /ˈfæktəri/ *noun* [count] (*plural* **fac·to·ries**)
a place where people make things, usually with machines: *He works at the automobile factory.*

fac·tu·al /ˈfæktʃuəl/ *adjective*
based on or containing facts: *a factual account of events*

fac·ul·ty /ˈfæklti/ *noun* [count, noncount] (*plural* **fac·ul·ties**)
the people who teach at a school, college, or university: *She is on the faculty at Columbia Business School.* ◆ *a faculty meeting*

fade /feɪd/ *verb* (fades, fad·ing, fad·ed)
to become lighter in color or less strong: *Will this shirt fade when I wash it?* • *The cheers of the crowd faded away.*

Fahr·en·heit /ˈfærənhaɪt/ *noun* [*noncount*] (abbreviation **F**)
(**GENERAL SCIENCE**) a way of measuring temperature. Water freezes at 32° **Fahrenheit** and boils at 212° **Fahrenheit**: *110°F* ⊃ Look at **Celsius**.

fail¹ /feɪl/ *verb* (fails, fail·ing, failed)
1 to not pass an exam or test: *She failed her driving test again.* • *How many students failed last year?* ⊃ ANTONYM **pass**
2 to try to do something but not be able to do it: *He played well but failed to win the match.* ⊃ ANTONYM **succeed**
3 to not do something that you should do: *The driver failed to stop at a red light.*

fail² /feɪl/ *noun*
without fail certainly: *Be there at twelve o'clock without fail!*

fail·ure /ˈfeɪlyər/ *noun*
1 [*noncount*] lack of success: *The search for the missing children ended in failure.*
2 [*count*] a person or thing that does not do well: *I felt that I was a failure because I didn't have a job.* ⊃ ANTONYM **success**

faint¹ /feɪnt/ *adjective* (faint·er, faint·est)
1 not clear or strong: *We could hear the faint sound of music in the distance.*
2 If you feel **faint**, you feel that you are going to fall, for example because you are sick or tired.

faint² /feɪnt/ *verb* (faints, faint·ing, faint·ed)
to suddenly become unconscious for a short time, for example because you are weak or sick: *She fainted as soon as she saw the blood.*

fair¹ /fɛr/ *adjective* (fair·er, fair·est)
1 treating people in an equal way or in the right way: *It's not fair! Why do I have to go to bed before my sister?* • *They didn't get a fair trial.* ⊃ ANTONYM **unfair**
2 good or big enough, but not very good or big: *They've invited a fair number of people to their party.* • *I would describe the service in this restaurant as fair.*
3 (used about a person's skin or hair) light in color: *He has fair hair.* ⊃ ANTONYM **dark**
4 (used about the weather) bright and not raining

fair² /fɛr/ *noun* [*count*]
1 a place outside where you can ride on big machines and play games to win prizes
2 (**BUSINESS**) a large event where people and businesses show and sell the things they make: *a book fair* • *a world trade fair*

fair·ly /ˈfɛrli/ *adverb*
1 more than a little, but not very: *She speaks French fairly well.* • *I'm fairly certain it was him.*
2 in a way that is right and honest: *This company treats its workers fairly.* ⊃ ANTONYM **unfairly**

fair·y /ˈfɛri/ *noun* [*count*] (*plural* fair·ies)
a very small person in stories. **Fairies** have wings and can do magic.

fair·y tale /ˈfɛri teɪl/ *noun* [*count*]
(**ENGLISH LANGUAGE ARTS**) a story for children that is about magic

faith /feɪθ/ *noun*
1 [*noncount*] feeling sure that someone or something is good, right, or honest: *I have great faith in your ability to do the job* (= I'm sure that you can do it).
2 [*count*] (**RELIGION**) a religion: *the Jewish faith*

faith·ful /ˈfeɪθfl/ *adjective*
always ready to support your friends; not changing: *a faithful friend*

fake /feɪk/ *noun* [*count*]
a copy of something that seems real but is not: *This painting is not really by Van Gogh – it's a fake.*
▶ **fake** *adjective*: *a fake passport*

fall¹ /fɔl/ *verb* (falls, fall·ing, fell /fɛl/, has fall·en /ˈfɔlən/)
1 to go down quickly toward the ground: *The book fell off the table.* • *She fell down the stairs and broke her arm.*
2 to suddenly stop standing: *He slipped on the ice and fell.* • *I fell over and hurt my leg.*
3 to become lower or less: *In the desert the temperature falls quickly at night.* • *Prices have fallen again.* ⊃ ANTONYM **rise**
fall apart to break into pieces: *The chair fell apart when I sat on it.*
fall asleep to start sleeping: *She fell asleep in the armchair.*
fall behind to become slower than others, or not do something when you should do it: *She's falling behind on her homework.*
fall for someone to begin to love someone: *He has fallen for someone he met on vacation.*
fall for something (*informal*) to believe something that someone tells you is true, although it is not true: *I can't believe you fell for that old excuse!*
fall in love with someone to begin to love someone: *He fell in love with Anna the first time they met.*
fall out with someone to argue with someone so that you stop being friends: *Jane has fallen out with her best friend.*
fall through If a plan **falls through**, it does not happen.

fall² /fɔl/ *noun*
1 [*count*] a sudden drop from a higher place to a lower place: *He had a bad fall from his horse.*
2 [*count*] becoming lower or less: *a fall in the price of oil* ⊃ **ANTONYM rise**
3 [*count, usually singular*] the part of the year between summer and winter: *In the fall, the leaves begin to fall from the trees.*
4 falls [*plural*] (**GEOGRAPHY**) a place where water falls from a high place to a low place: *Niagara Falls* ⊃ **SYNONYM waterfall**

fall·en form of **fall¹**

false /fɔls/ *adjective*
1 not true; wrong: *She gave a false name to the police.* ◆ *A spider has eight legs – **true or false?*** ⊃ **ANTONYM true** ⊃ Look at the note at **wrong¹**.
2 not real or not natural: *He has **false teeth** (=* teeth that are made of plastic).
a false alarm a warning about something bad that does not happen: *Everyone thought there was a fire, but it was a false alarm.*

fame /feɪm/ *noun* [*noncount*]
being known by many people: *The movie tells the story of her **rise to fame**.* ⊃ The adjective is **famous**.

fa·mil·iar /fəˈmɪlyər/ *adjective*
that you know well: *I heard a familiar voice in the next room.* ◆ *I'm not **familiar with** this computer.* ⊃ **ANTONYM unfamiliar**

fam·i·ly /ˈfæmli/ *noun* (*plural* **fam·i·lies**)
1 [*count, noncount*] a group of people who are connected to each other, especially parents and their children: *How many people are there in your family?* ◆ *Everyone in my family has red hair.* ◆ *His family lives on a farm.* ⊃ Look at **extended family**.
2 [*count*] (**BIOLOGY**) a group of plants or animals: *Lions belong to the cat family.*

fam·i·ly name /ˈfæmli ˌneɪm/ *noun* [*count*]
the name that is shared by members of a family ⊃ **SYNONYM last name** ⊃ Look at the note at **name¹**.

fam·i·ly tree /ˌfæmli ˈtri/ *noun* [*count*]
a plan that shows all the people in a family

fam·ine /ˈfæmən/ *noun* [*count, noncount*]
A **famine** happens when there is not enough food in a country: *How many people died in the famine?*

fa·mous /ˈfeɪməs/ *adjective*
known by many people: *New York is **famous for** its museums.* ◆ *She's a famous actress.* ⊃ The noun is **fame**.

fan¹ /fæn/ *noun* [*count*]
1 a person who likes someone or something, for example a singer or a sport, very much: *She is a big **fan of** modern art.* ◆ *football fans*
2 a thing that moves the air to make you cooler: *an electric fan*

fans

fan² /fæn/ *verb* (**fans, fan·ning, fanned**)
to make someone or something cooler by moving the air: *I fanned my face with the newspaper.*

fa·nat·ic /fəˈnæt̬ɪk/ *noun* [*count*]
a person who is very enthusiastic about something and may have extreme or dangerous opinions: *He's a baseball fanatic.* ◆ *a religious fanatic*

fan·cy /ˈfænsi/ *adjective* (**fan·ci·er, fan·ci·est**)
not simple or ordinary: *She wore a very fancy hat to the wedding.* ◆ *a fancy restaurant*

fang /fæŋ/ *noun* [*count*]
(**BIOLOGY**) a long, sharp tooth of a dog, a poisonous snake, etc.

fan·ny pack /ˈfæni pæk/ *noun* [*count*]
a small bag that you wear around the middle of your body to keep money, etc. in ⊃ Look at the picture at **bag**.

fan·tas·tic /fænˈtæstɪk/ *adjective* (*informal*)
very good; wonderful: *We had a fantastic vacation.* ⊃ **SYNONYM great**

fan·ta·sy /ˈfæntəsi/ *noun* [*count, noncount*] (*plural* **fan·ta·sies**)
something nice that you think about and that you hope will happen, although it is very unlikely: *It was just a fantasy.* ◆ *She was living in a fantasy world.* ⊃ **SYNONYM dream**

FAQ /ˌɛf eɪ ˈkyu/ *abbreviation*
(**COMPUTERS**) FAQ is used in writing to mean "frequently asked questions."

far¹ /fɑr/ *adverb* (**farther** /ˈfɑrðər/ or **further** /ˈfərðər/, **farthest** /ˈfɑrðəst/ or **furthest** /ˈfərðəst/)
1 a long way from somewhere: *My house isn't **far from** the station.* ◆ *It's much too far to drive in one day.* ⊃ Look at the note at **farther**.
2 You use **far** to ask about the distance from one place to another place: *How far is it to the coast from here?*

Grammar

■ We usually use **far** only in questions and negative sentences, and after **too** and **so**: *Is it far to walk?* ◆ *It's too far to walk.*
■ In other sentences we use **a long way**: *It's a long way to walk – let's take the bus.*

3 very much: *He's far taller than his brother.* ◆ *That's far too expensive.*

as far as... to a place: *We walked as far as the town and then came back.* ◆ *I read as far as the second chapter.*

as far as I know used when you think something is true, but you are not sure: *As far as I know, she's coming, but I may be wrong.*

by far You use **by far** to show that a person or thing is much better, bigger, etc. than anyone or anything else: *She's by far the best player on the team.*

far from something almost the opposite of something; not at all: *I'm far from certain.*

far from it (*informal*) certainly not; just the opposite: *"Are you upset?" "Far from it – I'm delighted."*

so far until now: *So far the work has been easy.*

far² /fɑr/ *adjective* (**far·ther** /ˈfɑrðər/ or **fur·ther** /ˈfərðər/, **far·thest** /ˈfɑrðəst/ or **fur·thest** /ˈfərðəst/)
1 a long way away: *Let's walk – it's not far.* ⊃ ANTONYM **near** ⊃ Look at the note at **far¹**, **farther**.
2 a long way from the center in the direction mentioned: *Who's that on the far left of the photo?*

fare /fɛr/ *noun* [*count*]
the money that you pay to travel by bus, train, airplane, etc.: *My bus fare went up.*

the Far East /ðə ˌfɑr ˈist/ *noun* [*singular*]
(GEOGRAPHY) China, Japan, and other countries in eastern Asia ⊃ Look at **the Middle East**.

fare·well /ˌfɛrˈwɛl/ *noun* [*count*] (*formal*)
goodbye: *We're having a farewell party for Megan.*

farm /fɑrm/ *noun* [*count*]
land and buildings where people keep animals and grow plants for food: *They work on a farm.* ◆ *farm animals*

farm·er /ˈfɑrmər/ *noun* [*count*]
a person who owns or works on a farm

farm·house /ˈfɑrmhaʊs/ *noun* [*count*]
the main house on a farm

farm·ing /ˈfɑrmɪŋ/ *noun* [*noncount*]
managing a farm or working on it: *farming methods*

farm·land /ˈfɑrmlænd/ *noun* [*noncount,plural*]
(GEOGRAPHY) land that is used for keeping animals or growing plants for food

farm·yard /ˈfɑrmyɑrd/ *noun* [*count*]
the area beside the main house on a farm, with buildings or walls around it

far·sight·ed /ˈfɑrˌsaɪt̬əd/ *adjective*
(HEALTH) If you are **farsighted**, you can see things clearly when they are far away but not

when they are close to you. ⊃ ANTONYM **nearsighted**

far·ther, far·thest /ˈfɑrðər; ˈfɑrðəst/ *adjective*, *adverb* forms of **far**

Which word?

Farther or further?

- In formal English, you should use **farther** to talk about distance in space: *I walked much farther than you did.*
- Use **further** to talk about distance in time: *I can't remember further back than 1990.*

---

fas·ci·nate /ˈfæsəneɪt/ *verb* (**fas·ci·nates, fas·ci·nat·ing, fas·ci·nat·ed**)
to attract or interest someone very much: *China has always fascinated me.* ◆ *I've always been fascinated by his ideas.*

fas·ci·nat·ing /ˈfæsəneɪt̬ɪŋ/ *adjective*
very interesting: *She told us fascinating stories about her life.*

fas·ci·na·tion /ˌfæsəˈneɪʃn/ *noun* [*count, noncount*]
when you find something or someone very interesting: *The girls listened in fascination.*

fash·ion /ˈfæʃn/ *noun* [*count, noncount*]
a way of dressing or doing something that people like and try to copy for a time: *Bright colors are back in fashion.* ◆ *Some styles never go out of fashion.* ◆ *a fashion show*

fash·ion·a·ble /ˈfæʃənəbl/ *adjective*
popular, or in a popular style at the time: *She was wearing a fashionable black hat.* ⊃ ANTONYM **old-fashioned, unfashionable**
▶ **fash·ion·a·bly** /ˈfæʃənəbli/ *adverb*: *He was always fashionably dressed.*

fash·ion de·sign·er /ˈfæʃn dɪˌzaɪnər/ *noun* [*count*]
a person whose job is to design clothes

fast¹ /fæst/ *adjective* (**fast·er, fast·est**)
1 moving, happening, or doing something very quickly: *the fastest rate of increase for many years* ◆ *a fast learner*

Which word?

Fast or quick?

- We say **fast** for a person or thing that moves at great speed: *a fast car* ◆ *a fast train* ◆ *a fast worker*
- We say **quick** for something that is done in a short time: *a quick answer* ◆ *a quick visit* ◆ *a quick meal*

---

2 If a clock or watch is **fast**, it shows a time that is later than the real time: *My watch is five minutes fast.* ⊃ ANTONYM **slow**

fast² 🔑 /fæst/ *adverb* (fast·er, fast·est)
1 quickly: *Don't drive so fast!* ◆ *I can't go any faster.* ⊃ ANTONYM **slowly**
2 completely or deeply: *The baby was fast asleep.* ◆ *The car was stuck fast in the mud.*

fast³ /fæst/ *verb* (fasts, fast·ing, fast·ed)
(**RELIGION**) to not eat food for a certain time: *Muslims fast during Ramadan.*

fas·ten 🔑 /'fæsn/ *verb* (fas·tens, fas·ten·ing, fas·tened)
1 to join or close something so that it will not come open: *Please fasten your seat belts.* ◆ *Can you fasten this suitcase for me?*
2 to attach or tie one thing to another thing: *Fasten this badge to your jacket.*

fas·ten·er /'fæsənər/ *noun* [count]
a thing that joins together two parts of something: *The fastener on my skirt just broke.*

fast food /,fæst 'fud/ *noun* [noncount]
hot food that is made and served very quickly in special restaurants, and often taken out

fat¹ 🔑 /fæt/ *adjective* (fat·ter, fat·test)
with a large round body: *You'll get fat if you eat too much.*

Thesaurus

fat is a general word to describe a person who has a large round body, but it is not polite to say to someone that they are fat: *Do I look fat in this dress?* ◆ *I'm getting fat!*
overweight is a little more polite, and is also a word used by doctors or health professionals: *She's a little overweight.* ◆ *He's only a few pounds overweight.*
heavy is often used when you want to be polite: *Donna's gotten a little heavier since the last time I saw her.*
obese means very fat, in a way that is not healthy. This word is often used by doctors and health professionals, but is also used in a general way to mean "very fat": *Obese patients are given advice on healthy eating.*

fat² 🔑 /fæt/ *noun*
1 [noncount] (**BIOLOGY**) the soft white substance under the skins of animals and people: *Cut the fat off the meat.*
2 [count, noncount] the substance containing oil that we get from animals, plants, or seeds and use for cooking: *foods that are low in fat* ◆ *Vegetable fats are healthier than animal fats.* ⊃ Look at **fatty**.

fa·tal /'feɪtl/ *adjective*
1 Something that is **fatal** causes death: *a fatal car accident*
2 Something that is **fatal** has very bad results: *I made the fatal mistake of signing a document without reading it carefully.*
▶ **fa·tal·ly** /'feɪtli/ *adverb*: *She was fatally injured in the crash.*

fate /feɪt/ *noun*
1 [noncount] the power that some people believe controls everything that happens: *It was fate that brought them together again after twenty years.*
2 [count] the things, especially bad things, that will happen or have happened to someone or something: *What will be the fate of the prisoners?*

fa·ther 🔑 /'fɑðər/ *noun* [count]
1 a man who has a child: *Where do your mother and father live?* ⊃ Look at **dad**, **daddy**.
2 **Father** (**RELIGION**) the title of certain priests: *Father O'Reilly*

fa·ther·hood /'fɑðərhʊd/ *noun* [noncount]
being a father

fa·ther-in-law /'fɑðər ɪn lɔ/ *noun* [count] (*plural* fa·thers-in-law)
the father of your husband or wife

fat·ty /'fæti/ *adjective* (fat·ti·er, fat·ti·est)
(used about food) having a lot of fat in it or on it: *Fatty foods are bad for you.*

fau·cet /'fɔsət/ *noun* [count]
a thing that you turn to make something like water or gas come out of a pipe: *Turn off the faucet – it's dripping.* ⊃ Look at the picture at **sink**.

fault 🔑 /fɔlt/ *noun*
1 [noncount] If something bad is your **fault**, you made it happen: *It's her fault that we're late.* ◆ *It's my fault for being careless.*
2 [count] something that is wrong or bad in a person or thing: *There is a serious fault in the machine.*
3 (**GEOGRAPHY**) a place where there is a long break (a **CRACK**) in the rock of the earth's surface: *the San Andreas fault in California*
be at fault to be wrong, or responsible for a mistake: *The other driver was at fault – he went through a red light.*

fault·less /'fɔltləs/ *adjective*
without any mistakes: *a faultless performance* ⊃ SYNONYM **perfect**

fault·y /'fɔlti/ *adjective*
not working well: *This light doesn't work – the switch is faulty.*

fa·vor 🔑 /'feɪvər/ *noun* [count]
something that you do to help someone: *Would you do me a favor and open the door?* ◆ *Can I ask you a favor – could you drive me to the airport this evening?*

be in favor of something to like or agree with something: *Are you in favor of higher taxes on cigarettes?*

fa·vor·a·ble /ˈfeɪvərəbl/ *adjective*
good or acceptable: *She made a favorable impression on his parents.*

fa·vor·ite¹ 🔑 /ˈfeɪvrət/ *adjective*
Your **favorite** person or thing is the one that you like more than any other: *What's your favorite food?*

fa·vor·ite² 🔑 /ˈfeɪvrət/ *noun* [count]
a person or thing that you like more than any other: *I like all chocolates but these are my favorites.*

fax /fæks/ *noun* [count, noncount] (plural **fax·es**)
a copy of a document that you send by telephone lines using a special machine (called a FAX MACHINE): *They need an answer today, so I'll send a fax.* ♦ *Can I send it by fax?*
▶ **fax** *verb* (**fax·es**, **fax·ing**, **faxed**)
to send someone a **fax**: *Can you fax the drawings to me?*

fear¹ 🔑 /fɪr/ *noun* [count, noncount]
the feeling that you have when you think that something bad might happen: *I have a terrible fear of dogs.* ♦ *He was shaking with fear.* ♦ *My fears for his safety were unnecessary.*

fear² 🔑 /fɪr/ *verb* (**fears**, **fear·ing**, **feared**)
1 to be afraid of someone or something: *We all fear illness and death.*
2 (formal) to feel that something bad might happen: *I fear we will be late.*

fear·ful /ˈfɪrfl/ *adjective* (formal)
afraid or worried about something: *They were fearful that they would miss their plane.*
▶ **fear·ful·ly** /ˈfɪrfəli/ *adverb*: *We watched fearfully.*

fear·less /ˈfɪrləs/ *adjective*
not afraid of anything
▶ **fear·less·ly** /ˈfɪrləsli/ *adverb*

feast /fist/ *noun* [count]
a large special meal for a lot of people: *a wedding feast*

feat /fit/ *noun* [count]
something you do that is difficult or dangerous: *Climbing Mount Everest was an amazing feat.*

feath·er 🔑 /ˈfɛðər/
noun [count]
one of the light, soft things that grow in a bird's skin and cover its body

feather

fea·ture¹ 🔑 **AWL** /ˈfitʃər/ *noun* [count]
1 an important part of something: *Pictures are a feature of this dictionary.*

2 one of the parts of your face, for example your eyes, nose, or mouth: *Her eyes are her best feature.*
3 a newspaper or magazine article, or TV program about something: *The magazine has a special feature on education.*

fea·ture² **AWL** /ˈfitʃər/ *verb* (**fea·tures**, **fea·tur·ing**, **fea·tured**)
to include someone or something as an important part: *Tonight's program features an interview with the actor Brad Pitt.*

Feb·ru·ary 🔑 /ˈfɛbyuˌɛri; ˈfɛbruˌɛri/ *noun* [count, noncount] (abbreviation **Feb.**)
the second month of the year

fed form of **feed**

fed·er·al **AWL** /ˈfɛdərəl/ *adjective*
(**POLITICS**) used for describing a political system in which a group of states or countries are joined together under a central government, but also have their own governments: *a federal system of rule* ♦ *the U.S. federal government*

fed·er·a·tion **AWL** /ˌfɛdəˈreɪʃn/ *noun* [count]
(**POLITICS**) a group of states or organizations that have joined together: *the American Federation of Teachers*

fed up /ˌfɛd ˈʌp/ *adjective* (informal)
bored or unhappy, especially with a situation that has continued for too long: *What's the matter? You look really fed up.* ♦ *I'm fed up with waiting – let's go.*

fee **AWL** /fi/ *noun* [count]
1 the money you pay for professional advice, or service from doctors, lawyers, schools, colleges, etc.: *We can't afford this lawyer's fees.* ♦ *Most ticket agencies will charge a small fee.* ⊃ Look at the note at **price**.
2 the money that you pay to do something, for example to join a club or visit a museum: *There is no entrance fee to the gallery.*

fee·ble /ˈfibl/ *adjective* (**fee·bler**, **fee·blest**)
not strong: *a feeble old man* ⊃ **SYNONYM weak**

feed 🔑 /fid/ *verb* (**feeds**, **feed·ing**, **fed** /fɛd/, **has fed**)
to give food to a person or an animal: *The baby's crying – I'll go and feed her.*

feed·back /ˈfidbæk/ *noun* [noncount]
advice or information about how well or badly you have done something: *The teacher will give you feedback on the test.*

feel¹ 🔑 /fil/ *verb* (**feels**, **feel·ing**, **felt** /fɛlt/, **has felt**)
1 to know something because your body tells you: *How do you feel?* ♦ *I don't feel well.* ♦ *I'm feeling tired.* ♦ *He felt someone touch his arm.*
2 used for saying how something seems when you touch it or experience it: *The water felt cold.*

• *This towel feels wet – can I have a dry one?* • *My coat feels like leather, but it's not.*
3 to touch something in order to find out what it is like: *Feel this wool – it's really soft.*
4 to have an opinion about something: *I feel that we should talk about this.* ⊃ SYNONYM **believe**
5 to try to find something with your hands instead of your eyes: *She felt in her pocket for some matches.*
feel like something to want something or want to do something: *I don't feel like going out tonight.*

feel² /fil/ *noun* [*singular*]
the impression you get when you touch something or when you are in a place: *I love the feel of silk.* • *The town has a friendly feel.*

feel·ing 🔑 /'filɪŋ/ *noun*
1 [*count*] something that you feel inside yourself, like happiness or anger: *a feeling of sadness*
2 [*noncount*] the ability to feel in your body: *I was so cold that I had no feeling in my feet.*
3 [*singular*] an idea that you are not certain about: *I have a feeling that she isn't telling the truth.*
hurt someone's feelings to do or say something that makes someone sad: *Don't tell him you don't like his shirt – you'll hurt his feelings.*

feet plural of **foot**

fe·line /'filaɪn/ *adjective*
connected with an animal of the cat family; like a cat

fell form of **fall¹**

fel·low¹ /'fɛloʊ/ *noun* [*count*] (*informal*)
a man: *He seems like a nice fellow.*

fel·low² /'fɛloʊ/ *adjective*
used for saying that someone is the same as you in some way: *your fellow students*

fel·o·ny /'fɛləni/ *noun* [*count*] (*plural* **fel·o·nies**)
a serious crime such as murder: *to be charged with a felony*

felt¹ form of **feel**

felt² /fɛlt/ *noun* [*noncount*]
a type of soft thick cloth

felt–tip pen /ˌfɛlt tɪp 'pɛn/ *noun* [*count*]
a pen with a soft point

fe·male 🔑 /'fimeɪl/ *adjective*
(BIOLOGY) belonging to the sex that can have babies: *female students*
▶ **fe·male** *noun* [*count*]: *My cat is a female.* ⊃ Look at **male**.

fem·i·nine /'fɛmənən/ *adjective*
1 typical of a woman or right for a woman: *feminine clothes*

2 (ENGLISH LANGUAGE ARTS) (in some languages) belonging to a certain class of nouns, adjectives, or pronouns: *The German word for a flower is feminine.* ⊃ Look at **masculine**.

fem·i·nism /'fɛmənɪzəm/ *noun* [*noncount*]
the belief that women should have the same rights and opportunities as men
▶ **fem·i·nist** /'fɛmənɪst/ *noun* [*count*], *adjective*

fence 🔑 /fɛns/ *noun* [*count*]
a thing like a wall that is made of pieces of wood or metal. **Fences** are put around yards and fields.

fenc·ing /'fɛnsɪŋ/ *noun* [*noncount*]
the sport of fighting with long, thin, pointed weapons (called SWORDS)

fern /fərn/ *noun* [*count*]
a plant with long thin leaves and no flowers, which grows in wet areas

fe·ro·cious /fə'roʊʃəs/ *adjective*
violent or cruel: *a ferocious wild animal* ⊃ SYNONYM **fierce**

fer·ry /'fɛri/ *noun* [*count*] (*plural* **fer·ries**)
a boat that takes people or things on short trips across a river or ocean: *We went by ferry.*

fer·tile /'fərtl̩/ *adjective*
1 If soil is **fertile**, plants grow well in it.
2 (BIOLOGY) Someone who is **fertile** is able to have babies.
▶ **fer·til·i·ty** /fər'tɪləti/ *noun* [*noncount*]: *Nowadays women can take drugs to increase their fertility* (= their chances of having a child).

fer·til·ize /'fərtl̩aɪz/ *verb* (**fer·til·iz·es, fer·til·iz·ing, fer·til·ized**)
1 (BIOLOGY) to put a male seed into an egg, a plant, or a female animal so that a baby, fruit, or young animal starts to develop
2 to put a substance on soil to make plants grow better

fer·til·iz·er /'fərtl̩aɪzər/ *noun* [*count, noncount*]
food for plants

fes·ti·val 🔑 /'fɛstəvl/ *noun* [*count*]
1 a series of public events, for example concerts and shows, in one place: *Do you like jazz festivals?*
2 (RELIGION) a time when people celebrate something, especially a religious event: *Christmas is an important Christian festival.*

fetch /fɛtʃ/ *verb* (**fetch·es, fetch·ing, fetched**)
to go and bring back something or someone: *She taught the dog to fetch the ball.*

fe·tus /'fitəs/ (*plural* **fe·tus·es**) *noun* [*count*]
(BIOLOGY) a young human or animal that is still growing inside its mother's body

feud /fyud/ *noun* [*count*]
a serious argument between people or groups that continues for a long time: *a family feud*

fe·ver /ˈfivər/ noun [count, noncount]
(**HEALTH**) If you have a **fever**, your body is too hot because you are sick: *to have a fever* ⟳ **SYNONYM temperature**
▶ **fe·ver·ish** /ˈfivərɪʃ/ adjective: *She felt feverish.*

few 🖊 /fyu/ adjective, pronoun (**few·er, few·est**)
not many: *Few people live to the age of 100.* ◆ *There are fewer buses in the evening.* ◆ *Few of the players played well.*
a few some, but not many: *Only a few people came to the meeting.* ◆ *I have read a few of her books.*
quite a few a lot, but not an extremely large amount or number of something: *It's been quite a few years since I saw him last.*

fi·an·cé /ˌfiɑnˈseɪ; fiˈɑnseɪ/ noun [count]
A woman's **fiancé** is the man she has promised to marry.

fi·an·cée /ˌfiɑnˈseɪ; fiˈɑnseɪ/ noun [count]
A man's **fiancée** is the woman he has promised to marry.

fi·as·co /fiˈæskoʊ/ noun [count] (plural **fi·as·cos** or **fi·as·coes**)
an event that does not succeed at all: *Our last party was a complete fiasco.*

fib /fɪb/ noun [count] (informal)
something you say that you know is not true; a small lie: *Don't tell fibs!*
▶ **fib** verb (**fibs, fib·bing, fibbed**) (informal)
to tell a small lie: *I was fibbing when I said I liked her hat.*

fi·ber /ˈfaɪbər/ noun
1 [noncount] (**BIOLOGY, HEALTH**) the part of your food that helps to move other food through your body and keep you healthy: *Dried fruits are high in fiber.*
2 [count] one of the many thin threads that form a material: *cotton fibers*

fic·tion /ˈfɪkʃn/ noun [noncount]
(**ENGLISH LANGUAGE ARTS**) stories that someone writes and that are not true: *I enjoy reading fiction.* ⟳ **ANTONYM nonfiction**

fid·dle /ˈfɪdl/ verb (**fid·dles, fid·dling, fid·dled**)
to touch something a lot with your fingers, because you are bored or nervous: *Stop fiddling with your pen and do some work!*

fidg·et /ˈfɪdʒət/ verb (**fidg·ets, fidg·et·ing, fidg·et·ed**)
to keep moving your body, hands, or feet because you are nervous, excited, or bored: *Sit still and stop fidgeting!*

field 🖊 /fild/ noun [count]
1 a piece of land used for animals or for growing plants for food, usually surrounded by a fence, trees, etc.
2 an area of study or knowledge: *Dr. Ramani is an expert in her field.*

3 a piece of land used for something special: *a soccer field* ◆ *an oil field* ◆ *an airfield* (= a place where airplanes land and take off)

Thesaurus

field an area of land used for playing team sports such as baseball, football, and soccer: *a baseball/football field* ◆ *The team ran out on the field.* ◆ *The school has its own playing field*.

court an area where certain ball games are played: *a basketball/tennis/squash court* ◆ *He won after only 52 minutes on the court.*

stadium a large place with seats around the sides where you can watch sports: *a football/sports stadium*

ballpark an area where baseball is played: *The batter hit one right out of the ballpark.*

track an area with a special surface for people or cars to have races on: *a running/racing track* ◆ *track and field events* (= which involve running, jumping, and throwing)

---

field hock·ey /ˈfild ˌhɑki/ noun [noncount]
(**SPORTS**) a game for two teams of eleven players who hit a small hard ball with long curved sticks on a field

field trip /ˈfild trɪp/ noun [count]
a trip that a school group takes in order to learn about something: *Our class went on a field trip to the art museum.*

fierce /fɪrs/ adjective (**fierc·er, fierc·est**)
1 angry and wild: *a fierce dog*
2 very strong: *the fierce heat of the sun*

fier·y /ˈfaɪəri/ adjective (**fier·i·er, fier·i·est**)
1 looking like fire: *fiery red hair*
2 quick to become angry: *a fiery temper*

fif·teen 🖊 /ˌfɪfˈtin/ number
15
▶ **fif·teenth** /ˌfɪfˈtinθ/ pronoun, adjective, adverb, noun [count]
15th: *her fifteenth birrthday*

fifth /fɪfθ/ pronoun, adjective, adverb, noun [count]
1 5th: *He came fifth in the race.*
2 one of five equal parts of something; ⅕

fif·ty 🖊 /ˈfɪfti/ number
1 50
2 **the fifties** [plural] the numbers, years, or temperature between 50 and 59: *He was born in the fifties* (= in the 1950s).
in your fifties between the ages of 50 and 59: *Her husband died when she was in her fifties.*
▶ **fif·ti·eth** /ˈfɪftiəθ/ pronoun, adjective, adverb, noun [count]
50th

fig /fɪg/ noun [count]
a soft, sweet fruit that is full of small seeds

---

fig. /fɪg/ abbreviation of **figure**[1](7): *See fig. 2.*

fight[1] /faɪt/ *verb* (fights, fight·ing, fought /fɔt/, has fought)
1 When people **fight**, they try to hurt or kill each other: *Our grandfather fought in the war.* • *My brothers are always fighting.*
2 to argue: *It's not worth fighting about money.*
3 to try very hard to stop something: *He fought against the illness for two years.*
4 to try very hard to do or get something: *The workers are fighting for better pay.*

fight[2] /faɪt/ *noun* [count]
1 when people try to hurt or kill each other: *Don't get into a fight.* • *A fight broke out between the two gangs.*
2 an angry argument about something: *I had a fight with my parents.*

fight·er /'faɪt̬ər/ *noun* [count]
1 a person who fights
2 (also **fight·er plane** /'faɪt̬ər pleɪn/) a fast airplane that shoots at other airplanes during a war

fig·u·ra·tive /'fɪgyərət̬ɪv/ *adjective*
(**ENGLISH LANGUAGE ARTS**) A **figurative** word or phrase is used in a different way from its usual meaning to create a particular effect: *"He exploded with rage" is a figurative use of the verb "to explode."* ⊃ Look at **literal**.
▶ **fig·u·ra·tive·ly** /'fɪgyərət̬ɪvli/ *adverb*: *I was using the expression figuratively.*

fig·ure[1] /'fɪgyər/ *noun* [count]
1 (**MATH**) one of the symbols (0–9) that we use to show numbers: *Should I write the numbers in words or figures?*
2 an amount or price: *What are our sales figures for this year?*
3 the shape of a person's body: *She has a good figure.*
4 a famous or important person: *He's an important historical figure.*
5 a shape of a person that you cannot see clearly: *I saw a tall figure outside the window.*
6 **figures** [plural] (**MATH**) working with numbers to find an answer: *I'm not very good at figures.* ⊃ **SYNONYM arithmetic**
7 (abbreviation **fig.**) a diagram or picture used in a book to explain something: *Figure 3 on page 2 shows the largest cities in the U.S.*

fig·ure[2] /'fɪgyər/ *verb* (fig·ures, fig·ur·ing, fig·ured) (*informal*)
to think or guess something: *I saw his car, so I figured he was here.*
it figures; that figures (*informal*) that is what I expected: *"John called in sick." "That figures. He wasn't feeling well yesterday."*

fig·ure of speech /ˌfɪgyər əv 'spitʃ/ *noun* [count] (*plural* **fig·ures of speech**)
(**ENGLISH LANGUAGE ARTS**) a word or phrase used in a different way from its usual meaning to create a particular effect: *I didn't really mean that he was insane – it was just a figure of speech.*

fig·ure skat·ing /'fɪgyər ˌskeɪt̬ɪŋ/ *noun* [noncount]
(**SPORTS**) a type of ICE SKATING in which you cut patterns in the ice using special moves ⊃ Look at **ice skate**.

file[1] **AWL** /faɪl/ *noun* [count]
1 a box or cover for keeping papers in
2 (**COMPUTERS**) a collection of information that is stored in a computer and that has a particular name: *Did you save your file?* • *You can delete that file now.*
3 a collection of papers or information about someone or something, which is kept inside a file: *The police are keeping a file on all suspected terrorists.*
4 a tool with rough sides that you use for making things smooth: *a nail file*
in single file in a line with each person following the one in front: *The children walked into the auditorium in single file.*

file[2] **AWL** /faɪl/ *verb* (files, fil·ing, filed)
1 to put papers in their correct place, for example in a cover or drawer: *Can you file these documents, please?*
2 to walk in a line, one behind the other: *The students filed into the classroom.*
3 to make something smooth using a tool with rough sides: *She filed her nails.*

file cab·i·net /'faɪl ˌkæbənət/ *noun* [count]
a piece of office furniture with large drawers, in which you keep documents

fill /fɪl/ *verb* (fills, fill·ing, filled)
1 to make something full: *Can you fill this glass with water, please?*
2 to become full: *His eyes filled with tears.*
fill something in to write facts or answers in the spaces that have been left for them: *Please fill in your name and address here.*
fill something out to complete an official document by writing facts or answers on it: *She filled out the application form for the job.*
fill up; fill something up to become full or to make something completely full: *The room soon filled up.* • *He filled up the tank with gas.*

fil·let (also **fi·let**) /fɪ'leɪ/ *noun* [count, noncount]
a piece of meat or fish with the bones taken out: *a fillet of sole*

fill·ing[1] /'fɪlɪŋ/ *noun*
1 [count] the substance that a dentist uses to fill a hole in your tooth: *I have three fillings in my teeth.*

2 [count, noncount] the food that is put inside a cake, between two pieces of bread (to make a SANDWICH), etc.: *a choice of sandwich fillings*

fill·ing² /ˈfɪlɪŋ/ *adjective*
(used about food) that makes you feel full: *Pasta is very filling.*

film¹ /fɪlm/ *noun*
1 [count, noncount] the thin plastic that you use in a camera for taking photographs: *I bought a roll of black and white film.*
2 [count] a movie: *It's a French film.*

film² /fɪlm/ *verb* (films, film·ing, filmed)
to use a camera to make a movie or video: *We filmed the monkeys at the zoo.* ✦ *A TV station is filming outside my house.*

fil·ter¹ /ˈfɪltər/ *noun* [count]
(GENERAL SCIENCE) a thing used for holding back the solid parts in a liquid or gas: *a coffee filter*

fil·ter² /ˈfɪltər/ *verb* (fil·ters, fil·ter·ing, fil·tered)
1 (GENERAL SCIENCE) to pass a liquid or gas through a FILTER: *You need to filter the water before you drink it.*
2 to move slowly or in small amounts: *Sunlight filtered through the curtains.* ✦ *People were filtering out of the theater after the show.*

filth·y /ˈfɪlθi/ *adjective* (filth·i·er, filth·i·est)
very dirty: *Go and wash your hands. They're filthy!*

fin /fɪn/ *noun* [count]
(BIOLOGY) one of the thin, flat parts on a fish that help it to swim ⊃ Look at the picture at **shark**.

fi·nal¹ AWL /ˈfaɪnl/ *adjective*
1 not followed by any others: *This will be our final class.* ⊃ SYNONYM **last**
2 not to be changed: *The judge's decision is final.*

fi·nal² AWL /ˈfaɪnl/ *noun* [count]
1 the last game or race in a competition, for the winners of the earlier games or races: *Her team made it to the finals.*
2 an important exam that you take at the end of a course in school: *I'm studying hard for my finals.* ✦ *She failed her chemistry final.*

fi·nal·ist /ˈfaɪnlɪst/ *noun* [count]
a person who is in the final game or stage of a competition: *an Olympic finalist*

fi·nal·ly AWL /ˈfaɪnl·i/ *adverb*
1 after a long time: *After a long wait the bus finally arrived.* ⊃ SYNONYM **in the end**
2 used before saying the last thing in a list: *And finally, I would like to thank my parents for all their help.*

fi·nance¹ AWL /ˈfaɪnæns; fəˈnæns/ *noun*
(BUSINESS)
1 [noncount] money, or the activity of managing money: *an expert in finance* ✦ *the Senate Finance Committee*

2 finances [plural] the money that you have and that you can spend: *You need to organize your finances.*

fi·nance² AWL /ˈfaɪnæns; fəˈnæns/ *verb*
(fi·nanc·es, fi·nanc·ing, fi·nanced)
(BUSINESS) to give the money that is needed to pay for something: *The building was financed by the government.*

fi·nan·cial AWL /fəˈnænʃl/ *adjective*
connected with money: *financial problems*
▸ **fi·nan·cial·ly** AWL /fəˈnænʃəli/ *adverb*:
financially independent

find /faɪnd/ *verb* (finds, find·ing, found /faʊnd/, has found)
1 to see or get something after looking or trying: *I can't find my glasses.* ✦ *She hasn't found a job yet.* ✦ *Did anyone find the answer to this question?*
2 to see or get something that you did not expect: *I found some money in the street.* ✦ *I woke up and found myself in the hospital.*
3 used for talking about your opinion or experience: *I didn't find that book very interesting.* ✦ *He finds it difficult to sleep at night.*
find something out to get information about something: *Can you find out what time the train leaves?* ✦ *Did she ever find out that you broke the window?*

fine¹ /faɪn/ *adjective* (fin·er, fin·est)
1 well or happy: *"How are you?" "Fine, thanks. And you?"*
2 used for saying that something is good or acceptable: *"Let's meet on Monday." "Fine."* ✦ *"Do you want some more milk in your coffee?" "No, that's fine."* ⊃ SYNONYM **OK**
3 very thin: *I have very fine hair.* ⊃ ANTONYM **thick**
4 made of very small pieces: *Salt is finer than sugar.* ⊃ ANTONYM **coarse**
5 beautiful or of good quality: *There's a fine view from the church.* ✦ *This is one of his finest paintings.*
6 (used about the weather) bright; not raining: *We had fine weather for our picnic.* ⊃ SYNONYM **sunny**

fine² /faɪn/ *noun* [count]
money that you must pay because you have done something wrong: *You'll get a fine if you park your car there.*
▸ **fine** *verb* (fines, fin·ing, fined)
to make someone pay a fine: *I was fined $50 for speeding* (= driving too fast).

fin·ger /ˈfɪŋɡər/ *noun* [count]
one of the five parts at the end of your hand ⊃ Look at the picture at **hand**.
keep your fingers crossed to hope that someone or something will be successful: *Good luck on the final exam – I'll keep my fingers crossed for you.*

fin·ger·nail /ˈfɪŋgərneɪl/ *noun* [count]
the thin, hard part at the end of your finger

fin·ger·print /ˈfɪŋgərprɪnt/ *noun* [count]
the mark that a finger makes when it touches something: *The police found his fingerprints on the gun.*

fin·ger·tip /ˈfɪŋgərtɪp/ *noun* [count]
the end of your finger

fin·ish¹ 🔑 /ˈfɪnɪʃ/ *verb* (fin·ish·es, fin·ish·ing, fin·ished)
1 to stop doing something: *I finish work at 5:30.* ◆ *Hurry up and finish your dinner!* ◆ *Have you finished cleaning your room?*
2 to stop happening: *School finishes at three o'clock.* ⊃ ANTONYM **begin**, **start**
finish something off to do or eat the last part of something: *He finished off the bread.*

fin·ish² /ˈfɪnɪʃ/ *noun* [count] (*plural* **fin·ish·es**)
the last part or the end of something: *There was a dramatic finish to the race.* ⊃ ANTONYM **start**

fin·ished /ˈfɪnɪʃt/ *adjective*
1 having reached the end of an activity or job: *When you're finished with your homework, you can watch TV.*
2 made; completed: *Is this the finished product?* ⊃ ANTONYM **unfinished**

fi·nite AWL /ˈfaɪnaɪt/ *adjective*
having a limit or a fixed size: *Our world's natural resources are finite.* ⊃ ANTONYM **infinite**

fir /fər/ (also **fir tree** /ˈfər tri/) *noun* [count]
a tall tree with thin, sharp leaves (called NEEDLES), which do not fall off in winter

fire¹ 🔑 /ˈfaɪər/ *noun*
1 [count, noncount] the heat and bright light that comes from burning things: *Many animals are afraid of fire.* ◆ *There was a big fire at the factory last night.*
2 [count] burning wood or another fuel (called COAL) that you use for keeping a place warm or for cooking: *They lit a fire to keep warm.*
3 [noncount] shooting from guns: *The soldiers were under fire.*
catch fire to start to burn: *She dropped her cigarette and the chair caught fire.*
on fire burning: *My house is on fire!*
put out a fire to stop something from burning: *We put out the fire with buckets of water.*
set fire to something; **set something on fire** to make something start to burn: *Someone set the house on fire.*

fire² 🔑 /ˈfaɪər/ *verb* (fires, fir·ing, fired)
1 to shoot with a gun: *The soldiers fired at the enemy.*
2 to tell someone to leave their job: *He was fired because he was always late for work.*

fire a·larm /ˈfaɪər əˌlɑrm/ *noun* [count]
a bell that rings to tell people that there is a fire

fire·crack·er /ˈfaɪərˌkrækər/ *noun* [count]
a small thing that explodes with a loud noise: *We lit firecrackers in the backyard on the Fourth of July.* ⊃ Look at **fireworks**.

fire de·part·ment /ˈfaɪər dɪˌpɑrtmənt/ *noun* [count]
a group of people whose job is to stop fires: *Call the fire department!*

fire drill /ˈfaɪər drɪl/ *noun* [count]
a practice of what people must do if there is a fire in a building

fire en·gine /ˈfaɪər ˌɛndʒən/ (also **fire truck** /ˈfaɪər ˌtrʌk/) *noun* [count]
a vehicle that carries people and equipment to stop fires

fire es·cape /ˈfaɪər ɪˌskeɪp/ *noun* [count]
stairs on the outside of a building that people can go down if there is a fire

fire ex·tin·guish·er /ˈfaɪər ɪkˌstɪŋgwɪʃər/ *noun* [count]
a metal container with water or chemicals inside for stopping small fires

fire·fight·er /ˈfaɪərˌfaɪt̬ər/ *noun* [count]
a person whose job is to stop fires

fire·house /ˈfaɪərhaʊs/ *noun* [count]
a building in a small town where fire engines are kept ⊃ SYNONYM **fire station**

fire hy·drant /ˈfaɪər ˌhaɪdrənt/ *noun* [count]
a piece of metal equipment on the street that is connected to a water pipe for stopping fires

fire hydrant

fire·man /ˈfaɪərmən/ *noun* [count] (*plural* **fire·men** /ˈfaɪərmən/)
a man whose job is to stop fires

fire·place /ˈfaɪərpleɪs/ *noun* [count]
the place in a room where you light a fire

fire·proof /ˈfaɪərpruf/ *adjective*
able to take a lot of heat without burning or being damaged: *a fireproof door*

fire sta·tion /ˈfaɪər ˌsteɪʃn/ *noun* [count]
a building where fire engines are kept

fire truck another word for **fire engine**

fire·works /ˈfaɪərwərks/ *noun* [plural]
things that explode with bright lights and loud noises, used for entertainment: *We watched a fireworks display in the park.*

firm[1] 🔊 /fərm/ *adjective* (**firm·er, firm·est**)
1 Something that is **firm** does not move easily when you press it: *Wait until the glue is firm.* ◆ *The shelf isn't very firm, so don't put too many books on it.*
2 strong and steady, and not likely to change: *She's very firm with her children* (= she makes them do what she wants). ◆ *a firm promise*
▶ **firm·ly** /'fərmli/ *adverb*: *Nail the pieces of wood together firmly.* ◆ *"No," she said firmly.*

firm[2] 🔊 /fərm/ *noun* [*count*]
(**BUSINESS**) a group of people working together in a business: *a law firm* (= that lawyers work for) ⊃ **SYNONYM company**

first[1] 🔊 /fərst/ *adjective*
before all the others: *January is the first month of the year.* ◆ *You won first prize!*
first thing early in the morning: *I'll call her first thing tomorrow morning.*

first[2] 🔊 /fərst/ *adverb*
1 before all the others: *I arrived at the house first.* ◆ *Mike finished first* (= he won) *in the competition.*
2 for the first time: *I first met Paul in 2006.*
3 before doing anything else: *First fry the onions, then add the potatoes.*
at first in the beginning: *At first she was afraid of the water, but she soon learned to swim.*
first of all before anything else: *I'm going to cook dinner, but first of all I need to buy some food.*

first[3] 🔊 /fərst/ *noun, pronoun*
1 the first [*count*] (*plural* **the first**) a person or thing that comes earliest or before all others: *I was the first to arrive at the party.*
2 a first [*singular*] an important event that is happening for the first time: *This operation is a first in medical history.*

first aid /ˌfərst 'eɪd/ *noun* [*noncount*]
(**HEALTH**) medical help that you give to someone who is hurt, before a doctor comes: *a first-aid kit*

first class /ˌfərst 'klæs/ *noun* [*noncount*]
1 the part of a train, airplane, etc. that is more expensive to travel in: *I got a seat in first class.*
2 a way of sending mail that you use if you want it to get special treatment
▶ **first class** *adverb*: *How much does it cost to fly first class?*

first-class /ˌfərst ˌklæs/ *adjective*
1 excellent: *a first-class player* ◆ *I know a place where the food is first-class.*
2 connected with the best and most expensive way of traveling on a train, airplane, or ship: *a first-class cabin*

first floor /ˌfərst 'flɔr/ (also **ground floor** /ˌgraʊnd 'flɔr/) *noun* [*count*]
the floor of a building that is level with the street: *I live in an apartment on the first floor.*

first la·dy /ˌfərst 'leɪdi/ *noun* [*usually singular*]
(**POLITICS**) the wife of the U.S. president, or of the leader of a state

first·ly /'fərstli/ *adverb*
used when you are giving the first thing in a list: *We were angry, firstly because he didn't come, and secondly because he didn't call.*

first name /ˌfərst 'neɪm/ (also **giv·en name**) *noun* [*count*]
the first of your names, which your parents give you when you are born: *"What is Mr. Carter's first name?" "Paul."* ⊃ Look at the note at **name**[1].

the first per·son /ðə ˌfərst 'pərsn/ *noun* [*singular*] (**ENGLISH LANGUAGE ARTS**)
1 the set of pronouns and verb forms that you use to talk about yourself: *"I am" is the first person singular of the verb "to be."* ◆ *"I," "me," and "we" are first-person pronouns.*
2 the style of telling a story as if it happened to you: *The author writes in the first person.*

first-rate /ˌfərst 'reɪt/ *adjective*
excellent: *a first-rate musician*

fish

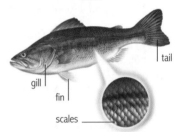

tail
gill
fin
scales

fish[1] 🔊 /fɪʃ/ *noun* [*count, noncount*] (*plural* **fish** or **fish·es**)
an animal that lives and breathes in water, and has thin flat parts (called **FINS**) that help it to swim: *I caught a big fish.* ◆ *We had fish for dinner.*

fish[2] /fɪʃ/ *verb* (**fish·es, fish·ing, fished**)
to try to catch fish
▶ **fish·ing** /'fɪʃɪŋ/ *noun* [*noncount*]: *I usually go fishing* (= as a sport) *on weekends.* ◆ *Fishing is a major industry in Maine.*

fish·er·man /'fɪʃərmən/ *noun* [*count*] (*plural* **fish·er·men** /'fɪʃərmən/)
a person who catches fish as a job or sport

fish·ing rod /'fɪʃɪŋ rɑd/ *noun* [*count*]
a long thin stick with a thin thread (called a **LINE**) and a hook, used for catching fish

fish stick /'fɪʃ stɪk/ *noun* [*count*]
a long piece of fish that is covered in very small pieces of dried bread: *a box of frozen fish sticks*

---

fish·y /ˈfɪʃi/ *adjective* (fish·i·er, fish·i·est)
1 tasting or smelling like fish: *a fishy smell*
2 (*informal*) seeming bad or dishonest: *I'm sure there's something fishy going on around here.*

fist /fɪst/ *noun* [count]
a hand with the fingers closed together tight: *She banged on the door with her fist.*

fit¹ 🔑 /fɪt/ *verb* (fits, fit·ting, fit·ted or fit)
1 to be the right size or shape for someone or something: *I tried the dress on, but it didn't fit.* ◆ *This key doesn't fit the lock.*
2 to put or attach something somewhere: *They fit a smoke alarm to the ceiling.* ◆ *Can you fit these pieces of the puzzle together?*
fit in (with someone or something) to be able to live in an easy and natural way with other people: *She found it hard to fit in at her new school.*
fit someone or **something in**
1 to find time to do something or see someone: *The doctor can fit you in at 10:30.*
2 to find or have enough space for someone or something: *We can't fit in any more chairs.*

fit² 🔑 /fɪt/ *adjective* (fit·ter, fit·test)
1 (HEALTH) healthy and strong: *I keep fit by jogging every day.*
2 good enough: *This food isn't fit to eat.* ◆ *Do you think she's fit for the job?* ⊃ SYNONYM **suitable** ⊃ ANTONYM **unfit**

fit³ /fɪt/ *noun*
1 [count] when you cannot stop laughing, coughing, or feeling angry: *fits of laughter* ◆ *a coughing fit.* ◆ *a fit of anger*
2 [singular] the way something fits you: *This coat is a really good fit.*

fit·ness /ˈfɪtnəs/ *noun* [noncount]
(HEALTH) being healthy and strong: *It's important to improve your fitness.*

five 🔑 /faɪv/ *number*
5

fix 🔑 /fɪks/ *verb* (fix·es, fix·ing, fixed)
1 to repair something: *The light isn't working – can you fix it?*
2 to decide a date or an amount for something: *They fixed a date for the wedding.* ⊃ SYNONYM **set**
3 to put something in a place so that it will not move: *We fixed the shelf to the wall.* ⊃ SYNONYM **attach**

fixed 🔑 /fɪkst/ *adjective*
1 already decided: *a fixed price*
2 not changing: *He has such fixed ideas that you can't discuss anything with him.*

fizz /fɪz/ *verb* (fizz·es, fizz·ing, fizzed)
When a liquid **fizzes**, it produces a lot of small bubbles and makes a long sound like an "s."
▶ **fizz** *noun* [noncount]: *This soda has lost its fizz.*

fizz·y /ˈfɪzi/ *adjective* (fiz·zi·er, fiz·zi·est)
(used about a drink) containing many small bubbles of gas: *fizzy mineral water*

flab·by /ˈflæbi/ *adjective* (flab·bi·er, flab·bi·est)
having too much soft fat instead of muscle: *a flabby stomach*

flag 🔑 /flæg/ *noun* [count]
a piece of cloth with a pattern on it, which is joined to a stick (called a FLAGPOLE). Every country has its own **flag**: *All the kids were waving flags.*

flair /flɛr/ *noun* [singular]
a natural ability to do something well: *She has a flair for languages.* ⊃ SYNONYM **talent**

flake /fleɪk/ *noun* [count]
a small thin piece of something: *huge flakes of snow*

flame 🔑 /fleɪm/ *noun* [count, noncount]
a hot, bright, pointed piece of fire: *The house was in flames* (= burning). ◆ *The paper burst into flames* (= began to burn).

fla·min·go /fləˈmɪŋgoʊ/ *noun* [count] (plural fla·min·gos or fla·min·goes)
a large pink and red bird that has long legs and stands in water

flam·ma·ble /ˈflæməbl/ *adjective*
(CHEMISTRY) A **flammable** substance burns easily: *highly flammable liquids* ⊃ SYNONYM **inflammable**

flan·nel /ˈflænl/ *noun* [noncount]
a type of soft wool or cotton cloth: *a flannel shirt*

flap¹ /flæp/ *noun* [count]
a piece of material, paper, etc. that is attached to something at one side only, often covering an opening: *the flap of an envelope*

flap² /flæp/ *verb* (flaps, flap·ping, flapped)
to move or to make something move up and down or from side to side: *The sails of the boat flapped in the wind.* ◆ *The bird flapped its wings.*

flare¹ /flɛr/ *verb* (flares, flar·ing, flared)
flare up
1 to suddenly burn more strongly
2 to suddenly start or get worse: *The pain flared up again.*

flare² /flɛr/ *noun* [count]
a thing that produces a bright light or flame, used especially as a signal

flash¹ 🔑 /flæʃ/ *verb* (flash·es, flash·ing, flashed)
1 to send out a bright light that comes and goes quickly; to make something do this: *The light kept flashing on and off.* ◆ *She flashed her headlights at the other driver.*
2 to appear and disappear very quickly, or to make something do this: *I saw something flash past the window.* ◆ *They flashed the answer up on the TV screen.*

| tʃ **ch**in | dʒ **J**une | v **v**an | θ **th**in | ð **th**en | s **s**o | z **z**oo | ʃ **sh**e |

flash² /flæʃ/ *noun* (*plural* **flash·es**)
1 [count] a bright light that comes and goes quickly: *a flash of lightning*
2 [count, noncount] a bright light that you use with a camera for taking photographs
in a flash very quickly: *The weekend was over in a flash.*

flash card /'flæʃ ˌkɑrd/ *noun* [count]
a card with words, numbers, or a picture on it, which you use to help you learn or remember something

flash drive /'flæʃ ˌdraɪv/ (also **USB flash drive**) *noun* [count]
(**COMPUTERS**) a small thing that stores information from a computer so that you can move it from one computer to another ➔ Look at the picture at **USB flash drive**.

flash·light /'flæʃlaɪt/ *noun* [count]
a small electric light that you can carry: *He shined the flashlight into the boys' faces.*

flashlight

flask /flæsk/ *noun* [count]
a container for keeping a liquid hot or cold: *a flask of coffee*

flat¹ 🖉 /flæt/ *adjective* (**flat·ter**, **flat·test**)
1 smooth, with no parts that are higher or lower than the rest: *The landscape in Kansas is very flat.* ◆ *a flat surface*
2 A tire that is **flat** does not have enough air inside it.
3 (symbol ♭) (**MUSIC**) half a note lower than a particular musical note: *B flat* ◆ *E flat* ➔ Look at **sharp¹**(6).

flat² /flæt/ *adverb*
with no parts that are higher or lower than the rest: *He lay flat on his back on the floor.*

flat·ten /'flætn/ *verb* (**flat·tens**, **flat·ten·ing**, **flat·tened**)
to make something flat: *I sat on the box and flattened it.*

flat·ter /'flæt̬ər/ *verb* (**flat·ters**, **flat·ter·ing**, **flat·tered**)
1 to say nice things about someone, because you want them to do something
2 If you are **flattered** by something, you like it because it makes you feel important: *I'm flattered that she wants my advice.*
▶ **flat·ter·ing** /'flæt̬ərɪŋ/ *adjective*: *flattering remarks*

flat·ter·y /'flæt̬əri/ *noun* [noncount]
nice things that someone says when they want you to do something

fla·vor 🖉 /'fleɪvər/ *noun* [count, noncount]
the taste of food: *They sell 20 different flavors of ice cream.*

▶ **fla·vor** *verb* (**fla·vors**, **fla·vor·ing**, **fla·vored**): *chocolate-flavored coffee*

fla·vor·ful /'fleɪvərfl/ *adjective*
having a lot of flavor: *a flavorful sauce*

fla·vor·ing /'fleɪvərɪŋ/ *noun* [count, noncount]
something that you add to food or a drink to give it a particular taste: *This product conatins no artificial flavorings.*

flaw /flɔ/ *noun* [count]
1 a mistake in something that means it is not correct or does not work correctly: *a flaw in his plan*
2 a mark or bad part in something that means it is not perfect: *There's a small flaw in the vase, so I got it cheaper.*
▶ **flawed** /flɔd/ *adjective*: *I think your plan is flawed.*

flea /fli/ *noun* [count]
a very small insect without wings, which can jump. It lives on and bites animals and people: *Our cat has fleas.* ➔ Look at the picture at **insect**.

flea mar·ket /'fli ˌmɑrkət/ *noun* [count]
a market, usually outside, where you can buy old and used objects

flee /fli/ *verb* (**flees**, **flee·ing**, **fled** /flɛd/, **has fled**)
to run away from something bad or dangerous: *During the war, thousands of people fled the country.*

fleece /flis/ *noun*
1 [count] the wool coat of a sheep
2 [noncount] a type of soft, warm cloth used for making jackets and other clothes

fleet /flit/ *noun* [count]
a big group of ships

flesh /flɛʃ/ *noun* [noncount]
1 the soft part of a human or animal body under your skin
2 the soft part of a fruit or vegetable that we eat: *the sweet flesh of a peach*
in the flesh If you see someone **in the flesh**, you are in the same place as them and actually see them rather than just seeing a picture of them.

flew form of **fly¹**

flex·i·ble 🆈 /'flɛksəbl/ *adjective*
1 able to change easily: *We can start earlier if you like – I can be flexible.* ◆ *flexible working hours*
2 able to bend easily without breaking ➔ **ANTONYM inflexible**
▶ **flex·i·bil·i·ty** 🆈 /ˌflɛksə'bɪləti/ *noun* [noncount]

flick /flɪk/ *verb* (**flicks**, **flick·ing**, **flicked**)
to move or make something move with a quick, light movement: *She flicked the dust off her coat.*
▶ **flick** *noun* [count]

---

flies
1 form of **fly**¹
2 plural of **fly**²

flight /flaɪt/ *noun*
1 [*count*] a trip in an airplane: *Our flight leaves at 10a.m.* ◆ *a direct flight from New York to Chicago.*
2 [*noncount*] flying: *Have you ever seen an eagle in flight?*
3 [*count*] a group of steps: *We carried the couch up a flight of stairs.*

flight at·tend·ant /'flaɪt ə,tɛndənt/ *noun* [*count*]
a person whose job is to serve and take care of passengers on an airplane

flim·sy /'flɪmzi/ *adjective* (**flim·si·er, flim·si·est**)
1 not strong; easy to break or tear: *a flimsy bookcase*
2 weak; not making you believe that it is true: *He gave a flimsy excuse for being late.*

fling /flɪŋ/ *verb* (**flings, fling·ing, flung** /flʌŋ/, **has flung**)
to throw something carelessly or with great force: *She flung her coat on the chair.*

flip-flop /'flɪp flɑp/ *noun* [*count*]
a simple open shoe with a narrow piece of material that goes between your big toe and the toe next to it

flip·pant /'flɪpənt/ *adjective*
not serious about important things: *a flippant answer*

flip·per /'flɪpər/ *noun* [*count*]
1 a flat part of the body of some animals, which they use for swimming in the ocean: *Seals and turtles have flippers*
2 a flat, rubber shoe that you wear to help you swim fast underwater ⊃ Look at the picture at **snorkel**.

flirt /flərt/ *verb* (**flirts, flirt·ing, flirt·ed**)
to behave as if you like someone in a romantic way: *Jan was flirting with him at the party.*
▶ **flirt** *noun* [*count*]
a person who **flirts** a lot with different people

float /floʊt/ *verb* (**floats, float·ing, float·ed**)
1 to stay on top of a liquid: *Wood floats on water.*
⊃ **ANTONYM sink**
2 to move slowly in the air: *Clouds were floating across the sky.*

flock /flɑk/ *noun* [*count*]
a group of sheep or birds: *a flock of geese* ⊃ Look at **herd**¹.

flood¹ /flʌd/ *noun* [*count*]
1 When there is a **flood**, a lot of water covers the land: *Many homes were destroyed in the flood.*
2 a lot of something: *She received a flood of letters after the accident.*

flood² /flʌd/ *verb* (**floods, flood·ing, flood·ed**)
to fill a place with water; to be filled or covered with water: *A pipe burst and flooded the kitchen.*

flood·light /'flʌdlaɪt/ *noun* [*count*]
a powerful light that is used outside, for example near a building or for sports

floor /flɔr/ *noun* [*count*]
1 [*usually singular*] the part of a room that you walk on: *There weren't any chairs so we sat on the floor.*
2 all the rooms at the same height in a building: *I live on the top floor.* ◆ *Our hotel room was on the sixth floor.* ⊃ Look at **first floor, ground floor**.

floor·board /'flɔrbɔrd/ *noun* [*count*]
a long flat piece of wood in a wooden floor

flop·py /'flɑpi/ *adjective* (**flop·pi·er, flop·pi·est**)
soft, loose, and hanging downward: *a floppy hat* ◆ *a dog with floppy ears*

flop·py disk /'flɑpi dɪsk/ *noun* [*count*] (also **flop·py** *plural* **flop·pies**)
(**COMPUTERS**) a small flat piece of plastic that stores information for a computer

flo·ral /'flɔrəl/ *adjective*
decorated with a pattern of flowers, or made with flowers: *a floral design*

flo·rist /'flɔrɪst/ *noun* [*count*]
a person who owns or works in a store that sells flowers

floss /flɑs/ *verb* (**floss·es, floss·ing, flossed**)
to use a special kind of string (called **DENTAL FLOSS**) to clean between your teeth: *You should floss daily.*

flour /'flaʊər/ *noun* [*noncount*]

ⓘ PRONUNCIATION
The word **flour** sounds just like **flower**.

soft, white or brown powder that we use to make bread, cakes, etc.

flour·ish /'flərɪʃ/ *verb* (**flour·ish·es, flour·ish·ing, flour·ished**)
to develop or grow successfully: *Their business is flourishing.* ◆ *These plants flourish in a sunny position.*

flow¹ /floʊ/ *verb* (**flows, flow·ing, flowed**)
to move in a steady, continuous way in one direction: *This river flows into the Atlantic Ocean.*

flow² /floʊ/ *noun* [*singular*]
a steady, continuous movement of something in one direction: *I used a handkerchief to stop the flow of blood.* ◆ *the steady flow of traffic through the city*

flow chart /'floʊ tʃart/ *noun* [*count*]
(**BUSINESS, GENERAL SCIENCE**) a diagram that shows the connections between the different stages of a process or parts of a system ⊃ Look at **pie chart**.

flowers

tulip　　sunflower　　rose

flow·er¹ 🔑 /ˈflaʊər/ *noun* [count]
the part of a plant that has a bright color, where the seeds or fruit come from: *She gave me a bunch of flowers.* ⊃ Look at the picture at **plant**.

flow·er² /ˈflaʊər/ *verb* (flow·ers, flow·er·ing, flow·ered)
(**BIOLOGY**) to produce flowers: *This plant flowers in late spring.*

flow·er bed /ˈflaʊər bɛd/ *noun* [count]
a piece of ground used for growing flowers

flow·er·pot /ˈflaʊərpɑt/ *noun* [count]
a container in which you grow plants

flow·er·y /ˈflaʊəri/ (also **flow·ered** /ˈflaʊərd/) *adjective*
covered or decorated with flowers: *She was wearing a flowery dress.*

flown form of **fly¹**

fl. oz. abbreviation of **fluid ounce**

flu /flu/ *noun* [noncount]
(**HEALTH**) an illness like a very bad cold that makes your body sore and hot: *I have the flu.*

fluc·tu·ate AWL /ˈflʌktʃueɪt/ *verb* (fluc·tu·ates, fluc·tu·at·ing, fluc·tu·at·ed)
to change often from one thing to another: *The number of students at the school fluctuates between 100 and 150.*

flu·en·cy /ˈfluənsi/ *noun* [noncount]
(**ENGLISH LANGUAGE ARTS**) the ability to speak or write a language well: *speaking activities to improve your fluency*

flu·ent /ˈfluənt/ *adjective*
1 able to speak easily and correctly: *Susan is fluent in English and Spanish.*
2 spoken easily and correctly: *She speaks fluent Japanese.*
▶ **flu·ent·ly** /ˈfluəntli/ *adverb*: *She speaks five languages fluently.*

fluff /flʌf/ *noun* [noncount]
very light and soft pieces of wool, cotton, or fur, or very light and soft new feathers

fluff·y /ˈflʌfi/ *adjective* (fluff·i·er, fluff·i·est)
feeling or looking very light and soft: *a fluffy kitten* • *fluffy clouds*

flu·id /ˈfluəd/ *noun* [count, noncount]
a substance that can flow; a liquid: *The doctor told her to drink plenty of fluids.*

flu·id ounce /ˌfluəd ˈaʊns/ (also **ounce**) *noun* [count] (abbreviation **fl. oz.**)
a measure of liquid (= 0.0296 liters). There are 16 **fluid ounces** in a **pint**, and 32 **fluid ounces** in a **quart**.

flung form of **fling**

flush /flʌʃ/ *verb* (flush·es, flush·ing, flushed)
1 to clean a toilet by pressing or pulling a handle that sends water through it: *Remember to flush the toilet.*
2 If you **flush**, your face becomes red because you are embarrassed or angry: *He flushed with anger.*

flushed /flʌʃt/ *adjective*
with a red face: *You look flushed. Are you feeling alright?*

flus·tered /ˈflʌstərd/ *adjective*
feeling nervous and confused because you have too much to do or not enough time: *She arrived late, looking hot and flustered.*

flute /flut/ *noun* [count]
(**MUSIC**) a musical instrument that you hold out to the side and play by blowing ⊃ Look at the picture at **instrument**.

flut·ter /ˈflʌtər/ *verb* (flut·ters, flut·ter·ing, flut·tered)
to make a quick, light movement through the air: *Flags fluttered in the breeze.*

fly¹ 🔑 /flaɪ/ *verb* (flies, fly·ing, flew /flu/, has flown /floʊn/)
1 to move through the air: *In the fall, some birds fly to warmer countries.*
2 to travel in an airplane: *I'm flying to Boston tomorrow.*
3 to make an airplane move through the air: *A pilot is a person who flies a plane.*
4 to move quickly: *The door suddenly flew open, and John came in.* • *A stone came flying through the window.*
5 to move around in the air: *Three flags were flying in front of the building.*

fly² /flaɪ/ *noun* (plural **flies**)
1 [count] a small insect with two wings ⊃ Look at the picture at **insect**.
2 [singular] the part where you fasten a pair of pants at the front: *Your fly is unzipped!*

fly·ing /ˈflaɪɪŋ/ *adjective*
able to fly: *flying insects*
with flying colors with great success; very well: *They all passed the exam with flying colors.*

fly·ing sau·cer /ˌflaɪɪŋ ˈsɔsər/ *noun* [*count*]
an object in the sky that some people think they
have seen, and that they think has come from
another planet

foal /foʊl/ *noun* [*count*]
a young horse ⊃ Look at the note at **horse**.

foam /foʊm/ *noun* [*noncount*]
1 a soft light material, full of small holes, which
is used inside seats, etc.: *a foam mattress*
2 a lot of very small white bubbles that you see
when you move liquid quickly

fo·cus¹ **AWL** /ˈfoʊkəs/ *verb* (fo·cus·es or
fo·cus·ses, fo·cus·ing or fo·cus·sing, fo·cused or
fo·cussed)
1 to give all your attention to something: *to
focus on a problem*
2 to move part of a camera, etc. so that you can
see things through it clearly

fo·cus² **AWL** /ˈfoʊkəs/ *noun* [*singular*]
the center of attention or interest; special
attention that is given to someone or
something: *It was the main focus of attention at
the meeting.*
in focus; **out of focus** If a photograph is **in
focus**, it is clear. If it is **out of focus**, it is not.

fog /fɔg; fɑg/ *noun* [*count, noncount*]
thick cloud that forms close to the ground, and
that is difficult to see through: *The fog will clear
by late morning.*
▶ **fog·gy** /ˈfɔgi; ˈfɑgi/ *adjective* (fog·gi·er,
fog·gi·est): *a foggy day* ◆ *It was very foggy this
morning.*

foil /fɔɪl/ *noun* [*noncount*]
thin metal paper that is used for covering food:
Wrap the meat in foil and put it in the oven.

fold¹ /foʊld/ *verb* (folds, fold·ing, fold·ed) (also
fold up)
1 to bend something so that one part is on top of
another part: *I folded the letter and put it in the
envelope.* ◆ *Fold up your clothes.* ⊃ **ANTONYM
unfold**
2 to be able to be made smaller in order to be
carried or stored more easily: *a folding chair* ◆
This table folds up flat.
fold your arms to cross one arm over the other
one in front of your chest: *She folded her arms
and waited.*

fold² /foʊld/ *noun* [*count*]
a line that is made when you bend cloth or
paper

fold·er /ˈfoʊldər/ *noun* [*count*]
1 a cover made of very thick paper or plastic, for
keeping papers in ⊃ Look at the picture at
stationery.
2 (**COMPUTERS**) a collection of information or
files that is stored together in a computer or on a
disk

fo·li·age /ˈfoʊliɪdʒ/ *noun* [*noncount*] (*formal*)
(**BIOLOGY**) all the leaves of a tree or plant

folk /foʊk/ *adjective*
typical of the ordinary people of a particular
country or community: *folk music* ◆ *a traditional
folk dance*

folks /foʊks/ *noun* [*plural*]
1 people in general: *There are a lot of old folks
living in this town.*
2 (*informal*) your parents: *How are your folks?*

fol·low /ˈfɑloʊ/ *verb* (fol·lows, fol·low·ing,
fol·lowed)
1 to come or go after someone or something:
Follow me and I'll show you the way. ◆ *I think that
car is following us!* ◆ *The movie will be **followed**
by the news.*
2 to go along a road, path, etc.: *Follow this road
for about a mile and then turn right.*
3 to do what someone says you should do: *I'd
like you all to **follow** my **instructions** carefully.*
4 to understand something: *Has everyone
followed the discussion so far?*
as follows as you will now hear or read: *The
dates of the meetings will be as follows: March 21,
April 3, April 19.*
▶ **fol·low·er** *noun* [*count*]
someone who follows or supports a person or a
belief

fol·low·ing /ˈfɑloʊɪŋ/ *adjective*
next: *I saw him the following day.*

fond /fɑnd/ *adjective* (fond·er, fond·est)
be fond of someone or **something** to like
someone or something a lot: *They are very fond
of their uncle.* ⊃ Look at the note at **like¹**.
▶ **fond·ly** /ˈfɑndli/ *adverb*: *I remember the place
fondly.*

food /fud/ *noun* [*noncount*]
things that people or animals eat: *Let's go and
get some food – I'm hungry.* ◆ *They gave the
horses food and water.* ◆ *My favorite food is pasta.*
⊃ Look at the note at **cooking**.

fool¹ /ful/ *noun* [*count*]
a person who is silly or who does something
silly: *You fool! You forgot to lock the door!*
make a fool of yourself to do something that
makes you look silly in front of other people: *He
always makes a fool of himself at parties.*

fool² /ful/ *verb* (fools, fool·ing, fooled)
to make someone believe something that is not
true: *You can't fool me! I know you're lying!* ⊃
SYNONYM trick
fool around to do silly things: *Stop fooling
around with those scissors.*

fool·ish /ˈfulɪʃ/ *adjective*
stupid or silly: *a foolish mistake*
▶ **fool·ish·ly** /ˈfulɪʃli/ *adverb*: *I foolishly forgot to
bring a coat.*

foot 🔊 /fʊt/ *noun* [*count*]
1 (*plural* **feet** /fit/) the part of your leg that you stand on: *I've been walking all day, and my feet hurt.* ⤳ Look at the picture at **leg**.
2 (*plural* **foot** or **feet**) (abbreviation **ft.**) a measure of length (=twelve inches or 30.48 centimeters). There are three **feet** in a **yard**: *"How tall are you?" "Five foot six* (= five feet and six inches)*."* ◆ *She is five feet tall.*
3 the lowest part of something: *She was standing **at the foot of** the stairs.* ⤳ **SYNONYM** **bottom**
on foot walking: *Should we go by car or on foot?*
put your foot down (*informal*) to say strongly that something must or must not happen: *My mom put her foot down when I asked if I could stay out after midnight.*
put your foot in your mouth (*informal*) to say or do something by accident that makes someone embarrassed or upset

foot·ball 🔊 /'fʊtbɔl/
noun (**SPORTS**)
1 [*noncount*] a game that is played by two teams of eleven players who throw, carry, or kick the ball to the end of the field. The players wear special clothing to protect their heads and bodies: *He played football in high school and college.* ◆ *a football game*
2 [*count*] a ball for playing this game

football

football
field

foot·print /'fʊtprɪnt/ *noun* [*count*]
a mark that your foot or shoe makes on the ground

foot·step /'fʊtstɛp/ *noun* [*count*]
the sound of a person walking: *I heard footsteps, and then a knock on the door.*

foot·wear /'fʊtwɛr/ *noun* [*noncount*]
shoes or boots: *The store has a large footwear department.*

for¹ 🔊 /fər; fɔr/ *preposition*
1 a word that shows who will get or have something: *These flowers are for you.*
2 a word that shows how something is used or why something is done: *We had fish for dinner.* ◆ *Take this medicine for your cold.* ◆ *He was sent to prison for murder.*
3 a word that shows where a person or thing is going: *Is this the train for New York?*
4 a word that shows how much something is: *I bought this book for $19.*
5 a word that shows that you like an idea: *Some people were for the strike and others were against it.* ⤳ **ANTONYM** **against**

6 with the meaning of: *What is the word for "small" in Spanish?*
7 on the side of someone or something: *He plays football for Cornell.*
8 a word that shows how long something has been happening: *She has lived here for 20 years.* ⤳ Look at the note at **since**.
9 a word that shows how far someone or something goes: *We walked for miles* (= a very long way).
10 a word that shows the person or thing you are talking about: *It's time for us to go.*

for² /fər; fɔr/ *conjunction* (*formal*)
because: *She was crying, for she knew they could never meet again.* ⤳ **SYNONYM** **as**

for·bid /fər'bɪd/ *verb* (**for·bids, for·bid·ding, for·bade** /fər'beɪd/, **has for·bid·den** /fər'bɪdn/)
to say that someone must not do something: *My parents have forbidden me to see him again.* ◆ *Smoking is forbidden* (= not allowed) *inside the building.* ⤳ **ANTONYM** **allow**

force¹ 🔊 /fɔrs/ *noun*
1 [*noncount*] power or strength: *He was killed by the force of the explosion.* ◆ *I lost the key so I had to open the door by force.*
2 [*count*] a group of people, for example police or soldiers, who do a special job: *the police force* ◆ *military forces*
3 [*count, noncount*] (**PHYSICS**) a power that can cause change or movement: *the force of gravity*

force² 🔊 /fɔrs/ *verb* (**forc·es, forc·ing, forced**)
1 to make someone do something that they do not want to do: *They forced him to give them the money.*
2 to do something by using a lot of strength: *The thief forced the window open.*

fore·cast¹ /'fɔrkæst/ *noun* [*count*]
what someone thinks will happen, based on the information that is available: *The weather forecast said that it would rain today.*

fore·cast² /'fɔrkæst/ *verb* (**fore·casts, fore·cast·ing, fore·cast, has fore·cast**)
to say what you think will happen, based on the information that is available: *They're forecasting rain for tomorrow.* ⤳ **SYNONYM** **predict**
▶ **fore·cast·er** /'fɔrkæstər/ *noun* [*count*]: *She's a weather forecaster on TV.*

fore·fa·ther /'fɔr,fɑðər/ *noun* [*count*] (*formal*)
(**HISTORY**) a person (especially a man) in your family who lived a long time ago ⤳ **SYNONYM** **ancestor**

fore·ground /'fɔrgraʊnd/ *noun* [*singular*]
(**ART**) the part of a picture that seems nearest to you: *The man in the foreground is my father.* ⤳ **ANTONYM** **background**

fore·head /'fɔrhɛd/ *noun* [*count*]
the part of your face above your eyes

for·eign 🔑 /ˈfɔrən; ˈfɑrən/ *adjective*
belonging to or connected with a country that is not your own: *We have some foreign students staying at our house.* • *a foreign language*

for·eign·er /ˈfɔrənər; ˈfɑrənər/ *noun* [count]
a person from another country

fore·see /fɔrˈsi/ *verb* (**fore·sees, fore·see·ing, fore·saw** /fɔrˈsɔ/, **has fore·seen** /fɔrˈsin/) (*formal*)
to know or guess what will happen in the future: *No one could have foreseen what would happen.*
⊃ **SYNONYM predict**

for·est 🔑 /ˈfɔrəst/ *noun* [count, noncount]
(**GEOGRAPHY**) a large area of land covered with trees: *We went for a walk in the forest.*

for·ev·er 🔑 /fəˈrɛvər/ *adverb*
1 for all time: *I will love you forever.* ⊃ **SYNONYM always**
2 (*informal*) very often: *I can't read because he's forever asking me questions!*

fore·word /ˈfɔrwərd/ *noun* [count]
(**ENGLISH LANGUAGE ARTS**) a piece of writing at the beginning of a book, which introduces it: *a collection of short stories, with a foreword by John Updike*

for·gave form of **forgive**

forge /fɔrdʒ/ *verb* (**forg·es, forg·ing, forged**)
to make an illegal copy of something in order to cheat people: *The passport had been forged.*
forge someone's signature to sign another person's name, pretending to be that person

for·ger·y /ˈfɔrdʒəri/ *noun* (*plural* **for·ger·ies**)
1 [noncount] the crime of making an illegal copy of something in order to cheat people
2 [count] something that has been copied in order to cheat people: *This painting is not really by Van Gogh – it's a forgery.*

for·get 🔑 /fərˈgɛt/ *verb* (**for·gets, for·get·ting, for·got** /fərˈgɑt/, **has for·got·ten** /fərˈgɑtn/)
1 to not remember something: *I forgot her name.* • *Don't forget to do your homework!*
2 to not bring something with you: *I had forgotten my glasses.*
3 to stop thinking about something: *Forget about your exams and enjoy yourself!* • *"I'm sorry I shouted at you." "Oh, forget it* (= don't worry about it).*"

for·get·ful /fərˈgɛtfl/ *adjective*
often forgetting things: *My grandmother had become very forgetful.* ⊃ **SYNONYM absentminded**

for·give 🔑 /fərˈgɪv/ *verb* (**for·gives, for·giv·ing, for·gave** /fərˈgeɪv/, **has for·giv·en** /fərˈgɪvn/)
to stop being angry with someone for a bad thing that they did: *I can't forgive him for behaving like that.*

for·give·ness /fərˈgɪvnəs/ *noun* [noncount]
the fact that you stop being angry with someone for a bad thing that they did: *He begged for forgiveness.*

for·got, for·got·ten forms of **forget**

fork 🔑 /fɔrk/ *noun* [count]
1 a thing with long points at one end, which you use for putting food in your mouth ⊃ Look at the picture at **knife**.
2 a large tool with points at one end, which you use for digging in the ground
3 a place where a road or river divides into two parts: *When you get to the fork in the road, go left.*

form¹ 🔑 /fɔrm/ *noun*
1 [count] a type of something: *Cars, trains, and buses are all forms of transportation.*
2 [count] a piece of paper with spaces for you to answer questions: *You need to fill out this form to get a new passport.*
3 [count, noncount] the shape of a person or thing: *a cake in the form of a car*
4 [count] (**ENGLISH LANGUAGE ARTS**) one of the ways you write or say a word: *"Forgot" is a form of "forget."*

form² 🔑 /fɔrm/ *verb* (**forms, form·ing, formed**)
1 to make something or to give a shape to something: *We formed a line outside the theater.* • *In English we usually form the past tense by adding "-ed."*
2 to grow or take shape: *Ice forms when water freezes.*
3 to start a group or an organization: *The club was formed last year.*

for·mal 🔑 /ˈfɔrml/ *adjective*
1 You use **formal** language or behave in a **formal** way at important or serious times and with people you do not know very well: *"Yours sincerely" is a formal way of ending a letter.* • *I wore a suit and tie because it was a formal dinner.*
2 official: *I'll be making a formal complaint to the hospital about my care.* ⊃ **ANTONYM informal**
▶ **for·mal·ly** /ˈfɔrməli/ *adverb*: *"How do you do?" she said formally.*

for·mat **AWL** /ˈfɔrmæt/ *noun* [count]
the shape of something, or the way it is arranged or produced: *It's the same book, but in a different format.*

for·mer /ˈfɔrmər/ *adjective*
of a time before now: *our former president*
▶ **for·mer·ly** /ˈfɔrmərli/ *adverb*: *The hotel was formerly a private house.*

the for·mer /ðə ˈfɔrmər/ *noun* [singular]
the first of two things or people: *He had to choose between losing his job and losing his family. He chose the former.* ⊃ **ANTONYM the latter**

for·mu·la AWL /ˈfɔrmyələ/ *noun* [*count*] (*plural* for·mu·las *or* for·mu·lae /ˈfɔrmyəli/)

1 (MATH, GENERAL SCIENCE) a group of letters, numbers, or symbols that show a rule in mathematics or science: *This formula is used to calculate the area of a circle.*

2 a list of the substances that you need to make something: *The formula for the new drug will not be made public.*

fort /fɔrt/ *noun* [*count*]
a strong building that was made to protect a place against its enemies

forth /fɔrθ/ *adverb*
back and forth ⊃ Look at **back³**.

for·ti·eth *number* form of **forty**

for·tress /ˈfɔrtrəs/ *noun* [*count*] (*plural* for·tress·es)
a large strong building that was made to protect a place against its enemies

for·tu·nate /ˈfɔrtʃənət/ *adjective*
lucky: *I was very fortunate to get the job.* ⊃
ANTONYM **unfortunate**
▸ **for·tu·nate·ly** /ˈfɔrtʃənətli/ *adverb*:
Fortunately, no one was hurt in the accident. ⊃
SYNONYM **luckily** ⊃ ANTONYM **unfortunately**

for·tune /ˈfɔrtʃən/ *noun*
1 [*count*] a lot of money: *He made a fortune selling old cars.*
2 [*noncount*] things that happen that you cannot control: *I had the good fortune to get the job.* ⊃
SYNONYM **luck**
tell someone's fortune to say what will happen to someone in the future: *She said she could tell my fortune by looking at my hand.*

for·ty 🖋 /ˈfɔrti/ *number*

> ℹ SPELLING
> Remember! There is a **U** in **four**, but no **U** in **forty**.

1 40
2 the forties [*plural*] the numbers, years, or temperatures between 40 and 49
in your forties between the ages of 40 and 49:
I think my teacher must be in his forties.
▸ **for·ti·eth** /ˈfɔrtiəθ/ *pronoun, adjective, adverb, noun* [*count*]
40th

for·ward¹ 🖋 /ˈfɔrwərd/ *adverb*
1 (also **for·wards** /ˈfɔrwərdz/) in the direction that is in front of you: *Move forward to the front of the train.*
2 in the direction of progress; ahead: *This new drug is a big step forward.* ⊃ ANTONYM **backward**
look forward to something to wait for something with pleasure: *We're looking forward to seeing you again.*

for·ward² /ˈfɔrwərd/ *verb* (for·wards, for·ward·ing, for·ward·ed)
to send a letter or e-mail that you receive at one address to another address: *Could you forward all my mail to me while I'm abroad?*

fos·sil /ˈfɑsl/ *noun* [*count*]
a part of a dead plant or an animal that has been in the ground for a very long time and has turned into rock

fos·sil fuel /ˈfɑsl ˌfyuəl/ *noun* [*count, noncount*]
fuel such as gas or oil that was formed over millions of years from dead animals or plants in the ground

fos·ter¹ /ˈfɑstər/ *verb* (fos·ters, fos·ter·ing, fos·tered) (*formal*)
to let a good feeling or situation develop: *The aim is to foster good relations between the two countries.*

fos·ter² /ˈfɑstər/ *adjective*
connected with taking a child who needs a home into your family, but without becoming their legal parent: *my foster parents* ◆ *a foster home*

fought form of **fight**

foul¹ /faʊl/ *adjective*
1 dirty, or with a bad smell or taste: *What a foul smell!*
2 very bad: *We had foul weather all week.*

foul² /faʊl/ (fouls, foul·ing, fouled) *verb*
(SPORTS) to do something to another player that is not allowed: *Johnson was fouled twice.*
▸ **foul** *noun* [*count*]: *He was sent off for a foul on the goalkeeper.*

found¹ AWL form of **find**

found² AWL /faʊnd/ *verb* (founds, found·ing, found·ed)
to start a new organization: *This school was founded in 1865.*
▸ **foun·der** AWL /ˈfaʊndər/ *noun* [*count*]
a person who starts a new organization: *the founder and president of the company*

foun·da·tion AWL /faʊnˈdeɪʃn/ *noun*
1 foundations [*plural*] the bricks or stones that form the solid base of a building, under the ground
2 [*count, noncount*] the idea or fact on which something is based: *Those skills are a good foundation for learning other subjects.* ◆ *That theory has no foundation.*
3 [*noncount*] the act of starting a new organization

foun·tain /ˈfaʊntn/ *noun* [*count*]
water that shoots up into the air and then falls down again. You often see **fountains** in parks and gardens.

four 🔑 /fɔr/ *number*
4
on all fours with your hands and knees on the ground: *We went through the tunnel on all fours.*
▶ **fourth** /fɔrθ/ *pronoun, adjective, adverb*
4th: *He finished fourth in the race.*

four·teen 🔑 /ˌfɔr'tin/ *number*
14
▶ **four·teenth** /ˌfɔr'tinθ/ *pronoun, adjective, adverb, noun* [count]
14th

the Fourth of Ju·ly /ðə ˌfɔrθ ʌv dʒʊ'laɪ/ *noun* [singular]
July 4; a national holiday in the U.S., when Americans celebrate the day in 1776 that America became an independent country ⊃ SYNONYM **Independence Day**

fox /faks/ *noun* [count]
(plural **fox·es**)
a wild animal like a small dog with a long thick tail and red fur

fox

foy·er /'fɔɪər/ *noun* [count]
an open area inside the entrance of a house or a large public building, for example a hotel or theater: *I'll meet you in the hotel foyer at seven thirty.*

frac·tion /'frækʃn/ *noun* [count] (MATH)
1 an exact part of a number: ¼ (= a quarter) *and* ⅓ (= a third) *are fractions.* ⊃ Look at **integer**.
2 a very small part of something: *For a fraction of a second I thought the car was going to crash.*

frac·ture /'fræktʃər/ *noun* [count]
(HEALTH) a break in one of your bones: *She had a fracture of the arm.*
▶ **frac·ture** *verb* (fractures, frac·tur·ing, fractured): *She fell and fractured her ankle.*

frag·ile /'frædʒl/ *adjective*
A thing that is **fragile** breaks easily: *Be careful with those glasses. They're very fragile.*

frag·ment /'frægmənt/ *noun* [count]
a very small piece that has broken off something: *There were **fragments of** glass everywhere.*

fra·grance /'freɪgrəns/ *noun* [count, noncount]
a pleasant smell: *The flowers are chosen for their delicate fragrance.*

fra·grant /'freɪgrənt/ *adjective*
having a pleasant smell: *The air was fragrant.*

frail /freɪl/ *adjective* (frail·er, frail·est)
not strong or healthy: *a frail old woman* ⊃ SYNONYM **weak**

frame¹ 🔑 /freɪm/ *noun* [count]
1 a thin piece of wood or metal around the edge of a picture, window, mirror, etc.

2 strong pieces of wood or metal that give something its shape: *the frame of the bicycle*
3 the metal or plastic around the edge of a pair of glasses ⊃ Look at the picture at **glasses**.
frame of mind the way that you feel at a particular time: *I'm not in the right frame of mind for a party.* ⊃ SYNONYM **mood**

frame² /freɪm/ *verb* (frames, fram·ing, framed)
to put a picture in a frame: *Let's have this photograph framed.*

frame·work AWL /'freɪmwərk/ *noun* [count]
1 the strong part of something that gives it shape: *The bridge has a steel framework.*
2 a set of rules or ideas which help you to decide what to do: *Your plan will provide a good framework.*

frank /fræŋk/ *adjective* (frank·er, frank·est)
saying exactly what you think: *To be frank, I don't like your shirt.* ⊃ SYNONYM **honest, truthful**
▶ **frank·ly** /'fræŋkli/ *adverb*: *Tell me frankly what you think of my work.*

fran·tic /'fræntɪk/ *adjective*
1 very busy or in a hurry: *a frantic search for the keys*
2 extremely worried or frightened: *Nancy was frantic when she couldn't find her son.* ◆ *frantic cries for help*
▶ **fran·ti·cal·ly** /'fræntɪkli/ *adverb*: *Tom searched frantically for his wallet.*

fraud /frɔd/ *noun*
1 [count, noncount] doing things that are not honest to get money: *His father was sent to prison for fraud.*
2 [count] a person or thing that is not what they seem to be: *He said he was a police officer, but I knew he was a fraud.*

fray /freɪ/ *verb* (frays, fray·ing, frayed)
If cloth **frays**, the threads become loose at the edges: *a frayed towel*

freak¹ /frik/ *noun* [count]
1 (informal) a person with a very strong interest in something: *a health freak* ◆ *a computer freak*
2 a person who looks strange or behaves in a very strange way

freak² /frik/ *adjective*
(used about an event or the weather) strange or unusual: *a freak accident* ◆ *a freak storm*

freck·les /'frɛklz/ *noun* [plural]
small light brown spots on a person's skin: *A lot of people with red hair have freckles.*

free¹ 🔑 /fri/ *adjective, adverb* (fre·er, fre·est)
1 able to go where you want and do what you want: *After five years in prison she was finally free.* ◆ *We set the bird free* (= let it go) *and it flew away.*

2 If something is **free**, you do not have to pay for it: *We have some free tickets for the concert.* ◆ *Children under twelve can stay here free.*
3 not busy: *Are you free this afternoon?* ◆ *I don't have much free time.*
4 not being used: *Excuse me, is this seat free?*
free from something; **free of something** without something bad: *She was finally free from pain.*

free² /friː/ *verb* (**frees, free·ing, freed**)
to make someone or something free: *He was freed after ten years in prison.*

Suffix

-free
(in adjectives) not containing the bad thing mentioned: *sugar-free cola* ◆ *fat-free yogurt* ◆ *a smoke-free environment* ◆ *a tax-free savings account*

free·dom /'friːdəm/ *noun*
1 [*noncount*] being free: *They gave their children too much freedom.*
2 [*count, noncount*] the right to do or say what you want: *freedom of speech*

free·way /'friːweɪ/ *noun* [*count*]
a wide road where vehicles can travel fast: *the freeways of southern California*

freeze /friːz/ *verb* (**freez·es, freez·ing, froze** /froʊz/, **has fro·zen** /'froʊzn/)
1 to become hard because it is so cold. When water **freezes**, it becomes ice.
2 to make food very cold so that it stays fresh for a long time: *frozen vegetables*
3 to stop suddenly and stay very still: *The cat froze when it saw the bird.*
freeze to death to be so cold that you die

freez·er /'friːzər/ *noun* [*count*]
an electric container that keeps food very cold (**FROZEN**) so that it stays fresh for a long time ⊃ Look at **refrigerator**.

freez·ing /'friːzɪŋ/ *adjective* (*informal*)
very cold: *Can you close the window? I'm freezing!* ⊃ Look at the note at **cold¹**.

freez·ing point /'friːzɪŋ ˌpɔɪnt/ (also **freez·ing**) *noun* [*count, noncount*]
(**PHYSICS**) the temperature at which a liquid freezes: *Water has a freezing point of 32° Fahrenheit, or 0° Celsius.* ◆ *Last night the temperature fell to six degrees below freezing.*

freight /freɪt/ *noun* [*noncount*]
things that trucks, ships, trains, and airplanes carry from one place to another: *a freight train*

French fries /ˌfrɛntʃ 'fraɪz/ (also **fries**) *noun* [*plural*]
thin pieces of potato cooked in hot oil: *a hamburger with French fries*

French toast /ˌfrɛntʃ 'toʊst/ *noun* [*noncount*]
bread that has been covered with a mixture of eggs and milk and then fried: *a piece of French toast*

fren·zy /'frɛnzi/ *noun* [*singular, noncount*]
a state of great emotion or activity that is not under control: *She was in a complete frenzy before the wedding.*

fre·quen·cy /'friːkwənsi/ *noun* (*plural* **fre·quen·cies**)
1 [*noncount*] the number of times something happens: *The frequency of fatal accidents has gone down.* ◆ *The frequency of cancer-related deaths near the factory is being investigated.*
2 [*count, noncount*] (**PHYSICS**) the rate at which a sound wave or radio wave moves up and down: *high-frequency sounds* ◆ *What frequency does the radio station broadcast on?*

fre·quent /'friːkwənt/ *adjective*
happening often: *His visits became less frequent.*
⊃ **ANTONYM infrequent**
▸ **fre·quent·ly** /'friːkwəntli/ *adverb*: *Steven is frequently late for school.* ⊃ **SYNONYM often**

fresh /frɛʃ/ *adjective* (**fresh·er, fresh·est**)
1 (used especially about food) made or picked not long ago; not frozen or in a can: *I'll make some fresh coffee.* ◆ *Eat plenty of fresh fruit and vegetables.*
2 new or different: *fresh ideas*
3 clean and cool: *Open the window and let some fresh air in.*
4 (used about water) not containing salt; not from the ocean: *fresh water*
▸ **fresh·ly** /'frɛʃli/ *adverb*: *freshly baked bread*

fresh·man /'frɛʃmən/ *noun* [*count*] (*plural* **fresh·men** /'frɛʃmən/)
a student who is in ninth grade in high school or the first year of college ⊃ Look at **junior²**, **senior²**(1), **sophomore**.

fret /frɛt/ *verb* (**fret, fret·ting, fret·ted**)
to be worried and unhappy about something: *I've been fretting about the exam all week.*

fric·tion /'frɪkʃn/ *noun* [*noncount*]
1 (**PHYSICS**) the action of one surface rubbing against another: *You have to put oil in the engine to reduce friction between the moving parts.*
2 disagreement between people or groups: *There was a lot of friction between the two families.*

Fri·day /'fraɪdeɪ; 'fraɪdi/ *noun* [*count, noncount*] (abbreviation **Fri.**)
the day of the week after Thursday and before Saturday

fridge /frɪdʒ/ *noun* [*count*] (*informal*)
= **refrigerator**

fried form of **fry**

friend 🔑 /frɛnd/ noun [count]

a person that you like and know very well: *David is my **best friend**.* • *We are very good friends.*
make friends with someone to become a friend of someone: *Have you made friends with any of the students in your class?*

friend·ly 🔑 /'frɛndli/ adjective (friend·li·er, friend·li·est)
kind and helpful: *My neighbors are very friendly.*
⊃ ANTONYM **unfriendly**
be friendly with someone to be someone's friend: *Jane is friendly with their daughter.*
▶ **friend·li·ness** /'frɛndlinəs/ noun [noncount]

friend·ship 🔑 /'frɛndʃɪp/ noun [count, noncount]
the state of being friends with someone: *a close friendship* • *Your friendship is very important to me.*

fries¹ /fraɪz/ noun [plural] = **French fries**: *a burger and fries*

fries² form of **fry**

fright /fraɪt/ noun [count, noncount]
a sudden feeling of fear: *I hope I didn't **give you a fright** when I shouted.* • *She cried out in fright.*

fright·en 🔑 /'fraɪtn/ verb (fright·ens, fright·en·ing, fright·ened)
to make someone feel afraid: *Sorry, did I frighten you?* ⊃ SYNONYM **scare**
▶ **fright·en·ing** /'fraɪtn·ɪŋ/ adjective: *That was the most frightening movie I have ever seen.* ⊃ SYNONYM **scary**

fright·ened /'fraɪtnd/ adjective
afraid: *He's **frightened of** spiders.* ⊃ SYNONYM **scared** ⊃ Look at the note at **afraid**.

frill /frɪl/ noun
1 [count] a narrow piece of cloth with a lot of folds, which decorates the edge of a shirt, dress, etc.: *a white blouse with frills at the cuffs*
2 frills [plural] nice things that are added to something, but that you feel are not necessary: *We want a simple meal – **no frills**.*
▶ **frill·y** /'frɪli/ adjective (frill·i·er, frill·i·est): *a frilly skirt*

fringe /frɪndʒ/ noun [count]
a line of loose strings (THREADS) that decorate the edge of a piece of cloth

friz·zy /'frɪzi/ adjective (friz·zi·er, friz·zi·est) adjective
(used about hair) with a lot of small CURLS (= curved pieces of hair)

fro /froʊ/ adverb
to and fro first one way and then the other way, many times: *She rocked the baby to and fro.*

frog /frɔg; frɑg/ noun [count]

frog

a small green animal that lives in and near water. **Frogs** have long back legs and they can jump.

from 🔑 /frəm; frʌm/ preposition
1 a word that shows where someone or something starts: *We traveled from New York to Boston.* • *She began to walk away from him.* • *The tickets cost from $15 to $35.*
2 a word that shows when something starts: *The store is open from 9:30 until 5:30.*
3 a word that shows who gave or sent something: *I got a letter from Lynn.* • *I borrowed a dress from my sister.*
4 a word that shows where someone lives or was born: *My family comes from Cuba.*
5 a word that shows what is used to make something: *Paper is made from wood.*
6 a word that shows how far away something is: *The house is two miles from here.*
7 a word that shows how something changes: *The sky changed from blue to gray.*
8 a word that shows why: *Children are dying from this disease.*
9 a word that shows difference: *My book is different from yours.*

front 🔑 /frʌnt/ noun [count, usually singular]
the side or part of something that faces forward and that you usually see first: *The book has a picture of a lion **on the front**.* • *John and I sat in the front of the car and the children sat in the back.*
in front of someone or **something**
1 farther forward than another person or thing: *Alice was sitting in front of her mother on the bus.*
2 when other people are there: *Please don't talk about it in front of my parents.*
▶ **front** adjective: *the front door* • *the front seat of a car*

fron·tier /frʌn'tɪr/ noun
1 [usually singular] (HISTORY) land that people are just beginning to live on, especially in the western U.S. in the 1800s: *frontier towns of the Wild West* ⊃ SYNONYM **border**
2 the frontiers [plural] the limit between what we know and what we do not know: *the frontiers of modern medicine*

frost /frɔst/ *noun* [count, noncount]
ice, like white powder, that covers the ground when the weather is very cold: *There was a frost last night.*
▶ **frosty** /'frɔsti/ *adjective* (frost·i·er, frost·i·est): *a frosty morning*

frost·ing /'frɔstɪŋ/ *noun* [noncount]
a sweet substance that you use for covering cakes: *chocolate frosting*

frown /fraʊn/ *verb* (frowns, frown·ing, frowned)
to show that you are angry or worried by making lines appear above your nose: *John frowned at me when I came in. "You're late," he said.*
▶ **frown** *noun* [count]: *She looked at me with a frown.*

froze form of **freeze**

fro·zen[1] form of **freeze**

fro·zen[2] /'froʊzn/ *adjective* (informal)
1 (used about food) kept at a very cold temperature so that it stays fresh for a long time: *frozen peas*
2 (used about water) turned to ice, or with a layer of ice on the top: *a frozen lake*

fruit

apples bananas cherries

grapefruit grapes kiwis

lemons limes oranges

pears pineapples plums

fruit /frut/ *noun* [count, noncount]

ⓘ PRONUNCIATION
The word **fruit** sounds like **boot**.

the part of a plant or tree that holds the seeds. Oranges and apples are types of **fruit**: *Would you like a **a piece of fruit**? • "Would you like **some fruit**?" "Yes please – I'll have a pear."*

fruit sal·ad /,frut 'sæləd/ *noun* [count, noncount]
a sweet dish made of small pieces of different kinds of fruit

frus·trat·ed /'frʌstreɪt̬əd/ *adjective*
feeling angry because you cannot do what you want to do: *She felt frustrated by her lack of progress.*

frus·trat·ing /'frʌstreɪt̬ɪŋ/ *adjective*
making you angry because you cannot do what you want to do: *It's very frustrating when you can't say what you mean in a foreign language.*

frus·tra·tion /frʌ'streɪʃn/ *noun* [noncount]
a feeling of anger because you cannot get or do something you want: *He got stuck in traffic and hit the steering wheel in frustration.*

fry /fraɪ/ *verb* (fries, fry·ing, fried, has fried)
to cook something in hot fat or oil: *Fry the onions in butter.* • *fried eggs* ⇒ Look at the note at **cook**[1].

fry·ing pan /'fraɪɪŋ pæn/ (also **skil·let** /'skɪlət/)
noun [count]
a flat, metal container with a long handle that you use for frying food

ft. abbreviation of **foot**(2)

fudge /fʌdʒ/ *noun* [noncount]
a type of soft, brown candy made from sugar, butter, milk, and usually chocolate

fuel /'fyuəl/ *noun* [noncount]
anything that you burn to make heat or power. Wood, gas, and oil are kinds of **fuel**.

fu·gi·tive /'fyudʒət̬ɪv/ *noun* [count]
a person who is running away or escaping, especially from the police: *a fugitive from the law*

Suffix

-ful

(in adjectives) full of something: *beautiful* • *helpful* • *powerful* • *truthful* • *useful*

ful·fill /fʊl'fɪl/ *verb* (ful·fills, ful·fill·ing, ful·filled)
to do what you have planned or promised to do: *Jane fulfilled her dream of traveling around the world.*
▶ **ful·fill·ment** /fʊl'fɪlmənt/ *noun* [noncount]: *the fulfillment of a promise*

full /fʊl/ *adjective*
(full·er, full·est)
1 with a lot of people or things in it, so that there is no more space: *My glass is full.* • *The bus was full so we waited for the next one.* • *These socks are full of holes.* ⇒ ANTONYM **empty**

full

full empty

2 having had enough to eat: *"Would you like anything else to eat?" "No thanks, I'm full."*
3 complete; with nothing missing: *Please tell me the full story.*
4 as much, big, etc. as possible: *The train was traveling at full speed.*
in full completely; with nothing missing: *Please write your name in full.*

full moon /ˌfʊl ˈmuːn/ *noun* [singular]
the time when you can see all of the moon

full-time /ˌfʊl ˈtaɪm/ *adjective, adverb*
for all the normal working hours of the day or week: *My mother has a full-time job.* ◆ *Do you work full-time?* ⊃ Look at **part-time**.

ful·ly 🔑 /ˈfʊli/ *adverb*
completely; totally: *I fully understand what you are saying.*

fumes /fyuːmz/ *noun* [plural]
smoke or gases that smell bad and that can be dangerous to breathe in: *toxic fumes*

fun¹ 🔑 /fʌn/ *noun* [noncount]
pleasure and enjoyment; something that you enjoy: *Sailing is great fun.* ◆ *I'm just learning Spanish for fun.* ◆ *Have fun* (= enjoy yourself)*!*
make fun of someone to laugh about someone in an unkind way: *The other children make fun of him because he wears glasses.*

fun² /fʌn/ *adjective*
enjoyable: *That party was really fun.* ◆ *to have a fun time*

func·tion¹ **AWL** /ˈfʌŋkʃn/ *noun* [count]
1 the special work that a person or thing does: *The function of the heart is to send blood around the body.*
2 an important social event: *The hall is often used for weddings and other functions.*

func·tion² **AWL** /ˈfʌŋkʃn/ *verb* (func·tions, func·tion·ing, func·tioned)
to work: *Car engines do not function without oil.*

fund¹ **AWL** /fʌnd/ *noun* [count]
money that will be used for something special: *a fund to help homeless people* ◆ *The school wants to raise funds for new computers.*

fund² **AWL** /fʌnd/ *verb* (funds, fund·ing, fund·ed)
(**BUSINESS**) to provide money for something official: *The government is funding a new study on nutrition.*

fun·da·men·tal **AWL** /ˌfʌndəˈmɛntl/ *adjective*
most important; from which everything else develops: *There is a fundamental difference between the two points of view.* ⊃ SYNONYM **basic**

fund-rais·ing /ˈfʌnd ˌreɪzɪŋ/ *noun* [noncount]
the activity of collecting money for a particular use: *fund-raising activities at the school*

fu·ner·al /ˈfyuːnərəl/ *noun* [count]
the time when a dead person is buried or burned

fun·gus /ˈfʌŋgəs/ *noun* [count, noncount] (plural fun·gi /ˈfʌndʒaɪ; ˈfʌŋgaɪ/)
(**BIOLOGY**) a living thing that is like a plant without leaves or flowers. **Fungi** grow on plants and wet surfaces: *Mushrooms are fungi.*

fun·nel /ˈfʌnl/ *noun* [count]
a tube that is wide at the top to help you pour things into bottles

fun·ny 🔑 /ˈfʌni/ *adjective* (fun·ni·er, fun·ni·est)
1 making you laugh or smile: *a funny story* ◆ *He's so funny!* ⊃ SYNONYM **amusing**
2 strange or surprising: *There's a funny smell in this room.*

fur 🔑 /fər/ *noun* [noncount]
the soft, thick hair that covers the bodies of some animals
▶ **fur·ry** /ˈfəri/ *adjective* (fur·ri·er, fur·ri·est): *a furry animal*

fu·ri·ous /ˈfyʊriəs/ *adjective*
very angry: *My parents were furious with me.* ⊃ Look at the note at **angry**.

fur·nace /ˈfərnəs/ *noun* [count]
a closed container with a fire inside it, used for heating buildings or for heating metals, making glass, etc.

fur·nish /ˈfərnɪʃ/ *verb* (fur·nish·es, fur·nish·ing, fur·nished)
to put furniture in a room, house, etc.: *The room was beautifully furnished.*
▶ **fur·nished** /ˈfərnɪʃt/ *adjective*
with furniture already in it: *I'm renting a furnished apartment.*

fur·nish·ings /ˈfərnɪʃɪŋz/ *noun* [plural]
the furniture, lamps, etc. in a room or house: *curtains, cushions, and other soft furnishings*

fur·ni·ture 🔑 /ˈfərnɪtʃər/ *noun* [noncount]
tables, chairs, beds, etc.: *They bought some furniture for their new house.* ◆ *All the furniture is very old.* ◆ *The only piece of furniture in the room was a large bed.*

fur·ther 🔑 /ˈfərðər/ *adjective, adverb*
1 more; extra: *Do you have any further questions?* ◆ *I have nothing further to say*
2 at or to a greater distance in time: *You need to plan a little further into the future.*
3 (informal) at or to a greater distance in space: *The hospital is further down the road.* ◆ *We couldn't go any further because the road was closed.* ⊃ SYNONYM **farther** ⊃ Look at the note at **farther**.

fur·ther·more **AWL** /ˈfərðərmɔr/ *adverb* (formal)
also; on top of what has already been written or said: *We will donate money to the disaster fund.*

Furthermore, we will send medical supplies immediately. ⊃ **SYNONYM moreover**

fur·thest form of **far**

fu·ry /ˈfyʊri/ *noun* [*noncount*] (*formal*)
very strong anger: *She was filled with fury.*

fuse /fyuz/ *noun* [*count*]
1 a small wire inside a piece of electrical equipment that stops it from working if too much electricity goes through it
2 a piece of string that is lit to make a bomb explode: *to light the fuse*

fu·sion /ˈfyuʒn/ *noun*
1 [*noncount, singular*] joining different things together to form one: *the fusion of two political systems*
2 [*noncount*] (**PHYSICS**) the process of combining atoms so that they release energy: *nuclear fusion*

fuss¹ /fʌs/ *noun* [*singular, noncount*]
a lot of excitement or worrying about small things that are not important: *He makes a fuss when I'm five minutes late.*
make a fuss over someone to pay a lot of attention to someone: *Grandpa always makes a fuss over me.*

fuss² /fʌs/ *verb* (**fuss·es, fuss·ing, fussed**)
1 to worry and get excited about small things that are not important: *Stop fussing!*

2 to pay too much attention to someone or something: *They were **fussing over** all the details of the party.*

fuss·y /ˈfʌsi/ *adjective* (**fuss·i·er, fuss·i·est**)
caring a lot about small things that are not important, and difficult to please: *Rob is fussy about his food* (= there are many things that he will not eat).

fu·tile /ˈfyutl̩/ *adjective*
A **futile** action has no chance of success: *They made a futile attempt to make him change his mind.*
▶ **fu·til·i·ty** /fyuˈtɪləti/ *noun* [*noncount*]: *the futility of war*

fu·ture¹ 𝄞 /ˈfyutʃər/ *noun*
1 [*singular, count*] the time that will come: *No one knows what will happen **in the future**.* • *The company's future is uncertain.*
2 the future (also **the fu·ture tense** /ðə ˌfyutʃər ˈtɛns/) [*singular*] (**ENGLISH LANGUAGE ARTS**) the form of a verb that shows what will happen after now ⊃ Look at **the past tense**, **present²**(3).

fu·ture² 𝄞 /ˈfyutʃər/ *adjective*
happening or existing in the time that will come: *Have you met John's future wife?*

fuzz·y /ˈfʌzi/ *adjective* (**fuzz·i·er, fuzz·i·est**)
not clear: *The photo was a little fuzzy, but I could still make out my mother in it.*

Gg

G, g /dʒi/ *noun* [*count, noncount*]
1 (*plural* **G's, g's** /dʒiz/) the seventh letter of the English alphabet: *"Girl" begins with a "G."*
2 g abbreviation of **gram**: *It weighs 100 g.*

gadg·et /'gædʒət/ *noun* [*count*]
a small machine or useful tool: *Their kitchen is full of electrical gadgets.*

gain 🖉 /geɪn/ *verb* (gains, gain·ing, gained)
1 to get something that you want or need: *I gained useful experience from that job.*
2 to get more of something: *I've **gained weight** recently.*

gal·ax·y /'gæləksi/ *noun* [*count*] (*plural* **gal·ax·ies**)
a very large group of stars and planets

gale /geɪl/ *noun* [*count*]
a very strong wind: *The trees were blown down in the gale.* ➔ Look at the note at **wind¹**.

gal·ler·y /'gæləri/ *noun* [*count*] (*plural* **gal·ler·ies**)
(**ART**) a place where people can look at or buy art: *an art gallery*

gal·lon 🖉 /'gælən/ *noun* [*count*]
a unit for measuring liquid (=8 pints, or around 3.8 liters). There are four **quarts** in a **gallon**.

gal·lop /'gæləp/ *verb* (gal·lops, gal·lop·ing, gal·loped)
When a horse **gallops**, it runs very fast: *The horses galloped around the field.*

gam·ble /'gæmbl/ *verb* (gam·bles, gam·bling, gam·bled)
1 to try to win money by playing games that need luck: *He gambled a lot of money on the last race.*
2 to take a risk, hoping that something will happen: *We **gambled on** the weather staying fine.*
▶ **gam·ble** *noun* [*count*]
something that you do without knowing if you will win or lose: *We **took a gamble**, and it paid off (= was successful).*
▶ **gam·bler** /'gæmblər/ *noun* [*count*]: *He was a gambler all his life.*

gam·bling /'gæmblɪŋ/ *noun* [*noncount*]
the activity of trying to win money by playing games that need luck: *He had heavy gambling debts.*

game 🖉 /geɪm/ *noun*
1 [*count*] something you play that has rules: *How about a **game** of tennis?* • *Let's play a **game**!* • *computer games*
2 [*noncount*] wild animals or birds that people kill for sport or food

game show /'geɪm ʃoʊ/ *noun* [*count*]
a television program in which people play games or answer questions to win prizes

gang¹ /gæŋ/ *noun* [*count*]
1 an organized group of criminals: *a **gang of** criminals*
2 a group of young people who spend a lot of time together and often cause trouble or fight against other groups: *street gangs*
3 (*informal*) a group of friends: *The whole gang is coming tonight.*

gang² /gæŋ/ *verb* (gangs, gang·ing, ganged)
gang up on or **against someone** to join together in a group to hurt or frighten someone: *At school the older boys ganged up on him and called him names.*

gang·ster /'gæŋstər/ *noun* [*count*]
a member of a group of criminals

gap /gæp/ *noun* [*count*]
a space in something or between two things; a space where something should be: *The goats got out through a **gap in** the fence.* • *Leave a **gap between** your car and the next one.*

gape /geɪp/ *verb* (gapes, gap·ing, gaped)
to look at someone or something with your mouth open because you are surprised: *She gaped at me in astonishment.*

gap·ing /'geɪpɪŋ/ *adjective*
wide open: *There was a gaping hole in the fence.*

ga·rage /gə'rɑʒ/ *noun* [*count*]
1 a building where you keep your car
2 a place where vehicles are repaired

ga·rage sale /gə'rɑʒ ˌseɪl/ *noun* [*count*]
a sale in someone's yard or **GARAGE** of used things that people do not want anymore: *I bought this old bike at a garage sale.* ➔ Look at **yard sale**.

gar·bage 🖉 /'gɑrbɪdʒ/ *noun* [*noncount*]
1 things that you do not want anymore; waste material: *Our garbage is picked up every Monday.*
2 the place where you put waste material: *Please **throw** your wrappers **in the garbage**.*
3 (*informal*) something that you think is bad, stupid, or wrong: *I don't know why you watch that garbage on TV.* • *You're talking garbage!* ➔ **SYNONYM** trash

gar·bage can
/'gɑrbɪdʒ ˌkæn/ *noun* [*count*]
a large container for garbage that you keep outside your house ➔ **SYNONYM** **trash can**

garbage can

ə **about**　y **yes**　w **woman**　t̬ **butter**　eɪ **say**　aɪ **five**　ɔɪ **boy**　aʊ **now**　oʊ **go**

gar·bage man /ˈgɑrbɪdʒ ˌmæn/ *noun* [count]
(*plural* **gar·bage men** /ˈgɑrbɪdʒ ˌmɛn/)
a man whose job is to take away the garbage from people's GARBAGE CANS

gar·bage truck /ˈgɑrbɪdʒ trʌk/ *noun* [count]
a large vehicle for collecting garbage from people's GARBAGE CANS

gar·den 🔑 /ˈgɑrdn/ *noun* [count]
a piece of land by your house where you can grow flowers, fruit, and vegetables: *I'm growing tomatoes in my garden.* • *a flower garden*
▶ **gar·den** *verb* (**gar·dens, gar·den·ing, gar·dened**)
to work in a garden: *My mother was gardening all weekend.*
▶ **gar·den·ing** /ˈgɑrdnɪŋ/ *noun* [noncount]
the work that you do in a garden to keep it looking attractive

gar·den·er /ˈgɑrdnər/ *noun* [count]
a person who works in a garden

gar·lic /ˈgɑrlɪk/ *noun* [noncount]
a plant like a small onion with a strong taste and smell, which you use in cooking

garlic

clove

gar·ment /ˈgɑrmənt/ *noun* [count] (*formal*)
a piece of clothing

gas 🔑 /gæs/ *noun* (*plural* **gas·es**)
1 [count, noncount] (**GENERAL SCIENCE**) a substance like air that is not a solid or a liquid: *Hydrogen and oxygen are gases.*
2 [noncount] a **gas** with a strong smell, which you burn to make heat: *Does your clothes dryer run on gas or electricity?* • *a gas stove*
3 [noncount] a liquid that you put in a car to make it go: *I hope the car doesn't run out of gas.* ⊃
SYNONYM gasoline
4 **the gas** [singular] (*informal*) = **gas pedal**: *Step on the gas, we're late!*

gas·e·ous /ˈgæsiəs; ˈgæʃəs/ *adjective*
(**CHEMISTRY**) like gas, or containing a gas: *a gaseous mixture*

gas·o·line /ˌgæsəˈlin/ *noun* [noncount]
a liquid that you put in a car to make it go ⊃
SYNONYM gas

gasp /gæsp/ *verb* (**gasps, gasp·ing, gasped**)
to breathe in quickly and noisily through your mouth: *She gasped in surprise when she heard the news.* • *He was gasping for air when they pulled him out of the water.*
▶ **gasp** *noun* [count]: *a gasp of surprise*

gas ped·al /ˈgæs ˌpɛdl/ *noun* [count] (also *informal* **the gas**)
the part of a vehicle that you press with your foot when you want it to go faster: *Take your foot off the gas pedal and step on the brake.* ⊃
SYNONYM accelerator

gas sta·tion /ˈgæs ˌsteɪʃn/ *noun* [count]
a place where you can buy fuel and other things for your car

gate 🔑 /geɪt/ *noun* [count]
1 a thing like a door in a fence or wall, which opens so that you can go through: *Please close the gate.*
2 a door in an airport that you go through to reach the airplane: *Please go to gate 15.*

gath·er /ˈgæðər/ *verb* (**gath·ers, gath·er·ing, gath·ered**)
1 to come together in a group: *We all gathered around to listen to the teacher.*
2 to bring together things that are in different places: *Can you gather up all the books and papers?*
3 to believe or understand something: *I gather that you know my sister.*

gath·er·ing /ˈgæðərɪŋ/ *noun* [count]
a time when people come together; a meeting: *a family gathering* • *There was a large gathering outside the stadium.*

gauge¹ /geɪdʒ/ *noun* [count]
an instrument that measures how much of something there is: *Where is the gas gauge in this car?*

gauge² /geɪdʒ/ *verb* (**gaug·es, gaug·ing, gauged**)
to judge, calculate, or guess something: *It was hard to gauge the mood of the audience.*

gave form of **give**

gay /geɪ/ *adjective*
1 attracted to people of the same sex ⊃ **SYNONYM homosexual**
2 an old-fashioned word meaning happy and full of fun

gaze /geɪz/ *verb* (**gaz·es, gaz·ing, gazed**)
to look at someone or something for a long time: *She sat and gazed out of the window.* • *He was gazing at her.*
▶ **gaze** *noun* [singular]

GDP /ˌdʒi di ˈpi/ *abbreviation*
(**BUSINESS**) the total value of all the goods and services produced by a country in one year. GDP is short for "gross domestic product." ⊃ Look at **GNP**.

gear /gɪr/ *noun*
1 [count] the parts in a car engine or a bicycle that control how fast the wheels turn around:

*You'll need to **change gears** to get up the hill in this car.*
2 [noncount] special clothes or equipment that you need for a job or sport: *camping gear*

gear·shift /'gɪrʃɪft/ *noun* [count]
a stick that you use for changing GEARS(1) in a car or other vehicle ⊃ Look at the picture at **steering wheel**.

GED /ˌdʒi i 'di/ *noun* [count]
an official certificate that people who did not finish high school can get, after taking a special test. **GED** is short for "General Equivalency Diploma.": *She dropped out of school when she was 16 but got her GED a few years later.*

gee /dʒi/ *exclamation*
a word that you say to show surprise, pleasure, etc.: *Gee, what a great idea!*

geek /gik/ *noun* [count] (informal)
a person who spends a lot of time on a particular interest and who is not popular or fashionable: *a computer geek* ⊃ SYNONYM **nerd**

geese plural of **goose**

gel /dʒɛl/ *noun* [count, noncount]
a thick substance that is between a liquid and a solid: *hair gel* • *shower gel*

gem /dʒɛm/ *noun* [count]
a stone that is very valuable and can be made into jewelry ⊃ SYNONYM **jewel**

gen·der AWL /'dʒɛndər/ *noun* [count, noncount]
1 (BIOLOGY) the fact of being male or female
2 (ENGLISH LANGUAGE ARTS) (in some languages) the division of nouns and some other words into MASCULINE and FEMININE; one of these types

gene /dʒin/ *noun* [count]
(BIOLOGY) one of the parts inside a cell that control what a living thing will be like. **Genes** are passed from parents to children: *The color of your eyes is decided by your genes.* ⊃ Look at **genetic**.

gen·er·al¹ /'dʒɛnərəl/ *adjective*
1 of, by, or for most people or things: *Is this parking lot **for general use**?*
2 not in detail: *Can you give me a **general idea** of what the book is about?*
in general usually: *I don't eat much meat in general.*

gen·er·al² /'dʒɛnərəl/ *noun* [count]
a very important officer in the army

gen·er·al·ize /'dʒɛnrəlaɪz/ *verb* (gen·er·al·iz·es, gen·er·al·iz·ing, gen·er·al·ized)
to form an opinion or make a statement using only a small amount of information: *You can't generalize about American culture based on one trip to New York.*
▶ **gen·er·al·i·za·tion** /ˌdʒɛnrələ'zeɪʃn/ *noun* [count, noncount]: *You shouldn't make*

generalizations until you know more about the subject.

gen·er·al knowl·edge /ˌdʒɛnərəl 'nɑlɪdʒ/ *noun* [noncount]
what you know about a lot of different things

gen·er·al·ly /'dʒɛnərəli/ *adverb*
usually; mostly: *I generally get up at about eight o'clock.*

gen·er·ate AWL /'dʒɛnəreɪt/ *verb* (gen·er·ates, gen·er·at·ing, gen·er·at·ed)
to make something such as heat or electricity: *Power plants generate electricity.*

gen·er·a·tion AWL /ˌdʒɛnə'reɪʃn/ *noun* [count]
all the people in a family, group, or country who were born at around the same time: *This photo shows three generations of my family.* • *The **younger generation** doesn't seem to be interested in politics.*

gen·er·a·tor /'dʒɛnəˌreɪtər/ *noun* [count]
(PHYSICS) a machine that produces electricity

gen·er·os·i·ty /ˌdʒɛnə'rɑsəti/ *noun* [noncount]
liking to give things to other people

gen·er·ous /'dʒɛnərəs/ *adjective*
always ready to give people things or to spend money: *a generous gift* • *It was **generous of** your parents to pay for the meal.* ⊃ ANTONYM **stingy**
▶ **gen·er·ous·ly** /'dʒɛnərəsli/ *adverb*: *Please give generously.*

ge·net·ic /dʒə'nɛtɪk/ *adjective*
(BIOLOGY) connected with the parts in the cells of living things (called GENES) that control what a person, animal, or plant will be like: *The disease has a genetic origin.*

ge·net·i·cal·ly mod·i·fied /dʒəˌnɛtɪkli 'mɑdəfaɪd/ *adjective* (abbreviation **GM**)
(BIOLOGY) (used about food and plants) grown from cells whose GENES (= the parts containing information) have been changed: *genetically modified crops*

ge·net·ic en·gi·neer·ing /dʒəˌnɛtɪk ˌɛndʒə'nɪrɪŋ/ *noun* [noncount]
(BIOLOGY) the science of changing the way a person, an animal, or a plant develops, by changing the information in its GENES (= the parts containing information)

ge·net·ics /dʒə'nɛtɪks/ *noun* [noncount]
(BIOLOGY) the scientific study of the way that the development of living things is controlled by qualities that have been passed on from parents to children ⊃ Look at **gene**.

ge·nie /'dʒini/ *noun* [count]
a spirit with magic powers, especially one that lives in a bottle or a lamp

gen·ius /'dʒinyəs/ *noun* [count] (plural gen·ius·es)
a very intelligent person: *Einstein was a genius.*

gen·re /ˈʒɑnrə/ *noun* [*count*]
(**ENGLISH LANGUAGE ARTS**) a particular type of writing, art, movie, or music: *The crime thriller is a very popular literary genre.*

gen·tle /ˈdʒɛntl/ *adjective* (**gen·tler**, **gen·tlest**)
1 quiet and kind: *Be gentle with the baby.* • *a gentle voice*
2 not strong or unpleasant: *It was a hot day, but there was a gentle breeze* (= a soft wind).
▶ **gen·tly** /ˈdʒɛntli/ *adverb*: *She stroked the kitten very gently.*

gen·tle·man /ˈdʒɛntəlmən/ *noun* [*count*]
(*plural* **gen·tle·men** /ˈdʒɛntəlmən/)
1 a man who is polite and kind to other people: *He's a real gentleman.*
2 (*formal*) a polite way of saying "man": *There is a gentleman here to see you.* • *Ladies and gentlemen …* (= at the beginning of a speech) ⊃ Look at **lady**.

gen·u·ine /ˈdʒɛnyuən/ *adjective*
real and true: *The painting was found to be genuine.* ⊃ **ANTONYM fake**
▶ **gen·u·ine·ly** /ˈdʒɛnyuənli/ *adverb*
really: *Do you think he's genuinely sorry?*

ge·og·ra·phy /dʒiˈɑgrəfi/ *noun* [*noncount*]
(**GEOGRAPHY**) the study of the earth and everything on it, such as mountains, rivers, land, and people
▶ **ge·o·graph·i·cal** /ˌdʒiəˈgræfɪkl/ *adjective*: *There is a list of geographical names* (= names of countries, oceans, etc.) *at the back of this dictionary.*

ge·ol·o·gy /dʒiˈɑlədʒi/ *noun* [*noncount*]
(**GENERAL SCIENCE**) the study of rocks and soil and how they were made
▶ **ge·o·log·i·cal** /dʒiəˈlɑdʒɪkl/ *adjective*: *a geological survey*
▶ **ge·ol·o·gist** /dʒiˈɑlədʒɪst/ *noun* [*count*]
a person who studies or knows a lot about **geology**

ge·om·e·try /dʒiˈɑmətri/ *noun* [*noncount*]
(**MATH**) the study in mathematics of things like lines, shapes, and angles
▶ **ge·o·met·ric** /dʒiəˈmɛtrɪk/ *adjective*
connected with **geometry**; consisting of regular shapes and lines: *a geometric design*

ge·ra·ni·um /dʒəˈreɪniəm/ *noun* [*count*]
a plant with red, white, or pink flowers

germ /dʒərm/ *noun* [*count*]
(**BIOLOGY**, **HEALTH**) a very small living thing that can make you sick: *flu germs*

ger·mi·nate /ˈdʒərməneɪt/ *verb* (**ger·mi·nates**, **ger·mi·nat·ing**, **ger·mi·nat·ed**)
(**BIOLOGY**) (used about a seed of a plant) to start growing; to cause a seed to do this
▶ **ger·mi·na·tion** /ˌdʒərməˈneɪʃn/ *noun* [*noncount*]

ger·und /ˈdʒɛrənd/ *noun* [*count*]
(**ENGLISH LANGUAGE ARTS**) a noun, ending in -ing, which has been made from a verb: *In the sentence "His hobby is fishing," "fishing" is a gerund.*

ges·ture¹ /ˈdʒɛstʃər/ *noun* [*count*]
a movement of your head or hand to show how you feel or what you want: *The boy made a rude gesture before running off.*

ges·ture² /ˈdʒɛstʃər/ *verb*
to point at something or make a sign to someone: *She asked me to sit down and* **gestured toward** *a chair.*

get /gɛt/ *verb* (**gets**, **get·ting**, **got** /gɑt/, **has got·ten** /ˈgɑtn/)
1 to become: *He is getting fat.* • *Mom got angry.* • *It's getting cold.*
2 to receive something: *I got a lot of presents for my birthday.*
3 to go and bring back someone or something: *Jenny will get the children from school.*
4 to buy or take something: *Will you get some bread when you go shopping?*
5 a word that you use with part of another verb to show that something happens to someone or something: *She got caught by the police.*
6 to start to have an illness: *I think I'm getting a cold.*
7 to arrive somewhere: *We* **got to** *Chicago at ten o'clock.*
8 to travel on something, such as a train or a bus: *I didn't walk – I got the bus.*
9 to make someone do something: *I* **got** *Peter* **to** *help me.*
10 to understand or hear something: *I don't* **get** *the joke.* • *Sorry, I didn't get that. Can you repeat what you just said?*
11 to have the opportunity to do something: *She was at the party, but I never* **got to** *speak to her.*
get ahead to become more successful in something, especially your work: *She wants to get ahead in her career.* • *He soon got ahead of the others in his class.*
get along words that you use to say or ask how well someone does something: *Josh is getting along well at school.*
get along with someone to live or work in a friendly way with someone: *We get along well with our neighbors.*
get around to something; **get around to doing something** to find the time to do something: *I haven't gotten around to e-mailing him yet.*
get away to manage to leave or escape from someone or a place: *The thieves got away in a stolen car.*
get away with something to do something bad and not be punished for it: *He lied but he got away with it.*

get back to return: *When did you get back from your vacation?*

get behind to fail to do something, pay something, etc. on time: *We got behind on our rent.*

get in to reach a place: *My train got in at 7:15.* ⊃ **SYNONYM arrive**

get in; get into something to climb into a car: *Tom got into the car.*

get off; get off something to leave something such as a train, bus, or bicycle: *Where did you get off the bus?*

get on to become old: *My grandfather is getting on – he's almost 80.*

get on; get onto something to climb onto a bus, train, or bicycle: *I got on the train.*

get out; get out of something to leave a car: *I opened the door and got out.*

get out of something; get out of doing something to not do something that you do not like: *I'll go swimming with you if I can get out of cleaning my room.*

get something out to take something from the place where it was: *She opened her bag and got out a pen.*

get over something to become well or happy again after you have been sick or sad: *He still hasn't gotten over his wife's death.*

get through to be able to speak to someone on the telephone: *I tried to call Kate, but I couldn't get through.*

get through something to use or finish a certain amount of something: *I got through a lot of work today.*

get together to meet; to come together in a group: *The whole family got together for Christmas.*

get up
1 to stand up: *He got up to let an elderly lady sit down.*
2 to get out of bed: *What time did you get up this morning?*

get up to something to reach a particular place, for example in a book: *We've gotten up to page 180.*

ⓘ **STYLE**

Got is sometimes used in the phrase **have got**. This is used in spoken English and means "to have": *She's got brown hair.* • *I've got a toothache.* Look at the entry for **have** for more examples.

---

ghet·to /ˈgɛt̮oʊ/ *noun* [count] (plural **ghet·tos** or **ghet·toes**)
a part of a city where many poor people live

ghost /goʊst/ *noun* [count]
the form of a dead person that a living person thinks they see: *Do you believe in ghosts?*

▶ **ghost·ly** /ˈgoʊstli/ *adjective* (**ghost·li·er**, **ghost·li·est**): *ghostly noises*

gi·ant¹ /ˈdʒaɪənt/ *noun* [count]
(in stories) a very big, tall person

gi·ant² /ˈdʒaɪənt/ *adjective*
very big: *a giant insect*

gift /gɪft/ *noun* [count]
1 something that you give to or get from someone: *This week's magazine comes with a special free gift.* ⊃ **SYNONYM present**
2 the natural ability to do something well: *She has a gift for languages.* ⊃ **SYNONYM talent**

gift·ed /ˈgɪftəd/ *adjective*
very intelligent, or having a strong natural ability: *Our school has a gifted and talented program.* • *a gifted musician*

gig·a·byte /ˈgɪgəbaɪt/ (abbreviation **GB**) *noun* [count]
(**COMPUTERS**) a unit of computer memory, equal to about a billion **BYTES** (= small units of information) ⊃ Look at **kilobyte**, **megabyte**.

gi·gan·tic /dʒaɪˈgæntɪk/ *adjective*
very big: *gigantic trees*

gig·gle /ˈgɪgl/ *verb* (**gig·gles**, **gig·gling**, **gig·gled**)
to laugh in a silly way: *The children couldn't stop giggling.*
▶ **gig·gle** *noun* [count]: *There was a giggle from the back of the class.*

gill /gɪl/ *noun* [count]
(**BIOLOGY**) the part on each side of a fish that it breathes through ⊃ Look at the picture at **fish**.

gin·ger /ˈdʒɪndʒər/ *noun* [noncount]
a plant with a hot strong taste, which is used in cooking: *ground ginger*

gin·ger ale /ˈdʒɪndʒər ˌeɪl/ *noun* [count, noncount]
a drink with bubbles in it that does not contain alcohol and is made with **GINGER**; a bottle or glass of this drink

gin·ger·bread /ˈdʒɪndʒərbrɛd/ *noun* [noncount]
a type of cookie or cake made with **GINGER**: *a gingerbread man* (= in the shape of a person)

gi·raffe /dʒəˈræf/ *noun* [count]
a big animal from Africa with a very long neck and long legs

girl /gərl/ *noun* [count]
a female child; a young woman: *They have three children, two girls and a boy.* • *I lived in this house as a girl.*

girl·friend /ˈgərlfrɛnd/ *noun* [count]
1 a girl or woman who someone has a romantic relationship with: *Do you have a girlfriend?*
2 a girl or woman's female friend: *I had lunch with a girlfriend.*

---

the Girl Scouts /ðə ˈgərl ˌskaʊts/ *noun* [singular]
a special club for girls, which does a lot of
activities with them and teaches them useful
skills
▶ **Girl Scout** *noun* [count]
a girl who is a member of **the Girl Scouts**

give 🔑 /gɪv/ *verb* (**gives**, **giv·ing**, **gave** /geɪv/,
has **giv·en** /ˈgɪvn/)
1 to let someone have something: *She gave me
a watch for my birthday.* ◆ *I **gave** my ticket **to** the
man at the door.* ◆ *Give the letter to your mother
after you read it.*
2 to make a sound or movement: *Jo gave me an
angry look.* ◆ *He gave a shout.* ◆ *She gave him a
kiss.*
3 to make someone have or feel something:
That noise is giving me a headache. ◆ *Whatever
gave you that idea?*
4 to perform something in public: *The visiting
professor gave a very interesting lecture.*
give something away to give something to
someone without getting money for it: *I gave all
my old clothes away.*
give someone back something; **give
something back to someone** to return
something to someone: *Can you give me back
that book I lent you?*
give in to accept or agree to something that you
did not want to accept or agree to: *My parents
finally gave in and said I could go to the party.*
give something out to give something to a lot
of people: *Could you give out these books to the
class, please?*
give up to stop trying to do something: *I give
up. What's the answer?*
give something up to stop doing or having
something: *He's trying to give up smoking.*

giv·en name /ˈgɪvən neɪm/ another word for **first
name** ⊃ Look at the note at **name**¹.

gla·cier /ˈgleɪʃər/ *noun* [count]
(**GEOGRAPHY**) a large area of ice that moves
slowly down a mountain

glad /glæd/ *adjective*
happy about something: *He was **glad** to see us.* ⊃
SYNONYM pleased
▶ **glad·ly** /ˈglædli/ *adverb*
If you do something **gladly**, you are happy to do
it: *I'll gladly help you.*

Word building

- You are usually **glad** or **pleased** about a
  particular event or situation: *I'm glad he's
  feeling better.* ◆ *I'm pleased to say that you
  passed your exam.*
- You use **happy** to describe a state of mind:
  I always feel happy when the sun is shining.
  You also use **happy** before a noun: *a happy
  child.*

glam·or·ous /ˈglæmərəs/ *adjective*
attractive in an exciting way: *a glamorous model*
◆ *Making movies is less glamorous than people
think.*

glam·our (also **glam·or**) /ˈglæmər/ *noun*
[noncount]
the quality of seeming to be more exciting and
attractive than ordinary things and people:
*Young people are attracted by the glamour of city
life.*

glance¹ /glæns/ *verb* (**glanc·es**, **glanc·ing**,
glanced)
to look quickly at someone or something: *Sue
glanced at her watch.*

glance² /glæns/ *noun* [count]
a quick look: *a **glance at** the newspaper*
at a glance immediately; with only a quick
look: *I could see at a glance that he was sick.*

gland /glænd/ *noun* [count]
(**BIOLOGY**) a small part inside your body that
produces a chemical substance for your body to
use: *sweat glands* ◆ *I have a sore throat and
swollen glands.*

glare¹ /glɛr/ *verb* (**glares**, **glar·ing**, **glared**)
1 to shine with a bright light that hurts your
eyes: *The sun glared down.*
2 to look at someone in an angry way: *He **glared**
at the children.*

glare² /glɛr/ *noun*
1 [noncount] strong light that hurts your eyes: *the
glare of the car's headlights*
2 [count] a long, angry look: *I tried to say
something, but he gave me a glare.*

glar·ing /ˈglɛrɪŋ/ *adjective*
1 A **glaring** light is very bright and hurts your
eyes: *a glaring white light*
2 very bad and easy to notice: *The article was
full of glaring mistakes.*

glass 🔑 /glæs/ *noun* (*plural* **glass·es**)
1 [noncount] hard material that you can see
through. Bottles and windows are made of
glass: *I cut myself on some broken glass.* ◆ *a glass
jar*
2 [count] a thing made of glass that you drink
from: *Could I have **a glass of** milk, please?* ◆ *a
wine glass*

glass·es 🔑 /ˈglæsəz/
noun [plural]
two pieces of glass or
plastic (called **LENSES**)
in a frame, which
people wear over
their eyes to help
them see better: *Does
she wear glasses?* ⊃ Look at **sunglasses**.

glasses

frame

lens

a pair of glasses

Grammar

- Be careful! **Glasses** is a plural noun so you cannot say "a glasses."
- Instead, you can say: *I need a new pair of glasses* or: *I need some new glasses.*

gleam /glim/ *verb* (gleams, gleam·ing, gleamed)
to shine with a soft light: *The moonlight gleamed on the lake.*
▸ **gleam** *noun* [*count, usually singular*]: *I could see a gleam of light through the trees.*

glee /gli/ *noun* [*noncount*]
a feeling of happiness, especially when something bad happens to someone else: *She couldn't hide her glee when her rival came last.*

glide /glaɪd/ *verb* (glides, glid·ing, glid·ed)
1 to move smoothly and quietly: *The dancers glided across the floor.*
2 to fly in a GLIDER: *I always wanted to go gliding.*

glid·er /ˈglaɪdər/ *noun* [*count*]
an airplane without an engine

glim·mer /ˈglɪmər/ *noun* [*count*]
1 a small, weak light
2 a small sign of something: *There's still a glimmer of hope.*
▸ **glim·mer** *verb* (glim·mers, glim·mer·ing, glim·mered): *A light glimmered in the distance.*

glimpse /glɪmps/ *noun* [*count*]
a view of someone or something that is quick and not clear: *I caught a glimpse of myself in the mirror.*
▸ **glimpse** *verb* (glimps·es, glimps·ing, glimpsed): *I just glimpsed him in the crowd.*

glis·ten /ˈglɪsn/ *verb* (glis·tens, glis·ten·ing, glis·tened)
(used about wet surfaces) to shine: *His eyes glistened with tears.*

glitch /glɪtʃ/ *noun* [*count*] (*plural* glitch·es)
(*informal*)
a small problem or fault that stops something from working correctly: *A software glitch caused my computer to crash.*

glit·ter /ˈglɪt̮ər/ *verb* (glit·ters, glit·ter·ing, glit·tered)
to shine with a lot of small flashes of bright light: *The broken glass glittered in the sun.*
▸ **glit·ter** *noun* [*noncount*]: *the glitter of jewels*

glit·ter·ing /ˈglɪt̮ərɪŋ/ *adjective*
1 shining with a lot of small flashes of bright light
2 very successful and exciting: *a glittering career*

gloat /gloʊt/ *verb* (gloats, gloat·ing, gloat·ed)
to show that you are happy about your own success or someone else's failure: *She is still gloating over her victory.*

glob·al 🔑 **AWL** /ˈgloʊbl/ *adjective*
of or about the whole world: *Pollution is a global problem.*
▸ **glob·al·ly** **AWL** /ˈgloʊbəli/ *adverb*: *We need to start thinking globally.*

glob·al·i·za·tion **AWL** /ˌgloʊbələˈzeɪʃn/ *noun*
[*noncount*]
(**BUSINESS**) the fact that different cultures and economic systems are becoming similar because of the influence of large international companies and of improved communications: *the globalization of world trade*

glob·al warm·ing /ˌgloʊbl ˈwɔrmɪŋ/ *noun*
[*noncount*]
the fact that the earth's atmosphere is getting hotter because of increases in certain gases ⊃ Look at **the greenhouse effect**.

globe **AWL** /gloʊb/ *noun*
1 [*count*] a round object with a map of the world on it
2 the globe [*singular*] the world: *He's traveled all over the globe.*

gloom /glum/ *noun* [*noncount*]
1 a state when it is almost completely dark: *It was hard to see anything in the gloom.*
2 a feeling of being sad and without hope: *The news brought deep gloom to the community.*

gloom·y /ˈglumi/ *adjective* (gloom·i·er, gloom·i·est)
1 dark and sad: *What a gloomy day!*
2 sad and without hope: *He's feeling very gloomy because he can't get a job.*
▸ **gloom·i·ly** /ˈgluməli/ *adverb*: *She looked gloomily out of the window at the rain.*

glo·ri·ous /ˈglɔriəs/ *adjective*
1 (*formal*) famous and full of GLORY: *a glorious history*
2 wonderful or beautiful: *The weather was glorious.*

glo·ry /ˈglɔri/ *noun* [*noncount*]
1 FAME (= being known by many people) and respect that you get when you do great things: *The winning team came home covered in glory.*
2 great beauty: *Fall is the best time to see the forest in all its glory.*

glos·sa·ry /ˈglɑsəri/ *noun* [*count*] (*plural* glos·sa·ries)
(**ENGLISH LANGUAGE ARTS**) a list of difficult words and their meanings, especially at the end of a book

gloss·y /ˈglɑsi/ *adjective* (gloss·i·er, gloss·i·est)
smooth and shiny: *glossy hair*

glove /glʌv/ *noun* [*count*]

gloves

glove   mitten

a thing that you wear to keep your hand warm or safe: *I need a new **pair of gloves**.* ◆ *rubber gloves*

glow /gloʊ/ *verb* (glows, glow·ing, glowed)

to send out soft light or heat without flames or smoke: *His cigarette glowed in the dark.*
▶ **glow** *noun* [*singular*]: *the glow of the sky at sunset*

glow·ing /ˈgloʊɪŋ/ *adjective*

saying that someone or something is very good: *His teacher wrote a glowing report about his work.*

glue¹ /glu/ *noun* [*noncount*]

a thick liquid that you use for sticking things together ⊃ Look at the picture at **stationery**.

glue² /glu/ *verb* (glues, glu·ing, glued)

to stick one thing to another thing with GLUE: *Glue the two pieces of wood **together**.*

glued to something (*informal*) giving all your attention to something and not wanting to leave it: *On election night we were all glued to the TV.*

glum /glʌm/ *adjective* (glum·mer, glum·mest)

sad and quiet: *Why are you looking so glum?*
▶ **glum·ly** /ˈglʌmli/ *adverb*

GM /ˌdʒi ˈɛm/ short for **genetically modified**: *GM crops*

gnaw /nɔ/ *verb* (gnaws, gnaw·ing, gnawed)

to bite something for a long time: *The dog was gnawing on a bone.*

GNP /ˌdʒi ɛn ˈpi/ *abbreviation*

(**BUSINESS**) the total value of everything that is produced by a country in one year, including the money earned from foreign countries. **GNP** is short for "gross national product." ⊃ Look at **GDP**.

go¹ /goʊ/ *verb* (goes, go·ing, went /wɛnt/, has gone /gɔn; gɑn/)

1 to move from one place to another: *I went to Boston by train.* ◆ *It's time to **go home**.* ◆ *Her new car goes very fast.* ⊃ Look at the note at **been**.
2 to travel to a place to do something: *Do you want to go shopping?* ◆ *Are you **going to** Dave's party?* ◆ *I'll go make some coffee.* ◆ *They went on vacation.*
3 to leave a place: *I have to go now – it's four o'clock.*
4 to lead to a place: *Does this road **go to** the airport?*
5 to have as its place: *"Where do these plates go?" "In that cabinet."*

6 to happen in a certain way: *How is your new job **going**?* ◆ *The week went very quickly.*
7 to become: *He's going bald.*
8 to make a certain sound: *Cows go "moo."*
9 to disappear: *My headache has gone.*
10 to be or look good with something else: *Does this sweater **go with** my skirt?* ◆ *I don't think those two colors go well **together**.* ⊃ SYNONYM **match**

be going to
1 words that show what you plan to do in the future: *Joe's going to cook dinner tonight.*
2 words that you use when you are sure that something will happen in the future: *It's going to rain.*

go ahead to begin or continue to do something: *"Can I borrow your pen?" "Sure, go ahead."*

go around to be enough for everyone: *Is there enough wine to go around?*

go away to leave a person or place; to leave the place where you live for at least one night: *Go away! I'm doing my homework.* ◆ *They went away for the weekend.*

go back to return to a place where you were before: *We're going back **to** school tomorrow.*

go by to pass: *The holidays went by very quickly.*

go down well to be something that people like: *The movie went down very well **with** the critics.*

Go for it! (*informal*) words you say to encourage someone to try hard to get or achieve something: *Go for it Jonathan! You know you can beat him.*

go off
1 to explode: *A bomb went off in the train station today.*
2 to make a sudden loud noise: *I woke up when the alarm went off.*

go on
1 to happen: *What's going on?*
2 to continue: *She went on writing.*
3 to start working: *I saw the lights go on in the house across the street.*

go out
1 to leave the place where you live or work for a short time, returning on the same day: *I went out for a walk.* ◆ *We're going out tonight.*
2 to stop shining or burning: *The fire's gone out.*
3 to have a romantic relationship with someone: *Evan and Amy just started going out.* ◆ *She's going out **with** a boy from school.*

go over to go to someone's home: *We're going over **to** Jo's this evening.*

go over something to look at or explain something carefully from the beginning to the end: *Go over your work before you hand it in to the teacher.* ⊃ SYNONYM **go through something**

go through something
1 to look in or at something carefully because you want to find something: *I went through all my pockets, but I couldn't find my wallet.*

2 to look at or explain something carefully from the beginning to the end: *Let's go through the plan one more time.* ⊃ SYNONYM **go over something**

3 to have a bad experience: *She went through a difficult time when her mother was sick.*

go up to become higher or more: *The price of gas has gone up again.* ⊃ SYNONYM **rise**

how's it going? (*informal*) how are you?: *"Hey, how's it going?" "I'm good. How about you?"*

to go remaining until something ends: *There were five minutes to go before the end of class.*

go² /goʊ/ *noun* [*count*] (*plural* **goes**) (*informal*)
a time when you try to do something: *I'm not sure if I can fix it, but I'll have a go. ◆ I can't get this bottle open. Can you give it a go?*

be on the go to be very active or busy: *I'm really tired. I've been on the go all day.*

goal ♪ **AWL** /goʊl/ *noun* [*count*]
1 something that you want to do very much: *She has finally achieved her goal of taking part in the Olympics.* ⊃ Look at the note at **purpose**.
2 (SPORTS) the place where the ball, etc. must go to win a point in sports such as SOCCER or HOCKEY: *He kicked the ball into the goal.* ⊃ Look at the picture at **soccer**.
3 (SPORTS) a point that a team wins when the ball, etc. goes into the **goal**: *The Bruins won by three goals to two.*

goal·keep·er /'goʊlˌkipər/ (also *informal* **goal·ie** /'goʊli/) *noun* [*count*]
(SPORTS) a player who tries to stop the ball from going into the goal in a game of SOCCER ⊃ Look at the picture at **soccer**.

goal·tend·er /'goʊlˌtɛndər/ (also *informal* **goal·ie** /'goʊli/) *noun* [*count*]
(SPORTS) a player who tries to stop the ball from going into the goal in a game of HOCKEY ⊃ Look at the picture at **ice hockey**.

goat /goʊt/ *noun*
[*count*]
an animal with horns. People keep **goats** for their milk.

goat

god ♪ /gɑd/ *noun*
(RELIGION)
1 **God** [*singular*] the one great spirit that Christians, Jews, and Muslims believe made the world: *Do you believe in God?*
2 [*count*] a spirit or force that people believe has power over them and nature: *Mars was the Roman god of war.*

god·child /'gɑdtʃaɪld/ *noun* [*count*] (*plural* **god·chil·dren** /'gɑdˌtʃɪldrən/) (also **god·son** /'gɑdsʌn/, **god·daugh·ter** /'gɑdˌdɔtər/)
(RELIGION) a child that a GODPARENT promises to help and teach about the Christian religion

god·dess /'gɑdəs/ *noun* [*count*] (*plural* **god·dess·es**)
(RELIGION) a female god: *Venus was the Roman goddess of love.*

god·par·ent /'gɑdˌpɛrənt/ (also **god·fa·ther** /'gɑdˌfɑðər/, **god·moth·er** /'gɑdˌmʌðər/) *noun* [*count*]
(RELIGION) a person that parents choose to help their child and teach them about the Christian religion

goes form of **go¹**

gog·gles /'gɑglz/
noun [*plural*]
big glasses that you wear so that water, dust, or wind cannot get in your eyes: *I always wear goggles when I swim.*

goggles

go·ing form of **go¹**

gold ♪ /goʊld/ *noun* [*noncount*] (symbol **Au**)
a yellow metal that is very valuable: *Is your ring made of gold? ◆ a gold watch*
▶ **gold** *adjective*
made of gold; with the color of gold: *gold jewelry ◆ gold paint*

gold·en /'goʊldən/ *adjective*
1 made of gold: *a golden crown*
2 with the color of gold: *golden hair*

gold·fish /'goʊldfɪʃ/ *noun* [*count*] (*plural* **gold·fish**)
a small orange fish that people keep as a pet

golf /gɑlf/ *noun* [*noncount*]
(SPORTS) a game that you play by hitting a small ball into holes with a long stick (called a GOLF CLUB): *My mother plays golf on Sundays.*
▶ **golf·er** /'gɑlfər/ *noun* [*count*]: *He's a professional golfer.*

golf course /'gɑlf kɔrs/ *noun* [*count*]
(SPORTS) a large piece of land, covered in grass, where people play GOLF

gone form of **go¹**

good¹ ♪ /gʊd/ *adjective* (**bet·ter**, **best**)
1 done or made very well: *It's a good knife – it cuts very well. ◆ The movie was really good.*
2 pleasant or enjoyable: *Did you have a good time? ◆ The weather was very good.* ⊃ SYNONYM **nice**
3 able to do something well: *She's a good driver. ◆ James is very good at tennis.*
4 kind, or doing the right thing: *It's good of you to help. ◆ The children were very good while you were out.*
5 having a useful or helpful effect: *Fresh fruit and vegetables are good for you.*
6 right or suitable: *This is a good place for a picnic.*

7 a word that you use when you are pleased: *Is everyone here? Good. Now, let's begin.* ⊃ The adverb is **well**.

good² 🔑 /gʊd/ *noun* [*noncount*]
something that is right or helpful: *They know the difference between good and bad.*
be no good; **not be any good** to not be useful: *This sweater isn't any good. It's too small.* • *It's no good asking Mom for money – she doesn't have any.*
do someone good to make someone well or happy: *It will do you good **to** go to bed early tonight.*
for good forever: *She has left home for good.*

good·bye 🔑 /ˌgʊdˈbaɪ/ *exclamation*
a word that you say when someone goes away, or when you go away: *Goodbye! See you tomorrow.* ⊃ Look at **bye**.

good-look·ing /ˌgʊd ˈlʊkɪŋ/ *adjective*
(used about people) nice to look at: *He's a good-looking boy.* ⊃ Look at the note at **attractive**.

good·ness /ˈgʊdnəs/ *noun* [*noncount*]
1 being good or kind
2 something in food that is good for your health: *Fresh vegetables have a lot of goodness in them.*
for goodness' sake words that show anger: *For goodness' sake, hurry up!*
goodness; **my goodness** words that show surprise: *Goodness! What a big cake!*
thank goodness words that show you are happy because a problem or danger has gone away: *Thank goodness it stopped raining.*

good night /ˌgʊd ˈnaɪt/ *exclamation*
words that you say when you leave someone in the evening or when someone is going to bed

goods 🔑 /gʊdz/ *noun* [*plural*]
things that you buy or sell: *That store sells electrical goods.*

goof /guf/ *verb* (goofs, goof·ing, goofed) (*informal*)
goof around to spend your time doing silly things: *We spent the summer just goofing around at the beach.*
goof off to spend your time doing nothing, especially when you should be working: *Stop goofing off and get back to work!*

goose /gus/ *noun*
[*count*] (*plural* **geese** /gis/)
a big bird with a long neck. People keep **geese** on farms for their eggs and meat.

goose

goose·bumps /ˈgusbʌmps/ *noun* [*plural*]
small points or lumps that appear on your skin because you are cold or scared: *I got **goosebumps** when she told me about the attack.*

go·pher /ˈgoʊfər/ *noun* [*count*]
a small animal with brown fur that digs holes in the ground

gopher

gorge /gɔrdʒ/ *noun* [*count*]
(GEOGRAPHY) a narrow valley with sides that go up very quickly (that are STEEP)

gor·geous /ˈgɔrdʒəs/ *adjective*
very good or attractive: *The weather was gorgeous!* • *She looked gorgeous in that dress.*

go·ril·la /gəˈrɪlə/ *noun* [*count*]
an African animal like a very big black MONKEY

gorilla

go·ry /ˈgɔri/ *adjective* (go·ri·er, go·ri·est)
full of violence and blood: *It's the goriest movie I've ever seen.*

gosh /gɑʃ/ *exclamation* (*informal*)
a word that shows surprise: *Gosh! What a big house!*

gos·pel /ˈgɑspl/ *noun*
1 **Gospel** [*count*] (RELIGION) one of the four books in the Bible that describe the life and ideas of Jesus Christ: *the Gospel of St. Matthew*
2 (also **gos·pel mu·sic**) [*noncount*] (MUSIC) a style of religious music that was developed by African-American Christians: *a gospel choir*

gos·sip /ˈgɑsəp/ *noun* [*noncount*]
talk about other people that is often unkind or not true: *Have you heard the latest gossip about her cousin?*
▶ **gos·sip** *verb* (gos·sips, gos·sip·ing, gos·siped): *They were **gossiping about** Karen's new boyfriend.*

got, got·ten forms of **get**

gov·ern 🔑 /ˈgʌvərn/ *verb* (gov·erns, gov·ern·ing, gov·erned)
(**POLITICS**) to officially rule or control a country, or part of a country: *Voters have the right to decide who will govern them.*

gov·ern·ment 🔑 /ˈgʌvərmənt/ *noun* [count]
(**POLITICS**) the group of people who officially rule or control a country: *The federal government will need to approve the project.* • *The government has failed to act.*

Word building

The U.S. Government
- The government in the U.S. is divided into three parts: the **legislative branch**, the **executive branch**, and the **judicial branch**.
- The legislative branch is responsible for making laws. This is the U.S. **Congress**, which is made up of two groups of people: the **Senate** and the **House of Representatives**.
- The executive branch is led by the **president**, and includes the **vice president** and the rest of the **Cabinet** (= other important politicians).
- The judicial branch includes the **Supreme Court**, which is the most important court in the country.

gov·er·nor /ˈgʌvənər/ *noun* [count]
(**POLITICS**) a person who rules a state in the U.S.: *the governor of California*

gown /gaʊn/ *noun* [count]
1 a long dress that a woman wears at a special time: *an evening gown*
2 a long, loose piece of clothing that people wear to do a special job. Judges and doctors sometimes wear **gowns**.

GPA /ˌdʒi pi ˈeɪ/ short for **grade point average**

grab /græb/ *verb* (grabs, grab·bing, grabbed)
to take something in a rough and sudden way: *The thief grabbed her bag and ran away.*

grace /greɪs/ *noun* [noncount]
1 a beautiful way of moving: *She dances with grace.*
2 (**RELIGION**) thanks to God that people say before or after they eat: *Let's say grace.*

grace·ful /ˈgreɪsfl/ *adjective*
A person or thing that is **graceful** moves in a smooth and beautiful way: *a graceful dancer*
▸ **grace·ful·ly** /ˈgreɪsfəli/ *adverb*: *He moves very gracefully.*

gra·cious /ˈgreɪʃəs/ *adjective*
(used about people's behavior) kind and polite: *a gracious smile*
▸ **gra·cious·ly** /ˈgreɪʃəsli/ *adverb*: *She accepted the invitation graciously.*

grade¹ 🔑 **AWL** /greɪd/ *noun* [count]
1 a number or letter that a teacher gives for your work to show how good it is: *She got very good grades on all her exams.*
2 one of the levels in a school, where all the children are the same age: *My sister is in the fifth grade.* ⊃ Look at the note at **elementary school**.
3 the level or quality of something: *We use only high-grade materials.*
make the grade (*informal*) to reach the expected standard; to succeed: *Around 10% of trainees fail to make the grade.*

grade² 🔑 **AWL** /greɪd/ *verb* (grades, grad·ing, grad·ed)
1 to look at the work that a student has done and give it a number or letter to show how good it is: *He stayed up late grading tests.*
2 to sort things or people into sizes or kinds: *The eggs are graded by size.*

grade point av·er·age /ˈgreɪd pɔɪnt ˌævrɪdʒ/ *noun* [count, usually singular] (abbreviation **GPA**)
a number that is calculated from the average of all the grades that a student receives in his or her courses: *Dylan graduated with a GPA of 3.7.*

grade school /ˈgreɪd skul/ *noun* [count, noncount] another word for **elementary school**

gra·di·ent /ˈgreɪdiənt/ *noun* [count]
how much and how quickly a road goes up and down: *This road has a steep gradient.*

grad·u·al /ˈgrædʒuəl/ *adjective*
happening slowly: *There has been a gradual increase in prices.* ⊃ **ANTONYM sudden**

grad·u·al·ly /ˈgrædʒuəli/ *adverb*
slowly, over a long period of time: *Life gradually returned to normal.*

grad·u·ate¹ /ˈgrædʒuət/ *noun* [count]
a person who has finished their studies at a university, college, or school: *a college graduate* • *a high school graduate* • *He's a graduate of Harvard.*

grad·u·ate² /ˈgrædʒueɪt/ *verb* (grad·u·ates, grad·u·at·ing, grad·u·at·ed)
to finish your studies at a school, college, or university and receive an official piece of paper (called a **DIPLOMA**): *I graduated from Rutgers University last year.*

grad·u·ate school /ˈgrædʒuət skul/ *noun* [count]
a part of a university where you can study for a second or higher degree: *I applied to several graduate schools to study for a master's degree in biology.*

grad·u·a·tion /ˌgrædʒuˈeɪʃn/ *noun*
1 [noncount] the act of successfully completing a high school, college, or university degree: *Are you planning to look for a job after graduation?*

2 [*singular*] a ceremony for people who have successfully completed a high school, college, or university degree: *My grandparents came to my high school graduation.*

graf·fi·ti /grəˈfiṭi/ *noun* [*noncount*]
words or pictures that people write or draw on walls: *The walls were covered with graffiti.*

grain 🔑 /greɪn/ *noun*
1 [*noncount*] the seeds of a plant that we eat, for example rice or WHEAT: *The animals are fed on grain.*
2 [*count*] a very small, hard piece of something: *a **grain** of sand* • *a few **grains** of rice*

gram 🔑 /græm/ (abbreviation **g**) *noun* [*count*]
a measure of weight. There are 1,000 **grams** in a **kilogram**: *30g of butter*

gram·mar 🔑 /ˈgræmər/ *noun* [*noncount*]

> ❶ **SPELLING**
> Remember! You spell **grammar** with **AR** at the end, not **ER**.

(**ENGLISH LANGUAGE ARTS**) the rules that tell you how to put words together when you speak or write

gram·mat·i·cal /grəˈmæṭɪkl/ *adjective* (**ENGLISH LANGUAGE ARTS**)
1 connected with grammar: *What is the grammatical rule for making plurals in English?*
2 correct because it follows the rules of grammar: *The phrase "they is happy" is not grammatical.*
▸ **gram·mat·i·cal·ly** /grəˈmæṭɪkli/ *adverb*: *The sentence is grammatically correct.*

grand /grænd/ *adjective* (**grand·er**, **grand·est**)
very big, important, or rich: *They live in a very grand house in the suburbs.*

grand·child 🔑 /ˈɡræntʃaɪld/ *noun* [*count*] (*plural* **grand·chil·dren** /ˈɡræn̩tʃɪldrən/)
the child of your son or daughter

grand·daugh·ter /ˈɡrænˌdɔṭər/ *noun* [*count*]
the daughter of your son or daughter

grand·fa·ther 🔑 /ˈɡrænˌfɑðər/ (also *informal* **grand·pa** /ˈɡrænpɑ; ˈɡræmpɑ/) *noun* [*count*]
the father of your mother or father

grand·moth·er 🔑 /ˈɡrænˌmʌðər/ (also *informal* **grand·ma** /ˈɡrænmɑ; ˈɡræmɑ/) *noun* [*count*]
the mother of your mother or father

grand·par·ent 🔑 /ˈɡrænˌpɛrənt/ *noun* [*count*]
the mother or father of your mother or father

grand·son /ˈɡrænsʌn/ *noun* [*count*]
the son of your son or daughter

grand·stand /ˈɡrændstænd/ *noun* [*count*]
(**SPORTS**) lines of seats, with a roof over them, where you sit to watch a sport

gra·no·la /grəˈnoʊlə/ *noun* [*noncount*]
food made with grains, nuts, etc. that you eat with milk for breakfast

grant¹ **AWL** /grænt/ *verb* (**grants**, **grant·ing**, **grant·ed**) (*formal*)
to give someone what they have asked for: *They granted him a visa to leave the country.*
take someone or **something for granted** to be so used to someone or something that you forget you are lucky to have them: *We tend to take our comfortable lives for granted.*

grant² **AWL** /grænt/ *noun* [*count*]
money that you are given for a special reason: *She receives a research grant* (= to help pay for research).

grape /greɪp/ *noun* [*count*]
a small green or purple fruit that we eat or make into wine: *a bunch of grapes* ⟳ Look at the picture at **fruit**.

grape·fruit /ˈɡreɪpfrut/ *noun* [*count*] (*plural* **grape·fruit** or **grape·fruits**)
a fruit that looks like a big orange, but is yellow ⟳ Look at the picture at **fruit**.

the grape·vine /ðə ˈɡreɪpvaɪn/ *noun* [*singular*]
the way that news is passed from one person to another: *I **heard through the grapevine** that you're getting married.*

graph /ɡræf/ *noun* [*count*]
(**MATH**) a picture that shows how numbers or amounts are different from each other

graph·ic /ˈɡræfɪk/ *adjective*
1 (**ART**) connected with drawings, diagrams, etc.: *She's studying **graphic design**.*
2 clear and giving a lot of detail, especially about something unpleasant: *He gave us a graphic description of the accident.*

graph·ics /ˈɡræfɪks/ *noun* [*plural*]
(**ART**, **COMPUTERS**) drawings, pictures, and diagrams: *computer graphics*

grasp /ɡræsp/ *verb* (**grasps**, **grasp·ing**, **grasped**)
1 to hold something firmly: *Claire grasped my arm to stop herself from falling.*
2 to understand something: *He couldn't grasp what I was saying.*
▸ **grasp** *noun* [*singular, noncount*]: *The ball fell from my grasp.*

grass 🔑 /ɡræs/ *noun* [*noncount*]
a plant with thin green leaves that covers fields and yards. Cows and sheep eat **grass**: *Don't walk on the grass.*
▸ **grass·y** /ˈɡræsi/ *adjective* (**grass·i·er**, **grass·i·est**)
covered with grass

grass·hop·per /ˈgræsˌhɑpər/ *noun* [count]
an insect that can jump high in the air and makes a sound with its back legs

grasshopper

grate /greɪt/ *verb* (grates, grat·ing, grat·ed)
If you **grate** food, you rub it over a metal tool (called a **GRATER**) so that it is in very small pieces: *Can you grate some cheese?* • *grated carrots*

grate·ful /ˈgreɪtfl/ *adjective*
If you are **grateful**, you feel or show thanks to someone: *We are grateful to you for the help you have given us.* ⊃ The noun is **gratitude**. ⊃ **ANTONYM ungrateful**
▸ **grate·ful·ly** /ˈgreɪtfəli/ *adverb*: *She nodded gratefully.*

grat·er /ˈgreɪtər/ *noun* [count]
a kitchen tool with holes in it, which is used to cut food into very small pieces by rubbing it across its surface

grater

grat·i·tude /ˈgrætətud/ *noun* [noncount]
the feeling of wanting to thank someone for something: *We gave David a present to show our gratitude for all his help.*

gra·tu·i·ty /grəˈtuəti/ *noun* [count] (plural **gra·tu·i·ties**) (formal)
a small amount of extra money that you give to someone who serves you, for example in a restaurant ⊃ **SYNONYM tip**

grave¹ /greɪv/ *noun* [count]
a hole in the ground where a dead person's body is buried: *We put flowers on the grave.* ⊃ Look at **tomb**.

grave² /greɪv/ *adjective* (grav·er, grav·est) (formal)
very bad or serious: *The children were in grave danger.*

grav·el /ˈgrævl/ *noun* [noncount]
very small stones that are used for making paths and roads

grave·stone /ˈgreɪvstoʊn/ *noun* [count]
a piece of stone on a **GRAVE¹** that shows the name of the dead person

grave·yard /ˈgreɪvyɑrd/ *noun* [count]
a piece of land, usually near a church, where dead people are buried

grav·i·ty /ˈgrævəti/ *noun* [noncount]
(PHYSICS) the force that pulls everything toward the earth

gra·vy /ˈgreɪvi/ *noun* [noncount]
a hot, brown sauce that you eat with meat

gray /greɪ/ *adjective* (gray·er, gray·est)
with a color like black and white mixed together: *a gray skirt* • *The sky was gray.* • *He's starting to get gray* (= to have gray hair).
▸ **gray** *noun* [count, noncount]: *He was dressed in gray.*

graze /greɪz/ *verb* (graz·es, graz·ing, grazed)
1 to eat grass: *The sheep were grazing in the fields.*
2 to hurt your skin by rubbing it against something rough: *He fell and grazed his arm.*
▸ **graze** *noun* [count]: *She has a graze on her knee.*

grease /gris/ *noun* [noncount]
fat from animals, or any thick substance that is like oil: *You will need very hot water to get the grease off these plates.*

greas·y /ˈgrisi/ *adjective* (greas·i·er, greas·i·est)
covered with or containing a lot of **GREASE**: *Greasy food is not good for you.* • *greasy hair*

great /greɪt/ *adjective* (great·er, great·est)

> **ⓘ PRONUNCIATION**
> The word **great** sounds like **late**.

1 very large: *It's a great pleasure to meet you.*
2 important or special: *Einstein was a great scientist.*
3 very; very good: *He knows a great many people.* • *There's a great big dog in the yard!* • *They are great friends.*
4 very nice or enjoyable: *I had a great weekend.* • *It's great to see you!* ⊃ **SYNONYM wonderful**

great- /greɪt/
a word that you put before other words to show some members of a family. For example, your **great-grandmother** is the mother of your grandmother or grandfather, and your **great-grandchildren** are the grandchildren of your son or daughter.

great·ly /ˈgreɪtli/ *adverb*
very much: *I wasn't greatly surprised to see her there.*

greed /grid/ *noun* [noncount]
the feeling that you want more of something than you need

greed·y /ˈgridi/ *adjective* (greed·i·er, greed·i·est)
A **greedy** person wants or takes more of something than they need: *She's so greedy – she ate all the chocolates!*
▸ **greed·i·ly** /ˈgridəli/ *adverb*

green¹ /grin/ *adjective* (green·er, green·est)
1 with the color of leaves and grass: *My brother has green eyes.* • *a dark green shirt*
2 covered with grass or other plants: *green fields*

3 connected with protecting the environment or the natural world: *green products* (= that do not damage the environment)

green² /grin/ *noun* [count, noncount]
the color of leaves and grass: *She was dressed in green.*

green card /'grin kɑrd/ *noun* [count]
an official card that shows that someone from another country is allowed to live and work in the U.S.: *to apply for a green card*

green·house /'grinhaʊs/ *noun* [count]
a building made of glass, where plants grow

the green·house ef·fect /ðə 'grinhaʊs ɪˌfɛkt/ *noun* [singular]
(GEOGRAPHY) the problem of the earth's atmosphere getting warmer all the time because of the harmful gases that go into the air ⊃ Look at **global warming**.

green·house gas /ˌgrinhaʊs 'gæs/ *noun* [count]
(*plural* **green·house gas·es**)
(GEOGRAPHY) one of the harmful gases that are making the earth's atmosphere get warmer

greet /grit/ *verb* (greets, greet·ing, greet·ed)
to welcome someone or say hello when you meet them: *He greeted me with a smile.*

greet·ing /'gritɪŋ/ *noun*
1 [count] friendly words that you say when you meet someone: *"Hello" and "Good morning" are greetings.*
2 **greetings** [plural] friendly words that you write to someone at a special time: *Greetings from sunny Arizona!*

gre·nade /grə'neɪd/ *noun* [count]
a small bomb that can be thrown by hand or fired from a gun: *a hand grenade*

grew form of **grow**

grid /grɪd/ *noun* [count]
lines that cross each other to make squares, for example on a map

grief /grif/ *noun* [noncount]
great sadness, especially because someone has died

grieve /griv/ *verb* (grieves, griev·ing, grieved)
to feel great sadness, especially because someone has died: *She is grieving for her dead child.*

grill¹ /grɪl/ *noun* [count]
a metal frame that you put food on to cook over a fire: *Dad's cooking burgers on the grill outside.*

grill² /grɪl/ *verb* (grills, grill·ing, grilled)
to cook food, such as meat and fish, on metal bars over a fire: *grilled steak* ⊃ Look at the note at **cook¹**.

grim /grɪm/ *adjective* (grim·mer, grim·mest)
1 (used about a person) very serious and not smiling: *a grim expression*
2 (used about a situation) very bad and making you feel worried: *The news is grim.*

grim·ace /'grɪməs/ *verb* (grim·ac·es, grim·ac·ing, grim·aced)
to show on your face that you are angry or that something is hurting you: *She grimaced in pain.*
▶ **grim·ace** *noun* [count]

grin /grɪn/ *verb* (grins, grin·ning, grinned)
to have a big smile on your face: *She grinned at me and waved.*
▶ **grin** *noun* [count]: *He had a big grin on his face.*

grind /graɪnd/ *verb* (grinds, grind·ing, ground /graʊnd/, **has ground**)
to make something into very small pieces or powder by crushing it: *They ground the wheat into flour.* ⊃ Look at **ground³**.

grip /grɪp/ *verb* (grips, grip·ping, gripped)
to hold something tight: *Marie gripped my hand as we crossed the road.*
▶ **grip** *noun* [singular]: *He kept a tight grip on the rope.*

grip·ping /'grɪpɪŋ/ *adjective*
very exciting, in a way that holds your attention: *a gripping adventure movie*

grit /grɪt/ *noun* [noncount]
very small pieces of stone or dirt

griz·zly bear /'grɪzli bɛr/ *noun* [count] (also **griz·zly** *plural* **griz·zlies**)
a large, brown, North American bear

groan /groʊn/ *verb* (groans, groan·ing, groaned)
to make a deep sad sound, for example because you are unhappy or in pain: *"I have a headache," he groaned.*
▶ **groan** *noun* [count]: *She gave a groan, then lay still.*

gro·cer·ies /'groʊsəriz/ *noun* [plural]
food and other things for the home that you buy regularly: *Can you help me unload the groceries from the car, please?*

gro·cer·y store /'groʊsəri ˌstɔr/ *noun* [count]
a store where food and other small things for the home are sold: *We need milk, bread, and detergent. Can you go to the grocery store and get some?*

groom /grum/ *noun* [count]
1 a man on the day of his wedding ⊃ SYNONYM **bridegroom** ⊃ Look at **bride**.
2 a person whose job is to take care of horses

groove /gruv/ *noun* [count]
a long, thin cut in the surface of something hard

grope /groʊp/ *verb* (gropes, grop·ing, groped)
to try to find something by using your hands, when you cannot see: *He groped around for the light switch.*

gross /groʊs/ *adjective* (gross·er, gross·est) (*informal*)
very bad or disgusting: *Yuck! That food smells gross!*

grouch·y /ˈgraʊtʃi/ *adjective* (grouch·i·er, grouch·i·est)
feeling angry and behaving in an angry way: *He's been grouchy all morning.*

ground¹ 🔑 /graʊnd/ *noun*
1 the ground [*singular*] the surface of the earth: *We sat on the ground to eat our picnic.* • *The ground was too dry for the plants to grow.*
2 [*count*] a piece of land that is used for something special: *a burial ground* • *a playground* (= a place where children play)
3 grounds [*plural*] the land around a large building: *the grounds of the hospital*

ground² form of **grind**

ground³ /graʊnd/ *adjective*
cut or crushed into very small pieces or powder: *ground beef* • *ground coffee*

ground floor /ˌgraʊnd ˈflɔr/ *noun* [*count*]
the part of a building that is at the same level as the street: *My office is on the ground floor.* ⊃ SYNONYM **first floor**

group¹ 🔑 /grup/ *noun* [*count*]
1 a number of people or things together: *A group of people were standing outside the store.* • *Our drama group meets every Tuesday.* • *Divide the class into groups of three.*
2 (MUSIC) a number of people who play music together ⊃ SYNONYM **band**

group² /grup/ *verb* (groups, group·ing, grouped)
to put things or people into groups, or to form a group: *Group these words according to their meaning.*

grow 🔑 /groʊ/ *verb* (grows, grow·ing, grew /gru/, has grown /groʊn/)
1 to become bigger: *Children grow very quickly.*
2 When a plant **grows** somewhere, it lives there: *Oranges grow in warm countries.*
3 to plant something in the ground and take care of it: *We grow vegetables in our garden.*
4 to allow your hair or nails to grow: *Mark has grown a beard.*
5 to become: *It was growing dark.* ⊃ SYNONYM **get**
grow into something to get bigger and become something: *Kittens grow into cats.*
grow out of something to become too big to do or wear something: *She's grown out of her shoes.*

grow up to become an adult; to change from a child to a man or woman: *I want to be a doctor when I grow up.*

growl /graʊl/ *verb* (growls, growl·ing, growled)
If a dog **growls**, it makes a low angry sound: *The dog growled at the stranger.*
▶ **growl** *noun* [*count*]: *The dog gave a low growl.*

grown /groʊn/ *adjective*
physically an adult: *a full-grown elephant*

grown-up /ˈgroʊn ʌp/ *noun* [*count*]
a man or woman, not a child: *Ask a grown-up to help you.* ⊃ SYNONYM **adult**
▶ **grown-up** *adjective*: *She has a grown-up son.*

growth 🔑 /groʊθ/ *noun* [*noncount*]
the process of getting bigger: *A good diet is important for children's growth.* • *population growth*

grub /grʌb/ *noun*
1 [*count*] (BIOLOGY) a young insect when it comes out of the egg
2 [*noncount*] (*informal*) food

grub·by /ˈgrʌbi/ *adjective* (grub·bi·er, grub·bi·est) (*informal*)
dirty: *grubby hands*

grudge /grʌdʒ/ *noun* [*count*]
a feeling of anger toward someone, because of something bad that they have done to you in the past: *I don't bear him a grudge about what happened.*

grue·some /ˈgrusəm/ *adjective*
very bad in a way that shocks you: *a gruesome murder*

grum·ble /ˈgrʌmbl/ *verb* (grum·bles, grum·bling, grum·bled)
to say many times that you do not like something: *She's always grumbling about her boss.*

grump·y /ˈgrʌmpi/ *adjective* (grump·i·er, grump·i·est) (*informal*)
a little angry: *She gets grumpy when she's tired.*

grunt /grʌnt/ *verb* (grunts, grunt·ing, grunt·ed)
to make a short rough sound, like a pig makes: *When I tried to ask her opinion, she just grunted at me.*
▶ **grunt** *noun* [*count*]

gua·ca·mo·le /ˌgwɑkəˈmoʊli/ *noun* [*noncount*]
a type of soft food that is made from a green fruit (an AVOCADO) that has been crushed

guar·an·tee¹ AWL /ˌgærənˈti/ *noun* [*count*, *noncount*]
1 (BUSINESS) a written promise by a company that it will repair or replace a thing you have bought, if it breaks or stops working: *a two-year guarantee* • *The watch comes with a money-back guarantee* (= you can get your money back if it stops working). ⊃ SYNONYM **warranty**

2 a promise that something will happen: *I want a guarantee that you will do the work today.*

guar·an·tee² AWL /ˌgærənˈti/ *verb* (guar·an·tees, guar·an·tee·ing, guar·an·teed)
1 (BUSINESS) to say that you will repair or replace a thing that someone has bought, if it breaks or stops working: *The television is guaranteed for three years.*
2 to promise that something will be done or will happen: *I can't guarantee that I will be able to help you, but I'll try.*

guard¹ /gɑrd/ *verb* (guards, guard·ing, guard·ed)
to keep someone or something safe from other people, or to stop someone from escaping: *The house was guarded by two large dogs.*

guard² /gɑrd/ *noun* [count]

> ⓘ PRONUNCIATION
> The word **guard** sounds like **yard**.

a person who keeps someone or something safe from other people, or who stops someone from escaping: *There are security guards outside the bank.*
be on guard to be ready if something bad happens: *The soldiers were on guard outside the palace* (= guarding the palace).

guard·i·an /ˈgɑrdiən/ *noun* [count]
a person who takes care of a child with no parents

guer·ril·la (also **gue·ril·la**) /gəˈrɪlə/ *noun* [count]
a person who is not in an army, but who fights secretly against the government or an army

guess /gɛs/ *verb* (guess·es, guess·ing, guessed)
to give an answer when you do not know if it is right: *Can you guess how old he is?*
I guess (*informal*) words you say when you think something is probably true, or you are not sure about something: *Mark isn't here, so I guess he's still at work.* ✦ *"Are you feeling okay?" "Yeah, I guess so."*
▶ **guess** *noun* [count] (*plural* guess·es): *If you don't know the answer, take a guess!*

guest /gɛst/ *noun* [count]
1 a person that you invite to your home or to a party or special event: *There were 200 guests at the wedding.*
2 a person who is staying in a hotel

guid·ance /ˈgaɪdns/ *noun* [noncount]
help and advice: *I want some guidance on how to find a job.*

guid·ance coun·se·lor /ˈgaɪdns ˌkaʊnsələr/ *noun* [count]
a person who works in a school and whose job

is to give students advice about college, personal problems, etc.

guide¹ /gaɪd/ *noun* [count]
1 a person who shows other people where to go and tells them about a place: *The guide took us around the castle.*
2 a book that tells you about something, or how to do something: *a guide to fishing*
3 another word for **guidebook**: *a guide to San Francisco*

guide² /gaɪd/ *verb* (guides, guid·ing, guid·ed)
to show someone where to go or what to do: *He guided us through the busy streets to our hotel.*

guide·book /ˈgaɪdbʊk/ (also **guide**) *noun* [count]
a book that tells you about a place you are visiting: *We looked in the guidebook to find a place to stay.*

guide·lines AWL /ˈgaɪdlaɪnz/ *noun* [plural]
official advice or rules on how to do something: *The government has issued new guidelines on food safety.*

guilt /gɪlt/ *noun* [noncount]
1 the bad feeling you have when you know that you have done something wrong: *She felt terrible guilt after stealing the money.*
2 the fact of having broken the law: *The police could not prove his guilt.* ➔ ANTONYM **innocence**

guilt·y /ˈgɪlti/ *adjective* (guilt·i·er, guilt·i·est)
1 If you feel **guilty**, you feel that you have done something wrong: *I feel guilty about lying to her.*
2 If you are **guilty**, you have broken the law: *He is guilty of murder.* ➔ ANTONYM **innocent**

guin·ea pig /ˈgɪni pɪg/ *noun* [count]
1 a small animal with short ears and no tail, which people often keep as a pet
2 (GENERAL SCIENCE) a person who is used in an experiment

guitars

acoustic   bass   electric
guitar   guitar   guitar

gui·tar /gɪˈtɑr/ *noun* [count]
(MUSIC) a musical instrument with strings: *I play the guitar in a band.* ✦ *an electric guitar*
▶ **gui·tar·ist** /gɪˈtɑrɪst/ *noun* [count]
(MUSIC) a person who plays the **guitar**

gulf /gʌlf/ *noun* [count]
(**GEOGRAPHY**) a large part of the ocean that has land almost all the way around it: *the Gulf of Mexico*

gull /gʌl/ *noun* [count]
a large gray or white bird that lives by the ocean ⊃ SYNONYM **seagull**

gulp /gʌlp/ *verb* (gulps, gulp·ing, gulped)
1 to eat or drink something quickly: *He **gulped down** a cup of coffee and left.*
2 to swallow because you are scared, surprised, etc.: *She gulped when the teacher called her name.*
▶ **gulp** *noun* [count]: *She took a gulp of coffee.*

gum /gʌm/ *noun*
1 [count] Your **gums** are the hard pink parts of your mouth that hold the teeth. ⊃ Look at the picture at **mouth**.
2 [noncount] (also **chew·ing gum** /'tʃuɪŋ gʌm/) a sweet, sticky candy that you keep in your mouth for a long time and bite many times but do not swallow: *a pack of gum*

gun ♪ /gʌn/ *noun* [count]
a weapon that shoots out pieces of metal (called **BULLETS**) to kill or hurt people or animals: *He aimed the gun at the bird and fired.*

gun·fire /'gʌn,faɪər/ *noun* [noncount]
the act of firing a gun or guns; the sound that this makes: *We heard gunfire and ran for safety.*

gun·man /'gʌnmən/ *noun* [count] (*plural* gun·men /'gʌnmən/)
a man who uses a gun to rob or kill people

gun·point /'gʌnpɔɪnt/ *noun*
at gunpoint while threatening someone, or being threatened with a gun: *He was robbed at gunpoint.*

gun·pow·der /'gʌn,paʊdər/ *noun* [noncount]
powder that explodes. It is used in guns and bombs.

gun·shot /'gʌnʃɑt/ *noun* [count]
the firing of a gun or the sound that this makes: *We heard gunshots.*

gu·ru /'guru; 'gʊru/ *noun* [count]
1 (**RELIGION**) a leader or teacher in the Hindu religion
2 (*informal*) a person who knows a lot about a subject and whose ideas are followed by many people: *a fashion guru*

gush /gʌʃ/ *verb* (gush·es, gush·ing, gushed)
to flow out suddenly and strongly: *Blood was **gushing from** the cut on her leg.*

gust /gʌst/ *noun* [count]
a sudden strong wind: *A **gust of** wind blew his hat off.*

guts /gʌts/ *noun* [plural]
1 (**BIOLOGY**) the stomach, and other parts near it, inside the body of people and animals
2 (*informal*) the courage to do something difficult or unpleasant: *It **takes guts** to admit you're wrong.*

gut·ter /'gʌtər/ *noun* [count]
1 a pipe under the edge of a roof to carry away water when it rains
2 the lower part at the edge of a road where water is carried away when it rains

guy /gaɪ/ *noun* (*informal*)
1 [count] a man: *He's a nice guy.*
2 **guys** [plural] used when speaking to a group of men and women or boys and girls: *Come on guys, let's go.*

gym /dʒɪm/ *noun*
1 (also *formal* **gym·na·si·um** /dʒɪm'neɪziəm/) [count] a room or building with equipment for doing physical exercise
2 [noncount] (**SPORTS**) a class in school in which you do physical exercises and play sports: *a gym class*

gym·nas·tics
/dʒɪm'næstɪks/
noun [noncount]
(**SPORTS**) exercises for
your body: *a gymnastics competition*
▶ **gym·nast**
/'dʒɪmnæst/
noun [count]
(**SPORTS**) a person who does **gymnastics**

gymnastics

gy·ne·col·o·gy /,gaɪnə'kɑlədʒi/ *noun* [noncount]
(**HEALTH**) the study and treatment of medical problems that only women have
▶ **gy·ne·col·o·gist** /,gaɪnə'kɑlədʒɪst/ *noun* [count]
a doctor who is trained in **gynecology**

gyp·sy /'dʒɪpsi/ *noun* [count] (*plural* gyp·sies)
Gypsies are people who travel around instead of living in one place.

Hh

H, h /eɪtʃ/ *noun* [count, noncount] (*plural* H's, h's /ˈeɪtʃəz/)
the eighth letter of the English alphabet: *"Hat" begins with an "H."*

hab·it 🔑 /ˈhæbət/ *noun* [count]
something that you do very often: *Smoking is a bad habit.* ♦ *She has a **habit of** calling me when I'm in bed.*

hab·i·tat /ˈhæbətæt/ *noun* [count]
(**BIOLOGY**) the natural place where a plant or an animal lives

hack /hæk/ *verb* (hacks, hack·ing, hacked)
1 to cut something or someone in a rough and violent way: *I hacked the dead branches off the tree.*
2 (**COMPUTERS**) to use a computer to get into someone else's computer in order to damage it or get secret information: *He **hacked into** the bank's computer system.*

hack·er /ˈhækər/ *noun* [count]
(**COMPUTERS**) a person who uses a computer to get into someone else's computer in order to damage it or get secret information

had /hæd/ form of **have**

had·n't /ˈhædənt/ short for **had not**

hag·gle /ˈhægl/ *verb* (hag·gles, hag·gling, hag·gled)
to argue with someone until you agree about the price of something: *Tourists were **haggling over** the price of a carpet.*

hail /heɪl/ *noun* [noncount]
frozen rain that falls in small hard balls (called HAILSTONES)
▶ **hail** *verb* (hails, hail·ing, hailed): *It's hailing.*

hair 🔑 /hɛr/ *noun*
1 [count] one of the long thin things that grow on the skin of people and animals: *There's a hair in my soup.*
2 [noncount] all the hairs on a person's head: *She has long black hair.*
let your hair down (*informal*) to relax and enjoy yourself: *She finds it hard to let her hair down.*

hair·brush /ˈhɛrbrʌʃ/ *noun* [count] (*plural* hair·brush·es)
a brush that you use to make your hair neat ⊃ Look at the picture at **brush**.

hair·cut /ˈhɛrkʌt/ *noun* [count]
1 when someone cuts your hair: *I need a haircut.*
2 the way that your hair is cut: *I like your new haircut.*

hair·dress·er /ˈhɛrdrɛsər/ *noun* [count]
a person whose job is to wash, cut, and arrange people's hair ⊃ Look at **barber**.

hair

She has curly hair.

bangs

She has braids.

She has a ponytail.

mustache

He is bald.

She has long, wavy hair.

He has short, spiky hair.

hair dry·er (also **hair dri·er**) /ˈhɛr ˌdraɪər/ *noun* [count]
a machine that dries your hair by blowing hot air on it

hair dryer

hair·style /ˈhɛrstaɪl/ *noun* [count]
the way that your hair is cut and arranged

hair·y /ˈhɛri/ *adjective* (hair·i·er, hair·i·est)
covered with a lot of hair: *He has very hairy legs.*

ha·lal /həˈlɑl/ *adjective*
(**RELIGION**) (used about meat) from an animal that has been killed according to Muslim law: *a halal butcher* (= a butcher who sells halal meat)

half¹ /hæf/ *adjective, pronoun, noun* [count] (*plural* **halves** /hævz/)

> ⓘ PRONUNCIATION
> The word **half** sounds like **staff**, because we don't say the letter l in this word.

one of two equal parts of something; ½: *Half of six is three.* ✦ *I lived in that apartment for two and a half years.* ✦ *The trip takes an hour and a half.* ✦ *I've been waiting more than half an hour.* ✦ *She gave me half of her apple.* ✦ *Half this money is yours.*
in half so that there are two equal parts: *Cut the cake in half.* ⊃ The verb is **halve**.

half² /hæf/ *adverb*
50%; not completely: *The bottle is half empty.* ✦ *He's half Italian* (= one of his parents is Italian).
half past (*formal*) 30 minutes after an hour on the clock: *It's half past nine* (= 9:30).

> ⓘ STYLE
> We usually say **nine thirty, two thirty**, etc.

half-broth·er (also **half broth·er**) /ˈhæf ˌbrʌðər/ *noun* [count]
Your **half-brother** shares one parent with you.

half-heart·ed /ˌhæf ˈhɑrt̬əd/ *adjective*
without interest or enthusiasm: *a half-hearted smile*

half-price /ˌhæf ˈpraɪs/ *adjective, adverb*
for half the usual price: *You can get half-price tickets one hour before the show.*

half-sis·ter (also **half sis·ter**) /ˈhæf ˌsɪstər/ *noun* [count]
Your **half-sister** shares one parent with you.

half·time /ˈhæftaɪm/ *noun* [noncount]
(**SPORTS**) a short time in the middle of a game like football, when play stops

half·way /ˌhæfˈweɪ/ *adverb*
in the middle: *They live **halfway between** New York and Boston.* ✦ *She left **halfway through** the class.*

hall /hɔl/ *noun* [count]
1 (also **hall·way**) a room or passage that leads to other rooms in a house or public building: *You can leave your coat in the hall.*
2 a big room or building where a lot of people meet: *a concert hall* ✦ *a dining hall* (= where people eat)

Hal·low·een /ˌhæləˈwin/ *noun* [singular]
the night of October 31

> ## Culture
>
> - In the past, people believed that dead people appeared from their graves on **Halloween**.
> - Nowadays, children dress up as witches, ghosts, etc. and go to people's houses saying "**trick or treat**," and the people give them candy.
> - People also make **jack-o'-lanterns**, where they cut shapes into a **pumpkin** (= a large orange vegetable) so that it looks like a face, and put a light inside.

hall·way /ˈhɔlweɪ/ *noun* [count] another word for **hall**(1)

halt /hɔlt/ *noun*
come to a halt to stop: *The car came to a halt in front of the school.*
▶ **halt** *verb* (halts, halt·ing, halt·ed) (*formal*): *She halted just outside the gate.*

halve /hæv/ *verb* (halves, halv·ing, halved)
to divide something into two parts that are the same: *There were two of us, so I halved the orange.* ⊃ The noun is **half**.

halves plural of **half**

ham /hæm/ *noun* [count, noncount]
meat from a pig's leg that you can keep for a long time because salt or smoke was used to prepare it: *a ham sandwich* ✦ *a delicious ham* ⊃ Look at the note at **pig**.

ham·burg·er /ˈhæmˌbərgər/ (also **burg·er** /ˈbərgər/) *noun* [count]
meat cut into very small pieces and made into a flat round shape. You often eat it in a round piece of bread (called a BUN): *A hamburger and fries, please.*

ham·mer¹ /ˈhæmər/ *noun* [count]
a tool with a handle and a heavy metal part, which you use for hitting nails into things

hammer

ham·mer² /'hæmər/ *verb* (ham·mers,
ham·mer·ing, ham·mered)
1 to hit something with a hammer: *I hammered
the nail into the wood.*
2 to hit something hard: *He hammered on the
door until someone opened it.*

ham·mock /'hæmək/ *noun* [count]
a bed made of cloth or rope that you hang up at
the two ends

ham·ster /'hæmstər/ *noun* [count]
a small animal that people keep as a pet. A
hamster can keep food in the sides of its mouth.

hand

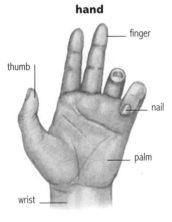

- finger
- thumb
- nail
- palm
- wrist

hand¹ /hænd/ *noun*
1 [count] the part at the end of your arm that has
four **fingers** and a **thumb**: *She held the letter in
her hand.*
2 a hand [singular] (informal) some help: *Could
you give me a hand with my homework? • Do you
need a hand?*
3 [count] one of the parts of a clock or watch that
move to show the time ⊃ Look at the picture at
watch.
by hand without using a machine: *The curtains
were made by hand.*
get out of hand to become difficult to control:
The party got out of hand.
hand in hand with your hand in another
person's hand: *They were walking hand in hand.*
hands up
1 words that mean "put one hand in the air if
you can answer the question"
2 words that mean "put your hands in the air"
because someone has a gun
hold hands to have another person's hand in
your hand
in good hands well taken care of: *Don't worry –
your son is in good hands.*
on hand near and ready to help: *There is a
doctor on hand 24 hours a day.*
on the one hand ... on the other hand words
that show the good and bad things about

something: *On the one hand, cars are very useful;
on the other hand, they cause a lot of pollution.*

hand² /hænd/ *verb* (hands, hand·ing, hand·ed)
to put something into someone's hand: *Can you
hand me the scissors, please? • I handed the
money to the cashier.*
hand something down to pass something
from an older person to a younger one: *He never
had any new clothes – they were all handed down
from his older brothers.*
hand something in to give something to
someone: *The teacher asked us to hand in our
homework.*
hand something out to give something to
many people: *Please hand out these books.*
hand something over to give something to
someone: *"Hand over your weapons!"*

hand·bag /'hændbæg/ *noun* [count]
a small bag that a woman uses for carrying
things like money and keys ⊃ SYNONYM **purse**

hand·book /'hændbʊk/ *noun* [count]
a book that gives useful information or advice
about something: *For information about school
policies, see the parent handbook.*

hand·cuffs /'hændkʌfs/ *noun* [plural]
two metal rings with a chain that the police put
on a prisoner's arms so that they cannot use
their hands

hand·ful /'hændfʊl/ *noun* [count]
1 as much as you can hold in one hand: *a
handful of stones*
2 a small number: *Only a handful of people
came to the meeting.*

hand·gun /'hændgʌn/ *noun* [count]
a gun that is small enough to hold in one hand:
The court issued a ban on handguns.

hand·i·cap /'hændikæp/ *noun* [count]
1 a physical or mental condition that means you
cannot use a part of your body completely or
easily, or that you cannot learn easily ⊃ SYNONYM
disability
2 something that makes it more difficult for you
to do something: *Not being able to drive is a real
handicap.*
▸ **hand·i·capped** /'hændikæpt/ *adjective*
not able to use a part of your body well ⊃
SYNONYM **disabled**

ⓘ STYLE
Some people do not like the words **handicap**
and **handicapped**, and prefer to use the
words **disability** and **disabled**.

hand·ker·chief /'hæŋkərtʃɪf/ *noun* [count]
a square piece of cloth or paper that you use for
clearing (BLOWING) your nose

han·dle¹ 🔑 /ˈhændl/ *noun* [*count*]
the part of a thing that you hold in your hand: *I turned the handle and opened the door.* ♦ *Hold that knife by the handle.* ⊃ Look at the picture at **cup**.

han·dle² 🔑 /ˈhændl/ *verb* (han·dles, han·dling, han·dled)
1 to touch something with your hands: *Always wash your hands before you handle food.*
2 to control or deal with someone or something: *He's not very good at handling pressure.*

han·dle·bars /ˈhændlbɑrz/ *noun* [*plural*]
the part at the front of a bicycle or motorcycle that you hold when you are riding it ⊃ Look at the picture at **bicycle**.

hand·made /ˌhændˈmeɪd/ *adjective*
made by a person, not by a machine: *handmade chocolates*

hand·out /ˈhændaʊt/ *noun* [*count*]
1 food, money, etc. that is given to people who need it: *Although she couldn't pay her rent, she was too proud to accept handouts.*
2 a printed sheet of paper that is given to people, for example to explain something in class: *Put all of your handouts in your notebook.*

hand·shake /ˈhændʃeɪk/ *noun* [*count*]
the action of shaking someone's right hand with your right hand: *a firm handshake*

hand·some /ˈhænsəm/ *adjective*
(usually used about a man) attractive: *a handsome man* ⊃ Look at the note at **attractive**.

hands-on /ˌhændz ˈɑn/ *adjective*
doing something yourself, instead of watching someone else do it: *She needs some **hands-on** experience.*

hand·writ·ing /ˈhændraɪtɪŋ/ *noun* [*noncount*]
the way you write: *Her handwriting is difficult to read.*

hand·writ·ten /ˈhændrɪtn/ *adjective*
written by hand, not typed or printed: *a handwritten note*

hand·y /ˈhændi/ *adjective* (hand·i·er, hand·i·est)
1 useful: *This bag will be **handy for** carrying my books.*
2 near and easy to find or reach: *Always keep a first-aid kit handy.*
come in handy to be useful: *Don't throw that box away – it might come in handy.*

hand·y·man /ˈhændimæn/ *noun* [*count*] (*plural* hand·y·men /ˈhændimɛn/)
a person whose job is to make or repair things, especially in a house or other building

hang 🔑 /hæŋ/ *verb*
1 (hangs, hang·ing, hung /hʌŋ/, has hung) to put something on a hook or fasten something to a wall: *Hang your coat **up** in the hall.* ♦ *I hung the picture over the fireplace.*
2 (hangs, hang·ing, hanged, has hanged) to kill yourself or another person by putting a rope around the neck and allowing the body to drop downward: *She was hanged for murder.*
hang around (*informal*) to stay somewhere with nothing special to do: *My plane was late so I had to hang around in the airport all morning.*
hang on (*informal*) to wait for a short time: *Hang on – I'm not ready.*
hang on to someone or **something** to hold someone or something firmly: *Hang on to your purse.*
hang out (*informal*) to spend a lot of time in a place, often not doing much: *On Saturdays I hang out with my friends at the mall.*
hang up to end a telephone call

hang·er /ˈhæŋər/ (also **coat hang·er** /ˈkoʊt ˌhæŋər/) *noun* [*count*]
a piece of metal, wood, or plastic with a hook. You use it for hanging clothes on.

hang glid·er /ˈhæŋ glaɪdər/ *noun* [*count*] (**SPORTS**)
1 a very large piece of material on a frame, which you hang from and fly through the air
2 a person who does HANG GLIDING

hang glider

▶ **hang glid·ing** /ˈhæŋ glaɪdɪŋ/ *noun* [*noncount*]: *I'd love to try hang gliding.*

hang·o·ver /ˈhæŋoʊvər/ *noun* [*count*]
pain in your head and a sick feeling, which you get if you have drunk too much alcohol the night before

Ha·nuk·kah /ˈhɑnəkə/ *noun* [*noncount*]
(**RELIGION**) a Jewish holiday that lasts for eight days in December

hap·pen 🔑 /ˈhæpən/ *verb* (hap·pens, hap·pen·ing, hap·pened)
to take place, usually without being planned first: *How did the accident happen?* ♦ *Did you hear what **happened to** me yesterday?*
happen to do something to do something by chance: *I happened to run into Tim yesterday.*

hap·pi·ness 🔑 /ˈhæpinəs/ *noun* [*noncount*]
the feeling of being happy ⊃ **ANTONYM unhappiness**

hap·py 🔑 /ˈhæpi/ *adjective* (hap·pi·er, hap·pi·est)
1 feeling pleased or showing that you are pleased: *She **looks** very **happy**.* ♦ *That was one of the happiest days of my life.* ⊃ **ANTONYM unhappy, sad** ⊃ Look at the note at **glad**.
2 a word that you use to say that you hope someone will enjoy a special time: *Happy New Year!* ♦ *Happy Birthday!* ♦ *Happy Holidays!*

▶ **hap·pi·ly** /ˈhæpəli/ *adverb*: *Everyone was smiling happily.*

ha·rass /həˈræs; ˈhærəs/ *verb* (**ha·rass·es, ha·rass·ing, ha·rassed**)
to bother or do unpleasant things to someone, especially over a period of time: *His ex-wife wouldn't stop harassing him.*

▶ **ha·rass·ment** /həˈræsmənt; ˈhærəsmənt/ *noun* [*noncount*]: *She accused her boss of harassment.*

har·bor /ˈhɑrbər/ *noun* [*count*]
a place where ships can stay safely in the water

hard¹ 🖉 /hɑrd/ *adjective* (**hard·er, hard·est**)
1 not soft: *These apples are very hard.* ◆ *I couldn't sleep because the bed was too hard.* ➔ **ANTONYM soft**
2 difficult to do or understand: *The exam was very hard.* ◆ *hard work* ➔ **ANTONYM easy**
3 full of problems: *He's had a hard life.* ➔ **ANTONYM easy**
4 not kind or gentle: *She is very hard on her children.* ➔ **ANTONYM soft**

hard² 🖉 /hɑrd/ *adverb* (**hard·er, hard·est**)
1 a lot: *She works very hard.* ◆ *You need to try harder!*
2 strongly: *It's raining hard.* ◆ *She hit him hard.*

hard·back /ˈhɑrdbæk/ *noun* [*count, noncount*]
a book with a hard cover: *I don't buy hardbacks – they're too expensive.* ◆ *Is this book available in hardback?* ➔ Look at **paperback**.

hard disk /ˈhɑrd dɪsk/ *noun* [*count*]
(**COMPUTERS**) a piece of hard plastic inside a computer that stores information and programs

hard·en /ˈhɑrdn/ *verb* (**hard·ens, hard·en·ing, hard·ened**)
to become hard: *Wait for the cement to harden.*

hard·ly 🖉 /ˈhɑrdli/ *adverb*
almost not; only just: *She spoke so quietly that I could hardly hear her.* ◆ *There's hardly any* (= almost no) *coffee left.* ◆ *We hardly ever go out anymore.*

hard·ware /ˈhɑrdwɛr/ *noun* [*noncount*]
1 (**COMPUTERS**) the machines that are part of a computer system, not the programs that work on it ➔ Look at **software**.
2 tools and equipment that are used to build or repair things in the house: *a hardware store*

hard–work·ing /ˌhɑrd ˈwərkɪŋ/ *adjective*
working with effort and energy: *a hard-working student*

hare /hɛr/ *noun* [*count*]
an animal like a RABBIT (= a small animal with long ears). **Hares** are bigger, have longer ears, and can run very fast.

harm¹ 🖉 /hɑrm/ *noun* [*noncount*]
damage or injury: *Eating a little red meat won't do you any harm.*

there is no harm in doing something
nothing bad will happen if you do something: *I don't know if she'll help you, but there's no harm in asking.*

harm² 🖉 /hɑrm/ *verb* (**harms, harm·ing, harmed**)
to hurt or damage someone or something: *These chemicals harm the environment.*

harm·ful 🖉 /ˈhɑrmfl/ *adjective*
Something that is **harmful** can hurt or damage people or things: *Fruit juice can be harmful to children's teeth.*

harm·less /ˈhɑrmləs/ *adjective*
not dangerous: *Don't worry – these insects are harmless.*

har·mo·ny /ˈhɑrməni/ *noun* (*plural* **har·mo·nies**)
1 [*noncount*] a state of agreement or of living together in peace: *The different species live together in harmony.*
2 [*count, noncount*] (**MUSIC**) musical notes that sound nice together: *They sang in harmony.* ◆ *beautiful harmonies*

harp /hɑrp/ *noun* [*count*]
(**MUSIC**) a large musical instrument that has many strings stretching from the top to the bottom of a frame. You play the **harp** with your fingers. ➔ Look at the picture at **instrument**.

harsh /hɑrʃ/ *adjective* (**harsh·er, harsh·est**)
1 not kind; cruel: *a harsh punishment*
2 rough and unpleasant to see or hear: *a harsh voice*

▶ **harsh·ly** /ˈhɑrʃli/ *adverb*: *Alec laughed harshly.*

har·vest /ˈhɑrvəst/ *noun*
1 [*count, noncount*] the time when grain, fruit, or vegetables are ready to cut or pick: *The apple harvest is in September.*
2 [*count*] all the grain, fruit, or vegetables that are cut or picked: *We had a good harvest this year.*

▶ **har·vest** *verb* (**har·vests, har·vest·ing, har·vest·ed**): *When do they harvest the wheat?*

has /hæz/ *form of* **have**

hash browns /ˈhæʃ braʊnz/ *noun* [*plural*]
a type of food made from potatoes that have been cut into small pieces and cooked in oil: *eggs, bacon, and hash browns*

has·n't /ˈhæzənt/ *short for* **has not**

has·sle /ˈhæsl/ *noun* [*count, noncount*] (*informal*)
a thing or situation that takes a lot of effort to do: *Traveling with all this luggage is a real hassle.*

haste /heɪst/ *noun* [*noncount*] (*formal*)
doing things too quickly, especially because you do not have enough time: *The letter was written in haste* (= quickly).

hast·y /ˈheɪsti/ *adjective* (hast·i·er, hast·i·est)
1 said or done quickly: *a hasty departure*
2 If you are **hasty**, you do something too quickly: *Don't be too hasty. This is a very important decision.*
▶ **hast·i·ly** /ˈheɪstəli/ *adverb*: *He hastily changed the subject.*

hats

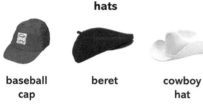

baseball cap　　beret　　cowboy hat

hat /hæt/ *noun* [count]
a thing that you wear on your head: *She's wearing a hat.*

hatch /hætʃ/ *verb* (hatch·es, hatch·ing, hatched)
(**BIOLOGY**) When baby birds, insects, or fish **hatch**, they come out of an egg.

hate¹ /heɪt/ *verb* (hates, hat·ing, hat·ed)
to have a very strong feeling of not liking someone or something: *Most cats hate water.* ◆ *I hate waking up early.* ⟳ **ANTONYM love**

Thesaurus

hate to have a strong feeling of not liking someone or something. This word is often used in informal English to talk about people or things that you really do not like: *I've always hated broccoli.* ◆ *He hates getting up early in the morning.* ◆ *I hate the way she always criticizes me.*

can't stand an expression used to mean that you really do not like someone or something. It is often used in informal spoken English: *I can't stand this music. Can we listen to something else?* ◆ *He can't stand waiting in line for things.* ◆ *I can't stand her brother, can you?*

dislike a slightly formal way of saying that you do not like someone or something, but not in a strong way. It is more usual to say "don't like": *I have always disliked flying.* ◆ *Why do you dislike him so much?*

despise to dislike someone or something very much and have no respect for them or it: *She despised any kind of gossip.* ◆ *He despised himself for being such a coward.*

loathe to hate someone or something very much: *They loathe each other.* ◆ *He loathed hypocrisy.*

hate² /heɪt/ *noun* [noncount]
a very strong feeling of not liking someone or something: *Her love for him turned to hate.* ⟳ **SYNONYM hatred** ⟳ **ANTONYM love**

ha·tred /ˈheɪtrəd/ *noun* [noncount]
a very strong feeling of not liking someone or something: *He had a deep **hatred** of injustice.* ⟳ **SYNONYM hate**

haul /hɔl/ *verb* (hauls, haul·ing, hauled)
to pull something heavy: *They hauled the boat out of the river.*

haunt /hɔnt/ *verb* (haunts, haunt·ing, haunt·ed)
1 If a place is **haunted**, people think that there are GHOSTS (= spirits of dead people) there: *A ghost haunts the castle.*
2 If something sad or unpleasant **haunts** you, you often think of it: *Her unhappy face still haunts me.*
▶ **haunt·ed** /ˈhɔntəd/ *adjective*: *a haunted house*

have

Full forms	Short forms	Negative short forms
present tense		
I **have**	I've	I **haven't**
you **have**	you've	you **haven't**
he/she/it **has**	he's/she's/it's	he/she/it **hasn't**
we **have**	we've	we **haven't**
they **have**	they've	they **haven't**
past tense		
had	I'd you'd, etc.	**hadn't**
present participle		
having		
past participle		
had		

have¹ /həv; hæv/ *verb*
a word that you use with parts of other verbs to show that something happened or started in the past: *I haven't seen that movie.* ◆ *Have you ever been to the Grand Canyon?* ◆ *We've been in New York for six months.* ◆ *When we arrived, Paul had already left.*

have² /hæv/ *verb*
1 (also **have got**) to own or keep something: *She has blue eyes.* ◆ *Do you have any brothers and sisters?* ◆ *He's got (= has got) short black hair.*
2 a word that you use with many nouns to talk about doing something: *What time do you have breakfast?* ◆ *Let's have a coffee.* ◆ *I had a meeting this morning.* ◆ *Jill and I had a fight.*
3 a word that you use with many nouns to talk about experiencing something: *Have fun!* ◆ *He had an accident.* ◆ *Did you have a good weekend?* ◆ *I have an idea.* ◆ *Do you have time to help me?*

4 (also **have got**) to be sick with something: *I have the flu.* ✦ *She's got* (= has got) *a headache.*
have something done to let someone do something for you: *I had my hair cut yesterday.* ✦ *Have you had your car repaired?*
have something on to be wearing something: *She had a green sweater on.* ✦ *What did the boy have on when you last saw him?*

haven't /ˈhævənt/ short for **have not**

have to /ˈhæftə; ˈhæftu/ *modal verb* (also **have got to**)
used for saying that someone must do something or that something must happen: *I have to go to the dentist today.* ✦ *We don't have to get up early tomorrow.* ✦ *Do we have to pay for this now?* ✦ *We had to do lots of boring exercises.* ⊃ Look at the note at **must**.

hawk /hɔk/ *noun* [count]
a large bird that catches and eats other birds and small animals

hay /heɪ/ *noun* [noncount]
dry grass that is used as food for farm animals

hay fe·ver /ˈheɪ ˌfivər/ *noun* [noncount]
(**HEALTH**) an illness like a cold. Grass and other plants can cause **hay fever**.

haz·ard /ˈhæzərd/ *noun* [count]
a danger: *Ice is a hazard for drivers.* ✦ *a fire hazard*
▶ **haz·ard·ous** /ˈhæzərdəs/ *adjective*: *hazardous chemicals*

haze /heɪz/ *noun* [noncount]
air that is difficult to see through because of heat, dust, or smoke

ha·zel·nut /ˈheɪzlnʌt/ *noun* [count]
a small nut that you can eat

haz·y /ˈheɪzi/ *adjective* (haz·i·er, haz·i·est)
1 not clear, especially because of heat: *Yesterday it was hot and hazy.*
2 difficult to remember or understand clearly: *I only have a hazy memory of our vacation in Seattle.*

he /hi/ *pronoun* (plural **they**)
the man or boy that the sentence is about: *I saw Mike when he was in town.* ✦ *"Where's John?" "He's* (= he is) *at home."*

head¹ /hɛd/ *noun*
1 [count] the part of your body above your neck: *She turned her head to look at me.* ✦ *He nodded his head* (= moved it up and down) *in agreement.* ✦ *"I disagree," she said, shaking her head.* ⊃ Look at the picture at **body**.
2 [count] your mind or brain: *A strange thought came into his head.* ✦ *Use your head* (= think)*!*
3 [singular] the top, front, or most important part: *She sat at the head of the table.*

4 [count, noncount] the person in charge of a group of people or organization: *The Pope is the head of the Catholic church.*
6 **heads** [noncount] the side of a coin that has the head of a person on it: *Heads or tails?* (= said when you are throwing a coin in the air to decide something) ⊃ **ANTONYM tails**
a head; **per head** for one person: *Dinner costs $50 a head.*
go to your head to make you too pleased with yourself: *Stop telling him how good-looking he is. It will go to his head!*
head first with your head before the rest of your body
keep your head to stay calm: *She needs to learn to keep her head when things get difficult.*
lose your head to become too excited, angry, etc.

head² /hɛd/ *verb* (heads, head·ing, head·ed)
1 to move in the direction mentioned: *Let's head for home.* ✦ *Where are you heading?*
2 to be the leader or most important person in a group: *Michael is heading the finance committee.*

head·ache /ˈhɛdeɪk/ *noun* [count]
(**HEALTH**) a pain in your head: *to have a headache*

head·ing /ˈhɛdɪŋ/ *noun* [count]
the words at the top of a piece of writing to show what it is about

head·light /ˈhɛdlaɪt/ (also **head·lamp** /ˈhɛdlæmp/) *noun* [count]
one of the two big bright lights on the front of a car ⊃ Look at the picture at **car**.

head·line /ˈhɛdlaɪn/ *noun*
1 [count] the words in big letters at the top of a newspaper story
2 **the headlines** [plural] the most important news on radio or television: *Here are the latest news headlines.*

head·phones /ˈhɛdfoʊnz/ *noun* [plural]
things that you put over your head and ears so that you can listen to music without other people hearing it ⊃ Look at **earphones**.

head·quar·ters /ˈhɛdˌkwɔrtərz/ *noun* [plural]
(abbreviation **HQ**)
the main offices where the leaders of an organization work: *The company's headquarters are in Detroit.*

head·set /ˈhɛdsɛt/ *noun* [count]
a piece of equipment that you wear on your head that includes a part for listening (called **HEADPHONES**) and a part for speaking into (called a **MICROPHONE**): *The pilot was talking into his headset.*

head·way /ˈhɛdweɪ/ *noun*
make headway to go forward or make progress: *We haven't made much headway in our discussions.*

heal /hil/ *verb* (heals, heal·ing, healed)
(**HEALTH**) to become well again; to make something well again: *The cut on his leg healed slowly.*

health /hɛlθ/ *noun* [noncount]
the condition of your body: *Smoking is bad for your health.* • *health insurance*

health·care /'hɛlθkɛr/ (also **health care**) *noun* [noncount]
(**HEALTH**) the service of providing medical care: *reforms to the healthcare system*

health food /'hɛlθ fud/ *noun* [count, noncount]
natural food that many people think is good for your health: *a health food store*

health·y /'hɛlθi/ *adjective* (health·i·er, health·i·est) (**HEALTH**)
1 well; not often sick: *healthy children*
2 helping to make or keep you well: *healthy food* ⊃ **ANTONYM unhealthy**

heap¹ /hip/ *noun* [count]
a lot of things on top of one another in a messy way: *She left her clothes in a heap on the floor.* ⊃ Look at the note at **pile¹**.

heap² /hip/ *verb* (heaps, heap·ing, heaped)
to put a lot of things on top of one another: *She heaped food onto my plate.*

hear /hɪr/ *verb* (hears, hear·ing, heard /hɑrd/, has heard)
1 to notice sounds with your ears: *Can you hear that noise?* • *I heard someone laughing in the next room.*

Which word?

Hear or listen?

■ When you **hear** something, sounds come to your ears: *I heard the door close.*
■ When you **listen to** something, you are trying to hear it: *I listen to the radio every morning.*

2 to be told about something: *Have you heard the news?*
hear from someone to get a letter or a phone call from someone: *Have you heard from your sister?*
hear of someone or **something** to know about someone or something: *Who is he? I've never heard of him.*
will not hear of something will not agree to something: *I wanted to get a motorcycle, but my parents wouldn't hear of it.*

hear·ing /'hɪrɪŋ/ *noun* [noncount]
the ability to hear: *Speak louder – her hearing isn't very good.*

hear·ing aid /'hɪrɪŋ eɪd/ *noun* [count]
a small machine that fits inside the ear and helps people to hear better

heart /hɑrt/ *noun*

ⓘ **PRONUNCIATION**
The word **heart** sounds like **start**.

1 [count] the part of the body that makes the blood go around inside: *Your heart beats faster when you run.* ⊃ Look at the picture at **body**.
2 [count] your feelings: *She has a big heart* (= she is kind and generous).
3 [singular] the center; the middle part: *They live in the heart of the city.*
4 [count] the shape ♡
5 hearts [plural] the group of playing cards (called a **SUIT**) that have red shapes like hearts on them: *the six of hearts* ⊃ Look at the picture at **playing card**.
break someone's heart to make someone very sad: *It broke his heart when his wife died.*
by heart so that you know every word: *I know that poem by heart.*
lose heart to stop hoping: *Don't lose heart – you can still win if you try.*
your heart sinks you suddenly feel unhappy: *My heart sank when I saw the first question on the test.*

heart·ache /'hɑrteɪk/ *noun* [count, noncount]
a strong feeling of sadness

heart at·tack /'hɑrt ə,tæk/ *noun* [count]
(**HEALTH**) a sudden dangerous illness, when your heart stops working normally: *She had a heart attack and died.*

heart·beat /'hɑrtbit/ *noun* [count]
(**HEALTH**) the movement or sound of your heart as it pushes blood around your body

heart·break /'hɑrtbreɪk/ *noun* [noncount]
a strong feeling of sadness or disappointment
▶ **heart·break·ing** /'hɑrt,breɪkɪŋ/ *adjective*
making you feel very sad: *a heartbreaking story about a homeless family*

heart·bro·ken /'hɑrt,broʊkən/ *adjective*
extremely sad because of something that has happened: *Maggie was heartbroken when her grandfather died.*

heart·less /'hɑrtləs/ *adjective*
not kind; cruel

heat¹ /hit/ *noun*
1 [noncount] the feeling of something hot: *the heat of the sun*
2 [noncount] hot weather: *I love the heat.* ⊃ **ANTONYM cold**
3 [noncount] a system for making a building warm: *Can you turn up the heat? I'm freezing!*
4 [count] (**SPORTS**) one of the first parts of a race or competition

heat² /hit/ (also **heat up**) *verb* (heats, heat·ing, heat·ed)
to make something hot; to become hot: *I heated the milk in the microwave.* ◆ *Wait for the oven to heat up before you put the cake in.*

heat·er /'hiṭər/ *noun* [count]
a thing that makes a place warm or that heats water: *a water heater* ◆ *The room was cold, so he bought a space heater* (= a small heater for one room).

heave /hiv/ *verb* (heaves, heav·ing, heaved)
to lift or pull something heavy: *We heaved the suitcase up the stairs.*

heav·en /'hɛvn/ *noun* [noncount]
(RELIGION) the place where many people believe God lives and where good people go to when they die ➔ Look at **hell**.

heav·y /'hɛvi/ *adjective* (heav·i·er, heav·i·est)
1 weighing a lot; difficult to lift or move: *I can't carry this bag – it's too heavy.* ➔ ANTONYM **light**
2 a word used to describe a person when you do not want to say that they are fat: *Ted's gotten a little heavier since the last time I saw him.* ➔ Look at the note at **fat¹**.
3 larger, stronger, or more than usual: *heavy rain* ◆ *The traffic was very heavy this morning.* ➔ ANTONYM **light**
▶ **heav·i·ly** /'hɛvəli/ *adverb*: *It was raining heavily.*

heav·y met·al /'hɛvi 'mɛtl/ *noun* [noncount]
(MUSIC) a kind of loud rock music

hec·tic /'hɛktɪk/ *adjective*
very busy: *I had a hectic day at work.*

he'd /hid/ short for **he had**, **he would**

hedge /hɛdʒ/ *noun* [count]
a line of small trees planted close together

heel /hil/ *noun* [count]
1 the back part of your foot ➔ Look at the picture at **leg**.
2 the back part of a shoe under the **heel** of your foot ➔ Look at the picture at **shoe**.
3 the part of a sock that covers the **heel** of your foot

height /haɪt/ *noun*

> **ⓘ PRONUNCIATION**
> The word **height** sounds like **white**.

1 [count, noncount] how far it is from the bottom to the top of someone or something: *What is the normal height of a basketball hoop?* ◆ *The wall is 12 feet in height.* ◆ *She asked me my height, weight, and age.* ➔ Look at the picture at **dimension**. ➔ The adjective is **high**.
2 [count] a high place: *I'm afraid of heights.*
3 [noncount] the strongest or most important part of something: *the height of summer*

heir /ɛr/ *noun* [count]
a person who gets money or property when another person dies: *He's the heir to a large fortune.*
▶ **heir·ess** /'ɛr·ɛs/ *noun* [count] (plural **heir·ess·es**)
an **heir** who is a woman

held form of **hold¹**

hel·i·cop·ter
/'hɛləkɑptər/ *noun* [count]
a vehicle that can go straight up in the air, with long metal parts on top that turn to help it fly

helicopter

he·li·um /'hiliəm/ *noun* [noncount] (symbol **He**)
(CHEMISTRY) a very light gas that is often used to fill BALLOONS (= things that float in the air)

hell /hɛl/ *noun* [noncount]
the place where some people believe that bad people go to when they die ➔ Look at **heaven**.

he'll /hil; hɪl/ short for **he will**

hel·lo /hə'loʊ/ *exclamation*
a word that you say when you meet someone or when you answer the telephone

> **ⓘ STYLE**
> We usually use **hi**, not **hello**, in less formal situations: *"Rob, this is my friend, Laura." "Hi, nice to meet you."* However, we always use **hello** when we answer the telephone.

helmets

hel·met /'hɛlmət/ *noun* [count]
a hard hat that keeps your head safe: *a bike helmet*

help¹ /hɛlp/ *verb* (helps, help·ing, helped)
1 to do something useful for someone; to make someone's work easier: *Will you help me with the laundry?* ◆ *She helped me carry the box.*
2 a word that you shout when you are in danger: *Help! I can't swim!*
can't help If you **can't help** doing something, you cannot stop yourself from doing it: *It was so funny that I couldn't help laughing.*
help yourself to take something that you want: *Help yourself to a drink.* ◆ *"Can I have a sandwich?" "Of course. Help yourself!"*

help² /hɛlp/ *noun*
1 [noncount] the act of helping someone: *Thank you for all your help.* ◆ *Do you need any help?*

2 [singular] a person or thing that helps: *He was a great help to me after I broke my leg.*

▶ **help·er** /ˈhɛlpər/ *noun* [count]
a person who helps

help·ful 🔎 /ˈhɛlpfl/ *adjective*
wanting to help; useful: *The saleswoman was very helpful.* • *helpful advice* ⊃ **ANTONYM unhelpful**

▶ **help·ful·ly** /ˈhɛlpfəli/ *adverb*

help·ing /ˈhɛlpɪŋ/ *noun* [count]
the amount of food on your plate: *I had a big helping of mashed potatoes.*

help·less /ˈhɛlpləs/ *adjective*
not able to do things without help: *Babies are totally helpless.*

▶ **help·less·ly** /ˈhɛlpləsli/ *adverb*

hem /hɛm/ *noun* [count]
the bottom edge of something, like a skirt or pants, which is folded and sewn

hem·i·sphere /ˈhɛməsfɪr/ *noun* [count]
(**GEOGRAPHY**) one half of the earth: *the northern hemisphere* ⊃ Look at the picture at **earth**.

hen /hɛn/ *noun* [count]
a female bird, especially a chicken, that people keep on farms for its eggs ⊃ Look at the note at **chicken**.

hep·a·ti·tis /ˌhɛpəˈtaɪt̮əs/ *noun* [noncount]
(**HEALTH**) a serious disease of the LIVER (= the part inside your body that cleans the blood)

her¹ 🔎 /hər/ *pronoun* (*plural* **them** /ðəm; ðɛm/)
a word that shows the woman or girl that you have just talked about: *Tell Jane that I'll see her tonight.* • *I wrote to her yesterday.*

her² 🔎 /hər/ *adjective*
of or belonging to the woman or girl that you have just talked about: *That's her book.* • *Jill hurt her leg.*

herb /ərb/ *noun* [count]
a plant whose leaves, seeds, etc. are used in cooking or in medicine ⊃ Look at **spice**.

her·bi·vore /ˈhərbɪvɔr/ *noun* [count]
(**BIOLOGY**) an animal that eats only grass and plants: *giraffes, elephants, and other herbivores* ⊃ Look at **carnivore**, **omnivore**.

▶ **her·biv·o·rous** /ˌhərˈbɪvərəs/ *adjective*: *herbivorous dinosaurs*

herd¹ /hərd/ *noun* [count]
a big group of animals of the same kind: *a herd of cattle* ⊃ Look at **flock**.

herd² /hərd/ *verb* (herds, herd·ing, herd·ed)
to move people or animals somewhere in a group: *The prisoners were herded into the van.*

here 🔎 /hɪr/ *adverb*
in, at, or to this place: *Your glasses are here.* • *Come here, please.* • *Here's my car.* • *Here comes the bus.* ⊃ Look at **there** (2).

here and there in different places: *There were groups of people here and there along the beach.*

here goes (*informal*) words that you say before you do something exciting or dangerous: *"Here goes," said Sue, and she jumped into the river.*

here you are; **here you go** (*informal*) words that you say when you give something to someone: *"Can I borrow a pen, please?" "Sure, here you go."*

her·i·tage /ˈhɛrət̮ɪdʒ/ *noun* [count, usually singular]
(**HISTORY**) the important traditions, qualities, and culture of a country: *The building is part of our national heritage.*

he·ro /ˈhɪroʊ/ *noun* [count] (*plural* **he·roes**)
1 a person, especially a man, who has done something brave or good: *Everyone said that Mark was a hero after he rescued his sister from the fire.*
2 (**ENGLISH LANGUAGE ARTS**) the most important man or boy in a book, play, or movie ⊃ Look at **heroine**.

he·ro·ic /həˈroʊɪk/ *adjective*
very brave

her·o·in /ˈhɛroʊən/ *noun* [noncount]
(**HEALTH**) a very strong illegal drug

her·o·ine /ˈhɛroʊən/ *noun* [count]
1 a woman who has done something brave or good
2 (**ENGLISH LANGUAGE ARTS**) the most important woman or girl in a book, play, or movie: *The heroine is played by Angelina Jolie.* ⊃ Look at **hero**.

her·o·ism /ˈhɛroʊɪzəm/ *noun* [noncount]
when someone does something very brave or good: *the heroism of New York's firefighters*

hers 🔎 /hərz/ *pronoun*
something that belongs to her: *Gina says this book is hers.* • *Are these keys hers?*

her·self 🔎 /hərˈsɛlf/ *pronoun* (*plural* **them·selves** /ðəmˈsɛlvz/)
1 a word that shows the same woman or girl that you have just talked about: *She fell and hurt herself.*
2 a word that makes "she" stronger: *"Who told you that Laura was married?" "She told me herself."*

by herself
1 without other people: *She lives by herself.* ⊃ **SYNONYM alone**
2 without help: *She can carry the box by herself.*

he's /hiz/ short for **he is**, **he has**

hes·i·tate /ˈhɛzəteɪt/ *verb* (hes·i·tates, hes·i·tat·ing, hes·i·tat·ed)
to stop for a moment before you do or say something, because you are not sure about it: *He hesitated before answering the question.*

▶ **hes·i·ta·tion** /ˌhɛzəˈteɪʃn/ *noun* [noncount]: *They agreed without hesitation.*

het·er·o·sex·u·al /ˌhɛtərəˈsɛkʃuəl/ *adjective*
attracted to people of the opposite sex ⟳
ANTONYM homosexual

hex·a·gon
/ˈhɛksəgɑn/ *noun*
[count]
(**MATH**) a shape with
six sides
▶ **hex·ag·o·nal**
/hɛkˈsægənl/ *adjective*
with six sides: *a
hexagonal box*

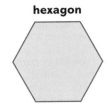

hexagon

hey /heɪ/ *exclamation* (*informal*)
a word that you say to make someone listen to
you, or when you are surprised: *Hey! Where are
you going?*

hi /haɪ/ *exclamation* (*informal*)
a word that you say when you meet someone:
Hi, Tony! How are you? ⟳ **SYNONYM hello**

hi·ber·nate /ˈhaɪbərneɪt/ *verb* (**hi·ber·nates,
hi·ber·nat·ing, hi·ber·nat·ed**)
(**BIOLOGY**) When an animal **hibernates**, it goes to
sleep for the winter.
▶ **hi·ber·na·tion** /ˌhaɪbərˈneɪʃn/ *noun* [noncount]

hic·cup /ˈhɪkʌp/ *noun* [count]
a sudden noise that you make in your throat.
You sometimes get the **hiccups** when you have
eaten or drunk too quickly.

hide /haɪd/ *verb* (**hides, hiding, hid** /hɪd/,
has hid·den /ˈhɪdn/)
1 to put something where people cannot find it:
I hid the money under the bed.
2 to be or get in a place where people cannot
see or find you: *Someone was hiding behind the
door.*
3 to not tell or show something to someone: *She
tried to hide her feelings.*

hide-and-seek /ˌhaɪd n ˈsik/ *noun* [noncount]
a children's game in which one player covers
his or her eyes while the other players hide, and
then tries to find them

hid·e·ous /ˈhɪdiəs/ *adjective*
very ugly: *That shirt is hideous!*

hid·ing /ˈhaɪdɪŋ/ *noun* [noncount]
be in hiding; go into hiding to be in, or go into
a place where people will not find you: *The
escaped prisoners are believed to be in hiding.*

hi·er·ar·chy AWL /ˈhaɪərɑrki/ *noun* [count] (*plural*
hi·er·ar·chies)
a system or organization that has many levels
from the lowest to the highest: *the hierarchy of
the Catholic Church*

hi·er·o·glyph·ics /ˌhaɪərəˈglɪfɪks/ *noun* [plural]
(**ENGLISH LANGUAGE ARTS**) the system of writing

that was used in ancient Egypt, in which a small
picture represents a word or sound

high¹ 🔊 /haɪ/ *adjective* (**high·er, high·est**)

> ⓘ **PRONUNCIATION**
> The word **high** sounds like **my**, because we
> don't say the letters **-gh** in this word.

1 Something that is **high** has a long distance
between the top and the bottom: *a high wall* ◆
*Mount Everest is the highest mountain in the
world.* ⟳ The noun is **height.** ⟳ **ANTONYM low**
2 You use **high** to say or ask how far something
is from the bottom to the top: *The table is 30
inches high.*

> ⓘ **STYLE**
> We use **tall**, not **high**, to talk about people:
> *How tall are you?* ◆ *He's six feet tall.*

3 far from the ground: *a high shelf* ⟳ **ANTONYM
low**
4 more than the usual level or amount: *The car
was traveling at high speed.* ◆ *high temperatures*
⟳ **ANTONYM low**
5 A **high** sound is not deep: *I heard the high
voice of a little girl.* ⟳ **ANTONYM low**

high² 🔊 /haɪ/ *adverb* (**high·er, high·est**)
a long way above the ground: *The plane flew
high above the clouds.* ⟳ **ANTONYM low**

high·er ed·u·ca·tion /ˌhaɪər ɛdʒəˈkeɪʃn/ *noun*
[noncount]
education at a college or university after the age
of 18 ⟳ Look at **continuing education**.

Collocations

Higher education
applying
- **apply for** college
- **apply to** a college/a university/Harvard
- **get into/go to** college/Princeton

studying
- **major in/minor in** biology/philosophy
- **work toward** a B.A./a law degree/a
  master's degree

finishing
- **finish/graduate from** college
- **earn/receive/get** a degree/a bachelor's
  degree/a master's degree

high jump /ˈhaɪ
dʒʌmp/ *noun* [singular]
(**SPORTS**) a sport
where people jump
over a high bar

high jump

high·lands /ˈhaɪləndz/ *noun* [*plural*]
(**GEOGRAPHY**) the part of a country with hills and mountains: *the Scottish Highlands*

high·light¹ **AWL** /ˈhaɪlaɪt/ *noun* [*count*]
the best or most exciting part of something: *The* **highlight** *of our vacation was seeing the Grand Canyon.*

high·light² **AWL** /ˈhaɪlaɪt/ *verb* (**high·lights**, **high·light·ing**, **high·light·ed**)
1 to give special importance to something so that people notice it: *The report highlighted the need for better inner-city schools.*
2 to mark important parts of a text in a bright color

high·light·er /ˈhaɪlaɪtər/ *noun* [*count*]
a special pen for marking important parts of a text in a bright color: *a yellow highlighter* ⊃ Look at the picture at **stationery**.

high·ly ⚲ /ˈhaɪli/ *adverb*
1 very or very much: *Their children are highly intelligent.* ◆ *She has a highly paid job.*
2 very well: *I* **think very highly of** *your work* (= I think it is very good).

High·ness /ˈhaɪnəs/ *noun* [*count*] (*plural* **High·ness·es**)
a word that you use when speaking to or about a royal person: *Yes, Your Highness.*

high school ⚲ /ˈhaɪ skul/ *noun* [*count, noncount*]
a school for young people between the ages of 14 and 18: *Beth and I went to the same high school.* ◆ *He's a senior in high school.* ⊃ Look at the note at **elementary school**.

high-tech (also **hi-tech**) /ˌhaɪ ˈtɛk/ *adjective* (*informal*)
using the most modern methods and machines, especially electronic ones: *He's got a lot of high-tech video equipment.*

high·way ⚲ /ˈhaɪweɪ/ *noun* [*count*]
a big road between towns or cities: *There was a lot of traffic on the highway.* ◆ *Take the highway and get off at exit 18.* ⊃ Look at the note at **road**.

hi·jack /ˈhaɪdʒæk/ *verb* (**hi·jacks**, **hi·jack·ing**, **hi·jacked**)
to take control of an airplane or a car, and make the pilot or driver take you somewhere
▶ **hi·jack·er** /ˈhaɪdʒækər/ *noun* [*count*]: *The hijackers threatened to blow up the plane.*
▶ **hi·jack·ing** /ˈhaɪdʒækɪŋ/ *noun* [*count, noncount*]: *the hijacking of a U.S. airplane*

hike /haɪk/ *noun* [*count*]
a long walk in the country: *We went on a ten-mile hike over the weekend.*

▶ **hike** *verb* (**hikes**, **hik·ing**, **hiked**): *They went* **hiking** *in the Blue Ridge Mountains.*

hi·lar·i·ous /hɪˈlɛriəs/ *adjective*
very funny: *That new TV show is hilarious.*

hill ⚲ /hɪl/ *noun* [*count*]
(**GEOGRAPHY**) a high piece of land that is not as high as a mountain: *I pushed my bike* **up the hill**.
◆ *Their house is* **at the top of the hill**. ⊃ Look at **uphill, downhill**.
▶ **hill·y** /ˈhɪli/ *adjective* (**hill·i·er**, **hill·i·est**): *Our neighborhood is very hilly.*

him ⚲ /hɪm/ *pronoun* (*plural* **them** /ðəm; ðɛm/)
a word that shows a man or boy: *Where's Andy? I can't see him.* ◆ *I spoke to him yesterday.*

him·self ⚲ /hɪmˈsɛlf/ *pronoun* (*plural* **them·selves** /ðəmˈsɛlvz/)
1 a word that shows the same man or boy that you have just talked about: *Paul looked at himself in the mirror.*
2 a word that makes "he" stronger: *Did he make this cake himself?*
by himself
1 without other people: *Dad went running by himself.* ⊃ **SYNONYM alone**
2 without help: *He did it by himself.*

hin·der /ˈhɪndər/ *verb* (**hin·ders**, **hin·der·ing**, **hin·dered**)
to make it more difficult to do something: *Teachers are hindered by a lack of resources.*

Hin·du /ˈhɪndu/ *noun* [*count*]
(**RELIGION**) a person who follows the religion of **HINDUISM**
▶ **Hin·du** *adjective*: *Hindu beliefs*

Hin·du·ism /ˈhɪnduɪzəm/ *noun* [*noncount*]
(**RELIGION**) the main religion of India

hinge /hɪndʒ/ *noun* [*count*]
a piece of metal that joins a lid to a box or a door to a frame so that you can open and close it

hinge

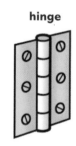

hint¹ /hɪnt/ *noun* [*count*]
1 something that you say, but not in a direct way: *Sam keeps* **dropping hints** (= making hints) *about wanting a bike for his birthday.*
2 a piece of advice or useful information: *helpful hints about how to lose weight*
3 a small amount of something: *There's a* **hint of** *garlic in the soup.*

hint² /hɪnt/ *verb* (hints, hint·ing, hint·ed)
to say something, but not in a direct way: *Sarah hinted that she might be leaving.*

hip /hɪp/ *noun* [count]
the place where your leg joins the side of your body ⊃ Look at the picture at **body**.

hip-hop /ˈhɪp hɑp/ *noun* [noncount]
(MUSIC) a type of dance music with spoken words and a strong beat, played on electronic instruments ⊃ Look at **rap**.

hip·pie (also **hippy**) /ˈhɪpi/ *noun* [count] (*plural* **hip·pies**)
a person from the 1960s or 1970s who was against war and often had long hair and wore clothes with bright colors

hip·po·pot·a·mus /ˌhɪpəˈpɑtəməs/ *noun* [count] (*plural* **hip·po·pot·a·mus·es** or **hip·po·pot·a·mi** /ˌhɪpəˈpɑtəmaɪ/) (also *informal* **hip·po** /ˈhɪpoʊ/)

hippopotamus

a large African animal that has thick skin and lives near water

hire /ˈhaɪər/ *verb* (hires, hir·ing, hired)
to give someone a job: *We hired a new salesperson for the northeast region.* ⋆ *They hired an architect to design their new house.*

his¹ /hɪz/ *adjective*
of or belonging to the man or boy that you have just talked about: *John came with his sister.* ⋆ *He hurt his arm.*

his² /hɪz/ *pronoun*
something that belongs to him: *Are these books yours or his?*

His·pan·ic /hɪˈspænɪk/ *adjective*
connected with or coming from a place where Spanish is spoken, especially Latin America: *Miami has a large Hispanic population.*
▶ **His·pan·ic** *noun* [count]: *the first Hispanic on the U.S. Supreme Court*

hiss /hɪs/ *verb* (hiss·es, hiss·ing, hissed)
to make a noise like a very long "s": *The cat hissed at me.*
▶ **hiss** *noun* [count] (*plural* **hiss·es**): *the hiss of steam*

his·to·ri·an /hɪˈstɔriən/ *noun* [count]
(HISTORY) a person who knows a lot about history

his·tor·ic /hɪˈstɔrɪk/ *adjective*
(HISTORY) important in history: *It was a historic moment when man first walked on the moon.*

his·tor·i·cal /hɪˈstɔrɪkl/ *adjective*
(HISTORY) connected with real people or events in the past: *She writes historical novels.*

his·to·ry /ˈhɪstəri/ *noun* [noncount]
1 all the things that happened in the past: *It was an important moment in history.*
2 the study of things that happened in the past: *History is my favorite subject.*

hit¹ /hɪt/ *verb* (hits, hit·ting, hit, has hit)
to touch someone or something hard: *He hit my ankle with his shopping cart.* ⋆ *The car hit a wall.* ⋆ *I hit my knee on the door.* ⋆ *I would never hit my children.*

hit² /hɪt/ *noun* [count]
1 touching someone or something hard: *That was a great hit!* (= in a game of baseball)
2 a person or a thing that a lot of people like: *That song was a hit in the 1990s.*
3 (COMPUTERS) a result of a search on a computer, especially on the Internet

hitch·hike /ˈhɪtʃhaɪk/ *verb* (hitch·hikes, hitch·hik·ing, hitch·hiked) (also **hitch** /hɪtʃ/) (hitch·es, hitch·ing, hitched)
to travel by asking for free rides in cars and trucks: *We hitchhiked across the country.*
▶ **hitch·hik·er** /ˈhɪtʃhaɪkər/ *noun* [count]: *We picked up a hitchhiker.*

hi-tech /ˌhaɪ ˈtɛk/ *adjective* another word for **high-tech**

HIV /ˌeɪtʃ aɪ ˈvi/ *abbreviation*
(HEALTH) the VIRUS (= a very small thing that can make you sick) that causes AIDS (= a serious illness that destroys the body's ability to fight infection)
be HIV-positive to have HIV

hive /haɪv/ (also **bee·hive** /ˈbihaɪv/) *noun* [count]
a thing that BEES (= black and yellow insects) live in

hoard /hɔrd/ *verb* (hoards, hoard·ing, hoard·ed)
to save and keep things secretly: *The old man hoarded the money in a box under his bed.*
▶ **hoard** *noun* [count]
a secret store of something, for example food or money: *a hoard of cash*

hoarse /hɔrs/ *adjective*
If your voice is **hoarse**, it is rough and quiet, for example because you have a cold: *He spoke in a hoarse whisper.*

hoax /hoʊks/ *noun* [count] (*plural* **hoax·es**)
a trick that makes someone believe something that is not true: *There wasn't really a bomb in the subway station – it was a hoax.*

hob·by /ˈhɑbi/ *noun* [count] (*plural* **hob·bies**)
something that you like doing in your free time: *My hobbies are reading and swimming.*

hock·ey /ˈhɑki/ *noun* [noncount] (also **ice hock·ey**)
(SPORTS) a game that is played on ice by two teams who try to hit a small flat rubber thing

(called a PUCK) into a goal with long wooden sticks ⊃ Look at **field hockey**.

hold¹ 🔑 /hoʊld/ verb (holds, hold·ing, held /hɛld/, has held)

1 to have something in your hand or arms: *She was holding a gun.* ◆ *He held the baby in his arms.*
2 to keep something in a certain way: ***Hold** your head **up** straight.* ◆ *Try to **hold** the camera **still**.*
3 to support the weight of someone or something: *Are you sure that branch will hold both of you?*
4 to have space for a certain number or amount: *The car holds five people.*
5 to make something happen: *The meeting was held in the conference room.* ◆ *It's impossible to hold a conversation with him.*
hold someone or **something back** to stop someone or something from moving forward: *The police held back the crowd.*
Hold it! (*informal*) words that you use to tell someone to wait or not to move
hold on
1 (*informal*) to wait: *Hold on, I'm coming.* ⊃
SYNONYM **hang on**
2 to keep holding something: *The little girl held on to her mother's hand.*
hold someone or **something up**
1 to make someone or something late: *The plane was held up for 40 minutes.*
2 to try to steal from a place, using a gun: *Two men held up a bank in Springfield today.*

hold² 🔑 /hoʊld/ noun
1 [*count, noncount*] taking or having something in your hands: *She had a firm hold on the rope.* ◆ *He **got hold of** the dog by its collar.*
2 [*count*] the part of a ship or an airplane where goods are kept
get hold of someone; **get a hold of someone** to find someone so that you can speak to them: *I'm trying to get a hold of Peter, but he's not home.*
get hold of something; **get a hold of something** to find something: *I can't get hold of the book I need.*
on hold waiting to speak to someone or continue a conversation on the telephone: *May I put you on hold while I find out that information?*

hold·up /ˈhoʊldʌp/ noun [*count*]
1 something that makes you wait: *There was a long holdup on the highway.* ⊃ SYNONYM **delay**
2 when someone tries to rob someone using a gun: *There was a holdup at the local supermarket yesterday.*

hole 🔑 /hoʊl/ noun [*count*]
an empty space or opening in something: *I'm going to **dig a hole** in the sand.* ◆ *My socks are full of holes.*

hol·i·day 🔑 /ˈhɑlədeɪ/ noun
1 [*count*] a day when most schools and offices are closed to celebrate a religious or national occasion: *Next Monday is a holiday.* ◆ *Memorial Day is a **national holiday**.*
2 **the holidays** [*plural*] the time in late December and early January that includes Christmas, Hanukkah, New Year's Day, etc.: *Are you doing anything special for the holidays?* ◆ *Happy holidays!*

hol·low /ˈhɑloʊ/ adjective
with an empty space inside: *A drum is hollow.*

hol·ly /ˈhɑli/ noun [*noncount*]
a plant that has leaves with a lot of sharp points, and red BERRIES (= small round fruit). People often use it to decorate their houses for Christmas.

ho·ly /ˈhoʊli/ adjective (ho·li·er, ho·li·est) (RELIGION)
1 very special because it is about God or a god: *The Bible is the holy book of Christians.*
2 A **holy** person lives a good and religious life.

home¹ 🔑 /hoʊm/ noun
1 [*count, noncount*] the place where you live: *Sam **left home** (= stopped living in his parents' house) at the age of 18.*
2 [*count*] a place to live for people who need special care: *My grandmother lives in a home for the elderly.* ⊃ Look at **nursing home**.
at home
1 in your house or apartment: *My son is 28 and still lives at home.*
2 comfortable, as if you were in your own home: *Please **make yourself at home**.*
3 (SPORTS) If a sports team plays a game **at home**, they play on their own field.

home² 🔑 /hoʊm/ adverb
to the place where you live

Grammar

■ Be careful! We do not use **to** before **home**: *Let's **go home**.* ◆ *What time did you **get home** last night?*

---

home³ /hoʊm/ adjective
1 connected with your home or your country: *What is your home address?* ◆ *home cooking*
2 (SPORTS) connected with your own sports team or field: *The home team has a lot of support.*

home·land /ˈhoʊmlænd/ noun [*count*]
the country where you were born

home·less /ˈhoʊmləs/ adjective
If you are **homeless**, you have nowhere to live: *The floods made many people homeless.* ◆ *helping **the homeless** (= people who have no home)*

home·made /ˌhoʊm'meɪd/ *adjective*
made in your house, not bought in a store: *homemade bread*

home page (also **home·page**) /'hoʊm peɪdʒ/ *noun* [*count*]
(**COMPUTERS**) the first of a number of pages of information on the Internet that belongs to a person or an organization. A **home page** contains connections to other pages of information.

home·room /'hoʊmrum/ *noun* [*count, noncount*]
a room in a school where students go at the beginning of each school day

home run /ˌhoʊm 'rʌn/ (also *informal* **ho·mer**) /'hoʊmər/ *noun* [*count*]
(**SPORTS**) a hit in baseball, which goes so far that the player can run around all four bases to score a point

home·sick /'hoʊmsɪk/ *adjective*
sad because you are away from home

home·work /'hoʊmwərk/ *noun* [*noncount*]
work that a teacher gives to you to do at home: *Have you done your math homework?* ➔ Look at the note at **exam**.

hom·i·cide /'hɑməsaɪd/ *noun* [*count, noncount*]
the crime of killing someone deliberately: *He was charged with homicide.* ➔ **SYNONYM murder**

ho·mo·sex·u·al /ˌhoʊmə'sɛkʃuəl/ *adjective*
attracted to people of the same sex ➔ **SYNONYM gay** ➔ **ANTONYM heterosexual**
▶ **ho·mo·sex·u·al·i·ty** /ˌhoʊməsɛkʃu'æləti/ *noun* [*noncount*]: *attitudes toward homosexuality*

hon·est /'ɑnəst/ *adjective*
A person who is **honest** says what is true and does not steal, lie, or cheat: *She's a very honest person.* • *Be honest – do you really like this dress?* ➔ **ANTONYM dishonest**
▶ **hon·est·ly** /'ɑnəstli/ *adverb*: *Try to answer the questions honestly.* • *Honestly, I don't know where your money is.*
▶ **hon·es·ty** /'ɑnəsti/ *noun* [*noncount*]: *I have serious doubts about his honesty.*

hon·ey /'hʌni/ *noun* [*noncount*]
the sweet food that is made by some insects (called BEES)

hon·ey·moon /'hʌnimun/ *noun* [*count*]
a vacation for two people who have just gotten married

honk /hɑŋk/ *verb* (honks, honk·ing, honked)
to make a loud noise with a car horn: *People honked their horns as they drove past.*

hon·or /'ɑnər/ *noun*
1 [*singular*] something that makes you proud and pleased: *It was a great honor to be invited to the White House.*

2 [*noncount*] respect from other people for something good that you have done: *They fought for the honor of their country.*
3 **honors** [*plural*] a class in school or at college that is at a higher level than other classes: *honors English* • *How many honors courses are you taking this year?*
in honor of someone or **something** to show that you respect someone or something: *There is a party tonight in honor of our visitors.*

hon·or roll /'ɑnər roʊl/ *noun* [*usually singular*]
a list of the students in a school who have received good grades for their work: *I made the honor roll this semester.*

hood /hʊd/ *noun* [*count*]
1 the part of a coat or jacket that covers your head and neck
2 the front part of a car, which covers the engine: *She checked under the hood to see what was making a noise.* ➔ Look at the picture at **car**.

hoof /hʊf/ *noun* [*count*] (*plural* **hoofs** or **hooves** /huvz/)
the hard part of the foot of horses and some other animals

hook ⌐ /hʊk/ *noun* [*count*]
a curved piece of metal or plastic for hanging things on, or for catching fish with: *Hang your coat on that hook.* • *a fish hook*
off the hook If a telephone is **off the hook**, the part that you speak into (called the RECEIVER) is not in place so that the telephone will not ring.

hoop /hup/ *noun* [*count*]
(**SPORTS**) the ring that you throw the ball through in a game of BASKETBALL: *Let's shoot some hoops* (= practice playing basketball). ➔ Look at the picture at **basket**.

hoo·ray (also **hur·ray**) /hʊ'reɪ/ (also **hur·rah** /hʊ'rɑ/) *exclamation*
a word that you shout when you are very pleased about something: *Hooray! She's won!*

hoot /hut/ *noun* [*count*]
the sound that an OWL (= a type of bird) makes
▶ **hoot** *verb* (hoots, hoot·ing, hoot·ed): *An owl hooted in the dark forest.*

hooves plural of **hoof**

hop /hɑp/ *verb* (hops, hop·ping, hopped)
1 (used about a person) to jump on one foot
2 (used about an animal or bird) to jump with two or all feet together: *The frog hopped onto the stone.*
3 (*informal*) to get into or out of a car, bus, etc.: *Hop in! I'll give you a ride downtown.* • *I hopped on the next bus.*
▶ **hop** *noun* [*count*]
a short jump

hope¹ 🔑 /hoʊp/ *verb* (hopes, hop·ing, hoped)
to want something to happen or be true: *I hope that you feel better soon.* • *I hope to see you tomorrow.* • *She's hoping for a bike for her birthday.* • *"Do you think it will rain?" "I hope not."* • *"Will you be at the party?" "I'm not sure – I hope so."*

hope² 🔑 /hoʊp/ *noun*
1 [count, noncount] a feeling of wanting something to happen and thinking that it will: *There's little hope of finding survivors.* • *Don't give up hope – you may still pass.*
2 [count, usually singular] a person or thing that gives you hope: *Can you help me? You're my only hope.*

hope·ful /'hoʊpfl/ *adjective*
If you are **hopeful**, you think that something that you want will happen: *I'm hopeful about getting a job.*

hope·ful·ly /'hoʊpfl·i/ *adverb*
1 (*informal*) I hope; we hope: *Hopefully he won't be late.*
2 hoping that what you want will happen: *The cat looked hopefully at our plates.*

hope·less /'hoʊpləs/ *adjective*
with no hope of success: *a hopeless situation*
▶ **hope·less·ly** /'hoʊpləsli/ *adverb*: *We got hopelessly lost in the forest.*

ho·ri·zon /hə'raɪzn/ *noun* [count, usually singular]
the line between the earth or ocean and the sky: *We could see a ship on the horizon.*

hor·i·zon·tal /ˌhɔrə'zɑntl/ *adjective*
going from side to side, not up and down: *a horizontal line* ➲ Look at **vertical**. ➲ Look at the picture at **line**.
▶ **hor·i·zon·tal·ly** /ˌhɔrə'zɑntəli/ *adverb*

hor·mone /'hɔrmoʊn/ *noun* [count]
(**BIOLOGY**) a substance in your body that influences the way you grow and develop

horn 🔑 /hɔrn/ *noun* [count]
1 one of the hard pointed things that some animals have on their heads ➲ Look at the picture at **antelope**.
2 a thing in a car or other vehicle that makes a loud sound to warn people: *Don't honk your horn late at night.* ➲ Look at the picture at **steering wheel**.
3 a musical instrument with a metal tube that you blow into

hor·o·scope /'hɔrəskoʊp/ *noun* [count]
something that tells you what will happen, using the planets and your date of birth: *Have you read your horoscope today?* (= in a newspaper, for example) ➲ Look at **astrology**.

hor·ri·ble /'hɔrəbl/ *adjective* (*informal*)
very bad or unpleasant: *What horrible weather!* • *I had a horrible dream.*

▶ **hor·ri·bly** /'hɔrəbli/ *adverb*: *horribly painful*

hor·rif·ic /hə'rɪfɪk/ *adjective*
causing fear or shock: *a horrific accident*

hor·ri·fy /'hɔrəfaɪ/ *verb* (hor·ri·fies, hor·ri·fy·ing, hor·ri·fied, has hor·ri·fied)
to shock and frighten someone: *Everyone was horrified by the murders.*

hor·ror /'hɔrər/ *noun* [noncount]
a feeling of fear or shock: *They watched in horror as he ran in front of the bus.*
horror movie a movie that tries to frighten or shock you for entertainment

horse 🔑 /hɔrs/ *noun* [count]
a big animal that can carry people and pull heavy things: *Do you know how to ride a horse?*

horse

Word building

- A male horse is a **stallion** and a female horse is a **mare**.
- A young horse is a **foal**.

horse·back /'hɔrsbæk/ *noun*
on horse·back sitting on a horse: *We saw a lot of policemen on horseback.*

horse·back rid·ing /'hɔrsbæk ˌraɪdɪŋ/ (also **rid·ing**) *noun* [noncount]
(**SPORTS**) the sport or activity of riding a horse: *She goes horseback riding every weekend.*

horse·shoe /'hɔrʃʃu/ *noun* [count]
a piece of metal shaped like a U that a horse wears on its foot

hose /hoʊz/ *noun* [count, noncount]
a long soft tube that you use to bring water, for example in the yard or when there is a fire

hose

hos·pi·ta·ble /hɑ'spɪt̮əbl/ *adjective*
friendly and helpful to visitors

hos·pi·tal 🔑 /'hɑspɪt̮l/ *noun* [count]
a place where doctors and nurses take care of people who are sick or hurt: *My brother is in the hospital with a broken leg.* • *The ambulance took her to the hospital.*

Word building

- If you are very sick or you **have an accident**, you go **to the hospital**.
- A doctor gives you **treatment** and you are

called a **patient**. You might need to **have surgery**.

hos·pi·tal·i·ty /ˌhɑspə'tæləti/ *noun* [noncount]
being friendly and helpful to people who are visiting you: *We thanked them for their hospitality.*

host /hoʊst/ *noun* [count]
a person who invites people to their house, for example to a party: *Mark, our host, introduced us to the other guests.* ⊃ Look at **hostess**.

hos·tage /'hɑstɪdʒ/ *noun* [count]
a prisoner that a person or group keeps until people give them what they want: *Several passengers were* **taken hostage**. ◆ *The group* **held** *his daughter* **hostage** *until he paid them the money.*

hos·tel /'hɑstl/ *noun* [count]
a place like a cheap hotel where people can stay: *a youth hostel*

host·ess /'hoʊstəs/ *noun* [count] (*plural* host·ess·es)
a woman who invites people to her house, for example to a party ⊃ Look at **host**.

hos·tile /'hɑstl/ *adjective*
very unfriendly: *a hostile crowd*
▶ **hos·til·i·ty** /hɑ'stɪləti/ *noun* [noncount]: *I could sense her hostility.*

hot 🔊 /hɑt/ *adjective* (**hot·ter**, **hot·test**)
1 having a high temperature: *I'm hot. Can you open the window?* ◆ *It's hot today, isn't it?* ◆ *hot water* ⊃ **ANTONYM cold**
2 **Hot** food has a strong, burning taste: *a hot sauce* ⊃ **SYNONYM spicy**

Thesaurus

hot having a high temperature; (used about a person) feeling heat in an uncomfortable way: *Do you like this hot weather?* ◆ *Be careful – the plates are hot.* ◆ *If you're hot, take off your sweater.*

warm with a temperature that is high but not very high, so that it feels pleasant; not hot and not cold: *Wash the blouse in warm soapy water.* ◆ *It's cold outside but it's nice and warm in here.* ◆ *Are you warm enough?* ◆ *I jumped up and down to keep warm.* ⊃ **ANTONYM cold, cool**

lukewarm slightly warm, often in an unpleasant way: *The food was only lukewarm.* ◆ *Add half a cup of lukewarm water to the mixture.*

boiling (*informal*) very hot in an unpleasant way: *You must be boiling in that heavy coat.* ◆ *Can you turn the heat down? It's* **boiling hot** *in here.* ⊃ **ANTONYM freezing**

hot-air bal·loon /ˌhɑt 'ɛr bəˌlun/ *noun* [count]
a big round thing that is filled with hot air so that it floats in the sky, carrying people in a container (called a **BASKET**) under it

hot-air balloon

hot dog /'hɑt dɔg/ *noun* [count]
a **SAUSAGE** (= meat made into a long, thin shape) that you eat in a long roll

ho·tel 🔊 /hoʊ'tɛl/ *noun* [count]
a place where you pay to sleep when you are traveling: *I stayed at a hotel near the airport.*

hot·line /'hɑtlaɪn/ (also **hot line**) *noun* [count]
a special telephone line that people can call to get advice or information

hour 🔊 /'aʊər/ *noun*
1 [count] (abbreviation **hr.**) a measure of time. There are 60 minutes in an **hour**: *The trip took two hours.* ◆ *I've been waiting for an hour.* ◆ *half an hour*
2 hours [plural] the time when someone is working, or when a store or office is open: *Our office hours are 9 a.m. to 5 p.m.*
3 the hour [singular] the time when a new **hour** starts (= 1 o'clock, 2 o'clock, etc.): *Buses leave* **on the hour.**
for hours (*informal*) for a long time: *I've been waiting for hours.*

hour·ly /'aʊərli/ *adjective*, *adverb*
happening or coming once an hour: *There is an hourly bus to the airport.* ◆ *Trains run hourly.*

house 🔊 /haʊs/ *noun* [count] (*plural* hous·es /'haʊzəz/)
1 a building where a person or a family lives: *How many rooms are there in your house?* ◆ *We're having dinner at Kate's house tonight.*
2 a building that has a special use: *an opera house*

house·hold /'haʊshoʊld/ *noun* [count]
all the people who live in one house and the work, money, etc. that is needed to take care of them: *household expenses*

house·keep·er /'haʊsˌkipər/ *noun* [count]
a person whose job is to do the cleaning, cooking, etc. in someone else's house

the House of Rep·re·sen·ta·tives /ðə ˌhaʊs əv ˌrɛprɪ'zɛntətɪvz/ *noun* [singular]
(**POLITICS**) one of the two parts of the government that makes the laws in the U.S. and some other countries ⊃ Look at **senate**. ⊃ Look at the note at **government**.

house·wife /'haʊswaɪf/ *noun* [count] (*plural* house·wives /'haʊswaɪvz/)
a woman who stays at home and takes care of her house and family

house·work /ˈhaʊswərk/ *noun* [noncount]
work that you do in your house, for example the cleaning and the laundry

hous·ing /ˈhaʊzɪŋ/ *noun* [noncount]
apartments and houses for people to live in: *low-income housing* (= for people who do not earn much money)

hov·er /ˈhʌvər/ *verb* (hov·ers, hov·er·ing, hov·ered)
to stay in the air in one place: *A helicopter hovered above the building.*

how /haʊ/ *adverb*
1 in what way: *How does this machine work?* • *She told me how to get to the train station.* • *Do you know how to spell "essential"?*
2 a word that you use to ask if someone is well or happy: *"How are you?" "Fine, thanks." • "How is your sister?" "She's much better, thank you."*

Which word?

- You use **how** only when you are asking about someone's health or happiness.
- When you are asking someone to describe another person or a thing you use **what … like?**: *"What is your sister like?" "Oh, she's very intelligent, and she's taller than me."*

---

3 a word that you use to ask if something is good: *How was the movie?*
4 a word that you use to ask questions about things like age, amount, or time: *How old are you?* • *How many brothers and sisters do you have?* • *How much does this cost?* • *How long have you lived here?*
5 a word that shows surprise or strong feeling: *How nice of you to help!*
how about …? words that you use when you suggest something: *How about a drink?* • *How about going for a walk?*
how do you do? (*formal*) polite words that you say when you meet someone for the first time

ⓘ **STYLE**

When someone says **How do you do?**, you also answer **How do you do?** and you shake hands.
Some people say **Nice to meet you** when they meet. This is less formal than **How do you do**.

how·ev·er /haʊˈɛvər/ *adverb*
1 but: *She's very intelligent. However, she's somewhat lazy.*
2 it does not matter how: *I never win, however hard I try.*

howl /haʊl/ *verb* (howls, howl·ing, howled)
to make a long, loud sound, like a dog makes: *The dogs howled all night.* • *The wind howled around the house.*
▸ **howl** *noun* [count]: *He let out a howl of anger.*

HQ /ˌeɪtʃ ˈkyu/ short for **headquarters**

hr. abbreviation of **hour**

hud·dle /ˈhʌdl/ *verb* (hud·dles, hud·dling, hud·dled)
to get close to other people because you are cold or scared: *We huddled together for warmth.*

hug /hʌɡ/ *verb* (hugs, hug·ging, hugged)
to put your arms around someone to show that you love them: *She hugged her parents and said goodbye.*
▸ **hug** *noun* [count]: *Come and give me a hug.*

huge /hyudʒ/ *adjective*
very big: *They live in a huge house.* ⊃ **SYNONYM enormous**
▸ **huge·ly** /ˈhyudʒli/ *adverb*
very or very much: *She is hugely popular.*

hum /hʌm/ *verb* (hums, hum·ming, hummed)
1 to sing with your lips closed: *You can hum the tune if you don't know the words.*
2 to make a low continuous sound: *The overhead wires hummed with power.*
▸ **hum** *noun* [singular]: *The computer was making a low hum.*

hu·man¹ /ˈhyumən/ *adjective*
connected with people, not animals or machines: *the human body*

hu·man² /ˈhyumən/ (also **hu·man be·ing** /ˌhyumən ˈbiɪŋ/) *noun* [count]
a person: *Dogs can hear much better than humans.*

hu·mane /hyuˈmeɪn/ *adjective*
showing kindness, especially to a person or animal that is suffering: *humane treatment of livestock* ⊃ **ANTONYM inhumane**
▸ **hu·mane·ly** /hyuˈmeɪnli/ *adverb*: *The prisoners were treated humanely.*

hu·man·i·tar·i·an /hyuˌmænəˈtɛriən/ *adjective*
concerned with trying to make people's lives better and helping them to suffer less: *Many countries have sent humanitarian aid to the earthquake victims.*

hu·man·i·ty /hyuˈmænəti/ *noun*
1 [noncount] all of the people in the world: *crimes against humanity*
2 [noncount] the quality of being kind and fair: *The prisoners were treated with humanity.*
3 humanities [plural] the subjects that are connected with the way people think and behave, for example history, literature, and languages

tʃ **chin**   dʒ **June**   v **van**   θ **thin**   ð **then**   s **so**   z **zoo**   ʃ **she**

the hu·man race /ðə ˌhyumən ˈreɪs/ *noun* [*singular*]
all the people in the world

hu·man rights /ˌhyumən ˈraɪts/ *noun* [*plural*]
(**POLITICS**) the basic freedoms that all people should have, for example the right to say what you think, to go to school, etc.: *an organization that campaigns for human rights*

hum·ble /ˈhʌmbl/ *adjective* (**hum·bler**, **hum·blest**)
1 A **humble** person does not think they are better or more important than other people: *Despite her success she is still very humble.*
2 poor or having a low social position: *He came from a humble background.*

hu·mid /ˈhyuməd/ *adjective*
(used about the weather or climate) warm and wet: *The island is hot and humid.* ⊃ **SYNONYM damp**
▶ **hu·mid·i·ty** /hyuˈmɪdəti/ *noun* [*noncount*]: *high levels of humidity*

hu·mil·i·ate /hyuˈmɪlieɪt/ *verb* (**hu·mil·i·ates**, **hu·mil·i·at·ing**, **hu·mil·i·at·ed**)
to make someone feel very embarrassed or ashamed: *I felt humiliated when he laughed at my work.*
▶ **hu·mil·i·at·ing** /hyuˈmɪlieɪtɪŋ/ *adjective*: *a humiliating defeat*
▶ **hu·mil·i·a·tion** /hyuˌmɪliˈeɪʃn/ *noun* [*count, noncount*]

hu·mor /ˈhyumər/ *noun* [*noncount*]
1 the quality of being funny: *a story full of humor*
2 the ability to laugh and know that something is funny: *Dave has a good sense of humor.*

hu·mor·ous /ˈhyumərəs/ *adjective*
making you smile or laugh: *a humorous story* ⊃ **SYNONYM funny**

hump /hʌmp/ *noun* [*count*]
a large round lump, for example on the back of a **CAMEL** (= an animal that lives in the desert)

hun·dred /ˈhʌndrəd/ *number*
1 100: *We invited a hundred people to the party.* • *two hundred dollars* • *four hundred and twenty*
2 **hundreds** (*informal*) a lot: *I have hundreds of e-mails in my inbox.*
▶ **hun·dredth** /ˈhʌndrədθ/ *pronoun, adjective, adverb, noun* [*count*]
100th

hung form of **hang**(1)

hun·ger /ˈhʌŋgər/ *noun* [*noncount*]
the feeling that you want or need to eat: *People were dying of hunger.* ⊃ Look at **thirst**.

hun·gry /ˈhʌŋgri/ *adjective* (**hun·gri·er**, **hun·gri·est**)
wanting to eat: *Let's eat soon – I'm hungry!* ⊃ Look at **thirsty**.

hunt /hʌnt/ *verb* (**hunts**, **hunt·ing**, **hunt·ed**)
1 to chase animals to kill them as a sport or for food: *Owls hunt at night.*
2 to try to find something: *I hunted everywhere for my watch, but I couldn't find it.*
▶ **hunt** *noun* [*count, usually singular*]: *a fox hunt* • *a hunt for the missing child*
▶ **hunting** /ˈhʌntɪŋ/ *noun* [*noncount*]
the activity of chasing and killing animals as a sport or for food: *to go hunting*

hunt·er /ˈhʌntər/ *noun* [*count*]
a person who hunts wild animals

hur·dle /ˈhərdl/ *noun* (**SPORTS**)
1 [*count*] a type of light fence that a person or a horse jumps over in a race
2 **hurdles** [*plural*] a race in which people or horses have to jump over **hurdles**: *the 200-meter hurdles*

hurl /hərl/ *verb* (**hurls**, **hurl·ing**, **hurled**)
to throw something very strongly: *She hurled the book across the room.*

hurrah, hurray = **hooray**

hur·ri·cane /ˈhərəkən/ *noun* [*count*]
(**GEOGRAPHY**) a storm with very strong winds: *Another hurricane hit the coast of Florida.* ⊃ Look at the note at **wind**[1].

hur·ry[1] /ˈhəri/ *verb* (**hur·ries**, **hur·ry·ing**, **hur·ried**, **has hur·ried**)
to move or do something quickly: *We hurried home after school.*
hurry up to move or do something more quickly because there is not much time: *Hurry up or we'll be late!*

hur·ry[2] /ˈhəri/ *noun* [*noncount*]
the need or wish to do something quickly: *Take your time. There's no hurry.*
in a hurry
1 quickly: *She got up late and left in a hurry.*
2 not having enough time to do something: *I can't talk to you now – I'm in a hurry.*

hurt[1] /hərt/ *verb* (**hurts**, **hurt·ing**, **hurt**, **has hurt**)
1 to make someone or something feel pain: *I fell and hurt my leg.* • *Did you hurt yourself?* • *These shoes hurt – they're too small.*
2 to feel pain: *My leg hurts.*
3 to make someone unhappy: *I never meant to hurt your feelings.*

Thesaurus

hurt is a general word meaning to feel pain, or to make someone or something else feel pain: *My feet hurt.* • *It hurts when I bend my knee.* • *Ouch! That really hurts!* • *Stop that – you're hurting me.* • *Did you hurt yourself when you fell?*

---

ache to feel a pain that is not strong, but that continues for a long time. This verb does not take an object, so you cannot put a noun directly after it: *His legs ached after playing soccer for two hours.* ◆ *Her eyes ached from lack of sleep.* ◆ *I'm aching all over.*

burn to feel very hot and painful; to hurt someone with fire or heat: *Your forehead's burning. You must have a fever.* ◆ *The water was so hot that I burned my hands.* ◆ *She was badly burned in the fire.*

sting to feel a sudden sharp pain; to make someone feel a pain like this: *My eyes were stinging from the soap.* ◆ *Ow! That antiseptic cream stings!*

hurt² /hərt/ *adjective*
1 physically harmed: *Was anyone hurt in the accident?* ⊃ SYNONYM **injured**
2 upset: *I was very hurt by what you said.*

hurt·ful /ˈhərtfl/ *adjective*
making someone feel upset: *What she said was really hurtful.*

hus·band 🔑 /ˈhʌzbənd/ *noun* [count]
the man that someone is married to ⊃ Look at **wife**.

hush /hʌʃ/ *verb* (**hush·es, hush·ing, hushed**)
a word that you use to tell someone to be quiet: *Hush now, and go to sleep.*
▶ **hush** *noun* [singular]
a situation in which it is completely quiet: *A hush fell over the room.* ⊃ SYNONYM **silence**

hut /hʌt/ *noun* [count]
a small, simple building with one room

hy·drau·lic /haɪˈdrɔlɪk/ *adjective*
Hydraulic equipment is worked by liquid moving under pressure: *hydraulic brakes*

hy·dro·e·lec·tric /ˌhaɪdroʊˈlɛktrɪk/ *adjective*
(PHYSICS) using the power of water to produce electricity: *hydroelectric power*

hy·dro·gen /ˈhaɪdrədʒən/ *noun* [noncount]
(symbol **H**)
(CHEMISTRY) a light gas that you cannot see or smell: *Water is made of hydrogen and oxygen.*

hy·giene /ˈhaɪdʒin/ *noun* [noncount]
(HEALTH) keeping yourself and things around you clean: *Good hygiene is very important when you are preparing food.*
▶ **hy·gi·en·ic** /haɪˈdʒɛnɪk; haɪˈdʒinɪk/ *adjective*: *hygienic conditions*

hymn /hɪm/ *noun* [count]
(RELIGION, MUSIC) a song that Christians sing in church

hype /haɪp/ *noun* [noncount] (*informal*)
advertisements that make you think something is better than it really is: *Don't believe the hype – the movie's terrible!*

hy·per·ac·tive /ˌhaɪpərˈæktɪv/ *adjective*
too active and only able to keep quiet and still for a short time: *a hyperactive child*

hy·phen /ˈhaɪfən/ *noun* [count]
(ENGLISH LANGUAGE ARTS) a mark (-) that you use in writing. It joins words together (for example "left-handed") or shows that a word continues on the next line.

hyp·no·sis /hɪpˈnoʊsəs/ *noun* [noncount]
when someone's mind and actions can be controlled by another person because they are in a kind of deep sleep: *She spoke about the attack **under hypnosis**.*

hyp·no·tize /ˈhɪpnətaɪz/ *verb* (**hyp·no·tiz·es, hyp·no·tiz·ing, hyp·no·tized**)
to put someone into a kind of deep sleep in which their mind and actions can be controlled by another person
▶ **hyp·no·tist** /ˈhɪpnətɪst/ *noun* [count]
a person who **hypnotizes** other people

hy·poc·ri·sy /hɪˈpɑkrəsi/ *noun* [noncount]
behavior in which someone pretends to have moral beliefs that they do not really have

hyp·o·crite /ˈhɪpəkrɪt/ *noun* [count]
a person who pretends to have moral beliefs that they do not really have
▶ **hy·po·crit·i·cal** /ˌhɪpəˈkrɪtɪkl/ *adjective*: *She's so hypocritical! She says she cares about the environment but she doesn't even recycle.*

hy·poth·e·sis AWL /haɪˈpɑθəsəs/ *noun* [count]
(*plural* **hy·poth·e·ses** /haɪˈpɑθəsiz/)
(GENERAL SCIENCE) an idea that is suggested as a way to explain something, but which has not yet been found to be true or correct: *to test a scientific hypothesis* (= to find out if it is true)

hy·po·thet·i·cal AWL /ˌhaɪpəˈθɛtɪkl/ *adjective*
based on situations that have not yet happened, not on facts: *a hypothetical situation*

hys·ter·i·cal /hɪˈstɛrɪkl/ *adjective*
so excited or upset that you cannot control yourself: *hysterical laughter*

I i

I, i /aɪ/ *noun* [*count, noncount*] (*plural* **I's, i's** /aɪz/)
the ninth letter of the English alphabet: *"Island" begins with an "I."*

I 🔑 /aɪ/ *pronoun* (*plural* **we** /wi/)
the person who is speaking: *I said I would call her later.* • *I'll (= I will) see you tomorrow.* • *I'm not going to fall, am I?*

ice 🔑 /aɪs/ *noun* [*noncount*]
water that has become hard because it is frozen: *Do you want ice in your drink?* • *I slipped on a patch of ice.*

ice·berg /'aɪsbərg/ *noun* [*count*]
(**GEOGRAPHY**) a very big piece of ice in the ocean

ice cream /'aɪs krim/ *noun* [*noncount*]
very cold, sweet food made from milk: *Do you like chocolate ice cream?* • *an ice-cream cone* (= a cone with ice cream in it)

ice cube /'aɪs kyub/ *noun* [*count*]
a small piece of ice that you put in a drink to make it cold

iced /aɪst/ *adjective*
(used about drinks) served very cold, with ice: *iced tea*

ice hockey

goaltender

puck

hockey stick

ice rink

ice hock·ey /'aɪs hɑki/ (also **hock·ey**) *noun*
[*noncount*]
(**SPORTS**) a game that is played on ice by two teams, who try to hit a small flat rubber thing (called a **PUCK**) into a goal with long wooden sticks

ice rink /'aɪs rɪŋk/ (also **skat·ing rink** /'skeɪtɪŋ rɪŋk/, **rink**) *noun* [*count*]
a special place where you can **ICE SKATE**

ice skate /'aɪs skeɪt/ *verb* (**ice skates, ice skat·ing, ice skat·ed**) (also **skate**)
to move on ice in special boots (called **ICE SKATES**), which have long sharp pieces of metal on the bottom ➲ Look at the picture at **skate**.

▶ **ice skat·ing** /'aɪs skeɪtɪŋ/ (also **skat·ing**) *noun*
[*noncount*]: *We go ice skating every weekend in the winter.* ➲ Look at **figure skating**.

i·ci·cle /'aɪsɪkl/ *noun* [*count*]
a long piece of ice that hangs down from something

ic·ing /'aɪsɪŋ/ *noun* [*noncount*]
a sweet substance that you use for covering cakes: *a cake with pink icing* ➲ Look at **frosting**.

i·con /'aɪkɑn/ *noun* [*count*]
1 a small picture on a computer screen that you can use to start a program or open a file: *Double-click on the icon.*
2 a famous person or thing that people admire: *Madonna and other pop icons*

ic·y /'aɪsi/ *adjective* (**ic·i·er, ic·i·est**)
1 very cold: *an icy wind*
2 covered with ice: *icy roads*

ID /ˌaɪ 'di/ *abbreviation* (*informal*)
a document that shows who you are: *Do you have any ID?* • *an ID card* ➲ **ID** is short for "identity" or "identification."

I'd /aɪd/ *short for* **I had, I would**

i·de·a 🔑 /aɪ'diə/ *noun* [*count*]
1 a plan or new thought: *It would be a good idea to get there early.* • *I have an idea. Let's have a party!*
2 a picture in your mind: *The movie gives you a good idea of what New Orleans is like.* • *I have no idea* (= I do not know) *where she is.*
3 an opinion or a belief: *She has her own ideas about how to bring up children.*

i·de·al /aɪ'diəl/ *adjective*
the best or exactly right: *This is an ideal place for a picnic.* ➲ **SYNONYM perfect**
▶ **i·de·al·ly** /aɪ'diəli/ *adverb*: *She's ideally suited to the job.*

i·de·al·ism /aɪ'diəlɪzəm/ *noun* [*noncount*]
the belief that a perfect life or situation is possible, even when this is not likely: *college students full of idealism*
▶ **i·de·al·ist** /aɪ'diəlɪst/ *noun* [*count*]: *He's an idealist.*

i·den·ti·cal **AWL** /aɪ'dɛntɪkl/ *adjective*
exactly the same: *These two cameras are identical.* • *identical twins*

i·den·ti·fi·ca·tion **AWL** /aɪˌdɛntəfə'keɪʃn/ *noun*
1 [*count, noncount*] the process of showing or finding out who someone or something is: *The identification of bodies after the accident was difficult.*
2 (abbreviation **ID**) [*noncount*] a document that shows who you are: *Do you have any identification?*

---

i·den·ti·fy 🖋 **AWL** /aɪˈdɛntəfaɪ/ *verb* (i·den·ti·fies, i·den·ti·fy·ing, i·den·ti·fied, has i·den·ti·fied)
to say or know who someone is or what something is: *The police have not identified the dead man yet.*
identify with someone to feel that you understand and share what someone else is feeling: *I found it hard to identify with the woman in the movie.*

i·den·ti·ty **AWL** /aɪˈdɛntəti/ *noun* [count, noncount] (*plural* i·den·ti·ties)
who or what a person or thing is: *The **identity of** the killer is not known.*

id·i·om /ˈɪdiəm/ *noun* [count]
(ENGLISH LANGUAGE ARTS) a group of words with a special meaning: *The idiom "break someome's heart" means "to make someone very unhappy."*

id·i·o·mat·ic /ˌɪdiəˈmætɪk/ *adjective*
(ENGLISH LANGUAGE ARTS) using language that contains natural expressions: *She speaks fluent and idiomatic English.*

id·i·ot /ˈɪdiət/ *noun* [count]
a person who is stupid or does something silly: *I was an idiot to believe what he said.*
▶ **id·i·ot·ic** /ˌɪdiˈɑtɪk/ *adjective*: *an idiotic mistake*

i·dol /ˈaɪdl/ *noun* [count]
1 a famous person that people love: *Noah was a Giants fan, and Eli Manning was his idol.*
2 (RELIGION) an object that people treat as a god

i·dol·ize /ˈaɪdl·aɪz/ *verb* (i·dol·iz·es, i·dol·iz·ing, i·dol·ized)
to love or admire someone very much or too much: *He has always idolized his uncle.*

i.e. /ˌaɪ ˈi/ *abbreviation*
used in writing to mean "that is" or "in other words": *the basic necessities of life, i.e. food, water, and somewhere to live*

if 🖋 /ɪf/ *conjunction*
1 a word that you use to say what is possible or true when another thing happens or is true: *If you press this button, the machine starts.* ◆ *If you see him, give him this letter.* ◆ *If your feet were smaller, you could wear my shoes.* ◆ *If I had a million dollars, I would buy a big house.* ◆ *I may see you tomorrow. If not, I'll see you next week.*
2 a word that shows a question: *Do you know if Paul is home?* ◆ *She asked me if I wanted to go to a party.* ➾ SYNONYM **whether**
3 every time: *If I forget to bring my lunch, I can buy it at the cafeteria.* ➾ SYNONYM **whenever**
as if in a way that makes you think something: *She looks as if she didn't get enough sleep last night.*
if I were you words that you use when you are giving someone advice: *If I were you, I would leave now.*

if only words that show that you want something very much: *If only I could drive!*

ig·loo /ˈɪglu/ *noun* [count] (*plural* ig·loos)
a small house that is made out of blocks of snow

ig·nite /ɪgˈnaɪt/ *verb* (ig·nites, ig·nit·ing, ig·nit·ed) (*formal*)
to start burning or to make something start burning: *The gas ignited and caused an explosion.*

ig·ni·tion /ɪgˈnɪʃn/ *noun* [count]
the part of a car where you put the key to start the engine: *I left my key in the ignition.*

ig·no·rance **AWL** /ˈɪgnərəns/ *noun* [noncount]
not knowing about something: *Her ignorance surprised me.*

ig·no·rant **AWL** /ˈɪgnərənt/ *adjective*
not knowing about something: *I'm very **ignorant about** computers.*

ig·nore 🖋 **AWL** /ɪgˈnɔr/ *verb* (ig·nores, ig·nor·ing, ig·nored)
to know about someone or something, but to not do anything about it: *He completely ignored his doctor's advice.* ◆ *I said "hello" to her, but she ignored me.*

Prefix

il–
(used with words beginning with "l") not; the opposite of: *illegal* ◆ *illegally* ◆ *illiterate* ◆ *illiteracy*

ill /ɪl/ *adjective*
(HEALTH) not well; not in good health: *He is seriously ill.* ◆ *a mentally ill patient* ➾ SYNONYM **sick** ➾ The noun is **illness**.

I'll /aɪl/ short for **I will**

il·le·gal 🖋 **AWL** /ɪˈligl/ *adjective*
not allowed by law: *It's illegal to drive through a red light.* ➾ ANTONYM **legal**
▶ **il·le·gal·ly** **AWL** /ɪˈligəli/ *adverb*: *She entered the country illegally.*

il·leg·i·ble /ɪˈlɛdʒəbl/ *adjective*
difficult or impossible to read: *Your handwriting is completely illegible.* ➾ ANTONYM **legible**

il·lit·er·ate /ɪˈlɪtərət/ *adjective*
not able to read or write ➾ ANTONYM **literate**
▶ **il·lit·er·a·cy** /ɪˈlɪtərəsi/ *noun* [noncount]: *the problem of adult illiteracy* ➾ ANTONYM **literacy**

ill·ness 🖋 /ˈɪlnəs/ *noun* (*plural* ill·ness·es)
(HEALTH)
1 [noncount] being sick: *I missed a lot of school because of illness last year.*
2 [count] a type or period of illness: *She died after a long illness.*

Collocations

Illness

getting sick
- **catch** a cold/the flu/a virus/a bug
- **get** sick/a cold/a headache
- **have** a cold/an infection/a fever/a toothache
- **feel** sick/hot/dizzy

treatment
- **examine** a patient
- **be on** medication/antibiotics
- **get/have** a shot/an injection/an X-ray
- **need/receive/get** treatment
- ⏵ Look at the note at **injury**.

il·log·i·cal AWL /ɪˈlɑdʒɪkl/ *adjective*
not sensible or reasonable: *I know you feel strongly about this, but your argument is illogical.*
⏵ ANTONYM **logical**

il·lu·sion /ɪˈluʒn/ *noun*
1 [count, noncount] a false idea or belief: *I have no illusions about the situation – I know it's serious.*
2 [count] something that your eyes tell you is there or is true but in fact is not: *That line looks longer, but in fact they're the same length. It's an optical illusion.*

il·lus·trate AWL /ˈɪləstreɪt/ *verb* (il·lus·trates, il·lus·trat·ing, il·lus·trat·ed)
1 to explain or make something clear by giving examples: *She gave some statistics to illustrate her point.*
2 (ART) to add pictures to show something more clearly: *The book is illustrated with color photographs.*

il·lus·tra·tion AWL /ˌɪləˈstreɪʃn/ *noun* [count]
(ART) a picture in a book: *This dictionary has a lot of illustrations.*

I'm /aɪm/ short for **I am**

Prefix

im-
(used with words beginning with "m" and "p") not; the opposite of: *impatient* ◆ *impatience* ◆ *impolite* ◆ *impurity* ◆ *immature* ◆ *immoral*

im·age 🔑 AWL /ˈɪmɪdʒ/ *noun* [count]
1 the impression that a person or an organization gives to the public: *He's very different from his public image.*
2 a picture in people's minds of someone or something: *A lot of people have an image of Seattle as cold and rainy.*
3 a picture on paper or in a mirror: *images of flowers*

im·age·ry AWL /ˈɪmɪdʒri/ *noun* [noncount]
(ENGLISH LANGUAGE ARTS) language that makes pictures in the minds of the people reading or listening: *poetic imagery*

i·mag·i·nar·y /ɪˈmædʒəˌnɛri/ *adjective*
not real; only in your mind: *The book is about an imaginary country.*

i·mag·i·na·tion 🔑 /ɪˌmædʒəˈneɪʃn/ *noun* [count, noncount]
the ability to think of new ideas or make pictures in your mind: *He has a big imagination.*
◆ *You didn't really see a ghost – it was just your imagination.*

i·mag·i·na·tive /ɪˈmædʒənəṭɪv/ *adjective*
having or showing imagination: *imaginative ideas*

i·mag·ine 🔑 /ɪˈmædʒən/ *verb* (i·mag·ines, i·mag·in·ing, i·mag·ined)
1 to make a picture of something in your mind: *Can you imagine life without electricity?* ◆ *I closed my eyes and imagined I was lying on a beach.*
2 to see, hear, or think something that is not true: *I never said that – you're imagining things.*
3 to think that something is probably true: *I imagine he'll be coming by car.*

im·i·tate /ˈɪməteɪt/ *verb* (im·i·tates, im·i·tat·ing, im·i·tat·ed)
to copy someone or something: *Children learn by imitating adults.*

im·i·ta·tion /ˌɪməˈteɪʃn/ *noun* [count]
something that you make to look like another thing: *It's not a real diamond – it's only an imitation.* ◆ *imitation leather* ⏵ SYNONYM **copy**

im·ma·ture AWL /ˌɪməˈtʃʊr; ˌɪməˈtʊr/ *adjective*
behaving in a way that is not sensible and is typical of younger people: *He's very immature for his age.* ⏵ ANTONYM **mature**

im·me·di·ate 🔑 /ɪˈmidiət/ *adjective*
happening now or very soon: *I can't wait – I need an immediate answer.*

im·me·di·ate·ly 🔑 /ɪˈmidiətli/ *adverb*

> ⓘ SPELLING
> Remember! You spell **immediately** with MM.

now: *Come to my office immediately!* ⏵ SYNONYM **at once**

im·mense /ɪˈmɛns/ *adjective*
very big: *immense problems*
▶ **im·mense·ly** /ɪˈmɛnsli/ *adverb*
very or very much: *We enjoyed the party immensely.*

im·merse /ɪˈmɜrs/ *verb* (im·mers·es, im·mers·ing, im·mersed)
1 to put something into a liquid so that it is covered: *Completely immerse the potatoes in boiling water.*

2 to give all your attention to something: *I was immersed in a book and didn't hear the phone.*

im·mi·grant AWL /ˈɪməgrənt/ *noun* [count]
a person who comes to another country to live there: *Many immigrants to the U.S. come from Mexico.*

im·mi·grate AWL /ˈɪməgreɪt/ *verb* (im·mi·grates, im·mi·grat·ing, im·mi·grat·ed)
to come to live in a country, after leaving your own country: *His family immigrated to Israel.* ➔ Look at **emigrate**.

im·mi·gra·tion AWL /ˌɪməˈgreɪʃn/ *noun* [noncount]
the process of coming to live in a country that is not your own: *The government is trying to control illegal immigration.*

im·mor·al /ɪˈmɔrəl/ *adjective*
(used about people and their behavior) not honest or good: *It's immoral to steal.* ➔ Look at **moral**.

im·mor·tal /ɪˈmɔrtl/ *adjective*
living or lasting forever

im·mune /ɪˈmyun/ *adjective*
(HEALTH) If you are **immune** to a disease, you cannot get it: *You're immune to the chicken pox if you've had it before.*
▶ **im·mu·ni·ty** /ɪˈmyunəti/ *noun* [noncount]: *You can build up your natural immunity to viruses.*

im·mune sys·tem /ɪˈmyun ˌsɪstəm/ *noun* [count]
(BIOLOGY, HEALTH) the system in your body that fights against infection and disease: *The virus attacks your immune system.*

im·mu·nize /ˈɪmyənaɪz/ *verb* (im·mu·niz·es, im·mu·niz·ing, im·mu·nized)
(HEALTH) to protect someone from a disease by putting a substance that protects the body (called a VACCINE) into their blood
▶ **im·mu·ni·za·tion** /ˌɪmyənəˈzeɪʃn/ *noun* [count, noncount]: *an immunization program*

im·pact AWL /ˈɪmpækt/ *noun* [count]
the effect that something has: *I hope this campaign will have an impact on young people.*

im·pa·tient 🔑 /ɪmˈpeɪʃnt/ *adjective*
not wanting to wait for something: *Don't be so impatient! The bus will be here soon.* ➔ ANTONYM **patient**
▶ **im·pa·tience** /ɪmˈpeɪʃns/ *noun* [noncount]: *He couldn't hide his impatience.*
▶ **im·pa·tient·ly** /ɪmˈpeɪʃntli/ *adverb*: *"Hurry up!" she said impatiently.*

im·peach /ɪmˈpitʃ/ *verb* (im·peach·es, im·peach·ing, im·peached)
(POLITICS) to officially accuse a public official of a crime or of doing something bad in their job
▶ **im·peach·ment** /ɪmˈpitʃmənt/ *noun* [count, noncount]

im·per·a·tive¹ /ɪmˈpɛrətɪv/ *noun* [count]
(ENGLISH LANGUAGE ARTS) the form of a verb that you use for telling someone to do something: *"Listen!" and "Go away!" are in the imperative.*

im·per·a·tive² /ɪmˈpɛrətɪv/ *adjective*
very important: *It is imperative that you see a doctor immediately.* ➔ SYNONYM **vital**

im·per·fect /ɪmˈpərfɪkt/ *adjective*
with mistakes or faults: *It's an imperfect system.* ➔ ANTONYM **perfect**
▶ **im·per·fec·tion** /ˌɪmpərˈfɛkʃn/ *noun* [count, noncount]: *a few slight imperfections* ➔ ANTONYM **perfection**

im·per·son·ate /ɪmˈpərsəneɪt/ *verb* (im·per·son·ates, im·per·son·at·ing, im·per·son·at·ed)
to copy the way another person speaks or behaves, usually in order to make people laugh: *Have you heard him impersonate the president?*

im·per·ti·nent /ɪmˈpərtn·ənt/ *adjective* (formal)
rude and not showing respect: *Don't be impertinent!*

im·ple·ment¹ AWL /ˈɪmpləmɛnt/ *noun* [count]
a tool that you use, especially for working outside: *farm implements*

im·ple·ment² AWL /ˈɪmpləmənt/ *verb* (im·ple·ments, im·ple·ment·ing, im·ple·ment·ed)
to start using a plan, system, etc.: *The bank has just implemented a new security system.*

im·pli·ca·tion AWL /ˌɪmpləˈkeɪʃn/ *noun*
1 [count] the effect that an action will have on something else in the future: *We need to discuss the implications of the new law.*
2 [count, noncount] something that is suggested, without actually being said: *He didn't actually say it, but the implication was that I am lazy.*

im·plic·it AWL /ɪmˈplɪsət/ *adjective*
not expressed in a direct way but understood by everyone: *an implicit agreement* ➔ Look at **explicit**.

im·ply AWL /ɪmˈplaɪ/ *verb* (im·plies, im·ply·ing, im·plied, has im·plied)
to suggest something without actually saying it: *He asked if I had any work to do. He was implying that I was lazy.*

im·po·lite /ˌɪmpəˈlaɪt/ *adjective*
not polite: *It was impolite of him to ask you to leave.*

im·port /ɪmˈpɔrt/ *verb* (im·ports, im·port·ing, im·port·ed)
to buy things from another country and bring them into your country: *The U.S. imports bananas from Ecuador.* ➔ ANTONYM **export**
▶ **im·port** /ˈɪmpɔrt/ *noun* [count]: *What are your country's main imports?*

ə **about**   y **yes**   w **woman**   t̬ **butter**   eɪ **say**   aɪ **five**   ɔɪ **boy**   aʊ **now**   oʊ **go**

► **im·port·er** /ɪmˈpɔrtər/ *noun* [*count*]: *an importer of electrical goods*

im·por·tance 🔑 /ɪmˈpɔrtns/ *noun* [*noncount*]
the quality of being important: *My doctor reminded me of the importance of exercise and a healthy diet.*

im·por·tant 🔑 /ɪmˈpɔrtnt/ *adjective*
1 If something is **important**, you must do, have, or think about it: *It is important to sleep well the night before an exam.* ◆ *I think that happiness is more important than money.*
2 powerful or special: *The president is a very important person.*

im·pose **AWL** /ɪmˈpoʊz/ *verb* (im·pos·es, im·pos·ing, im·posed)
to make a law, a rule, an opinion, etc. be accepted by using your power or authority: *A new tax was imposed on fuel.*

im·pos·si·ble 🔑 /ɪmˈpɑsəbl/ *adjective*
If something is **impossible**, you cannot do it, or it cannot happen: *It's impossible for me to finish this work by five o'clock.* ◆ *The house was impossible to find.* ⊃ ANTONYM **possible**

im·prac·ti·cal /ɪmˈpræktɪkl/ *adjective*
not sensible or realistic: *It would be impractical to take our bikes on the train.* ⊃ ANTONYM **practical**

im·pre·cise **AWL** /ˌɪmprɪˈsaɪs/ *adjective*
not clear or exact: *imprecise instructions* ⊃ ANTONYM **precise**

im·press 🔑 /ɪmˈprɛs/ *verb* (im·press·es, im·press·ing, im·pressed)
to make someone admire and respect you: *We were very impressed by your work.*

im·pres·sion 🔑 /ɪmˈprɛʃn/ *noun* [*count*]
feelings or thoughts you have about someone or something: *What was your first impression of the city?* ◆ *I get the impression that she's not very happy.* ◆ *He made a good impression on his first day at work.*

im·pres·sive /ɪmˈprɛsɪv/ *adjective*
If someone or something is **impressive**, you admire them: *an impressive building* ◆ *Your work is very impressive.*

im·pris·on /ɪmˈprɪzn/ *verb* (im·pris·ons, im·pris·on·ing, im·pris·oned)
to put someone in prison: *He was imprisoned for killing his wife.*
► **im·pris·on·ment** /ɪmˈprɪznmənt/ *noun* [*noncount*]: *two years' imprisonment*

im·prob·a·ble /ɪmˈprɑbəbl/ *adjective*
not likely to be true or to happen: *an improbable explanation* ⊃ ANTONYM **probable**

im·prove 🔑 /ɪmˈpruv/ *verb* (im·proves, im·prov·ing, im·proved)
to become better or to make something better:

Your English has improved a lot this year. ◆ *You need to improve your spelling.*

im·prove·ment 🔑 /ɪmˈpruvmənt/ *noun* [*count, noncount*]
a change that makes something better than it was before: *There has been a big improvement in Sam's work.*

im·pro·vise /ˈɪmprəvaɪz/ *verb* (im·pro·vis·es, im·pro·vis·ing, im·pro·vised)
to make or do something without any preparation: *I haven't prepared a speech, so I'll just have to improvise.*
► **im·prov·i·sa·tion** /ɪmˌprɑvəˈzeɪʃn/ *noun* [*count, noncount*]

im·pulse /ˈɪmpʌls/ *noun* [*count*]
a sudden strong wish to do something: *She felt an impulse to run away.*

im·pul·sive /ɪmˈpʌlsɪv/ *adjective*
doing things suddenly and without thinking carefully: *It was an impulsive decision.*

in¹ 🔑 /ɪn/ *preposition*
1 a word that shows where someone or something is: *a small town in Texas* ◆ *He put his hand in the water.* ◆ *She was lying in bed.*
2 making all or part of something: *There are 12 inches in a foot.*
3 a word that shows when something happens: *My birthday is in May.* ◆ *He graduated from high school in 2003.*
4 a word that shows how long something takes: *I'll be ready in ten minutes.*
5 a word that shows what clothes someone is wearing: *She was dressed in black for the funeral.*
6 a word that shows how someone or something is: *Jenny was in tears* (= she was crying). ◆ *Sit in a circle.*
7 a word that shows someone's job: *He's in the army.*
8 a word that shows in what way or in what language: *Write your name in capital letters.* ◆ *They were speaking in French.*

in² 🔑 /ɪn/ *adverb*
1 to a place, from outside: *I opened the door and went in.*
2 at home or at work: *I stopped by your house, but you weren't in.*

in³ /ɪn/ *adjective* (*informal*)
fashionable now: *This restaurant is the in place to go.* ◆ *The color gray is very in this season.*

in. abbreviation of **inch**

Prefix

in-
not; the opposite of: *inaccurate* ◆ *incomplete* ◆ *incorrectly* ◆ *independence* ◆ *invisible*

---

in·a·bil·i·ty /ˌɪnə'bɪləti/ *noun* [noncount, singular]
not being able to do something: *He has **an inability to** talk about his problems.* ➔ The adjective is **unable**.

in·ac·ces·si·ble AWL /ˌɪnæk'sɛsəbl/ *adjective*
very difficult or impossible to reach or contact: *That beach is inaccessible by car.* ➔ ANTONYM **accessible**

in·ac·cu·rate AWL /ɪn'ækyərət/ *adjective*
not correct; with mistakes in it: *The report in the newspaper was inaccurate.* ➔ ANTONYM **accurate** ➔ Look at the note at **wrong**[1].
▸ **in·ac·cu·rate·ly** /ɪn'ækyərətli/ *adverb*: *The message had been copied inaccurately.*

in·ac·tive /ɪn'æktɪv/ *adjective*
doing nothing; not active: *an inactive volcano* ➔ ANTONYM **active**

in·ad·e·quate AWL /ɪn'ædɪkwət/ *adjective*
not enough, or not good enough: *These shoes are **inadequate for** cold weather.* ➔ ANTONYM **adequate**
▸ **in·ad·e·quate·ly** AWL /ɪn'ædɪkwətli/ *adverb*

in·ap·pro·pri·ate AWL /ˌɪnə'proʊpriət/ *adjective*
not suitable: *Her dress was totally **inappropriate for** a funeral.* ➔ ANTONYM **appropriate**
▸ **in·ap·pro·pri·ate·ly** AWL /ˌɪnə'proʊpriətli/ *adverb*

in·au·gu·rate /ɪ'nɔgyəreɪt/ *verb* (in·au·gu·rates, in·au·gu·rat·ing, in·au·gu·rat·ed)
(**POLITICS**) to introduce a new public official or leader at a special ceremony: *President Obama was inaugurated on January 20, 2009.*
▸ **in·au·gu·ral** /ɪ'nɔgyərəl/ *adjective*: *the president's inaugural speech*
▸ **in·au·gu·ra·tion** /ɪˌnɔgyə'reɪʃn/ *noun* [count, noncount]: *the president's inauguration*

in·box /'ɪnbɑks/ *noun* [count] (*plural* in·box·es)
(**COMPUTERS**) the place on a computer where new e-mail messages are shown: *I have hundreds of e-mails in my inbox.*

Inc. (**BUSINESS**) abbreviation of **incorporated**

in·ca·pa·ble AWL /ɪn'keɪpəbl/ *adjective*
not able to do something: *He's **incapable of** lying.* ➔ ANTONYM **capable**

in·cen·tive AWL /ɪn'sɛntɪv/ *noun* [count, noncount]
something that makes you want to do something: *People need **incentives** to save money.*

inch /ɪntʃ/ *noun* [count] (*plural* inch·es)
(abbreviation **in.**)
a measure of length (=2.54 centimeters). There are twelve **inches** in a foot: *I am five feet six inches tall.* • *a twelve-inch ruler*

in·ci·dent AWL /'ɪnsədənt/ *noun* [count]
something that happens, especially something bad or unusual: *One particular incident sticks in my mind.*

in·ci·den·tal·ly AWL /ˌɪnsə'dɛntəli/ *adverb*
a word that you say when you are going to talk about something different: *Incidentally, have you been to that new Mexican restaurant yet?* ➔ SYNONYM **by the way**

in·cin·er·a·tor /ɪn'sɪnəreɪtər/ *noun* [count]
a container or machine for burning garbage or other things

in·clined AWL /ɪn'klaɪnd/ *adjective*
1 wanting to do something: *I know Andrew well, so I'm **inclined to** believe what he says.*
2 likely to do something: *She's **inclined to** change her mind very easily.*

in·clude 🔑 /ɪn'klud/ *verb* (in·cludes, in·clud·ing, in·clud·ed)
1 to have someone or something as one part of the whole: *The price of the room includes breakfast.*
2 to make someone or something part of a group: *Did you include the new girl on the list?* ➔ ANTONYM **exclude**

in·clud·ing 🔑 /ɪn'kludɪŋ/ *preposition*
with; if you count someone or something: *There were five people in the car, including the driver.* ➔ ANTONYM **excluding**

in·clu·sive /ɪn'klusɪv/ *adjective*
including everything or the thing mentioned: *The price is **inclusive of** meals.*

in·co·her·ent AWL /ˌɪnkoʊ'hɪrənt/ *adjective*
not clear or easy to understand; not saying something clearly: *I tried to understand what he was saying, but he was completely incoherent.* ➔ ANTONYM **coherent**
▸ **in·co·her·ent·ly** AWL /ˌɪnkoʊ'hɪrəntli/ *adverb*

in·come AWL /'ɪnkʌm/ *noun* [count, noncount]
all the money that you receive for your work, for example: *It's difficult for a family to live on one income.*

in·come tax /'ɪnkʌm tæks/ *noun* [count, noncount]
the money that you pay to the government from the money that you earn

in·com·pat·i·ble AWL /ˌɪnkəm'pætəbl/ *adjective*
very different, and so not able to exist or be used together: *The new software is **incompatible with** my computer.* ➔ ANTONYM **compatible**
▸ **in·com·pat·i·bil·i·ty** AWL /ˌɪnkəmˌpætə'bɪləti/ *noun* [count, noncount] (*plural* in·com·pat·i·bil·i·ties)

in·com·pe·tent /ɪn'kɑmpətənt/ *adjective*
not having the necessary skill to do something well: *That woman at the bank was completely incompetent.* ➔ ANTONYM **competent**

▶ **in·com·pe·tent·ly** /ɪnˈkɑmpətəntli/ *adverb*

in·com·plete /ˌɪnkəmˈplit/ *adjective*
not finished; with parts missing: *This list is incomplete.* ⊃ ANTONYM **complete**

in·com·pre·hen·si·ble /ɪnˌkɑmprɪˈhɛnsəbl/ *adjective*
impossible to understand: *an incomprehensible explanation*

in·con·sid·er·ate /ˌɪnkənˈsɪdərət/ *adjective*
(used about a person) not thinking or caring about other people and their feelings: *It's inconsiderate of you to make so much noise.* ⊃ ANTONYM **considerate**

in·con·sis·tent AWL /ˌɪnkənˈsɪstənt/ *adjective*
not always the same: *Her effort is inconsistent – sometimes she tries hard and sometimes she just gives up.* ◆ *These new facts are inconsistent with the earlier information.* ⊃ ANTONYM **consistent**

in·con·spic·u·ous /ˌɪnkənˈspɪkyuəs/ *adjective*
not easily seen or noticed: *He stood at the back and tried to look inconspicuous.* ⊃ ANTONYM **conspicuous**

in·con·ven·ient /ˌɪnkənˈvinyənt/ *adjective*
causing you problems or difficulty: *Is this an inconvenient time? If so, I can call back later.* ⊃ ANTONYM **convenient**
▶ **in·con·ven·ience** /ˌɪnkənˈvinyəns/ *noun* [count, noncount]: *We apologize for any inconvenience caused by the delay.*

in·cor·po·rate AWL /ɪnˈkɔrpəreɪt/ *verb* (in·cor·po·rates, in·cor·po·rat·ing, in·cor·po·rat·ed)
to make something a part of something else: *Can you incorporate this information into your report?* ⊃ SYNONYM **include**

in·cor·po·rat·ed AWL /ɪnˈkɔrpəreɪt̬əd/ *adjective* (abbreviation Inc.)
(BUSINESS) a word that is sometimes used after the name of a big company (a CORPORATION): *Apple, Inc.*

in·cor·rect /ˌɪnkəˈrɛkt/ *adjective*
not right or true: *There were several incorrect answers.* ⊃ ANTONYM **correct** ⊃ Look at the note at **wrong**[1].
▶ **in·cor·rect·ly** /ˌɪnkəˈrɛktli/ *adverb*: *Her name was spelled incorrectly.*

in·crease[1] 🔑 /ɪnˈkris/ *verb* (in·creas·es, in·creas·ing, in·creased)

> 🛈 **PRONUNCIATION**
> When **increase** is a verb, you say the second part of the word louder: **inCREASE**. When **increase** is a noun, you say the first part of the word louder: **INcrease**.

to become bigger or more; to make something bigger or more: *The number of working women*

has increased. ◆ *I'm going to increase your allowance to $10 a week.* ⊃ ANTONYM **decrease**

in·crease[2] 🔑 /ˈɪnkris/ *noun* [count, noncount]
when the amount, number, or level of something goes up: *There has been an increase in road accidents.* ◆ *recent price increases* ⊃ SYNONYM **rise** ⊃ ANTONYM **decrease**

in·creas·ing·ly /ɪnˈkrisɪŋli/ *adverb*
more and more: *This city is becoming increasingly dangerous.*

in·cred·i·ble /ɪnˈkrɛdəbl/ *adjective*
1 (informal) very large or very good: *She earns an incredible amount of money.* ◆ *The hotel was incredible.*
2 impossible or very difficult to believe: *I found his story completely incredible.* ⊃ SYNONYM **unbelievable**
▶ **in·cred·i·bly** /ɪnˈkrɛdəbli/ *adverb* (informal)
extremely: *He's incredibly smart.*

in·cu·ba·tor /ˈɪŋkyəbeɪt̬ər/ *noun* [count]
(HEALTH) a special machine that hospitals use to keep small or weak babies alive

in·cur·a·ble /ɪnˈkyʊrəbl/ *adjective*
(HEALTH) that cannot be made better: *an incurable disease* ⊃ ANTONYM **curable**

in·de·ci·sive /ˌɪndɪˈsaɪsɪv/ *adjective*
not able to make decisions easily ⊃ ANTONYM **decisive**

in·deed 🔑 /ɪnˈdid/ *adverb*
a word that you use to say strongly that something is true; in fact: *Exercise is important for your health. Indeed, it can lower the risk of heart disease.*

in·def·i·nite AWL /ɪnˈdɛfənət/ *adjective*
not clear or certain: *Our plans are still pretty indefinite.* ⊃ ANTONYM **definite**

in·def·i·nite ar·ti·cle /ɪnˌdɛfənət ˈɑrt̬ɪkl/ *noun* [count]
(ENGLISH LANGUAGE ARTS) the name for the words "a" and "an" ⊃ Look at **definite article**.

in·def·i·nite·ly AWL /ɪnˈdɛfənətli/ *adverb*
for a long time, perhaps forever: *I can't wait indefinitely.*

in·dent /ɪnˈdɛnt/ *verb* (in·dents, in·dent·ing, in·dent·ed)
to start a line of writing farther from the edge of the page than the other lines: *Indent the first line of your paragraph.*

in·de·pend·ence /ˌɪndɪˈpɛndəns/ *noun* [noncount]
being free from another person, thing, or country: *Moving into her own apartment gave her a real sense of independence.* ◆ *Cuba gained independence from Spain in 1898.*

In·de·pend·ence Day /ˌɪndɪˈpɛndəns deɪ/ *noun*
[noncount]
July 4; a national holiday in the U.S. On this day, Americans celebrate the day in 1776 when their country became independent from Britain. ⊃
SYNONYM the Fourth of July

in·de·pend·ent 🔑 /ˌɪndɪˈpɛndənt/ *adjective*

> ⓘ SPELLING
> Remember! You spell **independent** with three E's.

1 not controlled by another person, thing, or country: *Many former colonies became independent nations.*
2 not needing or wanting help: *She lives alone now and she is very independent.*
▶ **in·de·pend·ent·ly** /ˌɪndɪˈpɛndəntli/ *adverb*: *Hannah is able to work independently.*

in-depth /ˈɪndɛpθ/ *adjective*
full of detail: *We conducted an in-depth study.*

in·dex AWL /ˈɪndɛks/ *noun* [count] (*plural* **in·dex·es**)
a list of words from A to Z at the end of a book. It tells you what things are in the book and where you can find them.

in·dex fin·ger /ˈɪndɛks ˌfɪŋgər/ *noun* [count]
the finger next to your thumb

in·di·cate AWL /ˈɪndəkeɪt/ *verb* (**in·di·cates, in·di·cat·ing, in·di·cat·ed**)
1 to show that something is true, exists, or will happen: *Our records **indicate that** you are due for a checkup.*
2 to make someone notice something, especially by pointing to it: *The receptionist indicated the place where I should sign.*
▶ **in·di·ca·tor** AWL /ˈɪndəkeɪtər/ *noun* [count]
something that gives information or shows something; a sign: *Economic indicators suggest that housing prices are going to fall.*

in·di·ca·tion AWL /ˌɪndəˈkeɪʃn/ *noun* [count, noncount]
something that shows something: *He gave no indication that he was angry.* ⊃ **SYNONYM sign**

in·dif·fer·ent /ɪnˈdɪfrənt/ *adjective*
not interested in or caring about someone or something: *He seemed completely **indifferent to** my feelings.*

in·di·ges·tion /ˌɪndəˈdʒɛstʃən/ *noun* [noncount]
(HEALTH) pain in your stomach caused by something that you ate: *Onions **give me indigestion**.*

in·dig·nant /ɪnˈdɪgnənt/ *adjective*
angry because someone has done or said something that you do not like or agree with: *She was indignant when I said she was lazy.*

▶ **in·dig·nant·ly** /ɪnˈdɪgnəntli/ *adverb*: *"I'm not late," he said indignantly.*
▶ **in·dig·na·tion** /ˌɪndɪgˈneɪʃn/ *noun* [noncount]
a feeling of anger and surprise

in·di·rect /ˌɪndɪˈrɛkt/ *adjective*
not straight or direct: *We came by an indirect route.* ◆ *These problems are an indirect result of the war.* ⊃ **ANTONYM direct**
▶ **in·di·rect·ly** /ˌɪndɪˈrɛktli/ *adverb*: *These events affect us all, directly or indirectly.*

in·di·rect ob·ject /ˌɪndɪrɛkt ˈɑbdʒɛkt/ *noun* [count]
(ENGLISH LANGUAGE ARTS) a person or thing that an action is done to or for: *In the sentence "I sent him a letter," "him" is the indirect object.* ⊃ Look at **direct object**.

in·di·vid·u·al¹ 🔑 AWL /ˌɪndəˈvɪdʒuəl/ *adjective*
1 considered separately and not as part of a group: *The program evaluates the needs of each individual student.*
2 for only one person or thing: *individual servings of pasta*
▶ **in·di·vid·u·al·ly** AWL /ˌɪndəˈvɪdʒuəli/ *adverb*: *The teacher spoke to each student individually.*

in·di·vid·u·al² AWL /ˌɪndəˈvɪdʒuəl/ *noun* [count]
one person: *Teachers must treat each child as an individual.*

in·door /ˈɪndɔr/ *adjective*
done or used inside a building: *an indoor swimming pool* ◆ *indoor sports* ⊃ **ANTONYM outdoor**

in·doors /ˌɪnˈdɔrz/ *adverb*
in or into a building: *Let's **go indoors**. I'm cold.* ⊃ **SYNONYM inside** ⊃ **ANTONYM outdoors**

in·dulge /ɪnˈdʌldʒ/ *verb* (**in·dulg·es, in·dulg·ing, in·dulged**)
1 to do something special that you enjoy: *I **indulged myself** and spent a day at the spa.*
2 to give someone something that they really want: *After she retired, she had time to indulge her passion for traveling.*

in·dus·tri·al /ɪnˈdʌstriəl/ *adjective* (BUSINESS)
1 connected with making things in factories: *industrial machines*
2 with a lot of factories: *an industrial city*

in·dus·try 🔑 /ˈɪndəstri/ *noun* (*plural* **in·dus·tries**) (BUSINESS)
1 [noncount] the work of making things in factories: *Is there much industry in your country?*
2 [count] all the companies that make or do the same thing: *He'd like to find a job in the entertainment industry.*

in·ed·i·ble /ɪnˈɛdəbl/ *adjective*
not suitable to be eaten: *an inedible plant* ⊃ **ANTONYM edible**

in·ef·fec·tive /ˌɪnɪˈfɛktɪv/ *adjective*
not producing the effect or result that you want: *Efforts to reduce crime have been ineffective.* ⊃ ANTONYM **effective**

in·ef·fi·cient /ˌɪnɪˈfɪʃnt/ *adjective*
A person or thing that is **inefficient** does not work well or in the best way: *This washing machine is very old and inefficient.* ⊃ ANTONYM **efficient**

in·e·qual·i·ty /ˌɪnɪˈkwɑləti/ *noun* [count, noncount] (*plural* **in·e·qual·i·ties**)
not being the same or not having the same rights: *inequality between the sexes* ⊃ ANTONYM **equality**

in·er·tia /ɪˈnərʃə/ *noun* [noncount]
(**PHYSICS**) the physical force that stops things from moving, or keeps them moving in the same direction

in·ev·i·ta·ble AWL /ɪnˈɛvəṭəbl/ *adjective*
If something is **inevitable**, it will certainly happen: *The accident was inevitable – he was driving too fast.*
▶ **in·ev·i·ta·bly** AWL /ɪnˈɛvəṭəbli/ *adverb*: *Building the new hospital inevitably cost a lot of money.*

in·ex·pen·sive /ˌɪnɪkˈspɛnsɪv/ *adjective*
low in price: *an inexpensive restaurant* ⊃ SYNONYM **cheap** ⊃ ANTONYM **expensive**

in·ex·pe·ri·enced /ˌɪnɪkˈspɪriənst/ *adjective*
If you are **inexperienced**, you do not know about something because you have not done it many times before: *a young and inexperienced driver* ⊃ ANTONYM **experienced**

in·ex·pli·ca·ble /ˌɪnɪkˈsplɪkəbl/ *adjective*
Something that is **inexplicable** cannot be explained or understood: *I found his behavior inexplicable.*

in·fa·mous /ˈɪnfəməs/ *adjective*
famous for being bad: *The neighborhood is infamous for violent crime.* ⊃ SYNONYM **notorious**

in·fant /ˈɪnfənt/ *noun* [count] (*formal*)
a baby

in·fect /ɪnˈfɛkt/ *verb* (**in·fects**, **in·fect·ing**, **in·fect·ed**)
(**HEALTH**) to give a disease to someone: *Thousands of people have been infected with the virus.*

in·fect·ed /ɪnˈfɛktɪd/ *adjective*
(**HEALTH**) full of small living things (called GERMS) that can make you sick: *Clean that cut, or it could become infected.*

in·fec·tion 🔑 /ɪnˈfɛkʃn/ *noun* (**HEALTH**)
1 [noncount] the act of becoming or making someone sick: *A dirty water supply will spread infection.*

2 [count] an illness that affects one part of the body: *Mike has an ear infection.*

in·fec·tious /ɪnˈfɛkʃəs/ *adjective*
(**HEALTH**) An **infectious** disease goes easily from one person to another.

in·fer AWL /ɪnˈfər/ *verb* (**in·fers**, **in·fer·ring**, **in·ferred**)
to decide that something is true from the information you have: *I inferred from our conversation that he was unhappy with his job.*

in·fe·ri·or /ɪnˈfɪriər/ *adjective*
not as good or important as another person or thing: *There are so many smart women in my class that I always feel inferior.* ⊃ ANTONYM **superior**

in·fest·ed /ɪnˈfɛstəd/ *adjective*
If a place is **infested**, there are a lot of unpleasant animals or insects in it: *The basement was infested with mice.*

in·field /ˈɪnfild/ *noun* [singular]
(**SPORTS**) the central part of a baseball field ⊃ Look at **outfield**.

in·fi·nite AWL /ˈɪnfənət/ *adjective*
with no end; too much or too many to count or measure: *There are an infinite number of stars in the sky.* ⊃ ANTONYM **finite**

in·fi·nite·ly AWL /ˈɪnfənətli/ *adverb*
very much: *My new computer is infinitely better than my old one.*

in·fin·i·tive /ɪnˈfɪnəṭɪv/ *noun* [count]
(**ENGLISH LANGUAGE ARTS**) the simple form of a verb: *"Eat," "go," and "play" are all infinitives.*

Grammar

■ We sometimes use the **infinitive** with *to*, and sometimes without, depending on what comes before it: *He can sing. ◆ He wants to sing.*

in·fin·i·ty /ɪnˈfɪnəti/ *noun* [noncount]
space or time without end

in·flam·ma·ble /ɪnˈflæməbl/ *adjective*
(**CHEMISTRY**) An **inflammable** substance burns easily: *Gasoline is highly inflammable.* ⊃ SYNONYM **flammable**

in·flate /ɪnˈfleɪt/ *verb* (**in·flates**, **in·flat·ing**, **in·flat·ed**)
to fill something with air or gas: *He inflated the tire.* ⊃ SYNONYM **blow something up**
▶ **in·flat·a·ble** /ɪnˈfleɪṭəbl/ *adjective*
that can or must be filled with air: *an inflatable mattress*

in·fla·tion /ɪnˈfleɪʃn/ *noun* [noncount]
a general rise in prices in a country: *The government is trying to control inflation.*

---

in·flex·i·ble AWL /ɪnˈflɛksəbl/ adjective
1 not able to change easily: an inflexible attitude
2 not able to bend easily ⊃ **ANTONYM flexible**

in·flu·ence¹ 🔑 /ˈɪnfluəns/ noun
1 [count, noncount] the power to change what someone believes or does: Television has a strong **influence on** people. ◆ She was caught driving **under the influence of** alcohol.
2 [count] a person or thing that can change someone or something: Paul's new girlfriend is a good **influence on** him.

in·flu·ence² /ˈɪnfluəns/ verb (in·flu·enc·es, in·flu·enc·ing, in·flu·enced)
to change the way that someone thinks or the way that something happens: She is easily influenced by her friends.

in·flu·en·tial /ˌɪnfluˈɛnʃl/ adjective
having power or influence: Her father's very influential.

in·form 🔑 /ɪnˈfɔrm/ verb (in·forms, in·form·ing, in·formed)
to tell someone something: You should **inform** the police **of** the accident.

in·for·mal 🔑 /ɪnˈfɔrml/ adjective
relaxed and friendly; appropriate for a relaxed occasion: We had an informal discussion and came up with some great ideas. ◆ an informal dinner party

> ❶ **STYLE**
> Some words and expressions in this dictionary are marked **informal**. You use informal language when speaking and writing to people you know well, but not in serious writing or official letters.

▸ **in·for·mal·ly** /ɪnˈfɔrməli/ adverb: I was dressed informally, but everyone else had a suit on.

in·for·ma·tion 🔑 /ˌɪnfərˈmeɪʃn/ noun [noncount]
facts about people or things: Can you give me some **information about** tours of the city?

> **Grammar**
> ▪ Be careful! **Information** is a noncount noun, so you cannot say "an information" or "informations."
> ▪ You say **some information** or **a piece of information**: She gave me an interesting piece of information.

in·form·a·tive /ɪnˈfɔrmətɪv/ adjective
giving useful information: The talk was very informative.

in·fre·quent /ɪnˈfrikwənt/ adjective
not happening often: infrequent visits ⊃ **SYNONYM rare** ⊃ **ANTONYM frequent**
▸ **in·fre·quent·ly** /ɪnˈfrikwəntli/ adverb

in·fu·ri·ate /ɪnˈfyʊrieɪt/ verb (in·fu·ri·ates, in·fu·ri·at·ing, in·fu·ri·at·ed)
to make someone very angry: That sort of behavior really infuriates me!
▸ **in·fu·ri·at·ing** /ɪnˈfyʊrieɪtɪŋ/ adjective: an infuriating habit

> **Suffix**
>
> **-ing**
> (in adjectives) producing a particular state or effect: amaz**ing** ◆ disgust**ing** ◆ interest**ing** ◆ shock**ing**

in·gen·ious /ɪnˈdʒinyəs/ adjective
1 made or planned in an intelligent way: an ingenious plan
2 An **ingenious** person is good at finding answers to problems or thinking of new things.

in·gre·di·ent /ɪnˈgridiənt/ noun [count]
one of the things that you put in when you make something to eat: One of the main ingredients of this cereal is sugar.

in·hab·it /ɪnˈhæbət/ verb (in·hab·its, in·hab·it·ing, in·hab·it·ed)
to live in a place: Is the island inhabited (= does anyone live there)? ◆ The South Pole **is inhabited by** penguins.

in·hab·i·tant /ɪnˈhæbətənt/ noun [count]
a person or an animal that lives in a place: The town has 30,000 inhabitants.

in·hale /ɪnˈheɪl/ verb (in·hales, in·hal·ing, in·haled)
(**BIOLOGY**) to take air, smoke, etc. into your body by breathing: Be careful not to inhale the fumes from the paint. ⊃ **ANTONYM exhale**

in·her·it /ɪnˈhɛrət/ verb (in·her·its, in·her·it·ing, in·her·it·ed)
1 to get money or things from someone who has died: Katie **inherited** some money **from** her grandmother.
2 (**BIOLOGY**) to receive a quality, a physical characteristic, etc. from your parents or family: She inherited her father's gift for languages.
▸ **in·her·i·tance** /ɪnˈhɛrətəns/ noun [count, noncount]
money or things that you get from someone who has died: She spent her inheritance in just one year.

in·hu·mane /ˌɪnhyuˈmeɪn/ adjective
very cruel; not caring if people or animals suffer: the inhumane conditions of some zoo animals ⊃ **ANTONYM humane**

in·i·tial¹ AWL /ɪˈnɪʃl/ adjective
first: My initial reaction was to say "no."
▸ **in·i·tial·ly** AWL /ɪˈnɪʃl·i/ adverb: Initially, the system worked well. ⊃ **SYNONYM at first**

in·i·tial² AWL /ɪˈnɪʃl/ *noun* [count]
the first letter of a person's name: *John Walton's initials are J.W.*

in·i·ti·ate AWL /ɪˈnɪʃieɪt/ *verb* (in·i·ti·ates, in·i·ti·at·ing, in·i·ti·at·ed) (*formal*)
to start something: *to initiate peace talks*

in·i·ti·a·tion AWL /ɪˌnɪʃiˈeɪʃn/ *noun* [noncount]
an act of making someone part of a group, often with a special ceremony: *an initiation ceremony*

in·i·tia·tive AWL /ɪˈnɪʃət̮ɪv/ *noun*
1 [count] a new plan that is introduced to solve a problem: *a government initiative to help small business owners*
2 [noncount] the ability to see and do what is necessary without waiting for someone to tell you: *Don't keep asking me what to do – use your initiative.*

in·ject /ɪnˈdʒɛkt/ *verb* (in·jects, in·ject·ing, in·ject·ed)
(HEALTH) to put a drug into a person's body using a special needle (called a SYRINGE)
▶ **in·jec·tion** /ɪnˈdʒɛkʃn/ *noun* [count, noncount]: *a steroid injection* ➔ SYNONYM **shot**

in·jure 🖉 AWL /ˈɪndʒər/ *verb* (in·jures, in·jur·ing, in·jured)
(HEALTH) to hurt yourself or someone else, especially in an accident: *She injured her arm during a tennis match.* ◆ *Joe was injured in a car accident.*
▶ **in·jured** AWL /ˈɪndʒərd/ *adjective*: *The injured woman was taken to the hospital.*

in·ju·ry 🖉 AWL /ˈɪndʒəri/ *noun* [count, noncount] (*plural* in·ju·ries)
(HEALTH) damage to the body of a person or an animal: *He had serious head injuries.*

Collocations

Injuries

being injured
- **hurt/injure** yourself/your ankle/your arm
- **break** a bone/your leg/three ribs
- **bruise/cut/graze** your arm/your knee/ your shoulder
- **sprain/twist** your ankle/your wrist

treatment
- **examine/clean/disinfect** a wound
- **put on** a Band-Aid™/a bandage
- **be on/take** painkillers/antibiotics
➔ Look at the note at **illness**.

in·jus·tice /ɪnˈdʒʌstəs/ *noun* [count, noncount]
the fact of a situation not being fair or right: *the struggle against injustice*

ink /ɪŋk/ *noun* [count, noncount]
liquid for writing and printing: *Please write in black or blue ink.* ◆ *My printer has run out of ink.*

in·land /ˌɪnˈlænd/ *adverb*
in or toward the middle of a country: *The town is a few miles inland.*
▶ **in·land** /ˈɪnlənd/ *adjective*
in the middle of a country, not near the ocean: *an inland lake*

in-laws /ˈɪn lɔz/ *noun* [plural] (*informal*)
the parents of your husband or wife: *My in-laws are coming to visit this weekend.*

in·let /ˈɪnlɛt/ *noun* [count]
(GEOGRAPHY) a narrow area of water that goes into the land from the ocean or a lake

in-line skate /ˌɪnlaɪn ˈskeɪt/ *noun* [count]
a boot with a line of small wheels on the bottom: *a pair of in-line skates* ➔ SYNONYM **Rollerblade™**
➔ Look at the picture at **skate**.
▶ **in-line skating** /ˌɪnlaɪn ˈskeɪtɪŋ/ *noun* [noncount]

inn /ɪn/ *noun* [count]
a small hotel, usually in the country: *a romantic inn in Vermont*

in·ner /ˈɪnər/ *adjective*
inside; toward or close to the center: *the inner ear* ➔ ANTONYM **outer**

in·ner cit·y /ˌɪnər ˈsɪti/ *noun* [count] (*plural* in·ner cit·ies)
the poor areas near the center of a big city: *the problems of the inner cities*
▶ **in·ner-cit·y** *adjective*: *an inner-city school*

in·ning /ˈɪnɪŋ/ *noun* [count]
(SPORTS) one of the nine periods of a baseball game, in which each team has a turn to hit the ball: *At the end of the eighth inning, the Orioles were winning 4-2.*

in·no·cent /ˈɪnəsnt/ *adjective*
1 If you are **innocent**, you have not done anything wrong: *He claims he's innocent of the crime.* ➔ ANTONYM **guilty**
2 not knowing the bad things in life; believing everything you are told: *an innocent child* ➔ SYNONYM **naive**
▶ **in·no·cence** /ˈɪnəsns/ *noun* [noncount]: *The prisoner's family is convinced of her innocence.* ◆ *the innocence of childhood*

in·no·va·tion AWL /ˌɪnəˈveɪʃn/ *noun* [count, noncount]
the introduction of new things, ideas, etc., or something new that has been introduced: *a company with a reputation for innovation* ◆ *technological innovations in the music industry*

in·of·fen·sive /ˌɪnəˈfɛnsɪv/ *adjective*
not likely to make anyone feel upset or angry: *The joke was stupid but inoffensive.* ➔ ANTONYM **offensive**

insects

antenna | | wing

ant   **bee**   **beetle**   **flea**

fly   **ladybug**   **mosquito**   **wasp**

in·put `AWL` /'ɪnpʊt/ *noun* [*noncount*]
time, ideas, or work that you put into something to make it successful: *We'd like input from everyone on the committee.*

in·quire /ɪn'kwaɪər/ *verb* (in·quires, in·quir·ing, in·quired) (*formal*)
to ask for information about something: *I'm calling to* **inquire about** *my checking account.* ⊃ **SYNONYM ask**

in·quir·y /'ɪnkwəri; ɪn'kwaɪəri/ *noun* [*count*] (*plural* in·quir·ies) (*formal*)
a question that you ask to get information about something: *I'll* **make** *some* **inquiries** *about language programs.*

in·quis·i·tive /ɪn'kwɪzətɪv/ *adjective*
wanting to find out as much as possible about things: *He's very inquisitive and loves to read.*

in·sane /ɪn'seɪn/ *adjective*
1 (**HEALTH**) very sick in your mind: *The prisoners were slowly* **going insane.** ⊃ **SYNONYM crazy**
2 (*informal*) very stupid or dangerous: *His plan was insane!*
▶ **in·san·i·ty** /ɪn'sænəti/ *noun* [*noncount*]
the state of being **insane**

in·sect /'ɪnsɛkt/ *noun* [*count*]
(**BIOLOGY**) a very small animal that has six legs: *Ants, flies, butterflies, and beetles are all insects.*

in·sec·ti·cide /ɪn'sɛktəsaɪd/ *noun* [*count, noncount*]
a chemical substance that is used for killing insects ⊃ Look at **pesticide**.

in·se·cure `AWL` /ˌɪnsə'kyʊr/ *adjective*
1 worried and not sure about yourself: *Many teenagers feel* **insecure about** *their appearance.*
2 not safe or firm: *This ladder looks a little insecure.* ⊃ **ANTONYM secure**
▶ **in·se·cu·ri·ty** `AWL` /ˌɪnsə'kyʊrəti/ *noun* [*count, noncount*] (*plural* in·se·cu·ri·ties): *She had feelings of insecurity.*

in·sen·si·tive /ɪn'sɛnsətɪv/ *adjective*
not knowing or caring how another person feels: *That was a very insensitive remark.* • *She's*

completely insensitive to my feelings. ⊃ **ANTONYM sensitive**

in·sert `AWL` /ɪn'sərt/ *verb* (in·serts, in·sert·ing, in·sert·ed) (*formal*)
to put something into something or between two things: *Insert the CD into the computer.*

in·side¹ /ɪn'saɪd; 'ɪnsaɪd/ *preposition, adverb, adjective*
in, on, or to the inside of something: *What's inside the box?* • *It's raining – let's* **go inside** (= into the building). • *the inside pocket of a jacket* ⊃ Look at **outside**.

in·side² /ɪn'saɪd/ *noun* [*count*]
the part near the middle of something: *Do I need to clean the inside of my computer?* • *The door was locked* **from the inside.** ⊃ Look at **outside**.
inside out with the wrong side on the outside: *You have your sweater on inside out.*

in·sig·nif·i·cant `AWL` /ˌɪnsɪg'nɪfɪkənt/ *adjective*
of little value or importance: *an insignificant detail* ⊃ **ANTONYM significant**

in·sin·cere /ˌɪnsɪn'sɪr/ *adjective*
not being honest, and not meaning what you say or do: *His apology sounded insincere.* ⊃ **ANTONYM sincere**

in·sist /ɪn'sɪst/ *verb* (in·sists, in·sist·ing, in·sist·ed)
1 to say very strongly that something must happen or be done: *Paul* **insisted on** *driving me to the airport.*
2 to say very strongly that something is true, when someone does not believe you: *He* **insists** **that** *he didn't take the money.*

in·so·lent /'ɪnsələnt/ *adjective* (*formal*)
not showing respect: *He gave her an insolent stare.* ⊃ **SYNONYM rude**

in·som·ni·a /ɪn'samniə/ *noun* [*noncount*]
(**HEALTH**) a condition in which you are not able to sleep: *Do you ever suffer from insomnia?*

in·spect `AWL` /ɪn'spɛkt/ *verb* (in·spects, in·spect·ing, in·spect·ed)
to look at something carefully: *The teachers inspected our lockers.*

   ə **a**bout   y **y**es   w **w**oman   t̬ but**t**er   eɪ s**ay**   aɪ f**i**ve   ɔɪ b**oy**   aʊ n**ow**   oʊ g**o**

▶ **in·spec·tion** **AWL** /ɪnˈspɛkʃn/ noun [count, noncount]: The police made **an inspection of** the house.

in·spec·tor **AWL** /ɪnˈspɛktər/ noun [count]
1 a person whose job is to see that things are done correctly: health and safety inspectors
2 a police officer

in·spi·ra·tion /ˌɪnspəˈreɪʃn/ noun [count, noncount]
a person or thing that makes you want to do something or gives you good ideas: The beauty of the mountains is a great **inspiration to** many artists.
▶ **in·spi·ra·tion·al** /ˌɪnspəˈreɪʃənl/ adjective: inspirational music

in·spire /ɪnˈspaɪər/ verb (in·spires, in·spir·ing, in·spired)
1 to make someone want to do something: His wife **inspired** him **to** write this poem.
2 to make someone feel or think something: Her words **inspired** us all **with** hope.
▶ **in·spir·ing** /ɪnˈspaɪərɪŋ/ adjective: an inspiring teacher

in·stall /ɪnˈstɔl/ verb (in·stalls, in·stall·ing, in·stalled)
to put a new thing in its place so it is ready to use: to install software on the computer
▶ **in·stal·la·tion** /ˌɪnstəˈleɪʃn/ noun [count, noncount]

in·stall·ment /ɪnˈstɔlmənt/ noun [count]
1 a regular payment that you make for something: She's paying for her new car **in monthly installments**.
2 one part of a story on radio or television, or in a magazine: Don't miss next week's exciting installment.

in·stance **AWL** /ˈɪnstəns/ noun [count]
an example or a case of something: In most instances, the drug has no side effects.
for instance as an example: There are several interesting places to visit. Georgetown, for instance, has a lot of historic buildings.

in·stant¹ /ˈɪnstənt/ adjective
1 happening very quickly: The movie was an instant success.
2 (used about food) quick and easy to prepare: instant oatmeal
▶ **in·stant·ly** /ˈɪnstəntli/ adverb
immediately; at once: The driver was killed instantly.

in·stant² /ˈɪnstənt/ noun [singular]
a very short time: She thought **for an instant** before she answered. ➔ SYNONYM **moment**

in·stead /ɪnˈstɛd/ adverb, preposition
in the place of someone or something: We don't have any coffee. Would you like tea instead? ◆

He's been watching TV all afternoon **instead of** studying. ◆ Can you go to the meeting **instead of** me?

in·stinct /ˈɪnstɪŋkt/ noun [count, noncount]
(**BIOLOGY**) something that makes people and animals do certain things without thinking or learning about them: Birds build their nests **by instinct**.
▶ **in·stinc·tive** /ɪnˈstɪŋktɪv/ adjective: Animals have an instinctive fear of fire.

in·sti·tute **AWL** /ˈɪnstətut/ noun [count]
a group of people who meet to study or talk about a special thing; the building where they meet: the Institute of Science

in·sti·tu·tion **AWL** /ˌɪnstəˈtuʃn/ noun [count]
a big organization like a bank, hospital, prison, or school: Many financial institutions are based in New York.

in·struct **AWL** /ɪnˈstrʌkt/ verb (in·structs, in·struct·ing, in·struct·ed)
1 to tell someone what they must do: He instructed the driver **to** wait.
2 (formal) to teach someone something: Children must be **instructed in** road safety.

in·struc·tion **AWL** /ɪnˈstrʌkʃn/ noun
1 instructions [plural] words that tell you what you must do or how to do something: Read the instructions carefully. ◆ You should always **follow the instructions**.
2 [noncount] teaching or being taught something: driving instruction

in·struc·tor **AWL** /ɪnˈstrʌktər/ noun [count]
a person who teaches you how to do something: a driving instructor

in·stru·ment /ˈɪnstrəmənt/ noun [count]
1 (**MUSIC**) a thing that you use for playing music: Violins and trumpets are **musical instruments**. ◆ What instrument do you play?
2 a thing that you use for doing a special job: surgical instruments (= used by doctors)

in·stru·men·tal /ˌɪnstrəˈmɛntl/ adjective
1 helping to make something happen: She was **instrumental in** getting him the job.
2 (**MUSIC**) for musical instruments without voices: the instrumental version of a song

in·suf·fi·cient **AWL** /ˌɪnsəˈfɪʃnt/ adjective
not enough: We were given insufficient time to complete the report. ➔ ANTONYM **sufficient**

in·su·late /ˈɪnsəleɪt/ verb (in·su·lates, in·su·lat·ing, in·su·lat·ed)
to protect something with a material that stops electricity, heat, or sound from passing through: You can save energy by insulating your home.
▶ **in·su·la·tion** /ˌɪnsəˈleɪʃn/ noun [noncount]

instruments

saxophone

bow

violin   cello   double bass   harp

tuba

trombone

trumpet   flute   clarinet   oboe   recorder   piano

in·su·lin /'ɪnsələn/ *noun* [*noncount*]
(**HEALTH**, **BIOLOGY**) a substance that controls the
amount of sugar in the blood: *She has diabetes
and has to take insulin.*

in·sult 🔑 /ɪn'sʌlt/ *verb* (in·sults, in·sult·ing,
in·sult·ed)
to be deliberately rude to someone: *She insulted
my brother by saying he was fat.*
▶ **in·sult** /'ɪnsʌlt/ *noun* [*count*]: *The boys shouted
insults at each other.*
▶ **in·sult·ing** /ɪn'sʌltɪŋ/ *adjective*: *insulting
behavior*

in·sur·ance /ɪn'ʃʊrəns/ *noun* [*noncount*]
an agreement where you pay money to a
company so that it will give you money if
something bad happens: *My car was badly
damaged in the accident, but insurance paid for
the repairs.* ◆ *Does your salary include health
insurance?*

in·sure /ɪn'ʃʊr/ *verb* (in·sures, in·sur·ing,
in·sured)
1 to pay money to a company, so that it will give
you money if something bad happens: *Have you
insured your house against fire?*
2 another word for **ensure**

in·tact /ɪn'tækt/ *adjective*
complete; not damaged: *Very few of the
buildings remained intact after the earthquake.*

in·te·ger /'ɪntədʒər/ *noun* [*count*]
(**MATH**) a whole number, such as 3 or 4 but not
3.5 ⟳ Look at **fraction**(1).

integrate **AWL** /'ɪntəgreɪt/ *verb* (in·te·grates,
in·te·grat·ing, in·te·grat·ed)
1 to join things so that they become one thing,
or so that they work together: *The updates can
be integrated into your existing software.*
2 to become, or to make someone become
accepted as part of a group: *They have not made
any effort to integrate with the local community.* ⟳
Look at **segregate**.
▶ **in·te·grat·ed** **AWL** /'ɪntəgreɪtəd/ *adjective*: *an
integrated transportation system* (= including
buses, trains, taxis, etc.)
▶ **in·te·gra·tion** **AWL** /ˌɪntə'greɪʃn/ *noun*
[*noncount*]: *racial integration*

in·tel·lec·tu·al¹ /ˌɪntə'lɛktʃuəl/ *adjective*
connected with a person's ability to think and
understand things: *a child's intellectual
development*

in·tel·lec·tu·al² /ˌɪntə'lɛktʃuəl/ *noun* [*count*]
a person who enjoys thinking deeply about
things: *The café was a meeting place for artists
and intellectuals.*

in·tel·li·gence **AWL** /ɪn'tɛlədʒəns/ *noun*
[*noncount*]
1 being able to think, learn, and understand
quickly and well: *He is a man of great
intelligence.* ◆ *an intelligence test*
2 (**POLITICS**) important information about a
foreign country, especially one that is an
enemy: *intelligence reports*

in·tel·li·gent 🔑 **AWL** /ɪnˈtɛlədʒənt/ *adjective*
able to think, learn, and understand quickly and
well: *Their daughter is very intelligent.* ✦ *an
intelligent question*
▶ **in·tel·li·gent·ly** **AWL** /ɪnˈtɛlədʒəntli/ *adverb*:
They solved the problem very intelligently.

in·tend 🔑 /ɪnˈtɛnd/ *verb* (in·tends, in·tend·ing,
in·tend·ed)
to plan to do something: *When do you intend to
go to Portland?* ⟳ The noun is **intention**.
be intended for someone or **something** to
be planned or made for a particular person or
reason: *This dictionary is intended for learners of
English.*

in·tense **AWL** /ɪnˈtɛns/ *adjective*
very great or strong: *intense pain* ✦ *The heat from
the fire was intense.*
▶ **in·tense·ly** **AWL** /ɪnˈtɛnsli/ *adverb*: *I found the
movie intensely boring.*

in·ten·sive **AWL** /ɪnˈtɛnsɪv/ *adjective*
involving a lot of work in a short time: *an
intensive English course*
▶ **in·ten·sive·ly** **AWL** /ɪnˈtɛnsɪvli/ *adverb*

in·ten·tion 🔑 /ɪnˈtɛnʃn/ *noun* [count, noncount]
what you plan to do: *Our intention was to leave
early in the morning.* ✦ *They have no intention of
getting married.* ⟳ The verb is **intend**. ⟳ Look at the
note at **purpose**.

in·ten·tion·al /ɪnˈtɛnʃənl/ *adjective*
done on purpose, not by mistake: *I'm sorry I
upset you – it wasn't intentional!* ⟳ SYNONYM
deliberate
▶ **in·ten·tion·al·ly** /ɪnˈtɛnʃənəli/ *adverb*: *They
broke the window intentionally.* ⟳ SYNONYM
deliberately

in·ter·act **AWL** /ˌɪntərˈækt/ *verb* (in·ter·acts,
in·ter·act·ing, in·ter·act·ed)
to communicate or mix with someone: *She is
studying the way children interact with each
other.*
▶ **in·ter·ac·tion** **AWL** /ˌɪntərˈækʃn/ *noun* [count,
noncount]: *social interaction*

in·ter·ac·tive **AWL** /ˌɪntərˈæktɪv/ *adjective*
(COMPUTERS) involving direct communication
both ways, between a computer or other form of
technology and the person using it: *interactive
software for schools*

in·ter·est¹ 🔑 /ˈɪntrəst/ *noun*
1 [noncount, singular] wanting to know or learn
about someone or something: *He read the story
with interest.* ✦ *He shows no interest in politics.*
2 [count] something that you like doing or
learning about: *His interests are computers and
rock music.*
3 [noncount] (BUSINESS) the extra money that you
pay back if you borrow money or that you
receive if you put money in a bank ⟳ Look at the
note at **account¹**.

in·ter·est² 🔑 /ˈɪntrəst/ *verb* (in·ter·ests,
in·ter·est·ing, in·ter·est·ed)
to make someone want to know more: *Religion
doesn't interest her.*

in·ter·est·ed 🔑 /ˈɪntrəstəd/ *adjective*
wanting to know more about someone or
something: *Are you interested in cars?*

in·ter·est·ing 🔑 /ˈɪntrəstɪŋ/ *adjective*
A person or thing that is **interesting** makes you
want to know more about them: *This book is very
interesting.* ✦ *That's an interesting idea!* ⟳
ANTONYM **boring**

in·ter·fere /ˌɪntərˈfɪr/ *verb* (in·ter·feres,
in·ter·fer·ing, in·ter·fered)
1 to try to do something with or for someone,
when they do not want your help: *Don't
interfere! Let John decide what he wants to do.*
2 to stop something from being done well: *His
social life often interferes with his studies.*
▶ **in·ter·fer·ence** /ˌɪntərˈfɪrəns/ *noun* [noncount]

in·te·ri·or /ɪnˈtɪriər/ *noun* [count, usually singular]
the inside part: *We painted the interior of the
house white.*
▶ **in·te·ri·or** *adjective*: *interior walls* ⟳ ANTONYM
exterior

in·ter·jec·tion /ˌɪntərˈdʒɛkʃn/ *noun* [count]
(ENGLISH LANGUAGE ARTS) a short word or phrase
that you say suddenly to show surprise, pain,

happiness, or other feeling: *"Oh," "Hey," and "Wow" are interjections.* ➔ SYNONYM **exclamation**

in·ter·me·di·ate AWL /ˌɪntərˈmidiət/ *adjective*
coming between two things or levels: *She's in an intermediate class.*

in·ter·mis·sion /ˌɪntərˈmɪʃn/ *noun* [count]
a short period of time separating the parts of a play, concert, etc.

in·tern /ˈɪntərn/ *noun* [count]
1 (HEALTH) a doctor who has finished medical school and is working at a hospital to get practical training
2 a person, especially a student, who is working somewhere for a short time to learn about a particular job or career: *a summer intern at a law firm* ➔ Look at **internship**.

in·ter·nal AWL /ɪnˈtərnl/ *adjective*
of or on the inside: *He has internal injuries* (= inside his body). ➔ ANTONYM **external**
▶ **in·ter·nal·ly** AWL /ɪnˈtərnl·i/ *adverb*: *We dealt with the matter internally.*

in·ter·na·tion·al 🔑 /ˌɪntərˈnæʃənl/ *adjective*
between different countries: *international relations* • *an international flight* ➔ Look at **national**.
▶ **in·ter·na·tion·al·ly** /ˌɪntərˈnæʃənəli/ *adverb*: *an internationally famous musician*

In·ter·net 🔑 /ˈɪntərnɛt/ *noun* **the Internet** (also *informal* **the Net**) [singular]
(COMPUTERS) the international system of computers that makes it possible for you to see information from all around the world on your computer and to send information to other computers: *You can find out almost anything on the Internet.* • *Do you have Internet access?*

Collocations

The Internet

connecting
- **connect to/log on to/access** the Internet/ the Web
- **go/be** online/on the Internet

using
- **browse/surf/search** the Internet/the Web
- **check out/visit** a website/someone's blog
- **click/click on/follow** a link
- **start/have/write/read** a blog

chatting and sharing
- **chat with** someone/your friends online
- **meet someone in/enter** a chat room
- **download/upload** music/a song/a video/a photo
- **post** a comment/a message
- **share** information/files

in·tern·ship /ˈɪntərnʃɪp/ *noun* [count]
(BUSINESS) a period of time when someone, especially a student, works somewhere to learn about a particular job or career: *I'm doing a summer internship with a law firm.* ➔ Look at **intern**.

in·ter·pret AWL /ɪnˈtərprət/ *verb* (in·ter·prets, in·ter·pret·ing, in·ter·pret·ed)
1 to say in one language what someone has said in another language: *I can't speak Italian – can you interpret for me?*
2 to explain the meaning of something: *How would you interpret this poem?*

in·ter·pre·ta·tion AWL /ɪnˌtərprəˈteɪʃn/ *noun* [count, noncount]
an explanation of something: *What's your interpretation of these statistics?*

in·ter·pret·er /ɪnˈtərprətər/ *noun* [count]
a person whose job is to translate what someone is saying into another language

in·ter·ro·gate /ɪnˈtɛrəgeɪt/ *verb* (in·ter·ro·gates, in·ter·ro·gat·ing, in·ter·ro·gat·ed)
to ask someone a lot of questions over a long period of time: *The prisoner was interrogated for six hours.*
▶ **in·ter·ro·ga·tion** /ɪnˌtɛrəˈgeɪʃn/ *noun* [count, noncount]: *They took him away for interrogation.*

in·ter·rupt 🔑 /ˌɪntəˈrʌpt/ *verb* (in·ter·rupts, in·ter·rupt·ing, in·ter·rupt·ed)
1 to say or do something to stop someone from speaking or doing something: *Please don't interrupt me when I'm speaking.*
2 to stop something for a time: *The game was interrupted by rain.*
▶ **in·ter·rup·tion** /ˌɪntəˈrʌpʃn/ *noun* [count, noncount]: *I can't do my homework here. There are too many interruptions.*

in·ter·sec·tion /ˌɪntərˈsɛkʃn/ *noun* [count]
the place where two or more roads, lines, etc. meet and cross each other: *Turn right at the next intersection.*

in·ter·state /ˈɪntərsteɪt/ *noun* [count]
a wide road for fast traffic that goes between states in the U.S.: *Head south on Interstate 95 until you see the sign for Providence.*

in·ter·val AWL /ˈɪntərvl/ *noun* [count]
a period of time between two events: *There was an interval of several weeks between the attacks.*

in·ter·view¹ 🔑 /ˈɪntərvyu/ *noun* [count]
1 a meeting when someone asks you questions to decide if you will get a job: *I have a job interview tomorrow.*
2 a meeting when someone answers questions for a newspaper or for a television or radio program: *There was an interview with the candidate on TV last night.*

ə **about**   y **yes**   w **woman**   t̬ **butter**   eɪ **say**   aɪ **five**   ɔɪ **boy**   aʊ **now**   oʊ **go**

in·ter·view² /ˈɪntərvyu/ *verb* (in·ter·views, in·ter·view·ing, in·ter·viewed)
to ask someone questions in an interview: *They interviewed six people for the job.*
▸ **in·ter·view·er** /ˈɪntərvyuər/ *noun* [count]: *The interviewer asked me why I wanted the job.*

in·tes·tine /ɪnˈtɛstən/ *noun* [count]
(BIOLOGY) the tube in your body that carries food away from your stomach to the place where it leaves your body ⊃ Look at the picture at **body.**

in·ti·mate /ˈɪntəmət/ *adjective*
(used about people) having a close relationship: *They're intimate friends.* ⊃ SYNONYM **close**

in·tim·i·date /ɪnˈtɪmədeɪt/ *verb* (in·tim·i·dates, in·tim·i·dat·ing, in·tim·i·dat·ed)
to frighten someone so that they do what you want them to: *Don't let her threats intimidate you.*
▸ **in·tim·i·dat·ing** /ɪnˈtɪmədeɪtɪŋ/ *adjective*: *The new coach is really intimidating.*
▸ **in·tim·i·da·tion** /ɪnˌtɪmədeɪʃn/ *noun* [noncount]: *the intimidation of a witness*

in·to 🔑 /ˈɪntə; ˈɪntu/ *preposition*
1 to the middle or the inside of something: *Come into the kitchen.* • *I went into town.* • *He fell into the river.*
2 in the direction of something: *Please speak into the microphone.*
3 against something: *The car crashed into a tree.*
4 a word that shows how someone or something changes: *When it is very cold, water changes into ice.* • *They made the room into a bedroom.*
5 a word that you use when you divide a number: *4 into 12 is 3.*
be into something (*informal*) to like something; to be interested in something: *What kind of music are you into?*

in·tol·er·a·ble /ɪnˈtɑlərəbl/ *adjective*
so bad or difficult that you cannot accept it: *The situation was intolerable.* ⊃ SYNONYM **unbearable**

in·tra·net /ˈɪntrənɛt/ *noun* [count]
(COMPUTERS) a system of computers inside an organization that makes it possible for people to share information ⊃ Look at **Internet.**

in·tran·si·tive /ɪnˈtrænsətɪv/ *adjective*
(ENGLISH LANGUAGE ARTS) An intransitive verb does not have an object. ⊃ Look at **transitive.**

in·tri·cate /ˈɪntrɪkət/ *adjective*
having a lot of small parts or complicated details: *an intricate design*

in·trigue /ɪnˈtrig/ *verb* (in·trigues, in·trigu·ing, in·trigued)
to make someone very interested: *His story intrigued me.*
▸ **in·trigu·ing** /ɪnˈtrigɪŋ/ *adjective*: *I find his novels intriguing.*

in·tro·duce 🔑 /ˌɪntrəˈdus/ *verb* (in·tro·duc·es, in·tro·duc·ing, in·tro·duced)
1 to bring people together for the first time and tell each of them the name of the other: *She introduced me to her brother.* • *He introduced himself to me* (= told me his name).

> **ℹ️ STYLE**
> When we introduce people we say **this is** not "he is" or "she is" and not "here is": *Jan, **this is Bob.*** • *Bob, **this is Jan.***
> When you meet someone for the first time, you can say **Hello, how are you?** or **Nice to meet you.**

2 to bring in something new: *This law was introduced in 2002.*

in·tro·duc·tion 🔑 /ˌɪntrəˈdʌkʃn/ *noun*
1 [noncount] bringing in something new: *the introduction of computers into schools*
2 [count] bringing people together to meet each other
3 [count] a piece of writing at the beginning of a book that tells you about the book

in·tro·vert /ˈɪntrəvərt/ *noun* [count]
a quiet, shy person who finds it easier to be alone than with others ⊃ ANTONYM **extrovert**

in·trud·er /ɪnˈtrudər/ *noun* [count]
a person who enters a place without permission: *Police say the intruder was not armed.*

in·tu·i·tion /ˌɪntuˈɪʃn/ *noun* [count, noncount]
the feeling that you know something is true without being able to explain why: *He seemed like a nice guy, but my intuition told me not to trust him.*

In·u·it /ˈɪnuət; ˈɪnyuət/ *noun* [plural]
a race of people from northern Canada and parts of Greenland and Alaska

in·vade /ɪnˈveɪd/ *verb* (in·vades, in·vad·ing, in·vad·ed)
to go into another country to attack it: *Military forces invaded in March that year.* ⊃ The noun is **invasion.**
▸ **in·vad·er** /ɪnˈveɪdər/ *noun* [count]: *They prepared to fight the invaders.*

in·va·lid¹ /ɪnˈvæləd/ *adjective*
not legally or officially acceptable: *Your passport is invalid.* ⊃ ANTONYM **valid**

in·va·lid² /ˈɪnvələd/ *noun* [count]
(HEALTH) a person who has been very sick for a long time and needs another person to take care of them

in·val·u·a·ble /ɪnˈvælyəbl/ *adjective*
very useful: *Your help was invaluable.*

Which word?

- Be careful! **Invaluable** is not the opposite of **valuable**.
- The opposite of **valuable** is **worthless**.

in·var·i·a·bly `AWL` /ɪnˈvɛriəbli/ *adverb*
always or almost always: *He invariably arrives late.*

in·va·sion /ɪnˈveɪʒn/ *noun* [count, noncount]
a time when an army from one country goes into another country to attack it ⟳ The verb is **invade**.

in·vent 🔑 /ɪnˈvɛnt/ *verb* (in·vents, in·vent·ing, in·vent·ed)
1 to make or think of something for the first time: *Who invented the bicycle?*
2 to say something that is not true: *I realized that he had invented the whole story.*
▶ **in·ven·tor** /ɪnˈvɛntər/ *noun* [count]: *Marconi was the inventor of the radio.*

in·ven·tion /ɪnˈvɛnʃn/ *noun*
1 [count] a thing that someone has made for the first time
2 [noncount] inventing something: *The invention of the telephone changed the world.*

in·ver·te·brate /ɪnˈvərṭəbrət/ *noun* [count]
(**BIOLOGY**) any animal without a solid line of bones (a **BACKBONE**) going along its body: *worms and other invertebrates* ⟳ **ANTONYM vertebrate**

in·vest `AWL` /ɪnˈvɛst/ *verb* (in·vests, in·vest·ing, in·vest·ed)
(**BUSINESS**) to give money to a business or bank so that you will get more money back: *He invested all his money in the company.*
▶ **in·vest·ment** `AWL` /ɪnˈvɛstmənt/ *noun* [count, noncount]: *an investment of $10,000*
▶ **in·ves·tor** `AWL` /ɪnˈvɛstər/ *noun* [count]: *She was looking for investors for her new company.*

in·ves·ti·gate 🔑 `AWL` /ɪnˈvɛstəgeɪt/ *verb* (in·ves·ti·gates, in·ves·ti·gat·ing, in·ves·ti·gat·ed)
to try to find out about something: *The police are investigating the murder.*
▶ **in·ves·ti·ga·tion** `AWL` /ɪnˌvɛstəˈgeɪʃn/ *noun* [count, noncount]: *The company is under investigation for fraud.*

in·vis·i·ble `AWL` /ɪnˈvɪzəbl/ *adjective*
If something is **invisible**, you cannot see it: *Wind is invisible.* ⟳ **ANTONYM visible**

in·vi·ta·tion 🔑 /ˌɪnvəˈteɪʃn/ *noun* [count]
If you have an **invitation** to go somewhere, someone has spoken or written to you and asked you to go: *Joe sent me an invitation to his birthday party.*

in·vite 🔑 /ɪnˈvaɪt/ *verb* (in·vites, in·vit·ing, in·vit·ed)
to ask someone to come to a party, to your house, etc.: *Anna invited me to her party.* ◆ *Let's invite them over for dinner.*

in·voice /ˈɪnvɔɪs/ *noun* [count]
(**BUSINESS**) a list that shows how much you must pay for things that someone has sold you, or for work that someone has done for you

in·vol·un·tar·y /ɪnˈvɑləntɛri/ *adjective*
done without wanting or meaning to: *an involuntary gasp of pain*

in·volve 🔑 `AWL` /ɪnˈvɑlv/ *verb* (in·volves, in·volv·ing, in·volved)
1 to have something as a part: *The job involves using a computer.*
2 If you **involve** someone in something, you make them take part in it: *I want to involve more people in the concert.*

in·volved `AWL` /ɪnˈvɑlvd/ *adjective*
taking part in something; being part of something or connected with something: *I'm very involved in local politics.* ◆ *We need to interview the people involved.*

in·ward /ˈɪnwərd/ (also **in·wards** /ˈɪnwərdz/) *adverb*
toward the inside or center: *The doors open inward.* ⟳ **ANTONYM outward**

i·o·dine /ˈaɪədaɪn/ *noun* [noncount] (symbol **I**)
(**CHEMISTRY**) a dark substance that is found in the water in oceans. A liquid containing **iodine** is sometimes used to clean cuts on your skin.

IOU /ˌaɪ oʊ ˈyu/ *noun* [count] (*informal*)
a piece of paper that shows you promise to pay someone the money you owe them ⟳ **IOU** is a way of writing "I owe you."

IPA /ˌaɪ pi ˈeɪ/ *abbreviation*
(**ENGLISH LANGUAGE ARTS**) a system of symbols to show how words sound ⟳ **IPA** is short for "International Phonetic Alphabet."

IQ /ˌaɪ ˈkyu/ *noun* [count]
a way of measuring how intelligent someone is: *She has an IQ of 128.* ⟳ **IQ** is short for "intelligence quotient."

Prefix

ir-

(used with words beginning with "r") not; the opposite of: *irregular* ◆ *irrelevant* ◆ *irresponsible* ◆ *irresistible*

i·ron¹ /ˈaɪərn/ *noun*
1 [*noncount*] (symbol **Fe**) (**CHEMISTRY**) a strong hard metal: *The gates are made of iron.* • *an iron bar*
2 [*count*] a piece of electrical equipment that gets hot and that you use for making clothes smooth: *Don't forget to unplug the iron.*

iron
ironing board
iron

i·ron² /ˈaɪərn/ *verb* (**i·rons, i·ron·ing, i·roned**)
to make clothes smooth using an IRON¹(2): *Can you iron this shirt for me?*
▶ **i·ron·ing** /ˈaɪərnɪŋ/ *noun* [*noncount*] clothes that need to be **ironed**: *I usually do the ironing on Sunday night.*

i·ron·ic /aɪˈrɑnɪk/ *adjective*
meaning the opposite of what you say: *When I said it was a beautiful day, I was being ironic.*

i·ron·ing board /ˈaɪərnɪŋ bɔrd/ *noun* [*count*]
a special long table where you IRON clothes ⭗ Look at the picture at **iron**.

i·ro·ny /ˈaɪrəni/ *noun* [*count, noncount*] (*plural* **i·ro·nies**)
a strange or unusual part of a situation that is different from what you expect: *The irony is that when she finally got the job, she discovered she didn't like it.*

ir·ra·tion·al **AWL** /ɪˈræʃənl/ *adjective*
not based on facts; not sensible: *an irrational fear of worms* ⭗ **ANTONYM rational**
▶ **ir·ra·tion·al·ly** **AWL** /ɪˈræʃənəli/ *adverb*: *to behave irrationally*

ir·reg·u·lar /ɪˈrɛgyələr/ *adjective*
1 happening at different times: *Their visits were irregular.*
2 (**ENGLISH LANGUAGE ARTS**) A word that is **irregular** does not have the usual verb forms or plural: *"Catch" is an irregular verb.* ⭗ **ANTONYM regular**

ir·rel·e·vant **AWL** /ɪˈrɛləvənt/ *adjective*
not connected with something and not important: *Your point is completely irrelevant to the discussion.* ⭗ **ANTONYM relevant**

ir·re·sis·ti·ble /ˌɪrɪˈzɪstəbl/ *adjective*
so powerful or attractive that you cannot stop yourself from wanting or doing it: *Those chocolates look irresistible.*

ir·re·spon·si·ble /ˌɪrɪˈspɑnsəbl/ *adjective*
not thinking about the effect your actions will have; not sensible: *It was irresponsible of him to leave his little sister alone in the house.* ⭗ **ANTONYM responsible**

ir·ri·gate /ˈɪrəgeɪt/ *verb* (**ir·ri·gates, ir·ri·gat·ing, ir·ri·gat·ed**)
to supply water to land for growing food, using pipes or other equipment
▶ **ir·ri·ga·tion** /ˌɪrəˈgeɪʃn/ *noun* [*noncount*]

ir·ri·ta·ble /ˈɪrətəbl/ *adjective*
becoming angry easily: *He's very irritable in the morning.*

ir·ri·tate /ˈɪrəteɪt/ *verb* (**ir·ri·tates, ir·ri·tat·ing, ir·ri·tat·ed**)
1 to make someone angry: *He irritates me when he asks so many questions.*
2 (**HEALTH**) to make a part of your body hurt a little: *Cigarette smoke irritates my eyes.*
▶ **ir·ri·ta·tion** /ˌɪrəˈteɪʃn/ *noun* [*count, noncount*]: *This plant can cause irritation to your skin.*
▶ **ir·ri·tat·ing** /ˈɪrəteɪtɪŋ/ *adjective*

is /ɪz/ form of **be**

Suffix

-ish

1 (in adjectives and nouns) describing nationality or language: *English* • *Polish*
2 (in adjectives) similar to: *babyish* • *childish*
3 (in adjectives) fairly; kind of: *longish* • *brownish*

Is·lam /ˈɪslɑm; ˈɪzlɑm/ *noun* [*noncount*]
(**RELIGION**) the religion of Muslim people. **Islam** teaches that there is only one God and that Muhammad is his **PROPHET** (= the person that God has chosen to give his message to people).
▶ **Is·lam·ic** /ɪsˈlæmɪk; ɪzˈlæmɪk/ *adjective*: *the Islamic faith*

is·land /ˈaɪlənd/ *noun* [*count*]

> 🛈 **PRONUNCIATION**
> The word **island** sounds like **highland**, because we don't say the letter **s** in this word.

(**GEOGRAPHY**) a piece of land with water all around it: *the Caribbean islands*

isn't /ˈɪznt/ short for **is not**

i·so·late **AWL** /ˈaɪsəleɪt/ *verb* (**i·so·lates, i·so·lat·ing, i·so·lat·ed**)
to keep someone or something separate from other people or things: *If we isolate the animals that have the disease, the others won't catch it.*
▶ **i·so·la·tion** **AWL** /ˌaɪsəˈleɪʃn/ *noun* [*noncount*]: *The prisoner was kept in isolation for 24 hours.*

i·so·lat·ed **AWL** /ˈaɪsəleɪtəd/ *adjective*
far from other people or things: *an isolated house in the mountains*

is·sue¹ **AWL** /ˈɪʃu/ *noun* [*count*]
1 an important problem that people talk about: *Pollution is a serious issue.*

2 a magazine or newspaper of a particular day, week, or month: *Have you read this week's issue?*

is·sue² AWL /ˈɪʃu/ *verb* (is·sues, is·su·ing, is·sued)
to give or say something officially: *The soldiers were issued with uniforms.* ◆ *The police department has issued a statement.*

Suffix

–ist
(in nouns)
1 a person who has studied something or who does something as a job: *artist* ◆ *economist* ◆ *scientist*
2 a person who believes in something or belongs to a particular group: *capitalist* ◆ *communist* ◆ *feminist*

IT /ˌaɪ ˈti/ *noun* [noncount]
(**COMPUTERS**) the study or use of computers and other electronic equipment to store and send information ➔ IT is short for "Information Technology."

it 🔑 /ɪt/ *pronoun* (*plural* **they** /ðeɪ/, **them** /ðɛm/)
1 a word that shows a thing or animal: *I like your shirt. Is it new?* ◆ *Where's the coffee? I can't find it.*
2 a word that points to an idea that follows: *It's hard to learn a new language.*
3 a word that shows who someone is: *"Who's at the door?" "It's Joe."*
4 a word at the beginning of a sentence about time, the weather, or distance: *It's six o'clock.* ◆ *It's hot today.* ◆ *It's 100 miles from here to Philadelphia.*

i·tal·ics /ɪˈtælɪks/ *noun* [plural]
a type of writing or printing in which the letters do not stand straight up: *This sentence is in italics.*
▶ **i·tal·ic** /ɪˈtælɪk/ *adjective*: *italic writing*

itch /ɪtʃ/ *noun* [count] (*plural* **itch·es**)
the feeling on your skin that makes you want to rub or scratch it: *I have an itch on my back.*
▶ **itch** *verb* (itch·es, itch·ing, itched): *My nose itches.* ◆ *Mosquito bites really itch.*

itch·y /ˈɪtʃi/ *adjective* (itch·i·er, itch·i·est)
having or producing an ITCH: *an itchy sweater* ◆ *I feel itchy all over.*

it'd /ˈɪtəd/ short for **it had**, **it would**

i·tem 🔑 AWL /ˈaɪtəm/ *noun* [count]
1 one thing in a list or group of things: *What is the first item on the agenda?* ◆ *an item of clothing*

2 a piece of news: *There was an interesting news item about the Olympics.*

i·tin·er·ar·y /aɪˈtɪnərɛri/ *noun* [count] (*plural* i·tin·er·ar·ies)
a plan of a trip, including which way you will go, the places you will visit, etc.: *I'll e-mail you my itinerary for my trip to San Francisco.*

it'll /ˈɪtl/ short for **it will**

its 🔑 /ɪts/ *adjective*
of the thing or animal that you have just talked about: *The dog hurt its leg.* ◆ *The company has its annual meeting in June.*

Which word?

Its or it's?
- Be careful! **It's** is a short way of saying "it is" or "it has": **It's** (= it is) *cold today.* ◆ **It's** (= it has) *been raining.*
- **Its** means "belonging to it": *The bird had broken its wing.*

it's /ɪts/ short for **it is**, **it has**

it·self 🔑 /ɪtˈsɛlf/ *pronoun* (*plural* them·selves /ðəmˈsɛlvz/)
1 a word that shows the same thing or animal that you have just talked about: *The cat was washing itself.*
2 a word that makes "it" stronger: *The hotel itself was nice, but I didn't like the area.*
by itself
1 without being controlled by a person: *The machine will start by itself.*
2 alone: *The house stands by itself at the end of a dirt road.*

I've /aɪv/ short for **I have**

i·vo·ry /ˈaɪvəri/ *noun* [noncount]
the hard, white substance that the long teeth (called TUSKS) of an ELEPHANT (= a very large gray animal with big ears) are made of

i·vy /ˈaɪvi/ *noun* [noncount]
a plant with dark green leaves that climbs up walls or trees

the I·vy League /ði ˌaɪvi ˈlig/ *noun* [singular]
a group of eight private colleges and universities in the north of the U.S. that are old and respected: *an Ivy League education*

J j

J, j /dʒeɪ/ *noun* [count, noncount] (*plural* **J's, j's** /dʒeɪz/)
the tenth letter of the English alphabet: *"June" begins with a "J."*

jab /dʒæb/ *verb* (jabs, jab·bing, jabbed)
to push at someone with a sudden rough movement: *She **jabbed** me **in** the stomach with her elbow.*
▸ **jab** *noun* [count]: *I felt a jab in my ribs.*

jack /dʒæk/ *noun* [count]
the playing card that has a picture of a young man on it: *the jack of hearts*

jack·et 🔧 /'dʒækət/ *noun* [count]
a short coat with sleeves ⊃ Look at the picture at **clothes**.

jack·knife /'dʒæknaɪf/ *noun* [count] (*plural* jack·knives /'dʒæknaɪvz/)
a small knife with one or more sharp parts (called **BLADES**) that fold down into the handle ⊃ **SYNONYM pocketknife**

jack-o'-lan·tern /'dʒæk ə ˌlæntərn/ *noun* [count]
a large, round, orange vegetable (called a **PUMPKIN**) with a face cut into it, usually with a light inside. People make **jack-o'-lanterns** for **HALLOWEEN** (= October 31). ⊃ Look at the note at **Halloween**.

jack·pot /'dʒækpɑt/ *noun* [count]
the largest money prize you can win in a game: *The lottery jackpot is $5 million.*

jade /dʒeɪd/ *noun* [noncount]
a hard, green stone that is used for making jewelry: *a jade necklace*

jag·ged /'dʒægəd/ *adjective*
rough, with a lot of sharp points: *jagged rocks*

jag·uar /'dʒægwɑr/ *noun* [count]
a large wild cat with black spots that lives in Central and South America

jail /dʒeɪl/ *noun* [count, noncount]
a prison: *He was **sent to jail** for two years.*
▸ **jail** *verb* (jails, jail·ing, jailed): *She was **jailed for** fraud.*

jam¹ /dʒæm/ *noun*
1 [noncount] sweet food made from fruit and sugar. You eat **jam** on bread: *a jar of strawberry jam* ⊃ Look at **jelly**.
2 [count] a situation in which you cannot move because there are too many people or vehicles

jam² /dʒæm/ *verb* (jams, jam·ming, jammed)
1 to push something into a place where there is not much space: *She **jammed** all her clothes **into** a suitcase.*
2 to fix something or to become fixed so that you cannot move it: *I can't open the window. It's jammed.*

jan·i·tor /'dʒænətər/ *noun* [count]
a person whose job is to clean a large building

Jan·u·ar·y 🔧 /'dʒænyuɛri/ *noun* [count, noncount]
(abbreviation **Jan.**)
the first month of the year

jar /dʒɑr/ *noun* [count]
a glass container for food: *a jar of honey* ⊃ Look at the picture at **container**.

jar·gon /'dʒɑrgən/ *noun* [noncount]
(**ENGLISH LANGUAGE ARTS**) special or technical words that are used by a particular group of people, and that other people do not understand: *I tried to read the contract, but there was too much legal jargon for me.*

jave·lin /'dʒævələn/ *noun* (**SPORTS**)
1 [count] a long, pointed stick that people throw as a sport
2 the javelin [singular] the event or sport of throwing the javelin

the javelin

javelin

jaw /dʒɔ/ *noun* [count]
one of the two bones in the head of a person or animal that hold the teeth ⊃ Look at the picture at **face**.

jazz /dʒæz/ *noun* [noncount]
(**MUSIC**) a kind of music with a strong beat: *a jazz band*

jeal·ous /'dʒɛləs/ *adjective*
1 angry or sad because you want what another person has: *Ben was **jealous of** his brother's new car.* ⊃ **SYNONYM envious**
2 angry or sad because you are afraid of losing someone's love: *Sarah's boyfriend gets jealous if she talks to other guys.*
▸ **jeal·ous·y** /'dʒɛləsi/ *noun* [noncount]: *He felt sick with jealousy.*

jeans 🔧 /dʒinz/ *noun* [plural]
pants made of strong cotton material (called **DENIM**). **Jeans** are usually blue: *a pair of jeans* ✦ *He wore jeans and a T-shirt.* ⊃ Look at the picture at **clothes**.

Jeep™ /dʒip/ *noun* [count]
a strong car that can go well over rough land

---

jeer /dʒɪr/ *verb* (jeers, jeer·ing, jeered)
to laugh or shout at someone in an unkind way
that shows you do not respect them: *The crowd
jeered at him.*

jell·o (also **Jell-O™**) /ˈdʒɛloʊ/ *noun* [noncount]
a soft food with a fruit flavor, which shakes
when you move it

jel·ly /ˈdʒɛli/ *noun* [noncount]
a sweet, smooth food made from fruit, which
you eat on bread: *a peanut butter and jelly
sandwich* ◆ *grape jelly*

jel·ly·fish /ˈdʒɛlifɪʃ/
noun [count] (*plural*
jel·ly·fish or
jel·ly·fish·es)
an animal with a soft,
pale body that lives in
the ocean. **Jellyfish**
have long thin parts
that hang down and
can hurt (or STING) you.

jellyfish

jerk¹ /dʒɜrk/ *verb*
(jerks, jerk·ing, jerked)
to move quickly or suddenly; to pull or make
something move like this: *The car jerked
forward.* ◆ *She jerked the door open.*

jerk² /dʒɜrk/ *noun* [count]
1 (*informal*) a person who behaves in an unkind
or stupid way: *I'm sorry I hurt your feelings. I feel
like such a jerk.*
2 a sudden sharp movement: *The bus started
with a jerk.*

jer·sey /ˈdʒɜrzi/ *noun* [count] (*plural* jer·seys)
a shirt that is part of a sports uniform: *a football
jersey*

Je·sus /ˈdʒizəs/ (also **Je·sus Christ** /ˌdʒizəs
ˈkraɪst/) *noun*
(**RELIGION**) the man who Christians believe is the
Son of God

jet /dʒɛt/ *noun* [count]
1 a type of fast, modern airplane
2 liquid or gas that comes very fast out of a
small hole: *a jet of gas* ◆ *jets of water*

jet lag /ˈdʒɛt læg/ *noun* [noncount]
the feeling of being very tired after a long
airplane trip to a place where the local time is
different

Jew /dʒu/ *noun* [count]
(**RELIGION**) a person who follows the religion of
Judaism
▸ **Jew·ish** /ˈdʒuɪʃ/ *adjective*: *She is Jewish.* ◆ *the
Jewish holidays*

jew·el /ˈdʒuəl/ *noun* [count]
a beautiful stone that is very valuable:
diamonds, rubies, and other jewels ⊃ SYNONYM
gem

jew·el·er /ˈdʒuələr/ *noun* [count]
a person who sells, makes, or repairs jewelry
and watches

jewelry

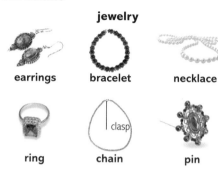

earrings   **bracelet**   **necklace**

ring   **chain**   **pin**

jew·el·ry /ˈdʒuəlri/ *noun* [noncount]
objects that people wear to decorate their
fingers, ears, arms, etc.: *a piece of gold jewelry* ◆
a jewelry store

jig·saw puz·zle
/ˈdʒɪgsɔ ˌpʌzl/ (also
puz·zle) *noun* [count]
a picture in many
pieces that you put
together

jig·saw puzzle

jin·gle /ˈdʒɪŋgl/ *verb*
(jin·gles, jin·gling,
jin·gled)
to make a pleasant
sound like small bells;
to cause something to
make this sound: *She jingled the coins in her
pocket.*

jinx /dʒɪŋks/ *noun* [singular]
bad luck, or a person or thing that brings bad
luck
▸ **jinx** *verb* (jinx·es, jinx·ing, jinxed)
to make someone have bad luck
▸ **jinxed** /dʒɪŋkst/ *adjective*
having a lot of bad luck: *After my third accident
in a month, I began to think I was jinxed.*

job ✎ **AWL** /dʒɑb/ *noun* [count]
1 the work that you do for money: *She got a job
as a waitress.* ◆ *Peter just lost his job.*

Word building

■ When you **apply for** a job, you **fill out** an
application form or you send a letter and
your **résumé** (= a list of your experience
and education).

■ You **have an interview**, and the **employer**
asks for **references** (= letters from other
people saying what you can do). Some jobs
are **full-time** and some are **part-time**.

■ If you **get fired**, you lose your job. When

you reach a certain age, you **retire** (= stop working).

■ To find out what someone's job is, we say: **What do you do?**

2 something that you must do: *I have a lot of jobs to do around the house.*

do a good job to do something well: *You did a good job on your homework.*

out of a job without paid work ➔ SYNONYM **unemployed**

Thesaurus

job the work that you do to earn money: *My dad told me to go out and get a job. • She's trying to find a full-time job. • I'm only doing my job (= I'm doing what I am paid to do). • He's looking for a job in teaching.*

work the job that you do to earn money. **Work** is a noncount noun, so you cannot say "a work" or "works": *It's very difficult to find work in this city. • I've been out of work (= without a job) for almost a year. • She goes jogging every morning before work.*

employment the state of having a job that you are paid to do. This is a noncount noun, and is a more formal word than **work** and **job**: *The company provides employment for 150 staff. • I'm only looking for part-time employment right now.*

career the jobs that someone has in a particular area of work over a period of time. Your **career** often involves several jobs, which usually involve more responsibility as time passes: *a teaching career • a career in politics • Why did you decide on a career as a vet?*

profession a job that needs special training and higher education: *the legal profession • She hopes to enter the medical profession. • He's a teacher by profession.*

jock·ey /ˈdʒɑki/ *noun* [count] (*plural* **jock·eys**) (SPORTS) a person who rides horses in races

jog /dʒɑg/ *verb* (jogs, jog·ging, jogged) to run slowly for exercise: *I jogged around the park. • I go jogging every morning.*
▶ **jog** *noun* [singular]: *She goes for a jog before breakfast.*
▶ **jog·ger** /ˈdʒɑgər/ *noun* [count] a person who goes **jogging** for exercise

join 🔎 /dʒɔɪn/ *verb* (joins, join·ing, joined)
1 to become a member of a group: *He joined the army. • Would you like to join our book club?*
2 to come together with someone or something: *Will you join us for dinner? • This road joins the main highway soon.*

3 to bring or fasten one thing to another thing: *The tunnel joins New York to New Jersey. • Join the two pieces of wood together.*
join in to do something with other people: *Everyone started singing, but he refused to join in.*

joint¹ /dʒɔɪnt/ *adjective* involving two or more people together: *The report was a joint effort (= we worked on it together). • My wife and I have a joint bank account.*

joint² /dʒɔɪnt/ *noun* [count]
1 a part of your body where two bones fit together and you are able to bend
2 a place where two parts of something join together: *the joints of the pipe*

joke¹ 🔎 /dʒoʊk/ *noun* [count] something that you say or do to make people laugh, for example a funny story that you tell: *She told us a joke. • I didn't get the joke (= understand it).*

joke² 🔎 /dʒoʊk/ *verb* (jokes, jok·ing, joked) to tell funny stories; to say things that are funny but not true: *They were laughing and joking together. • I didn't mean what I said – I was only joking.*

jok·er /ˈdʒoʊkər/ *noun* [count]
1 a person who likes to tell jokes or play tricks
2 an extra card which can be used instead of any card in some games: *Did you take the jokers out of the deck?*

jol·ly /ˈdʒɑli/ *adjective* (jol·li·er, jol·li·est) happy and full of fun

jolt /dʒoʊlt/ *verb* (jolts, jolt·ing, jolt·ed) to move or to make someone or something move in a sudden rough way: *The bus jolted to a stop. • The crash jolted us forward.* ➔ SYNONYM **jerk**
▶ **jolt** *noun* [count, usually singular]: *The train stopped with a jolt.*

jot /dʒɑt/ *verb* (jots, jot·ting, jot·ted)
jot something down to write something quickly: *I jotted down his phone number.*

jour·nal AWL /ˈdʒərnl/ *noun* [count]
1 a magazine about one particular thing: *a medical journal*
2 a book where you write what you have done each day: *Do you keep a journal?* ➔ SYNONYM **diary**

jour·nal·ism /ˈdʒərnəl·ɪzəm/ *noun* [noncount] the work of collecting and reporting news for newspapers, television, etc.

jour·nal·ist /ˈdʒərnəl·ɪst/ *noun* [count] a person whose job is to collect and report news for newspapers, television, etc.

jour·ney /ˈdʒɜrni/ *noun* [*count*] (*plural* **jour·neys**)
a long trip from one place to another: *The book is about her journey through South America.* ⊃ Look at the note at **trip**[1].

joy /dʒɔɪ/ *noun* [*noncount*]
a very happy feeling: *Their children give them so much joy.*
▶ **joy·ful** /ˈdʒɔɪfl/ *adjective*
very happy: *a joyful occasion*

joy·stick /ˈdʒɔɪstɪk/ *noun* [*count*]
a handle that you move to control something, for example a computer game

Jr. abbreviation of **Junior**: *Martin Luther King, Jr.*

Ju·da·ism /ˈdʒudɪˌɪzəm/ *noun* [*noncount*]
(**RELIGION**) the religion of the Jewish people

judge[1] /dʒʌdʒ/ *noun* [*count*]
1 the person in a court of law who decides how to punish someone: *The judge sent him to prison for 20 years.*
2 a person who chooses the winner of a competition

judge[2] /dʒʌdʒ/ *verb* (**judg·es, judg·ing, judged**)
1 to have or to form an opinion about someone or something: *It's difficult to judge how long the project will take.*
2 to decide who or what wins a competition: *The principal judged the poster competition.*

judg·ment (also **judge·ment**) /ˈdʒʌdʒmənt/ *noun*
1 [*noncount*] your ability to form opinions or make sensible decisions: *Use your judgment (= you decide).* ◆ *In my judgment, she will do the job very well.*
2 [*count, noncount*] the decision of a judge in a court of law

ju·di·cial /dʒuˈdɪʃl/ *adjective*
connected with a court of law, a judge, or a judgment: *the court's judicial powers* ◆ *the judicial branch of the federal government* ⊃ Look at the note at **government**.

ju·do /ˈdʒudoʊ/ *noun* [*noncount*]
(**SPORTS**) a sport where two people fight and try to throw each other onto the floor

jug /dʒʌg/ *noun* [*count*]
a container with a handle and a small hole at the top, which you use for holding liquids: *a jug of wine*

jug

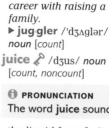

jug·gle /ˈdʒʌgl/ *verb* (**jug·gles, jug·gling, jug·gled**)
1 to keep two or more things in the air by throwing and catching them quickly

2 to try to do two or more important jobs or activities at the same time: *She's trying to juggle her career with raising a family.*
▶ **jug·gler** /ˈdʒʌglər/ *noun* [*count*]

juggler

juice /dʒus/ *noun* [*count, noncount*]

> ⓘ **PRONUNCIATION**
> The word **juice** sounds like **loose**.

the liquid from fruit and vegetables: *a glass of orange juice*

juic·y /ˈdʒusi/ *adjective* (**juic·i·er, juic·i·est**)
full of juice: *juicy tomatoes*

juke·box /ˈdʒukbɑks/ *noun* [*count*] (*plural* **juke·box·es**)
(**MUSIC**) a machine in a bar or restaurant that plays music when you put money in it

Ju·ly /dʒʊˈlaɪ/ *noun* [*count, noncount*]
(abbreviation **Jul.**)
the seventh month of the year

jum·ble /ˈdʒʌmbl/ *noun* [*singular*]
a lot of things that are mixed together in a messy way: *a jumble of old clothes and books*
▶ **jum·bled** /ˈdʒʌmbld/ *adjective*: *a jumbled heap of old toys*

jum·bo /ˈdʒʌmboʊ/ *adjective* (*informal*)
very large: *jumbo shrimp with garlic sauce*

jump /dʒʌmp/ *verb* (**jumps, jump·ing, jumped**)
1 to move quickly off the ground, using your legs to push you up: *The cat jumped onto the table.* ◆ *The horse jumped over the wall.*
2 to move quickly: *He jumped into the car and drove away.*
3 to move suddenly because you are surprised or scared: *A loud noise **made me jump**.*
4 to increase suddenly by a large amount: *His salary jumped by $20,000 when he got promoted.*
jump at something to accept an opportunity or an offer with enthusiasm: *Of course, I **jumped at the chance** to work in New York for a year.*
jump rope to jump many times over a rope that is turning, as a game or as a form of exercise: *The children are outside jumping rope.*
▶ **jump** *noun* [*count*]: *With a huge jump the horse cleared the fence.*

jump rope /ˈdʒʌmp roʊp/ *noun* [*count*]
a rope that you use for jumping over again and again as a game or as a form of exercise

jump·y /ˈdʒʌmpi/ *adjective* (jump·i·er, jump·i·est)
(*informal*)
nervous or worried: *Why are you so jumpy today?*

junc·tion /ˈdʒʌŋkʃn/ *noun* [count]
a place where roads or railroad lines meet: *There was an accident at the junction of Mill Road and Route 7.*

June 🔑 /dʒun/ *noun* [count, noncount]
(abbreviation **Jun.**)
the sixth month of the year

jun·gle /ˈdʒʌŋgl/ *noun* [count, noncount]
(**GEOGRAPHY**) a thick forest in a hot part of the world: *the jungles of South America*

jun·ior¹ /ˈdʒunyər/ *adjective*
1 connected with the third year of high school or college: *I spent my junior year abroad in Paris.*
2 **Junior** (abbreviation **Jr.**) a word that is used after the name of a son who has the same name as his father: *Martin Luther King, Jr.*
3 having a lower position or less experience in an organization: *a junior senator*
4 of or for children below a particular age: *the junior tennis championships* ⊃ Look at **senior**.

jun·ior² /ˈdʒunyər/ *noun* [count]
a student in eleventh grade in high school or the third year of college: *a high school junior* ⊃ Look at **freshman**, **senior²**(1), **sophomore**.

jun·ior col·lege /ˌdʒunyər ˈkɑlɪdʒ/ *noun* [count]
a college where you can study for two years to get a degree (called an **ASSOCIATE'S DEGREE**) or prepare for another college or university ⊃ Look at **community college**.

jun·ior high school /ˌdʒunyər ˈhaɪ skul/ (also **jun·ior high**) *noun* [count, noncount]
a school for children between the ages of about 11 and 14 ⊃ Look at the note at **elementary school**.

junk /dʒʌŋk/ *noun* [noncount]
things that are old or have no use: *The garage is full of junk.*

junk food /ˈdʒʌŋk fud/ *noun* [noncount] (*informal*)
food that is quick and easy to prepare and eat, but that is bad for your health

junk mail /ˈdʒʌŋk meɪl/ *noun* [noncount]
advertisements that companies send to people who have not asked for them ⊃ Look at **spam**.

ju·ry /ˈdʒʊri/ *noun* [count] (*plural* **ju·ries**)
a group of people in a court of law who decide if someone has done something wrong or not: *The jury decided that the woman was guilty of killing her husband.*

just¹ 🔑 /dʒʌst/ *adverb*
1 exactly: *This jacket is just my size.* ◆ *You're just in time.* ◆ *She looks just like her mother.*
2 a very short time before: *I just heard the news.* ◆ *Jim isn't here – he just went out.*
3 at this or that moment; now or very soon: *I'm just going to make some coffee.* ◆ *She called just as I was going to bed.*
4 a word that makes what you say stronger: *Just look at that funny little dog!*
5 only: *It's just a small gift.*
just about (*informal*) almost; very nearly: *I've met just about everyone.*
just a minute; **just a moment** used for asking someone to wait for a short time: *Just a moment – there's someone at the door.*

just² /dʒʌst/ *adjective*
fair and right: *a just punishment* ⊃ **ANTONYM** **unjust**

jus·tice /ˈdʒʌstəs/ *noun*
1 [noncount] treatment of people in a fair way: *the struggle for justice* ⊃ **ANTONYM** **injustice**
2 [noncount] the law: *the criminal justice system*
3 [count] a judge in an important court of law: *a Supreme Court justice*

jus·ti·fi·ca·tion **AWL** /ˌdʒʌstəfəˈkeɪʃn/ *noun* [count, noncount]
a good reason for doing something: *There's no justification for firing him.*

jus·ti·fy **AWL** /ˈdʒʌstəfaɪ/ *verb* (jus·ti·fies, jus·ti·fy·ing, jus·ti·fied, has jus·ti·fied)
to give or be a good reason for something: *Can you justify what you did?*

ju·ve·nile /ˈdʒuvənaɪl; ˈdʒuvənl/ *adjective* (*formal*)
connected with young people who are not yet adults: *juvenile crime*
▶ **ju·ve·nile** *noun* [count]

K k

K, k /keɪ/ *noun* [*count, noncount*] (*plural* **K's, k's** /keɪz/)
the eleventh letter of the English alphabet: *"King" begins with a "K."*

kan·ga·roo /ˌkæŋɡə'ru/ *noun* [*count*] (*plural* **kan·ga·roos**)
an Australian animal that jumps on its strong back legs and carries its babies in a pocket on its front

kangaroo

ka·ra·te /kə'rɑti/ *noun* [*noncount*]
(**SPORTS**) a Japanese sport where people fight with their hands and feet

kay·ak /'kaɪæk/ *noun* [*count*]
a light narrow boat for one person, which you move through the water using a piece of wood with a flat part at each end (called a **PADDLE**)

kayak

paddle

keen /kin/ *adjective* (**keen·er, keen·est**)
1 very good or strong: *keen eyesight*
2 wanting to do something: *Mike was keen to go out, but I wanted to stay at home.*

keep ♪ /kip/ *verb* (**keeps, keep·ing, kept** /kɛpt/, **has kept**)
1 to continue to have something: *You can keep that book – I don't need it.*
2 to stay in a particular state or condition: *We tried to keep warm.*
3 to make someone or something stay in a particular state or condition: *Keep this door closed.* ◆ *I'm sorry to keep you waiting.*
4 to put or store something in a particular place: *Where do you keep the coffee?*
5 to continue doing something; to do something many times: *Keep driving until you see the gas station, then turn left.* ◆ *She keeps forgetting my name.*
6 to do what you promised or arranged: *I always keep my promises.* ◆ *Can you keep a secret?*
7 to stay fresh: *Will this fish keep until tomorrow?*
keep away from someone or **something** to not go near someone or something: *Keep away from the river, children.*

keep someone from doing something to stop someone from doing something: *You can't keep me from going out!*
keep going to continue: *I was very tired, but I kept going to the end of the race.*
keep off something to not go on something: *Keep off the grass!*
keep on doing something to continue doing something; to do something many times: *That man keeps on looking at me.*
keep out to stay outside: *The sign on the door said "Danger. Keep out!"*
keep someone or **something out** to stop someone or something from going in: *We put a fence around the yard to keep the deer out.*
keep up with someone or **something** to go as fast as another person or thing so that you are together: *Don't walk so quickly – I can't keep up with you.*

ken·nel /'kɛnl/ *noun* [*count*]
a place where dogs can stay while their owners are away

kept form of **keep**

ker·o·sene /'kɛrəsin/ *noun* [*noncount*]
a type of oil that people burn to produce heat or light

ketch·up /'kɛtʃəp/ *noun* [*noncount*]
a cold sauce made from tomatoes

ket·tle /'kɛtl/ (also **tea·ket·tle** /'ti,kɛtl/) *noun* [*count*]
a container with a handle, for boiling water

keys

key ring

piano keys   **key**

key¹ ♪ /ki/ *noun* [*count*]
1 a piece of metal that opens or closes a lock: *Have you seen my car keys?*
2 something that helps you achieve or understand something: *A good education is the key to success.*
3 one of the parts of a computer, a piano, or other musical instrument that you press with your fingers: *Press the escape key to exit the program.* ◆ *Pianos have black and white keys.* ⊃ Look at the picture at **computer**.
4 (**MUSIC**) a set of musical notes that is based on one particular note: *This piece is in the key of A minor.*
5 answers to questions: *Check your answers with the key at the back of the book.*

tʃ **chin**   dʒ **June**   v **van**   θ **thin**   ð **then**   s **so**   z **zoo**   ʃ **she**

key² /ki/ *verb* (keys, key·ing, keyed)
key something in to put words or numbers into a computer by pressing the keys: *Key in your password.*

key·board /'kibɔrd/ *noun* [count]
1 all the keys on a computer or piano ⊃ Look at the picture at **computer**.
2 (MUSIC) a musical instrument like a small electrical piano

key·hole /'kihoʊl/ *noun* [count]
a hole in a lock where you put a key

key ring /'ki rɪŋ/ *noun* [count]
a metal ring that you keep keys on ⊃ Look at the picture at **key**.

kg abbreviation of **kilogram**

khak·i /'kæki/ *adjective*
having the pale brown-green or brown-yellow color of a soldier's uniform: *khaki pants*
▸ **khak·i** *noun* [noncount]

khak·is /'kækiz/ *noun* [plural]
a pair of pants that are a brown-green or light brown color: *a pair of khakis and a casual shirt*

kick¹ /kɪk/ *verb* (kicks, kick·ing, kicked)
1 to hit someone or something with your foot: *I kicked the ball to Chris.*
2 to move your foot or feet up and down quickly: *The little boy was kicking and screaming.*
kick off (*informal*) to begin an event: *He kicked off his latest tour in Chicago last week.*
kick someone out (*informal*) to make someone leave a place: *He was kicked out of school for fighting.*

kick² /kɪk/ *noun* [count]
1 a movement with your foot or your leg, usually to hit something with your foot: *If the door won't open, give it a kick.*
2 (*informal*) a feeling of excitement: *He gets a kick out of driving fast cars.*

kick·off /'kɪkɔf/ *noun* [count]
(SPORTS) the start of a game of football: *Kickoff is at 4 p.m.*

kid¹ /kɪd/ *noun* [count]
1 (*informal*) a child: *How old are your kids?* ◆ *He's a smart kid.*
2 a young GOAT (= an animal with horns that lives in mountain areas)

kid² /kɪd/ *verb* (kids, kid·ding, kid·ded)
(*informal*)
to say something that it not true, as a joke: *I didn't mean it. I was just kidding.*

kid·nap /'kɪdnæp/ *verb* (kid·naps, kid·nap·ping, kid·napped)
to take someone away and hide them, so that their family or friends will pay money to free them

▸ **kid·nap·per** /'kɪdnæpər/ *noun* [count]: *The kidnappers are demanding a ransom of $1 million.*
▸ **kid·nap·ping** /'kɪdnæpɪŋ/ *noun* [count, noncount]: *the kidnapping of 12 U.S. citizens*

kid·ney /'kɪdni/ *noun* [count] (*plural* **kid·neys**)
(BIOLOGY) one of the two parts inside your body that take waste liquid from your blood

kill /kɪl/ *verb* (kills, kill·ing, killed)
to make someone or something die: *Three people were killed in the accident.* ◆ *If you water this plant too much, you'll kill it.*
▸ **kill·er** /'kɪlər/ *noun* [count]
a person, animal, or thing that kills

ki·lo /'kiloʊ/ *noun* [count] (*plural* **ki·los**) short for **kilogram**

kil·o·byte /'kɪləbaɪt/ *noun* [count] (abbreviation **KB**)
(COMPUTERS) a unit of computer memory, equal to just over a thousand BYTES (= small units of information) ⊃ Look at **gigabyte**, **megabyte**.

kil·o·gram /'kɪləgræm/ (also **ki·lo**) *noun* [count] (abbreviation **kg**)
a measure of weight. There are 1,000 **grams**, or around 2.2 **pounds**, in a **kilogram**: *I bought two kilos of potatoes.*

kil·o·me·ter /kɪ'lɑmətər; 'kɪləmiːtər/ *noun* [count] (abbreviation **km**)
a measure of length. There are 1,000 **meters**, or around 0.62 **miles**, in a kilometer.

kin /kɪn/ *noun* [plural] (*formal*)
the people in your family: *Who is your **next of kin** (= your closest family member)?*

kind¹ /kaɪnd/ *noun* [count]
a group of things or people that are the same in some way: ***What kind of** music do you like?* ◆ *The bakery sells ten different **kinds of** bread.* ⊃
SYNONYM **type**
kind of (*informal*) a little; slightly: *He looks kind of tired.*

kind² /kaɪnd/ *adjective* (kind·er, kind·est)
friendly and good to other people: *"Can I carry your bag?" "Thanks. That's very **kind of** you."* ◆ *Be **kind to** animals.* ⊃ ANTONYM **unkind**
▸ **kind·ly** /'kaɪndli/ *adverb*: *She kindly drove me to the train station.*

kin·der·gar·ten /'kɪndər,gɑrtn/ *noun* [count, noncount]
the first year of school for children, which they start when they are around 5 years old: *Hannah's **in kindergarten** this year. Next year she'll start first grade.* ⊃ Look at the note at **elementary school**.

kind·ness /'kaɪndnəs/ *noun* [noncount]
the quality of being kind: *Thank you for your kindness.*

king 🔊 /kɪŋ/ *noun* [*count*]
a man from a royal family who rules a country: *the king of Jordan* ⊃ Look at **queen**.

king·dom /ˈkɪŋdəm/ *noun* [*count*]
a country where a king or queen rules: *the Kingdom of Saudi Arabia*

kiss 🔊 /kɪs/ *verb* (**kiss·es, kiss·ing, kissed**)
to touch someone with your lips to show love or to say hello or goodbye: *She kissed me on the cheek.* • *They kissed, and then he left.*
▶ **kiss** *noun* [*count*] (*plural* **kiss·es**): *Give me a kiss!*

kit /kɪt/ *noun* [*count*]
1 a set of equipment or tools that you need for a particular purpose: *a first-aid kit*
2 a set of small pieces that you put together to make something: *a model airplane kit*

kitchen utensils

sieve

can opener

corkscrew

ladle   whisk   ice-cream scoop

kitch·en /ˈkɪtʃən/ *noun* [*count*]
a room where you cook food

kite /kaɪt/ *noun* [*count*]
a toy that you fly in the wind on a long piece of string

kit·ten 🔊 /ˈkɪtn/ *noun* [*count*]
a young cat ⊃ Look at the picture at **cat**.

ki·wi /ˈkiwi/ *noun* [*count*] (*plural* **ki·wis**)
(also **ki·wi fruit** /ˈkiwi frut/ *plural* **ki·wi fruit**)
a small, green fruit with black seeds and rough, brown skin ⊃ Look at the picture at **fruit**.

Kleen·ex™ /ˈklinɛks/ *noun* [*count, noncount*]
(*plural* **Kleen·ex·es**)
a thin piece of soft paper that you use to clean your nose ⊃ **SYNONYM** tissue

kite

km abbreviation of **kilometer**

knead /nid/ *verb* (**kneads, knead·ing, knead·ed**)
to press and stretch a mixture of flour and water (called **DOUGH**) to make bread

> 🛈 **PRONUNCIATION**
> If a word starts with the letters **KN**, the K is always silent. So the word **knead** sounds like **need**, **know** sounds like **no**, and **knight** sounds like **night**.

knee 🔊 /ni/ *noun* [*count*]
the part in the middle of your leg where it bends: *I fell down and cut my knee.* ⊃ Look at the picture at **leg**.

knee·cap /ˈnikæp/ *noun* [*count*]
the bone that covers the front of your knee

kneel /nil/ *verb* (**kneels, kneel·ing, knelt** /nɛlt/ **or kneeled, has knelt or has kneeled**)
to bend your legs and rest on one or both of your knees: *He knelt down to pray.* • *She was kneeling on the floor.*

knew form of **know**

knife 🔊 /naɪf/ *noun* [*count*] (*plural* **knives** /naɪvz/)
a sharp, metal thing with a handle that you use to cut things or to fight: *a knife and fork*

knife

fork

knight /naɪt/ *noun* [*count*]
a soldier of a high level who rode a horse and fought for his king a long time ago

knit /nɪt/ *verb* (**knits, knit·ting, knit·ted or knit** /nɪt/, **has knit·ted or has knit**)
to make clothes from thick cotton or wool thread (called **YARN**) using **KNITTING NEEDLES**: *My grandmother is knitting a sweater for me.*
▶ **knit·ting** /ˈnɪtɪŋ/ *noun* [*noncount*]: *I brought some knitting to do while I was waiting.*

knit·ting nee·dle /ˈnɪtɪŋ ˌnidl/ *noun* [*count*]
one of two metal, plastic, or wooden sticks that you use to **KNIT** with

knives plural of **knife**

knob /nɑb/ *noun* [*count*]
1 a round handle on a door or drawer
2 a round thing that you turn to control part of a machine: *the volume control knob*

knock¹ 🔊 /nɑk/ *verb* (**knocks, knock·ing, knocked**)
1 to hit something and make a noise: *I knocked on the door, but no one answered.*
2 to hit something hard, usually by accident: *I knocked my head on the door.* • *She knocked a glass off the table.*

ə **about**   y **yes**   w **woman**   ṭ **butter**   eɪ **say**   aɪ **five**   ɔɪ **boy**   aʊ **now**   oʊ **go**

knock someone down; **knock someone over** to hit someone so that they fall onto the ground: *The boy was knocked down by a car.*
knock something down to break a building so that it falls down: *They're knocking down the old houses.* ➲ SYNONYM **demolish**
knock someone out to make someone fall asleep or become unconscious: *That cold medicine really knocked me out.*
knock something over to hit something so that it falls over: *I knocked over a vase of flowers.*

knock² 🔑 /nɑk/ *noun* [*count*]
the action of hitting something, or the sound that this makes: *I heard a* ***knock at*** *the door.*

knot¹ 🔑 /nɑt/ *noun* [*count*]
a place where you have tied two pieces of rope, string, etc. together: *I* ***tied a knot*** *in the rope.* ◆ *Can you undo this knot* (= make it loose)?

knot

knot² /nɑt/ *verb* (**knots**, **knot·ting**, **knot·ted**)
to tie a knot in something: *He knotted the ends of the rope together.*

know 🔑 /noʊ/ *verb* (**knows**, **know·ing**, **knew** /nu/, **has known** /noʊn/)
1 to have information in your head: *I don't know her name.* ◆ *He* ***knows*** *a lot* ***about*** *cars.* ◆ *Do you* ***know how to*** *use this machine?* ◆ *Did you* ***know that*** *he's moving to Los Angeles?*
2 to be familiar with a person or place: *I have known Mario for six years.* ◆ *I know Boston pretty well.* ◆ *I liked him when I* ***got to know him*** (= started to know him).
I know (*informal*) used to agree with something someone has just said: *"What a ridiculous situation!" "I know."*
let someone know to tell someone about something: *Let me know if you need any help.*
you know words that you use when you are thinking about what to say next, or to remind someone of something: *Well, you know, it's hard to explain.* ◆ *I just saw Maggie. You know – Jim's wife.*

know-how /ˈnoʊ haʊ/ *noun* [*noncount*] (*informal*)
practical knowledge, or the ability to do something: *I don't think we have the technical know-how for this job.*

knowl·edge 🔑 /ˈnɑlɪdʒ/ *noun* [*noncount*, *singular*]
what you know and understand about something: *He has a good* ***knowledge of*** *U.S. history.* ◆ *He did it* ***without my knowledge*** (= I did not know).

knowl·edge·a·ble /ˈnɑlɪdʒəbl/ *adjective*
knowing a lot: *She's very* ***knowledgeable about*** *history.*

known form of **know**

knuck·le /ˈnʌkl/ *noun* [*count*]
one of the parts where your fingers bend or where they join your hand

ko·a·la /koʊˈɑlə/ (also **ko·a·la bear** /koʊˌɑlə ˈbɛr/) *noun* [*count*]
an Australian animal with large ears and thick gray fur, which lives in trees

koala

the Ko·ran (also **the Qu·r'an, the Qu·ran**) /ðə kəˈræn; ðə kəˈrɑn/ *noun* [*singular*]
(RELIGION) the most important book in the Islamic religion

ko·sher /ˈkoʊʃər/ *adjective*
(used about food) prepared according to the rules of Jewish law

kung fu /ˌkʌŋ ˈfu/ *noun* [*noncount*]
(SPORTS) a Chinese style of fighting in which people use their hands and feet as weapons

L l

L, l /ɛl/ *noun* [*count, noncount*]
1 (*plural* **L's, l's** /ɛlz/) the twelfth letter of the English alphabet: *"Lake" begins with an "L."*
2 l abbreviation of **liter**

lab /læb/ *noun* [*count*] (*informal*) short for **laboratory**

la·bel¹ `AWL` /ˈleɪbl/ *noun* [*count*]
a piece of paper or material on something that tells you about it: *The label lists the nutritional information.* • *The washing instructions are on the label.*

la·bel² `AWL` /ˈleɪbl/ *verb* (**la·bels, la·bel·ing, la·beled**)
to put a **LABEL** on something: *I labeled all the boxes with my name and address.*

la·bor `AWL` /ˈleɪbər/ *noun* [*noncount*]
hard work that you do with your hands and body: *manual labor* (= work using your hands)

lab·o·ra·to·ry /ˈlæbrətɔri/ *noun* [*count*] (*plural* **lab·o·ra·to·ries**) (also *informal* **lab**)
a special room where scientists work: *a research laboratory*

La·bor Day /ˈleɪbər deɪ/ *noun* [*count, noncount*]
a holiday on the first Monday in September, when banks, schools, and many businesses are closed

la·bor·er /ˈleɪbərər/ *noun* [*count*]
a person who does hard work with their hands and body: *a farm laborer*

la·bor un·ion /ˈleɪbər ˌyunyən/ *noun* [*count*]
an organization for people who do the same type of work. **Labor unions** try to get better pay and working conditions for their members. ⊃ **SYNONYM union**

lace /leɪs/ *noun*
1 [*noncount*] very thin cloth with holes that form a pretty pattern: *lace curtains*
2 [*count*] a string that you use for tying your shoe: *Tie your laces or you'll trip over them.* ⊃ **SYNONYM shoelace**

lack¹ /læk/ *noun* [*noncount, singular*]
the state of not having something or of not having enough of something: *There is a **lack of** good teachers.*

lack² /læk/ *verb* (**lacks, lack·ing, lacked**)
to have none or not enough of something: *He lacked confidence.*

lad·der /ˈlædər/ *noun* [*count*]
a thing that you climb up when you want to reach a high place. A **ladder** is made of two tall pieces of metal or wood with shorter pieces between them (called **RUNGS**).

ladder

rung

ladies' room /ˈleɪdiz rum/ *noun* [*count*]
a room in a public building that has toilets for women to use: *Where is the ladies' room, please?* ⊃ Look at **men's room, restroom**.

la·dle /ˈleɪdl/ *noun* [*count*]
a spoon in the shape of a cup with a long handle, used for serving soup ⊃ Look at the picture at **kitchen**.

la·dy /ˈleɪdi/ *noun* [*count*] (*plural* **la·dies**)
1 a polite way of saying "woman": *an elderly lady* • *Good evening, **ladies** and gentlemen.* ⊃ Look at **gentleman**.
2 (*informal*) a rude way of talking to a woman who you do not know: *Hey lady, hurry up!*

la·dy·bug /ˈleɪdibʌg/ *noun* [*count*]
a small red or orange insect with black spots ⊃ Look at the picture at **insect**.

laid form of **lay¹**

laid-back /ˌleɪd ˈbæk/ *adjective* (*informal*)
calm and relaxed; not worried

lain form of **lie¹**

lake /leɪk/ *noun* [*count*]
(**GEOGRAPHY**) a big area of water with land all around it: *Lake Erie* • *We went swimming in the lake.*

lamb /læm/ *noun*

> **ℹ PRONUNCIATION**
> The word **lamb** sounds like **ham**, because we don't say the letter **b** in this word.

1 [*count*] a young sheep
2 [*noncount*] meat from a **lamb**: *We had roast lamb for dinner.*

lame /leɪm/ *adjective*
1 (**HEALTH**) not able to walk well: *My horse is lame.*
2 (*informal*) not very good, interesting, or exciting: *This party is so lame. Let's go home.*

lamp /læmp/ *noun* [*count*]
a thing that gives light: *It was dark, so I switched on the lamp.*

lamp

light bulb

lampshade

lamp·shade /ˈlæmpʃeɪd/ *noun* [*count*]
a cover for a lamp ⊃ Look at the picture at **lamp**.

land¹ 🔑 /lænd/ *noun* (**GEOGRAPHY**)
1 [*noncount*] the part of the earth that is not the ocean: *After two weeks in a boat, we were happy to be back on land.*
2 [*noncount*] a piece of ground: *They bought some land and built a house on it.* ◆ *land for farming*
3 [*count*] (*formal*) a country: *She returned to the land where she was born.*

land² 🔑 /lænd/ *verb* (**lands**, **land·ing**, **land·ed**)
1 to come down from the air or to bring something down to the ground: *The plane landed at La Guardia airport.* ◆ *The pilot landed the plane safely.* ◆ *He fell off the ladder and landed on his back.*
2 to go onto land or to put something onto land from a ship: *The Pilgrims landed in Massachusetts in 1620.*

land·fill /ˈlændfɪl/ *noun* [*count, noncount*]
a place where large amounts of garbage and other waste material are put into the ground and covered with earth

land·ing /ˈlændɪŋ/ *noun* [*count*]
1 coming down onto the ground in an airplane: *The plane made an **emergency landing** in a field.* ⊃ **ANTONYM takeoff**
2 the area at the top of stairs in a building: *There's a telephone on the landing.*

land·la·dy /ˈlændˌleɪdi/ *noun* [*count*] (*plural* **land·la·dies**)
a woman who rents a house or room to people for money

land·lord /ˈlændlɔrd/ *noun* [*count*]
a man who rents a house or room to people for money

land·mark /ˈlændmɑrk/ *noun* [*count*]
1 a big building or another thing that you can see easily from far away: *The Statue of Liberty is one of New York's most famous landmarks.*
2 an important stage in the development of something: *The Fourth of July celebrates an important landmark in American history.*

land·scape /ˈlænskeɪp/ *noun* [*count*]
everything you can see in an area of land: *The desert landscape is very beautiful.*

land·slide /ˈlændslaɪd/ *noun* [*count*]
(**GEOGRAPHY**) a sudden fall of earth, rocks, etc. down the side of a mountain

lane /leɪn/ *noun* [*count*]
1 one part of a wide road: *We were driving in the middle lane of the highway.* ⊃ Look at the note at **road**.
2 (**SPORTS**) a section of a swimming pool or sports track for one person to go along: *He'll be running in lane 2.*

3 a word used in the names of some streets in towns or cities: *We live at 1015 Beech Lane.* ⊃ The short way of writing "Lane" in street names is Ln.: *100 Roberts Ln.*

lan·guage 🔑 /ˈlæŋgwɪdʒ/ *noun* (**ENGLISH LANGUAGE ARTS**)
1 [*count*] words that people from a particular country say and write: *"Do you speak any foreign languages?" "Yes, I speak French and Italian."*
2 [*noncount*] words that people use to speak and write: *This word is not often used in spoken language.*

lan·tern /ˈlæntərn/ *noun* [*count*]
a light in a container made of glass or paper, which usually has a handle so you can carry it

lap /læp/ *noun* [*count*]
1 the flat part at the top of your legs when you are sitting: *The boy was sitting on his mom's lap.*
2 one trip around a track in a race: *There are three more laps to go in the race.*

lap·top /ˈlæptɑp/ *noun* [*count*]
(**COMPUTERS**) a small computer that is easy to carry

large 🔑 /lɑrdʒ/ *adjective* (**larg·er**, **larg·est**)
big: *They live in a large house.* ◆ *She has a large family.* ◆ *Do you have this shirt in a large size?* ⊃ **ANTONYM small**

large·ly /ˈlɑrdʒli/ *adverb*
mostly: *The room is largely used for meetings.* ⊃ **SYNONYM mainly**

lar·va /ˈlɑrvə/ *noun* [*count*] (*plural* **lar·vae** /ˈlɑrvi/)
(**BIOLOGY**) an insect at the stage when it has just come out of an egg, and has a short fat body and no legs

la·ser /ˈleɪzər/ *noun* [*count*]
(**PHYSICS**) an instrument that makes a very strong line of light (called a **LASER BEAM**). Some **lasers** are used to cut metal and others are used by doctors in operations.

lash /læʃ/ = **eyelash**

las·so /ˈlæsoʊ/ *noun* [*count*] (*plural* **las·sos** or **las·soes**)
a long rope with a circle at one end, which is used for catching cows and horses
▶ **las·so** *verb* (**las·sos** or **las·soes**, **las·so·ing**, **las·soed**)
to catch an animal with a **lasso**

last¹ 🔑 /læst/ *adjective*
1 after all the others: *December is the last month of the year.* ⊃ **ANTONYM first**
2 just before now; most recent: *It's June now, so last month was May.* ◆ *I was at school last week, but this week I'm on vacation.* ◆ *Did you go out last (= yesterday) night?*
3 the **last** person or thing is the only one left: *Who wants the last cookie?*

▶ **last·ly** /ˈlæstli/ *adverb*
finally, as the last thing: *Lastly, I want to thank my parents for all their help.*

last² 🔑 /læst/ *adverb*
1 after all the others: *He finished last in the race.*
2 at a time that is nearest to now: *I last saw Jim in 2009.*

last³ 🔑 /læst/ *verb* (lasts, last·ing, last·ed)
1 to continue for a time: *The concert lasted for three hours.* • *How long did the game last?*
2 to be enough for a certain time: *We have enough food to last us till next week.*

last⁴ 🔑 /læst/ *noun* [count] **the last** (*plural* **the last**)
a person or thing that comes after all the others; what comes at the end: *I was the last to arrive at the party.*
at last in the end; after some time: *She waited all week, and at last the letter arrived.* ⊃ **SYNONYM finally**

last·ing /ˈlæstɪŋ/ *adjective*
continuing for a long time: *Their trip to Niagara Falls made a lasting impression on them.*

last-min·ute /ˌlæst ˈmɪnət/ *adjective*
done or decided just before something happens or just before it is too late: *a last-minute change in plans* • *a few last-minute adjustments*

last name /ˈlæst ˌneɪm/ *noun* [count]
the part of your name that other members of your family also have: *My first name's Emma, my last name's Russell.* ⊃ **SYNONYM family name** ⊃ Look at the note at **name¹**.

late 🔑 /leɪt/ *adjective, adverb* (lat·er, lat·est)
1 after the usual or right time: *I went to bed late last night.* • *I was late for school today* (= I arrived late). • *My train was late.* ⊃ **ANTONYM early**
2 near the end of a time: *They arrived in the late afternoon.* • *She's in her late twenties* (= between the age of 25 and 29). ⊃ **ANTONYM early**
3 no longer alive; dead: *Her late husband was a doctor.*
a late night an evening when you go to bed later than usual
at the latest no later than a time or a date: *Please be here by twelve o'clock at the latest.*

late·ly /ˈleɪtli/ *adverb*
recently: *Have you seen Mark lately?* • *The weather has been very bad lately.*

lat·er¹ 🔑 /ˈleɪtər/ *adverb*
at a time in the future; after the time you are talking about: *See you later.* • *His father died later that year.* ⊃ **ANTONYM earlier**
later on (*informal*) at a time in the future; after the time you are talking about: *I'm going out later on.*

lat·er² /ˈleɪtər/ *adjective*
1 coming after something else or at a time in the future: *The game has been postponed to a later date.*
2 near the end of a period of time: *the later part of the twentieth century* ⊃ **ANTONYM earlier**

lat·est /ˈleɪtəst/ *adjective*
the newest or most recent: *the latest fashions*

Lat·in /ˈlætn/ *noun* [noncount]
(**ENGLISH LANGUAGE ARTS**) the language that people used a long time ago in ancient Rome: *Do you study Latin at school?*
▶ **Lat·in** *adjective*: *Latin poetry*

La·tin A·mer·i·ca /ˌlætn əˈmɛrɪkə/ *noun* [noncount]
the parts of the American continent where Spanish or Portuguese is the main language
▶ **La·tin A·mer·i·can** /ˌlætn əˈmɛrɪkən/ *adjective*: *Latin American music*

lat·i·tude /ˈlætɪtud/ *noun* [noncount] (**GEOGRAPHY**)
the distance of a place north or south of the line around the middle of the earth (called the **EQUATOR**). **Latitude** is measured in degrees. ⊃ Look at **longitude**. ⊃ Look at the picture at **earth**.

lat·te /ˈlɑteɪ/ *noun* [count]
a drink that is made by adding a small amount of strong coffee to a cup of hot milk: *This café is too expensive. They're charging $5 for a latte!* ⊃ Look at **cappuccino**, **espresso**.

the lat·ter /ðə ˈlætər/ *noun* [singular]
the second of two things or people: *I studied both French and German, but I preferred the latter.* ⊃ Look at **the former**.

laugh¹ 🔑 /læf/ *verb* (laughs, laugh·ing, laughed)
to make sounds to show that you are happy or that you think something is funny: *His jokes always make me laugh.*
laugh at someone or **something** to laugh to show that you think someone or something is funny or silly: *The children laughed at the clown.* • *They all laughed at me when I said I was afraid of spiders.*

laugh² /læf/ *noun* [count]
the sound you make when you are happy or when you think something is funny: *My brother has a loud laugh.* • *She told us a joke and we all had a good laugh* (= laughed a lot).
for a laugh as a joke; for fun: *The boys put a spider in her bed for a laugh.*

laugh·ter /ˈlæftər/ *noun* [noncount]
the sound of laughing: *I could hear laughter in the next room.*

launch /lɔntʃ/ *verb* (launch·es, launch·ing, launched)
1 to start something new: *The magazine was launched last year.*

2 to put a ship into the water or a SPACECRAFT (= a vehicle that travels in space) into the sky: *This ship was launched in 2005.*

Laun·dro·mat™ (also **laun·dro·mat**) /'lɔndrəmæt/ *noun* [*count*]
a place where you pay to wash and dry your clothes in machines

laun·dry 🔑 /'lɔndri/ *noun* [*noncount*]
clothes and sheets that you must wash or that you have washed: *a pile of dirty laundry*

la·va /'lɑvə/ *noun* [*noncount*]
(**GEOGRAPHY**) hot, liquid rock that comes out of a mountain with an opening at the top (called a VOLCANO) ➔ Look at the picture at **volcano**.

lav·a·to·ry /'lævətɔri/ *noun* [*count*] (*plural* lav·a·to·ries) (*formal*)
a room with a toilet in a public place like an airplane: *Where's the lavatory, please?*

lav·en·der /'lævəndər/ *noun* [*noncount*]
a plant with purple flowers that have a nice smell

law 🔑 /lɔ/ *noun* (**POLITICS**)
1 [*count*] a rule of a country that says what people may or may not do: *There is a law against carrying guns.*
2 the law [*noncount*] all the rules of a country: *Stealing is against the law* (= illegal). • *You're breaking the law* (= doing something illegal).
3 [*noncount*] the rules of a country as a subject of study: *She is studying law.*

lawn /lɔn/ *noun* [*count, noncount*]
an area of short grass next to or around a building: *They were sitting on the lawn.*

lawn·mow·er   **lawnmower**
/'lɔn,moʊər/
noun [*count*]
a machine that you
use to cut grass

law·suit /'lɔsut/ (also
suit) *noun* [*count*]
a legal argument that
a person or group
brings to a court of
law so that it can be
decided who is right and who is wrong

law·yer 🔑 /'lɔyər/ *noun* [*count*]
a person who has studied law and who helps people or talks for them in a court of law

lay¹ 🔑 /leɪ/ *verb* (lays, lay·ing, laid /leɪd/, has laid)
1 to put someone or something carefully on another thing: *I laid the papers on the desk.*

Which word?

Lay or lie?
■ **Lay** has an object: *He is laying a carpet in our new house.* The past tense is **laid**: *She laid the baby down gently on the bed.*
■ **Lie** does not have an object: *He is lying on the beach.* The past tense is **lay**: *She was tired so she lay on the bed.*

2 to make an egg: *Birds and insects lay eggs.*
lay someone off to stop giving work to someone, especially because there is not enough work to do: *The company had to lay off 500 auto workers.*

lay² form of **lie¹**

lay·er 🔑 **AWL** /'leɪər/ *noun* [*count*]
something flat that lies on another thing or that is between other things: *The table was covered with a thin layer of dust.* • *The cake has a layer of jam in the middle.* • *You'll need several layers of clothing.* ➔ Look at **the ozone layer**.

la·zy 🔑 /'leɪzi/ *adjective* (la·zi·er, la·zi·est)
1 A person who is **lazy** does not want to work: *Don't be so lazy – come and help me!* • *My teacher said I was lazy.*
2 making you feel that you do not want to do very much: *a lazy summer's day*
▶ **la·zi·ness** /'leɪzinəs/ *noun* [*noncount*]

lb. abbreviation of **pound**(1)

lead¹ 🔑 /lid/ *verb* (leads, lead·ing, led /lɛd/, has led)

ⓘ **PRONUNCIATION**
The word **lead** usually sounds like **need**. However, when it means a soft gray metal or the part inside a pencil, it sounds like **red**.

1 to take a person or an animal somewhere by going with them or in front of them: *He led me to the classroom.*
2 to go to a place: *This path leads to the river.*
3 to make something happen: *Smoking can lead to heart disease.*
4 to have a particular type of life: *They lead a very busy life.*
5 to be the first or the best, for example in a race or game: *Who's leading in the race?*
6 to control a group of people: *Who will lead the discussion?*

lead² /lid/ *noun*
1 the lead [*singular*] the first place or position in front of other people: *An American runner has taken the lead.* • *Who is in the lead* (= winning)?
2 [*singular*] the amount by which someone is in front of another person: *He has a lead of about ten minutes and is expected to win the race.*

---

3 [count] a piece of information that may help give the answer to a problem: *The police have a new lead on the murder case.*

lead³ /lɛd/ *noun*
1 [noncount] (symbol **Pb**) (**CHEMISTRY**) a soft, gray metal that is very heavy. **Lead** is used to make things like water pipes and roofs.
2 [count, noncount] the gray part inside a pencil

lead·er 🔑 /ˈlidər/ *noun* [count]
1 a person who controls a group of people: *They chose a new leader.*
2 a person or thing that is the first or the best: *The leader is ten yards in front of the other runners.*

lead·er·ship /ˈlidərʃɪp/ *noun* [noncount]
the state or position of being the person who controls a group of people: *The country is **under new leadership*** (= has new leaders).

lead·ing /ˈlidɪŋ/ *adjective*
best or most important: *He's one of the leading experts in this field.*

leaf 🔑 /lif/ *noun* [count] (*plural* **leaves** /livz/)
(**BIOLOGY**) one of the flat green parts that grow on a plant or tree: *Leaves are starting to fall from the trees.* ⊃ Look at the picture at **plant.**

leaf·let /ˈliflət/ *noun* [count]
a piece of paper with writing on it that gives information about something: *I picked up a leaflet on local museums and art galleries.*

league /lig/ *noun* [count]
1 (**SPORTS**) a group of teams that play against each other in a sport: *the National Football League*
2 a group of people or countries that work together to do something: *the League of Nations*

leak¹ /lik/ *verb* (**leaks, leak·ing, leaked**)
1 to have a hole that liquid or gas can go through: *The roof of our house leaks when it rains.* • *The boat is leaking.*
2 (used about liquid or gas) to go out through a hole: *Water is leaking from the pipe.*

leak² /lik/ *noun* [count]
a small hole that liquid or gas can get through: *There's a leak in the pipe.*
▶ **leak·y** /ˈliki/ *adjective* (**leak·i·er, leak·i·est**): *a leaky roof*

lean¹ 🔑 /lin/ *verb* (**leans, lean·ing, leaned**)
1 to not be straight; to bend forward, backward, or to the side: *She leaned out of the window and waved.*
2 to put your body or a thing against another thing: *Lean your bike against the wall.*

lean² /lin/ *adjective* (**lean·er, lean·est**)
1 thin and healthy: *He is tall and lean.* ⊃ Look at the note at **thin.**
2 **Lean** meat does not have very much fat.

leap /lip/ *verb* (**leaps, leap·ing, leaped** or **leapt** /lɛpt/, **has leaped** or **has leapt**)
to jump high or a long way: *The cat leaped onto the table.*
▶ **leap** *noun* [count]: *With one leap, he was over the top of the wall.*

leap year /ˈlip yɪr/ *noun* [count]
a year when February has 29 days. **Leap years** happen every four years.

learn 🔑 /lɜrn/ *verb* (**learns, learn·ing, learned**)

> ⓘ **PRONUNCIATION**
> The word **learn** sounds like **turn.**

1 to find out something, or how to do something, by studying or by doing it often: *When did you **learn** to swim?* • *I learned German at school.* • *Learn this list of words for homework* (= so you can remember them).
2 to hear about something: *I was sorry to **learn** of your father's death.*
▶ **learn·ing** /ˈlɜrnɪŋ/ *noun* [noncount]
the process of learning something: *new methods of language learning*

learn·er /ˈlɜrnər/ *noun* [count]
a person who is learning: *This dictionary is for learners of English.*

lease /lis/ *noun* [count]
an official written agreement between the owner of a building or land and the person who rents it: *I just signed the lease for my new apartment.*
▶ **lease** *verb* (**leas·es, leas·ing, leased**): *They lease the land from a local farmer.*

leash /liʃ/ *noun* [count] (*plural* **leash·es**)
a long piece of leather or a chain that you attach to a dog's neck so that it walks with you: *All dogs must be kept **on a leash.***

least 🔑 /list/ *adjective, pronoun, adverb*
1 the smallest amount of something: *Sue has a lot of money, Jan has less, and Kate has the least.* ⊃ **ANTONYM most**
2 less than all others: *I bought the least expensive tickets.* ⊃ **ANTONYM most**
at least
1 not less than: *It will cost at least $50.*
2 although other things are bad: *We're not rich, but at least we're happy.*
not in the least not at all: *"Are you angry?" "Not in the least!"*

leath·er 🔑 /ˈlɛðər/ *noun* [noncount]
the skin of an animal that is used to make things like shoes, jackets, or bags: *a leather jacket*

leave¹ 🔑 /liv/ *verb* (**leaves, leav·ing, left** /lɛft/, **has left**)
1 to go away from a place or a person: *The train leaves at 8:40.* • *He **left home** when he was 22.* • *We're **leaving for** Connecticut tomorrow.*

2 to let someone or something stay in the same place or in the same way: *Leave the door open, please.*
3 to forget to bring something with you: *I left my books at home.* • *I can't find my glasses. Maybe I left them behind at work.*
4 to make something stay; to not use something: *Leave some cake for me!*
5 to give something to someone when you die: *She left all her money to her two sons.*
6 to give the responsibility for something to another person: *I'll leave it to you to organize the food.*
be left to still be there after everything else has gone: *There is only one piece of cake left.*
leave someone or **something alone** to not touch, bother, or speak to someone or something: *Leave me alone – I'm busy!* • *Leave that bag alone – it's mine!*
leave someone or **something out** to not put in or do something; to not include someone or something: *The other children left him out of the game.* • *I left out question 3 in the exam because it was too difficult.*

leave² /liv/ *noun* [noncount]
a period of time when you are away from work for a special reason: *She's not working – she's on sick leave.* • *I'm taking a six-week leave of absence from work.*

leaves plural of **leaf**

lec·ture **AWL** /ˈlɛktʃər/ *noun* [count]
1 a talk to a group of people to teach them about something: *She gave an interesting lecture on the history of science.*
2 a serious talk to someone that explains what they have done wrong or how they should behave: *My parents gave me a lecture about staying out too late.*
▶ **lec·ture** **AWL** *verb* (lectures, lecturing, lectured): *Professor Sims lectures on modern art.* • *The police officer lectured the boys about running across the street.*

lec·tur·er **AWL** /ˈlɛktʃərər/ *noun* [count]
a person who gives talks to teach people about a subject, especially as a job in a college: *My history professor is a great lecturer.*

led form of **lead¹**

ledge /lɛdʒ/ *noun* [count]
a long, narrow, flat place, for example under a window or on the side of a mountain: *a window ledge*

leek /lik/ *noun* [count]
a vegetable like a long onion that is white at one end and green at the other: *leek and potato soup*

left¹ form of **leave¹**

left² /lɛft/ *adjective, adverb*
on the side where your heart is in the body: *I broke my left arm.* • ***Turn left*** *at the church.* ⊃ **ANTONYM right**

left³ /lɛft/ *noun* [singular]
1 the left side or direction: ***To the left*** *is the town library.* • *The house is **on your left**.* ⊃ **ANTONYM right**
2 the left (**POLITICS**) political groups who support changes in society to make people more equal: *The left proposes higher taxes for the rich.* ⊃ **ANTONYM the right**

left-hand /ˈlɛft hænd/ *adjective*
of or on the left: *Your heart is on **the left-hand side** of your body.* ⊃ **ANTONYM right-hand**

left-hand·ed /ˌlɛft ˈhændəd/ *adjective, adverb*
using your left hand more easily than your right hand, for example when you write: *Are you left-handed?* • *I can't write left-handed.* ⊃ **ANTONYM right-handed**

left·o·vers /ˈlɛftˌoʊvərz/ *noun* [plural]
food that has not been eaten at the end of a meal and is kept to be eaten later

left-wing /ˌlɛft ˈwɪŋ/ *adjective*
(**POLITICS**) having political ideas that support changes in society to make people more equal: *left-wing politicians* ⊃ **ANTONYM right-wing**

leg

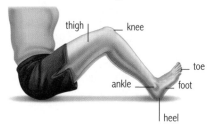

leg /lɛg/ *noun* [count]
1 one of the long parts of the body of a person or an animal that is used for walking and standing: *A spider has eight legs.* • *She sat down and crossed her legs.*
2 one of the parts of a pair of pants that covers your leg: *a pants leg*
3 one of the long parts that a table or chair stands on: *a table leg*

leg·a·cy /ˈlɛgəsi/ *noun* [count] (plural leg·a·cies)
a situation that exists because of something that happened in the past: *Future generations will be left with a legacy of pollution.*

le·gal **AWL** /ˈligl/ *adjective*
1 using or connected with the law: *legal advice*
2 allowed by the law: *In many parts of the U.S. it is legal to carry a gun.* ⊃ **ANTONYM illegal, against the law**
▶ **le·gal·ly** **AWL** /ˈligəli/ *adverb*: *They are not legally married.*

le·gal·ize /ˈligəlaɪz/ *verb* (**le·gal·iz·es, le·gal·iz·ing, le·gal·ized**)
to make something allowed by law

leg·end /ˈlɛdʒənd/ *noun* [*count*]
1 an old story that is perhaps not true: *the legend of Robin Hood*
2 a very famous person: *He was a legend in the world of music.*
▶ **leg·en·dar·y** /ˈlɛdʒəndɛri/ *adjective*: *the legendary tennis players Venus and Serena Williams*

leg·i·ble /ˈlɛdʒəbl/ *adjective*
clear enough to read: *legible writing* ⊃ **ANTONYM illegible**

leg·is·late **AWL** /ˈlɛdʒəsleɪt/ *verb* (**leg·is·lates, leg·is·lat·ing, leg·is·lat·ed**)
(**POLITICS**) to make a law about something: *to legislate against discrimination*

leg·is·la·tion **AWL** /ˌlɛdʒəsˈleɪʃn/ *noun* [*noncount*]
(**POLITICS**) a group of laws, or the process of making laws: *The government is planning to bring in new legislation to help small businesses.*

leg·is·la·tive **AWL** /ˈlɛdʒəsleɪṭɪv/ *adjective* (*formal*)
(**POLITICS**) connected with the act of making laws: *the legislative powers of Congress* ◆ *the legislative branch of the government* ⊃ Look at the note at **government**.

leg·is·la·ture **AWL** /ˈlɛdʒəsleɪtʃər/ *noun* [*count*]
(**POLITICS**) a group of people who have the power to make and change laws: *the Kansas state legislature*

le·git·i·mate /lɪˈdʒɪṭəmət/ *adjective*
1 reasonable or acceptable: *This program is not a legitimate use of taxpayers' money.*
2 allowed by law: *Are all of his business activities completely legitimate?*

lei·sure /ˈliʒər/ *noun* [*noncount*]
the time when you are not working and can do what you want: *leisure activities*

lei·sure·ly /ˈliʒərli/ *adjective*
done in a slow and calm way: *to walk at a leisurely pace*

lem·on 🔊 /ˈlɛmən/ *noun* [*count, noncount*]
a yellow fruit with **sour** (= sharp tasting) juice that is used for giving flavor to food and drink: *lemon juice* ⊃ Look at the picture at **fruit**.

lem·on·ade /ˌlɛməˈneɪd/ *noun* [*count, noncount*]
a drink that is made from fresh lemon juice, sugar, and water

lend 🔊 /lɛnd/ *verb* (**lends, lend·ing, lent** /lɛnt/, **has lent**)
to give something to someone for a short time: *I lent the book to Jo.* ◆ *Rick lent me his car for an hour.* ◆ *The bank will lend us up to $50,000.* ⊃ Look at the note at **borrow**.

length 🔊 /lɛŋθ/ *noun* [*count, noncount*]
how long something is: *The table is two yards in length.* ◆ *We measured the length of the garden.* ⊃ The adjective is **long**. ⊃ Look at the picture at **dimension**.

length·en /ˈlɛŋθən/ *verb* (**length·ens, length·en·ing, length·ened**)
to become or to make something longer: *I need to lengthen this skirt.*

length·wise /ˈlɛŋθwaɪz/ *adjective*
in a direction along the length of something: *Fold the paper lengthwise.*

length·y /ˈlɛŋθi/ *adjective* (**length·i·er, length·i·est**)
very long: *a lengthy meeting*

le·ni·ent /ˈliniənt/ *adjective*
If a punishment, or the person who gives the punishment, is **lenient**, it is not as strict as you expected: *The judge was too lenient. She should have gone to jail.*

lens /lɛnz/ *noun* [*count*] (*plural* **lens·es**)
(**PHYSICS**) a special piece of glass in things like cameras or glasses. It makes things look bigger, smaller, or clearer when you look through it. ⊃ Look at the picture at **glasses**, **microscope**.

lent form of **lend**

len·til /ˈlɛntl/ *noun* [*count*]
a small, round, dried seed. You cook **lentils** in water before you eat them: *lentil soup*

leop·ard /ˈlɛpərd/ *noun* [*count*]
a wild animal like a big cat with yellow fur and dark spots. **Leopards** live in Africa and southern Asia.

leopard

le·o·tard /ˈliətɑrd/ *noun* [*count*]
a piece of clothing that fits the body tightly from the neck to the tops of the legs. **Leotards** are worn by dancers or by women in some sports.

les·bi·an /ˈlɛzbiən/ *noun* [*count*]
a woman who is attracted to other women
▶ **les·bi·an** *adjective*: *a lesbian relationship*

less¹ 🔊 /lɛs/ *adjective, pronoun*
a smaller amount of something: *A poor person has less money than a rich person.* ◆ *The doctor advised him to drink less coffee.* ⊃ **ANTONYM more** ⊃ Look at **least**.

less² 🔊 /lɛs/ *adverb*
not so much: *It rains less in summer.* ◆ *I'm too fat – I must try to eat less.* ◆ *He's less intelligent than his sister.* ⊃ **ANTONYM more** ⊃ Look at **least**.

-less

(in adjectives) not having something; without:
hopeless ◆ painless ◆ thoughtless ◆ useless

less·en /ˈlɛsn/ *verb* (less·ens, less·en·ing, less·ened)
to become or to make something less: *This medicine will lessen the pain.*

les·son 🎵 /ˈlɛsn/ *noun* [count]
a time when you learn something with a teacher: *She gives piano lessons. ◆ I'm **taking** driving **lessons**.*

let 🎵 /lɛt/ *verb* (lets, let·ting, let, has let)
1 to allow someone or something to do something: *Her parents won't let her stay out after 11 o'clock. ◆ Let me carry your bag. ◆ Let the dog in (= let it come in).* ⊃ Look at the note at **allow**.
2 let's used for making suggestions about what you and other people can do: *Let's go to the movies tonight. ◆ Let's not go out this evening.*
let someone down to not do something that you promised to do for someone: *Claire let me down. We agreed to meet at eight o'clock but she didn't come.*
let go of someone or **something**; **let someone** or **something go** to stop holding someone or something: *Let go of my hand! ◆ Let me go. You're hurting me!*
let someone know to tell someone something: *If you need any help, let me know.*
let someone off to not punish someone: *He wasn't sent to prison – the judge let him off.*

le·thal /ˈliːθl/ *adjective*
Something that is **lethal** can cause a lot of damage or death: *a lethal weapon* ⊃ SYNONYM **deadly**

let·ter 🎵 /ˈlɛtər/ *noun* [count]
1 a piece of writing that one person sends to another person: *He got a letter from his cousin this morning. ◆ I'm writing a **thank-you letter** for the flowers she sent me.*
2 (ENGLISH LANGUAGE ARTS) a sign in writing that represents a sound in a language: *Z is the last letter in the English alphabet.*

let·tuce /ˈlɛtəs/ *noun* [count, noncount]
a plant with big green leaves that you eat cold in salads ⊃ Look at the picture at **vegetable**.

leu·ke·mi·a /luˈkimiə/ *noun* [noncount]
(HEALTH) a very serious disease of the blood

lev·ee /ˈlɛvi/ *noun* [count]
(GEOGRAPHY) a low wall built at the side of a river to prevent a flood

lev·el¹ 🎵 /ˈlɛvl/ *noun* [count]
1 the amount, size, or number of something: *a low **level of** unemployment*

2 how high something is: *The town is 1500 feet above **sea level**. ◆ a beginning-level Spanish class*

lev·el² /ˈlɛvl/ *adjective*
1 with no part higher than another part: *We need level ground to play soccer on. ◆ This shelf isn't level.* ⊃ SYNONYM **flat**
2 at the same height, standard, or position: *The two teams are level with 40 points each. ◆ His head is **level with** his mother's shoulder.*

lev·er /ˈlɛvər; ˈliːvər/ *noun* [count]
1 a handle that you pull or push to make a machine work: *Pull this lever.*
2 a bar for lifting something heavy or opening something. You put one end under the thing you want to lift or open, and push the other end.

li·a·ble /ˈlaɪəbl/ *adjective*
responsible for paying the cost of something: *Is the company liable for the damage?*
be liable to do something to be likely to do something: *We're all liable to have accidents when we're very tired.*

li·ar /ˈlaɪər/ *noun* [count]
a person who says or writes things that are not true (called LIES): *I don't believe her – she's a liar.* ⊃ The verb is **lie**.

li·bel /ˈlaɪbl/ *noun* [count, noncount]
the act of printing something about someone that is not true and would give people a bad opinion of him or her: *The actor is suing the newspaper for libel.*

lib·er·al AWL /ˈlɪbərəl/ *adjective*
1 A person who is **liberal** lets other people do and think what they want: *Kim's parents are very liberal, but mine are strict.*
2 (POLITICS) supporting political and social changes to make people more equal: *liberal democrats* ⊃ ANTONYM **conservative**

lib·er·al arts /ˌlɪbərəl ˈɑrts/ *noun* [plural]
subjects that develop your general knowledge and ability to think, for example history, languages, and literature

lib·er·ate AWL /ˈlɪbəreɪt/ *verb* (lib·er·ates, lib·er·at·ing, lib·er·at·ed)
to make someone or something free: *The city was liberated by the advancing army.*

lib·er·ty /ˈlɪbərti/ *noun* [count, noncount] (plural lib·er·ties)
being free to go where you want and do what you want: *the fight for justice and liberty ◆ civil liberties* ⊃ Look at **freedom**.

li·brar·i·an /laɪˈbrɛriən/ *noun* [count]
a person who works in a library

li·brar·y 🎵 /ˈlaɪbrɛri/ *noun* [count] (plural li·brar·ies)
a room or building where you go to borrow or read books

---

lice form of **louse**

li·cense¹ [AWL] /ˈlaɪsns/ *noun* [count]
an official piece of paper that shows you are allowed to do or have something: *Do you have a license for this gun?* ⊃ Look at **driver's license**.

li·cense² [AWL] /ˈlaɪsns/ *verb* (li·cens·es, li·cens·ing, li·censed)
to give someone official permission to do or have something: *This shop is licensed to sell guns.*

li·cense plate
/ˈlaɪsns pleɪt/ *noun* [count]
the flat piece of metal on the front or back of a car that has numbers and letters on it

license plate

lick /lɪk/ *verb* (licks, lick·ing, licked)
to move your tongue over something: *The cat was licking its paws.*
▶ **lick** *noun* [count]: *Can I have a lick of your ice cream?*

lic·o·rice /ˈlɪkərɪʃ/ *noun* [noncount]
a type of black candy with a strong flavor

lid 🔑 /lɪd/ *noun* [count]
the top part of a box, pot, or other container, which covers it and which you can take off ⊃ Look at the picture at **tub**.

lie¹ 🔑 /laɪ/ *verb* (lies, ly·ing, lay /leɪ/, has lain /leɪn/)
1 to put your body flat on something so that you are not sitting or standing: *He lay on the bed.* ⊃ Look at the note at **lay**.
2 to have your body flat on something: *The baby was lying on its back.*
3 to be or stay in a position or state: *The hills lie to the north of the town.*
lie down to put or have your body flat so that you can rest: *She lay down on the bed.*

lie² 🔑 /laɪ/ *verb* (lies, ly·ing, lied, has lied)
to say something that you know is not true: *He lied about his age. He said he was 16, but really he's 14.* • *Don't ever lie to me again!* ⊃ A person who lies is a **liar**.

lie³ 🔑 /laɪ/ *noun* [count]
something you say that you know is not true: *She told me a lie.*

lieu·ten·ant /luˈtɛnənt/ (abbreviation **Lt.**) *noun* [count]
an officer at a middle level in the army or navy

life 🔑 /laɪf/ *noun* (plural **lives** /laɪvz/)
1 [noncount] People, animals, and plants have **life** while they are alive, but things like stone, metal, and water do not: *Do you believe there is life after death?* • *Is there life on other planets?*

2 [count, noncount] being alive: *Many people lost their lives* (= died) *in the fire.* • *The doctor saved her life* (= stopped her from dying).
3 [count, noncount] the time that someone is alive: *He has lived here all his life.*
4 [count, noncount] the way that you live or the experiences that you have when you are alive: *They were very happy throughout their married life.* • *They lead a busy life.*
5 [noncount] energy; being busy and interested: *Young children are full of life.*

life·boat /ˈlaɪfboʊt/ *noun* [count]
a boat that goes to help people who are in danger in the ocean

life cycle /ˈlaɪf ˌsaɪkl/ *noun* [count]
(**BIOLOGY**) the stages of development that a plant or an animal goes through from the beginning of its life to the end: *the life cycle of a frog*

life·guard /ˈlaɪfgɑrd/ *noun* [count]
a person at a beach or a swimming pool whose job is to help people who are in danger in the water

life jack·et /ˈlaɪf ˌdʒækət/ (also **life vest** /ˈlaɪf vɛst/) *noun* [count]
a special jacket with no sleeves that can be filled with air. You wear it to help you float if you fall in the water.

life jacket

life·like /ˈlaɪflaɪk/ *adjective*
looking like the real person or thing: *That statue looks very lifelike.*

life·style /ˈlaɪfstaɪl/ *noun* [count, noncount]
the way that you live: *They have a healthy lifestyle.*

life·time /ˈlaɪftaɪm/ *noun* [count]
all the time that you are alive: *There have been a lot of changes in my grandma's lifetime.*

lift¹ 🔑 /lɪft/ *verb* (lifts, lift·ing, lift·ed)
1 to move someone or something to a higher position: *I can't lift this box. It's too heavy.* • *Lift your arm up.*
2 to end or remove a rule or law: *The ban on public meetings has been lifted.*
3 to go up and disappear into the air: *The clouds lifted toward the end of the day.*

lift² /lɪft/ *noun*
1 [singular] a feeling of happiness or excitement: *Her kind words gave us all a lift.*
2 [count] a free trip in another person's car: *Can you give me a lift downtown?* ⊃ **SYNONYM ride**

lift·off /ˈlɪftɔf/ *noun* [*count*]
the moment when a SPACECRAFT (= a vehicle that can travel into space) leaves the ground

light¹ 🔑 /laɪt/ *noun*
1 [*count, noncount*] the energy from the sun, a lamp, etc. that allows us to see things: *The light was not very good so it was difficult to read.* • *Strong sunlight is bad for the eyes.*
2 [*count*] a thing that gives light, for example an electric lamp

Word building

■ A light can be **on** or **off**.
■ You can **switch** or **turn** a light **on** or **off**: *Turn the lights off before you go to bed.* • *It's getting dark. Should I switch the light on?*

3 [*count*] something, for example a match, that you use to start a fire or start a cigarette burning: *Do you have a light?*

light² 🔑 /laɪt/ *adjective* (**light·er**, **light·est**)
1 full of natural light: *In summer it's light until about nine o'clock.* • *The room has a lot of windows so it's very light.* ⊃ ANTONYM **dark**
2 with a pale color: *a light blue shirt* ⊃ ANTONYM **dark**
3 easy to lift or move: *Will you carry this bag for me? It's very light.* ⊃ ANTONYM **heavy**
4 not very much or not very strong: *light rain* • *I had a light breakfast.*
▶ **light·ly** /ˈlaɪtli/ *adverb*: *She touched me lightly on the arm.*

light³ 🔑 /laɪt/ *verb* (**lights**, **light·ing**, **lit** /lɪt/ or **light·ed**, has **lit** or has **light·ed**)
1 to make something start to burn: *Will you light the fire?* • *She lit a candle.*
2 to give light to something: *The room is lit by two big lamps.*

light bulb /ˈlaɪt bʌlb/ *noun* [*count*]
the glass part of an electric lamp that gives light

light·en /ˈlaɪtn/ *verb* (**light·ens**, **light·en·ing**, **light·ened**)
to become lighter, or to make something lighter in color or weight
lighten up (*informal*) to become happier or less worried about something

light·er /ˈlaɪt̬ər/ *noun* [*count*]
a thing for lighting cigarettes

light·house /ˈlaɪthaʊs/ *noun* [*count*]
a tall building by or in the ocean, with a strong light to show ships that there are rocks ⊃ Look at the picture at **cliff**.

light·ing /ˈlaɪtɪŋ/ *noun* [*noncount*]
the kind of lights that a place has: *electric lighting*

light·ning /ˈlaɪtnɪŋ/
noun [*noncount*]
a sudden bright light in the sky when there is a storm: *He was struck* (= hit) *by lightning.* ⊃ Look at **thunder**.

lightning

light year /ˈlaɪt yɪr/ *noun* [*count*]
(**PHYSICS**) the distance that light travels in one year: *How many light years away from earth is the star?*

lik·a·ble (also **like·a·ble**) /ˈlaɪkəbl/ *adjective*
If a person is **likable**, they are friendly and easy to like.

like¹ 🔑 /laɪk/ *verb* (**likes**, **lik·ing**, **liked**)
1 to feel that someone or something is good, nice, or attractive; to enjoy something: *Do you like your new teacher?* • *I don't like carrots.* • *I like playing tennis.* ⊃ ANTONYM **dislike**
2 to want: *Do what you like, I don't care.* • *We can go whenever you like.*
if you like used to agree with someone or to suggest something: *"Should we go out tonight?" "Yes, if you like."*
would like a polite way of saying "want": *Would you like some coffee?* • *I'd like to speak to the manager.*

Thesaurus

like to feel that someone or something is good, nice, or attractive; to enjoy something: *He's nice. I like him a lot.* • *Which shirt do you like the best?* • *I don't like to see her cry.* • *He didn't like it when I shouted at him.*

love to like or enjoy someone or something very much: *I love this place.* • *My dad loves going to baseball games.* • *I love it when you bring me presents!*

be fond of to like or enjoy someone or something, especially if this has continued for a long time: *We were fond of the house and didn't want to leave.* • *We're all very fond of Mrs. Simpson.* • *I grew very fond of Turkish food while I was living in Istanbul.*

adore to love someone or something very much: *He simply adores his older brother.* • *She adores working with children.*

like² 🔑 /laɪk/ *preposition, conjunction*
1 the same as someone or something: *She is wearing a dress like mine.* • *John looks like his father.* ⊃ Look at **unlike**.
2 showing what is typical or usual for someone: *It's just like him to be late!*
3 in the same way as someone or something: *She acted like a child.*

4 for example: *I bought a lot of things, like books and clothes.*

what is … like? words that you say when you want to know more about someone or something: *"What's that book like?" "It's very interesting."*

like·a·ble /ˈlaikəbl/ = **likable**

like·li·hood /ˈlaiklihʊd/ *noun* [*noncount*]
the chance of something happening: *There is very little **likelihood of** you passing this exam* (= it is very unlikely that you will pass).

like·ly 🎵 /ˈlaikli/ *adjective* (**like·li·er**, **like·li·est**)
If something is **likely**, it will probably happen: *It's **likely that** she will agree.* • *They are **likely to** be late.* ⊃ **ANTONYM unlikely**

like·ness /ˈlaiknəs/ *noun* [*noncount, singular*]
being or looking the same: *There's a **strong likeness** between Dan and his brother.*

like·wise **AWL** /ˈlaikwaiz/ *adverb* (*formal*)
the same: *I sat down, and Molly did likewise.*

lik·ing /ˈlaikiŋ/ *noun* [*singular*]
the feeling that you like someone or something: *She has a **liking for** spicy food.*

lil·y /ˈlili/ *noun* [*count*] (*plural* **lil·ies**)
a plant with large flowers in the shape of a bell

limb /lim/ *noun* [*count*]
an arm or a leg

lime /laim/ *noun* [*count*]
a small green fruit like a lemon ⊃ Look at the picture at **fruit**.

lim·it¹ 🎵 /ˈlimət/ *noun* [*count*]
1 the most that is possible or allowed: *There is a **limit to** the amount of pain we can bear.* • *What is the **speed limit** (= how fast are you allowed to go)?*
2 the end or edge of something: *They live within the city limits.*
off-limits If a place is **off-limits**, it must not be entered: *The faculty room is off-limits to students.*

lim·it² 🎵 /ˈlimət/ *verb* (**lim·its**, **lim·it·ing**, **lim·it·ed**)
to do or have no more than a certain amount or number: *There are only 100 seats, so we must limit the number of tickets we sell.*
▶ **lim·it·ed** /ˈlimətəd/ *adjective*
small in number or amount: *We can't invite many people because space is limited.*

lim·ou·sine /ˈliməzin; ˌliməˈzin/ (*also informal* **lim·o** /ˈlimoʊ/) *noun* [*count*]
a long, expensive, and comfortable car

limousine

limp¹ /limp/ *adjective*
not firm or strong: *Her whole body went limp and she fell to the ground.*

limp² /limp/ *verb* (**limps**, **limp·ing**, **limped**)
to walk with difficulty because you have hurt your foot or leg
▶ **limp** *noun* [*singular*]: *He walks with a limp.*

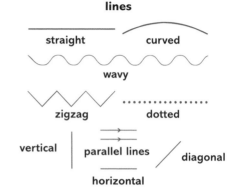

lines

straight   curved

wavy

zigzag   dotted

vertical   parallel lines   diagonal

horizontal

line¹ 🎵 /lain/ *noun* [*count*]
1 a long thin mark on the surface of something: *Draw a straight line.* • *The ball went over the line.*
2 people or things beside each other or one after the other: *There was a long **line of** people waiting at the post office.*
3 all the words that are beside each other on a page: *How many lines are there on this page?* • *I don't know the next line of the poem.*
4 a long piece of string or rope: *Hang the clothes on the line to dry.*
5 a very long wire for telephones or electricity: *The strong winds blew down many power lines.* • *I tried to call him, but the line was busy.*
6 a route that people or goods move along: *the Philadephia to Baltimore line* (= the railroad route) • *Before you travel on the subway, check which line you need.*

line² /lain/ *verb* (**lines**, **lin·ing**, **lined**)
1 to cover the inside of something with a different material: *The boots are **lined with** fur.*
2 to stand or be in lines along something: *People lined the streets to watch the race.*
line up to stand in a line or make a line: *We lined up to buy tickets.*

lin·en /ˈlinn/ *noun* [*noncount*]
1 a kind of strong cloth: *a white linen jacket*
2 the sheets, etc. that you put on a bed, or the cloth that you put on a table: *bed linen*

lin·er /ˈlainər/ *noun* [*count*]
1 a big ship that carries people a long way: *an ocean liner*
2 a bag that you put inside something to keep it clean: *a garbage can liner*

lin·ger /ˈliŋgər/ *verb* (**lin·gers**, **lin·ger·ing**, **lin·gered**)
to stay somewhere for a long time: *The smell of her perfume lingered in the room.*

lin·ge·rie /ˌlɑnʒəˈrei/ *noun* [noncount]
women's underwear

lin·guis·tics /lɪŋˈgwɪstɪks/ *noun* [noncount]
(**ENGLISH LANGUAGE ARTS**) the scientific study of language

lin·ing /ˈlaɪnɪŋ/ *noun* [count, noncount]
material that covers the inside of something: *My coat has a thick lining, so it's very warm.* ⊃ Look at the picture at **sleeping bag**.

link¹ **AWL** /lɪŋk/ *noun* [count]
1 something that joins things or people together: *There's **a link between** smoking **and** heart disease.*
2 (**COMPUTERS**) a place where one electronic document on the Internet is connected to another one: *To visit our other website, click on this link.*
3 one of the round parts in a chain

link² **AWL** /lɪŋk/ *verb* (links, link·ing, linked)
to join one person or thing to another: *The computers are linked together in a network.*

lion

mane — tail

paw —

li·on /ˈlaɪən/ *noun* [count]
a large animal of the cat family that lives in parts of Africa and Asia. **Lions** have yellow fur, and the males have a lot of hair around their head and neck (called a MANE).

Word building

- A female lion is called a **lioness**, and a young lion is called a **cub**.
- When a lion makes a loud noise, it **roars**.

lip /lɪp/ *noun* [count]
one of the two soft red parts above and below your mouth: *to kiss someone on the lips* ⊃ Look at the picture at **mouth**.

lip·stick /ˈlɪpstɪk/
noun [count, noncount]
a substance that is used for giving color to your lips: *She put on some lipstick.*

lipstick

liq·uid /ˈlɪkwəd/
noun [count, noncount]
(**PHYSICS**) anything that is not a solid or a gas. Water, oil, and milk are **liquids**.
▶ **liq·uid** *adjective*: *liquid soap*

liq·uor /ˈlɪkər/ *noun* [count, noncount]
strong alcoholic drinks: *a liquor store* (= where you can buy drinks like beer and wine)

list¹ /lɪst/ *noun* [count]
a lot of names or other things that you write or say, one after another: *a shopping list* (= of things that you need to buy)

list² /lɪst/ *verb* (lists, list·ing, list·ed)
to write or say things in a list: *Please list the items in alphabetical order.*

lis·ten /ˈlɪsn/ *verb* (lis·tens, lis·ten·ing, lis·tened)
to hear something when you are trying to hear it: *I was **listening to** the radio.* • *Listen! I want to tell you something.* ⊃ Look at the note at **hear**.
listen up (*informal*) words that you use when you want a group of people to give you their attention: *Okay, listen up everyone! I have an important announcement to make.*
▶ **lis·ten·er** /ˈlɪsnər/ *noun* [count]
a person who listens: *He's a good listener.*

lit form of **light³**

li·ter /ˈlitər/ *noun* [count] (abbreviation **l**)
a measure of liquid: *three liters of water*

lit·er·al /ˈlɪtərəl/ *adjective*
(used about the meaning of a word or phrase) original or basic: *The literal meaning of "petrified" is "turned to stone."* ⊃ Look at **figurative**.
▶ **lit·er·al·ly** /ˈlɪtərəli/ *adverb*: *You can't translate these expressions literally.*

lit·er·ar·y /ˈlɪtərɛri/ *adjective*
(**ENGLISH LANGUAGE ARTS**) connected with literature: *a literary journal*

lit·er·ate /ˈlɪtərət/ *adjective*
(**ENGLISH LANGUAGE ARTS**) able to read and write ⊃ **ANTONYM** **illiterate**
▶ **lit·er·a·cy** /ˈlɪtərəsi/ *noun* [noncount]: *literacy programs* ⊃ **ANTONYM** **illiteracy**

lit·er·a·ture /ˈlɪtərətʃər/ *noun* [noncount]
(**ENGLISH LANGUAGE ARTS**) books, plays, and poetry: *He is studying 19th-century English literature.*

lith·i·um /ˈlɪθiəm/ *noun* [noncount] (symbol **Li**)
(**CHEMISTRY**) a soft, very light, sliver-white metal that is used in BATTERIES (= things that give electricity)

lit·ter¹ /ˈlɪtər/ *noun*
1 [noncount] pieces of paper and other garbage that people leave in a public place: *The park was full of litter after the concert.*
2 [count] all the baby animals that are born to the same mother at the same time: *Our dog had a litter of six puppies.*

lit·ter² /ˈlɪtər/ verb (litters, lit·ter·ing, lit·tered)
to be or to make something messy with LITTER¹ (1): *My desk was* **littered** *with papers.*

lit·tle¹ ✏ /ˈlɪtl/ adjective
1 not big: *a little table* ➔ SYNONYM **small**
2 (used about distance or time) short: *Do you mind waiting* **a little while***?*
3 young: *a little girl* • *my* **little** (= younger) *brother*

lit·tle² ✏ /ˈlɪtl/ pronoun, adjective
not much: *I did very little today.* • *We have very little money.*
a little a small amount of something: *I have some ice cream. Would you like a little?* • *I speak a little French.*
little by little slowly: *Little by little she started to feel better.*

lit·tle³ /ˈlɪtl/ adverb
not much: *I'm tired – I slept very little last night.*
a little by a small amount; to a small degree: *This skirt is a little too short for me.* ➔ SYNONYM **a little bit**

live¹ ✏ /lɪv/ verb (lives, liv·ing, lived)
1 to have your home somewhere: *Where do you live?* • *He still lives with his parents.*
2 to be or stay alive: *You can't live without water.* • *He lived to the age of 93.*
3 to spend your life in a particular way: *They live a quiet life in the country.*
live on something
1 to eat something as your only food: *Cows live on grass.*
2 to have enough money to buy what you need to live: *They live on $500 a week.*
live up to something to be as good as you expected: *The restaurant didn't live up to our expectations.*

live² /laɪv/ adjective

ℹ **PRONUNCIATION**
When the word **live** is a verb, it sounds like **give**.
When the word **live** is an adjective, it sounds like **five**.

1 not dead: *Have you ever touched a* **real live** *snake?*
2 If a radio or television program is **live**, you see or hear it at the same time as it happens: *The game will be live on TV.*
3 performed when people are watching, not recorded: *The club has live music every Saturday.*
4 (PHYSICS) with electricity passing through it: *Don't touch that wire – it's live!*

live·ly /ˈlaɪvli/ adjective (live·li·er, live·li·est)
full of life; always moving or doing things: *The children are very lively.*

liv·er /ˈlɪvər/ noun
1 (BIOLOGY) [count] the part inside your body that cleans the blood ➔ Look at the picture at **body**.
2 [noncount] the **liver** of an animal that you can cook and eat as food

lives plural of **life**

live·stock /ˈlaɪvstɑk/ noun [noncount]
animals that are kept on a farm, such as cows, pigs, sheep, etc.

liv·ing¹ /ˈlɪvɪŋ/ adjective
alive; not dead: *Some people say he is the greatest living writer.*

liv·ing² /ˈlɪvɪŋ/ noun
1 [count, usually singular] money to buy the things you need in life: *How did he* **earn a living***?*
2 [noncount] the way that you live: *The* **cost of living** *has risen in recent years.*

liv·ing room /ˈlɪvɪŋ rum/ noun [count]
a room in a house where people sit together and watch television or talk, for example

liz·ard /ˈlɪzəd/ noun [count]
a small animal that has four legs, a long tail, and rough skin

lizard

load¹ ✏ /loʊd/ noun
1 [count] something that is carried: *The truck brought another load of wood.*
2 **loads** [plural] (informal) a lot: *We have loads of time.*

load² ✏ /loʊd/ verb (loads, load·ing, load·ed)
1 to put things in or on something, for example a car or a ship: *Two men loaded the furniture into the van.* • *They're loading the plane now.* ➔ ANTONYM **unload**
2 (COMPUTERS) to put a program into a computer: *Did you load the software correctly?*
3 to put bullets in a gun or film in a camera

loaf /loʊf/ noun [count] (plural loaves /loʊvz/)
bread that has been baked in one piece: *a loaf of bread* ➔ Look at the picture at **bread**.

loan¹ ✏ /loʊn/ noun [count]
money that someone lends you: *to* **take out a bank loan**

loan² /loʊn/ verb (loans, loan·ing, loaned)
to give something to someone for a period of time: *A friend loaned me $1,000.* ➔ SYNONYM **lend**

loathe /loʊð/ verb (loathes, loath·ing, loathed)
to hate someone or something very much: *I loathe modern art.* ➔ ANTONYM **love** ➔ Look at the note at **hate¹**.

loaves plural of **loaf**

lob·by[1] /ˈlɑbi/ *noun* [count] (*plural* **lob·bies**)
1 an area just inside a big building, where people can meet and wait: *a hotel lobby*
2 (**POLITICS**) a group of people who try to persuade the government to do something: *the gun control lobby*

lob·by[2] /ˈlɑbi/ *verb* (**lob·bies**, **lob·by·ing**, **lob·bied**)
(**POLITICS**) to try to persuade the government to do or not do something: *They lobbied Congress for more money for medical research.*
▶ **lob·by·ist** /ˈlɑbiɪst/ *noun* [count]: *environmental lobbyists*

lob·ster /ˈlɑbstər/ *noun* [count]
a large animal with a hard shell and eight legs, which lives in the ocean. Its shell is black but it turns red when it is cooked. ⊋ Look at the picture at **crustacean**.

lo·cal 🔑 /ˈloʊkl/ *adjective*
of a place near you: *Her children go to the local school.* • *a local newspaper* • *local government*
▶ **lo·cal·ly** /ˈloʊkəli/ *adverb*: *Do you work locally?*

lo·cate **AWL** /ˈloʊkeɪt/ *verb* (**lo·cates**, **lo·cat·ing**, **lo·cat·ed**)
to find the exact position of someone or something: *Rescue helicopters are trying to locate the missing sailors.*
▶ **lo·cat·ed** **AWL** /ˈloʊkeɪtəd/ *adjective*
in a place: *The factory is located near the river.*

lo·ca·tion **AWL** /loʊˈkeɪʃn/ *noun* [count]
a place: *The house is in a quiet location at the top of a hill.*

lock[1] 🔑 /lɑk/ *verb* (**locks**, **lock·ing**, **locked**)
to close something with a key: *Don't forget to lock the door when you leave.* ⊋ **ANTONYM unlock**
lock something away to put something in a place that you close with a key: *The paintings are locked away at night.*
lock someone in to lock a door so that someone cannot get out: *The prisoners are locked in.*
lock someone out to lock a door so that someone cannot get in
lock up to lock all the doors and windows of a building: *Make sure you lock up before you leave.*

lock[2] 🔑 /lɑk/ *noun* [count]
a metal thing that keeps a door, gate, or box closed so that you need a key to open it again: *I heard the key turn in the lock.*

lock·er /ˈlɑkər/ *noun* [count]
a small cabinet with a lock for keeping things in, for example in a school or a sports center

lock·er room /ˈlɑkər rum/ *noun* [count]
(**SPORTS**) a room with **LOCKERS** in it where people can change their clothes: *My gym has a really nice locker room.*

lodge[1] /lɑdʒ/ *verb* (**lodg·es**, **lodg·ing**, **lodged**)
to become stuck somewhere, or to make something do this: *The bullet lodged in her shoulder.*

lodge[2] /lɑdʒ/ *noun*
a small house in the country where people stay when they want to do outdoor activities: *a ski lodge*

lodg·ing /ˈlɑdʒɪŋ/ *noun* [count, noncount]
a place where you can stay: *The price includes food and lodging.*

loft /lɔft/ *noun* [count]
the room or space directly under the roof of a house: *My old books are in a box in the loft.*

log[1] /lɔg; lɑg/ *noun* [count]
1 a thick, round piece of wood from a tree: *Put another log on the fire.* ⊋ Look at the picture at **tree**.
2 an official written record of something: *The museum keeps a log of visitors.*

log[2] /lɔg; lɑg/ *verb* (**logs**, **log·ging**, **logged**)
to keep an official record of things that happen: *to log someone's phone calls* ⊋ **SYNONYM record**
log in; **log on** to type your name, etc. so that you can start using a computer: *You need a password to log on.*
log off; **log out** to stop using a computer: *Make sure you log out before you switch off the computer.*

log·ging /ˈlɔgɪŋ; ˈlɑgɪŋ/ *noun* [noncount]
the work of cutting down trees for their wood: *the logging industry*

log·ic **AWL** /ˈlɑdʒɪk/ *noun* [noncount]
a sensible reason or way of thinking: *There is no logic to your argument.*

log·i·cal **AWL** /ˈlɑdʒɪkl/ *adjective*
seeming natural or sensible: *There is only one logical conclusion.* ⊋ **ANTONYM illogical**
▶ **log·i·cal·ly** **AWL** /ˈlɑdʒɪkli/ *adverb*: *to think about things logically*

lo·go /ˈloʊgoʊ/ *noun* [count] (*plural* **lo·gos**)
(**BUSINESS**) a picture or a design that a company or an organization uses as its special sign: *You will find the company logo on all our products.*

lol·li·pop /ˈlɑlipɑp/ *noun* [count]
a big piece of hard candy on a stick

lone·ly 🔑 /ˈloʊnli/ *adjective* (**lone·li·er**, **lone·li·est**)
1 unhappy because you are not with other people: *She felt very lonely when she first went to live in the city.* ⊋ Look at **alone**.
2 far from other places: *a lonely house in the hills*
▶ **lone·li·ness** /ˈloʊnlinəs/ *noun* [noncount]

lone·some /ˈloʊnsəm/ *adjective*
unhappy because you are alone: *She felt lonesome after her daughter moved away.*

long[1] 🔊 /lɔŋ/ *adjective* (long·er /ˈlɔŋɡər/, long·est /ˈlɔŋɡəst/)
1 far from one end to the other: *Which is the longest river in the world?* ◆ *She has long black hair.* ◆ *His house is a long way from mine.* ○ **ANTONYM short** ○ Look at the note at **far**[1].
2 You use **long** to ask or talk about how far something is from one end to the other: *How long is the table?* ◆ *The wall is 10 feet long.* ○ The noun is **length**.
3 continuing for a lot of time: *a long concert* ◆ *He's lived here for a long time.* ○ **ANTONYM short**
4 You use **long** to ask or talk about the time from the beginning to the end of something: *How long is the class?*

long[2] 🔊 /lɔŋ/ *adverb* (long·er /ˈlɔŋɡər/, long·est /ˈlɔŋɡəst/)
for a lot of time: *I can't stay long.* ◆ *How long have you been waiting?* ◆ *She moved to the city long after her children were born.* ◆ *My grandfather died long before I was born.*
as long as; so long as only if: *You can borrow the book as long as you promise not to lose it.*
for long for a lot of time: *She went shopping but she was not out for long.*
long ago many years in the past: *Long ago there were no cars.*
no longer; not any longer not now; not as before: *She doesn't live here any longer.*
so long (*informal*) goodbye

long[3] /lɔŋ/ *verb* (longs, long·ing, longed)
to want something very much, especially if this does not seem likely: *I long to see my family again.* ◆ *She's longing for a phone call from her boyfriend.*

long-dis·tance /ˌlɔŋ ˈdɪstəns/ *adjective*
traveling or communicating between places that are far from each other: *a long-distance phone call*

long-haul /ˌlɔŋ ˈhɔl/ *adjective*
connected with carrying people or things over long distances: *a long-haul flight*

long·ing /ˈlɔŋɪŋ/ *noun* [count, noncount]
a strong feeling of wanting something: *a longing for peace* ○ **SYNONYM desire**

lon·gi·tude /ˈlɑndʒətud/ *noun* [noncount]
(**GEOGRAPHY**) the distance of a place east or west of a line from the North Pole to the South Pole that passes through Greenwich, England. **Longitude** is measured in degrees. ○ Look at **latitude**. ○ Look at the picture at **earth**.

long jump /ˈlɔŋ dʒʌmp/ *noun* [singular]
(**SPORTS**) a sport where you try to jump as far as you can

long-term /ˌlɔŋ ˈtərm/ *adjective*
of or for a long period of time: *long-term planning* ○ **ANTONYM short-term**

look[1] 🔊 /lʊk/ *verb* (looks, look·ing, looked)
1 to turn your eyes toward someone or something and try to see them: *Look at this picture.* ◆ *You should look both ways before you cross the street.*
2 to seem to be; to appear: *You look tired.* ◆ *It looks as if it's going to rain.*
3 You say **look** to make someone listen to you: *Look, I know you're busy, but I need your help.*
look after someone or **something** to take care of someone or something: *Can you look after my cat when I'm on vacation?*
look around something to visit a place: *We looked around the museum.*
look for someone or **something** to try to find someone or something: *I'm looking for my keys.*
look forward to something to wait for something with pleasure: *I'm looking forward to seeing you again.*
look into something to study or try to find out something: *We will look into the problem.*
look like someone or **something**
1 to seem to be something: *That looks like a good book.*
2 words that you use to ask about someone's appearance: *"What does he look like?" "He's tall with dark hair."*
3 to have the same appearance as someone or something: *She looks like her mother.*
look out! be careful: *Look out! There's a car coming!*
look out for someone or **something** to pay attention and try to see or find someone or something: *Look out for thieves!*
look something up to try to find information in a book: *I looked the word up in my dictionary.*
look up to someone to respect and admire someone

Thesaurus

look to turn your eyes toward someone or something, or in a particular direction: *She looked at me and smiled.* ◆ *Look out the window! There's a rainbow!*

watch to look at someone or something for some time, paying attention to what happens: *"Would you like to play?" "No thanks – I'll just watch."* ◆ *I only let my kids watch TV on weekends.* ◆ *He stood and watched as the taxi drove away.*

see to watch a movie, a television program, a game, a performance, etc. With this meaning, **see** is not used with the *-ing* form, so you can say "I saw a movie" but NOT "I was seeing a movie": *to see a movie/a TV program* ◆ *Did you see the game on TV yesterday?*

look² 🔑 /lʊk/ *noun*
1 [*count*] turning your eyes toward someone or something; looking: *Have a look at this article.* ◆ *Do you want to take a look around?*
2 [*count, usually singular*] trying to find someone or something: *I had a look for your pen, but I couldn't find it.*
3 [*count*] the expression on someone's face: *He had a worried look on his face.*
4 looks [*plural*] a person's appearance: *He has his father's good looks.*

look·out /'lʊkaʊt/ *noun*
be on the lookout for someone or **something** to pay attention in order to see, find, or avoid someone or something

loom /lum/ *noun* [*count*]
a machine that is used for making cloth by passing pieces of thread across and under other pieces

loop /lup/ *noun* [*count*]
a round shape made by something like string or rope

loop·hole /'luphoʊl/ *noun* [*count*]
a way of avoiding something because the words of a rule or law are not clear or wrong: *a loophole in the tax law*

loose 🔑 /lus/ *adjective* (loos·er, loos·est)

> ⓘ SPELLING
> Remember! Don't confuse **loose** with **lose**, which is a verb: *We can't lose this game.*

1 not tied or fixed: *The dog broke its chain and got loose.* ◆ *One of his teeth is loose.*
2 not fitting close against your body: *a loose white shirt* ⊃ ANTONYM **tight**
▶ **loose·ly** /'lusli/ *adverb*: *The rope was tied loosely around a tree.*

loos·en /'lusn/ *verb* (loos·ens, loos·en·ing, loos·ened)
to become looser or to make something looser: *Can you loosen this knot? It's too tight.* ⊃ ANTONYM **tighten**

lord /lɔrd/ *noun*
1 the Lord [*singular*] (RELIGION) God or Jesus Christ
2 [*count*] (in some countries) a man who has a high position in society: *Lord Fraser*

lose 🔑 /luz/ *verb* (los·es, los·ing, lost /lɔst/, has lost)
1 to not be able to find something: *I can't open the door because I lost my key.*
2 to not have someone or something that you had before: *I lost my job when the factory closed.*
3 to have less of something: *She's lost weight.* ◆ *to lose interest in something*
4 (SPORTS) to not win: *Our team lost the game.*

los·er /'luzər/ *noun* [*count*]
1 (SPORTS) a person who does not win a game, race, or competition ⊃ ANTONYM **winner**
2 (*informal*) a person who is never successful

loss 🔑 /lɔs/ *noun* (*plural* loss·es)
1 [*count, noncount*] losing something: *Has she told the police about the loss of her car?* ◆ *job losses*
2 [*count*] (BUSINESS) how much money a business loses: *The company announced a loss of $5 million.* ⊃ ANTONYM **profit**
at a loss If you are **at a loss**, you do not know what to do or say.

lost¹ form of **lose**

lost² 🔑 /lɔst/ *adjective*
1 If you are **lost**, you do not know where you are: *I took a wrong turn, and now I'm lost.* ◆ *Take this map so you don't get lost!*
2 If something is **lost**, you cannot find it.

lost-and-found /ˌlɔst ən 'faʊnd/ *noun* [*singular*]
a special area where lost things are kept for the owners to collect: *Look for your sweatshirt in the lost-and-found.*

lot¹ 🔑 /lɑt/ *pronoun* **a lot** (also *informal* **lots**)
very much; a large amount or number of things or people: *We ate a lot.*
a lot of; **lots of** a large number or amount of things or people: *She has a lot of friends.* ◆ *Lots of love from Jane* (= words at the end of a letter).

lot² 🔑 /lɑt/ *adverb* **a lot**
very much or often: *Your apartment is a lot bigger than mine.* ◆ *I go to the movies a lot.*

lot³ /lɑt/ *noun* [*count*]
an area of land that is used for a particular purpose: *a parking lot* ◆ *We're going to build a house on this lot.*

lo·tion /'loʊʃn/ *noun* [*count, noncount*]
liquid that you put on your skin: *hand lotion*

lot·ter·y /'lɑtəri/ *noun* [*count*] (*plural* lot·ter·ies)
a game where you buy a ticket with numbers on it. You win money if your numbers are chosen.

loud 🔑 /laʊd/ *adjective, adverb* (loud·er, loud·est)
making a lot of noise: *I couldn't hear what he said because the music was too loud.* ◆ *loud voices* ◆ *Please speak a little louder – I can't hear you.* ⊃ ANTONYM **quiet**
out loud so that other people can hear it: *I read the story out loud.*
▶ **loud·ly** /'laʊdli/ *adverb*: *She laughed loudly.*

loud·speak·er /'laʊdˌspikər/ *noun* [*count*]
a piece of equipment that makes sounds or voices louder: *Music was coming from the loudspeakers.*

æ cat   ɛ ten   i see   ɪ sit   ɑ hot   ɔ saw   ʌ cup   ʊ put   u too

lounge /laʊndʒ/ *noun* [*count*]
a comfortable room in an office, hotel, or other public place where you can sit and relax: *Let's go to the lounge to have coffee.*

louse /laʊs/ *noun* [*count*] (*plural* **lice** /laɪs/)
a small insect that lives on the bodies of people and animals

lous·y /ˈlaʊzi/ *adjective* (**lous·i·er, lous·i·est**)
(*informal*)
very bad: *The weather was lousy.* ⊃ SYNONYM **awful**

lov·a·ble /ˈlʌvəbl/ *adjective*
easy to love: *a lovable little boy*

love¹ 🔑 /lʌv/ *noun*
1 [*noncount*] the strong, warm feeling you have when you like someone or something very much: *Their **love** for each other was very strong.*
2 [*count*] a person, a thing, or an activity that you love: *Who was your first love?*
3 [*noncount*] (**SPORTS**) a word in the game of TENNIS that means zero: *The score is 15-love.*
be in love to love someone: *Have you ever been in love? • He says he is in love with her and they are going to get married.*
fall in love to begin to love someone: *He fell in love with Anna the first time they met.*
love; love from (*informal*) a way of ending a letter to someone that you know well: *See you soon. Love, Peter.*

love² 🔑 /lʌv/ *verb* (**loves, lov·ing, loved**)
1 to have a very strong, warm feeling for someone: *I love him very much. • She loves her parents.* ⊃ ANTONYM **hate**
2 to like something very much: *I love skiing. • I would love to go to Hawaii.* ⊃ ANTONYM **hate** ⊃
Look at the note at **like**¹.

love af·fair /ˈlʌv əˌfɛr/ *noun* [*count*]
a romantic or sexual relationship between two people who love each other but who are not married

love·ly /ˈlʌvli/ *adjective* (**love·li·er, love·li·est**)
beautiful or very nice: *That's a lovely dress. • We had a lovely Thanksgiving. • It's lovely to see you again.*

lov·er /ˈlʌvər/ *noun* [*count*]
1 If two people are **lovers**, they have a sexual relationship but they are not married.
2 a person who likes something very much: *a music lover*

lov·ing /ˈlʌvɪŋ/ *adjective*
feeling or showing love: *loving parents*

low 🔑 /loʊ/ *adjective* (**low·er, low·est**)

> 🛈 PRONUNCIATION
> The word **low** sounds like **go.**

1 near the ground: *There was a low wall around the garden. • a low bridge* ⊃ ANTONYM **high**
2 less than usual: *low temperatures • low pay* ⊃ ANTONYM **high**
3 deep or quiet: *a low sound • I heard low voices in the next room.*
▶ **low** *adverb*: *The plane flew low over the fields.*

low·er¹ /ˈloʊər/ *adjective*
that is under something or at the bottom of something: *She bit her lower lip.* ⊃ ANTONYM **upper**

low·er² /ˈloʊər/ *verb* (**low·ers, low·er·ing, low·ered**)
1 to move someone or something down: *They lowered the boat into the water.*
2 to make something less: *Please lower your voice* (= speak more quietly). ⊃ ANTONYM **raise**

low·er·case /loʊər'keɪs/ (also **low·er case**) *noun* [*noncount*]
(**ENGLISH LANGUAGE ARTS**) the small form of letters, for example a, b, c (not A, B, C): *My e-mail address is all in lowercase.* ⊃ ANTONYM **uppercase**

loy·al /ˈlɔɪəl/ *adjective*
A person who is **loyal** does not change their friends or beliefs: *a loyal friend • He is loyal to the company he works for.* ⊃ ANTONYM **disloyal**
▶ **loy·al·ty** /ˈlɔɪəlti/ *noun* [*count, noncount*] (*plural* **loy·al·ties**): *Loyalty to your friends is very important.*

luck 🔑 /lʌk/ *noun* [*noncount*]
1 good things that happen to you that you cannot control: *We **wish** you **luck** in your new career.*
2 things that happen to you that you cannot control; chance: *to have good luck*
bad luck; hard luck words that you say to someone when you are sorry that they did not have good luck
be in luck to have good things happen to you: *I was in luck – the store had the book I wanted.*
good luck words that you say to someone when you hope that they will do well: *Good luck! I'm sure you'll get the job.*

luck·y 🔑 /ˈlʌki/ *adjective* (**luck·i·er, luck·i·est**)
1 having good luck: *She is **lucky** to be alive after the accident.* ⊃ ANTONYM **unlucky**
2 bringing success or good luck: *My lucky number is 3.* ⊃ ANTONYM **unlucky**
▶ **luck·i·ly** /ˈlʌkəli/ *adverb*
it is lucky that: *I was late, but luckily they waited for me.*

lug·gage /ˈlʌgɪdʒ/ *noun* [*noncount*]
bags that you take with you when you travel: *How much luggage do you have?* ⊃ SYNONYM **baggage**

Grammar

- **Luggage** is a noncount noun, so you cannot say "a luggage" or "luggages."
- If you are talking about one suitcase or bag, you say **a piece of luggage**: *She brought five pieces of luggage with her and she was only staying for one week!*

luke·warm /ˌluk'wɔrm/ *adjective*
If a liquid is **lukewarm**, it is only slightly warm: *I had to have a lukewarm shower.* ⊃ Look at the note at **hot**(1).

lull·a·by /'lʌləbaɪ/ *noun* [*count*] (*plural* **lull·a·bies**)
(**MUSIC**) a gentle song that you sing to help a child go to sleep

lum·ber /'lʌmbər/ *noun* [*noncount*]
wood that is used for building

lum·ber·jack /'lʌmbərdʒæk/ *noun* [*count*]
a person whose job is to cut down trees to use for wood

lump 🔊 /lʌmp/ *noun* [*count*]
1 a hard piece of something: *a lump of coal* ⊃ Look at the note at **piece**.
2 (**HEALTH**) a part in or on your body that has become hard and bigger: *I have a lump on my head where I hit it.*

lump·y /'lʌmpi/ *adjective* (**lump·i·er, lump·i·est**)
full of or covered with LUMPS: *The sauce is lumpy.*
⊃ ANTONYM **smooth**

lu·nar /'lunər/ *adjective*
connected with the moon: *a lunar eclipse*

lu·na·tic /'lunətɪk/ *noun* [*count*] (*informal*)
a person who does stupid and often dangerous things

lunch 🔊 /lʌntʃ/ *noun* [*count, noncount*] (*plural* **lunch·es**)
a meal that you eat in the middle of the day: *What would you like for lunch? • What time do you usually have lunch?*

lunch·time /'lʌntʃtaɪm/ *noun* [*count, noncount*]
the time when you eat lunch: *I'll meet you at lunchtime.*

lung /lʌŋ/ *noun* [*count*]
(**BIOLOGY**) one of the two parts inside your body that you use for breathing ⊃ Look at the picture at **body**.

lunge /lʌndʒ/ *verb* (**lung·es, lung·ing, lunged**)
to move forward suddenly, especially in order to attack someone or take something: *Taylor lunged for the ball.*
▶ **lunge** *noun* [*count, usually singular*]: *He made a lunge for the gun.*

lurk /lərk/ *verb* (**lurks, lurk·ing, lurked**)
to wait somewhere secretly, especially because you are going to do something bad: *I thought I saw someone lurking behind the trees.*

lux·u·ri·ous /lʌgˈʒʊriəs/ *adjective*
very comfortable and expensive: *a luxurious hotel*

lux·u·ry /'lʌkʃəri/ *noun* (*plural* **lux·u·ries**)
1 [*noncount*] a way of living when you have all the expensive and beautiful things you want: *They live in luxury in a beautiful house in Malibu. • a luxury hotel*
2 [*count*] something very nice and expensive that you do not really need: *Eating in a restaurant is a luxury for most people.*

Suffix

–ly
(in adverbs) in a particular way: *quickly • happily • beautifully*

ly·ing form of **lie**

lyr·ics /'lɪrɪks/ *noun* [*plural*]
(**MUSIC**) the words of a song: *One member of the band writes the music, and another writes the lyrics.*

Mm

M, m /ɛm/ *noun* [count, noncount]
1 (*plural* M's, m's /ɛmz/) the thirteenth letter of the English alphabet: "*Milk*" *begins with an* "*M.*"
2 m abbreviation of **meter**

M.A. /ˌɛm ˈeɪ/ *noun* [count]
a second university degree that you receive when you complete a program of study at a university in an ARTS subject (= a subject that is not a science subject). M.A. is short for "Master of Arts": *She has an M.A. in art history.* ⊃ Look at **B. A.**, **M.S.**, **master's degree**.

ma'am /mæm/ *noun* [singular]
a polite way of speaking to a woman, instead of using her name: *Excuse me ma'am, can you tell me what time it is?* ⊃ Look at **sir**.

ma·ca·ro·ni /ˌmækəˈroʊni/ *noun* [noncount]
a type of PASTA (= Italian food made from flour and water) in the shape of short tubes: *macaroni and cheese* (= with a cheese sauce)

ma·chine 🔑 /məˈʃin/ *noun* [count]
a thing with moving parts that is made to do a job. **Machines** often use electricity: *a washing machine* • *This machine does not work.*

ma·chine gun /məˈʃin gʌn/ *noun* [count]
a gun that sends out a lot of bullets very quickly

ma·chin·er·y /məˈʃinəri/ *noun* [noncount]
machines in general, especially large ones; the moving parts of a machine: *industrial machinery*

ma·cho /ˈmɑtʃoʊ/ *adjective* (informal)
A man who is **macho** behaves in a strong and brave way, instead of showing that he is caring and sensitive.

mad /mæd/ *adjective* (mad·der, mad·dest)
1 (*informal*) very angry: *He was mad at me for losing his watch.* ⊃ Look at the note at **angry**.
2 (HEALTH) sick in your mind: *a mad scientist* ⊃ SYNONYM **crazy**
be mad about someone or **something** (*informal*) to like someone or something very much: *Marsha is mad about computer games.* • *He's mad about her.*
drive someone mad to make someone very angry: *This noise is driving me mad!*
like mad (*informal*) very hard, fast, much, etc.: *I had to run like mad to catch the bus.*

mad·am /ˈmædəm/ *noun* [singular]
1 (*formal*) a polite way of speaking to a woman: "*Can I help you, madam?*" *asked the salesclerk.* ⊃ Look at **ma'am**.

2 Madam (ENGLISH LANGUAGE ARTS) a word that you use at the beginning of a formal letter to a woman: *Dear Madam…* ⊃ Look at **sir**.

made form of **make**¹

mad·ly /ˈmædli/ *adverb*
1 in a wild way: *They were rushing around madly.*
2 (*informal*) very much: *Richard and Vanessa are madly in love.*

mad·ness /ˈmædnəs/ *noun* [noncount]
1 being sick in your mind; mental illness
2 stupid behavior that could be dangerous: *It would be madness to take a boat out in this terrible weather.*

mag·a·zine 🔑 /ˈmægəzin; ˌmægəˈzin/ *noun* [count]
a kind of thin book with a paper cover that you can buy every week or every month. It has a lot of different stories and pictures inside.

mag·ic 🔑 /ˈmædʒɪk/ *noun* [noncount]
1 a special power that can make strange or impossible things happen: *He suddenly appeared as if by magic.*
2 tricks that someone can do to entertain people
▶ **mag·ic** *adjective*: *magic tricks*

mag·i·cal /ˈmædʒɪkl/ *adjective*
1 seeming to have special powers: *a herb with magical powers to cure disease*
2 (*informal*) wonderful and exciting: *We spent a magical week in San Francisco.*

ma·gi·cian /məˈdʒɪʃn/ *noun* [count]
1 a person who does tricks to entertain people
2 a man in stories who has strange, unusual powers

mag·is·trate /ˈmædʒəstreɪt/ *noun* [count]
a judge in a court of law who decides how to punish people for small crimes

mag·ne·si·um /mægˈniziəm/ *noun* [noncount] (symbol **Mg**)
(CHEMISTRY) a metal that is silver in color and burns with a bright white light

mag·net /ˈmægnət/ *noun* [count]
(PHYSICS) a piece of metal that can make other metal things move toward it

magnet

mag·net·ic /mægˈnɛt̬ɪk/ *adjective*
(PHYSICS) having the ability to attract metal objects: *Is this metal magnetic?*

mag·net·ism /ˈmægnətɪzəm/ *noun* [noncount]
(PHYSICS) the power of some metals that makes other objects move toward or away from them

mag·nif·i·cent /mæg'nɪfəsənt/ *adjective*
very good or beautiful: *The library is a magnificent building.*

mag·ni·fy /'mægnəfaɪ/ *verb* (mag·ni·fies, mag·ni·fy·ing, mag·ni·fied, has mag·ni·fied)
to make something look bigger than it really is: *We magnified the insect under a microscope.*

mag·ni·fy·ing glass
/'mægnəfaɪɪŋ ˌglæs/
noun [count] (plural mag·ni·fy·ing glass·es)
a round piece of glass, usually with a handle, that makes things look bigger than they are when you look through it

magnifying glass

maid /meɪd/ *noun* [count]
a woman whose job is to clean in a hotel or a house

maid·en name /'meɪdn neɪm/ *noun* [count]
a woman's family name before she is married ⊃ Look at the note at **name¹**.

maid of hon·or /ˌmeɪd əv 'ɑnər/ *noun* [count]
(plural maids of hon·or)
(at a wedding) the most important BRIDESMAID (= someone who helps a woman on her wedding day): *My cousin Sarah was my maid of honor.* ⊃ Look at **bridesmaid**.

mail¹ /meɪl/ *noun* [noncount]
1 the way of sending and receiving letters and packages: *Your check is in the mail.* ◆ *to send a letter by airmail*
2 letters and packages that you send or receive: *Is there any mail for me?*
3 (COMPUTERS) computer messages sent by e-mail: *I need to check my mail.*

mail² /meɪl/ *verb* (mails, mail·ing, mailed)
1 to send a letter or package to someone: *to mail a package* ◆ *I'll **mail** the money **to** you.*
2 to send a message to someone by e-mail: *Mail me when you get to your hotel.* ⊃ SYNONYM e-mail

mailboxes

mail·box /'meɪlbɑks/ *noun* [count] (plural mail·box·es)
1 a private box outside a house, or a hole in a door for putting letters into

2 a box in the street where you put letters that you want to send
3 (COMPUTERS) a computer program that receives and stores e-mail

mail car·ri·er /'meɪl ˌkæriər/ *noun* [count]
a person whose job is to take (DELIVER) letters and packages to people's homes

mail·man /'meɪlmæn/ *noun* [count] (plural mail·men /'meɪlmən/)
a man whose job is to take (DELIVER) letters and packages to people's homes

mail or·der /'meɪl ˌɔrdər/ *noun* [noncount]
a way of shopping, in which you choose the things you want to buy and you are sent them by mail: *a mail order catalog*

main 🔑 /meɪn/ *adjective*
most important: *My main reason for learning new skills is to get a better job.* ◆ *I had fish for the **main course** (= the most important part of the meal).*

main·land /'meɪnlænd; 'meɪnlənd/ *noun* [singular]
(GEOGRAPHY) the main part of a country, not including the islands around it: *We took a ferry from the island to the mainland.*

main·ly 🔑 /'meɪnli/ *adverb*
mostly: *The students here are mainly from the East Coast.* ◆ *She eats mainly vegetables.*

main·stream /'meɪnstrim/ *noun* the mainstream [singular]
the ideas and opinions that are considered normal because they are shared by most people: *His extreme views put him outside the mainstream of American politics.*
▶ **main·stream** *adjective*: *mainstream education*

main·tain AWL /meɪn'teɪn/ *verb* (main·tains, main·tain·ing, main·tained)
1 to make something continue at the same level: *If he can maintain this speed, he'll win the race.*
2 to keep something working well: *The roads are well maintained.*

main·te·nance AWL /'meɪntn·əns/ *noun* [noncount]
keeping something in good condition: *car maintenance*

ma·jes·tic /mə'dʒɛstɪk/ *adjective*
making a strong impression because of its size or beauty: *a majestic mountain view*

maj·es·ty /'mædʒəsti/ *noun*
1 [noncount] the quality of being very big or very beautiful: *the majesty of the Grand Canyon*
2 Majesty [count] (plural Maj·es·ties) (formal) a word that you use to talk to or about a king or queen: *Her Majesty Queen Elizabeth II*

---

ma·jor¹ AWL /'meɪdʒər/ *adjective*
very large, important, or serious: *There are airports in all the major cities.* ◆ *major problems* ⊃ **ANTONYM minor**

ma·jor² AWL /'meɪdʒər/ *noun* [count]
1 the main subject that you study in college: *Her major is chemistry.* ⊃ Look at **minor²**(2).
2 an officer in the army

ma·jor³ AWL /'meɪdʒər/ *verb* (ma·jors, ma·jor·ing, ma·jored)
major in something to study something as your main subject in college: *She's majoring in chemistry.* ⊃ Look at **minor³**.

ma·jor·i·ty AWL /mə'dʒɔrəti/ *noun* [singular]
most things or people in a group: *The majority of people agreed with the new law.* ⊃ **ANTONYM minority**

ma·jor league /ˌmeɪdʒər 'lig/ *noun* [count]
(**SPORTS**) the groups of baseball teams that play at the highest level ⊃ Look at **minor league**.

make¹ 🔑 /meɪk/ *verb* (makes, mak·ing, made /meɪd/, has made)
1 to produce or create something: *They make cars in that factory.* ◆ *He made a box out of some pieces of wood.* ◆ *This shirt is made of cotton.*
2 to cause something to be or to happen; to perform an action: *The plane made a loud noise when it landed.* ◆ *Chocolate makes you fat.* ◆ *That story made me cry.* ◆ *I made a mistake.*
3 to force someone to do something: *My father made me stay at home.*
4 a word that you use with money and numbers: *She makes (= earns) a lot of money.* ◆ *Five and seven make twelve.*
5 to choose someone to do a job: *They made him president of the company.*
6 to have the right qualities to be something: *She'll make a great teacher.*
7 to be able to go somewhere: *I'm afraid I can't make the meeting on Friday.*
make do with something to use something that is not very good, because there is nothing better: *We didn't have a table, but we made do with some boxes.*
make something into something to change something so that it becomes a different thing: *They made the bedroom into an office.*
make it to manage to do something; to succeed: *She'll never make it as an actress.*
make something or **someone out** to be able to see, hear, or understand something or someone: *It was dark and I couldn't make out the words on the sign.*
make up to become friends again after an argument: *Laura and Tom had an argument last week, but they've made up now.* ◆ *Has she made up with him yet?*

make something up to invent something that is not true: *No one believes that story – he made it up!*

make² /meɪk/ *noun* [count]
(**BUSINESS**) the name of the company that made something: *"What make is your car?" "It's a Ford."*

make-be·lieve /'meɪk bɪˌliv/ *noun* [noncount]
imagining something, or the things that are imagined: *Don't believe his stories – they're all make-believe.*

make·o·ver /'meɪkˌoʊvər/ *noun* [count]
the process of improving the appearance of a person or a place: *She won a complete makeover in a magazine competition.*

mak·er /'meɪkər/ *noun* [count]
a person, company, or machine that makes something: *a filmmaker*

make·up /'meɪkʌp/ *noun* [noncount]
special powders and creams that you put on your face to make yourself more beautiful. Actors also wear **makeup** when they are acting: *She put on her makeup.*

ma·lar·i·a /mə'lɛriə/ *noun* [noncount]
(**HEALTH**) a serious disease that you get in hot countries from the bite of a small insect (called a **MOSQUITO**)

male 🔑 /meɪl/ *adjective*
(**BIOLOGY**) A **male** animal or person belongs to the sex that does not have babies: *A rooster is a male chicken.*
▶ **male** *noun* [count]: *The males of this species are bigger than the females.* ⊃ Look at **female**.

mal·ice /'mæləs/ *noun* [noncount]
a feeling of wanting to hurt other people: *He sent the e-mail out of malice.*
▶ **ma·li·cious** /mə'lɪʃəs/ *adjective*: *It's not true. It's just a malicious rumor.*

mall /mɔl/ (also **shop·ping mall** /'ʃɑpɪŋ mɔl/) *noun* [count]
a large building that has a lot of stores, restaurants, etc. inside it

mal·nu·tri·tion /ˌmælnu'trɪʃn/ *noun* [noncount]
(**HEALTH**) bad health that is the result of not having enough food or enough of the right kind of food: *Some of the children were suffering from malnutrition.*

mam·mal /'mæml/ *noun* [count]
(**BIOLOGY**) any animal that drinks milk from its mother's body when it is young: *Dogs, horses, whales, and people are all mammals.*

man¹ 🔑 /mæn/ *noun* (plural **men** /mɛn/)
1 [count] an adult male person: *I saw a tall man with dark hair.*
2 [noncount] all humans; people: *the damage man has caused to the environment*

3 [count] any person: *All men are created equal.*

man² /mæn/ *exclamation* (*informal*)
a word that you say when you are a little angry, or you are surprised, shocked, etc.: *Oh man! I can't believe I forgot my keys!* ◆ *Man, that's a great car!*

man·age 🔑 /'mænɪdʒ/ *verb* (**man·ag·es, man·ag·ing, man·aged**)
1 to be able to do something that is difficult: *The box was heavy but she managed to carry it out to the car.*
2 to be in charge of or control someone or something: *She manages a department of 30 people.*

man·age·a·ble /'mænɪdʒəbl/ *adjective*
not too big or too difficult to deal with: *I have a busy schedule, but it's manageable.*

man·age·ment /'mænɪdʒmənt/ *noun*
1 [noncount] the control of something, for example a business, and the people who work in it: *Teachers must show good classroom management.*
2 [count, noncount] (**BUSINESS**) all the people who control a business: *The hotel is now under new management.*

man·ag·er 🔑 /'mænɪdʒər/ *noun* [count]
(**BUSINESS**) a person who is in charge of a business, a store, an organization, or part of an organization: *He is the manager of a shoe store.* ◆ *a sales manager*

man·da·to·ry /'mændə,tɔri/ *adjective* (*formal*)
If something is **mandatory**, you have to do it: *mandatory drug testing for athletes* ➔ **SYNONYM compulsory**

mane /meɪn/ *noun* [count]
the long hair on the neck of some animals, for example horses and **LIONS** ➔ Look at the picture at **lion**.

ma·neu·ver /mə'nuvər/ *verb* (**ma·neu·vers, ma·neu·ver·ing, ma·neu·vered**)
to move to a different position using skill: *to maneuver into a parking space*
▶ **ma·neu·ver** *noun* [count, noncount]: *It's a complicated maneuver that you need to practice.*

man·go /'mæŋgoʊ/ *noun* [count] (*plural* **man·goes** or **man·gos**)
a fruit that is yellow or red on the outside and yellow on the inside. **Mangoes** grow in hot countries.

ma·ni·ac /'meɪniæk/ *noun* [count]
a person who behaves in a wild or dangerous way: *to drive like a maniac*

man·ic /'mænɪk/ *adjective* (*informal*)
full of activity and excitement: *Things are manic in the office right now.*

man·i·cure /'mænəkyʊr/ *noun* [count, noncount]
a treatment to make your hands and your **FINGERNAILS** (= the hard parts at the end of your fingers) look nice: *to have a manicure*

ma·nip·u·late **AWL** /mə'nɪpyəleɪt/ *verb* (**ma·nip·u·lates, ma·nip·u·lat·ing, ma·nip·u·lat·ed**)
to influence someone so that they do or think what you want: *Politicians know how to manipulate people's opinions.*
▶ **ma·nip·u·la·tion** **AWL** /mə,nɪpyə'leɪʃn/ *noun* [count, noncount]

man·kind /,mæn'kaɪnd/ *noun* [noncount]
all the people in the world

man–made /,mæn 'meɪd/ *adjective*
made by people; not formed in a natural way: *man-made materials* ➔ **SYNONYM artificial**

man·ner /'mænər/ *noun*
1 [singular] the way that you do something or the way that something happens: *Don't get angry. Let's try to talk about this in a calm manner.*
2 [singular] the way that someone behaves and speaks to other people: *He has a very friendly manner.*
3 manners [plural] the habits and customs of people in a particular country or culture: *It's bad manners to talk with your mouth full.*

man·ner·ism /'mænə,rɪzəm/ *noun* [count]
a particular way of speaking or behaving that someone has: *You don't look like your sister, but you have the same mannerisms.*

man·sion /'mænʃn/ *noun* [count]
a very big house

man·tel /'mæntl/ (also **man·tel·piece** /'mæntlpis/) *noun* [count]
a narrow shelf above the place where a fire is in a room (called the **FIREPLACE**): *She has photographs of her children on the mantel.*

man·u·al¹ **AWL** /'mænyuəl/ *adjective*
using your hands: *Do you prefer manual work or office work?*
▶ **man·u·al·ly** **AWL** /'mænyuəli/ *adverb*: *This machine is operated manually.*

man·u·al² **AWL** /'mænyuəl/ *noun* [count]
a book that tells you how to do something: *Where is the instruction manual for the DVD recorder?*

man·u·fac·ture /,mænyə'fæktʃər/ *verb* (**man·u·fac·tures, man·u·fac·tur·ing, man·u·fac·tured**)
to make things in a factory using machines: *The company manufactures radios.*
▶ **man·u·fac·ture** *noun* [noncount]: *the manufacture of cars*

man·u·fac·tur·er /ˌmænyəˈfæktʃərər/ *noun* [count]
a person or company that makes something: *If it doesn't work, send it back to the manufacturer.*

ma·nure /məˈnʊr/ *noun* [noncount]
animal waste that is put on soil to make plants grow better

man·u·script /ˈmænyəskrɪpt/ *noun* [count]
(**ENGLISH LANGUAGE ARTS**) a copy of a book, piece of music, etc. before it has been published: *an unpublished manuscript*

man·y 🔑 /ˈmɛni/ *adjective, pronoun* (**more** /mɔr/, **most** /moʊst/)
1 a large number of people or things: *Many people in this country are poor.* ◆ *There aren't many students in my class.* ◆ ***Many of** these books are very old.* ◆ *There are **too many** mistakes in your homework.*
2 a word that you use to ask or talk about the number of people or things: ***How many** brothers and sisters do you have?* ◆ *Take **as many** cookies **as** you want.* ⊃ Look at **much**.

map 🔑 /mæp/ *noun* [count]
a drawing of a city, a country, or the world that shows things like mountains, rivers, and roads: *Can you find Iowa **on the map?** ◆ a street **map of** Houston*

ma·ple /ˈmeɪpl/ *noun* [count]
a tree that has leaves with five points, which turn bright red or yellow in the fall: *pancakes with **maple syrup** (= the sweet liquid from this tree)*

mar·a·thon /ˈmærəˌθɑn/ *noun* [count]
(**SPORTS**) a very long race when people run about 26 miles

mar·ble /ˈmɑrbl/ *noun*
1 [noncount] a hard, attractive stone that is used to make STATUES (= models of people) and parts of buildings: *Marble is always cold when you touch it.*
2 [count] a small, glass ball that children play with: *The children are **playing marbles**.*

March 🔑 /mɑrtʃ/ *noun* [count, noncount]
(abbreviation **Mar.**)
the third month of the year

march¹ /mɑrtʃ/ *verb* (march·es, march·ing, marched)
1 to walk like a soldier: *The soldiers marched along the road.*
2 to walk through the streets in a large group to show that you do not agree with something: *They marched through the center of town shouting "Stop the war!"*
3 to walk somewhere quickly in a determined way: *She **marched up to** the manager and asked for her money back.*

march² /mɑrtʃ/ *noun* [count] (*plural* **march·es**)
1 an organized walk by a large group of people who want to show that they do not agree with something: *a peace march* ⊃ Look at **demonstration**(2).
2 a long trip made by soldiers walking together: *The soldiers were tired after the long march.*

mare /mɛr/ *noun* [count]
a female horse ⊃ Look at the note at **horse**.

mar·ga·rine /ˈmɑrdʒərən/ *noun* [noncount]
soft, yellow food that looks like butter, but is not made of milk. You put it on bread or use it in cooking.

mar·gin **AWL** /ˈmɑrdʒən/ *noun* [count]
1 the space at the side of a page that has no writing or pictures in it
2 the amount of space, time, etc. by which you win something: *He won the election by a wide margin.*

ma·rine¹ /məˈrin/ *adjective*
connected with the ocean: *the study of marine life*

ma·rine² /məˈrin/ *noun* [count]
a soldier who has been trained to fight on land or on the ocean

mark¹ 🔑 /mɑrk/ *noun* [count]
1 a spot or line that spoils the appearance of something: *There's **a dirty mark** on the front of your shirt.*
2 a shape or special sign on something: *This mark shows that the ring is made of silver.* ◆ *punctuation marks*
3 a number or letter that a teacher gives for your work to show how good it is: *She got a very **low mark** on her history test.* ◆ *He gets **good marks** in school.* ⊃ **SYNONYM grade**

mark² 🔑 /mɑrk/ *verb* (marks, mark·ing, marked)
1 to put a sign on something by writing or drawing on it: *The price is **marked on** the bottom of the box.*
2 to show where something is: *This cross marks the place where he died.*
3 to spoil the appearance of something by making a mark on it: *The white walls were dirty and marked.*
4 to celebrate or remember an important event: *The ceremony marked the tenth anniversary of the end of the war.*
5 to look at school work to see how good it is: *The teacher marked all my answers wrong.*

mar·ket¹ 🔑 /ˈmɑrkət/ *noun*
1 [count] a place where people go to buy and sell things, usually outside: *There is a fruit and vegetable market here on Fridays.*

2 [*count, noncount*] (**BUSINESS**) the people who want to buy something: *There is a big* ***market for*** *Spanish-language books in the U.S.*
on the market available to buy: *This is one of the best cameras on the market.*

mar·ket² /'mɑrkət/ *verb* (**mar·kets, mar·ket·ing, mar·ket·ed**)
(**BUSINESS**) to sell something using advertisements: *Companies spend millions marketing their products.*

mar·ket·ing /'mɑrkət̬ɪŋ/ *noun* [*noncount*]
(**BUSINESS**) using advertisements to help a company sell its products: *She works in the marketing department.*

ma·roon /mə'run/ *adjective*
having a color between brown and purple
▶ **ma·roon** *noun* [*noncount*]

mar·riage 🔑 /'mærɪdʒ/ *noun*
1 [*count, noncount*] the time when two people are together as husband and wife: *They had a long and happy marriage.*
2 [*count*] the time when a man and woman become husband and wife: *The marriage will take place at the church.* ➲ **SYNONYM wedding**

mar·ried 🔑 /'mærid/ *adjective*
having a husband or a wife: *Gary is* ***married to*** *Helen.* ➲ **ANTONYM single, unmarried**
get married to take someone as your husband or wife: *Fran and Paul* ***got married*** *last year.*

mar·ry 🔑 /'mæri/ *verb* (**mar·ries, mar·ry·ing, mar·ried, has mar·ried**)
to take someone as your husband or wife: *Will you marry me?* ◆ *They married when they were very young.*

marsh /mɑrʃ/ *noun* [*count, noncount*] (*plural* **marsh·es**)
(**GEOGRAPHY**) soft, wet ground
▶ **marsh·y** /'mɑrʃi/ *adjective*: *marshy ground*

mar·shal /'mɑrʃl/ *noun* [*count*]
1 an officer whose job is to do the things that are ordered by a court of law: *He was brought into the courtroom by two federal marshals.*
2 an important officer in some police and fire departments: *a fire marshal*

marsh·mal·low /'mɑrʃmɛloʊ/ *noun* [*count, noncount*]
a very soft, sweet, white food that comes in round pieces: *We toasted marshmallows over the fire.*

mar·tial arts /ˌmɑrʃl 'ɑrts/ *noun* [*plural*]
(**SPORTS**) fighting sports, in which you use your hands and feet as weapons: *judo, karate, and other martial arts*

mar·vel·ous /'mɑrvl·əs/ *adjective*
very good: *I had a marvelous vacation.* ➲ **SYNONYM wonderful**

mas·car·a /mæ'skærə/ *noun* [*noncount*]
a substance that you put on the hairs around your eyes (your **EYELASHES**) to make them look darker and thicker

mas·cot /'mæskɑt/ *noun* [*count*]
a person, animal, or thing that people think brings them good luck

mas·cu·line /'mæskyələn/ *adjective*
1 typical of a man, or right for a man: *a masculine voice*
2 (**ENGLISH LANGUAGE ARTS**) (in some languages) belonging to a certain class of nouns, adjectives, or pronouns: *The French word for "sun" is masculine.* ➲ Look at **feminine**(2).

mash /mæʃ/ *verb* (**mash·es, mash·ing, mashed**)
to press and mix food to make it soft: *mashed potatoes*

mask /mæsk/ *noun* [*count*]
a thing that you wear over your face to hide or protect it: *a gas mask* ◆ *The doctors and nurses all wore masks.* ◆ *a Halloween mask*

masks

mass /mæs/ *noun* (*plural* **mass·es**)
1 [*count*] a large amount or quantity of something without a clear shape: *a* ***mass of*** *rock*
2 [*noncount*] (**PHYSICS**) the amount of material that something contains: *to calculate the earth's mass*
3 Mass [*count, noncount*] (**RELIGION**) an important religious ceremony, especially in the Roman Catholic Church: *She goes to Mass every Sunday.*

mas·sa·cre /'mæsəkər/ *noun* [*count*]
the cruel killing of a lot of people
▶ **mas·sa·cre** *verb* (**mas·sa·cres, mas·sa·cring, mas·sa·cred**): *Hundreds of innocent people were massacred.*

mas·sage /mə'sɑʒ/ *noun* [*count, noncount*]
the act of rubbing someone's body to get rid of pain or help them relax: *Do you want me to* ***give*** *you* ***a massage****?*
▶ **mas·sage** *verb* (**mas·sag·es, mas·sag·ing, mas·saged**): *She massaged my back.*

mas·sive /'mæsɪv/ *adjective*
very big: *The house is massive – it has 16 bedrooms!* ➲ **SYNONYM enormous, huge**

mast /mæst/ *noun* [*count*]
1 a tall piece of wood or metal that holds the sails on a boat
2 a tall pole that holds a flag

mas·ter¹ /'mæstər/ *noun* [*count*]
1 a man who has people or animals in his control: *The dog ran to its master.*
2 a man who is very good at something: *paintings by the American masters*

mas·ter² /ˈmæstər/ *verb* (mas·ters, mas·ter·ing, mas·tered)
to learn how to do something well: *It takes a long time to master a foreign language.*

mas·ter·piece /ˈmæstərpis/ *noun* [count]
a great painting, book, movie, or play: *"The Grapes of Wrath" was Steinbeck's masterpiece.*

mas·ter's de·gree /ˈmæstərz dɪˌgri/ (also **mas·ter's**) *noun* [count]
a second or higher university degree. You usually get a **master's degree** by studying for one or two years after your first degree: *Ted has a master's degree in education.* ⊃ Look at **M.A., M.S., bachelor's degree**.

mat /mæt/ *noun* [count]
1 a small thing that covers a part of the floor: *Wipe your feet on the doormat before you go in.* • *an exercise mat for gymnasts* ⊃ Look at **rug**.
2 a small thing that you put under something on a table: *a place mat* (= that you put plates and dishes on)

match¹ /mætʃ/ *noun* (plural **match·es**)
1 [count] a short thin piece of wood that you use to light a fire or a cigarette: *He struck a match and lit his cigarette.* • *a box of matches*
2 [singular] something that looks good with something else, for example because it has the same color, shape, or pattern: *Your shoes and dress are a good match.*
3 [count] (**SPORTS**) a game between two people or teams: *a tennis match* • *a boxing match*

match² /mætʃ/ *verb* (match·es, match·ing, matched)
1 to have the same color, shape, or pattern as something else, or to look good with something else: *That scarf doesn't match your blouse.*
2 to find something that is like another thing or that you can put with it: *Match the word with the right picture.*
▸ **match·ing** /ˈmætʃɪŋ/ *adjective*: *She was wearing a blue skirt and matching jacket.*

mate¹ /meɪt/ *noun* [count]
1 a person who lives, works, or studies with you: *Andrew is one of my classmates.* • *a roommate*
2 (**BIOLOGY**) one of two animals that come together to make young animals: *In spring the birds look for mates.*

mate² /meɪt/ *verb* (mates, mat·ing, mat·ed)
(**BIOLOGY**) When animals **mate**, they come together to make young animals.

ma·te·ri·al /məˈtɪriəl/ *noun* [count, noncount]
1 cloth that you use for making clothes and other things: *I don't have enough material to make a dress.* ⊃ SYNONYM **fabric**

2 what you use for making or doing something: *Wood and stone are building materials.* • *writing materials* (= pens, paper, etc.)

ma·ter·nal /məˈtərnl/ *adjective*
1 behaving like a mother, or connected with being a mother: *She's not very maternal.* • *maternal love*
2 A **maternal** relation is from your mother's side of the family: *my maternal grandfather* (= my mother's father) ⊃ Look at **paternal**.

ma·ter·ni·ty /məˈtərnəti/ *adjective*
connected with women who are going to have or just had a baby: *maternity clothes* • *I get eight weeks of paid maternity leave* (= when I do not have to work).

math /mæθ/ *noun* [noncount] short for **mathematics**: *He's really good at math.* • *a math class*

math·e·ma·ti·cian /ˌmæθməˈtɪʃn/ *noun* [count]
(**MATH**) a person who studies or is an expert in mathematics

math·e·mat·ics /ˌmæθˈmætɪks/ (formal) (also **math**) *noun* [noncount]
(**MATH**) the study of numbers, measurements, and shapes: *Mathematics is my favorite subject.*
▸ **math·e·mat·i·cal** /ˌmæθˈmætɪkl/ *adjective*: *a mathematical problem*

mat·i·nee (also **mat·i·née**) /ˌmætnˈeɪ/ *noun* [count] (plural **mat·i·nees** or **mat·i·nées**)
an afternoon performance of a play or movie

mat·ter¹ /ˈmætər/ *noun*
1 [count] something that you must talk about or do: *There is a matter I would like to discuss with you.*
2 the matter [singular] the reason someone or something has a problem or is not good: *Julie's crying. What's the matter with her?* • *There is something the matter with my eye.*
3 [noncount] all physical substances, or a substance of a particular kind: *waste matter*
as a matter of fact words that you use when you say something true, important, or interesting: *I like Dave a lot. As a matter of fact, he's my best friend.*
no matter how, what, when, who, etc. words that you use to say that something is always true: *No matter how* (= however) *hard I try, I can't open the door.* • *I'll help you, no matter what* (= whatever) *happens.*

mat·ter² /ˈmætər/ *verb* (mat·ters, mat·ter·ing, mat·tered)
to be important: *It doesn't matter if you're late – we'll wait for you.*

mat·tress /ˈmætrəs/ *noun* [count] (plural **mat·tress·es**)
the thick, soft part of a bed

tʃ **ch**in   dʒ **J**une   v **v**an   θ **th**in   ð **th**en   s **s**o   z **z**oo   ʃ **sh**e

ma·ture AWL /mə'tʃʊr; mə'tʊr/ *adjective*
1 behaving in a sensible way like an adult
2 fully grown or fully developed ⊃ ANTONYM
immature
▸ **ma·ture** AWL *verb* (ma·tures, ma·tur·ing, ma·tured): *He has matured a lot since he went to college.*

mauve /moʊv/ *adjective, noun* [noncount]
pale purple

max·i·mum AWL /'mæksəməm/ *noun* [singular]
the biggest possible size, amount, or number: *This plane can carry a maximum of 150 people.*
▸ **max·i·mum** AWL *adjective*: *We drove at a maximum speed of 60 miles per hour.* ⊃ ANTONYM
minimum

May /meɪ/ *noun* [count, noncount]
the fifth month of the year

may /meɪ/ *modal verb*
1 a word that shows what will perhaps happen or what is possible: *I may go to Colorado next month.* ◆ *He may not be here.*
2 (*formal*) to be allowed to do something: *May I open the window?* ◆ *You may go now.* ⊃ Look at the note at **modal verb**.

may·be /'meɪbi/ *adverb*
a word that shows that something may happen or may be true: *"Are you going out tonight?" "Maybe." ◆ Maybe you should call him.* ⊃
SYNONYM **perhaps**

ℹ️ STYLE
You can use **maybe** when you want to sound polite: *Maybe you could help me with the cooking* (= Please help me with the cooking).

may·on·naise /ˌmeɪə'neɪz; 'meɪəneɪz/ *noun*
[noncount]
a cold, thick sauce made with eggs and oil

may·or /'meɪər/ *noun* [count]
(**POLITICS**) the leader of a group of people who control a city or town (called a COUNCIL)

maze /meɪz/ *noun* [count]
a system of paths that is confusing, so that it is difficult to find your way out

me /mi/ *pronoun* (*plural* **us** /ʌs/)
the person who is speaking: *He called me yesterday.* ◆ *Give it to me.* ◆ *Hello, it's me.*

mead·ow /'mɛdoʊ/ *noun* [count]
a field of grass

meal /mil/ *noun* [count]
food that you eat at a certain time of the day: *What's your favorite meal of the day?* ◆ *We had a nice meal in that restaurant.*

Culture

■ Breakfast, lunch, and dinner are the usual meals of the day.
■ We do not usually use "a" with the names

of meals: *Let's have lunch together tomorrow.*

meal·time /'miltaɪm/ *noun* [count]
the time at which a meal is usually eaten: *Our mealtimes are later on weekends.*

mean¹ /min/ *verb* (means, mean·ing, meant
/mɛnt/, has meant)
1 to have as a meaning: *What does "medicine" mean?* ◆ *The red light means that you have to stop here.*
2 to plan or want to say something: *She said "yes" but she really meant "no." ◆ I don't understand what you mean. ◆ We're going on Tuesday, I mean Thursday.*
3 to make something happen: *This snow means there will be no outdoor sports today.*
4 to plan or want to do something: *I didn't mean to hurt you. ◆ I meant to call you, but I forgot. ◆ It was meant as a joke.* ⊃ SYNONYM **intend**
5 to be important to someone: *My family means a lot to me.*
I mean words you use to explain or correct what you have just said: *It was so boring – I mean, nothing happened for an hour! ◆ She's from Carolina – California, I mean.*

mean² /min/ *adjective* (mean·er, mean·est)
1 (used about people or their behavior) unkind: *It was mean of you to say that Peter was fat.*
2 (**MATH**) average: *Use these statistics to calculate the mean annual temperature in Los Angeles.*

mean³ /min/ *noun* [count]
(**MATH**) the result you get when you add together all the numbers in a group and then divide the total by the number of amounts you added ⊃
SYNONYM **average**

mean·ing /'minɪŋ/ *noun*
1 [count] what something means or shows: *This word has two different meanings.*
2 [noncount] purpose or importance: *After his daughter's death, he felt that his life had no meaning.*

mean·ing·ful /'minɪŋfl/ *adjective*
useful, important, or interesting: *a meaningful relationship*

mean·ing·less /'minɪŋləs/ *adjective*
without meaning, reason, or sense: *These figures are meaningless if we have nothing to compare them with.*

means /minz/ *noun* [count] (*plural* **means**)
a way of doing something; a way of going somewhere: *Do you have a means of transportation* (= a car, a bicycle etc.)?
by all means (*formal*) of course; certainly: *"May I make a suggestion?" "By all means."*
by means of something (*formal*) by using something: *We crossed the river by means of a small bridge.*

by no means (*formal*) not at all: *I'm by no means sure that this is the right thing to do.*

meant form of **mean**[1]

mean·time /'mintaɪm/ *noun*
in the meantime in the time between two things happening: *Our house isn't ready, so we're living with my parents in the meantime.*

mean·while /'minwaɪl/ *adverb*
at the same time as another thing is happening, or in the time between two things happening: *Peter was at home studying. Dan, meanwhile, was out with his friends.* • *I'm going to buy a bed next week, but meanwhile I'm sleeping on the floor.*

mea·sles /'mizəlz/ *noun* [*noncount*]
(**HEALTH**) an illness that makes small red spots appear on your skin: *Did you ever have the measles?*

meas·ure[1] ♪ /'mɛʒər/ *verb* (**meas·ures, meas·ur·ing, meas·ured**)
1 to find the size, weight, or amount of someone or something: *Could you measure these windows for me?*
2 to be a certain size or amount: *This room measures 15 feet across.*

meas·ure[2] ♪ /'mɛʒər/ *noun* [*count*]
1 a way of showing the size or amount of something: *A yard is a measure of length.*
2 an action that someone does in order to achieve something: *The government has taken measures to resolve the crisis.*

meas·ure·ment ♪ /'mɛʒərmənt/ *noun* [*count*]
the size of something that is found by measuring it: *What are the measurements of the kitchen* (= how long and wide is it)?

meat ♪ /mit/ *noun* [*noncount*]
the parts of an animal or bird that you can eat: *I don't eat meat.* • *meat-eating animals*

meat·ball /'mitbɔl/ *noun* [*count*]
a small round ball of meat: *spaghetti and meatballs*

meat·loaf /'mitloʊf/ *noun* [*count, noncount*]
meat that has been cut into very small pieces and mixed with eggs, onions, etc. It is then formed into a long shape and baked: *a slice of meatloaf*

me·chan·ic /mə'kænɪk/ *noun* [*count*]
a person whose job is to repair or work with machines: *a car mechanic*

me·chan·i·cal /mə'kænɪkl/ *adjective*
moved, done, or made by a machine: *a mechanical toy*
▸ **me·chan·i·cal·ly** /mə'kænɪkli/ *adverb*: *The pump is operated mechanically.*

me·chan·ics /mə'kænɪks/ *noun* [*noncount*]
(**GENERAL SCIENCE**) the study of how machines work

mech·a·nism **AWL** /'mɛkənɪzəm/ *noun* [*count*]
a set of moving parts in a machine that does a particular job: *a car with an automatic locking mechanism*

med·al /'mɛdl/ *noun*
[*count*]
a piece of metal with words and pictures on it that you get for doing something very good: *She won a gold medal in the Olympic Games.*

medal

me·di·a **AWL** /'midiə/ *noun* [*plural*]
television, radio, and newspapers: *These events were widely reported in the media.*

med·i·cal ♪ **AWL** /'mɛdɪkl/ *adjective*
(**HEALTH**) connected with medicine, hospitals, or doctors: *a medical student* • *medical treatment*

med·i·ca·tion /,mɛdɪ'keɪʃn/ *noun* [*count, noncount*]
(**HEALTH**) medicine that you take to treat an illness: *flu medications* • *Have you been remembering to take your medication?*

med·i·cine ♪ /'mɛdɪsn/ *noun* (**HEALTH**)
1 [*noncount*] the science of understanding illnesses and making sick people well again: *He's studying medicine.*
2 [*count, noncount*] a special chemical substance that helps you to get better when you are sick: *Take this medicine every morning.*

me·di·e·val /,mɪd'ivl/ *adjective*
(**HISTORY**) connected with the years between about 1100 and 1500 in Europe: *a medieval castle* ⊃ Look at **the Middle Ages**.

me·di·o·cre /,midi'oʊkər/ *adjective*
not very good: *The restaurant looks great, but I thought the food was pretty mediocre.*

me·di·um ♪ **AWL** /'midiəm/ *adjective*
not big and not small: *Would you like a small, medium, or large Coke?* • *He is of medium height.*

meet ♪ /mit/ *verb* (**meets, meet·ing, met** /mɛt/, **has met**)
1 to come together by chance or because you have planned it: *I met Kate in the library today.* • *Let's meet outside the restaurant at seven o'clock.*
2 to see and speak to someone for the first time: *Have you met Anne?*
3 to go to a place and wait for someone to arrive: *Can you meet me at the airport?*
4 to join together with something: *The two rivers meet in St. Louis.*

ə **about**   y **yes**   w **woman**   t̬ **butter**   eɪ **say**   aɪ **five**   ɔɪ **boy**   aʊ **now**   oʊ **go**

meet with someone to have a meeting with someone, usually to talk about something: *I'm meeting with my son's teacher today.*

meet·ing 🔑 /ˈmiṭɪŋ/ *noun* [count]
1 a time when people come together for a special reason, usually to talk about something: *We had a meeting to talk about the plans for a new pool.*
2 a time when two or more people come together: *Do you remember your first meeting with your husband?*

meg·a·byte /ˈmɛgəbaɪt/ (abbreviation **MB**) *noun* [count]
(**COMPUTERS**) a unit of computer memory, equal to about one million **BYTES** (= small units of information) ⊃ Look at **gigabyte**, **kilobyte**.

mel·o·dy /ˈmɛlədi/ *noun* [count] (*plural* **mel·o·dies**)
(**MUSIC**) a group of musical notes that make a nice sound when you play or sing them together: *This song has a lovely melody.* ⊃
SYNONYM tune

mel·on /ˈmɛlən/ *noun* [count]
a big, round, yellow or green fruit with a lot of seeds inside

melons

melt 🔑 /mɛlt/ *verb* (melts, melt·ing, melt·ed)
to warm something so that it becomes liquid; to get warmer so that it becomes liquid: *Melt the butter in a saucepan.* ◆ *The snow melted in the sunshine.*

melt·ing pot /ˈmɛltɪŋ pɑt/ *noun* [count]
a place where a lot of different cultures, ideas, etc. come together: *New York is a real melting pot.*

mem·ber 🔑 /ˈmɛmbər/ *noun* [count]
a person who is in a group: *Is she a member of the family?*

mem·ber·ship /ˈmɛmbərʃɪp/ *noun* [noncount]
being in a group or an organization: *Membership in the club costs $100 a year.*

mem·brane /ˈmɛmbreɪn/ *noun* [count]
(**BIOLOGY**) a thin layer that is found inside a plant, or inside a person's or an animal's body

mem·o /ˈmɛmoʊ/ *noun* [count] (*plural* **mem·os**)
(**BUSINESS**) a note that you write to a person who works with you: *I sent you a memo about the meeting on Friday.*

mem·o·ra·ble /ˈmɛmrəbl/ *adjective*
easy to remember because it is special in some way: *Their wedding was a very memorable day.*

me·mo·ri·al /məˈmɔriəl/ *noun* [count]
something that people build or do to help us remember someone, or something that happened: *The statue is a memorial to all the soldiers who died in the war.*

mem·o·rize /ˈmɛməraɪz/ *verb* (mem·o·riz·es, mem·o·riz·ing, mem·o·rized)
to learn something so that you can remember it exactly: *We have to memorize a poem for homework.*

mem·o·ry 🔑 /ˈmɛməri/ *noun* (*plural* **mem·o·ries**)
1 [count] the ability to remember things: *Ruth has a very good memory – she never forgets people's names.*
2 [count] something that you remember: *I have very happy memories of that vacation.*
3 [count, noncount] (**COMPUTERS**) the part of a computer that holds information

men plural of **man**

mend /mɛnd/ *verb* (mends, mend·ing, mend·ed)
to repair a hole in a piece of clothing: *Can you mend this sock?*

men's room /ˈmɛnz rum/ *noun* [count]
a room in a public building that has toilets for men to use: *Excuse me – where is the men's room?* ⊃ Look at **ladies' room**, **restroom**.

men·stru·ate /ˈmɛnstrueɪt/ *verb* (men·stru·ates, men·stru·at·ing, men·stru·at·ed) (*formal*)
(**BIOLOGY**) (used about women) to lose blood from the body once a month ⊃ Look at **period** (3).

men·tal 🔑 **AWL** /ˈmɛntl/ *adjective*
of or in your mind: *mental illness* ◆ *mental arithmetic* (= done in your head)
▶ **men·tal·ly** **AWL** /ˈmɛntəli/ *adverb*: *He is mentally ill.*

men·tal·i·ty **AWL** /mɛnˈtæləti/ *noun* [count] (*plural* **men·tal·i·ties**)
a type of mind or way of thinking: *a criminal mentality*

men·tion 🔑 /ˈmɛnʃn/ *verb* (men·tions, men·tion·ing, men·tioned)
to speak or write about something without giving much information: *Liz mentioned that she was going to buy a new car.* ◆ *He didn't mention Anna in his letter.*
not to mention words you use to add something to what you have just said; and also: *He has a big apartment in the city, not to mention a new house on the beach.*

æ **cat**   ɛ **ten**   i **see**   ɪ **sit**   ɑ **hot**   ɔ **saw**   ʌ **cup**   ʊ **put**   u **too**   **285**

▸ **men·tion** *noun* [*count, noncount*]: *There was no mention of the accident in the newspaper.*

men·u /ˈmɛnyu/ *noun* [*count*] (*plural* **men·us**)
1 a list of the food that you can choose in a restaurant: *What's on the menu tonight?* • *Can I have the menu, please?*
2 (**COMPUTERS**) a list on the screen of a computer that shows what you can do: *Go to the menu and click "New."*

me·ow /miˈaʊ/ *noun* [*count*]
a sound that a cat makes
▸ **me·ow** *verb* (**me·ows, me·ow·ing, me·owed**): *Why is the cat meowing?* ⟳ Look at **purr**.

mer·chan·dise /ˈmɚtʃəndaɪz/ *noun* [*noncount*] (*formal*)
things that are for sale: *We have a wide selection of merchandise.*

mer·chant /ˈmɚtʃənt/ *noun* [*count*]
(**BUSINESS**) a person who buys and sells things, especially from and to other countries: *She's a wine merchant.*

mer·cu·ry /ˈmɚkyəri/ *noun* [*noncount*] (symbol **Hg**)
a silver, liquid metal

mer·cy /ˈmɚsi/ *noun* [*noncount*]
being kind and not hurting someone who has done wrong: *The prisoners begged for mercy.*
be at the mercy of someone or **something** to have no power against someone or something that is strong: *Farmers are at the mercy of the weather.*

mere /mɪr/ *adjective*
only; not more than: *She was a mere child when her parents died.*

mere·ly /ˈmɪrli/ *adverb* (*formal*)
only: *I don't want to buy the book – I am merely asking how much it costs.* ⟳ **SYNONYM just**

merge /mɚdʒ/ *verb* (**merg·es, merg·ing, merged**)
to join together with something else: *Three small companies merged into one large one.*

mer·it¹ /ˈmɛrət/ *noun* [*count*]
the thing or things that are good about someone or something: *What are the merits of this plan?*

mer·it² /ˈmɛrət/ *verb* (**mer·its, mer·it·ing, mer·it·ed**) (*formal*)
to be good enough for something: *This suggestion merits further discussion.* ⟳ **SYNONYM deserve**

mer·maid /ˈmɚmeɪd/ *noun* [*count*]
a woman in stories who has a fish's tail and lives in the ocean

mer·ry /ˈmɛri/ *adjective* (**mer·ri·er, mer·ri·est**)
happy: *Merry Christmas!*

mer·ry-go-round /ˈmɛri goʊ raʊnd/ *noun* [*count*]
a big, round machine with models of animals or cars on it. Children can ride on it as it turns. ⟳ **SYNONYM carousel**

mess¹ ♪ /mɛs/ *noun* [*noncount*]
1 a lot of things that are not organized or neat, and that may be dirty: *My bedroom is in a real mess.* • *Don't make a mess in the kitchen.*
2 a person or thing that is not neat and clean: *My hair is a mess!*
3 a difficult situation: *She's in a terrible mess – she has no money and nowhere to live.*

mess² /mɛs/ *verb* (**mess·es, mess·ing, messed**)
mess around to behave in a silly way: *Stop messing around and finish your work!*
mess something up
1 to make something dirty or not neat: *Don't mess my hair up!*
2 to do something badly or to spoil something: *The bad weather messed up our plans for the weekend.*

mes·sage ♪ /ˈmɛsɪdʒ/ *noun* [*count*]
words that one person sends to another: *Could you give a message to Carl, please?* • *Mr. Willis is not here right now. Can I take a message?*

mes·sen·ger /ˈmɛsəndʒɚ/ *noun* [*count*]
a person who brings a message

mess·y ♪ /ˈmɛsi/ *adjective* (**mess·i·er, mess·i·est**)
1 dirty or not neat: *a messy kitchen*
2 making you or something dirty or not neat: *Painting is a messy job.*

met form of **meet**

met·al ♪ /ˈmɛtl/ *noun* [*count*]
(**CHEMISTRY**) a solid substance that is usually hard and shiny, such as iron, silver, or gold: *This chair is made of metal.* • *a metal box*

me·tal·lic /məˈtælɪk/ *adjective*
(**CHEMISTRY**) looking like metal or making a noise like one piece of metal hitting another: *metallic paint*

met·a·mor·pho·sis /ˌmɛtəˈmɔrfəsəs/ *noun* [*count*] (*plural* **met·a·mor·pho·ses** /ˌmɛtəˈmɔrfəsiz/) (*formal*)
(**BIOLOGY**) a complete change of form, as part of a body's natural development: *the metamorphosis of a tadpole into a frog*

met·a·phor /ˈmɛtəfɔr/ *noun* [*count, noncount*]
(**ENGLISH LANGUAGE ARTS**) a word or phrase that is used to describe something by comparing it to something else: *"She has a heart of stone" is a metaphor.* ⟳ Look at **simile**.
▸ **met·a·phor·i·cal** /ˌmɛtəˈfɔrɪkl/ *adjective*: *metaphorical language*

me·te·or /ˈmiṭiər/ *noun* [*count*]
a small piece of rock in space that makes a bright line in the sky when it travels near the earth

me·te·or·ol·o·gy /ˌmiṭiəˈrɑlədʒi/ *noun* [*noncount*]
(**GENERAL SCIENCE**) the study of weather and climate

me·ter /ˈmiṭər/ *noun* [*count*]
1 (abbreviation **m**) a measure of length. There are 100 **centimeters**, or around 39 inches, in a **meter**: *The wall is eight meters long.*
2 a machine that measures or counts something: *an electricity meter*

meth·od 🔑 **AWL** /ˈmɛθəd/ *noun* [*count*]
a way of doing something: *What is the best method of cooking beef?*

me·thod·i·cal **AWL** /məˈθɑdɪkl/ *adjective*
doing things in an organized and careful way: *Paul is a methodical worker.*

meth·od·ol·o·gy **AWL** /ˌmɛθəˈdɑlədʒi/ *noun* [*count, noncount*] (*plural* **meth·od·ol·o·gies**)
a way of doing something that is based on particular ideas and methods: *language teaching methodologies*

met·ric /ˈmɛtrɪk/ *adjective*
using the system of meters, grams, and liters (the **METRIC SYSTEM**) to measure things

met·ro·pol·i·tan /ˌmɛtrəˈpɑlətn/ *adjective*
connected with a large city: *the Detroit metropolitan area* (= the city and the area around it)

mg abbreviation of **milligram**

mice plural of **mouse**

mi·cro·chip /ˈmaɪkroʊtʃɪp/ *noun* [*count*]
(**COMPUTERS**) a very small thing inside a computer or a machine that makes it work

mi·cro·phone /ˈmaɪkrəfoʊn/ (also *informal* **mike** /maɪk/) *noun* [*count*]
a piece of electrical equipment that makes sounds louder or records them so you can listen to them later

mi·cro·scope
/ˈmaɪkrəskoʊp/ *noun* [*count*]
(**GENERAL SCIENCE**) a piece of equipment with special glass in it that makes very small things look much bigger: *We looked at the hair under a microscope.*

microscope

lens

mi·cro·scop·ic /ˌmaɪkrəˈskɑpɪk/ *adjective*
so small that you cannot see it without a **MICROSCOPE**: *microscopic organisms*

mi·cro·wave /ˈmaɪkrəweɪv/ (also **mi·cro·wave ov·en** /ˌmaɪkrəweɪv ˈʌvən/) *noun* [*count*]
a type of oven that cooks or heats food very quickly using electric waves
▶ **mi·cro·wave** *verb* (**mi·cro·waves, mi·cro·wav·ing, mi·cro·waved**)
to cook or heat something in a **microwave**

Prefix

mid-
(used with nouns) in the middle of: *a midafternoon snack* • *It exploded in midair.* • *the Midwest* (= the northern central part of the U.S.) • *the mid-eighteenth century*

---

mid·day /ˌmɪdˈdeɪ/ *noun* [*noncount*]
twelve o'clock in the day: *We met at midday.* ⊃ **SYNONYM noun** ⊃ Look at **midnight**.

mid·dle 🔑 /ˈmɪdl/ *noun* [*singular*]
1 the part that is the same distance from the sides, edges, or ends of something: *A peach has a pit in the middle.*
2 the time after the beginning and before the end: *The phone rang in the middle of the night.*
be in the middle of doing something to be busy doing something: *I can't talk to you now – I'm in the middle of cooking dinner.*
▶ **mid·dle** *adjective*: *There are three houses, and ours is the middle one.*

mid·dle-aged /ˌmɪdl ˈeɪdʒd/ *adjective*
not old and not young; between the ages of around 40 and 60: *a middle-aged man*

the Mid·dle Ag·es /ðə ˌmɪdl ˈeɪdʒɪz/ *noun* [*plural*]
(**HISTORY**) the years between about 1100 and 1500 in Europe ⊃ Look at **medieval**.

the mid·dle class /ðə ˌmɪdl ˈklæs/ *noun* [*singular*]
the group of people in a society who are neither very rich nor very poor, and which includes business and professional people: *tax benefits for the middle class*
▶ **mid·dle-class** /ˌmɪdl ˈklæs/ *adjective*: *students from middle-class families* ⊃ Look at **the upper class, the working class**.

the Mid·dle East /ðə ˌmɪdl ˈist/ *noun* [*singular*]
(**GEOGRAPHY**) the group of countries in S.W. Asia and N.E. Africa ⊃ Look at **the Far East**.

mid·dle name /ˈmɪdl neɪm/ *noun* [*count*]
a name that comes between your first name and your family name ⊃ Look at the note at **name**[1].

mid·dle school /ˈmɪdl skul/ *noun* [*count*]
a school for children between the ages of about 11 and 14 ⊃ Look at the note at **elementary school**.

mid·night 🔑 /ˈmɪdnaɪt/ *noun* [*noncount*]
twelve o'clock at night: *We left the party at midnight.* ⊃ Look at **midday**.

mid·way /ˌmɪdˈweɪ/ adverb
in the middle: *Our farm is **midway** between Lincoln and Omaha.* ➔ SYNONYM **halfway**

the Mid·west /ðə ˌmɪdˈwɛst/ noun [singular]
(GEOGRAPHY) the northern central part of the U.S.: *I grew up in the Midwest.*

mid·wife /ˈmɪdwaɪf/ noun [count] (plural mid·wives /ˈmɪdwaɪvz/)
(HEALTH) a person whose job is to help women give birth to babies

might 🖋 /maɪt/ modal verb
1 a word that shows what will perhaps happen or what is possible: *Don't run, because you might fall.* ♦ *"Where's Anne?" "I don't know – she might be in the kitchen."*
2 used as the form of "may" when you repeat later what someone has said: *He said he might be late* (= his words were "I may be late").
3 (formal) a word that you use to suggest something in a polite way: *You might want to call him first.* ➔ Look at the note at **modal verb**.

might·y /ˈmaɪti/ adjective (might·i·er, might·i·est) (formal)
very great, strong, or powerful: *He hit him with a mighty blow across his shoulder.*

mi·graine /ˈmaɪɡreɪn/ noun [count, noncount]
(HEALTH) a very bad pain in your head that makes you feel sick

mi·grant AWL /ˈmaɪɡrənt/ noun [count]
a person who goes to another area or another country to find work: *migrant farm workers*

mi·grate AWL /ˈmaɪɡreɪt/ verb (mi·grates, mi·grat·ing, mi·grat·ed)
1 (BIOLOGY) (used about animals and birds) to move from one part of the world to another every year
2 (used about large numbers of people) to go to live and work in another place
▶ **mi·gra·tion** AWL /maɪˈɡreɪʃn/ noun [count, noncount]: *the annual migration of the reindeer*

mi·gra·to·ry AWL /ˈmaɪɡreɪtɔri/ adjective
(BIOLOGY) (used about animals and birds) moving from one part of the world to another every year: *migratory birds*

mike /maɪk/ noun [count] (informal) = **microphone**

mild /maɪld/ adjective (mild·er, mild·est)
1 not strong; not very bad: *a mild illness* ♦ *a mild winter*
2 (used about food) not having a strong flavor: *This cheese has a mild taste.*

mile 🖋 /maɪl/ noun
1 [count] a measure of length, equal to 1.6 kilometers. There are 1,760 yards, or 5,280 feet, in a mile: *We live three miles from the ocean.*
2 miles [plural] a long way: *We've already walked for miles.*

mile·age /ˈmaɪlɪdʒ/ noun [count, noncount]
the distance that a vehicle has traveled, measured in miles: *The car is five years old, but it has very low mileage.*

mile·stone /ˈmaɪlstoʊn/ noun [count]
a very important event in the development of something: *Finally passing the exam was a real milestone for her.*

mil·i·tar·y¹ AWL /ˈmɪləˌtɛri/ adjective
connected with soldiers or the army, navy, etc.: *a military camp* ♦ *military action*

mil·i·tar·y² AWL /ˈmɪləˌtɛri/ noun [singular] **the military**
a country's soldiers who fight on land, on water, or in the air: *Our son is **in the military**.* ♦ *to join the military* ➔ SYNONYM **the armed forces**

milk¹ 🖋 /mɪlk/ noun [noncount]
the white liquid that a mother makes in her body to give to her baby. People drink the **milk** of cows and some other animals: *Do you want milk in your coffee?*

milk² /mɪlk/ verb (milks, milk·ing, milked)
to take milk from a cow or another animal

milk·shake
/ˈmɪlkʃeɪk/ noun [count, noncount]
a drink made of milk with the flavor of chocolate or fruit added to it: *a strawberry milkshake*

milkshake

milk·y /ˈmɪlki/ adjective (milk·i·er, milk·i·est)
with a lot of milk in it: *milky coffee*

the Milk·y Way /ðə ˌmɪlki ˈweɪ/ noun [singular]
the system of stars that contains our sun and its planets, seen as a band of light in the night sky

mill /mɪl/ noun [count]
1 a building where a machine makes flour from grain ➔ Look at **windmill**.
2 (BUSINESS) a factory where one material is made, for example cloth or paper: *a paper mill*

mil·len·ni·um /məˈlɛniəm/ noun [count] (plural mil·len·ni·a /məˈlɛniə/ or mil·len·ni·ums)

> ❶ SPELLING
> Remember! You spell **millennium** with LL and NN.

a period of a thousand years

mil·li·gram /ˈmɪləɡræm/ (abbreviation **mg**) noun [count]
a measure of weight. There are 1,000 **milligrams** in a **gram**.

mil·li·li·ter /ˈmɪləliṭər/ *noun* [count] (abbreviation **ml**)
a measure of liquid. There are 1,000 **milliliters** in a **liter**.

mil·li·me·ter /ˈmɪləmiṭər/ (abbreviation **mm**) *noun* [count]
a measure of length. There are 1,000 **millimeters** in a **meter**: *60mm*

mil·lion 🔑 /ˈmɪlyən/ *number*
1 1,000,000; one thousand thousand: *About 4 million people live in this city* .

Grammar

- Be careful! When you use **million** with a number, don't add an "s": *six million dollars*
- If there is no number mentioned, then add an "s": *millions of dollars*

2 millions (*informal*) a lot: *I have millions of things to do.*
▶ **mil·lionth** /ˈmɪlyənθ/ *pronoun, adjective, pronoun, noun* [count]
1,000,000th: *Our millionth customer will receive a prize.* • *three millionths of a second*

mil·lion·aire /ˌmɪlyəˈnɛr/ *noun* [count]
a person who has more than one million dollars; a very rich person

mime /maɪm/ *noun* [count, noncount]
a way of telling a story or telling someone something by moving your face, hands, and body without speaking: *The show is a combination of dance and mime.*
▶ **mime** *verb* (mimes, mim·ing, mimed): *He mimed that he was hungry.*

mim·ic /ˈmɪmɪk/ (mim·ics, mim·ick·ing, mim·icked) *verb*
to copy the way someone moves and speaks in order to entertain people
▶ **mim·ic** *noun* [count]: *Sally's a great mimic.*

min. abbreviation of **minute**

mince /mɪns/ *verb* (minc·es, minc·ing, minced)
to cut food into very small pieces: *Mince the onions.*

mind¹ 🔑 /maɪnd/ *noun* [count]
the part of you that thinks and remembers: *He has a very quick mind.*
be or **go out of your mind** (*informal*) to be or become crazy: *Where were you? I was going out of my mind with worry.*
change your mind to have an idea, then decide to do something different: *I planned a vacation in California and then changed my mind and went to Texas.*
have something on your mind to be worried about something: *I have a lot on my mind right now.*

make up your mind to decide something: *Should I buy the blue shirt or the red one? I can't make up my mind.*

mind² 🔑 /maɪnd/ *verb* (minds, mind·ing, mind·ed)
to feel unhappy or angry about something: *Do you mind if I sit here?* • *I don't mind the heat at all.*
do you mind ...?; would you mind ...? please could you...?: *It's cold – would you mind closing the window?*
never mind don't worry; it doesn't matter: *"I forgot your book." "Never mind, I don't need it today."*

mine¹ 🔑 /maɪn/ *pronoun*
something that belongs to me: *That bike is mine.* • *Are those books mine or yours?*

mine² /maɪn/ *noun* [count]
1 a very big hole in the ground, where people work to get things like silver or gold: *a coal mine*
2 a bomb that is hidden under the ground or under water
▶ **mine** *verb* (mines, min·ing, mined): *Diamonds are mined in South Africa.*

min·er /ˈmaɪnər/ *noun* [count]
a person who works in a mine

min·er·al /ˈmɪnərəl/ *noun* [count]
Minerals are things like gold, salt, or oil that come from the ground and that people use.

min·er·al wa·ter /ˈmɪnərəl ˌwɔṭər/ *noun* [noncount]
water with MINERALS in it, which comes from the ground: *a bottle of mineral water*

min·gle /ˈmɪŋgl/ *verb* (min·gles, min·gling, min·gled)
to mix with other things or people: *The colors mingled together to make brown.* • *Police officers mingled with the crowd.*

Prefix

mini-
(in nouns) very small: *a minibus* • *a miniskirt*

min·i·a·ture /ˈmɪnətʃʊr/ *adjective*
very small; much smaller than usual: *a miniature railroad*

min·i·mal AWL /ˈmɪnəməl/ *adjective*
very small in amount: *The project has minimal support.*

min·i·mize AWL /ˈmɪnəmaɪz/ *verb* (min·i·miz·es, min·i·miz·ing, min·i·mized)
to make something as small as possible: *We want to minimize the risk to the public.*

min·i·mum AWL /'mɪnəməm/ noun [singular]
the smallest size, amount, or number that is possible: *We need a minimum of six people to play this game.*
▶ **min·i·mum** AWL adjective: *What is the minimum age for leaving school in your country?*
⊃ ANTONYM **maximum**

min·i·mum wage /ˌmɪnəməm 'weɪdʒ/ noun [singular]
the lowest amount of money that you can legally be paid for an hour of work: *He works in a gas station earning minimum wage.*

min·i·skirt /'mɪnɪskərt/ noun [count]
a very short skirt

min·is·ter /'mɪnəstər/ noun [count]
1 (RELIGION) a religious leader in some Christian churches
2 (POLITICS) one of the most important people in the government in some countries: *the Minister of Education*

min·is·try AWL /'mɪnəstri/ noun [count] (plural min·is·tries)
(POLITICS) (in some countries) a part of the government that controls one special thing: *the Ministry of Finance*

mi·nor¹ AWL /'maɪnər/ adjective
not very big or important: *Don't worry – it's only a minor problem.* ◆ *a minor road* ⊃ ANTONYM **major**

mi·nor² AWL /'maɪnər/ noun [count]
1 a person who is not old enough to do something legally: *She was arrested for selling alcohol to minors.*
2 a subject that you study in college, but not as your main subject: *Matthew majored in history, with a minor in Italian.* ⊃ Look at **major²**(1).

mi·nor³ AWL /'maɪnər/ verb (mi·nors, mi·nor·ing, mi·nored)
minor in something to study something in college, but not as your main subject: *Maggie majored in economics and minored in psychology.* ⊃ Look at **major³**.

mi·nor·i·ty AWL /mə'nɔrəti/ noun (plural mi·nor·i·ties)
1 [singular] the smaller part of a group: *Only a minority of the students speak English.* ⊃ ANTONYM **majority**
2 [count] a small group of people who are of a different race or religion from most of the people where they live: *ethnic minorities*

mi·nor league /ˌmaɪnər 'lig/ noun [count]
(SPORTS) the groups of baseball teams that do not play at the highest level: *He played in the minor league for three years.* ⊃ Look at **major league**.

mint /mɪnt/ noun
1 [noncount] a small plant with a strong fresh taste and smell, which you put in food and drinks: *mint tea*
2 [count] a candy made from this plant: *Would you like a mint?*

mi·nus¹ /'maɪnəs/ preposition
1 (MATH) less; when you take away: *Six minus two is four (6−2=4).* ⊃ ANTONYM **plus**
2 below zero: *The temperature will fall to minus ten degrees.*

mi·nus² /'maɪnəs/ adjective
1 (MATH) lower than zero: *a minus number*
2 (used after a letter grade on students' work) a little lower than: *I got an A minus (= A−) on the test.* ⊃ ANTONYM **plus**

mi·nus³ /'maɪnəs/ noun [count] (plural mi·nus·es)
1 (also **mi·nus sign** /'maɪnəs saɪn/) (MATH) the symbol (−), which is used to show that a number is below zero or that you should take the second number away from the first
2 a disadvantage: *Let's consider the pluses and minuses of moving out of the city.* ⊃ ANTONYM **plus**

mi·nute¹ /'mɪnət/ noun [count]
1 (abbreviation **min.**) a measure of time. There are 60 seconds in a **minute** and 60 **minutes** in an hour: *It's nine minutes after six.* ◆ *The train leaves in ten minutes.*
2 a short time: *Just a minute – I'll get my coat.* ◆ *Do you have a minute? I'd like to talk to you.* ⊃ SYNONYM **moment**
in a minute very soon: *I'll be ready in a minute.*
the minute as soon as: *Call me the minute you arrive.*

mi·nute² /maɪ'nut/ adjective
very small: *I can't read his writing – it's minute.* ⊃ SYNONYM **tiny**

mir·a·cle /'mɪrəkl/ noun [count]
a wonderful and surprising thing that happens and that you cannot explain: *It's a miracle that he wasn't killed.*

mi·rac·u·lous /mə'rækyələs/ adjective
wonderful and surprising: *a miraculous escape*
▶ **mi·rac·u·lous·ly** /mə'rækyələsli/ adverb: *Miraculously, no one was hurt.*

mir·ror /'mɪrər/ noun [count]
a piece of special glass where you can see yourself: *Look in the mirror.*

Prefix

mis-

(in verbs and nouns) bad or wrong; in a bad way or in the wrong way: *to misbehave* ◆ *to misunderstand* ◆ *a misunderstanding*

mis·be·have /ˌmɪsbɪˈheɪv/ verb (mis·be·haves, mis·be·hav·ing, mis·be·haved)
to behave badly: *Children who misbehaved were punished.* ➲ ANTONYM **behave**

mis·cel·la·ne·ous /ˌmɪsəˈleɪniəs/ (abbreviation **misc.**) adjective
consisting of many different types or things: *a box of miscellaneous items for sale*

mis·chief /ˈmɪstʃəf/ noun [noncount]
bad behavior that is not very serious: *Don't get into mischief while I'm out!*

mis·chie·vous /ˈmɪstʃəvəs/ adjective
A **mischievous** child likes to behave badly, but not in a serious way: *He gave a mischievous grin.* ➲ SYNONYM **naughty**

mis·er·a·ble /ˈmɪzərəbl/ adjective
1 feeling very sad: *I waited in the rain for an hour, feeling cold, wet, and miserable.*
2 making you feel sad: *miserable weather*

mis·er·y /ˈmɪzəri/ noun [noncount]
a strong feeling of sadness, pain etc.: *the misery of war*

mis·for·tune /ˌmɪsˈfɔrtʃən/ noun [count, noncount] (formal)
something bad that happens; bad luck: *He has known great misfortune.*

mis·lead /ˌmɪsˈlid/ verb (mis·leads, mis·lead·ing, mis·led, has mis·led)
to make someone believe something that is not true: *You misled me when you said you could give me a job.*
▶ **mis·lead·ing** /ˌmɪsˈlidɪŋ/ adjective: *a misleading advertisement*

mis·print /ˈmɪsprɪnt/ noun [count]
a mistake in printing or typing ➲ Look at **typo**.

Miss /mɪs/ noun
a word that you use before the name of a girl or woman who is not married: *Dear Miss Smith,…* ➲ Look at the note at **Ms**.

miss¹ /mɪs/ verb (miss·es, miss·ing, missed)
1 to not hit or catch something: *I tried to hit the ball, but I missed.*
2 to not see or hear something: *You missed a good program on TV last night.* ◆ *Our house is the one on the corner – you can't miss it.*
3 to be too late for a train, bus, airplane, or boat: *I just missed my bus.* ➲ ANTONYM **catch**
4 to feel sad about someone or something that has gone: *I'll miss you when you leave.*
miss out to not have a chance to have or do something: *You'll miss out on all the fun if you stay home!*

miss² /mɪs/ noun [count] (plural miss·es)
(SPORTS) a failure to hit, catch, or reach something you are trying to hit, catch, or reach:

After several misses, he finally managed to hit the target. ➲ Look at **catch²**(1).

mis·sile /ˈmɪsl/ noun [count]
1 a powerful weapon that can be sent long distances through the air and then explodes: *nuclear missiles*
2 a thing that you throw at someone to hurt them

mis·sing /ˈmɪsɪŋ/ adjective
lost, or not in the usual place: *The police are looking for the missing child.* ◆ *My bag is missing. Have you seen it?*

mis·sion /ˈmɪʃn/ noun [count]
a trip to do a special job: *They were sent on a mission to the moon.*

mis·sion·ar·y /ˈmɪʃəˌnɛri/ noun [count] (plural mis·sion·ar·ies)
(RELIGION) a person who goes to another country to teach people about a religion

mis·spell /ˌmɪsˈspɛl/ verb (mis·spells, mis·spell·ing, mis·spelled)
(ENGLISH LANGUAGE ARTS) to use one or more wrong letters when you are writing a word: *People often misspell the word "embarrassed."*

mist /mɪst/ noun [count, noncount]
thin clouds near the ground that are difficult to see through: *Early in the morning, the fields were covered in mist.*
▶ **mist·y** adjective (mist·i·er, mist·i·est): *a misty morning*

mis·take¹ /mɪˈsteɪk/ noun [count]
something that you think or do that is wrong: *You made a lot of spelling mistakes in this letter.* ◆ *It was a mistake to go by bus – the trip took two hours!*

Which word?

Mistake or fault?
- When you **make a mistake** you do something wrong: *Try not to make any mistakes on your exam.*
- If you do something bad it is **your fault**: *It's my fault we're late. I lost the tickets.*

---

by mistake when you did not plan to do it: *Sorry, I took your book by mistake.*

mis·take² /mɪˈsteɪk/ verb (mis·takes, mis·tak·ing, mis·took /mɪˈstʊk/, has mis·tak·en /mɪˈsteɪkən/)
to think that someone or something is a different person or thing: *I'm sorry – I mistook you for my cousin.*

mis·tak·en /mɪˈsteɪkən/ adjective
wrong: *I said she was 25 but I was mistaken – she's 27.* ◆ *a case of mistaken identity* (= when people think that a person is someone else) ➲ Look at the note at **wrong¹**.

---

mis·treat /ˌmɪsˈtrit/ *verb* (mis·treats, mis·treat·ing, mis·treat·ed)
to be cruel to a person or an animal

mis·un·der·stand /ˌmɪsʌndərˈstænd/ *verb* (mis·un·der·stands, mis·un·der·stand·ing, mis·un·der·stood /ˌmɪsʌndərˈstʊd/, has mis·un·der·stood)
to not understand something correctly: *I'm sorry, I misunderstood what you said.*

mis·un·der·stand·ing /ˌmɪsʌndərˈstændɪŋ/ *noun* [count]
a situation in which someone does not understand something correctly: *I think **there's been a misunderstanding**. I ordered two tickets, not four.*

mit·ten /ˈmɪtn/ *noun* [count]
a thing that you wear to keep your hand warm. It has one part for your thumb and another part for your other fingers. ⊃ Look at the picture at **glove**.

mix 🔑 /mɪks/ *verb* (mix·es, mix·ing, mixed)
1 to put different things together to make something new: *Mix yellow and blue paint **together** to make green.*
2 to join together to make something new: *Oil and water don't mix.*
3 to be with and talk to other people: *In my job, I **mix with** a lot of different people.*
mix someone or **something up** to think that one person or thing is a different person or thing: *People often mix Mark up **with** his brother.*
mix something up to put something in the wrong order or place: *Don't mix up my papers!*

mixed /mɪkst/ *adjective*
containing different kinds of people or things: *a mixed salad*

mix·er /ˈmɪksər/ *noun* [count]
a machine that mixes things together: *a cement mixer*

mix·ture 🔑 /ˈmɪkstʃər/ *noun* [count, noncount]
something that you make by mixing different things together: *Air is **a mixture of** gases.* ◆ *a cake mixture*

mix-up /ˈmɪks ʌp/ *noun* [count]
a confused situation, usually because someone has made a mistake: *There was a mix-up with the airline, and we got booked on the wrong flight.*

ml abbreviation of **milliliter**

mm abbreviation of **millimeter**

moan /moʊn/ *verb* (moans, moan·ing, moaned)
1 to make a long, sad sound when you are hurt or very unhappy: *He was **moaning with** pain.*
2 (*informal*) to talk a lot about what is wrong about something: *He's always **moaning about** the weather.* ⊃ SYNONYM **complain**
▸ **moan** *noun* [count]: *I heard a loud moan.*

mob /mɑb/ *noun* [count]
a big, noisy group of people who are shouting or fighting

mo·bile /ˈmoʊbl/ *adjective*
able to move easily from place to place: *A mobile library visits my neighborhood every week.*

mo·bile home
/ˌmoʊbl ˈhoʊm/ *noun* [count]
a small building for people to live in. It is made in a factory and can be moved with a truck. ⊃ SYNONYM **trailer**

mobile home

mock /mɑk/ *verb* (mocks, mock·ing, mocked) (*formal*)
to laugh at someone or something in an unkind way: *The other children mocked her old-fashioned clothes.*

mod·al verb /ˈmoʊdl vərb/ (also **mod·al**) *noun* [count]
(**ENGLISH LANGUAGE ARTS**) a verb, for example "might," "can," or "must," which you use with another verb

Grammar

- **Can, could, may, might, should, must, will, shall, would,** and **ought to** are modal verbs.
- Modal verbs do not have an "s" in the "he/she" form: *She can drive.* (NOT *She cans drive.*)
- After modal verbs (except **ought to**), you use the infinitive without "to": *I must go now.* (NOT *I must to go.*)
- You make questions and negative sentences without "do" or "did": *Will you come with me?* (NOT *Do you will come?*); *They might not know.* (NOT *They don't might know.*)

mode AWL /moʊd/ *noun*
1 [count] (*formal*) a type of something or way of doing something: *modes of transportation*
2 [count, noncount] one of the ways in which a machine can work: *My laptop's in **sleep mode** (= to save power).*

mod·el¹ 🔑 /ˈmɑdl/ *noun* [count]
1 a small copy of something: *a **model of** the Empire State Building* ◆ *a model airplane*
2 one of the cars, machines, etc. that a certain company makes: *Have you seen their **latest model**?*
3 a person or thing that is a good example to copy: *He's a model student.* ⊃ Look at **role model**.

4 a person who wears clothes at a special show or for photographs, so that people will see them and buy them

5 (ART) a person who sits or stands so that an artist can draw, paint, or photograph them

mod·el² /ˈmɑdl/ *verb* (mod·els, mod·el·ing, mod·eled)
to wear and show clothes as a model: *Kate modeled swimsuits at the fashion show.*

mo·dem /ˈmoʊdəm/ *noun* [count]
(COMPUTERS) a piece of equipment that uses a telephone line to connect two computers

mod·er·ate /ˈmɑdərət/ *adjective*
not too much and not too little: *Cook the vegetables over a moderate heat.*

mod·ern 🔑 /ˈmɑdərn/ *adjective*
of the present time; of the kind that is usual now: *modern art • The airport is very modern.*

mod·ern·ize /ˈmɑdərnaɪz/ *verb* (mod·ern·iz·es, mod·ern·iz·ing, mod·ern·ized)
to make something more modern and more suitable for use today: *We need to modernize our factories.*
▶ **mod·ern·i·za·tion** /ˌmɑdərnəˈzeɪʃn/ *noun* [noncount]

mod·est /ˈmɑdəst/ *adjective*
1 not talking much about good things that you have done or about things that you can do well: *You didn't tell me you could sing so well – you're very modest!*
2 not very big: *a modest increase in price*
▶ **mod·est·ly** /ˈmɑdəstli/ *adverb*: *He spoke quietly and modestly about his success.*
▶ **mod·es·ty** /ˈmɑdəsti/ *noun* [noncount]: *She accepted the prize with her usual modesty.*

mod·i·fy [AWL] /ˈmɑdəfaɪ/ *verb* (mod·i·fies, mod·i·fy·ing, mod·i·fied, has mod·i·fied)
to change something a little: *We need to modify the original plan.*
▶ **mod·i·fi·ca·tion** [AWL] /ˌmɑdəfəˈkeɪʃn/ *noun* [count, noncount]: *New modifications make the software run even faster.*

moist /mɔɪst/ *adjective*
a little wet: *Remember to keep the earth moist or the plant will die.*

mois·ture /ˈmɔɪstʃər/ *noun* [noncount]
small drops of water on something or in the air

mois·tur·ize /ˈmɔɪstʃəraɪz/ *verb* (mois·tur·iz·es, mois·tur·iz·ing, mois·tur·ized)
to put special cream on your skin to make it less dry

mo·lar /ˈmoʊlər/ *noun* [count]
(BIOLOGY) one of the large teeth in the back of your mouth

mold¹ /moʊld/ *noun*
1 [count] a container that you pour liquid into. The liquid then becomes hard (SETS) and takes the shape of the container: *They poured the chocolate into a heart-shaped mold.*
2 [noncount] a soft green, gray, or blue substance that grows on food that is too old
▶ **mold·y** /ˈmoʊldi/ (mold·i·er, mold·i·est) *adjective*: *moldy cheese*

mold² /moʊld/ *verb* (molds, mold·ing, mold·ed)
to make something soft into a certain shape: *The children molded animals out of clay.*

mole /moʊl/ *noun* [count]
1 a small gray or brown animal that lives under the ground and makes tunnels
2 a small dark spot on a person's skin

mol·e·cule /ˈmɑləkyul/ *noun* [count]
(CHEMISTRY) the smallest part into which a substance can be divided without changing its chemical nature ⊃ Look at **atom**.
▶ **mo·lec·u·lar** /məˈlɛkyələr/ *adjective*: *molecular biology*

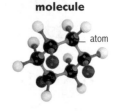

molecule

atom

mol·ten /ˈmoʊltn/ *adjective*
(CHEMISTRY) **Molten** metal or rock is liquid, because it is extremely hot: *molten lava*

mom 🔑 /mɑm/ *noun* [count] (informal)
mother: *This is my mom. • Can I have an apple, Mom?*

mo·ment 🔑 /ˈmoʊmənt/ *noun*
1 [count] a very short time: *He thought for a moment before he answered. • Can you wait a moment?*
2 [singular] a particular point in time: *At that moment, the phone rang.*
at the moment now: *She's on vacation at the moment, but she'll be back next week.*
in a moment very soon: *He'll be here in a moment.*
the moment as soon as: *Tell Jim to call me the moment he arrives.*

mo·men·tum /moʊˈmɛntəm/ *noun* [noncount]
the force that makes something move faster and faster: *The ball gained momentum as it rolled downhill.*

mom·my /ˈmɑmi/ *noun* [count] (plural mom·mies) (informal)
a word for "mother" that children use

Mon. abbreviation of **Monday**

mon·arch /ˈmɑnərk; ˈmɑnɑrk/ *noun* [count]
(POLITICS) a king or queen

---

mon·ar·chy /ˈmɑnərki/ *noun* [*count*] (*plural* **mon·ar·chies**)
(**POLITICS**) a country that has a king or queen ⊃ Look at **republic**.

mon·as·ter·y /ˈmɑnəˌstɛri/ *noun* [*count*] (*plural* **mon·as·ter·ies**)
(**RELIGION**) a place where religious men (called **MONKS**) live together ⊃ Look at **convent**.

Mon·day 🔊 /ˈmʌndeɪ; ˈmʌndi/ *noun* [*count, noncount*] (abbreviation **Mon.**)
the day of the week after Sunday and before Tuesday, the first day of the working week

money

bill

penny   **nickel**   **dime**   **quarter**

mon·ey 🔊 /ˈmʌni/ *noun* [*noncount*]

ⓘ PRONUNCIATION
The word **money** sounds like **funny**.

what you use when you buy or sell something: *How much money did you spend?* ◆ *This jacket cost a lot of money.* ◆ *The book made a lot of money.*

Word building

- Money consists of **coins** (= small, round, metal things) and **bills** (= pieces of paper). This is called **cash**: *I don't have much cash – can I pay by check?*
- The coins that you have in your bag or pocket are called **change**: *Do you have any change for the bus?*
- The money someone gives you in a store if you pay too much is also called **change**: *Here's your change.*

mon·i·tor¹ **AWL** /ˈmɑnəṭər/ *noun* [*count*]
(**COMPUTERS**) a machine that shows pictures or information on a screen like a television: *a PC with a 17-inch monitor* ⊃ Look at the picture at **computer**.

mon·i·tor² **AWL** /ˈmɑnəṭər/ *verb* (**mon·i·tors, mon·i·tor·ing, mon·i·tored**)
to check or watch something to see if it changes: *Scientists are monitoring pollution levels in the lake.*

monk /mʌŋk/ *noun* [*count*]
(**RELIGION**) a religious man who lives with other religious men in a special building (called a **MONASTERY**) ⊃ Look at **nun**.

mon·key /ˈmʌŋki/ *noun* [*count*] (*plural* **mon·keys**)
an animal that has a long tail and can climb trees

monkey

mon·o·logue (also **mon·o·log**) /ˈmɑnəlɔg; ˈmɑnəlɑg/ *noun* [*count*]
(**ENGLISH LANGUAGE ARTS**) a long speech by one person, for example in a play

mo·nop·o·ly /məˈnɑpəli/ *noun* [*count*] (*plural* **mo·nop·o·lies**)
(**BUSINESS**) the control of an industry or service by only one company: *The government passed a law to prohibit monopolies in the telephone industry.*

mo·not·o·nous /məˈnɑtn·əs/ *adjective*
always the same and therefore very boring: *It's a very monotonous job.*

mon·soon /ˌmɑnˈsun/ *noun* [*count*]
the season when very heavy rain falls in Southern Asia

mon·ster /ˈmɑnstər/ *noun* [*count*]
an animal in stories that is big, ugly, and scary

month 🔊 /mʌnθ/ *noun* [*count*]
1 one of the twelve parts of a year: *December is the last month of the year.* ◆ *We went to my brother's house last month.*

Word building

- The **months** of the year are: January, February, March, April, May, June, July, August, September, October, November, December.
- We use "in" with months: *My birthday is in September,* or "this," "next," or "last": *We're getting married next May.* ◆ *I graduated last June.*

2 about four weeks: *She was in the hospital for a month.*

month·ly /'mʌnθli/ adjective, adverb
happening or coming every month or once a month: *a monthly magazine* • *I am paid monthly.*

mon·u·ment /'mɑnyəmənt/ noun [count]
a thing that is built to help people remember a person or something that happened: *This is a monument to Paul Revere.*

moo /mu/ noun [count]
the sound that a cow makes
▶ **moo** verb (moos, moo·ing, mooed): *Cows were mooing in the barn.*

mood /mud/ noun [count, noncount]
the way that you feel at a particular time: *Dad is in a bad mood because he lost his glasses.* • *Our teacher was in a very good mood today.* • *I'm not in the mood for a party.*

mood·y /'mudi/ adjective (mood·i·er, mood·i·est)
If you are **moody**, you often change and become angry or unhappy without warning: *Teenagers can be very moody.*

moon /mun/ noun
1 the moon [singular] the big object that shines in the sky at night: *When was the first landing on the moon?*
2 [count] an object like the moon that moves around another planet: *How many moons does that planet have?*

moon·light /'munlaɪt/ noun [noncount]
the light from the moon

moor /mʊr/ verb (moors, moor·ing, moored)
to tie a boat or ship to something so that it will stay in one place

moose /mus/ noun
[count] (plural **moose**)
a type of large **DEER** with large flat horns (called **ANTLERS**)

moose

mop /mɑp/ noun
[count]
a thing with a long handle that you use for washing floors
▶ **mop** verb (mops, mop·ping, mopped): *I mopped the floor.*

mo·ped /'moʊpɛd/ noun [count]
a vehicle like a bicycle with a small engine

mor·al¹ /'mɔrəl/ adjective
connected with what people think is right or wrong: *Some people do not eat meat for moral reasons.* • *a moral problem* ⊃ Look at **immoral**.
▶ **mor·al·ly** /'mɔrəli/ adverb: *It's morally wrong to tell lies.*

mor·al² /'mɔrəl/ noun
1 morals [plural] ideas about what is right and wrong: *These people have no morals.*
2 [count] a lesson about what is right and wrong, which you can learn from a story or from something that happens: *The moral of the story is that we should be kind to animals.*

mo·rale /mə'ræl/ noun [noncount]
how happy, sad, etc. a group of people feel at a particular time: *After losing another game, the team's morale was low.*

more¹ /mɔr/ adjective, pronoun
a bigger amount or number of something: *You have more money than I have.* • *Can I have some more sugar in my tea?* • *We need two more chairs.* • *There aren't any more chocolates.* • *Tell me more about your job.* ⊃ Look at **most**. ⊃ **ANTONYM less, fewer**

more² /mɔr/ adverb
1 a word that makes an adjective or adverb stronger: *Your book was more expensive than mine.* • *Please speak more slowly.*
2 a bigger amount or number: *I like Anna more than her brother.* ⊃ Look at **most**. ⊃ **ANTONYM less**
more or less almost, but not exactly: *We are more or less the same age.* ⊃ **SYNONYM roughly**
once more (formal) again: *Spring will soon be here once more.* ⊃ Look at **anymore**.

more·o·ver /mɔr'oʊvər/ adverb (formal)
(used in writing to add another fact) also: *This group did the best work. Moreover, they completed the work quickly.* ⊃ **SYNONYM furthermore**

morn·ing /'mɔrnɪŋ/ noun [count]
the first part of the day, between the time when the sun comes up and the middle of the day: *I went swimming this morning.* • *I'm going to my aunt's house tomorrow morning.* • *The letter arrived on Tuesday morning.* • *I felt sick all morning.* • *I start work at nine o'clock in the morning.*
good morning (formal) words that you say when you see someone for the first time in the morning
in the morning tomorrow during the morning: *I'll see you in the morning.*

mort·gage /'mɔrgɪdʒ/ noun [count]
money that you borrow to buy a house

mo·sa·ic /moʊ'zeɪɪk/ noun [count, noncount]
(**ART**) a picture or pattern that is made by placing together small stones, pieces of glass, etc.

Mos·lem /'mɑzləm/ = **Muslim**

mosque /mɑsk/ noun [count]
(**RELIGION**) a building where Muslims go to say their prayers

mos·qui·to /məˈskiṭoʊ/ *noun* [*count*] (*plural* **mos·qui·toes** or **mos·qui·tos**)
a small insect that bites people and animals and drinks their blood ⊃ Look at the picture at **insect**.

moss /mɔs/ *noun* [*noncount*]
a soft green plant that grows in wet places on things like trees and stones

most¹ 🔑 /moʊst/ *adjective*, *pronoun*
the biggest amount or number of something: *Jo did a lot of work, but I did **the most**.* ◆ *He was away for **most of** last week.* ⊃ Look at **more**. ⊃ **ANTONYM least**
at most; **at the most** not more than a certain number, and probably less: *We can stay two days at the most.*
make the most of something to use something in the best way: *We only have one free day, so let's make the most of it.*

most² 🔑 /moʊst/ *adverb*
more than all others: *It's the most beautiful garden I've ever seen.* ◆ *Which part of the show did you enjoy most?* ⊃ **ANTONYM least**

most·ly 🔑 /ˈmoʊstli/ *adverb*
almost all: *The students in my class are mostly from this area.*

mo·tel /moʊˈtɛl/ *noun* [*count*]
a hotel where you can park your car outside your room

moth /mɔθ/ *noun* [*count*]
an insect with big wings that flies at night

moth

moth·er 🔑 /ˈmʌðər/ *noun* [*count*]
a woman who has a child: *My mother is a doctor.* ⊃ Look at **mom**, **mommy**.

moth·er·hood /ˈmʌðərhʊd/ *noun* [*noncount*]
the state of being a mother

moth·er-in-law /ˈmʌðər ɪn lɔ/ *noun* [*count*] (*plural* **moth·ers-in-law**)
the mother of your husband or wife

moth·er tongue /ˌmʌðər ˈtʌŋ/ *noun* [*count*]
(**ENGLISH LANGUAGE ARTS**) the first language you learn to speak as a child

mo·tion /ˈmoʊʃn/ *noun* [*noncount*]
movement: *The motion of the boat made her feel sick.* ◆ *Please remain seated while the bus is in motion* (= moving).

mo·tion·less /ˈmoʊʃənləs/ *adjective*
not moving; still: *to stand motionless*

mo·ti·vate **AWL** /ˈmoʊṭəveɪt/ *verb* (**mo·ti·vates**, **mo·ti·vat·ing**, **mo·ti·vat·ed**)
to make someone want to do something: *The best teachers know how to motivate children to learn.*

mo·ti·va·tion **AWL** /ˌmoʊṭəˈveɪʃn/ *noun* [*count*, *noncount*]
a reason for doing something, or a feeling of wanting to do something: *He's intelligent enough, but he seems to lack motivation.*

mo·tive **AWL** /ˈmoʊṭɪv/ *noun* [*count*]
a reason for doing something: *Was there a motive for the murder?*

mo·tor /ˈmoʊṭər/ *noun* [*count*]
(**PHYSICS**) the part inside a machine that makes it move or work: *an electric motor* ◆ *The washing machine doesn't work. It needs a new motor.*

> **ℹ STYLE**
> We usually use **engine**, not **motor**, when we are talking about cars and motorcycles.

mo·tor·boat /ˈmoʊṭərboʊt/ *noun* [*count*]
a small, fast boat that has a MOTOR

mo·tor·cy·cle 🔑
/ˈmoʊṭərˌsaɪkl/ *noun* [*count*]
a vehicle with two wheels and an engine
▶ **mo·tor·cy·clist** /ˈmoʊṭərˌsaɪklɪst/ *noun* [*count*]
a person who rides a **motorcycle**

motorcycle
engine

mo·tor home /ˈmoʊṭər hoʊm/ *noun* [*count*]
a large vehicle that you can live and sleep in when you are traveling or on vacation

motor home

mo·tor·ist /ˈmoʊṭərɪst/ *noun* [*count*]
a person who drives a car

mot·to /ˈmɑṭoʊ/ *noun* [*count*] (*plural* **mot·toes** or **mot·tos**)
a short phrase that states the main aims or beliefs of an organization, a group, a person, etc.: *Our company's motto is "The customer is always right."*

mound /maʊnd/ *noun* [*count*]
1 a small hill; a large pile of earth
2 a pile of things: *a mound of newspapers*

Mount /maʊnt/ (abbreviation **Mt.**) *noun* [*count*]
You use **Mount** before the name of a mountain: *Mount McKinley* ◆ *Mt. Rushmore*

mount /maʊnt/ *verb* (**mounts**, **mount·ing**, **mount·ed**)
1 (also **mount up**) to increase: *Tension in the area is mounting.* ◆ *My debts were beginning to mount up.*
2 to get on a horse or a bicycle

moun·tain 🔑 /'maʊntn/ *noun* [*count*]
a very high hill: *Granite Peak is the highest mountain in Montana.* • *We climbed the mountain.*

moun·tain bike /'maʊntn baɪk/ *noun* [*count*]
a bicycle with a strong frame and wide tires that you can use to ride over rough ground

moun·tain·eer /ˌmaʊntn·'ɪr/ *noun* [*count*]
a person who climbs mountains
▸ **moun·tain·eer·ing** /ˌmaʊntn·'ɪrɪŋ/ *noun* [*noncount*]: *He took up mountaineering as a boy.*

mountain lion

moun·tain lion /'maʊntn ˌlaɪən/ *noun* [*count*]
a large wild cat that lives in western North America ➲ **SYNONYM cougar**

moun·tain·ous /'maʊntn·əs/ *adjective*
(**GEOGRAPHY**) having many mountains: *a mountainous region*

mourn /mɔrn/ *verb* (**mourns, mourn·ing, mourned**)
to feel very sad, usually because someone has died: *She is still **mourning for** her husband.*
▸ **mourn·ing** /'mɔrnɪŋ/ *noun* [*noncount*]: *They are **in mourning for** their son.*

mouse 🔑 /maʊs/ *noun* [*count*] (*plural* **mice** /maɪs/)
1 a small animal with a long tail: *Our cat caught a mouse.*
2 (**COMPUTERS**) a thing that you move with your hand to tell a computer what to do ➲ Look at the picture at **computer**.

mouse pad /'maʊs pæd/ *noun* [*count*]
(**COMPUTERS**) a smooth piece of plastic that is the best kind of surface on which to use a computer mouse

mousse /mus/ *noun* [*count, noncount*]
1 a type of light food made by mixing together cream and eggs, and adding another food or flavor: *chocolate mousse*
2 a light, white substance that you use to make your hair stay in a particular style

mouth 🔑 /maʊθ/ *noun* [*count*] (*plural* **mouths** /maʊðz/)
1 the part of your face below your nose, which you use for eating and speaking: *Open your mouth, please!*
2 (**GEOGRAPHY**) the place where a river goes into the ocean: *the **mouth** of the Mississippi*

mouth·ful /'maʊθfʊl/ *noun* [*count*]
the amount of food or drink that you can put in your mouth at one time: *She only had a **mouthful of** cake.*

mouth·wash /'maʊθwɑʃ/ *noun* [*count, noncount*]
a liquid that you use to make your mouth fresh and healthy

mouth

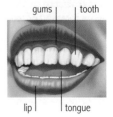

gums | tooth
lip | tongue

move¹ 🔑 /muv/ *verb* (**moves, mov·ing, moved**)
1 to go from one place to another; to change the way you are standing or sitting: *Don't get off the bus while it's moving.* • *We **moved to** the front of the theater.*
2 to put something in another place or another way: *Can you move your car, please?*
3 to go to live in another place: *They sold their house in Detroit and **moved to** Ann Arbor.*
4 to cause someone to have strong feelings, especially of sadness: *The news report **moved** me **to tears.***

move in to go to live in a house or apartment: *I have a new apartment – I'm moving in next week.*
move out to leave a house or apartment where you were living
move over to change your position in order to make space for someone or something: *Would you move over so I can sit down?*

move² 🔑 /muv/ *noun* [*count*]
1 a change of place or position: *The police are watching every move she makes.*
2 a change in the place where you live: *We need a big van for the move.*
get a move on (*informal*) hurry: *Get a move on or you'll be late for work!*

move·ment 🔑 /'muvmənt/ *noun* [*count*]
1 moving or being moved: *The old man's movements were slow and painful.*
2 a group of people who have the same ideas or beliefs: *a political movement*

mov·ie 🔑 /'muvi/ *noun*
1 [*count*] a story shown in moving pictures that you see in theaters or on television: *Would you like to **see a movie**?*
2 **the movies** [*plural*] the place where you go to watch a movie: *We **went to the movies** last night.*

Collocations

The movies

watching
- **go to** a movie
- **rent** a movie/a DVD
- **download** a movie/a video
- **watch** a movie/a DVD/a video/a preview

showing
- **show/screen** a movie
- **be released on/come out on/be out on** DVD

making
- **make/direct/produce/shoot** a movie/a sequel/a video
- **play** a character/the role of someone in a movie
- **write** the screenplay/soundtrack

movie star /'muvi star/ *noun* [*count*]
an actor or actress who is famous for being in movies

mov·ie the·a·ter /'muvi ˌθiəţər/ (also **the·a·ter**) *noun* [*count*]
a building where you go to see movies

mov·ing /'muvɪŋ/ *adjective*
making you feel something strongly, especially sadness: *It's a very moving story.*

mow /moʊ/ *verb* (mows, mow·ing, mowed, has mown /moʊn/)
to cut grass with a machine: *Sally is mowing the grass.*

mow·er /'moʊər/ *noun* [*count*]
a machine that cuts grass ⊃ **SYNONYM lawnmower**

MP3 play·er /ˌem pi 'θri ˌpleɪər/ *noun* [*count*]
a small piece of equipment that stores and plays music from computer files (called **MP3 FILES**)

mph /ˌem pi 'eɪtʃ/ *abbreviation*
a way of measuring how fast something is moving. **Mph** is short for **miles per hour**: *The train was traveling at 125mph.*

Mr. /'mɪstər/ *abbreviation*
a title that you use before the name of a man: *Mr. Richard Clay • Mr. Holland*

Mrs. /'mɪsəz/ *abbreviation*
a word that you use before the name of a woman who is married: *Mrs. Carol Garcia • Mrs. Nolan*

M.S. /ˌem 'es/ (also **M.Sc.** /ˌem es 'si/) *noun* [*count*]
a second university degree that you receive when you complete a program of study at a university in a science subject. **M.S.** is short for **Master of Science.** ⊃ Look at **M.A., B.S., master's degree.**

Ms. /mɪz/ *abbreviation*
a word that you can use before the name of any woman, instead of **Mrs.** or **Miss**: *Ms. Karen Green*

Grammar

- **Miss, Mrs., Ms.** and **Mr.** are all titles that we use in front of someone's family name.
- You do not use these titles in front of a person's first name, unless it is included with the family name: *Is there a Miss (Susan) Hudson here?* • *Hello, Miss Hudson, come this way* (NOT *Miss Susan*).

Mt. abbreviation of **Mount**

much¹ /mʌtʃ/ *adjective, pronoun* (**more** /mɔr/, **most** /moʊst/)
a big amount of something; a lot of something: *I don't have much money.* • *There was so much food that we couldn't eat it all.* • *Eat as much as you can.* • *How much paper do you want?* • *How much is this shirt?* ⊃ Look at **many.**

Grammar

- We usually use **much** only in negative sentences, in questions, and after "too," "so," "as," and "how."
- In other sentences we use **a lot (of)**: *She has a lot of money.*

much² /mʌtʃ/ *adverb*
a lot: *I don't like him very much.* • *Your apartment is much bigger than mine.* • *"Do you like it?" "No, not much."*

mud /mʌd/ *noun* [*noncount*]
soft wet earth: *Phil came home from the football game covered in mud.*

mud·dle /'mʌdl/ *verb* (mud·dles, mud·dling, mud·dled)
muddle through (*informal*) to manage to do something, even though you do not have the right equipment, skills, etc.: *I don't speak Spanish very well, but somehow I muddled through while I was in Mexico.*
▶ **mud·dle** *noun* [*count, noncount*]
a confused state: *I was in such a muddle that I couldn't find anything.*

mud·dy /'mʌdi/ *adjective* (mud·di·er, mud·di·est)
covered with mud: *When it rains, the roads get very muddy.*

muf·fin /'mʌfən/ *noun* [*count*]
a small sweet cake, sometimes with fruit in it: *We had blueberry muffins for breakfast.*

mug¹ /mʌg/ *noun* [*count*]
a big cup with straight sides and a handle: *a mug of tea* ⊃ Look at the picture at **cup.**

mug² /mʌg/ *verb* (mugs, mug·ging, mugged)
to attack someone in the street and take their money
▶ **mug·ger** /'mʌgər/ *noun* [*count*]: *Watch out for muggers, especially at night.*

mug·gy /'mʌgi/ *adjective* (mug·gi·er, mug·gi·est)
(used about the weather) warm and a little wet, so that you feel uncomfortable: *It was a muggy day in August.*

mule /myul/ *noun* [*count*]
an animal that is used for carrying heavy loads and whose parents are a horse and a DONKEY (= an animal like a small horse with long ears)

mul·ti·cul·tur·al /ˌmʌltiˈkʌltʃərəl/ *adjective*
for or including people from many different countries and cultures: *We live in **a multicultural** society.*

mul·ti·me·di·a /ˌmʌltiˈmidiə/ *adjective*
using sound, pictures, and film as well as words on a screen: *The company produces multimedia software for schools.*

mul·ti·ple /ˈmʌltəpl/ *noun* [*count*]
(**MATH**) a number that contains another number an exact number of times: *12, 18, and 24 are multiples of 6.*

mul·ti·ple-choice /ˌmʌltəpl ˈtʃɔɪs/ *adjective*
A **multiple-choice** exam or question gives you three or four different answers and you have to choose the right one.

mul·ti·ply 🔊 /ˈmʌltəplaɪ/ *verb* (mul·ti·plies, mul·ti·ply·ing, mul·ti·plied, has mul·ti·plied)
(**MATH**) to make a number bigger by a certain number of times: *Two **multiplied by** three is six* (= 2 x 3 = 6). • *Multiply three and seven **together**.* ⊃ Look at **divide**(3).
▶ **mul·ti·pli·ca·tion** /ˌmʌltəpləˈkeɪʃn/ *noun* [*noncount*]: *Today we did multiplication and division.*

mul·ti·ra·cial /ˌmʌltiˈreɪʃl/ *adjective*
including or involving different races of people: *We live in a multiracial society.*

mum·ble /ˈmʌmbl/ *verb* (mum·bles, mum·bling, mum·bled)
to speak quietly in a way that is not clear, so that people cannot hear you well: *She mumbled something, but I didn't hear what she said.*

mum·my /ˈmʌmi/ *noun* [*count*] (*plural* mum·mies)
a dead body of a person or animal that has been kept by rubbing it with oils and wrapping it in cloth: *an Egyptian mummy*

mumps /mʌmps/ *noun* [*noncount*]
(**HEALTH**) an illness that children can get, which causes the neck to get bigger (to SWELL)

munch /mʌntʃ/ *verb* (munch·es, munch·ing, munched)
to eat something in a noisy way: *The kids were munching on chips in front of the TV.*

mu·nic·i·pal /myuˈnɪsəpl/ *adjective*
(**POLITICS**) connected with the government of a city or town: *a municipal election*

mu·ral /ˈmyʊrəl/ *noun* [*count*]
(**ART**) a large picture painted on a wall

mur·der¹ 🔊 /ˈmərdər/ *noun* [*count*]
the crime of killing someone deliberately: *He was sent to prison for the **murder of** a police officer.*

mur·der² 🔊 /ˈmərdər/ *verb* (mur·ders, mur·der·ing, mur·dered)
to kill someone deliberately: *She was murdered with a knife.*
▶ **mur·der·er** /ˈmərdərər/ *noun* [*count*]: *The police have caught the murderer.*

mur·mur /ˈmərmər/ *verb* (mur·murs, mur·mur·ing, mur·mured)
to speak in a low quiet voice: *"I love you," she murmured.*
▶ **mur·mur** *noun* [*count*]: *I heard **the murmur of** voices from the next room.*

mus·cle 🔊 /ˈmʌsl/ *noun* [*count*]
(**BIOLOGY**) one of the parts inside your body that are connected to the bones and that help you to move: *Riding a bicycle is good for developing the leg muscles.*

mus·cu·lar /ˈmʌskyələr/ *adjective*
1 (**HEALTH**, **BIOLOGY**) connected with the muscles: *muscular pain*
2 having large, strong muscles: *a muscular body*

mu·se·um 🔊 /myuˈziəm/ *noun* [*count*]
a building where people can look at old or interesting things: *Have you ever been to the Museum of Modern Art?*

mush·room
/ˈmʌʃrum/ *noun* [*count*]
a type of plant with a flat top and no leaves, which you can eat as a vegetable

mushrooms

mu·sic 🔊 /ˈmyuzɪk/ *noun* [*noncount*] (**MUSIC**)
1 the sounds that you make by singing, or by playing instruments: *What sort of music do you like?*
2 signs on paper to show people what to sing or play: *Can you read music?*

Collocations

Music

listening
- **listen to/like/love/be into** music/classical music/jazz/pop/hip-hop, etc.
- **listen to** the radio/your MP3 player/a CD
- **put on/play** a song/a CD/some music
- **turn down/up** the radio/the volume

---

playing

- **play** an instrument/the piano/a note/a tune/a duet
- **sing** a song/a solo/the blues/in a choir
- **start/join/quit/leave** a band

writing

- **write/compose** music/a song/a melody/a piece of music/an opera
- **record/release** an album/a single/a CD

mu·si·cal¹ 🔊 /ˈmyuzɪkl/ *adjective* (**MUSIC**)
1 connected with music: *musical instruments* (= the piano, the guitar, the trumpet, etc.)
2 good at making music: *Sophie's very musical.*

mu·si·cal² /ˈmyuzɪkl/ *noun* [count]
(**MUSIC**) a play or movie in which the actors sing and dance: *We went to see a Broadway musical.*

mu·si·cian 🔊 /myuˈzɪʃn/ *noun* [count]
(**MUSIC**) a person who writes music or plays a musical instrument

Mus·lim /ˈmʌzləm; ˈmʊzləm/ *noun* [count]
(**RELIGION**) a person who follows the religion of Islam
▶ **Mus·lim** *adjective*: *the Muslim way of life*

mus·sel /ˈmʌsl/ *noun* [count]
a small animal that lives in the ocean. It has a black shell and a soft body that you can eat. ➷ Look at the picture at **shellfish**.

must 🔊 /məst; mʌst/ *modal verb*
1 (*formal*) a word that you use to tell someone what to do or what is necessary: *You must look before you cross the road.*

Grammar

- You use **must not** or the short form **mustn't** /ˈmʌsnt/ to tell people **not** to do something: *You mustn't be late.*
- When you want to say that someone can do something if they want, but that it is not necessary, you use **don't have to**: *You don't have to do your homework today* (= you can do it today if you want, but it is not necessary).

2 a word that shows that you are sure something is true: *You must be tired after your long trip.* ◆ *I can't find my keys. I must have left them at home.*
3 a word that you use to give someone advice: *You really must read this book – it's wonderful.* ➷ Look at the note at **modal verb**.

mus·tache /ˈmʌstæʃ/ *noun* [count]
the hair above a man's mouth, below his nose: *He has a mustache.* ➷ Look at the picture at **hair**.

mus·tard /ˈmʌstərd/ *noun* [noncount]
a thick, yellow sauce with a very strong taste, which you eat with meat

must·n't /ˈmʌsnt/ short for **must not**

mut·ter /ˈmʌtər/ *verb* (**mut·ters, mut·ter·ing, mut·tered**)
to speak in a low, quiet voice that is difficult to hear: *He muttered something about going home, and left the room.*

mu·tu·al **AWL** /ˈmyutʃuəl/ *adjective*
1 If a feeling or action is **mutual**, it is felt or done by both people involved: *We have a mutual agreement to help each other when necessary.* ◆ *I don't like her, and I'm sure **the feeling is mutual** (= she doesn't like me either).*
2 shared by two or more people: *We were introduced by a mutual friend.*

my 🔊 /maɪ/ *adjective*
of or belonging to me: *Where is my watch?* ◆ *These are my books, not yours.* ◆ *I hurt my arm.*

my·self 🔊 /maɪˈsɛlf/ *pronoun* (*plural* **our·selves** /aʊərˈsɛlvz/)
1 a word that shows the same person as the one who is speaking: *I hurt myself.* ◆ *I bought myself a new shirt.*
2 a word that makes "I" stronger: *"Did you buy this cake?" "No, I made it myself."*
by myself
1 without other people: *I live by myself.* ➷ **SYNONYM alone**
2 without help: *I made dinner by myself.*

mys·te·ri·ous 🔊 /mɪˈstɪriəs/ *adjective*
Something that is **mysterious** is strange and you do not know about it or understand it: *Several people said they had seen mysterious lights in the sky.*
▶ **mys·te·ri·ous·ly** /mɪˈstɪriəsli/ *adverb*: *The plane disappeared mysteriously.*

mys·ter·y /ˈmɪstəri/ *noun* [count] (*plural* **mys·ter·ies**)
something strange that you cannot understand or explain: *The police say that the man's death is still a mystery.*

myth /mɪθ/ *noun* [count]
1 (**ENGLISH LANGUAGE ARTS**) a very old story: *Greek myths*
2 a story or belief that is not true: *It's a myth that money makes you happy.*

my·thol·o·gy /mɪˈθɑlədʒi/ *noun* [noncount]
(**ENGLISH LANGUAGE ARTS**) the very old stories of a particular culture or society: *Greek and Roman mythology*
▶ **my·tho·log·i·cal** /ˌmɪθəˈlɑdʒɪkl/ *adjective*: *mythological creatures*

ə **about** y **yes** w **woman** t̬ **butter** eɪ **say** aɪ **five** ɔɪ **boy** aʊ **now** oʊ **go**

N n

N, n /ɛn/ *noun* [*count, noncount*] (*plural* **N's, n's** /ɛnz/)
the fourteenth letter of the English alphabet: *"Nice" begins with an "N."*

nag /næg/ *verb* (**nags, nag·ging, nagged**)
to keep asking someone to do something: *My parents are always nagging me to work harder.*

nail /neɪl/ *noun*
[*count*]

nails

1 the hard part at the end of a finger or toe: *toenails* ◆ *fingernails* ⊃
Look at the picture at **hand**.
2 a small, thin piece of metal with one sharp end, which you hit into wood (with a tool called a HAMMER) to attach things together
▶ **nail** *verb* (**nails, nail·ing, nailed**): *I nailed the pieces of wood together.*

nail clip·pers /'neɪl ˌklɪpərz/ *noun* [*plural*]
a metal tool you use for cutting the nails on your fingers and toes: *a pair of nail clippers*

nail file /'neɪl faɪl/ *noun* [*count*]
a small flat object with a rough surface that you use for shaping your nails

nail pol·ish /'neɪl pɑlɪʃ/ *noun* [*count*]
a liquid that people put on their nails to give them color

na·ive (also **na·ïve**) /nɑˈiv; naɪˈiv/ *adjective*
without enough experience of life and too ready to believe or trust other people: *I was too naive to understand what was really going on.* ◆ *a naive question*
▶ **na·ive·ly** (also **na·ïve·ly**) /nɑˈivli; naɪˈivli/ *adverb*: *She naively accepted the first price he offered.*

na·ked /'neɪkəd/ *adjective*
not wearing any clothes. ⊃ SYNONYM **nude**

name¹ /neɪm/ *noun*
1 [*count*] a word or words that you use to call or talk about a person or thing: *My name is Chris Eaves.* ◆ *What's your name?* ◆ *Do you know the name of this flower?*

Word building

- Your **first name** or **given name** is the name that your parents give you when you are born. Many people also have a **middle name**.
- Your **last name** or **family name** is the name

that everyone in your family has. When a woman gets married, she usually takes her husband's last name. Her old last name is then called her **maiden name**, and her new one is her **married name**.
- A **nickname** is a name that your friends or family sometimes call you instead of your real name: *His real name is Robert, but his nickname is Shorty.*

2 [*singular*] what people think or say about someone or something: *That area of town has a really bad name.* ⊃ SYNONYM **reputation**
3 [*count*] a famous person: *Some of the biggest names in Hollywood will be at the party.*
call someone names to say bad, unkind words about someone: *Joe cried because the other children were calling him names.*

name² /neɪm/ *verb* (**names, nam·ing, named**)
1 to give a name to someone or something: *They named their baby Sophie.* ◆ *They named him Michael after his grandfather* (= gave him the same name as his grandfather).
2 to know and say the name of someone or something: *The professor could name every one of his 60 students.*

name·ly /'neɪmli/ *adverb*
You use **namely** when you are going to name a person or thing that you have just said something about: *Only two students were late, namely Steven and Allan.*

nan·ny /'næni/ *noun* [*count*] (*plural* **nan·nies**)
a woman whose job is to take care of the children in a family

nap /næp/ *noun* [*count*]
a short sleep during the day: *I took a nap after lunch.*

nap·kin /'næpkən/ *noun* [*count*]
a piece of cloth or paper that you use when you are eating to clean your mouth and hands and to keep your clothes clean

nar·cot·ic /nɑrˈkɑtɪk/ *noun* [*count*]
a strong, illegal drug that affects your brain in a harmful way

nar·rate /'næreɪt/ *verb* (**nar·rates, nar·rat·ing, nar·rat·ed**) (*formal*) (**ENGLISH LANGUAGE ARTS**)
to tell a story: *Hoffman narrated the audio version of the book.*
▶ **nar·ra·tion** /næˈreɪʃn/ *noun* [*count, noncount*]: *the narration of events*
▶ **nar·ra·tor** /'næreɪtər/ *noun* [*count*]
the person who tells a story or explains what is happening in a play, movie, etc.

nar·ra·tive /'nærətɪv/ *noun* [*count*] (*formal*)
(**ENGLISH LANGUAGE ARTS**) the description of events in a story: *a historical narrative*

---

nar·row 🔊 /ˈnæroʊ/ adjective (nar·row·er, nar·row·est)
1 not far from one side to the other: *The bridge was very narrow.* • *a narrow ribbon* ➔ ANTONYM **broad**, **wide**
2 by a small amount: *We had a **narrow escape** – the car nearly hit a tree.* • *a narrow defeat*

nar·row·ly /ˈnæroʊli/ adverb
only by a small amount: *They narrowly escaped injury.*

nar·row-mind·ed /ˌnæroʊ ˈmaɪndəd/ adjective
not wanting to accept ideas or opinions that are different from your own: *The people in this town can be somewhat narrow-minded.* ➔ ANTONYM **open-minded**

na·sal /ˈneɪzl/ adjective
(BIOLOGY) connected with the nose: *the nasal passages*

nas·ty /ˈnæsti/ adjective (nas·ti·er, nas·ti·est)
bad; not nice: *There's a nasty smell in this room.* • *Don't be so nasty!* ➔ SYNONYM **horrible**

na·tion 🔊 /ˈneɪʃn/ noun [count]
(POLITICS) a country and all the people who live in it: *one of the richest nations in the world*

na·tion·al 🔊 /ˈnæʃənl/ adjective
(POLITICS) connected with all of a country; typical of a country: *She wore the Greek national costume.* • *national newspapers* ➔ Look at **international**.
▸ **na·tion·al·ly** /ˈnæʃənəli/ adverb: *to advertise something nationally*

na·tion·al an·them /ˌnæʃənl ˈænθəm/ noun [count]
(MUSIC) the official song of a country

na·tion·al·ism /ˈnæʃənlˌɪzəm/ noun [noncount]
(POLITICS) a feeling of love for your own country, or a feeling that your country is better than any other country
▸ **na·tion·al·is·tic** /ˌnæʃənəˈlɪstɪk/ adjective: *nationalistic beliefs* (= believing that your country is better than others)

na·tion·al·i·ty /ˌnæʃəˈnæləti/ noun [count] (plural na·tion·al·i·ties)
(POLITICS) the state of belonging to a certain country: *"What nationality are you?" "I'm American."*

na·tion·al park /ˌnæʃənl ˈpɑrk/ noun [count]
a large area of beautiful land that is protected by the government so that people can enjoy it

na·tive¹ /ˈneɪtɪv/ adjective
connected with the place where you were born: *I returned to my native country.* • *My native language is English.*

na·tive² /ˈneɪtɪv/ noun [count]
a person who was born in a place: *He's a native of Omaha.*

Na·tive A·mer·i·can /ˌneɪtɪv əˈmɛrɪkən/ noun [count]
a member of the group of people who were living in America before people from Europe arrived there

na·tive speak·er /ˌneɪtɪv ˈspikər/ noun [count]
(ENGLISH LANGUAGE ARTS) a person who speaks a language as their first language: *native speakers of English*

nat·u·ral 🔊 /ˈnætʃərəl/ adjective
1 made by nature, not by people: *This part of the state is an area of great natural beauty.* • *Earthquakes and floods are **natural disasters**.*
2 normal or usual: *It's **natural for** parents **to** feel sad when their children leave home.* ➔ ANTONYM **unnatural**
3 that you had from the time you were born, or that was easy for you to learn: *She has **a natural talent** for music.*

nat·u·ral·ize /ˈnætʃərəlaɪz/ verb (nat·u·ral·iz·es, nat·u·ral·iz·ing, nat·u·ral·ized)
(POLITICS) to make someone a citizen of a country where he or she was not born: *a naturalized American citizen*
▸ **nat·u·ral·i·za·tion** /ˌnætʃərələˈzeɪʃn/ noun [noncount]

nat·u·ral·ly /ˈnætʃrəli/ adverb
1 in a way that you would expect: *Naturally, I get upset when things go wrong.* ➔ SYNONYM **of course**
2 in a way that is not made or caused by people: *Is your hair naturally curly?*
3 in a normal way: *Try to stand naturally while I take a photo.*

na·ture 🔊 /ˈneɪtʃər/ noun
1 [noncount] all the plants, animals, etc. in the world and all the things that happen in it that are not made or caused by people: *the beauty of nature*
2 [count, noncount] the way a person or thing is: *Our cat has a very friendly nature.* • *It's **human nature** never to be completely satisfied.*

Collocations

The Natural World

animals
- animals **mate/breed/reproduce/feed (on something)**
- birds **fly/sing/nest/migrate**
- insects **crawl/fly/bite/sting**
- **hunt/capture/kill** prey
- **lay/fertilize** eggs

plants and fungi
- trees/plants **grow/bloom/blossom/flower**
- a seed **sprouts**

- leaves/buds/shoots **appear/develop/ form**
- a fungus **grows/spreads**
- **pollinate/fertilize** a flower/plant
- **produce/spread** pollen/seeds

naugh·ty /ˈnɔti/ adjective (naugh·ti·er, naugh·ti·est)
A **naughty** child does bad things or does not do what you ask them to do: She's the naughtiest child in the class.

nau·se·a /ˈnɔziə/ noun [noncount]
(**HEALTH**) the feeling that you are going to VOMIT (= bring up food from your stomach)

na·val /ˈneɪvl/ adjective
connected with a navy: a naval officer

na·vel /ˈneɪvl/ noun [count]
(**BIOLOGY**) the small hole in the middle of your stomach ⊃ SYNONYM **belly button**

nav·i·gate /ˈnævəɡeɪt/ verb (nav·i·gates, nav·i·gat·ing, nav·i·gat·ed)
to use a map or some other method to find which way a ship, an airplane, or a car should go: Long ago, explorers used the stars to navigate.
▶ **nav·i·ga·tion** /ˌnævəˈɡeɪʃn/ noun [noncount] deciding which way a ship or other vehicle should go by using a map, etc.: navigation skills
▶ **nav·i·ga·tor** /ˈnævəɡeɪtər/ noun [count]
a person who decides which way a vehicle should go: Dad's usually the navigator when we go somewhere in the car.

na·vy /ˈneɪvi/ noun [count] (plural na·vies)
the ships that a country uses when there is a war, and the people who work on them: Mark is **in the navy**. ◆ the U.S. Navy ⊃ Look at **army**.

na·vy blue /ˌneɪvi ˈblu/ (also **na·vy**) adjective, noun [noncount]
dark blue

near /nɪr/ adjective, adverb, preposition (near·er, near·est)
not far away in distance or time: Where's the nearest hospital? ◆ My parents live very near. ◆ I don't want to sit near the window. ◆ We're hoping to move to Arizona **in the near future**.

near·by /ˈnɪrbaɪ/ adjective
not far away; close: We took her to a nearby hospital.
▶ **near·by** /ˌnɪrˈbaɪ/ adverb: Let's go and see Tim – he lives nearby.

near·ly /ˈnɪrli/ adverb
almost; not completely or exactly: He's nearly 90 – it's his birthday next week. ◆ She was so sick that she nearly died.
not nearly not at all: The book wasn't nearly as good as the movie.

near·sight·ed /ˈnɪrˌsaɪtəd/ adjective
(**HEALTH**) If you are **nearsighted**, you can see things clearly when they are close to you but not when they are far away. ⊃ ANTONYM **farsighted**

neat /nit/ adjective (neat·er, neat·est)
1 with everything in the right place and done carefully: Keep your room **neat and clean**. ◆ She has very neat handwriting.
2 (informal) good; nice: That's a really neat car!
▶ **neat·ly** /ˈnitli/ adverb: Write your name neatly.

nec·es·sar·i·ly /ˌnɛsəˈsɛrəli/ adverb
not necessarily not always: Big men aren't necessarily strong.

nec·es·sar·y /ˈnɛsəˌsɛri/ adjective

ℹ SPELLING
Remember! You spell **necessary** with one C and SS.

If something is **necessary**, you must have it or do it: Warm clothes are necessary in winter.

ne·ces·si·ty /nəˈsɛsəti/ noun [count] (plural ne·ces·si·ties)
something that you must have: Food and clothes are necessities of life.

neck /nɛk/ noun [count]
1 the part of your body between your shoulders and your head: Helen wore a thick scarf around her neck. ⊃ Look at the picture at **body**.
2 the part of a piece of clothing that goes around your neck: The neck's too tight.
3 the thin part at the top of a bottle
neck and neck equal or level with someone or something in a race or competition: At the halfway point, the two cars were neck and neck.

neck·lace /ˈnɛkləs/ noun [count]
a piece of jewelry that you wear around your neck: a diamond necklace ⊃ Look at the picture at **jewelry**.

neck·tie /ˈnɛktaɪ/ noun [count]
a long, thin piece of cloth that you wear around your neck with a shirt ⊃ SYNONYM **tie**

nec·tar·ine /ˌnɛktəˈrin/ noun [count]
a soft, round, red and yellow fruit with smooth skin and a large hard part (called a PIT) in the center

need¹ /nid/ verb (needs, need·ing, need·ed)
1 If you **need** something, you must have it: All plants and animals need water. ◆ You don't need your coat – it's not cold.
2 If you **need** to do something, you must do it: James is very sick. He needs to go to the hospital. ◆ "Do we need to pay now, or can we pay next week?" "You don't need to pay now."

need² /nid/ noun
1 [noncount, singular] a situation in which you must have something or do something: She's **in**

need of a rest. ◆ There is a growing **need for** new books and equipment. ◆ **There's no need for** you to come.
2 needs [*plural*] the things that you must have: *He doesn't earn enough money to pay for his basic needs.* ◆ *a child's emotional and physical needs*
3 [*noncount*] the state of not having enough food, money, or support: *We are raising money to help families **in need**.*

nee·dle 🔑 /ˈnidl/ *noun* [*count*]
1 a small, thin piece of metal that you use for sewing cloth: *Put the thread through the eye* (= hole) *of the needle.* ⊃ Look at **knitting needle**. ⊃ Look at the picture at **thread**.
2 a small, thin piece of metal that forms part of an instrument: *The compass needle points north.* ◆ *a hypodermic needle* (= for taking blood or giving drugs) ⊃ Look at the picture at **syringe**.
3 a very thin, pointed leaf on a tree that stays green all year: *pine needles*

need·less /ˈnidləs/ *adjective*
not necessary; able to be avoided: *needless suffering* ◆ *The problem is the cost, **needless to say*** (= it is not necessary to say this, because it is obvious).
▶ **need·less·ly** /ˈnidləsli/ *adverb*: *Many people died needlessly.*

neg·a·tive¹ 🔑 **AWL** /ˈnɛɡəṭɪv/ *adjective*
1 bad or harmful: *The whole experience was definitely more positive than negative.*
2 only thinking about the bad qualities of someone or something: *If you go into the game with a negative attitude, you'll never win.*
3 using words like "no," "not," and "never": *"I don't like fish" is a negative sentence.*
4 (**HEALTH**) (used about a medical test) showing that something has not happened or is not there: *The result of the pregnancy test was negative.*
5 (**MATH**) (used about a number) less than zero ⊃ **ANTONYM positive**

neg·a·tive² **AWL** /ˈnɛɡəṭɪv/ *noun* [*count*]
1 a word, phrase, or sentence that says or means "no" or "not": *"Never" and "no one" are negatives.*
2 a piece of film that we use to make a photograph. On a **negative**, dark things are light and light things are dark.

ne·glect /nɪˈɡlɛkt/ *verb* (ne·glects, ne·glect·ing, ne·glect·ed)
1 to not take care of someone or something: *The dog was dirty and thin because its owner had neglected it.*
2 to not do something that you should do: *He neglected to tell her about the phone call from her boss.*
▶ **ne·glect** *noun* [*noncount*]: *The house was in a state of neglect.*

▶ **ne·glect·ed** /nɪˈɡlɛkṭəd/ *adjective*: *neglected children*

ne·go·ti·ate /nəˈɡoʊʃieɪt/ (ne·go·ti·ates, ne·go·ti·at·ing, ne·go·ti·at·ed) *verb*
to reach an agreement by talking with other people: *We have negotiated a deal.* ◆ *The unions were **negotiating with** the management **over** pay.*
▶ **ne·go·ti·a·tion** /nəˌɡoʊʃiˈeɪʃn/ *noun* [*count, noncount*]: *My salary is still **under negotiation**.*

neigh /neɪ/ *verb* (neighs, neigh·ing, neighed)
When a horse **neighs**, it makes a long, high sound.
▶ **neigh** *noun* [*count*]

neigh·bor 🔑 /ˈneɪbər/ *noun* [*count*]
1 a person who lives near you: *Don't make so much noise, or you'll wake the neighbors.* ◆ *our next-door neighbors*
2 a person or thing that is next to or near another: *The United States is Canada's neighbor.* ◆ *Try not to look at what your neighbor is writing.*

neigh·bor·hood /ˈneɪbərhʊd/ *noun* [*count*]
a part of a town or city; the people who live there: *They live in a friendly neighborhood.*

neigh·bor·ing /ˈneɪbərɪŋ/ *adjective*
near or next to: *people from neighboring areas*

nei·ther¹ 🔑 /ˈniðər/ *adjective, pronoun*
not one and not the other of two things or people: *Neither book is very interesting.* ◆ **Neither of** the boys was there.

nei·ther² 🔑 /ˈniðər/ *adverb*
also not: *Lydia can't swim and neither can I.* ◆ *"I don't like rice." "Neither do I."*
neither ... nor not ... and not: *Neither Paul nor I went to the party.*

ne·on /ˈniɑn/ *noun* [*noncount*] (symbol **Ne**)
a type of gas that is used in bright lights and signs

neph·ew /ˈnɛfyu/ *noun* [*count*]
the son of your brother or sister ⊃ Look at **niece**.

nerd /nərd/ *noun* [*count*] (*informal*)
a person who spends a lot of time on a particular interest and who is not popular or fashionable ⊃ **SYNONYM geek**
▶ **nerd·y** /ˈnərdi/ *adjective*: *He looked kind of nerdy.*

nerve 🔑 /nərv/ *noun*
1 [*count*] (**BIOLOGY**) one of the long thin things inside your body that carry feelings and messages to and from your brain
2 nerves [*plural*] feelings of being worried or afraid: *John breathed deeply to **calm** his **nerves**.*
3 [*noncount*] the state of being brave or calm when there is danger: *You need a lot of nerve to be a race car driver.*

ə **about**   y **yes**   w **woman**   ṭ **butter**   eɪ **say**   aɪ **five**   ɔɪ **boy**   aʊ **now**   oʊ **go**

get on someone's nerves to make someone feel a little angry: *Stop making that noise – you're getting on my nerves!*

nerve-rack·ing /ˈnərv ˌrækɪŋ/ *adjective*
making you very nervous or worried: *It was a nerve-racking drive up the mountain.*

nerv·ous 🔑 /ˈnərvəs/ *adjective*
1 worried or afraid: *I'm **nervous about** starting my new job.*
2 (**BIOLOGY**) connected with the **nerves** in your body: *the nervous system*
▶ **nerv·ous·ly** /ˈnərvəsli/ *adverb*: *He laughed nervously, not knowing what to say.*
▶ **nerv·ous·ness** /ˈnərvəsnəs/ *noun* [*noncount*]: *He tried to hide his nervousness.*

ner·vous break·down /ˌnərvəs ˈbreɪkdaʊn/ (also **break·down**) *noun* [*count*]
(**HEALTH**) a time when someone is so unhappy that they cannot live and work normally: *to have a nervous breakdown*

Suffix

-ness
(in nouns) a state or quality of something: *darkness* ◆ *happiness* ◆ *kindness* ◆ *sickness*

nest¹ /nɛst/ *noun* [*count*] (**BIOLOGY**)
1 a place where a bird keeps its eggs and babies ⊃ Look at the picture at **bird**.
2 the home of certain animals or insects: *a wasps' nest*

nest² /nɛst/ *verb* (nests, nest·ing, nest·ed)
(**BIOLOGY**) to make and live in a **nest**: *The ducks are nesting by the river.*

net 🔑 /nɛt/ *noun*
1 [*count*] material that has large spaces between the threads; a piece of this material that we use for a particular purpose: *a fishing net* ◆ *a tennis net* ◆ *He kicked the ball into the back of the net.* ⊃ Look at the picture at **tennis**.
2 the Net [*singular*] (**COMPUTERS**) = **the Internet**

net·work **AWL** /ˈnɛtwərk/ *noun* [*count*]
1 a number of things or people that form a single system or that are connected: *the rail network* ◆ *computer networks* ◆ *a **network of** friends*
2 a group of connected TV or radio companies that shows the same programs in different parts of a country: *a major television network*

neu·tral¹ **AWL** /ˈnutrəl/ *adjective*
1 not supporting either side in an argument or war: *I don't take sides when my brothers argue – I stay neutral.*
2 having or showing no strong qualities, emotions, or color: *a neutral tone of voice* ◆ *neutral colors*

neu·tral² **AWL** /ˈnutrəl/ *noun* [*noncount*]
the position in which no power is being sent from a vehicle's engine to its wheels: *Put the car in neutral.*

neu·tron /ˈnutrɑn/ *noun* [*count*]
(**CHEMISTRY**, **PHYSICS**) a very small piece of matter with no electric charge, found in all atoms ⊃ Look at **electron**, **proton**. ⊃ Look at the picture at **atom**.

nev·er 🔑 /ˈnɛvər/ *adverb*
not at any time; not ever: *She never works on Saturdays.* ◆ *I've never been to Oregon.* ◆ *I will never forget you.*

nev·er·the·less **AWL** /ˌnɛvərðəˈlɛs/ *adverb*
(*formal*)
despite what has just been said: *They played very well. Nevertheless, they didn't win.* ⊃ **SYNONYM nonetheless**

new 🔑 /nu/ *adjective* (new·er, new·est)
1 not existing before: *Have you seen his new movie?* ◆ *I bought a new pair of shoes yesterday.*
2 different from before: *Our new apartment is much bigger than our old one.* ◆ *The teacher usually explains the new words to us.*
3 doing something for the first time: *New parents are often tired.* ◆ *He's **new to** the job and still needs help.*

new·com·er /ˈnukʌmər/ *noun* [*count*]
a person who has just come to a place

new·ly /ˈnuli/ *adverb*
not long ago: *Our school is newly built.* ⊃ **SYNONYM recently**

new·ly·wed /ˈnuliwɛd/ *noun* [*count*]
a person who has recently married: *The newlyweds went to Italy for their honeymoon.*

news 🔑 /nuz/ *noun*
1 [*noncount*] information about things that have just happened: *Have you heard the news? Stewart is getting married.* ◆ *I have **some** good news for you.* ◆ *Julie told us an interesting **piece of** news.*
2 the news [*singular*] a program on television or radio that tells people about important things that have just happened: *We heard about the plane crash on the news.*
break the news to be the first person to tell someone about something important: *Have you broken the news to your wife?*

news·cast /ˈnuzkæst/ *noun* [*count*]
a news program on TV or radio
▶ **news·cast·er** /ˈnuzkæstər/ *noun* [*count*]
a person who reads the news on TV or radio

news·pa·per 🔑 /ˈnuzˌpeɪpər/ *noun*
1 (also **pa·per** /ˈpeɪpər/) [*count*] large pieces of paper with news, advertisements, and other things printed on them: *a daily newspaper*

2 [noncount] paper taken from old **newspapers**: *We wrapped the plates in newspaper before packing them.*

news·stand /'nuz,stænd/ *noun* [count]
a type of small store that is open at the front and sells newspapers, magazines, etc.

new year (also **New Year**) /'nu yɪr/ *noun* [singular]
the beginning of the year: *Happy New Year!* ◆ *We will get in touch in the new year.* ◆ *New Year's Eve* (= December 31) ◆ *New Year's Day* (= January 1)

next¹ 🔊 /nɛkst/ *adjective*
1 coming after this one: *I'm going on vacation next week.* ◆ *Take the next road on the right.*
2 nearest to this one: *I live in the next town.*
next to someone or something at the side of someone or something: *The bank is next to the post office.* ➔ SYNONYM **beside**

next² 🔊 /nɛkst/ *adverb*
straight after this: *I finished this work. What should I do next?*

next³ 🔊 /nɛkst/ *noun* [singular]
the person or thing that comes after this one: *Susy came first and Paul was the next to arrive.*

next door /,nɛkst 'dɔr/ *adverb*
in or to the nearest house: *Who lives next door?*
▶ **next-door** *adjective*: *They're my next-door neighbors.*

nib·ble /'nɪbl/ *verb* (nib·bles, nib·bling, nib·bled)
to eat something in very small bites: *The mouse nibbled the cheese.*

nice 🔊 /naɪs/ *adjective* (nic·er, nic·est)
pleasant, good, or kind: *Did you have a nice birthday?* ◆ *I met a nice boy at the party.* ◆ *It's nice to see you.*

> ℹ️ **STYLE**
> We often say **great, fantastic,** or **wonderful** instead of "very nice": *The party was great.* ◆ *We had a fantastic weekend.* ◆ *It was a wonderful show.*

nice and ... words that show that you like something: *It's nice and warm by the fire.*
▶ **nice·ly** /'naɪsli/ *adverb*: *You can have a cookie if you ask nicely* (= in a polite way).

nick·el /'nɪkl/ *noun*
1 [count] a coin that is worth five cents ➔ Look at the picture at **money**.
2 [noncount] (symbol **Ni**) (CHEMISTRY) a hard silver-white metal that is often mixed with other metals

nick·name /'nɪkneɪm/ *noun* [count]
a name that your friends or family sometimes call you instead of your real name ➔ Look at the note at **name¹**.

▶ **nick·name** *verb* (nick·names, nick·nam·ing, nick·named): *She was nicknamed "The Ice Queen."*

nic·o·tine /'nɪkətin/ *noun* [noncount]
(HEALTH) a poisonous chemical in cigarettes that makes it difficult to stop smoking

niece /nis/ *noun* [count]
the daughter of your brother or sister ➔ Look at **nephew**.

night 🔊 /naɪt/ *noun* [count, noncount]
1 the part of the day when it is dark and most people sleep: *These animals come out at night.* ◆ *The baby cried all night.* ◆ *She stayed at my house last night.*
2 the part of the day between the afternoon and when you go to bed: *We went to a party on Saturday night.* ◆ *He doesn't get home until 8 o'clock at night.* ➔ Look at **tonight**.

night·club /'naɪtklʌb/ *noun* [count]
a place where you can go late in the evening to listen to music, dance, etc. ➔ SYNONYM **club**

night·gown /'naɪtgaʊn/ *noun* [count]
a loose dress that a woman or girl wears in bed

night·life /'naɪtlaɪf/ *noun* [noncount]
things to do in the evenings in a particular area, such as dancing or going to clubs: *What's the nightlife like around here?*

night·ly /'naɪtli/ *adjective, adverb*
happening or coming every night: *a nightly TV show*

night·mare /'naɪtmɛr/ *noun* [count]
1 a dream that frightens you: *I had a nightmare last night.*
2 something that is very bad or that frightens you: *Traveling through the snow was a nightmare.*

night·time /'naɪt,taɪm/ *noun* [noncount]
the time when it is dark: *She is afraid to go out at nighttime.* ➔ ANTONYM **daytime**

nine 🔊 /naɪn/ *number*
9
▶ **ninth** /naɪnθ/ *pronoun, adjective, adverb, noun* [count]
9th

nine·teen 🔊 /,naɪn'tin/ *number*
19
▶ **nine·teenth** /,naɪn'tinθ/ *pronoun, adjective, adverb, noun* [count]
19th

nine·ty 🔊 /'naɪnti/ *number*
1 90
2 the nineties [plural] the numbers, years, or temperatures between 90 and 99
in your nineties between the ages of 90 and 99: *My grandmother is in her nineties.*

▶ **nine·ti·eth** /'naɪnʧiəθ/ *pronoun, adjective, adverb, noun* [*count*]
90th

nip /nɪp/ *verb* (nips, nip·ping, nipped)
to give someone a quick, painful bite: *The dog nipped his leg.*

nip·ple /'nɪpl/ *noun* [*count*]
one of the two small dark circles on either side of your chest. A baby can get milk from its mother through the **nipples**.

ni·trate /'naɪtreɪt/ *noun* [*count, noncount*]
(CHEMISTRY) a chemical substance that contains NITROGEN. **Nitrates** are often used to improve the quality of soil.

ni·tro·gen /'naɪtrədʒən/ *noun* [*noncount*] (symbol **N**)
(CHEMISTRY) the gas that forms about 80% of the earth's atmosphere

No. (also **no.**) abbreviation of **number**

no¹ 🔊 /noʊ/ *exclamation*
1 used for giving a negative reply or statement: *"Do you want a drink?" "No, thank you." ◆ "Can I borrow the car?" "No, you can't."* ⊃ ANTONYM **yes**
2 something that you say when something bad happens or something surprises or shocks you: *Oh no! I broke my watch!*

no² 🔊 /noʊ/ *adjective, adverb*
1 not one; not any: *I have no money – my purse is empty. ◆ No visitors may enter without a ticket. ◆ My house is no bigger than yours.*
2 used for saying that something is not allowed: *The sign said "No Swimming."*

no·ble /'noʊbl/ *adjective* (no·bler, no·blest)
1 good, honest, and caring about other people: *noble thoughts*
2 belonging to the highest social class, in some countries: *a man of noble birth*

no·bod·y¹ 🔊 /'noʊbʌdi; 'noʊbɑdi/ *pronoun*
no person; not anyone: *Nobody in our class speaks Greek. ◆ There was nobody home.* ⊃ SYNONYM **no one**

no·bod·y² 🔊 /'noʊbʌdi; 'noʊbɑdi/ *noun* [*count*] (plural no·bod·ies)
a person who is not important or famous: *She rose from being a nobody to become a superstar.*

nod /nɑd/ *verb* (nods, nod·ding, nod·ded)
to move your head down and up again quickly as a way of saying "yes" or "hello" to someone: *"Do you understand?" asked the teacher, and everyone nodded.*
nod off to go to sleep: *Grandma nodded off in her chair.*
▶ **nod** *noun* [*count*]: *Jim gave me a nod when I came in the room.*

noise 🔊 /nɔɪz/ *noun* [*count, noncount*]
a sound, especially one that is loud or unpleasant: *I heard a noise upstairs. ◆ Don't **make** so much **noise**!*

nois·y 🔊 /'nɔɪzi/ *adjective* (nois·i·er, nois·i·est)
making a lot of noise; full of noise: *The children are very noisy. ◆ The restaurant was too noisy.* ⊃ ANTONYM **quiet**
▶ **nois·i·ly** /'nɔɪzəli/ *adverb*: *He ate his dinner noisily.*

no·mad /'noʊmæd/ *noun* [*count*]
a member of a group of people that moves with its animals from place to place
▶ **no·mad·ic** /noʊ'mædɪk/ *adjective*: *nomadic tribes*

nom·i·nate /'nɑmɪneɪt/ *verb* (nom·i·nates, nom·i·nat·ing, nom·i·nat·ed)
(POLITICS) to suggest that someone or something should be given a job, a prize, etc.: *I would like to nominate Bill Jones as chairman. ◆ She was nominated for the Pulitzer Prize.*
▶ **nom·i·na·tion** /,nɑmə'neɪʃn/ *noun* [*count, noncount*]: *The closing date for nominations is September 8th.*

Prefix

non-

not: *a **non**smoker* (= a person who does not smoke) *◆ **non**alcoholic drinks* (= drinks containing no alcohol) *◆ a **non**stop flight*

non·al·co·hol·ic /,nɑnælkə'hɔlɪk; ,nɑnælkə'hɑlɪk/ *adjective*
(used about drinks) not containing alcohol: *nonalcoholic beer* ⊃ ANTONYM **alcoholic**

non·count noun /,nɑnkaʊnt 'naʊn/ (also **un·count·a·ble noun**) *noun* [*count*]
(ENGLISH LANGUAGE ARTS) **Noncount nouns** are ones that have no plural and cannot be used with "a" or "an": *The words "advice" and "furniture" are noncount nouns.* ⊃ Look at **count noun**.

none 🔊 /nʌn/ *pronoun*
not any; not one: *She's eaten all the chocolates – there are none in the box. ◆ I went to four stores, but none of them had the book I wanted.*

none·the·less AWL /,nʌnðə'lɛs/ *adverb* (formal)
anyway; despite what has just been said: *It won't be easy, but we're going to try nonetheless.* ⊃ SYNONYM **nevertheless**

non·ex·ist·ent /,nɑnɪg'zɪstənt/ *adjective*
not existing or not available: *In some areas, public transportation is completely nonexistent.*

non·fic·tion /,nɑn'fɪkʃn/ *noun* [*noncount*]
(ENGLISH LANGUAGE ARTS) writing that is about real people, events, and facts: *You'll find*

biographies in the nonfiction section of the library. ⊃ ANTONYM **fiction**

non·sense 🖉 /'nɑnsɛns/ noun [noncount]
1 words or ideas that have no meaning or that are not true: *It's nonsense to say that Jackie is lazy.*
2 silly or bad behavior: *Their new teacher doesn't allow any nonsense in class.*

noo·dles /'nudlz/ noun [plural]
long thin pieces of food made from flour, egg, and water that are cooked in water or used in soups: *Would you prefer rice or noodles?*

noon /nun/ noun [noncount]
twelve o'clock in the middle of the day: *I met him at noon.* ⊃ Look at **midnight**.

no one 🖉 /'noʊ wʌn/ pronoun
no person; not anyone: *There was no one in the classroom.* • *No one saw me go into the house.* ⊃
SYNONYM **nobody**

nor 🖉 /nɔr/ conjunction
used after "neither" and "not" to mean "also not": *Neither Tom nor I eat meat.* • *Allan won't go, and nor will Lucy.* • *"I don't like eggs." "Nor do I."*

norm **AWL** /nɔrm/ noun [count]
a way of behaving that is normal or accepted: *Is it the norm for children to have a TV in their bedroom?*

nor·mal 🖉 **AWL** /'nɔrml/ adjective
usual and ordinary; not different or special: *I will be home at the normal time.*

nor·mal·ly 🖉 **AWL** /'nɔrməli/ adverb
1 usually: *I normally go to bed at about eleven o'clock.*
2 in the usual or ordinary way: *He isn't behaving normally.*

north 🖉 /nɔrθ/ noun [singular] (abbreviation N.)
(GEOGRAPHY) the direction to your left when you watch the sun rise; a place in this direction: *the north of Alaska* ⊃ Look at the picture at **compass**.
▶ **north** adjective, adverb: *They live in North Minneapolis.* • *a north wind* (= that comes from the north) • *We traveled north from Raleigh to Philadelphia.*

north·east (also **North·east**) /,nɔrθ'ist/ noun [singular] (abbreviation N.E.)
(GEOGRAPHY) the direction between north and east; a place in this direction: *He lives in the Northeast.* ⊃ Look at the picture at **compass**.
▶ **north·east** adjective, adverb: *the northeast coast of Florida*
▶ **north·east·ern** /,nɔrθ'istərn/ adjective: *northeastern regions*

north·ern 🖉 /'nɔrðərn/ adjective
(GEOGRAPHY) connected with, in, or from the north: *Hartford is in northern Connecticut.*

north·ern·er (also **North·ern·er**) /'nɔrðərnər/ noun [count]
(GEOGRAPHY) a person who is from or who lives in the northern part of a country ⊃ ANTONYM **southerner**

the North Pole /ðə ,nɔrθ 'poʊl/ noun [singular]
(GEOGRAPHY) the point on the earth's surface which is farthest north ⊃ Look at **the South Pole**. ⊃ Look at the picture at **earth**.

north·west (also **North·west**) /,nɔrθ'wɛst/ noun [singular] (abbreviation N.W.)
(GEOGRAPHY) the direction between north and west; a place in this direction: *She's from the Northwest.* ⊃ Look at the picture at **compass**.
▶ **north·west** adjective, adverb: *If you look northwest, you can see the tower.*
▶ **north·west·ern** /,nɔrθ'wɛstərn/ adjective: *northwestern Pennsylvania*

nose 🖉 /noʊz/ noun [count]
1 the part of your face above your mouth, which you use for breathing and smelling: *Blow your nose!* (= Clear your nose by blowing through it.) ⊃ Look at the picture at **face**.
2 the front part of an airplane

nose·bleed /'noʊzblid/ noun [count]
(HEALTH) a flow of blood that comes from your nose: *I used to get nosebleeds as a child.*

nos·tal·gi·a /nɑ'stældʒə/ noun [noncount]
a feeling of pleasure, mixed with sadness, when you remember happy times in the past
▶ **nos·tal·gic** /nɑ'stældʒɪk/ adjective: *The reunion made Anne feel nostalgic for her college days.*

nos·tril /'nɑstrəl/ noun [count]
one of the two holes in your nose

nos·y /'noʊzi/ adjective (nos·i·er, nos·i·est)
too interested in other people's lives and business: *"Where are you going?" "Don't be so nosy!"*

not 🖉 /nɑt/ adverb
used for forming negative sentences or phrases: *I'm not hungry.* • *They did not arrive.* • *I can come tomorrow, but not on Tuesday.* • *"Are you angry with me?" "No, I'm not."*

Grammar

■ We often say and write **n't**: *John isn't* (= is not) *here.* • *I hope she won't* (= will not) *be late.*

not at all
1 used as a way of saying "no" or "definitely not": *"Are you tired?" "Not at all."* • *The instructions are not at all clear.*
2 used as a reply when someone has thanked you for something: *"Thanks for your help." "Oh, not at all."*

not only…but also words you use to show that there is something important to add: *Not only was he late, but also he was wearing jeans and a T-shirt!*

note¹ 🔑 /noʊt/ *noun* [count]
1 words that you write quickly to help you remember something: *I made a note of her address.* ✦ *The teacher told us to take notes.*
2 a short letter: *Dave sent me a note to thank me for the present.*
3 a short piece of extra information about something in a book: *Look at the note on page 39.*
4 (MUSIC) one sound in music; the written symbol for one sound: *I can play a few notes.* ✦ *What's this note?*

note² /noʊt/ *verb* (notes, not·ing, not·ed)
to notice and remember something: *Please note that all the stores are closed on Mondays.*
note something down to write something so that you can remember it: *The police officer noted down my name and address.*

note·book /'noʊtbʊk/ *noun* [count]
1 a small book that you can write in ⊃ Look at the picture at **stationery**.
2 (COMPUTERS) a very small computer that you can carry with you and use anywhere

note·pad /'noʊtpæd/ *noun* [count]
pieces of paper that you can write on, joined together in a block

note·pa·per /'noʊt,peɪpər/ *noun* [noncount]
paper that you write letters on

noth·ing 🔑 /'nʌθɪŋ/ *pronoun*
not anything; no thing: *There's nothing in this bottle – it's empty.* ✦ *I finished all my work and I have nothing to do.* ✦ *Don't leave the baby there with nothing on* (= not wearing any clothes); *he'll get cold.*
for nothing
1 for no money: *You can have these books for nothing. I don't want them.*
2 without a good result: *I went to the station for nothing – she wasn't on the train.*
have nothing to do with someone or **something** to have no connection with someone or something: *That question has nothing to do with what we're discussing.* ✦ *Keep out of this – it has nothing to do with you.*
nothing but only: *He eats nothing but salad.*
nothing like not the same as someone or something in any way: *He's nothing like his brother.*

no·tice¹ 🔑 /'noʊtəs/ *verb* (no·tic·es, no·tic·ing, no·ticed)
to see or pay attention to someone or something: *Did you notice what she was wearing?* ✦ *I noticed that he was driving a new pickup truck.*

no·tice² /'noʊtəs/ *noun*
1 [noncount] the act of paying attention to someone or something: *The protests are finally making the government take notice.* ✦ *I didn't take any notice of what she said.*
2 [count] a piece of writing that tells people something: *The notice on the wall says "NO SMOKING."*
3 [noncount] a warning that something will happen; the amount of time before it happens: *We only had two weeks' notice for the exam.* ✦ *We left for the station on very short notice, and I forgot my coat.* ✦ *He gave notice* (= he said officially that he will leave his job).

no·tice·a·ble /'noʊtəsəbl/ *adjective*
easy to see: *I have a mark on my shirt. Is it noticeable?*

no·tion **AWL** /'noʊʃn/ *noun* [count]
something that you have in your mind; an idea: *I had a notion that I had seen her before.*

no·to·ri·ous /noʊ'tɔriəs/ *adjective*
well known for being bad: *a notorious criminal* ⊃
SYNONYM infamous
▶ **no·to·ri·ous·ly** /noʊ'tɔriəsli/ *adverb*: *This road is notoriously dangerous.*

not·with·stand·ing **AWL** /,nɑtwɪθ'stændɪŋ/ *preposition, adverb* (formal)
despite something; not being affected by something: *The plane landed on time, notwithstanding the terrible weather conditions.*

noun /naʊn/ *noun* [count]
(ENGLISH LANGUAGE ARTS) a word that is the name of a person, place, thing, or idea: *"Anne," "Philadelphia," "cat," and "happiness" are all nouns.* ⊃ Look at **count noun, noncount noun**.

nour·ish /'nərɪʃ/ *verb* (nour·ish·es, nour·ish·ing, nour·ished)
to give someone or something the right kind of food so that they can grow and be healthy
▶ **nour·ish·ment** /'nərɪʃmənt/ *noun* [noncount]

Nov. abbreviation of **November**

nov·el¹ 🔑 /'nɑvl/ *noun* [count]
(ENGLISH LANGUAGE ARTS) a book that tells a story about people and things that are not real: *"To Kill a Mockingbird" is a novel by Harper Lee.*

nov·el² /'nɑvl/ *adjective*
new, different, and interesting: *a novel idea*

nov·el·ist /'nɑvəlɪst/ *noun* [count]
(ENGLISH LANGUAGE ARTS) a person who writes novels

nov·el·ty /'nɑvlti/ *noun* (plural nov·el·ties)
1 [noncount] the quality of being new and different: *The novelty of her new job soon faded.*
2 [count] something new and unusual: *It was a novelty for me not to have to get up early.*

æ **cat**   ɛ **ten**   i **see**   ɪ **sit**   ɑ **hot**   ɔ **saw**   ʌ **cup**   ʊ **put**   u **too**

No·vem·ber 🔊 /nouˈvɛmbər/ *noun* [count, noncount] (abbreviation **Nov.**)
the eleventh month of the year

now[1] 🔊 /naʊ/ *adverb*
1 at this time: *I can't see you now – can you come back later?* ◆ *She was in Washington, but she's living in Maryland now.* ◆ *Don't wait – do it now!* ◆ *From now on* (= after this time) *your teacher will be Mr. Hancock.*
2 used when you start to talk about something new, or to make people listen to you: *I finished writing that letter. Now, what should we have for dinner?* ◆ *Be quiet, now!*
now and then; **now and again** sometimes, but not often: *We go to that restaurant now and then.*

now[2] /naʊ/ (also **now that**) *conjunction*
because something has happened: *Now that Mark has arrived we can start dinner.*

now·a·days /ˈnaʊədeɪz/ *adverb*
at this time: *Most people work with computers nowadays.*

no·where 🔊 /ˈnoʊwɛr/ *adverb*
not anywhere; at, in, or to no place: *There's nowhere to stay in this town.*
nowhere near not at all: *Ruth's Spanish is nowhere near as good as yours.*

nu·cle·ar 🔊 **AWL** /ˈnukliər/ *adjective* (**PHYSICS**)
1 using the energy that is made when the central part of an atom is broken: *nuclear energy* ◆ *nuclear weapons*
2 connected with the center of atoms: *nuclear physics*

nu·cle·us /ˈnukliəs/ *noun* [count] (*plural* **nu·cle·i** /ˈnukliaɪ/)
(**PHYSICS**) the center of a cell or an atom ⊃ Look at the picture at **atom**.

nude /nud/ *adjective*
not wearing any clothes ⊃ **SYNONYM naked**
▸ **nu·di·ty** /ˈnudət̮i/ *noun* [noncount]: *The movie has scenes of nudity.*

nudge /nʌdʒ/ *verb* (**nudg·es, nudg·ing, nudged**)
to touch or push someone or something with your **ELBOW** (= the middle part of your arm where it bends): *Nudge me if I fall asleep in the theater.*
▸ **nudge** *noun* [count]: *Liz gave me a nudge.*

nug·get /ˈnʌgət/ *noun* [count]
a small lump of a valuable metal, especially gold, that is found in the earth

nui·sance /ˈnusns/ *noun* [count]
a person or thing that causes you trouble: *I lost my keys. What a nuisance!*

numb /nʌm/ *adjective*
not able to feel anything: *My fingers were numb with cold.*

num·ber[1] 🔊 /ˈnʌmbər/ *noun*
1 [count] (abbreviation **No.** or **no.**) a word or symbol that represents a quantity, for example "two" or "130": *Choose a number between ten and one hundred.* ◆ *What's your phone number?* ◆ *I live at no. 47.*
2 [count, noncount] a group of more than one person or thing: *A large number of our students come from large families.* ◆ *There are a number of ways you can cook an egg.*

num·ber[2] /ˈnʌmbər/ *verb* (**num·bers, num·ber·ing, num·bered**)
1 to give a number to something: *Number the pages from one to ten.*
2 a word you use to say how many people or things there are: *The army numbers over 500,000 men.*

nu·mer·al /ˈnumərəl/ *noun* [count]
(**MATH**) a sign or symbol that represents a quantity: *Roman numerals* (= I, II, III, IV, V, etc.)

nu·mer·a·tor /ˈnuməreɪt̮ər/ *noun* [count]
(**MATH**) the number above the line in a **FRACTION**, for example the 3 in ¾ ⊃ Look at **denominator**.

nu·mer·i·cal /nuˈmɛrɪkl/ *adjective*
connected with or shown by numbers: *to put items in numerical order*

nu·mer·ous /ˈnumərəs/ *adjective* (formal)
many

nun /nʌn/ *noun* [count]
(**RELIGION**) a woman who has given her life to God instead of getting married. Most **nuns** live together in a special building (called a **CONVENT**). ⊃ Look at **monk**.

nurse[1] 🔊 /nərs/ *noun* [count]
(**HEALTH**) a person whose job is to take care of people who are sick or hurt: *My sister works as a nurse in a hospital.*

nurse[2] /nərs/ *verb* (**nurs·es, nurs·ing, nursed**)
(**HEALTH**) to take care of someone who is sick or hurt: *I nursed my father when he was sick.*

nurs·er·y /ˈnərsəri/ *noun* [count] (*plural* **nurs·er·ies**)
1 a bedroom for a baby
2 a place where people grow and sell plants

nurs·er·y rhyme /ˈnərsəri raɪm/ *noun* [count]
a song or poem for young children

nurs·er·y school /ˈnərsəri skul/ *noun* [count, noncount]
a school for children between the ages of about two and five ⊃ **SYNONYM preschool**

nurs·ing /ˈnərsɪŋ/ *noun* [noncount]
(**HEALTH**) the job of being a nurse: *a career in nursing*

nurs·ing home /'nərsɪŋ hoʊm/ *noun* [count]
(**HEALTH**) a place where people who are too old or too sick to live on their own can live and be taken care of

nuts

pecan   peanut   chestnut

walnut   almond   hazelnut

nut 🔑 /nʌt/ *noun* [count]
1 a dry fruit that has a hard outside part with a seed inside. Many types of **nuts** can be eaten: *walnuts, hazelnuts, and peanuts*
2 a metal ring that you put on the end of a long piece of metal (called a BOLT) to fix things together ➲ Look at the picture at **bolt**.

nu·tri·ent /'nutriənt/ *noun* [count]
(**BIOLOGY, HEALTH**) a substance that someone or something needs to live and grow: *Plants draw minerals and other nutrients from the soil.*

nu·tri·tion /nu'trɪʃn/ *noun* [noncount]
(**HEALTH**) the food that you eat and the way that it affects your health: *We can offer you advice on diet and nutrition.*
▶ **nu·tri·tion·al** /nu'trɪʃənl/ *adjective*: *the nutritional value of green vegetables*

nu·tri·tious /nu'trɪʃəs/ *adjective*
(used about food) good for you: *tasty and nutritious meals*

nuts /nʌts/ *adjective* (informal)
crazy: *The kids are driving me nuts!*

ny·lon /'naɪlɑn/ *noun*
1 [noncount] very strong material that is made by machines and is used for making clothes, rope, brushes, and other things: *a nylon fishing line*
2 **nylons** [plural] another word for **pantyhose**

O o

O, o /oʊ/ *noun* [*count, noncount*] (*plural* O's, o's /oʊz/)
1 the fifteenth letter of the English alphabet: *"Orange" begins with an "O."*
2 a way of saying the number "0": *My number is seven three one, O two nine three* (= 731-0293).

oak /oʊk/ *noun*
1 [*count*] a kind of large tree
2 [*noncount*] the wood of an **oak** tree: *an oak table*

oar /ɔr/ *noun* [*count*]
a long stick with a flat end that you use for moving a boat through water (ROWING) ⊃ Look at the picture at **rowboat**.

o·a·sis /oʊˈeɪsəs/ *noun* [*count*] (*plural* o·a·ses /oʊˈeɪsiz/)
(GEOGRAPHY) a place in a desert that has trees and water

oath /oʊθ/ *noun* [*count*]
a formal promise: *He swore an oath of loyalty.*
under oath If you are **under oath**, you have made a formal promise to tell the truth in a court of law: *He was accused of lying under oath.*

oat·meal /ˈoʊtmil/ *noun* [*noncount*]
a soft, thick food that is made from OATS cooked with water or milk and eaten hot for breakfast: *a bowl of oatmeal with brown sugar*

oats /oʊts/ *noun* [*plural*]
a plant with seeds that we use as food for people and animals: *We make cereals from oats.*

o·be·di·ent /oʊˈbidiənt/ *adjective*
doing what someone tells you to do: *He was an obedient child.* ⊃ ANTONYM **disobedient**
▸ **o·be·di·ence** /oʊˈbidiəns/ *noun* [*noncount*]: *Most teachers expect complete obedience from their students.* ⊃ ANTONYM **disobedience**
▸ **o·be·di·ent·ly** /oʊˈbidiəntli/ *adverb*: *I called the dog and it followed me obediently.*

o·bese /oʊˈbis/ *adjective*
(HEALTH) (used about people) very fat, in a way that is not healthy ⊃ Look at the note at **fat¹**.
▸ **o·be·si·ty** /oʊˈbisəti/ *noun* [*noncount*]: *Obesity among children is increasing in this country.*

o·bey /oʊˈbeɪ/ *verb* (o·beys, o·bey·ing, o·beyed)
to do what someone tells you to do; to follow an order or rule: *He always obeyed his parents.* • *You must obey the law.*

ob·ject¹ ⚷ /ˈɑbdʒɛkt/ *noun* [*count*]

> **ⓘ PRONUNCIATION**
> When the word **object** is a noun, you say the first part of the word louder: **OBject**. When the word **object** is a verb, you say the second part of the word louder: **obJECT**.

1 a thing that you can see and touch: *There was a small round object on the table.*
2 what you plan to do: *His object in life is to become as rich as possible.* ⊃ SYNONYM **aim**
3 (ENGLISH LANGUAGE ARTS) the person or thing that is affected by an action. In the sentence "Susan painted the door," the **object** of the sentence is "the door." ⊃ Look at **subject**(3).

ob·ject² /əbˈdʒɛkt/ *verb* (ob·jects, ob·ject·ing, ob·ject·ed)
to not like something; to not agree with something: *I objected to their plan.*

ob·jec·tion /əbˈdʒɛkʃn/ *noun* [*count, noncount*]
a reason why you do not like something or do not agree with something: *I have no objections to the plan.*

ob·jec·tive¹ ⟨AWL⟩ /əbˈdʒɛktɪv/ *noun* [*count*]
something that you are trying to achieve ⊃ SYNONYM **aim**

ob·jec·tive² ⟨AWL⟩ /əbˈdʒɛktɪv/ *adjective*
based on the facts, not on your own feelings and opinions: *an objective report of what happened* ⊃ ANTONYM **subjective**
▸ **ob·jec·tive·ly** ⟨AWL⟩ /əbˈdʒɛktɪvli/ *adverb*

ob·li·gat·ed /ˈɑbləɡeɪtəd/ *adjective*
If you are **obligated** to do something, you have to do it because of a rule or law, or because it is the right thing to do: *She felt obligated to take care of her mother.*

ob·li·ga·tion /ˌɑbləˈɡeɪʃn/ *noun* [*count, noncount*]
something that you must do: *We have an obligation to help.*

ob·lig·a·to·ry /əˈblɪɡəˌtɔri/ *adjective* (*formal*)
If something is **obligatory**, you must do it because it is the law or a rule. ⊃ SYNONYM **compulsory**

o·blige /əˈblaɪdʒ/ *verb* (o·blig·es, o·blig·ing, o·bliged)
to force someone to do something: *Parents are obliged by law to send their children to school.*

o·bliv·i·ous /əˈblɪviəs/ *adjective*
not noticing or realizing something: *She was completely oblivious to all the trouble she had caused.*

ob·long /ˈɑblɔŋ/ *noun* [*count*]
any shape that is longer than it is wide: *An egg is an oblong.*
▸ **ob·long** *adjective*: *an oblong shape*

ə **a**bout   y **y**es   w **w**oman   t̬ **butter**   eɪ **say**   aɪ **five**   ɔɪ **boy**   aʊ **now**   oʊ **go**

ob·nox·ious /əbˈnɑkʃəs/ *adjective*
extremely unpleasant: *He really is an obnoxious person.*

o·boe /ˈoʊboʊ/ *noun* [count]
(MUSIC) a musical instrument made of wood that you play by blowing into it ⊃ Look at the picture at **instrument**.

ob·scene /əbˈsin/ *adjective*
connected with sex in a way that is rude or that shocks people: *He made an obscene gesture.*

ob·ser·vant /əbˈzərvənt/ *adjective*
good at noticing things: *That's very observant of you!*

ob·ser·va·tion /ˌɑbzərˈveɪʃn/ *noun*
1 [noncount] when you watch someone or something carefully: *The police kept the house under observation.* ◆ *His powers of observation are excellent.*
2 [count] something that you say or write: *He made an observation about the weather.* ⊃ SYNONYM **comment**

ob·serve /əbˈzərv/ *verb* (ob·serves, ob·serv·ing, ob·served) (*formal*)
to watch or see someone or something: *The police observed a man leaving the house.*
▶ **ob·serv·er** /əbˈzərvər/ *noun* [count]
a person who watches someone or something: *According to observers, the fire started around midnight.*

ob·sess /əbˈsɛs/ *verb* (ob·sess·es, ob·sess·ing, ob·sessed)
to completely fill your mind: *Don is obsessed with football.*

ob·ses·sion /əbˈsɛʃn/ *noun* [count]
a person or thing that you think about all the time: *Cars are his obsession.*

ob·sta·cle /ˈɑbstəkl/ *noun* [count]
something that makes it difficult for you to do something or go somewhere: *Not speaking a foreign language was a major obstacle to her career.*

ob·sti·nate /ˈɑbstənət/ *adjective*
not changing your ideas; not doing what other people want you to do: *He's too obstinate to say he's sorry.* ⊃ SYNONYM **stubborn**

ob·struct /əbˈstrʌkt/ *verb* (ob·structs, ob·struct·ing, ob·struct·ed)
to be in the way, so that someone or something cannot go past: *Please move your car – you're obstructing traffic.*
▶ **ob·struc·tion** /əbˈstrʌkʃn/ *noun* [count]
a thing that stops someone or something from going past: *The train had to stop because there was an obstruction on the tracks.*

ob·tain 🔑 **AWL** /əbˈteɪn/ *verb* (ob·tains, ob·tain·ing, ob·tained) (*formal*)
to get something: *to obtain permission*

ob·tuse an·gle /ɑbˈtus ˌæŋgl/ *noun* [count]
(MATH) an angle of more than 90° but less than 180° ⊃ Look at the picture at **angle**.

ob·vi·ous 🔑 **AWL** /ˈɑbviəs/ *adjective*
easy to see or understand: *It's obvious that she's not happy.* ⊃ SYNONYM **clear**
▶ **ob·vi·ous·ly** **AWL** /ˈɑbviəsli/ *adverb*: *There has obviously been a mistake.*

oc·ca·sion 🔑 /əˈkeɪʒn/ *noun* [count]
1 a time when something happens: *I've been to Chicago on three or four occasions.*
2 a special time: *A wedding is a big family occasion.*

oc·ca·sion·al /əˈkeɪʒnl/ *adjective*
happening sometimes, but not very often: *We get the occasional visitor.*

oc·ca·sion·al·ly /əˈkeɪʒnəli/ *adverb*
sometimes, but not often: *I go to Miami occasionally.*

oc·cu·pant **AWL** /ˈɑkyəpənt/ *noun* [count] (*formal*)
a person who lives or works in a particular room, house, or building: *The fire destroyed the building, but all the occupants escaped safely.*

oc·cu·pa·tion **AWL** /ˌɑkyəˈpeɪʃn/ *noun*
1 [count] (*formal*) a job: *What is your mother's occupation?*
2 [noncount] when a country or army takes or has control of an area or building

oc·cu·py **AWL** /ˈɑkyəpaɪ/ *verb* (oc·cu·pies, oc·cu·py·ing, oc·cu·pied, has oc·cu·pied)
1 to fill a space or period of time: *The bed seemed to occupy most of the room.* ⊃ SYNONYM **take up**
2 (*formal*) to live or work in a room or building: *The house next door has not been occupied for months.* ⊃ Look at **occupant**.
3 to keep someone busy: *She occupied herself reading.*
4 to take or have control of an area or building: *Protestors occupied the TV station.*
▶ **oc·cu·pied** **AWL** /ˈɑkyəpaɪd/ *adjective*
1 being used: *Excuse me – is this seat occupied?*
2 busy: *This work will keep me occupied all week.*

oc·cur 🔑 **AWL** /əˈkər/ *verb* (oc·curs, oc·cur·ring, oc·curred) (*formal*)
to happen: *The accident occurred this morning.*
occur to someone to come into someone's mind: *It occurred to me that you might like to come.*

oc·cur·rence **AWL** /əˈkərəns/ *noun* [count] (*formal*)
something that happens: *Identity theft is now a very common occurrence.*

o·cean 🔑 /ˈoʊʃn/ *noun* (GEOGRAPHY)
1 [noncount] the salt water that covers most of the surface of the earth: *People were swimming in the ocean.* ◆ *Ocean levels are rising.*

2 Ocean [count] one of the five large areas of salt water on Earth: *the Pacific Ocean*

o·clock 🔊 /əˈklɑk/ *adverb*
used after the numbers one to twelve for saying the time: *I left home at four o'clock and arrived in Los Angeles at five thirty.*

Grammar

- Be careful! **O'clock** is only used with full hours. You cannot say "at five thirty o'clock."

oc·ta·gon /ˈɑktəgɑn/ *noun* [count]
(**MATH**) a shape with eight straight sides
▶ **oc·tag·o·nal** /ɑkˈtægənl/ *adjective*: *an octagonal coin*

octagon

Oc·to·ber 🔊 /ɑkˈtoʊbər/ *noun*
[count, noncount] (abbreviation **Oct.**) the tenth month of the year

oc·to·pus /ˈɑktəpəs/ *noun* [count] (*plural* **oc·to·pus·es**)
an ocean animal with a soft body and eight long arms (called **TENTACLES**)

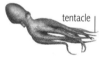 

tentacle

octopus   **squid**

odd 🔊 **AWL** /ɑd/ *adjective* (**odd·er, odd·est**)
1 strange or unusual: *It's odd that he left without telling anyone.* ⊃ **SYNONYM strange**
2 (**MATH**) not able to be divided by two: *1, 3, 5, and 7 are all odd numbers.* ⊃ **ANTONYM even**
the odd one out one that is different from all the others: *"Apple," "orange," "cabbage" – which is the odd one out?*

odd·ly /ˈɑdli/ *adverb*
in a strange or unusual way: *She behaved very oddly.* ⊃ **SYNONYM strangely**

odds **AWL** /ɑdz/ *noun* **the odds** [plural]
used for saying how likely something is: *The odds are that he'll win* (= he'll probably win). *The odds are against us* (= we will probably not succeed).
odds and ends (*informal*) different small things that are not important: *a box of odds and ends*

o·dor /ˈoʊdər/ *noun* [count] (*formal*)
a smell, especially a bad smell

of 🔊 /əv; ʌv/ *preposition*
1 belonging to or connected with someone or something: *the back of the chair* ◆ *What's the*

name of this mountain? ◆ *the time of the American Civil War* ◆ *the arrival of the president*
2 used for saying what something is or what something is made of: *a piece of wood* ◆ *a cup of coffee* ◆ *Is this shirt made of cotton?*
3 used for showing that someone or something is part of a group: *one of the girls* ◆ *some of his friends*
4 used after an amount, etc.: *a gallon of water* ◆ *the fourth of July*
5 used with some adjectives and verbs: *I'm proud of you.* ◆ *This perfume smells of roses.*
6 used for giving your opinion about someone's behavior: *That's very kind of you.*

off 🔊 /ɔf; ɑf/ *preposition, adverb*
1 down or away from something: *He fell off the roof.* ◆ *We got off the bus.* ◆ *The thief ran off.*
2 used for talking about removing something: *If you're hot, take your coat off.* ◆ *Can you clean that paint off the carpet?* ⊃ **ANTONYM on**
3 away from a place; at a distance in space or time: *I must be off* (= leave) *soon .* ◆ *Summer is still a long way off.*
4 joined to something and leading from it: *The bathroom is off the bedroom.*
5 not connected; not working: *Make sure the lights are off before you go.* ⊃ **ANTONYM on**
6 not at work or school: *I had the day off yesterday.*
7 (used about a plan or arrangement) not going to happen anymore; canceled: *The meeting next Monday is off.* ⊃ **ANTONYM on**

of·fend /əˈfɛnd/ *verb* (**of·fends, of·fend·ing, of·fend·ed**)
to make someone feel angry or unhappy; to hurt someone's feelings: *I hope they won't be offended if I don't come.*

of·fend·er /əˈfɛndər/ *noun* [count] (*formal*)
a person who breaks a law: *a juvenile* (= young) *offender*

of·fense 🔊 /əˈfɛns/ *noun*
1 [count] an illegal action: *He has committed an offense.* ⊃ **SYNONYM crime**
2 [noncount] when a person is angry or unhappy because of what someone has said or done: *He took offense when I refused his help.*
3 /ˈɑfɛns/ [noncount, singular] (**SPORTS**) the players on a sports team who try to score points

of·fen·sive /əˈfɛnsɪv/ *adjective*
1 rude in a way that makes someone feel upset, angry, or insulted: *offensive language* ⊃ **ANTONYM inoffensive**
2 used for or connected with attacking: *offensive weapons* ⊃ **ANTONYM defensive**

of·fer¹ 🔊 /'ɔfər; 'afər/ *verb* (of·fers, of·fer·ing, of·fered)
to say or show that you will do or give something if another person wants it: *She offered me a piece of cake.* ✦ *I **offered** to help her.*

of·fer² 🔊 /'ɔfər; 'afər/ *noun* [count]
1 when you offer to do or give something if another person wants it: *Thanks for the offer, but I don't need any help.* ✦ *I've received a **job offer**, but I'm not sure if I should accept it.*
2 an amount of money that you say you will give for something: *They **made an offer** for the house.*

of·fice 🔊 /'ɔfəs; 'afəs/ *noun*
1 [count] a place where people work, usually at desks: *I work in an office.*
2 [count] a place where you can buy something or get information ⊃ Look at **box office, post office, ticket office**.
3 [noncount] (POLITICS) an official position, often as part of a government or other organization: *How long has the president been **in office**?*

of·fi·cer 🔊 /'ɔfəsər; 'afəsər/ *noun* [count]
1 a person in the army, navy, or air force who gives orders to other people: *a naval officer*
2 a person who does important work, especially for the government: *an intelligence officer*
3 = **police officer**: *Sorry, officer, I didn't realize I was driving too fast.*

of·fi·cial¹ 🔊 /ə'fɪʃl/ *adjective*
connected with government, or with a particular organization or person in authority: *an official government report* ✦ *an official announcement*

of·fi·cial² 🔊 /ə'fɪʃl/ *noun* [count]
a person who does important work, especially for the government: *government officials*

of·fi·cial·ly 🔊 /ə'fɪʃəli/ *adverb*
done by the government, or by someone in authority: *He has now heard officially that he's got the job.*

of·ten 🔊 /'ɔfn; 'afn/ *adverb*
many times: *I don't see him very often.* ✦ *We often play tennis on Sunday.* ✦ *Write as often as you can.* ✦ ***How often** do you visit her?*
every so often sometimes, but not often: *Every so often she calls me.*

oh 🔊 /oʊ/ *exclamation*
1 used for showing a strong feeling, like surprise or fear: *Oh no! I've lost my keys!*
2 used before other words, for example when you are thinking of what to say: *"What time is it?" "Oh, about two o'clock."*
Oh well used when you are not happy about something, but you cannot change it: *"I'm too*

busy to go out tonight." "Oh well, I'll see you tomorrow then."

oil 🔊 /ɔɪl/ *noun* [noncount]
1 (CHEMISTRY) a thick liquid that comes from under the ground or the ocean. We use **oil** for energy and to make machines work smoothly.
2 (BIOLOGY) a thick liquid that comes from plants or animals and that we use in cooking: *Fry the onions in oil.* ✦ *olive oil*

oil paint·ing /'ɔɪl peɪntɪŋ/ *noun* [count]
(ART) a picture that has been done with paint made from oil

oil rig /'ɔɪl rɪg/ *noun* [count]
a large structure with special equipment for bringing oil out of the ground

oil well /'ɔɪl wɛl/ *noun* [count]
a hole that is made deep in the ground or under the ocean in order to get oil

oil·y /'ɔɪli/ *adjective* (oil·i·er, oil·i·est)
like oil, or covered with oil: *an oily liquid* ✦ *oily hands*

oint·ment /'ɔɪntmənt/ *noun* [count, noncount]
(HEALTH) a smooth substance that you put on sore skin or on an injury to help it get better

OK¹ 🔊 (also o·kay) /,oʊ'keɪ/ *exclamation* (informal)
yes: *"Should we go to the party?" "OK."* ⊃
SYNONYM **all right**

OK² 🔊 (also o·kay) /,oʊ'keɪ/ *adjective, adverb* (informal)
1 safe and well; calm or happy: *"How's your mom?" "OK, thanks."*
2 all right; acceptable: *Is it okay to sit here?* ⊃
SYNONYM **all right**

old 🔊 /oʊld/ *adjective* (old·er, old·est)
1 having lived for a long time: *My grandfather is very old.* ✦ *My sister is older than me.* ⊃ ANTONYM **young**
2 made or bought a long time ago: *an old house* ⊃ ANTONYM **new**
3 You use **old** to show the age of someone or something: *Dan is seven **years old**.* ✦ *How old are you?* ✦ *a four-year-old girl*
4 done or had before now: *My old job was more interesting than this one.* ⊃ ANTONYM **new**
5 known for a long time: *Jess is an old friend – we went to school together.*
▶ **the old** *noun* [plural]
old people

old age /,oʊld 'eɪdʒ/ *noun* [noncount]
the part of your life when you are old: *He's enjoying life **in his old age**.* ⊃ ANTONYM **youth**

old-fash·ioned 🔊 /,oʊld 'fæʃənd/ *adjective*
not modern: *old-fashioned clothes* ✦ *My parents are kind of old-fashioned.*

ol·ive /ˈɑlɪv/ *noun* [*count*]
a small green or black fruit that people eat or make into oil: *The salad dressing needs a little more olive oil.*

Suffix

-ology

(in nouns) the subject of study: *astrology* (= the study of the stars) • *biology* • *technology*

the O·lym·pic Games /ðɪ əˌlɪmpɪk ˈɡeɪmz/ (also **the O·lym·pics** /ðɪ əˈlɪmpɪks/) *noun* [*plural*]
(**SPORTS**) an international sports competition that is organized every four years in a different country
▶ **O·lym·pic** /əˈlɪmpɪk/ *adjective*: *Who holds the Olympic record for the 200 meters?*

om·e·let (also **om·e·lette**) /ˈɑmlət/ *noun* [*count*]
a dish made of eggs mixed together and then fried: *a cheese omelet*

o·mit /oʊˈmɪt/ *verb* (**o·mits**, **o·mit·ting**, **o·mit·ted**) (*formal*)
to not include something: *Omit question 2 and do question 3.* ⊃ **SYNONYM leave out**

om·ni·vore /ˈɑmnɪˌvɔr/ *noun* [*count*]
(**BIOLOGY**) an animal that eats both plants and meat ⊃ Look at **carnivore**, **herbivore**.
▶ **om·niv·o·rous** /ˌɑmˈnɪvərəs/ *adjective*: *an omnivorous diet*

on /ɑn; ɔn/ *preposition, adverb*
1 used for showing where something is: *Your book is on the table.* • *The number is on the door.* • *I have a cut on my hand.* • *There's a good movie on TV tonight.*
2 used with ways of traveling and types of travel: *He got on the bus.* • *I came here on foot* (= I walked).
3 used for showing when: *My birthday is on May 6.* • *I'll see you on Monday.*
4 working; being used: *All the lights were on.* ⊃ **ANTONYM off**
5 covering your body: *Put your coat on.*
6 about something: *a book on cars*
7 happening or planned: *What's on at the movie theater?* • *Is the meeting still on, or has it been canceled?* ⊃ **ANTONYM off**
8 using something: *I bought it on the Internet.* • *I was on the phone with Jania.* • *He saw it on TV.*
9 used for showing that someone or something continues: *The man shouted at us, but we just walked on.*
10 soon after: *She called me on her return from New York.*
on and on without stopping: *He went* (= talked) *on and on about his girlfriend.*

once¹ /wʌns/ *adverb*
1 one time: *I've only been to Europe once.* • *He calls us once a week* (= once every week).
2 at some time in the past: *This house was once a school.*
all at once all at the same time, or suddenly: *People began talking all at once.* • *All at once she got up and left the room.*
at once
1 (*formal*) immediately; now: *Come here at once!*
2 at the same time: *I can't do two things at once.*
for once this time only: *For once, I agree with you.*
once again; once more again; one more time: *Can you explain it to me once more?*
once and for all now and for the last time: *You have to make a decision once and for all.*
once in a while sometimes, but not often
once or twice a few times; not often: *I've only met them once or twice.*
once upon a time (used at the beginning of a children's story) a long time ago: *Once upon a time there was a beautiful princess…*

once² /wʌns/ *conjunction*
as soon as; when: *Once you've finished your homework you can go out.*

one¹ /wʌn/ *number, adjective*
1 the number 1: *One and one make two* (1 + 1 = 2). • *Only one person spoke.*
2 a person or thing, especially when they are part of a group: *One of my friends is sick.* • *I lost one of my books.*
3 only: *You are the one person I can trust.*
4 used for talking about a particular time, without saying exactly when: *I'll come over one evening.*
one by one first one, then the next, etc.; separately: *Please come in one by one.*
one or two a few: *There are one or two things I need to do this morning.*

one² /wʌn/ *pronoun*
1 used instead of the name of a person or thing: *I bought some bananas. Do you want one?* • *"Can I borrow a book?" "Yes. Which one?"* • *The questions are hard – leave the ones you can't do.*
2 (*formal*) people in general; I: *Exercise makes one physically fit.*

ⓘ STYLE
It is very formal to use **one** in this way and it sounds old-fashioned. We usually say "you" for "people in general" and "I" when you are talking about yourself.

one an·oth·er /ˌwʌn əˈnʌðər/ *pronoun*
each other: *We looked at one another.*

ə **about**   y **yes**   w **woman**   t̮ **butter**   eɪ **say**   aɪ **five**   ɔɪ **boy**   aʊ **now**   oʊ **go**

one·self /wʌnˈsɛlf/ *pronoun* (*formal*)
used with "one" for saying that an action involves the person doing it: *One has to ask oneself if such action is necessary.*
by oneself
1 alone; without other people
2 without help

one-way /ˌwʌn ˈweɪ/ *adjective*
allowing travel in one direction only: *a one-way street* ◆ *a one-way ticket* ⊃ Look at **round-trip**.

on·go·ing **AWL** /ˈɑngoʊɪŋ/ *adjective*
continuing to exist now: *It's an ongoing problem.*

on·ion 🔑 /ˈʌnyən/ *noun* [count, noncount]
a round vegetable with many layers and a strong smell. Cutting **onions** can make you cry. ⊃ Look at the picture at **vegetable**.

on·line /ˌɑnˈlaɪn/ (also **on-line**) *adjective, adverb*
(**COMPUTERS**) using a computer or the Internet: *Online shopping is both cheap and convenient.* ◆ *Reservations can be made online.* ⊃ Look at the note at **Internet**.

on·ly¹ 🔑 /ˈoʊnli/ *adjective, adverb*
1 with no others: *She's the only girl in her class.*
2 and no one or nothing else; no more than: *I invited twenty people to the party, but only five came.* ◆ *We can't have dinner now. It's only four o'clock!* ◆ *We only waited five minutes.*
if only words you use to say that you wish something would happen or be true: *If only he would call.*

on·ly² /ˈoʊnli/ *conjunction* (*informal*)
but: *I like this bag, only it's too expensive.*

on·ly child /ˌoʊnli ˈtʃaɪld/ *noun* [count] (*plural* **on·ly chil·dren** /ˌoʊnli ˈtʃɪldrən/)
a person who has no brothers or sisters: *I'm an only child.*

on·to 🔑 /ˈɑntə; ˈɑntu/ *preposition*
to a place on someone or something: *The bottle fell onto the floor.* ◆ *The cat jumped onto the table.*

on·ward /ˈɑnwərd/ (also **on·wards** /ˈɑnwərdz/) *adverb*
1 and after: *From September onward it usually gets a lot colder.*
2 forward: *The soldiers marched onwards until they came to a bridge.*

oops /ʊps/ *exclamation*
a word you say when you have, or almost have, a small accident, or when you break something, etc.: *Oops! Are you ok?*

ooze /uz/ *verb* (**ooz·es**, **ooz·ing**, **oozed**)
1 If a thick liquid **oozes** from something, it comes out slowly: *Blood was oozing from the wound.*
2 to show a lot of a particular quality: *She walked into the party oozing confidence.*

o·paque /oʊˈpeɪk/ *adjective*
If something is **opaque**, you cannot see through it: *a special piece of opaque glass* ⊃ **ANTONYM transparent**

o·pen¹ 🔑 /ˈoʊpən/ *adjective*
1 not closed, so that people or things can go in or out: *Leave the windows open.* ◆ *The book lay open on the table.* ◆ *an open box*
2 able to be used or done; available: *The bank is open from 9 a.m. to 4 p.m.* ◆ *The competition is open to all children under the age of 14.*
3 not hiding your thoughts and feelings: *She's a very open person.*
4 away from towns and people; with not many buildings or trees: *We were in open country.*
5 not yet decided: *"Where should we go on Friday?" "Let's leave it open."*
in the open air outside: *We had our lunch in the open air.*

o·pen² 🔑 /ˈoʊpən/ *verb* (**o·pens**, **o·pen·ing**, **o·pened**)
1 to move, or to move something, so that something is not closed or covered: *The door opened and a man came in.* ◆ *It was hot, so I opened a window.* ◆ *Open your eyes!* ◆ *Open your books to page 10.*
2 to make it possible for people to enter a place: *Banks don't open on Sundays.* ◆ *The president opened the new hospital.*
3 to start something; to start: *I'd like to open a bank account.* ◆ *How do you open a file in this program?* ◆ *The story opens with a murder.* ⊃ **ANTONYM close, shut**
open up to talk about what you feel and think: *It took him a long time to really open up to me.*

o·pen³ /ˈoʊpən/ *noun*
out in the open outside: *Children need to play out in the open.*
into the open not hidden or secret: *They intend to bring their complaints out into the open.*

open-air /ˌoʊpən ˈɛr/ *adjective*
not inside a building: *an open-air concert*

o·pen·er /ˈoʊpənər/ *noun* [count]
a small tool that you use for opening cans or bottles: *a can opener*

o·pen·ing /ˈoʊpənɪŋ/ *noun* [count]
1 a space in something where people or things can go in and out: *The cattle got out through an opening in the fence.* ⊃ **SYNONYM hole**
2 a ceremony to celebrate the start of a public event or the first time a new building, road, etc. is used: *the opening of the Olympic Games*

o·pen·ly /ˈoʊpənli/ *adverb*
not secretly; without trying to hide anything: *She told me openly that she didn't agree.*

---

open-minded /ˌoʊpən ˈmaɪndɪd/ *adjective*
ready to consider new ideas and opinions ⊃
ANTONYM **narrow-minded**

o·pe·ra /ˈɑprə/ *noun* [count, noncount]
(MUSIC) a play where the actors sing most of the
words to music: *Do you like opera?* ◆ *We went to
see an opera by Verdi.* ◆ *an opera house* (= a
buidling where you can see operas)

op·er·ate 🔑 /ˈɑpəreɪt/ *verb* (op·er·ates,
op·er·at·ing, op·er·at·ed)
1 to work; to make something work: *I don't
know how this machine operates.* ◆ *These
switches operate the heat.*
2 (HEALTH) to cut into someone's body to take
out or repair a part inside: *Doctors will operate
on her leg tomorrow.*

Word building

■ A doctor who **operates** on people in a
hospital is called a **surgeon**.
■ A surgeon's work is called **surgery**.

op·er·a·tion 🔑 /ˌɑpəˈreɪʃn/ *noun* [count]
1 (HEALTH) cutting into someone's body to take
out or repair a part inside: *He had an operation
on his eye.*
2 an event that needs a lot of people or
planning: *a military operation*

op·er·a·tor /ˈɑpəreɪt̬ər/ *noun* [count]
1 a person who makes a machine work: *a
machine operator*
2 a person who works for a telephone company
and helps to connect people making calls: *What
number do you dial for the operator?*
3 a person or company that runs a particular
business: *a tour operator*

o·pin·ion 🔑 /əˈpɪnyən/ *noun* [count]
what you think about something: *In my opinion,
she's wrong.* ◆ *What's your opinion of his work?* ◆
He had strong opinions on everything. ⊃
SYNONYM **view**

o·pos·sum /əˈpɑsəm/
noun [count]
a type of small animal
with fur and a long
tail that lives in trees

opossum

op·po·nent
/əˈpoʊnənt/ *noun*
[count]
(SPORTS) the person
against you in a fight or competition: *Flynn beat
his opponent easily.*

op·por·tu·ni·ty 🔑 /ˌɑpərˈtunət̬i/ *noun* [count,
noncount] (*plural* op·por·tu·ni·ties)
a chance to do something; a time when you can
do something that you want to do: *I didn't get*

the opportunity to visit them. ◆ *It was a golden* (=
perfect) *opportunity, and I decided to take it.*

op·pose /əˈpoʊz/ *verb* (op·pos·es, op·pos·ing,
op·posed)
to try to stop or change something because you
do not like it: *A lot of people opposed the new law.*

op·posed /əˈpoʊzd/ *adjective*
disagreeing strongly with something and trying
to stop it: *I am opposed to the plan.*
as opposed to (*formal*) words that you use to
show that you are talking about one thing, not
something different: *The flight cost $400, as
opposed to $200 last year.*

op·po·site¹ 🔑 /ˈɑpəzət/ *adjective, adverb,
preposition*

🛈 SPELLING
Remember! You spell **opposite** with PP.

1 as different as possible: *I can't walk with you,
because I'm going in the opposite direction.*
2 across from where someone or something is;
on the other side: *The church is on the opposite
side of the road from my house.* ◆ *The bank is
opposite the supermarket.*

op·po·site² 🔑 /ˈɑpəzət/ *noun* [count]
a word or thing that is as different as possible
from another word or thing: *"Hot" is the
opposite of "cold."*

op·po·si·tion /ˌɑpəˈzɪʃn/ *noun* [noncount]
disagreeing with something and trying to stop
it: *There was a lot of opposition to the plan.*

op·press /əˈprɛs/ *verb* (op·press·es,
op·press·ing, op·pressed)
(POLITICS) to treat someone in an unfair and
cruel way, and not give them the same freedom
and rights as other people
▶ **op·pressed** /əˈprɛst/ *adjective*: *an oppressed
minority*
▶ **op·pres·sion** /əˈprɛʃn/ *noun* [noncount]: *a
struggle against oppression*

opt /ɑpt/ *verb* (opts, opt·ing, opt·ed)
to choose to do something: *She opted for a
career in medicine.*

op·ti·cal /ˈɑptɪkl/ *adjective*
connected with the sense of sight: *optical effects*

op·ti·cian /ɑpˈtɪʃn/ *noun* [count]
a person who makes and sell glasses ⊃ Look at
optometrist.

op·ti·mism /ˈɑptəmɪzəm/ *noun* [noncount]
the feeling that good things will happen ⊃
ANTONYM **pessimism**

op·ti·mist /ˈɑptəmɪst/ *noun* [count]
a person who thinks that good things will
happen ⊃ ANTONYM **pessimist**

op·ti·mis·tic /ˌɑptəˈmɪstɪk/ *adjective*
If you are **optimistic**, you think that good things will happen: *I'm optimistic about winning.* ⊃ ANTONYM **pessimistic**

op·tion **AWL** /ˈɑpʃn/ *noun* [count]
a thing that you can choose: *You have the option of studying full-time or part-time.* ⊃ SYNONYM **choice**

op·tion·al **AWL** /ˈɑpʃənl/ *adjective*
If something is **optional**, you can choose it or not choose it: *All students must learn English, but Spanish is optional.* ⊃ ANTONYM **compulsory**

op·tom·e·trist /ɑpˈtɑmətrɪst/ *noun* [count]
(HEALTH) a person who tests your eyes and tells you which glasses, etc. you need ⊃ Look at **optician**.

or /ər; ɔr/ *conjunction*
1 a word that joins possibilities: *Is it blue or green?* ◆ *Are you coming or not?* ◆ *You can have soup, salad, or sandwiches.* ◆ *She hasn't called or written for weeks.*
2 if not: *Go now, or you'll be late.* ⊃ SYNONYM **otherwise**

o·ral /ˈɔrəl/ *adjective*
1 spoken; not written: *an oral exam*
2 connected with the mouth: *oral hygiene*

or·ange¹ /ˈɔrɪndʒ; ˈɑrɪndʒ/ *noun* [count, noncount]
1 a round fruit with a color between red and yellow, and a thick skin: *orange juice* ⊃ Look at the picture at **fruit**.
2 a color between red and yellow

or·ange² /ˈɔrɪndʒ; ˈɑrɪndʒ/ *adjective*
with a color that is between red and yellow: *orange paint*

or·bit /ˈɔrbət/ *noun* [count, noncount]
(PHYSICS) the path of a planet or an object that is moving around another thing in space
▶ **or·bit** *verb* (or·bits, or·bit·ing, or·bit·ed)
to move around something in space: *The spacecraft is orbiting the moon.*

or·chard /ˈɔrtʃərd/ *noun* [count]
a piece of land where fruit trees grow

or·ches·tra /ˈɔrkəstrə/ *noun* [count]
(MUSIC) a big group of people who play different musical instruments together

Word building

- An **orchestra** is made up of four sections.
- The **strings** section includes violins and cellos.
- The **woodwind** section includes clarinets and flutes.
- The **brass** section includes trumpets and trombones.

- The **percussion** section includes drums and cymbals.

or·deal /ɔrˈdil/ *noun* [count, usually singular]
a very bad experience: *He was lost in the mountains for a week without food or water – it was a terrible ordeal.*

or·der¹ /ˈɔrdər/ *noun*
1 [noncount] the way that you place people or things together: *The names are in alphabetical order.* ◆ *List the jobs in order of importance.*
2 [noncount] when everything is in the right place or everyone is doing the right thing: *Our teacher likes order in the classroom.* ◆ *Are these papers in order?* ⊃ ANTONYM **disorder**
3 [count] words that tell someone to do something: *He gave the order for work to begin.* ◆ *Soldiers have to obey orders.*
4 [count] when you ask a company to send or supply goods to you: *I'd like to place an order for some books.*
5 [count] when you ask for food or drink in a restaurant, bar, etc.: *The waiter took our order.*
in order so that you can do something: *We arrived early in order to buy our tickets.*
out of order (used about a machine, etc.) not working: *I couldn't call you – the phone was out of order.*

or·der² /ˈɔrdər/ *verb* (or·ders, or·der·ing, or·dered)
1 to tell someone that they must do something: *The student was ordered to leave the classroom.*
2 to ask a company to send or supply goods to you: *The store didn't have your book, so I ordered it for you.*
3 to ask for food or drink in a restaurant, bar, etc.: *I ordered some coffee.*

or·di·nal num·ber /ˈɔrdənl ˌnʌmbər/ *noun* [count]
(MATH) a number that shows the position of something in a series. "First," "second," "third," and "fourth" are ordinal numbers. ⊃ Look at **cardinal**(2).

or·di·nar·y /ˈɔrdnˌɛri/ *adjective*
not special or unusual: *It's interesting to see how ordinary people live in other countries.* ⊃ SYNONYM **normal**
out of the ordinary unusual: *Did you see anything out of the ordinary?* ⊃ SYNONYM **strange**

ore /ɔr/ *noun* [count, noncount]
(GEOGRAPHY) rock or earth from which you get metal: *iron ore*

or·gan /ˈɔrgən/ *noun* [count]
1 a part of your body that has a special purpose, for example your heart: *the body's internal organs*
2 (MUSIC) a musical instrument, usually in a church, that is played like a piano

or·gan·ic /ɔr'gænɪk/ *adjective*
1 grown in a natural way, without using chemicals: *organic vegetables*
2 (BIOLOGY) containing living things: *Improve the soil by adding* ***organic matter****.*
▶ **or·gan·i·cal·ly** /ɔr'gænɪkli/ *adverb*: *organically grown vegetables*

or·gan·ism /'ɔrgənɪzəm/ *noun* [*count*]
(BIOLOGY) a living thing, especially a very small one that you can only see with a special instrument (called a MICROSCOPE)

or·gan·i·za·tion 🔑 /ˌɔrgənə'zeɪʃn/ *noun*
1 [*count*] a group of people who work together for a special purpose: *He works for an organization that helps old people.*
2 [*noncount*] the activity of planning or arranging something; the way that something is planned or arranged: *She's busy with the organization of her daughter's wedding.*

or·gan·ize 🔑 /'ɔrgənaɪz/ *verb* (**or·gan·iz·es**, **or·gan·iz·ing**, **or·gan·ized**)
1 to plan or arrange something: *Our teacher organized a visit to the museum.*
2 to put or arrange things into a system or order: *You need to organize your work more carefully.*

or·gan·ized 🔑 /'ɔrgənaɪzd/ *adjective*
1 with everything planned or arranged: *a badly organized trip*
2 (used about a person) able to plan your work, life, etc. well: *Jenny's such an organized person.* ➲ ANTONYM **disorganized**

o·ri·ent·ed AWL /'ɔriɛntəd/ *adjective*
for, or interested in, a particular type of person or thing: *She's very career-oriented.* ◆ *a male-oriented career*

or·i·gin /'ɔrədʒɪn/ *noun* [*count, noncount*]
1 the time, way, or place that something first existed: *the* ***origins of*** *life on earth*
2 the country, race, culture, etc. that a person comes from: *His family is* ***of*** *Italian* ***origin****.*

o·rig·i·nal 🔑 /ə'rɪdʒənl/ *adjective*
1 first; earliest: *I have the car now, but my sister was the original owner.*
2 new and different: *His poems are very original.*
3 real, not copied: *original paintings*
▶ **o·rig·i·nal** *noun* [*count*]: *This is a copy of the painting – the original is in the Smithsonian.*

o·rig·i·nal·ly /ə'rɪdʒənəli/ *adverb*
in the beginning: *The school was originally very small.* ◆ *I'm from Texas originally.*

or·na·ment /'ɔrnəmənt/ *noun* [*count*]
a thing that we have because it is beautiful, not because it is useful: *glass ornaments*
▶ **or·na·men·tal** /ˌɔrnə'mɛntl/ *adjective*: *There is an ornamental pond in the yard.*

or·phan /'ɔrfən/ *noun* [*count*]
a child whose parents are dead

or·phan·age /'ɔrfənɪdʒ/ *noun* [*count*]
a home for children whose parents are dead

os·trich /'ɑstrɪtʃ/ *noun* [*count*] (*plural* **os·trich·es**)
a very big bird from Africa that cannot fly but can run fast because it has long legs

oth·er 🔑 /'ʌðər/ *adjective, pronoun*
as well as, or different from the one or ones I have said: *Carmen is Mexican, but the other students in my class are Korean.* ◆ *I can only find one shoe. Have you seen the other one?* ◆ *I saw her on the other side of the road.* ◆ *John and Claire arrived at nine o'clock, but the others* (= the other people) *were late.*
other than except for someone or something: *I haven't told anyone other than you.*
the other day not many days ago: *I saw your brother the other day.* ➲ SYNONYM **recently**

oth·er·wise 🔑 /'ʌðərwaɪz/ *adverb, conjunction*
1 in all other ways: *The house is small, but otherwise it's very nice.*
2 in a different way: *Most people agreed, but Rachel thought otherwise.*
3 if not: *Hurry up, otherwise you'll be late.* ➲ SYNONYM **or**

ot·ter /'ɑṭər/ *noun* [*count*]
a river animal with brown fur that eats fish

ouch /aʊtʃ/ *exclamation*
You say "**ouch**" when you suddenly feel pain: *Ouch! That hurts!* ➲ SYNONYM **ow**

ought to 🔑 /'ɔṭə; 'ɔt tu/ *modal verb*
1 words that you use to tell or ask someone what is the right thing to do: *It's late – you ought to go home.* ➲ SYNONYM **should**
2 words that you use to say what you think will happen or what you think is true: *Tom has worked very hard, so he ought to pass the exam.* ◆ *That movie ought to be good.* ➲ SYNONYM **should**
➲ Look at the note at **modal verb**.

ounce 🔑 /aʊns/ *noun* [*count*] (abbreviation **oz.**)
1 a measure of weight (=28.35 grams). There are 16 **ounces** in a **pound**: *eight* ***ounces of*** *flour*
2 another word for **fluid ounce**: *a 12-ounce can of cola.*

our 🔑 /ɑr; 'aʊər/ *adjective*
belonging to us: *This is our house.*

ours 🔑 /ɑrz; 'aʊərz/ *pronoun*
something that belongs to us: *Your car is the same as ours.*

our·selves 🔑 /ɑr'sɛlvz; aʊər'sɛlvz/ *pronoun* [*plural*]
1 used when you and another person or other people do an action and are also affected by it: *We made ourselves some coffee.*
2 a word that makes "we" stronger: *We built the house ourselves.*

by ourselves
1 without help
2 alone; without other people: *We went on vacation by ourselves.*

Suffix

-ous

(in adjectives) having a particular quality: *dangerous ◆ disastrous ◆ poisonous ◆ mysterious*

out /aʊt/ *adjective, adverb*
1 away from the inside of a place: *When you go out, please close the door.* ◆ *She opened the box and took out a picture.* ➷ **ANTONYM in**
2 not at home or not in the place where you work: *I called Steve but he was out.* ◆ *I went out to the movies last night.* ➷ **ANTONYM in**
3 not hidden; that you can see: *Look! The sun is out!* ◆ *All the flowers are out* (= open).
4 not burning or shining: *The fire went out.*
5 in a loud voice: *She cried out in pain.*
6 (used about a player in a game or sport) not allowed to continue playing: *If you get three answers wrong, you're out.* ➷ Look at **out of.**

out·age /'aʊtɪdʒ/ *noun* [count]
a time when there is no electricity in a building or an area: *There was a **power outage** across the whole city.*

out·break /'aʊtbreɪk/ *noun* [count]
the sudden start of something bad: *the **outbreak** of war*

out·come **AWL** /'aʊtkʌm/ *noun* [count]
the result or effect of an action or event: *What was the outcome of the investigation?*

out·door /'aʊtdɔr/ *adjective*
happening, existing, or used outside a building: *an outdoor swimming pool* ◆ *Bring outdoor clothing.* ➷ **ANTONYM indoor**

out·doors /ˌaʊt'dɔrz/ *adverb*
not in a building: *In summer we sometimes eat outdoors.* ➷ **SYNONYM outside** ➷ **ANTONYM indoors**

out·er /'aʊtər/ *adjective*
on the outside; far from the center: *Remove the outer leaves from the cabbage.* ◆ *the outer suburbs of the city* ➷ **ANTONYM inner**

out·er space /ˌaʊtər 'speɪs/ *noun* [noncount] = **space** (3)

out·field /'aʊtfild/ *noun* [singular]
(**SPORTS**) the part of a baseball field that is farthest away from where the ball is being hit ➷ Look at **infield.**

out·fit /'aʊtfɪt/ *noun* [count]
a set of clothes that you wear together: *I bought a new outfit for the party.*

out·go·ing /ˌaʊt'goʊɪŋ/ *adjective*
friendly and interested in other people and new experiences

out·grow /ˌaʊt'groʊ/ *verb* (out·grows, out·grow·ing, out·grew /ˌaʊt'gru/, has out·grown /ˌaʊt'groʊn/)
to become too big or too old for something: *She's outgrown her school uniform again.* ➷ **SYNONYM grow out of**

out·ing /'aʊtɪŋ/ *noun* [count]
a short trip for pleasure: *Mrs. Sharp's class is going on an outing to the zoo.* ➷ **SYNONYM trip**

out·law[1] /'aʊtlɔ/ *verb* (out·laws, out·law·ing, out·lawed)
to make something illegal: *The government has outlawed the use of cell phones while driving.*

out·law[2] /'aʊtlɔ/ *noun* [count]
(especially in the past) a person who has done something illegal and is hiding from the police

out·let /'aʊtlɛt/ *noun* [count]
a place on a wall where you can connect electrical equipment to a power supply: *Is there an outlet in here so I can plug in my phone?*

out·line /'aʊtlaɪn/ *noun* [count]
1 a line that shows the shape or edge of something: *It was dark, but we could see the dim outline of the castle.*
2 a description of the most important facts or ideas about something: *a brief outline of the events*

out·look /'aʊtlʊk/ *noun* [count]
1 the way you think or feel about life and the world: *I try to keep a positive outlook on life.*
2 what will probably happen: *The outlook for the economy is not good.*

out of /'aʊtəv/ *preposition*
1 words that show where from: *She took a cake out of the box.* ◆ *She got out of bed.* ➷ **ANTONYM into**
2 not in: *Fish can't live out of water.*
3 using something; from: *He made a table out of some old pieces of wood.*
4 from a number or set: *Nine out of ten people think that the government is right.*
5 without: *We're out of coffee.* ◆ *She's been out of work for six months.*
6 because of a particular feeling: *I was just asking out of curiosity.*

out of date /ˌaʊt əv 'deɪt/ *adjective*
old; not useful, wanted, or allowed now: *This map is out of date.* ➷ Look at **up to date.**

out·put **AWL** /'aʊtpʊt/ *noun* [count, noncount]
the amount of things that someone or something has made or done: *What was the factory's output last year?*

out·ra·geous /aʊt'reɪdʒəs/ *adjective*
that shocks you or makes you feel very angry:
His behavior was outrageous.

out·set /'aʊtsɛt/ *noun*
at or **from the outset** at or from the beginning
of something: *People were unhappy with the new
law from the outset.*

out·side¹ /'aʊtsaɪd; ˌaʊt'saɪd/ *noun* [count,
usually singular]
the part of something that is away from the
middle: *the outside of the package* • *We've only
seen the building from the outside.* ⊃ **ANTONYM
inside**

out·side² /'aʊtsaɪd/ *adjective*
away from the middle of something: *the outside
walls of the house* • *Could you turn on the outside
lights, please?* ⊃ **ANTONYM inside**

out·side³ /'aʊtsaɪd; ˌaʊt'saɪd/ *preposition,
adverb*
in or to a place that is not inside a building: *I left
my bicycle outside the store.* • *Come outside and
see the garden!* ⊃ **ANTONYM inside**

out·skirts /'aʊtsk�ərts/ *noun* [plural]
the edges of a town or city: *They live on the
outskirts of town.*

out·spo·ken /ˌaʊt'spoʊkən/ *adjective*
saying exactly what you think or feel: *Linda is
very outspoken in her criticism.*

out·stand·ing /ˌaʊt'stændɪŋ/ *adjective*
very good; much better than others: *Her work is
outstanding.* ⊃ **SYNONYM excellent**

out·ward¹ /'aʊtwərd/ *adjective*
1 connected with the way things seem to be:
*Despite her cheerful outward appearance, she
was in fact very unhappy.*
2 traveling away from a place that you will
return to later: *There were no delays on the
outward flight.*

out·ward² /'aʊtwərd/ (also **out·wards**
/'aʊtwərdz/) *adverb*
toward the outside: *The windows open outward.*
⊃ **ANTONYM inward**

o·val /'oʊvl/ *adjective*
(**MATH**) with a shape like an egg: *an oval mirror*
▶ **o·val** *noun* [count]: *Draw an oval.*

ov·en /'ʌvən/ *noun* [count]
a piece of equipment with a door that you use to
cook food in: *Take the bread out of the oven.*

o·ver¹ /'oʊvər/ *adverb, preposition*
1 above something; higher than something: *A
plane flew over our heads.* • *There is a picture over
the fireplace.*
2 on someone or something so that it covers
them: *She put a blanket over the sleeping child.*
3 across; to the other side of something: *The
dog jumped over the wall.*

4 to or in a place: *Come over and see us on
Saturday.* • *Come over here!* • *Go over there and
see if you can help.*
5 down or to the side: *I fell over in the street.* • *He
leaned over to speak to her.*
6 so that the other side is on top: *You may turn
your papers over and begin.*
7 more than a number, price, etc.: *She lived in
Spain for over 20 years.* • *This game is for children
aged ten and over.*
8 used for saying that someone repeats
something: *He said the same thing over and over*
(= many times). • *You'll have to start all over
again* (= from the beginning).
9 not used; remaining: *There is a lot of cake left
over from the party.*
all over everywhere; in every part: *Have you
seen my glasses? I've looked all over.* • *She travels
all over the world.*

o·ver² /'oʊvər/ *adjective*
finished: *The exams are over now.*

Prefix

over-

1 more than is good; too much: *overcook* •
oversleep • *overoptimistic* • *overweight*
2 on the outside; extra: *overcoat* • *overtime*

o·ver·all **AWL** /ˌoʊvər'ɔl/ *adjective*
including everything: *The overall cost of the
repairs will be about $350.* ⊃ **SYNONYM total**
▶ **o·ver·all** **AWL** *adverb*: *How much will it cost
overall?*

o·ver·alls /'oʊvərɔlz/ *noun* [plural]
pants with an extra part that covers your chest,
held up by a piece of cloth over each shoulder

o·ver·board /'oʊvərbɔrd/ *adverb*
over the side of a boat and into the water: *She
fell overboard.*

o·ver·cast /'oʊvərkæst/ *adjective*
(used about the sky) covered with clouds

o·ver·charge /ˌoʊvər'tʃɑrdʒ/ *verb*
(o·ver·charg·es, o·ver·charg·ing, o·ver·charged)
to ask someone to pay too much money for
something: *The taxi driver overcharged me.*

o·ver·coat /'oʊvərkoʊt/ *noun* [count]
a long warm coat: *Although it was a hot day, he
was wearing an overcoat.* ⊃ Look at the picture at
clothes.

o·ver·come /ˌoʊvər'kʌm/ *verb* (o·ver·comes,
o·ver·com·ing, o·ver·came /ˌoʊvər'keɪm/, has
o·ver·come)
to find an answer to a difficult thing in your life;
to control something: *He overcame his fear of
flying.*

o·ver·crowd·ed /ˌoʊvər'kraʊdəd/ *adjective*
too full of people: *The trains are overcrowded on
Friday evenings.*

tʃ **ch**in   dʒ **J**une   v **v**an   θ **th**in   ð **th**en   s **s**o   z **z**oo   ʃ **sh**e

o·ver·do /ˌoʊvər'du/ *verb* (o·ver·does /ˌoʊvər'dʌz/, o·ver·did /ˌoʊvər'dɪd/, o·ver·do·ing, has o·ver·done /ˌoʊvər'dʌn/) to use or do too much of something: *You should get a little exercise, but don't overdo it.*

o·ver·dose /'oʊvərdoʊs/ *noun* [count] (HEALTH) an amount of a drug or medicine that is too large and so is not safe: *He died of a **drug overdose**.*

o·ver·due /ˌoʊvər'du/ *adjective* not done by the expected time: *We had no money and the rent was overdue.* ⊃ SYNONYM late

o·ver·es·ti·mate AWL /ˌoʊvər'ɛstəmeɪt/ *verb* (o·ver·es·ti·mates, o·ver·es·ti·mat·ing, o·ver·es·ti·mat·ed) to think that someone or something is bigger, better, more important, etc. than they really are: *I overestimated how far we could get in a day.* ⊃ ANTONYM underestimate

o·ver·flow /ˌoʊvər'floʊ/ *verb* (o·ver·flows, o·ver·flow·ing, o·ver·flowed) to be so full that there is no space: *Someone left the faucet on and the bathtub overflowed.*

o·ver·grown /ˌoʊvər'groʊn/ *adjective* covered with plants that have grown too big: *The house was empty and the yard was overgrown.*

o·ver·head /'oʊvərhɛd/ *adjective* above your head: *an overhead light* ▶ **o·ver·head** /ˌoʊvər'hɛd/ *adverb*: *A plane flew overhead.*

o·ver·hear /ˌoʊvər'hɪr/ *verb* (o·ver·hears, o·ver·hear·ing, o·ver·heard /ˌoʊvər'hərd/) to hear what someone is saying when they are speaking to another person: *I overheard Louise saying that she was unhappy.*

o·ver·lap AWL /ˌoʊvər'læp/ *verb* (o·ver·laps, o·ver·lap·ping, o·ver·lapped) When two things **overlap**, part of one thing covers part of the other thing: *The tiles on the roof overlap.*

o·ver·look /ˌoʊvər'lʊk/ *verb* (o·ver·looks, o·ver·look·ing, o·ver·looked)
1 to not see or notice something: *He overlooked one important fact.*
2 to have a view over something: *My room overlooks the ocean.*

o·ver·night /ˌoʊvər'naɪt/ *adjective, adverb* for or during the night: *an overnight trip* ◆ *They stayed at our house overnight.*

o·ver·pass /'oʊvərpæs/ *noun* [count] (*plural* o·ver·pass·es) a bridge that carries a road over other roads ⊃ Look at **underpass**.

o·ver·seas AWL /ˌoʊvər'siz/ *adjective, adverb* in, to, or from another country across the ocean: *She travels overseas a lot.* ◆ *Much of the company's business comes from overseas markets.*

o·ver·sleep /ˌoʊvər'slip/ *verb* (o·ver·sleeps, o·ver·sleep·ing, o·ver·slept /ˌoʊvər'slɛpt/) to sleep too long and not wake up at the right time: *I overslept and was late for work.*

o·ver·throw /ˌoʊvər'θroʊ/ *verb* (o·ver·throws, o·ver·throw·ing, o·ver·threw /ˌoʊvər'θru/, has o·ver·thrown /ˌoʊvər'θroʊn/) (POLITICS) to remove a leader or government from power, by using force: *The dictator was overthrown in a military coup.*

o·ver·time /'oʊvərtaɪm/ *noun* [noncount]
1 extra time that you spend at work: *I have **done a lot of overtime** this week.*
2 (SPORTS) extra time that is added to the end of a sports game if there is no winner at the end of the normal period: *The game went into overtime.*

o·ver·weight /ˌoʊvər'weɪt/ *adjective* too heavy or fat: *The doctor said I was overweight and that I should eat less.* ⊃ ANTONYM underweight ⊃ Look at the note at **fat¹**.

o·ver·whelm·ing /ˌoʊvər'wɛlmɪŋ/ *adjective* very great or strong: *an overwhelming feeling of loneliness*

ow /aʊ/ *exclamation* You say "**ow**" when you suddenly feel pain: *Ow! You're standing on my foot.* ⊃ SYNONYM ouch

owe 🔑 /oʊ/ *verb* (owes, ow·ing, owed)

> ⓘ PRONUNCIATION
> The word **owe** sounds like **go**.

1 to have to pay money to someone: *I lent you $10 last week and $10 the week before, so you owe me $20.*
2 to have something because of a particular person or thing: *He **owes** his life **to** the man who pulled him out of the river.* ◆ *She owes her success to hard work.*

owl /aʊl/ *noun* [count] a bird that flies at night and eats small animals

own¹ 🔑 /oʊn/ *adjective, pronoun*

owl

> ⓘ PRONUNCIATION
> The word **own** sounds like **bone**.

a word that shows that something belongs to a particular person: *Is that **your own** camera or did you borrow it?* ◆ *I have **my own** room now that my sister has left home.* ◆ *I want a home **of my own**.*

Grammar

■ Be careful! You cannot use **own** after "a" or "the." You cannot say: *I would like an own room.* You say: *I would like my own room* or: *I would like a room of my own.*

on your own
1 alone: *She lives on her own.*
2 without help: *I can't move this box on my own – can you help me?*

own² 🔑 /oʊn/ *verb* (owns, own·ing, owned)
to have something that is yours: *We don't own our apartment – we rent it.* ◆ *I don't own a car.*
own up to say that you have done something wrong: *No one **owned up to** breaking the window.*

own·er 🔑 /'oʊnər/ *noun* [count]
a person who has something that belongs to them: *Who is the owner of that red car?*

ox /ɑks/ *noun* [count] (plural **ox·en** /'ɑksn/)
a large male cow that is used for pulling or carrying heavy things

ox·ide /'ɑksaɪd/ *noun* [count, noncount]
(CHEMISTRY) a combination of OXYGEN and another substance: *iron oxide*

ox·y·gen /'ɑksɪdʒən/ *noun* [noncount] (symbol **O**)
(CHEMISTRY) a gas in the air. Animals and plants need **oxygen** to live.

oys·ter /'ɔɪstər/ *noun* [count]
a small animal with a shell, which lives in the ocean. You can eat some types of **oyster**, and others produce shiny white things used to make jewelry (called PEARLS). ⊃ Look at the picture at **shellfish**.

oz. abbreviation of **ounce**

o·zone /'oʊzoʊn/ *noun* [noncount]
(CHEMISTRY) a poisonous gas that is a form of OXYGEN

o·zone-friend·ly /ˌoʊzoʊn 'frɛndli/ *adjective*
(used about cleaning products, etc.) not containing chemicals that could harm the OZONE LAYER: *Most aerosol sprays are now ozone-friendly.*

the o·zone lay·er /ði 'oʊzoʊn ˌleɪər/ *noun* [singular]
the layer of OZONE high above the surface of the earth, which helps to protect the earth from the bad effects of the sun

Pp

P, p /piː/ *noun* [*count, noncount*]
1 (*plural* **P's, p's** /piːz/) the sixteenth letter of the English alphabet: *"Pencil" begins with a "P."*
2 **p.** abbreviation of **page**

pace[1] /peɪs/ *noun*
1 [*singular*] how fast you do something or how fast something happens: *We started at a steady pace.*
2 [*count*] a step: *Take two paces forward.*
keep pace with someone or **something** to go as fast as someone or something: *She couldn't keep pace with the other runners.*

pace[2] /peɪs/ *verb*
to walk around in a nervous or angry way: *She paced up and down the sidewalk.*

pac·i·fi·er /ˈpæsəfaɪər/ *noun* [*count*]
a small, rubber object that you put in a baby's mouth to stop it from crying

pacifier

pack[1] /pæk/ *noun* [*count*]
1 a package or group of things that are sold together: *a pack of cigarettes*
2 a number of things that are wrapped or tied together: *The donkey had a heavy pack on its back.* ◆ *an ice pack*
3 a group of wild dogs or similar animals: *a pack of wolves*

pack[2] /pæk/ *verb* (**packs**, **pack·ing**, **packed**)
1 to put things into a bag, box, etc. before you go somewhere: *Have you packed your suitcase?* ◆ *Don't forget to pack your toothbrush.*
2 to put things into a box, bag, etc.: *Pack all these books into boxes.* ⊃ **ANTONYM unpack**
pack up to stop doing something: *At two o'clock we packed up and went home.*
▶ **pack·ing** /ˈpækɪŋ/ *noun* [*noncount*]: *I haven't done my packing and we're leaving tonight.*

pack·age /ˈpækɪdʒ/ *noun* [*count*]

package

MAIL TO:
Alison Shepard
1240 Courtney Avenue
Newton, New York
10063

1 something in a box, a bag, or wrapped in paper that is sent by mail: *I went to the post office to mail a package.*
2 a box, bag, etc. in which things are packed to be sold in a store: *a package of hamburger buns* ⊃ Look at the picture at **container**.

▶ **pack·age** *verb* (**pack·ag·es**, **pack·ag·ing**, **pack·aged**): *packaged food*

pack·ag·ing /ˈpækɪdʒɪŋ/ *noun* [*noncount*]
material like paper, plastic, etc. that is used to wrap things that you buy or that you send

packed /pækt/ *adjective*
full: *The train was packed.*

pack·et /ˈpækət/ *noun* [*count*]
a small flat bag that contains a small amount of something: *a packet of sunflower seeds*

pact /pækt/ *noun* [*count*]
an important agreement to do something: *They made a pact not to tell anyone.*

pad /pæd/ *noun* [*count*]
1 a thick flat piece of soft material: *Football players wear pads on their shoulders to protect them.* ◆ *I used a cotton pad to clean the cut.*
2 pieces of paper that are joined together at one end: *a writing pad*

pad·ded /ˈpædəd/ *adjective*
covered with or containing a layer of thick soft material: *a padded envelope*

pad·dle /ˈpædl/ *noun* [*count*]
a piece of wood with a flat end, which you use for moving a small boat through water ⊃ Look at the picture at **canoe**.
▶ **pad·dle** *verb* (**pad·dles**, **pad·dling**, **pad·dled**)
to move a small boat through water with a **paddle**: *We paddled up the river.*

pad·lock /ˈpædlɑk/ *noun* [*count*]
a lock that you use on things like gates and bicycles

padlock

key

page /peɪdʒ/ (abbreviation **p.**) *noun* [*count*]
one or both sides of a piece of paper in a book, magazine, or newspaper: *Please turn to page 120.* ◆ *What page is the story on?* ◆ *I'm reading a 600-page novel.*

paid form of **pay**[1]

pain /peɪn/ *noun*
1 [*count, noncount*] the feeling that you have in your body when you are hurt or sick: *I have a pain in my leg.* ◆ *He's in terrible pain.*
2 [*noncount*] unhappiness: *I could see the pain in her eyes.*
be a pain or **a pain in the neck** (*informal*) a person, thing, or situation that bothers you or makes you angry: *She can be a real pain when she's in a bad mood.*

pain·ful /ˈpeɪnfl/ *adjective*
1 giving pain: *I cut my leg – it's very painful.* ⊃
ANTONYM painless
2 making you feel upset or embarrassed: *Their divorce was painful for the kids.*
▸ **pain·ful·ly** /ˈpeɪnfl·i/ *adverb*

pain·kill·er /ˈpeɪnkɪlər/ *noun* [count]
(**HEALTH**) a drug that makes pain less strong: *She's on painkillers.*

pain·less /ˈpeɪnləs/ *adjective*
not causing pain: *a painless injection* ⊃ **ANTONYM painful**

pains·tak·ing /ˈpeɪnzteɪkɪŋ/ *adjective*
very careful and taking a long time: *a painstaking search of the area*

paint¹ /peɪnt/ *noun* [noncount]
(**ART**) a liquid that you put on things with a brush, to change the color or to make a picture: *red paint* • *Is the paint dry yet?*

paint² /peɪnt/ *verb* (**paints, paint·ing, paint·ed**)
1 to put paint on something to change the color: *We painted the walls gray.*
2 (**ART**) to make a picture of someone or something using paint: *I'm painting a picture of some flowers.* • *My sister paints very well.*

paint·brush /ˈpeɪntbrʌʃ/ *noun* [count] (*plural* **paint·brush·es**)
(**ART**) a brush that you use for painting ⊃ Look at the picture at **brush**.

paint·er /ˈpeɪntər/ *noun* [count]
1 a person whose job is to paint things like walls or houses
2 (**ART**) a person who paints pictures: *Picasso was a famous painter.* ⊃ **SYNONYM artist**

paint·ing /ˈpeɪntɪŋ/ *noun* [count]
(**ART**) a picture that someone makes with paint: *a painting by Norman Rockwell* • *He did a painting of the bridge.*

pair /pɛr/ *noun* [count]
1 two things of the same kind that you use together: *a pair of shoes* • *a new pair of earrings*
2 a thing with two parts that are joined together: *a pair of glasses* • *a pair of scissors* • *I bought two pairs of pants.*
3 two people or animals together: *a pair of ducks* ⊃ Look at **couple**.
in pairs with two things or people together: *Shoes are only sold in pairs.* • *The students were working in pairs.*

pa·ja·mas /pəˈdʒæməz/ *noun* [plural]
a loose jacket and pants that you wear in bed

pal /pæl/ *noun* [count] (*informal*)
a friend

pal·ace /ˈpæləs/ *noun* [count]
a very large house where a king or queen lives

pal·ate /ˈpælət/ *noun* [count]
the top part of the inside of your mouth

pale /peɪl/ *adjective* (**pal·er, pal·est**)
1 with not much color in your face: *Are you sick? You look pale.* • *She has very pale skin.* ⊃ **SYNONYM white**
2 with a light color; not strong or dark: *a pale blue dress* ⊃ **SYNONYM light** ⊃ **ANTONYM dark**

palm /pɑm/ *noun* [count]
1 the flat part of the front of your hand ⊃ Look at the picture at **hand**.
2 (also **palm tree** /ˈpɑm tri/) a tree that grows in hot countries, with no branches and a lot of big leaves at the top: *a coconut palm*

pam·phlet /ˈpæmflət/ *noun* [count]
a very thin book with a paper cover that gives information about something

pan /pæn/ *noun* [count]
a metal container that you use for cooking: *a frying pan* • *a saucepan*

pan·cake /ˈpænkeɪk/ *noun* [count]
a very thin round thing that you eat. You make **pancakes** with flour, eggs, and milk: *I had blueberry pancakes for breakfast.* ⊃ Look at the picture at **waffle**.

pan·da /ˈpændə/ *noun* [count]
a large black and white animal that lives in China

panda

pane /peɪn/ *noun* [count]
a piece of glass in a window: *a windowpane*

pan·el **AWL** /ˈpænl/ *noun* [count]
1 a group of people who give their opinions about something or discuss something: *Do you have any questions for our panel?* • *a panel of judges*
2 a flat piece of wood, metal, or glass that is part of a door, wall, or ceiling
3 a flat part on a machine, where there are things to help you control it: *the airplane's control panel*

pang /pæŋ/ *noun* [count]
a sudden strong and painful feeling: *hunger pangs* • *a pang of jealousy*

pan·ic /ˈpænɪk/ *noun* [count]
a sudden feeling of fear that you cannot control and that makes you do things without thinking carefully: *There was panic in the store when the fire started.*
▸ **pan·ic** *verb* (**pan·ics, pan·ick·ing, pan·icked**): *Don't panic!*

pan·ick·y /ˈpænɪki/ *adjective* (*informal*)
very worried about something; feeling or showing PANIC

pan·ic-strick·en /ˈpænɪk ˌstrɪkən/ *adjective*
very afraid, in a way that stops you from thinking clearly: *Panic-stricken shoppers fled from the scene.*

pant /pænt/ *verb* (**pants, pant·ing, pant·ed**)
to take in and let out air quickly through your mouth, for example after running or because you are very hot: *The dog was panting.*

pan·ther /ˈpænθər/
noun [*count*]
a wild animal like a big cat with black fur

pant·ies /ˈpæntiz/
noun [*plural*]
a piece of underwear for women that covers the lower part of the body but not the legs: *a pair of panties*

pan·try /ˈpæntri/ *noun* [*count*] (*plural* **pan·tries**)
a small room where you can keep food

pants 🔑 /pænts/ *noun* [*plural*]
a piece of clothing for your legs and the lower part of your body: *Your pants are on the chair.* ⊃ Look at the picture at **clothes**.

Grammar

- Be careful! **Pants** is a plural noun so you cannot say "a pants."
- You can say **a pair of pants** or **some pants**: *I bought a new pair of pants.* ♦ *I bought some new pants.*

pant·y·hose /ˈpæntihoʊz/ (also **ny·lons** /ˈnaɪlɑnz/) *noun* [*plural*]
a piece of very thin clothing that a woman wears over her feet and legs: *a pair of pantyhose*

pa·per 🔑 /ˈpeɪpər/ *noun*
1 [*noncount*] thin material for writing or drawing on, or for wrapping things in: *a sheet of paper* ♦ *a paper bag*
2 [*count*] a newspaper: *Have you seen today's paper?*
3 papers [*plural*] important pieces of paper with writing on them: *Her desk was piled high with papers.*
4 [*count*] a piece of writing that you do for class on a particular subject: *We have to write a ten-page history paper.*

pa·per·back /ˈpeɪpərbæk/ *noun* [*count, noncount*]
a book with a paper cover: *This novel is also available in paperback.* ⊃ Look at **hardback**.

pa·per clip /ˈpeɪpər klɪp/ *noun* [*count*]
a small metal object that you use for holding pieces of paper together ⊃ Look at the picture at **stationery**.

pa·per·work /ˈpeɪpərwərk/ *noun* [*noncount*]
the written work that you have to do as part of your job or to get something done: *Teachers have far too much paperwork.*

par·a·chute /ˈpærəʃut/ *noun* [*count*]
a thing that you have on your back when you jump out of an airplane and that opens, so that you fall to the ground slowly

pa·rade /pəˈreɪd/ *noun* [*count*]
a line of people who are walking together for a special reason, while other people watch them: *our town's Fourth of July parade*

par·a·dise /ˈpærədaɪs/ *noun*
1 [*noncount*] (**RELIGION**) the place where some people think good people go after they die ⊃ **SYNONYM heaven**
2 [*count*] a place that is very beautiful and seems perfect: *a tropical island paradise*

par·a·dox /ˈpærədɑks/ *noun* [*count*] (*plural* **par·a·dox·es**)
something that has two or more parts that seem strange or impossible together: *"A deafening silence" is a paradox.*

par·a·graph **AWL** /ˈpærəgræf/ *noun* [*count*]
(**ENGLISH LANGUAGE ARTS**) a group of sentences. A paragraph always begins on a new line.

par·al·lel **AWL** /ˈpærəlɛl/ *adjective, adverb*
(**MATH**) Parallel lines are straight lines that are always the same distance from each other: *The train tracks run parallel to the road.* ⊃ Look at the picture at **line**.

par·al·lel·o·gram /ˌpærəˈlɛləgræm/ *noun* [*count*]
(**MATH**) a flat shape with four straight sides. The opposite sides are PARALLEL and equal to each other. ⊃ Look at the picture at **shape**.

pa·ral·y·sis /pəˈræləsəs/ *noun* [*noncount*]
(**HEALTH**) not being able to move or feel your body, or a part of it: *The disease can cause paralysis.*

par·a·lyze /ˈpærəlaɪz/ *verb* (**par·a·lyz·ing, par·a·lyz·es, par·a·lyzed**)
(**HEALTH**) to make a person unable to move all or part of their body: *The injury paralyzed her legs.*
▸ **par·a·lyzed** /ˈpærəlaɪzd/ *adjective*: *After the accident, she was paralyzed from the waist down.*

par·a·med·ic /ˌpærəˈmɛdɪk/ *noun* [*count*]
(**HEALTH**) a person who is not a doctor or a nurse, but who takes care of people who are hurt or sick until they get to a hospital

panther

pa·ram·e·ter `AWL` /pə'ræmətər/ noun [count] (formal)
a rule or limit that controls the way in which something can be done: We had to work **within the parameters** set by the committee.

par·a·noid /'pærənɔɪd/ adjective
If you are **paranoid**, you believe that other people are trying to harm you or are saying bad things about you.
▶ **par·a·noi·a** /ˌpærə'nɔɪə/ noun [noncount]: a feeling of paranoia

par·a·phrase /'pærəfreɪz/ verb (par·a·phras·es, par·a·phras·ing, par·a·phrased)
(ENGLISH LANGUAGE ARTS) to say something again using different words so that it easier to understand: Paraphrase the author's main arguments.

par·a·site /'pærəsaɪt/ noun [count]
(BIOLOGY) a plant or animal that lives on another plant or animal and gets food from it: Some parasites cause disease.

par·cel /'pɑrsl/ noun [count]
something in a box, bag, or wrapped in paper that is sent by mail ➔ SYNONYM **package**

par·don¹ /'pɑrdn/ noun [count, noncount]
(POLITICS) an official decision not to punish someone for something bad they have done
I beg your pardon (formal)
1 words that you say to mean "I am sorry": I beg your pardon, I didn't mean to step on your foot.
2 words that you use to ask someone to say something again because you did not hear: I beg your pardon, could you say that again?

par·don² /'pɑrdn/ verb (par·dons, par·don·ing, par·doned) (formal)
to officially decide not to punish someone for something bad that they have done: Two hundred prisoners were pardoned by the president. ➔ SYNONYM **forgive**
pardon me
1 (also **pardon**) a polite way of asking someone to repeat what they just said: "You're very quiet." "Pardon me?" "I said, you're very quiet."
2 a polite way of saying you are sorry: Pardon me, I didn't see you standing there.

par·ent /'pɛrənt/ noun [count]
a mother or father: Her parents live in Massachusetts.
▶ **pa·ren·tal** /pə'rɛntl/ adjective: parental support

pa·ren·the·ses /pə'rɛnθəsiz/ noun [plural]
(ENGLISH LANGUAGE ARTS) a pair of marks, ( ), that you put around extra information in a piece of writing: Irregular plurals are given **in parentheses**.

par·ent·hood /'pɛrənthʊd/ noun [noncount]
being a parent

par·ish /'pærɪʃ/ noun [count] (plural **par·ish·es**)
an area that has its own church and priest

park¹ /pɑrk/ noun [count]
a place with grass and trees, where anyone can go to walk, play games, or relax: We had a picnic **in the park**. • Central Park ➔ Look at **national park**.

park² /pɑrk/ verb (parks, park·ing, parked)
to stop and leave a vehicle somewhere for a time: You can't park on this street. • My car is parked across from the bank.
▶ **park·ing** /'pɑrkɪŋ/ noun [noncount]: The sign says "No Parking." • I can't find a parking space.

par·ka /'pɑrkə/ noun [count]
a warm jacket or coat with a part that you pull up to cover your head (called a HOOD): a ski parka

park·ing lot /'pɑrkɪŋ lɑt/ noun [count]
an area or a building where you can leave your car for a time

park·ing me·ter /'pɑrkɪŋ ˌmitər/ noun [count]
a machine beside the road that you put money into when you park your car next to it

park·ing tick·et /'pɑrkɪŋ ˌtɪkət/ noun [count]
a piece of paper that orders you to pay money (called a FINE) for parking your car where it is not allowed

park·way /'pɑrkweɪ/ noun [count]
a wide street with trees and grass along the sides or middle: Rock Creek Parkway ➔ The short way of writing "Parkway" in street names is Pkwy.

par·lia·ment /'pɑrləmənt/ noun [count]
(POLITICS) the people that make the laws in some countries: the Canadian parliament

par·lor /'pɑrlər/ noun [count]
a store that sells a particular type of goods or services: an ice cream parlor • a beauty parlor

pa·ro·chi·al school /pə'roʊkiəl ˌskul/ noun [count]
a school that is connected with or run by a church

par·o·dy /'pærədi/ noun [count, noncount] (plural par·o·dies)
(ENGLISH LANGUAGE ARTS) a performance or a piece of writing, music, etc. that copies the style of someone or something in a funny way: a parody of disaster movies

pa·role /pə'roʊl/ noun [noncount]
permission that is given to a prisoner to leave prison early if he or she behaves well: He is being released **on parole**.

ə about   y yes   w woman   t̬ butter   eɪ say   aɪ five   ɔɪ boy   aʊ now   oʊ go

par·rot /ˈpærət/ *noun*
[count]

parrot

a bird with very bright feathers that can copy what people say

pars·ley /ˈpɑrsli/ *noun* [noncount]
a type of plant (called an HERB) with small green leaves, which you use in cooking or for decorating food

part¹ /pɑrt/ *noun* [count]
1 some, but not all of something; one of the pieces of something: *We spent **part of** the day on the beach.* ◆ *Which **part of** New Jersey do you come from?*
2 a piece of a machine: *Is there a store near here that sells bicycle parts?*
3 the person you are in a play or movie: *He played the **part of** Romeo.*
4 a line in your hair that you make by brushing it in different directions using a plastic or metal thing (called a COMB): *He has a side part.*
take part in something to do something together with other people: *All the students took part in the concert.*

part² /pɑrt/ *verb* (parts, part·ing, part·ed)
1 to go away from each other: *We parted at the airport.*
2 to move apart, or to make things or people move apart: *She parted her lips but said nothing.*
3 to make a line in your hair by brushing it in different directions using a plastic or metal thing (called a COMB): *Do you part your hair on the left or right side?*
part with something to give something to someone else, especially something that you would prefer to keep: *Read the contract very carefully before you part with any money.*

part³ /pɑrt/ *adverb*
not completely one thing and not completely another: *She's part French and part Chinese.*

par·tial /ˈpɑrʃl/ *adjective*
not complete: *The evening was only a partial success.*
▸ **par·tial·ly** /ˈpɑrʃəli/ *adverb*: *The road was partially blocked by a fallen tree.* ⊃ SYNONYM **partly**

par·tic·i·pant AWL /pɑrˈtɪsəpənt/ *noun* [count]
a person who does something together with other people: *All **participants in** the event will receive a certificate.*

par·tic·i·pate AWL /pɑrˈtɪsəpeɪt/ *verb*
(par·tic·i·pates, par·tic·i·pat·ing, par·tic·i·pat·ed) (*formal*)
to do something together with other people:

*Ten countries **participated in** the discussions.* ⊃ SYNONYM **take part**
▸ **par·tic·i·pa·tion** AWL /pɑrˌtɪsəˈpeɪʃn/ *noun* [noncount]: *Your participation is greatly appreciated.*

par·ti·ci·ple /ˈpɑrtəsɪpl/ *noun* [count]
(ENGLISH LANGUAGE ARTS) a form of a verb: *The present participle of "eat" is "eating" and the past participle is "eaten."*

par·ti·cle /ˈpɑrtɪkl/ *noun* [count]
a very small piece of something: *particles of dust*

par·tic·u·lar /pərˈtɪkyələr/ *adjective*
1 one only, and not any other: *You need a particular kind of flour to make bread.*
2 more than usual: *The road is very icy, so take particular care when you are driving.* ⊃ SYNONYM **special**
3 If you are **particular**, you want something to be exactly right: *He's very **particular about** the food he eats.*
in particular more than others: *Is there anything in particular you want to do this weekend?* ⊃ SYNONYM **especially**

par·tic·u·lar·ly /pərˈtɪkyələrli/ *adverb*
more than usual, or more than others: *I'm particularly interested in U.S. history.* ◆ *I don't particularly like fish.* ⊃ SYNONYM **especially**

par·ties plural of **party**

par·ti·tion /pɑrˈtɪʃn/ *noun* [count]
something that separates one part of a room from another: *a glass partition*

part·ly /ˈpɑrtli/ *adverb*
not completely, but in some way: *The window was partly open.* ◆ *The accident was partly my fault.*

part·ner AWL /ˈpɑrtnər/ *noun* [count]
1 your husband, wife, boyfriend, or girlfriend
2 (BUSINESS) one of the people who owns a business: *Tom and I are business partners.*
3 a person you are dancing with, or playing a game with

part·ner·ship AWL /ˈpɑrtnərʃɪp/ *noun* [count, noncount]
being partners: *The two sisters **went into partnership** and opened a store.*

part of speech /ˌpɑrt əv ˈspitʃ/ *noun* [count]
(*plural* **parts of speech**)
(ENGLISH LANGUAGE ARTS) one of the groups that words are divided into, for example "noun," "verb," "adjective," etc.

part-time /ˌpɑrt ˈtaɪm/ *adjective, adverb*
for only a part of the day or week: *I have a a **part-time** job as a salesclerk.* ◆ *My mom **works part-time**.* ⊃ Look at **full-time**.

par·ty 🔑 /ˈpɑrṭi/ *noun* [*count*] (*plural* **par·ties**)
1 a time when friends meet, usually in someone's home, to eat, drink, and enjoy themselves: *We're **having a party** this Saturday. Can you come?* • *a birthday party*
2 (**POLITICS**) a group of people who have the same ideas about politics: *He's a member of the Democratic Party.*

Culture

- There are two main **political parties** in the United States.
- These are the **Republican Party** and the **Democratic Party**.

---

3 a group of people who are traveling or working together: *a **party of** tourists*

pass¹ 🔑 /pæs/ *verb* (**pass·es**, **pass·ing**, **passed**)
1 to go by someone or something: *She passed me in the street.* • *Do you pass any stores on your way to the station?*
2 to go or move in a particular direction: *A plane **passed** overhead.* • *The train **passes through** our town on its way to Boston.*
3 to give something to someone: *Could you pass me the salt, please?*
4 (**SPORTS**) to kick, hit, or throw the ball to someone on your team
5 If time **passes**, it goes by: *A week passed before his letter arrived.*
6 to spend time: *How did you **pass the time** in the hospital?*
7 to do well enough on an examination or test: *Did you pass your driving test?* ⊃ **ANTONYM fail**
8 to officially approve a law by voting: *Congress is expected to pass the law.*
pass away to die: *The old man passed away in his sleep.*
pass something on to give or tell something to another person: *Will you pass on a message **to** Michael for me?*
pass out to suddenly become unconscious ⊃ **SYNONYM faint**

pass² /pæs/ *noun* [*count*] (*plural* **pass·es**)
1 (**SPORTS**) kicking, throwing, or hitting a ball to someone in a game
2 a special piece of paper or card that says you can go somewhere or do something: *You need a pass to get into the factory.*
3 a road or way through mountains: *The pass was blocked by snow.*

pas·sage 🔑 /ˈpæsɪdʒ/ *noun* [*count*]
1 a narrow way, for example between two buildings
2 (**ENGLISH LANGUAGE ARTS**) a short part of a book, a speech, or a piece of music: *We studied a passage from the story for homework.*

pas·sen·ger 🔑 /ˈpæsəndʒər/ *noun* [*count*]
a person who is traveling in a car, bus, train, or airplane but not driving or flying it: *The plane was carrying 200 passengers.*

pass·er·by /ˌpæsərˈbaɪ/ *noun* [*count*] (*plural* **pass·ers·by** /ˌpæsərzˈbaɪ/)
a person who is walking past you in the street: *I asked a passerby where the Science Museum was.*

pas·sion /ˈpæʃn/ *noun*
1 [*count, noncount*] a very strong feeling, usually of love, but sometimes of anger or hate
2 [*singular*] a strong feeling of liking something very much or being very interested in it: *He has **a passion for** baseball.*

pas·sion·ate /ˈpæʃnət/ *adjective*
having or showing very strong feelings: *a passionate kiss*
▶ **pas·sion·ate·ly** /ˈpæʃnətli/ *adverb*

pas·sive¹ **AWL** /ˈpæsɪv/ *adjective*
1 accepting what happens or what others do without trying to change things: *He remained passive though all our group meetings.*
2 (**ENGLISH LANGUAGE ARTS**) (used about a verb or a sentence) when the person or thing doing the action is the not the subject of the verb: *In the sentence "He was bitten by the dog," the verb is passive.* ⊃ **ANTONYM active**

pas·sive² **AWL** /ˈpæsɪv/ *noun* [*singular*]
(**ENGLISH LANGUAGE ARTS**) the form of a verb used when the action is done by another person or thing, not by the subject of the verb: *In the sentence "The car was stolen," the verb is **in the passive**.* ⊃ Look at **active**.

pass·port 🔑 /ˈpæsport/ *noun* [*count*]
a small book with your name and photograph in it. You must take it with you when you travel to other countries.

pass·word /ˈpæswərd/ *noun* [*count*]
a secret word that allows you to go into a place or start using a computer or a computer system: *Never tell anyone your password.*

past¹ 🔑 /pæst/ *noun*
1 **the past** [*singular*] the time before now, and the things that happened then: *We learn about the past in history classes.* • *In the past, many people had large families.* ⊃ **ANTONYM future**
2 [*count*] a person's life before now: *May I ask you a few questions about your past?*
3 **the past** [*singular*] (**ENGLISH LANGUAGE ARTS**) = **the past tense**

past² 🔑 /pæst/ *preposition, adverb*
1 from one side to the other of someone or something; on the other side of someone or something: *Go past the theater, then turn left.* • *The bus went past without stopping.*

---

tʃ **ch**in   dʒ **J**une   v **v**an   θ **th**in   ð **th**en   s **s**o   z **z**oo   ʃ **sh**e

2 a word that shows how many minutes after the hour: *It's two minutes past four.* ◆ *It's half past seven.*

past³ 🔑 /pæst/ *adjective*
1 connected with the time that has gone: *We will forget your past mistakes.*
2 just before now: *He's been sick for the past week.* ⊃ SYNONYM **last**

pas·ta /'pɑstə/ *noun* [noncount]
an Italian food that is made from flour and water, which comes in many different shapes: *pasta with tomato sauce*

paste¹ /peɪst/ *noun* [count, noncount]
a soft wet substance, usually made from powder and liquid, and sometimes used for sticking paper to things: *Mix the flour with milk to make a paste.* ◆ *wallpaper paste*

paste² /peɪst/ *verb* (pastes, past·ing, past·ed)
1 to stick something to another thing using PASTE: *Paste the picture into your books.*
2 (COMPUTERS) to copy or move writing or pictures into a computer document from somewhere else: *You can cut and paste the tables into your essay.*

pas·tel /pæ'stɛl/ *adjective*
(used about colors) pale, not strong: *My daughter wants to paint her room a pastel pink.*

pas·time /'pæstaɪm/ *noun* [count]
something that you like doing when you are not working: *Painting is her favorite pastime.* ⊃ SYNONYM **hobby**

past par·ti·ci·ple /ˌpæst 'pɑrtəsɪpl/ *noun* [count]
(ENGLISH LANGUAGE ARTS) the form of a verb that in English is used with "have" to make a tense (called the PERFECT TENSE): *"Broken" is the past participle of "break."*

the past per·fect /ðə ˌpæst 'pərfɪkt/ *noun* [singular]
(ENGLISH LANGUAGE ARTS) the form of a verb that describes an action that was finished before another thing happened: *The play had already started when we got there.*

the past tense /ðə ˌpæst 'tɛns/ (also **the past**) *noun* [singular]
(ENGLISH LANGUAGE ARTS) the form of a verb that you use to talk about the time before now: *The past tense of "sing" is "sang."* ⊃ Look at **future¹** (2), **present²** (3).

pas·ture /'pæstʃər/ *noun* [count, noncount]
a field or piece of land with grass where farm animals can eat

pat /pæt/ *verb* (pats, pat·ting, pat·ted)
to touch someone or something lightly with your hand flat: *She patted the dog on the head.*
▶ **pat** *noun* [count]: *He gave me a pat on the shoulder.*

patch /pætʃ/ *noun* [count] (*plural* patch·es)
1 a small piece of something that is not the same as the other parts: *a black cat with a white patch on its back*
2 a piece of cloth that you use to cover a hole in things like clothes: *I sewed a patch on my jeans.*

pat·ent /'pætnt/ *noun* [count]
(BUSINESS) the official right to be the only person or company to make or sell a product: *The company has the patent for the new software.*

pa·ter·nal /pə'tərnl/ *adjective*
1 behaving like a father, or connected with being a father: *paternal love*
2 A **paternal** relation is from your father's side of the family: *my paternal grandmother* (= my father's mother) ⊃ Look at **maternal**.

path 🔑 /pæθ/ *noun* [count] (*plural* paths /pæðz/)
1 a way across a piece of land, where people can walk: *a path through the woods*
2 the line along which someone or something moves: *The fire destroyed everything in its path.*

pa·thet·ic /pə'θɛtɪk/ *adjective* (*informal*)
very bad or weak: *That was a pathetic performance – they deserved to lose!*

pa·tience /'peɪʃns/ *noun* [noncount]
staying calm and not getting angry when you are waiting for something, or when you have problems: *Learning to play the piano takes hard work and patience.* ◆ *She was walking so slowly that her sister finally lost patience with her* (= became angry with her). ⊃ ANTONYM **impatience**

pa·tient¹ 🔑 /'peɪʃnt/ *adjective*
able to stay calm and not get angry when you are waiting for something or when you have problems: *Just sit there and be patient. Your mom will be here soon.* ⊃ ANTONYM **impatient**
▶ **pa·tient·ly** /'peɪʃəntli/ *adverb*: *She waited patiently for the bus.* ⊃ ANTONYM **impatiently**

pa·tient² 🔑 /'peɪʃnt/ *noun* [count]
(HEALTH) a sick person who is getting medical treatment from a doctor or nurse

pa·ti·o /'pætiou/ *noun* [count] (*plural* pat·i·os)
a flat, hard area outside a house where people can sit and eat: *to have breakfast on the patio*

pa·tri·ot /'peɪtriət/ *noun* [count]
(POLITICS) a person who loves his or her country: *the patriots who fought for American independence*
▶ **pa·tri·ot·ism** /'peɪtriətɪzəm/ *noun* [noncount]
love of your country

pa·tri·ot·ic /ˌpeɪtriˈɑṭɪk/ *adjective*
having or showing love for your country: *a patriotic song*

pa·trol /pəˈtroʊl/ *noun* [count]
a group of people or vehicles that go around a place to see that everything is all right: *an army patrol* ♦ *The police drive around the area in a patrol car.*
on patrol going around a place to see that everything is all right: *During the carnival there will be 30 police officers on patrol.*
▶ **pa·trol** *verb* (pa·trols, pa·trol·ling, pa·trolled): *A guard patrols the gate at night.*

pa·tron·ize /ˈpeɪtrənaɪz/ *verb* (pa·tron·iz·es, pa·tron·iz·ing, pa·tron·ized)
to treat someone in a way that shows you think you are better, more intelligent, etc. than them: *Don't patronize me.*
▶ **pa·tron·iz·ing** /ˈpeɪtrənaɪzɪŋ/ *adjective*: *I don't like her patronizing attitude.*

pat·ter /ˈpæṭər/ *noun* [singular]
quick, light sounds: *I heard the patter of children's feet on the stairs.*
▶ **pat·ter** *verb* (pat·ters, pat·ter·ing, pat·tered): *Rain pattered against the window.*

patterns

stripes

checks

plaid

pat·tern /ˈpæṭərn/ *noun* [count]
1 (ART) an arrangement of shapes and colors on something: *The curtains had a pattern of flowers and leaves.*
2 the way in which something happens or develops: *Her days all seemed to follow the same pattern.*
3 a thing that you copy when you make something: *I bought some material and a pattern to make a new skirt.*

pat·terned /ˈpæṭərnd/ *adjective*
decorated with shapes and colors: *a patterned shirt*

pause /pɔz/ *verb* (paus·es, paus·ing, paused)
to stop talking or doing something for a short time: *He paused for a moment before answering my question.*
▶ **pause** *noun* [count]
a period of time when you stop talking or stop what you are doing: *There was a long pause before she spoke.*

pave /peɪv/ *verb* (paves, pav·ing, paved)
to cover an area of ground with a hard surface: *There is a paved road near the house.*

pave·ment /ˈpeɪvmənt/ *noun* [noncount]
the hard surface of a road or street

paw /pɔ/ *noun* [count]
the foot of an animal, for example a dog or a cat
⊃ Look at the picture at **cat**.

pay[1] /peɪ/ *verb* (pays, pay·ing, paid /peɪd/, has paid)
to give someone money for something, for example something they are selling you or work that they do: *How much did you pay for your car?* ♦ *I paid the company for fixing the roof.* ♦ *She has a very well-paid job.*
pay someone back to hurt someone who has hurt you: *One day I'll pay her back for lying to me!*
pay someone or **something back** to give back the money that someone has lent to you: *Can you lend me $10? I'll pay you back next week.*

pay[2] /peɪ/ *noun* [noncount]
the money that you get for working: *It's a tough job, but the pay is good.*

pay·ment /ˈpeɪmənt/ *noun*
1 [noncount] paying or being paid: *This check is in payment for the work you have done.*
2 [count] an amount of money that you pay: *I make monthly payments of $50.*

pay phone /ˈpeɪ foʊn/ *noun* [count]
a telephone that you can use by putting in money or using a special card

PC /ˌpi ˈsi/ *abbreviation*
1 (COMPUTERS) a computer that you can use at home or in an office. PC is short for "personal computer."
2 short for **politically correct**

pea /pi/ *noun* [count]
a very small, round, green vegetable. Peas grow in long, thin cases (called PODS). ⊃ Look at the picture at **vegetable**.

peace /pis/ *noun* [noncount]
1 a time when there is no war or fighting between people or countries: *The two countries eventually made peace* (= agreed to stop fighting).
2 the state of being quiet and calm: *the peace and quiet of the countryside* ♦ *Go away and leave me in peace!*

peace·ful /ˈpisfl/ *adjective*
1 with no fighting: *a peaceful demonstration*
2 quiet and calm: *It's so peaceful here.*
▶ **peace·ful·ly** /ˈpisfli/ *adverb*: *She's sleeping peacefully.*

peach /pitʃ/ *noun* [count] (plural peach·es)
a soft round fruit with a yellow and red skin and a large hard part (called a PIT) in the center

peach

pit

pea·cock /ˈpikɑk/ *noun* [count]
a large bird with beautiful long blue and green feathers in its tail

peak /pik/ *noun* [count]
1 the time when something is highest, biggest, etc.: *Traffic is **at its peak** between five and six in the evening.*
2 (GEOGRAPHY) the pointed top of a mountain: *snowy mountain peaks*

pea·nut /ˈpinʌt/ *noun* [count]
a nut that you can eat: *salted peanuts* ⟳ Look at the picture at **nut**.

pea·nut but·ter /ˌpinʌt ˈbʌt̬ər/ *noun* [noncount]
a thick, soft substance made from PEANUTS, which you eat on bread

pear /pɛr/ *noun* [count]

ℹ PRONUNCIATION
The word **pear** sounds just like **pair**.

---

a fruit that is green or yellow on the outside and white on the inside ⟳ Look at the picture at **fruit**.

pearl /pərl/ *noun* [count]
a small, round, white thing that grows inside the shell of a fish (called an OYSTER). **Pearls** are valuable and are used to make jewelry: *a pearl necklace*

peas·ant /ˈpɛznt/ *noun* [count]
a poor person who lives in the country and works on a small piece of land

peb·ble /ˈpɛbl/ *noun* [count]
a small, round stone

pe·can /pəˈkɑn; pəˈkæn/ *noun* [count]
a type of nut that we eat. It has a smooth, red-brown shell and grows on trees in the southern U.S.: *pecan pie* ⟳ Look at the picture at **nut**.

peck /pɛk/ *verb* (pecks, peck·ing, pecked)
When a bird **pecks** something, it eats or bites it quickly: *The hens were **pecking at** the corn.*

pe·cu·liar /pɪˈkyulyər/ *adjective*
strange; not usual: *What's that peculiar smell?* ⟳
SYNONYM odd

ped·al /ˈpɛdl/ *noun* [count]
a part of a bicycle or other machine that you move with your feet ⟳ Look at the picture at **bicycle**.

pe·des·tri·an /pəˈdɛstriən/ *noun* [count]
a person who is walking in the street

pe·di·a·tri·cian /ˌpidiəˈtrɪʃn/ *noun* [count]
(HEALTH) a doctor who treats children

peek /pik/ *verb* (peeks, peek·ing, peeked)
to look at something quickly and secretly because you should not be looking at it: *No peeking at your presents before your birthday!*
▶ **peek** *noun* [singular]: *You can take a quick peek.*

peel¹ /pil/ *verb*
(peels, peel·ing, peeled)
1 to take the outside part off a fruit or vegetable: *Can you peel the potatoes?*
2 to come off in thin pieces: *The paint is **peeling off** the walls.*

peel

peel² /pil/ *noun* [noncount]
the outside part of some fruit and vegetables: *orange peel* ◆ *potato peel*

peep /pip/ *verb* (peeps, peep·ing, peeped)
to look at something quickly or secretly: *I **peeped through** the window and saw her.*

peer¹ /pɪr/ *noun* [count]
a person who is the same age as you: *Teenagers worry about being accepted by their peers* (= other teenagers).

peer² /pɪr/ *verb* (peers, peer·ing, peered)
to look carefully at something because you cannot see well: *I peered outside, but I couldn't see anything because it was dark.*

peg /pɛg/ *noun*
[count]
a small thing on a wall or door where you can hang things: *Your coat is hanging on the peg.*

pegs

pel·vis /ˈpɛlvəs/ *noun* [count] (plural pel·vis·es)
(BIOLOGY) the set of bones at the bottom of your back, which your leg bones are joined to ⟳ Look at the picture at **skeleton**.

pen /pɛn/ *noun* [count]
1 a thing that you use for writing with a liquid (called INK)
2 a small piece of ground with a fence around it for keeping farm animals in: *a pigpen*

pe·nal·ize /ˈpinl-aɪz/ *verb* (pe·nal·iz·es, pe·nal·iz·ing, pe·nal·ized)
1 to punish someone for breaking a rule or law: *He was penalized for touching the ball with his hands.*
2 to cause someone to suffer a disadvantage: *The new tax unfairly penalizes single parents.*

pen·al·ty /ˈpɛnlti/ *noun* [count] (plural pen·al·ties)
1 a punishment: *The **penalty for** parking here is $200* (= you must pay $200).
2 (SPORTS) a punishment for one team and an advantage for the other team because a player has broken a rule: *The referee **called a penalty for** an illegal pass.*

pen·cil /ˈpɛnsl/ *noun* [count, noncount]
an object that you use for writing or drawing. **Pencils** are made of wood and have a point that writes in gray or another color: *colored pencils* ◆

I wrote the note in pencil. ⊃ Look at the picture at **stationery**.

pen·e·trate /ˈpɛnətreɪt/ *verb* (**pen·e·trates, pen·e·trat·ing, pen·e·trat·ed**)
to go through or into something: *The knife penetrated deep into his chest.*

pen·guin /ˈpɛŋgwən/ *noun* [*count*]
a black and white bird that lives in very cold places. **Penguins** can swim, but they cannot fly.

penguin

pen·i·cil·lin /ˌpɛnəˈsɪlən/ *noun* [*noncount*]
(**HEALTH**) a type of drug that is used to stop infections and to treat illnesses

pen·in·su·la /pəˈnɪmsələ/ *noun* [*count*]
(**GEOGRAPHY**) an area of land that has water on three sides: *the Florida peninsula*

pe·nis /ˈpinəs/ *noun* [*count*] (*plural* **pe·nis·es**)
the part of a man's or a male animal's body that is used for getting rid of waste liquid and for having sex

pen·knife /ˈpɛn,naɪf/ *noun* [*count*] (*plural* **pen·knives** /ˈpɛn,naɪvz/)
a small knife that you can carry in your pocket

pen·ni·less /ˈpɛnɪləs/ *adjective*
having no money; poor

pen·ny /ˈpɛni/ *noun* [*count*] (*plural* **pen·nies**)
a small brown coin that is worth one cent ⊃ Look at the picture at **money**.

pen pal /ˈpɛn pæl/ *noun* [*count*]
a person that you make friends with by writing letters, but you have probably never met them

pen·sion /ˈpɛnʃn/ *noun* [*count*]
money that an old person (a person who is RETIRED) gets from the company where he or she used to work

pen·ta·gon /ˈpɛntəgɑn/ *noun*
1 [*count*] (**MATH**) a shape that has five straight and equal sides
2 the Pentagon [*singular*] (**POLITICS**) a large government building near Washington D.C. that contains the main offices of the U.S. military forces

pentagon

peo·ple 🎵 /ˈpipl/ *noun* [*plural*]
1 more than one person: *How many people came to the meeting?* ◆ *People often arrive late at parties.*

2 men and women who work in a particular activity: *sports people*
3 the people the ordinary citizens of a country: *He is a man of the people.*

pep·per /ˈpɛpər/ *noun*
1 [*noncount*] powder with a hot taste that you put on food: *salt and pepper*
2 [*count*] a red, green, or yellow vegetable that is almost empty inside ⊃ Look at the picture at **vegetables**.

pep·per·mint /ˈpɛpərmɪnt/ *noun*
1 [*noncount*] a plant with a strong, fresh taste and smell. It is used to make things like candies and medicines.
2 [*count*] a candy with the flavor of **peppermint**

pep·per·o·ni /ˌpɛpəˈrouni/ *noun* [*noncount*]
a type of hard, spicy SAUSAGE (= meat made into a long, thin shape): *pepperoni pizza*

per /pər/ *preposition*
for each; in each: *These apples cost $1.29 per pound.* ◆ *I was driving at 60 miles per hour.*

per·ceive **AWL** /pərˈsiv/ *verb* (**per·ceives, per·ceiv·ing, per·ceived**) (*formal*)
1 to notice or realize something: *Scientists failed to perceive the danger.*
2 to understand or think of something or someone in a particular way: *My comments were perceived as criticism.*

per·cent **AWL** /pərˈsɛnt/ *noun* [*count*] (*plural* **per·cent**) (symbol **%**)
(**MATH**) one part in every hundred: *90 percent of the people who work here are men* (= in 100 people, there are 90 men). ◆ *You get 10% off if you pay cash.*

per·cent·age **AWL** /pərˈsɛntɪdʒ/ *noun* [*count*]
(**MATH**) an amount of something, expressed as part of one hundred: *"What percentage of students passed the exam?" "About eighty percent."*

per·cep·tive /pərˈsɛptɪv/ *adjective*
quick to notice or understand things: *She made some very perceptive comments.*

perch¹ /pərtʃ/ *verb* (**perch·es, perch·ing, perched**)
to sit on something narrow or uncomfortable: *The bird perched on a branch.* ◆ *We perched on high stools.*

perch² /pərtʃ/ *noun* [*count*] (*plural* **perch·es**)
a place where a bird sits

per·cus·sion /pərˈkʌʃn/ *noun* [*noncount*]
(**MUSIC**) drums and other instruments that you play by hitting them: *the percussion section of an orchestra* ⊃ Look at the note at **orchestra**.

per·fect / ˈpərfɪkt/ *adjective*
1 so good that it cannot be better; with nothing wrong: *Her French is perfect.* ◆ *It's perfect weather for a picnic.*
2 (ENGLISH LANGUAGE ARTS) made from "has," "have," or "had" and the PAST PARTICIPLE of a verb: *"I've finished" is in the perfect tense.* ⊃ Look at **the past perfect**, **the present perfect**.

per·fec·tion /pərˈfɛkʃn/ *noun* [noncount]
the state of being perfect: *The meat was cooked to perfection.*

per·fect·ly / ˈpərfɪktli/ *adverb*
1 completely: *I'm perfectly all right.*
2 in a perfect way: *She played the piece of music perfectly.*

per·form / pərˈfɔrm/ *verb* (per·forms, per·form·ing, per·formed)
1 to do something such as a piece of work or a task: *Doctors performed a complicated operation to save her life.*
2 to be in something such as a play or a concert: *The band has never performed here before.* ◆ *The play will be performed every night next week.*

per·form·ance / pərˈfɔrməns/ *noun*
1 [count] a time when a play, etc. is shown, or music is played in front of a lot of people: *We went to the evening performance of the play.*
2 [noncount] how well you do something: *My parents were pleased with my performance on the exam.*

per·form·er /pərˈfɔrmər/ *noun* [count]
a person who is in something such as a play or a concert

per·fume / ˈpərfyum/ *noun* [count, noncount]
1 a liquid with a nice smell that you put on your body: *a bottle of perfume*
2 a nice smell

per·haps / pərˈhæps/ *adverb* (formal)
a word that you use when you are not sure about something: *I don't know where she is – perhaps she's still at work.* ◆ *There were three men, or perhaps four.* ⊃ SYNONYM **maybe**

pe·rim·e·ter /pəˈrɪmətər/ *noun* [count]
1 the outside edge or limit of an area of land: *the perimeter fence of an army camp*
2 (MATH) a measurement of the distance around an area or shape: *What is the perimeter of the triangle?*

pe·ri·od / ˈpɪriəd/ **AWL** *noun* [count]
1 an amount of time: *This is a difficult period for him.* ◆ *What period of history are you studying?*
2 one of the equal lengths of time that make a school day: *I have German during second period.*
3 (HEALTH) the time when a woman loses blood from her body each month

4 (ENGLISH LANGUAGE ARTS) a mark (.) that you use in writing to show the end of a sentence, or after the short form of a word

the pe·ri·od·ic ta·ble / ðə ˌpɪriɑdɪk ˈteɪbl/ *noun* [singular]
(CHEMISTRY) a list of all the chemical substances (called ELEMENTS)

perm /pərm/ *noun* [count]
the treatment of hair with special chemicals to make it curly: *I think I'm going to get a perm.*
▶ **perm** *verb* (perms, perm·ing, permed): *She had her hair permed.*

per·ma·nent / ˈpərmənənt/ *adjective*
continuing forever or for a very long time without changing: *I'm looking for a permanent job.* ⊃ Look at **temporary**.
▶ **per·ma·nent·ly** / ˈpərmənəntli/ *adverb*: *Has he left permanently?*

per·mis·sion / pərˈmɪʃn/ *noun* [noncount]
allowing someone to do something: *She gave me permission to leave early.* ◆ *You may not leave the school without permission.*

per·mit¹ /pərˈmɪt/ *verb* (per·mits, per·mit·ting, per·mit·ted) (formal)
to let someone do something: *You are not permitted to smoke in the hospital.* ⊃ SYNONYM **allow**

per·mit² / ˈpərmɪt/ *noun* [count]
a piece of paper that says you can do something or go somewhere: *Do you have a work permit?*

per·pen·dic·u·lar / ˌpərpənˈdɪkyələr/ *adjective*
(MATH) If two lines are **perpendicular**, one of the lines makes an angle of 90° with the other: *Are these lines perpendicular to each other?*

per·se·cute / ˈpərsəkyut/ *verb* (per·se·cutes, per·se·cut·ing, per·se·cut·ed)
to treat someone in a cruel and unfair way, especially because of their race or beliefs
▶ **per·se·cu·tion** / ˌpərsəˈkyuʃn/ *noun* [count, noncount]: *the persecution of minority groups*

per·se·vere / ˌpərsəˈvɪr/ *verb* (per·se·veres, per·se·ver·ing, per·se·vered)
to continue trying to do something that is difficult: *If you persevere with your studies, you'll get a good job.*

per·sist·ent **AWL** / pərˈsɪstənt/ *adjective*
1 determined to continue doing something, even though people tell you to stop: *She's a very persistent child – she just never gives up.*
2 lasting for a long time: *a persistent cough*

per·son / ˈpərsn/ *noun* [count] (plural peo·ple / ˈpipl/)
1 a man or woman: *I think she's the best person for the job.* ◆ *We invited a few people to dinner.*
2 (ENGLISH LANGUAGE ARTS) one of the three types of pronoun in grammar. "I" and "we" are the

first person, "you" is the second person, and "he," "she," "it," and "they" are the third person.
in person seeing someone, not just speaking on the telephone or writing a letter: *I want to speak to her in person.*

per·son·al / /'pərsənl/ *adjective*
1 of or for one person: *That letter is personal and you have no right to read it.* • *Please keep all your* **personal belongings** *with you.*
2 done by a particular person rather than someone who is acting for them: *The president made a personal visit to the victim's family.*

per·son·al com·pu·ter /ˌpərsənl kəm'pyuṭər/ *noun* [count] = **PC**

per·son·al·i·ty / /ˌpərsə'næləṭi/ *noun* [count] (*plural* **per·son·al·i·ties**)
1 the qualities that a person has that make them different from other people: *Mark has a great personality.*
2 a famous person: *a television personality*

per·son·al·ly /'pərsənəli/ *adverb*
1 You say **personally** when you are saying what you think about something: *Personally, I like her, but a lot of people don't.*
2 done by you yourself, and not by someone else acting for you: *I will deal with this matter personally.*

per·son·al pro·noun /ˌpərsənl 'proʊnaʊn/ *noun* [count]
(**ENGLISH LANGUAGE ARTS**) any of these pronouns: I, me, she, her, he, him, we, us, you, they, them

per·son·nel /ˌpərsə'nɛl/ *noun* [plural]
the people who work for a large business or organization: *military personnel*

per·spec·tive AWL /pər'spɛktɪv/ *noun*
1 [count, noncount] the ability to think about problems in a sensible way, without making them seem worse than they are: *You must try to* **keep** *things* **in perspective** (= do not exaggerate them).
2 [count] your way of thinking about something: *Try to look at this* **from my perspective***.*
3 (**ART**) [noncount] the way of drawing that makes some objects seem farther away than others

per·suade / /pər'sweɪd/ *verb* (**per·suades**, **per·suad·ing**, **per·suad·ed**)
to make someone think or do something by talking to them: *My friend* **persuaded** *me* **to** *buy the most expensive pair of jeans.*

per·sua·sion /pər'sweɪʒn/ *noun* [noncount]
the process of making someone think or do something: *After a lot of persuasion, she agreed to come.*

pes·si·mism /'pɛsəmɪzəm/ *noun* [noncount]
thinking that bad things will happen ➲ **ANTONYM optimism**

▶ **pes·si·mist** /'pɛsəmɪst/ *noun* [count]: *Lisa's such a pessimist.* ➲ **ANTONYM optimist**
▶ **pes·si·mis·tic** /ˌpɛsə'mɪstɪk/ *adjective*: *Don't be so pessimistic – of course it's not going to rain!* ➲ **ANTONYM optimistic**

pest /pɛst/ *noun* [count]
1 an insect or animal that damages plants or food
2 (*informal*) a person or thing that makes you angry: *My little sister's a real pest!*

pes·ter /'pɛstər/ *verb* (**pes·ters**, **pes·ter·ing**, **pes·tered**)
to make someone a little angry by asking them for something many times: *Journalists* **pestered** *the neighbors* **for** *information.*

pes·ti·cide /'pɛstəsaɪd/ *noun* [count, noncount]
a chemical substance that is used for killing insects and other animals that eat plants: *The crops are sprayed with pesticide.* ➲ Look at **insecticide**.

pet / /pɛt/ *noun* [count]
1 an animal that you keep in your home: *I have two pets – a cat and a goldfish.*
2 a child that a teacher or a parent likes best: *She's the* **teacher's pet***.*

pet·al /'pɛṭl/ *noun* [count]
(**BIOLOGY**) one of the parts of a flower that give it color ➲ Look at the picture at **plant**.

pe·tite /pə'tit/ *adjective*
(used about a girl or woman) small and thin: *a petite blonde*

pe·ti·tion /pə'tɪʃn/ *noun* [count]
a special letter from a group of people that asks for something: *Hundreds of people signed the* **petition for** *a new fence around the school.*

pe·tri·fied /'pɛtrəfaɪd/ *adjective*
very afraid: *I'm* **petrified of** *snakes.* ➲ **SYNONYM terrified**

pe·tro·le·um /pə'troʊliəm/ *noun* [noncount]
(**CHEMISTRY**) oil that is found under the ground or ocean and is used for making fuel for cars and other types of chemical substances

pet·ty /'pɛṭi/ *adjective* (**pet·ti·er**, **pet·ti·est**)
small and not important: *I'm not interested in the petty details.*

phan·tom /'fæntəm/ *noun* [count]
a spirit of a dead person that people think they see ➲ **SYNONYM ghost**

phar·aoh /'fɛroʊ/ *noun* [count]
(**HISTORY**) a person who ruled ancient Egypt

phar·ma·ceu·ti·cal /ˌfɑrmə'suṭɪkl/ *adjective*
(**HEALTH**) connected with making and selling medicines and drugs: *pharmaceutical companies*

phar·ma·cist /ˈfɑrməsɪst/ *noun* [count]
(**HEALTH**) a person who prepares and sells medicines

phar·ma·cy /ˈfɑrməsi/ *noun* [count] (*plural* phar·ma·cies)
(**HEALTH**) a store, or part of a store, which sells medicines and drugs

phase **AWL** /feɪz/ *noun* [count]
a time when something is changing or growing: *She's going through a difficult phase right now.*

Ph.D. /ˌpi eɪtʃ ˈdi/ *noun* [count]
a high level university degree that you get after doing research in a particular subject. Ph.D. is short for "Doctor of Philosophy": *She earned a Ph.D. in history.*

phe·nom·e·nal **AWL** /fəˈnɑmənl/ *adjective*
very great: *The product has been a phenomenal success.*
▶ **phe·nom·e·nal·ly** /fəˈnɑmənəli/ *adverb*: *a phenomenally successful movie*

phe·nom·e·non **AWL** /fəˈnɑmənɑn; fəˈnɑmənən/ *noun* [count] (*plural* phe·nom·e·na /fəˈnɑmənə/)
something that happens or exists in nature or society, especially something that is difficult to understand: *Earthquakes and tsunamis are natural phenomena.*

phi·los·o·pher **AWL** /fəˈlɑsəfər/ *noun* [count]
a person who studies PHILOSOPHY

phi·los·o·phy **AWL** /fəˈlɑsəfi/ *noun* (*plural* phi·los·o·phies)
1 [noncount] the study of ideas about the meaning of life
2 [count] a set of beliefs that a person has about life: *Enjoy yourself and don't worry about tomorrow – that's my philosophy!*
▶ **phil·o·soph·i·cal** **AWL** /ˌfɪləˈsɑfɪkl/ *adjective*: *a philosophical debate*

pho·bi·a /ˈfoʊbiə/ *noun* [count] (*plural* pho·bi·as)
a very strong fear that you cannot explain: *She has a phobia of spiders.* ◆ *claustrophobia* (= the fear of being in a small, closed space)

phone[1] /foʊn/ *noun* [count]
an instrument that you use for talking to someone who is in another place: *The phone's ringing – can you answer it?* ⊃ SYNONYM **telephone**
be on the phone to be using the phone: *Anna was on the phone for an hour.*

Collocations

Phones

making or receiving a call
- the phone/telephone **rings**
- **make/get/receive** a call/a phone call

- **dial** someone's number/an area code/the wrong number
- **call** someone/**speak to** someone on the phone
- **answer/pick up/hang up** the phone

cell phones
- **answer/use** your cell phone
- **send/get/receive** a text (message)
- **turn on/turn off** your cell phone
- **charge/recharge** your cell phone/the battery

phone[2] /foʊn/ *verb* (phones, phon·ing, phoned)
to speak to someone by phone: *I phoned my sister last night.* ⊃ SYNONYM **call**

phone book /ˈfoʊn bʊk/ (also **tel·e·phone book**) *noun* [count]
a book of people's names, addresses, and telephone numbers

phone booth /ˈfoʊn buθ/ (also **tel·e·phone booth**) *noun* [count]
a public telephone in the street

phone call /ˈfoʊn kɔl/ (also **tel·e·phone call**) *noun* [count]
when you use the phone to talk to someone: *I need to make a phone call.*

phone card /ˈfoʊn kɑrd/ *noun* [count]
a small plastic card that you buy and use to make calls to people from any telephone

phone num·ber /ˈfoʊn ˌnʌmbər/ (also **tel·e·phone num·ber**) *noun* [count]
the number of a particular phone that you use when you want to make a call to it: *What's your phone number?*

pho·net·ic /fəˈnɛtɪk/ *adjective*
(**ENGLISH LANGUAGE ARTS**) using special signs to show how to say words: *the phonetic alphabet used in a dictionary*

pho·net·ics /fəˈnɛtɪks/ *noun* [noncount]
(**ENGLISH LANGUAGE ARTS**) the study of the sounds that people make when they speak

pho·to /ˈfoʊtoʊ/ *noun* [count] (*plural* pho·tos)
a photograph: *Here's a photo of my sister.*

pho·to·cop·i·er /ˈfoʊtəkɑpiər/ *noun* [count]
a machine that makes copies of documents by photographing them

pho·to·cop·y /ˈfoʊtəkɑpi/ *noun* [count] (*plural* pho·to·cop·ies)
a copy of something on paper that you make with a PHOTOCOPIER
▶ **pho·to·cop·y** *verb* (pho·to·cop·ies, pho·to·cop·y·ing, pho·to·cop·ied, has pho·to·cop·ied): *Could you photocopy this letter for me?*

pho·to·graph 🖉 /'foʊtəgræf/ (also **pho·to**) *noun*
[*count*]
a picture that you take with a camera: *I took a photograph of the library.*
▶ **pho·to·graph** (pho·to·graphs, pho·to·graph·ing, pho·to·graphed) (*formal*): *The winner was photographed holding his prize.*

pho·tog·ra·pher /fə'tɑɡrəfər/ *noun* [*count*]
a person who takes photographs, especially as a job

pho·tog·ra·phy /fə'tɑɡrəfi/ *noun* [*noncount*]
taking photographs
▶ **pho·to·graph·ic** /ˌfoʊtə'ɡræfɪk/ *adjective*
connected with photographs or **photography**: *photographic equipment*

pho·to·syn·the·sis /ˌfoʊtoʊ'sɪnθəsɪs/ *noun* [*noncount*]
(**BIOLOGY**) the process by which green plants turn a gas in the air (**CARBON DIOXIDE**) and water into food, using light from the sun

phras·al verb /ˌfreɪzl 'vərb/ *noun* [*count*]
(**ENGLISH LANGUAGE ARTS**) a verb that joins with another word or words to make a verb with a new meaning: *"Pick someone up" and "take off" are phrasal verbs.*

phrase 🖉 /freɪz/ *noun* [*count*]
(**ENGLISH LANGUAGE ARTS**) a group of words that you use together as part of a sentence: *"First of all" and "a bar of chocolate" are phrases.*

phys·i·cal¹ 🖉 **AWL** /'fɪzɪkl/ *adjective*
connected with things that you feel or do with your body: *physical exercise*
▶ **phys·i·cal·ly** **AWL** /'fɪzɪkəli/ *adverb*: *I'm not physically fit.*

phys·i·cal² **AWL** /'fɪzɪkl/ *noun* [*count*]
(**HEALTH**) an examination of your body by a doctor to see if you are healthy: *I'm going in for my annual physical on Thursday.*

phys·i·cist /'fɪzəsɪst/ *noun* [*count*]
(**PHYSICS**) a person who studies or knows a lot about PHYSICS

phys·ics /'fɪzɪks/ *noun* [*noncount*]
the scientific study of things like heat, light, and sound

phy·sique /fə'zik/ *noun* [*count*]
the size and shape of a person's body: *a strong, muscular physique*

pi /paɪ/ *noun* [*singular*]
(**MATH**) the symbol π. It is used to show the relationship between the distance around a circle (its **CIRCUMFERENCE**) and the distance across it (its **DIAMETER**), which is about 3.14159.

pi·an·o 🖉 /pi'ænoʊ/ *noun* [*count*] (*plural* pi·an·os)
(**MUSIC**) a big musical instrument that you play by pressing black and white bars (called KEYS):

Can you play the piano? ⊃ Look at the picture at **instrument**.
▶ **pi·an·ist** /pi'ænɪst; 'piənɪst/ *noun* [*count*]
a person who plays the **piano**

pick¹ 🖉 /pɪk/ *verb* (picks, pick·ing, picked)
1 to take the person or thing you like best: *They picked Simon as their captain.* ⊃ SYNONYM **choose**
2 to take a flower, fruit, or vegetable from the place where it grows: *I picked some flowers for you.*
pick on someone (*informal*) to treat someone in an unfair or cruel way: *Sally gets picked on by the other kids.*
pick someone or **something out** to be able to see someone or something among a lot of others: *Can you pick out my father in this photo?*
pick someone or **something up**
1 to take and lift someone or something: *She picked up the kitten and stroked it.* ◆ *The phone stopped ringing just as I picked it up.*
2 to go to get someone or something, especially in a car: *My dad picks me up from school.* ◆ *Could you pick up something for dinner tonight?*
pick something up to learn something without really studying it: *I picked up some Spanish from the other kids in my neighborhood.*

pick² /pɪk/ *noun* [*singular*]
the one that you choose; your choice
take your pick to choose what you like: *We have orange juice, lemonade, or milk. Take your pick.*

pick·et /'pɪkət/ *noun* [*count*]
a person or group of people who stand outside the place where they work when there is a STRIKE (= an organized protest), and try to stop other people from going in
▶ **pick·et** *verb* (pick·ets, pick·et·ing, pick·et·ed): *Workers were picketing the factory.*

pick·le /'pɪkl/ *noun* [*count*]
a small green vegetable that is kept in a liquid with a strong sharp taste (called VINEGAR) before it is eaten: *a jar of pickles*

pick·pock·et /'pɪkpɑkət/ *noun* [*count*]
a person who steals things from people's pockets

pick·up /'pɪkʌp/ (also **pick·up truck**) *noun* [*count*]
a type of small truck that has an open part with low sides at the back

pickup

pic·nic /'pɪknɪk/ *noun* [*count*]
a meal that you eat outside, away from home: *We had a picnic by the river.*
▶ **pic·nic** *verb* (pic·nics, pic·nick·ing, pic·nicked): *We picnicked on the beach yesterday.*

pic·ture¹ 🔑 /'pɪktʃər/ *noun* [*count*]
1 a drawing, painting, or photograph: *Julie drew a picture of her dog.* ◆ *They showed us some pictures* (= photographs) *of their wedding.* ◆ *I took a picture* (= a photograph) *of the house.*
2 an idea or memory of something in your mind: *His novels give a good picture of what life was like back then.*

pic·ture² /'pɪktʃər/ *verb* (pic·tures, pic·tur·ing, pic·tured)
to imagine something in your mind: *I can just picture them lying on the beach.*

pie /paɪ/ *noun* [*count*]
a type of food made of fruit covered with PASTRY (= a mixture of flour, butter, and water): *an apple pie*

piece 🔑 /pis/ *noun* [*count*]
1 a part of something: *Would you like another piece of cake?* ◆ *a piece of broken glass* ◆ *The plate fell on the floor and smashed to pieces.*
2 one single thing: *Do you have a piece of paper?* ◆ *That's an interesting piece of news.*
3 a single work of art, music, etc.: *He played a piece by Chopin.*
in pieces broken: *The plate lay in pieces on the floor.*

pie chart /'paɪ tʃɑrt/ *noun* [*count*]
(**MATH**) a diagram that is a circle divided into pieces, showing the size of particular parts in relation to the whole ➔ Look at **flow chart**.

pier /pɪr/ *noun* [*count*]
a long structure that is built from the land into the ocean, where people can walk or get on and off boats

pierce /pɪrs/ *verb* (pierc·es, pierc·ing, pierced)
to make a hole in something with a sharp point: *The nail pierced her skin.* ◆ *I'm going to have my ears pierced.*

pierc·ing /'pɪrsɪŋ/ *adjective*
A **piercing** sound is very loud and unpleasant: *a piercing cry*

pig 🔑 /pɪg/ *noun* [*count*]
1 a fat animal that people keep on farms for its meat

pig

2 (*informal*) an unkind person, or a person who eats too much: *You ate all the cookies, you pig!*

pi·geon /'pɪdʒən/ *noun* [*count*]
a gray bird that you often see in cities

pigeon

pig·gy bank /'pɪgi bæŋk/ *noun* [*count*]
a small box, often shaped like a pig, that children save money in

pig·let /'pɪglət/ *noun* [*count*]
a young pig

pig·tail /'pɪgteɪl/ *noun* [*count*]
hair that you tie together at the sides of your head: *She wears her hair in pigtails.*

pile¹ 🔑 /paɪl/ *noun* [*count*]
a lot of things on top of one another; a large amount of something: *Clothes lay in piles on the floor.* ◆ *a pile of earth*

pile² /paɪl/ *verb* (piles, pil·ing, piled)
to put a lot of things on top of one another: *She piled the boxes on the table.*

pil·grim /'pɪlgrəm/ *noun* [*count*]
(**RELIGION**) a person who travels a long way to a place because it has a special religious meaning

pil·grim·age /'pɪlgrəmɪdʒ/ *noun* [*count*]
(**RELIGION**) a long trip that a PILGRIM makes

pill /pɪl/ *noun* [*count*]
(**HEALTH**) a small, round, hard piece of medicine that you swallow: *Take one of these pills before every meal.* ➔ SYNONYM **tablet**

pills

pil·lar /ˈpɪlər/ *noun* [count]
a tall strong piece of stone, wood, or metal that holds up a building

pil·low /ˈpɪloʊ/ *noun* [count]
a soft thing that you put your head on when you are in bed

pil·low·case /ˈpɪloʊkeɪs/ *noun* [count]
a cover for a PILLOW

pi·lot 🔑 /ˈpaɪlət/ *noun* [count]
a person who flies an airplane

pim·ple /ˈpɪmpl/ *noun* [count]
a small spot on your skin

PIN /pɪn/ (also **PIN num·ber** /ˈpɪn ˌnʌmbər/) *noun* [count]
a number that you use with a plastic card to take out money from a cash machine. PIN is short for "personal identification number."

pin¹ 🔑 /pɪn/ *noun* [count]

pins

1 a small, thin piece of metal with a round part at one end and a sharp point at the other. You use a **pin** for holding things together or fastening one thing to another. ➔ Look at **safety pin**.
2 a small piece of jewelry that you can wear on a shirt, jacket, etc.: *She wore a beautiful gold pin on her jacket.* ➔ Look at the picture at **jewelry**.
3 (**SPORTS**) a wooden object shaped like a bottle that you try to knock over in the sport of BOWLING

pin² /pɪn/ *verb* (pins, pin·ning, pinned)
1 to fasten things together with a pin or pins: *Could you **pin** this sign **to** the board?*
2 to hold someone or something so that they cannot move: *He tried to get away, but they pinned him against the wall.*

pinch¹ /pɪntʃ/ *verb* (pinch·es, pinch·ing, pinched)
to press someone's skin between your thumb and finger: *Don't pinch me – it hurts!*

pinch² /pɪntʃ/ *noun* [count] (plural pinch·es)
1 the act of pressing someone's skin between your thumb and finger: *He gave me a pinch on the arm to wake me up.*
2 an amount of something you can hold between your thumb and finger: *Add a **pinch of** salt to the soup.*

pine /paɪn/ *noun*
1 [count] (also **pine tree** /ˈpaɪn tri/) a tall tree with thin sharp leaves (called NEEDLES) that do not fall off in winter
2 the wood from this tree, which is often used for making furniture

pine·ap·ple /ˈpaɪnæpl/ *noun* [count, noncount]
a big fruit that is yellow inside and has a rough, brown skin ➔ Look at the picture at **fruit**.

pine cone /ˈpaɪn koʊn/ *noun* [count]
the hard, rough fruit of a PINE tree that contains the seeds: *We collected pine cones to use as Christmas decorations.*

Ping-Pong™ /ˈpɪŋpɑŋ/ (also **ta·ble ten·nis** /ˈteɪbl ˌtɛnəs/) *noun* [noncount]
(**SPORTS**) a game where players hit a small, light ball over a net on a big table

pink 🔑 /pɪŋk/ *adjective* (pink·er, pink·est)
with a light red color: *a pink blouse*
▶ **pink** *noun* [count, noncount]: *She was dressed in pink.*

pink·ie /ˈpɪŋki/ (also **pink·y**) *noun* [count] (plural pink·ies) (*informal*)
the smallest finger on your hand

pins and nee·dles /ˌpɪnz ən ˈnidlz/ *noun* [plural]
an uncomfortable feeling that you sometimes get in a part of your body when you have not moved it for a long time

pint 🔑 /paɪnt/ (abbreviation **pt.**) *noun* [count]
a measure of liquid (=0.47 liters). There are eight **pints** in a **gallon**: *a pint of beer* ♦ *two pints of milk*

pi·o·neer /ˌpaɪəˈnɪr/ *noun* [count]
a person who goes somewhere or does something before other people: *the pioneers of the American West*

pipe 🔑 /paɪp/ *noun* [count]
1 a long tube that takes something such as water, oil, or gas from one place to another: *A water pipe is leaking under the ground.*
2 a tube with a small bowl at one end that is used for smoking TOBACCO (= the dried leaves used for making cigarettes): *My grandfather smoked a pipe.*

pipe·line /ˈpaɪplaɪn/ *noun* [count]
a line of pipes that carry oil or gas a long way
in the pipeline If something is **in the pipeline**, it is being planned or prepared and will happen soon.

pi·rate¹ /ˈpaɪrət/ *noun* [count]
a person on a ship who robs other ships

pi·rate² /ˈpaɪrət/ *verb* (pi·rates, pi·rat·ing, pi·rat·ed)
to make an illegal copy of a book, a DVD, a CD, etc. in order to sell it: *Are you sure this isn't pirated software?*
▶ **pi·ra·cy** /ˈpaɪrəsi/ *noun* [noncount]
the crime of making illegal copies of things to sell

pis·tol /ˈpɪstl/ *noun* [count]
a small gun

pit /pɪt/ *noun* [*count*]
1 a deep hole in the ground: *We dug a deep pit in the yard.*
2 the hard part in the middle of some types of fruit: *Peaches and plums have pits.* ⊃ Look at the picture at **peach**.

pitch¹ /pɪtʃ/ *verb* (pitch·es, pitch·ing, pitched)
1 (SPORTS) (in baseball) to throw the ball to a person on the other team, who tries to hit it
2 to put up a TENT (= a small house made of cloth): *We pitched our tent under a big tree.*

pitch² /pɪtʃ/ *noun* (*plural* pitch·es)
1 [*count*] (SPORTS) an act of throwing a baseball to a player who tries to hit it: *He hit the first pitch of the game into center field.*
2 [*noncount*] (MUSIC) how high or low a sound is

pitch·er /'pɪtʃər/ *noun* [*count*]

pitcher

1 a container with a handle that you use for holding or pouring liquids: *a water pitcher* • *a pitcher of milk*
2 (SPORTS) (in baseball) the person who throws (PITCHES) the ball to a player on the other team, who tries to hit it ⊃ Look at the picture at **baseball**.

pit·y¹ /'pɪti/ *noun*
1 [*noncount*] a feeling of sadness for a person or an animal who is in pain or who has problems: *I feel no pity for him – it's his own fault.*
2 [*singular*] something that disappoints you or makes you feel a little sad: *It's a pity you can't come to the party.* ⊃ SYNONYM **shame**
take pity on someone to help someone because you feel sad for them: *I took pity on her and gave her some money.*

pit·y² /'pɪti/ *verb* (pit·ies, pit·y·ing, pit·ied, has pit·ied)
to feel sad for someone who is in pain or who has problems: *I really pity people who don't have anywhere to live.*

piz·za /'pitsə/ *noun* [*count, noncount*]
a flat, round piece of bread with tomatoes, cheese, and other things on top, which is cooked in an oven

piz·ze·ri·a /ˌpitsə'riə/ *noun* [*count*]
a restaurant that serves PIZZA

plac·ard /'plækərd/ *noun* [*count*]
a large sign that hangs in a public place or is carried on a stick: *The demonstrators' placards read "No more war."*

place¹ /pleɪs/ *noun* [*count*]
1 a particular area or position: *Put the book back in the right place.*

2 a particular building, city, town, country, etc.: *Boston is a very interesting place.* • *Do you know a good place to have lunch?*
3 a seat or space for one person: *An old man was sitting in my place.*
4 [*singular*] a person's home: *Do you want to come back to my place after lunch?*
5 the position that you have in a race, competition, or test: *Alice finished in second place.*
in place where it should be; in the right place: *Use tape to hold the picture in place.*
in place of someone or **something** instead of someone or something: *You can use milk in place of cream.*
out of place
1 not suitable for a particular situation: *My old furniture looks out of place in my new apartment.*
2 not in the correct or usual place: *Nothing is ever out of place in my father's office.*
take place to happen: *The wedding of John and Sara will take place on May 22.*

place² /pleɪs/ *verb* (plac·es, plac·ing, placed) (*formal*)
to put something somewhere: *The waiter placed the meal in front of me.*

pla·gia·rism /'pleɪdʒərɪzəm/ *noun* [*noncount*]
(ENGLISH LANGUAGE ARTS) the act of copying another person's ideas, words, or work and pretending they are your own: *to be accused of plagiarism*
▶ **pla·gia·rize** /'pleɪdʒəraɪz/ *verb* (pla·gia·riz·es, pla·gia·riz·ing, pla·gia·rized): *Most of his essay was plagiarized from the Internet.*

plague /pleɪg/ *noun* [*count*]
(HEALTH) a disease that spreads quickly and kills many people

plaid /plæd/ *noun* [*noncount*]
a pattern on material with squares and stripes that cross each other: *a plaid shirt* ⊃ Look at the picture at **pattern**.

plain¹ /pleɪn/ *adjective* (plain·er, plain·est)
1 simple and ordinary: *plain food*
2 with no pattern; all one color: *She wore a plain blue dress.*
3 easy to see, hear, or understand: *It's plain that he's unhappy.* ⊃ SYNONYM **clear**
4 not pretty: *She was a plain child.*

plain² /pleɪn/ *noun* [*count*]
a large piece of flat land

plain·ly /'pleɪnli/ *adverb*
in a way that is easy to see, hear, or understand: *They were plainly very angry.* ⊃ SYNONYM **clearly**

plan¹ /plæn/ *noun* [*count*]
1 something that you have decided to do and how you are going to do it: *What are your vacation plans?* • *They have plans to build a new school.* ⊃ Look at the note at **purpose**.

2 a map showing a building, a city, or a town: *a street plan of San Francisco*
3 a drawing that shows how a new building, room, or machine will be made: *Have you seen the plans for the new shopping center?*

plan² 🔊 /plæn/ *verb* (plans, plan·ning, planned)
1 to decide what you are going to do and how you are going to do it: *They're planning a long vacation next summer.* ◆ *I'm planning to go to college.*
2 to intend or expect to do something: *I'm planning on taking a vacation in July.*

plane 🔊 /pleɪn/ *noun* [count]
a vehicle with wings that can fly through the air: *I like traveling by plane.* ◆ *What time does your plane land?* ◆ *Our plane took off three hours late.* ◆ *I caught the next plane to Miami.* ⊃ SYNONYM **airplane**

plan·et 🔊 /ˈplænət/ *noun*
1 [count] a large round object in space that moves around the sun or another star: *Earth, Mars, and Venus are planets.*
2 the planet [singular] the world we live in, especially when we are talking about the environment: *the battle to save the planet*

plank /plæŋk/ *noun* [count]
a long, flat piece of wood

plank·ton /ˈplæŋktən/ *noun* [noncount, plural]
(**BIOLOGY**) the very small plants and animals that live in water: *fish that eat plankton*

plant

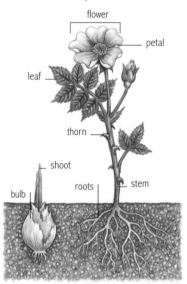

flower
petal
leaf
thorn
shoot
roots
stem
bulb

plant¹ 🔊 /plænt/ *noun* [count]
anything that grows from the ground: *Don't forget to water the plants.* ⊃ Look at the note at **nature**.

plant² 🔊 /plænt/ *verb* (plants, plant·ing, plant·ed)
to put plants or seeds in the ground: *We planted some roses in the garden.*

plan·ta·tion /plænˈteɪʃn/ *noun* [count]
a piece of land where things like tea, cotton, or rubber grow: *a sugar plantation*

plaque /plæk/ *noun*
1 [count] a flat piece of stone, metal, or wood with writing on it, which is attached to a wall or other surface: *The plaque on the wall commemorates the founder of the university.*
2 [noncount] (**HEALTH**) a harmful substance that forms on your teeth

plas·ter¹ /ˈplæstər/ *noun* [noncount]
a substance that is used for covering walls inside buildings

plas·ter² /ˈplæstər/ *verb* (plas·ters, plas·ter·ing, plas·tered)
1 to cover a wall with PLASTER to make it smooth
2 to cover a surface with a large amount of something: *She plastered herself with skin lotion.*

plas·tic 🔊 /ˈplæstɪk/ *noun* [noncount]
an artificial material that is used for making many different things: *These chairs are made of plastic.* ◆ *plastic cups*

plas·tic sur·ger·y /ˌplæstɪk ˈsərdʒəri/ *noun* [noncount]
(**HEALTH**) medical operations that doctors can do to improve a person's appearance

plate 🔊 /pleɪt/ *noun* [count]
a round dish that you put food on ⊃ Look at **license plate**.

pla·teau /plæˈtoʊ/ *noun* [count]
(**GEOGRAPHY**) a large area of high, flat land

plat·form /ˈplætfɔrm/ *noun* [count]
1 a surface that is higher than the floor, where people stand so that other people can see and hear them: *The principal went up to the platform to make his speech.*
2 the part of a train station where people get on and off trains: *The train to Washington leaves from platform 5.*

plat·i·num /ˈplætnəm/ *noun* [noncount] (symbol **Pt**)
(**CHEMISTRY**) an expensive gray-white metal that is often used for making jewelry: *a diamond ring with a platinum band*

play¹ 🔊 /pleɪ/ *verb* (plays, play·ing, played)
1 to have fun; to do something to enjoy yourself: *The children were playing with their toys.*
2 to take part in a game: *I like playing tennis.* ◆ *Do you know how to play chess?*
3 (**MUSIC**) to make music with a musical instrument: *My sister plays the piano very well.*

tʃ **ch**in   dʒ **J**une   v **v**an   θ **th**in   ð **th**en   s **s**o   z **z**oo   ʃ **sh**e

Grammar

- We usually say "play **the** violin, **the** piano, etc.": *I'm learning to play the clarinet.*
- When we talk about playing games or sports, we do not use "the": *Do you play basketball at school?* ◆ *Let's play cards!*

4 to put a CD, DVD, etc. in a machine and listen to it: *Should I play the CD again?*
5 to act the part of someone in a play: *Who wants to play the police officer?*

play² 🔑 /pleɪ/ *noun* (*plural* **plays**)
1 [*count*] a story that you watch in the theater or on television, or listen to on the radio: *We went to see a play by Arthur Miller.*
2 [*noncount*] games; what children do for fun: *work and play*

play·er 🔑 /ˈpleɪər/ *noun* [*count*]
1 a person who plays a game: *football players*
2 (**MUSIC**) a person who plays a musical instrument: *a trumpet player*

play·ful /ˈpleɪfl/ *adjective*
full of fun; not serious: *a playful puppy* ◆ *a playful remark*

play·ground /ˈpleɪɡraʊnd/ *noun* [*count*]
an area where children can play, for example at school

playing cards

spade
heart
diamond
club

deck of cards

play·ing card /ˈpleɪɪŋ kɑrd/ (also **card**) *noun* [*count*]
one of a set of 52 cards with numbers and pictures on them, which you use for playing games

play·ing field /ˈpleɪɪŋ fild/ *noun* [*count*]
a large area of grass where people play sports like football

play·off /ˈpleɪɔf/ *noun* [*count*]
(**SPORTS**) one or more games that are played by the best teams or players, in order to decide who the winner is

play·wright /ˈpleɪraɪt/ *noun* [*count*]
a person who writes plays: *the American playwright Arthur Miller*

pla·za /ˈplɑzə/ *noun* [*count*]
an open space in a city or town with offices or stores around it: *a shopping plaza*

plea /pli/ *noun* [*count*]
asking for something with strong feeling: *He made a **plea** for help.*

plead /plid/ *verb* (**pleads, plead·ing, plead·ed** or **pled** /plɛd/, **has plead·ed** or **has pled**)
1 to ask for something in a very strong way: *He **pleaded with** his parents **to** buy him a guitar.*
2 to say in a court of law that you did or did not do a crime: *She pleaded not guilty to murder.*

pleas·ant 🔑 /ˈplɛznt/ *adjective*
nice, enjoyable, or friendly: *The weather here is very pleasant.* ◆ *He's a very pleasant person.* ⊃
ANTONYM unpleasant
▶ **pleas·ant·ly** /ˈplɛzəntli/ *adverb*: *a pleasantly cool room*

please¹ 🔑 /pliz/ *exclamation*
a word that you use when you ask for something politely: *What time is it, please?* ◆ *Two cups of coffee, please.* ◆ *"Would you like some cake?" "Yes, please."*

please² 🔑 /pliz/ *verb* (**pleas·es, pleas·ing, pleased**)
to make someone happy: *I wore my best clothes to please my mother.*

pleased 🔑 /plizd/ *adjective*
happy: *He wasn't very **pleased** to see me.* ◆ *Are you **pleased with** your new watch?* ⊃ Look at the note at **glad**.

pleas·ure 🔑 /ˈplɛʒər/ *noun*
1 [*noncount*] the feeling of being happy or enjoying something: *She **gets** a lot of **pleasure** from her music.* ◆ *Are you in New York for business or for pleasure?*
2 [*count*] something that makes you happy: *It was a pleasure to meet you.*
it's a pleasure You say "it's a pleasure" as a polite way of answering someone who thanks you: *"Thank you for your help." "It's a pleasure."*
with pleasure You say "with pleasure" to show in a polite way that you are happy to do something: *"Can you help me move these boxes?" "Yes, with pleasure."*

pleat /plit/ *noun* [*count*]
a fold that is part of a skirt, a pair of pants, etc.
▶ **pleat·ed** /ˈpliṭəd/ *adjective*: *a short, pleated skirt*

pled form of **plead**

plen·ty 🔑 /ˈplɛnti/ *pronoun*
as much or as many as you need; a lot: *"Do we need more chairs?" "No, there are plenty."* ◆ *We have **plenty of** time to get there.*

pli·ers /ˈplaɪərz/ *noun* [*plural*]
a tool for holding small objects or for cutting wire: *Do you have **a pair of pliers**?*

plod /plɑd/ *verb* (plods, plod·ding, plod·ded)
to walk slowly in a heavy, tired way: *We plodded up the hill in the rain.*

plot¹ /plɑt/ *noun* [count]
1 (ENGLISH LANGUAGE ARTS) what happens in a story, play, or movie: *This book has a very exciting plot.*
2 a secret plan to do something bad: *a plot to kill the president*
3 a small piece of land that you use or you plan to use for a special purpose: *She bought a small plot of land to build a house on.* • *a vegetable plot*

plot² /plɑt/ *verb* (plots, plot·ting, plot·ted)
to make a secret plan to do something bad: *They plotted to rob the bank.*

plow /plaʊ/ *noun* [count]
a large farm tool that is pulled across a field to dig the soil ⊅ Look at **snowplow**.
▶ **plow** *verb* (plows, plow·ing, plowed): *The farmer plowed his fields.*

pluck /plʌk/ *verb* (plucks, pluck·ing, plucked)
to remove something by pulling it quickly: *He plucked the letter from her hands.* • *We needed to pluck the chicken* (= remove its feathers).

plug¹ /plʌg/ *noun* [count]
1 a thing with metal pins that joins a lamp, machine, etc. to a place in the wall (called an OUTLET) where there is electricity
2 a round thing that you put in the hole of a container to keep the water in: *She pulled out the plug and let the water drain away.* ⊅ Look at the picture at **sink**.

plug² /plʌg/ *verb* (plugs, plug·ging, plugged)
to fill a hole, so that nothing can get out: *He plugged the hole in the pipe with an old rag.*
plug something in to join a lamp, machine, etc. to the electricity, using a PLUG¹(1): *Can you plug in the television, please?* ⊅ ANTONYM **unplug**

plum /plʌm/ *noun* [count]
a soft round fruit with a hard round part (called a PIT) in the middle ⊅ Look at the picture at **fruit**.

plumb·er /ˈplʌmər/ *noun* [count]
a person whose job is to put in and repair things like water pipes and toilets

plumb·ing /ˈplʌmɪŋ/ *noun* [noncount]
1 the pipes that carry water into and around a building: *The builders are putting in the plumbing and central heating.*
2 the work of a PLUMBER

plump /plʌmp/ *adjective* (plump·er, plump·est)
a little fat, in a nice way: *a plump baby*

plunge /plʌndʒ/ *verb* (plung·es, plung·ing, plunged)
1 to jump or fall suddenly into something: *She plunged into the pool.*

2 to push something suddenly and strongly into something else: *I plunged my hand into the water.*

plu·ral /ˈplʊrəl/ *noun* [count]
(ENGLISH LANGUAGE ARTS) the form of a word that shows there is more than one: *The plural of "child" is "children."*
▶ **plu·ral** *adjective*: *Most plural nouns in English end in "s."* ⊅ Look at **singular**.

plus¹ AWL /plʌs/ *preposition*
(MATH) added to; and: *Two plus three is five (2 + 3 = 5).* • *All of our class plus half of another class are going.* ⊅ ANTONYM **minus**

plus² AWL /plʌs/ *noun* [count] (plural plus·es)
1 (also **plus sign** /ˈplʌs saɪn/) (MATH) the sign (+)
2 an advantage: *The job involves a lot of travel, which is a big plus.* ⊅ ANTONYM **minus**

plus³ AWL /plʌs/ *adjective*
1 (used after a number) or more: *He must earn $100,000 plus.*
2 (used after a letter grade on students' work) a little more than: *I got a B plus (= B+) on my essay.* ⊅ ANTONYM **minus**

plu·to·ni·um /pluˈtoʊniəm/ *noun* [noncount]
(symbol **Pu**)
(CHEMISTRY) a dangerous chemical substance that is used as a fuel in places where they make nuclear energy (called POWER PLANTS)

p.m. /ˌpi ˈɛm/ *abbreviation*
You use **p.m.** after a time to show that it is between 12 o'clock in the day and 12 o'clock at night: *The plane leaves at 3 p.m. (= 3 o'clock in the afternoon)* ⊅ Look at **a.m.**

pneu·mo·nia /nuˈmoʊnyə/ *noun* [noncount]
(HEALTH) a serious illness of the LUNGS (= the parts of your body that you breathe with)

poach /poʊtʃ/ *verb* (poach·es, poach·ing, poached)
1 to cook food gently in liquid: *I had a poached egg for breakfast.*
2 to kill and steal animals, birds, or fish from another person's land

P.O. Box /ˌpi ˈoʊ bɑks/ *noun* [count] (plural P.O. Box·es)
a box in a post office for keeping any mail sent to a person or an office: *The address to write to is P.O. Box 71.*

pock·et 🔑 /ˈpɑkət/ *noun* [count]
the part of a piece of clothing that you can put things in: *I put the key in my pocket.* ⊅ Look at the picture at **clothes**.
pick someone's pocket to steal money from someone's pocket or bag

pock·et·book /ˈpɑkətbʊk/
a small bag that a woman uses for carrying things like money and keys ⊅ SYNONYM **purse**

pock·et·knife /ˈpɑkətnaɪf/ *noun* [count] (*plural* pock·et·knives /ˈpɑkətnaɪvz/)
a small knife with one or more sharp parts (called BLADES) that fold down into the handle ⊃ SYNONYM **jackknife**

pod /pɑd/ *noun* [count]
(BIOLOGY) a long, thin case that some plants have, which is filled with seeds: *Peas grow in pods.* ⊃ Look at the picture at **vegetable**.

pod·cast /ˈpɑdkæst/ *noun* [count]
(COMPUTERS) something that has been recorded so that you can take it from the Internet and watch or listen to it on your computer or MP3 PLAYER (= a small device that stores and plays music and video): *I download podcasts of radio shows and listen to them in the car.*

po·di·um /ˈpoʊdiəm/ *noun* [count]
a tall, narrow desk that you stand behind when speaking to a large group of people

po·em /ˈpoʊəm/ *noun* [count]
(ENGLISH LANGUAGE ARTS) words arranged in lines in an artistic way, often with sounds repeated at the ends of lines: *He wrote poems about the beauty of the countryside.*

po·et /ˈpoʊət/ *noun* [count]
(ENGLISH LANGUAGE ARTS) a person who writes poems

po·et·ic /poʊˈɛt̮ɪk/ *adjective*
(ENGLISH LANGUAGE ARTS) like a poem: *poetic language*

po·et·ry /ˈpoʊətri/ *noun* [noncount]
(ENGLISH LANGUAGE ARTS) poems: *Whitman wrote beautiful poetry.*

point¹ /pɔɪnt/ *noun* [count]
1 a fact, an idea, or an opinion: *You made some interesting points* (= said some interesting things) *in your essay.* ⊃ Look at **point of view**.
2 the purpose of, or the reason for, doing something: *The point of going to school is to learn.* • *What's the point of going to her house? She's not at home.* • *There's no point in waiting for Julie – she isn't coming.*
3 a particular moment in time: *It started to rain, and at that point we decided to go home.*
4 a particular place: *No parking beyond this point.*
5 (MATH) a small round mark (.) that we use when writing part of a number (called a DECIMAL): *2.5* (= two point five)
6 the sharp end of something: *the point of a needle*
7 a unit that you win in a game or sport: *Our team scored six points.*
be on the point of doing something to be going to do something very soon: *I was on the point of leaving when he turned up.*

point² /pɔɪnt/ *verb* (points, point·ing, point·ed)
1 to show where something is using your finger, a stick, etc.: *I asked him where the bank was and he pointed across the road.* • *There was a sign pointing toward the museum.*
2 to hold something toward someone or something: *She was pointing a gun at his head.*
point something out to tell or show someone something: *Eva pointed out that my bag was open.*

point·ed /ˈpɔɪntəd/ *adjective*
with a sharp end: *a long, pointed nose*

point·less /ˈpɔɪntləs/ *adjective*
with no use or purpose: *It's pointless telling Paul anything – he never listens.*

point of view /ˌpɔɪnt əv ˈvyu/ *noun* [count] (*plural* **points of view**)
an opinion or way of thinking about something: *The book was written from the father's point of view.*

poi·son¹ /ˈpɔɪzn/ *noun* [count, noncount]
something that will kill you or make you very sick if you eat or drink it: *rat poison*

poi·son² /ˈpɔɪzn/ *verb* (poi·sons, poi·son·ing, poi·soned)
to use **poison** to kill or hurt someone or something

poi·son·ous /ˈpɔɪznəs/ *adjective*
Something that is **poisonous** will kill you or make you very sick if you eat or drink it: *Some mushrooms are poisonous.*

poke /poʊk/ *verb* (pokes, pok·ing, poked)
1 to push someone or something hard with your finger or another long thin thing: *She poked me in the eye with a pencil.*
2 to push something quickly somewhere: *Jeff poked his head out of the window.*
▶ **poke** *noun* [count]: *I gave her a poke to wake her up.*

pok·er /ˈpoʊkər/ *noun*
1 [noncount] a game that people play with cards, usually for money
2 [count] a metal stick that you use for moving the wood in a fire

po·lar /ˈpoʊlər/ *adjective*
(GEOGRAPHY) connected with the areas around the top and bottom of the earth (called the NORTH POLE and the SOUTH POLE): *the polar regions*

po·lar bear /ˈpoʊlər bɛr/ *noun* [count]
a large white animal that lives near the North Pole

pole /poʊl/ *noun* [count]
1 a long, thin piece of wood or metal. **Poles** are often used to hold something up: *a flagpole* • *a tent pole* • *tent poles*

2 (GEOGRAPHY) one of two places at the top and bottom of the earth: *the North Pole* • *the South Pole*

the pole vault /ðə ˈpoʊl vɔlt/ *noun* [singular] (SPORTS) the sport of jumping over a high bar using a long POLE to push yourself off the ground

po·lice 🔑 /pəˈlis/ *noun* [plural] the official organization whose job is to make sure that people do not break the laws of a country: *Have the police found the murderer?* • *a police car*

po·lice force /pəˈlis fɔrs/ *noun* [count] all the POLICE OFFICERS in a country or part of a country

po·lice·man /pəˈlismən/ *noun* [count] (plural po·lice·men /pəˈlismən/) a man who is a police officer

po·lice of·fi·cer /pəˈlis ˌɔfəsər/ (also **of·fi·cer**) *noun* [count] a man or woman who works in the police

po·lice sta·tion /pəˈlis ˌsteɪʃn/ *noun* [count] an office where police officers work: *They took the men to the police station for questioning.*

po·lice·wo·man /pəˈlisˌwʊmən/ *noun* [count] (plural po·lice·wo·men /pəˈlisˌwɪmən/) a woman who is a police officer

pol·i·cy 🔤 /ˈpɑləsi/ *noun* [count] (plural pol·i·cies) (POLITICS) the plans of a government or organization: *What is the government's policy on education?*

pol·ish¹ /ˈpɑlɪʃ/ *noun* [noncount] a cream or liquid that you put on something to make it shine: *furniture polish*

pol·ish² /ˈpɑlɪʃ/ *verb* (pol·ish·es, pol·ish·ing, pol·ished) to rub something so that it shines: *Have you polished your shoes?*

po·lite 🔑 /pəˈlaɪt/ *adjective* speaking or behaving in a way that shows respect: *It is polite to say "please" when you ask for something.* ⊃ ANTONYM **impolite, rude** ▸ **po·lite·ly** /pəˈlaɪtli/ *adverb*: *He asked politely for a glass of water.* ▸ **po·lite·ness** /pəˈlaɪtnəs/ *noun* [noncount]: *He stood up out of politeness and offered her his seat.*

po·lit·i·cal 🔑 /pəˈlɪtɪkl/ *adjective* (POLITICS) connected with politics or the government: *political parties* • *his political beliefs* ▸ **po·lit·i·cal·ly** /pəˈlɪtɪkli/ *adverb*: *a politically powerful country*

po·lit·i·cal·ly cor·rect /pəˌlɪtɪkli kəˈrɛkt/ *adjective* (abbreviation **PC**) words that are used to describe language or behavior that tries not to upset particular groups of people

po·lit·i·cal sci·ence /pəˌlɪtɪkl ˈsaɪəns/ *noun* [noncount] (POLITICS) the study of politics and systems of government

pol·i·ti·cian 🔑 /ˌpɑləˈtɪʃn/ *noun* [count] (POLITICS) a person who works in politics: *Politicians of all parties supported us.*

pol·i·tics 🔑 /ˈpɑlətɪks/ *noun* [noncount] (POLITICS) the work and ideas that are connected with government: *Are you interested in politics?* • *My son wants to go into politics* (= become a politician) ⊃ Look at the note at **party**(2).

poll /poʊl/ *noun* [count] **1** a way of discovering opinions by asking a group of people questions: *A recent poll showed that 73% of voters were unhappy with the government.* **2** (POLITICS) an election; the number of votes in an election: *The country will go to the polls* (= vote) *in November.*

pol·len /ˈpɑlən/ *noun* [noncount] (BIOLOGY) the yellow powder in flowers that is taken to other flowers by insects or by the wind

pol·li·nate /ˈpɑləneɪt/ *verb* (pol·li·nates, pol·li·nat·ing, pol·li·nat·ed) (BIOLOGY) to put POLLEN into a flower or plant so that it produces seeds: *Flowers are pollinated by bees.* ▸ **pol·li·na·tion** /ˌpɑləˈneɪʃn/ *noun* [noncount]

pol·lut·ant /pəˈlutnt/ *noun* [count] a substance that POLLUTES air, rivers, etc.

pol·lute /pəˈlut/ *verb* (pol·lutes, pol·lut·ing, pol·lut·ed) to make the air, rivers, etc. dirty and dangerous: *Many of our rivers are polluted with chemicals from factories.*

pol·lu·tion 🔑 /pəˈluʃn/ *noun* [noncount] **1** the action of making the air, rivers, etc. dirty and dangerous: *We must stop the pollution of our beaches.* **2** dirty and dangerous chemicals, gases, etc. that harm the environment: *Our rivers are full of pollution.* ⊃ Look at the note at **environment**.

pol·y·es·ter /ˌpɑliˈɛstər/ *noun* [noncount] an artificial material that is used for making clothes, etc.: *The sheets are a mixture of cotton and polyester.*

pol·y·gon /ˈpɑligɑn/ *noun* [count] (MATH) a flat shape with at least three straight sides and angles

pond /pɑnd/ *noun* [count] a small area of water: *We have a fish pond in our backyard.*

po·ny /ˈpoʊni/ *noun* [*count*] (*plural* **po·nies**)
a small horse

po·ny·tail /ˈpoʊniˌteɪl/ *noun* [*count*]
long hair that you tie at the back of your head so that it hangs down: *She wore her hair in a ponytail.* ⊃ Look at the picture at **hair**.

pool¹ /pul/ *noun*
1 [*count*] (also **swim·ming pool**) a place that has been built for people to swim in: *Karen dived into the pool.*
2 [*count*] a small area of liquid or light on the ground: *She was lying in a pool of blood.*
3 [*noncount*] a game in which two players try to hit balls into pockets on the edge of a table, using a long stick: *a pool table*

pool² /pul/ *verb* (**pools, pool·ing, pooled**)
to collect money or ideas together from different people: *First we'll work in pairs, then we'll pool our ideas.*

poor /pʊr/ *adjective* (**poor·er, poor·est**)
1 with very little money: *She was too poor to buy clothes for her children.* ◆ *She gave her life to helping the poor* (= poor people). ⊃ The noun is **poverty**. ⊃ **ANTONYM rich**
2 a word that you use when you feel sad because someone has problems: *Poor Tina! She's not feeling well.*
3 bad: *My grandfather is in very poor health.*

poor·ly /ˈpʊrli/ *adverb*
badly: *The street is poorly lit.*

pop¹ /pɑp/ *noun*
1 (also **pop mu·sic**) [*noncount*] (**MUSIC**) modern music that is most popular among young people: *What's your favorite pop group?* ◆ *a pop singer*
2 [*count*] a short, sharp sound: *The cork came out of the bottle with a loud pop.*

pop² /pɑp/ *verb* (**pops, pop·ping, popped**)
1 to burst, or to make something burst, with a short sharp sound: *The balloon will pop if you put a pin in it.*
2 to put something somewhere quickly: *Katie popped a candy into her mouth.*
pop up (*informal*) to appear suddenly: *The menu pops up when you double-click on the link.* ◆ *New restaurants were popping up everywhere.*

pop·corn /ˈpɑpkɔrn/ *noun* [*noncount*]
yellow grains from a tall plant (called **CORN**) that are heated until they burst and become light white balls

pope /poʊp/ *noun* [*count*]
(**RELIGION**) the head of the Roman Catholic Church: *Pope Benedict*

Pop·si·cle™ /ˈpɑpsɪkl/ *noun* [*count*]
a piece of sweet ice on a stick

pop·u·lar /ˈpɑpyələr/ *adjective*
liked by a lot of people: *Baseball is a popular sport in the U.S.* ⊃ **ANTONYM unpopular**

pop·u·lar·i·ty /ˌpɑpyəˈlærəti/ *noun* [*noncount*]
being liked by many people

pop·u·late /ˈpɑpyəleɪt/ *verb* (**pop·u·lates, pop·u·lat·ing, pop·u·lat·ed**)
(**GEOGRAPHY**) to fill a particular area with people: *Most of New England is heavily populated.*

pop·u·la·tion /ˌpɑpyəˈleɪʃn/ *noun* [*count*]
(**GEOGRAPHY**) the number of people who live in a place: *What is the population of your country?*

porch /pɔrtʃ/ *noun* [*count*] (*plural* **porch·es**)
a covered area with an open front, which is joined to a house on the ground floor

por·cu·pine
/ˈpɔrkyəpaɪn/ *noun* [*count*]
a small brown or black animal that is covered with long sharp parts (called **SPINES**)

porcupine

pore /pɔr/ *noun* [*count*]
one of the small holes in your skin that sweat passes through

pork /pɔrk/ *noun* [*noncount*]
meat from a pig: *pork sausages* ⊃ Look at the note at **pig**(1).

port /pɔrt/ *noun* [*count*]
a city or town by the ocean, where ships arrive and leave: *Baltimore is an important port.*

port·a·ble /ˈpɔrtəbl/ *adjective*
able to be moved or carried easily: *a portable television* ⊃ Look at the picture at **stereo**.

por·ter /ˈpɔrtər/ *noun* [*count*]
a person whose job is to carry people's bags in places like railroad stations and hotels

port·fo·li·o /pɔrtˈfoʊlioʊ/ *noun* [*count*] (*plural* **port·fo·li·os**)
1 a thin flat case for carrying documents, drawings, etc.
2 (**ART**) a collection of photographs, drawings, etc. that you show to people as an example of your work: *Please bring a portfolio of your work to the interview.*

por·tion **AWL** /ˈpɔrʃn/ *noun* [*count*]
1 a part of something larger: *He gave a portion of the money to each of his children.*
2 an amount of food for one person: *a large portion of rice*

por·trait /ˈpɔrtrət/ *noun* [*count*]
(**ART**) a painting or picture of a person

por·tray /pɔr'treɪ/ *verb* (por·trays, por·tray·ing, por·trayed)
1 to describe someone or something in a particular way: *The lawyer portrayed her client as an honest family man.*
2 to act the part of someone in a play or movie: *In his latest movie, he portrays a baseball coach.*
▸ **por·tray·al** /pɔr'treɪəl/ *noun* [count]: *She won an award for her portrayal of Virginia Woolf.*

pose¹ **AWL** /poʊz/ *verb* (pos·es, pos·ing, posed)
1 to cause or create something that someone must deal with: *This task poses several problems.*
2 (ART) to sit or stand in a particular position for a painting or photograph: *After the wedding ceremony, we all posed for pictures.*

pose² **AWL** /poʊz/ *noun* [count]
(ART) the position that someone stands or sits in, in order to be painted or photographed: *Just sit in a natural pose.*

posh /pɑʃ/ *adjective* (posh·er, posh·est)
expensive and of good quality: *a posh restaurant*

po·si·tion 🔑 /pə'zɪʃn/ *noun*
1 [count, noncount] the place where someone or something is: *Can you show me the position of your town on the map? • Is everyone in position (= in the right place)?*
2 [count, noncount] the way that someone or something is sitting, standing, facing, etc.: *She was still sitting in the same position when I came back. • Keep the box in an upright position.*
3 [count, noncount] how things are at a certain time: *He's in a difficult position – he doesn't have enough money to finish school.*
4 [count] a job: *There have been over a hundred applications for the position of Sales Manager.*

pos·i·tive 🔑 **AWL** /'pɑzət̬ɪv/ *adjective*
1 thinking or talking about the good parts of a situation: *It's important to stay positive. • The teacher was very positive about my work.* ⊃ ANTONYM **negative**
2 completely sure: *Are you positive that you closed the door?* ⊃ SYNONYM **sure**
3 (HEALTH) (used about a medical test) showing that something has happened or is there: *The result of the pregnancy test was positive.* ⊃ ANTONYM **negative**
4 (MATH) (used about a number) more than zero ⊃ ANTONYM **negative**

pos·i·tive·ly **AWL** *adverb* /'pɑzət̬ɪvli/ (*informal*)
really; extremely: *The idea is positively stupid.*

pos·sess /pə'zɛs/ *verb* (pos·sess·es, pos·sess·ing, pos·sessed) (*formal*)
to have or own something: *He lost everything that he possessed in the fire.*

pos·ses·sion /pə'zɛʃn/ *noun*

> ⓘ **SPELLING**
> Remember! You spell **possession** with SS and SS.

1 [noncount] (*formal*) the fact of having or owning something: *The possession of drugs is a crime.*
2 **possessions** [plural] the things that you have or own ⊃ SYNONYM **belongings**

pos·ses·sive /pə'zɛsɪv/ *adjective*
(ENGLISH LANGUAGE ARTS) used to describe words that show who or what a person or thing belongs to: *"Mine," "yours," and "his" are possessive pronouns.*

pos·si·bil·i·ty 🔑 /ˌpɑsə'bɪlət̬i/ *noun* [count] (*plural* pos·si·bil·i·ties)
something that might happen: *There's a possibility that it will rain, so take your umbrella.*

pos·si·ble 🔑 /'pɑsəbl/ *adjective*
able to happen or to be done: *Is it possible to get to your house by train? • I'll call you as soon as possible.* ⊃ ANTONYM **impossible**

pos·si·bly 🔑 /'pɑsəbli/ *adverb*
1 perhaps: *"Will you be free tomorrow?" "Possibly."*
2 in a way that can be done: *I'll come as soon as I possibly can.*

post¹ 🔑 /poʊst/ *noun* [count]
1 a piece of wood or metal that stands in the ground to hold something or to show where something is: *The sign had fallen off the post. • a fence post • a lamppost* ⊃ Look at **signpost**.
2 a job, especially an important one in a large organization: *a government post*

post² /poʊst/ *verb* (posts, post·ing, post·ed)
to put a notice where everyone can see it, for example in a public place or on the Internet: *The results will be posted on the college website.*

post·age /'poʊstɪdʒ/ *noun* [noncount]
money that you pay to send a letter or package

post·al /'poʊstl/ *adjective*
connected with sending and receiving letters, packages, etc.: *postal workers*

post·card /'poʊstkɑrd/ *noun* [count]
a card with a picture on one side, which you write on and send by mail: *She sent me a postcard from California.*

post·er /'poʊstər/ *noun* [count]
a big piece of paper on a wall, with a picture or words on it

post·grad·u·ate /ˌpoʊst'grædʒuət/ *adjective* (*formal*)
connected with studies that someone does at a university after they have received their first degree: *postgraduate courses in biology*

ə **a**bout   y **y**es   w **w**oman   t̬ bu**tt**er   eɪ **s**ay   aɪ f**i**ve   ɔɪ **b**oy   aʊ n**ow**   oʊ **g**o

post of·fice /ˈpoʊst ɔfəs/ *noun* [count]
a building where you go to send letters and packages and to buy stamps

post·pone /poʊsˈpoʊn/ *verb* (post·pones, post·pon·ing, post·poned)
to say that something will happen later than you planned: *The game was postponed because of the weather.*

pot /pɑt/ *noun* [count]
1 a deep, round container for cooking: *a big pot of soup*
2 a container that you use for a special thing: *a pot of coffee* ◆ *a plant pot* ⊃ Look at the picture at **cactus**.

po·tas·si·um /pəˈtæsiəm/ *noun* [noncount]
(symbol **K**)
(**CHEMISTRY**) a soft, silver-white metal that is used especially in mixtures (called **COMPOUNDS**)

po·ta·to /pəˈteɪṭoʊ/ *noun* [count, noncount]
(*plural* po·ta·toes)
a white vegetable with a brown or red skin that grows underground: *a baked potato* ◆ *mashed potato* ⊃ Look at **sweet potato**. ⊃ Look at the picture at **vegetable**.

po·ta·to chip /pəˈteɪṭoʊ tʃɪp/ *noun* [count]
a very thin piece of potato cooked in hot oil and eaten cold: *Do you want some potato chips with your sandwich?*

po·ten·tial¹ **AWL** /pəˈtɛnʃl/ *adjective*
possible; likely to happen or exist: *potential students*
▸ **po·ten·tial·ly** **AWL** /pəˈtɛnʃəli/ *adverb*: *This is a potentially dangerous situation* (= it could be dangerous).

po·ten·tial² **AWL** /pəˈtɛnʃl/ *noun* [noncount]
qualities or possibilities that exist and can be developed: *She has great potential as a musician.*

pot·ter·y /ˈpɑṭəri/ *noun* [noncount]
1 cups, plates, and other things that are made from CLAY (= heavy earth that becomes hard when it is baked in an oven): *This shop sells beautiful pottery.*
2 (**ART**) the activity of making cups, plates, and other things from CLAY: *Her hobby is pottery.*

poul·try /ˈpoʊltri/ *noun* [plural]
birds such as chickens that people keep on farms for their eggs or their meat

pounce /paʊns/ *verb* (pounc·es, pounc·ing, pounced)
to jump on someone or something suddenly: *The cat pounced on the bird.*

pound /paʊnd/ *noun* [count]
1 (symbol **lb.**) a measure of weight (=0.454 kilograms). There are 16 **ounces** in a pound:
You need half a pound of flour. ◆ *He weighs 195 pounds.* ◆ *2 lbs. sugar*
2 (symbol **£**) money that people use in Britain and some other countries: *The computer cost three hundred pounds.*

pour /pɔr/ *verb* (pours, pour·ing, poured)
1 to make liquid flow out of or into something: *She poured water into the teapot.* ◆ *She poured me a cup of coffee.* ◆ *Pour the sauce over the meat.*
2 to flow quickly: *Oil poured out of the damaged ship.* ◆ *Tears were pouring down her cheeks.*
3 to rain very hard: *Look at the weather. It's pouring.*

pov·er·ty /ˈpɑvərṭi/ *noun* [noncount]
the state of being poor: *There are many people living in poverty in this city.*

pow·der /ˈpaʊdər/ *noun* [count, noncount]
a dry substance like flour that is made of a lot of very small pieces: *Crush the spices to a powder.* ◆ *Can you get me some more chili powder, please?*

pow·er /ˈpaʊər/ *noun*
1 [noncount] the ability to control people or things; the ability to do things: *The president has a lot of power.* ◆ *I did everything in my power* (= everything I could do) *to help her.*
2 [noncount] the energy or strength that someone or something has: *The ship was helpless against the power of the storm.*
3 [noncount] energy that can be collected and used for making machines work, making electricity, etc.: *nuclear power*
4 [count] the right to do something: *Police officers have the power to arrest people.*
5 [count] a strong person or country: *There is a meeting of world powers next week.*
6 [count, usually singular] (**MATH**) the number of times that a number is to be multiplied by itself: *4 to the power of 3 is 4^3* (=$4×4×4=64$).

pow·er·ful /ˈpaʊərfl/ *adjective*
1 having a lot of strength or power: *The car has a very powerful engine.* ◆ *He is one of the most powerful people in the company.*
2 having a strong effect: *a powerful drug*

pow·er·less /ˈpaʊərləs/ *adjective*
not able to do anything: *I was powerless to help.*

pow·er plant /ˈpaʊər plænt/ *noun* [count]
a place where electricity is made

PR /ˌpi ˈɑr/ *short for* **public relations**

prac·ti·cal /ˈpræktɪkl/ *adjective*
1 connected with doing or making things, not just with ideas: *Do you have any practical experience in working on a farm?*
2 sensible or suitable; likely to be successful: *Your plan isn't practical.* ⊃ **ANTONYM impractical**
3 good at making and repairing things: *She's a very practical person and has made a lot of improvements to the house.*

prac·ti·cal joke /ˌpræktɪkl ˈdʒoʊk/ *noun* [count]
a trick that you play on someone that makes him or her look silly and makes other people laugh

prac·ti·cal·ly /ˈpræktɪkli/ *adverb*
almost; nearly: *Don't go out – lunch is practically ready!* • *It rained practically every day last week.*

prac·tice¹ 🖉 /ˈpræktəs/ *noun*
1 [noncount] action rather than ideas or thoughts: *Your plan sounds fine, but would it work in practice?*
2 [noncount] doing something many times so that you will do it well: *You need lots of practice when you're learning to play a musical instrument.*
3 [count] the business of a doctor, dentist, or lawyer: *Sarah wants to start her own practice when she graduates from law school.*
out of practice not good at something, because you have not done it for a long time

prac·tice² 🖉 /ˈpræktəs/ *verb* (prac·tic·es, prac·tic·ing, prac·ticed)
1 to do something many times so that you will do it well: *If you want to play the piano well, you must practice every day.*
2 to work as a doctor, dentist, or lawyer: *After graduating, she practiced medicine in Atlanta.*

prai·rie /ˈprɛri/ *noun* [count]
(GEOGRAPHY) a very large area of flat land that is covered in grass and few trees (especially in the middle of the U.S.)

praise /preɪz/ *verb* (prais·es, prais·ing, praised)
to say that someone or something is good: *She was praised for her hard work.*
▶ **praise** *noun* [noncount]: *The book has received a lot of praise.*

pray /preɪ/ *verb* (prays, pray·ing, prayed)
(RELIGION) to speak to God or a god: *They prayed to God for help.*

prayer 🖉 /prɛr/ *noun* (RELIGION)
1 [count] words that you say when you speak to God or a god: *They said a prayer for world peace.*
2 [noncount] the act of PRAYING: *the power of prayer* • *They knelt in prayer.*

preach /pritʃ/ *verb* (preach·es, preach·ing, preached)
(RELIGION) to talk about God or a god to a group of people

preach·er /ˈpritʃər/ *noun* [count]
(RELIGION) a person who gives religious talks in public: *Our preacher tonight is Reverend Jones.*

pre·cau·tion /prɪˈkɔʃn/ *noun* [count]
something that you do so that bad things will not happen: *I took the precaution of locking all the windows when I went out.*

pre·cede **AWL** /prɪˈsid/ *verb* (pre·cedes, pre·ced·ing, pre·ced·ed) (formal)
to happen or come before someone or something: *Look at the diagram on the preceding page.*

pre·cinct /ˈprisɪŋkt/ *noun* [count]
(GEOGRAPHY) one of the parts that a town or city is divided into

pre·cious /ˈprɛʃəs/ *adjective*
1 very valuable or expensive: *Diamonds are precious stones.*
2 that you consider to be very special: *My family is very precious to me.*

pre·cip·i·ta·tion /prɪˌsɪpəˈteɪʃn/ *noun* [noncount] (formal)
(GEOGRAPHY) rain or snow that falls to the ground

pre·cise **AWL** /prɪˈsaɪs/ *adjective*
exactly right: *I gave him precise instructions on how to get to my house.*
▶ **pre·cise·ly** **AWL** /prɪˈsaɪsli/ *adverb*: *They arrived at two o'clock precisely.*

pre·ci·sion **AWL** /prɪˈsɪʒn/ *noun* [noncount]
the quality of being clear or exact: *The plans were drawn with great precision.*

pred·a·tor /ˈprɛdətər/ *noun* [count]
(BIOLOGY) an animal that kills and eats other animals

pred·e·ces·sor /ˈprɛdəˌsɛsər/ *noun* [count]
the person who did a job before the person who does it now: *She was hired by my predecessor.*

pre·dic·a·ment /prɪˈdɪkəmənt/ *noun* [count]
an unpleasant and difficult situation that is hard to get out of

pre·dict **AWL** /prɪˈdɪkt/ *verb* (pre·dicts, pre·dict·ing, pre·dict·ed)
to say what you think will happen: *She predicted that it would rain, and she was right.*
▶ **pre·dict·a·ble** **AWL** /prɪˈdɪktəbl/ *adjective*
that was or could be expected to happen: *predictable results*

pre·dic·tion **AWL** /prɪˈdɪkʃn/ *noun* [count, noncount]
saying what will happen; what someone thinks will happen: *The results confirmed our predictions.*

pref·ace /ˈprɛfəs/ *noun* [count]
(ENGLISH LANGUAGE ARTS) a piece of writing at the beginning of a book that explains what it is about or why it was written

pre·fer 🖉 /prɪˈfər/ *verb* (pre·fers, pre·fer·ring, pre·ferred)
to like one thing or person better than another: *Would you prefer tea or coffee?* • *I would prefer to stay at home.* • *He prefers going out to studying.*

tʃ **ch**in   dʒ **J**une   v **v**an   θ **th**in   ð **th**en   s **s**o   z **z**oo   ʃ **sh**e

pref·er·a·ble /'prɛfərəbl/ *adjective*
better or more suitable: *I think living in the country is **preferable to** living in the city.*
▸ **pref·er·a·bly** /'prɛfərəbli/ *adverb*: *Call me Sunday morning, but preferably not too early!*

pref·er·ence /'prɛfərəns/ *noun* [*count, noncount*]
a feeling that you like one thing or person better than another: *We have lemonade and orange juice – do you have a preference?*

pre·fix /'prifɪks/ *noun* [*count*] (*plural* **pre·fix·es**)
(**ENGLISH LANGUAGE ARTS**) a group of letters that you add to the beginning of a word to make another word: *The prefix "im-" means "not," so "impossible" means "not possible."* ⊃ Look at **suffix**.

preg·nan·cy /'prɛgnənsi/ *noun* [*count, noncount*]
(*plural* **preg·nan·cies**)
(**HEALTH**) the state of being pregnant: *Many women feel sick **during pregnancy**.*

preg·nant 🔑 /'prɛgnənt/ *adjective*
(**HEALTH**) If a woman is **pregnant**, she has a baby growing in her body: *She's five months pregnant.*

pre·his·tor·ic /ˌprihɪˈstɔrɪk/ *adjective*
(**HISTORY**) from the time in history before events were written down: *prehistoric animals*

prej·u·dice /'prɛdʒədɪs/ *noun* [*count, noncount*]
a strong idea that you do not like someone or something, for a reason that is wrong or unfair: *She was a victim of racial prejudice.*
▸ **prej·u·diced** /'prɛdʒədɪst/ *adjective*: *He is prejudiced against me because I'm a woman.*

pre·lim·i·nar·y ⬛AWL⬛ /prɪˈlɪməˌnɛri/ *adjective*
happening before something else that is more important: *After a few preliminary remarks, the discussions began.*

pre·ma·ture /ˌpriməˈtʃʊr/ *adjective*
happening before the expected time: *Her baby was premature* (= born before the expected time).

pre·mier /prɪˈmɪr/ *noun* [*count*]
(**POLITICS**) the leader of the government in some countries: *the Russian premier, Vladimir Putin*

prep·a·ra·tion 🔑 /ˌprɛpəˈreɪʃn/ *noun*
1 [*noncount*] making something ready: *I packed my bags **in preparation for** the trip.*
2 preparations [*plural*] what you do to get ready for something: *They began to **make preparations for** the wedding last year.*

pre·pare 🔑 /prɪˈpɛr/ *verb* (**pre·pares, pre·par·ing, pre·pared**)
to make someone or something ready; to make yourself ready: *Martin is in the kitchen preparing dinner.* ◆ *I prepared well for the exam.*

pre·pared /prɪˈpɛrd/ *adjective*
ready; able to deal with something: *I wasn't **prepared for** all these problems.*

prepared to do something happy to do something: *I'm not prepared to give you any money.* ⊃ **SYNONYM willing**

prep·o·si·tion /ˌprɛpəˈzɪʃn/ *noun* [*count*]
(**ENGLISH LANGUAGE ARTS**) a word that you use before a noun or pronoun to show where, when, how, etc.: *In the sentence "He traveled from Orlando to Miami," "from" and "to" are prepositions.*

pre·school /'priskul/ *noun* [*count, noncount*]
a school for children between the ages of about two and five: *My daughter has another year of preschool before she starts kindergarten.* ⊃ **SYNONYM nursery school**

pre·scribe /prɪˈskraɪb/ *verb* (**pre·scribes, pre·scrib·ing, pre·scribed**)
(**HEALTH**) to say that someone must take a medicine: *The doctor prescribed some pills.*

pre·scrip·tion /prɪˈskrɪpʃn/ *noun* [*count, noncount*]
(**HEALTH**) a piece of paper that a doctor gives to you with the name of your medicine on it

pres·ence /'prɛzns/ *noun* [*noncount*]
the fact of being in a place: *an experiment to test for the **presence of** oxygen* ◆ *My grandmother did not allow arguing **in** her **presence*** (= when she was there).

pres·ent¹ 🔑 /'prɛznt/ *adjective*

ℹ **PRONUNCIATION**
When the word **present** is a noun or an adjective, you say the first part of the word louder: **PRESent**.
When the word **present** is a verb, you say the second part of the word louder: **preSENT**.

1 in a place: *The whole class was present.* ⊃ **ANTONYM absent**
2 being or happening now: *What is your present job?* ⊃ **SYNONYM current**

pres·ent² 🔑 /'prɛznt/ *noun*
1 [*count*] something that you give to someone or get from someone: *What can I get him for a birthday present?* ⊃ **SYNONYM gift**
2 [*noncount*] the time now: *I can't help you **at present** – I'm too busy.*
3 the present (also **the pre·sent tense**) [*singular*] the form of a verb that you use to talk about what is happening or what exists now ⊃ Look at **future¹**(2), **the past tense**.

pre·sent³ 🔑 /prɪˈzɛnt/ *verb* (**pre·sents, pre·sent·ing, pre·sent·ed**)
to give something to someone, especially in a formal ceremony: *The prizes were **presented to** the winners.* ◆ *They **presented** their teacher **with** some flowers.*

pres·en·ta·tion /ˌprɛznˈteɪʃn; ˌprɪznˈteɪʃn/ *noun*
1 [*count, noncount*] the act of giving something to someone, especially in a formal ceremony: *The presentation of prizes will take place at 7:30.*
2 [*count*] a meeting where someone shows or explains something to the people listening: *Each student has to give a short presentation on a subject of their choice.*

pres·ent par·ti·ci·ple /ˌprɛznt ˈpɑrtəsɪpl/ *noun* [*count*]
(**ENGLISH LANGUAGE ARTS**) the form of a verb that ends in "-ing"

the pres·ent per·fect /ðə ˌprɛznt ˈpərfɪkt/ *noun* [*singular*]
(**ENGLISH LANGUAGE ARTS**) the form of a verb for things that began in the past and continue now. We make it with the present tense of "have" and a past participle of the verb: *"They have disappeared"* is in the present perfect.

the pres·ent tense /ðə ˌprɛznt ˈtɛns/ (also **the pres·ent**) *noun* [*singular*]
(**ENGLISH LANGUAGE ARTS**) the form of a verb that you use to talk about what is happening or what exists now

pres·er·va·tion /ˌprɛzərˈveɪʃn/ *noun* [*noncount*]
the act of keeping something safe or in good condition: *the preservation of rare birds*

pre·ser·va·tive /prɪˈzɜrvətɪv/ *noun* [*count, noncount*]
a substance that is added to food so that it stays in good condition for longer: *Our juice is 100% natural, with no artificial colors or preservatives.*

pre·serve /prɪˈzɜrv/ *verb* (**pre·serves, pre·serv·ing, pre·served**)
to keep something safe or in good condition: *They managed to preserve most of the paintings.*

pres·i·den·cy /ˈprɛzədənsi/ *noun* (*plural* **pres·i·den·cies**) (**POLITICS**)
1 the presidency [*singular*] the position of being president
2 [*count*] the period of time that someone is president: *These events happened during the third year of his presidency.*

pres·i·dent /ˈprɛzədənt/ *noun* [*count*]
1 (**POLITICS**) the leader of the country in many countries of the world: *the president of the United States* ⊃ Look at the note at **government**.
2 (**BUSINESS**) the person with the highest position in an organization or a company
▶ **pres·i·den·tial** /ˌprɛzəˈdɛnʃl/ *adjective*: *the presidential elections*

Pres·i·dents' Day /ˈprɛzədənts deɪ/ *noun* [*count*]
a holiday on the third Monday in February to celebrate the birthdays of George Washington and Abraham Lincoln

press¹ /prɛs/ *noun* (*plural* **press·es**)
1 the press [*noncount*] newspapers and magazines and the people who write them: *She told her story to the press.*
2 [*count*] a machine for printing things like books and newspapers

press² /prɛs/ *verb* (**press·es, press·ing, pressed**)
1 to push something: *If you press this button, the door will open.* ◆ *She pressed her face against the window.* ⊃ Look at the picture at **squeeze**.
2 to make clothes flat and smooth using a piece of electrical equipment that gets hot (called an IRON): *This suit needs pressing.*

press con·fer·ence /ˈprɛs ˌkɑnfrəns/ *noun* [*count*]
a meeting when a famous or important person answers questions from news reporters

pres·sure¹ /ˈprɛʃər/ *noun*
1 [*noncount*] the force that presses on something: *The pressure of the water caused the dam to crack.*
2 [*count, noncount*] (**PHYSICS**) the force that a gas or liquid has when it is contained inside something: *He has high blood pressure* (= the force with which blood travels around your body). ◆ *You should check your tire pressure* (= the amount of air in your car tires) *regularly.*
3 [*count, noncount*] a feeling of being worried because of the things you have to do: *She's under a lot of pressure at work.* ◆ *financial pressures*

pres·sure² /ˈprɛʃər/ *verb* (**pres·sures, pres·sur·ing, pres·sured**)
to make someone do something that they do not really want to do: *Her parents pressured her into going to a college near home.*

pres·tige /prɛˈstiʒ/ *noun* [*noncount*]
the respect that someone or something has because they have a high social position or they have been very successful: *He dreamed of having a job with a lot of power and prestige.*
▶ **pres·ti·gious** /prɛˈstɪdʒəs/ *adjective*: *a prestigious university*

pre·sum·a·bly AWL /prɪˈzuməbli/ *adverb*
a word you use when you think that something is probably true: *Presumably, this rain means the parade will be canceled.*

pre·sume AWL /prɪˈzum/ *verb* (**pre·sumes, pre·sum·ing, pre·sumed**)
to think that something is true, although you are not sure: *She's not home yet, so I presume she's still at work.*

pre·tend /prɪˈtɛnd/ *verb* (**pre·tends, pre·tend·ing, pre·tend·ed**)
to try to make someone believe something that is not true: *He didn't want to talk, so he*

pretended to be asleep. ◆ *I pretended that I was enjoying myself.*

pre·ten·tious /prɪˈtɛnʃəs/ *adjective*
trying to appear more serious or important than you really are in order to impress other people

pre·text /ˈpritɛkst/ *noun* [count]
a reason that you give for doing something, which is not the real reason: *She left work early on the pretext of having a doctor's appointment.*

pret·ty¹ 🔑 /ˈprɪti/ *adjective* (**pret·ti·er**, **pret·ti·est**)
nice to look at: *a pretty little girl* ◆ *These flowers are very pretty.* ⊃ Look at the note at **attractive**.

pret·ty² 🔑 /ˈprɪti/ *adverb* (*informal*)
very, but not completely: *You should wear a heavier coat – it's pretty cold today.* ◆ *I'm pretty sure that Alex will agree.* ⊃ **SYNONYM quite**
pretty much; **pretty well** almost: *I won't be long. I'm pretty much finished.*

pret·zel /ˈprɛtsl/ *noun* [count]
a type of bread that is rolled and twisted into a special shape and baked with salt. **Pretzels** are often thin and hard: *a bag of pretzels*

pre·vent 🔑 /prɪˈvɛnt/ *verb* (**pre·vents**, **pre·vent·ing**, **pre·vent·ed**)
to stop someone from doing something; to stop something from happening: *Her parents want to prevent her from getting married.* ◆ *It is easier to prevent disease than to cure it.*

pre·ven·tion /prɪˈvɛnʃn/ *noun* [noncount]
stopping someone from doing something or stopping something from happening: *crime prevention* ◆ *the prevention of cruelty to animals*

pre·view /ˈprivyu/ *noun* [count]
1 a chance to see a play, movie, etc. before it is shown to the general public
2 a chance to see what something will be like before it happens or is shown: *Click on the print preview button.*

pre·vi·ous 🔑 **AWL** /ˈpriviəs/ *adjective*
coming or happening before or earlier: *Who was the previous owner of the car?*
▶ **pre·vi·ous·ly** **AWL** /ˈpriviəsli/ *adverb*: *I work in a factory now, but previously I was a salesclerk.*

prey /preɪ/ *noun* [noncount]
an animal or bird that another animal or bird kills for food: *Zebra are prey for lions.*

price 🔑 /praɪs/ *noun* [count]
how much money you pay to buy something: *The price is $15.* ◆ *Prices in this country are high.*

Thesaurus

price the money that you have to pay to buy something: *What's the price of gas now?* ◆ *We can't afford the car at that price.* ◆ *house prices*
cost the money that you need to buy, make,

or do something: *The cost of electricity is going up.* ◆ *A new computer system was installed at a cost of $80,000.* ◆ *the cost of living* (= the amount of money you need to pay for food, clothes, and a place to live)
charge the money that you pay for goods or services: *Is there a charge for parking here?* ◆ *Delivery is free of charge* (= costs nothing).
fee the money you pay to go into a place, or for professional advice or services from doctors, lawyers, colleges, etc.: *Some lawyers charge extremely high fees for their services.* ◆ *an annual membership fee* ◆ *tuition fees*
expense the money you spend on something, or something that makes you spend money: *The house was decorated at great expense.* ◆ *Owning a car is a big expense.*

price·less /ˈpraɪsləs/ *adjective*
extremely valuable: *priceless jewels*

pric·ey (also **pric·y**) /ˈpraɪsi/ *adjective* (**pric·i·er**, **pric·i·est**) (*informal*)
expensive: *The restaurant is great, but it's a little pricey.*

prick /prɪk/ *verb* (**pricks**, **prick·ing**, **pricked**)
to make a very small hole in something, or to hurt someone, with a sharp point: *I pricked my finger on a needle.*
▶ **prick** *noun* [count]: *She felt the prick of a needle.*

prick·ly /ˈprɪkli/ *adjective*
covered with sharp points: *a prickly cactus*

pride /praɪd/ *noun* [noncount]
1 the feeling that you are proud of something that you or others have or have done: *She showed us her painting with great pride.*
2 the feeling that you are better than other people ⊃ The adjective is **proud**.

priest 🔑 /prist/ *noun* [count]
a person who leads people in their religion: *a Roman Catholic priest*

pri·mar·i·ly **AWL** /praɪˈmɛrəli/ *adverb*
more than anything else; mainly: *The course is aimed primarily at people with no previous experience.*

pri·mar·y **AWL** /ˈpraɪˌmɛri/ *adjective*
first; most important: *The primary aim of this course is to improve your spoken French.*

pri·mar·y col·or /ˌpraɪmɛri ˈkʌlər/ *noun* [count]
(**ART**) any of the colors red, yellow, or blue. You can make any other color by mixing **primary colors** in diffferent ways.

prime **AWL** /praɪm/ *adjective*
1 most important: *My prime concern is to protect my property.*
2 of very good quality: *prime cuts of beef*

---

prime min·is·ter /ˌpraɪm ˈmɪnəstər/ *noun*
[count]
(**POLITICS**) the leader of the government in some countries, for example in Britain

prime num·ber /ˌpraɪm ˈnʌmbər/ *noun* [count]
(**MATH**) a number that can only be divided by itself and 1. The numbers 7, 17, and 41 are **prime numbers**.

prim·i·tive /ˈprɪmətɪv/ *adjective*
very simple; not developed: *The cooking facilities were very primitive.* ◆ *primitive beliefs*

prince /prɪns/ *noun* [count]
1 a man in a royal family, especially the son of a king or queen: *the Prince of Egypt*
2 (**POLITICS**) a man from a royal family who is the leader of a small country

prin·cess /ˈprɪnsɛs/ *noun* [count] (*plural* prin·cess·es)
a woman in a royal family, especially the daughter of a king or queen or the wife of a PRINCE

prin·ci·pal¹ 🔑 **AWL** /ˈprɪnsəpl/ *adjective*
most important: *My principal reason for going to the store was to buy shoes.*

prin·ci·pal² **AWL** /ˈprɪnsəpl/ *noun* [count]
a person who is in charge of a school: *The high school has a new principal.*

prin·ci·pal·ly **AWL** /ˈprɪnsəpli/ *adverb*
mainly; mostly: *She sometimes travels to Washington, but she works principally in Baltimore.*

prin·ci·ple **AWL** /ˈprɪnsəpl/ *noun* [count]
1 a rule about how you should live: *He has very strong principles.* ◆ *I refuse to lie about it; it's against my principles.*
2 a rule or fact about how something happens or works: *scientific principles*

print¹ 🔑 /prɪnt/ *verb* (**prints, print·ing, print·ed**)
1 to put words or pictures onto paper using a machine. Books, newspapers, and magazines are **printed**.
2 to write with letters that are not joined together: *Please print your name and address clearly.*
print something out to print information from a computer onto paper: *I'll just print out this document.* ⊃ The noun is **printout**.

print² /prɪnt/ *noun*
1 [noncount] letters that a machine makes on paper: *The print is too small to read without my glasses.*
2 [count] a mark where something has pressed on something: *footprints in the snow* ◆ *The police are looking for prints* (= fingerprints).
3 [count] (**ART**) a copy on paper of a painting or photograph

print·er /ˈprɪntər/
noun [count]
1 a machine that prints words from a computer
2 a person or company that prints things like books or newspapers

printer

print·out /ˈprɪntaʊt/ *noun* [count]
(**COMPUTERS**) information from a computer that is printed onto paper: *She gave me a printout of my reservation.*

pri·or **AWL** /ˈpraɪər/ *adjective*
coming or happening before or earlier: *No prior experience is necessary to do the job.* ⊃ SYNONYM **previous**

pri·or·i·tize **AWL** /praɪˈɔrətaɪz/ *verb*
(**pri·or·i·tiz·es, pri·or·i·tiz·ing, pri·or·i·tized**)
to organize things so that you can do the most important first: *You need to prioritize your work so you can meet your deadlines.*

pri·or·i·ty 🔑 **AWL** /praɪˈɔrəti/ *noun* (*plural* pri·or·i·ties)
1 [count] something that you think is more important than other things and that you must do first: *Education is a top priority.*
2 [noncount] being more important than someone or something or coming before someone or something else: *We give priority to families with small children.* ◆ *Emergency cases take priority over other patients in the hospital.*

prism /ˈprɪzəm/ *noun* [count]
(**PHYSICS**) a transparent glass or plastic object. It separates light that passes through it into the seven different colors.

pris·on 🔑 /ˈprɪzn/ *noun* [count]
a place where criminals must stay as a punishment: *He was sent to prison for robbing a bank.* ◆ *She was in prison for 15 years.* ⊃ SYNONYM **jail**

pris·on·er 🔑 /ˈprɪzn·ər/ *noun* [count]
a person who is in prison as a punishment; a person who is not free: *The number of prisoners serving life sentences has fallen.* ◆ *He was taken prisoner by rebel soldiers.*

pri·va·cy /ˈpraɪvəsi/ *noun* [noncount]
being alone and not watched or disturbed by other people: *He locked the door so he could have some privacy.*

pri·vate 🔑 /ˈpraɪvət/ *adjective*
1 for one person or a small group of people only, and not for anyone else: *You shouldn't read his letters – they're private.* ◆ *This is private property.*
2 alone; without other people: *I would like a private meeting with the manager.*

3 not connected with your job: *She never talks about her **private life** at work.*
4 not controlled or paid for by the government: *a private hospital ◆ private schools*
in private alone; without other people there: *Can I speak to you in private?* ➔ ANTONYM **in public**
▶ **pri·vate·ly** /ˈpraɪvətli/ *adverb*: *Let's go into my office – we can talk more privately there.*

priv·i·lege /ˈprɪvəlɪdʒ/ *noun* [count]
something special that only one person or a few people may do or have: *Prisoners who behave well have special privileges.*
▶ **priv·i·leged** /ˈprɪvəlɪdʒd/ *adjective*: *I feel very privileged to be playing for the national team.*

prize /praɪz/ *noun* [count]
something that you give to the person who wins a game, race, etc.: *I **won first prize** in the painting competition. ◆ Did you win a prize?*

prob·a·bil·i·ty /ˌprɑbəˈbɪləti/ *noun* [noncount, singular]
how likely something is to happen: *There was little probability of success.*

prob·a·ble /ˈprɑbəbl/ *adjective*
likely to happen or to be true: *It is probable that he will be late.* ➔ ANTONYM **improbable**

prob·a·bly /ˈprɑbəbli/ *adverb*
almost certainly: *I will probably see you on Thursday.*

prob·lem /ˈprɑbləm/ *noun* [count]
1 something that is difficult; something that makes you worry: *She has a lot of problems. Her husband is sick and she may lose her job. ◆ There is a problem with my phone – it doesn't work.*
2 a question that you must answer by thinking about it: *I can't **solve** this **problem**.*
no problem (*informal*) words you use to say that something is easy and you don't mind doing it: *"Can you fix this?" "Sure, no problem."*

prob·lem·at·ic /ˌprɑbləˈmæṭɪk/ *adjective*
causing a lot of problems, or full of problems: *Finding someone to do this work for you could be problematic.*

pro·ce·dure AWL /prəˈsidʒər/ *noun* [count, noncount]
the usual or correct way of doing something: *What is the procedure for applying for a student visa?*

pro·ceed AWL /prəˈsid; proʊˈsid/ *verb* (pro·ceeds, pro·ceed·ing, pro·ceed·ed) (*formal*)
1 to continue doing something: *We're not sure whether we want to **proceed with** the sale of the house.*
2 to do something next, after having done something else first: *Once he had calmed down, he **proceeded to** tell us what had happened.*

proc·ess AWL /ˈprɑsɛs/ *noun* [count] (plural proc·ess·es)
1 a number of actions, one after the other, for doing or making something: *He explained the **process of** building a boat. ◆ Learning a language is usually a slow process.*
2 a number of changes that happen in a natural way: *Trees go through the process of growing and losing leaves every year.*

pro·ces·sion /prəˈsɛʃn/ *noun* [count]
a line of people or cars that are moving slowly along: *We watched the funeral procession.*

pro·duce¹ /prəˈdus/ *verb* (pro·duc·es, pro·duc·ing, pro·duced)
1 to make or grow something: *This factory produces cars. ◆ What does the farm produce?*
2 to make something happen: *His hard work produced good results.*
3 to bring something out to show it: *She produced a ticket from her pocket.*
4 to organize something like a play or movie: *She is producing a play at our local theater.*

pro·duce² /ˈproʊdus/ *noun* [noncount]
food that you grow on a farm or in a garden to sell: *fresh farm produce*

pro·duc·er /prəˈdusər/ *noun* [count]
1 a person who organizes something like a play or movie: *a television producer*
2 a company or country that makes or grows something: *Brazil is an important producer of coffee.*

prod·uct /ˈprɑdʌkt/ *noun* [count]
1 something that people make or grow to sell: *The company has just launched a new product.*
2 (MATH) the amount you get if you multiply one number by another: *The product of three and five is fifteen.*

pro·duc·tion /prəˈdʌkʃn/ *noun*
1 [noncount] the action of making or growing something: *the production of oil*
2 [count] a play, movie, etc.

pro·duc·tive /prəˈdʌktɪv/ *adjective*
doing, achieving, or producing a lot: *The meeting was very productive.*

pro·fes·sion /prəˈfɛʃn/ *noun* [count]
a job that needs a lot of studying and special training: *She's a doctor **by profession**.* ➔ Look at the note at **job**.

pro·fes·sion·al¹ AWL /prəˈfɛʃənl/ *adjective*
1 connected with a profession: *I got professional advice from a lawyer.*
2 doing something for money as a job: *a professional tennis player* ➔ ANTONYM **amateur**
▶ **pro·fes·sion·al·ly** AWL /prəˈfɛʃənl·i/ *adverb*: *He plays the piano professionally.*

pro·fes·sion·al² AWL /prəˈfɛʃənl/ *noun* [*count*]
a person who works in a job that needs a lot of training or education: *doctors and other medical professionals*

pro·fes·sor /prəˈfɛsər/ *noun* [*count*]
a teacher at a college or university: *Professor Oliver • He's a psychology professor at Cornell University.*

pro·fi·cient /prəˈfɪʃnt/ *adjective*
able to do a particular thing well: *We are looking for someone who is **proficient in** Spanish.*
▸ **pro·fi·cien·cy** /prəˈfɪʃnsi/ *noun* [*noncount*]: *proficiency in English*

pro·file /ˈproʊfaɪl/ *noun* [*count*]
1 the shape of a person's face when you see it from the side
2 a short description of someone or something that gives useful information: *We're building up a profile of our typical customer.*

prof·it 🔑 /ˈprɑfət/ *noun* [*count*]
money that you get when you sell something for more than it cost to buy or make: *They **made a profit** of $10.*

prof·it·a·ble /ˈprɑfətəbl/ *adjective*
If something is **profitable**, it brings you money: *a profitable business*

pro·found /prəˈfaʊnd/ *adjective*
that you feel very strongly: *The experience had a profound influence on her.*

pro·gram¹ 🔑 /ˈproʊgræm/ *noun* [*count*]
1 something on television or radio: *Did you watch that program about cats on TV last night?* ⊃ Look at the note at **television**.
2 an official plan or system for doing something: *an intense training program • There are plans to expand the government programs for the elderly.*
3 (**COMPUTERS**) a set of instructions that you give to a computer: *He sells software programs for businesses.*
4 a piece of paper or a little book that tells people at a play or concert what they are going to see or hear

pro·gram² /ˈproʊgræm/ *verb* (**pro·grams**, **pro·gram·ming**, **pro·grammed**)
(**COMPUTERS**) to give a set of instructions to a computer: *It's easy to program the computer to recognize those symbols.*
▸ **pro·gram·ming** /ˈproʊgræmɪŋ/ *noun* [*noncount*]: *a degree in **computer programming***

pro·gram·mer /ˈproʊgræmər/ *noun* [*count*]
a person whose job is to write programs for a computer

pro·gress¹ 🔑 /ˈprɑgrəs/ *noun* [*noncount*]
1 improvement or development: *Jo has **made good progress** in math this year.*

2 movement forward: *She watched her father's slow progress down the steps.*
in progress happening now: *Quiet please – examination in progress.*

pro·gress² /prəˈgrɛs/ *verb* (**pro·gress·es**, **pro·gress·ing**, **pro·gressed**)
1 to improve or develop: *Students can progress at their own speed.*
2 to move forward; to continue: *She became more tired as the evening progressed.*

pro·hib·it AWL /proʊˈhɪbət/ *verb* (**pro·hib·its**, **pro·hib·it·ing**, **pro·hib·it·ed**) (*formal*)
to say that people must not do something: *The sign says that parking is prohibited here.* ⊃
SYNONYM forbid

pro·hi·bi·tion AWL /ˌproʊəˈbɪʃn/ *noun*
1 [*count, noncount*] (*formal*) a law or rule that says people must not do something: *a prohibition on carrying guns*
2 Prohibition [*noncount*] (**HISTORY**) the time between 1920 and 1933, when it was illegal to produce and sell alcoholic drinks in the U.S.

pro·ject¹ 🔑 AWL /ˈprɑdʒɛkt/ *noun* [*count*]
1 a big plan to do something: *a project to build a new airport • The research project will be funded by the government.*
2 a piece of work that you do at school. You find out a lot about something and write about it: *We **did a project on** the Civil War.*

pro·ject² AWL /prəˈdʒɛkt/ *verb* (**pro·jects**, **pro·ject·ing**, **pro·ject·ed**)
1 to plan something that will happen in the future: *the president's projected tour of Europe*
2 to make light, a moving picture, etc. appear on a flat surface or screen: *Colored lights were projected onto the dance floor.*
▸ **pro·jec·tion** AWL /prəˈdʒɛkʃn/ *noun* [*count, noncount*]

pro·jec·tor /prəˈdʒɛktər/ *noun* [*count*]
a machine that shows movies or pictures on a wall or screen

pro·lif·ic /prəˈlɪfɪk/ *adjective*
producing a lot of music, writing, art, etc.: *She is a prolific writer of short stories.*

pro·long /prəˈlɔŋ/ *verb* (**pro·longs**, **pro·long·ing**, **pro·longed**)
to make something last longer: *This treatment could prolong his life by around two years.*

prom /prɑm/ *noun* [*count*]
a formal dance for high school students that happens near the end of the school year: *the senior prom • Are you going to the prom this year?*

prom·i·nent /ˈprɑmənənt/ *adjective*
1 easy to see, for example because it is bigger than usual: *prominent teeth*
2 important and famous: *a prominent writer*

ə **about**   y **yes**   w **woman**   t̬ **butter**   eɪ **say**   aɪ **five**   ɔɪ **boy**   aʊ **now**   oʊ **go**

prom·ise¹ 🔑 /ˈprɑməs/ *verb* (prom·is·es, prom·is·ing, prom·ised)
1 to say that you will certainly do or not do something: *She promised to give me the money today.* • *I promise that I'll come.* • *Promise me you won't be late!*
2 to show signs that something will be good or successful: *The picnic promises to be a lot of fun.*

prom·ise² 🔑 /ˈprɑməs/ *noun* [count]
when you say that you will certainly do or not do something: *He kept his promise* (= did what he said). • *You broke your promise – how can I trust you?*

prom·is·ing /ˈprɑməsɪŋ/ *adjective*
showing signs of being very good or successful: *a promising young writer*

pro·mote **AWL** /prəˈmoʊt/ *verb* (pro·motes, pro·mot·ing, pro·mot·ed)
1 to give someone a more important job: *She worked hard, and after a year she was promoted to manager.* ⊃ ANTONYM **demote**
2 to help a product sell more or be more popular: *The band is on tour to promote their new album.*
▶ **pro·mo·tion** **AWL** /prəˈmoʊʃn/ *noun* [count, noncount]: *The new job is a promotion for me.*

prompt /prɑmpt/ *adjective*
quick: *She gave me a prompt answer.*

prompt·ly /ˈprɑmptli/ *adverb*
quickly; not late: *We arrived promptly at two o'clock.*

prone /proʊn/ *adjective*
likely to suffer from something or to do something bad: *Young people are especially prone to this disease.* • *to be accident-prone* (= to have a lot of accidents)

pro·noun /ˈproʊnaʊn/ *noun* [count]
(ENGLISH LANGUAGE ARTS) a word that you use in place of a noun: *"He," "it," "me," and "them" are all pronouns.*

pro·nounce /prəˈnaʊns/ *verb* (pro·nounc·es, pro·nounc·ing, pro·nounced)
to make the sound of a letter or word: *How do you pronounce your name?* • *You don't pronounce the "b" at the end of "comb."*

pro·nun·ci·a·tion 🔑 /prəˌnʌnsiˈeɪʃn/ *noun* [count, noncount]
how you say a word or words: *What's the correct pronunciation of this word?* • *Your pronunciation is very good.*

proof 🔑 /pruf/ *noun* [noncount]
information which shows that something is true: *Do you have any proof that you are the owner of this car?* ⊃ The verb is **prove**.

Suffix

-proof
(in adjectives) able to protect against the thing mentioned: *bulletproof* • *fireproof* • *waterproof*

proof·read /ˈprufrid/ *verb* (proof·reads, proof·read·ing, proof·read /ˈprufrɛd/, has proof·read)
to read and correct a piece of writing: *Did you proofread this essay?*

prop·a·gan·da /ˌprɑpəˈɡændə/ *noun* [noncount]
(POLITICS) information and ideas that may not be completely true, which are used by governments or organizations to influence people: *political propaganda*

pro·pel·ler /prəˈpɛlər/ *noun* [count]
a part that is connected to the engine on a ship or an airplane. It turns around very fast to make the ship or airplane move.

prop·er 🔑 /ˈprɑpər/ *adjective*
right or correct: *I don't have the proper tools to fix the car.*

prop·er·ly /ˈprɑpərli/ *adverb*
well or correctly: *Close the door properly.* • *I can't see properly without my glasses.*

prop·er name /ˌprɑpər ˈneɪm/ (also **prop·er noun** /ˌprɑpər ˈnaʊn/) *noun* [count]
(ENGLISH LANGUAGE ARTS) a word that is the name of a particular person or place: *"Mary," "Dallas," and "Empire State Building" are all proper names.*

prop·er·ty 🔑 /ˈprɑpərti/ *noun* (plural prop·er·ties)
1 [noncount] something that you have or own: *This book is the property of James Waters.* ⊃ Look at the note at **thing**.
2 [count] a building and the land around it
3 [count] a special quality or characterisitc that a substance has: *Some plants have healing properties.*

proph·et /ˈprɑfət/ *noun* [count]
a person that God chooses to give his message to people

pro·por·tion **AWL** /prəˈpɔrʃn/ *noun*
1 [count] a part of something: *A large proportion of* (= many) *people agree.*
2 [noncount] the amount or size of one thing compared to another thing: *What is the proportion of men to women in the factory?*

pro·pos·al /prəˈpoʊzl/ *noun* [count]
1 a plan or idea about how to do something: *a proposal to build a new station*
2 when you ask someone to marry you

pro·pose /prə'poʊz/ *verb* (pro·pos·es, pro·pos·ing, pro·posed)
1 (*formal*) to say what you think should happen or be done: *I propose that we meet again on Monday.* ➲ SYNONYM **suggest**
2 to ask someone to marry you: *He finally proposed to me!*

prop·o·si·tion /ˌprɑpə'zɪʃn/ *noun* [*count*]
1 (BUSINESS) a business idea, plan, or offer: *That sounds like an interesting proposition.*
2 (also **Proposition**) a suggested change to a law that people can vote on: *California voters approved Proposition 8 in 2008.*

prose /proʊz/ *noun* [*noncount*]
(ENGLISH LANGUAGE ARTS) writing that is not poetry: *He wrote poetry and prose.*

pros·e·cute /'prɑsəkyut/ *verb* (pros·e·cutes, pros·e·cut·ing, pros·e·cut·ed)
to say officially in a court of law that someone has done something illegal: *He was prosecuted for theft.*

pros·e·cu·tion /ˌprɑsə'kyuʃn/ *noun*
1 [*count, noncount*] the process of officially trying to show that someone has done something illegal, in a court of law
2 **the prosecution** [*singular*] the lawyers who are trying to show that someone is guilty in a court of law: *The prosecution claimed that he was lying.* ➲ Look at **defense**(3).

pros·pect AWL /'prɑspɛkt/ *noun*
1 [*singular*] a thought about what may or will happen in the future: *The prospect of becoming a father terrified him.*
2 **prospects** [*plural*] chances of being successful in the future: *A college degree will improve your job prospects.*

pros·per /'prɑspər/ *verb* (pros·pers, pros·per·ing, pros·pered)
to be successful, especially with money
▶ **pros·per·i·ty** /prɑ'spɛrəţi/ *noun* [*noncount*]: *Tourism brought great prosperity to the region.*

pros·per·ous /'prɑspərəs/ *adjective*
rich and successful

pros·ti·tute /'prɑstətut/ *noun* [*count*]
a person, especially a woman, who earns money by having sex with people

pro·tect /prə'tɛkt/ *verb* (pro·tects, pro·tect·ing, pro·tect·ed)
to keep someone or something safe: *Parents try to protect their children from danger.* ◆ *Wear a hat to protect your head against the sun.*

pro·tec·tion /prə'tɛkʃn/ *noun* [*noncount*]
keeping someone or something safe: *He was put under police protection.*

pro·tein /'proʊtin/ *noun* [*count, noncount*]
(BIOLOGY) a substance in foods such as meat, fish, and eggs. *Proteins helps you to grow and stay healthy.*

pro·test¹ /'proʊtɛst/ *noun* [*count*]
an action that shows publicly that you do not like or approve of something: *She took part in a protest against the war.*

pro·test² /prə'tɛst/ *verb* (pro·tests, pro·test·ing, pro·test·ed)
to say or show strongly that you do not like something: *They protested against the government's policy.*

Prot·es·tant /'prɑtəstənt/ *noun* [*count*]
(RELIGION) a person who believes in the Christian God and who is not a Roman Catholic

pro·ton /'proʊtɑn/ *noun* [*count*]
(CHEMISTRY, PHYSICS) a very small piece of matter with a positive electric charge, found in all atoms ➲ Look at **electron, neutron**. ➲ Look at the picture at **atom**.

pro·trac·tor /proʊ'træktər/ *noun* [*count*]
(MATH) a thing you use to measure and draw angles. It is usually a half circle of clear plastic with degrees (0° to 180°) marked on it.

proud /praʊd/ *adjective* (proud·er, proud·est)
1 pleased about something that you or others have done or about something that you have: *They are very proud of their new house.*
2 thinking that you are better than other people: *She was too proud to say she was sorry.* ➲ The noun is **pride**.
▶ **proud·ly** /'praʊdli/ *adverb*: *"I made this myself," he said proudly.*

prove /pruv/ *verb* (proves, prov·ing, proved, has proved or has prov·en /'pruvən/)
to show that something is true: *The blood on his shirt proves that he is the murderer.* ➲ ANTONYM **disprove** ➲ The noun is **proof**.

prov·erb /'prɑvərb/ *noun* [*count*]
(ENGLISH LANGUAGE ARTS) a short sentence that people often say, which gives help or advice: *"Waste not, want not" is an English proverb.*

pro·vide /prə'vaɪd/ *verb* (pro·vides, pro·vid·ing, pro·vid·ed)
to give something to someone who needs it: *I'll provide the food for the party.* ◆ *The company provided me with a car.*
provide for someone to give someone everything they need to live: *Robin has four children to provide for.*

pro·vid·ed /prə'vaɪdəd/ (also **pro·vid·ing** /prə'vaɪdɪŋ/) *conjunction*
only if: *I'll go provided that the children can come with me.* ◆ *Call me when you get home, providing it's not too late.*

tʃ **ch**in   dʒ **J**une   v **v**an   θ **th**in   ð **th**en   s **s**o   z **z**oo   ʃ **sh**e

prov·ince /ˈprɑvəns/ noun [count]
(**POLITICS**) a main part of some countries, which has its own government: *Canada has ten provinces.*
▶ **pro·vin·cial** /prəˈvɪnʃl/ adjective
connected with a **province**: *the provincial government*

pro·vi·sion /prəˈvɪʒn/ noun
1 [noncount] when something is given to someone who needs it: *The government is responsible for the provision of education.*
2 provisions [plural] (formal) supplies of food and drinks: *We stopped to buy provisions for our long trip.*

pro·voke /prəˈvoʊk/ verb (pro·vokes, pro·vok·ing, pro·voked)
1 to cause a particular feeling or reaction: *Dairy products may provoke allergic reactions in some people.*
2 to say or do something that you know will make a person angry or upset: *Be careful what you say and don't provoke him.*

prowl /praʊl/ verb (prowls, prowl·ing, prowled)
(used about an animal that is hunting or a person who is waiting for a chance to do something bad) to move around an area quietly so that no one sees or hears you: *I could hear someone prowling around outside.*

prune /prun/ noun [count]
a dried **PLUM** (= a soft round fruit that grows on trees)

pry /praɪ/ verb (pries, pry·ing, pried, has pried)
1 to try to find out about someone else's private life: *I don't mean to pry, but is everything okay between you and Sam?*
2 to use force to open something, remove a lid, etc.: *He pried the door open with a steel bar.*

P.S. /ˌpi ˈɛs/ abbreviation
You write **P.S.** at the end of a letter, after your name, when you want to add something: *... Love from Paul. P.S. I'll bring the car.*

pseu·do·nym /ˈsudənɪm/ noun [count]
a name used by someone, especially a writer, that is not their real name: *Samuel Clemens wrote **under the pseudonym** Mark Twain.*

psy·chi·a·trist /saɪˈkaɪətrɪst/ noun [count]
a doctor who helps people who have a mental illness

psy·chi·a·try /saɪˈkaɪətri/ noun [noncount]
(**HEALTH**) the study and treatment of mental illness: *During medical school, she decided to specialize in psychiatry.*

psy·chic /ˈsaɪkɪk/ adjective
having unusual powers that cannot be explained, for example knowing what someone else is thinking

psy·cho·log·i·cal **AWL** /ˌsaɪkəˈlɑdʒɪkl/ adjective
(**HEALTH**) connected with the mind or the way it works: *psychological problems*

psy·chol·o·gy **AWL** /saɪˈkɑlədʒi/ noun [noncount]
the study of the mind and how it works
▶ **psy·chol·o·gist** **AWL** /saɪˈkɑlədʒɪst/ noun [count]
a person who studies **psychology**

psy·cho·path /ˈsaɪkəpæθ/ noun [count]
a person who has a serious mental illness that makes them behave in a violent way toward other people

pt. abbreviation of **pint**

pu·ber·ty /ˈpyubərti/ noun [noncount]
(**BIOLOGY**) the time when a child's body is changing and becoming like that of an adult

pub·lic¹ /ˈpʌblɪk/ adjective
1 connected with everyone; for everyone: *Pollution is a danger to public health.* ◆ *a public park*
2 known by many people: *We're going to **make** the news **public** soon.*
▶ **pub·lic·ly** /ˈpʌblɪkli/ adverb
to everyone; not secretly: *She spoke publicly about her friendship with the actor.*

pub·lic² /ˈpʌblɪk/ noun **the public** [singular]
people in general; everyone: *The museum is open to the public between 10 a.m. and 4 p.m.*
in public when other people are there: *I don't want to talk about it in public.* ⊃ **ANTONYM in private**

pub·li·ca·tion **AWL** /ˌpʌbləˈkeɪʃn/ noun
1 [noncount] when a book, magazine, etc. is made and sold: *He became very rich after the **publication of** his first book.*
2 [count] a book, magazine, etc.

pub·lic·i·ty /pʌbˈlɪsəti/ noun [noncount]
giving information about something so that people know about it: *There was a lot of publicity for the new store.*

pub·li·cize /ˈpʌbləsaɪz/ verb (pub·li·ciz·es, pub·li·ciz·ing, pub·li·cized)
to attract people's attention to something and give them information about it: *We need to publicize the event if we want to sell more tickets.*

pub·lic re·la·tions /ˌpʌblɪk rɪˈleɪʃnz/ noun [noncount] (abbreviation **PR**)
the business of providing information about someone or something, in order to give people a good impression of them: *She works in public relations.*

pub·lic school /ˌpʌblɪk skul/ noun [count]
a free local school paid for by the government

pub·lic trans·por·ta·tion /ˌpʌblɪk ˌtrænspərˈteɪʃn/ *noun* [*noncount*]
buses and trains that everyone can use: *I usually travel by public transportation.*

pub·lish 🔑 **AWL** /ˈpʌblɪʃ/ *verb* (**pub·lish·es, pub·lish·ing, pub·lished**)
1 to prepare and print a book, magazine, or newspaper for selling: *This dictionary was published by Oxford University Press.*
2 to make information available to the public
▶ **pub·lish·er** **AWL** /ˈpʌblɪʃər/ *noun* [*count*]: *The publisher is OUP.*

puck /pʌk/ *noun* [*count*]
(**SPORTS**) a round, flat, rubber object that players hit with sticks in the sport of ICE HOCKEY ➲ Look at the picture at **ice hockey**.

pud·ding /ˈpʊdɪŋ/ *noun* [*noncount*]
a soft, thick, sweet food made with milk, eggs, and sugar: *chocolate pudding*

pud·dle /ˈpʌdl/ *noun* [*count*]
a small pool of rain or other liquid on the ground

puff¹ /pʌf/ *verb* (**puffs, puff·ing, puffed**)
1 to smoke a cigarette, pipe, etc.: *He sat puffing his cigar.*
2 (used about air, smoke, wind, etc.) to blow or come out in clouds: *Smoke was puffing out of the chimney.* ◆ *Stop puffing cigarette smoke in my face.*
3 (*informal*) to breathe quickly or loudly, especially after you have been running: *She was puffing as she ran up the hill.*

puff² /pʌf/ *noun* [*count*]
a small amount of air, wind, smoke, etc. that is blown from somewhere: *a puff of smoke*

pull¹ 🔑 /pʊl/ *verb* (**pulls, pull·ing, pulled**)
1 to move someone or something strongly toward you: *She pulled the drawer open.*
2 to go forward, moving something behind you: *The cart was pulled by two horses.*
3 to move something somewhere: *He pulled up his pants.*
pull in to drive a car to the side of the road and stop: *I pulled in to look at the map.*
pull someone's leg (*informal*) to try to make someone believe something that is not true, for fun: *I didn't really see an elephant – I was only pulling your leg!*
pull over to drive a car to the side of the road: *I pulled over to let the ambulance pass.*
pull out to drive a car away from the side of the road: *He suddenly pulled out in front of me and almost caused an accident.*
pull through to survive a dangerous illness or difficult time
pull yourself together to control your feelings after being upset: *Pull yourself together and stop crying.*

pull up to stop a car: *The driver pulled up at the traffic lights.*

pull² /pʊl/ *noun* [*count*]
an action of pulling something: *Give the rope a pull.*

pul·ley /ˈpʊli/ *noun* [*count*] (*plural* **pul·leys**)
a piece of equipment consisting of a wheel and a rope, which is used for lifting heavy things

pull·o·ver /ˈpʊloʊvər/ *noun* [*count*]
a warm piece of clothing with sleeves, which you wear on the top part of your body

pulse /pʌls/ *noun* [*count, usually singular*]
(**BIOLOGY**) the beating of your heart that you feel in different parts of your body, especially in your wrist: *The nurse felt* (= measured) *his pulse.*

pump¹ /pʌmp/ *noun* [*count*]
a machine that moves a liquid or gas into or out of something: *a bicycle pump* ◆ *a gasoline pump*

pump² /pʌmp/ *verb* (**pumps, pump·ing, pumped**)
to force a gas or a liquid to go in a particular direction: *Your heart pumps blood around your body.*
pump something up to fill something with air, using a PUMP: *I pumped up my bicycle tires.*

pump·kin /ˈpʌmpkɪn/ *noun* [*count*]
a very large, round vegetable with a thick orange skin: *pumpkin pie with cream*

pumpkin

pun /pʌn/ *noun* [*count*]
(**ENGLISH LANGUAGE ARTS**) a funny use of a word that has two meanings, or that sounds the same as another word

punch /pʌntʃ/ *verb* (**punch·es, punch·ing, punched**)
1 to hit someone or something hard with your closed hand (your FIST): *He punched me in the nose.*
2 to make a hole in something with a special tool: *The ticket collector punched my ticket.*
▶ **punch** *noun* [*count*] (*plural* **punch·es**): *a punch in the chin*

punc·tu·al /ˈpʌŋktʃuəl/ *adjective*
arriving or doing something at the right time; not late: *Please try to be punctual for your classes.*
▶ **punc·tu·al·ly** /ˈpʌŋktʃuəli/ *adverb*: *They arrived punctually at seven o'clock.*

punc·tu·ate /ˈpʌŋktʃueɪt/ *verb* (**punc·tu·ates, punc·tu·at·ing, punc·tu·at·ed**)
(**ENGLISH LANGUAGE ARTS**) to put periods, question marks, etc. in your writing

punc·tu·a·tion /ˌpʌŋktʃuˈeɪʃn/ *noun* [*noncount*]
(**ENGLISH LANGUAGE ARTS**) using PUNCTUATION MARKS when you are writing

punc·tu·a·tion mark /ˌpʌŋktʃuˈeɪʃn mɑrk/
noun [*count*]
(**ENGLISH LANGUAGE ARTS**) one of the marks that you use in your writing, for example a period or question mark

punc·ture /ˈpʌŋktʃər/ *verb* (**punc·tures, punc·tur·ing, punc·tured**)
to make a small hole in something: *A piece of glass punctured the tire.*
▶ **punc·ture** *noun* [*count*]

pun·ish ℘ /ˈpʌnɪʃ/ *verb* (**pun·ish·es, pun·ish·ing, pun·ished**)
to make someone suffer because they have done something wrong: *The children were **punished for** telling lies.*

pun·ish·ment ℘ /ˈpʌnɪʃmənt/ *noun* [*count, noncount*]
an act or a way of punishing someone: *What is the **punishment for** murder in your country? • The child was sent to bed **as a punishment** for being rude.*

pu·pil /ˈpyupl/ *noun* [*count*]
1 (*formal*) a child who is learning at school: *There are 30 pupils in the class.*
2 (**BIOLOGY**) the round, black part in the middle of your eye ➔ Look at the picture at **eye**.

pup·pet /ˈpʌpət/ *noun* [*count*]
a small model of a person or animal that you move by pulling strings or by putting your hand inside

pup·py /ˈpʌpi/ *noun* [*count*] (*plural* **pup·pies**)
a young dog ➔ Look at the picture at **dog**.

pur·chase¹ [AWL] /ˈpərtʃəs/ *noun* [*count*] (*formal*)
the action of buying something; something that you have bought: *She **made** several **purchases** and then left the store.*

pur·chase² [AWL] /ˈpərtʃəs/ *verb* (**pur·chas·es, pur·chas·ing, pur·chased**) (*formal*)
to buy something: *advice for people who are planning to purchase a new home*

pure ℘ /pyʊr/ *adjective* (**pur·er, pur·est**)
1 not mixed with anything else: *This shirt is pure cotton.*
2 clean and healthy: *pure mountain air*
3 complete or total: *What she said was pure nonsense.*

pure·ly /ˈpyʊrli/ *adverb*
only or completely: *He doesn't like his job – he does it purely for the money.*

pu·ri·fy /ˈpyʊrəfaɪ/ *verb* (**pu·ri·fies, pu·ri·fy·ing, pu·ri·fied**)
(**CHEMISTRY**) to remove dirty or harmful

substances from something: *purified water* ➔ The adjective is **pure**.

pur·ple ℘ /ˈpərpl/ *adjective*
with a color between red and blue
▶ **pur·ple** *noun* [*count, noncount*]: *She often wears purple.*

pur·pose ℘ /ˈpərpəs/ *noun* [*count*]
the reason for doing something: *The purpose of this meeting is to decide what we should do next.*
on purpose because you want to; not by accident: *"You broke my pen!" "I'm sorry, I didn't do it on purpose."* ➔ SYNONYM **deliberately**

Thesaurus

purpose the reason for doing something; what something is used for or is supposed to achieve: *What is **the purpose of** your visit? • The building is used **for** religious **purposes**.*

aim what someone is trying to achieve: *Our main aim is to increase sales. • He was willing to do almost anything to **achieve his aim** of winning first prize.*

plan what you have decided or arranged to do: *Do you have any plans for the weekend? • There are no plans to build new offices.*

intention what you want or intend to do: *Our intention was to leave early in the morning. • I **have no intention of** going to the wedding.*

goal (often used about your life or career plans) something that you hope to achieve: *What are your long-term goals? • I've finally **achieved my goal** of getting a college degree.*

pur·pose·ly /ˈpərpəsli/ *adverb*
on purpose; deliberately

purr /pər/ *verb* (**purrs, purr·ing, purred**)
When a cat **purrs**, it makes a low sound that shows that it is happy.

purse /pərs/ *noun* [*count*]
a bag that a woman uses for carrying things like money and keys ➔ Look at the picture at **bag**.

pur·sue [AWL] /pərˈsu/ *verb* (**pur·sues, pur·su·ing, pur·sued**) (*formal*)
to follow someone or something because you want to catch them: *The police pursued the stolen car for several miles.* ➔ SYNONYM **chase**

pur·suit [AWL] /pərˈsut/ *noun*
1 [*noncount*] the act of trying to achieve or get something: *the pursuit of wealth*
2 [*count*] an activity that you spend time doing: *leisure pursuits*

pus /pʌs/ *noun* [*noncount*]
(**HEALTH**) a thick, yellow liquid that sometimes forms in a part of your body that has been hurt

push /pʊʃ/ *verb* (push·es, push·ing, pushed)
1 to use force to move someone or something forward or away from you: *The car broke down so we had to push it to a garage.* • *He pushed me over!*
2 to move forward by pushing someone or something: *He pushed his way through the crowd.* • *to push past someone*
3 to press something with your finger: *Push the red button to stop the machine.*
4 to try to make someone do something: *Kim will not work hard unless you push her.*
push someone around to tell someone what to do in a rude and unpleasant way: *You shouldn't let him push you around like that.*
▶ **push** *noun* [count] (*plural* push·es): *She gave him a push and he fell.*

push·up /ˈpʊʃʌp/ *noun* [count]
a type of exercise in which you lie on your front and push your body up with your arms: *I do twenty pushups every morning.*

push·y /ˈpʊʃi/ *adjective* (push·i·er, push·i·est)
trying hard to get what you want in a way that seems rude: *a pushy salesman*

put /pʊt/ *verb* (puts, put·ting, put, has put)
1 to move something to a place or position: *She put the book on the table.* • *He put his hand in his pocket.*
2 to write something: *Put your name at the top of the page.*
3 to make someone feel something or be affected by something: *This kind of weather always puts me in a bad mood.* • *Don't put the blame on me!*
4 to say something: *I don't know how to put this, but I'm afraid we have a problem.*
put something away to put something back in its usual place: *She put the box away in the closet.*
put something down to stop holding something and put it on another thing, for example on the floor or a table: *Let me put my bags down first.*
put someone off to make someone not like someone or something: *The accident put me off driving.*
put something off to not do something until later: *He put off his vacation because the children were sick.* ➔ SYNONYM **delay**
put something on
1 to take clothes and wear them: *Put on your coat.* • *Put your shoes on.* ➔ ANTONYM **take something off**

2 to make a piece of electrical equipment start to work: *I put on the TV.* • *Put the lights on.* • *Should we put some music on?*
put something out to stop a fire or to stop a light from shining: *She put out the fire with a bucket of water.* • *Put the lights out before you go.*
put someone up to let someone sleep in your home: *Can you put me up for the night?*
put something up
1 to hold or lift something up: *Put up your hand if you know the answer.* ➔ SYNONYM **raise**
2 to build something: *to put up a fence*
3 to attach something to a wall, etc. so everyone can see it: *to put up a sign*
4 to increase something: *Most airlines put up their prices during the summer.*
put up with someone or **something** to have pain or problems without complaining: *We can't change the bad weather, so we have to put up with it.*

puz·zle¹ /ˈpʌzl/ *noun* [count]
1 a game that is difficult and makes you think a lot ➔ Look at **crossword puzzle**.
2 something that is difficult to understand or explain: *Janet's reason for leaving her job is a puzzle to me.*
3 = **jigsaw puzzle**

puz·zle² /ˈpʌzl/ *verb* (puz·zles, puz·zling, puz·zled)
to make you feel that you cannot understand or explain something: *Tim's illness puzzled his doctors.*
puzzle over something to think hard about something in order to understand it: *He was puzzling over a math problem for half an hour.*
▶ **puz·zling** /ˈpʌzlɪŋ/ *adjective*
difficult to understand or explain

puz·zled /ˈpʌzld/ *adjective*
not able to understand or explain something: *She had a puzzled look on her face.*

py·lon /ˈpaɪlɑn/ *noun* [count]
a tall metal tower that supports heavy electrical wires

pyr·a·mid /ˈpɪrəmɪd/ *noun* [count]
(MATH) a shape with a flat bottom and three or four sides that come to a point at the top: *the pyramids of Egypt* ➔ Look at the picture at **solid**.

py·thon /ˈpaɪθɑn/ *noun* [count]
a large snake that kills animals by squeezing them very hard

Q q

Q, q /kyu/ *noun* [*count, noncount*] (*plural* Q's, q's /kyuz/)
the seventeenth letter of the English alphabet: *"Question" begins with a "Q."*

qt. abbreviation of **quart**

Q-tip™ /'kyu tɪp/ *noun* [*count*]
a small, thin stick with cotton at each end: *I cleaned my ears with a Q-tip.*

quack /kwæk/ *noun* [*count*]
the sound that a DUCK (= a bird that lives on or near water) makes
▸ **quack** *verb* (quacks, quack·ing, quacked)

quad·ru·ple /kwɑ'drupl/ *verb* (quad·ru·ples, quad·ru·pling, quad·ru·pled)
(MATH) to multiply or be multiplied by four: *House prices have quadrupled in the past 20 years.*

quaint /kweɪnt/ *adjective* (quaint·er, quaint·est)
old-fashioned, usually in an attractive way: *a quaint little town*

qual·i·fi·ca·tion /ˌkwɑləfə'keɪʃn/ *noun* [*count*]
training, skill, or knowledge that you need to do something, such as a job: *He has all the right qualifications for the manager's job.*

qual·i·fied /'kwɑləfaɪd/ *adjective*
having the training, skill, or knowledge that you need to do something: *I don't feel qualified to comment – I know nothing about the subject.*

qual·i·fy /'kwɑləfaɪ/ *verb* (qual·i·fies, qual·i·fy·ing, qual·i·fied, has qual·i·fied)
1 to get the right knowledge, skill, and training so that you can do something: *These courses will qualify you to teach music.*
2 to have or give someone the right to have or do something: *You have to be a Texas resident to qualify for the scholarship.*

qual·i·ty 🖉 /'kwɑləti/ *noun* (*plural* qual·i·ties)
1 [*noncount*] how good or bad something is: *The quality of her work is excellent.* ◆ *This furniture isn't very good quality.*
2 [*count*] something that is part of a person's character: *Vicky has all the qualities of a good manager.*

quan·ti·ty 🖉 /'kwɑntəti/ *noun* [*count*] (*plural* quan·ti·ties)
how much of something there is: *I only bought a small quantity of cheese.* ⊃ SYNONYM **amount**

quar·an·tine /'kwɔrəntin/ *noun* [*noncount*]
(HEALTH) a period of time when a person or an animal is kept away from others so that they or it cannot pass on a disease: *The dog was kept in quarantine for six months.*

quar·rel¹ /'kwɔrəl/ *noun* [*count*]
an argument or a disagreement with someone: *He had a quarrel with his wife about money.* ⊃ SYNONYM **argument**

quar·rel² /'kwɔrəl/ *verb* (quar·rels, quar·rel·ing, quar·reled)
to argue or disagree with someone: *He quarreled with his wife about money.* ◆ *The children are always quarreling.* ⊃ SYNONYM **argue**

quar·ry /'kwɔri/ *noun* [*count*] (*plural* quar·ries)
a place where people cut stone, sand, etc. out of the ground

quart /kwɔrt/ *noun* [*count*] (abbreviation **qt.**)
a measure of liquid (=0.94 liters). There are two **pints** in a **quart** and four **quarts** in a **gallon**: *a quart of milk*

quar·ter 🖉 /'kwɔrtər/ *noun* [*count*]
1 (MATH) one of four equal parts of something; ¼: *a mile and a quarter* ◆ *Cut the apple into quarters.*
2 fifteen minutes before or after every hour: *It's quarter after two.* ◆ *I'll meet you at a quarter past.* ◆ *It's quarter to nine.* ◆ *I'll meet you outside the restaurant at a quarter of seven.*
3 a coin that is worth 25 cents: *The parking meter only takes quarters.* ⊃ Look at the picture at **money**.
4 three months: *You get a gas bill every quarter.*
5 one of the four parts that the academic year is divided into at many schools and colleges: *Report cards come out at the end of each quarter.*
6 (SPORTS) one of four equal time periods in a game of football or BASKETBALL: *The Eagles were leading 14-3 at the end of the first quarter.*

quar·ter·back /'kwɔrtərbæk/ *noun* [*count*]
(SPORTS) the player on a football team who tells the other players what to do and throws the ball to them

quar·tet /kwɔr'tɛt/ *noun* [*count*]
(MUSIC) a group of four people who play music or sing together: *a string quartet* ⊃ Look at **trio**.

queen 🖉 /kwin/ *noun* [*count*]
1 (POLITICS) a woman from a royal family who rules a country: *Queen Elizabeth II* (= the second)
2 the wife of a king

quench /kwɛntʃ/ *verb* (quench·es, quench·ing, quenched)
quench your thirst to drink as much as you need so that you stop feeling thirsty

que·ry¹ /'kwɪri/ *noun* [*count*] (*plural* que·ries)
a question: *Contact our office with any queries.*

que·ry² /'kwɪri/ *verb* (que·ries, que·ry·ing, que·ried)
to ask a question about something that you think is wrong: *I queried the invoice but the company said it was correct.*

ques·tion¹ 🔊 /ˈkwɛstʃən/ *noun* [*count*]
1 something that you ask: *They **asked** me a lot of questions.* ◆ *She didn't **answer** my question.* ◆ *What is the answer to question 3?*
2 something that you need to deal with; something that is being discussed: ***The question is**, how can we raise the money?* ◆ *It's **a question of** time – we need to finish the work today.*
in question (*formal*) that we are talking about: *On the day **in question** I was in Chicago.*
out of the question not possible: *No, I won't give you any more money. It's out of the question!*

ques·tion² 🔊 /ˈkwɛstʃən/ *verb* (**ques·tions, ques·tion·ing, ques·tioned**)
1 to ask someone questions about something: *The police **questioned** him **about** the stolen car.*
2 to feel doubt about something: *She said she just wanted to help, but I questioned her motives.*

ques·tion mark /ˈkwɛstʃən mɑrk/ *noun* [*count*]
the sign (?) that you write at the end of a question

ques·tion·naire /ˌkwɛstʃəˈnɛr/ *noun* [*count*]
a list of questions for people to answer so that information can be collected from the answers: *Please **fill out** (= write the answers on) the **questionnaire**.*

quick 🔊 /kwɪk/ *adjective, adverb* (**quick·er, quick·est**)
taking little time: *It's quicker to travel by plane than by train.* ◆ *Can I make a quick phone call?* ⊃ **SYNONYM fast** ⊃ **ANTONYM slow**

quick·ly 🔊 /ˈkwɪkli/ *adverb*
fast; in a short time: *Come as quickly as you can!* ⊃ **ANTONYM slowly**

qui·et¹ 🔊 /ˈkwaɪət/ *adjective* (**qui·et·er, qui·et·est**)
1 making very little noise: *Be quiet – the baby's asleep.* ◆ *a quiet voice* ⊃ **ANTONYM loud, noisy**
2 without many people or without many things happening: *It's very quiet downtown on Sundays.*
▶ **qui·et·ly** /ˈkwaɪətli/ *adverb*: *Please close the door quietly.*

qui·et² /ˈkwaɪət/ *noun* [*noncount*]
when there is no noise: *I need quiet when I'm working.* ◆ *I go to the library for a little **peace and quiet**.*

quilt /kwɪlt/ *noun* [*count*]
a bed cover with thick, warm material inside: *a baby quilt*

quit /kwɪt/ *verb* (**quits, quit·ting, quit, has quit**) (*informal*)
to leave a job or place; to stop doing something: *She quit her job to go to graduate school.* ◆ *You're almost finished – you can't quit now!*

quite 🔊 /kwaɪt/ *adverb*
very, but not extremely: *It's quite warm today, but it's not too hot.* ◆ *We waited quite a long time.* ⊃ **SYNONYM fairly**
not quite not completely: *Dinner is not quite ready.* ◆ *"Are you finished?" "Not quite."*
quite a few a lot, but not an extremely large amount or number: *There were quite a few people at the party.*

quiv·er /ˈkwɪvər/ *verb* (**quiv·ers, quiv·er·ing, quiv·ered**)
to shake slightly: *Her lip quivered and she started to cry.* ⊃ **SYNONYM tremble**

quiz¹ /kwɪz/ *noun* [*count*] (*plural* **quiz·zes**)
1 a short, informal test: *We have a math quiz this Friday.*
2 a set of questions that you try to answer in a game or competition: *a quiz show on TV*

quiz² /kwɪz/ *verb* (**quiz·zes, quiz·zing, quizzed**)
to ask someone questions in order to get information: *After I got home late, my mom quizzed me about where I had been.* ◆ *Can you quiz me on my math homework?*

quo·ta /ˈkwoʊtə/ *noun* [*count*]
the limited number or amount of people or things that is officially allowed: *We've already reached our quota – we can't take anyone else.*

quo·ta·tion **AWL** /kwoʊˈteɪʃn/ *noun* [*count*]
1 (*also informal* **quote**) (**ENGLISH LANGUAGE ARTS**) words you say or write that another person said or wrote before: *a quotation from a poem by Emily Dickinson*
2 (*also* **quote**) (**BUSINESS**) a statement that says how much a piece of work will probably cost: *We got quotations from three different builders.* ⊃ **SYNONYM estimate**

quo·ta·tion marks /kwoʊˈteɪʃn mɑrks/ (*also* **quotes**) *noun* [*plural*]
the signs (" ") that you use in writing before and after the exact words that someone has said

quote¹ **AWL** /kwoʊt/ *verb* (**quotes, quot·ing, quot·ed**)
to repeat exactly something that another person said or wrote: *She **quoted from** the Bible.* ◆ *I think she offered to help, but **don't quote me on that**.*

quote² **AWL** /kwoʊt/ *noun*
1 [*count*] another word for **quotation**: *I need to get some quotes for the roof repairs.*
2 **quotes** [*plural*] another word for **quotation marks**

quo·tient /ˈkwoʊʃnt/ *noun* [*count*]
(**MATH**) the amount you get if you divide one number by another: *The quotient of 48 divided by 12 is 4.* ⊃ Look at **IQ, product**(2).

the Qu·r'an (*also* **the Qu·ran**) /ðə kəˈræn; ðə kəˈrɑn/ *noun* [*singular*] (**RELIGION**) = **the Koran**

Rr

R, r /ɑr/ *noun* [*count*] (*plural* R's, r's /ɑrz/)
the eighteenth letter of the English alphabet:
"Rose" begins with an "R."

R & B /ˌɑr ən ˈbi/ *abbreviation* (**MUSIC**) short for
rhythm and blues

rab·bi /ˈræbaɪ/ *noun* [*count*] (*plural* **rab·bis**)
a leader or teacher of the Jewish religion

rab·bit /ˈræbət/ *noun* [*count*]
a small animal with long ears. **Rabbits** live in
holes under the ground.

ra·bies /ˈreɪbiz/ *noun* [*noncount*]
a serious disease that people can get if a dog or
another animal with the disease bites them: *The
dog had rabies.*

rac·coon /ræˈkun/
noun [*count*]
a small animal with
black fur around its
eyes, and rings of
black and white fur on
its tail

raccoon

race¹ /reɪs/ *noun* [*count*]
1 (**SPORTS**) a competition to see who can run,
drive, ride, etc. fastest: *Who **won** the **race**? ◆ a
horse race*
2 a group of people of the same kind, for
example with the same color skin, language, or
customs: *People of many different races live in
this neighborhood.*

race² /reɪs/ *verb* (**rac·es**, **rac·ing**, **raced**)
1 (**SPORTS**) to run, drive, ride, etc. in a
competition to see who is the fastest: *He'll be
racing against some of the finest runners in the
country.* ◆ *I'll race you to the other end of the pool.*
2 to move, or to move someone or something,
very fast: *He raced up the stairs.* ◆ *The ambulance
raced the injured woman to hospital.*

race·track /ˈreɪstræk/ *noun* [*count*]
a place where you go to see horse races

ra·cial /ˈreɪʃl/ *adjective*
connected with people's race; happening
between people of different races: *racial
differences*

rac·ing /ˈreɪsɪŋ/ *noun* [*noncount*]
the sport of taking part in races: *motor racing*

ra·cism /ˈreɪsɪzəm/ *noun* [*noncount*]
the belief that some groups (**RACES**) of people are
better than others
▸ **rac·ist** /ˈreɪsɪst/ *noun* [*count*]: *He's a total racist.*
▸ **rac·ist** /ˈreɪsɪst/ *adjective*: *a racist comment*

rack /ræk/ *noun* [*count*]
a kind of shelf made of bars, which you put
things on: *a towel rack*

rack·et /ˈrækət/ *noun*
1 [*singular*] (*informal*) a loud noise: *Stop making
that terrible racket!*
2 (also **rac·quet**) [*count*] (**SPORTS**) a thing that you
use for hitting the ball in sports such as TENNIS ⊃
Look at the picture at **tennis**.

ra·dar /ˈreɪdɑr/ *noun* [*noncount*]
a way of finding where a ship, airplane, or other
vehicle is and how fast it is traveling by using
radio waves

ra·di·a·tion /ˌreɪdiˈeɪʃn/ *noun* [*noncount*]
(**PHYSICS**) dangerous energy that some
substances send out: *High levels of radiation
have been recorded near the nuclear power plant.*

ra·di·a·tor /ˈreɪdiˌeɪtɑr/ *noun* [*count*]
1 a metal thing with hot water inside that makes
a room warm
2 a part of a car that has water in it to keep the
engine cold

rad·i·cal **AWL** /ˈrædɪkl/ *adjective*
(used about changes) very great; complete:
radical reforms in the welfare system

ra·di·o /ˈreɪdioʊ/ *noun* (*plural* **ra·di·os**)
1 [*count*] a piece of equipment that brings voices
or music from far away so that you can hear
them: *We heard the news **on the radio**. ◆ Can you
turn on the **radio**?*
2 [*noncount*] (**PHYSICS**) sending or receiving
sounds that travel a long way through the air by
special waves: *The captain of the ship sent a
message **by radio**.*

ra·di·o·ac·tive /ˌreɪdioʊˈæktɪv/ *adjective*
(**PHYSICS**) sending out dangerous energy: *the
disposal of **radioactive waste***

rad·ish /ˈrædɪʃ/ *noun* [*count*] (*plural* **rad·ish·es**)
a small, red vegetable that is white inside and
has a strong taste. You eat **radishes** in salads. ⊃
Look at the picture at **vegetable**.

ra·di·um /ˈreɪdiəm/ *noun* [*noncount*] (symbol **Ra**)
(**CHEMISTRY**) a chemical substance that is used in
the treatment of some serious diseases

ra·di·us /ˈreɪdiəs/ *noun* [*count*] (*plural* **ra·di·i**
/ˈreɪdiaɪ/)
(**MATH**) the length of a straight line from the
center of a circle to the outside ⊃ Look at the
picture at **circle**.

raf·fle /ˈræfl/ *noun* [*count*]
a way of making money for a charity by selling
tickets with numbers on them. Later some
numbers are chosen and the tickets with these
numbers on them win prizes.

raft /ræft/ *noun* [*count*]
a flat boat with no sides and no engine

rag /ræg/ *noun*
1 [*count*] a small piece of old cloth that you use for cleaning
2 rags [*plural*] clothes that are very old and torn: *She was dressed in rags.*

rage /reɪdʒ/ *noun* [*count, noncount*]
very strong anger: *He was trembling with rage.*

raid /reɪd/ *noun* [*count*]
a sudden attack on a place: *an air raid*
▶ **raid** *verb* (**raids, raid·ing, raid·ed**): *Police raided the house looking for drugs.*

rail /reɪl/ *noun*
1 [*count*] (also **rail·ing** /ˈreɪlɪŋ/) a long piece of wood or metal that is fastened to the wall or to something else: *Hold onto the rail as you go up the stairs.*
2 rails [*plural*] the long pieces of metal that trains go on
3 [*noncount*] trains as a way of traveling: *We decided to travel by rail.*

rail·road /ˈreɪlroʊd/ *noun* [*count*]
the system of trains, metal lines that they go on, and companies that own them: *railroad tracks*

rain¹ /reɪn/ *noun* [*noncount*]
the water that falls from the sky

rain² /reɪn/ *verb* (**rains, rain·ing, rained**)
When it **rains**, water falls from the sky: *It's raining.* • *It rained all day.*

rain·bow /ˈreɪnboʊ/ *noun* [*count*]
a half circle of colors in the sky when rain and sun come together

rain·coat /ˈreɪnkoʊt/ *noun* [*count*]
a light coat that you wear when it rains

rain·drop /ˈreɪndrɑp/ *noun* [*count*]
one drop of rain

rain·fall /ˈreɪnfɔl/ *noun* [*noncount*]
the total amount of rain that falls in a place: *The average annual rainfall here is less than two inches.*

rain for·est /ˈreɪn ˌfɔrəst/ (also **rain·for·est**) *noun* [*count*]
a forest in a hot part of the world where there is a lot of rain: *the Amazon rain forest*

rain·y /ˈreɪni/ *adjective* (**rain·i·er, rain·i·est**)
with a lot of rain: *a rainy day*

raise¹ /reɪz/ *verb* (**rais·es, rais·ing, raised**)
1 to move something or someone up: *Raise your hand if you want to ask a question.* ⊅
ANTONYM **lower**
2 to make something bigger, higher, stronger, etc.: *They raised the price of gas.* • *She raised her voice* (= spoke more loudly). ⊅ ANTONYM **lower**
3 to get money from other people for a particular purpose: *We raised $5,000 for the hospital.*

4 to start to talk about something: *He raised an interesting question.*
5 to take care of a child or an animal until they are an adult: *It's hard to raise a family on such a low salary.* • *He was born and raised in Memphis, Tennessee.*

raise² /reɪz/ *noun* [*count*]
an increase in the money you are paid for the work you do: *I'm going to ask my boss for a raise.*

rai·sin /ˈreɪzn/ *noun* [*count*]
a dried GRAPE (= a small green or purple fruit)

rake /reɪk/ *noun*
[*count*]
a tool with a long handle that you use for collecting leaves or for making the soil flat
▶ **rake** *verb* (**rakes, rak·ing, raked**): *I spent Sunday afternoon raking the leaves.*

rake

ral·ly /ˈræli/ *noun*
[*count*] (*plural* **ral·lies**)
a meeting of people to show that they feel strongly about something: *a peace rally*

RAM /ræm/ *noun* [*noncount*]
(**COMPUTERS**) the type of memory that allows a computer to work: *2 gigabytes of RAM*

ram /ræm/ *noun* [*count*]
a male sheep

Ram·a·dan /ˈrɑmədɑn/ *noun* [*count, noncount*]
(**RELIGION**) a month when Muslims do not eat or drink anything from early morning until the sun goes down in the evening

ramp /ræmp/ *noun* [*count*]
1 a path that you use instead of steps to go up or down: *I pushed the wheelchair up the ramp.*
2 a road that you use to join or leave a highway: *an entrance ramp* • *an exit ramp*

ran form of **run¹**

ranch /ræntʃ/ *noun* [*count*] (*plural* **ranch·es**)
a very large farm where cows, horses, or sheep are kept

ranch·er /ˈræntʃər/ *noun* [*count*]
a person who owns or manages a RANCH: *a cattle rancher*

ran·dom ᴀᴡʟ /ˈrændəm/ *adjective*
done or chosen without any special plan or pattern: *We interviewed a random selection of students.*
at random without thinking or deciding before: *She chose a few books at random.*
▶ **ran·dom·ly** ᴀᴡʟ /ˈrændəmli/ *adverb*: *The winning numbers are randomly selected by computer.*

rang form of **ring**²

range¹ AWL /reɪndʒ/ noun [count]
1 different things of the same kind: *This website sells a range of sports equipment.*
2 the amount between the highest and the lowest: *The age range of the children is between eight and twelve.* ◆ *That car is outside my price range.*
3 a line of mountains or hills
4 how far you can see, hear, shoot, travel, etc.: *The gun has a range of five miles.*

range² AWL /reɪndʒ/ verb (rang·es, rang·ing, ranged)
to be at different points between two things: *The ages of the students in the class range from 18 to 50.*

rank /ræŋk/ noun [count]
how important someone is in a group of people, for example in an army: *General is one of the highest ranks in the army.*

ran·som /ˈrænsəm/ noun [count]
the money that you must pay so that a criminal will free a person that they have taken: *The kidnappers have demanded a ransom of a million dollars.*

rap /ræp/ noun [count, noncount]
(MUSIC) a type of modern music, in which singers speak the words of a song: *a rap song* ➲ Look at **hip-hop**.
▶ **rap** verb (raps, rap·ping, rapped)
to speak the words of a rap song ➲ Look at **rapper**.

rape /reɪp/ verb (rapes, rap·ing, raped)
to force someone to have sex when they do not want to
▶ **rape** noun [count, noncount]: *He was sent to prison for rape.*

rap·id /ˈræpəd/ adjective
happening or moving very quickly: *She made rapid progress and was soon the best in the class.*
➲ ANTONYM **slow**
▶ **rap·id·ly** /ˈræpədli/ adverb: *The snow rapidly disappeared.*

rap·per /ˈræpər/ noun [count]
(MUSIC) a person who speaks the words of a RAP

rare 🔊 /rɛr/ adjective (rar·er, rar·est)
1 If something is **rare**, you do not find or see it often: *Pandas are rare animals.* ◆ *It's rare to see snow in Florida.* ➲ ANTONYM **common**
2 Meat that is **rare** is not cooked for very long, so that the inside is still red. ➲ Look at **well-done**.

rare·ly 🔊 /ˈrɛrli/ adverb
not very often: *We rarely agree with each other.*

rash¹ /ræʃ/ noun [count] (plural rash·es)
a lot of small red spots on your skin: *He had an itchy rash on his back.*

rash² /ræʃ/ adjective (rash·er, rash·est)
If you are **rash**, you do things too quickly and without thinking about the possible result: *You were very rash to leave your job before you found a new one.*

rasp·ber·ry /ˈræz,bɛri/ noun [count] (plural rasp·ber·ries)
a small soft red fruit that grows on bushes: *raspberry jam* ➲ Look at the picture at **berry**.

rat /ræt/ noun [count]
an animal like a big mouse

rate 🔊 /reɪt/ noun [count]
1 the speed of something or how often something happens: *The crime rate was lower in 2009 than in 2010.* ◆ *The nurse will check your heart rate.*
2 the amount that something costs or that someone is paid: *The basic rate of pay is $20 an hour.*
at any rate (informal) anyway; whatever happens: *I hope to be back before ten o'clock – I won't be late at any rate.*

rath·er 🔊 /ˈræðər/ adverb
more than a little but not very: *We were rather tired after our long trip.* ➲ SYNONYM **pretty**
rather than in the place of; instead of: *Could I have tea rather than coffee?*
would rather would prefer to do something: *I'd rather go by train than by bus.*

rat·ing /ˈreɪtɪŋ/ noun [count]
a measurement of how good, popular, difficult, etc. something is: *a hotel with a five star rating* ◆ *The new TV show got terrible ratings and was canceled.*

ra·tio AWL /ˈreɪʃioʊ/ noun [count]
(MATH) the relation between two numbers, which shows how much bigger one amount is than the other: *The ratio of boys to girls in the class is three to one* (= there are three boys to every one girl).

ra·tion¹ /ˈræʃn/ noun [count]
a small amount of something that you are allowed to have when there is not enough for everyone to have what they want: *food rations*

ra·tion² /ˈræʃn/ verb (ra·tions, ra·tion·ing, ra·tioned)
to control the amount of something that someone is allowed to have, for example because there is not enough for everyone to have as much as they want: *Eggs were rationed during the war.*

ra·tion·al AWL /ˈræʃənl/ adjective
based on facts; sensible: *There must be a rational explanation for why he's behaving like this.* ➲ ANTONYM **irrational**

ra·tion·ale /ˌræʃəˈnæl/ *noun* [count] (*formal*)
the reasons which explain a particular decision, belief, plan, etc.: *What is the rationale behind the new policy?*

rat·tle¹ /ˈrætl̩/ *verb* (**rat·tles, rat·tling, rat·tled**)
to make a sound like hard things hitting each other, or to shake something so that it makes this sound: *The windows were rattling all night in the wind.* ◆ *She rattled the ice cubes in her glass.*

rat·tle² /ˈrætl̩/ *noun* [count]
1 the noise of hard things hitting each other: *the rattle of empty bottles*
2 a toy that a baby can shake to make a noise

rat·tle·snake
/ˈrætl̩sneɪk/ *noun*
[count]
a poisonous snake
that makes a noise
like a RATTLE with its
tail when it is angry or
afraid

rattlesnake

ra·vine /rəˈvin/ *noun* [count]
(**GEOGRAPHY**) a small, deep, narrow valley

raw /rɔ/ *adjective*
1 not cooked: *raw meat*
2 in its natural state; not yet made into anything: *raw sugar*

ray /reɪ/ *noun* [count] (*plural* **rays**)
(**PHYSICS**) a line of light or heat: *the sun's rays*

ra·zor /ˈreɪzər/ *noun* [count]
a sharp thing that people use to cut hair off their bodies (to SHAVE)

ra·zor blade /ˈreɪzər
bleɪd/ *noun* [count]
the thin metal part of
a RAZOR that cuts

Rd. abbreviation of **road**

razor   **shaver**

Prefix

re-
(in verbs, and related nouns, adjectives, and adverbs) again: *rebuild something* (= *build it again*) ◆ *redo something* ◆ *repay someone* ◆ *a repayment*

reach¹ 🔑 /ritʃ/ *verb* (**reach·es, reach·ing, reached**)
1 to arrive somewhere: *It was dark when we reached the campsite.* ◆ *Have you reached the end of the book yet?*
2 to put out your hand to do or get something: *I reached for my phone.*
3 to be able to touch something: *Can you get that book from the top shelf? I can't reach it.*
4 to be able to contact someone by telephone: *You can reach me on my cell phone after 5p.m.*

reach² /ritʃ/ *noun*
beyond reach; out of reach too far away to touch: *Keep this medication out of the reach of children.*
within reach near enough to touch or go to: *Make sure you have your phone within reach.*

re·act **AWL** /riˈækt/ *verb* (**re·acts, re·act·ing, re·act·ed**)
to say or do something because something has happened: *How did Paul react to the news?*

re·ac·tion 🔑 **AWL** /riˈækʃn/ *noun* [count]
what you say or do because of something that has happened: *What was her reaction when you told her about the accident?* ◆ *What was his reaction to the news?*

read 🔑 /rid/ *verb* (**reads, read·ing, read** /rɛd/, **has read**)
1 to look at words and understand them: *Have you read this book? It's really interesting.*
2 to say words that you can see: *I read a story to the class.*
read something out to read something to other people: *The teacher read out the list of names.*
▶ **read·ing** /ˈridɪŋ/ *noun* [noncount]: *My interests are reading and baseball.*

read·er /ˈridər/ *noun* [count]
1 a person who reads something
2 a book for reading at school

read·i·ly /ˈrɛdl̩·i/ *adverb*
quickly and easily: *Most vegetables are readily available at this time of year.*

read·y 🔑 /ˈrɛdi/ *adjective*
1 prepared and able to do something: *I'll be ready to leave in five minutes.* ◆ *It's time to get ready for school.*
2 finished, so that you can use it: *Dinner will be ready soon.*
3 happy to do something: *He's always ready to help.* ⊃ SYNONYM **willing**

read·y-made /ˌrɛdi ˈmeɪd/ *adjective*
already prepared and ready to use: *ready-made meals*

real 🔑 /ril/ *adjective*
1 existing, not just imagined: *The movie is about events that happened in real life.*
2 actually true, not only what people think is true: *The name he gave to the police wasn't his real name.*
3 natural; not false or a copy: *This ring is real gold.*
4 big or complete: *I have a real problem.*

real es·tate /ˈril ɪˌsteɪt/ *noun* [noncount]
(**BUSINESS**) land and buildings: *Real estate prices fell again this month.* ◆ *a valuable piece of real estate*

real es·tate a·gent /'ril ɪˌsteɪt ˌeɪdʒənt/ (also **Re·al·tor™** /'riltər/) noun [count]
a person whose job is to sell buildings and land for other people

re·al·is·tic /ˌriəˈlɪstɪk/ adjective
1 sensible and accepting what is possible in a particular situation: We have to **be realistic** about our chances of winning.
2 showing things as they really are: a realistic painting

re·al·i·ty /riˈæləti/ noun [noncount]
the way that something really is, not how you would like it to be: I enjoyed my vacation, but now it's back to reality. • She looked very confident, but **in reality** she was extremely nervous.

re·al·ize /'riəlaɪz/ verb (re·al·iz·es, re·al·iz·ing, re·al·ized)
to understand or know something: When I got home, I realized that I had lost my key. • I didn't realize you were John's brother.
▸ **re·al·i·za·tion** /ˌriələˈzeɪʃn/ noun [noncount]: the sudden realization of what he had done

re·al·ly /'rili/ adverb
1 in fact; actually: Do you really mean it?
2 very or very much: I'm really hungry. • "Do you like this music?" "Not really."
3 a word that shows you are interested or surprised: "I'm going to Hawaii next year." "Really?"

Re·al·tor™ /'riltər/ noun [count] another word for **real estate agent**

rear¹ /rɪr/ noun [singular]
the back part of something: The kitchen is at **the rear** of the house. ⊃ ANTONYM **front**

rear² /rɪr/ adjective
at the back of something: the rear window of a car

rear³ /rɪr/ verb (rears, rear·ing, reared)
to care for and educate young children: She reared three children without any help. ⊃ SYNONYM **bring someone up**, **raise**

re·ar·range /ˌriəˈreɪndʒ/ verb (re·ar·rang·es, re·ar·rang·ing, re·ar·ranged)
to change the position or order of things: We rearranged the furniture in our living room to make more space. • I'll try to rearrange the meeting for next week.

rear·view mir·ror /ˌrɪrvyu ˈmɪrər/ noun [count]
the mirror inside a car that the driver uses to see the vehicle or road behind: She looked in her rearview mirror and saw the police car behind her.

rea·son /'rizn/ noun [count]
a cause or an explanation for why you do something or why something happens: The reason I'm calling is to ask you a favor. • Is there any **reason why** you were late? • She gave no **reasons for** her decision.

rea·son·a·ble /'riznəbl/ adjective
1 fair and ready to listen to what other people say: I tried to be reasonable, even though I was very angry.
2 fair or right in a particular situation: I think $100 is a reasonable price. ⊃ ANTONYM **unreasonable**

rea·son·a·bly /'riznəbli/ adverb
1 to a certain degree, but not very: The food was reasonably good. ⊃ SYNONYM **fairly**
2 in a reasonable way: Don't get angry – let's talk about this reasonably.

re·as·sure /ˌriəˈʃʊr/ verb (re·as·sures, re·as·sur·ing, re·as·sured)
to say or do something to make someone feel safer or happier: The doctor reassured her that she would be fine.
▸ **re·as·sur·ance** /ˌriəˈʃʊrəns/ noun [count, noncount]: He needs some reassurance that he made the right decision.

re·bate /'ribeɪt/ noun [count]
(BUSINESS) money that you get back because you have paid too much or because there is a special offer: We got a $500 rebate on our new car.

re·bel¹ /'rɛbl/ noun [count]
a person who fights against the people in control, for example the government

re·bel² /rɪˈbɛl/ verb (re·bels, re·bel·ling, re·belled)
to fight against the people in control, for example the government or your parents: She rebelled against her parents by refusing to go to college.

re·bel·lion /rɪˈbɛlyən/ noun [count, noncount]
(POLITICS) a time when some of the people in a country fight against their government: Hundreds of people died in the rebellion.

re·bel·lious /rɪˈbɛlyəs/ adjective
not doing what society or people in authority want you to do: rebellious teenagers

re·boot /ˌriˈbut/ verb (re·boots, re·boot·ing, re·boot·ed)
(COMPUTERS) to switch a computer off and then on again immediately: If the software doesn't work, you'll need to reboot your computer.

re·call /rɪˈkɔl/ verb (re·calls, re·call·ing, re·called)
(formal)
to remember something: I don't recall the name of the hotel.

re·ceipt /rɪˈsit/ noun [count]
a piece of paper that shows you have paid for something: "I would like to return this purse." "Do you have your receipt?"

---

re·ceive 🔊 /rɪˈsiv/ *verb* (re·ceives, re·ceiv·ing, re·ceived) *(formal)*

> ℹ️ **SPELLING**
>
> When the sound is /i/ (which is the vowel sound in the word "be"), there is a spelling rule: **I before E, except after C,** so you spell **receive** with **EI** (not IE).

to get or accept something that someone has given or sent to you: *Did you receive my letter?* ⟳
SYNONYM get

re·ceiv·er /rɪˈsivər/ *noun* [count]
the part of a telephone that you use for listening and speaking

re·cent 🔊 /ˈrisənt/ *adjective*
that happened or began only a short time ago: *Is this a recent photo of your son?*

re·cent·ly 🔊 /ˈrisəntli/ *adverb*
not long ago: *She worked here until pretty recently.*

re·cep·tion /rɪˈsɛpʃn/ *noun*
1 [count] a big, important party: *The wedding reception will be held at a hotel downtown.*
2 [noncount] how good telephone, television, and radio signals are: *We get much better reception with cable TV.*
3 [noncount] the place where you go first when you arrive at a hotel or an office building: *Please leave your key at the reception desk.*

re·cep·tion·ist /rɪˈsɛpʃn·ɪst/ *noun* [count]
a person in a hotel, an office, etc. whose job is to answer the telephone and to help people when they arrive

re·cess /ˈrisɛs/ *noun* [noncount]
the time at school when you can go out and play: *We played soccer at recess.*

re·ces·sion /rɪˈsɛʃn/ *noun* [count, noncount]
(**BUSINESS**) a time when the business and industry of a country are not successful: *The country is now in a recession.* ⟳ Look at **depression**(2).

re·charge /ˌriˈtʃɑrdʒ/ *verb* (re·charg·es, re·charg·ing, re·charged)
to fill something with electrical power: *He plugged in his phone to recharge it.* • *I need to recharge my camera batteries.*

rec·i·pe /ˈrɛsəpi/ *noun* [count]
a piece of writing that tells you how to cook something ⟳ Look at the note at **cooking.**

re·cite /rɪˈsaɪt/ *verb* (re·cites, re·cit·ing, re·cit·ed)
to say something, for example a poem or a list, from memory because you have learned it: *Can you recite the names of all of the U.S. presidents?*

reck·less /ˈrɛkləs/ *adjective*
A person who is **reckless** does dangerous things without thinking about what could happen: *reckless driving*

reck·on /ˈrɛkən/ *verb* (reck·ons, reck·on·ing, reck·oned)
1 (*informal*) to believe something because you have thought about it: *It's late. I reckon she isn't coming.*
2 to use numbers to find an answer: *We reckoned the trip would take about half an hour.*

rec·og·ni·tion /ˌrɛkəgˈnɪʃn/ *noun* [noncount]
1 knowing what something is or who someone is when you see it or them: *I said hello to her, but there was no sign of recognition on her face.*
2 public respect for something good that someone has done: *He received recognition for his work in the community.*

rec·og·nize 🔊 /ˈrɛkəgnaɪz/ *verb* (rec·og·niz·es, rec·og·niz·ing, rec·og·nized)
1 to know again someone or something that you have seen or heard before: *I didn't recognize you without your glasses.*
2 to know that something is true: *They recognize that there is a problem.*

rec·om·mend 🔊 /ˌrɛkəˈmɛnd/ *verb* (rec·om·mends, rec·om·mend·ing, rec·om·mend·ed)

> ℹ️ **SPELLING**
>
> Remember! You spell **recommend** with one **C** and **MM.**

1 to tell someone that a person or thing is good or useful: *Can you recommend a hotel near the airport?*
2 to tell someone in a helpful way what you think they should do: *I recommend that you see a doctor.* ⟳ **SYNONYM advise**

rec·om·men·da·tion /ˌrɛkəmənˈdeɪʃn/ *noun* [count, noncount]
saying that something is good or useful: *We followed their recommendation, and stayed at the new hotel.*

re·con·sid·er /ˌrikənˈsɪdər/ *verb* (re·con·sid·ers, re·con·sid·er·ing, re·con·sid·ered)
to think again about something because you may want to change your mind: *I think you should reconsider your decision.*

re·cord¹ 🔊 /ˈrɛkərd/ *noun* [count]

> ℹ️ **PRONUNCIATION**
>
> When the word **record** is a noun, you say the first part of the word louder: **RECord.** When the word **record** is a verb, you say the second part of the word louder: **reCORD.**

tʃ **ch**in   dʒ **J**une   v **v**an   θ **th**in   ð **th**en   s **s**o   z **z**oo   ʃ **sh**e

1 notes about things that have happened: *Keep a record of all the money you spend.*
2 (**SPORTS**) the best, fastest, highest, lowest, etc. that has been done in a sport: *She **holds the** world **record** for long jump.* ◆ *He did it **in record time** (= very fast).* ◆ *She's hoping to **break the record** for the mile (= to do it faster than anyone has done before).*
3 (**MUSIC**) a thin, round piece of black plastic that makes music when you play it on a special machine (called a RECORD PLAYER): *He still has his old record collection.*

re·cord² 🔊 /rɪˈkɔrd/ *verb* (re·cords, re·cord·ing, re·cord·ed)
1 to write notes about or make pictures of things that happen, so you can remember them later: *In his diary he recorded everything that he did.*
2 to save music or a movie using an electronic device, so that you can listen to or watch it later: *I recorded the show so I can watch it this weekend.*

re·cord·er /rɪˈkɔrdər/ *noun* [count]
1 a machine for recording sound and/or pictures: *an old tape recorder*
2 (**MUSIC**) a musical instrument that children often play. You blow through it and cover the holes in it with your fingers. ⟳ Look at the picture at **instrument**.

re·cord·ing /rɪˈkɔrdɪŋ/ *noun* [count]
music or speech that has been saved using an electronic device: *a new recording of Mozart's "Don Giovanni"*

rec·ord play·er /ˈrɛkərd ˌpleɪər/ *noun* [count]
(**MUSIC**) a machine that you use for playing records

re·cov·er 🔊 **AWL** /rɪˈkʌvər/ *verb* (re·cov·ers, re·cov·er·ing, re·cov·ered)
1 to become well or happy again after you have been sick or sad: *She is **recovering from** the flu.*
2 to get back something that was lost: *Police never recovered the stolen car.*

re·cov·er·y **AWL** /rɪˈkʌvəri/ *noun* [noncount]
when you feel well again after you have been sick: *He made a full recovery after his operation.*

re·cre·ate **AWL** /ˌrikriˈeɪt/ *verb* (re·cre·ates, re·cre·at·ing, re·cre·at·ed)
to make something that existed in the past exist again: *The movie recreates the glamour of 1940s Hollywood.*

rec·re·a·tion /ˌrɛkriˈeɪʃn/ *noun* [noncount]
relaxing and enjoying yourself, when you are not working: *recreation activities such as swimming and yoga*

re·cruit¹ /rɪˈkrut/ *verb* (re·cruits, re·cruit·ing, re·cruit·ed)
to find new people to join a company or an organization: *The army is recruiting new officers.*

re·cruit² /rɪˈkrut/ *noun* [count]
a person who has just joined the army, the navy, or the police: *the training of new recruits*

rec·tan·gle /ˈrɛktæŋgl/ *noun* [count]
(**MATH**) a shape with two long sides, two short sides, and four angles of 90 degrees ⟳ Look at the picture at **shape**.
▶ **rec·tan·gu·lar** /rɛkˈtæŋgyələr/ *adjective*: *This page is rectangular.*

re·cy·cle /riˈsaɪkl/ *verb* (re·cy·cles, re·cy·cling, re·cy·cled)
to do something to materials like paper and glass so that they can be used again: *Glass containers can be recycled.*
▶ **re·cy·cled** /riˈsaɪkld/ *adjective*
Something that is **recycled** has been used before: *recycled paper*

re·cy·cling /riˈsaɪklɪŋ/ *noun* [noncount]
1 the process of making objects and materials able to be used again: *the recycling of glass*
2 things that can be RECYCLED: *You need to separate your recycling into glass, plastic, and metal.*

red 🔊 /rɛd/ *adjective* (red·der, red·dest)
1 having the color of blood: *She's wearing a bright red dress.* ◆ *red wine*
2 **Red** hair has a color between red, orange, and brown.
▶ **red** *noun* [count, noncount]: *Lucy was dressed in red.*

re·do /ˌriˈdu/ *verb* (re·does /ˌriˈdʌz/, re·do·ing, re·did /ˌriˈdɪd/, re·done /ˌriˈdʌn/)
to do something again or in a different way: *My teacher asked me to redo the whole essay.*

re·duce 🔊 /rɪˈdus/ *verb* (re·duc·es, re·duc·ing, re·duced)
to make something smaller or less: *This shirt was reduced from $50 to $30.* ◆ *Reduce speed now (= words on a road sign).* ⟳ ANTONYM **increase**

re·duc·tion /rɪˈdʌkʃn/ *noun* [count]
making something smaller or less: *price reductions* ◆ *a reduction in the number of students*

red·wood /ˈrɛdwʊd/ *noun* [count]
a very tall tree that grows near the west coast of the U.S.

reed /rid/ *noun* [count]
a tall plant, like grass, that grows in or near water

redwood

reef /rif/ *noun* [count]
(**GEOGRAPHY**) a long line of rocks, plants, etc. near the surface of the ocean: *a coral reef*

reel /ril/ *noun* [count]
a thing with round sides that holds string for sewing or fishing, film for cameras or movies, etc.: *a fishing rod and reel*

re·fer /rɪˈfər/ *verb* (re·fers, re·fer·ring, re·ferred)
refer to someone or **something**
1 to talk about someone or something: *When I said that some people aren't working hard enough, I wasn't referring to you.*
2 to describe or be connected with someone or something: *The word "child" here refers to anyone under the age of 16.*
3 to look in a book or ask someone for information: *If you don't understand a word, you may refer to your dictionary.* ⊃ **SYNONYM consult**

ref·e·ree /ˌrɛfəˈri/ *noun* [count]
(**SPORTS**) a person who controls a game of football or some other sports, and makes sure the players follow the rules: *a basketball referee* ⊃ Look at **umpire**.

ref·er·ence /ˈrɛfrəns/ *noun*
1 [count] what someone says or writes about something: *The book is full of **references** to her childhood in India.*
2 [noncount] looking at something for information: *Keep these instructions **for future reference**.*
3 [count] If someone gives you a **reference**, they write or talk about you to someone who may give you a new job: *Did your boss give you a good reference?*

ref·er·ence book /ˈrɛfrəns bʊk/ *noun* [count]
a book where you look for information: *A dictionary is a reference book.*

ref·er·en·dum /ˌrɛfəˈrɛndəm/ *noun* [count] (plural **ref·er·en·dums** or **ref·er·en·da** /ˌrɛfəˈrɛndə/)
(**POLITICS**) an occasion when all the people of a country or state can vote on a political question: *to hold a referendum*

re·fill /ˌriˈfɪl/ *verb* (re·fills, re·fill·ing, re·filled)
to fill something again: *Can I refill your glass?*
▶ **re·fill** /ˈrifɪl/ *noun* [count]: *The diner has free refills on coffee.*

re·fin·er·y /rɪˈfaɪnəri/ *noun* [count] (plural **re·fin·er·ies**)
(**BUSINESS**) a factory where a particular substance is treated to make it more pure: *a sugar refinery • oil refineries*

re·flect /rɪˈflɛkt/ *verb* (re·flects, re·flect·ing, re·flect·ed)
1 to show a picture of someone or something in a mirror, water, or glass: *She could see herself reflected in the mirror.*

2 (**PHYSICS**) to send back light, heat, or sound: *The windows reflected the bright morning sunshine.*
3 to show something: *His music reflects his interest in African culture.*

re·flec·tion /rɪˈflɛkʃn/ *noun*
1 [count] a picture that you see in a mirror or on a shiny surface: *He admired his reflection in the mirror.*
2 [noncount] (**PHYSICS**) sending back light, heat, or sound
3 [count] a thing that shows what someone or something is like: *Your clothes are a **reflection of** your personality.*

re·form¹ /rɪˈfɔrm/ *verb* (re·forms, re·form·ing, re·formed)
to change something to make it better: *The government wants to reform the education system.*

re·form² /rɪˈfɔrm/ *noun* [count, noncount]
a change to something to make it better: *economic reform*

re·fresh /rɪˈfrɛʃ/ *verb* (re·fresh·es, re·fresh·ing, re·freshed)
to make someone feel less tired, less hot, or full of energy again: *A good night's sleep will refresh you after your long trip.*
▶ **re·freshed** /rɪˈfrɛʃt/ *adjective*: *He looked refreshed after a good night's sleep.*

re·fresh·ing /rɪˈfrɛʃɪŋ/ *adjective*
1 making you feel less tired or less hot: *a cold, refreshing drink*
2 new or different in a good way: *It's refreshing to meet someone who is so enthusiastic.*

re·fresh·ments /rɪˈfrɛʃmənts/ *noun* [plural]
food and drinks that are available at a theater or other public event: *Light refreshments will be served during the break.*

re·frig·er·ate /rɪˈfrɪdʒəreɪt/ *verb* (re·frig·er·ates, re·frig·er·at·ing, re·frig·er·at·ed)
to put food or a drink in a **REFRIGERATOR** in order to keep it cold and fresh: *Refrigerate after opening* (= on a food label).

re·frig·er·a·tor /rɪˈfrɪdʒəreɪtər/ (also informal **fridge** /frɪdʒ/) *noun* [count]
a metal container, usually electric, which keeps food cold but not frozen: *Can you put the milk in the refrigerator?* ⊃ Look at **freezer**.

ref·uge /ˈrɛfyudʒ/ *noun* [count]
a place where you are safe from someone or something: *We **took refuge** from the hot sun under a tree.*

ref·u·gee /ˌrɛfyuˈdʒi/ *noun* [count]
(**POLITICS**) a person who must leave their country because of danger, for example a war

re·fund¹ /ˈrifʌnd/ *noun* [count]
money that is paid back to you, because you have paid too much or because you are not happy with something you bought: *If you are not completely satisfied with the watch, you can return it for a full refund.*

re·fund² /rɪˈfʌnd/ *verb* (re·funds, re·fund·ing, re·fund·ed)
to give someone their money back, because they have paid too much or because they are not happy with something they bought: *We will refund your money in full.*

re·fus·al /rɪˈfyuzl/ *noun* [count, noncount]
saying "no" when someone asks you to do or have something: *a refusal to pay*

re·fuse¹ 🔑 /rɪˈfyuz/ *verb* (re·fus·es, re·fus·ing, re·fused)

> ⓘ **PRONUNCIATION**
> When **refuse** is a verb, you say the second part of the word louder: re**FUSE**. When **refuse** is a noun, you say the first part of the word louder: **RE**fuse.

to say "no" when someone asks you to do or have something: *I asked Matthew to help, but he refused.* ◆ *The company refused to give me my money back.*

ref·use² /ˈrɛfyus/ *noun* [noncount] (*formal*)
things that you throw away because you do not want them anymore ➔ SYNONYM **garbage**, **trash**

re·gard¹ /rɪˈgɑrd/ *verb* (re·gards, re·gard·ing, re·gard·ed)
to think about someone or something in a certain way: *I regard her as my best friend.*

re·gard² /rɪˈgɑrd/ *noun* (*formal*)
1 [noncount] attention to or care for someone or something: *She shows no regard for other people's feelings.*
2 [noncount] what you feel when you admire or respect someone or something: *I have great regard for his work* (= I think it is very good).
3 regards [plural] a word you use to send good wishes to someone at the end of a letter or an e-mail, or when you ask someone to give your good wishes to another person who is not there: *Kind regards,...* ◆ *Please give my regards to your parents.*
in regard to someone or **something**; **with regard to someone** or **something** (*formal*)
about someone or something: *I am writing to you in regard to your advertisement for a computer programmer.*

re·gard·ing /rɪˈgɑrdɪŋ/ *preposition* (*formal*)
about someone or something: *Please contact us if you require further information regarding this matter.* ➔ SYNONYM **concerning**

re·gard·less /rɪˈgɑrdləs/ *adverb*
not paying attention or being affected by someone or something: *Everyone will receive the same bonus, regardless of how long they have been working here.*

reg·gae /ˈrɛgeɪ/ *noun* [noncount]
(MUSIC) a type of Caribbean popular music

re·gime AWL /reɪˈʒim/ *noun* [count]
(POLITICS) a method or system of government, especially one that has not been elected in a fair way: *a military regime*

reg·i·ment /ˈrɛdʒəmənt/ *noun* [count]
a group of soldiers in an army

re·gion 🔑 AWL /ˈridʒən/ *noun* [count]
(GEOGRAPHY) a part of a country or of the world: *tropical regions of the world*

re·gion·al AWL /ˈridʒənl/ *adjective*
(GEOGRAPHY) belonging to a certain part of a country or of the world: *a regional dialect*

reg·is·ter¹ AWL /ˈrɛdʒəstər/ *verb* (reg·is·ters, reg·is·ter·ing, reg·is·tered)
1 to put a name on an official list: *I'm going to register for four classes this semester.*
2 to show a number or amount: *The thermometer registered 90°F.*

reg·is·ter² AWL /ˈrɛdʒəstər/ *noun* [count]
1 an official list of names: *the National Register of Historic Places*
2 = **cash register**

reg·is·trar /ˈrɛdʒəˌstrɑr/ *noun* [count]
a person whose job is to keep information about students at a college or university: *Contact the registrar for a copy of your certificate.*

reg·is·tra·tion AWL /ˌrɛdʒəˈstreɪʃn/ *noun*
1 [noncount] putting a name on an official list: *Registration for the fall semester will begin in August.*
2 [count] an official piece of paper with information about a vehicle and the name of its owner: *Can I see your driver's license and registration?*

re·gret¹ /rɪˈgrɛt/ *verb* (re·grets, re·gret·ting, re·gret·ted)
to feel sorry about something that you did or did not do: *He regrets selling his car.* ◆ *I don't regret what I said to her.*

re·gret² /rɪˈgrɛt/ *noun* [count, noncount]
a sad feeling about something that you did or did not do: *Do you have any regrets about quitting your job?*

reg·u·lar 🔑 /ˈrɛgyələr/ *adjective*
1 happening again and again with the same amount of space or time in between: *a regular heartbeat* ◆ *A light flashed at regular intervals.* ➔ ANTONYM **irregular**

2 going somewhere or doing something often: *I've never seen him before – he's not one of my regular customers.*

3 usual: *Who is your regular doctor?*

4 standard, average, or normal: *Would you like regular coffee or decaf?* ♦ *He's just a regular guy.*

5 (**ENGLISH LANGUAGE ARTS**) A word that is **regular** has the usual verb forms or plural: *"Work" is a regular verb.* ⟳ **ANTONYM irregular**

reg·u·lar·ly 🔑 /ˈrɛgyələrli/ *adverb*
If something happens **regularly**, it happens again and again with the same amount of time in between: *We meet regularly every Friday.*

reg·u·la·tion **AWL** /ˌrɛgyəˈleɪʃn/ *noun* [count]
an official rule that controls what people do: *You can't smoke here – it's against fire regulations.*

re·hears·al /rɪˈhərsl/ *noun* [count]
a time when you practice something, such as a play or a piece of music, before you do it in front of other people: *There's a play rehearsal tonight.*

re·hearse /rɪˈhərs/ *verb* (re·hears·es, re·hears·ing, re·hearsed)
to practice something, such as a play or a piece of music, before you do it in front of other people: *We are rehearsing for the concert.*

reign¹ /reɪn/ *noun* [count]
(**POLITICS**) a time when a king or queen rules a country: *The reign of Queen Elizabeth II began in 1952.*

reign² /reɪn/ *verb* (reigns, reign·ing, reigned)
(**POLITICS**) to be king or queen of a country: *Queen Victoria reigned for over sixty years.*

rein·deer /ˈreɪndɪr/ *noun* [count] (*plural* rein·deer)
a big animal that lives in very cold countries. **Reindeer** are brown and have long horns on their heads.

re·in·force **AWL** /ˌriɪnˈfɔrs/ *verb* (re·in·forc·es, re·in·forc·ing, re·in·forced)
to make something stronger: *They used steel bars to reinforce the concrete.*

reins /reɪnz/ *noun* [plural]
long, thin pieces of leather that a horse wears on its head so that the person riding it can control it

re·ject **AWL** /rɪˈdʒɛkt/ *verb* (re·jects, re·ject·ing, re·ject·ed)
to say that you do not want someone or something: *He rejected my offer of help.* ♦ *She got rejected from Princeton University.* ⟳ **ANTONYM accept**
▶ **re·jec·tion** **AWL** /rɪˈdʒɛkʃn/ *noun* [count, noncount]: *She doesn't handle rejection very well.* ♦ *David got rejection letters from eight law firms.*

re·late /rɪˈleɪt/ *verb* (re·lates, re·lat·ing, re·lat·ed)
to show or to make a connection between two or more things: *I found it difficult to relate the two ideas in my mind.* ⟳ **SYNONYM connect**
relate to someone or **something** to be connected to someone or something: *That's good advice, but it doesn't really relate to my situation.*

re·lat·ed /rɪˈleɪtəd/ *adjective*
in the same family; connected: *"Are those two boys related?" "Yes, they're brothers."*

re·la·tion 🔑 /rɪˈleɪʃn/ *noun*
1 **relations** [plural] the way that people, groups, or countries behave with each other or how they feel about each other: *diplomatic relations with other countries*
2 [noncount] a connection between two things: *The movie has no relation to the book.*
3 [count] a person in your family ⟳ **SYNONYM relative**

re·la·tion·ship 🔑 /rɪˈleɪʃnˌʃɪp/ *noun* [count]
1 the way people or groups behave with each other or how they feel about each other: *I have a good relationship with my parents.* ♦ *The book describes the relationship between the two communities.*
2 a romantic connection between two people: *to have a relationship with someone* ♦ *Are you in a relationship right now?*
3 the way that two or more things are connected: *Is there a relationship between stress and high blood pressure?*

rel·a·tive¹ /ˈrɛlətɪv/ *noun* [count]
a person in your family ⟳ **SYNONYM relation**

rel·a·tive² /ˈrɛlətɪv/ *adjective*
1 when compared with someone or something else: *the position of the earth relative to the sun* ♦ *They live in relative luxury.*
2 (**ENGLISH LANGUAGE ARTS**) referring to an earlier noun, sentence, or part of a sentence: *In the phrase "the woman who lives next door," "who" is a relative pronoun and "who lives next door" is a relative clause.*

rel·a·tive·ly /ˈrɛlətɪvli/ *adverb*
to a certain degree, especially when compared with others: *This room is relatively small.*

re·lax 🔑 **AWL** /rɪˈlæks/ *verb* (re·lax·es, re·lax·ing, re·laxed)
1 to rest and be calm; to become less worried or angry: *After a hard day at work, I just wanted to relax in front of the TV.*
2 to become less tight or to make something become less tight: *Let your body relax.*
▶ **re·lax·ing** **AWL** /rɪˈlæksɪŋ/ *adjective*: *We had a quiet, relaxing weekend.*

re·lax·a·tion AWL /ˌrilæk'seɪʃn/ *noun* [noncount]
time spent resting and being calm: *You need more rest and relaxation.*

re·laxed 🔑 AWL /rɪ'lækst/ *adjective*
calm and not worried: *She felt relaxed after her vacation.*

re·lay /'rileɪ/ (also **re·lay race** /'rileɪ reɪs/) *noun* [count]
(SPORTS) a race in which each member of the team runs, swims, etc. one part of the race

re·lease¹ 🔑 AWL /rɪ'lis/ *verb* (re·leas·es, re·leas·ing, re·leased)
1 to let a person or an animal go free: *He was released from prison last month.*
2 to allow something to be known by the public: *They have not released the victim's name.*
3 to make a movie, a song, a book, etc. available so people can see, hear, or buy it: *The movie is due to be released next month.*

re·lease² AWL /rɪ'lis/ *noun* [count, noncount]
1 when a person or an animal is allowed to go free: *the release of the prisoners*
2 a new movie, song, book, etc. that is available for people to see, hear, or buy: *this month's new movie releases*

rel·e·vant 🔑 AWL /'rɛləvənt/ *adjective*
connected with what you are talking or writing about; important: *We need someone who can do the job well – your age is not relevant.* ⮑ ANTONYM **irrelevant**
▶ **rel·e·vance** AWL /'rɛləvəns/ *noun* [noncount]: *I'm sorry, I don't see the relevance of your question.*

re·li·a·ble AWL /rɪ'laɪəbl/ *adjective*
that you can trust: *My car is very reliable.* ♦ *He's a reliable person.* ⮑ ANTONYM **unreliable** ⮑ The verb is **rely**.

re·li·ant AWL /rɪ'laɪənt/ *adjective*
not being able to live or work without someone or something: *She is totally reliant on her parents for money.* ⮑ The verb is **rely**.

re·lied AWL form of **rely**

re·lief 🔑 /rɪ'lif/ *noun* [noncount]
1 the good feeling you have when you are no longer worried or in pain: *It was a great relief to know she was safe.*
2 (POLITICS) food or money that is given to people who need it: *Many countries sent relief to the victims of the disaster.*

re·lies AWL form of **rely**

re·lieve /rɪ'liv/ *verb* (re·lieves, re·liev·ing, re·lieved)
to make a bad feeling or a pain stop or get better: *These pills should relieve the pain.*

re·lieved /rɪ'livd/ *adjective*
feeling happy because a problem or danger has gone away: *I was relieved to hear that you weren't hurt in the accident.*

re·lig·ion 🔑 /rɪ'lɪdʒən/ *noun* (RELIGION)
1 [noncount] believing in a god or gods and the activities connected with this
2 [count] one of the ways of believing in a god or gods: *Christianity, Islam, and other world religions*

re·lig·ious 🔑 /rɪ'lɪdʒəs/ *adjective* (RELIGION)
1 connected with religion: *a religious leader*
2 having a strong belief in a religion: *My parents are very religious.*

re·luc·tance AWL /rɪ'lʌktəns/ *noun* [noncount]
not wanting to do something: *He agreed, but with great reluctance.*

re·luc·tant AWL /rɪ'lʌktənt/ *adjective*
If you are **reluctant** to do something, you do not want to do it: *He was **reluctant to** give me the money.*
▶ **re·luc·tant·ly** AWL /rɪ'lʌktəntli/ *adverb*: *She reluctantly agreed to help.*

re·ly 🔑 AWL /rɪ'laɪ/ *verb* (re·lies, re·ly·ing, re·lied, has re·lied)
rely on someone or **something**
1 to need someone or something: *I rely on my parents for money.* ⮑ SYNONYM **depend on** ⮑ The adjective is **reliant**.
2 to feel sure that someone or something will do what they say they will do: *You can rely on him to help you.* ⮑ The adjective is **reliable**.

re·main 🔑 /rɪ'meɪn/ *verb* (re·mains, re·main·ing, re·mained) (*formal*)
1 to stay in the same way; to not change: *I asked her a question, but she remained silent.*
2 to stay after other people or things have gone: *After the fire, very little remained of the house.*

re·main·der /rɪ'meɪndər/ *noun* [singular] (*formal*)
the people, things, etc. that are left after the others have gone or been used: *The remainder of the week should be warm and sunny.* ⮑ SYNONYM **rest**

re·main·ing /rɪ'meɪnɪŋ/ *adjective*
continuing to exist or stay after other people or things have gone or been used: *They spent the remaining two days of their vacation at the beach.*

re·mains /rɪ'meɪnz/ *noun* [plural]
what is left when most of something has gone: *the remains of an old church*

re·mark¹ 🔑 /rɪ'mɑrk/ *noun* [count]
something that you say: *He made a remark about the food.* ⮑ SYNONYM **comment**

re·mark² /rɪˈmɑrk/ *verb* (re·marks, re·mark·ing, re·marked)
to say something: *"It's cold today," he remarked.*
➔ **SYNONYM comment**

re·mark·a·ble /rɪˈmɑrkəbl/ *adjective*
unusual and surprising in a good way: *a remarkable discovery*
▶ **re·mark·a·bly** /rɪˈmɑrkəbli/ *adverb*: *She speaks French remarkably well.*

re·mar·ry /riˈmæri/ *verb* (re·mar·ries, re·mar·ry·ing, re·mar·ried)
to marry again: *After her husband died, she didn't think she'd ever remarry.*

re·me·di·al /rɪˈmidiəl/ *adjective*
for people who need extra help to learn something: *remedial English classes*

rem·e·dy /ˈrɛmədi/ *noun* [count] (*plural* rem·e·dies)
1 (HEALTH) something that makes you better when you are sick or in pain: *a remedy for asthma*
2 a way of solving a problem: *There is no easy remedy for unemployment.*

re·mem·ber /rɪˈmɛmbər/ *verb* (re·mem·bers, re·mem·ber·ing, re·mem·bered)
to keep something in your mind or bring something back into your mind: *Can you remember his name?* • *I remember mailing the letter.* • *Did you remember to buy milk?* ➔
ANTONYM forget

re·mind /rɪˈmaɪnd/ *verb* (re·minds, re·mind·ing, re·mind·ed)
1 to help someone remember something that they must do: *Please remind me to buy some bread on the way home.*
2 to make someone remember someone or something: *She reminds me of her mother.*

re·mind·er /rɪˈmaɪndər/ *noun* [count]
something that makes you remember something: *Eddie kept the ring as a reminder of happier days.*

re·morse /rɪˈmɔrs/ *noun* [noncount]
the feeling you have when you are sorry for doing something wrong: *She was filled with remorse for what she had done.* ➔ Look at **guilt**.

re·mote /rɪˈmoʊt/ *adjective* (re·mot·er, re·mot·est)
1 far away from where other people live: *a remote island in the Pacific Ocean*
2 far away in time: *the remote past*

re·mote con·trol /rɪˌmoʊt kənˈtroʊl/ *noun* (also informal **re·mote**) [count]
a piece of equipment that you use for controlling a television, a toy, or other machine from a distance: *Pass me the remote control – I want to see what else is on TV.*

re·mote·ly /rɪˈmoʊtli/ *adverb*
at all; in any way: *I'm **not remotely** interested in your opinions.*

re·mov·al AWL /rɪˈmuvl/ *noun* [noncount]
when you take something off or away: *the removal of a car that was blocking the exit*

re·move AWL /rɪˈmuv/ *verb* (re·moves, re·mov·ing, re·moved)
to take someone or something off or away from someone or something: *The statue was removed from the museum.* • *Please remove your shoes before entering the temple.* ➔ **SYNONYM take away, take off**

re·new /rɪˈnu/ *verb* (re·news, re·new·ing, re·newed)
1 to start something again: *We renewed our friendship after many years.*
2 to make something acceptable or able to be used for a further period of time: *You can renew your library books over the Internet.* • *If you want to stay in the country you must renew your visa.*

re·new·a·ble /rɪˈnuəbl/ *adjective*
1 (used about sources of energy) that will always exist: *renewable energy sources, such as solar power and wind*
2 that can be continued or replaced with a new one for another period of time: *Your work permit is not renewable.*

ren·o·vate /ˈrɛnəveɪt/ *verb* (ren·o·vates, ren·o·vat·ing, ren·o·vat·ed)
to repair an old building so that it is in good condition again
▶ **ren·o·va·tion** /ˌrɛnəˈveɪʃn/ *noun* [count, noncount]: *The museum is closed during renovation.*

rent¹ /rɛnt/ *noun* [count]
the money that you pay to live in a place or to use something that belongs to another person: *How much is your rent?* • *Megan couldn't afford to pay her rent this month.*
for rent available to rent: *Do you have any apartments for rent?*

rent² /rɛnt/ *verb* (rents, rent·ing, rent·ed)
1 to pay to live in a place, or to use something for a short time: *We're renting an apartment near campus.* • *We rented a car in Denver.*
2 (also **rent something out**) to let someone live in a place or use something for a short time in return for money: *He rents out his house to students during the summer.* • *Do you rent bikes by the hour?*

rent·al /ˈrɛntl/ *noun*
1 [noncount] the act of renting something or an arrangement to rent something: *You can arrange your car rental over the Internet.*

2 [count, noncount] the amount of money that you pay when you rent something: *Bike rental is $40 per day.*

3 [count] a house, car, or piece of equipment that you can rent: *"Is this your own car?" "No, it's a rental."*

Rep. abbreviation of **Representative**

re·paid form of **repay**

re·pair¹ 🔎 /rɪˈpɛr/ *verb* (re·pairs, re·pair·ing, re·paired)
to make something that is broken or damaged good again: *How much will it cost to repair the car?* ⊃ SYNONYM **fix**

re·pair² /rɪˈpɛr/ *noun* [count, noncount]
something you do to fix something that is broken or damaged: *The hotel is closed for repairs.* ◆ *The bridge is **under repair**.*

re·pay /rɪˈpeɪ/ *verb* (re·pays, re·pay·ing, re·paid /riˈpeɪd/, has re·paid)
1 to pay back money to someone: *to repay a loan*
2 to do something for someone to show your thanks: *How can I **repay** you **for** all your help?*

re·pay·ment /rɪˈpeɪmənt/ *noun* [count, noncount]
paying someone back, or the money that you pay them: *monthly repayments*

re·peat 🔎 /rɪˈpit/ *verb* (re·peats, re·peat·ing, re·peat·ed)
1 to say or do something again: *He didn't hear my question, so I repeated it.*
2 to say what another person has said: *Repeat this sentence after me.*
▸ **re·peat** *noun* [count]: *I think I've seen this episode before – it must be a repeat.*

re·peat·ed /rɪˈpitəd/ *adjective*
happening or done many times: *There have been repeated accidents on this stretch of road.*
▸ **re·peat·ed·ly** /rɪˈpitədli/ *adverb*: *I've asked him repeatedly not to leave his bike here.*

rep·e·ti·tion /ˌrɛpəˈtɪʃn/ *noun* [count, noncount]
saying or doing something again: *to learn by repetition*

re·pet·i·tive /rɪˈpɛt̬ətɪv/ *adjective*
not interesting because the same thing is repeated many times: *The job paid well, but I found it a little repetitive.*

re·place 🔎 /rɪˈpleɪs/ *verb* (re·plac·es, re·plac·ing, re·placed)
1 to take the place of someone or something: *Teachers will never be replaced by computers in the classroom.*
2 to put a new or different person or thing in the place of another: *I need to replace my watch battery.*

3 to put something back in the place where it was before: *Please replace the books on the shelf when you are finished with them.*

re·place·ment /rɪˈpleɪsmənt/ *noun* [count]
a new or different person or thing that takes the place of another: *Sue is leaving the company next month so we need to find a replacement.*

re·play /ˈripleɪ/ *noun* [count] (plural **re·plays**)
(SPORTS) something on television, etc. that you watch or listen to again, especially a small part of a sports game: *I missed the touchdown but saw the replay.*

rep·li·ca /ˈrɛplɪkə/ *noun* [count]
an exact copy of something: *a replica of the Empire State Building*

re·ply¹ 🔎 /rɪˈplaɪ/ *verb* (re·plies, re·ply·ing, re·plied, has re·plied)
to say or write something as an answer to someone or something: *I wrote to Jane, but she hasn't replied.*

re·ply² 🔎 *noun* [count, noncount] (plural **re·plies**)
an answer: *Have you had a **reply to** your letter?* ◆ *What did you say **in reply** to his question?*

re·port¹ 🔎 /rɪˈpɔrt/ *verb* (re·ports, re·port·ing, re·port·ed)
to give people information about something that has happened: *We **reported** the accident **to** the police.*

re·port² 🔎 /rɪˈpɔrt/ *noun* [count]
something that someone says or writes about something that has happened: *Did you read the newspaper reports about the earthquake?*

re·port card /rɪˈpɔrt kɑrd/ *noun* [count]
a written statement about a student's work with a grade for each subject: *He had four A's and two B's on his report card.*

re·port·ed speech /rɪˌpɔrtɪd ˈspitʃ/ *noun* [noncount]
(ENGLISH LANGUAGE ARTS) saying what someone has said, rather than repeating their exact words. In **reported speech**, "I'll come later" becomes "He said he'd (= he would) come later."

re·port·er 🔎 /rɪˈpɔrtər/ *noun* [count]
a person who writes for a newspaper or speaks on the radio or television about things that have happened ⊃ Look at **journalist**.

rep·re·sent 🔎 /ˌrɛprɪˈzɛnt/ *verb* (rep·re·sents, rep·re·sent·ing, rep·re·sent·ed)
1 to speak or do something in place of another person or other people: *It is an honor for athletes to represent their country.*
2 to be an example or a sign of something: *The yellow lines on the map represent roads.*

rep·re·sen·ta·tion /ˌrɛprɪzɛnˈteɪʃn/ *noun*
1 [noncount] (formal) having someone act or speak for you: *Do you have any legal representation* (= someone to speak for you in a court of law)?
2 [count, noncount] the way that someone or something is shown or described: *The article complains about the representation of women in advertising.*

rep·re·sen·ta·tive /ˌrɛprɪˈzɛntətɪv/ *noun* [count]
1 a person who speaks or does something for a group of people: *There were representatives from every department at the meeting.*
2 Representative (abbreviation **Rep.**) (**POLITICS**) a member of the House of Representatives in the U.S. Congress ⟳ Look at the note at **government**.

rep·ri·mand /ˈrɛprəmænd/ *verb* (rep·ri·mands, rep·ri·mand·ing, rep·ri·mand·ed)
to tell someone officially that they have done something wrong: *She was reprimanded for being late.*
▶ **rep·ri·mand** *noun* [count]: *a severe reprimand*

re·pro·duce /ˌriprəˈdus/ *verb* (re·pro·duc·es, re·pro·duc·ing, re·pro·duced)
1 to make a copy of something
2 (**BIOLOGY**) When people, animals, or plants **reproduce**, they have young ones.

re·pro·duc·tion /ˌriprəˈdʌkʃn/ *noun* [noncount]
(**BIOLOGY**) producing babies, or young animals or plants: *We are studying plant reproduction at school.*

rep·tile /ˈrɛptaɪl/ *noun* [count]
any animal with cold blood that lays eggs. Snakes are **reptiles**.

re·pub·lic /rɪˈpʌblɪk/ *noun* [count]
(**POLITICS**) a country where people choose the government and the leader (the **PRESIDENT**): *the Republic of Ireland* ⟳ Look at **monarchy**.

Re·pub·li·can /rɪˈpʌblɪkən/ *noun* [count]
(**POLITICS**) a person in THE REPUBLICAN PARTY in the U.S.
▶ **Re·pub·li·can** *adjective*: *Republican voters* ⟳ Look at **Democrat**.

the Re·pub·li·can Par·ty /ðə rɪˈpʌblɪkən ˌparti/ *noun* [singular]
(**POLITICS**) one of the two main political parties in the U.S. ⟳ Look at **the Democratic Party**.

re·pul·sive /rɪˈpʌlsɪv/ *adjective*
disgusting or very unpleasant: *What a repulsive smell!*

rep·u·ta·tion /ˌrɛpyəˈteɪʃn/ *noun* [count]
what people think or say about someone or something: *This restaurant has a good reputation.*

re·quest¹ /rɪˈkwɛst/ *noun* [count]
asking for something in a polite or formal way: *They made a request for money.*

re·quest² /rɪˈkwɛst/ *verb* (re·quests, re·quest·ing, re·quest·ed) (formal)
to ask for something: *I requested a private room at the hospital.*

re·quire **AWL** /rɪˈkwaɪər/ *verb* (re·quires, re·quir·ing, re·quired) (formal)
1 to need something: *Please contact us if you require further information.*
2 to officially demand or order something: *Passengers are required by law to wear seat belts.*

re·quire·ment **AWL** /rɪˈkwaɪərmənt/ *noun* [count]
something that you need or that you must do or have: *course requirements for graduation*

re·sched·ule **AWL** /ˌriˈskɛdʒəl/ *verb* (re·sched·ules, re·sched·ul·ing, re·sched·uled)
to change the time of something so that it happens later: *I'm going to have to reschedule our meeting for next week.*

res·cue¹ /ˈrɛskyu/ *verb* (res·cues, res·cu·ing, res·cued)
to save someone or something from danger: *She rescued the boy when he fell in the river.*

res·cue² /ˈrɛskyu/ *noun* [count, noncount]
saving someone or something from danger: *When she was attacked, no one came to her rescue.* ◆ *The attempted rescue of the climbers failed when it started to snow.*

re·search¹ **AWL** /ˈrisərtʃ/ *noun* [noncount]
studying something carefully to find out more about it: *scientific research*

re·search² **AWL** /rɪˈsərtʃ/ *verb* (re·search·es, re·search·ing, re·searched)
to study something carefully to find out more about it: *Scientists are researching the causes of the disease.*
▶ **re·search·er** **AWL** /rɪˈsərtʃər/ *noun* [count]: *a medical researcher*

re·sem·blance /rɪˈzɛmbləns/ *noun* [count, noncount]
looking like someone or something else: *There's no resemblance between my two brothers.*

re·sem·ble /rɪˈzɛmbl/ *verb* (re·sem·bles, re·sem·bling, re·sem·bled)
to look like someone or something else: *Lisa resembles her mother.*

re·sent /rɪˈzɛnt/ *verb* (re·sents, re·sent·ing, re·sent·ed)
to feel angry about something because you think it is not fair: *I resented her criticism of my work.*
▶ **re·sent·ful** /rɪˈzɛntfl/ *adjective*: *He felt resentful at being criticized unfairly.*

re·sent·ment /rɪˈzɛntmənt/ *noun* [*noncount, singular*]
a feeling of anger about something that you think is not fair

res·er·va·tion 🔑 /ˌrɛzərˈveɪʃn/ *noun* [*count*]
1 a room, seat, table, or another thing that you have asked someone to keep for you: *I called the restaurant and made a reservation for a table for two.*
2 a feeling of doubt about something: *I still have some reservations about taking the job.*
3 an area of land in the U.S. that is kept separate for Native Americans to live in

re·serve¹ /rɪˈzərv/ *verb* (re·serves, re·serv·ing, re·served)
1 to ask for a seat, table, room, etc. to be kept for you at a future time: *I'd like to reserve a room for tomorrow night.* ⟶ SYNONYM **book**
2 to keep something for a special reason or to use later: *Those seats are reserved.*

re·serve² /rɪˈzərv/ *noun* [*count*]
1 something that you keep to use later: *reserves of food*
2 an area of land where the animals and plants are protected by law: *a nature reserve*
in reserve that you keep and do not use unless you need to: *Don't spend all the money – keep some in reserve.*

re·served /rɪˈzərvd/ *adjective*
If you are **reserved**, you keep your feelings hidden from other people.

res·er·voir /ˈrɛzərvwɑr/ *noun* [*count*]
(GEOGRAPHY) a big lake where a city or town keeps water to use later

res·i·dence AWL /ˈrɛzədəns/ *noun*
1 [*count*] (*formal*) a large house, usually where an important or famous person lives: *a diplomat's residence*
2 [*noncount*] having your home in a particular place: *The family applied for permanent residence in the United States.*

res·i·dent AWL /ˈrɛzədənt/ *noun* [*count*]
a person who lives in a place

res·i·den·tial AWL /ˌrɛzəˈdɛnʃl/ *adjective*
A **residential** area is one where there are houses rather than offices or factories.

re·sign /rɪˈzaɪn/ *verb* (re·signs, re·sign·ing, re·signed)
to leave your job: *The director resigned last week.*
resign yourself to something to accept something that you do not like but that you cannot change: *There were a lot of people in line, so John resigned himself to a long wait.*

res·ig·na·tion /ˌrɛzɪgˈneɪʃn/ *noun* [*count, noncount*]
saying that you want to leave your job: *a letter of resignation* ♦ *to hand in your resignation* (= to give your company a letter saying that you want to leave your job)

re·signed /rɪˈzaɪnd/ *adjective*
accepting something that is bad, but cannot be changed: *Ben was **resigned to the fact** that he would never be a professional athlete.*

re·sist /rɪˈzɪst/ *verb* (re·sists, re·sist·ing, re·sist·ed)
1 to try to stop something from happening or to fight against someone or something: *The board of directors is resisting pressure to fire the company president.*
2 to stop yourself from doing or having something that you want to do or have: *I can't resist chocolate.*

re·sis·tance /rɪˈzɪstəns/ *noun* [*noncount*]
when people try to stop something from happening; fighting against someone or something: *There was a lot of **resistance to** the plan to build a new airport.*

res·o·lu·tion AWL /ˌrɛzəˈluʃn/ *noun*
1 [*count*] something that you decide to do or not to do: *Julie **made a resolution** to study harder.*
2 [*count*] (POLITICS) a formal decision that is made after a vote by a group of people: *a United Nations resolution to send more troops to the region*
3 [*noncount*] a solution to a problem or an argument

re·solve AWL /rɪˈzɑlv/ *verb* (re·solves, re·solv·ing, re·solved) (*formal*)
1 to find a solution to a problem: *All of the technical problems have been resolved.*
2 to decide to do or not do something: *He resolved never to do it again.*

re·sort /rɪˈzɔrt/ *noun* [*count*]
a place where a lot of people go on vacation: *a popular beach resort*
a last resort the only person or thing left that can help: *As a last resort, I asked my parents for money.*

re·source AWL /ˈrisɔrs/ *noun* [*count*]
something that a person, an organization, or a country has and can use: *Oil is one of our most important natural resources.*

re·spect¹ 🔑 /rɪˈspɛkt/ *noun* [*noncount*]
1 feeling that you have a good opinion of someone: *I **have** a lot of **respect for** your father.*
2 being polite to someone or something: *You should treat old people with more respect.*

re·spect² 🔑 /rɪˈspɛkt/ *verb* (re·spects, re·spect·ing, re·spect·ed)
1 to have a good opinion of someone or something: *I respect him for his honesty.* ⟶ SYNONYM **admire**

2 to pay attention to or be careful about something: *We should respect other people's cultures and values.*

re·spect·a·ble /rɪˈspɛktəbl/ *adjective*
If a person or thing is **respectable**, people think they are good or correct: *She comes from a respectable family.*

re·spect·ful /rɪˈspɛktfl/ *adjective*
If you are **respectful**, you are polite to other people and in different situations: *The crowd listened in respectful silence.*

res·pi·ra·to·ry /ˈrɛsprəˌtɔri/ *adjective*
(**BIOLOGY**, **HEALTH**) connected with breathing: *He suffers from respiratory problems.*
▸ **res·pi·ra·tion** /ˌrɛspəˈreɪʃn/ *noun* [noncount] (*formal*)
breathing

re·spond **AWL** /rɪˈspɑnd/ *verb* (**re·sponds**, **re·spond·ing**, **re·spond·ed**) (*formal*)
to do or say something to answer someone or something: *I said "hello," but he didn't respond.* ⊃ **SYNONYM reply**

re·sponse **AWL** /rɪˈspɑns/ *noun* [count]
an answer to someone or something: *I wrote to them but I haven't had a response.* ⊃ **SYNONYM reply**

re·spon·si·bil·i·ty /rɪˌspɑnsəˈbɪləţi/ *noun* [count, noncount] (*plural* **re·spon·si·bil·i·ties**)
a duty to deal with or take care of someone or something: *Who **has responsibility for** the new students?* • *The dog is my brother's responsibility.* • *You need to **take responsibity** for your own actions.*

re·spon·si·ble /rɪˈspɑnsəbl/ *adjective*
1 having the duty to take care of someone or something: *The driver is **responsible for** the lives of the people on the bus.*
2 being the person who made something bad happen: *Who was **responsible for** the accident?*
3 A **responsible** person is someone that you can trust: *We need a responsible person to take care of our son.* ⊃ **ANTONYM irresponsible**

rest¹ /rɛst/ *noun*
1 the rest [singular] the part that is left or the ones that are left: *If you don't want the rest, I'll eat it.* • *I liked the beginning, but **the rest of** the movie wasn't very good.* • *Jason watched TV and the rest of us went for a walk.*
2 [count, noncount] a time when you relax, sleep, or do nothing: *After walking for an hour, we stopped for a rest.* • *Try to **get some rest** now.*

rest² /rɛst/ *verb* (**rests**, **rest·ing**, **rest·ed**)
1 to relax, sleep, or do nothing after an activity or an illness: *We worked all morning and then rested for an hour before starting work again.*

2 to be on something; to put something on or against another thing: *His arms were resting on the table.*

res·tau·rant /ˈrɛstərɑnt/ *noun* [count]
a place where you buy a meal and eat it

rest·ful /ˈrɛstfl/ *adjective*
making you feel relaxed and calm: *a restful weekend*

rest·less /ˈrɛstləs/ *adjective*
not able to stay still or relax because you are bored or nervous: *The kids always get restless on long drives.*

re·store **AWL** /rɪˈstɔr/ *verb* (**re·stores**, **re·stor·ing**, **re·stored**)
to make something as good as it was before: *The old hotel has been restored.*
▸ **res·to·ra·tion** **AWL** /ˌrɛstəˈreɪʃn/ *noun* [count, noncount]: *an historic house in need of restoration*

re·strain **AWL** /rɪˈstreɪn/ *verb* (**re·strains**, **re·strain·ing**, **re·strained**)
to stop someone or something from doing something; to control someone or something: *I couldn't restrain my anger.*

re·strict **AWL** /rɪˈstrɪkt/ *verb* (**re·stricts**, **re·strict·ing**, **re·strict·ed**)
to allow only a certain amount, size, sort, etc.: *Our house is very small, so we had to restrict the number of people we invited to the party.* ⊃ **SYNONYM limit**

re·stric·tion **AWL** /rɪˈstrɪkʃn/ *noun* [count]
a rule to control someone or something: *There are a lot of parking restrictions downtown.*

rest·room /ˈrɛstrum/ *noun* [count]
a room with a toilet in a public place, for example a restaurant or theater

re·sult¹ /rɪˈzʌlt/ *noun* [count]
1 something that happens because of something else: *The accident was a result of bad driving.* • *I woke up late and was late for school **as a result**.*
2 the score at the end of a game, competition, or exam: *election results* • *When will you know your exam results?*

re·sult² /rɪˈzʌlt/ *verb* (**re·sults**, **re·sult·ing**, **re·sult·ed**)
result in something to make something happen: *The accident resulted in the death of two drivers.* ⊃ **SYNONYM cause**

re·sume /rɪˈzum/ *verb* (**re·sumes**, **re·sum·ing**, **re·sumed**) (*formal*)
to start something again after stopping for a period of time: *to resume negotiations*

ré·su·mé (also **re·su·me**) /ˈrɛzəmeɪ/ *noun* [count]
a written list of your education and work experience that you send when you are trying to

ə **about**   y **yes**   w **woman**   ţ **butter**   eɪ **say**   aɪ **five**   ɔɪ **boy**   aʊ **now**   oʊ **go** get a new job: *To apply for the job, send your résumé and cover letter to Judy Williams.*

re·tail¹ /'riteɪl/ *noun* [noncount]
(**BUSINESS**) the business of selling goods to people in stores, etc.: *the recommended retail price*

re·tail² /'riteɪl/ *verb* (re·tails, re·tail·ing, re·tailed)
(**BUSINESS**) to be sold at a particular price: *This camera retails for $199.99.*

re·tail·er /'riteɪlər/ *noun* [count]
(**BUSINESS**) a person or company that sells things to people: *a furniture retailer* ◆ *Online retailers (= who sell on the Internet) often have the best prices.*

re·tain **AWL** /rɪ'teɪn/ *verb* (re·tains, re·tain·ing, re·tained) (*formal*)
to keep or continue to have something: *The Democrats retained control of the Senate after the election.*

re·tal·i·ate /rɪ'tælieɪt/ *verb* (re·tal·i·ates, re·tal·i·at·ing, re·tal·i·at·ed)
to do something bad to someone because they did something bad done to you: *to retaliate against an attack*

ret·i·na /'rɛtn·ə/ *noun* [count]
(**BIOLOGY**) the part of your eye that sends an image of what you see to your brain

re·tire /rɪ'taɪər/ *verb* (re·tires, re·tir·ing, re·tired)
to stop working because you are a certain age: *My grandfather retired when he was 65.*
▶ **re·tired** /rɪ'taɪərd/ *adjective*: *a retired teacher*

re·tire·ment /rɪ'taɪərmənt/ *noun* [noncount]
the time in a person's life after they have reached a certain age and have stopped working: *We all wish you a long and happy retirement.*

re·treat /rɪ'trit/ *verb* (re·treats, re·treat·ing, re·treat·ed)
to move back or away from someone or something, for example because you have lost a fight: *The enemy is retreating.*
▶ **re·treat** *noun* [count, noncount]: *The army is now in retreat.*

re·turn¹ 🔊 /rɪ'tərn/ *verb* (re·turns, re·turn·ing, re·turned)
1 to come or go back to a place: *They returned from California last week.*
2 to give, put, send, or take something back: *Will you return this book to the library?*

re·turn² 🔊 /rɪ'tərn/ *noun*
1 [singular] coming or going back to a place: *the talk show host's return to daytime TV*
2 [noncount] giving, putting, sending, or taking something back: *the return of the stolen money*

in return as a way of thanking someone for something they have done for you or paying them for something they have given you: *Can I buy you lunch in return for all your help?*

re·un·ion /ri'yunyən/ *noun* [count]
a meeting of people who have not seen each other for a long time: *We had a family reunion on my aunt's birthday.* ◆ *a high school reunion*

re·u·nite /ˌriyu'naɪt/ *verb* (re·u·nites, re·u·nit·ing, re·u·nit·ed)
to come together or to bring people together again: *The missing child was found and reunited with his parents.*

Rev. abbreviation of **Reverend**

re·veal **AWL** /rɪ'vil/ *verb* (re·veals, re·veal·ing, re·vealed)
to tell something that was a secret or show something that was hidden: *She refused to reveal any names to the police.*

re·venge /rɪ'vɛndʒ/ *noun* [noncount]
something bad that you do to someone who has done something bad to you: *He wants to take his revenge on the judge who sent him to prison.*

rev·e·nue **AWL** /'rɛvənu/ *noun* [noncount]
(**BUSINESS**) money that a government receives from taxes, or a company receives from its business: *Revenue from income tax rose last year.*

Rev·er·end /'rɛvərənd/ *adjective* (abbreviation **Rev.**)
(**RELIGION**) the title of a Christian priest

re·ver·sal **AWL** /rɪ'vərsl/ *noun* [count, noncount]
the action of changing something to the opposite of what it was before: *This is a complete reversal of your recent decision.*

re·verse¹ **AWL** /rɪ'vərs/ *verb* (re·vers·es, re·vers·ing, re·versed)
to change a decision or process to the opposite: *The court reversed the decision.*

re·verse² **AWL** /rɪ'vərs/ *noun* [noncount]
1 the complete opposite of what someone just said, or of what you expect: *It should have been a relaxing vacation, but it was just the reverse.*
2 the control in a car or other vehicle that allows it to move backward: *Put the car in reverse, and back into the parking space.*

re·view¹ /rɪ'vyu/ *noun*
1 [count, noncount] looking at something or thinking about something again to see if it needs changing: *There will be a review of your contract after six months.*
2 [count] a piece of writing in a newspaper or magazine that says what someone thinks about a book, movie, play, etc.: *The movie got very good reviews.*

re·view² /rɪˈvyu/ *verb* (re·views, re·view·ing, re·viewed)
1 to look at something or think about something again to see if it needs changing: *Your salary will be reviewed after one year.*
2 to study something to make sure you remember it or understand it: *Let's review what we've studied so far.* ◆ *She reviewed her notes before the meeting.*
3 to write about a new book, movie, etc., giving your opinion of it: *The play was reviewed in yesterday's newspaper.*

re·view·er /rɪˈvyuər/ *noun* [count]
a person who writes about new books, movies, games, etc.

re·vise **AWL** /rɪˈvaɪz/ *verb* (re·vis·es, re·vis·ing, re·vised)
to change something to make it better or more correct: *The book has been revised for this new edition.*
▸ **re·vi·sion** **AWL** /rɪˈvɪʒn/ *noun* [count, noncount]: *The whole system is in need of revision.* ◆ *Several revisions have been made.*

re·vive /rɪˈvaɪv/ *verb* (re·vives, re·viv·ing, re·vived)
to become or make someone or something well or strong again: *They tried to revive him, but he was already dead.*

re·volt /rɪˈvoʊlt/ *verb* (re·volts, re·volt·ing, re·volt·ed)
to fight against the people in control: *The army is **revolting against** the government.*
▸ **re·volt** *noun* [count, noncount]: *The army quickly stopped the revolt.*

rev·o·lu·tion **AWL** /ˌrɛvəˈluʃn/ *noun* [count]
1 (POLITICS) a fight by people against their government in order to put a new government in its place: *The American Revolution was in the late 18th century.*
2 a big change in the way of doing things: *the Industrial Revolution*

rev·o·lu·tion·ar·y **AWL** /ˌrɛvəˈluʃnˌɛri/ *adjective*
1 (POLITICS) connected with a political REVOLUTION(1)
2 producing great changes; very new and different: *a revolutionary new idea to reduce carbon emissions*

rev·o·lu·tion·ize **AWL** /ˌrɛvəˈluʃnˌaɪz/ *verb* (rev·o·lu·tion·iz·es, rev·o·lu·tion·iz·ing, rev·o·lu·tion·ized)
to change something completely, usually making it better: *a discovery that could revolutionize the treatment of cancer*

re·volve /rɪˈvɑlv/ *verb* (re·volves, re·volv·ing, re·volved)
to move around in a circle: *The earth **revolves around** the sun.*

re·volv·er /rɪˈvɑlvər/ *noun* [count]
a type of small gun

re·ward¹ /rɪˈwɔrd/ *noun*
1 [count, noncount] something that someone gives you because you have done something good or worked hard: *My mom bought me a new cell phone as a reward for working hard in school.*
2 [count] money that someone gives you for helping the police, finding something that was lost, etc.: *She is offering a $100 reward to anyone who finds her dog.*

re·ward² /rɪˈwɔrd/ *verb* (re·wards, re·ward·ing, re·ward·ed)
to give something to someone because they have done something well or worked hard: *His company rewarded him with a bonus at the end of the year.*

re·ward·ing /rɪˈwɔrdɪŋ/ *adjective*
making you feel satisfied or happy because you think it is important or useful: *Teaching doesn't pay well, but it's very rewarding.*

re·wind /ˌriˈwaɪnd/ *verb* (re·winds, re·wind·ing, re·wound /ˌriˈwaʊnd/, has re·wound)
to make a video or music tape go backward: *Rewind the video – I want to see that touchdown again!*

re·write /ˌriˈraɪt/ *verb* (re·writes, re·writ·ing, re·wrote /ˌriˈroʊt/, has re·writ·ten /ˌriˈrɪtn/)
(ENGLISH LANGUAGE ARTS) to write something again in a different or better way: *to rewrite an essay*

rhe·tor·i·cal ques·tion /rɪˌtɔrɪkl ˈkwɛstʃən/ *noun* [count]
(ENGLISH LANGUAGE ARTS) a question that does not expect an answer

rhi·no /ˈraɪnoʊ/ *noun* [count] (plural rhi·nos)
(informal) short for **rhinoceros**

rhi·noc·er·os
/raɪˈnɑsərəs/ *noun* [count] (plural rhi·noc·er·os or rhi·noc·er·os·es)
a big, wild animal from Africa or Asia, with thick skin and a horn on its nose

rhinoceros

rhom·bus /ˈrɑmbəs/ *noun* [count] (plural rhom·bus·es)
(MATH) a flat shape with four sides that are the same length and four angles that are not 90°

rhombus

rhyme¹ /raɪm/ *noun* [count] (**ENGLISH LANGUAGE ARTS**)
1 a word that has the same sound as another word, for example "bell" and "well"
2 a short piece of writing where the lines end with the same sounds: *a children's rhyme*

rhyme² /raɪm/ *verb* (rhymes, rhym·ing, rhymed) (**ENGLISH LANGUAGE ARTS**)
1 to have the same sound as another word: *"Chair" rhymes with "bear."*
2 to have lines that end with the same sounds: *This poem doesn't rhyme.*

rhythm /ˈrɪðəm/ *noun* [count]
(**MUSIC**) a regular pattern of sounds that come again and again: *This music has a good rhythm.*

rhythm and blues /ˌrɪðəm ən ˈbluz/ *noun* [noncount] (abbreviation **R & B**)
(**MUSIC**) a type of popular music that has a strong beat. It is a mixture of two different styles of music (called BLUES and JAZZ).

rib /rɪb/ *noun* [count]
1 one of the bones around your chest ⊃ Look at the picture at **skeleton**.
2 a piece of meat with one or more bones from the **ribs** of a cow or a pig: *barbecued ribs*

rib·bon /ˈrɪbən/ *noun* [count]
1 a long, thin piece of material for tying things or making something look pretty: *She wore a pink ribbon in her hair.*
2 a piece of **ribbon** that is given as a prize in a competition: *Carol's apple pie won a blue ribbon (= first prize) at the county fair.*

rib cage /ˈrɪb keɪdʒ/ *noun* [count]
(**BIOLOGY**) the structure of curved bones (called RIBS) around your chest

rice /raɪs/ *noun* [noncount]
short, thin, white or brown grain from a plant that grows on wet land in hot countries. We cook and eat **rice**: *Would you like rice or potatoes with your chicken?*

rich /rɪtʃ/ *adjective* (rich·er, rich·est)
1 having a lot of money: *a rich family* ⋆ *It's a favorite resort for the rich (= people who are rich) and famous.* ⊃ **ANTONYM poor**
2 containing a lot of something: *Oranges are rich in vitamin C.*
3 Food that is **rich** has a lot of fat or sugar in it and makes you feel full quickly: *a rich chocolate cake*

rid /rɪd/ *adjective*
get rid of someone or **something** to make yourself free of someone or something that you do not want: *This dog is following me – I can't get rid of it.* ⋆ *I got rid of my old coat and bought a new one.*

rid·den form of **ride¹**

rid·dle /ˈrɪdl/ *noun* [count]
a difficult question that has a funny answer: *Here's a riddle: What has four legs but can't walk? The answer is a chair!*

ride¹ /raɪd/ *verb* (rides, rid·ing, rode /roʊd/, has rid·den /ˈrɪdn/)
1 to sit on a horse or bicycle and control it as it moves: *I'm learning how to ride (= a horse).* ⋆ *Don't ride your bike on the grass!*
2 to travel in a car, bus, or train: *He's too young to ride in the front seat.*

ride² /raɪd/ *noun* [count]
1 a trip on a horse or bicycle, or in a car, bus, or train: *We went for a bike ride.* ⋆ *Can I have a ride home after class tonight?*
2 a large machine that people ride on for fun: *I can't wait to go on the rides at the school fair.*

rid·er /ˈraɪdər/ *noun* [count]
a person who rides a horse or bicycle

ridge /rɪdʒ/ *noun* [count]
(**GEOGRAPHY**) a long, thin part of something that is higher than the rest, for example along the top of hills or mountains: *We walked along the ridge looking down at the valley below.*

ri·dic·u·lous /rɪˈdɪkyələs/ *adjective*
so silly that it makes people laugh: *I look ridiculous in this hat.*
▶ **ri·dic·u·lous·ly** /rɪˈdɪkyələsli/ *adverb*: *It's ridiculously expensive.*

rid·ing /ˈraɪdɪŋ/ *noun* [noncount]
the sport of riding a horse ⊃ **SYNONYM horseback riding**

ri·fle /ˈraɪfl/ *noun* [count]
a long gun that you hold against your shoulder to shoot with

right¹ /raɪt/ *adjective*
1 correct or true: *That's not the right answer.* ⋆ *"Are you Mr. Johnson?" "Yes, that's right."* ⊃ **ANTONYM wrong**
2 best: *Is she the right person for the job?* ⊃ **ANTONYM wrong**
3 good; fair or what the law allows: *It's not right to leave young children alone in the house.* ⊃ **ANTONYM wrong**
4 on or of the side of the body that faces east when a person faces north: *Most people write with their right hand.* ⊃ **ANTONYM left**

right² /raɪt/ *adverb*
1 exactly: *He was sitting right next to me.*
2 correctly: *Have I spelled your name right?* ⊃ **ANTONYM wrong**
3 all the way; completely: *Go right to the end of the road.*
4 to the right side: *Turn right at the end of street.* ⊃ **ANTONYM left**

5 immediately: *Wait here – I'll be* **right back.** ◆ *Call the doctor* **right away.**

right now
1 at this moment; exactly now: *We can't discuss this right now.*
2 around the present time: *Many people are unemployed right now.*

right³ 🔊 /raɪt/ *noun*
1 [*singular*] the right side or direction: *We live in the first house* **on the right.** ⟳ ANTONYM **left**
2 [*count*] what you are allowed to do, especially by law: *In the U.S., everyone* **has the right to** *a fair trial.*
3 [*noncount*] what is good or fair: *Young children have to learn the difference between right and wrong.* ⟳ ANTONYM **wrong**
4 the right [*singular*] (POLITICS) political groups who do not support many or sudden changes in society: *The right is opposed to the tax increase.* ⟳ ANTONYM **the left**

right an·gle /'raɪt æŋgl/ *noun* [*count*]
(MATH) an angle of 90 degrees. A square has four **right angles.** ⟳ Look at the picture at **angle.**

right-hand /ˌraɪt 'hænd/ *adjective*
of or on the right: *The supermarket is on the* **right-hand side** *of the road.*

right-hand·ed /ˌraɪt 'hændəd/ *adjective*
If you are **right-handed,** you use your right hand more easily than your left hand, for example for writing.

right·ly /'raɪtli/ *adverb*
correctly: *If I remember rightly, the party is on June 15th.*

right-wing /ˌraɪt 'wɪŋ/ *adjective*
(POLITICS) having political ideas that support low taxes and few changes in society: *right-wing politics* ⟳ ANTONYM **left-wing**

rig·id AWL /'rɪdʒɪd/ *adjective*
1 not able or not wanting to be changed: *The school has very rigid rules.*
2 hard and not easy to bend or move: *She was rigid with fear.*

rig·or·ous /'rɪgərəs/ *adjective*
careful, with a lot of attention to detail: *Rigorous tests have been done to make sure the drinking water is safe.*
▶ **rig·or·ous·ly**
/'rɪgərəsli/ *adverb*:
The software has been rigorously checked.

rim /rɪm/ *noun* [*count*]
the edge of something round: *the rim of a cup*

rim

| rim

rind /raɪnd/ *noun* [*count*]
the thick, hard skin of some fruits or cheeses: *lemon rind*

ring¹ 🔊 /rɪŋ/ *noun* [*count*]
1 a circle of metal that you wear on your finger: *a wedding ring* ⟳ Look at the picture at **jewelry.**
2 a circle: *The coffee cup left a ring on the table.*
3 a space with seats around it, used for a competition or a performance: *a boxing ring*
4 the sound that a bell makes: *There was a ring at the door.*

ring² 🔊 /rɪŋ/ *verb* (rings, ring·ing, rang /ræŋ/, has rung /rʌŋ/)
1 to make a sound like a bell: *My phone is ringing.*
2 to press or move a bell so that it makes a sound: *We rang the doorbell again but no one answered.*
ring a bell (*informal*) to sound familiar: *"Do you know Chris Oliver?" "The name rings a bell."*

ring·tone /'rɪŋtoʊn/ *noun* [*count*]
the sound a cell phone makes when someone is calling you: *You can download ringtones from the Internet.*

rink /rɪŋk/ *noun* [*count*]
1 short for **ice rink**
2 short for **skating rink**

rinse /rɪns/ *verb* (rins·es, rins·ing, rinsed)
to wash something with water to take away dirt or soap: *Wash your hair and rinse it well.*

ri·ot /'raɪət/ *noun* [*count*]
when a group of people fight and make a lot of noise and trouble: *Riots have broken out downtown.*
▶ **ri·ot** *verb* (ri·ots, ri·ot·ing, ri·ot·ed): *The prisoners are rioting.*

rip /rɪp/ *verb* (rips, rip·ping, ripped)
to pull or tear something quickly and suddenly: *I ripped my shirt on a nail.* ◆ *Joe* **ripped** *the letter* **open.**
rip someone off (*informal*) to cheat someone by making them pay too much for something: *Tourists complained that they were being ripped off by local taxi drivers.* ⟳ The noun is **rip-off.**
rip something up to tear something into small pieces: *She ripped up the photo.*

ripe /raɪp/ *adjective* (rip·er, rip·est)
Fruit that is **ripe** is ready to eat: *These bananas aren't ripe – they're still green.*

rip-off /'rɪp ɔf/ *noun* [*count*] (*informal*)
something that costs a lot more than it should: *$70 for a T-shirt! What a rip-off!*

rip·ple /'rɪpl/ *noun* [*count*]
a small wave or movement on the surface of water

► **rip·ple** *verb* (rip·ples, rip·pling, rip·pled)
to move in small waves

rise¹ 🔑 /raɪz/ *noun* [count]
when the amount, number, or level of
something goes up: *There has been **a sharp rise
in** the price of oil.* • *a rise in unemployment* ⊃
SYNONYM increase ⊃ **ANTONYM fall**

rise² 🔑 /raɪz/ *verb* (ris·es, ris·ing, rose /roʊz/,
has ris·en /'rɪzn/)
1 to go up; to become higher or more: *Smoke
was rising from the chimney.* • *Prices have risen
by 20%.*
2 to get up from a sitting or lying position: *She
rose to her feet.*
3 If the sun or moon rises, it moves up in the
sky: *The sun rises in the east, and sets* (= goes
down) *in the west.*

risk¹ 🔑 /rɪsk/ *noun* [count]
the possibility that something bad may happen;
a dangerous situation: *Smoking can increase the
risk of heart disease.*
at risk in danger: *Children are most at risk from
this disease.*
take a risk or **risks** to do something when you
know that something bad may happen because
of it: *Don't take risks when you're driving.*

risk² 🔑 /rɪsk/ *verb* (risks, risk·ing, risked)
1 to put something or yourself in danger: *He
risked his life to save the child from the burning
house.*
2 to do something when you know that
something bad may happen because of it: *If you
don't work harder, you risk failing the exam.*

risk·y /'rɪski/ *adjective* (risk·i·er, risk·i·est)
dangerous

rit·u·al /'rɪtʃuəl/ *noun* [count, noncount]
(**RELIGION**) an action, a ceremony, or a process
which is usually done the same way: *religious
rituals*

ri·val /'raɪvl/ *noun* [count]
a person who wants to do better than you, or
who is trying to take what you want: *Today the
New York Yankees are playing their main rivals,
the Boston Red Sox.*

ri·val·ry /'raɪvlri/ *noun* [count, noncount] (*plural*
ri·val·ries)
a situation in which people are trying to do
better than each other, or trying to be the first to
do or get something: *There was a lot of rivalry
between the sisters.*

riv·er 🔑 /'rɪvər/ *noun* [count]
(**GEOGRAPHY**) a long, wide line of water that flows
into the ocean or a lake: *the Shenandoah River*

roach /roʊtʃ/ *noun* [count] (*plural* roach·es)
(*informal*) = **cockroach**

road 🔑 /roʊd/ *noun* [count]
the way from one place to another, where cars
can go: *Will this road to take me to the highway?* •
*Route 27 is the **main road** into the city.*
on the road traveling for a long distance: *We
were on the road for 14 hours.*

Thesaurus

road a hard surface made for vehicles to
travel on. The short way of writing "Road" in
addresses is **Rd.**: *My address is 32 Danfield
Rd., St Louis.* • *country/mountain roads* •
Where does this road go? • *I live on a very
busy road.* • *Take the first road on the left.*
street a road in a city or town that has
buildings on one or both sides. The short
way of writing "Street" in addresses is **St.**:
1281 Tobin St. • *a street map of San
Francisco* • *You can't drive down there. It's a
one-way street.* • *They live across the street
from us.*
highway a big road that connects cities and
towns: *Highway 101 between Ventura and
Los Angeles* • *Take the highway to Flagstaff.*
• *There was a traffic jam on the highway.*
lane one part of a larger road, marked with
painted lines to keep lines of traffic
separate: *a four-lane highway* • *You're in the
wrong lane for turning right.*
avenue a wide street in a city or town. This
word is often used in the names of city
streets, and can be written as **Ave.**: *109
Fifth Ave.* • *We stayed at a hotel on
Lexington Avenue.*

road trip /'roʊd trɪp/ *noun* [count] (*informal*)
a long trip made in a car

roam /roʊm/ *verb* (roams, roam·ing, roamed)
to walk or travel with no special plan: *Dogs were
roaming the streets looking for food.*

roar¹ /rɔr/ *verb* (roars, roar·ing, roared)
to make a loud, deep sound: *The lion roared.* •
*Everyone **roared with laughter**.*

roar² /rɔr/ *noun* [count]
a loud, deep sound: *the lion gave a huge roar* •
the roar of an airplane's engines

roast /roʊst/ *verb* (roasts, roast·ing, roast·ed)
to cook or be cooked in an oven or over a fire:
Roast the chicken in a hot oven. ⊃ Look at the note
at **cook¹**.
► **roast** *adjective*: *roast beef*

rob 🔑 /rɑb/ *verb* (robs, rob·bing, robbed)
to take something that is not yours from a
person or place: *They robbed a bank.* ⊃ Look at the
note at **steal**.

rob·ber /ˈrɑbər/ *noun* [count]
a person who steals things from a person or a place: *a bank robber* ⊃ Look at the note at **thief**.

rob·ber·y /ˈrɑbəri/ *noun* [count, noncount] (*plural* **rob·ber·ies**)
taking something that is not yours from a person or a place: *What time did the robbery take place?*

robe /roʊb/ *noun* [count]
1 a long, loose thing that you wear on your body, for example at a special ceremony: *a judge's robe*
2 a piece of clothing like a loose coat with a belt, which you wear before or after a bath, before you get dressed in the morning, etc.: *I was still in my robe when the doorbell rang.* ⊃ SYNONYM **bathrobe**

rob·in /ˈrɑbən/ *noun* [count]
a small brown bird with a red front

robin

ro·bot /ˈroʊbɑt/ *noun* [count]
a machine that can work like a person: *This car was built by robots.*

rock¹ 🔊 /rɑk/ *noun*
1 [noncount] the very hard material that is in the ground and in mountains
2 [count] a big piece of rock: *The ship hit the rocks.*
3 (also **rock mu·sic**) [noncount] (MUSIC) a type of popular music with a strong beat: *a radio station that plays classic rock*

rock² /rɑk/ *verb* (**rocks**, **rock·ing**, **rocked**)
to move slowly backward and forward or from side to side; to make someone or something do this: *The boat was rocking gently on the lake.* ◆ *I rocked the baby until she went to sleep.*

rock and roll /ˌrɑk ənd ˈroʊl/ (also **rock 'n' roll** /ˌrɑkn̩ˈroʊl/) *noun* [noncount]
(MUSIC) a type of music with a strong beat that was most popular in the 1950s

rock·et /ˈrɑkət/ *noun* [count]
1 a vehicle that is used for traveling into space: *to launch a rocket* ◆ *a space rocket*
2 a weapon that travels through the air and carries a bomb ⊃ SYNONYM **missile**
3 an object that shoots high into the air and then explodes with bright lights in different colors (a type of FIREWORK)

rock mu·sic /ˈrɑk ˌmyuzɪk/ = **rock¹**(3)

rock·y /ˈrɑki/ *adjective* (**rock·i·er**, **rock·i·est**)
with a lot of rocks: *a rocky path*

rod /rɑd/ *noun* [count]
a long, thin, straight piece of wood or metal: *a fishing rod*

rode form of **ride¹**

ro·dent /ˈroʊdnt/ *noun* [count]
a type of small animal that has strong, sharp front teeth, for example a mouse or a RAT

ro·de·o /ˈroʊdioʊ; roʊˈdeɪoʊ/ *noun* [count] (*plural* **ro·de·os**)
a competition in which people ride wild horses, catch cows with a rope, etc.

role 🔊 AWL /roʊl/ *noun* [count]
1 what a person does, for example in an organization or a relationship: *Your role is to welcome guests as they arrive.*
2 a person's part in a play or movie: *He played the role of the king.*

role mod·el /ˈroʊl ˌmɑdl/ *noun* [count]
a person that you admire and try to copy

roll¹ 🔊 /roʊl/ *noun* [count]
1 something made into a long, round shape by turning it around itself many times: *a roll of toilet paper*
2 a small, round piece of bread made for one person: *a basket of warm rolls*

rolls

roll² 🔊 /roʊl/ *verb* (**rolls**, **roll·ing**, **rolled**)
1 to move along by turning over and over; to make something move in this way: *The pencil rolled off the table onto the floor.* ◆ *We rolled the rock down the path.*
2 to turn your body over when you are lying down: *She **rolled over** onto her back.*
3 to move on wheels: *The car rolled down the hill.*
4 to make something into a long, round shape or the shape of a ball: *Can you help me **roll up** this rug?*
5 to make something flat by moving something heavy on top of it: *Roll the dough into a large circle.*

Roll·er·blade™ /ˈroʊlərbleɪd/ *noun* [count]
a boot with a line of small wheels on the bottom ⊃ SYNONYM **in-line skate** ⊃ Look at **roller skate**.
▸ **Roll·er·blad·ing** /ˈroʊlərbleɪdɪŋ/ *noun* [noncount]: *to go Rollerblading*

roll·er coast·er /ˈroʊlər koʊstər/ *noun* [count]
a small train on a metal track that goes up and down and around bends, which people ride on for fun

roll·er skate /ˈroʊlər skeɪt/ (also **skate**) *noun* [count]
a boot with small wheels on the bottom ⊃ Look at the picture at **skate**.
▸ **roll·er-skating** /ˈroʊlər ˌskeɪtɪŋ/ (also **skating**) *noun* [noncount]: *When we were kids, we used to **go roller-skating** every weekend.*

Ro·man /ˈroʊmən/ *adjective*
(**HISTORY**) connected with ancient Rome: *the remains of a Roman villa*
▶ **Ro·man** *noun* [count]

Ro·man Cath·o·lic /ˌroʊmən ˈkæθlɪk/ *noun* [count], *adjective* (**RELIGION**) = **Catholic**

ro·mance /roʊˈmæns; ˈroʊmæns/ *noun*
1 [noncount] a time when two people are in love: *The article suggests ways to put the romance back into your marriage.*
2 [count] (**ENGLISH LANGUAGE ARTS**) a story about love: *She writes romances.*

Ro·man nu·mer·al /ˌroʊmən ˈnumərəl/ *noun* [count]
one of the letters that were used in Roman times as numbers: *The number 16 is XVI in Roman numerals.*

ro·man·tic 🖋 /roʊˈmæntɪk/ *adjective*
about love; full of feelings of love: *a romantic dinner*

roof 🖋 /ruf/ *noun* [count] (*plural* **roofs**)
the top of a building or car, which covers it

rook·ie /ˈrʊki/ *noun* [count]
a person who has just started doing a job or playing a professional sport: *a rookie police officer*

room 🖋 /rum/ *noun*
1 [count] one of the spaces in a building that has walls around it: *How many rooms do you have in your house?* • *a classroom*
2 [noncount] space; enough space: *There's no room for you in the car.*

room·mate /ˈrumˌmeɪt/ *noun* [count]
a person that you share a room, an apartment, or a house with: *Joey was my college roommate.*

roost·er /ˈrustər/ *noun* [count]
an adult male chicken
➷ Look at the note at **chicken**.

rooster

root 🖋 /rut/ *noun* [count]
the part of a plant that is under the ground ➷ Look at the picture at **plant**.

root beer /ˈrut bɪr/ *noun* [count]
a type of sweet, brown drink that has bubbles in it, but no alcohol

rope 🖋 /roʊp/ *noun* [count]
very thick, strong string

rope

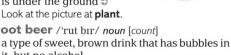

rose¹ form of **rise²**

rose² /roʊz/ *noun* [count]
a flower with a sweet smell. It grows on a bush that has sharp points (called **THORNS**) on it. ➷ Look at the picture at **flower**.

ros·y /ˈroʊzi/ *adjective* (**ros·i·er**, **ros·i·est**)
pink and looking healthy: *rosy cheeks*

rot /rɑt/ *verb* (**rots**, **rot·ting**, **rot·ted**)
to become bad and soft, as things do when they die: *the smell of rotting fruit* ➷ **SYNONYM decay**

ro·tate /ˈroʊteɪt/ *verb* (**ro·tates**, **ro·tat·ing**, **ro·tat·ed**)
to move in circles: *The earth rotates around the sun.*
▶ **ro·ta·tion** /roʊˈteɪʃn/ *noun* [count, noncount]: *the rotation of the earth*

rot·ten /ˈrɑtn/ *adjective*
1 old and not fresh; bad: *These eggs are rotten – they smell awful!*
2 (*informal*) very bad; not nice: *That was a rotten thing to say!*

rough 🖋 /rʌf/ *adjective* (**rough·er**, **rough·est**)

> **ⓘ PRONUNCIATION**
> The word **rough** sounds like **stuff**, because sometimes the letters **-gh** sound like **f**, in words like **enough** and **tough**.

1 not smooth or flat: *It was difficult to walk on the rough ground.*
2 not gentle or calm: *a rough neighborhood* (= where there is a lot of crime) • *The ferry was canceled because the ocean was too rough.*
3 not exactly correct; made or done quickly: *Can you give me a rough idea how much it will cost?* • *a rough drawing*

rough·ly /ˈrʌfli/ *adverb*
1 about; not exactly: *The drive should take roughly two hours.* ➷ **SYNONYM approximately** ➷ **ANTONYM exactly**
2 not gently: *He pushed me away roughly.*

round¹ 🖋 /raʊnd/ *adjective*
having the shape of a circle or a ball: *a round table*

round² /raʊnd/ *noun* [count]
1 a number or set of events: *another round of peace talks*
2 a lot of visits, one after another, for example as part of your job: *The mail carrier starts his round at seven o'clock.*
3 one part of a game or competition: *the third round of the boxing match*

round-trip /ˈraʊnd trɪp/ *adjective*
for a trip to a place and back again: *How much is a round-trip ticket to Portland?* ➷ Look at **one-way**.

route 🖋 **AWL** /rut; raʊt/ *noun* [count]
a way from one place to another: *What is the quickest route from Philadelphia to Boston?*

rou·tine¹ /ru'tin/ *noun* [*count*]
your usual way of doing things: *Make exercise a part of your **daily routine.***

rou·tine² /ru'tin/ *adjective*
normal and regular: *a routine medical exam*

row¹ 🔊 /roʊ/ *noun* [*count*]

> ⓘ **PRONUNCIATION**
> The word **row** sounds like **no.**

a line of people or things: *We sat in the **front row** of the theater* (= the front line of seats). ◆ *a **row** of books*
in a row one after another: *It rained for four days in a row.*

row² /roʊ/ *verb* (rows, row·ing, rowed)
to move a boat through water using long pieces of wood with flat ends (called **OARS**): *We rowed across the lake.*
▸ **row·ing** /'roʊwɪŋ/ *noun* [*noncount*]: *a rowing machine*

rowboat

row·boat /'roʊboʊt/ *noun* [*count*]
a small boat that you move through water using long, thin pieces of wood with flat ends (called **OARS**)

row·dy /'raʊdi/ *adjective* (row·di·er, row·di·est)
(used about people) noisy and likely to cause trouble: *The crowd was getting rowdy.*

roy·al 🔊 /'rɔɪəl/ *adjective*
(**POLITICS**) connected with a king or queen: *the royal family*

roy·al·ty /'rɔɪəlti/ *noun* [*noncount*]
kings, queens, and their families

RSVP /ˌɑr ɛs vi 'pi/ *abbreviation*
You write **RSVP** on an invitation to mean "please reply."

rub 🔊 /rʌb/ *verb* (rubs, rub·bing, rubbed)
to move something backward and forward on another thing: *I rubbed my hands together to keep them warm.* ◆ *The cat rubbed its head against my leg.*

rub·ber 🔊 /'rʌbər/ *noun* [*noncount*]
a strong material that we use to make things like car tires: *a pair of rubber gloves*

rub·ber band /ˌrʌbər 'bænd/ *noun* [*count*]
a thin circle of rubber that you use for holding things together

ru·by /'rubi/ *noun* [*count*] (*plural* ru·bies)
a dark red stone that is used in jewelry: *a ruby ring*

rud·der /'rʌdər/ *noun* [*count*]
a flat piece of wood or metal at the back of a boat or an airplane. It moves to make the boat or airplane go left or right.

rude 🔊 /rud/ *adjective* (rud·er, rud·est)
not polite: *It's rude to walk away when someone is talking to you.* ⊃ **SYNONYM impolite**
▸ **rude·ly** /'rudli/ *adverb*: *"Shut up!" she said rudely.*
▸ **rude·ness** /'rudnəs/ *noun* [*noncount*]: *I would like to apologize for my rudeness.*

rug /rʌg/ *noun* [*count*]
a piece of thick material that you put on the floor ⊃ Look at **carpet**.

rug·by /'rʌgbi/ *noun* [*noncount*]
(**SPORTS**) a game like football for two teams of 13 or 15 players. In **rugby**, you can kick and carry the ball.

rug

rug·ged /'rʌgəd/ *adjective*
Rugged land is not smooth, and has a lot of rocks and not many plants on it.

ru·in¹ 🔊 /'ruɪn/ *verb* (ru·ins, ru·in·ing, ru·ined)
to damage something badly so that it is no longer good; to destroy something completely: *I spilled coffee on my jacket and ruined it.* ◆ *The rain ruined our picnic.*

ru·in² /'ruɪn/ *noun* [*count*]
a building that has been badly damaged: *The old castle is now a ruin.*
in ruins badly damaged or destroyed: *The city was in ruins after the war.*

rule¹ 🔊 /rul/ *noun*
1 [*count*] something that tells you what you must or must not do: *It's **against the rules** to smoke.* ◆ *to **break a rule*** (= do something that you should not do)
2 [*noncount*] government: *The country is **under** military **rule.***

rule² 🔊 /rul/ *verb* (rules, rul·ing, ruled)
(**POLITICS**) to control a country: *The queen ruled for many years.*

rul·er /'rulər/ *noun* [*count*]
1 a long piece of plastic, metal, or wood that you use for drawing straight lines or for measuring things ⊃ Look at the picture at **stationery**.
2 (**POLITICS**) a person who rules a country

rum /rʌm/ *noun* [*count, noncount*]
a strong alcoholic drink that is made from the sugar plant

rum·ble /'rʌmbl/ *verb* (rum·bles, rum·bling, rum·bled)
to make a long, deep sound: *I'm so hungry that my stomach is rumbling.*
▶ **rum·ble** *noun* [*singular*]: *a rumble of thunder*

ru·mor /'rumər/ *noun* [*count, noncount*]
something that a lot of people are talking about that is perhaps not true: *There's a rumor that our teacher is leaving.*

run¹ 🔑 /rʌn/ *verb* (runs, run·ning, ran /ræn/, has run)
1 to move very quickly on your legs: *I was late, so I ran to the bus stop.*
2 to control something and make it work: *Who runs the business?*
3 to work or make something work: *The car had stopped but the engine was still running.* ◆ *You can run this software on your home computer.*
4 to go; to make a trip: *The buses don't run on Sundays.*
5 to move something somewhere: *He ran his fingers through his hair.*
6 to pass or go somewhere: *The road runs across the fields.*
7 to flow: *The Mississippi River runs into the Gulf of Mexico.*
8 to be one of the people who is trying to win an election: *He ran for senator in Ohio.*
run after someone or **something** to try to catch a person or an animal: *The dog ran after a rabbit.* ⟳ SYNONYM **chase**
run away to go quickly away from a place: *She ran away from home when she was 14.* ⟳
SYNONYM **escape**
run into someone to meet someone by chance: *Guess who I ran into today?*
run into someone or **something** to crash into someone or something: *The bus went out of control and ran into a line of people.*
run out of something to have no more of something: *We've run out of coffee. Will you go and buy some?*
run over someone or **something** to hit a person or an animal with your car or other vehicle: *The dog was run over by a bus.*

run² 🔑 /rʌn/ *noun* [*count*]
1 an act of moving very quickly on your legs: *I go for a run every morning.*
2 (SPORTS) a point in the game of baseball: *Our team won by two runs.*

run-down /ˌrʌn 'daʊn/ *adjective*
1 (used about a building or place) in bad condition: *a run-down apartment building*

2 (HEALTH) (used about a person) very tired and not healthy, especially because you have been working too hard

rung¹ form of **ring²**

rung² /rʌŋ/ *noun* [*count*]
one of the steps of a LADDER (= a piece of equipment that is used for climbing up something) ⟳ Look at the picture at **ladder**.

run·ner /'rʌnər/ *noun* [*count*]
(SPORTS) a person who runs

run·ner-up /ˌrʌnər 'ʌp/ *noun* [*count*] (*plural* run·ners-up)
(SPORTS) a person or team that comes second in a race or competition

run·ning /'rʌnɪŋ/ *noun* [*noncount*]
(SPORTS) the sport of running: *Let's go running tomorrow morning.*

run·ny /'rʌni/ *adjective* (run·ni·er, run·ni·est)
1 If you have a **runny** nose, a lot of liquid comes out of it, for example because you have a cold.
2 If a substance is **runny**, it has more liquid than is usual: *The cake batter is too runny.*

run·way /'rʌnweɪ/ *noun* [*count*] (*plural* run·ways)
a long piece of ground where airplanes take off and land

ru·ral /'rʊrəl/ *adjective*
connected with the country, not the city: *rural areas* ⟳ Look at **urban**.

rush¹ 🔑 /rʌʃ/ *verb* (rush·es, rush·ing, rushed)
1 to move or do something very quickly or too quickly: *The children rushed out of school.* ◆ *We rushed to finish the work on time.*
2 to take someone or something quickly to a place: *She was rushed to the hospital.*
rush into something to do something without thinking about it enough first: *We shouldn't have rushed into buying this house.*

rush² /rʌʃ/ *noun* [*singular*]
1 a sudden quick movement: *At the end of the football game there was a rush for the exits.*
2 a situation when you need to move or do something very quickly: *I can't stop now – I'm in a rush.* ◆ *Don't eat so fast. There's no rush.* ⟳
SYNONYM **hurry**

rush hour /'rʌʃ ˌaʊər/ *noun* [*count*]
the time when the roads are busy because a lot of people are going to or coming from work

rust /rʌst/ *noun* [*noncount*]
(CHEMISTRY) a red-brown substance that you sometimes see on metal that has been wet
▶ **rust** *verb* (rusts, rust·ing, rust·ed): *My bike rusted because I left it out in the rain.*

rus·tle /'rʌsl/ *verb* (rus·tles, rus·tling, rus·tled)
to make a sound like dry leaves moving together; to make something make this sound:

Stop rustling your newspaper – I can't hear the radio!
▶ **rus·tle** *noun* [*singular*]: *the rustle of leaves*

rust·y /'rʌsti/ *adjective* (rust·i·er, rust·i·est)
(used about things made of metal) covered with a red-brown substance (called RUST) because it got wet: *a rusty nail*

rut /rʌt/ *noun* [*count*]
a deep track that a wheel makes in the ground
be in a rut to have a boring life that is difficult to change: *I quit my job because I felt I was stuck in a rut.*

ruth·less /'ruθləs/ *adjective*
hard and cruel; determined to get what you want without caring for others: *a ruthless dictator*
▶ **ruth·less·ly** /'ruθləsli/ *adverb*

rye /raɪ/ *noun* [*noncount*]
a plant that is grown for its grain, which is used to make flour and a type of alcoholic drink (called WHISKEY): *rye bread*

Ss

S, s /ɛs/ *noun* [*count, noncount*] (*plural* S's, s's /'ɛsəz/)
the nineteenth letter of the English alphabet: *"Sun" begins with an "S."*

the Sab·bath /ðə 'sæbəθ/ *noun* [*singular*]
(**RELIGION**) the day of the week for rest and prayer in some religions. This is usually Sunday for Christians and Saturday for Jews.

sack /sæk/ *noun* [*count*]
a big, strong bag for carrying heavy things: *a sack of potatoes*

sa·cred /'seɪkrəd/ *adjective*
(**RELIGION**) with a special religious meaning: *A church is a sacred building.*

sac·ri·fice¹ /'sækrəfaɪs/ *noun* [*count, noncount*]
1 when you stop doing or having something important so that you can get or do something else: *They made a lot of sacrifices to pay for their son to go to college.*
2 (**RELIGION**) an animal or other thing that is given to a god

sac·ri·fice² /'sækrəfaɪs/ *verb* (sac·ri·fic·es, sac·ri·fic·ing, sac·ri·ficed)
1 to stop doing or having something important so that you can help someone or to get something else: *During the war, many people sacrificed their lives for their country.*
2 (**RELIGION**) to kill an animal as a gift to a god: *They sacrificed a lamb.*

sad /sæd/ *adjective* (sad·der, sad·dest)
unhappy, or making you feel unhappy: *We are very sad to hear that you are leaving.* ◆ *a sad story*
▶ **sad·ness** /'sædnəs/ *noun* [*noncount, singular*]: *Thoughts of him filled her with sadness.*

sad·dle /'sædl/ *noun* [*count*]
a seat on a horse or bicycle ⊃ Look at the picture at **bicycle.**

sad·ly /'sædli/ *adverb*
1 in a sad way: *She looked sadly at the empty house.*
2 a word you use to show that you are not happy about a situation or fact: *Sadly, there was nothing we could do to help.* ⊃ **SYNONYM** **unfortunately**

sa·fa·ri /sə'fɑri/ *noun* [*count, noncount*] (*plural* sa·fa·ris)
a trip to look at or hunt wild animals, usually in Africa

safe¹ /seɪf/ *adjective* (saf·er, saf·est)
1 not in danger; not hurt: *Don't go out alone at night – you won't be safe.*

2 not dangerous: *Is it safe to swim in this river?* ◆ *Always keep medication in a safe place.*
safe and sound not hurt or broken: *The children were found safe and sound.*
▶ **safe·ly** /'seɪfli/ *adverb*: *Call your parents to tell them you arrived safely.*

safe² /seɪf/ *noun* [*count*]
a strong, metal box with a lock where you keep money or things like jewelry

safe·ty /'seɪfti/ *noun* [*noncount*]
being safe: *He is worried about the safety of his children.*

safe·ty belt /'seɪfti bɛlt/ *noun* [*count*]
a long, thin piece of material that you put around your body in a car or an airplane to keep you safe in an accident ⊃ **SYNONYM** **seat belt**

safe·ty pin /'seɪfti pɪn/ *noun* [*count*]
a pin that you use for joining pieces of cloth together. It has a cover over the point so that it is not dangerous.

safety pin

sag /sæg/ *verb* (sags, sag·ging, sagged)
to bend or hang down: *The bed is very old and it sags in the middle.*

said form of **say¹**

sail¹ /seɪl/ *verb* (sails, sail·ing, sailed)
1 to travel on water: *The ship sailed along the coast.*
2 to control a boat with sails: *We sailed the yacht down the river.*
▶ **sail·ing** /'seɪlɪŋ/ *noun* [*noncount*]
the sport of controlling a boat with sails: *We often go sailing on weekends.*

sail² /seɪl/ *noun* [*count*]
a big piece of cloth on a boat, which catches the wind and moves the boat along

sail·boat /'seɪlboʊt/ *noun* [*count*]
a boat that uses one or more **SAILS** to catch the wind

sail·or /'seɪlər/ *noun* [*count*]
a person who sails ships or boats as their job or as a sport

saint /seɪnt/ *noun* [*count*] (abbreviation **St.**)
(**RELIGION**) (in the Christian religion) a dead person who lived their life in a very good way: *Saint Nicholas* ◆ *St. Louis, Missouri*

sake /seɪk/ *noun*
for goodness' sake; for Heaven's sake (*informal*) something that you say to show you are angry or surprised
for the sake of someone or **something; for someone's** or **something's sake** to help someone or something; because of someone or

something: *The couple stayed together for the sake of their children.*

sal·ad 🔑 /'sæləd/ *noun* [*count, noncount*]
a dish of cold vegetables that have not been cooked: *Do you want soup or salad with your chicken?*

sal·ad dress·ing /'sæləd ˌdrɛsɪŋ/ (also **dress·ing**) *noun* [*count, noncount*]
a sauce used to add flavor to salads: *What type of dressing would you like on your salad?*

sa·la·mi /sə'lɑmi/ *noun* [*count, noncount*] (*plural* **sa·la·mis**)
a type of large SAUSAGE (= a mixture of meat and spices in a long shape) with a strong flavor, usually eaten in thin slices: *a salami sandwich*

sal·a·ry /'sæləri/ *noun* [*count, noncount*] (*plural* **sal·a·ries**)
money that you receive regularly for the work that you do: *How much is your annual salary?*

sale 🔑 /seɪl/ *noun*
1 [*count, noncount*] selling something: *The sale of alcohol to children is illegal.*
2 sales [*plural*] the number of items sold: *The company reported excellent sales figures.*
3 [*count*] a time when a store sells things for less money than usual: *I'm not going to buy a coat now – I'll wait until there's a sale.*
for sale If something is **for sale**, its owner wants to sell it: *Is this house for sale?*
on sale
1 offered at a lower price than usual: *I bought these shoes on sale for $75.*
2 available for someone to buy in stores: *Tickets for the concert go on sale tomorrow morning.*

sales·clerk /'seɪlzklərk/ (also **sales clerk**) *noun* [*count*]
a person whose job is to sell things to people in a store: *She worked as a salesclerk on the weekends.*

sales·man /'seɪlzmən/ *noun* [*count*] (*plural* **sales·men** /'seɪlzmən/)
a man whose job is to sell things

sales·per·son /'seɪlzpərsn/ *noun* [*count*] (*plural* **sales·peo·ple** /'seɪlzpipl/)
a man or a woman whose job is to sell things

sales rep·re·sen·ta·tive /'seɪlz rɛprɪˌzɛntətɪv/ (also *informal* **sales rep** /'seɪlz rɛp/) *noun* [*count*]
someone who works for a company and travels around a particular area selling the company's products: *a sales rep for a computer software company*

sales·wom·an /'seɪlzwʊmən/ *noun* [*count*] (*plural* **sales·wom·en**) /'seɪlzwɪmən/
a woman whose job is to sell things

sa·li·va /sə'laɪvə/ *noun* [*noncount*]
(**BIOLOGY**) the liquid in your mouth that helps you to swallow food

salm·on /'sæmən/ *noun* [*count, noncount*] (*plural* **salm·on**)
a big fish with pink meat that lives in the ocean and in rivers

sa·lon /sə'lɑn/ *noun* [*count*]
a place where you can have your hair cut or have other beauty treatments: *a hair salon* ♦ *I got my nails done at the beauty salon.*

sal·sa /'sɔlsə/ *noun* [*noncount*]
1 a type of Mexican sauce made from tomatoes, onions, and other vegetables: *chips and salsa*
2 (**MUSIC**) a type of Latin American dance music with a strong beat

salt 🔑 /sɔlt/ *noun* [*noncount*]
a white substance that comes from ocean water and from the earth. We put it on food to give it flavor: *Add a little salt and pepper.*
▶ **salt·y** /'sɔlti/ *adjective* (**salt·i·er, salt·i·est**)
tasting of salt or containing salt: *I don't like this sauce – it's too salty.*

sa·lute /sə'lut/ *verb* (**sa·lutes, sa·lut·ing, sa·lut·ed**)
to make the special sign that soldiers use to show respect, by lifting their hand to their head: *The soldiers saluted as the general walked past.*
▶ **sa·lute** *noun* [*count*]: *The soldier gave a salute.*

same¹ 🔑 /seɪm/ *adjective*
the same not different; not another: *Emma and I like the same kind of music.* ♦ *I've lived in the same town all my life.* ♦ *He went to the same school as me.*

same² 🔑 /seɪm/ *pronoun*
all or **just the same** despite this: *I understand why you're angry. All the same, I think you should say sorry.*
same to you (*informal*) words that you use for saying to someone what they have said to you: *"Have a good weekend." "Same to you."*
the same not a different person or thing: *Do these two words mean the same?* ♦ *I'd like one the same as yours.*
▶ **same** *adverb* **the same**
in the same way: *We treat boys exactly the same as girls.*

sam·ple /'sæmpl/ *noun* [*count*]
a small amount of something that shows what the rest is like: *a free sample of perfume* ♦ *a blood sample*

sand 🔑 /sænd/ *noun* [*noncount*]
(**GEOGRAPHY**) powder made of very small pieces of rock, which you find on beaches and in deserts: *Concrete is a mixture of sand and cement.*

san·dal /ˈsændl/ *noun* [count]
a light open shoe that you wear in warm
weather ⊃ Look at the picture at **shoe**.

sand·wich
/ˈsænwɪtʃ/ *noun*
[count] (*plural*
sand·wich·es)
two pieces of bread
with other food
between them: *a
cheese sandwich*

sandwich

pickle

sand·y /ˈsændi/ *adjective* (sand·i·er, sand·i·est)
with sand: *a sandy beach*

sane /seɪn/ *adjective* (san·er, san·est)
with a normal, healthy mind; not crazy ⊃
ANTONYM insane

sang form of **sing**

san·i·ty /ˈsænəti/ *noun* [noncount]
the state of having a normal, healthy mind ⊃
ANTONYM insanity

sank form of **sink¹**

San·ta Claus /ˈsæntə klɔz/ *noun* [count]
an old man with a red coat and a long white
beard. Children believe that he brings presents
at Christmas.

sap /sæp/ *noun* [noncount]
(**BIOLOGY**) the liquid in a plant or tree

sap·phire /ˈsæfaɪər/ *noun* [count, noncount]
a bright blue valuable stone that is often used in
jewelry: *sapphire earrings*

sar·casm /ˈsɑrkæzəm/ *noun* [noncount]
saying the opposite of what you mean because
you want to be rude to someone or to show
them you are angry
▶ **sar·cas·tic** /sɑrˈkæstɪk/ *adjective*: *There's no
need to be sarcastic.*

sar·dine /sɑrˈdin/ *noun* [count]
a very small ocean fish that you can eat. You
often buy **sardines** in cans.

sa·ri /ˈsɑri/ *noun* [count] (*plural* sa·ris)
a long piece of material that women, especially
Indian women, wear around their bodies as a
dress

SAT™ /ˌɛs eɪ ˈti/ *abbreviation*
a test taken by high school students who want to
go to college: *to take the SAT • SAT scores*

Sat. abbreviation of **Saturday**

sat form of **sit**

sat·el·lite /ˈsæt̬l·aɪt/ *noun* [count]
1 a piece of electronic equipment that people
send into space. **Satellites** travel around the
earth and send back pictures or television and
radio signals: *satellite television*

2 a natural object that moves around a bigger
object in space: *Our moon is one of the largest
satellites in the solar system.*

sat·el·lite dish /ˈsæt̬l·aɪt ˌdɪʃ/ *noun* [count]
a piece of equipment that people put on the
outside of their houses so that they can receive
television signals from a SATELLITE

sat·in /ˈsætn/ *noun* [noncount]
very shiny smooth cloth

sat·ire /ˈsætaɪər/ *noun*
1 [noncount] using humor to attack someone or
something that you think is bad or silly: *political
satire*
2 [count] (**ENGLISH LANGUAGE ARTS**) a piece of
writing or a play, movie, etc. that uses **satire**:
*The play is a **satire on** political life.*

sat·is·fac·tion /ˌsætəsˈfækʃn/ *noun* [noncount]
being pleased with what you or other people
have done: *She finished painting the picture and
looked at it **with satisfaction**.*

sat·is·fac·to·ry /ˌsætəsˈfæktəri/ *adjective*
good enough, but not very good: *Her work is not
satisfactory.* ⊃ **ANTONYM unsatisfactory**

sat·is·fied /ˈsætəsfaɪd/ *adjective*
pleased because you have had or done what
you wanted: *The teacher was not **satisfied with**
my work.* ⊃ **ANTONYM dissatisfied**

sat·is·fy /ˈsætəsfaɪ/ *verb* (sat·is·fies, sat·is·fy·ing,
sat·is·fied, has sat·is·fied)
to give someone what they want or need; to be
good enough to make someone pleased:
Nothing he does satisfies his father.
▶ **sat·is·fy·ing** /ˈsætəsfaɪɪŋ/ *adjective*: *a satisfying
result*

sat·u·rat·ed fat /ˌsætʃəreɪt̬əd ˈfæt/ *noun* [count,
noncount]
(**HEALTH**) a type of fat that is found in some foods,
for example meat, butter, and fried food. Eating
too many **saturated fats** is bad for your body.

Sat·ur·day /ˈsæt̬ərdeɪ; ˈsæt̬ərdi/ *noun* [count,
noncount] (abbreviation **Sat.**)
the day of the week after Friday and before
Sunday

sauce /sɔs/ *noun* [count, noncount]
a thick liquid that you eat on or with other food:
pasta with tomato sauce

sauce·pan /ˈsɔspæn/ (also **pan**) *noun* [count]
a round metal container for cooking

sau·cer /ˈsɔsər/ *noun* [count]
a small round plate that you put under a cup:
cups and saucers ⊃ Look at the picture at **cup**.

sau·na /ˈsɔnə/ *noun* [count]
a room that is hot and filled with steam, where
people sit to relax and feel healthy: *a hotel with a
swimming pool and sauna*

sau·sage /ˈsɔsɪdʒ/ *noun* [*count, noncount*]
a mixture of meat, spices, etc. that is pressed into a long, thin skin: *garlic sausage* • *sausages and eggs*

sav·age /ˈsævɪdʒ/ *adjective*
wild or violent: *He was the victim of a savage attack by a large dog.*

save 🖊 /seɪv/ *verb* (**saves, sav·ing, saved**)
1 to take someone or something away from danger: *He saved me from the fire.* • *The doctor saved her life.*
2 (also **save up**) to keep or not spend money so that you can buy something later: *I've saved enough money to buy a car.* • *I'm saving up for a new bike.*
3 to keep something to use in the future: *Save some of the meat for tomorrow.*
4 to use less of something: *She saves money by making her own clothes.*
5 (**COMPUTERS**) to store information in a computer by giving it a special instruction: *Don't forget to save the file before you close it.*
6 (**SPORTS**) to stop someone from scoring a goal in sports such as HOCKEY or SOCCER

sav·ings /ˈseɪvɪŋz/ *noun* [*plural*]
money that you are keeping to use later: *I keep my savings in the bank.* ⊃ Look at the note at **account¹**.

saw¹ form of **see**

saw² /sɔ/ *noun* [*count*]
a metal tool for cutting wood
▶ **saw** *verb* (**saws, saw·ing, sawed, has sawed** or **has sawn** /sɔn/): *She sawed a branch off the tree.*

saw

saw·dust /ˈsɔdʌst/ *noun* [*noncount*]
powder that falls when you cut wood with a SAW

sax·o·phone /ˈsæksəfoʊn/ (also *informal* **sax** /sæks/) *noun* [*count*]
(**MUSIC**) a musical instrument made of metal that you play by blowing into it ⊃ Look at the picture at **instrument**.

say¹ 🖊 /seɪ/ *verb* (**says** /sɛz/, **say·ing, said** /sɛd/, **has said**)
1 to make words with your mouth: *You say "please" when you ask for something.* • *"This is my room," he said.* • *She said that she was cold.*

Which word?

Say or tell?

■ We use **say** with the actual words that are spoken, or before **that** in reported speech: *"I'm ready," Tom said.* • *Tom said that he was ready.*

■ Notice that you **say** something **to** someone: *Tom said to Kate that he was ready,* but you **tell** someone something (without **to**): *Tom told Kate that he was ready.*

2 to give information in writing, numbers, or pictures: *The notice on the door said "Private."* • *The clock says three-thirty.*
that is to say what I mean is…: *I'll see you in a week, that's to say next Monday.*

say² /seɪ/ *noun*
have a say to have the right to help decide something: *I'd like to have a say in who we invite to the party.*

say·ing /ˈseɪɪŋ/ *noun* [*count*]
a sentence that people often say, which gives advice about something: *"Love is blind" is an old saying.*

scab /skæb/ *noun* [*count*]
(**HEALTH**) a hard covering that grows over your skin where it is cut or broken

scaf·fold·ing /ˈskæfəldɪŋ/ *noun* [*noncount*]
metal bars and pieces of wood joined together, where people can stand when they are working on high parts of a building

scald /skɔld/ *verb* (**scalds, scald·ing, scald·ed**)
(**HEALTH**) to burn someone or something with very hot liquid

scale 🖊 /skeɪl/ *noun*
1 [*count*] a set of levels or numbers used for measuring something: *Their work is assessed on a scale from 1 to 10.*
2 [*count, noncount*] the size or level of something: *It was not until morning that the full scale of the damage could be seen.*
3 [*count*] a machine for showing how heavy people or things are: *a bathroom scale*
4 [*count*] how distances are shown on a map: *This map has a scale of one inch to ten miles.*
5 (**MUSIC**) [*count*] a series of musical notes that go up or down in a fixed order: *the scale of C major*
6 [*count*] one of the flat hard things that cover the body of animals like fish and snakes ⊃ Look at the picture at **fish**.

scal·lop /ˈskæləp; ˈskɑləp/ *noun* [*count*]
a small animal that lives in the ocean and that you can eat. It has two round shells that fit together.

scalp /skælp/ *noun* [*count*]
the skin on the top of your head, under your hair

scan¹ /skæn/ *verb* (**scans, scan·ning, scanned**)
1 to look at or read every part of something quickly until you find what you are looking for: *Vic scanned the list until he found his own name.*

2 (used about a machine) to examine what is inside a person's body or inside an object: *All luggage is scanned before it is loaded onto the plane.*
3 (COMPUTERS) to pass light over a picture or document using an electronic machine (called a SCANNER) in order to copy it and put it in the memory of a computer

scan² /skæn/ *noun* [count]
(HEALTH) a medical test in which a machine produces a picture of the inside of a person's body on a computer screen: *to have a full body scan* ◆ *a brain scan*

scan·dal /'skændl/ *noun*
1 [count] something that shocks people and makes them talk about it because they think it is bad: *a political scandal*
2 [noncount] unkind talk about someone that gives you a bad idea of them

scan·ner /'skænər/ *noun* [count]
1 (COMPUTERS) a piece of equipment that copies words or pictures from paper into a computer
2 (HEALTH) a machine that gives a picture of the inside of something. Doctors use one kind of **scanner** to look inside people's bodies.

scape·goat /'skeɪpɡoʊt/ *noun* [count]
a person who is blamed for something bad that is usually not their fault: *She felt that she was a scapegoat for her manager's mistakes.*

scar /skɑr/ *noun* [count]
(HEALTH) a mark that is left on your skin by an old cut or wound: *The operation didn't leave a very big scar.*
▶ **scar** *verb* (scars, scar·ring, scarred): *His face was badly scarred by the accident.*

scarce /skɛrs/ *adjective* (scarc·er, scarc·est)
difficult to find; not enough: *Food for wild birds and animals is scarce in the winter.*

scarce·ly /'skɛrsli/ *adverb*
almost not; just: *He was so afraid that he could scarcely speak.*

scare¹ 🔑 /skɛr/ *verb* (scares, scar·ing, scared)
to make someone feel afraid: *That noise scared me!* ⇒ SYNONYM **frighten**

scare² /skɛr/ *noun* [count]
1 a feeling of being afraid: *You gave me a scare!*
2 a situation where many people are afraid or worried about something: *a health scare*

scare·crow /'skɛrkroʊ/ *noun* [count]
a thing that looks like a person, which farmers put in their fields to frighten birds

scared 🔑 /skɛrd/ *adjective*
afraid: *Claire is scared of the dark.* ⇒ Look at the note at **afraid**.

scarf /skɑrf/ *noun*
[count] (plural **scarves** /skɑrvz/)
a piece of material that you wear around your neck to keep warm

scarf

scar·let /'skɑrlət/ *adjective*
having a bright red color
▶ **scar·let** *noun* [noncount]

scar·y 🔑 /'skɛri/ *adjective* (scar·i·er, scar·i·est)
making you feel afraid: *a scary ghost story*

scat·ter /'skæṭər/ *verb* (scat·ters, scat·ter·ing, scat·tered)
1 to move quickly in different directions: *The crowd scattered when it started to rain.*
2 to throw things so that they fall in a lot of different places: *Scatter the grass seed over the lawn.*

sce·nar·i·o AWL /sə'nɛrioʊ/ *noun* [count] (plural sce·nar·i·os)
one way that things may happen in the future: *A likely scenario is that we will have to close down the factory.*

scene /sin/ *noun* [count]
1 the place where something happened: *The police arrived* **at the scene** *of the crime.*
2 part of a play or movie: *Today we're going to look at Act 1, Scene 2 of the play.*
3 what you see in a place: *He painted scenes of life on a farm.*

scen·er·y /'sinəri/ *noun* [noncount]
1 the things like mountains, rivers, and trees that you see around you in the country: *What beautiful scenery!*
2 things on the stage of a theater that make it look like a real place

sce·nic /'sinɪk/ *adjective*
having beautiful views of things such as mountains, rivers, and trees: *We took a scenic drive along the coast.*

scent /sɛnt/ *noun* [count, noncount]
1 a pleasant smell: *These flowers have no scent.*
2 the smell that an animal leaves behind and that other animals can follow
▶ **scent·ed** /'sɛntəd/ *adjective*
having a nice smell: *scented candles*

sched·ule 🔑 AWL /'skɛdʒəl/ *noun* [count]
1 a plan or list of times when things will happen or be done: *I have a busy schedule next week.* ◆ *We're* **behind schedule** (= late) *with the project.* ◆ *Filming began* **on schedule** (= at the planned time).
2 a list that shows when planes, buses, etc. arrive at and leave a particular place: *Do you have a train schedule?*

scheme¹ AWL /skim/ *noun* [*count*]
a plan to do something, especially something bad or illegal: *Police discovered a scheme to steal paintings worth nearly a million dollars.*

scheme² AWL /skim/ *verb* (schemes, schem·ing, schemed)
to make secret or dishonest plans to do something: *She felt that they were all scheming against her.*

schiz·o·phre·ni·a /ˌskɪtsəˈfriniə/ *noun* [*noncount*]
(HEALTH) a serious mental illness in which a person confuses the real world and the world of the imagination
▸ **schiz·o·phre·nic** /ˌskɪtsəˈfrɛnɪk/ *adjective*

schol·ar /ˈskɑlər/ *noun* [*count*]
1 a person who has learned a lot about a particular subject: *a famous history scholar*
2 a person who has been given a SCHOLARSHIP to help pay for their studies

schol·ar·ship /ˈskɑlərʃɪp/ *noun* [*count*]
an amount of money that is given to a student to help them pay for their education: *Adrian got a scholarship to Rutgers University.*

school /skul/ *noun*
1 [*count, noncount*] a place where children go to learn: *The kids are at school.* ◆ *Which school do you go to?*
2 [*noncount*] being at **school**: *I hate school!* ◆ *He left school when he was 16.* ◆ *School starts at nine o'clock.*

Grammar

- You usually talk about **school** without "the" or "a": *I enjoyed being at school.* ◆ *Do you walk to school?*
- You use "a" or "the" when more information about the school is given: *Harry goes to the school that his father went to.* ◆ *She teaches at a school for deaf children.*

3 [*count*] a place where you go to learn a special thing: *a language school*
4 [*count, noncount*] a college or university, or the time that you spend there: *Mike had to quit school and get a job.*

Collocations

School

learning
- **go to/attend** school/(a) class
- **take** a course/classes (in law, biology, etc.)

school
- **be in (the)** first/second, etc. grade
- **study** history/chemistry/German, etc.

- **drop out of/quit** school
- **graduate (from)/finish** high school

problems at school
- **skip** class/school
- **cheat on** an exam/a test
- **get** detention (for doing something wrong)
- **be suspended from/expelled from** school
⊃ Look at the note at **exam**.

school·child /ˈskultʃaɪld/ *noun* [*count*] (*plural* school·chil·dren /ˈskultʃɪldrən/)
a boy or girl who goes to school

sci·ence /ˈsaɪəns/ *noun* [*count, noncount*]
the study of natural things: *I'm interested in science.* ◆ *Biology, chemistry, and physics are all sciences.*

sci·ence fic·tion /ˌsaɪəns ˈfɪkʃn/ (also *informal* **sci-fi** /ˈsaɪ faɪ/) *noun* [*noncount*]
(ENGLISH LANGUAGE ARTS) stories about things like travel in space, life on other planets, or life in the future

sci·en·tif·ic /ˌsaɪənˈtɪfɪk/ *adjective*
(GENERAL SCIENCE) of or about science: *We need more grants for scientific research.*

sci·en·tist /ˈsaɪəntɪst/ *noun* [*count*]
(GENERAL SCIENCE) a person who studies science or works with science

scis·sors /ˈsɪzərz/
noun [*plural*]
a tool for cutting that has two sharp parts that are joined together: *These scissors aren't very sharp.* ◆ *I need some scissors. Do you have any?* ◆ *a pair of scissors*

scissors

a pair of scissors

scold /skoʊld/ *verb* (scolds, scold·ing, scold·ed)
to tell a child in an angry way that they have done something wrong: *His mother scolded him for not putting away his toys.*

scoop¹ /skup/ *noun* [*count*]
1 a thing like a spoon that is used for picking up ice cream, flour, etc. ⊃ Look at the picture at **kitchen**.
2 the amount that a **scoop** holds: *Two scoops of ice cream, please.*

scoop² /skup/ *verb* (scoops, scoop·ing, scooped)
to use a spoon or your hands to take something up or out: *I scooped some ice cream out of the bowl.*

scoot·er /ˈskuţər/ *noun* [*count*]
1 a light motorcycle with a small engine
2 a child's vehicle with two wheels that you stand on and move by pushing one foot against the ground

ə about   y yes   w woman   ţ butter   eɪ say   aɪ five   ɔɪ boy   aʊ now   oʊ go

scope AWL /skoʊp/ *noun*
1 [*noncount*] the chance or opportunity to do something: *The job offers plenty of scope for creativity.*
2 [*singular*] the different subjects that are being discussed: *How wide is the scope of the government's investigation?*

score¹ 🔊 /skɔr/ *noun* [*count*]
(**SPORTS**) the number of points, goals, etc. that you get in a game or competition: *The winner got a score of 320.* • *What's the score now?*

score² 🔊 /skɔr/ *verb* (**scores, scor·ing, scored**)
1 (**SPORTS**) to get points, goals, etc. in a game or competition: *The Bulls scored 30 points in the fourth quarter.*
2 to give a number that shows how well someone does on a test, a competition, etc.: *The written driving test is scored by computer.*

score·board /'skɔrbɔrd/ *noun* [*count*]
(**SPORTS**) a large board that shows the score during a game or competition

scorn /skɔrn/ *noun* [*noncount*]
a strong feeling that someone or something is stupid or not good enough: *He was full of scorn for my idea.*
▶ **scorn·ful** /'skɔrnfl/ *adjective*: *She gave him a scornful look.*

scor·pi·on
/'skɔrpiən/ *noun* [*count*]
a small animal that looks like an insect and can hurt (**STING**) you with its tail

scorpion

— sting

Scotch tape™
/'skɑtʃ teɪp/ *noun* [*noncount*]
a type of clear tape that is sticky on one side, which you buy in a roll

scowl /skaʊl/ *verb* (**scowls, scowl·ing, scowled**)
to look at someone in an angry way: *His teacher scowled at him for being late.*
▶ **scowl** *noun* [*count*]: *He looked up at me with a scowl.*

scram·ble /'skræmbl/ *verb* (**scram·bles, scram·bling, scram·bled**)
to move quickly up or over something, using your hands to help you: *They scrambled over the wall.*

scram·bled eggs /ˌskræmbəld 'ɛgz/ *noun* [*plural*]
eggs that you mix together with milk and cook in a pan with butter

scrap /skræp/ *noun*
1 [*count*] a small piece of something: *a scrap of paper*

2 [*noncount*] something you do not want any more but that is made of material that can be used again: *scrap metal*

scrap·book /'skræpbʊk/ *noun* [*count*]
a large book with empty pages that you can stick pictures or newspaper articles in

scrape /skreɪp/ *verb* (**scrapes, scrap·ing, scraped**)
1 to move a rough or sharp thing across something: *I scraped the mud off my shoes with a knife.*
2 to hurt or damage something by moving it against a rough or sharp thing: *I fell and scraped my knee on the wall.*

scratch¹ 🔊 /skrætʃ/ *verb* (**scratch·es, scratch·ing, scratched**)
1 to move your nails across your skin: *She scratched her head.*
2 to cut or make a mark on something with a sharp thing: *The cat scratched me!*

scratch² 🔊 /skrætʃ/ *noun* [*count*] (*plural* **scratch·es**)
a cut or mark that a sharp thing makes: *Her hands were covered in scratches from the cat.*
from scratch from the beginning: *I threw away the letter I was writing and started again from scratch.*

scream¹ /skrim/ *verb* (**screams, scream·ing, screamed**)
to make a loud, high noise with your voice that shows you are afraid or hurt: *She saw the snake and screamed.* • *He screamed for help.*

scream² /skrim/ *noun* [*count*]
a loud, high noise you make with your voice: *a scream of pain*

screech /skritʃ/ *verb* (**screech·es, screech·ing, screeched**)
to make an unpleasant, loud, high sound: *The car's brakes screeched as it stopped suddenly.*

screen 🔊 /skrin/ *noun* [*count*]
1 (**COMPUTERS**) the flat, square part of a television or computer where you see pictures or words ⊃ Look at the picture at **computer**.
2 the flat thing on the wall of a theater, where you see movies
3 a kind of thin wall that you can move around. **Screens** are used to keep away cold, light, etc. or to stop people from seeing something: *The nurse put a screen around the bed.*

screen sav·er /'skrɪn ˌseɪvər/ *noun* [*count*]
(**COMPUTERS**) a picture that appears on your computer screen when you are not using it

screws   **screwdriver**

screw¹ /skru/ *noun* [*count*]
a small metal thing with a sharp end, which you use for fastening things together. You push it into something by turning it with a special tool (called a SCREWDRIVER).

screw² /skru/ *verb* (**screws, screw·ing, screwed**)
1 to attach something to another thing using a SCREW: *The cabinet is screwed to the wall.*
2 to turn something to attach it to another thing: *Screw the lid on the jar.*

screw·driv·er /'skrudraɪvər/ *noun* [*count*]
a tool for turning SCREWS ⊃ Look at the picture at **screw**.

scrib·ble /'skrɪbl/ *verb* (**scrib·bles, scrib·bling, scrib·bled**)
to write something or make marks on paper quickly and without care: *The children scribbled in my book.*

script /skrɪpt/ *noun* [*count*]
the written words that actors speak in a play or movie

scrip·ture (also **Scrip·ture**) /'skrɪptʃər/ *noun* [*noncount*]
(**RELIGION**) the book or books that a particular religion is based on

scroll /skroʊl/ *verb* (**scrolls, scroll·ing, scrolled**)
(**COMPUTERS**) to move what you can see on a computer screen up or down so that you can look at different parts of it: *Scroll down to the bottom of the document.*

scrub /skrʌb/ *verb* (**scrubs, scrub·bing, scrubbed**)
to rub something hard to clean it, usually with a brush and soap and water: *He scrubbed the floor.*

scruff·y /'skrʌfi/ *adjective* (**scruff·i·er, scruff·i·est**)
messy and perhaps dirty: *She was wearing scruffy jeans.*

scu·ba div·ing /'skubə ˌdaɪvɪŋ/ *noun* [*noncount*]
swimming underwater using special equipment for breathing: *You should never go scuba diving alone.*

sculp·tor /'skʌlptər/ *noun* [*count*]
(**ART**) a person who makes shapes from materials like stone or wood

sculp·ture /'skʌlptʃər/ *noun* [*count, noncount*]
(**ART**) the art of making shapes from stone, wood, or other material; a work of art that has been made in this way: *He's studying sculpture at college.* ◆ *a marble sculpture of the goddess Venus*

sea /si/ *noun* (**GEOGRAPHY**)
1 **Sea** [*count*] a big area of salt water: *the Black Sea* ⊃ Look at **ocean**.
2 [*noncount*] the ocean: *The pieces of wood floated out to sea.*
at sea traveling on the ocean: *We spent three weeks at sea.*

sea·food /'sifud/ *noun* [*noncount*]
fish and small animals from the ocean that we eat, especially SHELLFISH (= animals with shells that live in water)

sea·gull /'sigʌl/ *noun* [*count*]
a big, gray or white bird that lives near the ocean and makes a loud sound

seal¹ /sil/ *noun* [*count*]
1 an animal with short fur that lives in and near the ocean, and that eats fish
2 a piece of paper or plastic on a package or bottle, which you have to break before you can open it

seal² /sil/ *verb* (**seals, seal·ing, sealed**)
to close something by sticking two parts together: *She sealed the envelope.*

seam /sim/ *noun* [*count*]
a line where two pieces of cloth are joined together

search¹ /sərtʃ/ *verb* (**search·es, search·ing, searched**)
to look carefully because you are trying to find someone or something: *I searched everywhere for my pen.* ◆ *I searched the document to find the names.*

search² /sərtʃ/ *noun* [*count, noncount*] (*plural* **search·es**)
when you try to find someone or something: *I found my key after a long search.* ◆ *We drove around the town in search of a cheap restaurant.* ◆ *The search for the murder weapon goes on.*

search en·gine /'sərtʃ ˌɛndʒən/ *noun* [*count*]
(**COMPUTERS**) a computer program that searches the Internet for information

sea·shell /'siʃɛl/ *noun* [*count*]
the empty shell of a small animal that lives in the ocean

seashell

sea·shore /'siʃɔr/ *noun* the seashore [*singular*]
(**GEOGRAPHY**) the land next to the ocean: *We were looking for seashells on the seashore.*

sea·sick /'sisɪk/ *adjective*
(**HEALTH**) If you are **seasick**, you feel sick because the boat you are on is moving a lot.

sea·son 🔑 /'sizn/ *noun* [count]
1 one of the four parts of the year (called SPRING, SUMMER, FALL, and WINTER)
2 a special time of the year for something: *The football season starts in September.*

sea·son·ing /'sizn·ɪŋ/ *noun* [count, noncount]
a substance used to add flavor to food, for example salt, PEPPER (= powder with a hot taste) or spices: *Add some seasoning to the chicken, then put it in the oven.*

seat 🔑 /sit/ *noun* [count]
something that you sit on: *the back seat of a car* ◆ *We had seats at the front of the theater.* ◆ *Please take a seat* (= sit down).

seat belt /'sit bɛlt/ *noun* [count]
a long, thin piece of material that you put around your body in a car, bus, or airplane to keep you safe

sea·weed /'siwid/ *noun* [noncount]
a plant that grows in the ocean. There are many different types of **seaweed**.

sec. abbreviation of **second**

se·clud·ed /sə'kludəd/ *adjective*
far away from other people, roads, etc.: *a secluded beach*

sec·ond¹ 🔑 /'sɛkənd/ *adjective, adverb, noun* [singular]
next after first; 2nd: *February is the second month of the year.* ◆ *She finished second in the race.* ◆ *Today is the second of April* (= April 2nd). ◆ *I was the first to arrive, and Jim was the second.*

sec·ond² 🔑 /'sɛkənd/ *noun* [count]
1 (abbreviation **sec.**) a measure of time. There are 60 **seconds** in a minute.
2 a very short time: *Wait a second!* ◆ *I'll be ready in a second.*

sec·ond·ar·y school /'sɛkən,dɛri ,skul/ *noun* [count]
a school for children between the ages of about 12 and 18

sec·ond-class /,sɛkənd 'klæs/ *adjective*
less important than other people or things: *Older people should not be treated as second-class citizens.*

sec·ond·hand /,sɛkənd'hænd/ (also **sec·ond-hand**) *adjective, adverb*
not new; used by another person before: *secondhand books* ◆ *I bought this car secondhand.*

sec·ond·ly /'sɛkəndli/ *adverb*
a word that you use when you are giving the second thing in a list: *Firstly, it's too expensive, and secondly, we don't really need it.*

se·cre·cy /'sikrəsi/ *noun* [noncount]
not telling other people: *They worked in secrecy.*

se·cret¹ 🔑 /'sikrət/ *noun* [count]
something that you do not or must not tell other people: *I can't tell you where I'm going – it's a secret.* ◆ *Can you keep a secret* (= not tell other people)?
in secret without other people knowing: *They met in secret.*

se·cret² 🔑 /'sikrət/ *adjective*
If something is **secret**, other people do not or must not know about it: *They kept their wedding secret* (= they did not tell anyone about it). ◆ *a secret meeting*

sec·re·tar·i·al /,sɛkrə'tɛriəl/ *adjective*
connected with the work of a secretary: *a secretarial job*

sec·re·tar·y 🔑 /'sɛkrə,tɛri/ *noun* [count] (plural **sec·re·tar·ies**)
1 a person who types letters, answers the telephone, and does other things in an office
2 a person who is in charge of a large department in the U.S. government: *the Secretary of Defense* ◆ *the Agriculture Secretary*

se·cre·tive /'sikrətɪv/ *adjective*
If you are **secretive**, you do not like to tell other people about yourself or your plans: *Mark is very secretive about his job.*

se·cret·ly 🔑 /'sikrətli/ *adverb*
without other people knowing: *We are secretly planning a big party for her.*

sect /sɛkt/ *noun* [count]
(POLITICS, RELIGION) a group of people who have particular beliefs about religion or politics. A **sect** has often separated from a larger group: *a religious sect*

sec·tion 🔑 AWL /'sɛkʃn/ *noun* [count]
one of the parts of something: *This section of the road is closed.*

sec·tor AWL /'sɛktər/ *noun* [count]
1 (BUSINESS) a part of the business activity of a country: *The manufacturing sector is growing.*
2 (MATH) a part of a circle that is between two straight lines drawn from the center to the edge ⊃ Look at the picture at **circle**.

se·cure AWL /sə'kyʊr/ *adjective*
1 If you are **secure**, you feel safe and you are not worried: *Do you feel secure about the future?* ⊃ ANTONYM **insecure**
2 safe: *Don't climb that ladder – it's not very secure* (= it may fall). ◆ *Her job is secure* (= she will not lose it).
3 well locked or protected so that no one can go in or out: *This gate isn't very secure.*
▶ **se·cure·ly** AWL /sə'kyʊrli/ *adverb*: *Are all the windows securely closed?*

se·cu·ri·ty AWL /sə'kyʊrəti/ *noun* [noncount]
1 the feeling of being safe: *Children need love and security.* ⊃ ANTONYM **insecurity**

2 things that you do to keep a place safe: *We need better security at airports.*

se·date /sə'deɪt/ *verb* (se·dates, se·dat·ing, se·dat·ed)

(**HEALTH**) to give someone medicine or a drug to make them feel calm or want to sleep: *The vet sedated the horse before examining it.*

sed·a·tive /'sɛdətɪv/ *noun* [*count*]

(**HEALTH**) a drug or medicine that makes you feel calm or want to sleep

see 🖉 /si/ *verb* (sees, see·ing, saw /sɔ/, has seen /sin/)

1 to know or notice something using your eyes: *It was so dark that I couldn't see anything.* ◆ *Can you see that plane?*

2 to watch a movie, play, or television program: *I'm going to see a movie tonight.* ⊃ Look at the note at **look**[1].

3 to find out about something: *Go and see what time the train leaves.*

4 to visit or meet someone: *We're going to see my grandma on the weekend.* ◆ *I'll see you outside the train station at ten o'clock.*

5 to understand something: *"You have to turn the key this way." "I see."*

6 to make certain about something: *Please see that you lock the door.*

I'll see; **we'll see** words that mean "I will think about what you have said and tell you what I have decided later": *"Will you lend me the money?" "I'll see."*

let's see; **let me see** words that you use when you are thinking or trying to remember something: *Let's see, where did I put the keys?*

see someone off to go to an airport or a station to say goodbye to someone who is leaving

see to something to do what you need to do for someone or something: *Sit down – I'll see to the dinner.*

see you; **see you later** (*informal*) goodbye: *"Bye Dave!" "See you!"*

seed 🖉 /sid/ *noun* [*count*]

(**BIOLOGY**) the small, hard part of a plant from which a new plant grows

seek **AWL** /sik/ *verb* (seeks, seek·ing, sought /sɔt/, has sought) (*formal*)

to try to find or get something: *You should seek help.*

seem 🖉 /sim/ *verb* (seems, seem·ing, seemed)

to give the impression of being or doing something: *She seems tired.* ◆ *My mother seems to like you.* ◆ *Helen seems like* (= seems to be) *a nice girl.*

seen form of **see**

seep /sip/ *verb* (seeps, seep·ing, seeped)

(used about a liquid) to flow very slowly through small holes in something: *Water started seeping in through the cracks.*

see·saw /'sisɔ/ (also **see-saw**) *noun* [*count*]

a piece of equipment for children to play on. It is made of a piece of wood or metal, which moves up and down when a child sits on each end.

seg·ment /'sɛgmənt/ *noun* [*count*]

1 a part of something: *I divided the sheet of paper into three segments.*

2 one of the sections of an orange, a lemon, etc.

3 (**MATH**) a part of a circle that is separated from the rest with one line ⊃ Look at the picture at **circle**.

seg·re·gate /'sɛgrəgeɪt/ *verb* (seg·re·gates, seg·re·gat·ing, seg·re·gat·ed)

to separate one group of people from the rest, for example because of their race, religion, or sex ⊃ Look at **integrate** (2).

▶ **seg·re·ga·tion** /ˌsɛgrə'geɪʃn/ *noun* [*noncount*]: *racial segregation* (= separating people of different races)

seize /siz/ *verb* (seiz·es, seiz·ing, seized)

1 to take something quickly and firmly: *The thief seized her bag and ran away.* ⊃ **SYNONYM** **grab**

2 to take control of something, or to take something away from someone: *The police seized 50 pounds of illegal drugs.*

sei·zure /'siʒər/ *noun*

1 [*noncount*] the act of taking something away or taking control of something

2 [*count*] a sudden attack of an illness, when a person becomes unconscious and their body may make violent movements

sel·dom /'sɛldəm/ *adverb*

not often: *It seldom snows here in March.* ⊃ **SYNONYM** **rarely**

se·lect **AWL** /sə'lɛkt/ *verb* (se·lects, se·lect·ing, se·lect·ed) (*formal*)

to take the person or thing that you like best: *We select only the finest fruits.* ⊃ **SYNONYM** **choose**

se·lec·tion **AWL** /sə'lɛkʃn/ *noun*

1 [*noncount*] taking the person or thing you like best: *The manager is responsible for team selection.*

2 [*count*] a group of people or things that someone has chosen, or a group of things that you can choose from: *The store has a good selection of toys.*

self /sɛlf/ *noun* [*count*] (*plural* **selves** /sɛlvz/)

a person's own nature or qualities: *It's good to see you back to your old self again* (= well or happy again).

Prefix

self-

(in nouns and adjectives) by yourself or itself; for yourself or itself: *self-control* ◆ *self-service* ◆ *self-employed* ◆ *He is self-taught* (= *he taught himself*).

self·con·fi·dent /ˌsɛlf ˈkɑnfədənt/ *adjective*
sure about yourself and what you can do
▶ **self·con·fi·dence** /ˌsɛlf ˈkɑnfədəns/ *noun* [noncount]: *Failing that exam made her lose a lot of self-confidence.*

self·con·scious /ˌsɛlf ˈkɑnʃəs/ *adjective*
worried about what other people think of you: *She walked into her new school feeling very self-conscious.*

self·con·trol /ˌsɛlf kənˈtroʊl/ *noun* [noncount]
the ability to control yourself and your emotions

self·de·fense /ˌsɛlf dɪˈfɛns/ *noun* [noncount]
the use of force to protect yourself: *I only hit him in self-defense.*

self·em·ployed /ˌsɛlf ɛmˈplɔɪd/ *adjective*
working for yourself, not for someone else: *He's a self-employed electrician.*

self·es·teem /ˌsɛlf ɪˈstim/ *noun* [noncount]
a good opinion of your own character and abilities: *to suffer low self-esteem*

self·ish /ˈsɛlfɪʃ/ *adjective*
thinking too much about what you want and not about what other people want: *I'm sick of your selfish behavior!*
▶ **self·ish·ly** /ˈsɛlfɪʃli/ *adverb*: *He behaved very selfishly.*
▶ **self·ish·ness** /ˈsɛlfɪʃnəs/ *noun* [noncount]: *Her selfishness made me very angry.*

self·pit·y /ˌsɛlf ˈpɪti/ *noun* [noncount]
when you think too much about your own problems and feel sorry for yourself

self·serv·ice /ˌsɛlf ˈsərvəs/ *adjective*
In a **self-service** store or restaurant you take what you want and then pay for it: *The café is self-service.*

sell /sɛl/ *verb* (sells, sell·ing, sold /soʊld/, has sold)
to give something to someone who pays you money for it: *I sold my guitar for $400.* ◆ *He sold me a ticket.* ◆ *Drugstores usually sell cigarettes.* ⊃ Look at **buy**.
sell out; be sold out to be sold completely so that there are no more left: *I went to the store to buy a newspaper, but they had all sold out.* ◆ *The concert was sold out weeks ago.*
sell out of something to sell all that you have of something: *I'm afraid we're sold out of milk.*

sell·er /ˈsɛlər/ *noun* [count] (BUSINESS)
1 a person or company that sells something: *a flower seller*
2 something that is sold in the amount or way mentioned: *This magazine is a big seller in the 25-40 age group.* ⊃ Look at **best seller**.

se·mes·ter /səˈmɛstər/ *noun* [count]
one of the two periods that the school or college year is divided into: *I'm taking an art history course next semester.*

Prefix

semi-

(in adjectives and nouns) half or part: *to be semiretired* (= *to only work some of the time*) ◆ *a semipermanent arrangement* ◆ *a semicircle*

sem·i·cir·cle /ˈsɛmiˌsərkl/ *noun* [count]
half a circle: *The children sat in a semicircle.* ⊃ Look at the picture at **circle**.

sem·i·co·lon /ˈsɛmiˌkoʊlən/ *noun* [count]
(ENGLISH LANGUAGE ARTS) a mark (;) that you use in writing to separate parts of a sentence

sem·i·fi·nal /ˈsɛmifaɪnl; ˌsɛmiˈfaɪnl/ *noun* [count]
(SPORTS) one of the two games that are played in a competition to find out who will play in the last part of the competition (the FINAL)

sem·i·nar /ˈsɛmənɑr/ *noun* [count]
a class at a college, etc. in which a small group of students discuss or study a subject with a teacher

sen·ate /ˈsɛnət/ *noun* [count] **the Senate**
(POLITICS) one of the two parts of the government that makes the laws in the U.S. and some other countries ⊃ Look at **the House of Representatives**. ⊃ Look at the note at **government**.

sen·a·tor /ˈsɛnətər/ *noun* [count]
(POLITICS) a member of the SENATE

send /sɛnd/ *verb* (sends, send·ing, sent /sɛnt/, has sent)
1 to make something go somewhere, especially a letter or a message: *I sent a message to John.* ◆ *Did you send your parents a postcard?*
2 to make someone go somewhere: *My company is sending me to New York.* ◆ *He was sent to prison for ten years.*
send for someone or **something** to ask for someone or something to come to you: *Send for an ambulance!*
send something off to mail something: *I'll send off that letter off today.*

sen·ior¹ /ˈsinyər/ *adjective*
1 having a higher position in an organization: *a senior officer in the army*

2 connected with the last year of high school or college

3 Senior (abbreviation **Sr.**) a word that is used after the name of a father who has the same name as his son: *His father is John Brown, Sr.* ⊃ Look at **junior**.

sen·ior² /ˈsinyər/ *noun* [count]
1 a student in the final year of high school or college: *He's a senior at Yale.* ⊃ Look at **freshman**, **junior²**, **sophomore**.
2 another word for **senior citizen**: *Tickets are $10, but only $7 for seniors and students.*

sen·ior cit·i·zen /ˌsinyər ˈsɪtəzn/ (also **sen·ior**) *noun* [count]
a person who has reached the age when you can stop work

sen·ior·i·ty /ˌsinˈyɔrəti/ *noun* [noncount]
the position that you have in a company or organization because of how long you have worked there: *Promotion is not always based only on seniority.*

sen·sa·tion /sɛnˈseɪʃn/ *noun* [count]
1 a physical feeling: *I felt a burning sensation on my skin.*
2 great excitement or interest: *The movie caused a sensation.*

sen·sa·tion·al /sɛnˈseɪʃn·l/ *adjective*
1 very exciting or interesting: *sensational news*
2 very good or beautiful: *You look sensational tonight!*

sense¹ /sɛns/ *noun*
1 [noncount,singular] the ability to feel or understand something: *The boy had no sense of right and wrong.* • *I like him – he has a great sense of humor.*
2 [noncount,singular] the ability to think carefully about something and to do the right thing: *Did anyone have the sense to call the police?*
3 [count] (BIOLOGY) the power to see, hear, smell, taste, or touch: *Dogs have a very good sense of smell.*
4 [count] a meaning: *This word has four senses.*
make sense to be possible to understand: *What does this sentence mean? It doesn't make sense to me.*

sense² /sɛns/ *verb* (sens·es, sens·ing, sensed)
to understand or feel something: *I sensed that he was worried.*

sen·si·ble /ˈsɛnsəbl/ *adjective*
able to think carefully about something and to do the right thing: *It wasn't very sensible of you to run away.* • *a sensible answer* ⊃ ANTONYM **silly**
▶ **sen·si·bly** /ˈsɛnsəbli/ *adverb*: *I hope you'll behave sensibly.*

sen·si·tive /ˈsɛnsətɪv/ *adjective*
1 understanding other people's feelings and being careful about them: *He's a very sensitive man.* ⊃ ANTONYM **insensitive**
2 easily becoming worried or unhappy about something, or about things in general: *Don't say anything about her hair – she's very sensitive about it.*
3 easily hurt or damaged: *She has very sensitive skin.*

sent form of **send**

sen·tence¹ /ˈsɛntns/ *noun* [count]
1 (ENGLISH LANGUAGE ARTS) a group of words that tells you something or asks a question. When a **sentence** is written, it always begins with a capital letter and usually ends with a period: *You don't need to write a long letter. A couple of sentences will be enough.*
2 the punishment that a judge gives to someone in a court of law: *Twenty years in prison was a very harsh sentence.*

sen·tence² /ˈsɛntns/ *verb* (sen·tenc·es, sen·tenc·ing, sen·tenced)
to tell someone in a court of law what their punishment will be: *The judge sentenced the man to two years in prison.*

sen·ti·men·tal /ˌsɛntəˈmɛntl/ *adjective*
producing or showing feelings, such as romantic love or happy memories, that are too strong or not appropriate: *a sentimental love story* • *I'm so sentimental – I always cry at weddings!*

sep·a·rate¹ /ˈsɛprət/ *adjective*
1 away from something; not together or not joined: *The cup broke into three separate pieces.* • *In my school, the older children are separate from the younger ones.*
2 different; not the same: *We stayed in separate rooms in the same hotel.*
▶ **sep·a·rate·ly** /ˈsɛprətli/ *adverb*: *Should we pay separately or together?*

sep·a·rate² /ˈsɛpəreɪt/ *verb* (sep·a·rates, sep·a·rat·ing, sep·a·rat·ed)
1 to stop being together: *My parents separated when I was a baby.* ⊃ SYNONYM **split up**
2 to divide people or things; to keep people or things away from each other: *The teacher separated the class into two groups.* ⊃ SYNONYM **split**
3 to be between two things: *The river separates the two sides of the city.*
▶ **sep·a·ra·tion** /ˌsɛpəˈreɪʃn/ *noun* [count, noncount]: *The separation from my family and friends made me very unhappy.*

Sep·tem·ber /sɛpˈtɛmbər/ *noun* [count, noncount] (abbreviation **Sept.**)
the ninth month of the year

tʃ **chin**   dʒ **June**   v **van**   θ **thin**   ð **then**   s **so**   z **zoo**   ʃ **she**

se·quel /'sikwəl/ *noun* [*count*]
(**ENGLISH LANGUAGE ARTS**) a movie, book, etc. that continues the story of the one before: *Have you seen the Batman sequel?*

se·quence **AWL** /'sikwəns/ *noun* [*count*]
a number of things that happen or come one after another: *an extraordinary sequence of events* ♦ *Complete the following sequence: 2, 4, 8…*

ser·geant /'sɑrdʒənt/ *noun* [*count*]
an officer in the army or the police

se·ri·al /'sɪriəl/ *noun* [*count*]
a story that is told in parts on television or in a magazine

se·ries 🔑 **AWL** /'sɪriz/ *noun* [*count*] (*plural* se·ries)
1 a number of things of the same kind that come one after another: *I heard a series of shots, and then silence.*
2 a number of television or radio programs, often on the same subject, that come one after another: *The first episode of the new series is on Saturday.* ♦ *a TV series on dinosaurs*
3 (**SPORTS**) a number of games that are played one after another by the same two teams: *The Yankees won the World Series.*

se·ri·ous 🔑 /'sɪriəs/ *adjective*
1 very bad: *That was a serious mistake.* ♦ *They had a serious accident.*
2 important: *a serious decision*
3 not funny: *a serious play*
4 If you are **serious**, you are not joking or playing: *Are you serious about going to live in Vermont?* ♦ *You look very serious. Is something wrong?*
▶ **se·ri·ous·ness** /'sɪriəsnəs/ *noun* [*noncount*]: *The boy didn't understand the seriousness of his crime.*

se·ri·ous·ly /'sɪriəsli/ *adverb*
in a serious way: *She's seriously injured.* ♦ *You're not seriously expecting me to believe that?* ♦ *Smoking can seriously damage your health.*
take someone or **something seriously** to show that you know someone or something is important: *Don't take what he says too seriously – he's always joking.*

ser·mon /'sərmən/ *noun* [*count*]
(**RELIGION**) a talk that a priest gives in church

ser·vant /'sərvənt/ *noun* [*count*]
a person who works in a rich person's house, doing work like cooking and cleaning

serve 🔑 /'sərv/ *verb* (**serves, serv·ing, served**)
1 to give food or drink to someone: *Breakfast is served from 7:30a.m. to 9:00a.m.*
2 to do work for other people: *During the war he served in the army.*

it serves you right words that you use to tell someone that it is right that a bad thing has happened to them: *"I feel really sick." "It serves you right for eating so much!"*

serv·ice 🔑 /'sərvəs/ *noun*
1 [*count*] a business that does useful work for all the people in a country or an area: *The company is starting a new delivery service.* ♦ *financial services*
2 [*noncount*] the work that someone does for customers in a store, restaurant, or hotel: *The food was good but the service was very slow.*
3 [*count, noncount*] help or work that you do for someone: *She left the company after ten years of service.*
4 [*count*] the time when someone looks at a car or machine to see that it is working well: *She takes her car to the garage for a service every six months.*
5 the services [*plural*] the army, navy, and air force
6 [*count*] (**RELIGION**) a meeting in a church with prayers and singing: *We went to the evening service.*

serv·ice sta·tion /'sərvəs ˌsteɪʃn/ *noun* [*count*]
a place where you can buy fuel and other things for your car ➔ **SYNONYM gas station**

ses·sion /'sɛʃn/ *noun* [*count*]
a period of time spent doing a particular activity: *The first computer training session is at nine o'clock.*

set¹ 🔑 /sɛt/ *verb* (**sets, set·ting, set, has set**)
1 to put something somewhere: *Dad set the plate in front of me.*
2 (**ENGLISH LANGUAGE ARTS**) to put the action of a play, book, or movie in a particular time and place: *The movie is set in Chicago in the 1920s.*
3 to make something happen: *They set the school on fire* (= made it start to burn).
4 to make something ready to use, or to make something start working: *I set my alarm clock for seven o'clock.* ♦ *I set the machine to record my favorite TV program.*
5 to decide what something will be; to fix something: *Let's set a date for the meeting.*
6 to become hard or solid: *Wait for the cement to set.*
7 When the sun **sets**, it goes down from the sky. ➔ **ANTONYM rise**
set off; set out to start a trip: *We set off for the beach at two o'clock.*
set the table to put knives, forks, plates, and other things on the table before you eat
set something up to start something: *The company was set up in 2001.*

set² 🔑 /sɛt/ *noun* [*count*]
1 a group of things of the same kind, or a group of things that you use together: *a set of six glasses* ♦ *a tool set*
2 a piece of equipment for receiving electronic signals: *a TV set*
3 a place where actors perform a play or part of a movie or TV program: *Everyone needs to be on the set in five minutes, please.*
4 (**SPORTS**) a group of games that form part of a match in TENNIS or VOLLEYBALL: *He won in straight sets* (= without losing a set).

set·back /'sɛtbæk/ *noun* [*count*]
a problem that stops you from making progress: *The team suffered a major setback when their best player was injured.*

set·ting /'sɛtɪŋ/ *noun* [*count*]
1 the place where something is or where something happens: *The house is in a beautiful setting on top of a hill.*
2 one of the positions of the controls of a machine: *What setting should the oven be on?*

set·tle 🔑 /'sɛtl/ *verb* (**set·tles, set·tling, set·tled**)
1 to decide something after talking with someone; to end a discussion or an argument: *That's settled then, we'll go on Monday.* ♦ *Have you settled your argument with Ray?*
2 to go to live in a new place and stay there: *The family left Minnesota and finally settled in Iowa.*
3 to come down and rest somewhere: *The bird settled on a branch.*
4 to pay something: *Have you settled your bill?*
settle down
1 to sit down or lie down so that you are comfortable: *I settled down in front of the television.*
2 to become calm and quiet: *The children settled down and went to sleep.*
3 to begin to have a calm life in one place: *When are you going to get married and settle down?*
settle in to start to feel happy in a new place: *We only moved to this apartment last week, and we haven't settled in yet.*

set·tle·ment /'sɛtlmənt/ *noun* [*count*]
1 an agreement about something after talking or arguing: *After days of talks, the two sides reached a settlement.*
2 (**GEOGRAPHY**) a group of homes in a place where no people have lived before: *a settlement in the forest*

set·tler /'sɛtlər/ *noun* [*count*]
(**HISTORY**) a person who goes to live in a place where not many people live: *early settlers in Virginia*

sev·en 🔑 /'sɛvən/ *number*
7

sev·en·teen 🔑 /,sɛvən'tin/ *number*
17

▶ **sev·en·teenth** /,sɛvən'tinθ/ *pronoun, adjective, adverb, noun* [*count*]
17th

sev·enth /'sɛvənθ/ *pronoun, adjective, adverb, noun* [*count*]
1 7th
2 one of seven equal parts of something; ⅐

sev·en·ty 🔑 /'sɛvənti/ *number*
1 70
2 the seventies [*plural*] the numbers, years, or temperature between 70 and 79
in your seventies between the ages of 70 and 79

▶ **sev·en·ti·eth** /'sɛvənṭiəθ/ *pronoun, adjective, adverb, noun* [*count*]
70th

sev·er·al 🔑 /'sɛvrəl/ *adjective, pronoun*
more than two but not many: *I've read this book several times.* ♦ *Several letters arrived this morning.* ♦ *If you need a pen, there are several on the table.*

se·vere /sə'vɪr/ *adjective* (**se·ver·er, se·ver·est**)
1 not kind or gentle: *a severe punishment*
2 very bad: *She suffers from severe headaches.* ♦ *We're expecting a severe* (= very cold) *winter.*
▶ **se·vere·ly** /sə'vɪrli/ *adverb*: *They punished him severely.* ♦ *She was severely injured in the accident.*

sew 🔑 /soʊ/ *verb* (**sews, sew·ing, sewed, has sewed** or **has sewn** /soʊn/)

ⓘ **PRONUNCIATION**
The word **sew** sounds just like **so**.

to use a needle and cotton to join pieces of material together or to join something to material: *He sewed a button on his shirt.* ♦ *Can you sew?*

sew·age /'suɪdʒ/ *noun* [*noncount*]
the waste material from people's bodies that is carried away from their homes in underground pipes

sew·er /'suər/ *noun* [*count*]
an underground pipe that carries human waste to a place where it can be treated

sewing

sewing machine

sew·ing /'soʊɪŋ/ *noun* [*noncount*]
the activity of sewing; something that you sew: *a sewing machine*

sewn form of **sew**

sex 🔑 **AWL** /sɛks/ *noun* (*plural* **sex·es**)
1 [*count, noncount*] (**BIOLOGY**) the state of being a male or a female: *What sex is your dog?* ◆ *the male sex*
2 [*noncount*] when two people put their bodies together, sometimes to make a baby: *to have sex*

sex·ism **AWL** /'sɛksɪzəm/ *noun* [*noncount*]
the unfair treatment of people, especially women, because of their sex; the attitude that causes this: *sexism in the workplace*
▸ **sex·ist** /'sɛksɪst/ *adjective*: *a sexist attitude toward women*

sex·u·al 🔑 **AWL** /'sɛkʃuəl/ *adjective*
connected with sex: *a campaign for sexual equality* ◆ *sexual organs*
▸ **sex·u·al·ly** **AWL** /'sɛkʃuəli/ *adverb*: *to be sexually active*

sex·y /'sɛksi/ *adjective* (**sex·i·er, sex·i·est**)
attractive or exciting in a sexual way: *a sexy guy* ◆ *sexy clothes*

sh! (also **shh!**) /ʃ/ *exclamation*
be quiet!: *Sh! You'll wake the baby up!*

shab·by /'ʃæbi/ *adjective* (**shab·bi·er, shab·bi·est**)
old and in bad condition because it has been used a lot: *This coat's getting a little shabby.*
▸ **shab·bi·ly** /'ʃæbəli/ *adverb*: *She was shabbily dressed.*

shack /ʃæk/ *noun* [*count*]
a small building that has not been built well

shade¹ 🔑 /ʃeɪd/ *noun*
1 [*noncount*] a place where it is dark and cool because the sun does not shine there: *We sat in the shade of a big tree.*
2 [*count*] a thing that keeps strong light from your eyes: *I bought a new shade for the lamp.*
3 [*count*] how light or dark a color is: *I'm looking for a shirt in a darker shade of green.*

shade

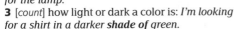

shadow | shade

shade² /ʃeɪd/ *verb* (**shades, shad·ing, shad·ed**)
to stop light from shining on something: *He shaded his eyes with his hand.*

shad·ow 🔑 /'ʃædoʊ/ *noun* [*count*]
a dark shape that you see near someone or something that is in front of the light: *The dog was chasing its own shadow.* ⊃ Look at the picture at **shade**.

shad·y /'ʃeɪdi/ *adjective* (**shad·i·er, shad·i·est**)
not in the sun: *We sat in a shady part of the garden.*

shake 🔑 /ʃeɪk/ *verb* (**shakes, shak·ing, shook** /ʃʊk/, **has shak·en** /'ʃeɪkən/)
1 to move quickly from side to side or up and down; to make something do this: *The house shakes when trains go past.* ◆ *He was shaking with fear.* ◆ *Shake the bottle before opening it.* ◆ *An explosion shook the windows.*
2 to disturb or upset someone or something: *The scandal shook the whole country.*
3 to cause something to be less certain: *Nothing could shake her belief that she was right.*
shake hands to hold someone's hand and move it up and down when you meet them
shake your head to move your head from side to side to say "no"

shak·y /'ʃeɪki/ *adjective* (**shak·i·er, shak·i·est**)
1 shaking because you are sick or afraid: *You have shaky hands.*
2 not firm; not strong: *That ladder looks a little shaky.*

shall /ʃəl; ʃæl/ *modal verb*
1 a word that you use in questions when you are asking, offering, or suggesting something: *Shall we go now?*
2 (*formal*) a word that you use to say that something must happen, or will definitely happen: *You shall not steal.* ⊃ Look at the note at **modal verb**.

shal·low /'ʃæloʊ/ *adjective* (**shal·low·er, shal·low·est**)
1 not deep; with not much water: *This part of the river is shallow – we can walk across.*
2 not interested in serious thought: *a shallow person* ⊃ **ANTONYM deep**

shame 🔑 /ʃeɪm/ *noun*
1 [*noncount*] the unhappy feeling that you have when you have done something wrong or stupid: *She was filled with shame after she lied to her parents.* ⊃ The adjective is **ashamed**.
2 [*singular*] a fact or situation that disappoints you or makes you feel sad: *It's a shame you can't come to the party.* ◆ *"Sally's not well." "What a shame!"* ⊃ **SYNONYM pity**

shame·ful /'ʃeɪmfl/ *adjective*
that someone should feel bad about: *a shameful waste of money*

shame·less /'ʃeɪmləs/ *adjective*
doing bad things without caring what other people think: *It was a shameless attempt to copy someone else's work.*

sham·poo /ʃæm'pu/ *noun* [*count, noncount*]
(*plural* **sham·poos**)
a special liquid for washing your hair: *a bottle of shampoo*
▸ **sham·poo** *verb* (**sham·poos, sham·poo·ing, sham·pooed**): *How often do you shampoo your hair?*

shapes

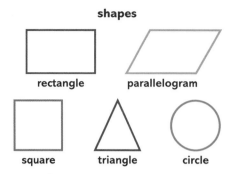

rectangle   parallelogram

square   triangle   circle

shape¹ 🔑 /ʃeɪp/ *noun*
1 [*count, noncount*] what you see if you draw a line around something; the form of something: *What shape is the table – round or square?* ◆ *I bought a bowl in the shape of a fish.* ◆ *Circles, squares, and triangles are all different shapes.*
2 [*noncount*] the physical condition of someone or something: *He was in bad shape after the accident.* ◆ *I like to keep in shape* (= stay in good physical condition) *by exercising every day.*
out of shape (used about a person) not in good physical condition: *I didn't realize how out of shape I was!*
take shape to start to develop well: *Plans for the new building are beginning to take shape.*

shape² 🔑 /ʃeɪp/ *verb* (**shapes, shap·ing, shaped**)
to give a particular shape to something: *She shaped the clay into a pot.*

shaped 🔑 /ʃeɪpt/ *adjective*
having a certain shape: *He gave me a birthday card shaped like a cat.* ◆ *a heart-shaped box of chocolates*

share¹ 🔑 /ʃɛr/ *verb* (**shares, shar·ing, shared**)
1 to divide something between two or more people: *Share this candy with your friends.* ◆ *We shared a large pizza between three of us.*
2 to have or use something with another person: *I share a bedroom with my sister.*

share² 🔑 /ʃɛr/ *noun*
1 [*singular*] a part of something bigger that each person has: *Here is your share of the money.* ◆ *I did my share of the work.*
2 [*count*] (**BUSINESS**) one of equal parts which the value of a company is divided into, and which are sold to people who want to own part of the company: *She owns shares in the company.*

share·hold·er /ʃɛrhoʊldər/ *noun* [*count*]
(**BUSINESS**) a person who owns shares in a company

shark /ʃɑrk/ *noun*
[*count*]
a big fish that lives in the ocean. **Sharks** have sharp teeth and are often dangerous.

shark

fin

sharp¹ 🔑 /ʃɑrp/ *adjective* (**sharp·er, sharp·est**)
1 with an edge or point that cuts or makes holes easily: *a sharp knife* ◆ *a sharp needle* ⊃ **ANTONYM blunt**
2 clear and easy to see: *We could see the sharp outline of the mountains against the sky.*
3 strong and sudden: *a sharp bend in the road* ◆ *I felt a sharp pain in my leg.*
4 able to see, hear, or learn well: *She has a very sharp mind.* ◆ *sharp eyes*
5 sudden and angry: *sharp words*
6 (symbol ♯) (**MUSIC**) half a note higher than a particular musical note: *C sharp* ⊃ Look at **flat¹**(3).
▶ **sharp·ly** /ʃɑrpli/ *adverb*: *The road bends sharply to the left.* ◆ *"Go away!" he said sharply.*

sharp² /ʃɑrp/ *adverb*
1 exactly: *Be here at six o'clock sharp.*
2 with a big change of direction: *Turn sharp right at the next corner.*

sharp·en /ʃɑrpən/ *verb* (**sharp·ens, sharp·en·ing, sharp·ened**)
to make something sharp or sharper: *They sharpened all the knives.*

sharp·en·er /ʃɑrpənər/ *noun* [*count*]
a thing that you use for making something sharp: *a pencil sharpener* ⊃ Look at the picture at **stationery**.

shat·ter /ʃætər/ *verb* (**shat·ters, shat·ter·ing, shat·tered**)
1 to break into very small pieces; to break something into very small pieces: *The glass hit the floor and shattered.* ◆ *The explosion shattered the windows.*
2 to destroy something completely: *Her hopes were shattered by the terrible news.*

shave /ʃeɪv/ *verb* (**shaves, shav·ing, shaved**)
to cut hair off your face or body by cutting it very close with a special knife (called a **RAZOR**): *He shaves every morning.*
▶ **shave** *noun* [*count*]: *I didn't have a shave this morning.*

shav·er /ʃeɪvər/ *noun* [*count*]
an electric tool that you use for **SHAVING** ⊃ Look at the picture at **razor**.

shawl /ʃɔl/ *noun* [*count*]
a big piece of cloth that a woman wears around her shoulders, or that you put around a baby

she /ʃi/ *pronoun* (*plural* **they** /ðeɪ/)
a woman or girl who the sentence is about:
"Where's your sister?" "She's (= she is) *at work."*

shear /ʃɪr/ *verb* (**shears, shear·ing, sheared,**
has shorn /ʃɔrn/ **or has sheared**)
to cut the wool off a sheep

shears /ʃɪrz/ *noun*
[*plural*]
a tool like a very large
pair of scissors that
you use for cutting
plants, flowers, etc.: *a*
pair of shears

shears

— handle

blade

a pair of shears

shed¹ /ʃɛd/ *noun*
[*count*]
a small building where you keep things or
animals: *We keep our tools in the shed.*

shed² /ʃɛd/ *verb* (**sheds, shed·ding, shed, has**
shed)
to lose something because it falls off: *The snake*
shed its skin.

she'd /ʃid/ short for **she had, she would**

sheep /ʃip/ *noun*
[*count*] (*plural* **sheep**)
an animal that people
keep on farms for its
meat and its wool ⊃
Look at **lamb**.

sheep

sheer /ʃɪr/ *adjective*
1 used to show the
large size, amount, or
level of something:
sheer nonsense ♦ *The first thing you notice is the*
sheer size of the building.
2 going down quickly from a high place to a low
place: *It was a sheer drop to the ocean.*

sheet /ʃit/ *noun* [*count*]
1 a big piece of thin material for a bed: *I put*
some clean sheets on the bed.
2 a thin, flat piece of something like paper,
glass, or metal: *a sheet of writing paper*

shelf /ʃɛlf/ *noun* [*count*] (*plural* **shelves**
/ʃɛlvz/)
a long, flat piece of wood on a wall or in a
cabinet where things can stand: *Put the plates*
on the shelf. ♦ *bookshelves*

shell /ʃɛl/ *noun* [*count*]
1 (**BIOLOGY**) the hard outside part of birds' eggs,
nuts, and some animals: *Turtles have a hard*
shell. ⊃ Look at **seashell**. ⊃ Look at the picture at
crustacean.
2 a metal container that explodes when it
comes out of a large gun

she'll /ʃil/ short for **she will**

shellfish

mussel   **oyster**

shell·fish /'ʃɛlfɪʃ/ *noun* [*count*] (*plural* **shell·fish**)
a kind of animal that lives in water and that has
a shell

shel·ter¹ /'ʃɛltər/ *noun*
1 [*noncount*] protection from bad weather or
danger: *We took shelter from the rain under a*
tree. ♦ *People ran for shelter when the bombs*
started to fall.
2 [*count*] a place that protects people or animals
from bad weather, danger, etc.: *a bus shelter* (=
for people who are waiting at a bus stop)

shel·ter² /'ʃɛltər/ *verb* (**shel·ters, shel·ter·ing,**
shel·tered)
1 to make someone or something safe from bad
weather or danger: *The trees shelter the house*
from the wind.
2 to go to a place where you will be safe from
bad weather or danger: *Let's shelter from the*
rain under that tree.

shelves plural of **shelf**

shep·herd /'ʃɛpərd/ *noun* [*count*]
a person who takes care of sheep

sher·iff /'ʃɛrəf/ *noun* [*count*]
an officer of the law, who is in charge of the
police force of a U.S. county

she's /ʃiz/ short for **she is, she has**

shield¹ /ʃild/ *noun* [*count*]
a big piece of metal, wood, or leather that
soldiers carried in front of their bodies when
they were fighting in wars long ago. Some
police officers carry **shields** now.

shield² /ʃild/ *verb* (**shields, shield·ing,**
shield·ed)
to keep someone or something safe from
danger or from being hurt: *She shielded her eyes*
from the sun with her hand.

shift¹ **AWL** /ʃɪft/ *verb* (**shifts, shift·ing, shift·ed**)
1 to move something from one place to
another: *Can you help me to shift the bed? I want*
to sweep the floor.
2 to change the way you think about
something: *Attitudes toward marriage have*
shifted over the years.
3 to change the position of **GEARS** in a car (= the
parts that control how fast the wheels turn): *He*
shifted into first gear and drove off.

shift² AWL /ʃɪft/ noun [count]
1 a change in what people think about something: *There has been a **shift in** public opinion away from the war.*
2 a group of workers who begin work when another group finishes: *the night shift*

shin /ʃɪn/ noun [count]
the bone in the front part of your leg from your knee to your foot

shine /ʃaɪn/ verb (shines, shin·ing, shone /ʃoʊn/ or shined, has shone or has shined)
1 to give out light: *The sun is shining.*
2 to be bright: *I polished the silver until it shone.*
3 to direct a light at someone or something: *Don't **shine** your flashlight **in** my eyes!*

shin·y /ˈʃaɪni/ adjective (shin·i·er, shin·i·est)
causing a bright effect when in the sun or in light: *The new shampoo leaves your hair soft and shiny.* ♦ *He has a shiny new car.*

ship¹ /ʃɪp/ noun [count]
a big boat for carrying passengers and goods on the ocean: *We went to India **by ship**.*

ship² /ʃɪp/ verb (ships, ship·ping, shipped)
to send or carry goods from one place to another: *The fruit is shipped from Hawaii by airplane.*

ship·ment /ˈʃɪpmənt/ noun
1 [count] a quantity of goods that is sent from one place to another: *a shipment of grain*
2 [noncount] the transportation of goods from one place to another: *Is the cargo ready for shipment?*

ship·ping /ˈʃɪpɪŋ/ noun [noncount]
1 the activity of carrying goods from one place to another: *Your books are all packed and ready for shipping.*
2 ships in general or considered as a group: *The port is now open to shipping.* ♦ *a shipping company*

ship·wreck /ˈʃɪprɛk/ noun [count]
an accident on the ocean when a ship is destroyed in bad weather or on rocks
be shipwrecked to be on a ship when it is in a shipwreck: *They were shipwrecked off the coast of Maine.*

shirt /ʃərt/ noun [count]

🛈 **PRONUNCIATION**
The word **shirt** sounds like **hurt**.

a thin piece of clothing that you wear on the top part of your body ⊃ Look at the picture at **clothes**.

shiv·er /ˈʃɪvər/ verb (shiv·ers, shiv·er·ing, shiv·ered)
to shake because you are cold, afraid, or sick: *We were shivering with cold.*
▶ **shiv·er** noun [count]

shoal /ʃoʊl/ noun [count]
(**BIOLOGY**) a large group of fish that feed and swim together

shock¹ /ʃɑk/ noun
1 [count] a very bad surprise: *The news of his death **came as a shock to** all of us.*
2 [noncount] (**HEALTH**) a medical condition that makes you very weak, caused by damage to the body: *After the accident, two people were taken to the hospital suffering from shock.*
3 [count] a sudden pain when electricity goes through your body: *Don't touch that wire – you'll get an **electric shock**.*

shock² /ʃɑk/ verb (shocks, shock·ing, shocked)
to give someone a very bad surprise; to upset someone: *I was shocked by his behavior.*
▶ **shock·ing** /ˈʃɑkɪŋ/ adjective: *a shocking crime*

shocked /ʃɑkt/ adjective
feeling surprised in a bad way, and upset or angry: *Don't look so shocked – I did warn you!*

shoes

sneakers   sandal

heel

shoe   slippers

shoes   boot

shoe /ʃu/ noun [count]
a covering made of leather or plastic that you wear on your foot: *a pair of shoes* ♦ *What size shoes do you take?* ♦ *a shoe store*

shoe·lace /ˈʃuleɪs/ (also **lace** /leɪs/) noun [count]
a long, thin piece of material like string that you tie to close a shoe: *Tie your shoelaces.*

shone form of **shine**

shook form of **shake**

shoot¹ 🔑 /ʃut/ *verb* (shoots, shoot·ing, shot /ʃɑt/, has shot)
1 to fire a gun or another weapon; to hurt or kill a person or an animal with a gun: *She shot a bird.* ◆ *The police officer was shot in the arm.*
2 to move quickly or suddenly: *The car shot past us at 75 miles per hour.*
3 to make a movie: *They're shooting a movie about the war.*
4 (**SPORTS**) (in some sports) to throw, hit, or kick a ball toward or into the area where you score points: *He shot the ball right past me.*
shoot up to increase very quickly: *Prices have shot up in the past year.*

shoot² /ʃut/ *noun* [count]
(**BIOLOGY**) a new part of a plant: *The first shoots appear in spring.* ⟳ Look at the picture at **plant**.

shoot·ing /ˈʃutɪŋ/ *noun* [count]
a situation in which someone is shot with a gun: *Two people were injured in the shooting.*

shop¹ 🔑 /ʃɑp/ *verb* (shops, shop·ping, shopped)
to go to buy things from stores: *I'm **shopping** for some new clothes.* ⟳ Look at **shopper**, **shopping**.
shop around to look at the price and quality of an item in different stores before you decide where to buy it: *We shopped around for the best deal on a new car.*

shop² /ʃɑp/ *noun* [count]
1 a small store which usually sells only one type of product: *a gift shop*
2 a place where things are made or repaired: *Our car will be in the shop until Friday.*

shop·lift·ing /ˈʃɑplɪftɪŋ/ *noun* [noncount]
the crime of stealing things from stores: *He was accused of shoplifting.*
▶ **shop·lift·er** /ˈʃɑplɪftər/ *noun* [count]: *Shoplifters will be prosecuted.*

shop·per /ˈʃɑpər/ *noun* [count]: *The streets were full of shoppers.*

shop·ping 🔑 /ˈʃɑpɪŋ/ *noun* [noncount]
1 buying things from stores: *She **does** her **shopping** after work.* ◆ *I usually **go shopping** on the weekend.*
2 the things that you have bought in a store: *Will you carry my shopping for me?*

Collocations

Shopping

shopping
- **go/go out** shopping/grocery shopping
- **go to** the grocery store/the drug store/the mall

at the store
- **try on** clothes/shoes
- **stand in/wait in** the checkout line

buying
- **accept/take** credit cards
- **pay** in cash/by check/by (credit) card
- **ask for/get** a receipt/a refund/a discount
- **return/exchange** an item/a product

shop·ping cen·ter /ˈʃɑpɪŋ ˌsɛntər/ *noun* [count]
a place where there are many stores, either outside or in a covered building

shop·ping mall /ˈʃɑpɪŋ mɔl/ *noun* [count] = **mall**

shore /ʃɔr/ *noun* [count]
(**GEOGRAPHY**) the land next to the ocean or a lake: *The swimmer kept close to the shore.*

shorn form of **shear**

short 🔑 /ʃɔrt/ *adjective* (short·er, short·est)
1 a small distance from one end to the other: *Her hair is very short.* ◆ *We live a short distance from the beach.* ⟳ **ANTONYM long**
2 less tall than most people: *I'm too short to reach the top shelf.* ◆ *a short, fat man* ⟳ **ANTONYM tall**
3 lasting for only a little time: *The play was very short.* ◆ *a short vacation* ⟳ **ANTONYM long**
be short for something to be a short way of saying or writing something: *"Tom" is short for "Thomas."*
be short of something to not have enough of something: *I'm short of money this month.*
for short as a short way of saying or writing something: *My name's Jennifer, but everyone calls me "Jen" for short.*

short·age /ˈʃɔrtɪdʒ/ *noun* [count]
a situation where there is not enough of something: *a water shortage* ◆ *There is a shortage of good teachers.*

short cir·cuit /ˌʃɔrt ˈsərkət/ *noun* [count]
(**PHYSICS**) a bad electrical connection that causes a machine to stop working

short·cut /ˈʃɔrtkʌt/ *noun* [count]
a shorter way to get somewhere or to do something: *We **took a shortcut** to school across the field.*

short·en /ˈʃɔrtn/ *verb* (short·ens, short·en·ing, short·ened)
to become shorter or to make something shorter: *The pants were too long, so I shortened them.*

short·ly /ˈʃɔrtli/ *adverb*
soon: *The doctor will see you shortly, Mr. Smith.* ◆ *We left shortly after six o'clock.*

shorts /ʃɔrts/ *noun* [plural]
1 short pants that end above your knees: *a pair of shorts* ⟳ Look at the picture at **clothes**.
2 a piece of loose clothing that men wear under their pants

short sto·ry /ˌʃɔrt 'stɔri/ *noun* [count] (*plural* short sto·ries)
(**ENGLISH LANGUAGE ARTS**) a piece of writing that is shorter than a novel

short-term /ˌʃɔrt 'tərm/ *adjective*
of or for a short period of time: *What are your short-term plans?* ⊃ **ANTONYM long-term**

shot¹ form of **shoot¹**

shot² /ʃɑt/ *noun* [count]
1 the action of firing a gun, or the noise that this makes: *He fired a shot.*
2 (**SPORTS**) the action of throwing, hitting, or kicking a ball in certain sports: *He took a shot at the basket.*
3 a photograph: *This is a good shot of you.*
4 (**HEALTH**) the act of putting a drug into your body using a needle: *a flu shot*

shot·gun /ʃɑtgʌn/ *noun* [count]
a long gun that is used for shooting small animals and birds

should /ʃəd; ʃʊd/ *modal verb*

🛈 **PRONUNCIATION**
The word **should** sounds like **good**, because we don't say the letter l in this word.

1 a word that you use to give or ask someone for advice: *You should try that new restaurant.* ◆ *Should I invite him to the party?*
2 a word that you use to tell or ask someone what is the right thing to do: *If you feel sick, you should stay in bed.* ◆ *You shouldn't eat so much chocolate.* ◆ *I'm tired. I shouldn't have gone to bed so late.* ⊃ **SYNONYM ought to**
3 a word that you use to say what you think will happen or what you think is true: *They should be here soon.* ⊃ Look at the note at **modal verb**.

shoul·der /ʃoʊldər/ *noun* [count]

🛈 **PRONUNCIATION**
The word **shoulder** sounds like **older**.

1 the part of your body between your neck and your arm ⊃ Look at the picture at **body**.
2 a narrow part along the side of a road where cars can stop: *The car was making a strange noise, so we drove onto the shoulder.*

shoul·der bag /ʃoʊldər bæg/ *noun* [count]
a type of bag that you carry over one shoulder with a long, narrow piece of cloth or leather

shoul·der blade /ʃoʊldər bleɪd/ *noun* [count]
(**BIOLOGY**) one of the two large, flat bones on each side of your back

shoul·der-length /ʃoʊldər lɛŋθ/ *adjective*
(used about hair) long enough to reach your shoulders

should·n't /ʃʊdnt/ short for **should not**

should've /ʃʊdəv/ short for **should have**

shout /ʃaʊt/ *verb* (shouts, shout·ing, shout·ed)
to speak very loudly: *Don't shout at me!* ◆ *"Go back!" she shouted.* ◆ *He shouted out instructions to everyone on the team.*
▶ **shout** *noun* [count]: *We heard a shout for help.*

shove /ʃʌv/ *verb* (shoves, shov·ing, shoved)
to push someone or something in a rough way: *They shoved him through the door.*
▶ **shove** *noun* [usually singular]: *She gave the door a shove with her shoulder.*

shov·el¹ /ʃʌvl/ *noun* [count]
a tool that you use for picking up and moving earth, sand, or snow

shovel

shov·el² *verb* (shov·els, shov·el·ing, shov·eled)
to move something with a **shovel**: *We shoveled the snow off the path.*

show¹ /ʃoʊ/ *verb* (shows, show·ing, showed, has shown /ʃoʊn/ or has showed)
1 to let someone see something: *She showed me her family photos.* ◆ *You have to show your ticket on the train.* ◆ *They're showing that movie at a theater near my house.*
2 to make something clear; to explain something to someone: *Can you show me how to use the computer?* ◆ *Research shows that most people get too little exercise.*
3 to appear or be seen: *The anger showed in his face.*
4 to lead someone to a place: *Let me show you to your room.*
show someone around to go with someone and show them everything in a building: *David showed me around the school.*
show off to talk loudly or do something silly to make people notice you: *Joyce was showing off by driving too fast.*
show something off to let people see something that is new or beautiful: *James wanted to show off his new jacket.*
show up (*informal*) to arrive: *What time did they show up?*

show² /ʃoʊ/ *noun* [count]
1 something that you watch at the theater or on television: *a comedy show* ◆ *Did you enjoy the show?*
2 a group of things in one place that people go to see: *a flower show* ◆ *The paintings are on show at the Museum of Art until May.*

show busi·ness /'ʃoʊ ˌbɪznəs/ *noun* [*noncount*]
the business of entertaining people in the theater, in movies, on television, etc.: *He wants a career in show business.*

show·er /'ʃaʊər/ *verb* (show·ers, show·er·ing, show·ered)
1 to wash yourself under a shower: *After my run, I showered and went back to work.*
2 to cover someone or something with a lot of small falling objects: *Ash from the volcano showered down on the town.*

show·er¹ 🔊 /'ʃaʊər/ *noun* [*count*]
1 a place where you can wash by standing under water that falls from above you: *There's a shower in the bathroom.*
2 the act of washing yourself in a shower: *I took a shower after the tennis match.*
3 rain that falls for a short time: *The day will be cloudy, with occasional heavy showers.*
4 a party where people give presents to a woman who is going to get married or have a baby: *I'm going to my friend's baby shower next week.*

shown form of **show¹**

shrank form of **shrink**

shred /ʃrɛd/ *noun* [*count*]
a small, thin piece of material that has been cut or torn off: *shreds of paper*

shrewd /ʃrud/ *adjective* (shrewd·er, shrewd·est)
able to make good decisions because you understand people or situations well: *She's a very shrewd businesswoman.*

shriek /ʃrik/ *verb* (shrieks, shriek·ing, shrieked)
to make a loud, high sound: *She shrieked with fear* (= because she was afraid).
▶ **shriek** *noun* [*count*]: *He gave a shriek of pain.*

shrill /ʃrɪl/ *adjective* (shrill·er, shrill·est)
A **shrill** sound is high and loud: *a shrill whistle*

shrimp /ʃrɪmp/ *noun* [*count*]
a small animal with a soft shell and a lot of legs that lives in the ocean. It turns pink when you cook it.

shrine /ʃraɪn/ *noun* [*count*]
(**RELIGION**) a special place that is important to people for religious reasons

shrink /ʃrɪŋk/ *verb* (shrinks, shrink·ing, shrank /ʃræŋk/ or shrunk /ʃrʌŋk/, has shrunk)
to become smaller or to make something smaller: *My jeans shrank when I washed them.*

shriv·el /'ʃrɪvl/ *verb* (shriv·els, shriv·el·ing, shriv·eled)
to become smaller, especially because of dry conditions: *The plants shriveled up and died in the hot weather.*

shrub /ʃrʌb/ *noun* [*count*]
a plant like a small low tree

shrug /ʃrʌg/ *verb* (shrugs, shrug·ging, shrugged)
to move your shoulders to show that you do not know or do not care about something: *I asked her where Sam was, but she just shrugged.*
▶ **shrug** *noun* [*count*]: *He answered my question with a shrug.*

shrunk form of **shrink**

shud·der /'ʃʌdər/ *verb* (shud·ders, shud·der·ing, shud·dered)
to shake because you are cold or afraid, or because of a strong feeling: *He shuddered when he saw the snake.*
▶ **shud·der** *noun* [*count*]

shuf·fle /'ʃʌfl/ *verb* (shuf·fles, shuf·fling, shuf·fled)
1 to walk slowly, without taking your feet off the ground: *The old man shuffled along the road.*
2 to mix playing cards before a game: *She shuffled the cards carefully before dealing them.*

shut¹ 🔊 /ʃʌt/ *verb* (shuts, shut·ting, shut, has shut)
to move, or to move something, so that it is not open: *Could you shut the door, please?* ◆ *The door shut behind me.* ⊃ SYNONYM **close**
shut down to close and stop working; to make something close and stop working: *The factory shut down last year.* ⊃ SYNONYM **close down**
shut something off to stop a supply of electricity, water, or gas: *They shut off the gas to our building while they repaired the leak.*
shut up (*informal*) words you use to tell someone to be quiet in a rude way: *Shut up and listen!*

shut² /ʃʌt/ *adjective*
not open: *Is the door shut?* ⊃ SYNONYM **closed**

shut·ter /'ʃʌtər/ *noun* [*count*]
a wooden or metal thing that covers the outside of a window: *Close the shutters at night.*

shut·tle /'ʃʌtl/ *noun* [*count*]
1 an airplane, a bus, or a train that travels regularly between two places
2 = space shuttle

shy 🔊 /ʃaɪ/ *adjective* (shy·er, shy·est)
not able to talk easily to people you do not know: *He was too shy to speak to her.* ◆ *a shy smile*
▶ **shy·ness** /'ʃaɪnəs/ *noun* [*noncount*]: *As a child, she suffered from terrible shyness.*

sib·ling /'sɪblɪŋ/ *noun* [*count*] (*formal*)
a brother or a sister: *Do you have any siblings?*

sick 🔊 /sɪk/ *adjective* (sick·er, sick·est)
(**HEALTH**) not well: *She's taking care of her sick mother.* ◆ *Joe's been out sick* (= away because of illness) *all week.* ⊃ Look at the note at **illness**.
be sick When you **are sick**, food comes up from your stomach and out of your mouth: *He was sick twice during the night.* ⊃ SYNONYM **vomit**

be sick of something to have had or done too much of something, so that you do not want it any longer: *I'm sick of watching TV – let's go out.*
feel sick to feel that food is going to come up from your stomach

sick·ness /ˈsɪknəs/ *noun* [*noncount*]
(**HEALTH**) being or feeling sick: *He could not work for a long time because of sickness.*

side 🔊 /saɪd/ *noun* [*count*]
1 one of the flat outside parts of something: *A box has six sides.*
2 the part of something that is not the front, back, top, or bottom: *There is a door at the side of the house.* • *There's a scratch on the side of my car.*
3 the part of something that is near the edge and away from the middle: *I stood at the side of the road.*
4 the right or left part of something: *He lay on his side.* • *You will see the restaurant on the left side of the street.*
5 one of two groups of people who fight, argue, or play a game against each other: *I thought you were on my side* (= agreed with me). • *Which side won the debate?*
side by side next to each other: *They walked side by side.*
take sides to show that you agree with one person, and not the other, in a fight or an argument

side·burns /ˈsaɪdbərnz/ *noun* [*plural*]
hair that grows down the sides of a man's face, in front of his ears

side ef·fect /ˈsaɪd ɪˌfɛkt/ *noun* [*count*]
(**HEALTH**) an extra and usually bad effect that a drug has on you, as well as its useful effects: *Side effects of the drug may include headaches.*

side·walk /ˈsaɪdwɔk/ *noun* [*count*]
the part at the side of a road where people can walk: *The kids rode their bikes on the sidewalk.*

side·ways /ˈsaɪdweɪz/ *adjective, adverb*
1 to or from the side: *She looked sideways at the girl next to her.*
2 with one of the sides first: *We carried the table sideways through the door.*

siege /sidʒ/ *noun* [*count*]
a situation when an army stays outside a town, or police stay outside a building for a long time so that no one can get in or out

si·es·ta /siˈɛstə/ *noun* [*count*]
a short sleep or rest that people take in the afternoon, especially in hot countries: *to have a siesta*

sieve /sɪv/ *noun* [*count*]
a type of kitchen tool that you use to remove lumps from food such as flour or soup ⊃ Look at the picture at **kitchen**.

sigh /saɪ/ *verb* (sighs, sigh·ing, sighed)
to let out a deep breath, for example because you are sad, tired, or pleased
▶ **sigh** *noun* [*count*]: *"I wish I had more money,"* he said with a sigh.

sight 🔊 /saɪt/ *noun*
1 [*noncount*] the ability to see: *She has poor sight* (= she cannot see well). ⊃ **SYNONYM** eyesight
2 [*noncount*] seeing someone or something: *We had our first sight of the city from the plane.*
3 [*count*] something that you see: *The mountains were a beautiful sight.*
4 **sights** [*plural*] the interesting places, especially in a city or town, that are often visited by tourists: *When you come to St. Louis, I'll show you the sights.*
5 [*noncount*] a position where you can see someone or something: *We watched until they were out of sight* (= until we could not see them). • *Eventually the town came into sight* (= we could see it).
at first sight when you see someone or something for the first time: *He fell in love with her at first sight.*
catch sight of someone or **something** to see someone or something suddenly: *I caught sight of Faye in the crowd.*
lose sight of someone or **something** to no longer be able to see someone or something: *After sailing for an hour we lost sight of land.*

sight·see·ing /ˈsaɪtsiɪŋ/ *noun* [*noncount*]
the activity of visiting interesting buildings and places as a tourist: *to go sightseeing* • *Did you have a chance to do any sightseeing?*
▶ **sight·se·er** /ˈsaɪtsiər/ *noun* [*count*]: *The city was full of sightseers.* ⊃ **SYNONYM** tourist

sign¹ 🔊 /saɪn/ *noun* [*count*]
1 a thing with writing or a picture on it that tells you something: *The sign said "No Smoking."* • *a road sign*

sign

SAN DIEGO
235 miles

2 something that tells you that something exists, is happening, or may happen in the future: *Dark clouds are a sign of rain.*
3 a mark, shape, or movement that has a special meaning: *In mathematics, a cross is a plus sign.* • *I put up my hand as a sign for him to stop.*

sign² 🔊 /saɪn/ *verb* (signs, sign·ing, signed)
to write your name in your own way on something: *Sign here, please.* • *I signed the check.* ⊃ The noun is **signature**.

sig·nal 🔑 /'sɪgnəl/ *noun* [*count*]
1 a light, sound, or movement that tells you something without words: *A red light is a signal for cars to stop.*
2 an electrical wave that carries a sound, a picture, or a message: *I can't get a signal on my cell phone.*
▶ **sig·nal** *verb* (**sig·nals**, **sig·nal·ing**, **sig·naled**): *The police officer **signaled to** the children **to** cross the road.*

sig·na·ture /'sɪgnətʃər/ *noun* [*count*]
your name as you usually write it, for example at the end of a letter ⊃ The verb is **sign**.

sig·nif·i·cance **AWL** /sɪg'nɪfəkəns/ *noun* [*noncount*]
the importance or meaning of something: *What is **the significance of** this discovery?*

sig·nif·i·cant **AWL** /sɪg'nɪfəkənt/ *adjective*
1 important or large enough to be noticed: *a significant increase in the number of accidents*
2 having a particular meaning: *It is significant that he changed his will just before he died.*

sign lan·guage /'saɪn ˌlæŋgwɪdʒ/ *noun* [*noncount*]
(**ENGLISH LANGUAGE ARTS**) a language that uses movements of the hands. It is used especially by people who cannot hear.

sign·post /'saɪnpoʊst/ *noun* [*count*]
a sign beside a road that shows the way to a place and how far it is

Sikh /sik/ *noun* [*count*]
(**RELIGION**) a person who follows one of the religions of India (called **SIKHISM**)
▶ **Sikh** *adjective*

si·lence 🔑 /'saɪləns/ *noun*
1 [*noncount*] a situation in which there is no sound: *I can only work **in** complete **silence**.*
2 [*count, noncount*] a time when no one speaks or makes a noise: *There was a long silence before she answered the question.* ◆ *We ate our dinner **in** silence.*

si·lent /'saɪlənt/ *adjective*
1 with no sound; completely quiet: *Everyone was asleep, and the house was silent.*
2 If you are **silent**, you are not speaking: *I asked him a question and he was silent for a moment before he answered.*
▶ **si·lent·ly** /'saɪləntli/ *adverb*: *The cat moved silently toward the bird.*

sil·hou·ette /ˌsɪlu'ɛt/ *noun* [*count*]
the dark shape of something that you can see against a light surface: *the silhouette of buildings against the sky*

sil·i·con /'sɪlɪkən; 'sɪlɪkɑn/ *noun* [*noncount*]
(symbol **Si**)
(**CHEMISTRY**) a chemical substance that is used for making computer parts and glass

silk /sɪlk/ *noun* [*noncount*]
a soft, smooth cloth made from a substance that an insect (called a **SILKWORM**) makes: *This scarf is made of silk.* ◆ *a silk shirt*

silk·y /'sɪlki/ *adjective* (**silk·i·er**, **silk·i·est**)
soft, smooth, and shiny like **SILK**: *silky hair*

sill /sɪl/ *noun* [*count*]
a narrow shelf at the bottom of a window

sil·ly 🔑 /'sɪli/ *adjective* (**sil·li·er**, **sil·li·est**)
not sensible or serious; stupid: *Don't be so silly!* ◆ *It was **silly of** you **to** leave the door open when you went out.*

sil·ver¹ 🔑 /'sɪlvər/ *noun* [*noncount*]
1 (symbol **Ag**) (**CHEMISTRY**) a shiny gray metal that is valuable: *a silver necklace*
2 things that are made of silver, for example knives, forks, and dishes: *The thieves stole some valuable silver.*

sil·ver² /'sɪlvər/ *adjective*
with the color of silver: *Our new car is silver.*

sil·ver·ware /'sɪlvərwɛr/ *noun* [*noncount*]
forks, knives, and spoons that are made of silver or some other metal

sim·i·lar 🔑 **AWL** /'sɪmələr/ *adjective*
the same in some ways but not completely the same: *Rats are **similar to** mice, but they are bigger.* ◆ *Jane and her sister look very similar.*

sim·i·lar·i·ty **AWL** /ˌsɪmə'lærəti/ *noun* [*count*]
(*plural* **sim·i·lar·i·ties**)
a way that people or things are the same: *There are a lot of **similarities between** the two countries.*
⊃ **ANTONYM difference**

sim·i·le /'sɪməli/ *noun* [*count, noncount*]
(**ENGLISH LANGUAGE ARTS**) a word or phrase that compares one thing with something else, using the words "like" or "as": *"As white as snow" and "a face like a mask" are similes.* ⊃ Look at **metaphor**.

sim·mer /'sɪmər/ *verb* (**sim·mers**, **sim·mer·ing**, **sim·mered**)
to cook gently in water that is almost boiling: *Simmer the vegetables for ten minutes.*

sim·ple 🔑 /'sɪmpl/ *adjective* (**sim·pler**, **sim·plest**)
1 easy to do or understand: *This dictionary is written in simple English.* ◆ *"How do you open this?" "I'll show you – it's simple."* ⊃ **ANTONYM difficult**
2 without a lot of different parts or extra things: *She wore a simple black dress.* ◆ *a simple meal* ⊃ **SYNONYM plain**

sim·plic·i·ty /sɪm'plɪsəti/ *noun* [*noncount*]
the quality of being simple: *I like the simplicity of these paintings.*

sim·pli·fy /'sɪmpləfaɪ/ *verb* (**sim·pli·fies**, **sim·pli·fy·ing**, **sim·pli·fied**, **has sim·pli·fied**)
to make something easier to do or understand:

The story has been simplified so that the children can understand it.

sim·ply /ˈsɪmpli/ *adverb*
1 a word that you use when you want to show how easy or basic something is: *Simply add water and stir.* ⊃ **SYNONYM just**
2 in a simple way: *Please explain it more simply.*
3 really: *The weather was simply terrible – it rained every day!*

sim·u·late **AWL** /ˈsɪmyəleɪt/ *verb* (sim·u·lates, sim·u·lat·ing, sim·u·lat·ed)
to create the effect or appearance of something else: *The astronauts trained in a machine that simulates conditions in space.*
▸ **sim·u·la·tion** **AWL** /ˌsɪmyəˈleɪʃn/ *noun* [count, noncount]: *a computer simulation of a nuclear attack*

si·mul·ta·ne·ous /ˌsaɪmlˈteɪniəs/ *adjective*
happening at exactly the same time: *The city was hit by three simultaneous explosions.*
▸ **si·mul·ta·ne·ous·ly** /ˌsaɪmlˈteɪniəsli/ *adverb*: *"I'm sorry!" they said simultaneously.*

sin /sɪn/ *noun* [count, noncount]
(**RELIGION**) something that your religion says you should not do, because it is very bad: *Stealing is a sin.*
▸ **sin** *verb* (sins, sin·ning, sinned): *He knew that he had sinned.*

since /sɪns/ *adverb, preposition, conjunction*
1 from a time in the past until a later time in the past or until now: *He's been sick since Sunday.* ◆ *I haven't seen him since 2007.* ◆ *She's lived here since she was a child.* ◆ *George went to Alaska in 1994 and has lived there ever since* (= in all the time from then until now). ◆ *Andy left three years ago and we haven't seen him since.*

Which word?

For or since?
■ We use **for** to say how long something has continued, for example in **hours**, **days**, or **years**: *She's been sick for three days.* ◆ *I've lived in this house for ten months.* ◆ *We have been married for ten years.*
■ We use **since** with points of time in the past, for example a **time** on the clock, a **date**, or an **event**: *I've been here since six o'clock.* ◆ *She has been alone since her husband died.* ◆ *We've been married since 1996.*

2 because: *Since it's your birthday, I'll buy you a coffee.* ⊃ **SYNONYM as**
3 at a time after another time in the past: *They got married five years ago and have since had three children.*

sin·cere /sɪnˈsɪr/ *adjective*
being honest and meaning what you say: *Were*

you being sincere when you said that you loved me? ⊃ **ANTONYM insincere**

sin·cere·ly /sɪnˈsɪrli/ *adverb*
1 in a sincere way: *I am sincerely grateful to you.*
2 **Sincerely** a word that you write at the end of a formal letter, before your name

sing /sɪŋ/ *verb* (sings, sing·ing, sang /sæŋ/, has sung /sʌŋ/)
(**MUSIC**) to make music with your voice: *She sang a song.* ◆ *The birds were singing.*

sing·er /ˈsɪŋər/ *noun* [count]
(**MUSIC**) a person who sings, or whose job is singing, especially in public: *an opera singer*

sin·gle¹ /ˈsɪŋɡl/ *adjective*
1 only one: *He gave her a single red rose.*
2 a word that makes "every" stronger: *You answered every single question correctly.*
3 not married: *Are you married or single?*
4 for one person: *I would like a single room, please.* ◆ *a single bed* ⊃ Look at **double¹**(3).

sin·gle² /ˈsɪŋɡl/ *noun* [count]
1 (**MUSIC**) one song, which you can buy on a CD, or from the Internet, etc.: *Have you heard the band's new single?* ⊃ Look at **album**(1).
2 a piece of paper money that is worth one dollar

sin·gle par·ent /ˌsɪŋɡl ˈpɛrənt/ *noun* [count]
a person who takes care of their child or children alone, without help from the other parent

sin·gu·lar /ˈsɪŋɡyələr/ *noun* [noncount]
(**ENGLISH LANGUAGE ARTS**) the form of a word that you use for one person or thing: *The singular of "men" is "man."*
▸ **sin·gu·lar** *adjective*: *"Table" is a singular noun.* ⊃ Look at **plural**.

sin·is·ter /ˈsɪnəstər/ *adjective*
making you feel that something bad will happen: *a sinister atmosphere*

sink¹ /sɪŋk/ *verb* (sinks, sink·ing, sank /sæŋk/, has sunk /sʌŋk/)
1 to go down under water: *If you throw a stone into water, it sinks.* ◆ *The fishing boat sank to the bottom of the ocean.* ⊃ Look at **float**(1).
2 to make a ship go down under water: *The ship was sunk by a torpedo.*
3 to go down: *The sun sank slowly behind the hills.*

sink² /sɪŋk/ *noun* [count]
a large container in a kitchen where you wash dishes, or in a bathroom where you wash your hands and face

sink

faucet | sink

plug

sip /sɪp/ *verb* (sips, sip·ping, sipped)
to drink something slowly, taking only a little each time: *She sipped her coffee.*
▶ **sip** *noun* [count]: *Can I have **a sip of** your lemonade?*

sir 🔑 /sər/ *noun* [singular]
1 a polite way of speaking to a man, instead of using his name: *"Can I help you, sir?" asked the salesclerk.* ⊃ Look at **ma'am.**
2 Sir a word that you use at the beginning of a formal letter to a man: *Dear Sir…* ⊃ Look at **madam** (2).

si·ren /ˈsaɪrən/ *noun* [count]
a machine that makes a long, loud sound to warn people about something. Police cars and fire engines have **sirens.**

sis·ter 🔑 /ˈsɪstər/ *noun* [count]
1 a girl or woman who has the same parents as you: *I have two sisters and one brother.* ◆ *Jane and Anne are sisters.*
2 Sister (RELIGION) a female member of a religious group ⊃ SYNONYM **nun**

sis·ter-in-law /ˈsɪstər ɪn lɔ/ *noun* [count] (plural sis·ters-in-law)
1 the sister of your wife or husband
2 the wife of your brother

sit 🔑 /sɪt/ *verb* (sits, sit·ting, sat /sæt/, has sat)
1 to rest your weight on your bottom, for example in a chair: *We sat in the garden all afternoon.* ◆ *Come and sit next to me.* ◆ *She was sitting on the sofa.*
2 to be in a particular place or position: *The letter sat on the table for two days.*
sit down to move your body downward so you are sitting: *She came into the room and sat down.*
sit up to sit when you have been lying: *He sat up in bed and looked at the clock.*

sit·com /ˈsɪtkɑm/ *noun* [count, noncount]
a funny program on television that shows the same people in a different situation each week. Sitcom is short for "situation comedy."

site AWL /saɪt/ *noun* [count]
1 a place where a building is, was, or will be: *a building site* ◆ *This house was built on the site of an old theater.*
2 a place where something happened: *the site of a famous battle*
3 (COMPUTERS) a place on the Internet that you can look at to find out information about something ⊃ SYNONYM **website**

sit·u·at·ed /ˈsɪtʃueɪt̮əd/ *adjective*
in a place: *The hotel is situated close to the beach.*

sit·u·a·tion 🔑 /ˌsɪtʃuˈeɪʃn/ *noun* [count]
the things that are happening in a particular place or at a particular time: *We are **in a difficult situation** at the moment.*

sit-up /ˈsɪt ʌp/ *noun* [count]
an exercise for the stomach muscles in which you lie on your back, then lift the top half of your body from the floor: *To keep fit, she does twenty sit-ups every morning.*

six 🔑 /sɪks/ *number* (plural six·es)
6

six·teen 🔑 /sɪkˈstin/ *number*
16
▶ **six·teenth** /sɪkˈstinθ/ *pronoun, adjective, adverb, noun* [count]
1 16th
2 one of sixteen equal parts of something; $\frac{1}{16}$

sixth /sɪksθ/ *pronoun, adjective, adverb, noun* [count]
1 6th
2 one of six equal parts of something; $\frac{1}{6}$

six·ty 🔑 /ˈsɪksti/ *number*
1 60
2 the sixties [plural] the numbers, years, or temperatures between 60 and 69
in your sixties between the ages of 60 and 69: *My mom's in her sixties.*
▶ **six·ti·eth** /ˈsɪkstiəθ/ *pronoun, adjective, adverb, noun* [count]
60th

size 🔑 /saɪz/ *noun*
1 [noncount] how big or small something is: *My bedroom is the same size as yours.*
2 [count] an exact measurement: *Do you have these shoes in a bigger size?*

siz·zle /ˈsɪzl/ *verb* (siz·zles, siz·zling, siz·zled)
to make the sound of food frying in hot fat: *The bacon was sizzling in the pan.*

skate¹ /skeɪt/ *verb* (skates, skat·ing, skat·ed)
(SPORTS) to move over ice or the ground wearing SKATES: *Can you skate?* ◆ *They skated across the frozen lake.* ⊃ Look at **ice skate, roller skate.**
▶ **skat·ing** /ˈskeɪt̮ɪŋ/ *noun* [noncount]: *We go skating every weekend.*

skates

  ice skates   **in-line skates**   **roller skates**

skate² /skeɪt/ *noun* [count]
1 a boot with a long sharp piece of metal under it, which you wear for moving on ice
2 a boot with wheels on the bottom, which you wear for moving quickly on smooth ground

skate·board

skateboard

/'skeɪtbɔrd/ *noun*
[*count*]
a long piece of wood
or plastic on wheels.
You stand on it as it moves over the ground.
▶ **skate·board·ing** /'skeɪtbɔrdɪŋ/ *noun*
[*noncount*]: *Dave **goes** skateboarding every weekend.*

skat·ing rink /'skeɪʈɪŋ rɪŋk/ (also **rink**) *noun*
[*count*]
1 a special place where you can SKATE on ice
2 a special place where you can ROLLER SKATE (=
move around in boots with small wheels on the
bottom)

skeleton

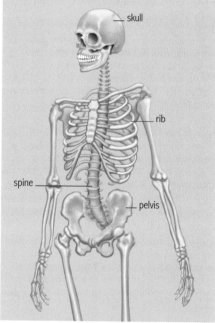

skull

rib

spine

pelvis

skel·e·ton /'skɛlətn/ *noun* [*count*]
the bones of a whole animal or person

skep·ti·cal /'skɛptɪkl/ *adjective*
having doubts that something is true or that
something will happen: *I am **skeptical about** his
chances of winning.*

sketch /skɛtʃ/ *noun* [*count*] (*plural* **sketch·es**)
(**ART**) a picture that you draw quickly: *The artist is
making sketches for his next painting.*
▶ **sketch** *verb* (**sketch·es, sketch·ing, sketched**):
He quickly sketched the view from the window.

ski /ski/ *noun* [*count*] (*plural* **skis**)
(**SPORTS**) one of a pair of long flat pieces of wood,
metal, or plastic that you attach to boots so that
you can move over snow: *a pair of skis*

▶ **ski** *verb* (skis,
ski·ing, skied, has
skied): *Can you ski?* ◆
*We **went skiing** in
Colorado.*
▶ **ski·er** /'skiər/ *noun*
[*count*]: *Marie's a good
skier.*

ski

goggles

pole

ski

skid /skɪd/ *verb* (skids,
skid·ding, skid·ded)
If a vehicle such as a car or truck **skids**, it moves
suddenly and in a dangerous way to the side,
for example because the road is wet: *The truck
skidded on the icy road.*

skies plural of **sky**

skill /skɪl/ *noun*
1 [*noncount*] the ability to do something well:
Flying a plane takes great skill.
2 [*count*] a thing that you can do well: *What skills
do you need for this job?*

skilled /skɪld/ *adjective*
good at something because you have learned
about or done it for a long time: *skilled workers*

skil·let /'skɪlət/ *noun* [*count*] another word for
frying pan

skill·ful /'skɪlfl/ *adjective*
very good at doing something: *a very skillful
tennis player*
▶ **skill·ful·ly** /'skɪlfəli/ *adverb*: *He chopped the
vegetables quickly and skillfully.*

skim /skɪm/ *verb* (skims, skim·ming, skimmed)
1 to remove something from the surface of a
liquid: *to skim the fat off the gravy*
2 to read something quickly in order to get the
main idea: *Skim the text and answer the
questions below.*

skim milk /ˌskɪm 'mɪlk/ *noun* [*noncount*]
milk that contains less fat than normal because
the cream has been removed from it

skin /skɪn/ *noun* [*count*]
1 the substance that covers the outside of a
person or an animal's body: *She has dark skin.* ◆
animal skins ⊃ Look at the note at **appearance**.
2 the outside part of some fruits and vegetables:
a banana skin

skin·ny /'skɪni/ *adjective* (skin·ni·er, skin·ni·est)
too thin: *He's so skinny – he doesn't eat enough.* ⊃
Look at the note at **thin**.

skip /skɪp/ *verb* (skips, skip·ping, skipped)
1 to move along quickly with little jumps from
one foot to the other: *The children were skipping
along the road.*
2 to not do or have something that you should
do or have: *I skipped my class today and went
swimming.*

▶ **skip** *noun* [count]: *She gave a skip and a jump and was off down the street.*

skirt 🔑 /skərt/ *noun* [count]

> ℹ **PRONUNCIATION**
> The word **skirt** sounds like **hurt**.

a piece of clothing for a woman or girl that hangs from the middle of the body (the WAIST) and covers part of the legs ⊃ Look at the picture at **clothes**.

ski slope /'ski sloʊp/ *noun* [count]
a part of a mountain where you can SKI

skull /skʌl/ *noun* [count]
the bones in the head of a person or an animal ⊃ Look at the picture at **skeleton**.

sky 🔑 /skaɪ/ *noun* [count, noncount] (*plural* **skies**)
the space above the earth where you can see the sun, moon, and stars: *a beautiful blue sky* • *There are no clouds in the sky.*

sky·div·ing /'skaɪ ˌdaɪvɪŋ/ *noun* [noncount]
(**SPORTS**) a sport in which you jump from an airplane and fall through the sky before you open your PARACHUTE (= a large piece of cloth that lets you fall to the ground slowly)

skydiving

sky·line /'skaɪlaɪn/ *noun* [count]
the shape that is made by tall buildings, trees, hills, etc. against the sky: *the Manhattan skyline*

sky·scrap·er /'skaɪskreɪpər/ *noun* [count]
a very tall building: *He works on the 49th floor of a skyscraper.*

skyscraper

slab /slæb/ *noun* [count]
a thick, flat piece of something: *stone slabs* • *a big slab of cheese* ⊃ Look at the note at **piece**.

slack /slæk/ *adjective*
1 loose: *Suddenly the rope went slack.* ⊃ ANTONYM **tight**
2 not busy: *Business has been very slack.*

slacks /slæks/ *noun* [plural]
pants, especially not very formal or informal ones: *He wore a pair of slacks and a sweater.*

slam /slæm/ *verb* (slams, slam·ming, slammed)
to close something or put something down with a loud noise: *She slammed the door angrily.* • *He slammed the book on the table and went out.*

slang /slæŋ/ *noun* [noncount]
very informal words that people use when they are talking. You do not use **slang** when you need to be polite, and you do not usually use it in writing.

slant /slænt/ *verb* (slants, slant·ing, slant·ed)
Something that **slants** has one side higher than the other or does not stand straight up: *My handwriting slants to the left.*
▶ **slant** *noun* [singular]: *Cut the flower stems on the slant.*

slap /slæp/ *verb* (slaps, slap·ping, slapped)
to hit someone with the flat, inside part of your hand: *He slapped me on the face.*
▶ **slap** *noun* [count]: *She gave me a slap across the face.*

slash /slæʃ/ *noun* [count] (*plural* **slash·es**)
(**ENGLISH LANGUAGE ARTS**) a mark (/) that you use in writing. It shows different possibilities, for example "lunch and/or dinner," and also to write FRACTIONS, for example ¾.

slaugh·ter /'slɔtər/ *verb* (slaugh·ters, slaugh·ter·ing, slaugh·tered)
1 to kill an animal for food
2 to kill a lot of people in a cruel way
▶ **slaugh·ter** *noun* [noncount]: *We must act to stop this slaughter.*

slave¹ /sleɪv/ *noun* [count]
a person who belongs to another person and must work for that person for no money

slave² /sleɪv/ *verb* (slaves, slav·ing, slaved)
to work very hard: *I've been slaving away all day.*

slav·er·y /'sleɪvəri/ *noun* [noncount]
(**HISTORY**) the system of having SLAVES: *When did slavery end in America?*

sled /slɛd/ *noun* [count]
a small vehicle with pieces of metal or wood instead of wheels, which you sit in to move over snow ⊃ Look at **sleigh**.

sleep¹ 🔑 /slip/ *verb* (sleeps, sleep·ing, slept /slɛpt/, has slept)
to rest with your eyes closed, as you do at night: *I sleep for eight hours every night.* • *Did you sleep well?* ⊃ Look at the note at **asleep**.
sleep over to sleep at someone else's house

sleep² 🔑 /slip/ *noun*
1 [noncount] the natural condition of rest when your eyes are closed and your mind and body are not active or conscious: *I didn't get any sleep last night.*
2 [singular] a period of sleep: *I sometimes have a short sleep in the afternoon.*
go to sleep to start to sleep: *I got into bed and soon went to sleep.* ⊃ SYNONYM **fall asleep** ⊃ Look at the note at **asleep**.

sleep·ing bag
/'slipɪŋ bæg/ *noun*
[count]
a big, warm bag that
you sleep in when
you go camping

sleeping bag

lining

sleep·less /'sliplǝs/
adjective
without sleep: *I had a sleepless night.*

sleep·y /'slipi/ *adjective* (sleep·i·er, sleep·i·est)
1 tired and ready to sleep: *I feel sleepy after that big meal.*
2 quiet, with not many things happening: *a sleepy little town*

sleet /slit/ *noun* [noncount]
snow and rain together

sleeve /sliv/ *noun* [count]
the part of a coat, dress, shirt, etc. that covers
your arm: *a shirt with short sleeves* ⊃ Look at the
picture at **clothes**.

sleigh /sleɪ/ *noun*
[count]
a large vehicle with
pieces of metal or
wood instead of
wheels that you sit in
to move over snow. A
sleigh is usually pulled by animals. ⊃ Look at
sled.

sleigh

slen·der /'slɛndǝr/ *adjective*
thin, in an attractive way: *She has long, slender
legs.*

slept form of sleep

slice /slaɪs/ *noun* [count]
a thin piece that you cut off bread, meat, or
other food: *Would you like a slice of cake?* • *She
cut the bread into slices.* ⊃ Look at the picture at
bread. ⊃ Look at the note at **piece**.
▶ slice *verb* (slic·es, slic·ing, sliced): *Slice the
onions.* ⊃ Look at the note at **cut¹**.

slide¹ /slaɪd/ *verb* (slides, slid·ing, slid /slɪd/,
has slid)
to move smoothly or to make something move
smoothly across something: *She fell and slid
along the ice.*

slide² /slaɪd/ *noun*
[count]
1 a long, metal thing
that children play on.
They climb up steps,
sit down, and then
SLIDE down the other
side.
2 a small photograph that you show on a
screen, using a special machine (called a
PROJECTOR): *a slide show*

slide

slight /slaɪt/ *adjective* (slight·er, slight·est)
small; not important or serious: *I have a slight
problem.* • *a slight headache*

slight·ly /'slaɪtli/ *adverb*
a little: *I'm feeling slightly better today.*

slim /slɪm/ *adjective* (slim·mer, slim·mest)
thin, but not too thin: *a tall slim man* ⊃ Look at the
note at **thin**.

slime /slaɪm/ *noun* [noncount]
a thick liquid that looks or smells bad: *The pond
was covered in green slime.*
▶ slim·y /'slaɪmi/ *adjective* (slim·i·er, slim·i·est): *a
slimy surface*

sling¹ /slɪŋ/ *noun* [count]
(HEALTH) a piece of cloth that you wear to hold up
an arm that is hurt: *Her arm is in a sling.*

sling² /slɪŋ/ *verb* (slings, sling·ing, slung /slʌŋ/,
has slung) (informal)
to throw something without care: *He slung his
bag over his shoulder.*

slip¹ /slɪp/ *verb* (slips, slip·ping, slipped)
1 to move smoothly over something by
accident and fall or almost fall: *He slipped on the
ice and broke his leg.*
2 to move out of the correct position or out of
your hand by accident: *Sorry, the glass just
slipped out of my hand.*
3 to go quickly and quietly so that no one sees
you: *Ann **slipped out** of the room.* • *We **slipped
away** when no one was looking.*
4 to put something in a place quickly and
quietly: *He **slipped** the money **into** his pocket.*
slip up (informal) to make a mistake

slip² /slɪp/ *noun* [count]
1 a small mistake: *It was just a slip.*
2 a small piece of paper: *Write your address on
this slip of paper.*

slip·per /'slɪpǝr/ *noun* [count]
a light, soft shoe that you wear in the house: *a
pair of slippers* ⊃ Look at the picture at **shoe**.

slip·per·y /'slɪpǝri/ *adjective*
so smooth or wet that you cannot move on it or
hold it easily: *a slippery floor* • *The road was wet
and slippery.*

slit /slɪt/ *noun* [count]
a long, thin hole or cut
▶ slit *verb* (slits, slit·ting, slit, has slit): *I slit the
envelope **open** with a knife.*

slith·er /'slɪðǝr/ *verb* (slith·ers, slith·er·ing,
slith·ered)
to move by sliding from side to side along the
ground like a snake: *I saw a snake slithering
down a rock.*

slob /slɑb/ *noun* [count] (informal)
a lazy, messy person: *My brother's such a slob –
he never cleans his room.*

slo·gan /ˈsloʊɡən/ noun [count]
a short sentence or group of words that is easy to remember. **Slogans** are used to make people believe something or buy something: *antigovernment slogans* • *an advertising slogan*

slope¹ /sloʊp/ noun [count]
a piece of ground that has one end higher than the other, like the side of a hill: *We walked down the mountain slope.* ⊃ Look at **ski slope**.

slope² /sloʊp/ verb (slopes, slop·ing, sloped)
to have one end higher than the other: *The field* **slopes down** *to the river.* • *a sloping roof*

slop·py /ˈslɑpi/ adjective (slop·pi·er, slop·pi·est)
showing a lack of care or effort; careless or messy: *a sloppy piece of work*

slot /slɑt/ noun [count]
a long, thin hole that you push something through: *Put your money in the slot and take your ticket.*

slot ma·chine /ˈslɑt məˌʃin/ noun [count]
a machine in which you put money and play a game to win money

slow¹ /sloʊ/ adjective (slow·er, slow·est)
1 not moving or doing something quickly: *a slow train* • *She hasn't finished her work yet – she's very slow.*
2 If a clock or watch is **slow**, it shows a time that is earlier than the real time: *My watch is five minutes slow.* ⊃ ANTONYM **fast**

slow² /sloʊ/ adverb
slowly: *Please drive slower.* • *slow-moving traffic*

slow³ /sloʊ/ verb (slows, slow·ing, slowed)
slow down; slow someone or **something down** to start to go more slowly; to make someone or something start to go more slowly: *The train slowed down as it came into the station.* • *Don't talk to me when I'm working – it slows me down.*

slow·ly /ˈsloʊli/ adverb
at a slow speed; not quickly: *The old lady walked slowly up the hill.*

slug /slʌɡ/ noun [count]
a small, soft animal that moves slowly and eats plants ⊃ Look at the picture at **snail**.

slum /slʌm/ noun [count]
(GEOGRAPHY) a poor part of a city where people live in old, dirty buildings

slump /slʌmp/ verb (slumps, slump·ing, slumped)
1 (BUSINESS) (used about prices, sales, and the economy) to fall suddenly and by a large amount: *Shares* **slumped to** *their lowest ever level.*
2 to fall or sit down suddenly because you are sick, weak, or tired: *Suddenly the old man* **slumped to** *the floor.*

slung form of **sling²**

slush /slʌʃ/ noun [noncount]
snow on the ground that has partly melted and is usually dirty

sly /slaɪ/ adjective
A person who is **sly** tricks people or does things secretly. ⊃ SYNONYM **cunning**

smack /smæk/ verb (smacks, smack·ing, smacked)
to hit someone with the inside part of your hand: *I would never smack my children.*
▸ **smack** noun [count]: *She gave her son* **a smack**.

small /smɔl/ adjective (small·er, small·est)
1 not big; little: *This dress is too small for me.* • *My house is smaller than yours.*
2 young: *They have two small children.*

smart /smɑrt/ adjective (smart·er, smart·est)
1 able to learn and think quickly; intelligent: *He's a very smart boy.* ⊃ Look at the note at **intelligent**.
2 (informal) saying things or making jokes in a way that shows you do not have respect for someone: *Don't* **get smart with** *me!*

smart·phone /ˈsmɑrtfoʊn/ noun [count]
a cell phone that can do many of the things that a computer does

smash /smæʃ/ verb (smash·es, smash·ing, smashed)
1 to break into many pieces, or to break something in this way: *The plate fell on the floor and smashed.* • *The boys smashed the window with their ball.* ⊃ Look at the note at **break¹**.
2 to move with great force in a particular direction: *He smashed his hand through the window.*

smear /smɪr/ verb (smears, smear·ing, smeared)
to spread a soft substance on something, making it dirty: *The child had* **smeared** *chocolate* **all over** *his clothes.*
▸ **smear** noun [count]: *She had smears of paint on her dress.*

smell /smɛl/ verb (smells, smell·ing, smelled)
1 to have a particular smell: *Dinner smells good!* • *The perfume* **smells of** *roses.*
2 to notice something with your nose: *Can you* **smell** *smoke?*
3 to have a bad smell: *Your feet smell!*
▸ **smell** noun [count, noncount]: *There's a* **smell of** *gas in this room.*

smell·y /ˈsmɛli/ adjective (smell·i·er, smell·i·est)
having a bad smell: *smelly socks*

smile¹ /smaɪl/ verb (smiles, smil·ing, smiled)
to move your mouth to show that you are happy or that you think something is funny: *He* **smiled at** *me.*

smile² /smaɪl/ noun [count]
an expression on your face in which the corners of your mouth turn up, showing that you think

something is good, funny, etc.: *She had a big smile on her face.* • *"It's good to see you," he said with a smile.*

smog /smɑg/ *noun* [noncount]
dirty, poisonous air that can cover a whole city

smoke¹ /smoʊk/ *noun* [noncount]
the gray, white, or black gas that you see in the air when something is burning: *The room was full of smoke.* • *cigarette smoke*

smoke² /smoʊk/ *verb* (smokes, smok·ing, smoked)
1 to breathe in smoke through a cigarette, etc. and let it out again; to use cigarettes, etc. in this way, as a habit: *He was smoking a cigar.* • *Do you smoke?*
2 to send out smoke: *The oil in the pan started to smoke.*
▶ **smok·er** /smoʊkər/ *noun* [count]
a person who **smokes**: *Her parents used to be heavy smokers* (= they used to smoke a lot).

smoked /smoʊkt/ *adjective*
Smoked food is put over a wood fire to give it a special taste: *smoked salmon*

smok·ing /ˈsmoʊkɪŋ/ *noun* [noncount]
the activity or habit of smoking cigarettes, etc.: *She's trying to quit smoking.*

smok·y /ˈsmoʊki/ *adjective* (smok·i·er, smok·i·est)
full of smoke: *a smoky room*

smol·der /ˈsmoʊldər/ *verb* (smoul·ders, smoul·der·ing, smoul·dered)
to burn slowly without a flame: *A cigarette was smoldering in the ashtray.*

smooth /smuð/ *adjective* (smooth·er, smooth·est)
1 having a completely flat surface: *Babies have such smooth skin.* • *The surface should be completely smooth.* ⊃ ANTONYM **rough**
2 with no big pieces in it: *Beat the sauce until it is smooth.* ⊃ ANTONYM **lumpy**
3 A **smooth** movement or trip is even and comfortable: *The weather was good, so we had a very smooth flight.* ⊃ ANTONYM **bumpy**
4 without any problems: *The move to the new house was fairly smooth.*
▶ **smooth·ly** /ˈsmuðli/ *adverb*: *The plane landed smoothly.*

smoth·er /ˈsmʌðər/ *verb* (smoth·ers, smoth·er·ing, smoth·ered)
1 to kill someone by covering their face so that they cannot breathe
2 to cover a thing with too much of something: *He smothered his skin with cream.*

smudge /smʌdʒ/ *verb* (smudg·es, smudg·ing, smudged)
If something **smudges** or you **smudge** it, it becomes dirty or messy because you have

touched it: *Leave the painting to dry or you'll smudge it.* • *My lipstick has smudged.*
▶ **smudge** *noun* [count]: *There's a smudge on your cheek.*

smug /smʌg/ *adjective* (smug·ger, smug·gest)
too pleased with yourself, in a way that bothers other people: *He gave her a smug look.*

smug·gle /ˈsmʌgl/ *verb* (smug·gles, smug·gling, smug·gled)
to take things secretly into or out of a country when this is against the law: *They were trying to **smuggle** drugs **into** the country.*
▶ **smug·gler** /ˈsmʌglər/ *noun* [count]: *drug smugglers*

snack /snæk/ *noun* [count]
a small, quick meal: *We had a snack on the train.*

snack bar /ˈsnæk bɑr/ *noun* [count]
a place where you can buy and eat SNACKS

snag /snæg/ *noun* [count]
a small problem: *It's a beautiful bike – **the only snag is** it's very expensive.*

shell

snail

slug

snail /sneɪl/ *noun* [count]
a small, soft animal with a hard shell on its back. **Snails** move very slowly.

snake /sneɪk/ *noun* [count]
an animal with a long, thin body and no legs: *Do these snakes bite?*

snap¹ /snæp/ *verb* (snaps, snap·ping, snapped)
1 to break something suddenly with a sharp noise; to be broken in this way: *He snapped the pencil in two.* • *Suddenly, the rope snapped.* ⊃ Look at the note at **break¹**.
2 to say something in a quick, angry way: *"Go away – I'm busy!" she snapped.*
3 to try to bite someone or something: *The dog snapped at my leg.*
snap your fingers to make a sharp noise by moving your middle finger quickly against your thumb

snap² /snæp/ *noun* [count]
1 a sudden sound of something breaking
2 a small, round, metal object with two parts that you press together to fasten a piece of clothing

snap·shot /ˈsnæpʃɑt/ *noun* [count]
a photograph that you take quickly

snarl /snɑrl/ *verb* (snarls, snarl·ing, snarled)
When an animal **snarls**, it shows its teeth and makes a low, angry sound: *The dogs **snarled at** the stranger.*

snatch /snætʃ/ *verb* (snatch·es, snatch·ing, snatched)
to take something with a quick, rough movement: *A thief snatched her bag and ran away.* ⊃ SYNONYM **grab**

sneak /snik/ *verb* (sneaks, sneak·ing, sneaked or snuck /snʌk/, has sneaked or has snuck)
to go somewhere very quietly so that no one sees or hears you: *She sneaked out of the house without telling her parents.*

sneak·er /'snikər/ *noun* [count]
a soft shoe that you wear for playing sports or with informal clothes: *a pair of sneakers* ⊃ Look at the picture at **shoe**.

sneer /snɪr/ *verb* (sneers, sneer·ing, sneered)
to speak or smile in an unkind way to show that you do not like someone or something, or that you think they are not good enough: *I told her about my idea, but she just sneered at it.*
▸ **sneer** *noun* [count]: *His lips curled in a sneer.*

sneeze /sniz/ *verb* (sneez·es, sneez·ing, sneezed)
(HEALTH) to make air come out of your nose and mouth with a sudden loud noise, for example because you have a cold: *Pepper makes you sneeze.*
▸ **sneeze** *noun* [count]: *That was a loud sneeze!*

sniff /snɪf/ *verb* (sniffs, sniff·ing, sniffed)
1 to make a noise by suddenly taking in air through your nose. People sometimes **sniff** when they have a cold or when they are crying: *I wish you'd stop sniffing!*
2 to smell something: *The dog was sniffing the meat.*
▸ **sniff** *noun* [count]: *I heard a loud sniff.*

snip /snɪp/ *verb* (snips, snip·ping, snipped)
to cut something using scissors, with a short quick action: *I sewed on the button and snipped off the end of the thread.*

snip·er /'snaɪpər/ *noun* [count]
a person who shoots at someone from a hidden place: *Three soldiers were killed by snipers.*

snob /snɑb/ *noun* [count]
a person who likes people with a high social position and thinks they are better than other people: *Jack's such a snob – he's always talking about his rich relatives.*

snooze /snuz/ *verb* (snooz·es, snooz·ing, snoozed) (*informal*)
to sleep for a short time
▸ **snooze** *noun* [count]: *I had a snooze after lunch.*

snore /snɔr/ *verb* (snores, snor·ing, snored)
to make a noise in your nose and throat when you are asleep: *He was snoring loudly.*
▸ **snore** *noun* [count]: *a loud snore*

snorkeling

① snorkel
② mask
③ swimsuit
④ flipper

snor·kel /'snɔrkl/ *noun* [count]
a short tube that a person swimming just below the surface of the water can use to breathe through
▸ **snor·kel·ing** /'snɔrkəlɪŋ/ *noun* [noncount]
(SPORTS): *to go snorkeling*

snort /snɔrt/ *verb* (snorts, snort·ing, snort·ed)
to make a noise by blowing air through the nose: *The horse snorted.*

snout /snaʊt/ *noun* [count]
(BIOLOGY) the long nose of certain animals: *a pig's snout*

snow ♫ /snoʊ/ *noun* [noncount]
soft, white pieces of frozen water that fall from the sky when it is very cold
▸ **snow** *verb* (snows, snow·ing, snowed): *It often snows in January and February.* • *It's snowing!*
be snowed in to not be able to leave home or travel because there is too much snow: *We've been snowed in since Monday.*

snow·ball /'snoʊbɔl/ *noun* [count]
a ball of snow that children throw at each other: *The kids were having a snowball fight* (= throwing snowballs at each other).

snow·board·ing
/'snoʊbɔrdɪŋ/ *noun*
[noncount]
(SPORTS) the sport of moving down mountains that are covered in snow using a large board (called a SNOWBOARD) that you fasten to both your feet

snowboarding

snowboard

snow·fall /'snoʊfɔl/ *noun* [count, noncount]
the snow that falls on one occasion, or the amount of snow that falls in a place: *heavy snowfalls* • *What is the average snowfall for this region?*

snow·flake /'snoʊfleɪk/ *noun* [count]
one piece of falling snow

snow·man /'snoʊmæn/ *noun* [count] (*plural* snow·men*) /'snoʊmɛn/
the figure of a person that children make out of snow

snow·plow /'snoʊplaʊ/ *noun* [count]
a large vehicle that clears snow away from roads

snow·storm /'snoʊstɔrm/ *noun* [*count*]
a winter storm with a lot of snow and strong winds ⊃ SYNONYM **blizzard**

snow·y /'snoʊi/ *adjective* (snow·i·er, snow·i·est)
with a lot of snow: *snowy weather*

snuck form of **sneak**

so¹ /soʊ/ *adverb*
1 a word that makes an adjective or adverb stronger, especially when this produces a particular result: *This bag is so heavy that I can't carry it.* ◆ *I'm so tired I can't keep my eyes open.* ◆ *Why are you so late?*

Grammar

So or such?

- You use **so** before an adjective that is used without a noun: *It was so cold that we stayed home.* ◆ *This book is so exciting.*
- You use **such** before a noun that has an adjective in front of it: *It was such a cold night that we stayed home.* ◆ *This is such an exciting book!*

2 You use "so" instead of saying words again: *"Is John coming?" "I think so* (= I think that he is coming)*." ◆ "I got it wrong, didn't I?" "I'm afraid so* (= you did get it wrong)*."*
3 also: *Julie is a teacher and so is her husband.* ◆ *"I like this music." "So do I."* ⊃ Look at **neither**.
and so on and other things like that: *The store sells pens, paper, and so on.*
or so words that you use to show that a number is not exactly right: *Forty or so people came to the party.*
so long (*informal*) goodbye: *So long! See you soon.*

so² /soʊ/ *conjunction*
1 because of this or that: *The store is closed, so I can't buy any bread.*
2 (also **so that**) in order that: *Speak louder so that everyone can hear you.* ◆ *I'll give you a map so you can find my house.*
3 a word you use when you want to start talking about something: *So, Susan, how's school this year?*
so what?; so? (*informal*) why is that important or interesting?: *"It's late." "So what? There's no school tomorrow."*

soak /soʊk/ *verb* (soaks, soak·ing, soaked)
1 to make someone or something very wet: *Soak the plants thoroughly once a week.*
2 to be in a liquid; to let something stay in a liquid: *Leave the dishes to soak in hot water.*
soak something up to take in a liquid: *Soak up the water with a cloth.*

soaked /soʊkt/ *adjective*
very wet: *You're soaked! Come in and get dry.*

soak·ing /'soʊkɪŋ/ *adjective*
very wet: *This towel is soaking.*

soap /soʊp/ *noun* [*noncount*]
a substance that you use with water for washing and cleaning: *a bar of soap*
▶ **soap·y** /'soʊpi/ *adjective* (soap·i·er, soap·i·est): *soapy water*

soap

a bar of soap

soap op·er·a /'soʊp ˌɑprə/ *noun* [*count*]
a story about the lives of a group of people, which is on TV every day or several times each week: *Do you watch the soaps?*

soar /sɔr/ *verb* (soars, soar·ing, soared)
1 to fly high in the sky
2 to go up very fast: *Prices are soaring.*

sob /sɑb/ *verb* (sobs, sob·bing, sobbed)
to cry loudly, making short sounds
▶ **sob** *noun* [*count*]: *I could hear her sobs through the wall.*

so·ber /'soʊbər/ *adjective*
not having drunk too much alcohol ⊃ ANTONYM **drunk**

so-called AWL /ˌsoʊ 'kɔld/ *adjective*
a word that you use to show that you do not think another word is correct: *Her so-called friends did not help her* (= they are not really her friends)*.*

soc·cer /'sɑkər/ *noun* [*noncount*]
(SPORTS) a game for two teams of eleven players who try to kick a round ball into the other team's goal: *a soccer game*

soccer
goal   goalkeeper

so·cia·ble /'soʊʃəbl/ *adjective*
friendly and enjoying being with other people

so·cial /'soʊʃl/ *adjective*
connected with people together in society; connected with being with other people: *the social problems of big cities* ◆ *Anne has a busy social life* (= she goes out with friends a lot)*.*
▶ **so·cial·ly** /'soʊʃəli/ *adverb*: *We work together, but I don't know him socially.*

so·cial·ism /'soʊʃlˌɪzəm/ *noun* [*noncount*]
(POLITICS) the political idea that is based on the belief that all people are equal and that money and property should be equally divided ⊃ Look at **capitalism**, **communism**.
▶ **so·cial·ist** /'soʊʃlˌɪst/ *noun* [*count*], *adjective*: *socialist beliefs*

so·cial·ize /'souʃl·aɪz/ *verb* (so·cial·iz·es, so·cial·iz·ing, so·cial·ized)
to meet and spend time with people in a friendly way: *I enjoy **socializing with** friends.*

so·cial net·work·ing /ˌsouʃəl 'nɛtwərkɪŋ/ *noun* [noncount]
the activity of meeting and communicating with people using a website or other service on the Internet

so·cial sci·ence /ˌsouʃəl 'saɪəns/ *noun* [noncount] (also **so·cial stud·ies** /'souʃəl ˌstʌdiz/) [plural]
the study of people in society

So·cial Se·cu·ri·ty /ˌsouʃl sə'kyʊrəţi/ *noun* [noncount]
(**POLITICS**) money that a government pays to people who are elderly or cannot work: *In a few years I will be **on Social Security**.*

so·cial work·er /'souʃl ˌwərkər/ *noun* [count]
a person whose job is to help people who have problems, for example because they are poor or sick

so·ci·e·ty /sə'saɪəţi/ *noun* (plural so·ci·e·ties)
1 [noncount] a large group of people who live in the same country or area and have the same ideas about how to live: *They carried out research into the roles of men and women in today's society.*
2 [count] a group of people who are interested in the same thing: *a music society*

so·ci·ol·o·gy /ˌsousi'ɑlədʒi/ *noun* [noncount]
the study of human societies and the way people behave

sock /sɑk/ *noun* [count]
a thing that you wear on your foot, inside your shoe: *a pair of socks*

sock·et /'sɑkət/ *noun* [count]
a place in a wall where you can connect electrical equipment to a power supply ⊃ **SYNONYM outlet**

so·da /'soudə/ *noun* [noncount]
1 a sweet flavored drink with bubbles in it, which does not contain alcohol
2 (also **so·da wa·ter**) water with bubbles in it that is used for mixing with other drinks: *whiskey and soda* ⊃ **SYNONYM club soda**

so·di·um /'soudiəm/ *noun* [noncount] (symbol **Na**)
(**CHEMISTRY**) a soft silver-white metal that is found in salt and other chemical mixtures (**COMPOUNDS**)

so·fa /'soufə/ *noun* [count]
a long, soft seat for more than one person: *Emily and Bob were sitting on the sofa.* ⊃ **SYNONYM couch** ⊃ Look at the picture at **chair**.

soft /sɔft/ *adjective* (soft·er, soft·est)
1 not hard or firm; that moves when you press it: *Warm butter is soft.* ♦ *a soft bed*

2 smooth and nice to touch; not rough: *soft skin*
♦ *My cat's fur is very soft.*
3 not bright or strong: *the soft light of a candle*
4 quiet or gentle; not loud: *soft music* ♦ *He has a very soft voice.*
5 kind and gentle; not strict: *She's too soft with her class and they don't do any work.*

soft·ball /'sɔfbɔl/ *noun* [noncount]
(**SPORTS**) a team game that is similar to baseball, but played with a larger ball on a smaller field

soft drink /'sɔft drɪŋk/ *noun* [count]
a sweet flavored drink with bubbles, which does not have alcohol in it ⊃ **SYNONYM soda**

soft·en /'sɔfn/ *verb* (soft·ens, soft·en·ing, soft·ened)
to become softer or more gentle, or to make something softer or more gentle: *This cream softens the skin.*

soft·ly /'sɔfli/ *adverb*
gently or quietly: *She spoke very softly.*

soft·ware /'sɔftwɛr/ *noun* [noncount]
(**COMPUTERS**) programs for a computer: *There's a lot of new educational software available now.*

sog·gy /'sɑgi/ *adjective* (sog·gi·er, sog·gi·est)
very wet

soil /sɔɪl/ *noun* [noncount]
what plants and trees grow in; earth

so·lar /'soulər/ *adjective*
of or using the sun: *solar energy*

the so·lar sys·tem /ðə 'soulər ˌsɪstəm/ *noun* [singular]
the sun and the planets that move around it

sold form of **sell**

sol·dier /'souldʒər/ *noun* [count]
a person in an army

sole¹ **AWL** /soul/ *adjective*
only: *His sole interest is football.*

sole² **AWL** /soul/ *noun*
1 [count] the bottom part of your foot or of a shoe: *These boots have leather soles.*
2 [count, noncount] (plural **sole**) a flat fish that is used for food

sole·ly **AWL** /'soulli/ *adverb*
only, and not involving anyone or anything else: *I agreed to come solely because of Frank.*

sol·emn /'sɑləm/ *adjective*
serious: *slow, solemn music*
▶ **sol·emn·ly** /'sɑləmli/ *adverb*: *"I have some bad news for you," he said solemnly.*

sol·id¹ /'sɑləd/ *adjective*
1 hard, not like a liquid or a gas: *Water becomes solid when it freezes.*
2 with no empty space inside; made of the same material inside and outside: *a solid rubber ball* ♦ *This ring is solid gold.*

solids

cone   cube   cylinder

pyramid   sphere

sol·id² /'sɑləd/ *noun* [count]
1 something that is hard; not a liquid or gas: *Milk is a liquid and cheese is a solid.*
2 (MATH) an object that has length, height, and WIDTH, not a flat shape: *A cube is a solid.*

so·lid·i·fy /sə'lɪdəfaɪ/ *verb* (so·lid·i·fies, so·lid·i·fy·ing, so·lid·i·fied, has so·lid·i·fied)
to become hard or solid

sol·i·tar·y /'sɑlə,tɛri/ *adjective*
without others; alone: *She went for a long, solitary walk.*

sol·i·tude /'sɑlətud/ *noun* [noncount]
the state of being alone, especially because you want to be: *He lived in solitude.*

so·lo¹ /'soʊloʊ/ *adjective, adverb*
alone; without other people: *She flew solo across the Atlantic.*

so·lo² /'soʊloʊ/ *noun* [count] (*plural* so·los)
(MUSIC) a piece of music for one person to sing or play: *a guitar solo* ⊃ Look at **duet**.

sol·u·ble /'sɑlyəbl/ *adjective*
(CHEMISTRY) If something is **soluble**, when you put it in a liquid it becomes part of the liquid: *These tablets are soluble in water.*

so·lu·tion /sə'luʃn/ *noun* [count]
1 the answer to a question or problem: *I can't find a **solution to** this problem.*
2 the correct answer to a game, a competition, etc.: *The **solution to** the crossword will be published next week.*
3 a liquid that has a solid substance mixed completely (DISSOLVED) into it: *He made a solution of sugar and water.*

solve /sɑlv/ *verb* (solves, solv·ing, solved)
to find the answer to a question or a problem: *The police are still trying to solve the crime.* ◆ *Have you solved the puzzle yet?*

some /səm; sʌm/ *adjective, pronoun*

ⓘ PRONUNCIATION
The word **some** sounds just like **sum**.

1 a number or an amount of something: *I bought some tomatoes and some butter.* ◆ *This cake is delicious. Do you want some?*

Which word?

Some or any?
- We use **some** in statements, and in questions where we expect the answer to be "Yes": *He gave me some good advice.* ◆ *Would you like some coffee?*
- We use **any** in questions, and after "not" and "if": *Did you buy any apples?* ◆ *I didn't buy any meat.* ◆ *If you have any questions, please ask me at the end of the class.*

2 part of a number or an amount of something: *Some of the children can swim, but the others can't.*
3 I do not know which: *There's some man at the door who wants to see you.*
some more a little more or a few more: *Have some more coffee.* ◆ *Some more people arrived.*
some time a long time: *We waited for some time but she did not come.*

some·bod·y /'sʌmbʌdi; 'sʌmbɑdi/ another word for **someone**

some·day /'sʌmdeɪ/ *adverb*
at some time in the future: *I hope you'll come back and visit someday.*

some·how /'sʌmhaʊ/ *adverb*
in some way that you do not know: *We must find her somehow.*

some·one /'sʌmwʌn/ (also **some·bod·y**) *pronoun*
a person; a person that you do not know: *There's someone at the door.* ◆ *Someone has broken the window.* ◆ *Ask **someone else** (= another person) to help you.* ◆ *Somebody help me!*

some·place /'sʌmpleɪs/ *adverb* another word for **somewhere**

som·er·sault /'sʌmərsɔlt/ *noun* [count]
a movement when you turn your body with your feet going over your head: *The children were doing somersaults on the carpet.*

some·thing /'sʌmθɪŋ/ *pronoun*
a thing; a thing you cannot name: *There's something under the table. What is it?* ◆ *I want to tell you something.* ◆ *Would you like **something else** (= another thing) to eat?*
or something (*informal*) words that you use to show you are not sure about what you have just said: *I think he's a teacher or something.*

something like the same as someone or something in some ways, but not in every way: *A rat is something like a mouse, but bigger.*

some·time /ˈsʌmtaɪm/ *adverb*
at a time that you do not know exactly: *I'll call you sometime tomorrow.* ◆ *Will you come and see me sometime?*

some·times 🔑 /ˈsʌmtaɪmz/ *adverb*
not very often: *He sometimes writes to me.* ◆ *Sometimes I drive to work and sometimes I go by bus.*

some·what 🅰🆆🅻 /ˈsʌmwʌt/ *adverb*
a little: *Somewhat to my surprise, he apologized.* ◆ *We were somewhat confused by her instructions.*

some·where 🔑 /ˈsʌmwɛr/ *adverb* (also **some·place**)
1 at, in, or to a place that you do not know exactly: *They live somewhere near Detroit.* ◆ *"Did she go to California last year?" "No, I think she went somewhere else* (= to another place).*"*
2 a word that you use when you do not know the exact time, number, etc.: *Your weight should be somewhere around 150 pounds.*

son 🔑 /sʌn/ *noun* [count]

ℹ **PRONUNCIATION**
The word **son** sounds just like **sun**.

a boy or man who is someone's child: *They have a son and two daughters.*

song 🔑 /sɔŋ/ *noun* (**MUSIC**)
1 [count] a piece of music with words that you sing: *a pop song*
2 [noncount] singing; music that a person or bird makes: *The story is told through song and dance.*

son-in-law /ˈsʌn ɪn lɔ/ *noun* [count] (*plural* **sons-in-law**)
the husband of your daughter ⊃ Look at **daughter-in-law**.

son·net /ˈsɑnət/ *noun* [count]
(**ENGLISH LANGUAGE ARTS**) a poem that has 14 lines and a fixed pattern of which lines end with the same sound as others: *Shakespeare's sonnets*

soon 🔑 /sun/ *adverb*
not long after now, or not long after a particular time: *John will be home soon.* ◆ *She arrived soon after two o'clock.* ◆ *Goodbye! See you soon!*
as soon as at the same time that; when: *Call me as soon as you get home.*
sooner or later at some time in the future: *Don't worry – I'm sure he'll write to you sooner or later.*

soot /sʊt/ *noun* [noncount]
black powder that comes from smoke

soothe /suð/ *verb* (**soothes, sooth·ing, soothed**)
1 to make someone feel calmer and less unhappy: *The baby was crying, so I tried to soothe her by singing to her.*
2 to make something less painful: *This cream will soothe your skin.*
▶ **sooth·ing** /ˈsuðɪŋ/ *adjective*: *soothing music* ◆ *a soothing massage*

so·phis·ti·cat·ed /səˈfɪstəkeɪt̬əd/ *adjective*
1 having a lot of experience of the world and social situations; knowing about things like fashion and culture: *She's a very sophisticated young woman.*
2 (used about machines, systems, etc.) advanced and complicated: *highly sophisticated computer systems*

soph·o·more /ˈsɑfmɔr/ *noun* [count]
a student who is in the tenth grade in high school or the second year of college: *Jamie is a sophomore at the University of Maryland.* ⊃ Look at **freshman, junior², senior²**(1).

so·pran·o /səˈprænoʊ/ *noun* [count] (*plural* **so·pran·os**)
(**MUSIC**) the highest singing voice; a woman or child with this voice

sore 🔑 /sɔr/ *adjective*
If a part of your body is **sore**, it gives you pain: *My feet were sore after the long walk.* ◆ *I have a sore throat.*

sor·row /ˈsɑroʊ; ˈsɔroʊ/ *noun* [noncount] (formal)
sadness

sor·ry 🔑 /ˈsɑri; ˈsɔri/ *adjective* (**sor·ri·er, sor·ri·est**)
1 a word that you use when you feel bad about something you have done: *I'm sorry I didn't call you.* ◆ *Sorry I'm late!* ◆ *I'm sorry for losing your pen.*
2 feeling sad: *I'm sorry you can't come to the party.*
3 a word that you use to say "no" politely: *I'm sorry – I can't help you.*
4 a word that you use when you did not hear what someone said and you want them to say it again: *"My name is Linda Willis." "Sorry? Linda who?"*
feel sorry for someone to feel sad because someone has problems: *I felt sorry for her and gave her some money.*

sort¹ 🔑 /sɔrt/ *noun* [count]
a group of things or people that are the same in some way; a type or kind: *What sort of music do you like best – pop or classical?* ◆ *We found all sorts of shells on the beach.*
sort of (informal) words that you use when you are not sure about something: *It's sort of long and thin, a little like a sausage.*

sort² 🔑 /sɔrt/ *verb* (**sorts, sort·ing, sort·ed**)
to put things into groups: *The machine sorts the eggs into large ones and small ones.*
sort something out to find an answer to a problem: *They didn't know what to do, so I offered to help sort things out.*
sort through something to look through a lot of things in order to organize them or to find something that you are looking for: *I need to sort through this desk drawer.*

SOS /ˌɛs oʊ 'ɛs/ *noun* [*singular*]
a call for help from a ship or an airplane that is in danger

so-so /'soʊ ˌsoʊ/ *adjective, adverb* (*informal*)
OK, but not very good: *"How are you feeling?" "So-so."*

sought **AWL** form of **seek**

soul /soʊl/ *noun*
1 [*count*] the part of a person that some people believe does not die when the body dies: *Christians believe that your soul goes to heaven when you die.*
2 (also **soul mu·sic**) [*noncount*] a kind of music that was made popular by African-American musicians: *a soul singer*
not a soul not one person: *I looked everywhere, but there wasn't a soul in the building.*

sound¹ 🔑 /saʊnd/ *noun* [*count*]
something that you hear: *I heard the sound of a baby crying.* ◆ *Light travels faster than sound.*

sound² 🔑 /saʊnd/ *verb* (**sounds, sound·ing, sound·ed**)
1 to seem a particular way when you hear it: *He sounded angry when I spoke to him on the phone.* ◆ *That sounds like a good idea.* ◆ *She told me about the book – it sounds interesting.*
2 to make a sound, or to cause something to make a sound: *He sounded the car horn.*

sound³ /saʊnd/ *adjective*
1 right and good: *She gave me some sound advice.*
2 healthy or strong: *sound teeth*

sound⁴ /saʊnd/ *adverb*
sound asleep sleeping very well: *The children are sound asleep.*

sound·ly /'saʊndli/ *adverb*
completely and deeply: *I slept very soundly last night.*

sound·proof /'saʊndpruf/ *adjective*
made so that no sound can get in or out: *a soundproof room*

sound·track /'saʊndtræk/ *noun* [*count*]
(**MUSIC**) the music that has been recorded for a movie: *The movie soundtrack is available to buy now.*

soup 🔑 /sup/ *noun* [*noncount*]
liquid food that you make by cooking things like vegetables or meat in water: *tomato soup*

sour /'saʊər/ *adjective*
1 with a sharp taste like a lemon: *If it's too sour, put some sugar in it.* ⊃ **SYNONYM tart**
2 Sour milk tastes bad because it is not fresh: *This milk has gone sour.*

source **AWL** /sɔrs/ *noun* [*count*]
a place where something comes from: *Our information comes from many sources.*

south 🔑 /saʊθ/ *noun* [*singular*] (abbreviation **S.**)
(**GEOGRAPHY**) the direction that is on your right when you watch the sun come up in the morning ⊃ Look at the picture at **compass**.
▶ **south** *adjective, adverb*: *Brazil is in South America.* ◆ *the south coast of the island* ◆ *Birds fly south in the winter.*

south·east (also **South·east**) /ˌsaʊθ'ist/ *noun* [*singular*] (abbreviation **S.E.**)
(**GEOGRAPHY**) the direction between south and east; a place in this direction: *He lives in the Southeast.* ⊃ Look at the picture at **compass**.
▶ **south·east** *adjective, adverb*: *the coast of southeast Florida*
▶ **south·east·ern** /ˌsaʊθ'istərn/ *adjective*: *the southeastern states of the U.S.*

south·ern 🔑 /'sʌðərn/ *adjective*
(**GEOGRAPHY**) connected with, in, or from the south: *Los Angeles is in southern California.*

south·ern·er (also **South·ern·er**) /'sʌðərnər/ *noun* [*count*]
(**GEOGRAPHY**) a person who is from or who lives in the southern part of a country ⊃ **ANTONYM northerner**

the South Pole /ðə ˌsaʊθ 'poʊl/ *noun* [*singular*]
(**GEOGRAPHY**) the point on the earth's surface which is farthest south ⊃ Look at **the North Pole**. ⊃ Look at the picture at **earth**.

south·west (also **South·west**) /ˌsaʊθ'wɛst/ *noun* [*singular*] (abbreviation **S.W.**)
(**GEOGRAPHY**) the direction between south and west; a place in this direction: *He's from the Southwest.* ⊃ Look at the picture at **compass**.
▶ **south·west** *adjective, adverb*: *Our garden faces southwest.*
▶ **south·west·ern** /ˌsaʊθ'wɛstərn/ *adjective*

sou·ve·nir /ˌsuvə'nɪr/ *noun* [*count*]
something that you keep to remember a place or a special event: *I brought back this cowboy hat as a souvenir of Texas.*

sow /soʊ/ *verb* (**sows, sow·ing, sowed, has sown** /soʊn/ **or has sowed**)
to put seeds in the ground: *The farmer sowed the field with corn.*

soy·bean /ˈsɔɪbin/ *noun* [*count*]
a type of BEAN that can be cooked and eaten, or used to make different kinds of food, for example oil and a type of milk

spa /spɑ/ *noun* [*count*]
a place where people go to relax, take exercise, and have health and beauty treatments

space /speɪs/ *noun*
1 [*noncount*] a place that is big enough for someone or something to go into or onto: *Is there space for me in your car?* ⊃ SYNONYM **room**
2 [*count*] an empty place between things: *a parking space* • *There is a space here for you to write your name.*
3 (also **out·er space**) [*noncount*] the area outside the earth's atmosphere where all the other planets and stars are: *space travel*

space·craft /ˈspeɪskræft/ *noun* [*count*] (*plural* **space·craft**)
a vehicle that travels in space

space·ship /ˈspeɪsʃɪp/ *noun* [*count*]
a vehicle that travels in space

space shut·tle /ˈspeɪs ˌʃʌt̮l/ (also **shut·tle**) *noun* [*count*]
a vehicle that can travel into space and land like an airplane when it returns to Earth

spa·cious /ˈspeɪʃəs/ *adjective*
with a lot of space inside: *a spacious kitchen*

spade /speɪd/ *noun*
1 [*count*] a tool that you use for digging
2 spades [*plural*] the playing cards that have the shape ♠ on them: *the queen of spades* ⊃ Look at the picture at **playing card**.

spade

spa·ghet·ti /spəˈɡɛt̮i/ *noun* [*noncount*]
a kind of food made from flour and water (called PASTA) that looks like long pieces of string: *I'll cook some spaghetti.*

spam /spæm/ *noun* [*noncount*] (*informal*)
(COMPUTERS) advertisements that companies send by e-mail to people who have not asked for them ⊃ Look at **junk mail**.

span¹ /spæn/ *noun* [*count*]
1 the length of something from one end to another: *The bird's wingspan is 30 inches.*
2 the length of time that something continues: *We are looking at a time span of several months.*

span² /spæn/ *verb* (**spans**, **span·ning**, **spanned**)
1 to continue for a particular length of time: *His career spanned more than 50 years.*
2 to form a bridge over something: *The river is spanned by a beautiful iron bridge.*

spare¹ /spɛr/ *adjective*
1 not needed now, but kept because it may be needed in the future: *Do you have a spare tire in your car?* • *You can stay with us tonight. We have a spare room.*
2 Spare time is time when you are not working: *What do you do in your spare time?*

spare² /spɛr/ *verb* (**spares**, **spar·ing**, **spared**)
to be able to give something to someone: *I can't spare the time to help you today.*
to spare more than is needed: *There's no time to spare. We have to leave right away.*

spark /spɑrk/ *noun* [*count*]
a very small piece of something that is burning

spar·kle /ˈspɑrkl/ *verb* (**spar·kles**, **spar·kling**, **spar·kled**)
to shine with a lot of very small points of light: *The lake sparkled in the sunlight.* • *Her eyes sparkled with excitement.*
▶ **spar·kle** *noun* [*noncount*]: *the sparkle of diamonds*

spar·kling /ˈspɑrklɪŋ/ *adjective*
1 shining with a lot of very small points of light: *sparkling blue eyes*
2 Sparkling wine or water has a lot of small bubbles in it.

spar·row /ˈspæroʊ/ *noun* [*count*]
a small, brown bird

sparse /spɑrs/ *adjective*
small in quantity or amount: *a sparse crowd*
▶ **sparse·ly** /ˈspɑrsli/ *adverb*: *a sparsely populated area*

spat form of **spit**

speak /spik/ *verb* (**speaks**, **speak·ing**, **spoke** /spoʊk/, has **spo·ken** /ˈspoʊkən/)
1 to say things; to talk to someone: *Please speak more slowly.* • *Can I speak to John Smith, please?* (= words that you say on the telephone) • *The mayor spoke for over an hour.* ⊃ Look at the note at **talk¹**.
2 to know and use a language: *I can speak French and Italian.*
speak up to talk louder: *Can you speak up? I can't hear you!* ⊃ The noun is **speech**.

speak·er /ˈspikər/ *noun* [*count*]
1 a person who is talking to a group of people
2 the part of something such as a radio or CD player where the sound comes out ⊃ Look at the picture at **stereo**.

spear /spɪr/ *noun* [*count*]
a long stick with a sharp point at one end, used for hunting or fighting

spe·cial¹ /ˈspɛʃl/ *adjective*
1 not usual or ordinary; important for a reason: *It's my birthday today, so we're having a special dinner.*

2 for a particular person or thing: *He goes to a special school for deaf children.*

spe·cial² /'spɛʃl/ *noun* [count]
something that is not usually available but that is offered for a short time: *Tonight's special is roast beef* (= in a restaurant, for example).

spe·cial·ist /'spɛʃl·ɪst/ *noun* [count]
a person who knows a lot about something: *She's a specialist in American art.*

spe·cial·ize /'spɛʃl·aɪz/ *verb* (spe·cial·iz·es, spe·cial·iz·ing, spe·cial·ized)
specialize in something to study or know a lot about one subject, type of product, etc.: *He specialized in criminal law.*

spe·cial·ly /'spɛʃl·i/ *adverb*
for a particular purpose or reason: *These dogs have been specially trained to find illegal drugs.* ◆ *a specially designed chair*

spe·cial·ty /'spɛʃl·ti/ *noun* [count] (*plural* spe·cial·ties)
1 something that is made by a person or place that is very good and that they or it is known for: *The chef's specialty is baked salmon in a cream sauce.* ◆ *local specialties*
2 an area of study or a subject that you know a lot about

spe·cies /'spiʃiz/ *noun* [count] (*plural* spe·cies)
(BIOLOGY) a group of animals or plants that are the same and can BREED (= make new animals or plants) together: *a rare species of frog* ◆ *The panda is an endangered species* (= in danger of disappearing).

spe·cif·ic AWL /spə'sɪfɪk/ *adjective*
1 exact and clear: *He gave us specific instructions on how to get there.*
2 particular: *Is there anything specific that you want to talk about?*
▶ **spe·cif·i·cal·ly** AWL /spə'sɪfɪkli/ *adverb*: *I specifically asked you to buy butter, not margarine.*

spec·i·fy AWL /'spɛsəfaɪ/ *verb* (spec·i·fies, spec·i·fy·ing, spec·i·fied)
to say something clearly or in detail: *He said he'd be arriving in the morning, but didn't specify the time.*

spec·i·men /'spɛsəmən/ *noun* [count] (GENERAL SCIENCE)
1 one example of a group of things: *specimens of different types of rock*
2 a small amount or part of something that shows what the rest is like: *The doctor took a specimen of blood for testing.* ⊃ SYNONYM **sample**

speck /spɛk/ *noun* [count]
a very small spot, mark, or piece of something: *specks of dust*

spec·ta·cle /'spɛktəkl/ *noun* [count]
something that is exciting and unusual to look at: *the thrilling spectacle of the New Year's Day parade*

spec·tac·u·lar /spɛk'tækyələr/ *adjective*
wonderful to see: *There was a spectacular view from the top of the mountain.*
▶ **spec·tac·u·lar·ly** /spɛk'tækyələrli/ *adverb*: *This is a spectacularly beautiful area.*

spec·ta·tor /'spɛkteɪtər/ *noun* [count]
a person who is watching an event, especially a sports event: *There were 2,000 spectators at the football game.*

spec·trum /'spɛktrəm/ *noun* [count, usually singular] (*plural* **spec·tra** /'spɛktrə/ or **spec·trums**)
(PHYSICS) the set of seven colors into which white light can be separated: *You can see the colors of the spectrum in a rainbow.*

spec·u·late /'spɛkyəleɪt/ *verb* (spec·u·lates, spec·u·lat·ing, spec·u·lat·ed)
to make a guess about something without knowing all of the facts: *I would rather not speculate about what may happen next year.*
▶ **spec·u·la·tion** /ˌspɛkyə'leɪʃn/ *noun* [count, noncount]: *There was speculation that she was going to resign.*

sped form of **speed²**

speech 🖉 /spitʃ/ *noun* (*plural* speech·es)
1 [count] a talk that you give to a group of people: *The president made a speech.*
2 [noncount] the power to speak, or the way that you speak: *He has problems with his speech.*

speed¹ 🖉 /spid/ *noun* [count, noncount]
how fast something goes: *The car was traveling at a speed of 50 miles an hour.* ◆ *a high-speed train* (= that goes very fast)

speed² /spid/ *verb* (speeds, speed·ing, sped /spɛd/ or speed·ed, has sped or has speed·ed)
1 to go or move very quickly: *He sped past me on his bike.*
2 to drive too fast: *The police stopped me because I was speeding.*
speed up; speed something up to go faster; to make something go faster: *What can we do to speed up the process?*

speed·boat /'spidbout/ *noun* [count]
a small fast boat with an engine

speed lim·it /'spid lɪmət/ *noun* [count]
the fastest that you are allowed to travel on a road: *The speed limit on the highway is 60 miles an hour.*

speed·om·e·ter /spɪ'dɑmətər/ *noun* [count]
a piece of equipment in a vehicle that tells you how fast you are traveling ⊃ Look at the picture at **steering wheel**.

spell¹ 🔊 /spɛl/ *verb* (spells, spell·ing, spelled)
(**ENGLISH LANGUAGE ARTS**)
1 to use the right letters to make a word: *"How do you spell your name?" "A-Z-I-Z." • You've spelled this word wrong.*
2 (used about a set of letters) to form a particular word: *B-A-L-L spells "ball."*

spell² /spɛl/ *noun* [count]
1 a short period of time: *a spell of cold weather*
2 magic words that make someone change or make them do what you want: *The witch cast a spell on the prince.*

spell·ing /'spɛlɪŋ/ *noun* (**ENGLISH LANGUAGE ARTS**)
1 [count, noncount] the right way of writing a word: *Look in your dictionary to find the right spelling.*
2 [noncount] the ability to spell correctly: *You need to work on your spelling.*

spend 🔊 /spɛnd/ *verb* (spends, spend·ing, spent /spɛnt/, has spent)
1 to pay money for something: *Louise spends a lot of money on clothes.*
2 to pass time: *I spent the summer in New Hampshire. • He spent a lot of time sleeping.*

sperm /spɚm/ *noun* [count] (*plural* sperm)
(**BIOLOGY**) a cell that is produced by a male and that can join with a female egg to produce young

sphere **AWL** /sfɪr/ *noun* [count]
(**MATH**) any round object that is like a ball: *The earth is a sphere.* ⊃ Look at the picture at **solid**.
▶ **spher·i·cal** **AWL** /'sfɪrɪkl; 'sfɛrɪkl/ *adjective*: *a spherical object*

spice 🔊 /spaɪs/ *noun* [count]
a powder of the seeds from a plant, which you can put in food to give it a stronger taste: *They use a lot of spices, such as chili and ginger.*
▶ **spic·y** /'spaɪsi/ *adjective* (spic·i·er, spic·i·est): *spicy food*

spi·der 🔊 /'spaɪdɚ/ *noun* [count]
a small animal with eight legs, which catches and eats insects: *Spiders spin webs to catch flies.*

spider

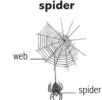

web

spider

spied form of **spy²**

spies
1 plural of **spy¹**
2 form of **spy²**

spike /spaɪk/ *noun* [count]
a piece of metal with a sharp point: *The fence has spikes along the top.*

spik·y /'spaɪki/ *adjective* (spik·i·er, spik·i·est)
1 having sharp points: *spiky leaves*

2 Spiky hair sticks straight up in the air. ⊃ Look at the picture at **hair**.

spill /spɪl/ *verb* (spills, spill·ing, spilled)
If you **spill** a liquid, it flows out of something by accident: *I spilled my coffee!*

spin /spɪn/ *verb* (spins, spin·ning, spun /spʌn/, has spun)
1 to turn around quickly; to turn something around quickly: *She spun around as he entered the room. • Spin the wheel.*
2 to make thread from wool or cotton: *She spun and dyed the wool herself.*
3 If a spider **spins** a WEB (= a thin net that it makes to catch flies), it produces thread from its own body to make it.

spin·ach /'spɪnɪtʃ/ *noun* [noncount]
a vegetable with big, green leaves

spine /spaɪn/ *noun* [count] (**BIOLOGY**)
1 the line of bones in your back ⊃ Look at the picture at **skeleton**.
2 one of the sharp points on some plants and animals: *Porcupines use their spines to protect themselves.*

spi·ral /'spaɪrəl/ *noun* [count]
a long shape that goes around and around as it goes up: *A spring is a spiral.*
▶ **spi·ral** *adjective*: *a spiral staircase*

spire /'spaɪɚ/ *noun* [count]
a tall, pointed structure on top of a church

spir·it 🔊 /'spɪrɪt/ *noun*
1 [count] the part of a person that is not the body. Some people think that your **spirit** does not die when your body dies.
2 **spirits** [plural] the way that a person feels: *She's in high spirits (= happy) today.*
3 **spirits** [plural] strong alcoholic drinks such as WHISKEY

spir·i·tu·al /'spɪrɪtʃuəl/ *adjective*
1 connected with deep thoughts and feelings rather than the physical body: *Our society often neglects people's spiritual needs.*
2 (**RELIGION**) connected with religion: *a spiritual leader*

spit /spɪt/ *verb* (spits, spit·ting, spit or spat /spæt/, has spit or has spat)
to send liquid or food out from your mouth: *The baby spit her food out. • He spat on the ground.*

spite /spaɪt/ *noun* [noncount]
when someone deliberately says or does unkind things: *She broke my watch out of spite.*
in spite of something although something is true; not noticing or caring about something: *I slept well in spite of the noise. • In spite of the bad weather, we went out.* ⊃ **SYNONYM despite**

spite·ful /'spaɪtfl/ *adjective*
saying or doing unkind things

splash¹ /splæʃ/ *verb* (splash·es, splash·ing, splashed)
to throw drops of liquid over someone or something; to make this happen: *The car splashed us as it drove past.* ◆ *The children were splashing around in the pool.*

splash² /splæʃ/ *noun* [count] (*plural* splash·es)
1 the sound that a person or thing makes when they fall into water: *Tom jumped into the river with a big splash.*
2 a small amount of liquid: *There were splashes of paint on the floor.*

splen·did /'splɛndəd/ *adjective*
very beautiful or very good: *a splendid palace* ◆ *a splendid example of early American art*

splin·ter /'splɪntər/ *noun* [count]
a very small, thin, sharp piece of wood, metal, or glass that has broken off a bigger piece: *I have a splinter in my finger.*

split¹ /splɪt/ *verb* (splits, split·ting, split, has split)
1 to divide or separate; to make this happen: *I split the wood with an ax.* ◆ *We **split** the money **between** us.* ◆ *The teacher told us to **split into** groups.*
2 to tear or break apart; to make this happen: *His jeans split when he sat down.* ◆ *How did you split your lip?*
split up to stop being together: *He has split up with his girlfriend.*

split² /splɪt/ *noun* [count]
1 a long cut or hole in something: *There's a big split in the tent.*
2 a disagreement that divides a group of people

spoil 🔑 /spɔɪl/ *verb* (spoils, spoil·ing, spoiled)
1 to make something less good than before: *The mud spoiled my shoes.* ◆ *Did the bad weather spoil your vacation?*
2 to give a child too much so that they think they can always have what they want: *She spoils her grandchildren.*
▶ **spoiled** /spɔɪld/ *adjective*
(used about a child) rude and badly behaved because people give them everything they ask for: *a spoiled child*

spoke¹ form of **speak**

spoke² /spoʊk/ *noun* [count]
one of the thin bars that join the middle part of a wheel to the outside part ⊃ Look at the picture at **bicycle**.

spo·ken form of **speak**

spokes·man /'spoʊksmən/ (also **spokes·wom·an** /'spoʊkswʊmən/) *noun* [count]
(*plural* spokes·men /'spoʊksmən/ , spokes·wom·en /'spoʊkswɪmən/)
a person who tells someone what a group of people has decided

spokes·per·son /'spoʊkspɜrsn/ *noun* [count]
(spokes·per·sons or spokes·peo·ple /'spoʊkspipl/)
a person who tells someone what a group of people has decided

sponge /spʌndʒ/ *noun* [count]
a soft thing with a lot of small holes in it that you use for washing yourself or cleaning things

sponge

spong·y /'spʌndʒi/ *adjective* (spong·i·er, spong·i·est)
soft, like a SPONGE: *The ground was spongy.*

spon·sor¹ /'spɑnsər/ *noun* [count]
1 a person or a company that gives money so that an event will take place: *The race organizers are trying to attract sponsors.*
2 a person who agrees to pay money to a charity if someone else completes a particular activity: *I need sponsors for a 25-mile bike ride to raise money for cancer research.*

spon·sor² /'spɑnsər/ *verb* (spon·sors, spon·sor·ing, spon·sored)
1 to give money so that an event will take place: *The local team was sponsored by a large company.*
2 to agree to pay money to a charity if someone else completes a particular activity: *a sponsored walk to raise money for children in need*

spon·ta·ne·ous /spɑn'teɪniəs/ *adjective*
done or happening suddenly; not planned: *The audience burst into spontaneous applause.*
▶ **spon·ta·ne·ous·ly** /spɑn'teɪniəsli/ *adverb*: *to laugh spontaneously*

spook·y /'spuki/ *adjective* (spook·i·er, spook·i·est) (*informal*)
making you feel nervous or afraid: *It's spooky being alone in the house at night.* ⊃ SYNONYM **creepy**

spoon 🔑 /spun/ *noun* [count]
a thing with a round end that you use for eating, serving, or mixing food: *a wooden spoon* ◆ *You need a knife, fork, and spoon.*

spoons

tablespoon

teaspoon

spoon·ful /'spunfʊl/ *noun* [count]
the amount that you can put in one spoon: *a spoonful of sugar*

sport 🔑 /spɔrt/ *noun* [count, noncount]
a physical game or activity that you do to keep your body strong or because you enjoy it: *Jane **plays** a lot of **sports**.* ◆ *Soccer is my favorite sport.*

sports car /'spɔrts kɑr/ *noun* [count]
a fast car, usually with a roof that you can open

sports car

sports·man /'spɔrtsmən/ (also **sports·wom·an** /'spɔrtswʊmən/) *noun* [count] (plural **sports·men** /'spɔrtsmən/, **sports·wom·en** /'spɔrtswɪmən/)
a person who plays sports

sport·y /'spɔrti/ *adjective* (sport·i·er, sport·i·est)
liking or good at sports

spot[1] /spɑt/ *noun* [count]
1 a small, round mark: *a white dog with black spots*
2 a place: *This is a good spot for a picnic.*

spot[2] /spɑt/ *verb* (spots, spot·ting, spot·ted)
to see someone or something suddenly: *She spotted her friend in the crowd.*

spot·less /'spɑtləs/ *adjective*
completely clean: *She keeps the house spotless.*

spot·light /'spɑtlaɪt/ *noun* [count]
a strong light that shines a bright light on a small area. **Spotlights** are often used in theaters.

spot·ty /'spɑti/ *adjective* (spot·ti·er, spot·ti·est)
good in some parts, but not in others: *I have a spotty knowledge of French.*

spouse /spaʊs/ *noun* [count] (formal)
your husband or wife

spout /spaʊt/ *noun* [count]
the narrow part of a container that you pour liquid out of

sprain /spreɪn/ *verb* (sprains, sprain·ing, sprained)
to hurt part of your body by turning it suddenly: *Scott fell and sprained his ankle.*

sprang form of **spring**[2]

sprawl /sprɔl/ *verb* (sprawls, sprawl·ing, sprawled)
to sit or lie with your arms and legs spread out: *The kids were sprawled on the floor, watching TV.*

spray[1] /spreɪ/ *noun*
1 [noncount] liquid in very small drops that flies through the air: *spray from the ocean*
2 [count, noncount] liquid in a container that comes out in very small drops when you press a button: *a can of hair spray*

spray[2] /spreɪ/ *verb* (sprays, spray·ing, sprayed)
to make very small drops of liquid fall on something: *Someone sprayed paint on my car.*

spread /sprɛd/ *verb* (spreads, spread·ing, spread, has spread)
1 to open something so that you can see all of it: *The bird spread its wings and flew away.* ♦ *Spread out the map on the table.*
2 to put a soft substance all over something: *I spread butter on the bread.*
3 to reach more people or places; to make something do this: *Fire quickly spread to other parts of the building.* ♦ *Rats spread disease.*
▸ **spread** *noun* [noncount]: *Doctors are trying to stop the spread of the disease.*

spread·sheet /'sprɛdʃit/ *noun* [count]
(COMPUTERS) a computer program for working with rows of numbers, used especially for doing accounts

spree /spri/ *noun* [count] (informal)
a time when you go out and do a lot of something that you enjoy, often doing too much of it: *We went on a big shopping spree yesterday.*

spring[1] /sprɪŋ/ *noun*
1 [count, noncount] the part of the year after winter, when plants start to grow: *flowers that bloom in spring*
2 [count] a long, thin piece of metal that is twisted around and around. A **spring** will go back to the same size and shape after you push or pull it.
3 [count] (GEOGRAPHY) a place where water comes out of the ground: *a mountain spring*

spring

spring[2] /sprɪŋ/ *verb* (springs, spring·ing, sprang /spræŋ/ or sprung /sprʌŋ/, has sprung)
to jump or move suddenly: *He sprang to his feet.* ♦ *Everyone has sprung into action.*
spring up to appear or develop quickly or suddenly: *New buildings are springing up all over the city.*

sprin·kle /'sprɪŋkl/ *verb* (sprin·kles, sprin·kling, sprin·kled)
to shake small pieces of something or drops of a liquid on another thing: *Sprinkle some sugar on the fruit.*

sprin·kler /'sprɪŋklər/ *noun* [count]
a thing that sends out water in small drops. **Sprinklers** are used on grass and for stopping fires in buildings.

sprint /sprɪnt/ *verb* (sprints, sprint·ing, sprint·ed)
to run a short distance very fast

sprout[1] /spraʊt/ *verb* (sprouts, sprout·ing, sprout·ed)
(BIOLOGY) to start to grow: *New leaves are sprouting on the trees.*

sprout[2] /spraʊt/ *noun* [count]
a new part that has grown on a plant

sprung form of **spring**[2]

spun form of **spin**

spy¹ /spaɪ/ *noun* [count] (*plural* **spies**)
a person who tries to learn secrets about another country, person, or company

spy² /spaɪ/ *verb* (**spies, spy·ing, spied, has spied**)
to watch a country, person, or company and try to learn their secrets: *He spied for his government for more than ten years.*
spy on someone or **something** to watch someone or something secretly: *Have you been spying on me?*

squab·ble /'skwɑbl/ *verb* (**squab·bles, squab·bling, squab·bled**)
to argue about something that is not important: *The children were **squabbling over** the last piece of cake.* ◆ *Stop **squabbling with** your brother!*
▶ **squab·ble** *noun* [count]: *It was a silly squabble about what game to play.*

squad /skwɑd/ *noun* [count]
a small group of people who work together: *a women's soccer squad* ◆ *a squad of police officers*

square¹ 🔊 /skwɛr/ *noun* [count]
1 a shape with four straight sides that are the same length ⊃ Look at the picture at **shape**.
2 an open space in a town or city, with buildings around it: *Times Square is in New York City.* ◆ *the town square*
3 (MATH) the number that you get when you multiply another number by itself: *Four is the **square of** two* (= 2x2=4).

square² 🔊 /skwɛr/ *adjective* (MATH)
1 with four straight sides that are the same length: *a square table*
2 (abbreviation **sq.**) used for talking about the area of something: *If a room is 5 yards long and 4 yards wide, its area is 20 **square yards**.*
3 (used about something that is square in shape) having sides of a particular length: *The picture is twenty inches square* (= each side is 20 inches long).

squared /skwɛrd/ *adjective*
(MATH) (used about a number) multiplied by itself: *Four squared is sixteen.*

square root /ˌskwɛr 'rut/ *noun* [count]
(MATH) a number that produces another particular number when it is multiplied by itself: *The square root of sixteen is four.*

squash¹ /skwɑʃ/ *verb* (**squash·es, squash·ing, squashed**)
1 to press something hard and make it flat: *She sat on my hat and squashed it.* ⊃ Look at the picture at **squeeze**.
2 to push a lot of people or things into a small space: *We **squashed** five people **into** the back of the car.*

squash² /skwɑʃ/ *noun*
1 [noncount] (SPORTS) a game where two players hit a small ball against the wall in a special room: *the squash courts*
2 [count, noncount] (*plural* **squash**) a type of vegetable with a hard skin that grows on the ground: *pumpkins, zucchini, and other kinds of squash*

squat /skwɑt/ *verb* (**squats, squat·ting, squat·ted**)
to bend your knees and sit just above the ground: *I **squatted down** to light the fire.*

squeak /skwik/ *verb* (**squeaks, squeak·ing, squeaked**)
to make a short, high sound like a mouse: *The door was squeaking, so I put some oil on it.*
▶ **squeak** *noun* [count]: *the squeak of a mouse*
▶ **squeak·y** /'skwiki/ *adjective* (**squeak·i·er, squeak·i·est**): *She has a squeaky voice.*

squeal /skwil/ *verb* (**squeals, squeal·ing, squealed**)
to make a loud, high sound: *The children **squealed with** excitement.*
▶ **squeal** *noun* [count]: *squeals of delight*

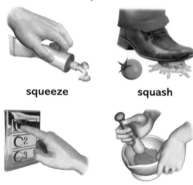

squeeze

squeeze   squash

press   crush

squeeze /skwiz/ *verb* (**squeez·es, squeez·ing, squeezed**)
1 to press something hard: *Squeeze the lemons and add the juice to the mixture.* ◆ *She squeezed his hand.*
2 to go into a small space; to push too much into a small space: *Fifty people **squeezed into** the small room.* ◆ *Can you **squeeze** another person **into** your car?*
▶ **squeeze** *noun* [count]: *She **gave** my arm a **squeeze**.*

squid /skwɪd/ *noun* [count] (*plural* **squid** or **squids**)
an animal that lives in the ocean. It has a soft body and ten long parts (called TENTACLES). ⊃ Look at the picture at **octopus**.

squint /skwɪnt/ *verb* (squints, squint·ing, squint·ed)
to look at something with your eyes almost closed: *to squint in bright sunlight*

squir·rel /'skwərəl/ *noun* [count]
a small gray, brown, or black animal with a big, thick tail. **Squirrels** live in trees and eat nuts.

squirrel

squirt /skwərt/ *verb* (squirts, squirt·ing, squirt·ed)
(used about a liquid) to suddenly come out and go onto something or toward something; to make this happen: *I bit into the orange and juice squirted out.* ◆ *He squirted me with water.*

Sr. abbreviation of **Senior**: *John Brown, Sr.*

St.
1 abbreviation of **saint**
2 abbreviation of **street**

stab /stæb/ *verb* (stabs, stab·bing, stabbed)
to push a knife or another sharp thing into someone or something: *He was stabbed in the back.*

sta·bil·i·ty AWL /stə'bɪləti/ *noun* [noncount]
being steady and not changing: *After so many changes, we need a period of stability.*

sta·bi·lize AWL /'steɪbl·aɪz/ *verb* (sta·bi·liz·es, sta·bi·liz·ing, sta·bi·lized)
to become or to make something firm, steady, or not likely to change: *The patient's condition has stabilized.*

sta·ble¹ AWL /'steɪbl/ *adjective*
not likely to move, fall, or change: *Don't stand on that chair – it's not very stable.* ⊃ ANTONYM **unstable**

sta·ble² AWL /'steɪbl/ *noun* [count]
a building where you keep horses

stack¹ /stæk/ *noun* [count]
a lot of things on top of one another: *a stack of books* ⊃ SYNONYM **pile**

stack² /stæk/ *verb* (stacks, stack·ing, stacked)
to put things on top of one another: *I stacked up the chairs after the concert.*

sta·di·um /'steɪdiəm/ *noun* [count]
(SPORTS) a place with seats around it where you can watch sports: *a football stadium* ⊃ Look at the note at **field**.

staff /stæf/ *noun* [plural]
the people who work in a place: *The hotel staff were very friendly.*

stage /steɪdʒ/ *noun* [count]
1 a particular time in a longer set of things that happen: *The first stage of the project lasts for two weeks.* ◆ *At this stage, I don't know what I'll do when I leave school.*
2 the part of a theater where the actors, dancers, etc. perform: *The audience threw flowers onto the stage.* ◆ *There were more than 50 people on stage in one scene.*

stag·ger /'stægər/ *verb* (stag·gers, stag·ger·ing, stag·gered)
to walk as if you are going to fall: *He staggered across the room with the heavy box.*

stag·nant /'stægnənt/ *adjective*
If water is **stagnant**, it is not moving, so it is dirty and smells bad.

stain /steɪn/ *verb* (stains, stain·ing, stained)
to leave a dirty mark on something, which is difficult to remove: *The spilled wine stained the carpet red.*
▶ **stain** *noun* [count]: *She had blood stains on her shirt.*

stain·less steel /ˌsteɪnləs 'stil/ *noun* [noncount]
a metal that does not RUST (= change color or get damaged by water): *stainless steel pots and pans*

stair /stɛr/ *noun*
1 **stairs** [plural] steps that lead up and down inside a building: *I ran up the stairs to the bedroom.* ⊃ Look at **downstairs**, **upstairs**.
2 one of the steps in a set of **stairs**: *How many stairs are there up to the top floor?*

stair·case /'stɛrkeɪs/ (also **stair·way**) /'stɛrweɪ/ *noun* [count]
a large set of stairs

stale /steɪl/ *adjective* (stal·er, stal·est)
not fresh: *stale bread* ◆ *stale air*

stalk /stɔk/ *noun* [count]
one of the long, thin parts of a plant that the flowers, leaves, or fruit grow on

stall /stɔl/ *noun* [count]
1 a big table with things on it that someone wants to sell, for example in a street or market: *a fruit stall*
2 a small area with walls around it and a shower or toilet in it: *a shower stall*
3 a small area with walls around it for one animal, especially a horse

stal·lion /'stælyən/ *noun* [count]
an adult male horse ⊃ Look at the note at **horse**.

stam·i·na /'stæmənə/ *noun* [noncount]
the ability to do something difficult for a long time: *You need a lot of stamina to run a marathon.*

stam·mer /ˈstæmər/ *verb* (stam·mers, stam·mer·ing, stam·mered)
to say the same sound many times when you are trying to say a word: *"B-b-b-but wait for me," she stammered.* ⊃ SYNONYM **stutter**

▸ **stam·mer** *noun* [singular]: *to have a stammer*

stamp¹ 🔊 /stæmp/ *noun* [count]
1 a small piece of paper that you put on a letter to show that you have paid to send it: *Could I have three postcard stamps, please?* • *He has been collecting stamps since he was eight.*
2 a small piece of wood or metal that you press on paper to make marks or words: *a date stamp*

stamp² /stæmp/ *verb* (stamps, stamp·ing, stamped)
1 to put your foot down very hard: *She stamped on the spider and killed it.*
2 to walk by putting your feet down hard and loudly: *Mike stamped angrily out of the room.*
3 to press a small piece of wood or metal on paper to make marks or words: *They stamped my passport at the airport.*

stam·pede /stæmˈpid/ *noun* [count]
a situation when a lot of animals or people start running in the same direction because they are frightened or excited: *There was a stampede when the doors finally opened.*

▸ **stam·pede** *verb* (stam·pedes, stam·ped·ing, stam·ped·ed): *a herd of stampeding buffalo*

stand¹ 🔊 /stænd/ *verb* (stands, stand·ing, stood /stʊd/, has stood)
1 to be on your feet: *She was standing by the door.* • *Stand still while I take your photograph.*
2 (also **stand up**) to get up on your feet: *The teacher asked us all to stand up.*
3 to be in a place: *The castle stands on a hill.*
4 to put something somewhere: *I stood the ladder against the wall.*
5 to be able to survive difficult conditions: *Camels can stand extremely hot and cold temperatures.*
can't stand someone or **something** to hate someone or something: *I can't stand this music.* ⊃ Look at the note at **hate¹**.
stand back to move back: *The police told the crowd to stand back.*
stand by
1 to watch but not do anything: *How can you stand by while those boys kick the cat?*
2 to be ready to do something: *Stand by until I call you!*
stand by someone to help someone when they need it: *Julie's parents stood by her when she was in trouble.*
stand for something to be a short way of saying or writing something: *U.S. stands for "United States."*
stand out to be easy to see: *Joe stands out in a crowd because of his red hair.*

stand someone up (*informal*) to not keep an appointment with someone: *Jan's date stood her up, so she went to the movie alone.*
stand up for someone or **something** to say that someone or something is right; to support someone or something: *Everyone else said I was wrong, but my sister stood up for me.*
stand up to someone to argue or fight with a more powerful person who is attacking you

stand² 🔊 /stænd/ *noun*
1 [count] a table or small store where you can buy things or get information: *a newsstand (= where you can buy newspapers and magazines)*
2 [count] a piece of furniture that you can put things on: *an umbrella stand*
3 **stands** [plural] (**SPORTS**) a large structure where people can watch sports from seats arranged in rows that are low near the front and high near the back

stan·dard¹ 🔊 /ˈstændərd/ *noun*
1 [count] how good someone or something is: *Her work is of a very high standard.*
2 **standards** [plural] a level of behavior that people think is acceptable: *Many people are worried about falling standards in modern society.*

stan·dard² 🔊 /ˈstændərd/ *adjective*
normal; not special: *Clothes are sold in standard sizes.*

stan·dard·ize /ˈstændərdaɪz/ *verb* (stan·dard·iz·es, stan·dard·iz·ing, stan·dard·ized)
to make things of a certain type the same as each other

stand·ard of liv·ing /ˌstændərd əv ˈlɪvɪŋ/ *noun* [count] (*plural* **stand·ards of liv·ing**)
how rich or poor you are: *They have a low standard of living (= they are poor).*

stand·by /ˈstændbaɪ/ *noun* [count] (*plural* **stand·bys**)
a person or thing that is ready to be used if needed
on standby ready and waiting to do something immediately if needed: *We were put on standby for the flight to Miami.*

stand·still /ˈstænstɪl/ *noun* [singular]
a situation when there is no activity or progress: *Traffic came to a complete standstill.*

stank form of **stink**

sta·ple /ˈsteɪpl/ *noun* [count]
a small piece of metal that you use for fastening pieces of paper together. You press the **staples** through the paper, using a **STAPLER** ⊃ Look at the picture at **stationery**.

▸ **sta·ple** *verb* (sta·ples, sta·pling, sta·pled): *Staple the pieces of paper together.*

---

sta·pler /'steɪplər/ *noun* [count]
a tool that you use for fastening pieces of paper together with metal STAPLES ⊃ Look at the picture at **stationery**.

star¹ 🔊 /stɑr/ *noun* [count]
1 one of the small, bright lights that you see in the sky at night
2 a shape with points: *a horse with a white star on its forehead*
3 a famous person who performs something or plays sports, for example an actor: *a basketball star*

star² /stɑr/ *verb* (stars, star·ring, starred)
1 to be the main actor in a play or movie: *He has starred in many movies.*
2 to have someone as a star: *The movie stars George Clooney.*

starch /stɑrtʃ/ *noun* [count, noncount]
(**BIOLOGY, CHEMISTRY**) a white substance that is found in foods such as potatoes, rice, and bread

stare 🔊 /stɛr/ *verb* (stares, star·ing, stared)
to look at someone or something for a long time: *Everyone stared at her hat.* ◆ *He was staring out of the window.*

star·fish /'stɑrfɪʃ/
noun [count] (*plural* star·fish)
a flat animal that lives in the ocean and is shaped like a star

starfish

the Stars and Stripes /ðə ˌstɑrz ən 'straɪps/ *noun* [singular]
the national flag of the U.S.

start¹ 🔊 /stɑrt/ *verb* (starts, start·ing, start·ed)
1 to begin to do something: *I start work at nine o'clock.* ◆ *It started raining.* ◆ *She started to cry.*
2 to begin to happen; to make something begin to happen: *The concert starts at 8:00.* ◆ *The police do not know who started the fire.*
3 to begin to work or move; to make something begin to work or move: *The engine won't start.* ◆ *I can't start the car.*
start off to begin: *The teacher started off by asking us our names.*
start over to begin again: *I've made a lot of mistakes, so I'd better start over.*

start² 🔊 /stɑrt/ *noun* [count]
1 the beginning or first part of something: *She arrived after the start of the meeting.*
2 the act of starting something: *There's lots of work to do, so let's make a start.*
for a start (*informal*) words that you use when you give your first reason for something: *"Why can't we go on vacation?" "Well, for a start, we don't have enough money."*

star·tle /'stɑrt̮l/ *verb* (star·tles, star·tling, star·tled)
to make someone suddenly surprised or afraid: *You startled me when you knocked on the window.*
▸ **star·tled** /'stɑrt̮ld/ *adjective*: *He was so startled he dropped the glass.*

starve /stɑrv/ *verb* (starves, starv·ing, starved)
(**HEALTH**) to die because you do not have enough to eat: *Millions of people are starving in some parts of the world.*
be starving (*informal*) to be very hungry: *When will dinner be ready? I'm starving!*
▸ **star·va·tion** /stɑr'veɪʃn/ *noun* [noncount]: *The child died of starvation.*

state¹ 🔊 /steɪt/ *noun*
1 how someone or something is: *The house was in a terrible state.* ◆ *What state of mind is he in?*
2 (**POLITICS**) a part of a country, especially one of the 50 parts of the United States: *Texas is a state in the U.S.*
3 (**POLITICS**) a country and its government: *Many social programs are run by the state.*
4 the States [plural] (*informal*) the United States

state² 🔊 /steɪt/ *verb* (states, stat·ing, stat·ed)
to say or write something, especially officially: *I stated in my letter that I was looking for a job.*

state·ment 🔊 /'steɪtmənt/ *noun* [count]
something that you say or write, especially officially: *The driver made a statement to the police about the accident.*

states·man /'steɪtsmən/ *noun* [count] (*plural* states·men /'steɪtsmən/)
(**POLITICS**) a politician with a lot of experience who the public respects

stat·ic /'stæt̮ɪk/ *noun* [noncount] (**PHYSICS**)
1 sudden noises on a radio or television, caused by electricity in the atmosphere: *Change the station – there's too much static on this one.*
2 (also **stat·ic e·lec·tric·i·ty** /ˌstæt̮ɪk ɪlɛk'trɪsət̮i/) electricity that collects on the surface of something: *My hair gets full of static when I brush it.*

sta·tion 🔊 /'steɪʃn/ *noun* [count]
1 a place where trains stop so that people can get on and off: *the train station*
2 a place where buses start and end their trips: *the bus station*
3 a building for some special work: *the police station* ◆ *the fire station* ◆ *a gas station*
4 a television or radio company

sta·tion·ar·y /'steɪʃnˌɛri/ *adjective*
not moving: *a stationary vehicle*

sta·tion·er·y /'steɪʃnˌɛri/ *noun* [noncount]
paper, pens, and other things that you use for writing

stationery

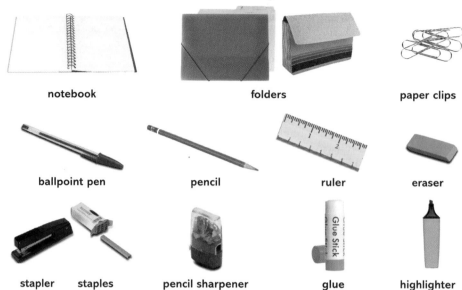

notebook   folders   paper clips

ballpoint pen   pencil   ruler   eraser

stapler   staples   pencil sharpener   glue   highlighter

---

sta·tion wag·on
/'steɪʃn ˌwægən/ *noun* [*count*]
a long car with a door at the back and space behind the back seat for carrying things

station wagon

stat·is·ti·cian **AWL** /ˌstætɪ'stɪʃn/ *noun* [*count*]
a person who studies or works with STATISTICS

sta·tis·tics **AWL** /stə'tɪstɪks/ *noun* [*plural*] (**MATH**)
1 numbers that give information about something: **Statistics show** that women live longer than men.
2 the science of studying and collecting these numbers: *I'm taking a statistics course in college.*
▶ **sta·tis·ti·cal** **AWL** /stə'tɪstɪkl/ *adjective*: *statistical analysis*

stat·ue /'stætʃu/ *noun* [*count*]
a model of a person or an animal, made from stone or metal: *the Statue of Liberty in New York*

sta·tus **AWL** /'stætəs; 'steɪtəs/ *noun*
1 [*noncount*] the legal position of a person, group, or country: *Please write your name, age, and **marital status** (= whether you are married or single).*
2 [*singular*] your social or professional position compared to other people: *Teachers have a very high status in many countries.*

stay¹ 🔊 /steɪ/ *verb* (stays, stay·ing, stayed)
1 to be in the same place and not go away: *Stay here until I come back.* ◆ *I stayed in bed until ten o'clock.*

2 to continue in the same way and not change: *I tried to stay awake.*
3 to live somewhere for a short time: *I stayed with my friend in Atlanta.* ◆ *Which hotel are you staying at?*
stay behind to be somewhere after other people have gone: *The teacher asked me to stay behind after class.*
stay in to be at home and not go out: *I'm staying in this evening because I'm tired.*
stay up to not go to bed: *We stayed up until after midnight.*

stay² /steɪ/ *noun* [*count*] (*plural* stays)
a short time when you live somewhere: *Did you enjoy your stay in Las Vegas?*

stead·y¹ 🔊 /'stɛdi/ *adjective* (stead·i·er, stead·i·est)
1 not moving or shaking: *Hold the ladder steady while I stand on it.*
2 developing or changing at a regular speed: *a steady increase*
3 not changing or stopping: *She now has a steady job.* ◆ *His breathing was steady.*
▶ **stead·i·ly** /'stɛdəli/ *adverb*: *Prices are falling steadily.*

stead·y² /'stɛdi/ *verb* (stead·ies, stead·y·ing, stead·ied, has stead·ied)
to stop yourself, someone, or something from moving, shaking, or falling: *She thought she was going to fall, so she put out a hand to steady herself.*

---

steak /steɪk/ *noun* [*count*]
a wide, flat piece of meat, especially meat from a cow (called BEEF): *I'd like steak and potatoes, please.*

steal /stil/ *verb* (steals, steal·ing, stole /stoʊl/, has sto·len /'stoʊlən/)
to secretly take something that is not yours: *Her money has been stolen.*

Which word?

- A person who steals is called a **thief**. A thief **steals** things: *They **stole** my camera.*
- A thief **robs** people and places: *I've been robbed.* ◆ *They **robbed** a bank.*

steam¹ /stim/ *noun* [*noncount*]
the gas that water becomes when it gets very hot: *There was steam coming from my coffee.*

steam² /stim/ *verb* (steams, steam·ing, steamed)
1 to send out steam: *a steaming bowl of soup*
2 to cook something in steam: *steamed vegetables*

steel /stil/ *noun* [*noncount*]
very strong metal that is used for making things like knives, tools, and machines

steep /stip/ *adjective* (steep·er, steep·est)
A **steep** hill, mountain, or road goes up quickly from a low place to a high place: *I can't ride my bike up the hill – it's too steep.*
▶ **steep·ly** /'stipli/ *adverb*: *The path climbed steeply up the side of the mountain.*

stee·ple /'stipl/ *noun* [*count*]
a tall, pointed structure on the top of a church

steer /stɪr/ *verb* (steers, steer·ing, steered)
to make a car, boat, bicycle, etc. go left or right by turning a wheel or handle

steering wheel

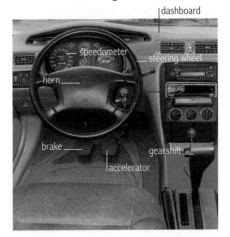

dashboard
speedometer
steering wheel
horn
brake
gearshift
accelerator

steer·ing wheel /'stɪrɪŋ wil/ *noun* [*count*]
the wheel that you turn to make a car go left or right

stem /stɛm/ *noun* [*count*]
(BIOLOGY) the long, thin part of a plant that the flowers and leaves grow on ⊃ Look at the picture at **plant**.

sten·cil /'stɛnsl/ *noun* [*count*]
(ART) a thin piece of metal, plastic, or heavy paper with a design cut out of it. You put it against a surface and paint over it so that the design is left on the surface; a design that is produced in this way

step¹ /stɛp/ *noun* [*count*]
1 a movement when you move your foot up and put it down in another place to walk, run, or dance: *She took a step forward and then stopped.*
2 a place to put your foot when you go up or down: *These steps go down to the garden.*
3 one thing in a list of things that you must do: *What's the first step in planning a vacation?*
step by step doing one thing after another; slowly: *This book shows you how to play the guitar, step by step.*

step² /stɛp/ *verb* (steps, step·ping, stepped)
to move your foot up and put it down in another place when you walk, run, or dance: *You stepped on my foot!*
step out to leave a place for a short time: *Mr. Anderson just stepped out. Can I help you?*

step·father /'stɛpfɑðər/ *noun* [*count*]
a man who has married your mother but who is not your father ⊃ Look at the note at **stepmother**.

step·lad·der /'stɛplædər/ *noun* [*count*]
a type of LADDER (= a thing that helps you to climb up something) with two parts, one with steps. The parts are joined together at the top so that it can stand on its own and be folded up when you are not using it.

step·mother /'stɛpmʌðər/ *noun* [*count*]
a woman who has married your father but who is not your mother

Word building

- The child of your stepmother or stepfather is called your **stepbrother** or **stepsister**.
- The child from an earlier marriage of your husband or wife is called your **stepson** or **stepdaughter**.

ster·e·o /'stɛrioʊ/ *noun* [*count*] (*plural* ster·e·os)
a machine for playing CDs, tapes, or records, with two parts (called SPEAKERS)

stereo

speaker

portable stereo

where the sound comes from: *a car stereo*
▶ **ster·e·o** *adjective*: *a stereo broadcast*

ster·e·o·type /ˈstɛriətaɪp/ *noun* [count]
an idea that a lot of people have about a particular type of person or thing, which is often not really true: *a cultural stereotype*

ster·ile /ˈstɛrəl/ *adjective* (**BIOLOGY**, **HEALTH**)
1 not able to produce young animals or babies
2 completely clean and free from things that can cause disease (**BACTERIA**): *All medical instruments must be sterile.*

stern¹ /stɜrn/ *adjective* (**stern·er**, **stern·est**)
serious and strict with people; not smiling or friendly: *a stern expression*
▶ **stern·ly** /ˈstɜrnli/ *adverb*: *"Go to your room," he said sternly.*

stern² /stɜrn/ *noun* [count]
the back end of a ship or boat ⟹ Look at **bow²**(2).

steth·o·scope
/ˈstɛθəskoʊp/ *noun*
[count]
(**HEALTH**) the thing that a doctor uses to listen to your heart and breathing

stethoscope

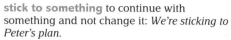

stew /stu/ *noun* [count, noncount]
food that you make by cooking meat or vegetables in liquid for a long time: *beef stew*
▶ **stew** *verb* (**stews**, **stew·ing**, **stewed**): *stewed fruit*

stew·ard /ˈstuərd/ *noun* [count]
a man whose job is to serve and help people on a ship or an airplane ⟹ Look at **flight attendant**.

stew·ard·ess /ˈstuərdəs/ *noun* [count] (*plural* **stew·ard·ess·es**)
a woman whose job is to serve and help people on a ship or an airplane ⟹ Look at **flight attendant**.

stick¹ /stɪk/ *verb* (**sticks**, **stick·ing**, **stuck** /stʌk/, **has stuck**)
1 to push a pointed thing into something: *Stick a fork into the meat to see if it's cooked.*
2 to join something to something else with a sticky substance; to become joined in this way: *I stuck a stamp on the envelope.*
3 to be fixed in one place; to not be able to move: *This door always sticks.*
4 (*informal*) to put something somewhere: *Stick that box on the floor.*
stick out to come out of the side or top of something so that you can see it easily: *The boy's head was sticking out of the window.*
stick something out to push something out: *Don't stick your tongue out!*

stick to something to continue with something and not change it: *We're sticking to Peter's plan.*
stick together (used about a group of people) to stay friendly and support each other
stick up for someone or **something** to say that someone or something is right: *Everyone else said I was wrong, but Kim stuck up for me.*

stick² /stɪk/ *noun* [count]
1 a long, thin piece of wood: *We found some sticks and made a fire.*
2 a long, thin object that is used in some sports to hit or control the ball: *a hockey stick*
3 a long, thin piece of something: *a stick of celery*

stick·er /ˈstɪkər/ *noun* [count]
a small piece of paper with a picture or words on it, which you can stick onto things

stick·y /ˈstɪki/ *adjective* (**stick·i·er**, **stick·i·est**)
able to stick to things; covered with a substance that can stick to things: *Glue is sticky.* ◆ *sticky fingers*

stiff /stɪf/ *adjective* (**stiff·er**, **stiff·est**)
not easy to bend or move: *stiff cardboard*

still¹ /stɪl/ *adverb*
1 a word that you use to show that something has not changed: *Do you still live in Denver?* ◆ *Is it still raining?*
2 although that is true: *She felt sick, but she still went to the party.*
3 a word that you use to make another word stronger: *It was cold yesterday, but today it's colder still.*

still² /stɪl/ *adjective*
without moving: *Please stand still while I take a photo.* ◆ *The water was perfectly still.*
▶ **still·ness** /ˈstɪlnəs/ *noun* [noncount]: *the stillness of the night*

stim·u·late /ˈstɪmyəleɪt/ *verb* (**stim·u·lates**, **stim·u·lat·ing**, **stim·u·lat·ed**)
1 to make something active or more active: *to stimulate the economy*
2 to make someone feel interested in or excited about something: *History classes don't really stimulate her.*
▶ **stim·u·lat·ing** /ˈstɪmyəleɪtɪŋ/ *adjective*: *a stimulating discussion*

sting¹ /stɪŋ/ *verb* (**stings**, **sting·ing**, **stung** /stʌŋ/, **has stung**)
1 (**HEALTH**) If an insect or a plant **stings** you, it hurts you by pushing a small sharp part into your skin: *I've been stung by a bee!*
2 to feel a sudden sharp pain: *The smoke made my eyes sting.* ⟹ Look at the note at **hurt¹**.

sting² /stɪŋ/ *noun* [count]
1 (also **sting·er** /'stɪŋər/) the sharp part of some insects, which can hurt you: *A wasp's sting is in its tail.* ⊃ Look at the picture at **scorpion**.
2 (HEALTH) a place on your skin where an insect or a plant has STUNG you: *a bee sting*

stin·gy /'stɪndʒi/ *adjective* (stin·gi·er, stin·gi·est)
A **stingy** person does not like to give or spend money. ⊃ ANTONYM **generous**

stink¹ /stɪŋk/ *verb* (stinks, stink·ing, stank /stæŋk/, has stunk /stʌŋk/) (*informal*)
1 to have a very bad smell: *That fish stinks!*
2 to seem to be very bad or unpleasant: *This job really stinks!*

stink² /stɪŋk/ *noun* [count] (*informal*)
a very bad smell: *What a terrible stink!*

stir /stər/ *verb* (stirs, stir·ring, stirred)
1 to move a spoon or another thing around and around to mix something: *He put sugar in his coffee and stirred it.*
2 to move a little; to make something move a little: *The wind stirred the leaves.*

stir-fry¹ /'stər fraɪ/ *verb* (stir-fries, stir-fry·ing, stir-fried, has stir-fried)
to cook thin pieces of vegetables, fish, or meat quickly by moving them around in very hot oil: *Stir-fry the chicken for two minutes, then add the sauce.* • *stir-fried vegetables*

stir-fry² /'stər fraɪ/ *noun* [count, noncount] (*plural* stir-fries)
a hot dish of pieces of vegetables, fish, or meat that have been STIR-FRIED: *I'd like the shrimp stir-fry with rice, please.*

stitch¹ /stɪtʃ/ *noun* [count] (*plural* stitch·es)
1 a small line or circle of thread that joins or decorates cloth
2 a circle of wool that you put around a needle when you are KNITTING (= making clothes from wool)
3 (HEALTH) a short piece of special thread that doctors use to sew the edges of a cut together: *The cut needed eight stitches.*

stitch² /stɪtʃ/ *verb* (stitch·es, stitch·ing, stitched)
to sew something: *I stitched a button on my skirt.*

stock¹ /stɑk/ *noun* [count, noncount] (BUSINESS)
1 things that a store keeps ready to sell: *We have a large stock of tables and chairs.* • *I'll see if we have your size in stock.* • *That book's out of stock at the moment.*
2 a share in a company or business that someone has bought, or the value of those shares: *to buy stocks in a company* ⊃ Look at **stock exchange**.

stock² /stɑk/ *verb* (stocks, stock·ing, stocked)
to keep something ready to sell: *Sorry, we don't stock umbrellas.*

stock up to collect a large amount of something that you can use in the future: *We'd better stock up on food before the snowstorm.*

stock·bro·ker /'stɑkbroʊkər/ *noun* [count]
(BUSINESS) a person whose job is to buy and sell shares in companies for other people

stock ex·change /'stɑk ɪks,tʃeɪndʒ/ (also **stock mar·ket** /'stɑk ,mɑrkət/) *noun* [count]
(BUSINESS) a place where people buy and sell shares in companies; the business of doing this: *the New York Stock Exchange* • *to lose money in the stock market*

stock·ing /'stɑkɪŋ/ *noun* [count]
a long, thin piece of clothing that a woman wears over her leg and foot: *a pair of stockings*

stock·pile /'stɑkpaɪl/ *noun* [count]
a large amount of something that you keep to use in the future if needed
▶ **stock·pile** *verb* (stock·piles, stock·pil·ing, stock·piled): *to stockpile canned food and water*

stole, sto·len forms of **steal**

stom·ach 🔊 /'stʌmək/ *noun* [count]
1 (BIOLOGY) the part inside your body where food goes after you eat it ⊃ Look at the picture at **body**.
2 the front part of your body below your chest and above your legs ⊃ Look at the picture at **body**.

stom·ach·ache /'stʌmək,eɪk/ *noun* [count]
(HEALTH) a pain in your stomach: *I have a stomachache.*

stone 🔊 /stoʊn/ *noun*
1 [noncount] the very hard material that is in the ground. **Stone** is sometimes used for building: *a stone wall*
2 [count] a small piece of **stone**: *The children were throwing stones into the river.*
3 [count] a small piece of beautiful rock that is very valuable: *A diamond is a precious stone.*

ston·y /'stoʊni/ *adjective* (ston·i·er, ston·i·est)
containing a lot of stones; covered with a lot of stones: *stony ground*

stood form of **stand¹**

stool /stul/ *noun* [count]
a small seat with no back ⊃ Look at the picture at **chair**.

stoop /stup/ *verb* (stoops, stoop·ing, stooped)
If you **stoop**, you bend your body forward and down: *She stooped to pick up the baby.*

stop¹ 🔊 /stɑp/ *verb* (stops, stop·ping, stopped)
1 to finish moving or working; to become still: *The train stopped at every station.* • *The clock has stopped.* • *I stopped to mail a letter.*
2 to not do something anymore; to finish: *Stop making that noise!*

3 to make someone or something finish moving or doing something: *Ring the bell to stop the bus.*

stop by to make a short visit somewhere: *I'll stop by this evening on my way home from work.*
stop someone from doing something to not let someone do something: *My dad stopped me from going out.*

stop² /stɑp/ *noun* [count]
1 the moment when someone or something finishes moving: *The train came to a stop.*
2 a place where buses or trains stop so that people can get on and off: *I'm getting off at the next stop.*
put a stop to something to make something finish: *A teacher put a stop to the fight.*

stop·light /'stɑplaɪt/ *noun* [count]
a light that changes from red to yellow to green, to tell cars and other vehicles when to stop and start ⊃ **SYNONYM traffic light**

stor·age /'stɔrɪdʒ/ *noun* [noncount]
the process of keeping of things somewhere until they are needed: *We're using this room for storage at the moment.*

store¹ /stɔr/ *noun* [count]
1 a building or part of a building where things are bought and sold: *He went to the store to buy bread and milk.* ◆ *a furniture store* ⊃ Look at **grocery store**, **department store**, **convenience store**.
2 things that you are keeping to use later: *a secret store of food*
in store going to happen in the future: *There's a surprise in store for you when you get home!*

store² /stɔr/ *verb* (stores, stor·ing, stored)
to keep something to use later: *The information is stored on a computer.* ⊃ The noun is **storage**.

store·keep·er /'stɔrkipər/ *noun* [count]
a person who owns a small store

storm¹ /stɔrm/ *noun* [count]
very bad weather with strong winds and rain: *a thunderstorm*

Word building

- When there is a storm, you hear **thunder** and see **lightning** in the sky.
- **Cyclones**, **hurricanes**, **tornadoes**, and **typhoons** are large, violent storms.

storm² /stɔrm/ *verb* (storms, storm·ing, stormed)
to move in a way that shows you are angry: *He stormed out of the room.*

storm·y /'stɔrmi/ *adjective* (storm·i·er, storm·i·est)
with strong wind and rain: *a stormy night*

sto·ry /'stɔri/ *noun* [count] (*plural* sto·ries)
1 words that tell you about people and things that are not real: *He has written many stories for children.* ◆ *a ghost story*
2 words that tell you about things that really happened: *My grandmother told me stories about when she was a child.*
3 one level in a building: *The building has four stories.* ⊃ **SYNONYM floor**

stove /stoʊv/ *noun* [count]
1 a piece of kitchen equipment for cooking with electricity or gas. It has places for heating pots on the top and an oven for cooking food inside it: *You can cook the beans on top of the stove.*
2 a closed metal box in which you burn wood or other fuel to heat a room: *a wood-burning stove*

straight¹ /streɪt/ *adjective* (straight·er, straight·est)
1 with no curves; going in one direction only: *Use a ruler to draw a straight line.* ◆ *His hair is curly, and mine is straight.* ⊃ Look at the picture at **line**.
2 with one side as high as the other: *This picture isn't straight.*
3 honest and direct: *a straight answer to a straight question*
4 (*informal*) attracted to people of the opposite sex ⊃ **SYNONYM heterosexual** ⊃ **ANTONYM gay**
get something straight to make sure that you understand something completely: *Let's get this straight. Are you sure you left your bike by the theater?*
get straight A's to get the grade "A" (= the best grade) in all of your classes

straight² /streɪt/ *adverb*
1 in a straight line: *Look straight in front of you.* ◆ *Go straight until you come to the bank, then turn left.*
2 without stopping or doing anything else; directly: *Come straight home.* ◆ *She walked straight past me.*

straight·en /'streɪtn/ *verb* (straight·ens, straight·en·ing, straight·ened)
to become or to make something straight
straighten something out to make a situation less difficult or confused: *We can't make a decision until we straighten things out.*

straight·for·ward **AWL** /ˌstreɪt'fɔrwərd/ *adjective*
easy to understand or do: *a straightforward question*

strain¹ /streɪn/ *noun* [count]
1 physical force: *The rope broke under the strain.*
2 a feeling of being very worried, or the problems that cause you to feel this way: *His illness put a great strain on their marriage.*

3 an injury to part of your body, caused by making it work too hard: *back strain*

strain² /streɪn/ *verb* (strains, strain·ing, strained)
1 to try very hard: *Her voice was so quiet that I had to strain to hear her.*
2 to hurt a part of your body by making it work too hard: *Don't read in the dark. You'll strain your eyes.*
3 to pour a liquid through something with small holes in it, to remove any solid pieces

strand /strænd/ *noun* [count]
one piece of thread or hair

strand·ed /'strændəd/ *adjective*
left in a place that you cannot get away from: *The car broke down and I was stranded on a lonely road.*

strange /streɪndʒ/ *adjective* (strang·er, strang·est)
1 unusual or surprising: *Did you hear that strange noise?*
2 that you do not know: *We were lost in a strange city.*

strange·ly /'streɪndʒli/ *adverb*
in a surprising or unusual way: *He was acting very strangely.* ◆ *She was strangely quiet.*

strang·er /'streɪndʒər/ *noun* [count]
1 a person who you do not know
2 a person who is in a place that they do not know: *I'm a **stranger to** this city.* ➲ Look at **foreigner**.

stran·gle /'stræŋgl/ *verb* (stran·gles, stran·gling, stran·gled)
to kill someone by pressing their neck so that they cannot breathe

strap¹ /stræp/ *noun* [count]
a long, flat piece of material that you use for carrying something or for keeping something in place: *a leather watch strap* ➲ Look at the picture at **bag**.

strap² /stræp/ *verb* (straps, strap·ping, strapped)
to hold something in place with a STRAP: *I strapped the bag onto the back of my bike.*

stra·te·gic **AWL** /strə'tidʒɪk/ *adjective*
helping you to achieve a plan: *They made a strategic decision to sell part of the company.*

strat·e·gy **AWL** /'strætədʒi/ *noun* [count] (plural strat·e·gies)
a plan; planning: *What's your **strategy for** passing the exam?*

straw /strɔ/ *noun*
1 [noncount] dried plants that animals sleep on or that people use for making things like hats and floor coverings: *a straw hat*
2 [count] a thin paper or plastic tube that you can drink through
the last straw; the final straw the last of several bad things; the thing that finally makes a situation impossible for you

straw·ber·ry /'strɔ,bɛri/ *noun* [count] (plural straw·ber·ries)
a soft, red fruit with seeds near the surface ➲ Look at the picture at **berry**.

stray /streɪ/ *adjective*
A **stray** animal is lost or does not have a home: *a stray dog*
▶ **stray** *noun* [count] (plural strays)
an animal that has no home

streak /strik/ *noun* [count]
a long, thin line that is a different color from the surface it is on: *She has **streaks of** gray in her hair.* ◆ *a streak of lightning*

stream¹ /strim/ *noun* [count]
1 (GEOGRAPHY) a small river: *a mountain stream*
2 moving liquid, or moving things or people: *a stream of blood* ◆ *I've had a **steady stream** of visitors.*

stream² /strim/ *verb* (streams, stream·ing, streamed)
1 to move like water: *Tears were **streaming down** his face.*
2 (COMPUTERS) to play video or sound on a computer while you are receiving it from the Internet: *I suggest you stream the song instead of downloading it.*

stream·line /'strimlaɪn/ *verb* (stream·lines, stream·lin·ing, stream·lined)
1 to give something like a car or boat a long, smooth shape so that it can go fast through air or water
2 to make an organization or a way of doing things work better by making it simpler

street /strit/ *noun* [count] (abbreviation **St.**)
a road in a city or town with buildings along the sides: *I saw Anna walking down the street.* ◆ *I live on Main Street.* ◆ *264 Chestnut St.* ➲ Look at the note at **road**.

street·car /'stritkɑr/ *noun* [count]
an electric bus that runs along metal tracks (called RAILS) in the road ➲ SYNONYM **trolley**

street·light /'stritlaɪt/ *noun* [count]
a light on a tall post in the street

strength /strɛŋkθ/ *noun* [noncount]
1 how strong or powerful you are: *I don't have the **strength to** lift this box – it's too heavy.*
2 how strong a feeling or an opinion is: *I was surprised at the strength of her feelings.*
3 a good quality or ability that someone or something has: *His greatest strength is his honesty.* ➲ ANTONYM **weakness**

---

streng·then /ˈstrɛŋkθən/ *verb* (streng·thens, streng·then·ing, streng·thened)
to become or to make someone or something stronger: *The wind had strengthened overnight.*

stress¹ 🖉 **AWL** /strɛs/ *noun* (plural stress·es)
1 [count, noncount] a feeling of being very worried because of problems in your life: *Mom's been suffering from stress since Dad got sick.*
2 [noncount] special attention that you give to something because you think it is important: *There should be more stress on learning foreign languages in school.*
3 [count, noncount] (**ENGLISH LANGUAGE ARTS**) saying one word or part of a word more strongly than another: *In the word "dictionary," the stress is on the first part of the word.*

stress² **AWL** /strɛs/ *verb* (stress·es, stress·ing, stressed)
1 to say something strongly to show that it is important: *I must stress how important this meeting is.* ⊃ **SYNONYM emphasize**
2 to say one word or part of a word more strongly than another: *You should stress the first part of the word "happy."*
stress out; **stress someone out** (*informal*) to feel worried and unable to relax; to cause someone to feel this way: *Sam's really stressing out over his biology exam.*

stress·ful **AWL** /ˈstrɛsfl/ *adjective*
causing you to worry a lot: *a stressful job*

stretch¹ 🖉 /strɛtʃ/ *verb* (stretch·es, stretch·ing, stretched)
1 to pull something to make it longer or wider; to become longer or wider: *The T-shirt stretched when I washed it.*
2 to push your arms and legs out as far as you can: *Joe got out of bed and stretched.* ◆ *The cat stretched out in front of the fire and went to sleep.*
3 to cover a large area of land or a long period of time: *The beach stretches for miles.*

stretch² /strɛtʃ/ *noun* [count] (plural stretch·es)
1 a piece of land or water: *This is a beautiful stretch of countryside.*
2 the act of pushing out your arms, legs, etc. as far as you can: *Give your legs a good stretch before you start running.*

stretch·er /ˈstrɛtʃər/ *noun* [count]
a kind of bed for carrying someone who is sick or hurt: *They carried him to the ambulance on a stretcher.*

strict 🖉 /strɪkt/ *adjective* (strict·er, strict·est)
If you are **strict**, you make people do what you want and do not allow them to behave badly: *Her parents are very strict – she always has to be home before ten o'clock.* ◆ *strict rules*

strict·ly /ˈstrɪkli/ *adverb*
1 definitely; in a strict way: *Smoking is strictly forbidden.*
2 exactly: *That is not strictly true.*

stride /straɪd/ *verb* (strides, strid·ing, strode /stroʊd/)
to walk with long steps: *The police officer strode across the road.*
▶ **stride** *noun* [count]: *He walked with long strides.*

strike¹ /straɪk/ *verb* (strikes, strik·ing, struck /strʌk/, has struck)
1 (*formal*) to hit someone or something: *A stone struck me on the back of the head.*
2 to attack someone or something suddenly: *The earthquake struck just after midnight.* ◆ *The building was struck by lightning.*
3 to come suddenly into your mind: *It suddenly struck me that she looked like my sister.*
4 (**BUSINESS**) to stop working because you want more money or are angry about something: *The nurses are striking for better pay.*
5 If a clock **strikes**, it rings a bell a certain number of times so that people know what time it is: *The clock struck nine.*
strike a match to make fire with a match

strike² /straɪk/ *noun* [count]
1 a time when people are not working because they want more money or are angry about something: *The hospital workers are on strike.*
2 a sudden military attack

strik·ing /ˈstraɪkɪŋ/ *adjective*
If something is **striking**, you notice it because it is very unusual, interesting, or attractive: *That's a very striking hat.*

string 🖉 /strɪŋ/ *noun*
1 [count] very thin rope that you use for tying things: *I tied up the package with string.* ◆ *The key was hanging on a string.*
2 [count] (**MUSIC**) a piece of thin wire on a musical instrument: *guitar strings*
3 the strings [plural] (**MUSIC**) the group of musical instruments that have strings ⊃ Look at the note at **orchestra**.
4 [count] a line of things on a piece of thread: *a string of blue beads*

string

strip¹ /strɪp/ *verb* (strips, strip·ping, stripped)
1 to take off your clothes; to take off another person's clothes: *She stripped and ran into the ocean.* ◆ *They were stripped and searched by the police officers.*
2 to take off something that is covering something: *I stripped off the wallpaper.*

tʃ chin   dʒ June   v van   θ thin   ð then   s so   z zoo   ʃ she

strip² /strɪp/ *noun* [*count*]
a long, thin piece of something: *a strip of paper*

stripe /straɪp/ *noun* [*count*]
a long, thin line of color: *Zebras have black and white stripes.* ⊃ Look at the picture at **pattern**.
▸ **striped** /straɪpt/ *adjective*: *He wore a blue and white striped shirt.*

strive /straɪv/ *verb* (**strives, striv·ing, strove** /stroʊv/ or **strived, striv·en** /ˈstrɪvn/ or **strived**) (*formal*)
to try very hard to do or get something: *Athletes often strive for perfection.*

strode form of **stride**

stroke¹ /stroʊk/ *noun* [*count*]
1 (**ART**) one of the movements you make when you are writing or painting: *a brush stroke*
2 (**SPORTS**) a movement that you make with your arms, for example when you are swimming or playing sports such as TENNIS
3 (**HEALTH**) a sudden illness affecting the brain that can cause a person to be unable to move part of their body: *He had a stroke.*
4 a gentle movement of your hand over a surface: *He gave the cat a stroke.*
5 [*singular*] a sudden successful action or event: *It was a stroke of luck finding your ring again so quickly.*

stroke² /stroʊk/ *verb* (**strokes, strok·ing, stroked**)
to move your hand gently over someone or something to show love: *to stroke a cat*

stroll /stroʊl/ *verb* (**strolls, stroll·ing, strolled**)
to walk somewhere in a slow, relaxed way: *We strolled along the beach.*
▸ **stroll** *noun* [*count*]: *We went for a stroll by the river.*

stroll·er /ˈstroʊlər/ *noun* [*count*]
a chair on wheels in which a young child is pushed along

stroller

strong /strɔŋ/ *adjective* (**strong·er, strong·est**)
1 A **strong** person has a powerful body, and can carry heavy things: *I need someone strong to help me move this piano.*
2 A **strong** object does not break easily: *Don't stand on that chair – it's not very strong.*
3 A **strong** opinion or belief is not easy to change: *There was strong opposition to the plan.*
4 powerful: *strong winds* • *The current was very strong.*
5 having a big effect on the mind or the body: *I like strong coffee* (= with not much milk in it). • *a strong smell of oranges*

▸ **strong·ly** /ˈstrɔŋli/ *adverb*: *I strongly believe that he is wrong.*

strove form of **strive**

struck form of **strike¹**

struc·ture ✍ **AWL** /ˈstrʌktʃər/ *noun*
1 [*noncount*] the way that something is made: *We are studying the structure of a bird's wing.*
2 [*count*] a building or another thing that people have made with many parts: *The new post office is a tall glass and brick structure.*

strug·gle ✍ /ˈstrʌɡl/ *verb* (**strug·gles, strug·gling, strug·gled**)
1 to try very hard to do something that is not easy: *We struggled to lift the heavy box.*
2 to move your arms and legs a lot when you are fighting or trying to get free: *She struggled with her attacker.*
▸ **strug·gle** *noun* [*count*]: *In 1862 the American slaves won their struggle for freedom.*

stub·born /ˈstʌbərn/ *adjective*
A **stubborn** person does not change their ideas easily or do what other people want them to do: *She's too stubborn to say sorry.* ⊃ **SYNONYM** **obstinate**
▸ **stub·born·ly** /ˈstʌbərnli/ *adverb*: *He stubbornly refused to apologize.*

stuck¹ form of **stick¹**

stuck² /stʌk/ *adjective*
1 not able to move: *This drawer is stuck – I can't open it.* • *I was stuck in Italy with no money.*
2 not able to do something because it is difficult: *If you get stuck, ask your teacher for help.*

stu·dent ✍ /ˈstudnt/ *noun* [*count*]
a person who is studying at a school, college, or university: *Tom is a history student.*

stu·di·o /ˈstudioʊ/ *noun* [*count*] (*plural* **stu·di·os**)
1 a room where an artist works
2 a room where people make movies, radio and television programs, or records: *a television studio*
3 (also **stu·di·o a·part·ment** /ˌstudioʊ əˈpɑrtmənt/) an apartment with only one main room: *Our first home was a tiny studio in New York.*

stud·y¹ ✍ /ˈstʌdi/ *verb* (**stud·ies, study·ing, stud·ied, has stud·ied**)
1 to spend time learning about something: *He studied French in college.*
2 to look at something carefully: *We should study the map before we leave.*

stud·y² ✍ /ˈstʌdi/ *noun* (*plural* **stud·ies**)
1 [*noncount*] the activity of learning about something: *Biology is the study of living things.*
2 **studies** [*plural*] the subjects that you study: *He's taking a class in business studies.*

3 [count] a room in a house where you go to study, read, or write
4 [count] a piece of research that is done to learn more about a question or subject: *They are doing a study of the causes of heart disease.*

stuff¹ 🔊 /stʌf/ *noun* [noncount] (*informal*)
1 any material, substance, or group of things: *What's this blue stuff on the carpet?* • *Put your stuff in this bag.* ⊃ Look at the note at **thing**.
2 a word you use to talk about things that people do, say, think, etc.: *I have a whole bunch of stuff to do this weekend.*

Thesaurus

stuff (*informal*) a substance or a group of things or activities: *What's that green stuff at the bottom of the bottle?* • *You can just put your stuff on the chair over there.* • *I can't go out. I have lots of stuff to do at home.*
things objects, clothes, or tools that you own or that you use for something: *Bring your swimming things.* • *Where can I put my things?* • *Put your things (= coat, etc.) on and let's go.*
belongings the things you own that can be moved: *She packed her belongings in a bag, and left.* • *Please make sure you have all your belongings with you when leaving the plane.*
property (*formal*) a thing or things that belong to someone: *This building is government property.* • *The bag contained stolen property.*

stuff² /stʌf/ *verb* (stuffs, stuff·ing, stuffed)
1 to fill something with something: *The pillow was stuffed with feathers.*
2 (*informal*) to push something quickly into another thing: *He took the money quickly and stuffed it into his pocket.*

stuff·ing /'stʌfɪŋ/ (also **dress·ing** /'drɛsɪŋ/) *noun* [noncount]
a mixture of small pieces of food such as bread and onions, which you put inside a chicken, vegetable, etc. before cooking it: *turkey with stuffing*

stuff·y /'stʌfi/ *adjective* (stuff·i·er, stuff·i·est)
If a room is **stuffy**, it has no fresh air in it: *Open the window – it's very stuffy in here.*

stum·ble /'stʌmbl/ *verb* (stum·bles, stum·bling, stum·bled)
to hit your foot against something when you are walking or running, and almost fall: *The old lady stumbled as she was going upstairs.*

stump /stʌmp/ *noun* [count]
the small part that is left when something is cut off or broken: *a tree stump*

stun /stʌn/ *verb* (stuns, stun·ning, stunned)
1 to hit a person or an animal on the head so hard that they cannot see, think, or make a sound for a short time
2 to make someone very surprised: *His sudden death stunned his family and friends.*

stung form of **sting¹**

stunk form of **stink¹**

stun·ning /'stʌnɪŋ/ *adjective*
very beautiful; wonderful: *a stunning dress* • *She looked stunning.*

stunt /stʌnt/ *noun* [count]
something dangerous or difficult that a person does, especially as part of a movie: *James Bond movies are full of exciting stunts.*

stu·pid 🔊 /'stupəd/ *adjective*
not intelligent; silly: *Don't be so stupid!* • *What a stupid question!*
▶ **stu·pid·i·ty** /stu'pɪdəti/ *noun* [noncount]: *There are no limits to his stupidity!*
▶ **stu·pid·ly** /'stupədli/ *adverb*: *I stupidly forgot to close the door.*

stur·dy /'stɑrdi/ *adjective* (stur·di·er, stur·di·est)
strong and healthy; not easy to break: *sturdy legs* • *sturdy shoes*

stut·ter /'stʌtər/ *verb* (stut·ters, stut·ter·ing, stut·tered)
to say the same sound many times when you are trying to say a word: *"I d-d-don't understand," he stuttered.* ⊃ **SYNONYM stammer**
▶ **stut·ter** *noun* [singular]: *to have a stutter*

style 🔊 **AWL** /staɪl/ *noun*
1 [count, noncount] a way of doing, making, or saying something: *I don't like his style of writing.*
2 [count, noncount] the shape or kind of something: *This store has all the latest styles.* • *I love your new hairstyle.*
3 [noncount] an ability to do things in a way that other people admire: *She does everything with style and elegance.*

styl·ish **AWL** /'staɪlɪʃ/ *adjective*
fashionable and attractive: *Kate's very stylish.*

styl·ist /'staɪlɪst/ *noun* [count]
a person whose job is to cut and shape people's hair

sty·lus /'staɪləs/ *noun* [count] (*plural* **sty·lus·es** or **sty·li** /'staɪlaɪ/)
(**COMPUTERS**) a special pen you use to write or draw on some computer screens

sty·ro·foam™ /'staɪrəfoʊm/ *noun* [noncount]
a very light, soft plastic that is usually white. It is used for packing things so they do not get broken.

sub·ject 🔊 /'sʌbdʒɪkt/ *noun* [count]
1 the person or thing that you are talking or writing about: *What is the subject of the talk?*

2 something you study at school, college, or university: *I'm studying three subjects: Math, Physics, and Chemistry.*
3 (**ENGLISH LANGUAGE ARTS**) the word in a sentence that does the action of the verb: *In the sentence "Sue ate the cake," "Sue" is the subject.* ⊃ Look at **object**¹(3).

sub·jec·tive /səb'dʒɛktɪv/ *adjective*
based on your own feelings and opinions, not on the facts: *a highly subjective point of view* ⊃ **ANTONYM objective**
▶ **sub·jec·tive·ly** /səb'dʒɛktɪvli/ *adverb*

sub·let /sʌb'lɛt/ *verb* (**sub·lets, sub·let·ting, sub·let, has sub·let**)
to rent to someone a room, an apartment, etc. that you are renting from someone else

sub·ma·rine   **submarine**
/'sʌbmə,rin/
noun [count]
a ship that can travel underwater

sub·mit **AWL**
/səb'mɪt/ *verb*
(**sub·mits, sub·mit·ting, sub·mit·ted**)
to give a plan, a document, etc. to an official organization so that it can be looked at or considered: *I submitted my college applications last month.*

sub·scrip·tion /səb'skrɪpʃn/ *noun* [count]
money that you pay, for example to get the same magazine each month or to join a club: *I have a subscription to "Vogue" magazine.*

sub·se·quent **AWL** /'sʌbsəkwənt/ *adjective*
(*formal*)
coming after something: *the damage caused by the heavy rains and subsequent flooding*
▶ **sub·se·quent·ly** **AWL** /'sʌbsəkwəntli/ *adverb*: *The rumors were subsequently found to be untrue.*

sub·stance /'sʌbstəns/ *noun* [count]
any solid, liquid, or gas: *Stone is a hard substance.* ◆ *chemical substances*

sub·stan·tial /səb'stænʃl/ *adjective*
large in amount or importance: *The storms caused substantial damage.*
▶ **sub·stan·tial·ly** /səb'stænʃl·i/ *adverb*: *House prices have fallen substantially.*

sub·sti·tute **AWL** /'sʌbstətut/ *noun* [count]
a person or thing that you put in the place of another: *a substitute teacher*
▶ **sub·sti·tute** **AWL** *verb* (**sub·sti·tutes, sub·sti·tut·ing, sub·sti·tut·ed**): *You can substitute margarine for butter.*

sub·ti·tles /'sʌbtaɪt̮lz/ *noun* [plural]
words at the bottom of a movie or TV program that tell you what people are saying: *It was a French movie with English subtitles.*

sub·tle /'sʌt̮l/ *adjective*
not large, bright, or easy to notice: *subtle colors* ◆ *There has been a subtle change in her behavior.*

sub·to·tal /'sʌbtoʊt̮l/ *noun* [count]
(**MATH**) the amount you have after adding some numbers, which is then added to other amounts to give a final total

sub·tract /səb'trækt/ *verb* (**sub·tracts, sub·tract·ing, sub·tract·ed**)
(**MATH**) to take a number away from another number: *If you subtract 6 from 9, you get 3.* ⊃ **SYNONYM take away** ⊃ **ANTONYM add**
▶ **sub·trac·tion** /səb'trækʃn/ *noun* [noncount]: *The children are learning how to do subtraction.* ⊃ Look at **addition**(1).

sub·urb /'sʌbərb/ *noun* [count]
(**GEOGRAPHY**) an area where people live that is outside the central part of a city: *We live in the suburbs.*
▶ **sub·ur·ban** /sə'bərbən/ *adjective*: *suburban areas*

sub·way /'sʌbweɪ/ *noun* [count] (*plural* **sub·ways**)
an underground train system in a city: *the New York City subway* ◆ *a subway station*

suc·ceed /sək'sid/ *verb* (**suc·ceeds, suc·ceed·ing, suc·ceed·ed**)
to do or get what you wanted to do or get: *She finally succeeded in getting a job.* ◆ *I tried to get a ticket for the concert but I didn't succeed.* ⊃ **ANTONYM fail**

suc·cess /sək'sɛs/ *noun* (*plural* **suc·cess·es**)
1 [noncount] doing or getting what you wanted; doing well: *I wish you success with your studies.*
2 [count] someone or something that does well or that people like a lot: *The party was a great success.* ⊃ **ANTONYM failure**

suc·cess·ful /sək'sɛsfl/ *adjective*

> ⓘ **SPELLING**
> Remember! You spell **successful** with **CC** and **SS**.

If you are **successful**, you have or have done what you wanted, or you have become popular, rich, etc.: *a successful actor* ◆ *The play was very successful.* ⊃ **ANTONYM unsuccessful**
▶ **suc·cess·ful·ly** /sək'sɛsfəli/ *adverb*: *The lawyer successfully argued that his client was innocent.*

such /sʌtʃ/ *adjective*
1 a word that makes another word stronger: *He wears such strange clothes.* ◆ *It was such a nice day that we decided to go to the beach.* ⊃ Look at the note at **so**¹(1).
2 like this or that: *There's no such thing as ghosts.* ◆ *"Can I speak to Mrs. Graham?" "I'm sorry. There's no such person here."*

such as words that you use to give an example: *Sweet foods such as chocolate can make you fat.* ⊃ **SYNONYM** like

suck 🖉 /sʌk/ *verb* (sucks, suck·ing, sucked)
1 to pull something into your mouth, using your lips: *The baby sucked milk from its bottle.*
2 to hold something in your mouth and touch it a lot with your tongue: *She was sucking a lollipop.*

sud·den 🖉 /'sʌdn/ *adjective*
happening quickly when you do not expect it: *His death was very sudden.* • *a sudden change in the weather*
all of a sudden suddenly: *We were watching TV when all of a sudden the lights went out.*

sud·den·ly 🖉 /'sʌdnli/ *adverb*
quickly, and when you are not expecting it: *He left very suddenly.* • *Suddenly there was a loud noise.*

sue /su/ *verb* (sues, su·ing, sued)
to go to a court of law and ask for money from a person who has done something bad to you: *She sued the company for loss of earnings.*

suede /sweɪd/ *noun* [noncount]
a type of soft leather with a rough surface: *suede boots*

suf·fer 🖉 /'sʌfər/ *verb* (suf·fers, suf·fer·ing, suf·fered)
to feel pain, sadness, or another unpleasant feeling: *She suffers from bad headaches.* • *It's not right for children to suffer.*
▶ **suf·fer·ing** /'sʌfərɪŋ/ *noun* [noncount]: *They have experienced so much suffering.*

suf·fi·cient **AWL** /sə'fɪʃnt/ *adjective* (formal)
as much or as many as you need or want: *There was sufficient food to last two weeks.* ⊃ **SYNONYM** enough ⊃ **ANTONYM** insufficient
▶ **suf·fi·cient·ly** **AWL** /sə'fɪʃəntli/ *adverb*

suf·fix /'sʌfɪks/ *noun* [count] (*plural* suf·fix·es)
(**ENGLISH LANGUAGE ARTS**) letters that you add to the end of a word to make another word: *If you add the suffix "-ly" to the adjective "quick," you make the adverb "quickly."* ⊃ Look at **prefix**.

suf·fo·cate /'sʌfəkeɪt/ *verb* (suf·fo·cates, suf·fo·cat·ing, suf·fo·cat·ed)
to die or to make someone die because there is no air to breathe
▶ **suf·fo·ca·tion** /,sʌfə'keɪʃn/ *noun* [noncount]

sug·ar 🖉 /'ʃʊgər/ *noun* [noncount]
a sweet substance that comes from certain plants: *Do you take sugar in your coffee?* • *Would you like cream and sugar in your coffee?*
▶ **sug·ar·y** /'ʃʊgəri/ *adjective*: *I try to avoid sugary foods.*

sug·gest 🖉 /səg'dʒɛst; sə'dʒɛst/ *verb* (sug·gests, sug·gest·ing, sug·gest·ed)
to say what you think someone should do or what should happen: *I suggest that you stay here tonight.* • *Simon suggested going for a walk.* • *What do you suggest?*

sug·ges·tion 🖉 /səg'dʒɛstʃən; sə'dʒɛstʃən/ *noun* [count]
a plan or an idea that someone thinks of for someone else to discuss and consider: *I don't know what to buy Ally for her birthday. Do you have any suggestions?* • *May I make a suggestion?*

su·i·cide /'suəsaɪd/ *noun* [count, noncount]
the act of killing yourself: *He committed suicide at the age of 23.*

suit¹ 🖉 /sut/ *noun* [count]

> ℹ️ **PRONUNCIATION**
> The word **suit** sounds like **boot**.

1 a jacket and pants, or a jacket and skirt, that you wear together and that are made from the same material ⊃ Look at the picture at **clothes**.
2 one of the 4 sets that PLAYING CARDS (= cards with numbers and pictures on them that you use for playing games) are divided into: *The four suits are hearts, clubs, diamonds, and spades.*
3 another word for **lawsuit**: *a divorce suit*

suit² /sut/ *verb* (suits, suit·ing, suit·ed)
1 If something **suits** you, it looks good on you: *Does this hat suit me?*
2 to be right for you; to be what you want or need: *Would it suit you if I came at five o'clock?*

suit·a·ble 🖉 /'sutəbl/ *adjective*
right for someone or something: *This movie isn't suitable for children.* ⊃ **ANTONYM** unsuitable
▶ **suit·a·bly** /'sutəbli/ *adverb*: *Tony wasn't suitably dressed for a party.*

suit·case /'sutkeɪs/ *noun* [count]
a large bag with flat sides that you carry your clothes in when you travel ⊃ Look at the picture at **bag**.

suite /swit/ *noun* [count]
a set of connected rooms in a hotel: *We stayed in the honeymoon suite.*

sul·fur /'sʌlfər/ *noun* [noncount] (symbol **S**)
(**CHEMISTRY**) a natural yellow substance that smells like bad eggs

sulk /sʌlk/ *verb* (sulks, sulk·ing, sulked)
to not speak because you are angry about something: *She's been sulking all day because her mom wouldn't let her go to the party.*
▶ **sulk·y** /'sʌlki/ *adjective* (sulk·i·er, sulk·i·est): *I don't like sulky teenagers.*

sul·len /'sʌlən/ *adjective*
looking upset and not wanting to speak to
people: *a sullen expression*

sum¹ 🔑 **AWL** /sʌm/ *noun* [count]
1 an amount of money: *$100,000 is a large sum
of money*.
2 (MATH) the answer that you have when you
add numbers together: *The sum of two and five
is seven*.

sum² **AWL** /sʌm/ *verb* (sums, sum·ming,
summed)
sum up; **sum something up** to describe in a
few words the main ideas of what someone has
said or written: *To sum up, there are three ways
of dealing with the problem...* ◆ *Can I just sum up
what we've agreed so far?*

sum·ma·rize **AWL** /'sʌməraɪz/ *verb*
(sum·ma·riz·es, sum·ma·riz·ing, sum·ma·rized)
to describe the main ideas or points of
something: *You need to summarize your
arguments in the final paragraph of the essay*.

sum·ma·ry **AWL** /'sʌməri/ *noun* [count] (*plural*
sum·ma·ries)
a short description of something that gives only
the most important information: *Here is a
summary of the news...*

sum·mer 🔑 /'sʌmər/ *noun* [count, noncount]
the part of the year between spring and fall: *I'm
going to Spain in the summer*. ◆ *a summer
vacation*

sum·mit /'sʌmət/ *noun* [count]
(GEOGRAPHY) the top of a mountain

sum·mon /'sʌmən/ *verb* (sum·mon,
sum·mon·ing, sum·moned) (*formal*)
to order a person to come to a place: *The boys
were summoned to the head teacher's office*.

sun 🔑 /sʌn/ *noun*
1 the sun [singular] the big round object in the
sky that gives us light in the day, and heat: *The
sun is shining*.
2 [noncount, singular] light and heat from the sun:
We sat in the sun all morning.

Sun. abbreviation of **Sunday**

sun·bathe /'sʌnbeɪð/ *verb* (sun·bathes,
sun·bath·ing, sun·bathed)
to lie in the sun so that your skin becomes
darker: *We sunbathed on the beach*.
▶ **sun·bath·ing** /'sʌnbeɪðɪŋ/ *noun* [noncount]:
Sunbathing is bad for your skin.

sun·block /'sʌnblɑk/ *noun* [noncount]
a cream that you put on your skin to protect it
completely from the sun

sun·burn /'sʌnbɜrn/ *noun* [noncount]
(HEALTH) red, painful skin that you get when you
have been in the sun for too long ⊃ Look at
suntan.

▶ **sun·burned** /'sʌnbɜrnd/ (also **sunburnt**
/'sʌnbɜrnt/) *adjective*: *sunburned shoulders*

sun·dae /'sʌndeɪ/ *noun* [count]
a very cold, sweet food (ICE CREAM) with pieces of
fruit, nuts, sweet sauce, etc. on the top

Sun·day 🔑 /'sʌndeɪ; 'sʌndi/ *noun* [count,
noncount] (abbreviation **Sun.**)
the day of the week after Saturday and before
Monday, thought of as either the first or the last
day of the week

sun·flow·er /'sʌnflaʊər/ *noun* [count]
a very tall plant with large yellow flowers, which
farmers grow for their seeds and oil, which are
used in cooking ⊃ Look at the picture at **flower**.

sung form of **sing**

sun·glass·es /'sʌnglæsəs/ *noun* [plural]
dark glasses that you wear in strong light: *a pair
of sunglasses*

sunk form of **sink**¹

sun·light /'sʌnlaɪt/ *noun* [noncount]
the light from the sun: *The room was full of
sunlight*.

sun·ny /'sʌni/ *adjective* (sun·ni·er, sun·ni·est)
bright and warm with light from the sun: *a
sunny day* ◆ *Tomorrow will be warm and sunny*.

sun·rise /'sʌnraɪz/ *noun* [count, noncount]
the time in the morning when the sun comes
up: *They were up before sunrise*. ⊃ SYNONYM
dawn

sun·screen /'sʌnskrin/ *noun* [noncount]
a cream that you put on your skin to protect it
from the sun

sun·set /'sʌnsɛt/ *noun*
[count, noncount]
the time in the
evening when the sun
goes down: *The park
closes at sunset*.

sunset

sun·shine /'sʌnʃaɪn/
noun [noncount]
the light and heat from the sun: *We sat outside in
the sunshine*.

sun·tan /'sʌntæn/ (also **tan**) *noun* [count]
When you have a **suntan**, your skin is brown
because you have been in the hot sun: *I'm trying
to get a suntan*. ⊃ Look at **sunburn**.
▶ **sun·tanned** /'sʌntænd/ (also **tanned** /tænd/)
adjective: *suntanned arms*

su·per /'supər/ *adjective* (*informal*)
very good: *That was a super meal*. ⊃ SYNONYM
wonderful

su·perb /su'pɜrb/ *adjective*
very good or beautiful: *a superb vacation* ◆ *The
view from the window is superb*.

su·per·fi·cial /ˌsupərˈfɪʃl/ *adjective*
not knowing or thinking about something in a deep or complete way: *She only had a superficial knowledge of the subject.*

su·per·in·ten·dent /ˌsupərɪnˈtɛndənt/ *noun* [count]
1 a person who is in charge of all the schools in a particular area
2 a person who is in charge of a building, and makes small repairs to it

su·pe·ri·or /səˈpɪriər/ *adjective*
better or more important than another person or thing: *I think ground coffee is **superior to** instant coffee.* ⊃ **ANTONYM** inferior

su·per·la·tive /səˈpərlətɪv/ *noun* [count]
(ENGLISH LANGUAGE ARTS) the form of an adjective or adverb that shows the most of something: *"Most intelligent," "best," and "fastest" are all superlatives.* ⊃ Look at **comparative**.
▶ **su·per·la·tive** *adjective*: *"Youngest" is the superlative form of "young."*

su·per·mar·ket /ˈsupərˌmɑrkət/ *noun* [count]
a big store where you can buy food and other things for your home ⊃ Look at **grocery store**.

Word building

- In a supermarket, you put the things you want to buy in a **shopping cart** or a **basket**.
- You pay for your **shopping** at the **checkout**.

su·per·nat·u·ral /ˌsupərˈnætʃərəl/ *adjective*
that cannot be explained by the laws of science: *It's a story about a boy with supernatural powers.*

su·per·son·ic /ˌsupərˈsɑnɪk/ *adjective*
(PHYSICS) faster than the speed of sound: *a supersonic jet*

su·per·star /ˈsupərstɑr/ *noun* [count]
a person, such as a singer or movie star, who is very famous and successful

su·per·sti·tion /ˌsupərˈstɪʃn/ *noun* [count, noncount]
a belief in good and bad luck and other things that cannot be explained: *People say that walking under a ladder brings bad luck, but it's just a superstition.*
▶ **su·per·sti·tious** /ˌsupərˈstɪʃəs/ *adjective*: *A lot of people are **superstitious about** the number 13.*

su·per·vise /ˈsupərvaɪz/ *verb* (su·per·vis·es, su·per·vis·ing, su·per·vised)
to watch someone or something in order to see that people are working or behaving correctly: *It was his job to supervise the builders.*
▶ **su·per·vi·sion** /ˌsupərˈvɪʒn/ *noun* [noncount]: *Children must not use the pool without supervision.*

▶ **su·per·vi·sor** /ˈsupərvaɪzər/ *noun* [count]: *a factory supervisor*

sup·per /ˈsʌpər/ *noun* [count]
the last meal of the day: *We had supper and then went to bed.* ⊃ Look at the note at **meal**.

sup·ply¹ /səˈplaɪ/ *verb* (sup·plies, sup·ply·ing, sup·plied, has sup·plied)
to give or sell something that someone needs: *The school **supplies** us **with** books. • The lake **supplies** water **to** thousands of homes.*
▶ **sup·pli·er** /səˈplaɪər/ *noun* [count]: *We are the region's biggest supplier of computer equipment.*

sup·ply² /səˈplaɪ/ *noun* [count] (*plural* sup·plies)
a store or an amount of something that you need: *Food supplies were dropped by helicopter. • The water supply was cut off.*

sup·port¹ /səˈpɔrt/ *verb* (sup·ports, sup·port·ing, sup·port·ed)
1 to hold someone or something up, so that they do not fall: *The bridge isn't strong enough to support heavy vehicles.*
2 to say that someone or something is right or the best: *Everyone else said I was wrong, but Paul supported me. • a political candidate who supports tougher drug laws*
3 to help someone to live by giving things like money, a home, or food: *She has three children to support.*

sup·port² /səˈpɔrt/ *noun*
1 [noncount] help: *Thank you for all your support.*
2 [count] something that holds up another thing: *a roof support*

sup·port·er /səˈpɔrtər/ *noun* [count]
a person who supports a politician, a plan, etc.: *The political candidate thanked all of his supporters.*

sup·por·tive /səˈpɔrt̮ɪv/ *adjective*
giving help or support to someone in a difficult situation: *My friends were very supportive when I lost my job.*

sup·pose /səˈpoʊz/ *verb* (sup·pos·es, sup·pos·ing, sup·posed)
1 to think that something is probably true or will probably happen: *"Where's Jenny?" "I don't know – I suppose she's still at work."*
2 a word that you use when you agree with something but are not happy about it: *"Can I borrow your pen?" "Yes, I suppose so – but don't lose it."*
be supposed to
1 If you **are supposed to** do something, you should do it: *They were supposed to meet us here. • You're not supposed to smoke in this room.*
2 If something **is supposed to** be true, people say it is true: *This is supposed to be a good restaurant.*

sup·pos·ing /sə'poʊzɪŋ/ conjunction
if something happens or is true: *Supposing we miss the bus, how will we get to the airport?*

su·preme /sə'prim/ adjective
highest or most important: *the supreme champion*

Su·preme Court /sə,prim 'kɔrt/ noun [singular]
the most important court of law in a country or state ◑ Look at the note at **government**.

su·preme·ly /sə'primli/ adverb (formal)
extremely: *He is supremely confident that he can win.*

sure 🔑 /ʃʊr/ adjective (sur·er, sur·est) adverb
1 knowing that something is true or right: *I'm sure I've seen that man before. ◆ If you're not sure how to do it, ask your teacher.* ◑ SYNONYM **certain**
2 If you are **sure** to do something, you will certainly do it: *If you work hard, you're **sure to** pass the exam.*
3 (informal) a word you use to make what you say stronger: *It sure is hot today.*
for sure without any doubt: *I think he's coming to the party, but I don't know for sure.*
make sure to check something so that you are certain about it: *I think the party starts at eight, but I'll call to make sure. ◆ Make sure you don't leave your bag on the bus.*
sure (informal) yes: *"Can I borrow this book?" "Sure."*
sure enough as I thought: *I said they would be late, and sure enough they were.*

sure·ly /'ʃʊrli/ adverb
a word that you use when you think that something must be true, or when you are surprised: *This will surely cause problems. ◆ Surely you're not going to walk all the way home?*

surf¹ /sərf/ verb (surfs, surf·ing, surfed)
(SPORTS) to stand or lie on a long piece of wood or plastic (called a SURFBOARD) and ride on a wave
surf the Net; surf the Internet to use the Internet: *He spends hours every day surfing the Net.*
▸ **surf·er** /'sərfər/ noun [count]: *The beach is popular with surfers.* ◑ Look at the picture at **surfing**.

surf² /sərf/ noun [noncount]
(GEOGRAPHY) the white part on the top of waves in the ocean

sur·face 🔑 /'sərfəs/ noun [count]
1 the outside part of something: *the earth's surface*
2 the top of water: *She dove below the surface.*

surf·board /'sərfbɔrd/ noun [count]
(SPORTS) a long piece of wood or plastic that you sit or lie on to ride on a wave ◑ Look at the picture at **surfing**.

surf·ing /'sərfɪŋ/ noun
[noncount]
(SPORTS) the sport of riding on waves while standing on a SURFBOARD: *His hobbies include surfing and photography. ◆ We went surfing in Hawaii.*

surfing

surge /sərdʒ/ noun [count]
a sudden strong movement in a particular direction by a lot of people or things: *There has been a recent surge (= an increase) in demand for electricity.*
▸ **surge** verb (surg·es, surg·ing, surged): *The crowd surged forward.*

sur·geon /'sərdʒən/ noun [count]
(HEALTH) a doctor who cuts your body to take out or repair a part inside: *a brain surgeon*

sur·ger·y /'sərdʒəri/ noun [count, noncount] (plural sur·ger·ies)
(HEALTH) cutting a person's body to take out or repair a part inside: *He needed surgery after the accident.*

sur·plus /'sərpləs/ noun [count, noncount] (plural surplus·es)
an amount that is more than you need: *Many rich countries have a food surplus.*

sur·prise¹ 🔑 /sə'praɪz/ noun
1 [noncount] the feeling that you have when something happens suddenly that you did not expect: *He looked up in surprise when I walked in. ◆ To my surprise, everyone agreed with me.*
2 [count] something that happens when you do not expect it: *Don't tell him about the party – it's a surprise.*
take someone by surprise to happen when someone does not expect it: *The news took me completely by surprise.*

sur·prise² 🔑 /sə'praɪz/ verb (sur·pris·es, sur·pris·ing, sur·prised)
to do something that someone does not expect: *I arrived early to surprise her.*

sur·prised 🔑 /sə'praɪzd/ adjective
If you are **surprised**, you feel or show surprise: *I was surprised to see Jack yesterday – I thought he was in Florida.*

sur·pris·ing /sə'praɪzɪŋ/ adjective
making you feel surprised: *The news was surprising.*
▸ **sur·pris·ing·ly** /sər'praɪzɪŋli/ adverb: *The exam was surprisingly easy.*

sur·ren·der /sə'rɛndər/ verb (sur·ren·ders, sur·ren·der·ing, sur·ren·dered)
to stop fighting because you cannot win: *After six hours on the roof, the man surrendered to the police.*

▶ **sur·ren·der** *noun* [noncount]: *We will not even consider surrender.*

sur·round 🔑 /səˈraʊnd/ *verb* (sur·rounds, sur·round·ing, sur·round·ed)
to be or go all around something: *The lake is **surrounded by** trees.* ◆ *The police have surrounded his house.*

sur·round·ings /səˈraʊndɪŋz/ *noun* [plural]
everything around you, or the place where you live: *I don't like seeing animals in a zoo – I prefer to see them **in their natural surroundings.***

sur·vey **AWL** /ˈsərveɪ/ *noun* [count] (*plural* sur·veys)
asking questions to find out what people think or do: *We did a survey of people's favorite TV shows.*

sur·viv·al **AWL** /sərˈvaɪvl/ *noun* [noncount]
the state of continuing to live or exist, especially when this is difficult: *Food and water are necessary for survival.*

sur·vive 🔑 **AWL** /sərˈvaɪv/ *verb* (sur·vives, sur·viv·ing, sur·vived)
to continue to live in or after a difficult or dangerous time: *Camels can survive for many days without water.* ◆ *Only one person survived the plane crash.*
▶ **sur·vi·vor** **AWL** /sərˈvaɪvər/ *noun* [count]: *The government sent help to the survivors of the earthquake.*

sus·pect¹ /səˈspɛkt/ *verb* (sus·pects, sus·pect·ing, sus·pect·ed)
1 to think that something is true, but not be sure: *She **suspected that** he was lying.*
2 to think that someone has done something wrong but not be sure: *They **suspect** Helen **of** stealing the money.* ⊃ The noun is **suspicion**, and the adjective is **suspicious**.

sus·pect² /ˈsʌspɛkt/ *noun* [count]
a person who is thought to be guilty of a crime: *The police have arrested two suspects.*

sus·pend **AWL** /səˈspɛnd/ *verb* (sus·pends, sus·pend·ing, sus·pend·ed)
1 to hang something from something else: *Colored flags were suspended from the ceiling.*
2 to stop something from happening for a time: *The bus service was suspended because of bad weather conditions.*
3 to send someone away from their school, job, etc. for a period of time, usually as a punishment: *Gary was **suspended from** school for fighting.*

sus·pense /səˈspɛns/ *noun* [noncount]
the feeling that you have when you are waiting for news or for something exciting or important to happen: *Don't **keep** me **in suspense** – did you pass?*

sus·pen·sion **AWL** /səˈspɛnʃn/ *noun*
1 [count, noncount] not being allowed to go to school or work for a period of time, usually as a punishment: *Smoking on school property will result in immediate suspension.*
2 [noncount, singular] delaying something for a period of time: *The judge announced a suspension of the trial.*

sus·pi·cion /səˈspɪʃn/ *noun*
1 [count, noncount] a feeling that someone has done something wrong: *He was arrested **on suspicion of** murder.*
2 [count] an idea that is not totally certain: *We have a **suspicion that** she is unhappy.* ⊃ The verb is **suspect**.

sus·pi·cious /səˈspɪʃəs/ *adjective*
1 If you are **suspicious**, you do not believe someone or something, or you feel that something is wrong: *The police are **suspicious of** her story.*
2 A person or thing that is **suspicious** makes you feel that something is wrong: *Anyone who sees anything suspicious should contact the police.*
▶ **sus·pi·cious·ly** /səˈspɪʃəsli/ *adverb*: *"What are you doing here?" the woman asked suspiciously.*

sus·tain·a·ble **AWL** /səˈsteɪnəbl/ *adjective*
1 using natural products and energy in a way that does not harm the environment: *sustainable farming methods*
2 that can continue for a long time: *sustainable economic growth*

SUV /ˌɛs yu ˈvi/ *noun* [count]
a type of large, strong car that can go well over rough ground but that many people drive in cities

SUV

swal·low¹ 🔑 /ˈswɑloʊ/ *verb* (swal·lows, swal·low·ing, swal·lowed)
to make food or drink move down your throat from your mouth: *I can't swallow these pills without water.*

swal·low² /ˈswɑloʊ/ *noun* [count]
a small bird with a long tail

swam form of **swim**

swamp /swɑmp/ *noun* [count, noncount]
(**GEOGRAPHY**) an area of soft, wet ground

swan /swɑn/ *noun* [count]
a big, white bird with a very long neck. **Swans** live on rivers and lakes.

swan

tʃ **chin**   dʒ **June**   v **van**   θ **thin**   ð **then**   s **so**   z **zoo**   ʃ **she**

swap /swɑp/ *verb* (swaps, swap·ping, swapped)
to change one thing for another thing; to give one thing and get another thing for it: *Do you want to* **swap** *chairs* **with** *me* (= you have my chair and I'll have yours)?* ◆ *I* **swapped** *my CD for Tom's* (= I took his and he took mine).
▶ **swap** *noun* [*singular*]

swarm¹ /swɔrm/ *noun* [*count*]
a big group of insects that fly: *a swarm of bees*

swarm² /swɔrm/ *verb* (swarms, swarm·ing, swarmed)
to fly or move quickly in a big group: *The fans swarmed into the stadium.*

sway /sweɪ/ *verb* (sways, sway·ing, swayed)
to move slowly from side to side: *The trees were swaying in the wind.*

swear /swɛr/ *verb* (swears, swear·ing, swore /swɔr/, has sworn /swɔrn/)
1 to say bad words: *Don't* **swear** *at your mother!*
2 to make a serious promise: *He* **swears** *that he is telling the truth.*

swear word /'swɛr wərd/ *noun* [*count*]
a bad word

sweat /swɛt/ *verb* (sweats, sweat·ing, sweat·ed)
to produce liquid through your skin because you are hot, sick, or afraid: *The room was so hot that everyone was sweating.*
▶ **sweat** *noun* [*count, noncount*]: *He wiped the sweat from his forehead.*

sweat·er /'swɛtər/ *noun* [*count*]
a warm piece of clothing with long sleeves, often made of wool, which you wear on the top part of your body ᗡ Look at the picture at **clothes**.

sweat·pants /'swɛtpænts/ *noun* [*plural*]
loose, warm pants made of thick cotton, which you wear on the bottom part of your body for playing sports or relaxing

sweat·shirt /'swɛtʃərt/ *noun* [*count*]
a warm piece of clothing with long sleeves made of thick cotton, which you wear on the top part of your body

sweat·suit /'swɛtsut/ *noun* [*count*]
a SWEATSHIRT and SWEATPANTS worn together, for playing sports or relaxing in

sweat·y /'swɛti/ *adjective* (sweat·i·er, sweat·i·est)
covered with sweat: *sweaty socks* ◆ *I'm all hot and sweaty – I need a shower.*

sweep /swip/ *verb* (sweeps, sweep·ing, swept /swɛpt/, has swept)
1 to clean something by moving dirt, dust, or garbage away with a brush: *I swept the floor.*
2 to push something along or away quickly and strongly: *The bridge was* **swept away** *by the floods.*

sweep up; **sweep something up** to remove dirt, dust, or garbage using a brush: *I swept up the broken glass.*

sweet /swit/ *adjective* (sweet·er, sweet·est)
1 containing or tasting of sugar: *Honey is sweet.*
2 having or showing a kind character: *It was* **sweet of** *you* **to** *help me.*
3 with a good smell: *the sweet smell of roses*

sweet·en /'switn/ *verb* (sweet·ens, sweet·en·ing, sweet·ened)
to make something sweet: *The tea is sweetened with sugar.*

sweet·heart /'swithɑrt/ *noun* [*singular*]
a word that you use when speaking to a person that you love: *Do you want a drink, sweetheart?*

sweet·ly /'switli/ *adverb*
in a pretty, kind, or nice way: *She smiled sweetly.*

sweet po·ta·to /'swit pə,teɪtoʊ/ *noun* [*count, noncount*] (*plural* **sweet po·ta·toes**)
a vegetable that looks like a red potato, but that is orange inside and tastes sweet ᗡ Look at the picture at **vegetable**.

swell /swɛl/ *verb* (swells, swell·ing, swelled, has swol·len /'swoʊlən/ or has swelled)
swell up to become bigger or thicker than normal: *After he hurt his ankle, it began to swell up.* ᗡ Look at the picture at **swollen**².

swell·ing /'swɛlɪŋ/ *noun* [*count*]
(HEALTH) a place on the body that is bigger or fatter than it usually is: *The fall caused a swelling on my knee.*

swept form of **sweep**

swerve /swərv/ *verb* (swerves, swerv·ing, swerved)
to change direction suddenly so that you do not hit someone or something: *The driver swerved when he saw the child in the road.*

swift /swɪft/ *adjective* (swift·er, swift·est)
quick or fast: *We made a swift decision.*
▶ **swift·ly** /'swɪftli/ *adverb*: *She ran swiftly up the stairs.*

swim /swɪm/ *verb* (swims, swim·ming, swam /swæm/, has swum /swʌm/)
to move your body through water: *Can you swim?* ◆ *I swam across the lake.*
▶ **swim** *noun* [*singular*]: *Let's go for a swim.*
▶ **swim·mer** /'swɪmər/ *noun* [*count*]: *He's a good swimmer.*

swim·ming /'swɪmɪŋ/ *noun* [*noncount*]
the sport or activity of swimming: *Swimming is my favorite sport.* ◆ *I* **go swimming** *every day.*

swim·ming pool /'swɪmɪŋ pul/ (*also* **pool**) *noun* [*count*]
a place that is built for people to swim in: *an indoor swimming pool*

swim·suit /ˈswɪmsut/ *noun* [count]
a piece of clothing that you wear to go
swimming ⊃ **SYNONYM bathing suit** ⊃ Look at the
picture at **snorkel**.

swim trunks /ˈswɪm trʌŋks/ (also **swim·ming
trunks** /ˈswɪmɪŋ trʌŋks/) *noun* [plural]
short pants that a man or boy wears for
swimming: *a pair of swim trunks* ⊃ Look at the
picture at **dive**.

swing¹ /swɪŋ/ *verb* (swings, swing·ing, swung
/swʌŋ/, has swung)
1 to move backward and forward or from side
to side through the air; to make someone or
something do this: *Monkeys were swinging from
the trees.* • *He swung his arms as he walked.*
2 to move in a curve: *The door swung open.*

swing² /swɪŋ/ *noun*
[count]
a seat that hangs down
and that children can
sit on to move
backward and forward
through the air

swings

swipe /swaɪp/ *verb*
(swipes, swip·ing,
swiped) (*informal*)
1 (*informal*) to steal something
2 to hit or try to hit something by swinging your
arm: *He swiped at the ball and missed.*
3 to pass a plastic card that has information on
it through a machine that can read it: *Swipe your
credit card here to pay.*

switch¹ 🔑 /swɪtʃ/
noun [count] (*plural*
switch·es)
a small thing that you
press to turn
electricity on or off:
*Where is the light
switch?*

switch

switch² 🔑 /swɪtʃ/
verb (switch·es,
switch·ing, switched)
to change to something different: *I switched to
another seat because I couldn't see the screen.*
switch something off to make a light or a
machine stop working by pressing a switch: *I
switched the TV off.* • *Don't forget to switch off the
lights!* ⊃ **SYNONYM turn something off**
switch something on to make a light or a
machine work by pressing a switch: *Switch the
radio on.* ⊃ **SYNONYM turn something on**

switch·board /ˈswɪtʃbɔrd/ *noun* [count]
the place in a large company where someone
answers telephone calls and sends them to the
right people

swol·len¹ form of **swell**

swol·len² /ˈswoʊlən/
adjective
(**HEALTH**) (used about a
part of the body)
thicker or fatter than it
usually is: *a swollen
ankle* ⊃ The verb is
swell.

swollen

a swollen ankle

swoop /swup/ *verb*
(swoops, swoop·ing,
swooped)
to fly down quickly:
The plane swooped down low over the buildings.

sword /sɔrd/ *noun* [count]

> **ⓘ PRONUNCIATION**
> The word **sword** sounds like **cord**, because
> we don't say the **w** in this word.

a weapon that looks like a very long, sharp knife

swore, sworn forms of **swear**

swum form of **swim**

swung form of **swing¹**

syl·la·ble /ˈsɪləbl/ *noun* [count]
(**ENGLISH LANGUAGE ARTS**) a part of a word that
has one VOWEL sound when you say it. "Swim"
has one **syllable** and "system" has two
syllables.

syl·la·bus /ˈsɪləbəs/ *noun* [count] (*plural*
syl·la·bus·es or syl·la·bi /ˈsɪləbaɪ/)
a list of all the things that you must study in a
class

sym·bol 🔑 **AWL** /ˈsɪmbl/ *noun* [count]
a mark, sign, or picture that has a special
meaning: *O is the symbol for oxygen.* • *A dove is
the symbol of peace.*

sym·bol·ize **AWL** /ˈsɪmbəlaɪz/ *verb*
(sym·bol·iz·es, sym·bol·iz·ing, sym·bol·ized)
to be a symbol of something: *The use of light and
dark symbolizes good and evil.* ⊃ **SYNONYM
represent**

sym·met·ri·cal /sɪˈmɛtrɪkl/ (also **sym·met·ric**
/sɪˈmɛtrɪk/) *adjective*
having two halves that are exactly the same:
symmetrical patterns

sym·me·try /ˈsɪmətri/ *noun* [noncount]
the state of having two halves that are exactly
the same: *We admired the perfect symmetry of
the garden's design.*

sym·pa·thet·ic /ˌsɪmpəˈθɛtɪk/ *adjective*
showing that you understand other people's
feelings when they have problems: *Everyone
was very sympathetic when I was sick.* ⊃ **ANTONYM
unsympathetic**

▶ **sym·pa·thet·i·cal·ly** /ˌsɪmpəˈθεṭɪkli/ *adverb*: *He smiled sympathetically.*

sym·pa·thize /ˈsɪmpəθaɪz/ *verb* (**sym·pa·thiz·es, sym·pa·thiz·ing, sym·pa·thized**)
to show that you understand someone's feelings when they have problems: *I sympathize with you – I have a lot of work to do, too.*

sym·pa·thy /ˈsɪmpəθi/ *noun* [*noncount*]
understanding of another person's feelings and problems: *Everyone feels a lot of sympathy for the victims.*

sym·pho·ny /ˈsɪmfəni/ *noun* [*count*] (*plural* **sym·pho·nies**)
(**MUSIC**) a long piece of music for a lot of musicians playing together: *Beethoven's fifth symphony*

symp·tom /ˈsɪmptəm/ *noun* [*count*]
(**HEALTH**) something that shows that you have an illness: *A sore throat is often a symptom of a cold.*

syn·a·gogue /ˈsɪnəgɑg/ *noun* [*count*]
(**RELIGION**) a building where Jewish people go to say prayers and learn about their religion

syn·o·nym /ˈsɪnənɪm/ *noun* [*count*]
(**ENGLISH LANGUAGE ARTS**) a word that means the same as another word: *"Big" and "large" are synonyms.* ⊃ Look at **antonym**.

syn·tax /ˈsɪntæks/ *noun* [*noncount*]
(**ENGLISH LANGUAGE ARTS**) the system of rules for the structure of a sentence

syn·the·siz·er /ˈsɪnθəsaɪzər/ *noun* [*count*]
(**MUSIC**) an electronic musical instrument that can produce a lot of different sounds

syn·thet·ic /sɪnˈθεṭɪk/ *adjective*
made by people, not natural: *Nylon is a synthetic material, but wool is natural.* ⊃ SYNONYM **artificial**

sy·ringe /səˈrɪndʒ/ *noun* [*count*]
(**HEALTH**) a plastic or glass tube with a needle that is used for taking blood out of the body or putting drugs into the body

syringe

needle

syr·up /ˈsɪrəp/ *noun* [*noncount*]
a thick, sweet liquid made by boiling sugar with water or fruit juice: *pancakes with maple syrup*

sys·tem 🔑 /ˈsɪstəm/ *noun* [*count*]
1 a group of things or parts that work together: *the subway system* • *We have a new computer system at work.*
2 a group of ideas or ways of doing something: *What system of government do you have in your country?*

sys·tem·at·ic /ˌsɪstəˈmæṭɪk/ *adjective*
done in a careful and organized way: *The police began a systematic search for the missing boy.*
▶ **sys·tem·at·i·cal·ly** /ˌsɪstəˈmæṭɪkli/ *adverb*

Tt

T, t /ti/ *noun* [*count, noncount*] (*plural* T's, t's /tiz/)
the twentieth letter of the English alphabet:
"Table" begins with a "T."

ta·ble 🎵 /'teɪbl/ *noun* [*count*]
1 a piece of furniture with a flat top on legs: *a coffee table*
2 a list of facts or numbers: *There is a table of irregular verbs at the back of this dictionary.*

ta·ble·cloth /'teɪblklɔθ/ *noun* [*count*]
a cloth that you put over a table when you have a meal

ta·ble·spoon /'teɪblspun/ *noun* [*count*]
1 a large spoon that you use for serving or measuring food ⊃ Look at the picture at **spoon**.
2 (also **ta·ble·spoon·ful** /'teɪbl,spunfʊl/) the amount that a **tablespoon** holds: *Add two tablespoons of sugar.* ⊃ Look at **teaspoon**.

tab·let /'tæblət/ *noun* [*count*]
(**HEALTH**) a small, hard piece of medicine that you swallow: *Take two of these tablets before every meal.* ⊃ **SYNONYM pill**

ta·ble ten·nis /'teɪbl ,tɛnəs/ *noun* [*noncount*]
another word for **Ping-Pong™**

tab·loid /'tæblɔɪd/ *noun* [*count*]
a newspaper with small pages, a lot of pictures, and short, simple articles

tack /tæk/ *noun* [*count*] another word for
thumbtack

tack·le¹ /'tækl/ *verb* (**tack·les, tack·ling, tack·led**)
1 to try to deal with a difficult problem or situation: *How should we tackle this problem?*
2 (**SPORTS**) to stop another player by pulling him down in a game of football

tack·le² /'tækl/ *noun* [*count*]
(**SPORTS**) the act of stopping another player by pulling him down in a game of football

tack·y /'tæki/ *adjective* (**tack·i·er, tack·i·est**)
(*informal*)
cheap and of bad quality: *a store selling tacky souvenirs*

tact /tækt/ *noun* [*noncount*]
knowing how and when to say things so that you do not hurt people: *She handled the situation with great tact.*

tact·ful /'tæktfl/ *adjective*
careful not to say or do things that may make people unhappy or angry: *That wasn't a very tactful thing to say!* ⊃ **ANTONYM tactless**
▶ **tact·ful·ly** /'tæktfəli/ *adverb*: *He tactfully suggested I should lose some weight.*

tac·tic /'tæktɪk/ *noun* [*count*]
a method that you use to achieve something: *I don't think this tactic will work.*

tact·less /'tæktləs/ *adjective*
saying or doing things that may make people unhappy or angry: *It was tactless of you to ask how old she was.* ⊃ **ANTONYM tactful**
▶ **tact·less·ly** /'tæktləsli/ *adverb*

tad·pole /'tædpoʊl/ *noun* [*count*]
a small animal with a large black head and a long tail that lives in water. It is the young form of a **FROG**.

tag /tæg/ *noun*
1 [*count*] a small piece of paper or material attached to something, which tells you about it: *I looked at the price tag to see how much the dress cost.*
2 [*noncount*] a children's game in which one child chases the others and tries to touch one of them

tail 🎵 /teɪl/ *noun*
1 [*count*] the long, thin part at the end of an animal's body: *The dog wagged its tail.* ⊃ Look at the picture at **lion**.
2 [*count*] the part at the back of something: *the tail of an airplane*
3 **tails** [*plural*] the side of a coin that does not have the head of a person on it ⊃ **ANTONYM heads**

tai·lor /'teɪlər/ *noun* [*count*]
a person whose job is to make clothes for men

tail·pipe /'teɪlpaɪp/ *noun* [*count*]
a pipe through which waste gases come out, for example on a car

take 🎵 /teɪk/ *verb* (**takes, tak·ing, took** /tʊk/, **has tak·en** /'teɪkən/)
1 to move something or go with someone to another place: *Mark took me to the train station.* ◆ *Take your coat with you – it's cold.* ⊃ Look at the note at **bring**.
2 to put your hand around something and hold it: *Take this money – it's yours.* ◆ *She took my hand and led me outside.*
3 to remove something from a place or a person, often without asking them: *Someone has taken my bike.*
4 to agree to have something; to accept something: *If you take my advice, you'll forget all about him.* ◆ *Do you take credit cards?*
5 to need an amount of time: *The trip took four hours.* ◆ *It takes a long time to learn a language.*
6 to travel in a bus, train, etc.: *I took a taxi to the hospital.*
7 to swallow or put a medicine or drug into your body: *Don't forget to take your medicine.*
8 a word that you use with many nouns to talk about doing something: *Let's take a walk.* ◆ *I*

tʃ **ch**in   dʒ **J**une   v **v**an   θ **th**in   ð **th**en   s **s**o   z **z**oo   ʃ **sh**e

need to take a shower. • *Take a look at this picture.*

take after someone to be or look like an older member of your family: *She takes after her mother.*

take something away to remove someone or something: *I took the scissors away from the child.*

take something back to return something to the place you got it from: *I took those pants back to the store – they were too small.*

take something down to write something that someone says: *He took down my address.*

take off When an airplane **takes off**, it leaves the ground and starts to fly. ɔ ANTONYM **land**

take something off
1 to remove clothes from your body: *Take off your coat.* ɔ ANTONYM **put something on**
2 to have time as a vacation, not working: *I am taking a week off in June.*

take over; take something over to get control of something or responsibility for something: *Robert took over the business when his father died.*

take up something to use or fill time or space: *The bed takes up half the room.* • *The new baby takes up all her time.*

take·off /'teɪkɔf; 'teɪkɑf/ *noun* [count, noncount] the time when an airplane leaves the ground and starts to fly ɔ ANTONYM **landing**

take·out /'teɪkaʊt/ (also **take-out**) *noun* [noncount] food that you buy already cooked from a restaurant to eat somewhere else: *It's too late to start cooking now. Let's get some takeout.*
▶ **take·out** *adjective*: *a takeout dinner* • *a takeout restaurant*

tale /teɪl/ *noun* [count] (ENGLISH LANGUAGE ARTS) a story, usually about things that are not true: *fairy tales*

tal·ent /'tælənt/ *noun* [count, noncount] a natural ability to do something very well: *She has a talent for drawing.*

tal·ent·ed /'tæləntəd/ *adjective* having a natural ability to do something well: *a talented musician*

talk¹ /tɔk/ *verb* (**talks, talk·ing, talked**) to speak to someone; to say words: *She is talking to her friend on the telephone.* • *We talked about our vacation.*

talk something over to discuss something with someone, especially to try to decide or agree on something: *I'm not sure what to do – I need to talk it over with my parents.*

Thesaurus

talk to say words to another person or other people. You **talk** to someone in order to give information, show feelings, or share ideas: *They talked on the phone for over an hour.* • *Can I talk to you for a minute?* • *When they get together, all they talk about is basketball.* • *We need to talk* (= about something serious or important).

speak to talk to someone about something; to have a conversation with someone. You **speak** to someone in order to try to achieve something or to tell them to do something. **Speak** is a little more formal than **talk**: *Can I speak with you for a minute?* • *I've spoken to his parents about his behavior.* • *The boss would like to speak to you.*

discuss to talk and share ideas with other people about a subject or problem, especially in order to decide something. The word **discuss** is more formal than **speak**: *I need to discuss the matter with my manager before I make a decision.* • *I am not prepared to discuss this on the phone.*

communicate to share and exchange information or ideas with someone. **Communicate** is a little formal, and is often used when the method of communication is important: *She's very good at communicating her ideas to the team.* • *We only communicate by e-mail these days.*

talk² /tɔk/ *noun* [count]
1 when two or more people talk about something: *Dave and I had a long talk about the problem.* • *The two countries are holding talks to try and end the war.* ɔ Look at the note at **discussion**.
2 when a person speaks to a group of people: *Professor Wilson gave an interesting talk on Chinese art.*

talk·a·tive /'tɔkəṭɪv/ *adjective* A person who is **talkative** likes to talk a lot.

talk show /'tɔk ʃoʊ/ *noun* [count] a television program on which famous people are asked questions and talk about their lives

tall /tɔl/ *adjective* (**tall·er, tall·est**)
1 higher than other people or things: *a tall tree* • *Richard is taller than his brother.* ɔ ANTONYM **short**
2 You use **tall** to say or ask how far it is from the bottom to the top of someone or something: *How tall are you?* • *She's only 5 feet tall.* ɔ Look at the note at **high**.

tam·bou·rine /ˌtæmbəˈrin/ *noun* [count]
(**MUSIC**) a round musical instrument with metal disks around the edge. To play it, you hit it or shake it with your hand.

tambourine

tame¹ /teɪm/ *adjective* (tam·er, tam·est)
A **tame** animal is not wild and is not afraid of people: *The birds are so tame they will eat from your hand.*

tame² /teɪm/ *verb* (tames, tam·ing, tamed)
to make a wild animal easy to control; to make something TAME

tam·pon /ˈtæmpɑn/ *noun* [count]
a small roll of cotton material that a woman puts inside her body to take in and hold the blood that she loses once a month

tan¹ /tæn/ (also **sun·tan**) *noun*
1 [count] a darker color that your skin has when you have spent time in the sun: *to get a tan*
2 [noncount] a color between yellow and brown
▶ **tan** *adjective:* *You're very tan – have you been on vacation?* • *a tan coat*

tan² /tæn/ *verb* (tans, tan·ning, tanned)
If your skin **tans**, it becomes darker because you have spent time in the sun: *My skin tans really easily.*

tan·ger·ine /ˌtændʒəˈrin/ *noun* [count]
a fruit like a small sweet orange, with a skin that is easy to take off

tan·gle /ˈtæŋgl/ *noun* [count]
many things that have become twisted together so that you cannot easily separate the different parts: *My hair is full of tangles.*
▶ **tan·gle** *verb* (tan·gles, tan·gling, tan·gled): *Does your hair tangle easily?*
▶ **tan·gled** /ˈtæŋgld/ *adjective:* *The string is all tangled.*

tank /tæŋk/ *noun* [count]
1 a large container for holding liquid or gas: *a fuel tank* (= in a car)
2 a strong, heavy vehicle with big guns. **Tanks** are used by armies in wars.

tank·er /ˈtæŋkər/ *noun* [count]
a ship or truck that carries oil or gas in large amounts: *an oil tanker*

tan·trum /ˈtæntrəm/ *noun* [count]
If a child has a **tantrum**, they cry and shout because they are angry.

tap¹ /tæp/ *verb* (taps, tap·ping, tapped)
to hit or touch someone or something quickly and lightly: *She tapped me on the shoulder.* • *I tapped on the window.*

tap² /tæp/ *noun* [count]
1 a light hit with your hand or fingers: *They heard a tap at the door.*
2 a thing that you turn to make something like water or gas come out of a pipe: *Turn off the tap.*
⊃ **SYNONYM faucet**

tap dance /ˈtæp dæns/ *noun* [noncount]
a type of dance in which you wear special shoes with pieces of metal on them that make sounds as you dance
▶ **tap-dance** *verb* (tap-danc·es, tap-danc·ing, tap-danced)

tape¹ 🔑 **AWL** /teɪp/ *noun*
1 [noncount] a long, thin piece of material or paper, used for sticking things together: *His glasses were held together by tape.*
2 [count, noncount] a long, thin piece of plastic material that is used for recording sound, music, or moving pictures, so you can listen to or watch it later: *I have the concert on tape.* • *Rewind the tape when you're finished.*

tape² **AWL** /teɪp/ *verb* (tapes, tap·ing, taped)
1 to fasten something to something else using TAPE¹(1): *Tape the label to the package before you mail it.*
2 to put sound, music, or moving pictures on TAPE¹(2) so that you can listen to or watch it later
⊃ **SYNONYM record**

tape meas·ure /ˈteɪp ˌmɛʒər/ *noun* [count]
a long, thin piece of plastic, cloth, or metal for measuring things

tape measure

tape re·cord·er /ˈteɪp rɪˌkɔrdər/ *noun* [count]
a machine that you use for recording and playing sound or music on tape

tap·es·try /ˈtæpəstri/ *noun* [count, noncount] (*plural* tap·es·tries)
(**ART**) a piece of cloth with pictures on it made from thread in different colors

tar /tɑr/ *noun* [noncount]
a black substance that is thick and sticky when it is hot, and hard when it is cold. **Tar** is used for making roads.

ta·ran·tu·la /təˈræntʃələ/ *noun* [count]
a large spider covered with hair. **Tarantulas** live in hot countries and sometimes have a poisonous bite.

tar·get **AWL** /ˈtɑrgət/ *noun* [count]
1 a person, place, or thing that you try to hit when you are shooting or attacking: *The bomb hit its target.*
2 a result that you are trying to achieve: *Our target is to finish the job by Friday.*

ə **about** y **yes** w **woman** t̬ **butter** eɪ **say** aɪ **five** ɔɪ **boy** aʊ **now** oʊ **go**

3 a round object with circles on it, which you try to hit in shooting practice

tart¹ /tɑrt/ *adjective*
with a sharp taste like a lemon: *This apple is really tart!* ⊃ SYNONYM sour

tart² /tɑrt/ *noun* [count]
an open PIE (= a type of baked food) filled with sweet food such as fruit: *Would you like a piece of apple tart?*

task 🔑 **AWL** /tæsk/ *noun* [count]
a piece of work that you must do; a job: *I had the task of cleaning the floors.*

taste¹ 🔑 /teɪst/ *noun*
1 [*singular*] the feeling that a certain food or drink gives in your mouth: *Sugar has a sweet taste, and lemons have a sour taste.* ◆ *I don't like the taste of this cheese.*
2 [*noncount*] the power to know about food and drink with your mouth: *When you have a cold, you often lose your sense of taste.*
3 [*count, usually singular*] a small amount of food or drink: *Have a taste of this fish to see if you like it.*
4 [*noncount*] being able to choose nice things: *She has good taste in clothes.*

taste² 🔑 /teɪst/ *verb* (tastes, tast·ing, tast·ed)
1 to have a particular flavor: *This tastes like oranges.* ◆ *Honey tastes sweet.*
2 to feel or know a particular food or drink in your mouth: *Can you taste onions in this soup?*
3 to eat or drink a small amount of something, to test its flavor: *Taste some of this cheese to see if you like it.*

taste·ful /'teɪstfl/ *adjective*
attractive and of good quality, and showing that you can choose nice things: *tasteful furniture* ⊃ ANTONYM **tasteless**
▶ **taste·ful·ly** /'teɪstfəli/ *adverb*: *The room was tastefully decorated.*

taste·less /'teɪstləs/ *adjective*
1 likely to make someone feel angry or upset: *That was a really tasteless joke.*
2 having little or no flavor: *a bowl of tasteless soup* ⊃ ANTONYM **tasty**
3 of bad quality and not attractive, showing that you cannot choose nice things: *tasteless jewelry* ⊃ ANTONYM **tasteful**

tast·y /'teɪsti/ *adjective* (tast·i·er, tast·i·est)
good to eat: *The soup was very tasty.*

tat·too /tæ'tu/ *noun* [count] (*plural* tat·toos)
a picture on someone's skin, made with a needle and liquid: *She has a tattoo of a tiger on her shoulder.*
▶ **tat·too** *verb* (tat·toos, tat·too·ing, tat·tooed): *He had a snake tattooed on his arm.*

taught form of **teach**

taut /tɔt/ *adjective*
stretched very tight; not loose: *The rope should be taut before you attach it.*

tax¹ 🔑 /tæks/ *noun* [count] (*plural* tax·es)
money that you have to pay to the government. You pay **tax** from the money you earn or when you buy things: *There is a tax on cigarettes in this country.* ◆ *The president announced plans to cut taxes.*

tax² /tæks/ *verb* (tax·es, tax·ing, taxed)
to make someone pay tax

tax·a·tion /tæk'seɪʃn/ *noun* [noncount]
the government system that takes money from people to pay for public services, or the money that people have to pay as taxes: *The government has promised to reduce taxation.*

tax·i /'tæksi/ (also **tax·i·cab** /'tæksi,kæb/, **cab**) *noun* [count]
a car that you can travel in if you pay the driver: *I took a taxi to the airport.* ◆ *I came by taxi.*

tea 🔑 /ti/ *noun*
1 [*count, noncount*] a brown drink that you make with hot water and the dry leaves of a special plant; a cup of this drink: *Would you like a cup of tea?* ◆ *Two teas, please.*
2 [*noncount*] the dry leaves of a special plant that you use to make **tea** to drink

tea bag /'ti bæg/ *noun* [count]
a small paper bag with tea leaves inside. You use it to make tea.

teach 🔑 /titʃ/ *verb* (teach·es, teach·ing, taught /tɔt/, has taught)
1 to give lessons to students, for example in a school or college: *He teaches English to international students.*
2 to show someone how to do something: *My mother taught me how to drive.*
▶ **teach·ing** /'titʃɪŋ/ *noun* [noncount]: *modern teaching methods*

teach·er 🔑 /'titʃər/ *noun* [count]
a person whose job is to teach: *He's my English teacher.*

tea·ket·tle /'ti,kɛtl/ *noun* [count] another word for **kettle**

team 🔑 **AWL** /tim/ *noun* [count]
1 (SPORTS) a group of people who play a sport or a game together against another group: *Which team do you play for?* ◆ *a football team*
2 a group of people who work together: *a team of doctors*

team·mate /'timmeɪt/ *noun* [count]
a member of your team or group

tea·pot /'tipɑt/ *noun* [count]
a container for making and pouring tea

tear¹ 🔊 /tɪr/ *noun* [count]

ℹ **PRONUNCIATION**
With this meaning, **tear** sounds like **near** or **cheer**.

a drop of water that comes from your eye when you cry: *I was in tears* (= crying) *at the end of the movie.* ◆ *She read the letter and burst into tears* (= suddenly started to cry).

tear² 🔊 /tɛr/ *verb* (**tears**, **tear·ing**, **tore** /tɔr/, has **torn** /tɔrn/)

ℹ **PRONUNCIATION**
The verb and noun **tear²** and **tear³** sound like **hair** or **care**.

1 to damage something by pulling it apart or making a hole in it: *She tore her dress on a nail.* ◆ *I tore the piece of paper in half.* ◆ *I can't use this bag – it's torn.*
2 to come apart; to break: *Paper tears easily.*
3 to take something from someone or something in a quick and violent way: *He tore the bag out of her hands.*
4 to move somewhere very fast: *He tore down the street.*
tear something down to destroy a building: *They tore down the old houses and built a shopping mall.*
tear something up to destroy something by pulling it into small pieces: *I tore the letter up and threw it away.*

tear³ /tɛr/ *noun* [count]
a hole in something like paper or material that is caused by tearing: *You have a tear in your jeans.*

tease /tiz/ *verb* (**teas·es**, **teas·ing**, **teased**)
to laugh at someone in a friendly way or in order to upset them: *Don't pay any attention to him – he's only teasing you.*

tea·spoon /'tispun/ *noun* [count]
1 a small spoon that you use for putting sugar into tea or coffee ⊃ Look at the picture at **spoon**.
2 (also **tea·spoon·ful** /'tispunfʊl/) the amount that a **teaspoon** holds ⊃ Look at **tablespoon**.

tech·ni·cal 🔊 **AWL** /'tɛknɪkl/ *adjective*
connected with the machines and materials used in science and in making things: *The train was delayed due to a technical problem.*

tech·ni·cian /tɛk'nɪʃn/ *noun* [count]
a person who works with machines or instruments: *a laboratory technician*

tech·nique **AWL** /tɛk'nik/ *noun* [count]
a special way of doing something: *new techniques for learning languages*

tech·nol·o·gy 🔊 **AWL** /tɛk'nɑlədʒi/ *noun* [count, noncount] (*plural* **tech·nol·o·gies**)
knowing about science and about how things work, and using this to build and make things: *science and technology* ◆ *recent developments in computer technology*

ted·dy bear /'tɛdi bɛr/ *noun* [count]
a toy for children that looks like a **BEAR**

teddy bear

te·di·ous /'tidiəs/ *adjective*
very long and not interesting: *a tedious speech* ⊃ **SYNONYM boring**

teen /tin/ *noun* [count]
a person who is between 13 and 19 years old
▶ **teen** *adjective*: *He's been on the cover of several teen magazines.*

teen·ag·er /'tineɪdʒər/ *noun* [count]
a person who is between 13 and 19 years old
▶ **teen·age** /'tineɪdʒ/ (also **teen·aged** /'tineɪdʒd/) *adjective*: *comic books for teenage boys*

teens /tinz/ *noun* [plural]
the time when you are between the ages of 13 and 19: *She is in her teens.*

tee·pee /'tipi/ *noun* [count] = **tepee**

teeth plural of **tooth**

tel·e·phone¹ 🔊 /'tɛləfoʊn/ *noun* [count]
a piece of equipment that you use for talking to someone who is in another place: *What's your telephone number?* ◆ *Can I make a telephone call?* ◆ *The telephone's ringing – can you answer it?* ⊃ **SYNONYM phone**
on the telephone using a telephone to speak to someone: *He's on the telephone with his wife.*

tel·e·phone² /'tɛləfoʊn/ *verb* (**tel·e·phones**, **tel·e·phon·ing**, **tel·e·phoned**) (*formal*)
to use a telephone to speak to someone: *I must telephone my parents.* ⊃ **SYNONYM phone, call**

tel·e·phone di·rec·to·ry /'tɛləfoʊn də,rɛktəri/ *noun* [count] (*plural* **tel·e·phone di·rec·to·ries**) (*formal*)
a book of people's names, addresses, and telephone numbers ⊃ **SYNONYM phone book**

tel·e·scope /'tɛləskoʊp/ *noun* [count]
a long, round piece of equipment with special glass inside it. You look through it to make things that are far away appear bigger.

telescope

---

tʃ **ch**in　　dʒ **J**une　　v **v**an　　θ **th**in　　ð **th**en　　s **s**o　　z **z**oo　　ʃ **sh**e

tel·e·vise /ˈtɛləvaɪz/ *verb* (tel·e·vis·es, tel·e·vis·ing, tel·e·vised)
to show something on television: *All of the president's speeches are televised.*

tel·e·vi·sion 🔑 /ˈtɛləvɪʒn/ *noun* (abbreviation **TV**)
1 (also **tel·e·vi·sion set** /ˈtɛləvɪʒn sɛt/) [*count*] a piece of electrical equipment with a screen that shows moving pictures with sound: *Can you turn the television on, please?*
2 [*noncount*] things that you watch on a television: *I watched television last night.* ◆ *What's on TV?* ◆ *a television program*
3 [*noncount*] a way of sending pictures and sounds so that people can watch them on television: *a television documentary* ◆ *cable TV*

Collocations

Television

watching
- **watch** television/TV/a show/a program/a documentary/a repeat
- **see** a commercial/the news
- **change/switch** the channel
- **turn on/turn off** the television/the TV

showing
- **show** a program/a documentary/a commercial/an episode
- **get** low/high ratings

appearing
- **be on/appear on** television/TV/a show/a talk show
- **take part in** a show/a game show
- **do/make** a show/a commercial/a documentary

tell 🔑 /tɛl/ *verb* (tells, tell·ing, told /toʊld/, has told)
1 to give information to someone by speaking or writing: *I told her my new address.* ◆ *This book tells you how to make bread.* ◆ *He told me that he was tired.*
2 to say what someone must do: *Our teacher told us to read this book.*
3 to know, guess, or understand something: *I can tell that she's been crying because her eyes are red.* ◆ *I can't tell the difference between James and his brother. They look exactly the same!*
tell someone off to speak to someone in an angry way because they have done something wrong: *I told the children off for making so much noise.* ⊃ Look at the note at **say**.

tel·ler /ˈtɛlər/ *noun* [*count*]
a person who works in a bank and whose job is to receive and pay out money

tem·per /ˈtɛmpər/ *noun* [*count, noncount*]
If you have a **temper**, you get angry very easily: *She must learn to control her temper.*

lose your temper to suddenly become angry: *She lost her temper with a customer and shouted at him.*

tem·per·a·ment /ˈtɛmprəmənt/ *noun* [*count, noncount*]
a person's character, especially how it affects the way they behave and feel: *We're lucky that the baby has such a calm temperament.*

tem·per·a·ture 🔑 /ˈtɛmprətʃər/ *noun* [*count*]
how hot or cold a thing or a place is: *On a hot day, the temperature can reach 100°F.* ◆ *a low temperature*
have a temperature to feel hotter than normal because you are sick
take someone's temperature to see how hot someone is, using a special instrument (called a THERMOMETER)

tem·ple /ˈtɛmpl/ *noun* [*count*]
a building where people go to say prayers to a god or gods

tem·po /ˈtɛmpoʊ/ *noun* [*count*] (*plural* **tem·pos**)
(MUSIC) the speed of a piece of music: *music with a slow tempo*

tem·po·rar·i·ly AWL /ˌtɛmpəˈrɛrəli/ *adverb*
for a short time only: *The road is temporarily closed for repairs.* ⊃ Look at **permanently**.

tem·po·rar·y 🔑 AWL /ˈtɛmpəˌrɛri/ *adjective*
Something that is **temporary** lasts for a short time: *I had a temporary job over the summer.* ⊃ Look at **permanent**.

tempt /tɛmpt/ *verb* (tempts, tempt·ing, tempt·ed)
to make someone want to do or have something, especially something that is wrong: *He saw the money on the table, and he was tempted to take it.*
▶ **tempt·ing** /ˈtɛmptɪŋ/ *adjective*: *That cake looks very tempting!*

temp·ta·tion /tɛmpˈteɪʃn/ *noun*
1 [*noncount*] a feeling that you want to do something that you know is wrong: *I couldn't resist the temptation to open the letter.*
2 [*count*] a thing that makes you want to do something wrong: *Don't leave the money on your desk – it's a temptation to thieves.*

ten 🔑 /tɛn/ *number*
10

ten·ant /ˈtɛnənt/ *noun* [*count*]
a person who pays money (called RENT) to live in or use a place

tend 🔑 /tɛnd/ *verb* (tends, tend·ing, tend·ed)
to usually do or be something: *Men tend to be taller than women.*

ten·den·cy /ˈtɛndənsi/ *noun* [*count*] (*plural* ten·den·cies)
something that a person or thing usually does: *He **has a tendency to** be late.*

ten·der /ˈtɛndər/ *adjective*
1 kind, gentle, and loving: *a tender look*
2 Tender meat is soft and easy to cut or bite. ⊃ **ANTONYM tough**
3 If a part of your body is **tender**, it hurts when you touch it. ⊃ **SYNONYM sore**
▸ **ten·der·ly** /ˈtɛndərli/ *adverb*
in a kind and gentle way: *He touched her arm tenderly.*
▸ **ten·der·ness** /ˈtɛndərnəs/ *noun* [*noncount*]: *a feeling of tenderness*

ten·nis /ˈtɛnəs/ *noun* [*noncount*]
(**SPORTS**) a game for two or four players, who hit a ball to each other over a net using a piece of equipment (called a **RACKET**): *Let's play tennis. • a tennis court* (= a place where you play tennis)

tennis

court
net
racket

ten·or /ˈtɛnər/ *noun* [*count*]
(**MUSIC**) a singing voice for a man; a man with this voice: *Pavarotti was a famous tenor.*

tense¹ **AWL** /tɛns/ *adjective*
1 (used about a person) worried or nervous, and not able to relax: *I always feel very tense before exams.* ⊃ **ANTONYM relaxed**
2 (used about a part of the body) tight; not relaxed: *tense muscles*
3 (used about a situation, a time, etc.) in which people feel worried and not relaxed: *The atmosphere in the meeting was very tense.*

tense² **AWL** /tɛns/ *noun* [*count, noncount*]
(**ENGLISH LANGUAGE ARTS**) the form of a verb that shows if something happens in the past, present, or future

ten·sion **AWL** /ˈtɛnʃn/ *noun* [*noncount*]
being worried or nervous, and not able to relax: *Tension can give you headaches.*

tent /tɛnt/ *noun* [*count*]
a kind of small house made of cloth. You sleep in a **tent** when you go camping: *We put up our tent.*

ten·ta·cle /ˈtɛntɪkl/ *noun* [*count*]
one of the long, thin parts like legs on the body of some ocean animals: *An octopus has eight tentacles.* ⊃ Look at the picture at **octopus**.

tenth /tɛnθ/ *pronoun, adjective, adverb, noun* [*count*]
1 10th
2 one of ten equal parts of something; ¹⁄₁₀

te·pee (also **tee·pee, ti·pi**) /ˈtipi/ *noun* [*count*]
a type of **TENT** with a round bottom and a pointed top, used by Native Americans in the past

term /tərm/ *noun*
1 [*count*] a word or group of words connected with a special subject: *a computing term*
2 [*count*] one of the periods of time which the academic year is divided into at some colleges and universities: *The summer term is from April to July.*
3 terms [*plural*] the things that people must agree to when they make an arrangement or an agreement: ***Under the terms of** the contract, you must complete all the work by the end of the year.*

ter·mi·nal **AWL** /ˈtərmənl/ *noun* [*count*]
a building where people begin and end their trips by bus, train, airplane, or ship: *The flight to Phoenix departs from Terminal 3.*

ter·mi·nate **AWL** /ˈtərməneɪt/ *verb* (ter·mi·nates, ter·mi·nat·ing, ter·mi·nat·ed) (*formal*)
to end, or to make something end: *We had no other option but to terminate the contract.*

ter·mi·nol·o·gy /ˌtərməˈnɑlədʒi/ *noun* [*count, noncount*] (*plural* ter·mi·nol·o·gies)
the special words that are used in a particular job, subject, or activity: *That journal uses a lot of medical terminology.*

term pa·per /ˈtərm ˌpeɪpər/ *noun* [*count*]
a long piece of writing that a student does for a particular class

ter·race /ˈtɛrəs/ *noun* [*count*]
a flat place outside a house or restaurant: *We had our lunch on the terrace.*

ter·rain /təˈreɪn/ *noun* [*noncount*]
(**GEOGRAPHY**) a type of land: *That trail has a lot of rough terrain.*

ter·ri·ble 🔑 /ˈtɛrəbl/ *adjective*
very bad: *She had a terrible accident. • The food in that restaurant is terrible!*

ter·ri·bly /ˈtɛrəbli/ *adverb*
1 very: *I'm terribly sorry!*
2 very badly: *He played terribly.*

ter·ri·fic /təˈrɪfɪk/ *adjective* (*informal*)
very good; excellent: *What a terrific idea!*

ter·ri·fied /ˈtɛrəfaɪd/ *adjective*
very afraid: *He is **terrified of** dogs.* ⊃ Look at the note at **afraid**.

ter·ri·fy /ˈtɛrəfaɪ/ *verb* (ter·ri·fies, ter·ri·fying, ter·ri·fied, has ter·ri·fied)
to make someone feel very afraid: *Spiders terrify Joan.*

▶ **ter·ri·fy·ing** /ˈtɛrəfaɪɪŋ/ *adjective*: *It was a terrifying experience.*

ter·ri·to·ry /ˈtɛrəˌtɔri/ *noun* [count, noncount] (*plural* **ter·ri·to·ries**)
(**POLITICS**) the land that belongs to one country: *This island was once French territory.*

ter·ror /ˈtɛrər/ *noun* [noncount]
very great fear: *He screamed in terror as the rats came toward him.*

ter·ror·ism /ˈtɛrərɪzəm/ *noun* [noncount]
when a group of people hurt or kill other people, for example by putting a bomb in a public place, in order to try to make a government do what they want: *the fight against terrorism*

ter·ror·ist /ˈtɛrərɪst/ *noun* [count]
a person who hurts or kills people, for example by putting a bomb in a public place, in order to try to make the government do what they want: *a terrorist attack*

test¹ /tɛst/ *noun* [count]
1 an exam that you do in order to show what you know or what you can do: *We have a spelling test every Friday.*
2 (**HEALTH**) a short medical examination of a part of your body: *to have an eye test* ◆ *The doctors took a blood test.*

test² /tɛst/ *verb* (**tests, test·ing, test·ed**)
1 to ask someone questions to find out what they know or what they can do: *The teacher tested us on our spelling.*
2 to use or look at something carefully to find out how good it is or if it works well: *I don't think drugs should be tested on animals.* ◆ *The doctor tested my eyes.*

test tube /ˈtɛst tub/ *noun* [count]
(**GENERAL SCIENCE**) a long, thin glass tube that you use in chemical experiments

text¹ **AWL** /tɛkst/ *noun*
1 [noncount] (**ENGLISH LANGUAGE ARTS**) the words in a book, newspaper, or magazine: *This book has a lot of pictures but not much text.*
2 [count] another word for **text message**
3 [count] (**ENGLISH LANGUAGE ARTS**) a book or a short piece of writing that you study: *Read the text and answer the questions.*

text² **AWL** /tɛkst/ *verb* (**texts, text·ing, text·ed**)
to send someone a written message on a cell phone: *He texted me to say he'd arrived in Dallas.*

text·book /ˈtɛksbʊk/ *noun* [count]
a book that teaches you about something: *a biology textbook*

text mes·sage /ˈtɛkst ˌmɛsɪdʒ/ (also **text**) *noun* [count]
a message that you send in writing from one cell phone to another

tex·ture /ˈtɛkstʃər/ *noun* [count, noncount]
the way that something feels when you touch it: *Silk has a smooth texture.*

than /ðən; ðæn/ *conjunction, preposition*
You use "than" when you compare people or things: *I'm older than him.* ◆ *You speak Spanish much better than she does.* ◆ *We live less than a mile from the beach.*

thank /θæŋk/ *verb* (**thanks, thank·ing, thanked**)
to tell someone that you are pleased because they gave you something or helped you: *I thanked her for my birthday present.* ⊃ Look at **thanks, thank you.**

thank·ful /ˈθæŋkfl/ *adjective*
happy that something good has happened or that something bad has not happened: *I was thankful for a rest after the long walk.*
▶ **thank·ful·ly** /ˈθæŋkfəli/ *adverb*: *There was an accident, but thankfully no one was hurt.*

thanks /θæŋks/ *exclamation, noun* [plural]
a word that shows you are pleased because someone gave you something or helped you: *Please give my thanks to your sister for her help.* ◆ *"Here's a cup of coffee for you." "Thanks a lot."*
thanks to someone or **something** because of someone or something: *We're late, thanks to you!* ⊃ Look at **thank, thank you.**

Thanks·giv·ing /ˌθæŋksˈgɪvɪŋ/ (also **Thanks·giv·ing Day**) *noun* [count, noncount]
a public holiday in November in the U.S., and in October in Canada: *Are you going home to your parents for Thanksgiving this year?*

Culture

- **Thanksgiving** is an important holiday in the U.S. and Canada.
- People celebrate Thanksgiving by getting together with their families and by thinking about the good things in their lives, especially their families, homes, and food.
- Families eat **Thanksgiving dinner** together. This is a special meal of **turkey** with **cranberry sauce, sweet potatoes, corn,** and other vegetables. This is often followed by **pumpkin pie.**

thank you /ˈθæŋk yu/ *exclamation, noun* [count]
words that show you are pleased because someone gave you something or helped you: *Thank you for your letter.* ◆ *"How are you?" "I'm fine, thank you."* ⊃ SYNONYM **thanks**
no, thank you; no, thanks You use these words to say that you do not want something: *"Would you like some more coffee?" "No, thank you."*

that / ðət; ðæt/ *adjective, pronoun, conjunction, adverb*
1 (*plural* **those** /ðoʊz/) a word that you use to talk about a person or thing that is there or then: *"Who is that boy in the yard?" "That's my brother."* • *She got married two years ago. At that time, she was a teacher.*
2 the person or thing already mentioned: *A lion is an animal that lives in Africa.* • *The people that I met were very nice.* • *I'm reading the book that you gave me.*
3 a word that you use to join two parts of a sentence: *Jo said that she was unhappy.* • *I'm sure that he will come.* • *I was so hungry that I ate all the food.*
4 as much as that: *The next town is ten miles from here. I can't walk that far.*

thaw /θɔ/ *verb* (thaws, thaw·ing, thawed)
to warm something that is frozen so that it becomes soft or liquid; to get warmer and so become soft or liquid: *The ice is thawing.* ⇨ **ANTONYM freeze**

the / ðə; ði/ *article*
1 a word that you use before the name of someone or something when it is clear what person or thing you mean: *I bought a shirt and some pants. The shirt is blue.* • *The sun is shining.*
2 a word that you use before numbers and dates: *Friday the thirteenth* • *I grew up in the nineties.*
3 a word that you use to talk about a group of people or things of the same kind: *the French* (= all French people) • *Do you play the piano?*
4 a word that you use before the names of rivers, oceans, etc. and some countries: *the Mississippi* • *the Atlantic* • *the United States of America*
the…, the… words that you use to talk about two things happening together because of each other: *The more you eat, the fatter you get.*

the·a·ter / ˈθiətər/ *noun*
1 [count] a building where you go to see plays: *I'm going to the theater this evening.*
2 [count] a building where you go to see movies ⇨ **SYNONYM movie theater**
3 [noncount, singular] the work of acting in or creating plays: *He's worked in theater for many years.*

theft /θɛft/ *noun* [count, noncount]
the crime of stealing something from a person or a place: *She was sent to prison for theft.* • *I told the police about the theft of my car.* ⇨ Look at **thief.**

their / ðɛr/ *adjective*

> ⓘ **PRONUNCIATION**
> The word **their** sounds just like **there** and **they're.**

of or belonging to them: *What is their address?*

theirs / ðɛrz/ *pronoun*
something that belongs to them: *Our house is smaller than theirs.*

them / ðəm; ðɛm/ *pronoun* [plural]
1 a word that shows more than one person, animal, or thing: *I e-mailed them and then I called them.* • *I'm looking for my keys. Have you seen them?*
2 him or her: *If anyone calls, tell them I'm busy.*

theme AWL /θim/ *noun* [count]
something that you talk or write about: *The theme of his speech was "the future of our planet."*

theme park / ˈθim pɑrk/ *noun* [count]
a place with a lot of things to do, see, ride on, etc., which are all based on a single idea: *The Disney theme parks are famous worldwide.*

them·selves / ðəmˈsɛlvz/ *pronoun* [plural]
1 a word that shows the same people, animals, or things that you have just talked about: *They bought themselves a new car.*
2 a word that makes "they" stronger: *Did they build the house themselves?*
by themselves
1 alone; without other people: *The children went out by themselves.*
2 without help: *They cooked dinner by themselves.*

then / ðɛn/ *adverb*
1 at that time: *I became a teacher in 1999. I lived in Chicago then, but now I live in Atlanta.* • *I'm going tomorrow. Can you wait **until then**?*
2 next; after that: *We had dinner, and then watched a movie.*
3 if that is true: *If you miss that train then you'll have to get a bus.*

the·ol·o·gy /θiˈɑlədʒi/ *noun* [noncount]
(**RELIGION**) the study of religion

the·o·ry AWL / ˈθɪri; ˈθiəri/ *noun* [count] (*plural* the·o·ries)
an idea that tries to explain something: *There are a lot of different theories about how life began.*

ther·a·pist / ˈθɛrəpɪst/ *noun* [count]
a person who treats a particular type of illness or problem, or who uses a particular type of treatment: *a speech therapist*

ther·a·py / ˈθɛrəpi/ *noun* [noncount]
a way of helping people who are sick in their body or mind, usually without drugs: *speech therapy*

there / ðɛr/ *adverb, pronoun*
1 a word that you use with verbs like "be," "seem," and "appear" to show that something is true or that something is happening: ***There's*** (= there is) *a man at the door.* • ***Is there*** *a movie on TV tonight?* • ***There aren't*** *any stores in this town.*

tʃ **ch**in   dʒ **J**une   v **v**an   θ **th**in   ð **th**en   s **s**o   z **z**oo   ʃ **sh**e

2 in, at, or to that place: *Don't put the box there – put it here.* ♦ *Have you been to Portland? I'm going there next week.* ⟹ Look at **here**.
3 a word that makes people look or listen: *Oh look, there's Kate.*
there you are words that you say when you give something to someone: *"There you are," she said, giving me a cookie.*

there·fore 🔑 /ˈðɛrfɔr/ *adverb*
for that reason: *Simon was busy, and therefore could not come to the meeting.*

ther·mal /ˈθərml/ *adjective*
(**PHYSICS**) connected with heat: *thermal energy*

ther·mom·e·ter
/θərˈmɑmətər/ *noun* [*count*]
an instrument that shows how hot or cold something is

thermometers

Ther·mos™
/ˈθərməs/ *noun* [*count*]
(*plural* **Ther·mos·es**)
a container like a bottle that keeps a liquid hot or cold

ther·mo·stat /ˈθərməstæt/ *noun* [*count*]
a thing that controls the heat in a house or a machine by switching it on or off

the·sau·rus /θɪˈsɔrəs/ *noun* [*count*] (*plural* **the·sau·ri** /θɪˈsɔraɪ/ or **the·sau·rus·es**)
a book that has lists of words and phrases with similar meanings

these 🔑 /ðiz/ *adjective, pronoun* [*plural*]
a word that you use to talk about people or things that are here or now. **These** is the plural form of "this": *These books are mine.* ♦ *Do you want these?*

the·sis **AWL** /ˈθisəs/ *noun* [*count*] (*plural* **the·ses** /ˈθisiz/)
a long piece of writing on a particular subject, which you do as part of a college or university degree: *She wrote her thesis on early American literature.*

they 🔑 /ðeɪ/ *pronoun* [*plural*]
1 the people, animals, or things that the sentence is about: *Jo and David came at two o'clock and they left at six o'clock.* ♦ *"Where are my keys?" "They're* (= they are) *on the table."*
2 people: *They say it will be cold this winter.*
3 a word that you use instead of "he" or "she": *Someone called for you – they said they would call again later.*

they'd /ðeɪd/ short for **they had, they would**

they'll /ðeɪl/ short for **they will**

they're /ðɛr/ short for **they are**

they've /ðeɪv/ short for **they have**

thick 🔑 /θɪk/ *adjective* (**thick·er, thick·est**)
1 far from one side to the other: *The walls are very thick.* ♦ *It's cold outside, so wear a thick coat.* ⟹ **ANTONYM thin**
2 You use **thick** to say or ask how far something is from one side to the other: *The ice is six inches thick.*
3 with a lot of people or things close together: *thick, dark hair*
4 If a liquid is **thick**, it does not flow easily: *This paint is too thick.* ⟹ **ANTONYM thin**
5 difficult to see through: *thick smoke*
▶ **thick·ness** /ˈθɪknəs/ *noun* [*count, noncount*]: *The wood is 3 inches in thickness.*

thick·en /ˈθɪkən/ *verb* (**thick·ens, thick·en·ing, thick·ened**)
to become thick, or to make something thick: *Keep stirring the mixture until it thickens.*

thick·ly /ˈθɪkli/ *adverb*
in a way that makes a wide piece or a thick layer of something: *Spread the butter thickly.* ♦ *thickly sliced bread* ⟹ **ANTONYM thinly**

thief /θif/ *noun* [*count*] (*plural* **thieves** /θivz/)
a person who steals something: *A thief stole my wallet.*

Word building

- A **thief** is a general word for a person who steals things, usually secretly and without violence. The name of the crime is **theft**.
- A **robber** steals from a bank, store, etc. and often uses violence or threats.
- A **burglar** takes things from your house when you are out or asleep: *We had burglars while we were on vacation and all my jewelry was stolen.*

thigh /θaɪ/ *noun* [*count*]
the part of your leg above your knee ⟹ Look at the picture at **leg**.

thin 🔑 /θɪn/ *adjective* (**thin·ner, thin·nest**)
1 not far from one side to the other: *The walls in this house are very thin.* ♦ *I cut the bread into thin slices.* ⟹ **ANTONYM thick**
2 not fat: *He's tall and thin.*
3 not close together: *My father's hair is getting thin.* ⟹ **ANTONYM thick**
4 If a liquid is **thin**, it flows easily like water: *The soup was very thin.* ⟹ **ANTONYM thick**

Thesaurus

thin is a general word to describe a person who is not fat. It can be used with a positive, negative, or neutral meaning: *He's tall and thin.* ♦ *She has long, thin legs.* ♦ *You need to eat more. You're too thin!* ♦ *She was looking pale and thin.* ⟹ **ANTONYM fat**

ər **bird**   ɪr **near**   ɛr **hair**   ɑr **car**   ɔr **north**   ʊr **tour**   ʒ **vision**   h **hat**   ŋ **sing**   463

slim is a positive word, meaning thin in an attractive way. It is often used to describe women: *How do you manage to stay so slim?* • *He put his arm around her slim waist.*

skinny is a more informal word meaning very thin. It can be used with a negative meaning to describe someone who is too thin: *a skinny movie star* • *He was such a skinny kid.* • *skinny legs/arms*

lean is a positive word, and means thin and healthy. It is often used to describe men: *He had a lean, muscular body.* • *He's tall, lean, and handsome.*

underweight describes a person who weighs less than the normal or expected amount. It is used by doctors or health professionals: *She's dangerously underweight.* ⊃ ANTONYM **overweight**

thing 🔊 /θɪŋ/ *noun*
1 [count] an object: *What's that red thing?*
2 [count] what happens or what you do: *A strange thing happened to me yesterday.* • *That was a difficult thing to do.*
3 [count] an idea or a subject: *We talked about a lot of things.*
4 things [plural] objects, clothes, or tools that belong to you or that you use for something: *Have you packed your things for the trip?* ⊃ Look at the note at **stuff.**
5 things [plural] the situation or conditions of your life: *How are things with you?*

think 🔊 /θɪŋk/ *verb* (thinks, think·ing, thought /θɔt/, has thought)
1 to have an opinion about something; to believe something: *I think it's going to rain.* • *"Do you think Sara will come tomorrow?" "Yes, I think so."* (= I think that she will come) • *I think they live in Boston, but I'm not sure.* • *What do you think of this music?*
2 to use your mind: *Think before you answer the question.* • *I often think about that day.*
3 to intend or plan to do something: *He's thinking about leaving his job.* • *We're thinking of moving to Canada.*
think of something to have something in your mind: *I can't think of her name.*
think something over to consider something carefully: *I'll think over your offer and let you know tomorrow.*
think something up to create something in your mind: *I need to think up a title for my book.*

thin·ly /ˈθɪnli/ *adverb*
in a way that makes a thin piece of something: *Slice the potatoes thinly.* ⊃ ANTONYM **thickly**

third 🔊 /θɜrd/ *pronoun, adjective, adverb, noun* [count]
1 3rd
2 one of three equal parts of something; ⅓

the Third World /ðə ˌθɜrd ˈwɜrld/ *noun* [singular]
a way of describing the poorer countries of the world

thirst /θɜrst/ *noun* [noncount]
the feeling you have when you want to drink something

thirst·y 🔊 /ˈθɜrsti/ *adjective* (thirst·i·er, thirst·i·est)
If you are **thirsty**, you want to drink something: *I'm thirsty. Can I have a drink of water, please?* ⊃ Look at **hungry.**

thir·teen 🔊 /ˌθɜrˈtin/ *number*
13
▶ **thir·teenth** /ˌθɜrˈtinθ/ *pronoun, adjective, adverb, noun* [count]
13th

thir·ty 🔊 /ˈθɜrti/ *number*
1 30
2 the thirties [plural] the numbers, years, or temperatures between 30 and 39
in your thirties between the ages of 30 and 39
▶ **thir·ti·eth** /ˈθɜrtiəθ/ *pronoun, adjective, adverb, noun* [count]
30th

this¹ 🔊 /ðɪs/ *adjective, pronoun* (*plural* these /ðiz/)
1 a word that you use to talk about a person or thing that is close to you in time or space: *Come and look at this photo.* • *This is my sister.* • *These boots are really comfortable.* • *How much does this cost?*
2 a word that you use with periods of time that are connected to the present time: *I am on vacation this week.* • *What are you doing this evening* (= today in the evening)?

this² /ðɪs/ *adverb*
so: *The road is not usually this busy* (= not as busy as it is now).

this·tle /ˈθɪsl/ *noun* [count]
a plant with sharp, pointed leaves and purple flowers

thong /θɔŋ/ *noun* [count]
1 a simple, open shoe with a narrow part that goes between your big toe and the toe next to it
2 a type of underwear that has a very narrow piece of cloth, like a string, at the back

thorn /θɔrn/ *noun* [count]
a sharp point that grows on a plant: *Rose bushes have thorns.* ⊃ Look at the picture at **plant.**

thor·ough /ˈθərou/ *adjective*
careful and complete: *The police made a thorough search of the house.*

thor·ough·ly /ˈθərəli; ˈθərouli/ *adverb*
1 carefully and completely: *He cleaned the room thoroughly.*

2 completely; very or very much: *I thoroughly enjoyed the movie.*

those 🔊 /ðoʊz/ *adjective, pronoun* [*plural*]
a word that you use to talk about people or things that are there or then. **Those** is the plural form of "that": *I don't know those boys. • She went to college in the 1980s. In those days, students didn't have their own computers. • Can I have one of those?*

though 🔊 /ðoʊ/ *conjunction, adverb*

ℹ️ **PRONUNCIATION**
The word **though** sounds like **go**.

---

1 despite something: *I was very cold, though I was wearing my coat. • Though she was in a hurry, she stopped to talk. • I went to the party, even though I was tired.* ⊃ **SYNONYM although**
2 but: *I thought it was right, though I wasn't sure.*
3 however: *I like him very much. I don't like his wife, though.*
as though in a way that makes you think something: *The house looks as though no one lives there. • I'm so hungry – I feel as though I haven't eaten for days!*

thought¹ form of **think**

thought² 🔊 /θɔt/ *noun*
1 [*count*] an idea: *Have you had any thoughts about what you want to do when you leave school?*
2 [*noncount*] thinking: *After a lot of thought, I decided not to take the job.*

thought·ful /ˈθɔtfl/ *adjective*
1 thinking carefully: *She listened with a thoughtful look on her face.*
2 thinking about other people: *It was very thoughtful of you to cook us dinner.* ⊃ **SYNONYM kind, considerate**

thought·less /ˈθɔtləs/ *adjective*
not thinking about other people: *It was very thoughtless of them to leave the room in such a mess.* ⊃ **SYNONYM inconsiderate**

thou·sand 🔊 /ˈθaʊznd/ *number*
1,000: *a thousand people • two thousand and fifteen • There were thousands of birds on the lake.*
▶ **thou·sandth**
/ˈθaʊznθ/ *pronoun, adjective, adverb, noun* [*count*]
1,000th

thread¹ 🔊 /θrɛd/
noun [*count, noncount*]

ℹ️ **PRONUNCIATION**
The word **thread** sounds like **red**.

---

a long, thin piece of cotton, wool, etc.: *I need a needle and thread.*

thread² /θrɛd/ *verb* (threads, thread·ing, thread·ed)
to put thread through the hole in a needle: *to thread a needle*

threat 🔊 /θrɛt/ *noun* [*count*]
1 a promise that you will hurt someone if they do not do what you want: *He was accused of making threats against the police.*
2 a person or thing that may damage or hurt someone or something: *Pollution is a threat to the lives of animals and people.*

threat·en 🔊 /ˈθrɛtn/ *verb* (threat·ens, threat·en·ing, threat·ened)
1 to say that you will hurt someone if they do not do what you want: *They threatened to kill everyone on the plane. • She threatened him with a knife.*
2 to seem ready to do something bad: *The dark clouds threatened rain.*
▶ **threat·en·ing** /ˈθrɛtnɪŋ/ *adjective*: *threatening behavior*

three 🔊 /θri/ *number*
3

threw form of **throw**

thrift store /ˈθrɪft stɔr/ *noun* [*count*]
a store that sells clothes and other goods given by people, in order to make money for charity

thrill¹ /θrɪl/ *noun* [*count*]
a sudden strong feeling of excitement: *It gave me a big thrill to meet my favorite actor in person.*

thrill² /θrɪl/ *verb* (thrills, thrill·ing, thrilled)
to make someone feel very excited or pleased: *This band has thrilled audiences all over the world.*
▶ **thrill·ing** /ˈθrɪlɪŋ/ *adjective*: *a thrilling adventure*

thrilled /θrɪld/ *adjective*
very happy and excited: *We are all thrilled that you won the prize.*

thrill·er /ˈθrɪlər/ *noun* [*count*]
an exciting book, movie, or play about a crime

throat 🔊 /θroʊt/ *noun* [*count*]
1 the front part of your neck
2 the part inside your neck that takes food and air down from your mouth into your body: *I have a sore throat.* ⊃ Look at the picture at **body**.

throb /θrɑb/ *verb* (throbs, throb·bing, throbbed)
to make strong, regular movements or noises; to beat strongly: *His finger was throbbing with pain.*

throne /θroʊn/ *noun* [*count*]
a special chair where a king or queen sits

thread

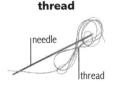

needle

thread

---

through 🔑 /θru/ *preposition, adverb*

1 from one side or end of something to the other side or end: *We drove through the tunnel.* • *What can you see through the window?* • *She opened the gate, and we walked through.*
2 from the beginning to the end of something: *We traveled through the night.*
3 until, and including: *We'll be in New York Tuesday through Friday.*
4 because of someone or something: *She got the job through her father.*
5 connected by telephone: *Can you put me through to Jill Knight, please?* • *I tried to call you but I couldn't get through.*
be through with someone or **something** to be finished with someone or something: *Are you through with that magazine?*

through·out /θru'aʊt/ *preposition, adverb*
1 in every part of something: *We painted the house throughout.* • *She is famous throughout the world.*
2 from the beginning to the end of something: *They talked throughout the movie.*

throw 🔑 /θroʊ/ *verb* (throws, throw·ing, threw /θru/, has thrown /θroʊn/)

1 to send something through the air by pushing it out of your hand: ***Throw** the ball **to** Alex.* • *The boys were **throwing** stones **at** people.*
2 to do something quickly and without care: *She threw on her coat (= put it on quickly) and ran out of the house.*
3 to move your body or part of it quickly: *He threw his arms up.*
throw something away or **out** to get rid of garbage or something that you do not want: *Don't throw that box away.*
throw someone out to force someone to leave a place: *They'll throw you out if you don't pay the rent!*
throw up to bring food up from the stomach and out of the mouth: *I feel like I'm going to throw up.* ⊃ **SYNONYM vomit**
▶ **throw** *noun* [count]: *What a good throw!*

thrust /θrʌst/ *verb* (thrusts, thrust·ing, thrust, has thrust)
to push someone or something suddenly and strongly: *She **thrust** the money **into** my hand.*
▶ **thrust** *noun* [count]: *He killed her with a thrust of the knife.*

thud /θʌd/ *noun* [count]
the sound that a heavy thing makes when it hits something: *The book hit the floor with a thud.*

thug /θʌg/ *noun* [count]
a violent person

thumb 🔑 /θʌm/ *noun* [count]

the short thick finger at the side of your hand ⊃ Look at the picture at **hand**.

thumb·tack
/'θʌmtæk/ (also **tack**) *noun* [count]
a short pin with a flat round top, which you use for fastening paper to a wall or board: *I fastened the card to the board with a thumbtack.*

thumbtacks

thump /θʌmp/ *verb* (thumps, thump·ing, thumped)
1 to hit someone or something hard with your hand or a heavy thing: *He thumped on the door.*
2 to make a loud sound by hitting or beating hard: *Her heart was thumping with fear.*

thun·der¹ /'θʌndər/ *noun* [noncount]
a loud noise in the sky when there is a storm: *There was **thunder and lightning**.* ⊃ Look at the note at **storm¹**.

thun·der² /'θʌndər/ *verb* (thun·ders, thun·der·ing, thun·dered)
1 When it **thunders**, there is a loud noise in the sky during a storm: *It thundered all night.*
2 to make a very loud, deep noise: *The trucks thundered along the road.*

thun·der·storm /'θʌndər,stɔrm/ *noun* [count]
a storm with a lot of rain, THUNDER, and flashes of light (called LIGHTNING) in the sky ⊃ Look at the note at **storm¹**.

Thurs·day 🔑 /'θərzdeɪ; 'θərzdi/ *noun* [count, noncount] (abbreviation **Thurs.**)
the day of the week after Wednesday and before Friday

thus /ðʌs/ *adverb* (formal)
1 because of this: *He was very busy and was thus unable to come to the meeting.*
2 in this way: *Hold the wheel in both hands, thus.*

tick¹ /tɪk/ *verb* (ticks, tick·ing, ticked)
(used about a clock) to make short, repeated sounds: *I could hear a clock ticking.*

tick² /tɪk/ *noun* [count]
1 one of the short, repeated sounds that a clock makes
2 a very small animal with eight legs, like an insect, which bites animals or people and sucks their blood

tick·et 🔑 /'tɪkət/ *noun* [*count*]
1 a piece of paper or card that you buy to travel, to go into a theater, to watch a sports event, etc.: *Do you want a one-way or a round-trip ticket?* ◆ *a theater ticket*
2 an official piece of paper that you get when you park in the wrong place, drive too fast, etc. The **ticket** tells you how much money you have to pay as a punishment: *He got a ticket for speeding on the highway.*

tick·et of·fice /'tɪkət ˌɒfəs/ *noun* [*count*]
a place where you buy tickets

tick·le /'tɪkl/ *verb* (tick·les, tick·ling, tick·led)
1 to touch someone lightly with your fingers to make them laugh: *She tickled the baby's feet.*
2 to have the feeling that something is touching you lightly: *My nose tickles.*

tick·lish /'tɪklɪʃ/ *adjective*
If a person is **ticklish**, they laugh easily when someone TICKLES them.

tic-tac-toe /ˌtɪk tæk 'toʊ/ *noun* [*noncount*]
a game for two players in which each person tries to win by writing three O's or three X's in a line

tide /taɪd/ *noun* [*count*]
(**GEOGRAPHY**) the movement of the ocean toward the land and away from the land: *The tide is coming in.* ◆ *The tide is going out.*

Word building

- **High tide** is when the ocean is nearest the land
- **Low tide** is when the ocean is farthest from the land.

ti·dy /'taɪdi/ *adjective* (ti·di·er, ti·di·est)
with everything in the right place: *Her room is very tidy.* ➲ SYNONYM **neat** ➲ ANTONYM **messy**

tie¹ 🔑 /taɪ/ *verb* (ties, ty·ing, tied, has tied)
1 to attach or fasten something using rope, string, etc.: *I tied my hair back with a ribbon.* ◆ *I tied a scarf around my neck.* ◆ *The prisoner was tied to a chair.*
2 (**SPORTS**) to end a game or competition with the same number of points for both teams or players: *Jenny tied with Sara for third place.*
tie someone up to put a piece of rope around someone so that they cannot move: *The robbers tied up the owner of the store.*
tie something up to put a piece of string or rope around something to hold it in place: *I tied up the package with string.* ◆ *The dog was tied up in the yard.* ➲ ANTONYM **untie**

tie² 🔑 /taɪ/ *noun*
1 [*count*] a long, thin piece of cloth that you wear around your neck with a shirt ➲ SYNONYM **necktie** ➲ Look at the picture at **clothes**.

2 [*count*] (**SPORTS**) when two teams or players have the same number of points at the end of a game or competition: *The game ended in a tie.*
3 ties [*plural*] a connection between people or organizations: *Police believe he had ties to the Mafia.*

ti·ger /'taɪgər/ *noun*
[*count*]
a wild animal like a big cat, with yellow fur and black lines (STRIPES). **Tigers** live in Asia.

tiger

tight 🔑 /taɪt/ *adjective* (tight·er, tight·est)
1 fastened firmly, so that you cannot move it easily: *a tight knot* ◆ *I can't open this jar – the lid is too tight.* ➲ ANTONYM **loose**
2 Tight clothes fit very close in a way that is often uncomfortable: *These shoes are too tight.* ◆ *tight pants*
▶ **tight** (also **tight·ly** /'taɪtli/) *adverb*: *Hold tight!* ◆ *I tied the string tightly around the box.*

tight·en /'taɪtn/ *verb* (tight·ens, tight·en·ing, tight·ened)
to become tighter, or to make something tighter: *Can you tighten this screw?* ➲ ANTONYM **loosen**

tight·rope /'taɪtroʊp/ *noun* [*count*]
a rope or wire high above the ground. People (called ACROBATS) walk along **tightropes** as a form of entertainment.

tights /taɪts/ *noun* [*plural*]
a thin piece of clothing that a woman or girl wears over her feet and legs: *a pair of tights*

tile /taɪl/ *noun* [*count*]
a flat, square object. We use **tiles** for covering roofs, walls, and floors.
▶ **tile** *verb* (tiles, til·ing, tiled): *Dad is tiling the bathroom.*

till /tɪl/ *conjunction, preposition* (*informal*) = **until**: *They didn't arrive till six o'clock.*

tilt /tɪlt/ *verb* (tilts, tilt·ing, tilt·ed)
to have one side higher than the other; to move something so that it has one side higher than the other: *She tilted the tray, and all the glasses fell off.*

tim·ber /'tɪmbər/ *noun* [*noncount*]
wood that we use for building and making things

time¹ 🔑 /taɪm/ *noun*
1 [*noncount, singular*] a period of seconds, minutes, hours, days, weeks, months, or years: *Time passes quickly when you're busy.* ◆ *They have lived here for some time* (= for a long time). ◆ *I don't have time to help you now – I'm late for school.* ◆ *It takes a long time to learn a language.*

2 [count, noncount] a certain point in the day or night, which you say in hours and minutes: *"What time is it?" "It's twenty after six."* ◆ *What's the time?* ◆ *Can you tell me the times of buses to Boston, please?* ◆ *It's time to go home.* ◆ *By the time* (= when) *we arrived they had eaten all the food.*

3 [count] a certain moment or occasion: *I've seen this movie four times.* ◆ *Come and visit us next time you're in Seattle.*

4 [count] an experience; something that you do: *We had a great time on vacation.*

5 [count] a period in the past; a part of history: *In Shakespeare's time, not many people could read.*

all the time very often, or always: *"Do you ever go to the movies?" "Oh, all the time."*

at a time together; on one occasion: *The elevator can carry six people at a time.*

at one time in the past, but not now: *We were in the same class at one time.*

at the time then: *My family moved to Brooklyn in 1996 – I was four at the time.*

at times sometimes: *A teacher's job can be very difficult at times.*

for the time being now, but not for long: *You can stay here for the time being, until you find an apartment.*

free time; **spare time** time when you do not have to work or study: *What do you do in your free time?*

from time to time sometimes; not often: *I see my cousin from time to time.*

have a good time enjoy yourself: *Have a good time at the party!*

in time not late: *If you hurry, you'll arrive in time for the movie.*

in a week's, two months', a year's time after a week, two months, a year: *I'll see you in two weeks' time.*

it's about time (*informal*) words that you use to say that something should be done now: *It's about time you started studying if you want to pass the exam.*

on time not late or early: *My train was on time.*

spend time to use time to do something: *I spend a lot of time playing tennis.*

take your time to do something slowly

tell time to read the time from a clock or watch: *Can your children tell time?*

time after time; **time and time again** many times

time² /taɪm/ *verb* (times, tim·ing, timed)

1 to plan something so that it will happen when you want: *The bomb was timed to explode at six o'clock.*

2 to measure how much time it takes to do something: *We timed the walk – it took two hours.*

time lim·it /ˈtaɪm ˌlɪmət/ *noun* [count]
an amount of time in which something must be done: *The time limit for the test is one hour.*

time-out /ˌtaɪm ˈaʊt/ (also **time-out**) *noun* [count]
(**SPORTS**) a short period of rest during a sports game

tim·er /ˈtaɪmər/ *noun* [count]
a machine, or part of a machine, that measures time

times¹ /taɪmz/ *preposition* (symbol **x**)
(**MATH**) multiplied by: *Three times four is twelve (3x4 = 12).*

times² /taɪmz/ *noun* [plural]
a word that you use to show how much bigger, smaller, more expensive, etc. one thing is than another: *Los Angeles is six times bigger than Memphis.*

time zone /ˈtaɪm zoʊn/ *noun* [count]
one of the 24 areas that the world is divided into, each with its own time: *New York is in the Eastern time zone.*

tim·id /ˈtɪməd/ *adjective*
shy and easily afraid ➔ **SYNONYM shy**
▶ **tim·id·ly** /ˈtɪmədli/ *adverb*: *She opened the door timidly and came in.*

tin /tɪn/ *noun* [noncount] (symbol **Sn**)
(**CHEMISTRY**) a soft, white metal: *a tin roof*

tin·gle /ˈtɪŋgl/ *verb* (tin·gle, tin·gling, tin·gled)
If a part of your body **tingles**, it feels like a lot of small sharp points are pushing into your skin: *His cheeks tingled as he came in from the cold.*

ti·ny /ˈtaɪni/ *adjective* (ti·ni·er, ti·ni·est)
very small: *Ants are tiny insects.*

tip¹ /tɪp/ *noun* [count]
1 the pointed or thin end of something: *the tips of your fingers*
2 a small, extra amount of money that you give to someone who has done a job for you: *I left a tip on the table.*
3 a small piece of advice: *She gave me some useful tips on how to pass the exam.*

tip² /tɪp/ *verb* (tips, tip·ping, tipped)
1 to move so that one side goes up or down; to move something so that one side goes up or down: *Don't tip your chair back.*
2 to turn something so that the things inside fall out: *She opened a can of beans and tipped them into a bowl.*
3 to give someone an extra amount of money to thank them for something they have done for you as part of their job: *Do you tip taxi drivers in your country?*

tip over; **tip something over** to turn over; to make something turn over: *The boat tipped over and we all fell in the water.* ◆ *Don't tip your drink over!*

ti·pi /ˈtipi/ *noun* [count] (*plural* **ti·pis**) = **tepee**

tip·toe /ˈtɪptoʊ/ *verb* (tip·toes, tip·toe·ing, tip·toed)
to walk quietly on your toes: *He tiptoed into the bedroom.*
on tiptoe standing or walking on your toes with the rest of your feet off the ground: *I can reach it if I stand on tiptoe.*

tire 🔎 /ˈtaɪər/ *noun* [count]
a circle of rubber around the outside of a wheel, for example on a car or bicycle: *I think we have a flat tire* (= a tire with not enough air inside). ➪ Look at the picture at **car**.

tired 🔎 /ˈtaɪərd/ *adjective*
needing to rest or sleep: *I've been working all day, and I'm tired.* ◆ *He's feeling tired.*
be tired of something to have had or done too much of something, so that you do not want it any longer: *I'm tired of watching TV – let's go out.*

tir·ing /ˈtaɪərɪŋ/ *adjective*
making you feel tired: *a tiring trip*

tis·sue /ˈtɪʃu/ *noun*
1 [count] a thin piece of soft paper that you use to clean your nose: *a box of tissues* ➪ **SYNONYM Kleenex™**
2 [noncount] (**BIOLOGY**) all the cells that form the bodies of humans, animals, and plants

tis·sue pa·per /ˈtɪʃu ˌpeɪpər/ *noun* [noncount]
thin paper that you use for wrapping things

ti·ta·ni·um /ˌtaɪˈteɪniəm/ *noun* [noncount] (symbol **Ti**)
(**CHEMISTRY**) a hard, silver-gray metal that is often used with other metals to make strong, light materials

ti·tle 🔎 /ˈtaɪt̬l/ *noun* [count]
1 the name of something, for example a book, movie, or picture: *What is the title of this poem?*
2 a word like "Mr.," "Mrs.," or "Doctor" that you put in front of a person's name

TM abbreviation of **trademark**

to 🔎 /tə; tu/ *preposition*
1 a word that shows direction: *She went to Italy.* ◆ *James has gone to school.* ◆ *This bus goes to the city center.*
2 a word that shows the end or limit of something: *The museum is open from 9:30 to 5:30.* ◆ *Jeans cost from $20 to $45.*
3 a word that shows the person or thing that receives something: *I gave the book to Paula.* ◆ *He sent a letter to his parents.* ◆ *Be kind to animals.*
4 on or against something: *He put his hands to his ears.* ◆ *They were sitting back to back.*
5 a word that shows how something changes: *The sky changed from blue to gray.*
6 a word that you use for comparing things: *I prefer football to tennis.*

7 a word that shows why: *I came to help.*
8 a word that shows how many minutes it is before the hour: *It's two minutes to six.*
9 (**ENGLISH LANGUAGE ARTS**) a word that you use before verbs to make the INFINITIVE (= the simple form of a verb): *I want to go home.* ◆ *Don't forget to write.* ◆ *She asked me to go but I didn't want to* (= to go).

toad /toʊd/ *noun* [count]
a small animal with rough skin that lives in or near water ➪ Look at **frog**.

toad

toast /toʊst/ *noun*
1 [noncount] a thin piece of bread that you have cooked so that it is brown: *I had a slice of toast and butter for breakfast.*
2 [count] the act of holding up a glass of wine and wishing someone happiness or success before you drink: *They drank a toast to the new president.*
▶ **toast** *verb* (toasts, toast·ing, toast·ed): *toasted sandwiches* ◆ *We all toasted the bride and groom* (= at a wedding).

toast·er /ˈtoʊstər/ *noun* [count]
a machine for making TOAST (1)

toaster

toast ___

to·bac·co /təˈbækoʊ/ *noun* [noncount]
special dried leaves that people smoke in cigarettes and pipes

to·bog·gan /təˈbɑgən/ *noun* [count]
a type of flat board that people use for traveling down hills on snow for fun

to·day 🔎 /təˈdeɪ/ *adverb*, *noun* [noncount]
1 this day; on this day: *What should we do today?* ◆ *Today is Friday.*
2 the present time; at the present time: *Most families in the U.S. today have a car.* ➪ **SYNONYM nowadays**

tod·dler /ˈtɑdlər/ *noun* [count]
a young child who has just started to walk

toe 🔎 /toʊ/ *noun* [count]
1 one of the five parts at the end of your foot ➪ Look at the picture at **leg**.
2 the part of a shoe or sock that covers the end of your foot

toe·nail /ˈtoʊneɪl/ *noun* [count]
the hard part at the end of your toe

to·geth·er 🔎 /təˈgɛðər/ *adverb*
1 with each other or close to each other: *John and Lisa usually walk home together.* ◆ *Stand with your feet together.* ◆ *They live together.*

2 so that two or more things are joined to or mixed with each other: *Tie the ends of the rope together.* ◆ *Add these numbers together.* ◆ *Mix the eggs and sugar together.*

toi·let 🔊 /ˈtɔɪlət/ *noun* [*count*]
a large bowl with a seat, which you use when you need to get rid of waste from your body

toi·let pa·per /ˈtɔɪlət ˌpeɪpər/ *noun* [*noncount*]
paper that you use to clean your body after using the toilet

toi·let·ries /ˈtɔɪlətriz/ *noun* [*plural*]
things such as soap or a brush that you use when you wash yourself, do your hair, etc.

to·ken /ˈtoʊkən/ *noun* [*count*]
1 a small thing that you use to show something else: *This gift is a token of our friendship.*
2 a piece of paper, plastic, or metal that you use instead of money to pay for something: *a book token*

told form of **tell**

tol·er·ant /ˈtɑlərənt/ *adjective*
letting people do things even though you do not like or understand them: *We must be tolerant of other people's beliefs.*
▶ **tol·er·ance** /ˈtɑlərəns/ *noun* [*noncount*]: *tolerance of other religions*

tol·er·ate /ˈtɑləreɪt/ *verb* (tol·er·ates, tol·er·at·ing, tol·er·at·ed)
to let people do something even though you do not like or understand it: *He won't tolerate rudeness.*

toll /toʊl/ *noun* [*count*]
1 money that you pay to use a road or bridge: *The highway toll is $4.*
2 [*usually singular*] the number of people who were killed or injured by something: *The death toll has now reached 5,000.*

to·ma·to 🔊 /təˈmeɪtoʊ/ *noun* [*count*] (*plural* to·ma·toes*)
a soft, red fruit that you eat cold in salads or cook as a vegetable: *tomato soup* ⮕ Look at the picture at **vegetable**.

tomb /tum/ *noun* [*count*]
a place where a dead person's body is buried, often one with a stone above it

tomb·stone /ˈtumstoʊn/ *noun* [*count*]
a large, flat stone on the place where a person is buried (their GRAVE) showing their name and the dates when they lived

to·mor·row 🔊 /təˈmɑroʊ/ *adverb*, *noun* [*noncount*]
the day after today; on the day after today: *Let's go swimming tomorrow.* ◆ *I'll see you tomorrow morning.* ◆ *We are going home the day after tomorrow.*

ton /tʌn/ *noun*
1 [*count*] a unit for measuring weight, equal to 2,000 pounds
2 **tons** [*plural*] (*informal*) a lot: *He has tons of money.*

tone /toʊn/ *noun*
1 [*count, noncount*] the way that someone's voice sounds: *I knew he was angry by the tone of his voice.*
2 [*singular*] the general quality or style of something: *The tone of the meeting was optimistic.*
3 [*count*] a sound that you hear on the telephone: *Please speak after the tone.*

tongs /tɑŋz/ *noun* [*plural*]
a tool with two parts that you use for holding things or picking things up

tongs

tongue 🔊 /tʌŋ/ *noun* [*count*]

> 🛈 **PRONUNCIATION**
> The word **tongue** sounds like **young**.

the soft part inside your mouth that moves when you talk or eat ⮕ Look at the picture at **mouth**.

tongue-twist·er /ˈtʌŋ ˌtwɪstər/ *noun* [*count*]
words that are difficult to say together quickly: *"She sells seashells by the seashore" is a tongue-twister.*

to·night 🔊 /təˈnaɪt/ *adverb*, *noun* [*noncount*]
the evening or night of today; on the evening or night of today: *I'm going to a party tonight.* ◆ *Tonight is the last night of our vacation.*

too 🔊 /tu/ *adverb*
1 also: *Green is my favorite color, but I like blue too.*
2 more than you want or need: *These shoes are too big.* ◆ *She put too much milk in my coffee.*

took form of **take**

tool 🔊 /tul/ *noun* [*count*]
a thing that you hold in your hand and use to do a special job: *Hammers and saws are tools.*

tooth 🔊 /tuθ/ *noun* [*count*] (*plural* teeth /tiθ/)
1 one of the hard, white things in your mouth that you use for eating: *I brush my teeth after every meal.* ⮕ Look at the picture at **mouth**.
2 one of the long, narrow, pointed parts of an object such as a COMB (= a thing that you use for making your hair neat)

tooth·ache /ˈtuθeɪk/ *noun* [*count*]
(**HEALTH**) a pain in your tooth: *I have a toothache.*

tooth·brush /ˈtuθbrʌʃ/ *noun* [*count*] (*plural* tooth·brush·es)
a small brush for cleaning your teeth ⮕ Look at the picture at **brush**.

tooth·paste
/'tuθpeɪst/ *noun*
[*noncount*]
a substance that you
put on your
TOOTHBRUSH and use
for cleaning your
teeth

toothpaste

tooth·pick /'tuθpɪk/ *noun* [*count*]
a short, pointed piece of wood that you use to
get pieces of food out from between your teeth

top¹ /tɑp/ *noun*
1 [*count*] the highest part of something: *There's a
church* **at the top of** *the hill.* ⇒ ANTONYM **bottom**
2 [*singular*] the highest or most important
position: *to be at the top of your profession*
3 [*count*] a cover that you put on something to
close it: *Where's the top of this jar?*
4 [*count*] a piece of clothing that you wear on the
top part of your body: *I like your top – is it new?*
on top on its highest part: *The cake had cream
on top.*
on top of something on or over something: *A
tree fell on top of my car.*

top² /tɑp/ *adjective*
highest or best: *Put this book on the top shelf.* ◆
She's one of the country's top athletes.

top·ic AWL /'tɑpɪk/ *noun* [*count*]
something that you talk, learn, or write about:
The topic of the discussion was climate change. ⇒
SYNONYM **subject**

top·i·cal AWL /'tɑpɪkl/ *adjective*
connected with something that is happening
now: *a topical joke*

torch /tɔrtʃ/ *noun* [*count*] (*plural* **torch·es**)
a long piece of wood with burning material at
the end that you carry to give light: *the Olympic
torch*

tore, torn forms of **tear**²

tor·na·do /tɔr'neɪdoʊ/ *noun* [*count*] (*plural*
tor·na·does)
a violent storm with a very strong wind that
blows in a circle ⇒ Look at the note at **wind**¹.

tor·pe·do /tɔr'pidoʊ/ *noun* [*count*] (*plural*
tor·pe·does)
a type of bomb in the shape of a long tube,
which is fired from a ship that travels under the
water (called a SUBMARINE)

tor·rent /'tɔrənt/ *noun* [*count*]
a large amount of water moving very quickly:
The rain was coming down **in torrents**.
▶ **tor·ren·tial** /tə'rɛnʃl/ *adjective*: *torrential rain*

tor·so /'tɔrsoʊ/ *noun* [*count*] (*plural* **tor·sos**)
the main part of your body, not your head,
arms, and legs

tor·til·la /tɔr'tiyə/ *noun* [*count*]
a type of very thin, round Mexican bread. It is
usually eaten hot and filled with meat, cheese,
etc.

tor·toise /'tɔrtəs/ *noun* [*count*]
an animal with a hard shell on its back, which
lives on land and moves very slowly ⇒ Look at
turtle.

tor·ture /'tɔrtʃər/ *noun* [*noncount*]
the act of making someone feel great pain,
often to make them give information: *His
confession was obtained* **under torture**.
▶ **tor·ture** *verb* (**tor·tures, tor·tur·ing, tor·tured**):
Many of the prisoners had been tortured.

toss /tɔs/ *verb* (**toss·es, toss·ing, tossed**)
1 to throw something quickly and without care:
I tossed the paper into the trash.
2 to move quickly up and down or from side to
side; to make something do this: *The boat was
being tossed by the huge waves.*

to·tal¹ /'toʊtl/ *adjective*
complete; if you count everything or everyone:
There was total silence in the classroom. ◆ *What
was the total number of people at the meeting?*

to·tal² /'toʊtl/ *noun* [*count*]
(MATH) the number you have when you add
everything together: *Enter the total at the bottom
of the page.*

to·tal·ly /'toʊtl·i/ *adverb*
completely: *I totally agree.*

touch¹ /tʌtʃ/ *verb* (**touch·es, touch·ing,
touched**)

> ⓘ **PRONUNCIATION**
> The word **touch** sounds like **much**.

1 to put a part of your body, usually your hand
or finger, onto someone or something: *Don't
touch the paint – it's still wet.* ◆ *He touched me on
the arm.*
2 to be so close to another thing or person that
there is no space in between: *The two wires were
touching.* ◆ *Her coat was so long that it touched
the ground.*
3 to make someone feel sad, sorry for someone,
grateful, etc: *She told us a sad story that touched
our hearts.*

touch² /tʌtʃ/ *noun* (*plural* **touch·es**)
1 [*count, usually singular*] the action of putting a
hand or finger on someone or something: *I felt
the* **touch** *of his hand on my arm.*
2 [*noncount*] the feeling in your hands and skin
that tells you about something: *We had to feel
our way* **by touch**.
be or **keep in touch with someone** to meet,
call, or write to someone often: *Are you still in
touch with Kevin?* ◆ *Let's keep in touch.*

get in touch with someone to write to, or call someone: *I'm trying to get in touch with my cousin.*

lose touch with someone to stop meeting, calling, or writing to someone: *I've lost touch with all my old friends from school.*

touch·down /'tʌtʃdaʊn/ *noun*
1 [count] (**SPORTS**) (in football) an act of scoring points by carrying the ball over the other team's line, or receiving the ball when you are in this position
2 [count, noncount] the moment when a plane lands ⊃ **SYNONYM landing**

tough /tʌf/ *adjective* (**tough·er, tough·est**)
1 difficult: *This is a tough job.* ⊃ **SYNONYM hard**
2 strict or firm: *He's very **tough on** his children.* ⊃ **SYNONYM hard** ⊃ **ANTONYM soft**
3 very strong: *You need to be tough to go climbing in winter.*
4 difficult to break or tear: *a tough pair of boots*
5 Tough meat is difficult to cut and eat. ⊃ **ANTONYM tender**

tough·en /'tʌfn/ *verb* (**tough·ens, tough·en·ing, tough·ened**)
to become or to make something stronger: *toughened glass*

tou·pee /tu'peɪ/ *noun* [count]
a piece of artificial hair that a man wears to cover a part of his head where he has no hair

tour /tʊr/ *noun* [count]
1 a short visit to see a building or city: *They gave us **a tour** of the house.*
2 a trip to see a lot of different places: *We went on a tour of Europe.*
▶ **tour** *verb* (**tours, tour·ing, toured**): *We toured Europe for three weeks.*

tour·ism /'tʊrɪzəm/ *noun* [noncount]
the business of arranging vacations for people: *The country earns a lot of money from tourism.*

tour·ist /'tʊrɪst/ *noun* [count]
a person who visits a place on vacation

tour·na·ment /'tʊrnəmənt/ *noun* [count]
(**SPORTS**) a sports competition with a lot of players or teams: *a tennis tournament*

tow /toʊ/ *verb* (**tows, tow·ing, towed**)
to pull a vehicle using a rope or chain: *My car was towed to a garage.*

toward /tord; tə'word/ (also **to·wards** /tordz; tə'wordz/) *preposition*
1 in the direction of someone or something: *We walked toward the river.* • *I couldn't see her face – she had her back toward me.*
2 to someone or something: *The people here are always very friendly toward tourists.*
3 to help pay for something: *Tom gave me $10 toward Sam's birthday present.*

4 near a time or a date: *Let's meet toward the end of the week.* • *It gets cooler toward evening.*

tow·el /'taʊəl/ *noun* [count]
a piece of cloth that you use for drying yourself: *I washed my hands and dried them on a towel.*

tow·er /'taʊər/ *noun* [count]
a tall, narrow building or a tall part of a building: *Chicago's Sears Tower* • *a church tower*

town /taʊn/ *noun* [count]
(**GEOGRAPHY**) a place where there are a lot of houses, stores, and other buildings: *I grew up in a small town in New Jersey.* • *I'm **going into town** to do some shopping.*

town hall /ˌtaʊn 'hɔl/ *noun* [count]
a large building that contains the local government offices of a town ⊃ Look at **city hall**.

tox·ic /'taksɪk/ *adjective*
(**HEALTH, CHEMISTRY**) containing poison: *Toxic waste had been dumped on the site.* ⊃ **SYNONYM poisonous**

tox·in /'taksɪn/ *noun* [count]
a poisonous substance: *Pesticides can release toxins into the environment.*

toys

model train   **doll**

toy /tɔɪ/ *noun* [count]
a thing for a child to play with: *a toy soldier* • *The children are in the yard playing with their toys.*

trace¹ **AWL** /treɪs/ *noun*
1 [count, noncount] a mark or sign that shows that a person or thing has been in a place: *The police could not find any **trace** of the missing child.* • *to disappear **without trace***
2 [count] a very small amount of something: *Traces of blood were found at the crime scene.*

trace² **AWL** /treɪs/ *verb* (**trac·es, trac·ing, traced**)
1 to look for and find someone or something: *The police **traced** the gang **to** a house in Rochester.*
2 to put thin paper over a picture and draw over the lines to make a copy

track¹ /træk/ *noun*
1 tracks [plural] a line of marks that an animal, a person, or a vehicle makes on the ground: *We saw tracks in the snow.*
2 [count, noncount] the metal lines that a train runs on: *The train had left the tracks.*

3 (SPORTS) [count] a special road for races: *a racing track* ⊃ Look at the note at **field**.
4 [count] (MUSIC) one song or piece of music on a CD, tape, or record: *Which is your favorite track?*
5 (SPORTS) = **track and field**
keep track of someone or **something** to have information about what is happening or where someone or something is
lose track of someone or **something** to not have information about what is happening or where someone or something is: *I lost all track of time* (= forgot what time it was).
on the right or **wrong track** having the right or wrong idea about something: *That's not the answer, but you're on the right track.*

track² /træk/ *verb* (tracks, track·ing, tracked)
track someone or **something down** to find someone or something after looking in several different places: *The police have so far failed to track down the attacker.*

track and field /ˌtræk ən 'fild/ (also **track**) *noun* [noncount]
(SPORTS) sports such as running, jumping, and throwing

track record /'træk ˌrɛkərd/ *noun* [singular]
all the successes and failures a person or organization has had in the past: *We are looking for someone with an excellent track record.*

trac·tor /'træktər/
noun [count]
a big, strong vehicle that people use on farms to pull heavy things

tractor

trade¹ /treɪd/ *noun*
1 [noncount] (BUSINESS)
the buying and selling of things: *trade between the U.S. and Japan*
2 [count] an act of exchanging something for something else: *I made a trade of my apple for his cookie.*
3 [count, noncount] a job for which you need special skills, especially with your hands: *Dave is a plumber by trade.* ◆ *to learn a trade*
4 [count] a particular type of business: *the building trade*

trade² /treɪd/ *verb* (trades, trad·ing, trad·ed)
1 (BUSINESS) to buy and sell things: *Japan trades with many different countries.*
2 to exchange something for something else: *I'll trade my sandwich for yours.*

trade·mark /'treɪdmɑrk/ *noun* [count]
(abbreviation **TM**)
a special mark or name that a company puts on the things it makes and that other companies must not use

trad·er /'treɪdər/ *noun* [count]
(BUSINESS) a person who buys and sells things

tra·di·tion 🔑 AWL /trə'dɪʃn/ *noun* [count, noncount]
something that people in a particular place have done or believed for a long time: *In the U.S. it's a tradition to eat turkey on Thanksgiving.* ◆ *cultural traditions*

tra·di·tion·al AWL /trə'dɪʃənəl/ *adjective*
connected with the things that a particular group of people have done or believed for a long time: *It is traditional to eat turkey on Thanksgiving.* ◆ *traditional holiday decorations*
▶ **tra·di·tion·al·ly** AWL /trə'dɪʃənəli/ *adverb*: *Driving trains was traditionally a man's job.*

traf·fic¹ 🔑 /'træfɪk/ *noun* [noncount]
all the cars and other vehicles that are on a road: *There was a lot of traffic on the way to work this morning.*

traf·fic² /'træfɪk/ *verb* (traf·fics, traf·fick·ing, traf·ficked)
to buy and sell something illegally: *He was arrested for trafficking drugs.*
▶ **traf·fick·er** /'træfɪkər/ *noun* [count]: *a drugs trafficker*

traf·fic jam /'træfɪk dʒæm/ *noun* [count]
a long line of cars and other vehicles that cannot move or can only move slowly

traf·fic light /'træfɪk laɪt/ (also **traf·fic sig·nal** /'træfɪk ˌsɪgnəl/) *noun* [count]
a light that changes from red to yellow to green, to tell cars and other vehicles when to stop and start ⊃ SYNONYM **stoplight**

trag·e·dy /'trædʒədi/ *noun* [count] (plural trag·e·dies)
1 a very sad thing that happens: *Her early death was a tragedy.*
2 (ENGLISH LANGUAGE ARTS) a serious and sad play: *Shakespeare's "King Lear" is a tragedy.* ⊃ Look at **comedy**.

trag·ic /'trædʒɪk/ *adjective*
very sad: *a tragic accident*
▶ **trag·i·cal·ly** /'trædʒɪkli/ *adverb*: *He died tragically at the age of 25.*

trail¹ /treɪl/ *noun* [count]
1 a line of marks that show which way a person or thing has gone: *There was a trail of blood across the floor.*
2 a path in the country: *We followed the trail through the forest.*

trail² /treɪl/ *verb* (trails, trail·ing, trailed)
to pull something along behind you; to be pulled along behind someone or something: *Her skirt was too long, and it trailed along the ground.*

æ **cat**   ɛ **ten**   i **see**   ɪ **sit**   ɑ **hot**   ɔ **saw**   ʌ **cup**   ʊ **put**   u **too**

trail·er /ˈtreɪlər/ *noun* [*count*]
1 a container with wheels that a vehicle pulls along: *The car was towing a boat on a trailer.*
2 a vehicle without an engine, which can be pulled by a car or truck or used as a home when it is parked
3 a small building for people to live in. It is made in a factory and can be moved with a truck. ⟳ SYNONYM **mobile home**

trail·er park /ˈtreɪlər pɑrk/ *noun* [*count*]
an area of land where there are many small buildlngs (called TRAILERS) that people live in

train¹ 🔑 /treɪn/ *noun* [*count*]
a number of vehicles that are pulled by an engine along a special track (a RAILROAD line): *I'm going to Boston by train.* ◆ *We caught the 7:15 train to Philadelphia.* ◆ *You need to change trains at Chicago.*

train² 🔑 /treɪn/ *verb* (trains, train·ing, trained)
1 to teach a person or an animal to do something: *He was trained as a pilot.*
2 to make yourself ready for something by studying or doing something a lot: *Ann is training to be a doctor.* ◆ *She's training for the Olympics.*
▶ **train·er** /ˈtreɪnər/ *noun* [*count*]
a person who teaches people or animals to do something

train·ee /treɪˈni/ *noun* [*count*]
(BUSINESS) a person who is learning how to do a job: *The company hired him as a management trainee.*

train·ing 🔑 /ˈtreɪnɪŋ/ *noun* [*noncount*]
the process of getting ready for a sport or job: *She is in training for the Olympic Games.*

trai·tor /ˈtreɪtər/ *noun* [*count*]
a person who harms their own country or group in order to help another country or group

tramp /træmp/ *noun* [*count*]
a person with no home or job, who goes from place to place

tram·ple /ˈtræmpl/ *verb* (tram·ples, tram·pling, tram·pled)
to walk on something and damage it with your feet: *Don't trample on the flowers!*

tram·po·line /ˌtræmpəˈlin/ *noun* [*count*]
a piece of equipment for jumping up and down on

trance /træns/ *noun* [*count*]
a mental state in which you do not notice what is happening around you: *He was staring straight ahead, lost in a trance.*

tran·qui·li·zer /ˈtræŋkwəlaɪzər/ *noun* [*count*]
(HEALTH) a drug that is used to make you feel calm or help you to sleep

trans·fer¹ AWL /ˈtrænsfər; trænsˈfər/ *verb* (trans·fers, trans·fer·ring, trans·ferred)
to move someone or something to a different place: *I want to transfer $500 to my savings account.*

trans·fer² AWL /ˈtrænsfər/ *noun*
1 [*count, noncount*] moving or being moved to a different place or situation: *a transfer of funds*
2 [*count*] a ticket that allows you to change from one bus or train to another without paying more money

trans·form AWL /trænsˈfɔrm/ *verb* (trans·forms, trans·form·ing, trans·formed)
to change a person or thing completely: *The Internet has transformed people's lives.*
▶ **trans·for·ma·tion** AWL /ˌtrænsfərˈmeɪʃn/ *noun* [*count, noncount*]: *The city's transformation has been amazing.*

tran·sis·tor /trænˈzɪstər/ *noun* [*count*]
a small electronic part inside something such as a radio, a television, or a computer

tran·si·tion AWL /trænˈzɪʃn/ *noun* [*count, noncount*]
a change from one state or form to another: *the transition from childhood to adolescence*

tran·si·tive /ˈtrænsətɪv/ *adjective*
(ENGLISH LANGUAGE ARTS) A transitive verb has an object: *In the sentence "Keith opened the door," "opened" is a transitive verb.* ⟳ ANTONYM **intransitive**

trans·late 🔑 /ˈtrænzleɪt; trænsˈleɪt/ *verb* (trans·lates, trans·lat·ing, trans·lat·ed)
to change what someone has said or written in one language to another language: *Can you translate this letter into English for me?*
▶ **trans·la·tion** /trænsˈleɪʃn; trænzˈleɪʃn/ *noun* [*count, noncount*]: *a translation from English into French* ◆ *I've only read his books in translation.*
▶ **trans·la·tor** /ˈtrænsleɪtər; ˈtrænzleɪtər/ *noun* [*count*]: *She works as a translator.*

trans·mit AWL /trænsˈmɪt; trænzˈmɪt/ *verb* (trans·mits, trans·mit·ting, trans·mit·ted)
to send out television or radio signals: *The concert was transmitted live all over the world.*
▶ **trans·mit·ter** /trænsˈmɪtər; trænzˈmɪtər/ *noun* [*count*]
a piece of equipment that sends out television or radio signals

trans·par·ent 🔑 /trænsˈpærənt/ *adjective*
If something is **transparent**, you can see through it: *Glass is transparent.* ⟳ ANTONYM **opaque**

trans·plant /ˈtrænsplænt/ *noun* [*count*]
(HEALTH) a medical operation where a body part is taken from one person and put into another person: *to have a kidney transplant*

tʃ **ch**in   dʒ **J**une   v **v**an   θ **th**in   ð **th**en   s **so**   z **zoo**   ʃ **she**

▶ **trans·plant** /træns'plænt/ *verb* (trans·plants, trans·plant·ing, trans·plant·ed): to transplant a liver into another body

trans·port AWL /træn'spɔrt/ *verb* (trans·ports, trans·port·ing, trans·port·ed)
to carry people or things from one place to another: *The goods were transported by air.*

trans·por·ta·tion 🔑 AWL /ˌtrænspɔr'teɪʃn/ *noun* [noncount]
1 carrying people or things from one place to another: *the **transportation of** passengers to and from the airport*
2 vehicles that you travel in: *I usually take **public transportation** to work.* • *There is free transportation to the stadium from downtown.*

trap¹ /træp/ *noun* [count]
1 a thing that you use for catching animals: *The rabbit's leg was caught in a trap.*
2 a plan to trick someone: *I knew the question was a trap, so I didn't answer it.*

trap² /træp/ *verb* (traps, trap·ping, trapped)
1 to keep someone in a place that they cannot escape from: *They were trapped in the burning building.*
2 to catch or trick someone or something: *Police are hoping this new evidence could help trap the killer.*

trap·e·zoid
/'træpəzɔɪd/ *noun* [count]
(**MATH**) a flat shape with four straight sides. One pair of opposite sides are PARALLEL (= always the same distance from each other), and the other pair are not.

trapezoid

trash 🔑 /træʃ/ *noun* [noncount]
1 things that you do not want anymore: *old boxes, bottles, and other trash* • *Don't forget to take out the trash (= carry it outside to be collected).*
2 something that you think is bad, stupid, or wrong: *How can you watch that trash on TV?* ⊃ SYNONYM **garbage**

trash can /'træʃ ˌkæn/ *noun* [count]
a large container for garbage that you keep outside your house ⊃ SYNONYM **garbage can**

trash·y /'træʃi/ *adjective* (trash·i·er, trash·i·est)
of bad quality: *trashy novels*

trau·ma /'trɔmə; 'traʊmə/ *noun* [count, noncount]
a state of great shock or sadness, or an event that causes this feeling: *the trauma of losing your parents*
▶ **trau·mat·ic** /trə'mætɪk; trɔ'mætɪk/ *adjective*: *a traumatic experience*

trav·el¹ 🔑 /'trævl/ *verb* (trav·els, trav·el·ing, trav·eled)
to go from one place to another: *I would like to travel around the world.* • *I travel to school by bus.* • *She traveled 500 miles in one day.*

trav·el² 🔑 /'trævl/ *noun*
1 [noncount] the action of going from one place to another: *My hobbies are music and travel.*
2 travels [plural] a person's trips to different places, especially places that are far away: *You must have seen a lot of interesting places **on your travels**.* ⊃ Look at the note at **trip¹**.

trav·el a·gen·cy /'trævl ˌeɪdʒənsi/ *noun* [count] (plural trav·el a·gen·cies)
a company that plans vacations and trips for people

trav·el a·gent /'trævl ˌeɪdʒənt/ *noun* [count]
a person who works in a TRAVEL AGENCY

trav·el·er /'trævlər/ *noun* [count]
a person who is traveling

trav·el·er's check /'trævlərz ˌtʃɛk/ *noun* [count]
a special check that you can use when you go to other countries

tray /treɪ/ *noun* [count]
a flat object that you use for carrying food or drinks

trea·son /'trizn/ *noun* [noncount]
the crime of harming your country by helping its enemies

treas·ure¹ /'trɛʒər/ *noun* [noncount]
a collection of gold, silver, jewelry, or other things that are worth a lot of money: *They were searching for **buried treasure**.*

treas·ure² /'trɛʒər/ *verb* (treas·ures, treas·ur·ing, treas·ured)
to think that someone or something is very special and important: *I will treasure those memories forever.*

treas·ur·er /'trɛʒərər/ *noun* [count]
a person who is in charge of the money of a club or an organization

treat¹ 🔑 /trit/ *verb* (treats, treat·ing, treat·ed)
1 to behave in a certain way toward someone or something: *How does your boss treat you?* • *Treat these glasses **with** care.*
2 to think about something in a certain way: *They **treated** my idea **as** a joke.*
3 to try to make a sick person well again: *Several people are being **treated for** burns.*
4 to give yourself or another person something special or enjoyable: *I **treated** the children **to** ice cream.*

treat² /trit/ *noun* [count]
something special or enjoyable that makes someone happy: *My parents took me to the theater **as a treat** for my birthday.*

treat·ment 🦴 /ˈtritmənt/ *noun*
1 [*count, noncount*] (**HEALTH**) the things that a doctor does to try to make a sick person well again: *a new **treatment** for cancer* ⊃ Look at the note at **illness**, **injury**.
2 [*noncount*] the way that you behave toward someone or something: *Their **treatment** of the animals was very cruel.*

trea·ty /ˈtriti/ *noun* [*count*] (*plural* **trea·ties**)
a written agreement between countries: *The two countries signed a peace treaty.*

tree

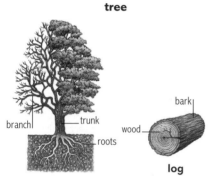

branch | trunk
bark
wood
roots

log

tree 🦴 /tri/ *noun* [*count*]
(**BIOLOGY**) a big plant that can live for a long time. Trees have a central part (called a **TRUNK**) and many smaller parts (called **BRANCHES**): *an oak tree* • *Apples grow on trees.*

trem·ble /ˈtrɛmbl/ *verb* (**trem·bles, trem·bling, trem·bled**)
to shake, for example because you are cold, afraid, or sick: *She was **trembling with** fear.*

tre·men·dous /trɪˈmɛndəs/ *adjective*
1 very big or very great: *The new trains travel at a tremendous speed.*
2 very good: *The game was tremendous.*
▶ **tre·men·dous·ly** /trɪˈmɛndəsli/ *adverb*: *The movie was tremendously exciting.*

trench /trɛntʃ/ *noun* [*count*] (*plural* **trench·es**)
a long, narrow hole that is dug in the ground, for example to put pipes or wires in

trend **AWL** /trɛnd/ *noun* [*count*]
a change to something different: *new **trends** in science*

trend·y /ˈtrɛndi/ *adjective* (**trend·i·er, trend·i·est**) (*informal*)
fashionable: *a trendy new bar*

tres·pass /ˈtrɛspæs/ *verb* (**tres·pass·es, tres·pass·ing, tres·passed**)
to go on someone's land without asking them if you can
▶ **tres·pass·er** /ˈtrɛspæsər/ *noun* [*count*]: *A sign on the gate said "No Trespassers."*

tri·al 🦴 /ˈtraɪəl/ *noun* [*count, noncount*]
1 the process in a court of law when people (called the **JUDGE** and the **JURY**) can decide if a person has done something wrong and what the punishment will be: *He was **on trial for** murder.*
2 the process of testing something to see if it is good or bad: *They are conducting trials of a new drug.*

tri·an·gle /ˈtraɪæŋgl/ *noun* [*count*]
(**MATH**) a shape with three straight sides ⊃ Look at the picture at **shape**.
▶ **tri·an·gu·lar** /traɪˈæŋgyələr/ *adjective*: *triangular shapes*

tribe /traɪb/ *noun* [*count*]
a small group of people who have the same language and customs and who have a leader (called a **CHIEF**): *the Zulu tribes of Africa*
▶ **trib·al** /ˈtraɪbl/ *adjective*: *tribal dances*

trib·ute /ˈtrɪbyut/ *noun* [*count, noncount*]
something that you do, say, or give to show that you respect or admire someone: *The concert was a **tribute to** the musician on his 80th birthday.*

trick¹ 🦴 /trɪk/ *noun* [*count*]
1 something that you do to make someone believe something that is not true: *They used a trick to get past the guards.*
2 something that you have learned to do, especially as a form of entertainment: *Do you know any card tricks?*
play a trick on someone to do something that makes someone look silly, in order to make other people laugh: *The children played a trick on their teacher by hiding her books.*

trick² 🦴 /trɪk/ *verb* (**tricks, trick·ing, tricked**)
to do something that is not honest to get what you want from someone: *He **tricked** the old lady **into** giving him all her money.*

trick·le /ˈtrɪkl/ *verb* (**trick·les, trick·ling, trick·led**)
to move slowly like a thin line of water: *Tears trickled down her cheeks.*
▶ **trick·le** *noun* [*count, usually singular*]: *a trickle of blood*

trick·y /ˈtrɪki/ *adjective* (**trick·i·er, trick·i·est**)
difficult; hard to do: *a tricky question*

tri·cy·cle /ˈtraɪsɪkl/ *noun* [*count*]
a type of bicycle with three wheels

tried, tries forms of **try**

trig·ger¹ **AWL** /ˈtrɪgər/ *noun* [*count*]
the part of a gun that you move with your finger to fire it

trig·ger² **AWL** /ˈtrɪgər/ *verb* (**trig·gers, trig·ger·ing, trig·gered**)
to make something happen suddenly: *Her cigarette smoke triggered the fire alarm.*

trig·o·nom·e·try /ˌtrɪɡəˈnɑmətri/ *noun*
[*noncount*]
(**MATH**) the type of mathematics that deals with
the relationship between the sides and angles
of **TRIANGLES** (= shapes with three sides)

tril·lion /ˈtrɪlyən/ *number*
1,000,000,000,000; one million million: *The
country is trilllions of dollars in debt.*

tril·o·gy /ˈtrɪlədʒi/ *noun* [*count*] (*plural* **tril·o·gies**)
(**ENGLISH LANGUAGE ARTS**) a group of three books,
plays, or movies that form a set

trim /trɪm/ *verb* (**trims, trim·ming, trimmed**)
to cut a small amount off something to make it
neat: *He trimmed my hair.*
▸ **trim** *noun* [*count*]: *My hair needs a trim.*

tri·o /ˈtrioʊ/ *noun* [*count*] (*plural* **tri·os**)
a group of three people who play music or sing
together ⊃ Look at **quartet**.

trip¹ 🔈 /trɪp/ *noun* [*count*]
a visit to a place; an act of traveling: *We went on
a trip to the mountains.* ◆ *How was your trip?* ⊃
Look at **round-trip**.

Thesaurus

trip an act of traveling from one place to
another, and usually back again. A **trip** can
be short or long, and can be for business or
pleasure: *a business trip* ◆ *a round-the-
world trip* ◆ *a trip to the grocery store* ◆ *They
took a trip down the river.* ◆ *We just got back
from our trip to Japan. We had a great time.*

travel the general activity of moving from
place to place. With this meaning, **travel** is a
noncount noun. A person's **travels** are the
time he or she spends traveling, especially
in foreign countries and for pleasure: *air/
rail/space travel* ◆ *Foreign travel is very
popular these days.* ◆ *The book is about her
travels around Europe.*

journey a long and often difficult trip from
one place to another: *It was a dangerous
journey across the mountains.* ◆ *They
continued their journey on foot.*

expedition a long, organized trip to find out
about a place or to do something special:
He led the first expedition to the North Pole.
◆ *She made two expeditions to Brazil to
study the wild plants.*

voyage a long trip by water or in space: *The
Titantic sank on its first voyage.* ◆ *The
spacecraft began its voyage to Jupiter.*

trip² 🔈 /trɪp/ *verb* (**trips, trip·ping, tripped**)
to hit your foot against something so that you
fall or almost fall: *She tripped over the step.*

trip someone up to make someone fall or
almost fall: *He put out his foot and tripped me up.*

tri·ple /ˈtrɪpl/ *adjective*
with three parts, happening three times, or
containing three times as much as usual: *a triple
murder* (= in which three people were killed)
▸ **tri·ple** *verb* (**tri·ples, tri·pling, tri·pled**)
to become or to make something three times
bigger: *Sales have tripled this year.*

tri·umph /ˈtraɪʌmf/ *noun* [*count, noncount*]
great success: *The race ended in triumph for his
team.*

tri·um·phant /traɪˈʌmfənt/ *adjective*
very happy because you have won or
succeeded at something
▸ **tri·um·phant·ly** /traɪˈʌmfəntli/ *adverb*: *The
winning team ran triumphantly around the
stadium.*

triv·i·al /ˈtrɪviəl/ *adjective*
not important: *She gets angry about trivial
things.*

trol·ley /ˈtrɑli/ *noun* [*count*] (*plural* **trol·leys**)
an electric bus that runs along metal tracks
(called **RAILS**) in the road ⊃ **SYNONYM** **streetcar**

trom·bone /trɑmˈboʊn/ *noun* [*count*]
(**MUSIC**) a large musical instrument. You play it
by blowing and moving a long tube up and
down. ⊃ Look at the picture at **instrument**.

troop /trup/ *noun*
1 **troops** [*plural*] soldiers: *We sent packages to
U.S. troops.*
2 [*count*] a large group of people or animals: *a
troop of elephants*

tro·phy /ˈtroʊfi/ *noun*
[*count*] (*plural* **tro·phies**)
a thing, for example a
silver cup, that you
get when you win a
competition: *a tennis
trophy*

trophy

trop·i·cal /ˈtrɑpɪkl/
adjective
connected with, or
coming from the parts
of the world where it is
very hot and wet: *tropical fruit* ◆ *a tropical island*

the trop·ics /ðə ˈtrɑpɪks/ *noun* [*plural*]
(**GEOGRAPHY**) the part of the world where it is
very hot and wet

trot /trɑt/ *verb* (**trots, trot·ting, trot·ted**)
to run with short quick steps: *The horse trotted
along the road.*
▸ **trot** *noun* [*singular*]: *We rode at a steady trot.*

trou·ble¹ 🔑 /ˈtrʌbl/ *noun*
1 [count, noncount] a difficulty or problem: *We had a lot of **trouble** finding the book you wanted.*
2 [noncount] extra work or effort: *"Thanks for your help!" "Oh, it was **no trouble**."* ◆ *He **took the trouble** to thank everyone individually for their help.*
3 [count, noncount] a situation in which people are fighting or arguing: *There was trouble after the football game last Saturday.*
4 [noncount] (HEALTH) pain or illness: *He has heart trouble.*
be in trouble to have problems, for example because you have done something wrong: *I'll be in trouble if I'm home late again.*
get into trouble to get into a situation which is dangerous or in which you may be punished: *He got into trouble **with** the police.*
go to a lot of trouble to do extra work: *They went to a lot of trouble to help me.*

trou·ble² /ˈtrʌbl/ *verb* (trou·bles, trou·bling, trou·bled)
1 to worry someone: *I was troubled by the news.*
2 (formal) a word that you use when you need to disturb someone by asking them something: *I'm **sorry to trouble you**, but you're sitting in my seat.* ◑ SYNONYM **bother**

trou·ble·mak·er /ˈtrʌblˌmeɪkər/ *noun* [count]
a person who deliberately causes trouble

trou·ble·shoot·er /ˈtrʌblˌʃutər/ *noun* [count]
(BUSINESS) a person who helps to solve problems in a company or an organization
▶ **trou·ble·shoot·ing** /ˈtrʌblˌʃutɪŋ/ *noun* [noncount]

trough /trɔf/ *noun* [count]
a long, open container that holds food or water for animals

trou·sers /ˈtraʊzərz/ *noun* [plural] (formal)
a piece of clothing for your legs and the lower part of your body ◑ SYNONYM **pants**

trout /traʊt/ *noun* [count, noncount] (plural **trout**)
a fish that lives in rivers and that you can eat

tru·ant /ˈtruənt/ *noun* [count]
a child who stays away from school when they should be there

truce /trus/ *noun* [count]
an agreement to stop fighting for a short time

truck 🔑 /trʌk/ *noun*
[count]
a big vehicle for
carrying heavy
things: *a truck driver*

truck

true 🔑 /tru/ *adjective*
1 right or correct: *Is it **true that** you are leaving?* ◆ *Seattle is in Oregon: true or false?* ◑ ANTONYM **untrue, false**

2 real: *A true friend will always help you.* ◆ *It's a **true story** (= it really happened).* ◑ The noun is **truth**.
come true to happen in the way that you hoped or imagined: *Her dream came true.*

tru·ly /ˈtruli/ *adverb*
really: *I'm truly sorry.*
Yours truly (formal) words that you can use at the end of a formal letter before you write your name

trum·pet /ˈtrʌmpət/ *noun* [count]
(MUSIC) a musical instrument that is made of metal and that you blow ◑ Look at the picture at **instrument**.

trunk /trʌŋk/ *noun*
1 the thick part of a tree, which grows up from the ground ◑ Look at the picture at **tree**.
2 the part at the back of a car where you can put bags and boxes ◑ Look at the picture at **car**.
3 the long nose of an ELEPHANT (= a very large gray animal) ◑ Look at the picture at **elephant**.
4 a big, strong box for carrying things when you travel ◑ Look at **swim trunks**.

trust¹ 🔑 /trʌst/ *noun* [noncount]
the belief that someone is honest and good, and will not hurt you in any way: *He put his **trust in** God.*

trust² 🔑 /trʌst/ *verb* (trusts, trust·ing, trust·ed)
to believe that someone is honest and good, and will not hurt you in any way: *I just don't trust him.* ◆ *You can **trust** Pat **to** do the job well.*

trust·wor·thy /ˈtrʌstwərði/ *adjective*
A **trustworthy** person is someone that you can trust.

truth 🔑 /truθ/ *noun* [noncount, singular]
being true; what is true: *There is **no truth in** these rumors.* ◆ *We need to find out the **truth about** what happened.* ◆ *Are you **telling** me the truth?*

truth·ful /ˈtruθfl/ *adjective*
1 true: *a truthful answer*
2 A person who is **truthful** tells the truth.
▶ **truth·ful·ly** /ˈtruθfəli/ *adverb*: *You must answer me truthfully.*

try 🔑 /traɪ/ *verb* (tries, try·ing, tried, has tried)
1 to make an effort to do something: *I **tried to** remember her name, but I couldn't.* ◆ *I'm not sure if I can help you, but I'll try.*
2 to do, use, or test something in order to see how good or successful it is: *Have you ever tried Japanese food?* ◆ *If that doesn't work, try turning it off and then on again.*
3 to ask someone questions in a court of law to decide if they have done something wrong: *He was **tried for** murder.*
try and do something (informal) to try to do something: *I'll try and come early tomorrow.*

try something on to put on a piece of clothing to see if you like it and if it is big enough: *I tried the jeans on but they were too small.*

try something out to test something to find out if it is good enough: *I think I'll try out a new recipe tonight.*

▶ **try** *noun* [count] (*plural* **tries**): *I don't know if I can lift the box, but I'll give it a try.*

T-shirt /ˈtiʃərt/ *noun* [count]
a kind of shirt with short sleeves and no COLLAR (= the folded part that fits around the neck) ⊃ Look at the picture at **clothes**.

tsu·na·mi /tsuˈnɑmi/ *noun* [count] (*plural* **tsu·na·mis**)
(**GEOGRAPHY**) a very large wave in the ocean, usually caused by the sudden strong shaking of the ground (called an EARTHQUAKE)

tub /tʌb/ *noun* [count]
1 (*informal*) another word for **bathtub**
2 a round container: *a tub of margarine*

tub

— lid

Sunny Spread

tu·ba /ˈtubə/ *noun* [count]
(**MUSIC**) a large musical instrument that makes a low sound when you blow through it: *Frank plays the tuba in the band.* ⊃ Look at the picture at **instrument**.

tube /tub/ *noun* [count]
1 a long, thin pipe for liquid or gas
2 a long, thin, soft container with a hole and a covering (called a CAP) at one end: *a tube of toothpaste* ⊃ Look at the picture at **container**.

tuck /tʌk/ *verb* (**tucks, tuck·ing, tucked**)
1 to put or push the edges of something inside or under something else: *He tucked his shirt into his pants.*
2 to put something in a small place, especially to hide it or keep it safe: *She tucked the letter behind the books.*

tuck someone in to make someone feel comfortable in bed by pulling the covers around them: *I'll come up later and tuck you in.*

Tues·day /ˈtuzdeɪ; ˈtuzdi/ *noun* [count, noncount] (abbreviation **Tues.**)
the day of the week after Monday and before Wednesday

tuft /tʌft/ *noun* [count]
a small amount of something, such as hair or grass, growing together

tug¹ /tʌg/ *verb* (**tugs, tug·ging, tugged**)
to pull something hard and quickly: *I tugged at the rope, and it broke.*

tug² /tʌg/ *noun* [count]
1 a sudden hard pull: *The little girl gave my hand a tug.*

2 (also **tug·boat** /ˈtʌgboʊt/) a small, strong boat that pulls big ships

tu·i·tion /tuˈɪʃn/ *noun* [noncount]
money that you pay in order to take classes at a college, university, or private school: *He works part-time to help pay his college tuition.*

tu·lip /ˈtuləp/ *noun* [count]
a flower that comes in spring and is shaped like a cup ⊃ Look at the picture at **flower**.

tum·ble /ˈtʌmbl/ *verb* (**tum·bles, tum·bling, tum·bled**)
to fall suddenly: *He tumbled down the steps.*

tum·bler /ˈtʌmblər/ *noun* [count]
a tall glass with straight sides, a flat bottom, and no handle

tum·my /ˈtʌmi/ *noun* [count] (*plural* **tum·mies**) (*informal*)
the part of your body between your chest and your legs ⊃ SYNONYM **stomach**

tu·mor /ˈtumər/ *noun* [count]
(**HEALTH**) a group of cells in the body that is not growing normally because of a disease: *a brain tumor*

tu·na /ˈtunə/ *noun* [count, noncount] (*plural* **tu·na**)
a large fish that lives in the ocean and that you can eat

tune¹ /tun/ *noun* [count]
(**MUSIC**) a group of musical notes that make a nice sound when you play or sing them together: *I know the tune, but I don't know the words.*

tune² /tun/ *verb* (**tunes, tun·ing, tuned**)
(**MUSIC**) to make small changes to a musical instrument so that it makes the right sounds: *She tuned her guitar.*

tune in to listen to a radio program or watch a television program: *Tune in at the same time next week for the next episode.*

tun·nel /ˈtʌnl/ *noun* [count]
a long hole under the ground or ocean for a road or railroad: *The train went through a tunnel.*
▶ **tun·nel** *verb* (**tun·nels, tun·nel·ing, tun·neled**)
to dig a **tunnel** under or through the ground

tur·ban /ˈtərbən/ *noun* [count]
a covering that some men wear on their heads for religious reasons. You make a **turban** by folding a long piece of material around and around.

tur·key /ˈtərki/ *noun* [count] (*plural* **tur·keys**)
a big bird that people keep on farms, or the meat of this bird. People eat **turkey** at Thanksgiving.

turkey

turn¹ 🔊 /tərn/ *verb* (**turns**, **turn·ing**, **turned**)
1 to move around, or to move something around: *The wheels are turning.* ◆ *Turn the key.* ◆ *She turned around and walked toward the door.*
2 to move in a different direction: *Turn left at the traffic lights.*
3 to become different: *The weather has turned cold.*
4 to make someone or something change: *The sun turned her hair blond.*
5 to find a certain page in a book: *Please turn to page 97.*
turn someone away to not allow someone to go into a place: *The theater had to turn away some people because there were no tickets left.*
turn something down
1 to say "no" to what someone wants to do or to give you: *They offered me the job, but I turned it down.*
2 to make something produce less sound or heat by moving a switch: *I'm too hot – can you turn the heat down?*
turn something in to give your work to a teacher: *I have to turn in my essay by Wednesday.*
turn into something to become different; to change someone or something into something different: *Water turns into ice when it gets very cold.*
turn something off to move the handle or switch that controls something, so that it stops: *Turn the faucet off.* ◆ *She turned off the television.*
turn something on to move the handle or switch that controls something, so that it starts: *Could you turn the light on?*
turn out to be something in the end: *It turned out to be a fantastic day.*
turn something out to switch off a light: *Can you turn the lights out before you leave?*
turn over; **turn something over** to move so that the other side is on top; to move something in this way: *She turned over and went back to sleep.* ◆ *If you turn over the page you'll find the answers on the other side.*
turn to someone or **something** to go to someone or something to get help or advice
turn up
1 (used about a person) to arrive: *Has David turned up yet?*
2 to be found: *I lost my glasses last week and they haven't turned up yet.*
turn something up to make something produce more sound or heat by moving a switch: *Turn up the TV – I can't hear it.*

turn² 🔊 /tərn/ *noun* [count]
1 the action of turning something around: *Give the screw a few turns.*
2 a change of direction: *Take a left turn at the end of this road.*
3 the time when you can or should do something: *It's your turn to do the laundry!*

in turn one after the other: *I spoke to each of the students in turn.*
take turns to do something one after the other: *You can't both use the computer at the same time. Why don't you take turns?*

turn·ing point /'tərnɪŋ pɔɪnt/ *noun* [count]
a time when an important change happens: *Getting that job was a turning point in her career as a journalist.*

tur·nip /'tərnəp/ *noun* [count]
a round, white vegetable that grows under the ground

turn·pike /'tərnpaɪk/ *noun* [count]
a wide, fast road that drivers have to pay money to use

turn sig·nal /'tərn sɪgnəl/ *noun* [count]
the flashing light on a car that shows that it is going to turn right or left

tur·quoise /'tərkwɔɪz/ *adjective*
having a bright color between blue and green
▶ **tur·quoise** *noun* [noncount]

tur·tle /'tərtl/ *noun* [count]
an animal that lives mainly in the water, moves slowly, and has a hard shell on its back

tusk /tʌsk/ *noun* [count]
a long, pointed tooth that grows beside the mouth of an ELEPHANT (= a very big gray animal that lives in Africa and Asia) ➲ Look at the picture at **elephant**.

tu·tor¹ /'tutər/ *noun* [count]
a teacher who teaches one person or a small group in a particular subject

tu·tor² /'tutər/ *verb* (**tu·tors**, **tu·tor·ing**, **tu·tored**)
to give one student or a small group of students extra help in a particular subject: *He tutors students in mathematics.*

tux·e·do /tʌk'sidoʊ/ *noun* [count] (*plural* **tux·e·dos**)
a black or white jacket and pants that a man can wear to a formal dinner, a wedding, or other occasion

TV 🔊 /ˌti'vi/ *noun* [count, noncount]
television: *All rooms have a large TV.* ◆ *What's on TV tonight?* ◆ *cable TV*

tweez·ers /'twizərz/ *noun* [plural]
a small tool made of two pieces of metal joined at one end. You use **tweezers** for holding or pulling out very small things: *She pulled the splinter out of her finger with a pair of tweezers.*

tweezers

twelfth /twɛlfθ/ *pronoun*, *adjective*, *adverb*, *noun* [count]
12th

twelve 🔑 /twɛlv/ *number*
12

twen·ty 🔑 /'twɛnti/ *number*
1 20
2 the twenties [*plural*] the numbers, years, or temperatures between 20 and 29
in your twenties between the ages of 20 and 29
▶ **twen·ti·eth** /'twɛntiəθ/ *adjective, adverb, pronoun, noun* [*count*]
20th

twice 🔑 /twaɪs/ *adverb*
two times: *I've been to Philadelphia twice.* ◆ *He ate twice as much as I did.*

twig /twɪg/ *noun* [*count*]
a small, thin branch of a tree

twi·light /'twaɪlaɪt/ *noun* [*noncount*]
the time after the sun has gone down and before it gets completely dark ⟳ Look at **dusk**.

twin /twɪn/ *noun* [*count*]
1 one of two people who have the same mother and were born at the same time: *David and John are twins.* ◆ *I have a twin sister.*
2 one of two things that are the same: *a room with twin beds*

twin·kle /'twɪŋkl/ *verb* (twin·kles, twin·kling, twin·kled)
to shine with a small, bright light that comes and goes: *Stars twinkled in the night sky.*

twirl /twɜrl/ *verb* (twirls, twirl·ing, twirled)
to turn around and around quickly; to make someone or something do this: *She twirled around in front of the mirror.*

twist¹ 🔑 /twɪst/ *verb* (twists, twist·ing, twist·ed)
1 to change the shape of something by turning it in different directions; to turn in many directions: *She **twisted** the metal **into** strange shapes.* ◆ *The path **twists and turns** through the forest.*
2 to turn something with your hand: *Twist the lid off the jar.*
3 to turn something around another object many times: *They **twisted** the sheets **into** a rope, and escaped through the window.*
4 to hurt part of your body by suddenly turning it in a way that is not natural: *She fell and twisted her ankle.*

twist² *noun* [*count*]
1 the action of turning something with your hand, or of turning part of your body: *She gave the handle a hard twist.*

2 a change in a story or situation that you do not expect: *It's a story with a twist at the end, which surprised us all.*
3 a place where a road or river bends: *The car followed the **twists and turns** of the mountain road.*

twitch /twɪtʃ/ *verb* (twitch·es, twitch·ing, twitched)
to make a sudden quick movement with a part of your body: *Rabbits twitch their noses.*
▶ **twitch** *noun* [*count*] (*plural* **twitch·es**): *He has a nervous twitch.*

two 🔑 /tu/ *number*
2
in two into two pieces: *The cup fell on the floor and broke in two.*

ty·ing form of **tie¹**

type¹ 🔑 /taɪp/ *noun*
1 [*count*] a group of things that are the same in some way: *An almond is a **type of** nut.* ◆ *What type of music do you like?* ⟳ **SYNONYM kind, sort**
2 [*noncount*] the letters that a machine makes on paper: *The type was so small I couldn't read it.*

type² 🔑 /taɪp/ *verb* (types, typ·ing, typed)
to write something using a machine that has keys, such as a computer or a **TYPEWRITER**: *Yesterday I typed another chapter of my book.* ◆ *Can you type?*

type·writ·er /'taɪpraɪtər/ *noun* [*count*]
a machine with keys that you use for writing: *an old electric typewriter*

ty·phoon /taɪ'fun/ *noun* [*count*]
(**GEOGRAPHY**) a violent storm with strong winds in a hot country ⟳ Look at the note at **storm¹**.

typ·i·cal 🔑 /'tɪpɪkl/ *adjective*
Something that is **typical** is a good example of its kind: *It is a typical small town.*
▶ **typ·i·cal·ly** /'tɪpɪkli/ *adverb*: *The workers here typically earn about $15 per hour.*

ty·po /'taɪpoʊ/ (*plural* **ty·pos**)
a small mistake in something that has been typed: *Check for any typos in your résumé before you send it.* ⟳ Look at **misprint**.

ty·rant /'taɪrənt/ *noun* [*count*]
(**POLITICS**) a person with a lot of power, who uses it in a cruel way
▶ **ty·ran·ni·cal** /tɪ'rænɪkl/ *adjective*: *He was a tyrannical ruler.*

U u

U, u /yu/ *noun* [count, noncount] (*plural* U's, u's /yuz/)
the twenty-first letter of the English alphabet: *"Ugly" begins with a "U."*

UFO /ˌyu ɛf ˈoʊ/ *abbreviation* (*plural* UFOs)
a strange object that some people think they have seen in the sky and that may come from another planet. **UFO** is short for "unidentified flying object."

ug·ly 🔑 /ˈʌgli/ *adjective* (**ug·li·er, ug·li·est**)
not pleasant to look at: *an ugly face* • *The house was really ugly.* ⊃ ANTONYM **beautiful**

ul·cer /ˈʌlsər/ *noun* [count]
(HEALTH) a painful area on your skin or inside your body: *a mouth ulcer*

ul·ti·mate AWL /ˈʌltəmət/ *adjective*
happening at the end of a long process: *Our ultimate goal is independence.*

ul·ti·ma·tum /ˌʌltəˈmeɪtəm/ *noun* [count]
a warning to someone that, if they do not do what you ask, you will punish them: *The landlord gave them an ultimatum: pay the rent or get out of the apartment.*

ul·tra·vi·o·let /ˌʌltrəˈvaɪələt/ *adjective*
(abbreviation **UV**)
(PHYSICS) **Ultraviolet** light cannot be seen, and makes your skin darker: *You must protect your skin from harmful ultraviolet rays.*

um·brel·la /ʌmˈbrɛlə/ *noun* [count]
a thing that you hold over your head to keep you dry when it rains: *It started to rain, so I put my umbrella up.*

um·pire /ˈʌmpaɪər/ *noun* [count]
(SPORTS) a person who watches a game such as baseball or TENNIS, to make sure the players follow the rules ⊃ Look at **referee**.
▸ **um·pire** *verb* (**um·pires, um·pir·ing, um·pired**): *The game was umpired by Jones.*

Prefix

un-

not; the opposite of: *unhappy* • *untrue* (= not true) • *unlock* • *undress* (= to take clothes off)

the UN /ðə ˌyu ˈɛn/ short for **the United Nations**

un·a·ble 🔑 /ʌnˈeɪbl/ *adjective*
not able to do something: *John is unable to come to the meeting because he is sick.* ⊃ ANTONYM **able**
⊃ The noun is **inability**.

un·ac·cept·a·ble /ˌʌnəkˈsɛptəbl/ *adjective*
If something is **unacceptable**, you cannot accept or allow it: *This behavior is completely unacceptable.* ⊃ ANTONYM **acceptable**

u·nan·i·mous /yuˈnænəməs/ *adjective*
with the agreement of every person: *The decision was unanimous.*

un·armed /ˌʌnˈɑrmd/ *adjective*
not carrying a gun or any weapon: *an unarmed police officer* ⊃ ANTONYM **armed**

un·at·trac·tive /ˌʌnəˈtræktɪv/ *adjective*
not nice to look at ⊃ ANTONYM **attractive**

un·a·void·a·ble /ˌʌnəˈvɔɪdəbl/ *adjective*
If something is **unavoidable**, you cannot stop it or get away from it: *This tragic accident was unavoidable.* ⊃ ANTONYM **avoidable**

un·a·ware AWL /ˌʌnəˈwɛr/ *adjective*
not knowing about or not noticing someone or something: *I was unaware of the danger.* ⊃ ANTONYM **aware**

un·bear·a·ble /ʌnˈbɛrəbl/ *adjective*
If something is **unbearable**, you cannot accept it because it is so bad: *Everyone left the room because the noise was unbearable.*
▸ **un·bear·a·bly** /ʌnˈbɛrəbli/ *adverb*: *It was unbearably hot.*

un·be·liev·a·ble /ˌʌnbɪˈlivəbl/ *adjective*
very surprising or difficult to believe ⊃ SYNONYM **incredible**

un·bi·ased AWL /ʌnˈbaɪəst/ *adjective*
fair and not affected by your own or someone else's opinions, needs, etc.: *We need an unbiased selection process.* ⊃ ANTONYM **biased**

un·born /ˌʌnˈbɔrn/ *adjective*
not yet born: *her unborn child*

un·cer·tain /ʌnˈsɜrtn/ *adjective*
not sure; not decided: *I'm uncertain about what to do.* • *an uncertain future* ⊃ SYNONYM **unsure** ⊃ ANTONYM **certain**
▸ **un·cer·tain·ty** /ʌnˈsɜrtnti/ *noun* [count, noncount] (*plural* **un·cer·tain·ties**): *This decision should put an end to all the uncertainty.*

un·cle 🔑 /ˈʌŋkl/ *noun* [count]
the brother of your mother or father, or the husband of your aunt: *Uncle John*

un·clear /ˌʌnˈklɪr/ *adjective*
1 not easy to see, hear, know, or understand: *It is unclear what the results will show.*
2 not completely understanding something; not sure about something: *I'm unclear about what you want me to do.* ⊃ ANTONYM **clear**

un·com·fort·a·ble 🔑 /ʌnˈkʌmfərtəbl/ *adjective*
1 not pleasant to wear, sit on, lie on, etc.: *The chair was hard and uncomfortable.* ⊃ ANTONYM **comfortable**

tʃ **chin**   dʒ **June**   v **van**   θ **thin**   ð **then**   s **so**   z **zoo**   ʃ **she**

2 feeling worried or embarrased, or making someone feel this way: *I felt really uncomfortable when they started arguing in front of me.* ✦ *There was an uncomfortable silence.*
▸ **un·com·fort·a·bly** /ʌnˈkʌmfərtəbli/ *adverb*: *The room was uncomfortably hot.*

un·com·mon /ʌnˈkɑmən/ *adjective*
not usual: *This tree is uncommon in America.* ⊃ **SYNONYM rare** ⊃ **ANTONYM common**

un·con·scious 🔑 /ʌnˈkɑnʃəs/ *adjective*
1 If you are **unconscious**, you are in a kind of sleep and you do not know what is happening: *She hit her head, and was unconscious for three days.*
2 If you are **unconscious** of something, you do not know about it: *Mike seemed unconscious that I was watching him.* ⊃ **ANTONYM conscious**
▸ **un·con·scious·ly** /ʌnˈkɑnʃəsli/ *adverb*
▸ **un·con·scious·ness** /ʌnˈkɑnʃəsnəs/ *noun*
[*noncount*]: *She slipped into unconsciousness.*

un·con·sti·tu·tion·al **AWL** /ˌʌnkɑnstəˈtuʃnl/ *adjective*
(**POLITICS**) not allowed by the basic laws or rules (the **CONSTITUTION**) of a country or organization

un·con·trol·la·ble /ˌʌnkənˈtroʊləbl/ *adjective*
If a feeling is **uncontrollable**, you cannot control or stop it: *I suddenly got an uncontrollable urge to sneeze.*
▸ **un·con·trol·la·bly** /ˌʌnkənˈtroʊləbli/ *adverb*: *He started laughing uncontrollably.*

un·con·ven·tion·al **AWL** /ˌʌnkənˈvɛnʃənl/ *adjective*
not following what is considered normal or acceptable by most people: *She dresses in a very unconventional way.* ⊃ **ANTONYM conventional**

un·con·vinced **AWL** /ˌʌnkənˈvɪnst/ *adjective*
not believing or not certain that something is true: *She seemed unconvinced by their promises.* ⊃ **ANTONYM convinced**

un·cool /ʌnˈkul/ *adjective* (*informal*)
not considered acceptable or fashionable: *I'm not wearing those shoes – they're so uncool.* ⊃ **ANTONYM cool**

un·count·a·ble noun /ˌʌnˌkaʊntəbl ˈnaʊn/ *noun* [*count*] (**ENGLISH LANGUAGE ARTS**) another word for **noncount noun**

un·cov·er /ʌnˈkʌvər/ *verb* (**un·cov·ers**, **un·cov·er·ing**, **un·cov·ered**)
1 to take something from on top of another thing: *Uncover the pan and cook the soup for 30 minutes.* ⊃ **ANTONYM cover**
2 to find out something that was secret: *Police uncovered a plot to steal the painting.*

un·de·ni·a·ble **AWL** /ˌʌndɪˈnaɪəbl/ *adjective*
clear, true, or certain: *It is undeniable that girls mature faster than boys.*

un·der 🔑 /ˈʌndər/ *preposition, adverb*
1 in or to a place that is lower than or below something: *The cat is under the table.* ✦ *We sailed under the bridge.* ✦ *The boat filled with water, then went under.*
2 less than something: *If you are under 16, you are not allowed to drive a car.*
3 covered by something: *I'm wearing a T-shirt under my sweater.* ⊃ **SYNONYM underneath**
4 controlled by someone or something: *The team is playing well under the new captain.*
5 in a particular state or condition: *The building is still under construction* (= being built).

Prefix

under-
1 (in nouns and adjectives) below: *underwater* ✦ *underwear* (= clothes that you wear under your other clothes)
2 (in nouns) lower in age, level, or position: *an undergraduate*
3 (in adjectives and verbs) not enough: *undercooked* ✦ *underpaid*

un·der·age /ˌʌndərˈeɪdʒ/ *adjective*
too young to be allowed by law to do something: *underage drinking*

un·der·cov·er /ˌʌndərˈkʌvər/ *adjective*
working or happening secretly: *an undercover detective*

un·der·dog /ˈʌndərdɔg/ *noun* [*count*]
a person, team, etc. that is weaker than the others, and is not expected to be successful: *The underdogs scored at the last minute and won the game.*

un·der·es·ti·mate **AWL** /ˌʌndərˈɛstəmeɪt/ *verb*
(**un·der·es·ti·mates**, **un·der·es·ti·mat·ing**, **un·der·es·ti·mat·ed**)
to think that someone or something is smaller, weaker, less important, etc. than they really are: *Don't underestimate her – she's actually very smart.* ✦ *We underestimated how much food we would need.* ⊃ **ANTONYM overestimate**

un·der·go **AWL** /ˌʌndərˈgoʊ/ *verb* (**un·der·goes**, **un·der·go·ing**, **un·der·went** /ˌʌndərˈwɛnt/, has **un·der·gone** /ˌʌndərˈgɔn; ˌʌndərˈgɑn/)
to have a difficult or unpleasant experience: *She is in the hospital undergoing an operation.*

un·der·grad·u·ate /ˌʌndərˈgrædʒuət/ *noun* [*count*]
a student in college who is studying for their first degree (called a **BACHELOR'S DEGREE**) ⊃ Look at **graduate**[1].

un·der·ground 🔑 /ˈʌndərgraʊnd/ *adjective*
under the ground: *an underground parking garage*

▶ **un·der·ground** /ˌʌndərˈɡraʊnd/ *adverb*: *Moles spend most of their time underground.*

un·der·growth /ˈʌndərɡroʊθ/ *noun* [noncount]
bushes and other plants that grow under trees: *There was a path through the undergrowth.*

un·der·line /ˈʌndərlaɪn/ *verb* (un·der·lines, un·der·lin·ing, un·der·lined)
to draw a line under a word or words. This sentence is underlined.

un·der·ly·ing **AWL** /ˈʌndərˌlaɪɪŋ/ *adjective*
important but hidden: *the underlying cause of the disaster*

un·der·neath /ˌʌndərˈniθ/ *preposition, adverb*
under or below something: *The dog sat underneath the table.* ◆ *She wore a black jacket with a red sweater underneath.*

un·der·pants /ˈʌndərpænts/ *noun* [plural]
a piece of clothing that men or women wear under pants, a skirt, etc.

un·der·pass /ˈʌndərpæs/ *noun* [count] (plural un·der·pass·es)
a road or path that goes under another road ⊃ Look at **overpass**.

un·der·shirt /ˈʌndərˌʃɜrt/ *noun* [count]
a piece of clothing that you wear under your other clothes on the top part of your body

un·der·stand 🔑 /ˌʌndərˈstænd/ *verb*
(un·der·stands, un·der·stand·ing, un·der·stood /ˌʌndərˈstʊd/, has un·der·stood)
1 to know what something means or why something happens: *I didn't understand what the teacher said.* ◆ *He doesn't understand Spanish.* ◆ *I don't understand why you're so angry.*
2 (formal) to know something because someone has told you about it: *I understand that you would like to see the manager.* ⊃ **SYNONYM believe**
make yourself understood to make people understand you: *My Italian isn't very good, but I can usually make myself understood.*

un·der·stand·ing¹ /ˌʌndərˈstændɪŋ/ *noun* [noncount, singular]
knowing about something: *He has a good **understanding** of computers.*

un·der·stand·ing² /ˌʌndərˈstændɪŋ/ *adjective*
ready to listen to other people's problems and try to understand them: *My parents are very understanding.* ⊃ **SYNONYM sympathetic**

un·der·state·ment /ˈʌndərsteɪtmənt/ *noun* [count]
something you say that makes something seem less important, large, etc. than it really is: *It would be an understatement to say the Sahara Desert is hot.*

un·der·stood form of **understand**

un·der·tak·er /ˈʌndərteɪkər/ *noun* [count]
a person whose job is to organize FUNERALS (= the time when dead people are buried or burned)

un·der·wa·ter 🔑 /ˌʌndərˈwɔtər/ *adjective, adverb*
below the surface of water: *Can you swim underwater?* ◆ *an underwater camera*

un·der·wear 🔑 /ˈʌndərwɛr/ *noun* [noncount]
clothes that you wear next to your body, under your other clothes

un·der·weight /ˌʌndərˈweɪt/ *adjective*
weighing less than is normal or correct ⊃ **ANTONYM overweight** ⊃ Look at the note at **thin**.

un·der·went **AWL** form of **undergo**

un·do /ʌnˈdu/ *verb* (un·does /ʌnˈdʌz/, un·do·ing, un·did /ʌnˈdɪd/, has un·done /ʌnˈdʌn/)
to open something that was tied or fastened: *I can't undo this knot.* ◆ *to undo a jacket*

un·done /ʌnˈdʌn/ *adjective*
not tied or fastened: *Your shoelaces are undone.*

un·doubt·ed·ly /ʌnˈdaʊt̬ədli/ *adverb*
certainly; without doubt: *She is undoubtedly very intelligent.*

un·dress /ʌnˈdrɛs/ *verb* (un·dress·es, un·dress·ing, un·dressed)
to take clothes off yourself or another person: *He undressed and got into bed.* ◆ *She undressed her baby.* ⊃ **ANTONYM dress**
▶ **un·dressed** /ʌnˈdrɛst/ *adjective*: *I got undressed and took a shower.*

un·eas·y /ʌnˈizi/ *adjective*
worried that something is wrong: *I started to feel uneasy when the children were late coming home.*
▶ **un·eas·i·ly** /ʌnˈizəli/ *adverb*: *She looked uneasily around the room.*

un·ed·u·cat·ed /ʌnˈɛdʒəkeɪt̬əd/ *adjective*
having had little or no formal education: *an uneducated, but very intelligent woman* ⊃ **ANTONYM educated**

un·em·ployed /ˌʌnɪmˈplɔɪd/ *adjective*
If you are **unemployed**, you can work but you do not have a job: *She has been unemployed for over a year.* ◆ *a new training program for **the unemployed** (= people who do not have a job)*

un·em·ploy·ment 🔑 /ˌʌnɪmˈplɔɪmənt/ *noun* [noncount]
1 when there are not enough jobs for the people who want to work: *If the factory closes, unemployment in the town will increase.* ⊃ **ANTONYM employment**
2 money that the government pays to people after they lose their jobs: *people living on unemployment*

un·e·qual /ˌʌnˈikwəl/ *adjective*
different in size, amount, value, or level as
something or someone else: *an unequal
distribution of power* ⟩ ANTONYM **equal**

un·e·ven /ˌʌnˈivən/ *adjective*
not smooth or flat: *We had to drive slowly
because the road was so uneven.* ⟩ ANTONYM **even**

un·ex·pect·ed /ˌʌnɪkˈspɛktəd/ *adjective*
surprising because you did not expect it: *an
unexpected visit*
▶ **un·ex·pect·ed·ly** /ˌʌnɪkˈspɛktədli/ *adverb*: *She
arrived unexpectedly.*

un·fair /ˌʌnˈfɛr/ *adjective*
Something that is **unfair** does not treat people
in the same way or in the right way: *It was **unfair**
to give chocolates to some of the children and not
to the others.* ⟩ ANTONYM **fair**
▶ **un·fair·ly** /ˌʌnˈfɛrli/ *adverb*: *He left his job
because the boss was treating him unfairly.*

un·faith·ful /ˌʌnˈfeɪθfl/ *adjective*
having a sexual relationship with someone who
is not your husband, wife, or partner ⟩ ANTONYM
faithful

un·fa·mil·iar /ˌʌnfəˈmɪlyər/ *adjective*
that you do not know; strange: *I woke up in an
unfamiliar room.* • *I'm **unfamiliar with** this
author's work.* ⟩ ANTONYM **familiar**

un·fash·ion·a·ble /ˌʌnˈfæʃnˈəbl/ *adjective*
not popular at a particular time: *unfashionable
clothes* ⟩ ANTONYM **fashionable**

un·fas·ten /ˌʌnˈfæsn/ *verb* (un·fas·tens,
un·fas·ten·ing, un·fas·tened)
to open something that was tied or attached: *to
unfasten your seatbelt* ⟩ ANTONYM **fasten**

un·fin·ished /ˌʌnˈfɪnɪʃt/ *adjective*
not complete; not finished: *We have some
unfinished business to discuss.*

un·fit /ˌʌnˈfɪt/ *adjective*
1 not good enough or not right for something:
*This house is **unfit for** people to live in.*
2 not healthy or strong: *She doesn't get enough
exercise – that's why she's so unfit.* ⟩ ANTONYM **fit**

un·fold /ʌnˈfoʊld/ *verb* (un·folds, un·fold·ing,
un·fold·ed)
to open something to make it flat; to open out
and become flat: *Marie unfolded the newspaper,
and started to read.* • *The sofa unfolds to make a
bed.* ⟩ ANTONYM **fold**

un·for·tu·nate /ʌnˈfɔrtʃənət/ *adjective*
not lucky: *It's unfortunate that you were sick on
your birthday.* ⟩ ANTONYM **fortunate**

un·for·tu·nate·ly /ʌnˈfɔrtʃənətli/ *adverb*
a word that you use to show that you are not
happy about a situation or fact: *I'd like to give
you some money, but unfortunately I don't have
any.* ⟩ ANTONYM **fortunately**

un·friend·ly /ˌʌnˈfrɛndli/ *adjective*
not friendly; not kind or helpful to other people
⟩ ANTONYM **friendly**

un·grate·ful /ʌnˈɡreɪtfl/ *adjective*
If you are **ungrateful**, you do not show thanks
when someone helps you or gives you
something: *Don't be so ungrateful! I tried hard to
find the right present for your birthday.* ⟩
ANTONYM **grateful**

un·hap·py /ʌnˈhæpi/ *adjective* (un·hap·pi·er,
un·hap·pi·est)
not happy: *He was very unhappy after his wife left
him.* ⟩ SYNONYM **sad** ⟩ ANTONYM **happy**
▶ **un·hap·pi·ly** /ʌnˈhæpəli/ *adverb*: *"I failed the
exam," she said unhappily.*
▶ **un·hap·pi·ness** /ʌnˈhæpinəs/ *noun* [noncount]:
John had a lot of unhappiness in his life.

un·health·y /ʌnˈhɛlθi/ *adjective* (un·health·i·er,
un·health·i·est) (HEALTH)
1 not well; often sick: *an unhealthy child*
2 that can make you sick: *unhealthy food* ⟩
ANTONYM **healthy**

un·help·ful /ʌnˈhɛlpfl/ *adjective*
not wanting to help someone; not useful: *I spoke
to a ticket agent about changing our flight, but
she was completely unhelpful.* ⟩ ANTONYM **helpful**

u·ni·corn /ˈyunəkɔrn/ *noun* [count]
an animal that only exists in stories. It looks like
a white horse with one horn on its head.

u·ni·form¹ AWL /ˈyunəfɔrm/ *noun* [count]
the special clothes that some people in the same
job, team, etc. wear: *Police officers wear blue
uniforms.*

u·ni·form² AWL /ˈyunəfɔrm/ *adjective*
not changing; always the same shape, size,
level, etc.: *We need to establish a uniform
standard for testing new products.*

un·im·por·tant /ˌʌnɪmˈpɔrtnt/ *adjective*
not important ⟩ ANTONYM **important**

un·in·hab·it·ed /ˌʌnɪnˈhæbətəd/ *adjective*
where no one lives: *an uninhabited island*

un·ion /ˈyunyən/ *noun*
1 [noncount, singular] coming together: *the union
of the groups into one organization*
2 [count] (POLITICS) a group of people or
countries that have joined together: *the
European Union*
3 [count] an organization for people who do the
same type of work. **Unions** try to get better pay
and working conditions for their members: *the
National Writers' Union* ⟩ SYNONYM **labor union**

u·nique AWL /yuˈnik/ *adjective*
not like anyone or anything else: *Everyone in the
world is unique.*

u·ni·sex /'yunəsɛks/ *adjective*
designed for and used by both men and women: *a unisex bathroom*

u·nit /'yunɪt/ *noun* [count]
1 one complete thing or group that may be part of something larger: *The book has twelve units.*
2 a measurement: *A foot is a unit of length, and a pound is a unit of weight.*

u·nite /yu'naɪt/ *verb* (u·nites, u·nit·ing, u·nit·ed)
to join together to do something together; to put two things together: *We must unite to defeat our enemies.*

u·nit·ed /yu'naɪṭəd/ *adjective*
1 (used about countries) joined together: *the United States of America*
2 (used about people or groups) working together to achieve the same things: *We need to become a more united team.*

the U·nit·ed Na·tions /ðə yu,naɪṭəd 'neɪʃnz/ *noun* [singular] (abbreviation **the UN**)
(**POLITICS**) the organization that tries to stop world problems and to give help to countries that need it

the U·nit·ed States /ðə yu,naɪṭəd 'steɪts/ (also **the U·nit·ed States of A·mer·i·ca** /ðə yu,naɪṭəd ,steɪts əv ə'mɛrɪkə/) *noun* [singular] (abbreviation **the U.S.** or **the U.S.A.**)
a large country in North America made up of 50 states and the District of Columbia

u·ni·ver·sal /,yunə'vərsl/ *adjective*
connected with, done by, or for everyone: *The environment is a universal issue.*
▶ **u·ni·ver·sal·ly** /,yunə'vərsəli/ *adverb*: *to be universally accepted* (= accepted everywhere and by everyone)

the u·ni·verse /ðə 'yunəvərs/ *noun* [singular]
the earth and all the stars, planets, and everything else in space

u·ni·ver·si·ty /,yunə'vərsəṭi/ *noun* [count]
(*plural* u·ni·ver·si·ties)
a place where people go to study more difficult subjects after they have left high school or college: *the University of Michigan* • *My sister was accepted to one of the best universities in the country.* ⊃ Look at the note at **higher education**.

Which word?

University or college?
■ **Universities** and **colleges** both offer courses for students who are studying for their first degree (a **bachelor's degree**).
■ **Universities** also offer courses for people who are studying for more advanced degrees, for example a **master's degree** or a **Ph.D.**
■ **College** is often the word we use in general conversation when we are talking about a

place of higher education, even when the place we are talking about is a university: *a college student* • *"Where did you go to college?" "Ohio State University."*

un·just /,ʌn'dʒʌst/ *adjective* (formal)
not fair or right: *This tax is unjust, because poor people pay as much as rich people.* ⊃ **SYNONYM** **unfair**

un·jus·ti·fied **AWL** /,ʌn'dʒʌstəfaɪd/ *adjective*
not fair or necessary: *Her criticism was totally unjustified.*

un·kind /,ʌn'kaɪnd/ *adjective*
unpleasant and not friendly: *It was unkind of you to laugh at her.* ⊃ **ANTONYM** **kind**

un·known /,ʌn'noʊn/ *adjective*
1 that you do not know: *She left the job for unknown reasons.*
2 not famous: *an unknown actor* ⊃ **ANTONYM** **famous, well-known**

un·lead·ed /,ʌn'lɛdəd/ *adjective*
Unleaded fuel does not contain any **LEAD** (= a soft, heavy, gray metal).

un·less /ən'lɛs/ *conjunction*
if not; except if: *You will be late unless you leave now.* • *Unless you work, harder you'll fail the exam.*

un·like /ʌn'laɪk/ *preposition*
1 different from: *She is unlike anyone I've ever met.*
2 not typical of someone or something: *It's unlike him to be late. I wonder where he is.* ⊃ **ANTONYM** **like**

un·like·ly /ʌn'laɪkli/ *adjective* (un·like·li·er, un·like·li·est)
If something is **unlikely**, it will probably not happen: *It is unlikely that it will rain.* • *He is unlikely to pass the exam.* ⊃ **ANTONYM** **likely**

un·load /,ʌn'loʊd/ *verb* (un·loads, un·load·ing, un·load·ed)
to take things that have been carried somewhere off or out of a car, truck, ship, or airplane: *I unloaded the suitcases from the car.* • *They unloaded the ship at the dock.* ⊃ **ANTONYM** **load**

un·lock /,ʌn'lɑk/ *verb* (un·locks, un·lock·ing, un·locked)
to open something with a key: *I unlocked the door, and went in.* ⊃ **ANTONYM** **lock**

un·luck·y /ʌn'lʌki/ *adjective* (un·luck·i·er, un·luck·i·est)
having or bringing bad luck: *They were unlucky that it rained on their wedding day.* • *Some people think the number 13 is unlucky.* ⊃ **ANTONYM** **lucky**

un·mar·ried /,ʌn'mærɪd/ *adjective*
not married; without a husband or wife ⊃ **SYNONYM** **single**

un·mis·tak·a·ble /ˌʌnmɪˈsteɪkəbl/ *adjective*
If something is **unmistakable**, it is easy to recognize and will not be confused with anything else: *Her southern accent was unmistakable.*

un·nat·u·ral /ʌnˈnætʃərəl/ *adjective*
different from what is normal or expected: *There was an unnatural silence.* ⟳ ANTONYM **natural**

un·nec·es·sar·y /ʌnˈnɛsəˌsɛri/ *adjective*

> ℹ️ SPELLING
> Remember! You spell **unnecessary** with **NN**, one **C**, and **SS**.

not needed, or more than is needed: *All this fuss is totally unnecessary.* ⟳ ANTONYM **necessary**
▶ **un·nec·es·sar·i·ly** /ʌnˌnɛsəˈsɛrəli/ *adverb*: *His explanation was unnecessarily complicated.*

un·of·fi·cial /ˌʌnəˈfɪʃl/ *adjective*
not accepted or approved by a person in authority: *Unofficial reports say that four people died in the explosion.* ⟳ ANTONYM **official**
▶ **un·of·fi·cial·ly** /ˌʌnəˈfɪʃəli/ *adverb*

un·pack /ˌʌnˈpæk/ *verb* (un·packs, un·pack·ing, un·packed)
to take all the things out of a bag, box, etc.: *Have you unpacked your suitcase? ◆ We arrived at the hotel, unpacked, and then went to the beach.* ⟳ ANTONYM **pack**

un·paid /ˌʌnˈpeɪd/ *adjective*
not yet paid: *unpaid bills*

un·pleas·ant 🎵 /ʌnˈplɛznt/ *adjective*
not pleasant; not nice: *There was an unpleasant smell of bad fish.* ⟳ ANTONYM **pleasant**
▶ **un·pleas·ant·ly** /ʌnˈplɛzntli/ *adverb*: *It was unpleasantly hot in that room.* ⟳ ANTONYM **pleasantly**

un·plug /ˌʌnˈplʌg/ *verb* (un·plugs, un·plug·ging, un·plugged)
to take out a piece of electrical equipment (called a PLUG) from the electricity supply: *Can you unplug the TV, please?* ⟳ ANTONYM **plug something in**

un·pop·u·lar /ˌʌnˈpɑpyələr/ *adjective*
not liked by many people; not popular: *He's unpopular at work because he's lazy.* ⟳ ANTONYM **popular**

un·pre·dict·a·ble AWL /ˌʌnprɪˈdɪktəbl/ *adjective*
If something is **unpredictable**, you cannot say how it will change in the future: *The weather is very unpredictable at this time of year.* ⟳ ANTONYM **predictable**

un·pro·fes·sion·al /ˌʌnprəˈfɛʃənl/ *adjective*
not behaving in way that is appropriate for a person in a particular job: *Criticizing her client*

like that was really unprofessional. ⟳ ANTONYM **professional**

un·qual·i·fied /ʌnˈkwɑləfaɪd/ *adjective*
not having the knowledge or training to do something: *She is totally unqualified for this job.* ⟳ ANTONYM **qualified**

un·rea·son·a·ble /ʌnˈrizn·əbl/ *adjective*
expecting too much: *an unreasonable request* ⟳ ANTONYM **reasonable**

un·re·li·a·ble AWL /ˌʌnrɪˈlaɪəbl/ *adjective*
If something or someone is **unreliable**, you cannot trust it or them: *Don't lend her any money – she's very unreliable. ◆ an unreliable car* ⟳ ANTONYM **reliable**

un·rest /ˌʌnˈrɛst/ *noun* [noncount]
a situation in which people are angry or unhappy, and are likely to protest or fight: *There has been a lot of political unrest since the last election.*

un·ru·ly /ʌnˈruli/ *adjective*
difficult to control: *an unruly crowd*

un·safe /ˌʌnˈseɪf/ *adjective*
dangerous; not safe: *Don't climb on that wall – it's unsafe.* ⟳ ANTONYM **safe**

un·sat·is·fac·to·ry /ˌʌnsætəsˈfæktəri/ *adjective*
not good enough; not acceptable: *Your work is unsatisfactory. Please do it again.* ⟳ ANTONYM **satisfactory**

un·screw /ˌʌnˈskru/ *verb* (un·screws, un·screw·ing, un·screwed)
to open or remove something by turning it: *Could you unscrew the top of this jar for me?*

un·skilled /ˌʌnˈskɪld/ *adjective*
not having or needing special skills or training: *unskilled workers ◆ unskilled jobs* ⟳ ANTONYM **skilled**

un·sta·ble AWL /ˌʌnˈsteɪbl/ *adjective*
Something that is **unstable** may fall, move, or change: *This bridge is unstable. ◆ an unstable government* ⟳ ANTONYM **stable**

un·stead·y /ʌnˈstɛdi/ *adjective*
not completely in control of your movements, so that you may fall: *She's still a little unsteady on her feet after the operation.* ⟳ ANTONYM **steady**

un·suc·cess·ful /ˌʌnsəkˈsɛsfl/ *adjective*
not having or resulting in success: *an unsuccessful attempt to climb the mountain* ⟳ ANTONYM **successful**
▶ **un·suc·cess·ful·ly** /ˌʌnsəkˈsɛsfəli/ *adverb*: *He tried unsuccessfully to lift the box.*

un·suit·a·ble /ʌnˈsuɪtəbl/ *adjective*
not suitable; not right for someone or something: *This movie is unsuitable for children.* ⟳ ANTONYM **suitable**

un·sure /ˌʌnˈʃʊr/ *adjective*
not sure about something: *We were unsure what to do.* ➔ ANTONYM **sure**

un·sym·pa·thet·ic /ˌʌnsɪmpəˈθɛtɪk/ *adjective*
If you are **unsympathetic**, you are not kind to someone who is hurt or sad, and you show that you do not understand their feelings and problems. ➔ ANTONYM **sympathetic**

un·tan·gle /ˌʌnˈtæŋgl/ *verb* (un·tan·gles, un·tan·gling, un·tan·gled)
to separate threads, hair, etc. that are twisted together in a messy way: *The wires got mixed up, and it took me a long time to untangle them.*

un·tie /ˌʌnˈtaɪ/ *verb* (un·ties, un·ty·ing, un·tied, has un·tied)
to remove a knot; to take off the string or rope that is holding something: *Can you untie this knot?* • *I untied the boat and started rowing away from the dock.* ➔ ANTONYM **tie something up**

un·til 🔑 /ənˈtɪl/ (also informal **till** /tɪl/) *conjunction, preposition*

> ⓘ SPELLING
> Remember! You spell **until** with one L, but you spell **till** with LL.

up to a certain time or event: *The store is open until 7:00.* • *Stay in bed until you feel better.* • *I can't come until tomorrow.*

un·true /ˌʌnˈtru/ *adjective*
not true or correct: *What you said was completely untrue.* ➔ ANTONYM **true**

un·u·su·al 🔑 /ʌnˈyuʒuəl/ *adjective*
If something is **unusual**, it does not often happen or you do not often see it: *It's unusual for Joe to be late.* • *What an unusual name!*
▶ **un·u·su·al·ly** /ʌnˈyuʒuəli/ *adverb*: *It was an unusually hot summer.*

un·want·ed /ˌʌnˈwɑntəd/ *adjective*
not wanted: *an unwanted gift*

un·wel·come /ʌnˈwɛlkəm/ *adjective*
If someone or something is **unwelcome**, you are not happy to have or see them: *an unwelcome visitor* ➔ ANTONYM **welcome**

un·will·ing /ʌnˈwɪlɪŋ/ *adjective*
If you are **unwilling** to do something, you are not ready or happy to do it: *He was unwilling to lend me any money.* ➔ ANTONYM **willing**

un·wind /ˌʌnˈwaɪnd/ *verb* (un·winds, un·wind·ing, un·wound /ˌʌnˈwaʊnd/, has un·wound)
1 to open out something that has been wrapped into a ball or around something else: *to unwind a ball of string*
2 to start to relax, after working hard or worrying about something: *Watching TV helps me unwind after a busy day.*

un·wise /ˌʌnˈwaɪz/ *adjective*
showing that you do not make good decisions: *It would be unwise to tell anyone about our plan yet.* ➔ SYNONYM **foolish** ➔ ANTONYM **wise**
▶ **un·wise·ly** /ˌʌnˈwaɪzli/ *adverb*: *Unwisely, I agreed to help her.*

un·wrap /ˌʌnˈræp/ *verb* (un·wraps, un·wrap·ping, un·wrapped)
to take off the paper or cloth that is around something: *I unwrapped the present.* ➔ ANTONYM **wrap**

un·zip /ˌʌnˈzɪp/ *verb* (un·zips, un·zip·ping, un·zip·ped)
to open a piece of clothing, a bag, etc. by pulling the long thing that fastens it (the ZIPPER)

up 🔑 /ʌp/ *preposition, adverb*
1 in or to a higher place: *We climbed up the mountain.* • *Put your hand up if you know the answer.* ➔ ANTONYM **down**
2 from sitting or lying to standing: *Stand up, please.* • *What time do you get up (= out of bed)?* • *"Is Joe up (= out of bed)?" "No, he's still asleep."*
3 to the place where someone or something is: *She came up to me and asked me the time.*
4 a word we use to show an increase in something: *Prices are going up.* • *Please turn the radio up – I can't hear it.* ➔ ANTONYM **down**
5 into pieces: *Cut the meat up.*
6 so that it is finished: *Eat up – it's time to go to school now.*
7 in a certain direction: *She lives up the street from us.* ➔ ANTONYM **down**
be up to someone to be the person who should do or decide something: *"What do you want to do tonight?" "I don't care. It's up to you."*
up to
1 as far as; until: *Up to now, she has worked very hard.*
2 as much or as many as: *Up to 300 people came to the meeting.*
3 doing something, especially something bad: *What is that man up to?*

up·bring·ing /ˈʌpbrɪŋɪŋ/ *noun* [singular]
the way that you are treated and taught to behave by your parents: *He had a very religious upbringing.* ➔ The verb is **bring someone up**.

up·date /ʌpˈdeɪt/ *verb* (up·dates, up·dat·ing, up·dat·ed)
to make something more modern or add new things to it: *The information on our website is updated every week.*
▶ **up·date** /ˈʌpdeɪt/ *noun* [count]: *an update on a news story (= the latest information)*

up·grade /ʌpˈgreɪd/ *verb* (up·grades, up·grad·ing, up·grad·ed)
to change something so that it is better: *I just upgraded my home computer.*

► **up·grade** /'ʌpgreɪd/ *noun* [*count*]: *to install an upgrade*

up·hill /ˌʌp'hɪl/ *adverb*
going up, toward the top of a hill: *I have to ride my bike uphill to get to school.* ⊃ **ANTONYM downhill**

up·hol·ster·y /ə'poʊlstəri/ *noun* [*noncount*]
the thick, soft material that is used to cover chairs, car seats, etc.

up·load /'ʌploʊd/ *verb* (up·loads, up·load·ing, up·load·ed)
(**COMPUTERS**) to copy a computer file from a small computer system to a larger one ⊃ Look at **download**.

up·on /ə'pɑn/ *preposition* (*formal*)
on: *The decision was based upon the doctor's evidence.*

up·per 🔑 /'ʌpər/ *adjective*
in a higher place than something else: *the upper lip* ⊃ **ANTONYM lower**

up·per·case /ˌʌpər'keɪs/ (also **up·per case**) *noun* [*noncount*]
(**ENGLISH LANGUAGE ARTS**) the large form of letters, for example A, B, C (not a, b, c): *NATO is written in uppercase.* ⊃ **ANTONYM lowercase**

the up·per class /ði ˌʌpər 'klæs/ *noun* [*singular*]
the group of people in a society with the highest social position, who have more money and power than other people
► **up·per-class** /ˌʌpər 'klæs/ *adjective*: *an upper-class accent* ⊃ Look at **the middle class, the working class.**

up·right /'ʌpraɪt/ *adjective, adverb*
standing straight up, not lying down: *Put the ladder upright against the wall.*

up·ris·ing /'ʌpraɪzɪŋ/ *noun* [*count*]
(**POLITICS**) a situation in which a group of people start to fight against the government in their country

up·set¹ 🔑 /ˌʌp'sɛt/ *verb* (up·sets, up·set·ting, up·set, has up·set)
1 to make someone feel unhappy or worried: *You upset Tom when you said he was fat.*
2 to make something change in a way that you do not like: *The bad weather upset our plans for the weekend.*
► **up·set·ting** /ˌʌp'sɛtɪŋ/ *adjective*
making you feel unhappy or worried: *The experience was very upsetting for all of us.*

up·set² 🔑 /ˌʌp'sɛt/ *adjective*
1 unhappy or worried: *The kids were really upset when the dog died.*
2 (**HEALTH**) a little sick: *an upset stomach*

up·side down /ˌʌpsaɪd 'daʊn/ *adverb*
with the top part at the bottom: *The picture is upside down.*

up·stairs 🔑 /ˌʌp'stɛrz/ *adverb*
to or on a higher floor of a building: *I went upstairs to bed.*
► **up·stairs** /'ʌpstɛrz/ *adjective*: *An upstairs window was open.* ⊃ **ANTONYM downstairs**

up to date /ˌʌp tə 'deɪt/ *adjective*
modern; using new information: *Is this information up to date?* • *up-to-date equipment* ⊃ Look at **out of date**.

up·town /ˌʌp'taʊn/ *adjective, adverb*
in or to the parts of a city or town that are away from the center, where people live: *She lives uptown, so she has to take the subway to work.* ⊃ Look at **downtown**.

up·ward 🔑 /'ʌpwərd/ (also **up·wards** /'ʌpwərdz/) *adverb*
up; toward a higher place: *We climbed upward, toward the top of the mountain.* ⊃ **ANTONYM downward**

u·ra·ni·um /yʊ'reɪniəm/ *noun* [*noncount*] (symbol U)
(**CHEMISTRY**) a metal that can be used to produce nuclear energy: *Uranium is highly radioactive.*

ur·ban /'ərbən/ *adjective*
(**GEOGRAPHY**) connected with a city: *urban areas* ⊃ Look at **rural**.

urge¹ /ərdʒ/ *verb* (urg·es, urg·ing, urged)
to try to make someone do something: *I urged him to stay for dinner.*

urge² /ərdʒ/ *noun* [*count*]
a strong feeling that you want to do something: *I had a sudden urge to laugh.*

ur·gen·cy /'ərdʒənsi/ *noun* [*noncount*]
the need to do something quickly because it is very important

ur·gent 🔑 /'ərdʒənt/ *adjective*
so important that you must do it or answer it quickly: *Is your message urgent?*
► **ur·gent·ly** /'ərdʒəntli/ *adverb*: *I must see you urgently.*

u·ri·nate /'yʊrəneɪt/ *verb* (u·ri·nates, u·ri·nat·ing, u·ri·nat·ed) (*formal*)
(**BIOLOGY**) to pass URINE from the body

u·rine /'yʊrɪn/ *noun* [*noncount*]
(**BIOLOGY**) the waste liquid that passes from your body when you use the toilet

URL /ˌyu ɑr 'ɛl/ *abbreviation*
(**COMPUTERS**) the address of a website: *What's the URL for that website?*

U.S.A. /ˌyu ɛs 'eɪ/ short for **United States of America**

U.S. /ˌyu 'ɛs/ short for **United States**: *the smallest state in the U.S.* • *the U.S. dollar*

us·a·ble /ˈyuzəbl/ *adjective*
in good enough condition to be used: *My old bike is a little rusty, but it's still usable.*

us·age /ˈyusɪdʒ/ *noun*
1 [*noncount*] the way that something is used; the amount that something is used: *Internet usage*
2 [*count, noncount*] (**ENGLISH LANGUAGE ARTS**) the way that words are normally used in a language

USB /ˌyu es ˈbi/ *abbreviation*
(**COMPUTERS**) the system for connecting other pieces of equipment to a computer: *You'll need a USB cable to connect your cell phone to the computer.*

us 🔑 /əs; ʌs/ *pronoun* [*plural*]
me and another person or other people; me and you: *She invited us to dinner.* • *Come with us.*

USB flash drive
/ˌyu es bi ˈflæʃ draɪv/
(also **flash drive**) *noun*
[*count*]

USB flash drive

(**COMPUTERS**) a small thing that stores information from a computer so that you can move it from one computer to another

use¹ 🔑 /yuz/ *verb* (us·es, us·ing, used)

> ⓘ **PRONUNCIATION**
> When the word **use** is a verb, it sounds like **shoes** or **choose**.
> When **use** is a noun, it sounds like **juice** or **loose**.

1 to do a job with something: *Could I use your phone?* • *Do you know how to use this machine?* • *Wood is used to make paper.*
2 to take something: *Don't use all the milk.*
use something up to use something until you have no more: *I used up all the coffee, so I had to buy some more.*

use² 🔑 /yus/ *noun*
1 [*noncount*] using something or being used: *This pool is for the use of hotel guests only.*
2 [*count*] what you can do with something: *This machine has many uses.*
3 [*noncount*] the opportunity to use something, for example something that belongs to someone else: *I have the use of Jim's car while he's away.*
it's no use doing something it will not help to do something: *It's no use telling her anything – she never listens.*
make use of something to find a way of using something: *If you don't want that box, I can make use of it.*

used¹ 🔑 /yuzd/ *adjective*
that had another owner before; not new: *I bought a used car.* ⊃ **SYNONYM secondhand** ⊃ **ANTONYM new**

used² 🔑 /yust/ *adjective*
be used to something to know something well because you have seen, heard, tasted, done, etc. it a lot: *I'm used to walking because I don't have a car.*
get used to something to begin to know something well after a time: *I'm getting used to my new job.*

used to 🔑 /ˈyustə; ˈyustu/ *modal verb*
words that tell us about something that happened often or that was true in the past: *She used to smoke when she was younger.* • *I used to be afraid of dogs, but now I like them.*

Grammar

- To form questions, we use **did** with **use to**: *Did she use to smoke when she was younger?*
- We form negatives with **didn't use to**: *I didn't use to like fish, but I do now.*

use·ful 🔑 /ˈyusfl/ *adjective*
good and helpful for doing something: *This bag will be useful for carrying my books.*
▶ **use·ful·ly** /ˈyusfəli/ *adverb*

use·less /ˈyusləs/ *adjective*
1 not good for anything: *A car is useless without gas.*
2 that does not do what you hoped: *It's useless to complain – they won't give you your money back.*

us·er 🔑 /ˈyuzər/ *noun* [*count*]
a person who uses something: *computer users*

us·er-friend·ly /ˌyuzər ˈfrɛndli/ *adjective*
easy to understand and use: *Computers are much more user-friendly than they used to be.*

u·su·al 🔑 /ˈyuʒuəl/ *adjective*
that happens most often: *He arrived home later than usual.* ⊃ **SYNONYM normal**
as usual in the way that happens most often: *Julie was late, as usual.*

u·su·al·ly 🔑 /ˈyuʒuəli/ *adverb*
in the way that is usual; most often: *I'm usually home by six o'clock.*

u·ten·sil /yuˈtɛnsl/ *noun* [*count*]
a tool that is used in the home: *cooking utensils* ⊃ Look at the picture at **kitchen**.

u·ter·us /ˈyutərəs/ *noun* [*count*] (*plural* u·ter·us·es) (*formal*)
(**BIOLOGY**) the part of a woman or female animal where a baby develops before it is born ⊃ **SYNONYM womb**

u·to·pi·a (also **U·to·pi·a**) /yuˈtoʊpiə/ *noun* [*count, noncount*]
a place where everything is perfect, but that does not exist

tʃ **ch**in   dʒ **J**une   v **v**an   θ **th**in   ð **th**en   s **s**o   z **z**oo   ʃ **sh**e

ut·ter¹ /ˈʌtər/ *adjective*
complete: *He felt an utter fool.*
▶ **ut·ter·ly** /ˈʌtərli/ *adverb*: *That's utterly impossible!*

ut·ter² /ˈʌtər/ *verb* (ut·ters, ut·ter·ing, ut·tered)
(*formal*)
to say something or make a sound with your mouth: *She did not **utter a word**.*

U-turn /ˈyu tərn/
a type of movement where a car, etc. turns around so that it goes back in the direction it came from

UV /ˌyu ˈvi/ (**PHYSICS**) short for **ultraviolet**

V v

V, v /viː/ noun [count, noncount]
1 (plural **V's, v's** /viːz/) the twenty-second letter of the English alphabet: *"Voice" begins with a "V."*
2 V abbreviation of **volt**
3 v. (also **vs.**) abbreviation of **versus**: *the Supreme Court case Roe v. Wade*

va·can·cy /ˈveɪkənsi/ noun [count] (plural **va·can·cies**)
1 a room in a hotel that no one is using: *The sign outside the hotel says "no vacancies"* (= the hotel is full).
2 a job that no one is doing: *We have a **vacancy** for a secretary in our office.*

va·cant /ˈveɪkənt/ adjective
1 empty or not being used: *a vacant room*
2 If a job in a company is **vacant**, no one is doing it and it is available for someone to do.

va·ca·tion 🔑 /veɪˈkeɪʃn/ noun [count, noncount]
a time when you do not go to work or school, and often go and stay away from home: *They're **on vacation** in Hawaii.* • *You've been working too hard. You need a vacation!* • *We're going to the beach for our **summer vacation**.*

vac·ci·nate /ˈvæksn·eɪt/ verb (**vac·ci·nates, vac·ci·nat·ing, vac·ci·nat·ed**)
(HEALTH) to put a substance into a person's or an animal's blood using a needle, to stop them from getting a disease: *Have you been **vaccinated against** measles?*

vac·ci·na·tion /ˌvæksn·ˈeɪʃn/ noun [count, noncount]
(HEALTH) when a substance is put into a person's or an animal's blood with a needle, to stop them from getting a disease: *a vaccination against measles*

vac·cine /ˌvækˈsin/ noun [count]
(HEALTH) a substance that is put into a person's or an animal's blood using a needle, to stop them from getting a disease

vac·u·um¹ /ˈvækyum/ noun [count]
1 (PHYSICS) a space with no air, gas, or anything else in it
2 another word for **vacuum cleaner**

vac·u·um² /ˈvækyum/ verb (**vac·u·ums, vac·u·um·ing, vac·u·umed**)
to clean a floor using a VACUUM CLEANER

vac·u·um clean·er /ˈvækyum ˌklinər/
(also **vac·u·um**) noun [count]
a machine that cleans floors by sucking up dirt

va·gi·na /vəˈdʒaɪnə/ noun [count]
(BIOLOGY) the part of a woman's or a female animal's body that leads to the place where a baby grows (called the UTERUS)

vacuum cleaner

vague /veɪg/ adjective (**vagu·er, vagu·est**)
not clear or not exact: *I couldn't find the house because he gave me very vague directions.*
▶ **vague·ly** /ˈveɪgli/ adverb: *I vaguely remember what happened.*

vain /veɪn/ adjective (**vain·er, vain·est**)
1 too proud of what you can do or how you look ⊃ The noun is **vanity**.
2 not producing the result you want: *They made a **vain attempt** to save his life.* ⊃ SYNONYM **useless**
in vain without success: *I tried in vain to sleep.*

val·e·dic·to·ri·an /ˌvælədɪkˈtɔriən/ noun [count]
the student who received the highest grades in their class in high school or college

Val·en·tine's Day /ˈvæləntaɪnz ˌdeɪ/ noun [singular]
the day (February 14) when people send a card (called a VALENTINE) to the person that they love

val·id AWL /ˈvæləd/ adjective
able to be used; acceptable: *Your bus ticket is valid for one week.* ⊃ ANTONYM **invalid**

val·ley 🔑 /ˈvæli/ noun [count] (plural **val·leys**)
(GEOGRAPHY) the low land between mountains; the land that a river flows through

val·u·a·ble 🔑 /ˈvælyəbl/ adjective
1 worth a lot of money: *Is this ring valuable?*
2 very useful: *The book contains some valuable information.*

val·u·a·bles /ˈvælyəblz/ noun [plural]
the small things that you own that are worth a lot of money, for example jewelry or a cell phone: *You should put your valuables in the hotel safe.*

val·ue¹ 🔑 /ˈvælyu/ noun
1 [count] how much money you can sell something for: *The thieves stole goods with a total **value** of $100,000.*
2 [count, noncount] how much something is worth compared with its price: *The hotel is a **good value**, with rooms at $80 a night.*
3 [noncount] how useful or important something is: *Their help was **of great value**.*

4 values [*plural*] your beliefs about what is the right and wrong way to behave: *Do young people today have a different set of values?*

val·ue² /ˈvælyu/ *verb* (val·ues, valu·ing, val·ued)
1 to think that something is very important: *I value my freedom.*
2 to say how much money something is worth: *The house was valued at $800,000.*

valve /vælv/ *noun* [*count*]
(**PHYSICS**) a part in a pipe or tube which lets air, liquid, or gas flow in one direction only

vam·pire /ˈvæmpaɪər/ *noun* [*count*]
a person in stories who drinks people's blood

van /væn/ *noun* [*count*]
a kind of big car or small truck for carrying people or things

van

van·dal /ˈvændl/ *noun* [*count*]
a person who deliberately damages public property: *Vandals broke the benches in the park.*

van·dal·ize /ˈvændl·aɪz/ *verb* (van·dal·iz·es, van·dal·iz·ing, van·dal·ized)
to destroy or damage public property deliberately
▶ **van·dal·ism** /ˈvændl·ɪzəm/ *noun* [*noncount*]: *Vandalism is a problem in this part of the city.*

va·nil·la /vəˈnɪlə/ *noun* [*noncount*]
a substance from a plant that gives a taste to some sweet foods: *vanilla ice cream*

van·ish /ˈvænɪʃ/ *verb* (van·ish·es, van·ish·ing, van·ished)
to go away; to stop being seen: *The thief ran into the crowd and vanished.* ➔ **SYNONYM disappear**

van·i·ty /ˈvænəti/ *noun* [*noncount*]
being too proud of what you can do or how you look ➔ The adjective is **vain**.

va·por /ˈveɪpər/ *noun* [*count, noncount*]
(**GENERAL SCIENCE**) very small drops of liquid that look like a gas: *water vapor*

var·i·a·ble **AWL** /ˈvɛriəbl/ *adjective*
not staying the same; often changing: *variable temperatures*

var·i·a·tion **AWL** /ˌvɛriˈeɪʃn/ *noun* [*count, noncount*]
a change or difference in the amount or level of something: *There was a lot of variation in the test scores.*

var·ied¹ **AWL** /ˈvɛrid/ *adjective*
including a lot of different things: *I try to make my classes as varied as possible.*

var·ied² **AWL** form of **vary**

var·ies **AWL** form of **vary**

va·ri·e·ty 🔑 /vəˈraɪəti/ *noun* (plural va·ri·e·ties)
1 [*singular*] a lot of different things: *There's a wide variety of dishes on the menu.*
2 [*noncount*] the fact that you are not always doing the same things: *There's a lot of variety in my new job.*
3 [*count*] a type of something: *This variety of apple is very sweet.*

var·i·ous 🔑 /ˈvɛriəs/ *adjective*
several different: *We sell this shirt in various colors and sizes.*

var·nish /ˈvɑrnɪʃ/ *noun* [*noncount*]
a clear paint with no color, which you put on something to make it shine
▶ **var·nish** *verb* (var·nish·es, var·nish·ing, var·nished): *The doors are then stained and varnished.*

var·si·ty /ˈvɑrsəti/ *noun* [*count, noncount*] (plural var·si·ties)
the main sports team that of a high school or college

var·y 🔑 **AWL** /ˈvɛri/ *verb* (var·ies, var·y·ing, var·ied, has var·ied)
1 to be different from each other, or to change according to the situation: *Class sizes vary from 8 to 15.* ◆ *The price varies according to the quality.*
2 to make something different by changing it often in some way: *We try to vary the class to suit students' needs.*

vase /veɪs/ *noun* [*count*]
a pot that you put cut flowers in

vast /væst/ *adjective*
very big: *Australia is a vast country.* ➔ **SYNONYM enormous, huge**

VCR /ˌvi si ˈɑr/ *noun* [*count*]
a machine connected to a television, which you use for recording or showing programs. **VCR** is short for "video cassette recorder."

veal /vil/ *noun* [*noncount*]
meat from a young cow (a **CALF**) ➔ Look at the note at **cow**.

veg·an /ˈvigən/ *noun* [*count*]
a person who does not eat meat or any other foods that come from animals, such as eggs or milk

veg·e·ta·ble 🔑 /ˈvɛdʒtəbl/ *noun* [*count*]
a plant or part of a plant that we eat: *The students grow vegetables such as cabbages, beans, and carrots.*

veg·e·tar·i·an /ˌvɛdʒəˈtɛriən/ *noun* [*count*]
a person who does not eat meat or fish
▶ **veg·e·tar·i·an** *adjective*: *a vegetarian restaurant*

veg·e·ta·tion /ˌvɛdʒəˈteɪʃn/ *noun* [*noncount*]
(*formal*)
all the plants that are found in a particular place: *the thick vegetation of the rain forest*

vegetables

peppers   broccoli   cabbage   carrots   cauliflower

celery   cucumbers   lettuce   onions   peas

potatoes   sweet potatoes   tomatoes   zucchini   radishes

---

ve·hi·cle 🔑 **AWL** /ˈviɪkl/ *noun* [count] (*formal*)
a car, bus, truck, bicycle, etc.; a thing that takes people or things from place to place: *Are you the owner of this vehicle?*

veil /veɪl/ *noun* [count]
a piece of material that a woman puts over her head and face

vein /veɪn/ *noun* [count]
one of the small tubes in your body that carry blood to the heart ⊃ Look at the picture at **body**.

Vel·cro™ /ˈvɛlkroʊ/ *noun* [noncount]
two bands of special material that stick together to fasten clothes, shoes, etc.

ve·loc·i·ty /vəˈlɑsət̮i/ *noun* [noncount]
(**PHYSICS**) the speed at which something moves in a particular direction: *wind velocity*

vel·vet /ˈvɛlvət/ *noun* [noncount]
cloth that is soft and thick on one side: *red velvet curtains*

vend·ing ma·chine /ˈvɛndɪŋ ˌməʃin/ *noun* [count]
a machine that you put money in to buy food or drinks: *Can I have a dollar to buy a snack from the vending machine?*

ve·ne·tian blind /vəˌniʃn ˈblaɪnd/ *noun* [count]
a covering for a window that is made of flat pieces of plastic or metal, which can be turned to let more or less light into the room

vent /vɛnt/ *noun* [count]
a hole in the wall of a room or machine that lets air come in, and lets smoke, steam, or smells go out: *an air vent*

ven·ti·late /ˈvɛntəleɪt/ *verb* (ven·ti·lates, ven·ti·lat·ing, ven·ti·lat·ed)
to allow air to move through a room or building

▸ **ven·ti·la·tion** /ˌvɛntəˈleɪʃn/ *noun* [noncount]:
The only ventilation was one tiny window.

ven·ue /ˈvɛnyu/ *noun* [count]
the place where an event happens, for example a concert or a sports game: *Please note the change of venue for this event.*

verb /vərb/ *noun* [count]
(**ENGLISH LANGUAGE ARTS**) a word that tells you what someone does or what happens. "Go," "sing," "do," and "be" are all **verbs**.

ver·bal /ˈvərbl/ *adjective* (*formal*)
1 connected with words, or using words: *He has good verbal skills.*
2 spoken, not written: *We made a verbal agreement.*
▸ **ver·bal·ly** /ˈvərbəli/ *adverb*

ver·dict /ˈvərdɪkt/ *noun* [count]
a decision in a court of law about whether someone is guilty or not: *The jury returned a verdict of "not guilty."*

verge /vərdʒ/ *noun*
on the verge of something; on the verge of doing something very near to doing something, or to something happening: *Scientists are on the verge of finding a cure.*

ver·i·fy /ˈvɛrəfaɪ/ *verb* (ver·i·fies, ver·i·fy·ing, ver·i·fied) (*formal*)
to check or say that something is true: *We are unable to verify this statement.*
▸ **ver·i·fi·ca·tion** /ˌvɛrəfəˈkeɪʃn/ *noun* [noncount]

verse /vərs/ *noun*
1 [noncount] (**ENGLISH LANGUAGE ARTS**) words arranged in lines with a definite beat, often with sounds repeated at the ends of lines: *The play is written in verse.* ⊃ SYNONYM **poetry**

---

tʃ **ch**in   dʒ **J**une   v **v**an   θ **th**in   ð **th**en   s **s**o   z **z**oo   ʃ **sh**e

2 [count] (**MUSIC, ENGLISH LANGUAGE ARTS**) a group of lines in a song or poem: *This song has five verses.*

ver·sion [AWL] /'vɜrʒn/ *noun* [count]
1 a form of something that is different in some way: *the latest version of the software*
2 what one person says or writes about something that happened: *His version of the accident is different from mine.*

ver·sus /'vɜrsəs/ *preposition* (abbreviation **vs.** or **v.**)
(**SPORTS**) on the other side in a sport: *There's a good baseball game on TV tonight – the Dodgers versus the Giants.* ➔ **SYNONYM against**

ver·te·bra /'vɜrtəbrə/ *noun* [count] (*plural* **ver·te·brae** /'vɜrtəbreɪ/)
(**BIOLOGY**) any of the small bones that are connected together to form the line of bones down the middle of your back

ver·te·brate /'vɜrtəbrət/ *noun* [count]
(**BIOLOGY**) any animal, bird, or fish that has a line of bones down the middle of its back (called a **backbone**) ➔ **ANTONYM invertebrate**

ver·ti·cal /'vɜrtɪkl/ *adjective*
going straight up or down at an angle of 90° from the ground: *a vertical line* ➔ Look at **horizontal**. ➔ Look at the picture at **line**.
▸ **ver·ti·cal·ly** /'vɜrtɪkli/ *adverb*

ver·y¹ 🔑 /'vɛri/ *adverb*
You use "very" before another word to make it stronger: *Very few people know that.* ◆ *She speaks very quietly.* ◆ *I like chocolate very much.* ◆ *I'm not very hungry.*

ver·y² /'vɛri/ *adjective*
exact; same: *You are the very person I wanted to see!* ◆ *We climbed to the very top of the mountain.*

vest /vɛst/ *noun*
[count]
1 a piece of clothing like a jacket with no sleeves
2 a special piece of clothing that covers the top part of the body: *a bulletproof vest*

vest

vet /vɛt/ *noun* [count] (*informal*)
1 short for **veteran**: *a Vietnam vet*
2 short for **veterinarian**

vet·er·an /'vɛtərən/ *noun* [count] (also *informal* **vet**)
a person who has been in the army, navy, or air force during a war: *a veteran of the Gulf War*

vet·er·i·nar·i·an /ˌvɛtərə'nɛriən/ (also *informal* **vet**) *noun* [count]
a doctor for animals

▸ **vet·er·i·nar·y** /'vɛtərəˌnɛri/ *adjective*: *a veterinary surgeon*

ve·to /'vitoʊ/ *verb* (**ve·toes**, **ve·to·ing**, **ve·toed**)
(**POLITICS**) to refuse to give official permission for an action or plan, when other people have agreed to it: *The governor vetoed the proposal to reduce taxes.*

vi·a [AWL] /'viə; 'vaɪə/ *preposition*
1 going through a place: *We flew from New York to Los Angeles via Chicago.*
2 using something: *These pictures come to you via satellite.*

vi·brate /'vaɪbreɪt/ *verb* (**vi·brates**, **vi·brat·ing**, **vi·brat·ed**)
to move very quickly from side to side or up and down: *The house vibrates every time a train goes past.*
▸ **vi·bra·tion** /vaɪ'breɪʃn/ *noun* [count, noncount]: *You can feel the vibrations from the engine when you're in the car.*

vice /vaɪs/ *noun*
1 [noncount] criminal activities involving sex or drugs: *detectives from the vice squad*
2 [count] a moral weakness or bad habit: *His only vice was the occasional glass of wine.*

vice pres·i·dent /ˌvaɪs 'prɛzədənt/ *noun* [count]
1 (**POLITICS**) the person below the president of a country in importance, who can control the country if the president cannot ➔ Look at the note at **government**.
2 a person who controls a particular part of a large business organization: *the vice president of sales*

vice ver·sa /ˌvaɪs 'vɜrsə/ *adverb*
in the opposite way to what has just been said: *You can translate any document from Spanish into English and vice versa (= from English into Spanish).*

vi·cin·i·ty /və'sɪnəti/ *noun*
in the vicinity (*formal*) in an area; near a place: *There are three parks in the vicinity of the school.*

vi·cious /'vɪʃəs/ *adjective*
violent and cruel: *a vicious attack*

vic·tim /'vɪktəm/ *noun* [count]
a person or thing that is hurt, damaged, or killed by someone or something: *the innocent victims of crime*

vic·to·ri·ous /vɪk'tɔriəs/ *adjective*
successful in a fight, game, or war: *the victorious team*

vic·to·ry /'vɪktəri/ *noun* [count, noncount] (*plural* **vic·to·ries**)
success in a fight, game, or war: *the Yankees' 6-2 victory over the Red Sox* ➔ **ANTONYM defeat**

vid·e·o 🔑 /ˈvɪdioʊ/ *noun* (plural **vid·e·os**)
1 [count, noncount] a kind of tape that is used for recording moving pictures and sound; a box containing this tape: *You can get this movie on video or on DVD.* ✦ *They made a video of the wedding.* ➔ SYNONYM **videotape**
2 [count] a copy of a movie, program, etc. that is recorded on VIDEOTAPE: *We stayed at home and watched a video.*
3 [noncount] the system of recording and showing moving pictures and sound using a camera: *video equipment*

vid·e·o game /ˈvɪdioʊ ɡeɪm/ *noun* [count]
a game that you play using a TV or computer screen

vid·e·o·tape /ˈvɪdioʊteɪp/ *noun* [count, noncount]
a kind of tape that is used for recording moving pictures and sound; a box containing this tape: *I replaced all of my old videotapes with DVDs.*
▸ **vid·e·o·tape** *verb* (**vid·e·o·tapes**, **vid·e·o·tap·ing**, **vid·e·o·taped**): *The interview was videotaped.*

view¹ 🔑 /vyu/ *noun*
1 [count] what you believe or think about something: *He has strong views on marriage.* ✦ *In my view, she has done nothing wrong.* ➔ SYNONYM **opinion**
2 [count] what you can see from a place: *There were beautiful views of the mountains all around.*
3 [noncount] the ability to see something from a particular place: *A large truck was blocking her view.*
in view of something (formal) because of something: *In view of the bad weather we decided to cancel the game.*
on view in a place for people to see: *Her paintings are on view at the museum.*

view² /vyu/ *verb* (**views**, **view·ing**, **viewed**) (formal)
1 to think about something in a particular way: *She viewed vacations as a waste of time.*
2 to watch or look at something: *Viewed from this side, the building looks much taller than it really is.*

view·er /ˈvyuər/ *noun* [count]
a person who watches a television program

vig·i·lant /ˈvɪdʒələnt/ *adjective* (formal)
careful and looking out for danger

vig·or·ous /ˈvɪɡərəs/ *adjective*
strong and active: *vigorous exercise*
▸ **vig·or·ous·ly** /ˈvɪɡərəsli/ *adverb*: *She shook my hand vigorously.*

vile /vaɪl/ *adjective* (**vil·er**, **vil·est**)
very unpleasant: *What a vile smell!* ➔ SYNONYM **horrible**

vil·la /ˈvɪlə/ *noun* [count]
a pleasant house in the country, especially somewhere warm

vil·lage /ˈvɪlɪdʒ/ *noun* [count]
(GEOGRAPHY) a very small town: *She lives in a village in the mountains.*

vil·lain /ˈvɪlən/ *noun* [count]
a bad person, usually in a book, play, or movie

vine /vaɪn/ *noun* [count]
the plant that produces GRAPES (= small fruits that we eat or use to make wine)

vin·e·gar /ˈvɪnɪɡər/ *noun* [noncount]
a liquid with a strong, sharp taste that is used in cooking: *I mixed some oil and vinegar to put on the salad.*

vine·yard /ˈvɪnyərd/ *noun* [count]
a piece of land where GRAPES (= small round green or purple fruits) are grown to make wine

vi·o·la /viˈoʊlə/ *noun* [count]
(MUSIC) a musical instrument like a large VIOLIN

vi·o·lence 🔑 /ˈvaɪələns/ *noun* [noncount]
1 violent behavior: *There's too much violence on TV.*
2 force or power: *the violence of the storm*

vi·o·lent 🔑 /ˈvaɪələnt/ *adjective*
strong and dangerous; causing physical harm: *Her husband was a violent man.* ✦ *The protest march started peacefully but later turned violent.*
▸ **vi·o·lent·ly** /ˈvaɪələntli/ *adverb*: *Did she behave violently toward you?*

vi·o·let /ˈvaɪələt/ *noun*
1 [count] a small, purple flower
2 [count, noncount] a color that is between dark blue and purple
▸ **vi·o·let** *adjective*: *violet eyes*

vi·o·lin /ˌvaɪəˈlɪn/ *noun* [count]
(MUSIC) a musical instrument that you hold under your chin and play by moving a stick (called a BOW) across the strings ➔ Look at the picture at **instrument**.

VIP /ˌvi aɪ ˈpi/ *noun* [count]
a person who is famous or important. VIP is short for "very important person."

vir·gin /ˈvərdʒən/ *noun* [count]
a person who has never had sex

vir·tu·al AWL /ˈvərtʃuəl/ *adjective*
1 being almost or very nearly something: *He married a virtual stranger.*
2 (COMPUTERS) made to appear to exist by a computer
▸ **vir·tu·al·ly** AWL /ˈvərtʃuəli/ *adverb*: *The two boys look virtually (= almost) the same.*

vir·tu·al re·al·i·ty /ˌvərtʃuəl riˈæləṭi/ *noun* [noncount]
(COMPUTERS) computer images that seem to be all around you and seem almost real

vir·tue /'vərtʃu/ *noun* [count]
behavior that shows high moral standards; a good quality or habit: *a life of virtue* ◆ *He has many virtues.*

vi·rus /'vaɪrəs/ *noun* [count] (*plural* **vi·rus·es**)
1 (**HEALTH**, **BIOLOGY**) a living thing that is too small to see, but that can make you sick: *a flu virus*
2 (**COMPUTERS**) a program that enters your computer and stops it from working correctly

vi·sa /'vizə/ *noun* [count]
an official piece of paper or mark in your passport to show that you can go into a country

vis·i·ble **AWL** /'vɪzəbl/ *adjective*
If something is **visible**, you can see it: *Stars are only visible at night.* ➔ **ANTONYM invisible**

vi·sion **AWL** /'vɪʒn/ *noun*
1 [noncount] the power to see: *He wears glasses because he has poor vision.* ➔ **SYNONYM sight**
2 [count] a picture in your mind; a dream: *They have a vision of a world without war.*

vis·it 🔑 /'vɪzət/ *verb* (**vis·its**, **vis·it·ing**, **vis·it·ed**)
to go to see a person or place for a short time: *When you go to Chicago you must visit the Field Museum.* ◆ *She visited me in the hospital.*
▶ **vis·it** *noun* [count]: *This is my first **visit** to New York.* ◆ *He promised to **pay** us **a visit** next year.*

vis·i·tor 🔑 /'vɪzəţər/ *noun* [count]
a person who goes to see another person or a place for a short time: *The old lady never has any visitors.* ◆ *Millions of visitors come to Orlando every year.*

vi·sor /'vaɪzər/ *noun* [count]
1 a part of a hard hat (a **HELMET**) that you can pull down to protect your eyes or face
2 a piece of plastic, cloth, etc. on a hat or in a car, which stops the sun from shining in your eyes

vi·su·al **AWL** /'vɪʒuəl/ *adjective*
connected with seeing: *Painting and photography are visual arts.*

vi·su·al·ize **AWL** /'vɪʒuəlaɪz/ *verb* (**vi·su·al·iz·es**, **vi·su·al·iz·ing**, **vi·su·al·ized**)
to have a picture in your mind of someone or something: *It's hard to visualize what this place looked like before the factory was built.* ➔ **SYNONYM imagine**

vi·tal /'vaɪţl/ *adjective*
very important or necessary: *It's vital that she sees a doctor – she's very sick.* ➔ **SYNONYM essential**
▶ **vi·tal·ly** /'vaɪţəli/: *vitally important*

vi·ta·min /'vaɪţəmən/ *noun* [count]
(**HEALTH**) one of the things in food that you need to be healthy: *Oranges are full of vitamin C.*

viv·id /'vɪvəd/ *adjective*
1 making a very clear picture in your mind: *I had a very vivid dream last night.*
2 having a strong, bright color: *vivid yellow*
▶ **viv·id·ly** /'vɪvədli/ *adverb*: *I remember my first day at school vividly.*

vo·cab·u·lar·y /voʊ'kæbyə,lɛri/ *noun* [count, noncount] (*plural* **vo·cab·u·lar·ies**) (**ENGLISH LANGUAGE ARTS**)
1 all the words that someone knows or that are used in a particular book or subject: *He has an amazing vocabulary for a five-year-old.*
2 the words that people use when they are talking about a particular subject: *technical vocabulary*

vo·cal /'voʊkl/ *adjective*
connected with the voice: *the vocal organs* (= the tongue, lips, etc.)

vocal cords /'voʊkl kɔrdz/ *noun* [plural]
(**BIOLOGY**) the thin bands of muscle in the back of your throat that move to produce the voice

vo·ca·tion /voʊ'keɪʃn/ *noun* [count, noncount] (*formal*)
a type of work or way of life that you do because you believe it is especially right for you: *Peter has found his vocation as a priest.*

vo·ca·tion·al school /voʊ'keɪʃn·l ˌskul/ *noun* [count, noncount]
a school that teaches students skills that are necessary for particular jobs: *He went to a vocational school to study carpentry.*

vogue /voʊɡ/ *noun* [count, noncount]
a fashion for something: *a vogue for large cars* ◆ *Black is always in vogue.*

voice 🔑 /vɔɪs/ *noun* [count]
the sounds that you make when you speak or sing: *Steve has a very deep voice.*
lose your voice to not be able to speak, usually because of illness: *He had a bad cold and lost his voice.*
raise your voice to speak more loudly

voice mail /'vɔɪs meɪl/ (also **voice·mail**) *noun* [noncount]
an electronic system that lets you leave or listen to telephone messages: *Have you checked your voice mail?*

vol·ca·no /vɑl'keɪnoʊ/ *noun* [count] (*plural* **vol·ca·noes**) (**GEOGRAPHY**) a mountain with a hole in the top where fire, gas, and hot liquid rock (called **LAVA**) sometimes come out

volcano

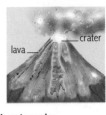
lava — crater

▶ **vol·can·ic** /vɑl'kænɪk/ *adjective*: *volcanic rocks*

vol·ley·ball /'vɑlibɔl/ *noun* (**SPORTS**)
1 [*noncount*] a game where two teams try to hit a ball over a high net with their hands: *We played volleyball on the beach.*
2 [*count*] a ball for playing this game

volt /voʊlt/ *noun* [*count*] (abbreviation **V**) (**PHYSICS**) a measure of electricity

vol·ume 🔑 **AWL** /'vɑlyəm; 'vɑlyum/ *noun*
1 [*noncount, singular*] (**MUSIC**) the amount of sound that something makes: *I can't hear the radio. Can you turn up the volume?*
2 [*count, noncount*] (**MATH, PHYSICS**) the amount of space that something fills, or the amount of space inside something: *What is the volume of this box?*
3 [*count, noncount*] the large quantity or amount of something: *a high volume of traffic on the roads*
4 [*count*] a book, especially one of a set: *The encyclopedia is in two volumes.*

vol·un·tar·y **AWL** /'vɑlən,tɛri/ *adjective*
If something is **voluntary**, you do it because you want to, not because you must: *She made a voluntary decision to leave the job.* ⊃ **ANTONYM compulsory**
▶ **vol·un·tar·i·ly** **AWL** /,vɑlən'tɛrəli/ *adverb*: *She left the job voluntarily.*

vol·un·teer¹ **AWL** /,vɑlən'tɪr/ *noun* [*count*]
a person who says that they will do a job without being forced or without being paid: *They're asking for volunteers to help at the Christmas party.* ◆ *He does volunteer work at a children's hospital.*

vol·un·teer² **AWL** /,vɑlən'tɪr/ *verb* (**vol·un·teers, vol·un·teer·ing, vol·un·teered**)
to say that you will do a job without being forced or without being paid: *I volunteered to do the dishes.* ◆ *She volunteers at her daughter's school.*

vom·it /'vɑmət/ *verb* (**vom·its, vom·it·ing, vom·it·ed**)
(**HEALTH**) When you **vomit**, food comes up from your stomach and out of your mouth.
▶ **vom·it** *noun* [*noncount*]

the food that comes up from your stomach when you **vomit**

vote¹ 🔑 /voʊt/ *noun* [*count*]
when you choose someone or something by writing on a piece of paper or by putting up your hand: *There were 96 votes for the plan, and 25 against.* ◆ *We couldn't agree on a title for the project, so we decided to take a vote.*

vote² 🔑 /voʊt/ *verb* (**votes, vot·ing, vot·ed**)
to choose someone or something by writing on a piece of paper or by putting up your hand: *Who did you vote for in the election?* ◆ *They voted to ban the use of cell phones inside the building.*
▶ **vot·er** /'voʊtər/ *noun* [*count*]
a person who votes in a political election

vouch·er /'vaʊtʃər/ *noun* [*count*]
a piece of paper that you can use instead of money to pay for something

vow /vaʊ/ *noun* [*count*]
a formal and serious promise to do something: *The monks made a vow of silence.*

vow·el /'vaʊəl/ *noun* [*count*]
(**ENGLISH LANGUAGE ARTS**) one of the letters "a," "e," "i," "o," or "u" ⊃ Look at **consonant**.

voy·age /'vɔɪɪdʒ/ *noun* [*count*]
a long trip by boat or in space: *Columbus made his first voyage to the New World in 1492.* ⊃ Look at the note at **trip¹**.

vs. abbreviation of **versus**

vul·gar /'vʌlgər/ *adjective*
not showing good judgment about what is attractive or appropriate; not polite or well behaved: *a vulgar joke*

vul·ner·a·ble /'vʌlnərəbl/ *adjective*
likely to be hurt or damaged: *The soldiers' position meant that they were vulnerable to attack.* ◆ *When she first moved to the city, she felt lonely and vulnerable.*

vul·ture /'vʌltʃər/ *noun* [*count*]
a type of bird that eats dead animals

W w

W, w /'dʌblyu/ *noun* [*count, noncount*]
1 (*plural* **W's, w's** /'dʌblyuz/) the twenty-third letter of the English alphabet: *"Water" begins with a "W."*
2 W short for **watt**

wack·y /'wæki/ *adjective* (**wack·i·er, wack·i·est**) (*informal*)
funny in a slightly crazy way: *She has some pretty wacky ideas!*

wad /wɑd/ *noun* [*count*]
a lot of pieces of paper folded or rolled together: *He pulled a wad of dollar bills out of his pocket.*

wade /weɪd/ *verb* (**wades, wad·ing, wad·ed**)
to walk through water: *Can we wade across the river, or is it too deep?*

pancakes   **waffles**

waf·fle /'wɑfl/ *noun* [*count*]
a flat cake with a pattern of squares on it that is often eaten with a sweet sauce (called SYRUP)

wag /wæg/ *verb* (**wags, wag·ging, wagged**)
If a dog **wags** its tail, its tail moves from side to side several times.

wage /weɪdʒ/ *noun* [*singular*] (also **wag·es** [*plural*])
the money that you receive for the work that you do: *the minimum wage* (= the lowest amount that someone is allowed to be paid for each hour that they work) ◆ *to work for low wages*

wag·on /'wægən/ *noun* [*count*]
1 a vehicle with four wheels that a horse pulls
2 a child's toy like an open box on four wheels, with a long handle for pulling it

wail /weɪl/ *verb* (**wails, wail·ing, wailed**)
to make a long, sad noise: *The little boy fell off his bike and started wailing.*

waist /weɪst/ *noun* [*count*]
the narrow part around the middle of your body

waist·line /'weɪstlaɪn/ *noun* [*count, usually singular*]
the measurement of the body around the waist, used to talk about how fat or thin a person is: *an expanding waistline*

wait¹ /weɪt/ *verb* (**waits, wait·ing, wait·ed**)
to stay in one place until something happens or until someone or something comes: *If I'm late, please wait for me.* ◆ *Have you been waiting long?* ◆ *The doctor kept me waiting* (= made me wait) *for half an hour.*
can't wait used when someone is very excited about something that is going to happen: *I can't wait to see you again!*
wait and see to be patient and find out later: *"What are we having for dinner?" "Wait and see!"*
wait on someone to serve someone food or drinks, usually in a restaurant
wait up to not go to bed until someone comes home: *I'll be home late tonight so don't wait up for me.*

wait² /weɪt/ *noun* [*count, usually singular*]
a time when you wait: *We had a long wait for the bus.*

wait·er /'weɪtər/ *noun* [*count*]
a man who brings food and drinks to your table in a restaurant

wait·ing room /'weɪtɪŋ ˌrum/ *noun* [*count*]
a room where people can sit and wait, for example to see a doctor

wait·ress /'weɪtrəs/ *noun* [*count*] (*plural* **wait·ress·es**)
a woman who brings food and drinks to your table in a restaurant

wake /weɪk/ (also **wake up**) *verb* (**wakes, wak·ing, woke** /woʊk/, **has wok·en** /'woʊkən/)
1 to stop sleeping: *What time did you wake up this morning?*
2 to make someone stop sleeping: *The noise woke me up.* ◆ *Don't wake the baby.*

walk¹ /wɔk/ *verb* (**walks, walk·ing, walked**)
to move on your legs, but not run: *I usually walk to work.* ◆ *We walked 10 miles today.*
walk out to leave suddenly because you are angry: *He walked out of the meeting.*

walk² /wɔk/ *noun* [*count*]
a trip on foot: *The beach is a short walk from our house.* ◆ *I took the dog for a walk.* ◆ *It was a beautiful day, so we went for a walk in the park.*

walk·er /'wɔkər/ *noun* [*count*]
a person who is walking

walk·ie-talk·ie /ˌwɔki 'tɔki/ *noun* [*count*] (*informal*)
a small radio that you can carry with you and use to send and receive messages

wall /wɔl/ *noun* [*count*]
1 a side of a building or room: *There's a picture on the wall.*
2 a thing made of stones, bricks, etc. that is built around an area: *an old stone wall* ◆ *A high wall surrounded the prison.*

wallets

wal·let /'wɑlət/ *noun* [count]
a small, flat case for money and bank cards: *A pickpocket stole my wallet.*

wall·pa·per /'wɔl,peɪpər/ *noun* [noncount]
special paper that you use for covering the walls of a room
▸ **wall·pa·per** *verb* (wall·pa·pers, wall·pa·per·ing, wall·pa·pered)
to put **wallpaper** onto the walls of a room: *We wallpapered the living room ourselves.*

Wall Street /'wɔl strit/ *noun* [noncount]
(**BUSINESS**) a street in New York City that has many important banks and companies, and the business that is done there

wal·nut /'wɔlnʌt/ *noun* [count]
a type of nut that we eat ⊃ Look at the picture at **nut**.

wal·rus /'wɔlrəs; 'wɑlrəs/ *noun* [count] (*plural* **wal·rus·es**)
an animal with short fur that lives in and near the ocean, and that eats fish. It has two very long teeth (called **TUSKS**).

waltz /wɔlts/ *noun* [count] (*plural* **waltz·es**)
(**MUSIC**) a dance for two people to music that has a pattern of three beats; the music for this dance

wand /wɑnd/ *noun* [count]
a thin stick that people hold when they are doing magic tricks

wan·der /'wɑndər/ *verb* (wan·ders, wan·der·ing, wan·dered)
to walk slowly with no special plan: *We wandered around town until the stores opened.*

want 🔊 /wɑnt; wɔnt/ *verb* (wants, want·ing, want·ed)
to wish to have or do something: *He wants a bike for his birthday.* • *I want to go out tonight.* • *She wanted me to give her some money.*

Which word?

Want or would like?
- **Would like** is more polite than **want**.
- Look at these examples: *"I want a drink!"* screamed the child. • *Would you like some more coffee?*

war 🔊 /wɔr/ *noun* [count, noncount]
fighting between countries or between groups of people: *War broke out* (= started). • *The two*

countries have been **at war** (= fighting) *for five years.* • *to* **declare war** *on another country*

ward /wɔrd/ *noun* [count]
(**HEALTH**) a room in a hospital that has beds for the patients: *He worked as a nurse on the children's ward.*

Suffix

-ward

(in adjectives and adverbs) in the direction of: **backward** • **downward** • **eastward** • **outward**

war·den /'wɔrdn/ *noun* [count]
a person whose job is to manage a prison

ward·robe /'wɔrdroʊb/ *noun* [count]
1 a person's collection of clothes: *I need a whole new winter wardrobe!*
2 a piece of furniture where you can hang your clothes

ware·house /'wɛrhaʊs/ *noun* [count]
a big building where people keep things before they sell them: *a furniture warehouse*

war·fare /'wɔrfɛr/ *noun* [noncount]
the activity and ways of fighting a war: *naval warfare*

warm¹ 🔊 /wɔrm/ *adjective* (warm·er, warm·est)

🛈 PRONUNCIATION
The word **warm** sounds like **storm**.

1 having a pleasant temperature that is high but not very high; between cool and hot: *It's warm by the fire.* ⊃ Look at the note at **hot**.
2 Warm clothes are clothes that stop you from feeling cold: *It's cold in the mountains, so take some warm clothes with you.*
3 friendly and kind: *Martha is a very warm person.* ⊃ **ANTONYM cold**
▸ **warm·ly** /'wɔrmli/ *adverb*: *The children were warmly dressed.* • *He thanked me warmly.*

warm² 🔊 /wɔrm/ *verb* (warms, warm·ing, warmed)
warm up; warm someone or **something up**
to become warmer, or to make someone or something warmer: *I warmed up some soup for lunch.* • *It was cold this morning, but it's warming up now.*

warm-blood·ed /,wɔrm 'blʌdəd/ *adjective*
(**BIOLOGY**) having a body temperature that does not change if the temperature of the air changes: *Mammals are warm-blooded.* ⊃ Look at **cold-blooded**.

warmth /wɔrmθ/ *noun* [noncount]
1 a pleasant temperature that is not too hot: *the warmth of the sun*
2 the quality of being kind and friendly: *the warmth of her smile*

warm-up /'wɔrm ʌp/ (also **warm-up**) *noun* [*count*]
a set of exercises that you do to prepare yourself for an activity, such as a sports game

warn 🔊 /wɔrn/ *verb* (**warns, warn·ing, warned**)
to tell someone about danger or about something bad that may happen: *I warned him not to go too close to the fire.*

warn·ing /'wɔrnɪŋ/ *noun* [*count, noncount*]
something that tells you about danger or about something bad that may happen: *There is a warning on every pack of cigarettes.* ✦ *The storm came **without warning**.*

war·rant /'wɔrənt/ *noun* [*count*]
an official document giving someone permission to do something: *Police have issued a **warrant for** his arrest.*

war·ran·ty /'wɔrənti/ *noun* [*count, noncount*]
(*plural* **war·ran·ties**)
(**BUSINESS**) a written promise by a company that it will repair or replace a thing you have bought, if it breaks or stops working: *My new car comes with a 2-year warranty.* ✦ *Is this cell phone still **under warranty**?* ⊃ **SYNONYM guarantee**

war·ri·or /'wɔriər/ *noun* [*count*] (*formal*)
(especially in the past) a person who fights in a war; a soldier

wart /wɔrt/ *noun* [*count*]
(**HEALTH**) a small, hard, dry lump that sometimes grows on the face or body

was /wəz; wʌz/ form of **be**

wash¹ 🔊 /wɑʃ/ *verb* (**wash·es, wash·ing, washed**)
1 to clean someone, something, or yourself with water: *Did you wash the car?* ✦ *Wash your hands before you eat.* ✦ *I washed and dressed quickly.*
2 (used about water) to flow somewhere: *The waves washed over my feet.*
wash someone or **something away** (used about water) to move or carry someone or something to another place: *The house was washed away by the river.*
wash up to wash your face and hands: *Go and wash up, and put on some clean clothes.*

wash² /wɑʃ/ *noun*
1 [*noncount*] clothes that are being washed or that need to be washed: *All my socks are in the wash!*
2 [*usually singular*] cleaning something with water: *The car needs a good wash.*

wash·a·ble /'wɑʃəbl/ *adjective*
Something that is **washable** can be washed without being damaged: *This sweater is **machine washable** (= it can be washed in the washing machine).*

wash·cloth /'wɑʃklɔθ/ *noun* [*count*]
a small, square piece of cloth that you use to wash your face and body

wash·ing ma·chine /'wɑʃɪŋ məʃin/ (also **wash·er** /'wɑʃər/) *noun* [*count*]
a machine that washes clothes

was·n't /'wʌznt; 'wɑznt/ short for **was not**

wasp /wɑsp/ *noun* [*count*]
a yellow and black insect that flies and can hurt (**STING**) you by pushing a sharp part into your skin ⊃ Look at the picture at **insect**.

waste¹ 🔊 /weɪst/ *verb* (**wastes, wast·ing, wast·ed**)
to use too much of something or not use something in a good way: *She **wastes** a lot of money **on** candy.* ✦ *He wasted his **time** at college – he didn't do any work.*

waste² 🔊 /weɪst/ *noun*
1 [*singular*] not using something in a useful way: *It's a waste to throw away all this food!* ✦ *This watch was **a waste of money** – it's broken already!*
2 [*noncount*] material, food, etc. that people no longer use or need: *A lot of waste from the factories goes into this river.*

waste³ 🔊 /weɪst/ *adjective*
not useful or needed: *Plants produce oxygen as a waste product.*

waste·bas·ket /'weɪst,bæskət/ *noun* [*count*]
a container where you put things like paper that you do not want

wastebasket

waste·ful /'weɪstfl/ *adjective*
using more of something than you need; causing waste

watch¹ 🔊 /wɑtʃ/ *verb* (**watch·es, watch·ing, watched**)
1 to look at someone or something for some time: *We **watched television** all evening.* ✦ *Watch how I do this.* ⊃ Look at the note at **look¹**.
2 to take care of something or someone for a short time: *Could you watch my bags while I buy a ticket?*
3 to be careful about someone or something: *You'd better watch what you say to her.*
watch out to be careful because of someone or something dangerous: *Watch out! There's a car coming.* ⊃ **SYNONYM look out**
watch out for someone or **something** to look carefully and be ready for someone or something dangerous: *Watch out for ice on the roads.*

watch² /wɑtʃ/
noun (*plural* watch·es)
1 [*count*] a thing that you wear on your wrist so you know what time it is: *She kept looking at her watch nervously.* ⊃ Look at the note at **clock**.
2 [*noncount*] the action of watching something in case of danger or problems: *The soldier was keeping watch at the gate.*

watch

hand

wa·ter¹ /ˈwɔṭər/ *noun* [*noncount*]
the liquid that is in rivers, lakes, and oceans: *I'd like a glass of water.* • *After the heavy rain a lot of the fields were under water.*

wa·ter² /ˈwɔṭər/ *verb* (wa·ters, wa·ter·ing, wa·tered)
1 to give water to plants: *Did you water the plants?*
2 (used about the eyes or mouth) to fill with liquid: *The smoke made my eyes water.* • *The food smelled so good that it made my mouth water.*

wa·ter·col·or /ˈwɔṭərkʌlər/ *noun* (**ART**)
1 watercolors [*plural*] paints that you mix with water
2 [*count*] a picture that you paint with watercolors

wa·ter cool·er /ˈwɔṭər ˌkulər/ *noun* [*count*]
a machine that you can get cold drinking water from, for example in an office

wa·ter·fall /ˈwɔṭərfɔl/
noun [*count*]
(**GEOGRAPHY**) a place where water falls from a high place to a low place

waterfall

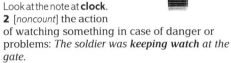

wa·ter·front
/ˈwɔṭərfrʌnt/ *noun*
[*count, usually singular*]
a part of a town or an area that is next to an ocean, a river, or a lake: *a waterfront apartment*

wa·ter·ing can /ˈwɔṭərɪŋ kæn/ *noun* [*count*]
a container that you use for watering plants

wa·ter·mel·on /ˈwɔṭərˌmɛlən/ *noun* [*count*]
a big, round fruit with a thick, green skin. It is pink inside with a lot of black seeds.

wa·ter·proof /ˈwɔṭərpruf/ *adjective*
If something is **waterproof**, it does not let water go through it: *a waterproof jacket*

wa·ter·ski·ing /ˈwɔṭərskiɪŋ/ *noun* [*noncount*]
(**SPORTS**) the sport of moving fast over water on long boards (called WATERSKIS), pulled by a boat

watt /wɑt/ *noun* [*count*] (abbreviation **W**)
(**PHYSICS**) a unit of electrical power: *a 60-watt light bulb*

wave¹ /weɪv/ *noun* [*count*]
1 (**GEOGRAPHY**) one of the high lines of water that moves across the top of the ocean: *Waves crashed against the cliffs.*
2 a sudden increase of a feeling or type of behavior: *There was a wave of sympathy for the victims.*
3 a movement of your hand from side to side in the air to say hello or goodbye, or to make a sign to someone: *With a wave of his hand, he said good night and left the room.*
4 a gentle curve in hair ⊃ Look at **wavy**.
5 (**PHYSICS**) the form that some types of energy such as heat, light, and sound take: *radio waves*

wave² /weɪv/ *verb* (waves, wav·ing, waved)
1 to move your hand from side to side in the air to say hello or goodbye, or to make a sign to someone: *She waved to me as the train left the station.* • *Who are you waving at?*
2 to move something quickly from side to side in the air: *The children waved flags as the mayor rode past.*
3 to move up and down or from side to side: *The flags were waving in the wind.*

wavelength

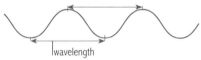

wavelength

wave·length /ˈweɪvlɛŋθ/ *noun* [*count*]
(**PHYSICS**) the size of a radio wave that a particular radio station uses to send out its programs
be on the same wavelength (*informal*) to have the same way of thinking as another person: *We get along OK, but we're not really on the same wavelength.*

wav·y /ˈweɪvi/ *adjective* (wav·i·er, wav·i·est)
having curves; not straight: *a wavy line* • *She has wavy black hair.* ⊃ Look at the picture at **hair**, **line**.

wax /wæks/ *noun* [*noncount*]
the substance that is used for making CANDLES (= tall sticks that you burn to give light) or for making things shine: *I bought wax for the floor.*

way /weɪ/ *noun* (*plural* ways)
1 [*count*] a method or style of doing something: *What is the best way to learn a language?* • *He smiled in a friendly way.*
2 [*count, usually singular*] a road or path that you must follow to go to a place: *Can you tell me the way to the station, please?* • *I lost my way, and I had to look at the map.* • *We stopped for a meal on the way to the show.* • *Here's the museum. Where's the way in?* • *I can't find the way out.*

3 [*singular*] a direction; where someone or something is going or looking: *Come this way.* ✦ *She was looking the other way.* ✦ *Is this picture the right way up?* ✦ *Those two words should be the other way around.*
4 [*singular*] distance: *It's a long way from Houston to Amarillo.*

by the way words that you say when you are going to talk about something different: *By the way, I got an e-mail from Ann yesterday.*
give way
1 to break: *The ladder gave way and Ben fell to the ground.*
2 to agree with someone when you did not agree before: *My parents finally gave way and said I could go out with my friends.*
in the way in front of someone so that you stop them from seeing something or moving: *I can't see – you're in the way.*
no way (*informal*) a way of saying "no" more strongly: *"Can I borrow your bike?" "No way!"*
out of the way no longer stopping someone from moving or doing something: *Get out of the way! There's a car coming!*
way of life how people live: *Is the way of life in Europe different from America?*

we 🔊 /wi/ *pronoun* [*plural*]
I and another person or other people; you and I: *Mick and I went out last night – we went to the theater.* ✦ *Are we late?*

weak 🔊 /wik/ *adjective* (weak·er, weak·est)
1 not powerful or strong: *She felt very weak after her long illness.* ✦ *He is too weak to be a good leader.* ⊃ **ANTONYM strong**
2 Something that is **weak** can break easily: *The bridge is too weak to carry heavy traffic.*
3 (used about a drink) containing a lot of water; not strong in taste: *I'd like some weak tea.* ⊃
ANTONYM strong
▸ **weak·ly** /'wikli/ *adverb*: *She smiled weakly at them.*

weak·en /'wikən/ *verb* (weak·ens, weak·en·ing, weak·ened)
to become less strong, or to make someone or something less strong: *He was weakened by the illness.*

weak·ness 🔊 /'wiknəs/ *noun* (*plural* weak·ness·es)
1 [*noncount*] the state of not being strong: *He thought that crying was a sign of weakness.*
2 [*count*] something that is wrong or bad in a person or thing ⊃ **ANTONYM strength**

wealth /wɛlθ/ *noun*
1 [*noncount*] a lot of money, land, or property: *He is a man of great wealth.*
2 [*singular*] a large number or amount of something: *He has a wealth of teaching experience.*

▸ **wealth·y** /'wɛlθi/ *adjective* (wealth·i·er, wealth·i·est): *a wealthy family* ⊃ **SYNONYM rich**

weap·on 🔊 /'wɛpən/ *noun* [*count*]
something, such as a gun, that is used for fighting or killing people: *nuclear weapons* ✦ *The police still haven't found the murder weapon.*

wear¹ 🔊 /wɛr/ *verb* (wears, wear·ing, wore /wɔr/, has worn /wɔrn/)

ⓘ PRONUNCIATION
The word **wear** sounds just like **where**.

to have clothes, jewelry, etc. on your body: *She was wearing a red dress.* ✦ *I wear glasses.*
wear off to become less strong: *The pain is wearing off.*
wear out; wear something out to become thin or damaged because you have used it a lot; to make something do this: *Children's shoes usually wear out very quickly.*
wear someone out to make someone very tired: *She wore herself out by working too hard.*

wear² /wɛr/ *noun* [*noncount*]
1 clothes: *sportswear*
2 long use which damages something: *This carpet is showing signs of wear.*

wea·ry /'wɪri/ *adjective* (wea·ri·er, wea·ri·est)
very tired: *a weary traveler*
▸ **wea·ri·ly** /'wɪrəli/ *adverb*: *She sank wearily into a chair.*

wea·sel /'wizl/ *noun* [*count*]
a small wild animal with red-brown fur, a long thin body, and short legs. **Weasels** eat smaller animals.

weath·er 🔊 /'wɛðər/ *noun* [*noncount*]
(**GEOGRAPHY**) how much sun, rain, or wind there is at a certain time, or how hot or cold it is: *What's the weather like where you are?* ✦ *We had bad weather last week.*

Collocations

The weather

good weather
- the sun **shines**
- a gentle/cool/warm breeze **blows**

bad weather
- snow **falls/covers everything**
- the rain **falls/pours down**
- the wind **blows/howls**
- snow/wet weather/a storm/a hurricane **is approaching/is forecast**
- **forecast/expect/predict** rain/snow/wet weather/a storm/a hurricane
- thunder **rumbles**
- lightning **strikes**

weath·er fore·cast /'wɛðər ˌfɔrkæst/ *noun* [count]
words on television, radio, or in a newspaper that tell you what the weather will be like: *The weather forecast says it will be sunny and dry tomorrow.*

weath·er·vane /'wɛðərveɪn/ *noun* [count]
a thing on the roof of a building that turns to show which direction the wind is blowing from

weave /wiv/ *verb* (weaves, weav·ing, wove /woʊv/, has wo·ven /'woʊvən/)
to make cloth by putting threads over and under one another: *These scarves are woven by hand.*

web /wɛb/ *noun*
1 [count] a thin net that a spider makes to catch insects ⊃ Look at the picture at **spider**.
2 the Web [singular] (COMPUTERS) the system that makes it possible for you to see information from all over the world on your computer ⊃ SYNONYM the World Wide Web ⊃ Look at the note at **Internet**.

web·cam /'wɛbkæm/ *noun* [count]
(COMPUTERS) a video camera that is connected to a computer so that you can watch what it records on a website as it is happening

web page /'wɛb peɪdʒ/ *noun* [count]
(COMPUTERS) a part of a website that you can see on your computer screen: *We learned how to create and register a new web page.*

web·site /'wɛbsaɪt/ *noun* [count]
(COMPUTERS) a place on the Internet that you can look at to find out information about something: *I found this information on their website.* ◆ *Visit our website to learn more.*

we'd /wid/ short for **we had**, **we would**

wed·ding /'wɛdɪŋ/ *noun* [count]
a time when a man and a woman get married: *Billy and Elena invited me to their wedding.* ◆ *She just bought a wedding dress.*

Word building

- At a **wedding**, two people **get married**.
- On their **wedding day**, the woman is called the **bride** and the man is the **groom** (or **bridegroom**).
- The groom is helped by his **best man**. The bride is helped by her **bridesmaids**. The most important bridesmaid is the **maid of honor**.
- After the ceremony, there is usually a **wedding reception** (= a formal party). Many **couples** go on a **honeymoon** (= a vacation) after getting married.
- **Marriage** is the relationship between a **husband** and a **wife**: *They had a long and happy marriage.*

wedge /wɛdʒ/ *noun* [count]
a piece of wood or other material, with one thick and one thin, pointed end: *Push a wedge under the door to keep it open.*

Wednes·day /'wɛnzdeɪ; 'wɛnzdi/ *noun* [count, noncount] (abbreviation **Weds.**)
the day of the week after Tuesday and before Thursday

weed¹ /wid/ *noun* [count]
a wild plant that grows where you do not want it: *The garden of the old house was full of weeds.*

weed² /wid/ *verb* (weeds, weed·ing, weed·ed)
to pull WEEDS out of the ground

week /wik/ *noun* [count]
1 a time of seven days, usually from Sunday to the next Saturday: *I'm going to Sue's house next week.* ◆ *I play tennis twice a week.* ◆ *I saw him two weeks ago.*
2 the part of the week when people go to work, especially Monday to Friday: *I work during the week but not on weekends.*

week·day /'wikdeɪ/ *noun* [count]
any day except Saturday or Sunday: *I only work on weekdays.*

week·end /'wikɛnd/ *noun* [count]
Saturday and Sunday: *What are you doing over the weekend?*

week·ly /'wikli/ *adjective, adverb*
happening or coming every week or once a week: *a weekly magazine* ◆ *I am paid weekly.*

week·night /'wiknaɪt/ *noun* [count]
any night of the week except Saturday, Sunday, and sometimes Friday night: *My parents don't let me go out on weeknights.*

weep /wip/ *verb* (weeps, weep·ing, wept /wɛpt/, has wept) (formal)
to cry, usually because you are sad

weigh /weɪ/ *verb* (weighs, weigh·ing, weighed)

> ℹ **PRONUNCIATION**
> The word **weigh** sounds just like **way**.

1 to measure how heavy someone or something is using a machine (called a SCALE): *The clerk weighed the package.*
2 to have or show a certain weight: *"How much do you weigh?" "I weigh 155 pounds."*

weight /weɪt/ *noun*
1 [noncount] how heavy someone or something is: *Do you know the weight of the letter?* ◆ *I'm getting fat – I need to lose weight* (= get thinner)! ◆ *He put on weight* (= got fatter).

2 [count] a piece of metal that weighs a particular amount and is used to measure the weight of something, or which people lift in order to improve their strength and as a sport: *She lifts weights as part of her training.*

weight·lift·ing /ˈweɪtˌlɪftɪŋ/ *noun* [noncount] (SPORTS) a sport in which people lift heavy metal weights

weird /wɪrd/ *adjective* (weird·er, weird·est) very strange: *I had a weird dream.*

weird·o /ˈwɪrdoʊ/ *noun* [count] (*plural* weird·os) (*informal*)
a person who looks strange or behaves in a strange way

wel·come¹ 🔑 /ˈwɛlkəm/ *verb* (wel·come, wel·com·ing, wel·comed)
1 to be friendly to someone when they arrive somewhere: *He came to the door to welcome us.*
2 to be happy to receive or accept something: *I really don't know what to do next, so I'd welcome any suggestions.*
▶ **wel·come** *noun* [count]: *They gave us a warm welcome.*

wel·come² /ˈwɛlkəm/ *adjective*
1 If someone or something is **welcome**, you are happy to see them or it: *The cool drinks were welcome on such a hot day.* ◆ *Welcome to America!*
2 (*informal*) used to say that you are happy for someone to do something if they want to: *If you come to the States again, you're welcome to stay with us.*
make someone welcome to show a visitor that you are happy to see them
you're welcome polite words that you say when someone has said "thank you": *"Thank you." "You're welcome."*

weld /wɛld/ *verb* (welds, weld·ing, weld·ed)
to join pieces of metal by heating them and pressing them together: *All the parts of the sculpture have to be welded together.*

wel·fare AWL /ˈwɛlfɛr/ *noun* [noncount]
1 the health and happiness of a person: *The school is responsible for the welfare of its students.*
2 money that the government pays to people who need it: *There are many familes on welfare.*

we'll /wil/ short for **we will**

well¹ 🔑 /wɛl/ *adverb* (bet·ter, best)
1 in a good or right way: *You speak English very well.* ◆ *These shoes are really well made.* ⊃ ANTONYM **badly**
2 completely or very much: *I don't know Cathy very well.* ◆ *You'll need to shake the bottle well before you open it.*
as well also: *"I'm going out." "Can I come as well?"* ⊃ SYNONYM **too**

as well as and also: *She has an apartment in Florida as well as a house in Maine.*
do well to be successful: *He did well on his exams.*
may or **might as well** words that you use to say that you will do something, often because there is nothing else to do: *If you've finished your work, you may as well go home.*
well done! words that you say to someone who has done something good: *"I got the job!" "Well done!"*

well² 🔑 /wɛl/ *adjective* (bet·ter, best)
healthy: *"How are you?" "I'm very well, thanks."* ⊃ ANTONYM **sick**

well³ 🔑 /wɛl/ *exclamation*
1 a word that you often say when you are starting to speak: *"Do you like it?" "Well, I'm not really sure."*
2 a word that you use to show surprise: *Well, that's strange!*
3 a word that you use when you are waiting for someone to say something: *Well? Are you going to tell me what happened?*
4 (also **oh well**) a word that you use when you know there is nothing you can do to change a situation: *Well, we made a mistake and there's nothing we can do about it now.*

well⁴ /wɛl/ *noun* [count]
a deep hole for getting water or oil from under the ground: *an oil well*

well-be·haved /ˌwɛl bɪˈheɪvd/ *adjective*
behaving in a way that most people think is good: *Their children are very well behaved.*

well-be·ing /ˌwɛl ˈbiɪŋ/ *noun* [noncount]
a feeling of being healthy and happy

well-done /ˌwɛl ˈdʌn/ *adjective*
Meat that is **well done** has been cooked for a long time. ⊃ Look at **rare** (2).

well-dressed /ˌwɛl ˈdrɛst/ *adjective*
wearing attractive or expensive clothes: *a well-dressed young man*

well-known /ˌwɛl ˈnoʊn/ *adjective*
famous: *She's very well known in this part of the country.* ◆ *a well-known writer* ⊃ ANTONYM **unknown**

well off /ˌwɛl ˈɔf/ *adjective*
rich: *They must be very well off – their house is huge.* ⊃ SYNONYM **rich**, **wealthy**

went form of **go¹**

wept form of **weep**

we're /wɪr/ short for **we are**

were /wər/ form of **be**

weren't /wərnt/ short for **were not**

were·wolf /ˈwɛrwʊlf/ *noun* [count] (plural **were·wolves** /ˈwɛrwʊlvz/)
(in stories) a person who sometimes changes into a wild animal like a big dog (called a WOLF), especially at the time of the full moon

west 🔑 /wɛst/ *noun* [singular] (abbreviation **W.**) (**GEOGRAPHY**)
1 the direction you look in to see the sun go down: *Which way is west?* • *They live in the west of Montana.* ➷ Look at the picture at **compass**.
2 the west or **the West** the part of any country, city, etc. that is further to the west than the other parts: *the history of the American West*
3 the West the countries of North America and western Europe
▶ **west** *adjective, adverb*: *A west wind is blowing.* • *The town is five miles west of here.*

west·ern¹ 🔑 /ˈwɛstərn/ *adjective* (**GEOGRAPHY**)
1 in or of the west of a place: *Western parts of the country will be very cold.*
2 Western from or connected with the western part of the world, especially Europe and North America

west·ern² /ˈwɛstərn/ *noun* [count]
a movie, TV program, or book about life in the past in the west of the U.S.

wet¹ 🔑 /wɛt/ *adjective* (**wet·ter, wet·test**)
1 covered in water or another liquid: *This towel is wet – can I have a dry one?* • *There was a strong smell of wet paint.*
2 with a lot of rain: *a wet day* ➷ **ANTONYM dry**

wet² /wɛt/ *verb* (**wets, wet·ting, wet** or **wet·ted, has wet** or **has wet·ted**)
to make something wet: *Wet your hair before you put shampoo on it.*

wet·lands /ˈwɛtləndz/ *noun* [plural]
(**GEOGRAPHY**) an area of land that is always wet: *The wetlands are home to a large variety of wildlife.*

wet·suit /ˈwɛtsut/ *noun* [count]
a rubber suit that covers the whole body, which you wear for swimming underwater or playing sports in the water

we've /wiv/ short for **we have**

whale /weɪl/ *noun*
[count]
a very big animal that lives in the ocean and looks like a very big fish

whale

wharf /wɔrf/ *noun* [count] (plural **wharves** /wɔrvz/)
a long structure that is built from the land into the ocean, where people can tie up their boats

what 🔑 /wʌt; wət/ *pronoun, adjective*
1 a word that you use when you ask about someone or something: *What's your name?* •

What are you reading? • *What time is it?* • *What kind of music do you like?*
2 the thing that: *I don't know what this word means.* • *Tell me what to do.*
3 a word that you use to show surprise or other strong feelings: *What a terrible day!* • *What beautiful flowers!*

what? (*informal*)
1 a word that you use when you did not hear something correctly: *What? I can't hear you.*
2 a word that you use when you want to know what someone wants: *"Mom!" "What?" "Can I have a drink?"*

what about...? words that you use when you suggest something: *What about going to a restaurant tonight?* ➷ **SYNONYM how about...?**

what...for? for what purpose or reason?: *What did you say that for?* • *What's this machine for?*

what if...? what would happen if...?: *What if the car breaks down?*

what is...like? words that you use when you want to know more about someone or something: *"What's her brother like?" "He's very nice."*

what's on? words that you use when you want to know what television programs are being shown: *What's on TV tonight?*

what's up? (*informal*)
1 used to say "hello" to someone: *"Hey Chris, what's up?" "Not much. How about you?"*
2 what is wrong?: *You look sad. What's up?*

what·ev·er 🔑 /wʌtˈɛvər; wɑtˈɛvər/ *adjective, pronoun, adverb*
1 any or every; anything or everything: *These animals eat whatever food they can find.* • *I'll do whatever I can to help you.*
2 it does not matter what: *Whatever you do, don't be late.*
3 (*informal*) a word that you say to show that you do not mind what you do or have: *"What should we do tomorrow?" "Whatever."*

what's /wʌts; wɑts/ short for **what is, what has**

wheat /wit/ *noun* [noncount]
a type of grain that can be made into flour

wheel¹ 🔑 /wil/ *noun* [count]
a thing like a circle, which turns around to move something such as a car or a bicycle: *His favorite toy is a dog on wheels.* ➷ Look at the picture at **car**.

wheel² /wil/ *verb* (**wheels, wheel·ing, wheeled**)
to push along something that has wheels: *I wheeled my bicycle up the hill.*

wheel·bar·row
/ˈwilˌbæroʊ/ *noun*
[count]
a container with one wheel and two handles that you use outside for carrying things

wheelbarrow

wheel·chair
/'wiltʃɛr/ noun [count]
a chair with wheels
for someone who
cannot walk

wheelchair

wheeze /wiz/ verb
(wheezes, wheez·ing,
wheezed)
to breathe in a noisy
way, for example
because you have an
illness in your chest: *She's been wheezing and
coughing all day.*

when 🔑 /wɛn/ adverb, conjunction
1 at what time: *When did she arrive?* • *I don't
know when his birthday is.*
2 at the time that: *It was raining when we left
school.* • *I saw her in May, when she was in
Denver.* • *He came when I called him.*
3 since; considering that: *Why do you want
another dog when you have two already?*

when·ev·er 🔑 /wɛn'ɛvər/ conjunction
1 at any time that: *Come and see us whenever
you want.*
2 every time that: *Whenever I see her, she talks
about her boyfriend.*

where 🔑 /wɛr/ adverb, conjunction
1 in or to what place: *Where do you live?* • *I asked
her where she lived.* • *Where's he going?*
2 in which; at which: *This is the street where I
live.*

where·as AWL /wɛr'æz/ conjunction
a word that you use between two different
ideas: *John likes traveling, whereas I don't.*

where·by AWL /wɛr'baɪ/ adverb (formal)
by which; because of which: *They are
introducing a program whereby all staff can have
regular training.*

wher·ev·er 🔑 /wɛr'ɛvər/ adverb, conjunction
at, in, or to any place: *Sit wherever you like.*

wheth·er 🔑 /'wɛðər/ conjunction
1 a word that we use to talk about choosing
between two things: *I don't know **whether** to go
or not.*
2 if: *She asked me whether I was married.*

which 🔑 /wɪtʃ/ pronoun, adjective
1 what person or thing: *Which color do you like
best – blue or green?* • *Which apartment do you
live in?*
2 a word that shows exactly what thing or
things you are talking about: *Did you read the
poem which Louise wrote?*
3 a word that you use before you say more
about something: *Her new dress, which she
bought for $200, is really beautiful.*

which·ev·er /wɪtʃ'ɛvər/ adjective, pronoun
any person or thing: *Here are two books – take
whichever you want.*

while¹ 🔑 /waɪl/ conjunction
1 during the time that; when: *The telephone
rang while I was taking a shower.*
2 at the same time as: *I listen to the radio while
I'm eating my breakfast.*

while² 🔑 /waɪl/ noun [singular]
a period of time: *Let's sit here **for a while**.* • *I'm
going home **in a while** (= soon).*

whim·per /'wɪmpər/ verb (whim·pers,
whim·per·ing, whim·pered)
to make a soft crying noise, because you are
hurt or afraid: *"Don't leave me alone," he
whimpered.*
▸ **whim·per** noun [count]: *The dog gave a
whimper.*

whine /waɪn/ verb (whines, whin·ing, whined)
1 to complain about things in an unpleasant,
crying voice: *The children were whining all
afternoon.*
2 to make a long, high, sad sound: *The dog was
whining outside the door.*

whip¹ /wɪp/ noun [count]
a long piece of leather or rope with a handle,
used for making animals move faster or for
hitting people

whip² /wɪp/ verb (whips, whip·ping, whipped)
1 to hit an animal or a person with a WHIP: *The
rider whipped the horse to make it go faster.*
2 to mix food very quickly with a fork, for
example, until it is light and thick: *whipped
cream*

whirl /wɔrl/ verb (whirls, whirl·ing, whirled)
to move around and around very quickly: *The
dancers whirled around the room.*

whirl·pool /'wɔrlpul/ noun [count]
(**GEOGRAPHY**) a place in a river or the ocean
where the water moves around in a circle very
quickly

whisk¹ /wɪsk/ verb (whisks, whisk·ing, whisked)
1 to mix eggs or cream very quickly with a fork
or a WHISK
2 to take someone or something somewhere
very quickly: *The president was **whisked away** in
a helicopter.*

whisk² /wɪsk/ noun [count]
a tool that you use for mixing eggs or cream
very quickly ⊃ Look at the picture at **kitchen**.

whisk·er /'wɪskər/ noun [count]
one of the long hairs that grow near the mouth
of a cat, a mouse, and some other animals ⊃
Look at the picture at **cat**.

---

whis·key /'wɪski/ *noun* [*count, noncount*] (*plural* whis·keys)
a strong alcoholic drink; a glass of this drink

whis·per /'wɪspər/ *verb* (whis·pers, whis·per·ing, whis·pered)
to speak very quietly to someone, so that other people cannot hear what you are saying: *He whispered so that he would not wake the baby up.*
▶ **whis·per** *noun* [*count*]: *She spoke in a whisper.*

whis·tle¹ /'wɪsl/ *noun* [*count*]
1 a small musical instrument that makes a long, high sound when you blow it: *The referee blew his whistle to start the game.*
2 the long, high sound that you make when you blow air out between your lips or when you blow a **whistle**

whis·tle² /'wɪsl/ *verb* (whis·tles, whis·tling, whis·tled)
to make a long, high sound by blowing air out between your lips or through a WHISTLE: *He whistled a tune to himself.*

white¹ /waɪt/ *adjective* (whit·er, whit·est)
1 with the color of snow or milk: *He wore a white shirt and a blue tie.*
2 with pale skin
3 White wine is wine with a light color.

white² /waɪt/ *noun*
1 [*noncount*] the color of snow or milk: *She was dressed in white.*
2 [*count*] a person with pale skin
3 [*count, noncount*] the part inside an egg that is around the yellow middle part: *Add the whites of two eggs.* ⊃ Look at the picture at **egg**.

white·board /'waɪtbɔrd/ *noun* [*count*]
a large, white board that people like teachers write on with special pens ⊃ Look at **blackboard**.

white-col·lar /ˌwaɪt 'kɑlər/ *adjective*
(BUSINESS) connected with people who do office work rather than physical work: *white-collar jobs* ⊃ Look at **blue-collar**.

the White House /ðə 'waɪt haʊs/ *noun* [*singular*] (POLITICS)
1 the large building in Washington, D.C. where the U.S. president lives and works
2 the U.S. president and his or her officials: *The White House has issued a statement.*

whiz (also **whizz**) /wɪz/ *verb* (whiz·zes, whiz·zing, whizzed) (*informal*)
to move very quickly: *The bullet whizzed past his head.*

who /hu/ *pronoun*
1 a word we use in questions to ask about the name, position, etc. of one or more people: *Who is that girl?* ◆ *I don't know who did it.*
2 a word that shows which person or people you are talking about: *I like people who say what*

they think. ◆ *The woman who I work for is very nice.*

who'd /hud/ short for **who had**, **who would**

who·ev·er /hu'ɛvər/ *pronoun*
1 the person who; any person who: *Whoever broke the glass must pay for it.*
2 a way of saying "it does not matter who": *I don't want to see anyone – whoever it is.*

whole¹ /hoʊl/ *adjective*

> ℹ PRONUNCIATION
> The word **whole** sounds just like **hole**, because we don't say the **w** in this word.

complete; with no parts missing: *He ate the whole cake!* ◆ *We are going to Australia for a whole month.*

whole² /hoʊl/ *noun* [*singular*]
1 a thing that is complete: *Two halves make a whole.*
2 all of something: *I spent the whole of the weekend in bed.*
on the whole generally, but not always completely true: *On the whole, I think it's a good idea.*

whole·some /'hoʊlsəm/ *adjective*
1 good for your health: *simple, wholesome food for the whole family*
2 having good moral values: *We prefer more wholesome entertainment for our kids.*

who'll /hul/ short for **who will**

whol·ly /'hoʊli/ *adverb* (*formal*)
completely: *He is not wholly to blame for the situation.* ⊃ SYNONYM **totally**

whom /hum/ *pronoun* (*formal*)
a word we use instead of "who" as the object of a verb or PREPOSITION: *To whom did you give the money?* ◆ *She's the woman whom I met in Greece.*

whoop /wup; hup/ *verb* (whoops, whoop·ing, whooped)
to shout loudly because you are happy or excited
▶ **whoop** *noun* [*count*]: *He let out a whoop of laughter.*

who's /huz/ short for **who is**, **who has**

whose /huz/ *adjective, pronoun*
1 used to ask who something belongs to: *Whose car is this?*
2 used to say exactly which person or thing you mean, or to give extra information about a person or thing: *That's the boy whose sister is a singer.*

who've /huv/ short for **who have**

why /waɪ/ *adverb*
for what reason: *Why are you late?* ◆ *I don't know why she's angry.*

why not? words that you use to make or agree to a suggestion: *Why not ask Kate to go with you?* • *"Let's go see a movie." "Sure, why not?"*

wick·ed /'wɪkəd/ *adjective*
very bad: *a story about a wicked witch* ➔ SYNONYM **evil**

wide¹ 🖉 /waɪd/ *adjective* (wid·er, wid·est)
1 far from one side to the other: *We drove down a wide road.* ➔ ANTONYM **narrow**
2 You use **wide** to say or ask how far something is from one side to the other: *The table was 6 feet wide.* • *How wide is the river?*
3 completely open: *The children's eyes were wide with excitement.* ➔ The noun is **width**.

wide² /waɪd/ *adverb*
completely; as far or as much as possible: *Open your mouth wide.* • *I'm wide awake!* • *She stood with her feet wide apart.*

wide·ly /'waɪdli/ *adverb*
by a lot of people; in or to a lot of places: *He has traveled widely in Asia.*

wid·en /'waɪdn/ *verb* (wid·ens, wid·en·ing, wid·ened)
to become wider; to make something wider: *They are widening the road.*

wide·spread AWL /'waɪdsprɛd/ *adjective*
If something is **widespread**, it is happening in many places: *The disease is becoming more widespread.*

wid·ow /'wɪdoʊ/ *noun* [count]
a woman whose husband is dead

wid·ow·er /'wɪdoʊər/ *noun* [count]
a man whose wife is dead

width /wɪdθ/ *noun* [count]
how far it is from one side of something to the other; how wide something is: *The room is fifteen feet in width.* ➔ The adjective is **wide**. ➔ Look at the picture at **dimension**.

wife 🖉 /waɪf/ *noun* [count] (plural **wives** /waɪvz/)
the woman that someone is married to ➔ Look at **husband**.

wig /wɪg/ *noun* [count]
a covering for your head made of hair that is not your own

wi·ki /'wɪki/ *noun* [count] (plural **wi·kis**)
a website that allows any user to change or add to the information it contains

wild¹ 🖉 /waɪld/ *adjective* (wild·er, wild·est)
1 Wild plants and animals live or grow in nature, not with people: *We picked some wild flowers.*
2 excited; not controlled: *She was wild with anger.* • *The crowd went wild with excitement.*
3 (informal) exciting and interesting, because it is unusual: *a totally wild outfit*

wild² /waɪld/ *noun* **the wild** [singular]
a natural area that is not controlled by people: *In Africa we saw gorillas in the wild.*

wil·der·ness /'wɪldərnəs/ *noun* [count, usually singular]
a large area of land that has never been used for building on or for growing things: *We love to go camping in the wilderness.*

wild·life /'waɪldlaɪf/ *noun* [noncount]
animals and plants in nature ➔ Look at the note at **nature**.

will¹ 🖉 /wəl; wɪl/ *modal verb*

Grammar

- The negative form of **will** is **will not** or the short form **won't** /woʊnt/: *They won't be there.*
- The short form of **will** is **'ll**. We often use this: *You'll* (= you will) *be late.* • *He'll* (= he will) *drive you to the station.*

1 a word that shows the future: *Do you think she will come tomorrow?*
2 a word that you use when you agree or promise to do something: *I'll carry your bag for you.*
3 a word that you use when you ask someone to do something: *Will you open the window, please?* ➔ Look at the note at **modal verb**.

will² 🖉 /wɪl/ *noun*
1 [count, noncount] the power of your mind that makes you choose, decide, and do things: *She has a very strong will, and no one can stop her from doing what she wants.*
2 [singular] what someone wants to happen: *The man made him get into the car against his will* (= when he did not want to).
3 [count] a legal document that says who will have your money, house, etc. when you die: *My grandmother left me $2,000 in her will.*

will·ing /'wɪlɪŋ/ *adjective*
ready and happy to do something: *I'm willing to work weekends.* ➔ ANTONYM **unwilling**
▶ **will·ing·ly** /'wɪlɪŋli/ *adverb*: *I'll willingly help you.*
▶ **will·ing·ness** /'wɪlɪŋnəs/ *noun* [noncount, singular]: *He showed no willingness to help.*

wil·low /'wɪloʊ/ *noun* [count]
a tree with long, thin branches that hang down. **Willow** trees grow near water.

will·pow·er /'wɪl,paʊər/ *noun* [noncount]
the ability to keep trying to succeed, even when something is hard to do: *It takes willpower to quit smoking.*

wimp /wɪmp/ *noun* [count] (informal)
a person who is weak or afraid to do things

---

win 🔑 /wɪn/ *verb* (wins, win·ning, won /wʌn/, has won)
1 to be the best or the first in a game, race, or competition: *Who won the race?* • *Tom won and I was second.* ⊃ ANTONYM **lose**
2 to receive something because you did well or tried hard: *I won a prize in the competition.* • *Who won the gold medal?*
▸ **win** *noun* [count]: *Our team has had five wins this year.* ⊃ Look at **winning, winner.**

wind¹ 🔑 /wɪnd/ *noun* [count, noncount]
(GEOGRAPHY) air that moves: *The wind blew his hat off.* • *Strong winds caused a lot of damage to buildings.*

Thesaurus

wind air that moves quickly outside: *The wind was blowing hard.* • *The trees were swaying in the wind.* • *Several trees were blown over in the strong winds.* • *A gust of wind blew my hat off.*
hurricane a violent storm with very strong winds, which starts over the ocean: *Many of the buildings here were destroyed in the hurricane.* • *Hurricane Rita is now approaching the coast of Florida.*
tornado a violent storm with very strong winds that move in a circle. There is often also a tall cloud which is narrow at the bottom and wide at the top: *A tornado tore through the town yesterday.* • *The hotel was completely destroyed by a tornado.* • *a tornado warning*
breeze a light wind: *A light breeze was blowing.* • *The flowers were gently moving in the breeze.* • *a cool/warm breeze*
gale a very strong wind: *The roof of the school was torn off by the gale.* • *The gale blew down several trees.*

wind² /waɪnd/ *verb* (winds, wind·ing, wound /waʊnd/, has wound)

ⓘ PRONUNCIATION
The verb **wind** sounds like **find**, and the past forms sound like **found.**

1 to make something long go around and around another thing: *The nurse wound the bandage around my knee.*
2 to turn a key or handle to make something work or move: *The clock will stop if you don't wind it up.*
3 A road or river that **winds** has a lot of bends and turns: *The path winds through the forest.*

wind·chill /'wɪndtʃɪl/ *noun* [noncount]
the effect of a cold temperature together with wind: *The windchill factor makes it feel even colder outside today.*

wind in·stru·ment /'wɪnd ˌɪnstrəmənt/ *noun* [count]
(MUSIC) a musical instrument that you play by blowing through it

wind·mill /'wɪndmɪl/ *noun* [count]
a tall building with long, flat parts that turn in the wind

win·dow 🔑 /'wɪndoʊ/ *noun* [count]
1 an opening in a building or in a car door, for example, with glass in it: *It was cold, so I closed the window.* • *She looked out of the window.*
2 (COMPUTERS) an area on a computer screen that shows a particular type of information or program: *to open or close a window*

win·dow·pane /'wɪndoʊpeɪn/ *noun* [count]
a piece of glass in a window

win·dow·sill /'wɪndoʊsɪl/ *noun* [count]
a shelf under a window

wind·shield /'wɪndʃild/
the big window at the front of a car ⊃ Look at the picture at **car.**

wind·shield wip·er /'wɪndʃild ˌwaɪpər/ (also **wip·er**) *noun* [count]
a thing that cleans rain and dirt off the WINDSHIELD while you are driving

wind·surf·ing
/'wɪndsərfɪŋ/ *noun* [noncount]
(SPORTS) the sport of moving over water on a special board with a sail: *We like to go windsurfing on the weekend.*

windsurfing

▸ **wind·surf·er** /'wɪndsərfər/ *noun* [count]: *This beach is popular with windsurfers.*

wind·y /'wɪndi/ *adjective* (wind·i·er, wind·i·est)
with a lot of wind: *It's very windy today!*

wine 🔑 /waɪn/ *noun* [count, noncount]
an alcoholic drink made from small green or purple fruit (called GRAPES): *Would you like red or white wine?* • *She ordered a glass of wine.*

wing 🔑 /wɪŋ/ *noun* [count]
1 one of the two parts that a bird or an insect uses to fly: *The chicken ran around flapping its wings.* ⊃ Look at the picture at **bird.**
2 one of the two long parts at the sides of an airplane that support it in the air
3 a part of a building that was added to the main part: *He's in the new wing of the hospital.*

wing·span /'wɪŋspæn/ *noun* [count]
the distance between the end of one wing and the end of the other: *Eagles can have a wingspan of over seven feet.*

| tʃ **chin** | dʒ **June** | v **van** | θ **thin** | ð **then** | s **so** | z **zoo** | ʃ **she** |

wink /wɪŋk/ *verb* (winks, wink·ing, winked)
to close and open one eye quickly as a friendly
or secret sign to someone: *She winked at me.*
▸ **wink** *noun* [*count*]: *He gave me a wink.* ⊃ Look at
blink.

win·ner 🔎 /'wɪnər/ *noun* [*count*]
a person or an animal that wins a game, race, or
competition: *The winner was given a prize.* ⊃
ANTONYM loser

win·ning /'wɪnɪŋ/ *adjective*
The **winning** person or team is the one that
wins a game, race, or competition: *the winning
team*

win·ter 🔎 /'wɪntər/ *noun* [*count, noncount*]
the coldest part of the year, which comes
between fall and spring: *It often snows in the
winter.*

wipe¹ /waɪp/ *verb* (wipes, wip·ing, wiped)
1 to make something clean or dry with a cloth: *I
washed my hands and wiped them on a towel.* ◆
The waitress wiped off the table.
2 to take away something by rubbing it: *She
wiped the dirt off her shoes.* ◆ *I wiped up the milk
on the floor.*
wipe something out to destroy a place
completely: *The bombs wiped out whole towns.*

wipe² /waɪp/ *noun* [*count*]
1 the action of WIPING something: *He gave the
table a quick wipe.*
2 a piece of paper or thin cloth with a special
liquid on it that you use for cleaning things: *a
box of face wipes* (= for cleaning your face)

wip·er /'waɪpər/ *noun* [*count*] = **windshield wiper**

wire 🔎 /'waɪər/ *noun* [*count*]
a long piece of very thin metal: *The box was
fastened with a piece of wire.* ◆ *The telephone
wires had been cut.* ⊃ Look at the picture at **cord**.

wis·dom /'wɪzdəm/ *noun* [*noncount*]
knowing and understanding a lot about many
things: *Some people think that old age brings
wisdom.* ⊃ The adjective is **wise**.

wis·dom tooth /'wɪzdəm tuθ/ *noun* [*count*]
(*plural* **wis·dom teeth** /'wɪzdəm tiθ/)
(**BIOLOGY**) one of the four large teeth at the back
of your mouth that appear when you are about
20 years old

wise /waɪz/ *adjective* (wis·er, wis·est)
knowing and understanding a lot about many
things: *a wise old man* ◆ *Do you think this is wise?*
▸ **wise·ly** /'waɪzli/ *adverb*: *Many people wisely
stayed at home in the bad weather.*

wish¹ 🔎 /wɪʃ/ *verb* (wish·es, wish·ing, wished)
1 to want something that is not possible or that
will probably not happen: *I wish I could fly!* ◆ *I
wish I had passed the exam!* ◆ *I wish we were rich.*

2 to say to yourself that you want something
and hope that it will happen: *You can't have
everything you wish for.*
3 (*formal*) to want to do or have something: *I
wish to see the manager.*
4 to say that you hope someone will have
something: *I wished her a happy birthday.*

wish² 🔎 /wɪʃ/ *noun* [*count*] (*plural* **wish·es**)
1 a feeling that you want to do or have
something: *I have no wish to go.*
2 an act of trying to make something happen by
saying you want it to happen or by hoping that it
will happen: *Close your eyes and make a wish!*
best wishes words that you write at the end of a
letter, before your name, to show that you hope
someone is well and happy: *See you soon. Best
wishes, Lucy.*

wit /wɪt/ *noun*
1 [*noncount*] speaking or writing in an
intelligent and funny way
2 **wits** [*plural*] the ability to think quickly and in
an intelligent way: *He needed all his wits to find
his way out.*

witch /wɪtʃ/ *noun* [*count*] (*plural* **witch·es**)
a woman in stories who uses magic to do bad
things ⊃ Look at **wizard**.

with 🔎 /wɪð; wɪθ/ *preposition*
1 a word that shows people or things are
together: *I live with my parents.* ◆ *Mix the flour
with milk.* ◆ *I agree with you.*
2 having or carrying: *He's an old man with gray
hair.* ◆ *I want to live in a house with a garden.* ◆ *I
passed a woman with an enormous suitcase.*
3 using: *I cut it with a knife.* ◆ *Fill the bottle with
water.*
4 against: *I played tennis with my sister.*
5 agreeing with or supporting someone or
something: *Are you with us on this plan?* ⊃
ANTONYM against
6 because of: *Her hands were blue with cold.*

with·draw /wɪð'drɔ; wɪθ'drɔ/ *verb* (with·draws,
with·draw·ing, with·drew /wɪð'dru; wɪθ'dru/, has
with·drawn /wɪð'drɔn; wɪθ'drɔn/)
1 to move back or away: *The army withdrew
from the town.*
2 to say that you will not take part in something:
Rob has withdrawn from the race.
3 to take something out or away: *I withdrew
$100 from my bank account.*

with·er /'wɪðər/ *verb* (with·ers, with·er·ing,
with·ered)
If a plant **withers**, it becomes dry and dies: *The
plants withered in the hot sun.*

with·in 🔎 /wɪ'ðɪn; wɪ'θɪn/ *preposition*
1 before the end of: *I'll be back within an hour.*
2 not farther than: *We live within a mile of the
train station.*

3 (*formal*) inside: *There are 400 prisoners within the prison walls.*

with·out 🔑 /wɪˈðaʊt; wɪˈθaʊt/ *preposition, adverb*
1 not having, showing, or using something: *It's cold – don't go out without your coat.* ◆ *I drink coffee without sugar.*
2 not being with someone or something: *He left without me.*
do without to manage when something is not there: *There isn't any milk, so we'll have to do without.*
without doing something not doing something: *They left without saying goodbye.*

wit·ness /ˈwɪtnəs/ *noun* [count] (*plural* **wit·ness·es**)
1 a person who sees something happen and can tell other people about it later: *There were two witnesses to the accident.*
2 a person who goes to a court of law to tell people what he or she saw: *a witness for the defense*
▶ **wit·ness** *verb* (**wit·ness·es**, **wit·ness·ing**, **wit·nessed**): *She witnessed a murder.*

wit·ty /ˈwɪt̮i/ *adjective* (**wit·ti·er**, **wit·ti·est**)
intelligent and funny: *a witty answer*

wives plural of **wife**

wiz·ard /ˈwɪzərd/ *noun* [count]
a man in stories who has magic powers ⊃ Look at **witch**.

wob·ble /ˈwɑbl/ *verb* (**wob·bles**, **wob·bling**, **wob·bled**)
to move a little from side to side: *That chair wobbles when you sit on it.*
▶ **wob·bly** /ˈwɑbli/ *adjective* (**wob·bli·er**, **wob·bli·est**): *a wobbly table*

wok /wɑk/ *noun* [count]
a large pan that is shaped like a bowl and used for cooking Chinese food

woke, wok·en forms of **wake**

wolf /wʊlf/ *noun*
[count] (*plural* **wolves** /wʊlvz/)
a wild animal like a big dog

wolf

wom·an 🔑 /ˈwʊmən/ *noun* [count] (*plural* **wom·en** /ˈwɪmən/)
an adult female person: *men, women, and children* ◆ *Would you prefer to see a woman doctor?*

womb /wum/ *noun* [count]
the part of a woman or a female animal where a baby develops before it is born ⊃ SYNONYM **uterus**

won form of **win**

won·der¹ 🔑 /ˈwʌndər/ *verb* (**won·ders**, **won·der·ing**, **won·dered**)
to ask yourself something; to want to know something: *I wonder what that noise is.* ◆ *I wonder why he didn't come.*
I wonder if… words that you use to ask a question politely: *I wonder if I could use your phone.*

won·der² /ˈwʌndər/ *noun*
1 [noncount] a feeling that you have when you see or hear something very strange, surprising, or beautiful: *The children stared in wonder at the elephants.*
2 [count] something that gives you this feeling: *the wonders of modern medicine*
it's a wonder… it is surprising that…: *It's a wonder you weren't killed in the accident.*
no wonder it is not surprising: *She didn't sleep last night, so no wonder she's tired.*

won·der·ful 🔑 /ˈwʌndərfl/ *adjective*
very good: *What a wonderful present!* ◆ *This food is wonderful.* ⊃ SYNONYM **fantastic**

won't /woʊnt/ short for **will not**

wood 🔑 /wʊd/ *noun*
1 [count, noncount] the hard substance that trees are made of: *Put some more wood on the fire.* ◆ *The table is made of wood.* ⊃ Look at the picture at **tree**.
2 [count] a big group of trees, smaller than a forest: *a large wood* ◆ *a walk in the woods*

wood·en 🔑 /ˈwʊdn/ *adjective*
made of wood: *The toys are kept in a large wooden box.*

wood·land /ˈwʊdlənd/ *noun* [count, noncount]
an area of land that is covered with trees: *The house is surrounded by woodlands.*

wood·peck·er /ˈwʊdˌpɛkər/ *noun* [count]
a bird that makes holes in trees when it is looking for insects to eat

wood·wind /ˈwʊdwɪnd/ *noun* [count]
(MUSIC) a type of musical instrument that is often made of wood and that you play by blowing into it ⊃ Look at the note at **orchestra**.

wool 🔑 /wʊl/ *noun* [noncount]
1 the soft, thick hair of sheep
2 thread or cloth that is made from the hair of sheep: *The cat was playing with a ball of wool.* ◆ *This sweater is made of pure wool.*

wool·en /ˈwʊlən/ *adjective*
made of wool: *woolen socks*

wool·ly (also **wool·y**) /ˈwʊli/ *adjective* (**wool·li·er**, **wool·li·est**)
made of wool, or like wool: *a woolly hat*

word 🔑 /wərd/ *noun*
1 [count] (ENGLISH LANGUAGE ARTS) a sound that you make, or a letter or group of letters that you

ə **about**   y **yes**   w **woman**   t̮ **butter**   eɪ **say**   aɪ **five**   ɔɪ **boy**   aʊ **now**   oʊ **go**

write, which has a meaning: *What's the Italian word for "dog"? • Do you know the words of this song?*

2 [*count*] something that you say: *Can I have a word with you? • Don't say a word about this to anyone.*

3 [*singular*] a promise: *She gave me her word that she wouldn't tell anyone. • Claire said she would come, and she kept her word* (= did what she had promised).

in other words saying the same thing in a different way: *Joe doesn't like hard work – in other words, he's lazy!*

take someone's word for it to believe what someone says

word for word using exactly the same words: *Mike repeated word for word what you told him.*

word proc·es·sor /'wərd ˌprɑsɛsər/ *noun* [*count*]

(**COMPUTERS**) a small computer that you can use for writing

▶ **word proc·es·sing** /'wərd ˌprɑsɛsɪŋ/ *noun* [*noncount*]: *I mainly use the computer for word processing.*

wore form of **wear¹**

work¹ /wərk/ *verb* (**works**, **work·ing**, **worked**)

1 to be busy doing or making something: *You will need to work hard if you want to pass the exam. • I'm going to work on my essay this evening.*

2 to do something as a job and get money for it: *Suzy works for the government. • I work at the car factory.*

3 to go correctly or to do something correctly: *We can't watch TV – it isn't working. • How does this camera work?*

4 to make something do something: *Can you show me how to work the coffee machine?*

5 to have the result you wanted: *I don't think your plan will work.*

work out

1 to have the result you wanted: *I hope things work out for you.*

2 to do exercises to keep your body strong and healthy: *She works out every day.* ⊃ The noun is **workout**.

work something out to find the answer to something: *We worked out the cost of a new kitchen.*

work² /wərk/ *noun*

1 [*noncount*] the job that you do to earn money: *I'm looking for work • What time do you start work? • How long have you been out of work* (= without a job)? ⊃ Look at the note at **job**.

2 [*noncount*] the place where you have a job: *I called him at work. • I'm not going to work today.*

3 [*noncount*] doing or making something: *Digging the garden is hard work. • She's so lazy –*

she never does any work. • The group is at work on (= making) *a new show.*

4 [*noncount*] something that you make or do: *The teacher corrected the student's work. • The artist only sells her work to friends.*

5 [*count*] (**ART, ENGLISH LANGUAGE ARTS, MUSIC**) a book, painting, or piece of music: *He's read the complete works of Hawthorne. • A number of priceless works of art were stolen from the gallery.*

6 works [*plural*] a place where people make things with machines: *My grandfather worked at the steelworks.*

get to work to start doing something: *Let's get to work on this project.*

work·a·hol·ic /ˌwərkə'hɑlɪk/ *noun* [*count*] a person who works a lot and feels that they need to work all the time

work·book /'wərkbʊk/ *noun* [*count*] a book where you write answers to questions, which you use when you are studying something

work·er /'wərkər/ *noun* [*count*] a person who works: *an office worker*

the work·ing class /ðə ˌwərkɪŋ 'klæs/ *noun* [*singular*] the group of people in a society who do not have much money or power and who usually do physical work

▶ **work·ing-class** /ˌwərkɪŋ 'klæs/ *adjective*: *working-class families* ⊃ Look at **the middle class**, **the upper class**.

work·man /'wərkmən/ *noun* [*count*] (*plural* **work·men** /'wərkmən/) a man who works with his hands to build or repair something

work·out /'wərkaʊt/ *noun* [*count*] physical exercise that you do when you are training for a sport or trying to stay healthy: *She does a 20-minute workout every morning.*

work·sheet /'wərkʃit/ *noun* [*count*] a piece of paper where you write answers to questions, which you use when you are studying something

work·shop /'wərkʃɑp/ *noun* [*count*]

1 a place where people make or repair things

2 a time when people meet and work together to learn about something: *We went to a drama workshop.*

world /wərld/ *noun*

1 the world [*singular*] (**GEOGRAPHY**) the earth with all its countries and people: *There was a map of the world on the classroom wall. • Which is the biggest city in the world?*

2 [*singular*] the life and activities of people; their experience: *It's time you learned something about the real world! • the modern world*

3 [count] a particular area of activity or group of people, animals, or things: *the world of politics* • *the plant world*
think the world of someone or **something** to like someone or something very much: *She thinks the world of her grandchildren.*

world-fa·mous /ˌwɜrld ˈfeɪməs/ *adjective*
known everywhere in the world: *a world-famous writer*

the World Series /ðə ˌwɜrld ˈsɪriz/ *noun* [*singular*]
(**SPORTS**) a number of baseball games played every year that decide which is the best team in the U.S. and Canada that year

world·wide /ˌwɜrldˈwaɪd/ *adjective, adverb*
existing or happening everywhere in the world: *Pollution is a worldwide problem.* • *They sell their computers worldwide.*

the World Wide Web /ðə ˌwɜrld ˌwaɪd ˈwɛb/
(also **the Web**) *noun* [*singular*] (abbreviation WWW)
(**COMPUTERS**) the system of computers that makes it possible to see information from all over the world on your computer ➔ Look at **the Internet**.

worm /wɜrm/ *noun* [*count*]
a small animal that lives in the ground, with a long thin body, and no legs

worn form of **wear¹**

worn out /ˌwɔrn ˈaʊt/ *adjective*
1 old and completely finished because you have used it a lot: *These shoes are completely worn out.* • *worn-out carpets*
2 very tired: *He's worn out after his long trip.* ➔ **SYNONYM exhausted**

wor·ried /ˈwɜrid/ *adjective*
unhappy because you think that something bad will happen or has happened: *Jill is worried that she's going to fail the exam.* • *I'm worried about my brother – he looks sick.*

wor·ry¹ /ˈwɜri/ *verb* (**wor·ries, wor·ry·ing, wor·ried, has wor·ried**)
to feel that something bad will happen or has happened; to make someone feel this: *I always worry when Mark doesn't come home at the usual time.* • *Don't worry if you don't know the answer.* • *There's nothing to worry about.* • *What worries me is how we are going to get home.*
▶ **wor·ry·ing** /ˈwɜriɪŋ/ *adjective*: *It's been a worrying time for all of us.*

wor·ry² /ˈwɜri/ *noun* (*plural* **wor·ries**)
1 [*noncount*] a feeling that something bad will happen or has happened: *Her face showed signs of worry.*
2 [*count*] something that makes you feel worried: *I have a lot of worries.*

worse /wɜrs/ *adjective, adverb* (bad, worse, worst)
1 not as good or as well as something else: *The weather today is **worse than** yesterday.* • *Her Spanish is bad, but her Italian is **even worse**.*
2 sicker or more unhappy than before: *If you **get worse**, you must go to the doctor.* ➔ **ANTONYM better**

wors·en /ˈwɜrsn/ *verb* (**wors·ens, wors·en·ing, wors·ened**)
to get worse, or to make something worse: *Relations between the two countries worsened after the election.*

wor·ship /ˈwɜrʃəp/ *verb* (**wor·ships, wor·ship·ing** or **wor·ship·ping, wor·shiped** or **wor·shipped**)
1 (**RELIGION**) to show that you believe in God or a god by saying prayers: *Christians usually worship in churches.*
2 to love someone very much or think that someone is wonderful: *She worships her grandchildren.*
▶ **wor·ship** *noun* [*noncount*]: *A mosque is a place of worship.*

worst¹ /wɜrst/ *adjective, adverb* (bad, worse, worst)
the least pleasant or suitable; the least well: *He's the worst player on the team!* • *That was the worst day of my life.* • *Everyone played badly, but I played worst of all.* ➔ **ANTONYM best**

worst² /wɜrst/ *noun* [*singular*]
something or someone that is as bad as it or they can be: *I'm **the worst** in the class **at** grammar.* ➔ **ANTONYM best**
if worst comes to worst if something very bad happens: *If worst comes to worst and I fail the exam, I'll take it again next year.*

worth¹ /wɜrθ/ *adjective*
1 having a particular value: *This house is worth $700,000.*
2 good or useful enough to do or have: *Is this movie worth seeing?* • *It's not worth asking Lynn for money – she never has any.*

worth² /wɜrθ/ *noun* [*noncount*]
1 the value of someone or something: *The painting is **of** little **worth**.*
2 how much or how many of something an amount of money will buy: *I'd like ten dollars' worth of gas, please.*

worth·less /ˈwɜrθləs/ *adjective*
having no value or use: *A check is worthless if you don't sign it.*

worth·while /ˌwɜrθˈwaɪl/ *adjective*
good or useful enough for the time that you spend or the work that you do: *Passing the exam made all my hard work worthwhile.*

| tʃ **ch**in | dʒ **J**une | v **v**an | θ **th**in | ð **th**en | s **s**o | z **z**oo | ʃ **sh**e

wor·thy /ˈwərði/ *adjective* (wor·thi·er, wor·thi·est)
good enough for something or to have something: *He always felt he was not **worthy** of her.*

would 🖉 /wəd; wʊd/ *modal verb*

Grammar

- The negative form of **would** is **would not**, or the short form **wouldn't** /ˈwʊdnt/: *He wouldn't help me.*
- The short form of **would** is **'d**. We often use this: *I'd* (= I would) *like to meet her.* ◆ *They'd* (= they would) *help if they had the time.*

1 a word that you use to talk about a situation that is not real: *If I had a lot of money, I would buy a big house.*
2 the past form of "will": *He said he would come.* ◆ *They wouldn't tell us where she was.*
3 a word that you use with "like" or "love" to ask or say what someone wants: *Would you like a cup of coffee?* ◆ *I'd love to go to Alaska.*
4 a word that you use to ask something in a polite way: *Would you close the door, please?*
5 a word that you use to talk about something that happened many times in the past: *When I was young, my grandparents would visit us every Sunday.* ⊃ **SYNONYM used to** ⊃ Look at the note at **modal verb**.

would've /ˈwʊdəv/ short for **would have**

wound¹ /wund/ *noun* [count]
(**HEALTH**) a hurt place in your body made by something like a gun or a knife: *He had knife wounds in his chest.*

wound² /wund/ *verb* (wounds, wound·ing, wound·ed)
(**HEALTH**) to hurt someone with a weapon: *The bullet wounded him in the leg.*
▶ **wound·ed** /ˈwundəd/ *adjective*: *She nursed the wounded soldier.*

wound³ form of **wind²**

wove, wo·ven forms of **weave**

wow /waʊ/ *exclamation* (*informal*)
a word that shows surprise and pleasure: *Wow! What a great car!*

wrap 🖉 /ræp/ *verb* (wraps, wrap·ping, wrapped)
to put paper or cloth around someone or something: *The baby was **wrapped in** a blanket.* ◆ *She **wrapped** the glasses **up** in paper.* ⊃ **ANTONYM unwrap**

wrap·per /ˈræpər/ *noun* [count]
a piece of paper or plastic that covers and protects something when you buy it: *Don't throw your candy wrappers on the floor!*

wrap·ping /ˈræpɪŋ/ *noun* [count, noncount]
a piece of paper, plastic, etc. that is used for covering something to protect it: *I took the wrapping off the box.*

wrap·ping pa·per /ˈræpɪŋ ˌpeɪpər/ *noun* [noncount]
special paper that you use to wrap presents

wreath /riθ/ *noun* [count] (*plural* wreaths /riðz; riθs/)
a circle of flowers or leaves: *She put a wreath on the grave.*

wreck¹ /rɛk/ *noun* [count]
1 a ship, car, or airplane that has been very badly damaged in an accident: *a shipwreck* ◆ *The car was a wreck, but no one was hurt.*
2 an accident that badly damages a car, ship, or airplane: *The highway wreck killed two people.*

wreck² /rɛk/ *verb* (wrecks, wreck·ing, wrecked)
to break or destroy something completely: *The fire had completely wrecked the hotel.* ◆ *Our vacation was wrecked by the strike.*

wreck·age /ˈrɛkɪdʒ/ *noun* [noncount]
the broken parts of something that has been badly damaged: *A few survivors were pulled from the wreckage of the train.*

wrench /rɛntʃ/ *noun* [count] (*plural* wrench·es)
a tool that you use for turning small metal rings (called NUTS) and pins (called BOLTS), used for holding things together

wrench

wres·tle /ˈrɛsl/ *verb* (wres·tles, wres·tling, wres·tled)
(**SPORTS**) to fight by trying to throw someone to the ground, especially as a sport
▶ **wres·tler** /ˈrɛslər/ *noun* [count]: *He used to be a professional wrestler.*
▶ **wres·tling** /ˈrɛslɪŋ/ *noun* [noncount]: *a wrestling match*

wrig·gle /ˈrɪgl/ *verb* (wrig·gles, wrig·gling, wrig·gled)
to turn your body quickly from side to side: *The teacher told the children to stop wriggling.*

wring /rɪŋ/ *verb* (wrings, wring·ing, wrung /rʌŋ/, has wrung)
to press and twist something with your hands to make water come out: *He **wrung** the towel **out** and hung it out to dry.*

wring

wrin·kle /ˈrɪŋkl/ *noun* [count]
a small line in something, for example in the skin of your face or in clothes: *My grandmother has a lot of wrinkles.* ◆ *Iron out the wrinkes in the fabric.*
▶ **wrin·kled** /ˈrɪŋkəld/ *adjective*: *His face is very wrinkled.*

wrist /rɪst/ *noun* [count]
the part of your body where your arm joins your hand ⊃ Look at the picture at **hand**.

write /raɪt/ *verb* (writes, writ·ing, wrote /roʊt/, has writ·ten /ˈrɪtn/)
1 to make letters or words on paper using a pen or pencil: *Write your name at the top of the page.* ◆ *He can't read or write.*
2 (ENGLISH LANGUAGE ARTS, MUSIC) to create a story, book, song, piece of music, etc.: *Eugene O'Neill wrote many plays.* ◆ *I wrote a poem for you.*
3 to write and send a letter to someone: *My Auntie Maggie **writes to** me every Christmas.* ◆ *I wrote her a postcard.*
write something down to write something on paper so that you can remember it: *I wrote down his telephone number.*

writ·er /ˈraɪt̮ər/ *noun* [count]
(ENGLISH LANGUAGE ARTS) a person who writes books, stories, etc.: *Mark Twain was a famous writer.*

writ·ing /ˈraɪt̮ɪŋ/ *noun* [noncount]
1 the activity or skill of putting words on paper: *Today we're going to practice our writing.* ◆ *a sheet of writing paper* (= for writing letters on)
2 words that someone puts on paper; the way a person writes: *I can't read your writing – it's too small.*
in writing written on paper: *They offered me the job over the phone, but not in writing.*

writ·ten form of **write**

wrong¹ /rɔŋ/ *adjective*
1 not true or not correct: *She gave me the wrong key, so I couldn't open the door.* ◆ *This clock is wrong.* ⊃ ANTONYM **right**
2 not the best or not suitable: *We took the wrong road and got lost.* ⊃ ANTONYM **right**
3 not as it should be, or not working well: *There's something **wrong with** my car – it won't start.* ◆ *"What's **wrong with** Judith?" "She has a cold."*
4 bad, or not what the law allows: *Stealing is wrong.* ◆ *I haven't **done** anything wrong.* ⊃ ANTONYM **right**

Thesaurus

wrong not right or correct; (used about a person) not right about someone or something: *I'm afraid that's the wrong answer.* ◆ *He was driving on the wrong side of the road.* ◆ *That picture is **the wrong way around**.* ◆ *We were **wrong about** her – she's actually very kind.* ⊃ ANTONYM **right**

false (used about facts) not true or correct: *A whale is a fish. **True or false?*** ◆ *She gave false information to the insurance company.* ⊃ ANTONYM **true**

incorrect wrong according to the facts; containing mistakes. This word is a little formal: *an incorrect spelling* ◆ *Incorrect answers should be marked with a cross.* ⊃ ANTONYM **correct**

mistaken (used about a person) wrong in your opinion or judgment: *I thought I saw Jackie sitting over there, but I must have been mistaken.* ◆ *It was a case of **mistaken identity*** (= people thought that a particular person was someone else). ⊃ ANTONYM **right**, **correct**

inaccurate (used about something such as a newspaper report, a map, etc.) wrong according to the facts; containing mistakes: *an inaccurate statement* ◆ *All the maps we had were completely inaccurate.* ◆ *The report was badly researched and inaccurate.* ⊃ ANTONYM **accurate**

wrong² /rɔŋ/ *adverb*
not correctly; not right: *You spelled my name wrong.* ⊃ ANTONYM **right**
go wrong
1 to not happen as you hoped or wanted: *All our plans went wrong.*
2 to stop working well: *Don't worry – nothing will go wrong with this equipment.*

wrong³ /rɔŋ/ *noun* [noncount]
what is bad or not right: *Babies don't know the difference between right and wrong.* ⊃ ANTONYM **right**

wrong·ly /ˈrɔŋli/ *adverb*
not correctly: *He was wrongly accused of stealing the money.*

wrote form of **write**

wrung form of **wring**

WWW /ˌdʌblyu ˌdʌblyu ˈdʌblyu/ short for **the World Wide Web**

X x

X, x /ɛks/ *noun* [count, noncount] (*plural* X's, x's /'ɛksəz/)
the twenty-fourth letter of the English alphabet: *"X-ray"begins with an "X."*

xe·non /'zɛnɑn/ *noun* [noncount] (symbol **Xe**)
(**CHEMISTRY**) a gas that exists in the air and that is sometimes used in electric lamps

X·mas (*informal*) abbreviation of **Christmas**: *Merry Xmas and a Happy New Year!*

X-ray /'ɛksreɪ/ *noun* [count]
(**HEALTH, PHYSICS**) a photograph of the inside of your body that is made by using a special light that you cannot see: *The doctor **took an X-ray of my shoulder.***
▶ **X-ray** *verb* (X-rays, X-ray·ing, X-rayed): *She had her leg X-rayed.*

xy·lo·phone
/'zaɪləfoʊn/ *noun*
[count]
(**MUSIC**) a musical instrument with metal or wooden bars that you hit with small hammers

xylophone

Y y

Y, y /waɪ/ *noun* [count, noncount] (*plural* Y's, y's /waɪz/)
the twenty-fifth letter of the English alphabet: *"Yawn" begins with a "Y."*

yacht /yɑt/ *noun* [count]

> ℹ **PRONUNCIATION**
> The word **yacht** sounds like **hot**.

1 a boat with sails that people go on for pleasure: *a yacht race*
2 a big boat with an engine that people go on for pleasure: *a millionaire's yacht*

yam /yæm/ *noun* [count, noncount]
a large root with a rough skin, that is cooked and eaten as a vegetable

yank /yæŋk/ *verb* (yanks, yank·ing, yanked)
(*informal*)
to pull something suddenly, quickly, and hard: *She yanked on the dog's leash.*

yard /yɑrd/ *noun* [count]
1 an area next to a building or house, sometimes with grass and trees on it and a wall around it: *The children were playing in the school yard.* ✦ *a farmyard*
2 (abbreviation **yd.**) a measure of length (=36 inches or 0.9144 meters). There are three **feet** in a **yard**.

yard sale /'yɑrd seɪl/ *noun* [count]
a sale that you hold outside your house, where you sell used things that you do not want anymore ⊃ Look at **garage sale**.

yarn /yɑrn/ *noun* [noncount]
thick thread made of wool or cotton that you use for making cloth or clothes: *She knitted a scarf using red, white, and blue yarn.*

yawn /yɔn/ *verb* (yawns, yawn·ing, yawned)
to open your mouth wide and breathe in deeply because you are tired
▶ **yawn** *noun* [count]: *"I'm going to bed now," she said with a yawn.*

yd. abbreviation of **yard**

yeah /yɛə/ *exclamation* (*informal*)
yes

year /yɪr/ *noun* [count]
1 a period of 365 or 366 days from January 1 to December 31. A year has twelve months and 52 weeks: *Where are you going on vacation **this year**?* ✦ *"What year were you born?" "1993."* ✦ *I left school **last year.***
2 any period of twelve months: *I've known Chris for three years.* ✦ *My son is seven years old.* ✦ *I have a seven-year-old son.* ✦ *a group of twelve-year-olds*

> ℹ **STYLE**
> Be careful! You can say **She's ten** or **She's ten years old** (but NOT "She's ten years").

all year round for the whole year: *The swimming pool is open all year round.* ⊃ Look at **leap year, new year.**

year·book /'yɪrbʊk/ *noun* [count]
a book that is produced each year by the students at a school or college, with pictures of

students, teachers, sports teams, and events that happened during the year

year·ly /ˈyɪrli/ *adjective, adverb*
happening or coming every year or once a year: *a yearly visit* ◆ *We meet twice yearly.*

yeast /yist/ *noun* [*noncount*]
a substance that you use for making bread rise

yell /yɛl/ *verb* (**yells, yell·ing, yelled**)
to shout loudly: *Stop yelling at me!*
▶ **yell** *noun* [*count*]: *Give a yell when you hear your name.*

yel·low /ˈyɛloʊ/ *adjective*
with the color of a lemon or of butter: *She was wearing a yellow shirt.*
▶ **yel·low** *noun* [*count, noncount*]: *Yellow is my favorite color.*

yes /yɛs/ *exclamation*
a word that you use for answering a question. You use "yes" to agree, to say that something is true, or to say that you would like something: *"Do you have the key?" "Yes, here it is."* ◆ *"Would you like some coffee?" "Yes, please."*

yes·ter·day /ˈyɛstərdeɪ; ˈyɛstərdi/ *adverb, noun* [*count, noncount*]
(on) the day before today: *Did you see Tom yesterday?* ◆ *I called you yesterday afternoon, but you were out.* ◆ *I sent the letter the day before yesterday.* ⊃ Look at **tomorrow**.

yet /yɛt/ *adverb, conjunction*
1 a word that you use for talking about something that has not happened but that you expect to happen: *I haven't finished the book yet.* ◆ *Have you seen that show yet?* ⊃ Look at the note at **already**.
2 now; as early as this: *You don't need to go yet – it's only seven o'clock.*
3 in the future: *They may win yet.*
4 until now: *This is her best performance yet.*
5 but; despite that: *We arrived home tired yet happy.*
yet again once more: *John is late yet again!*
yet another words you use to show surprise that there is one more of something: *They're opening yet another restaurant on this street.*

yield /yild/ *verb* (**yields, yield·ing, yield·ed**)
1 to produce something, such as vegetables or results: *The survey yielded some interesting information.*
2 to allow someone to have power or control: *The government eventually yielded to the rebels.*
⊃ **SYNONYM give in**
3 to allow other cars on a bigger road to go first: *You have to yield to traffic from the left here.*

yo·ga /ˈyoʊɡə/ *noun* [*noncount*]
(**SPORTS**) a system of exercises that helps you relax both your body and your mind

yo·gurt /ˈyoʊɡərt/ *noun* [*count, noncount*]
a thick, liquid food made from milk: *strawberry yogurt* ◆ *Do you want a yogurt?*

yolk /yoʊk/ *noun* [*count, noncount*]
the yellow part in an egg ⊃ Look at the picture at **egg**.

you /yu/ *pronoun*
1 the person or people that I am speaking to: *You are late.* ◆ *I called you yesterday.*
2 any person; a person: *You can buy stamps at a post office.*

you'd /yud/ short for **you had**, **you would**

you'll /yul/ short for **you will**

young¹ /yʌŋ/ *adjective* (**young·er** /ˈyʌŋɡər/, **young·est** /ˈyʌŋɡəst/)
in the early part of life; not old: *They have two young children.* ◆ *You're younger than me.* ⊃
ANTONYM old

young² /yʌŋ/ *noun* [*plural*]
1 baby animals: *Birds build nests for their young.*
2 **the young** children and young people: *a television program for the young*

young·ster /ˈyʌŋstər/ *noun* [*count*]
a young person: *There isn't much for youngsters to do here.*

your /yər; yɔr/ *adjective*
1 of or belonging to the person or people I am talking to: *Where's your car?* ◆ *Do you all have your books?* ◆ *Show me your hands.*
2 belonging to or connected with people in general: *You should have your teeth checked every six months.*

you're /yɔr/ short for **you are**

yours /yɔrz/ *pronoun*
1 something that belongs to you: *Is this pen yours or mine?*
2 **Yours** a word that you write at the end of a letter before you write your name

your·self /yərˈsɛlf/ *pronoun* (*plural* **your·selves** /yərˈsɛlvz/)
1 a word that shows "you" when I have just talked about you: *Did you hurt yourself?* ◆ *Make yourselves a drink.*
2 a word that makes "you" stronger: *Did you make this cake yourself?* ◆ *"Who told you?" "You told me yourself!"*
by yourself; **by yourselves**
1 alone; without other people: *Do you live by yourself?*
2 without help: *You can't carry all those bags by yourself.* ⊃ **SYNONYM on your own**

youth /yuθ/ *noun* (*plural* **youths** /yuðz/)
1 [*noncount*] the part of your life when you are young: *She regrets that she spent her youth traveling and not studying.* ◆ *He was a fine musician in his youth.* ⊃ **ANTONYM old age**

   tʃ **ch**in   dʒ **J**une   v **v**an   θ **th**in   ð **th**en   s **s**o   z **z**oo   ʃ **sh**e

2 [count] a boy or young man: *The fight was started by a gang of youths.*

3 the youth [noncount] young people: *We must do more for the youth of this country.*

you've /yuv/ short for **you have**

yo-yo /'yoʊ yoʊ/ *noun* [count] (*plural* **yo-yos**)
a toy which is a round piece of wood or plastic with a string around the middle. You put the string on your finger and make the **yo-yo** go up and down.

yuck /yʌk/ *exclamation* (*informal*)
a word that you say when you think something looks or tastes disgusting: *Yuck! I hate cabbage!*
▸ **yuck·y** /'yʌki/ *adjective* (**yuck·i·er, yuck·i·est**): *This soup tastes yucky.* ◆ *That's a really yucky color.* ⊃ SYNONYM **disgusting** ⊃ ANTONYM **yummy**

yum·my /'yʌmi/ *adjective* (**yumm·i·er, yumm·i·est**) (*informal*)
tasting very good: *This cake is yummy.* ⊃ SYNONYM **delicious** ⊃ ANTONYM **yucky**

Zz

Z, z /zi/ *noun* [count, noncount] (*plural* **Z's, z's** /ziz/)
the twenty-sixth and last letter of the English alphabet: *"Zoo" begins with a "Z."*

ze·bra /'zibrə/ *noun* [count] (*plural* **ze·bras** or **ze·bra**)
an African wild animal like a horse, with black and white lines on its body

zebra

ze·ro /'zɪroʊ/ *number* (*plural* **ze·ros**)
1 the number 0
2 nothing at all; none: *My chances of passing the test are almost zero.*
3 (PHYSICS) 0° Fahrenheit or Celsius: *The temperature is five degrees below zero.*

zig·zag /'zɪgzæg/ *noun* [count]
a line that goes up and down, like a lot of letter W's, one after the other ⊃ Look at the picture at **line**.

zinc /zɪŋk/ *noun* [noncount] (symbol **Zn**)
(CHEMISTRY) a blue-white metal

zip /zɪp/ *verb* (**zips, zip·ping, zipped**)
to fasten something together with a ZIPPER: *She zipped up her dress.*

zip code (also **ZIP code**) /'zɪp koʊd/ *noun* [count]
a group of numbers that you write at the end of an address: *I want to send you a package – what's your ZIP code?*

zipper

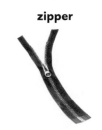

zip·per /'zɪpər/ *noun* [count]
a long metal or plastic thing with a small part that you pull to close and open things like clothes and bags that you pull to close and open things like clothes and bags

the zo·di·ac /ðə 'zoʊdiæk/ *noun* [singular]
a diagram of the positions of the planets and stars, which is divided into twelve equal parts. Each part has a special name and symbol: *the twelve signs of the zodiac* ⊃ Look at **astrology**.

zom·bie /'zɑmbi/ *noun* [count]
(in stories) a dead body that has been made alive again by magic: *a movie about zombies*

zone /zoʊn/ *noun* [count]
a special area that is different from other areas around it: *Do not enter the danger zone!*

zoo /zu/ *noun* [count] (*plural* **zoos**)
a place where wild animals are kept, and people can go to look at them

zo·ol·o·gy /zoʊ'ɑlədʒi/ *noun* [noncount]
(BIOLOGY) the scientific study of animals

zoom /zum/ *verb* (**zooms, zoom·ing, zoomed**)
to move very fast: *The traffic zoomed past us.*
zoom in; zoom out to make something that you are looking at through a camera bigger or smaller by changing the picture controls: *The camera zoomed in on a face in the crowd.* ◆ *If you zoom out, you'll get more background to the picture.*

zuc·chi·ni /zu'kini/ (*plural* **zuc·chi·ni** or **zuc·chi·nis**) *noun* [count]
a long vegetable that is green on the outside and white on the inside ⊃ Look at the picture at **vegetable**.

Reference Section

Contents

2000 Keywords

This is a list of the 2,000 most important and useful words to learn at this stage in your language learning. These words have been carefully chosen by a group of language experts and experienced teachers, who have judged the words to be important and useful for three reasons:

- Words that are used very **frequently** (= very often) in English are included in this list. Frequency information has been gathered from the American English section of the Oxford English Corpus, which is a collection of written and spoken texts containing over 2 billion words.
- The keywords are frequent across a **range** of different types of text. This means that the keywords are often used in a variety of contexts, not just in newspapers or in scientific articles for example.
- The list includes some important words which are very **familiar** to most users of English, even though they are not used very frequently. These include, for example, words which are useful for explaining what you mean when you do not know the exact word for something.

In order to make the definitions in this dictionary easy to understand, we have written them using these 2,000 words. When we needed to use a word that is not on the list, the word is shown in SMALL CAPITALS, with an explanation of the word's meaning.

The 2,000 keywords are shown in the main section of the dictionary in a different color from other words, and are marked with a key symbol 🔑. These keywords are an excellent starting point for improving your vocabulary.

Names of people, places, etc. beginning with a capital letter are not included in the list of 2,000 keywords. Keywords which are marked in the dictionary, but not included in the list are numbers, days of the week, and the months of the year. In addition, there is a list of **language study terms** on the CD-ROM of this dictionary. These words are connected with language learning, and knowing these will help you use your *Oxford Basic American Dictionary* more effectively.

A

a, an *indefinite article*
ability *n.*
able *adj.*
about *adv., prep.*
above *prep., adv.*
absolutely *adv.*
academic *adj.*
accept *v.*
acceptable *adj.*
accident *n.*
  by accident
according *to prep.*
account *n.*
accurate *adj.*
accuse *v.*
achieve *v.*
achievement *n.*
acid *n.*
across *adv., prep.*
act *n., v.*
action *n.*
active *adj.*
activity *n.*
actor, actress *n.*
actual *adj.*
actually *adv.*
add *v.*
address *n.*
admire *v.*

admit *v.*
adult *n.*
advanced *adj.*
advantage *n.*
adventure *n.*
advertisement *n.*
advice *n.*
advise *v.*
affect *v.*
afford *v.*
afraid *adj.*
after *prep., conj., adv.*
afternoon *n.*
afterward *adv.*
again *adv.*
against *prep.*
age *n.*
  aged *adj.*
ago *adv.*
agree *v.*
agreement *n.*
ahead *adv.*
aim *n., v.*
air *n.*
airplane *n.*
airport *n.*
alarm *n.*
alcohol *n.*
alcoholic *adj.*
alive *adj.*

all *adj., pron., adv.*
allow *v.*
all right *adj., adv.,*
  exclamation
almost *adv.*
alone *adj., adv.*
along *prep., adv.*
alphabet *n.*
already *adv.*
also *adv.*
although *conj.*
always *adv.*
among *prep.*
amount *n.*
amuse *v.*
analyze *v.*
analysis *n.*
ancient *adj.*
and *conj.*
anger *n.*
angle *n.*
angry *adj.*
animal *n.*
announce *v.*
another *adj., pron.*
answer *n., v.*
any *adj., pron., adv.*
anybody *pron.*
anymore *(also any*
  more) adv.

anyone *pron.*
anything *pron.*
anyway *adv.*
anywhere *adv.*
apart *adv.*
apartment *n.*
apparently *adv.*
appear *v.*
appearance *n.*
apple *n.*
apply *v.*
appointment *n.*
appreciate *v.*
appropriate *adj.*
approve *v.*
area *n.*
argue *v.*
argument *n.*
arm *n.*
army *n.*
around *adv., prep.*
arrange *v.*
arrangement *n.*
arrest *v.*
arrive *v.*
arrow *n.*
art *n.*
article *n.*
artificial *adj.*
artist *n.*

artistic *adj.*
as *prep., conj.*
ashamed *adj.*
ask *v.*
asleep *adj.*
at *prep.*
atmosphere *n.*
atom *n.*
attach *v.*
attack *n., v.*
attention *n.*
attitude *n.*
attract *v.*
attractive *adj.*
aunt *n.*
authority *n.*
available *adj.*
average *adj., n.*
avoid *v.*
awake *adj.*
aware *adj.*
away *adv.*

B
baby *n.*
back *n., adj., adv.*
backward *adv.*
bad *adj.*
badly *adv.*
bag *n.*
bake *v.*
balance *n.*
ball *n.*
band *n.*
bank *n.*
bar *n.*
base *n., v.*
baseball *n.*
basic *adj.*
basis *n.*
bath *n.*
bathroom *n.*
be *v.*
beach *n.*
bear *v.*
beard *n.*
beat *v.*
beautiful *adj.*
beauty *n.*
because *conj.*
become *v.*
bed *n.*
bedroom *n.*
beer *n.*
before *prep., conj., adv.*
begin *v.*
beginning *n.*
behave *v.*
behavior *n.*
behind *prep., adv.*
belief *n.*
believe *v.*
bell *n.*

belong *v.*
below *prep., adv.*
belt *n.*
bend *v.*
benefit *n.*
beside *prep.*
best *adj., adv., n.*
better *adj., adv.*
between *prep., adv.*
beyond *prep., adv.*
bicycle *n.*
big *adj.*
bill *n.*
bird *n.*
birth *n.*
birthday *n.*
bite *v.*
bitter *adj.*
black *adj.*
blame *v.*
block *n.*
blood *n.*
blow *v., n.*
blue *adj., n.*
board *n.*
boat *n.*
body *n.*
boil *v.*
bomb *n., v.*
bone *n.*
book *n.*
boot *n.*
border *n.*
bored *adj.*
boring *adj.*
born: be born *v.*
borrow *v.*
boss *n.*
both *adj., pron.*
bother *v.*
bottle *n.*
bottom *n.*
bowl *n.*
box *n.*
boy *n.*
boyfriend *n.*
brain *n.*
branch *n.*
brave *adj.*
bread *n.*
break *v.*
breakfast *n.*
breath *n.*
breathe *v.*
brick *n.*
bridge *n.*
brief *adj.*
bright *adj.*
bring *v.*
broken *adj.*
brother *n.*
brown *adj., n.*
brush *n., v.*
bubble *n.*

build *v.*
building *n.*
bullet *n.*
burn *v.*
burst *v.*
bury *v.*
bus *n.*
bush *n.*
business *n.*
busy *adj.*
but *conj.*
butter *n.*
button *n.*
buy *v.*
by *prep.*
bye *exclamation*

C
cabinet *n.*
cake *n.*
calculate *v.*
call *v., n.*
calm *adj.*
camera *n.*
camp *n., v.*
can *modal v., n.*
cancel *v.*
candy *n.*
capable *adj.*
capital *n.*
car *n.*
card *n.*
care *n., v.*
   take care of
   care for
career *n.*
careful *adj.*
carefully *adv.*
careless *adj.*
carelessly *adv.*
carry *v.*
case *n.*
   in case (of)
cash *n.*
cat *n.*
catch *v.*
cause *n., v.*
CD *n.*
ceiling *n.*
celebrate *v.*
cell *n.*
cell phone *n.*
cent *n.*
center *n.*
centimeter *n.*
central *adj.*
century *n.*
ceremony *n.*
certain *adj.*
certainly *adv.*
chain *n., v.*
chair *n.*
challenge *n.*
chance *n.*

change *v., n.*
character *n.*
characteristic *n.*
charge *n., v.*
charity *n.*
chase *v., n.*
cheap *adj.*
cheat *v.*
check *v., n.*
cheek *n.*
cheese *n.*
chemical *adj., n.*
chemistry *n.*
chest *n.*
chicken *n.*
chief *adj., n.*
child *n.*
childhood *n.*
chin *n.*
chocolate *n.*
choice *n.*
choose *v.*
church *n.*
cigarette *n.*
circle *n.*
citizen *n.*
city *n.*
class *n.*
clean *adj., v.*
clear *adj., v.*
clearly *adv.*
climate *n.*
climb *v.*
clock *n.*
close /kloʊs/ *adj., adv.*
close /kloʊz/ *v.*
closed *adj.*
cloth *n.*
clothes *n.*
clothing *n.*
cloud *n.*
club *n.*
coast *n.*
coat *n.*
coffee *n.*
coin *n.*
cold *adj., n.*
collect *v.*
collection *n.*
college *n.*
color *n., v.*
column *n.*
combination *n.*
combine *v.*
come *v.*
comfortable *adj.*
command *n.*
comment *n., v.*
common *adj.*
communicate *v.*
communication *n.*
community *n.*
company *n.*
compare *v.*

comparison n.
competition n.
complain v.
complaint n.
complete adj.
completely adv.
complicated adj.
computer n.
concentrate v.
concert n.
conclusion n.
condition n.
confidence n.
confident adj.
confuse v.
confused adj.
connect v.
connection n.
conscious adj.
consider v.
consist v.
constant adj.
contact n., v.
contain v.
container n.
continent n.
continue v.
continuous adj.
contract n.
contrast n.
contribute v.
control n., v.
convenient adj.
conversation n.
convince v.
cook v.
cookie n.
cooking n.
cool adj.
copy n., v.
corner n.
correct adj., v.
correctly adv.
cost n., v.
cotton n.
cough v.
could modal v.
count v.
country n.
county n.
couple n.
course n.
  of course
court n.
cousin n.
cover v., n.
covering n.
cow n.
crack v.
crash n., v.
crazy adj.
cream n., adj.
create v.
credit card n.

crime n.
criminal adj., n.
crisis n.
criticism n.
criticize v.
cross v.
crowd n.
cruel adj.
crush v.
cry v.
culture n.
cup n.
curly adj.
curve n.
curved adj.
custom n.
customer n.
cut v., n.

D

dad n.
damage n., v.
dance n., v.
dancer n.
danger n.
dangerous adj.
dark adj., n.
date n.
daughter n.
day n.
dead adj.
deal v.
dear adj.
death n.
debt n.
decide v.
decision n.
decorate v.
deep adj.
deeply adv.
defeat v.
definite adj.
definitely adv.
definition n.
degree n.
deliberately adv.
deliver v.
demand n., v.
dentist n.
deny v.
department n.
depend v.
depression n.
describe v.
description n.
desert n.
deserve v.
design n., v.
desk n.
despite prep.
destroy v.
detail n.
  in detail
determination n.

determined adj.
develop v.
development n.
device n.
diagram n.
dictionary n.
die v.
difference n.
different adj.
difficult adj.
difficulty n.
dig v.
dinner n.
direct adj., adv., v.
direction n.
directly adv.
dirt n.
dirty adj.
disadvantage n.
disagree v.
disagreement n.
disappear v.
disappoint v.
disaster n.
discover v.
discuss v.
discussion n.
disease n.
disgusting adj.
dish n.
dishonest adj.
disk n.
distance n.
distant adj.
disturb v.
divide v.
division n.
divorce n., v.
do v., auxiliary v.
doctor n. (abbr. Dr.)
document n.
dog n.
dollar n.
door n.
dot n.
double adj.
doubt n.
down adv., prep.
downstairs adv., adj.
downward adv.
draw v.
drawer n.
drawing n
dream n., v.
dress n., v.
drink n., v.
drive v., n.
driver n.
drop v., n.
drug n.
dry adj., v.
during prep.
dust n.
duty n.

DVD n.

E

each adj., pron.
each other pron.
ear n.
early adj., adv.
earn v.
earth n.
easily adv.
east n., adj., adv.
eastern adj.
easy adj.
eat v.
economic adj.
economy n.
edge n.
educate v.
education n.
effect n.
effort n.
e.g. abbr.
egg n.
either adj., pron., adv.
election n.
electric adj.
electrical adj.
electricity n.
electronic adj.
else adv.
e-mail (also email) n., v.
embarrass v.
embarrassed adj.
emergency n.
emotion n.
employ v.
employment n.
empty adj.
encourage v.
end n., v.
  in the end
enemy n.
energy n.
engine n.
enjoy v.
enjoyable adj.
enjoyment n.
enough adj., pron., adv.
enter v.
entertain v.
entertainment n.
enthusiasm n.
enthusiastic adj.
entrance n.
environment n.
equal adj.
equipment n.
error n.
escape v.
especially adv.
essential adj.
etc. abbr.
even adv.
evening n.

event *n.*
ever *adv.*
every *adj.*
everybody *pron.*
everyone *pron.*
everything *pron.*
everywhere *adv.*
evidence *n.*
evil *adj.*
exact *adj.*
exactly *adv.*
exaggerate *v.*
exam *n.*
examination *n.*
examine *v.*
example *n.*
excellent *adj.*
except *prep.*
exchange *v., n.*
excited *adj.*
excitement *n.*
exciting *adj.*
excuse *n., v.*
exercise *n.*
exist *v.*
exit *n.*
expect *v.*
expensive *adj.*
experience *n., v.*
experiment *n.*
expert *n.*
explain *v.*
explanation *n.*
explode *v.*
explore *v.*
explosion *n.*
expression *n.*
extra *adj., adv.*
extreme *adj.*
extremely *adv.*
eye *n.*

F

face *n., v.*
fact *n.*
factory *n.*
fail *v.*
failure *n.*
fair *adj.*
fall *v., n.*
false *adj.*
familiar *adj.*
family *n.*
famous *adj.*
far *adv., adj.*
farm *n.*
farmer *n.*
fashion *n.*
fashionable *adj.*
fast *adj., adv.*
fasten *v.*
fat *adj., n.*
father *n.*
fault *n.*

favor *n.*
   in favor
favorite *adj., n.*
fear *n., v.*
feather *n.*
feature *n.*
feed *v.*
feel *v.*
feeling *n.*
female *adj.*
fence *n.*
festival *n.*
few *adj., pron.*
   a few
field *n.*
fight *v., n.*
figure *n.*
file *n.*
fill *v.*
film *n.*
final *adj.*
finally *adv.*
financial *adj.*
find *v.*
   find out sth
fine *adj.*
finger *n.*
finish *v.*
fire *n., v.*
firm *n., adj.*
firmly *adv.*
first *adj., adv., n.*
   at first
fish *n.*
fit *v., adj.*
fix *v.*
fixed *adj.*
flag *n.*
flame *n.*
flash *v.*
flat *adj.*
flavor *n.*
flight *n.*
float *v.*
flood *n.*
floor *n.*
flour *n.*
flow *v.*
flower *n.*
fly *v.*
fold *v.*
follow *v.*
food *n.*
foot *n.*
football *n.*
for *prep.*
force *n., v.*
foreign *adj.*
forest *n.*
forever *adv.*
forget *v.*
forgive *v.*
fork *n.*
form *n., v.*

formal *adj.*
forward *adv.*
frame *n.*
free *adj., v., adv.*
freedom *n.*
freeze *v.*
fresh *adj.*
friend *n.*
friendly *adj.*
friendship *n.*
frighten *v.*
from *prep.*
front *n., adj.*
   in front
frozen *adj.*
fruit *n.*
fry *v.*
fuel *n.*
full *adj.*
fully *adv.*
fun *n., adj.*
funny *adj.*
fur *n.*
furniture *n.*
further *adj. , adv.*
future *n., adj.*

G

gain *v.*
gallon *n.*
game *n.*
garbage *n.*
garden *n.*
gas *n.*
gate *n.*
general *adj.*
   in general
generally *adv.*
generous *adj.*
gentle *adj.*
gently *adv.*
gentleman *n.*
get *v.*
gift *n.*
girl *n.*
girlfriend *n.*
give *v.*
glass *n.*
glasses *n.*
global *adj.*
glove *n.*
go *v.*
goal *n.*
god *n.*
gold *n., adj.*
good *adj., n.*
goodbye *exclamation*
goods *n.*
govern *v.*
government *n.*
grade *n., v.*
grain *n.*
gram *n.*
grammar *n.*

grandchild *n.*
grandfather *n.*
grandmother *n.*
grandparent *n.*
grass *n.*
grateful *adj.*
gray *adj., n.*
great *adj.*
green *adj., n.*
groceries *n.*
ground *n.*
group *n.*
grow *v.*
growth *n.*
guard *n., v.*
guess *v.*
guest *n.*
guide *n.*
guilty *adj.*
gun *n.*

H

habit *n.*
hair *n.*
half *n., adj., pron., adv.*
hall *n.*
hammer *n.*
hand *n.*
handle *v., n.*
hang *v.*
happen *v.*
happiness *n.*
happy *adj.*
hard *adj., adv.*
hardly *adv.*
harm *n., v.*
harmful *adj.*
hat *n.*
hate *v., n.*
have *v.*
   have to *modal v.*
he *pron.*
head *n.*
health *n.*
healthy *adj.*
hear *v.*
heart *n.*
heat *n., v.*
heavy *adj.*
height *n.*
hello *exclamation*
help *v., n.*
helpful *adj.*
her *pron., adj.*
here *adv.*
hers *pron.*
herself *pron.*
hide *v.*
high *adj., adv.*
highly *adv.*
high school *n.*
highway *n.*
hill *n.*
him *pron.*

himself *pron.*
hire *v.*
his *adj., pron.*
history *n.*
hit *v., n.*
hold *v., n.*
hole *n.*
holiday *n.*
home *n., adv..*
honest *adj.*
hook *n.*
hope *v., n.*
horn *n.*
horse *n.*
hospital *n.*
hot *adj.*
hotel *n.*
hour *n.*
house *n.*
how *adv.*
however *adv.*
huge *adj.*
human *adj., n.*
humor *n.*
hungry *adj.*
hunt *v.*
hurry *v., n.*
hurt *v.*
husband *n.*

I

I *pron.*
ice *n.*
idea *n.*
identify *v.*
if *conj.*
ignore *v.*
illegal *adj.*
illegally *adv.*
illness *n.*
image *n.*
imagination *n.*
imagine *v.*
immediate *adj.*
immediately *adv.*
impatient *adj.*
importance *n.*
important *adj.*
impossible *adj.*
impress *v.*
impression *n.*
improve *v.*
improvement *n.*
in *prep., adv.*
inch *n.*
include *v.*
including *prep.*
increase *v., n.*
indeed *adv.*
independent *adj.*
individual *adj.*
industry *n.*
infection *n.*
influence *n.*

inform *v.*
informal *adj.*
information *n.*
injure *v.*
injury *n.*
insect *n.*
inside *prep., adv., n., adj.*
instead *adv., prep.*
instruction *n.*
instrument *n.*
insult *v., n.*
intelligent *adj.*
intend *v.*
intention *n.*
interest *n., v.*
interested *adj.*
interesting *adj.*
international *adj.*
Internet *n.*
interrupt *v.*
interview *n.*
into *prep.*
introduce *v.*
introduction *n.*
invent *v.*
investigate *v.*
invitation *n.*
invite *v.*
involve *v.*
iron *n.*
island *n.*
issue *n.*
it *pron.*
item *n.*
its *adj.*
itself *pron.*

J

jacket *n.*
jeans *n.*
jewelry *n.*
job *n.*
join *v.*
joke *n., v.*
judge *n., v.*
judgment *(also judgement) n.*
juice *n.*
jump *v.*
just *adv.*

K

keep *v.*
key *n.*
kick *v., n.*
kid *n., v.*
kill *v.*
kilogram *(also* kilo*) n.*
kilometer *n.*
kind *n., adj.*
kindness *n.*
king *n.*
kiss *v., n.*

kitchen *n.*
knee *n.*
knife *n.*
knock *v., n.*
knot *n.*
know *v.*
knowledge *n.*

L

lack *n.*
lady *n.*
lake *n.*
lamp *n.*
land *n., v.*
language *n.*
large *adj.*
last *adj., adv., n., v.*
late *adj., adv.*
later *adv.*
laugh *v.*
laundry *n.*
law *n.*
lawyer *n.*
lay *v.*
layer *n.*
lazy *adj.*
lead /lid/ *v.*
leader *n.*
leaf *n.*
lean *v.*
learn *v.*
least *adj., pron., adv.*
  at least
leather *n.*
leave *v.*
left *adj., adv., n.*
leg *n.*
legal *adj.*
legally *adv.*
lemon *n.*
lend *v.*
length *n.*
less *adj., pron., adv.*
lesson *n.*
let *v.*
letter *n.*
level *n.*
library *n.*
lid *n.*
lie *v., n.*
life *n.*
lift *v.*
light *n., adj., v.*
lightly *adv.*
like *prep., v., conj.*
likely *adj.*
limit *n., v.*
line *n.*
lip *n.*
liquid *n., adj.*
list *n., v.*
listen *v.*
liter *n.*
literature *n.*

little *adj., pron., adv.*
  a little
live /lIv/ *v.*
living *adj.*
load *n., v.*
loan *n.*
local *adj.*
lock *v., n.*
lonely *adj.*
long *adj., adv.*
look *v., n.*
loose *adj.*
lose *v.*
loss *n.*
lost *adj.*
lot *pron., adv.*
  a lot (of)
  lots (of)
loud *adj.*
loudly *adv.*
love *n., v.*
low *adj., adv.*
luck *n.*
lucky *adj.*
lump *n.*
lunch *n.*

M

machine *n.*
magazine *n.*
magic *n., adj.*
mail *n., v.*
main *adj.*
mainly *adv.*
make *v.*
male *adj., n.*
man *n.*
manage *v.*
manager *n.*
many *adj., pron.*
map *n.*
mark *n., v.*
market *n.*
marriage *n.*
married *adj.*
marry *v.*
match *n., v.*
material *n.*
math *n.*
mathematics *n.*
matter *n., v.*
may *modal v.*
maybe *adv.*
me *pron.*
meal *n.*
mean *v.*
meaning *n.*
measure *v., n.*
measurement *n.*
meat *n.*
medical *adj.*
medicine *n.*
medium *adj.*
meet *v.*

meeting n.
melt v.
member n.
memory n.
mental adj.
mention v.
mess n.
message n.
messy adj.
metal n.
method n.
meter n.
middle n., adj.
midnight n.
might modal v.
mile n.
milk n.
mind n., v.
mine pron.
minute n.
mirror n.
Miss n.
miss v.
missing adj.
mistake n.
mix v.
mixture n.
model n.
modern adj.
mom n.
moment n.
money n.
month n.
mood n.
moon n.
moral adj.
morally adv.
more adj., pron., adv.
morning n.
most adj., pron., adv.
mostly adv.
mother n.
motorcycle n.
mountain n.
mouse n.
mouth n.
move v., n.
movement n.
movie n.
Mr. abbr.
Mrs. abbr.
Ms. abbr.
much adj., pron., adv.
mud n.
multiply v.
murder n., v.
muscle n.
museum n.
music n.
musical adj.
musician n.
must modal v.
my adj.
myself pron.

mysterious adj.

N

nail n.
name n., v.
narrow adj.
nation n.
national adj.
natural adj.
nature n.
navy n.
near adj., adv., prep.
nearby adj., adv.
nearly adv.
neat adj.
neatly adv.
necessary adj.
neck n.
need v., n.
needle n.
negative adj.
neighbor n.
neither adj., pron., adv.
nerve n.
nervous adj.
net n.
never adv.
new adj.
news n.
newspaper n.
next adj., adv., n.
nice adj.
night n.
no exclamation, adj.
nobody pron.
noise n.
noisy adj.
noisily adv.
none pron.
nonsense n.
no one pron.
nor conj.
normal adj.
normally adv.
north n., adj., adv.
northern adj.
nose n.
not adv.
note n.
nothing pron.
notice v.
novel n.
now adv.
nowhere adv.
nuclear adj.
number (abbr. No.,
   no.) n.
nurse n.
nut n.

O

object n.
obtain v.
obvious adj.
occasion n.

occur v.
ocean n.
o'clock adv.
odd adj.
of prep.
off adv., prep.
offense n.
offer v., n.
office n.
officer n.
official adj., n.
officially adv.
often adv.
oh exclamation
oil n.
OK (also okay)
   exclamation, adj., adv.
old adj.
old-fashioned adj.
on prep., adv.
once adv., conj.
one number, adj., pron.
onion n.
only adj., adv.
onto prep.
open adj., v..
operate v.
operation n.
opinion n.
opportunity n.
opposite adj., adv., n.,
   prep.
or conj.
orange n., adj.
order n., v.
ordinary adj.
organization n.
organize v.
organized adj.
original adj., n.
other adj., pron.
otherwise adv.
ought to modal v.
ounce n.
our adj.
ours pron.
ourselves pron.
out adj., adv.
out of prep.
outside n., adj., prep.,
   adv.
oven n.
over adv., prep.
owe v.
own adj., pron., v.
owner n.

P

pack v., n.
package n.
page n.
pain n.
painful adj.
paint n., v.

painter n.
painting n.
pair n.
pale adj.
pan n.
pants n.
paper n.
parent n.
park n., v.
part n.
   take part (in)
particular adj.
particularly adv.
partly adv.
partner n.
party n.
pass v.
passage n.
passenger n.
passport n.
past adj., n., prep., adv.
path n.
patient n., adj.
pattern n.
pause v.
pay v., n.
payment n.
peace n.
peaceful adj.
pen n.
pencil n.
people n.
perfect adj.
perform v.
performance n.
perhaps adv.
period n.
permanent adj.
permission n.
person n.
personal adj.
personality n.
persuade v.
pet n.
phone n.
photo n.
photograph n.
phrase n.
physical adj.
physically adv.
piano n.
pick v.
   pick sth up
picture n.
piece n.
pig n.
pile n.
pilot n.
pin n.
pink adj., n.
pint n.
pipe n.
place n., v.
   take place

plain *adj.*
plan *n., v.*
plane *n.*
planet *n.*
plant *n., v.*
plastic *n.*
plate *n.*
play *v., n.*
player *n.*
pleasant *adj.*
please *exclamation, v.*
pleased *adj.*
pleasure *n.*
plenty *pron.*
pocket *n.*
poem *n.*
poetry *n.*
point *n., v.*
pointed *adj.*
poison *n., v.*
poisonous *adj.*
police *n.*
polite *adj.*
politely *adv.*
political *adj.*
politician *n.*
politics *n.*
pollution *n.*
pool *n.*
poor *adj.*
popular *adj.*
port *n.*
position *n.*
positive *adj.*
possibility *n.*
possible *adj.*
possibly *adv.*
post *n.*
pot *n.*
potato *n.*
pound *n.*
pour *v.*
powder *n.*
power *n.*
powerful *adj.*
practical *adj.*
practice *n., v.*
prayer *n.*
prefer *v.*
pregnant *adj.*
preparation *n.*
prepare *v.*
present *adj., n., v.*
president *n.*
press *n., v.*
pressure *n.*
pretend *v.*
pretty *adv., adj.*
prevent *v.*
previous *adj.*
price *n.*
priest *n.*
principal *adj.*
print *v.*

priority *n.*
prison *n.*
prisoner *n.*
private *adj.*
prize *n.*
probable *adj.*
probably *adv.*
problem *n.*
process *n.*
produce *v.*
product *n.*
production *n.*
professional *adj.*
profit *n.*
program *n.*
progress *n.*
project *n.*
promise *v., n.*
pronunciation *n.*
proof *n.*
proper *adj.*
property *n.*
protect *v.*
protection *n.*
protest *n.*
proud *adj.*
prove *v.*
provide *v.*
public *adj., n.*
    publicly *adv.*
publish *v.*
pull *v.*
punish *v.*
punishment *n.*
pure *adj.*
purple *adj., n.*
purpose *n.*
    on purpose
push *v., n.*
put *v.*

Q
quality *n.*
quantity *n.*
quarter *n.*
queen *n.*
question *n., v.*
quick *adj.*
quickly *adv.*
quiet *adj.*
quietly *adv.*
quite *adv.*

R
race *n., v.*
radio *n.*
railroad *n.*
rain *n., v.*
raise *v.*
rare *adj.*
rarely *adv.*
rate *n.*
rather *adv.*
reach *v.*
reaction *n.*

read *v.*
ready *adj.*
real *adj.*
reality *n.*
realize *v.*
really *adv.*
reason *n.*
reasonable *adj.*
receive *v.*
recent *adj.*
recently *adv.*
recognize *v.*
recommend *v.*
record *n., v.*
recover *v.*
red *adj., n.*
reduce *v.*
refer to *v.*
refuse *v.*
region *n.*
regular *adj.*
regularly *adv.*
relation *n.*
relationship *n.*
relax *v.*
relaxed *adj.*
release *v.*
relevant *adj.*
relief *n.*
religion *n.*
religious *adj.*
rely *v.*
remain *v.*
remark *n.*
remember *v.*
remind *v.*
remove *v.*
rent *n., v.*
repair *v., n.*
repeat *v.*
replace *v.*
reply *n., v.*
report *v., n.*
reporter *n.*
represent *v.*
request *n., v.*
require *v.*
rescue *v.*
research *n., v.*
reservation *n.*
respect *n., v.*
responsibility *n.*
responsible *adj.*
rest *n., v.*
restaurant *n.*
result *n., v.*
return *v., n.*
rice *n.*
rich *adj.*
rid *adj.:* get rid of
ride *v., n.*
right *adj., adv., n.*
ring *n., v.*
rise *n., v.*

risk *n., v.*
river *n.*
road *n.*
rob *v.*
rock *n.*
role *n.*
roll *n., v.*
romantic *adj.*
roof *n.*
room *n.*
root *n.*
rope *n.*
rough *adj.*
round *adj.*
route *v.*
row *n.*
royal *adj.*
rub *v.*
rubber *n.*
rude *adj.*
    rudely *adv.*
ruin *v.*
rule *n., v.*
run *v., n.*
rush *v.*

S
sad *adj.*
sadness *n.*
safe *adj.*
safely *adv.*
safety *n.*
sail *v.*
salad *n.*
sale *n.*
salt *n.*
same *adj., pron.*
sand *n.*
satisfaction *n.*
satisfied *adj.*
sauce *n.*
save *v.*
say *v.*
scale *n.*
scare *v.*
scared *adj.*
scary *adj.*
schedule *n.*
school *n.*
science *n.*
scientific *adj.*
scientist *n.*
scissors *n.*
score *n., v.*
scratch *v., n.*
screen *n.*
search *n., v.*
season *n.*
seat *n.*
second *adj., adv., n.*
secret *adj., n.*
secretary *n.*
secretly *adv.*
section *n.*

see v.
seed n.
seem v.
sell v.
send v.
senior adj.
sense n.
sensible adj.
sensitive adj.
sentence n.
separate adj., v.
separately adv.
series n.
serious adj.
serve v.
service n.
set n., v.
settle v.
several adj., pron.
sew v.
sex n.
sexual adj.
shade n.
shadow n.
shake v.
shame n.
shape n., v.
  shaped adj.
share v., n.
sharp adj.
she pron.
sheep n.
sheet n.
shelf n.
shell n.
shine v.
shiny adj.
ship n.
shirt n.
shock n., v.
shoe n.
shoot v.
shop v.
shopping n.
short adj.
shot n.
should modal v.
shoulder n.
shout v., n.
show v., n.
shower n.
shut v.
shy adj.
sick adj.
side n.
sight n.
sign n., v.
signal n.
silence n.
silly adj.
silver n., adj.
similar adj.
simple adj.
since prep., conj., adv.

sing v.
singer n.
single adj.
sink v.
sir n.
sister n.
sit v.
situation n.
size n.
skill n.
skin n.
skirt n.
sky n.
sleep v., n.
sleeve n.
slice n.
slide v.
slightly adv.
slip v.
slow adj.
slowly adv.
small adj.
smell v., n.
smile v., n.
smoke n., v.
smooth adj.
  smoothly adv.
snake n.
snow n., v.
so adv., conj.
soap n.
social adj.
society n.
sock n.
soft adj.
soil n.
soldier n.
solid adj., n.
solution n.
solve v.
some adj., pron.
somebody pron.
somehow adv.
someone pron.
something pron.
sometimes adv.
somewhere adv.
son n.
song n.
soon adv.
  as soon as
sore adj.
sorry adj.
sort n., v.
sound n., v.
soup n.
south n., adj., adv.
southern adj.
space n.
speak v.
speaker n.
special adj.
speech n.
speed n.

spell v.
spend v.
spice n.
spider n.
spirit n.
spoil v.
spoon n.
sport n.
spot n.
spread v.
spring n.
square adj., n.
stage n.
stair n.
stamp n..
stand v., n.
standard n., adj.
star n.
stare v.
start v., n.
state n., v.
statement n.
station n.
stay v.
steady adj.
steal v.
steam n.
step n., v.
stick v., n.
sticky adj.
still adv., adj.
stomach n.
stone n.
stop v., n.
store n., v.
storm n.
story n.
stove n.
straight adv., adj.
strange adj.
street n.
strength n.
stress n.
stretch v.
strict adj.
string n.
strong adj.
strongly adv.
structure n.
struggle v., n.
student n.
study n., v.
stuff n.
stupid adj.
style n.
subject n.
substance n.
succeed v.
success n.
successful adj.
successfully adv.
such adj.
  such as
suck v.

sudden adj.
suddenly adv.
suffer v.
sugar n.
suggest v.
suggestion n.
suit n.
suitable adj.
sum n.
summer n.
sun n.
supply n.
support n., v.
suppose v.
sure adj., adv.
surface n.
surprise n., v.
surprised adj.
surround v.
survive v.
swallow v.
swear v.
sweat n., v.
sweet adj.
swim v.
switch n., v.
symbol n.
system n.

T
table n.
tail n.
take v.
talk v., n.
tall adj.
tape n.
task n.
taste n., v.
tax n.
tea n.
teach v.
teacher n.
team n.
tear /tɛr/ v.
tear /tɪr/ n.
technical adj.
technology n.
telephone n.
television n.
tell v.
temperature n.
temporary adj.
tend v.
terrible adj.
test n., v.
text n.
than prep., conj.
thank v.
thanks n.
thank you n.
that adj., pron., conj.
the definite article
theater n.
their adj.

theirs *pron.*
them *pron.*
themselves *pron.*
then *adv.*
there *adv.*
therefore *adv.*
these *adj., pron.*
they *pron.*
thick *adj.*
thin *adj.*
thing *n.*
think *v.*
thirsty *adj.*
this *adj., pron.*
those *adj., pron.*
though *conj., adv.*
thought *n.*
thread *n.*
threat *n.*
threaten *v.*
throat *n.*
through *prep., adv.*
throw *v.*
thumb *n.*
ticket *n.*
tie *v., n.*
tight *adj., adv.*
time *n.*
tire *n.*
tired *adj.*
title *n.*
to *prep., infinitive*
    marker
today *adv., n.*
toe *n.*
together *adv.*
toilet *n.*
tomato *n.*
tomorrow *adv., n.*
tongue *n.*
tonight *adv., n.*
too *adv.*
tool *n.*
tooth *n.*
top *n., adj.*
topic *n.*
total *adj., n.*
totally *adv.*
touch *v., n.*
tour *n.*
tourist *n.*
toward *prep.*
towel *n.*
town *n.*
toy *n.*
track *n.*
tradition *n.*
traffic *n.*
train *n., v.*
training *n.*
translate *v.*
transparent *adj.*
transportation *n.*
trash *n.*

travel *v., n.*
treat *v.*
treatment *n.*
tree *n.*
trial *n.*
trick *n.*
trip *n., v.*
trouble *n.*
truck *n.*
true *adj.*
trust *n., v.*
truth *n.*
try *v.*
tube *n.*
tune *n.*
tunnel *n.*
turn *v., n.*
TV *n.*
twice *adv.*
twist *v.*
type *n., v.*
typical *adj.*

U
ugly *adj.*
unable *adj.*
uncle *n.*
uncomfortable *adj.*
unconscious *adj.*
under *prep., adv.*
underground *adj., adv.*
understand *v.*
underwater *adj., adv.*
underwear *n.*
unemployment *n.*
unexpected *adj.*
unexpectedly *adv.*
unfair *adj.*
unfortunately *adv.*
unfriendly *adj.*
unhappy *adj.*
uniform *n.*
union *n.*
unit *n.*
universe *n.*
university *n.*
unkind *adj.*
unknown *adj.*
unless *conj.*
unlikely *adj.*
unlucky *adj.*
unpleasant *adj.*
until *conj., prep.*
unusual *adj.*
up *adv., prep.*
upper *adj.*
upset *v., adj.*
upstairs *adv., adj.*
upward *adv.*
urgent *adj.*
us *pron.*
use *v., n.*
used *adj.*
used to *modal v.*

useful *adj.*
user *n.*
usual *adj.*
usually *adv.*

V
vacation *n.*
valley *n.*
valuable *adj.*
value *n.*
variety *n.*
various *adj.*
vary *v.*
vegetable *n.*
vehicle *n.*
very *adv.*
video *n.*
view *n.*
violence *n.*
violent *adj.*
visit *v., n.*
visitor *n.*
voice *n.*
volume *n.*
vote *n., v.*

W
wait *v.*
wake (up) *v.*
walk *v., n.*
wall *n.*
want *v.*
war *n.*
warm *adj., v.*
warn *v.*
wash *v.*
waste *v., n., adj.*
watch *v., n.*
water *n.*
wave *n., v.*
way *n.*
we *pron.*
weak *adj.*
weakness *n.*
weapon *n.*
wear *v.*
weather *n.*
website *n.*
wedding *n.*
week *n.*
weekend *n.*
weigh *v.*
weight *n.*
welcome *v.*
well *adv., adj.,*
    exclamation
    as well (as)
west *n., adj., adv.*
western *adj.*
wet *adj.*
what *pron., adj.*
whatever *adj., pron.,*
    adv.
wheel *n.*
when *adv., conj.*

whenever *conj.*
where *adv., conj.*
wherever *conj.*
whether *conj.*
which *pron., adj.*
while *conj., n.*
white *adj., n.*
who *pron.*
whoever *pron.*
whole *adj., n.*
whose *adj., pron.*
why *adv.*
wide *adj.*
wife *n.*
wild *adj.*
will *modal v., n.*
win *v.*
wind /wɪnd/ *n.*
window *n.*
wine *n.*
wing *n.*
winner *n.*
winter *n.*
wire *n.*
wish *v., n.*
with *prep.*
within *prep.*
without *prep.*
woman *n.*
wonder *v.*
wonderful *adj.*
wood *n.*
wooden *adj.*
wool *n.*
word *n.*
work *v., n.*
worker *n.*
world *n.*
worried *adj.*
worry *v.*
worse *adj., adv.*
worst *adj., adv., n.*
worth *adj.*
would *modal v.*
wrap *v.*
wrist *n.*
write *v.*
writer *n.*
writing *n.*
wrong *adj., adv.*

Y
yard *n.*
year *n.*
yellow *adj., n.*
yes *exclamation*
yesterday *adv., n.*
yet *adv.*
you *pron.*
young *adj.*
your *adj.*
yours *pron.*
yourself *pron.*
youth *n.*

The Academic Word List

Averil Coxhead, Victoria University of Wellington, New Zealand

What is the Academic Word List (AWL)?

The Academic Word List (AWL) is a list of 570 word families. It was developed to help teachers and learners decide which words to spend time on in class. In particular, the AWL is for learners who are preparing to study in English at university, but we now know that these words are also used in secondary school texts as well as newspapers. All AWL words in this dictionary are marked with an **AWL** symbol, like this:

> **con·cept** **AWL** /ˈkɑnsɛpt/ *noun* [*count*]
> an idea, or a basic truth about something: *This course teaches the basic concepts of mathematics.*
> • *It's hard to understand the concept of infinity.*

You can find the list of AWL words in this dictionary on the CD-ROM, and download the full AWL from this website:
www.victoria.ac.nz/lals/resources/academicwordlist

The most important thing about the AWL is that the words in the list make up around 10% of the words in an academic written text. That is, in such a text, at least ten words in a hundred are in the AWL. Let's compare that number with the words in the first 2,000 words of English. Up to seventy or more words in a hundred will come from that list. That leaves around 20% of the text, which consists of a number of proper nouns, technical words, and words that are not used very often. We can see that most of the words, however, are among the 2,000 most frequent words or in the AWL, so this is an important group of words for learning.

How was the AWL developed?

The AWL was developed by looking at the words in written academic texts from a variety of university subjects, such as Biology, Commercial Law, Computer Science, Economics, Education, International Law, Management, Physics, and Psychology. These subjects were put together under four main areas of study: Arts, Commerce, Law, and Science. Words that were used often in all four subject areas were selected for the list. The list does not include words that are in the first 2,000 words of English or proper nouns like "Los Angeles" or "London."

The AWL has 570 word families. A word family has a head word, for example, *require*, and family members such as *requires*, *required*, *requiring*, and *requirement*. The AWL is organized into ten smaller lists called "sublists." Each sublist has 60 families, except for the tenth sublist which has 30. The first sublist has the words that are used the most often in the written academic texts. It has words such as *require* and *area*. The second sublist has the words that are less frequent than the first list but more frequent than the third list, and so on. The tenth list has the least frequent words in the AWL.

How can learners use the AWL?

Start with Sublist 1 because it contains the most frequent words in the AWL. If you know these words, move on to Sublist 2 and so on. Focus first on the meaning of the words and then work on developing your knowledge of the words, such as how they are spelled and pronounced, what their common word family members are, what other words appear with them in common patterns, and so on.

Some learners like to start with the head words starting with the letter "A" and carry on down the list. This is not a very useful way to learn because words that have similar meanings or look the same can be very confusing. Instead, work on words that you need to use in speaking and writing and that you find often in your reading and listening.

Here are three things you could do with the words from the AWL:

1 Study words from the list directly. Use word cards and look carefully at the words when you meet them in your reading.
2 Make sure you read academic texts because they contain academic vocabulary. Check that these texts are not too difficult. If over 5% of the words in the texts are new words for you, the text is too difficult. Also, listen to academic lectures and discussions.
3 Try to speak in academic discussions and write academic texts as much as possible. While you are speaking and writing, try to use academic vocabulary and look for opportunities for feedback from other people on how you are using these words.

You can use the information in this dictionary on the AWL words to help you with your learning. This information includes the meaning of words, how they are used in example sentences, and more. It takes time to build knowledge about words and using tools like this dictionary and the AWL is a good place to start.

Irregular Verbs

In this list you will find the infinitive form of the irregular verb followed by the past tense and the past participle. Look up the infinitive form in the main part of the dictionary for how to pronounce the verb forms and other information.

Infinitive	Past tense	Past participle	Infinitive	Past tense	Past participle
arise	arose	arisen	find	found	found
babysit	babysat	babysat	fit	fitted, fit	fitted, fit
bear	bore	borne	flee	fled	fled
beat	beat	beaten	fling	flung	flung
become	became	become	fly	flew	flown
begin	began	begun	forbid	forbàde	forbidden
bend	bent	bent	forecast	forecast	forecast
bet	bet	bet	foresee	foresaw	foreseen
bid	bid	bid	forget	forgot	forgotten
bind	bound	bound	forgive	forgave	forgiven
bite	bit	bitten	freeze	froze	frozen
bleed	bled	bled	get	got	gotten
blow	blew	blown	give	gave	given
break	broke	broken	go	went	gone
breed	bred	bred	grind	ground	ground
bring	brought	brought	grow	grew	grown
broadcast	broadcast	broadcast	hang	hung, hanged	hung, hanged
build	built	built	hear	heard	heard
burn	burned, burnt	burned, burnt	hide	hid	hidden
burst	burst	burst	hit	hit	hit
buy	bought	bought	hold	held	held
cast	cast	cast	hurt	hurt	hurt
catch	caught	caught	keep	kept	kept
choose	chose	chosen	kneel	knelt, kneeled	knelt, kneeled
cling	clung	clung	knit	knitted, knit	knitted, knit
come	came	come	know	knew	known
cost	cost	cost	lay	laid	laid
creep	crept	crept	lead	led	led
cut	cut	cut	lean	leaned	leaned
deal	dealt	dealt	leap	leaped, leapt	leaped, leapt
dig	dug	dug	leave	left	left
dive	dived, dove	dived	lend	lent	lent
draw	drew	drawn	let	let	let
dream	dreamed, dreamt	dreamed, dreamt	lie	lay	lain
			light	lit, lighted	lit, lighted
drink	drank	drunk	lose	lost	lost
drive	drove	driven	make	made	made
eat	ate	eaten	mean	meant	meant
fall	fell	fallen	meet	met	met
feed	fed	fed	mislead	misled	misled
feel	felt	felt	mistake	mistook	mistaken
fight	fought	fought	misunderstand	misunderstood	misunderstood

Infinitive	Past tense	Past participle	Infinitive	Past tense	Past participle
mow	mowed	mown	spend	spent	spent
outgrow	outgrew	outgrown	spin	spun	spun
overcome	overcame	overcome	spit	spit, spat	spit, spat
overdo	overdid	overdone	split	split	split
overhear	overheard	overheard	spread	spread	spread
oversleep	overslept	overslept	spring	sprang, sprung	sprung
overthrow	overthrew	overthrown	stand	stood	stood
pay	paid	paid	steal	stole	stolen
plead	pleaded, pled	pleaded, pled	stick	stuck	stuck
proofread	proofread	proofread	sting	stung	stung
prove	proved	proved, proven	stink	stank	stunk
put	put	put	stride	strode	–
quit	quit	quit	strike	struck	struck
read	read	read	strive	strove, strived	striven, strived
redo	redid	redone	sublet	sublet	sublet
rewind	rewound	rewound	swear	swore	sworn
rewrite	rewrote	rewritten	sweep	swept	swept
ride	rode	ridden	swell	swelled	swollen, swelled
ring	rang	rung	swim	swam	swum
rise	rose	risen	swing	swung	swung
run	ran	run	take	took	taken
saw	sawed	sawed, sawn	teach	taught	taught
say	said	said	tear	tore	torn
see	saw	seen	tell	told	told
seek	sought	sought	think	thought	thought
sell	sold	sold	throw	threw	thrown
send	sent	sent	thrust	thrust	thrust
set	set	set	undergo	underwent	undergone
sew	sewed	sewed, sewn	understand	understood	understood
shake	shook	shaken	undo	undid	undone
shear	sheared	shorn, sheared	unwind	unwound	unwound
shed	shed	shed	upset	upset	upset
shine	shone, shined	shone, shined	wake	woke	woken
shoot	shot	shot	wear	wore	worn
show	showed	shown, showed	weave	wove	woven
shrink	shrank, shrunk	shrunk	weep	wept	wept
shut	shut	shut	wet	wet, wetted	wet, wetted
sing	sang	sung	win	won	won
sink	sank	sunk	wind	wound	wound
sit	sat	sat	withdraw	withdrew	withdrawn
sleep	slept	slept	wring	wrung	wrung
slide	slid	slid	write	wrote	written
sling	slung	slung			
slit	slit	slit			
sneak	sneaked, snuck	sneaked, snuck			
sow	sowed	sown, sowed			
speak	spoke	spoken			
speed	sped, speeded	sped, speeded			

Punctuation

● Period

A **period** (.) is used at the end of a sentence, unless the sentence is a question or an exclamation:
- We went shopping.
- He tried to go.

It is also used after an abbreviation:
- Mr. Smith   Main St.   etc.   a.m.

❓ Question mark

A **question mark** (?) is used at the end of a direct question:
- How old are you?
- "When did they go?" Todd asked.

It is not used after an indirect question:
- Todd asked when they went.

❗ Exclamation point

An **exclamation point** (!) is used with sentences that express strong emotion, such as surprise, excitement, or shock:
- I can't believe it!
- That's wonderful!

It is also used after an exclamation:
- Bye!   Ouch!

, Comma

A **comma** (,) separates items in a series:
- I can speak English, Spanish, and Italian.
- Do you want coffee, tea, or orange juice?
- She was a tall, slim, beautiful woman.

Commas are also used to separate different parts of a sentence:
- He wanted to go, but he didn't have time.
- Although she is small, she is very strong.

They appear before or around extra information in a sentence:
- They don't like our dog, which barks all day.
- Michael Jackson, the American pop star, was famous all over the world.

A comma also usually comes before or after a quotation:
- David said, "I'll see you Saturday."
- "I'll see you on Saturday," David said.

It goes before or after a name when a person is being spoken to directly:
- Stuart, would you like to go?
- I'm sorry, Jess.

Commas also separate cities and towns from states:
- Des Moines, Iowa
- Juneau, Alaska

: Colon

A **colon** (:) is used to introduce explanations, long quotations, or a series:
- She had three pets: a dog, a cat, and a horse.

It can also introduce a quotation:
- As Thomas Jefferson said: "All men are born equal."

; Semicolon

A **semicolon** (;) is used to separate two contrasting parts of a sentence:
- Humans use moral judgment; animals do not.

It is also used in a series that has commas in it:
- The menu featured hamburger, potato, and carrot casserole; and pecan pie.

' Apostrophe

An **apostrophe** (') shows that one or more letters are missing in a short form:
- don't (= do not)
- he's (= he is or he has)
- I'm (= I am)
- they'd (= they had or they would)
- they're (= they are)
- we've (= we have)

It also shows that a person or thing belongs to someone:
- Kerri's car
- Robin's sister
- James' teacher or James's teacher

The apostrophe goes after the "s" if the noun is plural:
- the boy's room (= one boy)
- the boys' room (= two or more boys)

❝❞ Quotation marks

Quotation marks (" ") are used to show what someone said:

> "Let's see a movie," Roger suggested.

They also show thoughts that are presented like speech:

> "I should leave now," she thought.

Quotations marks are also used around the titles of essays, songs, poems, etc.:

> They always play "The Star-Spangled Banner" before baseball games.

⊖ Hyphen

A **hyphen** (-) connects two or more ideas that form one idea:

> a twelve-year-old boy
> a well-known actor

It joins a prefix to a word that begins with a capital letter:

> anti-European   pro-American

A hyphen is also used with compound numbers:

> ninety-nine   twenty-seven

The hyphen is used to divide a word at the end of a line:

> I had known her ever since we were child-ren, and we were very close.

⊖ Dash

A **dash** (–) separates a word or phrase from the rest of the sentence. It is often used near the end of a sentence to sum up or emphasize an idea:

> I lost my keys, forgot my homework, and missed class – it was an awful day.

A dash also shows that an idea has been interrupted in the middle of a sentence or thought:

> If only she would love me, I would – Oh, what's the use? It will never happen.

⓪ Parentheses

Parentheses ( ) separate extra information from the rest of the sentence:

> The recipe calls for 1 pound (450 grams) of flour.
> Tony (the smallest boy in class) was hurt playing football.

Parentheses are often used around numbers and letters in sentences, especially with lists or choices:

> If you had a choice, would you rather live in (a) the U.S.A., (b) Canada, or (c) China?

Geographical Names

This list shows the English spelling and pronunciation of geographical names and the adjectives that go with them.

Inclusion in this list does not imply status as a sovereign nation.

Noun	Adjective
Afghanistan /æfˈgænəˌstæn/	Afghan /ˈæfgæn/
Africa /ˈæfrɪkə/	African /ˈæfrɪkən/
Albania /ælˈbeɪniə/	Albanian /ælˈbeɪniən/
Algeria /ælˈdʒɪriə/	Algerian /ælˈdʒɪriən/
America /əˈmɛrɪkə/	American /əˈmɛrɪkən/
Andorra /ænˈdɔrə/	Andorran /ænˈdɔrən/
Angola /æŋˈgoʊlə/	Angolan /æŋˈgoʊlən/
Antarctica /æntˈɑrktɪkə; -ˈɑrt̬ɪkə/	Antarctic /æntˈɑrktɪk; -ˈɑrt̬ɪk/
Antigua and Barbuda /ænˌtigə ən barˈbudə/	Antiguan /ænˈtigən/, Barbudan /barˈbudn/
(the) Arctic /ˈɑrktɪk; ˈɑrt̬ɪk/	Arctic /ˈɑrktɪk; ˈɑrt̬ɪk/
Argentina /ˌɑrdʒənˈtinə/	Argentine /ˈɑrdʒənˌtin; -ˌtaɪn/
	Argentinian /ˌɑrdʒənˈtɪniən/
Armenia /ɑrˈminiə/	Armenian /ɑrˈminiən/
Asia /ˈeɪʒə/	Asian /ˈeɪʒn/
Australia /ɔˈstreɪlyə/	Australian /ɔˈstreɪlyən/
Austria /ˈɔstriə/	Austrian /ˈɔstriən/
Azerbaijan /ˌæzərbaɪˈdʒɑn; ˌɑzər-/	Azerbaijani /ˌæzərbaɪˈdʒɑni; ˌɑzər-/
(the) Bahamas /bəˈhɑməz/	Bahamian /bəˈheɪmiən/
Bahrain /bɑˈreɪn/	Bahraini /bɑˈreɪni/
Bangladesh /ˌbɑŋɡləˈdɛʃ; ˌbæŋ-/	Bangladeshi /ˌbɑŋɡləˈdɛʃi; ˌbæŋ-/
Barbados /barˈbeɪdoʊs/	Barbadian /barˈbeɪdiən/
Belarus /ˌbɛləˈrus/	Belarusian /ˌbɛləˈrusiən/, Belorussian /ˌbɛləˈrʌʃn/
Belgium /ˈbɛldʒəm/	Belgian /ˈbɛldʒən/
Belize /bəˈliz/	Belizean /bəˈliziən/
Benin /bəˈnin/	Beninese /ˌbɛnəˈniz; -ˈnis/
Bhutan /buˈtɑn/	Bhutanese /ˌbutnˈiz; -ˈis/
Bolivia /bəˈlɪviə/	Bolivian /bəˈlɪviən/
Bosnia and Herzegovina /ˌbɑzniə ən ˌhɛrtsəgoʊˈvinə/	Bosnian /ˈbɑzniən/, Herzegovinian /ˌhɛrtsəgəˈvɪniən/
Botswana /bɑtˈswɑnə/	Botswanan /bɑtˈswɑnən/
Brazil /brəˈzɪl/	Brazilian /brəˈzɪlyən/
Brunei /bruˈnaɪ /	Bruneian /bruˈnaɪən/
Bulgaria /bʌlˈgɛriə/	Bulgarian /bʌlˈgɛriən/
Burkina Faso /bərˌkinə ˈfɑsoʊ/	Burkinabe /bərˌkinəˈbeɪ/
Burma /ˈbərmə/ (now officially Myanmar)	Burmese /ˌbərˈmiz; -ˈmis/
Burundi /bʊˈrʊndi; -ˈrun-/	Burundian /bʊˈrʊndiən; -ˈrun-/
Cambodia /kæmˈboʊdiə/	Cambodian /kæmˈboʊdiən/
Cameroon /ˌkæməˈrun /	Cameroonian /ˌkæməˈruniən/
Canada /ˈkænədə/	Canadian /kəˈneɪdiən/
Cape Verde /ˌkeɪp ˈvərd/	Cape Verdean /ˌkeɪp ˈvərdiən/
(the) Central African Republic /ˌsɛntrəl ˌæfrɪkən rɪˈpʌblɪk/	Central African /ˌsɛntrəl ˈæfrɪkən/
Chad /tʃæd/	Chadian /ˈtʃædiən/
Chile /ˈtʃɪli/	Chilean /ˈtʃɪliən; tʃɪˈleɪən/
China /ˈtʃaɪnə/	Chinese /ˌtʃaɪˈniz; -ˈnis/
Colombia /kəˈlʌmbiə/	Colombian /kəˈlʌmbiən/
Comoros /ˈkɑməˌroʊz/	Comoran /ˈkɑmərən; kəˈmɔrən/
Congo /ˈkɑŋgoʊ/	Congolese /ˌkɑŋgəˈliz; -ˈlis/
Costa Rica /ˌkoʊstə ˈrikə; ˌkɑstə-/	Costa Rican /ˌkoʊstə ˈrikən; ˌkɑstə-/
Côte d'Ivoire /ˌkoʊt diˈvwar/	Ivorian /aɪˈvɔriən/
Croatia /kroʊˈeɪʃə/	Croatian /kroʊˈeɪʃn/

Noun	Adjective
Cuba /ˈkyubə/	Cuban /ˈkyubən/
Cyprus /ˈsaɪprəs/	Cypriot /ˈsɪpriət/
(the) Czech Republic /ˌtʃɛk rɪˈpʌblɪk/	Czech /tʃɛk/
(the) Democratic Republic of the Congo /ˌdɛməˌkrætɪk rɪˌpʌblɪk əv ðə ˈkaŋgoʊ/	Congolese /ˌkaŋgəˈliz; -ˈlis/
Denmark /ˈdɛnmark/	Danish /ˈdeɪnɪʃ/
Djibouti /dʒɪˈbuṭi/	Djiboutian /dʒɪˈbuṭiən/
Dominica /ˌdaməˈnikə/	Dominican /ˌdaməˈnikən/
(the) Dominican Republic /dəˌmɪnɪkən rɪˈpʌblɪk/	Dominican /dəˈmɪnɪkən/
East Timor /ˌist ˈtimɔr/	East Timorese /ˌist ˌtimɔˈriz; -ˈris/
Ecuador /ˈɛkwəˌdɔr/	Ecuadorian, Ecuadorean /ˌɛkwəˈdɔriən/
Egypt /ˈidʒɪpt/	Egyptian /ɪˈdʒɪpʃn/
El Salvador /ɛl ˈsælvəˌdɔr/	Salvadoran /ˌsælvəˈdɔrən/
England /ˈɪŋglənd/	English /ˈɪŋglɪʃ/
Equatorial Guinea /ˌikwəˌtɔriəl ˈgɪni; ˌɛkwə-/	Equatorial Guinean /ˌikwəˌtɔriəl ˈgɪniən; ˌɛkwə-/
Eritrea /ˌɛrəˈtriə/	Eritrean /ˌɛrəˈtriən/
Estonia /ɛˈstoʊniə/	Estonian /ɛˈstoʊniən/
Ethiopia /ˌiθiˈoʊpiə/	Ethiopian /ˌiθiˈoʊpiən/
Europe /ˈyʊrəp/	European /ˌyʊrəˈpiən/
Fiji /ˈfidʒi/	Fijian /ˈfidʒiən; fɪˈdʒiən/
Finland /ˈfɪnlənd/	Finnish /ˈfɪnɪʃ/
France /fræns/	French /frɛntʃ/
(the) Former Yugoslav Republic of Macedonia /ˌfɔrmər ˌyugəslav rɪˈpʌblɪk əv ˌmæsəˈdoʊniə/	Macedonian /ˌmæsəˈdoʊniən/
Gabon /gæˈboʊn/	Gabonese /ˌgæbəˈniz; -ˈnis/
(the) Gambia /ˈgæmbiə/	Gambian /ˈgæmbiən/
Georgia /ˈdʒɔrdʒə/	Georgian /ˈdʒɔrdʒən/
Germany /ˈdʒərməni/	German /ˈdʒərmən/
Ghana /ˈganə/	Ghanaian /gɑˈneɪən/
Great Britain /ˌgreɪt ˈbrɪtn/	British /ˈbrɪtɪʃ/
Greece /gris/	Greek /grik/
Grenada /grəˈneɪdə/	Grenadian /grəˈneɪdiən/
Guatemala /ˌgwaṭəˈmɑlə/	Guatemalan /ˌgwaṭəˈmɑlən/
Guinea /ˈgɪni/	Guinean /ˈgɪniən/
Guinea-Bissau /ˌgɪni bɪˈsaʊ/	Guinean /ˈgɪniən/
Guyana /gaɪˈænə; -ˈɑnə/	Guyanese /ˌgaɪəˈniz; -ˈnis/
Haiti /ˈheɪṭi/	Haitian /ˈheɪʃn/
Holland /ˈhalənd/ → (the) Netherlands	
Honduras /hanˈdʊrəs/	Honduran /hanˈdʊrən/
Hungary /ˈhʌŋgəri/	Hungarian /hʌŋˈgɛriən/
Iceland /ˈaɪslənd/	Icelandic /aɪsˈlændɪk/
India /ˈɪndiə/	Indian /ˈɪndiən/
Indonesia /ˌɪndəˈniʒə/	Indonesian /ˌɪndəˈniʒn/
Iran /ɪˈran; ɪˈræn/	Iranian /ɪˈreɪniən; ɪˈra-/
Iraq /ɪˈrak; ɪˈræk/	Iraqi /ɪˈraki; ɪˈræki/
Israel /ˈɪzriəl; ˈɪzreɪl/	Israeli /ɪzˈreɪli/
Italy /ˈɪṭl•i/	Italian /ɪˈtælyən/
(the) Ivory Coast /ˌaɪvri ˈkoʊst; ˌaɪvəri-/ → Côte d'Ivoire	
Jamaica /dʒəˈmeɪkə/	Jamaican /dʒəˈmeɪkən/
Japan /dʒəˈpæn/	Japanese /ˌdʒæpəˈniz; -ˈnis/
Jordan /ˈdʒɔrdn/	Jordanian /dʒɔrˈdeɪniən/
Kazakhstan /ˌkazakˈstan/	Kazakh /kəˈzak/, Kazakhstani /ˌkazakˈstani/
Kenya /ˈkɛnyə; ˈkin-/	Kenyan /ˈkɛnyən; ˈkin-/
Kiribati /ˈkɪrəˌbæs; ˌkɪrəˈbaṭi/	I-Kiribati /ˌi ˈkɪrəˌbæs; ˌi ˌkɪrəˈbaṭi/
Korea /kəˈriə/ → North Korea, South Korea	Korean /kəˈriən/
Kuwait /kʊˈweɪt/	Kuwaiti /kʊˈweɪṭi/
Kyrgyzstan /ˈkɪrgɪstæn; -ˌstan/	Kyrgyz /kɪrˈgiz/, Kyrgyzstani /ˌkɪrgɪˈstani; -ˈstæni/

Noun	Adjective
Laos /laʊs; ˈlɑoʊs/	Laotian /leɪˈoʊʃn/, Lao /laʊ/
Latvia /ˈlætviə/	Latvian /ˈlætviən/
Lebanon /ˈlɛbəˌnɑn; -nən/	Lebanese /ˌlɛbəˈniz; -ˈnis/
Lesotho /ləˈsoʊtoʊ; ləˈsutu/	Basotho /bəˈsoʊtoʊ; -ˈsutu/
Liberia /laɪˈbɪriə/	Liberian /laɪˈbɪriən/
Libya /ˈlɪbiə/	Libyan /ˈlɪbiən/
Liechtenstein /ˈlɪktənˌstaɪn; -ˌʃtaɪn/	Liechtenstein /ˈlɪktənˌstaɪn; -ˌʃtaɪn/
Lithuania /ˌlɪθuˈeɪniə/	Lithuanian /ˌlɪθuˈeɪniən/
Luxembourg /ˈlʌksəmˌbərg/	Luxembourg /ˈlʌksəmˌbərg/
Macedonia /ˌmæsəˈdoʊniə/	Macedonian /ˌmæsəˈdoʊniən/
Madagascar /ˌmædəˈgæskər/	Madagascan /ˌmædəˈgæskən/
Malawi /məˈlawi/	Malawian /məˈlawiən/
Malaysia /məˈleɪʒə/	Malaysian /məˈleɪʒn/
(the) Maldives /ˈmɔldivz; -daɪvz/	Maldivian /mɔlˈdɪviən/
Mali /ˈmali/	Malian /ˈmaliən/
Malta /ˈmɔltə/	Maltese /ˌmɔlˈtiz; -ˈtis/
(the) Marshall Islands /marʃl ˈaɪləndz/	Marshallese /ˌmarʃəˈliz; -ˈlis/
Mauritania /ˌmɔrəˈteɪniə/	Mauritanian /ˌmɔrəˈteɪniən/
Mauritius /mɔˈrɪʃəs/	Mauritian /mɔˈrɪʃn/
Mexico /ˈmɛksɪˌkoʊ/	Mexican /ˈmɛksɪkən/
Micronesia /ˌmaɪkrəˈniʒə/	Micronesian /ˌmaɪkrəˈniʒn/
Moldova /malˈdoʊvə; mɔl-/	Moldovan /malˈdoʊvn, mɔl-/
Monaco /ˈmanəˌkoʊ/	Monegasque /ˌmanɪˈgæsk/, Monacan /ˈmanəkən/
Mongolia /manˈgoʊliə/	Mongolian /manˈgoʊliən/
Montenegro /ˌmantəˈnɛgroʊ; -ˈnigroʊ/	Montenegrin /ˌmantəˈnɛgrən; -ˈnigrən/
Morocco /məˈrakoʊ/	Moroccan /məˈrakən/
Mozambique /ˌmoʊzæmˈbik; -zəm-/	Mozambican /ˌmoʊzæmˈbikən; -zəm-/
Myanmar /ˈmyanmar; ˈmyæn-/	Burmese /ˌbərˈmiz; -ˈmis/
Namibia /nəˈmɪbiə/	Namibian /nəˈmɪbiən/
Nauru /naˈuru/	Nauruan /naˈuruən/
Nepal /nəˈpɔl; nəˈpal/	Nepalese /ˌnɛpəˈliz; -ˈlis/
(the) Netherlands /ˈnɛðərləndz/	Dutch /dʌtʃ/
New Zealand /ˌnu ˈzilənd/	New Zealand /ˌnu ˈzilənd/
Nicaragua /ˌnɪkəˈragwə/	Nicaraguan /ˌnɪkəˈragwən/
Niger /niˈʒɛr; ˈnaɪdʒər/	Nigerien /niˈʒɛriən; naɪˌdʒɪriˈɛn/
Nigeria /naɪˈdʒɪriə/	Nigerian /naɪˈdʒɪriən/
Northern Ireland /ˌnɔrðərn ˈaɪərlənd/	Northern Irish /ˌnɔrðərn ˈaɪrɪʃ/
North Korea /ˌnɔrθ kəˈriə/	North Korean /ˌnɔrθ kəˈriən/
Norway /ˈnɔrweɪ/	Norwegian /nɔrˈwidʒən/
Oceania /ˌoʊʃiˈæniə/	Oceanian /ˌoʊʃiˈæniən/
Oman /oʊˈman/	Omani /oʊˈmani/
Pakistan /ˈpækəˌstæn; ˈpakəˌstan/	Pakistani /ˌpækəˈstæni; ˌpakəˈstani/
Palau /pəˈlaʊ/	Palauan /pəˈlaʊən/
Panama /ˈpænəˌma/	Panamanian /ˌpænəˈmeɪniən/
Papua New Guinea /ˌpæpyuə nu ˈgɪni; ˌpæpuə-/	Papua New Guinean /ˌpæpyuə nu ˈgɪniən; ˌpæpuə-/
Paraguay /ˈpærəˌgwaɪ; -ˌgweɪ/	Paraguayan /ˌpærəˈgwaɪən; -ˈgweɪ-/
Peru /pəˈru/	Peruvian /pəˈruviən/
(the) Philippines /ˈfɪləˌpinz; ˌfɪləˈpinz/	Philippine /ˈfɪləˌpin/
Poland /ˈpoʊlənd/	Polish /ˈpoʊlɪʃ/
Portugal /ˈpɔrtʃəgl/	Portuguese /ˌpɔrtʃəˈgiz; -ˈgis; ˈpɔrtʃəˌgiz; -ˌgis/
Qatar /ˈkatar; -tər/	Qatari /kəˈtari/
(the) Republic of Ireland /rɪˌpʌblɪk əv ˈaɪərlənd/	Irish /ˈaɪrɪʃ/
Romania /ruˈmeɪniə; roʊ-/	Romanian /ruˈmeɪniən; roʊ-/
Russia /ˈrʌʃə/	Russian /ˈrʌʃn/
Rwanda /ruˈandə/	Rwandan /ruˈandən/
Saint Kitts and Nevis /seɪnt ˌkɪts ən ˈnivəs/	Kittitian /kəˈtɪʃn/, Nevisian /nəˈvɪʒn/
Saint Lucia /ˌseɪnt ˈluʃə/	Saint Lucian /ˌseɪnt ˈluʃən/

Noun	Adjective
Saint Vincent and the Grenadines /seɪnt vɪnsnt ən ðə 'grɛnədinz/	Saint Vincentian /ˌseɪnt vɪn'sɛnʃn/, Vincentian /vɪn'sɛnʃn/
Samoa /sə'moʊə/	Samoan /sə'moʊən/
San Marino /ˌsæn mə'rinoʊ/	Sammarinese /ˌsæmˌmærə'niz; -'nis/
São Tomé and Principe /ˌsaʊ tə'meɪ ən 'prɪnsəpi; ˌsaʊn- /	São Tomean /ˌsaʊ tə'meɪən; ˌsaʊn-/
Saudi Arabia /ˌsaʊdi ə'reɪbiə; ˌsɔdi-/	Saudi /'saʊdi; 'sɔdi/, Saudi Arabian /ˌsaʊdi ə'reɪbiən; ˌsɔdi-/
Scandinavia /ˌskændə'neɪviə/	Scandinavian /ˌskændə'neɪviən/
Scotland /'skatlənd/	Scottish /'skatɪʃ/, Scots /skats/
Senegal /'sɛnəgɔl; -gal/	Senegalese /ˌsɛnəgə'liz; -'lis/
Serbia /'sərbiə/	Serbian /'sərbiən/
(the) Seychelles /seɪ'ʃɛlz; -'ʃɛl/	Seychellois /ˌseɪʃɛl'wa/
Sierra Leone /si,ɛrə li'oʊn/	Sierra Leonean /si,ɛrə li'oʊniən/
Singapore /'sɪŋəˌpɔr/	Singaporean /ˌsɪŋə'pɔriən/, Singapore /'sɪŋəˌpɔr/
Slovakia /sloʊ'vakiə/	Slovak /'sloʊvak/, Slovakian /sloʊ'vakiən/
Slovenia /sloʊ'viniə/	Slovenian /sloʊ'viniən/
(the) Solomon Islands /ˌsaləmən 'aɪləndz/	—
Somalia /sə'maliə/	Somali /sə'mali/
South Africa /ˌsaʊθ 'æfrɪkə/	South African /ˌsaʊθ 'æfrɪkən/
South Korea /ˌsaʊθ kə'riə/	South Korean /ˌsaʊθ kə'riən/
Spain /speɪn/	Spanish /'spænɪʃ/
Sri Lanka /ˌsri 'laŋkə; ˌʃri-/	Sri Lankan /ˌsri 'laŋkən; ˌʃri-/
Sudan /su'dæn/	Sudanese /ˌsudn'iz; -'is/
Suriname /'sʊrəˌnam; -ˌnæm; ˌsʊrə'namə/	Surinamese /ˌsʊrənə'miz; -'mis/
Swaziland /'swaziˌlænd/	Swazi /'swazi/
Sweden /'swidn/	Swedish /'swidɪʃ/
Switzerland /'swɪtsərlənd/	Swiss /swɪs/
Syria /'sɪriə/	Syrian /'sɪriən/
Tajikistan /tə'dʒikəˌstæn; -'dʒikə-; -ˌstan/	Tajik /ta'dʒik; ta'dʒɪk/, Tajikistani /təˌdʒikə'stani; -ˌdʒikə-; -'stæni
Tanzania /ˌtænzə'niə/	Tanzanian /ˌtænzə'niən/
Thailand /'taɪlænd/	Thai /taɪ/
Togo /'toʊgoʊ/	Togolese /ˌtoʊgə'liz; -'lis/
Tonga /'taŋgə/	Tongan /'taŋgən/
Trinidad and Tobago /ˌtrɪnədæd ən tə'beɪgoʊ/	Trinidadian /ˌtrɪnə'dædiən/, Tobagonian /ˌtoʊbə'goʊniən/
Tunisia /tu'niʒə/	Tunisian /tu'niʒn/
Turkey /'tərki/	Turkish /'tərkɪʃ/
Turkmenistan /tərk'mɛnəstæn; -stan/	Turkmen /'tərkmɛn; -mən/
Tuvalu /tu'valu/	Tuvaluan /tu'valuən/
Uganda /yu'gændə/	Ugandan /yu'gændən/
Ukraine /yu'kreɪn; 'yukreɪn/	Ukrainian /yu'kreɪniən/
(the) United Arab Emirates /yʊˌnaɪtəd ˌærəb 'ɛmərəts/	Emirati /ˌɛmə'rati/
(the) United Kingdom /yʊˌnaɪtəd 'kɪŋdəm/	British /'brɪtɪʃ/
(the) United States of America /yʊˌnaɪtəd ˌsteɪts əv ə'mɛrɪkə/	American /ə'mɛrɪkən/
Uruguay /'yʊrəˌgwaɪ; -ˌgweɪ/	Uruguayan /ˌyʊrə'gwaɪən; -'gweɪ-/
Uzbekistan /ʊz'bɛkəstæn; -stan/	Uzbek /'ʊzbɛk/, Uzbekistani /ʊzˌbɛkə'stani/
Vanuatu /ˌvanu'atu; ˌvænu-/	Ni-Vanuatu /ˌni ˌvanu'atu; -ˌvænu-/
(the) Vatican City /ˌvæṭɪkən 'sɪṭi/	—
Venezuela /ˌvɛnə'zweɪlə/	Venezuelan /ˌvɛnə'zweɪlən/
Vietnam /ˌviɛt'nam; -'næm/	Vietnamese /ˌviɛtnə'miz; viˌɛt-; -'mis/
Wales /weɪlz/	Welsh /wɛlʃ/
(the) West Indies /ˌwɛst 'ɪndiz/	West Indian /ˌwɛst 'ɪndiən/
Yemen /'yɛmən/	Yemeni /'yɛməni/
Zambia /'zæmbiə/	Zambian /'zæmbiən/
Zimbabwe /zɪm'babweɪ; -wi/	Zimbabwean /zɪm'babweɪən; -wiən/

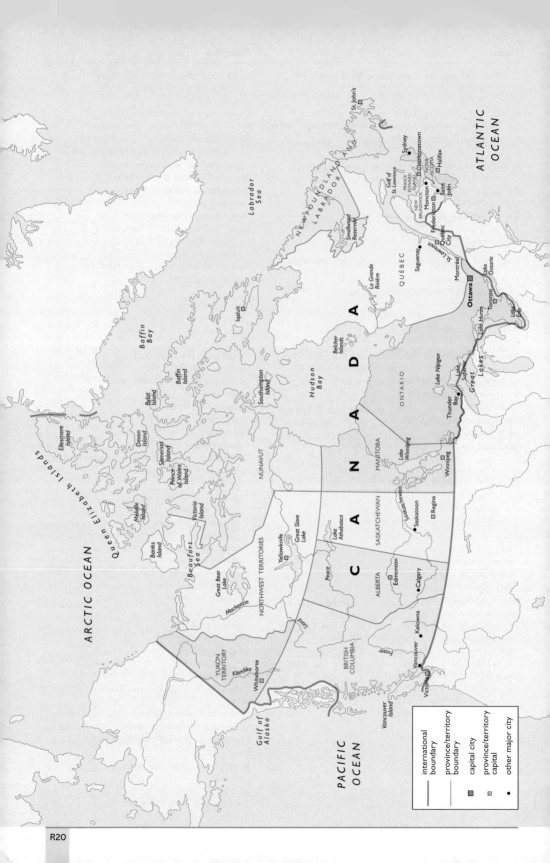

ARCTIC OCEAN

Queen Elizabeth Islands

Ellesmere
Island

Devon
Island

Somerset
Island

Prince
of Wales
Island

Melville
Island

Banks
Island

Victoria
Island

Beaufort
Sea

Bylot
Island

Baffin
Island

Baffin
Bay

Southampton
Island

Iqaluit

Labrador
Sea

NEW FOUNDLAND

LABRADOR

St. John's

ATLANTIC
OCEAN

Smallwood
Reservoir

Sydney
Charlottetown

Gulf of
St. Lawrence

PRINCE
EDWARD
ISLAND

NOVA
SCOTIA

Halifax

Moncton

NEW
BRUNSWICK

Saint
John

Fredericton

Québec
City

St. Lawrence

Saguenay

QUÉBEC

La Grande
Rivière

Montréal

Belcher
Islands

Hudson
Bay

Ottawa

Lake
Ontario

Toronto

ONTARIO

Lake Huron

Lake
Erie

Great
Lakes

Lake
Superior

Lake Nipigon

Thunder
Bay

Great Slave
Lake

Great Bear
Lake

Mackenzie

NORTHWEST TERRITORIES

Yellowknife

NUNAVUT

C A N A D A

MANITOBA

Lake
Winnipeg

Winnipeg

Lake
Athabasca

Saskatchewan

SASKATCHEWAN

Saskatoon

Regina

Peace

ALBERTA

Edmonton

Calgary

Liard

YUKON
TERRITORY

Klondike

Whitehorse

BRITISH
COLUMBIA

Fraser

Kelowna

Vancouver

Vancouver
Island

Victoria

Gulf of
Alaska

PACIFIC
OCEAN

legend:

international
boundary

province/territory
boundary

capital city

province/territory
capital

other major city

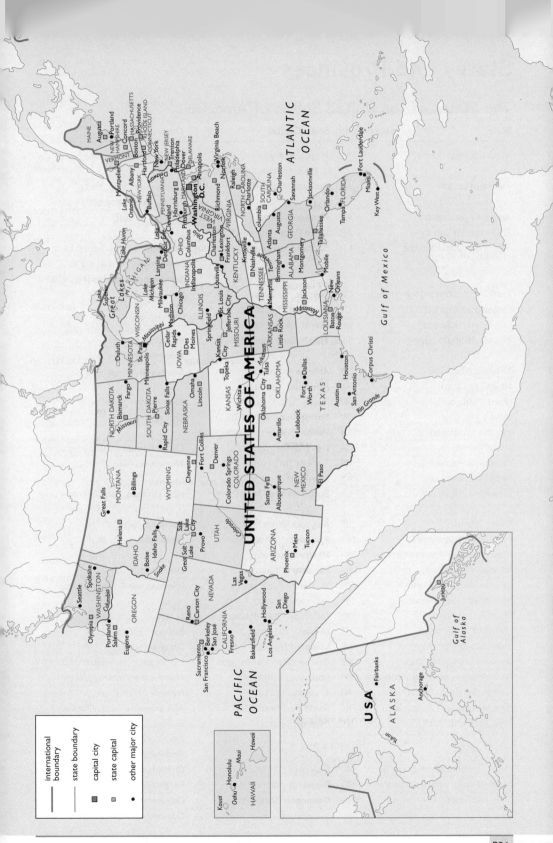

UNITED STATES OF AMERICA

ATLANTIC OCEAN

PACIFIC OCEAN

Gulf of Mexico

Legend

international boundary

state boundary

capital city

state capital

other major city

USA / ALASKA

Gulf of Alaska

HAWAII

States and Provinces

The States of the United States of America

State	abbreviation	State Capital	Other Major Cities
Alabama /ˌæləˈbæmə/	AL	Montgomery /məntˈɡʌməri; mɑnt-/	Birmingham /ˈbərmɪŋˌhæm/
Alaska /əˈlæskə/	AK	Juneau /ˈdʒunoʊ/	Anchorage /ˈæŋkərɪdʒ/ Fairbanks /ˈfɛrbæŋks/
Arizona /ˌærəˈzoʊnə/	AZ	Phoenix /ˈfinɪks/	Tucson /ˈtusɑn/
Arkansas /ˈɑrkənˌsɔ/	AR	Little Rock /ˈlɪtl̩ ˌrɑk/	
California /ˌkæləˈfɔrnyə/	CA	Sacramento /ˌsækrəˈmɛntoʊ/	Los Angeles /lɔs ˈændʒələs/ San Diego /ˌsæn diˈeɪɡoʊ/ San Francisco /ˌsæn frənˈsɪskoʊ/
Colorado /ˌkɑləˈrædoʊ; -ˈrɑdoʊ/	CO	Denver /ˈdɛnvər/	
Connecticut /kəˈnɛtɪkət/	CT	Hartford /ˈhɑrtfərd/	
Delaware /ˈdɛləˌwɛr/	DE	Dover /ˈdoʊvər/	
Florida /ˈflɔrədə; ˈflɑr-/	FL	Tallahassee /ˌtæləˈhæsi/	Miami /maɪˈæmi/ Orlando /ɔrˈlændoʊ/
Georgia /ˈdʒɔrdʒə/	GA	Atlanta /ətˈlæntə/	Savannah /səˈvænə/
Hawaii /həˈwaɪi/	HI	Honolulu /ˌhɑnəˈlulu/	
Idaho /ˈaɪdəˌhoʊ/	ID	Boise /ˈbɔɪzi; -si/	Idaho Falls /ˌaɪdəhoʊ ˈfɔlz/
Illinois /ˌɪləˈnɔɪ/	IL	Springfield /ˈsprɪŋfild/	Chicago /ʃɪˈkɑɡoʊ; -ˈkɔɡoʊ/
Indiana /ˌɪndiˈænə/	IN	Indianapolis /ˌɪndiəˈnæpələs/	
Iowa /ˈaɪəwə/	IA	Des Moines /də ˈmɔɪn/	Cedar Rapids /ˌsidər ˈræpədz/
Kansas /ˈkænzəs/	KS	Topeka /təˈpikə/	Wichita /ˈwɪtʃəˌtɔ/
Kentucky /kənˈtʌki/	KY	Frankfort /ˈfræŋkfərt/	
Louisiana /luˌiziˈænə/	LA	Baton Rouge /ˌbætn̩ ˈruʒ/	New Orleans /ˌnu ˈɔrlənz; -ɔrˈlinz/
Maine /meɪn/	ME	Augusta /ɔˈɡʌstə; ə-/	Portland /ˈpɔrtlənd/
Maryland /ˈmɛrələnd/	MD	Annapolis /əˈnæpələs/	Baltimore /ˈbɔltəˌmɔr/
Massachusetts /ˌmæsəˈtʃusəts/	MA	Boston /ˈbɔstən/	
Michigan /ˈmɪʃɪɡən/	MI	Lansing /ˈlænsɪŋ/	Detroit /dɪˈtrɔɪt/
Minnesota /ˌmɪnəˈsoʊtə/	MN	St. Paul /ˌseɪnt ˈpɔl/	Minneapolis /ˌmɪniˈæpələs/
Mississippi /ˌmɪsəˈsɪpi/	MS	Jackson /ˈdʒæksn̩/	
Missouri /məˈzʊri/	MO	Jefferson City /ˌdʒɛfərsn̩ ˈsɪti/	St. Louis /ˌseɪnt ˈluəs/
Montana /mɑnˈtænə/	MT	Helena /ˈhɛlənə/	Billings /ˈbɪlɪŋz/
Nebraska /nəˈbræskə/	NE	Lincoln /ˈlɪŋkən/	Omaha /ˈoʊməˌhɑ; -ˌhɔ/
Nevada /nəˈvædə; -ˈvɑdə/	NV	Carson City /ˌkɑrsn̩ ˈsɪti/	Las Vegas /lɑs ˈveɪɡəs/
New Hampshire /ˌnu ˈhæmpʃər/	NH	Concord /ˈkɑŋkərd/	Manchester /ˈmænˌtʃɛstər/
New Jersey /ˌnu ˈdʒərzi/	NJ	Trenton /ˈtrɛntn̩/	Newark /ˈnuərk/
New Mexico /ˌnu ˈmɛksɪˌkoʊ/	NM	Santa Fe /ˌsæntə ˈfeɪ/	Albuquerque /ˈælbəˌkərki/
New York /ˌnu ˈyɔrk/	NY	Albany /ˈɔlbəni/	Buffalo /ˈbʌfəˌloʊ/ New York /ˌnu ˈyɔrk/ Rochester /ˈrɑtʃəstər; -ˌtʃɛstər/
North Carolina /ˌnɔrθ kærəˈlaɪnə/	NC	Raleigh /ˈrɔli; ˈrɑli/	Charlotte /ˈʃɑrlət/
North Dakota /ˌnɔrθ dəˈkoʊtə/	ND	Bismarck /ˈbɪzmɑrk/	Fargo /ˈfɑrɡoʊ/
Ohio /oʊˈhaɪoʊ/	OH	Columbus /kəˈlʌmbəs/	Cleveland /ˈklivlənd/ Cincinnati /ˌsɪnsəˈnæti/

State	abbreviation	State Capital	Other Major Cities
Oklahoma /ˌoʊkləˈhoʊmə/	OK	Oklahoma City /ˌoʊkləhoʊmə ˈsɪt̬i/	Tulsa /ˈtʌlsə/
Oregon /ˈɔrəgən; ˈɑr-; -ˌgɑn/	OR	Salem /ˈseɪləm/	Portland /ˈpɔrtlənd/
Pennsylvania /ˌpɛnslˈveɪnyə/	PA	Harrisburg /ˈhærəsˌbərg/	Philadelphia /ˌfɪləˈdɛlfiə/ Pittsburgh /ˈpɪtsbərg/
Rhode Island /ˌroʊd ˈaɪlənd/	RI	Providence /ˈprɑvədəns/	
South Carolina /ˌsaʊθ kærəˈlaɪnə/	SC	Columbia /kəˈlʌmbiə/	Charleston /ˈtʃɑrlstən/
South Dakota /ˌsaʊθ dəˈkoʊt̬ə/	SD	Pierre /pɪr/	Sioux Falls /ˌsu ˈfɔlz/
Tennessee /ˌtɛnəˈsi/	TN	Nashville /ˈnæʃvɪl/	Memphis /ˈmɛmfəs/
Texas /ˈtɛksəs/	TX	Austin /ˈɔstən/	Dallas /ˈdæləs/ Fort Worth /ˌfɔrt ˈwərθ/ Houston /ˈhyustən/ San Antonio /ˌsæn ænˈtoʊnioʊ/
Utah /ˈyutɔ; ˈyutɑ/	UT	Salt Lake City /ˌsɔlt leɪk ˈsɪt̬i/	Provo /ˈproʊvoʊ/
Vermont /vərˈmɑnt/	VT	Montpelier /mɑntˈpilyər/	
Virginia /vərˈdʒɪnyə/	VA	Richmond /ˈrɪtʃmənd/	Norfolk /ˈnɔrfək/
Washington /ˈwɑʃɪŋtən; ˈwɔ-/	WA	Olympia /əˈlɪmpiə/	Seattle /siˈæt̬l/
West Virginia /ˌwɛst vərˈdʒɪnyə/	WV	Charleston /ˈtʃɑrlstən/	
Wisconsin /wɪsˈkɑnsn/	WI	Madison /ˈmædəsn/	Milwaukee /mɪlˈwɔki/
Wyoming /waɪˈoʊmɪŋ/	WY	Cheyenne /ʃaɪˈæn/	

The Great Lakes

Lake Erie /ˌleɪk ˈɪri/
Lake Ontario /ˌleɪk ɑnˈtɛrioʊ/
Lake Huron /ˌleɪk ˈhyʊrɑn; -ən/
Lake Superior /ˌleɪk səˈpɪriər/
Lake Michigan /ˌleɪk ˈmɪʃɪgən/

The Provinces and Territories of Canada

Province/Territory	Provincial/Territorial Capital	Other Major Cities
Alberta /ælˈbərt̬ə/	Edmonton /ˈɛdməntən/	Calgary /ˈkælgəri/
British Columbia /ˌbrɪt̬ɪʃ kəˈlʌmbiə/	Victoria /vɪkˈtoriə/	Vancouver /vænˈkuvər/
Manitoba /ˌmænəˈtoʊbə/	Winnipeg /ˈwɪnəˌpɛg/	
New Brunswick /ˌnu ˈbrʌnzwɪk/	Fredericton /ˈfrɛdrɪktən/	
Newfoundland and Labrador /nufəndlənd ən ˈlæbrədɔr/	St. John's /ˌseɪnt ˈdʒɑnz/	
Northwest Territories /ˌnɔrθwɛst ˈtɛrətɔriz/	Yellowknife /ˈyɛloʊˌnaɪf/	
Nova Scotia /ˌnoʊvə ˈskoʊʃə/	Halifax /ˈhæləˌfæks/	
Nunavut /ˈnunəˌvʊt/	Iqaluit /ɪˈkæluət/	
Ontario /ɑnˈtɛrioʊ/	Toronto /təˈrɑntoʊ/	Ottawa /ˈɑt̬əwə/
Prince Edward Island /ˌprɪns ˌɛdwərd ˈaɪlənd/	Charlottetown /ˈʃɑrlətˌtaʊn/	
Québec /kwɪˈbɛk; kəˈbɛk/	Québec City /kwɪˌbɛk ˈsɪt̬i; kəˌbɛk-/	Montréal /ˌmɑntriˈɔl/
Saskatchewan /sæˈskætʃəwən; -ˌwɑn/	Regina /rɪˈdʒaɪnə/	Saskatoon /ˌsæskəˈtun/
Yukon Territory /ˌyukɑn ˈtɛrətɔri/	Whitehorse /ˈwaɪthɔrs/	

Canadian English

Katherine Barber, editor of the *Canadian Oxford Dictionary*.

Canadian English is a lot like American English. Almost all the words are the same, and the pronunciation is very similar. Canadians spell and say some words differently than Americans, though, and they have some words that Americans do not use. Here are some examples.

Spelling

Some words that end in *–or* (**color, neighbor**, etc.) are more often spelled with *–our* than with *–or*: **colour, neighbour**, etc. Be careful: some words are always spelled with *-or* in all varieties of English: **actor, doctor, error**, etc.

Some words that end in *–ter* (**center, theater**, etc.) are more often spelled *–tre*: **centre, theatre**, etc. Be careful: some words are spelled with *-ter* in all varieties of English: **enter, character**, etc.

When adding *-ing*, *-ed*, or *-er* to words ending in *l* or *p* that are not stressed on the final syllable, the *l* or *p* is doubled: **cancelling, worshipped, traveller**.

For words ending in *-dge*, the *-e* is kept when *-ment* is added: **judgement, acknowledgement**.

In Canadian English, **licence** and **practice** are nouns while **license** and **practise** are verbs. American English uses **license** and **practice** for both noun and verb.

The piece of paper you use to pay money out of your bank account is a **cheque** (American English **check**).

A book that contains information about all the things you can buy from a company is a **catalogue** (American English usually **catalog**).

Pronunciation

Shone, the past tense of **shine**, rhymes with *on*. (For Americans, it sounds like *shown*.)

The vowel in **roof** is the same as the vowel in **boot**. (Some Americans use the same vowel as in *book*.)

The second syllable in **anti-** and **multi-** rhymes with *tea*. (Some Americans say *tie*.)

Most Canadians say **route** like *root*, though some say it to rhyme with *out* (as many Americans also do).

About half of Canadians pronounce the "h" in **herb** while the other half don't. (Americans don't.)

About half start the word **schedule** with a "sh" and the other half with a "sk". (Americans say "sk".)

Some say the word **been** like *bean* and others like *bin*. Some use both of these pronunciations. (Americans say *bin*.)

Words

Most Canadians call the letter Z **zed**, and tend to get upset with Canadians who call it **zee** like the Americans.

A police officer of the lowest rank is a **constable**.

A **serviette** is a table napkin, especially if it is made of paper.

The favorite tag ending for Canadians is **eh** (rather than the American **huh**), as in *"Nice day, eh?"*

Washroom is the polite word for a toilet; to **go to the washroom** means to use the toilet.

A **toque** (also spelled **tuque**) is a knitted cap.

The native peoples of Canada are called **First Nations** (previously called Indians), **Inuit** (previously called Eskimos) and **Métis** (people who have both European and native ancestors).

Hydro is electricity.

A type of apartment which is one big room for sleeping, eating, cooking, and sitting is a **bachelor**.

A **loonie** is a one-dollar coin; a **toonie** is a two-dollar coin.

Weights and Measures

	U.S. Standard System	Metric System

Weight

	1 ounce (oz.)	= 28.35 grams (g)
16 ounces	= 1 pound (lb.)	= 0.454 kilogram (kg)
2,000 pounds	= 1 ton	= 907 kilograms

> *I weigh 195 pounds.*
> *The truck weighs over four tons.*
> *We added eight ounces of nuts to the cookies.*

Length

	1 inch (in.)	= 2.54 centimeters (cm)
12 inches	= 1 foot (ft.)	= 30.48 centimeters
3 feet	= 1 yard (yd.)	= 0.9144 meter (m)
1,760 yards	= 1 mile	= 1.609 kilometers (km)

> *The bus stop is only 30 yards away from our house.*
> *There are 5,280 feet in one mile.*

Area

	1 square inch (sq. inch)	= 6.45 square centimeters (cm²)
144 square inches	= 1 square foot (sq. foot)	= 929.03 square centimeters
9 square feet	= 1 square yard (sq. yard)	= 0.836 square meter (m²)
4,840 square yards	= 1 acre	= 0.405 hectare
640 acres	= 1 square mile	= 2.59 square kilometers (km²) or 259 hectares

> *Our backyard measures 700 square feet.*
> *How many square inches are in a square yard?*

Capacity

	1 fluid ounce (fl. oz.)	= 29.573 milliliters (ml)
16 fluid ounces	= 1 pint (pt.)	= 0.473 liter (l)
2 pints	= 1 quart (qt.)	= 0.946 liter
4 quarts	= 1 gallon (gal.)	= 3.785 liters
	1 teaspoon (tsp.)	= 5 milliliters
1 tablespoon (tbsp.)	= 3 teaspoons	= 15 milliliters
1 cup (c.)	= 8 ounces	= 237 milliliters
2 cups	= 1 pint	= 473 milliliters

> *I bought a gallon of milk and some bananas at the supermarket.*
> *How many pints are there in a gallon?*
> *To make bread, you will need 2 cups of flour and 1 tablespoon of yeast.*

Temperature

The Fahrenheit (°F) scale is usually used to measure temperature in the U.S.:

> *Temperatures went up to over a hundred (= 100°F).*
> *She's sick in bed with a temperature of a hundred and two (= 102°F).*

The Celsius or Centigrade (°C) scale is used in scientific contexts:

> *Water freezes at 0°C (= zero degrees Celsius) and boils at 100°C (= one hundred degrees Celsius).*

ACKNOWLEDGMENTS

Illustrations and photographs by: AA Reps 49 (internal organs), 66 (car), 165 (eye), 190 (empty, full), 263 (leg), 268 (limousine), 296 (motor home), 297 (mouth), 416 (skeleton), 437 (portable stereo), 438 (stethoscope), 439 (station wagon), 453 (syringe), 478 (truck), 493 (van); Alamy Ltd. 84 (clothes, dress), 138 (dominoes), 212 (hang glider), 247 (iron), 292 (mobile home), 338 (pickup), 436 (glue), 450 (SUV), 490 (USB flash drive); Beehive Illustration 267 (lightning); CAMP/ RelaXimages/ Photolibrary Group Ltd. 388 (rowboat); Corbis 33 (bagel), 250 (jigsaw puzzle); Corel 37 (basket), 82 (cliff), 138 (donkey), 177 (fire hydrant), 179 (flashlight), 194 (garbage can), 269 (lipstick), 288 (milkshake), 329 (parrot), 360 (pumpkin), 398 (seashell), 417 (skyscraper), 445 (submarine), 447 (sunset), 467 (tiger), 502 (waterfall); Dennis Kitchen Studio 33 (backpack, purse), 58 (bucket), 63 (calculator), 84 (T-shirt), 98 (jars), 145 (dustpan), 250 (chain, engagement ring, pin), 266 (life jacket), 301 (nails), 354 (printer), 387 (rope), 391 (safety pin), 396 (a pair of scissors), 398 (screwdriver, screws), 408 (Loafers™), 418 (sleeping bag), 430 (sponge), 436 (stapler/ staples), 443 (stroller), 456 (tape measure), 458 (teddy bear), 479 (tub), 492 (vacuum cleaner); Digital vision 417 (skydiving); Garth Glazier 49 (the body); Getty 219 (high jump); Hemera CDs 64 (camel), 78 (chopsticks), 120 (deer), 326 (panda), 408 (sandal, shoe, slippers, sneakers), 415 (ice skates, roller skates), 416 (skateboard), 418 (slide), 421 (sleigh), 452 (swings), 466 (thumbtacks); Hemera Technologies Inc. 11 (alarm clock), 16 (anchor), 18 (antelope), 22 (arch), 33 (briefcase, fanny pack, grocery bag, suitcase), 34 (banjo), 37 (bathrobe), 41 (bench), 43 (bicycle, binoculars); 46 (blimp), 54 (a loaf of bread), 57 (broom), 58 (buffalo, hairbrush, paintbrushes, toothbrush), 59 (bulldozer), 63 (cactus), 65 (candle), 68 (luggage cart, shopping cart), 69 (cat, kitten), 72 (armchair, chair, sofa/couch, stool), 83 (clipboard), 84 (clothes, jacket, overcoat, shorts), 91 (compass), 106 (bull, cow), 108 (crib), 114 (cymbals), 115 (dagger), 137 (dolphin), 142 (electric drill), 143 (drum, duck), 145 (dustpan), 149 (egg), 168 (fans), 200 (glove, mitten), 201 (goose), 204 (grater), 207 (acoustic guitar, bass guitar, electric guitar), 210 (hammer), 214 (baseball cap, beret, cowboy hat), 217 (helmets), 224 (hose), 225 (hot-air balloon), 242 (cello, clarinet, flute, harp, piano, recorder, saxophone, trombone, trumpet, violin), 250 (bracelet, earrings), 252 (juggler), 254 (kayak), 256 (can opener, corkscrew, ice cream scoop, ladle, sieve, whisk), 258 (ladder), 261 (lawnmower), 277 (magnifying glass, mailboxes), 281 (masks), 284 (medal), 296 (motorcycle), 284 (pacifier, padlock), 340 (pins), 341 (pitcher), 343 (deck of cards), 366 (rake), 388 (rug), 394 (saw), 395 (scarf), 407 (shears, mussel, oyster), 408 (cowboy boot), 410 (shovel), 415 (in-line skates), 427 (spade), 430 (tablespoon, teaspoon), 436 (folders, notebook, paper clips, pencil), 442 (string), 450 (swan), 456 (tambourine), 458 (telescope), 465 (thread), 470 (tongs), 473 (tractor), 477 (trophy), 480 (tweezers), 495 (vest), 502 (watch), 506 (wheelbarrow), 507 (wheelchair), 515 (wrench), 519 (zebra, zipper); Illustration Ltd. 294 (bill, coins), 436 (ballpoint pen, eraser, pencil sharpener); JB Illustrations 23 (armadillo), 37 (bat), 38 (bear), 39 (beaver), 77 (chimpanzee, chipmunk), 106 (coyote), 150 (elephant), 166 (face), 186 (fox), 201 (gopher,

gorilla) , 211 (hand), 221 (hippopotamus), 254 (kangaroo), 257 (koala), 264 (leopard), 269 (lion), 294 (monkey), 297 (mountain lion), 318 (opossum), 327 (panther), 347 (porcupine), 365 (raccoon), 382 (rhinoceros) , 431 (sports car), 433 (squirrel) , 501 (wastebasket), 512 (wolf); Jae Wagoner Artists Rep. 76 (chess), 128 (dice), 147 (easel), 343 (playing cards), 472 (doll, model train); Meiklejohn Illustrations 46 (blind), 52 (bows), 199 (a pair of glasses), 209 (spiky hair, ponytail, braids, curly hair, wavy hair, bald head), 254 (key), 258 (lamp), 276 (magnet), 287 (microscope), 405 (shadow/shade), 431 (spring), 432 (crush, press, squash, squeeze), 515 (wring); Mendola Art 112 (cup and saucer, mug), 256 (knives), 325 (package); Munro Campagna 42 (blueberries, raspberries, strawberries), 76 (chilies), 86 (coconuts), 103 (corn), 190 (apples, bananas, cherries, grapefruit, grapes, kiwis, lemons, limes, oranges, pears, pineapples, plums), 194 (garlic), 285 (melons), 299 (mushrooms), 494 (broccoli, cabbage, carrots, cauliflower, celery, cucumbers, lettuce, onions, peas, peppers, potatoes, radishes, sweet potatoes, tomatoes, zucchini; NB Illustration 500 (wallets); OUP 4 (acorn), 16 (angles), 27 (atom), 29 (avocado), 30 (graph axes), 33 (bald eagle), 34 (Band-Aid™, bandage), 35 (barbed wire, bar code), 36 (baseball), 44 (bird), 50 (bolts), 52 (bow, bowling), 61 (butterfly), 76 (chicken) , 79 (circle), 88 (comb), 98 (bags, bottles, boxes, cans, cartons, packages, tubes), 103 (cord), 109 (alligator, crocodile), 111 (crab, lobster), 129 (dimensions), 135 (diving), 137 (dog, puppy), 140 (dragonfly), 146 (the earth), 147 (solar eclipse), 148 (eel), 171 (feather), 181 (rose, sunflower, tulip), 188 (frog), 201 (goat, goggles), 204 (grasshopper), 208 (gymnastics), 210 (hair dryer), 219 (hexagon), 220 (hinge) , 224 (horse), 240 (ant, bee, beetle, flea, fly, ladybug, mosquito, wasp), 249 (javelin), 250 (jellyfish, necklace), 252 (jugs), 257 (knot), 266 (license plate), 268 (lines), 270 (lizard), 293 (molecule), 295 (moose), 296 (moth), 311 (almond, chestnut, hazelnut, peanut, pecan, walnut), 314 (octopus, squid), 323 (owl), 332 (checks, peach, plaid, stripes), 333 (peel), 334 (penguin), 339 (pig, pigeon, pills), 342 (plant), 368 (electric razor, rattlesnake, razor), 371 (redwood), 382 (rhombus), 386 (robin), 387 (rooster), 397 (scorpion), 406 (shapes, shark), 407 (sheep), 412 (sign), 414 (sink), 416 (ski), 420 (snail, slug), 421 (snorkeling, snowboarding), 422 (bar of soap, soccer), 424 (cone, cube, cylinder, pyramid, sphere), 429 (spider), 435 (starfish), 436 (highlighter, ruler), 452 (a swollen ankle, switch), 460 (tennis), 469 (toad), 471 (toothpaste), 475 (trapezoid), 476 (log, tree), 479 (turkey), 497 (volcano), 502 (wavelength), 506 (whale), 510 (windsurfing); OUP (OXED) 15 (amoeba), 463 (thermometers); OUP (digital camera) 84 (turtleneck); Photodisc/Getty 242 (double bass, oboe), 517 (xylophone); Photolibrary Group Ltd. 65 (canoe), 93 (computer), 217 (helicopter), 242 (tuba), 404 (sewing), 449 (surfing); Q2A Solutions 156 (equilateral triangle), 178 (fish), 254 (piano keys), 333 (pegs), 384 (rim); Ravenhill Represents 75 (cheesecake), 386 (rolls), 393 (sandwich), 499 (pancakes, waffles); Reppans 110 (crossword); Roger Motzkus 183 (football), 229 (ice hockey); Sparks Literary Agency 437 (inside of car); Stockbyte/Getty 256 (kite), 469 (toaster)

Maps © Oxford University Press

Minimum system requirements

Windows XP, Windows Vista®, Windows® 7; 350 MHz, 256 MB RAM

Macintosh OS 10.4; 500 MHz, 256 MB RAM

Minimum installation of the software requires 200 MB available on hard disk.

Macintosh users must perform a complete installation of the software requiring 700 MB available on hard disk.

Oxford University Press
Software Licence

Please read these terms before using the CD-ROM

This CD-ROM contains copyright material and by using it you agree to be bound by the terms of this Licence. If you do not accept the terms set out below then do not use the CD-ROM.

The literary material and computer software programs in this CD-ROM ('the Software') and any associated documentation are protected by copyright laws worldwide. The copyright is owned or licensed to Oxford University Press ('OUP').

1   Licence

OUP grants you the non-exclusive non-transferable right to use the Software on a single computer of the type specified in the packaging. You may not network the

except as expressly
adapt, distribute, transmit, transfer,
..ware or any associated documentation.
..usiness which would flow from unauthorized
,ociated documentation, you will make every
and associated documentation secure both during the
_nce and after its termination.

this licence at any time by destroying the Software and any
.nentation. This licence will also terminate if you breach any of its

warrants that the Software will be free from defects in materials and
kmanship under normal use and will conform to the published specification
90 days from the date you receive it.

₁he above warranty is in lieu of all other warranties express or implied and
representations and in particular but without limitation to the foregoing:

₄.2.1   OUP gives no warranties and makes no representations that the Software will be suitable for any particular purpose or for use under any specific conditions notwithstanding that such purpose or conditions may be known either to OUP or the dealer from whom you acquired the CD-ROM;

4.2.2   OUP accepts no responsibility for any mathematical or technical limitations of the Software;

4.2.3   OUP does not warrant that the operation of the Software will be uninterrupted or free from errors.

5   Limitation of liabil

5.2 Save ₁
suppliers
damages fo₁
consequential lo_
Software or any asso₁

5.3 Links to any third party
OUP disclaims any respon_.
to which a link is provided.

6   Law

This licence is governed by English law and the English Courts shall have jurisdiction.

Your key to academic success!

■ Understand What Words Mean

> **27,000** words, phrases, and meanings

> **15,000** examples show how words are used

> **500** color illustrations

> **25** reference pages on irregular verbs, punctuation, and more

■ Build Your Vocabulary and Achieve Academic Success

> Focus on the **2,000** most important words to know

> Learn words from the Academic Word List

> Develop content area vocabulary in math, science, social studies, and more

> Expand your knowledge of synonyms, antonyms, affixes, and words that go together

■ Develop Your Language Skills with the CD-ROM

> Search the A-Z dictionary

> Listen to words and sentences

> Record your pronunciation

> Focus on content area vocabulary

> Make your own word lists

Oxford American Dictionaries help you at every stage of your language learning·

OXFORD
UNIVERSITY PRESS

www.oup.com

ISBN 978-0-19-439969-2

9 780194 399692